deleted

GOTHIC LITERATURE

A Gale Critical Companion

GOTHIC LITERATURE

A Gale Critical Companion

Volume 3: Authors L-Z

Foreword by **Jerrold E. Hogle, Ph.D.**
University of Arizona

Jessica Bomarito, Project Editor

THOMSON

GALE

Detroit • New York • San Francisco • San Diego • New Haven, Conn. • Waterville, Maine • London • Munich

THOMSON

™

GALE

Gothic Literature, Vol. 3

Project Editor
Jessica Bomarito

Editorial
Regan Blinder, Kathy D. Darrow, Jeffrey W. Hunter, Jelena O. Krstović, Julie Landelius, Michelle Lee, Ellen McGeagh, Rachelle Mucha, Thomas J. Schoenberg, Noah Schusterbauer, Lawrence J. Trudeau, Russel Whitaker

Indexing Services
Factiva

Production Services
Zott Solutions, Inc.

Permissions
Margaret Abendroth, Lori Hines, Shalice Shah-Caldwell, Kim Smilay, Andrew Specht

Imaging and Multimedia
Lezlie Light, Daniel Newell, Kelly A. Quin

Product Design
Michael Logusz, Pamela Galbreath

Composition and Electronic Capture
Carolyn Roney

Manufacturing
Rhonda Dover

Product Managers
Marc Cormier, Janet Witalec

LIBRARY OF CONGRESS CATALOGING-IN-PUBLICATION DATA

Gothic literature : a Gale critical companion / foreword by Jerrold E. Hogle ; Jessica Bomarito, project editor.
    p. cm. -- (Gale critical companion collection)
    Includes bibliographical references and index.
    ISBN 0-7876-9470-3 (set hardcover : alk. paper) -- ISBN 0-7876-9471-1 (v. 1 : alk. paper) -- ISBN 0-7876-9472-X (v. 2 : alk. paper) -- ISBN 0-7876-9473-8 (v. 3 : alk. paper)
    1. English literature--History and criticism--Handbooks, manuals, etc. 2. Gothic revival (Literature)--Great Britain--Handbooks, manuals, etc. 3. Gothic revival (Literature)--United States--Handbooks, manuals, etc. 4. Horror tales, American--History and criticism--Handbooks, manuals, etc. 5. Horror tales, English--History and criticism--Handbooks, manuals, etc. 6. American literature--History and criticism--Handbooks, manuals, etc. I. Bomarito, Jessica, 1975- II. Series.
    PR408.G68G675 2006
    820.9'11--dc22
                                        2005011420

CONTENTS

VOLUME 2

CONTENTS

These very useful Critical Companion volumes offer a wide range of historical accounts about, literary excerpts from, and critical interpretations of a long-standing mode of fiction-making that has come to be called "the Gothic." Though this label has most often been attached to "terrifying" or "horrific" pieces of prose fiction ever since Horace Walpole's *The Castle of Otranto* (the founding text of this form, first published in 1764) added the subtitle *A Gothic Story* to its Second British Edition of 1765, the hyperbolic and haunting features of this highly popular, but often controversial, mode have proliferated across the last two-and-a-half centuries in an increasing array of forms: novels, prose "romances," plays, paintings, operas, short stories, narrative and lyric poems, "shilling shocker" tales, newspaper serials and crime-reports, motion pictures, television shows, comic books, "graphic" novels, and even video games. That variety of presentation is what now makes "*the* Gothic" the best phrase for describing this ongoing phenomenon. It has proven to be a set of transportable features more than it has been a single genre. Its variations are not so much similar in compositional form as they are inclined to share certain settings, symbols, situations, psychological states, and emotional effects on readers or audiences, all of which appear at least somewhat in *The Castle of Otranto* but have gone on to vary greatly in their manifestations over time. The incompatible generic ingredients of the

Gothic initially—Walpole saw it as a combination of the supernatural "ancient" and the more realistic "modern" romance—have made it unstable from the start and so have led it to "expatiate" widely and wildly (Walpole's own word in his 1765 Preface) and hence to carry its volatile inconsistency into every form it has assumed, from its beginnings in mid-eighteenth century England to its current profusion throughout the Western world at the dawn of the twenty-first century.

Yet what are the traits that hold "the Gothic" together, if only just barely, as it spreads itself like one of its specters or monstrosities across literary, dramatic, and other audio-visual forms? As the following essays and excerpts show, all truly Gothic stories or stagings take place, at least part of the time, in some sort of antiquated (sometimes falsely antiquated) space, be it a castle, ruin, crumbling abbey, graveyard, old manor house or theater, haunted wilderness or neighborhood, cellar or attic full of artifacts—*or* aging train station, rusted manufacturing plant, or outdated spaceship. This space, reminiscent of *medieval* "Gothic" castles or churches but often existing long after those in more modern recastings of their features, threatens to overwhelm and engulf protagonists (including readers or viewers) in the setting's vastness, darkness, and vaguely threatening, even irrational, depths. That is usually because this space is haunted or invaded by some form of ghost, specter, or monster, a frightening crosser of the supposed boundaries between life and death, natural and supernatural, or "normal" and "abnormal." Usually this figure betokens some hidden "primal crime" buried from sight ages ago or having occurred in the recent past, the truth about which at least seems to lie in the darkest depths, or deepest darkness, of the antiquated space. Gothic protagonists and their readers or viewers, faced with this haunting in such a setting, are thus pulled back and forth (like the Gothic as a mode) between older and newer states of being, longing to escape into the seeming safety of one or the other but kept in a tug-of-war of terrifying suspense between the powers of the past and the present, darkness and daylight, insane incoherence and rational order.

At the same time, the extreme *fictionality* of all these elements is so emphasized in the melodramatic exaggeration of Gothic description and characterizations that the threats in these situations are made to seem both imminent (about to appear) and immanent (sequestered within) *and yet* safely distant, at least for readers or audiences. As in the "scary movies" of more recent times, many of which employ or derive from the Gothic, the spectators of such fictions can experience the thrill of fear that the threats really arouse and at the same time feel entirely safe from those threats because it is all so obviously artificial and unlikely to become real or lead to real consequences. Any fiction that does not have all these basic features to some extent is not really "Gothic" through and through, although many adjacent fictions (such as those of Charles Dickens or Herman Melville or most films directed by Alfred Hitchcock or M. Night Shyamalan) use *pieces* of the Gothic to arouse some of the suggestions and effects associated with it.

Even when fictions are thoroughly Gothic, however, as are the ones most emphasized in these volumes, they can vary widely across a continuum between *terror* and *horror*. Near the end of her life and career, Ann Radcliffe, arguably the most influential British author of Gothic romances in the turbulent 1790s (including *The Mysteries of Udolpho* and *The Italian*), composed a dialogue "On the Supernatural in Poetry" that appeared posthumously with her last novel, *Gaston de Blondeville*, in 1826. There her fictional interlocutors make a clear distinction between devices that invoke "the terrible" (a suspenseful uncertainty about hidden possibilities that *could* be violent or repulsive or supernatural but rarely appear in such extreme forms) and blatant descriptions that

expose "the horrible" (the unambiguously violent, deadly, grotesque, and even horrifically supernatural, so much so that the line between what is "sanctioned" and "forbidden" has been crossed without a doubt). Radcliffe herself, as her novels show, clearly prefers the suggestiveness of terror, to the point where her violence is more potential than actual and the apparently supernatural is always explained away, as is the case with many of her successors in Gothic writing. She thereby places herself and her imitators squarely in the tradition of the "sublime" defined as the safely fearful or awesome by Edmund Burke in his 1757 *A Philosophical Enquiry into the Origin of Our Ideas of the Sublime and Beautiful.*

Gothic "horror," by contrast, became most epitomized in Radcliffe's time by Matthew Lewis's *The Monk* (1796), filled as it is, not just with a vociferous anti-Catholicism that Radcliffe shares, but with explicit sexual intercourse, incestuous rape and murder, the brutal dismembering of a tyrannical nun by a mob, and the physical appearance of Satan himself as homosexually seductive. The blatantly stagey hyperbole of Lewis's style makes all this less immediate than it might otherwise be, but it also defines the "horrible" extreme of the Gothic continuum that locates the mere potentiality of "terror" at its opposite end. It thus helps establish a polarity across which the Gothic has played ever since, as it wafts between, say, Daphne du Maurier's Radcliffean *Rebecca* (1938) and William Peter Blatty's horrific *The Exorcist* (1971) and their ongoing imitators of both types. The Gothic is set off from other forms of fiction by its Walpolean features but also demarcated within itself by its leanings at times towards "terrific" suspense, on the one hand, and graphic "horror," on the other. The two come together mostly in extreme cases such as Stoker's original novel *Dracula* (1897), where suspenseful intimations about the Count's vampiric nature in "sublime" Transylvania give way to his graphic gorging of himself with the blood of a married woman before witnesses in Victorian London, after which he breaks all "normal" gender boundaries by drawing the same woman to *his* breast to suck up his own already vampiric blood. It is this whole range of Gothic possibilities that the following excerpts and accounts explore, since this anamorphic (or self-distorting) and metamorphic (or shape-shifting) form of fiction has been pulled between these extremes, we now see, from its earliest manifestations.

The tension between the terrifying and the horrible in the Gothic, moreover, has developed into another continuum of symbolic possibilities—the "psychological" versus "ontological" or supernatural Gothic—especially since 1800. If Radcliffe's heroines in the 1790s think themselves into states of fear that are finally based on associations of ideas not corroborated by the outside world, it is a small step from there to the projection of a whole state of mind into an external space that is vast, dark, and threatening more because of drives inside the observer than its own separate features. Hence the tormenting Spirits that rise in the Higher Alps at the bidding of the title character in Lord Byron's Gothic verse-drama *Manfred* (1817) are, as he admits, "The mind, the spirit, the Promethean spark, / The lightning of my being" as much as anything else. At about the same time, though, Dr. John Polidori, Byron's personal physician and occasional lover, forecasts the late Victorian coming of Dracula with his Byronic novella *The Vampyre* (1819), in which the predatory Lord Ruthven seems threatening at first only in the suspicious thoughts of the hero (Aubrey) until the latter faces the horror that his own sister "has glutted the thirst of a VAMPYRE," which Ruthven turns out to have been for centuries. In this latter case, Gothic monstrosity is granted the ontological state of being quite outside any observer, a distinct existence confirmed from multiple points of view, as in Stoker's *Dracula*. Throughout the nineteenth century, starting with the Romantic era of Byron and Polidori, the Gothic careens incessantly between the strictly psychological, where ghosts or monsters are more mental than physical, and the unabashedly supernatural in which an other-worldly horror violently invades the space of the self from outside its boundaries. When both are involved, though, the nineteenth century tilts more often towards rooting the supernatural in the psyche. That is certainly the case in Mary Shelley's *Frankenstein* (1818), now the most famous Gothic tale in history, where the half-fantastic creature composed from multiple carcasses is mostly an outsized sewing-together of his creator's most repressed, libidinous, and boundary-crossing impulses.

As supernatural levels of being have become increasingly doubted in the post-Renaissance world of the West, the terrors or horrors generated from within have become a staple of the Gothic and projected onto its haunted settings, just as much as older beliefs in seductive Satan-figures have continued to be in the vein of *The Monk, The Exorcist,* or Anne Rice's *Vampire Chronicles* (1976-2001). The most debated Gothic story in Western history may be Henry James's *The Turn of the Screw* (1898), in which the highly repressed governess of two children in a castellated old estate-house is convinced she sees the ghosts of her predecessor, Miss Jessel, and Jessel's lower-class lover, Peter Quint, but may just as likely be projecting them onto the estate-world she observes as she sublimates her own desires for an absentee Master far above her in social station. Even today, as parts of these volumes show, readers and viewers cannot be sure when they begin Gothic tales or films—though they often find out in "twist" endings (in such pictures as *The Sixth Sense* and *The Others*)—whether the haunting specters they see are the delusions of characters or unambiguously other-worldly, outside any psychological point of view. We sometimes long for the comfort of supernatural visitations but fear how much this longing comes from irrational psychic forces in ourselves and others, and the Gothic plays on and explores these apprehensions, as it has for over two hundred years.

But this last point demands a fuller answer to the most lingering question about the conflicted oddity that is the Gothic as it multiplies into all the forms explored in these volumes: Why do we have this malleable symbolic mode in Anglo-European Western culture and its former colonies, and why does this anamorphic form, torn as it is between extremes (supernatural/realistic, horrible/terrifying, really frightening/merely fictional, ontological/psychological, and others), persist from *The Castle of Otranto* in the 1760s through *Frankenstein* and *Dracula* to films, novels, and video games of today, some of which keep repeatedly adapting some of those older stories for new audiences? Numerous answers are offered in the definitional and interpretive essays that follow, as well as in some Gothic tales themselves, here excerpted at their most indicative moments. But I would like to begin the discussion by suggesting the most overriding reasons why the Gothic has arisen and why it persists as a cultural formation clearly *needed*, as well as wanted, by Western readers and audiences.

To begin with, "the Gothic" comes about at a time in the West when the oldest structures of Christian religiosity (including Roman Catholicism) and social hierarchies seemingly predetermined to the advantage of hereditary aristocrats (symbolized by their castles or estate-houses) are starting to fragment and decay, as in Walpole's principal Ghost (who appears initially in pieces), even as these receding forms hang on as standard grounds of being in the minds of many. At such a time, the older symbols of power seem increasingly hollowed out, like the ruins of medieval Gothic structures, while they also seem locations that vaguely harbor historical foundations for human minds newly liberated by the rational and scientific Enlightenment that is overthrowing the older orders by degrees in the eighteenth century. In this situation, while beliefs about the self-determining (rather than strictly hereditary) individual start to gain ascendancy and give greater weight to personal psychology over predetermined roles, Westerners face an existential anxiety about where they really come from and the orders to which they belong when the best-known external indicators of those groundings are becoming empty repositories, realms filled up with the nostalgic desires projected into them more than the metaphysical and cultural certainties once manifested by them.

As Leslie Fiedler has shown by exposing the basis of the American Gothic in *Love and Death in the American Novel* (1960), this uprooted, yet root-seeking, condition for Westerners around 1765 makes them hover between longings for past securities, though these are also seen as primitively irrational and confining, and longings for rebellion against those patriarchal schemes, which simultaneously produce a sense of guilt about the overthrow of those "fathers," making that revolution a sort of "primal crime." Guilt, after all, is what Walpole's Prince Manfred feels when he finds that his own grandfather once murdered the original founder of Otranto and usurped its birthright from the latter's heirs, the same way as the rising middle class of the eighteenth century (the main readership of the Gothic as time went on) probably felt about gradually decimating the very power-bases it now sought to occupy in place of the aristocracy. In addition, Fiedler writes, this sense of haunted guilt and uncertainties about middle-class entitlement raised "the fear that in destroying the old ego-ideals of Church and State, the West has opened a way for the inruption of darkness: for insanity and the disintegration of the self." The Gothic of Walpole and its acceleration by the 1790s in Radcliffe and Lewis come about, since fictions always respond to the needs of their audiences, to address and symbolize this cultural and psychological condition of early capitalist and pre-industrial modernity. That is why the early Gothic places both desires for lost foundations *and* fears about the irrational darkness lying outside the limits of newly enlightened reason in the same antiquated spaces and their mysterious depths, which Gothic characters from Manfred to Lewis's monk then seek to penetrate

or recover and escape or destroy so as to construct a sense of identity that is somehow both grounded and self-determined. The Gothic is a powerful symbolic indicator, then, of the social and psychic contradictions out of which the modern Western self emerged and keeps emerging, and we need and want it, I would argue, to keep retelling that story that is so basic to our modern sense of ourselves.

The story has kept developing in the West, however, and the Gothic has developed with it. As the ideological belief in personal self-making becomes even more accepted towards the end of the eighteenth and the beginning of the nineteenth centuries, the individual mind comes to be viewed as the dynamic, but also anxious, site of its own "ghosts" and increasing depths. Ann Radcliffe and many of her contemporaries accept the basic premises of empirical psychology, which claims (since John Locke in the 1690s, anyway) that the human mind begins as a near-vacancy and gradually accumulates and organizes the memories it retains (hence the "ghosts") of earlier and more recent sense-perceptions. Adult observations in later life are therefore colored by the associations of previous, and now ghost-like, impressions that are applied to the intake of newer phenomena. Terry Castle can consequently see in *The Female Thermometer* (1995) that the Radcliffean Gothic turns landscapes as well as characters into "spectralized" thoughts within reflective states of mind that make nature seem already painted (and thus filtered by perceivers) and people already colored by older sayings and texts about their "types." To observe at any moment in the Gothic from the 1790s on is to call attention, at least some of the time, to the lenses of perception and the gradually accumulated psychic layers of associated memories that are projected onto any object contemplated or produced by the perceiving self. Ruins and old houses, as well as Frankenstein-ian creatures, are now filled with dark indications of deep past threats because the mind transfers its own layers of developing perceptions, as well as middle-class guilt, into what it sees and thus confronts its own "doubling" there, its deepest internal memories reembodied in perceptions of external depths now haunted by mental ghosts. When Victor Frankenstein first sees the face of his finished creature in Mary Shelley's Gothic book, he falls into a regressive dream in which the mottled visage of his fabrication from dead bodies becomes linked to his longing for his own deceased mother, whose corpse he preconsciously has seen himself re-embracing while he tries to make life out of death without the biological involvement of a woman. By 1820 at least, the Gothic has become the fictional *locus* where outward quests for self-completion now are seen as mainly inward probings through the archaic layers of the self. Gothic "objects," from antiquated locations to other people to mere things, have thus become manifestations of the perceiver's own growing depths of thought in which the desire for pre-rational foundations is actually pursuing "the mother" conceived of as the initial interplay of self and other that produces the confused beginnings, later repressed, of all thought, sensation, and memory.

It is no wonder, then, that the Gothic comes to be torn constantly between terror and horror, on one level, and the psychological and the clearly supernatural, on another. Terror offers the uneasy comfort that what we fear, being mentally constructed for the most part, could be non-existent in the end (as in Radcliffe's conclusions), except in our own minds. Such solipsism, however, can also be seen as a myopic middle-class or even aristocratic avoidance of the violent upheavals and even greater displacements of older orders brought on by the exploding mercantile and industrial economies—and the racist imperialism that went with them—in the nineteenth century. Consequently, this era's Gothic invasions of the isolated psyche by "horror," the external violence and many forms of non-middle-class "ugliness" that cannot be wished away as mere thought, force this counter-awareness on audiences, albeit through extreme fictionality, increasingly so in the form of the vampire made prominent by Polidori. By the time of the serialized *Varney the Vampire* (1847), usually attributed to Thomas Peckett Prest, and the many stagings of vampire plays in Victorian England, France, and America, this Gothic monster can symbolize many potential invaders of middle-class security simultaneously, from vengeful old aristocrats to foreign and racial "others" to diseases of the blood made more virulent by urban growth, foreign tourism, and the expansion of prostitution. The nineteenth century in the West, we can say, needs the Gothic to carry out and fictively obscure the cultural hesitation at the time between middle-class withdrawal into increasing private spaces, including sheer thought (which thereby confronts its own deep irrationalities), and the need of the same people to face the horrors of growing cities and empires with their illnesses, "unclean" impoverished laborers, exploited women, and enslaved "colored" races.

What the Gothic does in part, among its reaction to these changes, is to increase the struggle between its psychological and supernatural tendencies. First, it becomes the source of many symbols for the concept of the "unconscious" that Sigmund Freud, building on many others, brought into wide prominence by the end of the nineteenth century and the early decades of the twentieth. Especially insofar as the Gothic has gradually become a realm of mental projection and of the mind forced back to the beginnings and hauntings of its own development, it has provided the archaic depths, dim repositories, memory-traces, accumulations of memories layer upon layer, and primal states (including regressions back to "mother" or sheer vacancy) from which Freud and his contemporaries craft their description of the unconscious and its sublimation by pre-conscious and conscious levels of thought. In the early twentieth century, the Gothic therefore comes to be seen as primarily psychological in the sense of *psychoanalytic,* as long having manifested in its haunted spaces and the mental quandaries of its characters the processes of thought described by Freud, even though it is more accurate to say that the Gothic first helped make Freud's schemes conceivable and expressible. Back in Freud's formative period, though, the assertion of the human species's long physical evolution by Charles Darwin and others from the 1850s on challenges the layerings of personal consciousness with a biologically historical progression beyond, yet still working inside, individual people. The Gothic reacts by reinvoking its old invasions of supernatural, or at least trans-individual, forces to show psychological projections running up against pervasive external drives that may really control the psyche after all. Robert Louis Stevenson's *Strange Case of Dr. Jekyll and Mr. Hyde* (1886) may seem to suggest a psychological bifurcation in the Victorian self, with Jekyll as internalized *superego* and Hyde as raging *libido,* but the Doctor's attempts to control this internal split finally cannot prevent the "troglodytic" emergence of all that remains primitively *de*volved in his superficially *e*volved condition. Even more dramatically, Stoker's Count Dracula arouses and enacts unconscious libidinal desires by being a devolved, "child-brain" force supernaturally driving across centuries that invades "civilized" England with all the diseases and the racial and animalistic "others" that the supposedly evolved want to keep distant from themselves and cannot. *The Turn of the Screw* plays out an undecidability between the dominance of the psychological and the power of the supernatural because the nineteenth-century West in its final years needs ways to articulate that it is frantically at odds with itself over what to believe about the deepest foundations of life.

The Gothic from its beginnings and as it evolves with the cultural changes around it, in other words, turns out to be the modern Western world's most striking, if most conflicted, symbolic method for both confronting and disguising its own unresolved struggles with incompatible beliefs about what it means to be human. Walpole's *Castle* starts the tradition by leaving its readers caught where most of them already were: between longings for a fading hierarchical order underwritten by supernatural assurances ("ancient romance") and desires for greater self-determination based on free re-imaginings of uprooted older perceptions ("modern romance"). Radcliffe and Lewis, during the revolutionary 1790s, help readers confront and prevent cultural dissolution by offering reassurances that spectral perceptions of danger to the self can finally control the terror those specters produce *and* shocking revelations *at the same time* that current upheavals are but symptoms of multiple irrationalities that established religion and governments have tried to repress only to force them towards more extreme violence. *Frankenstein* offers a condemnation and a celebration of the scientific and industrial advances puzzled over by its readers, along with symbols for the unsettled debate over whether life is externally infused (by, say, some ultimate Father) or internally generated (primarily within the mother whom Victor both remembers and tries to forget). *Jekyll and Hyde* and *Dracula* both blame individual free will for inviting its underlying depravities into consciousness and point to attacks on the evolved Anglo race by "devolved" levels of humanity from other times and places. In extreme forms of expression that allow us to perceive or avoid such levels in our thinking, the Gothic holds up to us our conflicted conservative *and* progressive tendencies in the full cry of their unresolved tug-of-war in our culture and in ourselves. Our hesitation between psychological and supernatural causes for events *or*

between inherited and self-determined foundations of identity *or* between feeling controlled by our pasts and asserting our capacities to alter ourselves decisively in the present: all these still-active antinomies of modern existence are what the Gothic is fundamentally generated to articulate *and* to obscure.

Over one hundred years after Stoker's *Dracula*, of course, the kinds of tendencies we are torn between have changed somewhat, as the more recent Gothic certainly shows. We both want to transcend, even forget, and want to throw ourselves fully into the past (or is it fully past?) condition of slavery and racism that haunts the history of America in William Faulkner's *Absalom, Absalom!* (1936) and Toni Morrison's *Beloved* (1987). We want to preserve childhood innocence and see it as really filled with dark drives to be conquered and controlled in Stephen King's *The Shining* (1977) and Daniel Mann's *Willard* (1982) as well as *The Exorcist* and its "prequels" and sequels on film. We paranoiacally want to find evidence of old conspiracies that explain our current confusions of values and see them as but the imaginings of diseased nostalgic minds in the quite Gothic *X-Files* television series (1993-2002) or the four *Alien* films (1979-97) full of Gothic echoes. Still, the Gothic, as the accounts and excerpts in these volumes will reveal in fuller detail, remains one of the key ways we come to terms, while also avoiding direct confrontation, with the betwixt-and-between, regressive-progressive, seemingly predetermined-hopefully *un*determined nature of modern life. The Gothic is complex and tangled in its proliferations, but fairly simple in its aims: it allows us to play with our inexplicable and haunted modern lives in some fictional safety while concurrently helping us give shape and form to the conflicted beings we really are. I therefore invite our readers to enjoy and ponder the following descents into the Gothic maelstrom of pleasure and fear that reveals so much about modern Western existence.

—*Jerrold E. Hogle, Ph.D.*
University of Arizona

The Gale Critical Companion Collection

In response to a growing demand for relevant criticism and interpretation of perennial topics and important literary movements throughout history, the Gale Critical Companion Collection (GCCC) was designed to meet the research needs of upper high school and undergraduate students. Each edition of GCCC focuses on a different literary movement or topic of broad interest to students of literature, history, multicultural studies, humanities, foreign language studies, and other subject areas. Topics covered are based on feedback from a standing advisory board consisting of reference librarians and subject specialists from public, academic, and school library systems.

The GCCC is designed to complement Gale's existing Literary Criticism Series (LCS), which includes such award-winning and distinguished titles as *Nineteenth-Century Literature Criticism* (*NCLC*), *Twentieth-Century Literary Criticism* (*TCLC*), and *Contemporary Literary Criticism* (*CLC*). Like the LCS titles, the GCCC editions provide selected reprinted essays that offer an inclusive range of critical and scholarly response to authors and topics widely studied in high school and undergraduate classes; however, the GCCC also includes primary source documents, chronologies, sidebars, supplemental photographs, and other material not included in the LCS products. The graphic and supplemental material is designed to extend the usefulness of the critical essays and provide students with historical and cultural context on a topic or author's work. GCCC titles will benefit larger institutions with ongoing subscriptions to Gale's LCS products as well as smaller libraries and school systems with less extensive reference collections. Each edition of the GCCC is created as a stand-alone set providing a wealth of information on the topic or movement. Importantly, the overlap between the GCCC and LCS titles is 15% or less, ensuring that LCS subscribers will not duplicate resources in their collection.

Editions within the GCCC are either single-volume or multi-volume sets, depending on the nature and scope of the topic being covered. Topic entries and author entries are treated separately, with entries on related topics appearing first, followed by author entries in an A-Z arrangement. Each volume is approximately 500 pages in length and includes approximately 50 images and sidebar graphics. These sidebars include summaries of important historical events, newspaper clippings, brief biographies of important figures, complete poems or passages of fiction written by the author, descriptions of events in the related arts (music, visual arts, and dance), and so on.

The reprinted essays in each GCCC edition explicate the major themes and literary techniques of the authors and literary works. It is important to note that approximately 85% of the essays reprinted in GCCC editions are full-text, meaning that they are reprinted in their entirety, including footnotes and lists of abbreviations. Essays are selected based on their coverage of the seminal works and themes of an author, and based on the importance of those essays to an appreciation of the author's contribution to the movement and to literature in general. Gale's editors select those essays of most value to upper high school and undergraduate students, avoiding narrow and highly pedantic interpretations of individual works or of an author's canon.

Scope of Gothic Literature

Gothic Literature, the fourth set in the Gale Critical Companion Collection, consists of three volumes. Each volume includes a detailed table of contents, a foreword on the subject of Gothic literature written by noted scholar Jerrold E. Hogle, and a descriptive chronology of key events throughout the history of the genre. The main body of volume 1 consists of entries on five topics relevent to Gothic literature and art, including 1) Gothic Literature: An Overview; 2) Society, Culture, and the Gothic; 3) Gothic Themes, Settings, and Figures; 4) Performing Arts and The Gothic; and 5) Visual Arts and the Gothic. Volumes 2 and 3 include entries on thirty-seven authors and literary figures associated with the genre, including such notables as Matthew Gregory Lewis, Stephen King, Edgar Allan Poe, Ann Radcliffe, Mary Wollstonecraft Shelley, and Bram Stoker, as well as entries on individuals who have garnered less attention, but whose contributions to the genre are noteworthy, such as Joanna Baillie, Daphne du Maurier, Washington Irving, Edith Wharton, and Oscar Wilde.

Organization of Gothic Literature

A *Gothic Literature* topic entry consists of the following elements:

- The **Introduction** defines the subject of the entry and provides social and historical information important to understanding the criticism.

- The list of **Representative Works** identifies writings and works by authors and figures associated with the subject. The list is divided into alphabetical sections by name; works listed under each name appear in chronological order. The genre and publication date of each work is given. Unless otherwise indicated, plays are dated by first performance, not first publication.

- Entries generally begin with a section of **Primary Sources,** which includes essays, speeches, social history, newspaper accounts and other materials that were produced during the time covered.

- Reprinted **Criticism** in topic entries is arranged thematically. Topic entries commonly begin with general surveys of the subject or essays providing historical or background information, followed by essays that develop particular aspects of the topic. For example, the Gothic Themes, Settings, and Figures entry in volume 1 of *Gothic Literature* begins with a section providing primary source material that demonstrates gothic themes, settings, and figures. This is followed by a section providing topic overviews, and three other sections: Haunted Dwellings and the Supernatural; Psychology and the Gothic; and Vampires. Each section has a separate title heading and is identified with a page number in the table of contents. The critic's name and the date of composition or publication of the critical work are given at the beginning of each piece of criticism. Unsigned criticism is preceded by the title of the source in which it appeared. Footnotes are reprinted at the end of each essay or excerpt. In the case of excerpted criticism, only those footnotes that pertain to the excerpted texts are included.

- A complete **Bibliographical Citation** of the original essay or book precedes each piece of criticism.

- Critical essays are prefaced by brief **Annotations** explicating each piece. Unless the descriptor "excerpt" is used in the annotation, the essay is being reprinted in its entirety.

- An annotated bibliography of **Further Reading** appears at the end of each entry and suggests resources for additional study. In some cases, significant essays for which the editors could not obtain reprint rights are included here.

A *Gothic Literature* author entry consists of the following elements:

- The **Author Heading** cites the name under which the author most commonly wrote, followed by birth and death dates. Also located here are any name variations under which an author wrote. If the author wrote consistently under a pseudonym, the pseudonym will be listed in the author heading and the author's actual name given in parenthesis on the first line of the biographical and critical information. Uncertain birth or death dates are indicated by question marks.

- A *Portrait of the Author* is included when available.

- The *Introduction* contains background information that introduces the reader to the author that is the subject of the entry.

- The list of *Principal Works* is ordered chronologically by date of first publication and lists the most important works by the author. The genre and publication date of each work is given. Unless otherwise indicated, plays are dated by first performance, not first publication.

- Author entries are arranged into three sections: *Primary Sources, General Commentary,* and *Title Commentary.* The Primary Sources section includes letters, poems, short stories, journal entries, and essays written by the featured author. General Commentary includes overviews of the author's career and general studies; Title Commentary includes in-depth analyses of seminal works by the author. Within the Title Commentary section, the reprinted criticism is further organized by title, then by date of publication. The critic's name and the date of composition or publication of the critical work are given at the beginning of each piece of criticism. Unsigned criticism is preceded by the title of the source in which it appeared All titles by the author featured in the text are printed in boldface type. However, not all boldfaced titles are included in the author and subject indexes; only substantial discussions of works are indexed. Footnotes are reprinted at the end of each essay or excerpt. In the case of excerpted criticism, only those footnotes that pertain to the excerpted texts are included.

- A complete *Bibliographical Citation* of the original essay or book precedes each piece of criticism.

- Critical essays are prefaced by brief *Annotations* explicating each piece. Unless the descriptor "excerpt" is used in the annotation, the essay is being reprinted in its entirety.

- An annotated bibliography of *Further Reading* appears at the end of each entry and suggests resources for additional study. In some cases, significant essays for which the editors could not obtain reprint rights are included here. A list of *Other Sources from Thomson Gale* follows the Further Reading section and provides references to other biographical and critical sources on the author in series published by Gale.

Indexes

The *Author Index* lists all of the authors featured in the *Gothic Literature* set, with references to the main author entries in volumes 2 and 3 as well as commentary on the featured author in other author entries and in the topic volumes. Page references to substantial discussions of the authors appear in boldface. Authors featured in sidebars are indexed as well. The Author Index also includes birth and death dates and cross references between pseudonyms and actual names, and cross references to other Gale series in which the authors have appeared. A complete list of these sources is found facing the first page of the Author Index.

The *Title Index* alphabetically lists the titles of works written by the authors featured in volumes 2 and 3 and provides page numbers or page ranges where commentary on these titles can be found. Page references to substantial discussions of the titles appear in boldface. English translations of foreign titles and variations of titles are cross-referenced to the title under which a work was originally published. Titles of novels, plays, nonfiction books, films, and poetry, short story, or essay collections are printed in italics, while individual poems, short stories, and essays are printed in roman type within quotation marks.

The *Subject Index* includes the authors and titles that appear in the Author Index and the Title Index as well as the names of other authors and figures that are discussed in the set. The Subject Index also lists hundreds of literary terms and topics covered in the criticism. The index provides page numbers or page ranges where subjects are discussed and is fully cross referenced.

Citing Gothic Literature

When writing papers, students who quote directly from the *GL* set may use the following general format to footnote reprinted criticism. The first example pertains to material drawn from periodicals, the second to material reprinted from books.

Markley, A. A. "The Godwinian Confessional Narrative and Psychological Terror in *Arthur Gordon Pym." The Edgar Allan Poe Review* 4, no. 1 (spring 2003): 4-16; reprinted in *Gothic Literature: A Gale Critical Companion,* vol. 3, ed. Jessica Bomarito (Farmington Hills, Mich.: Thomson Gale, 2006), 29-42.

Mishra, Vijay. "Theorizing the (Gothic) Sublime," in *The Gothic Sublime* (Albany: State University of New York Press, 1994), 19-43; reprinted in *Gothic Literature: A Gale Critical Companion,* vol. 1, ed. Jessica Bomarito (Farmington Hills, Mich.: Thomson Gale, 2006), 211-17.

Gothic Literature *Advisory Board*

The members of the *Gothic Literature* Advisory Board—reference librarians and subject specialists from public, academic, and school library systems—offered a variety of informed perspectives on both the presentation and content of the *Gothic Literature* set. Advisory board members assessed and defined such quality issues as the relevance, currency, and usefulness of the author coverage, critical content, and topics included in our product; evaluated the layout, presentation, and general quality of our product; provided feedback on the criteria used for selecting authors and topics covered in our product; identified any gaps in our coverage of authors or topics, recommending authors or topics for inclusion; and analyzed the appropriateness of our content and presentation for various user audiences, such as high school students, undergraduates, graduate students, librarians, and educators. We wish to thank the advisors for their advice during the development of *Gothic Literature*

Suggestions are Welcome

Readers who wish to suggest new features, topics, or authors to appear in future volumes of the Gale Critical Companion Collection, or who have other suggestions or comments are cordially invited to call, write, or fax the Product Manager.

Product Manager, Gale Critical Companion
　　Collection
Thomson Gale
27500 Drake Road
Farmington Hills, MI 48331-3535
1-800-347-4253 (GALE)
Fax: 248-699-8054

The editors wish to thank the copyright holders of the excerpted criticism included in this volume and the permissions managers of many book and magazine publishing companies for assisting us in securing reproduction rights. We are also grateful to the staffs of the Detroit Public Library, the Library of Congress, the University of Detroit Mercy Library, Wayne State University Purdy/ Kresge Library Complex, and the University of Michigan Libraries for making their resources available to us. Following is a list of the copyright holders who have granted us permission to reproduce material in this edition of *Gothic Literature*. Every effort has been made to trace copyright, but if omissions have been made, please let us know.

Copyrighted material in Gothic Literature *was reproduced from the following periodicals:*

Americana: The Journal of American Popular Culture (1900-present), v. 2, spring, 2003. Copyright © 2003 Americana: The Institute for the Study of American Popular Culture. Reproduced by permission.—*American Transcendental Quarterly*, v. 9, March 1, 1995; v. 1, 2001. Copyright © 1995, 2001 by The University of Rhode Island. Both reproduced by permission.—*Arizona Quarterly*, v. 34, 1978 for "The Gothic Formula of 'Bartleby'" by Steven T. Ryan. Copyright © 1978 by Arizona Board of Regents, The University of Arizona, Tucson, AZ. Reproduced by permission of the publisher and author.—*Bucknell Review*, v. XII, May, 1964. Reproduced by permission.—*College English*, v. 27, March 1, 1966 for "Dr. Jekyll and the Emergence of Mr. Hyde" by Masao Miyoshi. Republished in *The Divided Self: A Perspective on the Literature of the Victorians*, New York University Press, 1969, University of London Press, 1969. Copyright © 1966 by the National Council of Teachers of English. Reproduced by permission of the publisher and author.—*Comparative Literature Studies*, v. 24, 1987. Copyright © 1987 by The Pennsylvania State University. Reproduced by permission of the publisher.—*Costerus*, v. I, 1972. Copyright © Editions Rodopi B.V. Reproduced by permission.—*Critical Survey*, v. 15, September, 2003. Copyright © 2003 by Critical Survey. Republished with permission of Critical Survey, conveyed through Copyright Clearance Center, Inc.—*Dalhousie Review*, v. 47, summer, 1967 for "Terror Made Relevant: James's Ghost Stories" by Raymond Thorberg. Reproduced by permission of the publisher and author.—*Deutsche Vierteljahrsschrift für Literaturwissenschaft und Geistesgeschichte*, March 1, 2001 for "The Gothic IMAGINARY: Goethe in Strasbourg" by Kenneth S. Calhoon. Reproduced by permission of the author.—*Dickens Quarterly*, September 1, 1989; v. 16, September 1, 1999. Copyright © 1989, 1999 by the Dickens Society. Both reproduced by permission.—*Dickens Studies Newsletter*, v. VI, September 1, 1975. Copyright © by the Dickens Society. Reproduced by permission.—*Dickensian*, September 1, 1977 for "The Fall of the House of Clennam: Gothic Conventions in Little Dorrit" by

David Jarrett. Reproduced by permission of the author.—*The Edgar Allan Poe Review,* v. IV, spring, 2003 for "The Godwinian Confessional Narrative and Psychological Terror in Arthur Gordon Pym" by A.A. Markley. Copyright © 2003 The Pennsylvania State University. Reproduced by permission of the publisher and author.—*Eighteenth-Century Fiction,* v. 15, January 1, 2003. Copyright © 2003 Eighteenth-Century Fiction, McMaster University. Reproduced by permission.—*ELH,* v. 48, autumn, 1981; v. 59, spring, 1992; v. 70, winter, 2003. Copyright © 1981, 1992, 2003 The Johns Hopkins University Press. All reproduced by permission.—*ESQ: A Journal of the American Renaissance,* v. 18, 1972 for "Poe and the Gothic Tradition" by Maurice Lévy. Translated by Richard Henry Haswell. Reproduced by permission of the publisher and the translator.—*European Romantic Review,* v. 13, June 1, 2002 for "Interracial Sexual Desire in Charlotte Dacre's Zofloya" by Anne K. Mellor. Copyright © 2002 Taylor & Francis Ltd. Reproduced by permission of the publisher and author. http://www.tandf.co.uk/journals—*Faulkner Journal,* v. II, fall, 1986. Copyright © 1987 by Ohio Northern University. Reproduced by permission.—*German Life and Letters,* v. XVIII, 1964-1965. Copyright © 1964-1965 Basil Blackwell Ltd. Reproduced by permission of Blackwell Publishers.—*Gothic. New Series,* v. I, 1986; 1987; v. II, 1987. Copyright © 1986, 1987 by Gary William Crawford. All reproduced by permission of the author.—*Journal of Evolutionary Psychology,* v. X, August 1, 1989. Copyright © 1989 by the Institute for Evolutionary Psychology. Reproduced by permission.—*Journal of Popular Culture,* v. 13, 1979; v. 26, winter, 1992; v. 30, spring, 1997. Copyright © 1979, 1992, 1997 Basil Blackwell Ltd. All reproduced by permission of Blackwell Publishers.—*Literature/Film Quarterly,* v. 21, 1993. Copyright © 1993 Salisbury State College. Reproduced by permission.—*Malahat Review,* 1977 for "Atwood Gothic" by Eli Mandel. Copyright © The Malahat Review, 1977. All rights reserved. Reproduced by permission of the Literary Estate of the author.—*Mississippi Quarterly,* v. XLII, summer, 1989. Copyright © 1989 by Mississippi State University. Reproduced by permission.—*Modern Fiction Studies,* v. XVII, summer, 1971; v. 46, fall, 2000. Copyright © 1971, 2000 The Johns Hopkins University Press. Both reproduced by permission.—*Mosaic,* v. 35, 2002; v. 35, March 1, 2002. Copyright © Mosaic 2002. All acknowledgment of previous publication is herewith made.—*Narrative,* v. 12, January 1, 2004. Copyright © 2004 by the Ohio State University. Reproduced by permission.—*The Nation and The Athenaeum,* v. XXXIII, May 26, 1923. Copyright 1923 New Statesman, Ltd. Reproduced by permission.—*New York Times Book Review,* March 8, 1953 for "The Macabre and the Unexpected" by John Barkham. Copyright 1953, renewed 1981 by The New York Times Company. Reproduced by permission of the Literary Estate of John Barkham.—*Papers on Language and Literature,* v. 20, winter, 1984; v. 37, winter, 2001. Copyright © 1984, 2001 by The Board of Trustees, Southern Illinois University at Edwardsville. Both reproduced by permission.—*Princeton University Library Chronicle,* v. XLIV, spring, 1983 for "A Story Replete with Horror" by Williston R. Benedict. Copyright © 1983 by Princeton University Library. Reproduced by permission of the author.—*Prism(s): Essays in Romanticism,* v. 9, 2001. Copyright © 2001 by the American Conference on Romanticism. Reproduced by permission.—*Review of Contemporary Fiction,* fall, 1994. Copyright © 1994 The Review of Contemporary Fiction. Reproduced by permission.—*Review of English Studies,* v. XIX, 1968. Reproduced by permission of the publisher.—*The Saturday Review of Literature,* v. XVIII, September 24, 1938 for "Sinister House," by Basil Davenport. Copyright © 1938, renewed 1966 Saturday Review Magazine, © 1979 General Media International, Inc. Reproduced by permission of the publisher.—*Studies in American Fiction,* v. 7, spring, 1979. Copyright © 1979 Northeastern University. Reproduced by permission.—*Studies in English Literature 1500-1900,* v. 39, autumn, 1999. Copyright © 1999 The Johns Hopkins University Press. Reproduced by permission.—*Studies in the Literary Imagination,* v. VII, spring, 1974. Copyright © 1974 Department of English, Georgia State University. Reproduced by permission.—*Studies in the Novel,* v. IX, summer, 1977. Copyright © 1977 by North Texas State University. Reproduced by permission.—*Studies in Romanticism,* v. 40, spring, 2001. Copyright 2001 by the Trustees of Boston University. Reproduced by permission.—*Studies in Scottish Literature,* v. XXVIII, 1993. Copyright © G. Ross Roy 1993. Reproduced by permission of the editor.—*Studies in Short Fiction,* v. 21, fall, 1984. Copyright © 1984 by Studies in Short Fiction. Reproduced by permission.—*Studies in Weird Fiction,* spring, 1990; winter, 1994; v. 24, winter, 1999. Copyright © 1990, 1994, 1999 Necronomicon Press. All reproduced by permission of the author.—*Studies on Voltaire and the Eighteenth Century, Transactions of the Eighth International Congress on the Enlightenment III,* v. 305, 1992 for "The Gothic Caleb Williams" by Betty Rizzo. Copyright © 1992 University of Oxford. Reproduced by permission of the publisher and author.—*Victorian Newsletter,* fall, 2002 for "Who Is Heathcliff? The Shadow Knows" by Marilyn Hume. Reproduced by permission of the publisher and author.—*West Virginia University Philological Papers*, v. 42-43, 1997-1998. Reproduced by permission.—*Wordsworth Circle*, v. 31, summer, 2000; v. 34, spring, 2003. Copyright © 2000, 2003 Marilyn Gaull. Both reproduced by permission of the editor.

Copyrighted material in Gothic Literature *was reproduced from the following books:*

Andriano, Joseph. From *Our Ladies of Darkness: Feminine Daemonology in Male Gothic Fiction.* The Pennsylvania State University Press, 1993. Copyright © 1993 by The Pennsylvania State University. Reproduced by permission of the publisher.—Atwood, Margaret. From *The Animals in That Country.* Atlantic-Little Brown Books, 1969. Copyright © 1968 by Oxford University Press (Canadian Branch). All rights reserved. Reproduced by permission of Houghton Mifflin Company, in Canada by Oxford University Press.—Auerbach, Nina. From *Our Vampires, Ourselves.* University of Chicago Press, 1995. Copyright © 1995 by The University of Chicago. All rights reserved. Reproduced by permission of the publisher and the author.—Baldick, Chris. From an Introduction to *Melmoth the Wanderer.* Edited by Douglas Grant. Oxford University Press, 1989. © Oxford University Press 1968, Introduction and Select Biography © Chris Beldick 1989. Reproduced by permission of Oxford University Press.—Bayer-Berenbaum, Linda. From *The Gothic Imagination: Expansion in Gothic Literature and Art.* Fairleigh Dickinson University Press, 1982. Copyright © 1982 by Associated University Presses, Inc. Reproduced by permission.—Bell, Michael Davitt. From *The Development of American Romance: The Sacrifice of Relation.* The University of Chicago Press, 1980. Copyright © 1980 by The University of Chicago. All rights reserved. Reproduced by permission.—Bleiler, E. F. From "Introduction: William Beckford and *Vathek,*" in *Three Gothic Novels:* **The Castle of Otranto, Vathek, The Vampyre.** Edited by E.F. Bleiler. Dover Publications, 1966. Copyright © 1966 by Dover Publications, Inc. Reproduced by permission.—Botting, Fred. From *Gothic.* Routledge, 1996. Copyright © 1996 Fred Botting. Reproduced by permission of the publisher and author.—Botting, Fred. From "Reflections of Excess: Frankenstein, the French Revolution, and Monstrosity," in *Reflections of Excess: Frankenstein, the French Revolution and Monstrosity.* Edited by Allison Yarrington and Kelvin Everest. Routledge, 1993. Reproduced by permission of Taylor & Francis, the editor, and author.—Botting, Fred. From *Gothic.* Routledge, 1996. Copyright © 1996 by Fred Botting. All rights reserved. Reproduced by permission of the pub-

lisher and the author.—Brantly, Susan C. From *Understanding Isak Dinesen.* University of South Carolina Press, 2002. Copyright © 2002 University of South Carolina Press. Reproduced by permission.—Brennan, Matthew C. From *The Gothic Psyche: Disintegration and Growth in Nineteenth-Century English Literature.* Camden House, 1997. Copyright © 1997 by the Editor and Contributors. All rights reserved. Reproduced by permission.—Brown, Jane K. and Marshall Brown. From "Faust and the Gothic Novel," in *Interpreting Goethe's Faust Today.* Edited by Jane K. Brown, Meredith Lee, and Thomas P. Saine. Camden House, 1994. Copyright © 1994 by Camden House, Inc. Reproduced by permission.—Bulwer-Lytton, Edward George. From "Glenallan," in *Gothic Tales of Terror. Volume One: Classic Horror Stories from Great Britain.* Taplinger Publishing Company, Inc., 1972. Copyright © 1972 selection and original material by Peter Haining. Reproduced by permission of the editor.—Burns, Sarah. From *Painting the Dark Side: Art and the Gothic Imagination in Nineteenth-Century America.* University of California Press, 2004. Copyright © 2004 by The Regents of the University of California. Reproduced by permission.—Casebeer, Edwin F. From "Stephen King's Canon: The Art of Balance," in *A Dark Night's Dreaming: Contemporary American Horror Fiction.* Edited by Tony Magistrale and Michael A. Morrison. University of South Carolina Press, 1996. Copyright © 1996 by the University of South Carolina. Reproduced by permission.—Clery, E. J. From "The Politics of the Gothic Heroine in the 1790s," in *Reviewing Romanticism.* Edited by Philip W. Martin and Robin Jarvis. MacMillan Academic and Professional Ltd., 1992. Editorial matter and selection Copyright © Philip W. Martin and Robin Jarvis, 1992. Text Copyrights © Macmillan Academic and Professional Ltd, 1992. Reproduced with permission of Palgrave Macmillan.—Clery, E. J. From *Women's Gothic: From Clara Reeve to Mary Shelley.* Northcote House Publishers, Ltd., 2000, 2004. Copyright © 2000 and 2004 by E. J. Clery. Reproduced by permission.—Clery, Emma. From "Against Gothic," in *Gothick Origins and Innovations.* Edited by Allan Lloyd Smith and Victor Sage. Rodopi, 1994. Copyright © Editions Rodopi B.V. Reproduced by permission.—Conger, Syndy M. From "An Analysis of *The Monk* and Its German Sources," in *Matthew G. Lewis, Charles Robert Maturin and the Germans: An Interpretive Study of the Influence of German Literature on Two Gothic Novels.* Edited by Dr. James Hogg. Institut Fur Englische Sprache Und Literatur, 1977. Copyright © 1976 by Syndy M. Conger. Reproduced by permission.—Conger, Syndy McMillen. From "The Reconstruction of the Gothic Feminine

Ideal in Emily Brontë's *Wuthering Heights,"* in *The Female Gothic.* Edited by Juliann E. Fleenor. Eden Press, 1983. Copyright © 1983 Eden Press, Inc. Reproduced by permission of the author.—Davenport-Hines, Richard. From *Gothic.* North Point Press, 1998. Copyright © 1998 by Richard Davenport-Hines. Reprinted by permission of North Point Press, a division of Farrar, Straus and Giroux LLC. In the United Kingdom, Canada and the British Commonwealth by the author.—Dinesen, Isak. From "The Monkey," in *Seven Gothic Tales.* Harrison Smith and Robert Haas, Inc., 1934; The Modern Library 1939. Copyright © 1934 by Harrison Smith and Robert Haas, Inc. Renewed 1961 by Isak Dinesen. Reproduced by permission of the Rungstedlund Foundation. In the United States by Random House, Inc.—du Maurier, Daphne. From *Rebecca.* Doubleday & Company, Inc., 1938. Copyright 1938 Doubleday, Doran and Company, Inc. Renewed 1965 by Daphne du Maurier Browning. Reproduced with permission of Curtis Brown Ltd., London on behalf of The Chichester Partnership.—Duthie, Peter. From *Plays on the Passions.* Broadview Press, Ltd., 2001. Copyright © 2001 Peter Duthie. All rights reserved. Reproduced by permission.—Faulkner, William. From "A Rose for Emily," in *Collected Stories of William Faulkner.* Vintage International, 1995. Copyright 1930, renewed 1958 by William Faulkner. Used by permission of Random House, Inc. In the United Kingdom by the Literary Estate of William Faulkner.—Fedorko, Kathy A. From *Gender and the Gothic in the Fiction of Edith Wharton.* The University of Alabama Press, 1995. Copyright © 1995 The University of Alabama Press. All rights reserved. Reproduced by permission.—Fiedler, Leslie. From *Love and Death in the American Novel. Revised edition.* Stein and Day, 1966. Reproduced by permission of the Estate of Leslie Fiedler.—Fisher, IV, Benjamin F. From "Gothic Possibilities in *Moby-Dick,"* in *Gothick Origins and Innovations.* Edited by Allan Lloyd Smith and Victor Sage. Rodopi, 1994. Copyright © Editions Rodopi B.V. Reproduced by permission.—Frank, Frederick S. From "The Gothic *Vathek*: The Problem of Genre Resolved," in *AMS Studies in Eighteenth Century: Vathek and the Escape from Time: Bicentenary Revaluations.* Edited by Kenneth W. Graham. AMS, 1990. Copyright © 1990 by AMS Press, Inc. Reproduced by permission.—Freud, Sigmund. From *The Uncanny.* Translated by David McLintock. Penguin, 2003. Translation and editorial matter Copyright © 2003 by David McLintock. Reproduced by permission of Penguin Books, Ltd. In the United States and the Philippines by the Literary Estate of David McLintock.—Frisch, Shelley L. From "Poetics of the Uncanny: E. T. A. Hoffmann's 'Sand-

man,'" in *The Scope of the Fantastic: Theory, Technique, Major Authors.* Edited by Robert A. Collins and Howard D. Pearce. Greenwood Press, 1985. Copyright © 1985 by The Thomas Burnett Swann Fund. All rights reserved. Reproduced by permission of Greenwood Publishing Group, Inc., Westport, CT.—Gamer, Michael. From an Introduction to *The Castle of Otranto.* Edited, with an Introduction and Notes by Michael Gamer. Penguin Books, 2001. Editorial matter copyright © Michael Gamer, 2001. Reproduced by permission of the author.—Geary, Robert F. From "Carmilla and the Gothic Legacy: Victorian Transformations of Supernatural Horror," in *The Blood Is the Life: Vampires in Literature.* Edited by Leonard G. Heldreth and Mary Pharr. Bowling Green State University Popular Press, 1999. Copyright © 1999 Bowling Green State University Press. Reproduced by permission.—Goddu, Teresa A. From *Gothic America: Narrative, History, and the Nation.* Columbia University Press, 1997. Copyright © 1997 Columbia University Press. Reprinted with permission of the publisher.—Goethe, Johann Wolfgang von. From *Faust: Part One.* Translated by David Luke. Oxford University Press, 1987. Copyright © 1987 by Oxford University Press. Reproduced by permission of Oxford University Press.—Graham, Kenneth W. From "Emily's Demon-Lover: The Gothic Revolution and *The Mysteries of Udolpho,"* in *Gothic Fictions: Prohibition/Transgression.* Edited by Kenneth W. Graham. AMS Press, 1989. Copyright © 1989 by AMS Press, Inc. Reproduced by permission.—Griffith, Clark. From "Poe and the Gothic," in *Papers on Poe: Essays in Honor of John Ward Ostrom.* Edited by Richard P. Veler. Chantry Music Press, Inc., 1972. Copyright © 1972 by Chantry Music Press, Inc. Reproduced by permission of the Literary Estate of Clark Griffith.—Gross, Louis S. From *Redefining the American Gothic: From* Wieland *to* Day of the Dead. UMI Research Press, 1989. Copyright © 1989 Louis Samuel Gross. All rights reserved. Reproduced by permission of the author.—Hannaham, James. From "'Bela Lugosi's Dead and I Don't Feel So Good Either': Goth and the Glorification of Suffering in Rock Music," in *Gothic: Transmutations of Horror in Late Twentieth Century Art.* Edited by Christoph Grunenberg. MIT Press, 1997. Copyright © 1997 The Institute of Contemporary Art, Boston. Reproduced by permission of The MIT Press, Cambridge, MA.—Haslam, Richard. From "Maturin and the 'Calvinist Sublime,'" in *Gothick Origins and Innovations.* Edited by Allan Lloyd Smith and Victor Sage. Rodopi, 1994. Copyright © Editions Rodopi B.V. Reproduced by permission.—Heilman, Robert B. From "Charlotte Brontë's 'New' Gothic," in *From Jane Austen to Joseph Conrad: Essays

Collected in Memory of James T. Hillhouse.
Edited by Robert C. Rathburn and Martin Stein-
mann, Jr. University of Minnesota Press, 1958.
Copyright © 1958 by the University of Minnesota.
Renewed 1986 by Robert Charles Rathburn and
Martin Steinmann, Jr. All rights reserved. Repro-
duced by permission.—Heller, Tamar. From *Dead
Secrets: Wilkie Collins and the Female Gothic.*
Yale University Press, 1992. Copyright © 1992 by
Yale University. All rights reserved. Reproduced by
permission.—Hoeveler, Diane Long. From "Mary
Shelley and Gothic Feminism: The Case of 'The
Mortal Immortal,'" in *Iconoclastic Departures:
Mary Shelley after Frankenstein: Essays in Honor
of the Bicentenary of Mary Shelley's Birth.* Edited
by Syndy M. Conger, Frederick S. Frank, and
Gregory O'Dea. Fairleigh Dickinson University
Press, 1997. Copyright © 1997 by Associated
University Presses, Inc. Reproduced by permis-
sion.—Hoffmann, E. T. A. From an Introduction
to *The Best Tales of Hoffmann.* Edited by E. F.
Bleiler. Dover Publications, Inc., 1967. Copyright
© 1967 by Dover Publications, Inc. All rights
reserved. Reproduced by permission.—Hoffmann,
E. T. A. From "The Sand-Man," in *The Best Tales
of Hoffmann.* Edited and with an introduction by
E. F. Bleiler. Translated by J. T. Bealby. Dover
Publications, Inc., 1967. Copyright © 1967 by
Dover Publications, Inc. All rights reserved. Repro-
duced by permission.—Hogle, Jerrold E. From
"Stoker's Counterfeit Gothic: *Dracula* and Theatri-
cality at the Dawn of Simulation," in *Bram
Stoker: History, Psychoanalysis, and the Gothic.*
Edited by William Hughes and Andrew Smith.
MacMillan Press Ltd., 1998. Selection and edito-
rial matter Copyright © William Hughes and
Andrew Smith, 1998. Text Copyright © Macmillan
Press Ltd., 1998. Reproduced with permission of
Palgrave Macmillan.—Horner, Sue and Zlosnik,
Avril. From "Daphne du Maurier and Gothic
Signatures: Rebecca as Vamp(ire)," in *Body Mat-
ters: Feminism, Textuality, Corporeality.* Edited
by Avril Horner and Angela Keane. Manchester
University Press, Manchester, UK, 2000. Copyright
© 2000 by Manchester University Press. Reproduced by permission of the publisher and au-
thors.—Howells, Coral Ann. From *Margaret At-
wood.* Macmillan Press Ltd., 1996. Copyright ©
1996 Coral Ann Howells. All rights reserved.
Reproduced with permission of Palgrave Macmillan.—Ingebretsen, Edward J. From "Anne Rice:
Raising Holy Hell, Harlequin Style," in *The Gothic
World of Anne Rice.* Edited by Gary Hoppenstand
and Ray B. Browne. Bowling Green State University Popular Press, 1996. Copyright © 1996 by
Bowling Green State University Popular Press.
Reproduced by permission.—James, Sibyl. From
"Gothic Transformations: Isak Dinesen and the

Gothic," in *The Female Gothic.* Edited by Juliann
E. Fleenor. Eden Press, 1983. Copyright © 1983 by
Eden Press, Inc. Reproduced by permission of the
author.—Johnson, Greg. From *Joyce Carol Oates:
A Study of the Short Fiction.* Twayne Publishers,
1994. Copyright © 1994 by Twayne Publishers.
Reproduced by permission of Thomson Gale.—
Keats, John. From "A letter to Richard Woodhouse
on September 21, 1819," in *Selected Letters of
John Keats, Revised Edition.* Edited by Grant F.
Scott. Harvard University Press, 2002. Copyright
© 1958 by the President and Fellows of Harvard
College. Copyright © renewed 1986 by Herschel
C. Baker, the Executor of the author Hyder Edward
Rollins. Copyright © 2002 by the President and
Fellows of Harvard College. All rights reserved.
Reproduced by permission of Harvard University
Press.—Kerr, Elizabeth M. From "Otranto to
Yoknapatawpha: Faulkner's Gothic Heritage," in
William Faulkner's Gothic Domain. National
University Publications, Kennikat Press, 1979.
Copyright © 1979 by Kennikat Press Corp. All
rights reserved. Reproduced by permission of the
Literary Estate of the author.—King, Stephen.
From "The Modern American Horror Movie—Text
and Subtext," in *Stephen King's Danse Macabre.*
Everest House, 1982, Berkeley Books, 2001. Copy-
right © 1981 by Stephen King. All other rights
expressly reserved. Used by permission of Penguin
Group (USA) Inc., 345 Hudson Street, New York,
NY 10014. In North America with permission of
the author.—King, Stephen. From *Stephen King's
Danse Macabre.* Everest Publishing Group, 1982.
Copyright © 1981 by Stephen King. All other
rights expressly reserved. Used by permission of
Penguin Group (USA) Inc., 345 Hudson Street,
New York, NY 10014. In North American with
permission of the author.—Lamont, Claire. From
"Jane Austen's Gothic Architecture," in *Exhibited
by Candlelight: Sources and Developments in the
Gothic Tradition.* Edited by Valeria Tinkler-Villani
and Peter Davidson, with Jane Stevenson. Rodopi,
1995. Copyright © Editions Rodopi B.V. Repro-
duced by permission.—Lanone, Catherine. From
"Verging on the Gothic: Melmoth's Journey to
France," in *European Gothic: A Spirited Ex-
change, 1760-1960.* Edited by Avril Horner.
Manchester University Press, Manchester, UK,
1996. Copyright © 1996 by Manchester University
Press. Reproduced by permission of the publisher
and the author.—Lawler, Donald. From "The
Gothic Wilde," in *Rediscovering Oscar Wilde.*
Edited by C. George Sandulescu. Colin Smythe,
1994. Copyright © 1994 by The Princess Grace
Irish Library, Monaco. Reproduced by permis-
sion.—Le Tellier, Robert Ignatius. From *Sir Walter
Scott and the Gothic Novel.* Edwin Mellen Press,
1995. Copyright © 1995 The Edwin Mellen Press.

All rights reserved. Reproduced by permission.—Leatherdale, Clive. From *Dracula: The Novel and the Legend: A Study of Bram Stoker's Gothic Masterpiece.* Third Edition. Desert Island Books, 2001. Copyright © 2001 by Clive Leatherdale. Reproduced by permission.—Lougy, Robert E. From *Charles Robert Maturin.* Bucknell University Press, 1975. Copyright © 1975 by Associated University Presses, Inc. Reproduced by permission.—Mack, Douglas S. From "Aspects of the Supernatural in the Shorter Fiction of James Hogg," in *Exhibited by Candlelight: Sources and Developments in the Gothic Tradition.* Edited by Valeria Tinkler-Villani and Peter Davidson, with Jane Stevenson. Rodopi, 1995. Copyright © Editions Rodopi B.V. Reproduced by permission.—Magistrale, Tony. From "'More Demon than Man': Melville's Ahab as Gothic Villain," in *Spectrum of the Fantastic: Selected Essays from the Sixth International Conference on the Fantastic in the Arts.* Edited by Donald Palumbo. Greenwood Press, 1988. Copyright © 1988 by Donald Palumbo. Reproduced by permission of Greenwood Publishing Group, Inc., Westport, CT.—Martindale, Andrew. From *Gothic Art.* Thames and Hudson, 1967. Copyright © 1967 Thames and Hudson Ltd, London. All rights reserved. Reproduced by permission.—Maturin, Charles Robert. From "Leixlip Castle," in *Gothic Tales of Terror: Classic Horror Stories from Great Britain, Europe, and the United States, 1765-1840.* Edited by Peter Haining. Taplinger Publishing Company, Inc., 1972. Selection and original copyright © 1972 by Peter Haining. Reproduced by permission of the editor.—Miall, David S. From "The Preceptor as Fiend: Radcliffe's Psychology of the Gothic," in *Jane Austen and Mary Shelley and Their Sisters.* Edited by Laura Dabundo. University Press of America, 2000. Copyright © 2000 by University Press of America, Inc. All rights reserved. Reproduced by permission.—Mighall, Robert. From *A Geography of Victorian Gothic Fiction: Mapping History's Nightmares.* Oxford University Press, 1999. Copyright © 1999 Robert Mighall. All rights reserved. Reproduced by permission of Oxford University Press.—Milbank, Alison. From "From the Sublime to the Uncanny: Victorian Gothic and Sensation Fiction," in *Gothick Origins and Innovations.* Edited by Allan Lloyd Smith and Victor Sage. Rodopi, 1994. Copyright © Editions Rodopi B.V. Reproduced by permission.—Mishra, Vijay. From *The Gothic Sublime.* State University of New York Press, 1994. Copyright © 1994 State University of New York. All rights reserved. Reproduced by permission of the State University of New York Press.—Morrison, Toni. From *Playing in the Dark: Whiteness and the Literary Imagination.* Vintage Books, 1993. Copyright © 1992 by Toni Morrison. Reprinted by permission of International Creative Management, Inc.—Morrison, Toni. From *Beloved.* Vintage Books, 2004. Copyright © 1987, 2004 by Toni Morrison. Reprinted by permission of International Creative Management, Inc.—Neumeier, Beate. From "Postmodern Gothic: Desire and Reality in Angela Carter's Writing," in *Modern Gothic: A Reader.* Edited by Victor Sage and Allan Lloyd Smith. Manchester University Press, 1996. Copyright © 1996 by Manchester University Press. Reproduced by permission of the publisher and author.—Oates, Joyce Carol. From "Temple," from *Demon and Other Tales.* Necronomicon Press, 1996. Copyright © 1996 by The Ontario Review, Inc. Reproduced by permission of The Ontario Review, Inc.—Oates, Joyce Carol. From *The Strange Case of Dr. Jekyll and Mr. Hyde.* University of Nebraska Press, 1990. Copyright © 1990 by Pennyroyal Press, Inc. All rights reserved. Reproduced by permission of the University of Nebraska Press.—Oates, Joyce Carol. From "Afterword: Reflections on the Grotesque," in *Haunted: Tales of the Grotesque.* Dutton, 1994. Copyright © 1994 by The Ontario Review, Inc. Used by permission of Dutton, a division of Penguin Group (USA) Inc. In the United Kingdom by John Hawkins & Associates, Inc.—Polidori, John. From "The Vampyre: A Tale," in *The Vampyre and Other Tales of the Macabre.* Edited by Robert Morrison and Chris Baldick. Oxford University Press, 1997. Editorial Matter Copyright © 1997 by Robert Morrison and Chris Baldick. All rights reserved. Reproduced by permission of Oxford University Press.—Prawer, S. S. From *Caligari's Children: the Film as Tale of Terror.* Da Capo Press, 1989. Copyright © 1980 S. S. Prawer. Reproduced by permission of the author.—Punter, David. From *The Literature of Terror: A History of Gothic Fictions from 1765 to the Present Day. Vol. 2.* Longman, 1996. Copyright © 1996 Addison Wesley Longman, Ltd. All rights reserved. Reproduced by permission of Pearson Education Limited.—Punter, David. From *The Literature of Terror: A History of Gothic Fictions from 1765 to the Present Day. Vol. 2.* Longman, 1996. Copyright © 1996 Addison Wesley Longman Limited. All rights reserved. Reproduced by permission of Pearson Education Limited.—Punter, David. From "Narrative and Psychology in Gothic Fiction," in *Gothic Fictions: Prohibition/Transgression.* Edited by Kenneth W. Graham. AMS, 1989. Copyright © 1989 by AMS Press, Inc. Reproduced by permission.—Radcliffe, Ann. From "The Haunted Chamber," in *Gothic Tales of Terror, Volume One: Classic Horror Stories from Great Britain.* Edited by Peter Haining. 1972. Taplinger Publishing Company, Inc., 1972. Selection and original material copyright © Peter Haining, 1972. Reproduced by permission of the editor.—Railo, Eino. From *The Haunted Castle: A Study of the Elements of English Romanticism.* Routledge, 1927. Reproduced by permission of the publisher.—Ranger, Paul. From *Terror and Pity Reign in Every Breast: Gothic Drama in the London Patent Theatres, 1750-1820.* The Society for Theatre Research, 1991. Copyright © 1991 Paul Ranger. Reproduced by permission.—Rank, Otto. From "The Double as Immortal Self," in *Beyond Psychology.* E, Hauser, 1941. Copyright © 1941 by Estelle B. Rank. Renewed 1969 by Estelle B. Simon. Reproduced by permission of the Literary Estate of the author.—Robertson, Fiona. From *Legitimate Histories: Scott, Gothic, and the Authorities of Fiction.* Clarendon Press, 1994. Copyright © 1994 by Fiona Robertson. Reproduced by permission of Oxford University Press.—Sage, Victor. From *Le Fanu's Gothic: The Rhetoric of Darkness.* Palgrave MacMillan, 2004. Copyright © 2004 by Victor Sage. Reproduced with permission of Palgrave Macmillan.—Savoy, Eric. From "The Face of the Tenant: A Theory of American Gothic," in *American Gothic: New Interventions in a National Narrative.* Edited by Robert K. Martin and Eric Savoy. University of Iowa Press, 1998. Copyright © 1998 by the University of Iowa Press. All rights reserved. Reproduced by permission.—Senf, Carol A. From *The Vampire in Nineteenth-Century English Literature.* Bowling Green University Popular Press, 1988. Copyright © 1988 by Bowling Green State University Popular Press. Reproduced by permission.—Shelley, Percy Bysshe. From "The Assassins," in *Gothic Tales of Terror. Volume One: Classic Horror Stories from Great Britain.* Copyright © 1972 selection and original material copyright by Peter Haining. Reproduced by permission of the editor.—Shetty, Nalini V. From "Melville's Use of the Gothic Tradition," *Studies in American Literature: Essays in Honour of William Mulder.* Edited by Jagdish Chander and Narindar S. Pradhan. Oxford University Press, 1976. Copyright © Oxford University Press 1976. All rights reserved. Reproduced by permission of Oxford University Press India, New Delhi.—Showalter, Elaine. From *Sister's Choice: Tradition and Change in American Women's Writing.* Clarendon Press, 1991. Copyright © 1991 Elaine Showalter. Reproduced by permission of Oxford University Press.—Summers, Montague. From *The Gothic Quest: A History of the Gothic Novel.* The Fortune Press, 1938. Reproduced by permission.—Thomas, Ronald R. From *Dreams of Authority: Freud and the Fictions of the Unconscious.* Cornell University Press, 1990. Copyright © 1990 by Cornell University. Used by permission of the publisher, Cornell University Press.—Tillotson, Marcia. From "'A Forced Solitude': Mary Shelley and the Creation of Frankenstein's Monster," in *The Female Gothic.* Edited by Juliann E. Fleenor. Eden Press, 1983. Copyright © 1983 by Eden Press, Inc. Reproduced by permission of the Literary Estate of Marcia Tillotson.—Valente, Joseph. From *Dracula's Crypt: Bram Stoker, Irishness, and the Question of Blood.* University of Illinois Press, 2002. Copyright © 2001 by the Board of Trustees of the University of Illinois. Used with permission of the University of Illinois Press.—Vincent, Sybil Korff. From "The Mirror and the Cameo: Margaret Atwood's Comic/Gothic Novel, *Lady Oracle,*" in *The Female Gothic.* Edited by Juliann E. Fleenor. Elden Press, 1983. Copyright © 1983 Eden Press, Inc. All rights reserved. Reproduced by permission of the author.—Warfel, Harry R. From *Charles Brockden Brown: American Gothic Novelist.* 1949. University of Florida Press, 1949. Copyright © 1949 University of Florida. Renewed 1977 by Jean Dietze. All rights reserved. Reproduced by permission.—Weissberg, Liliane. From "Gothic Spaces: The Political Aspects of Toni Morrison's *Beloved,*" in *Modern Gothic: A Reader.* Edited by Victor Sage and Allan Lloyd Smith. Manchester University Press, 2004. Copyright © 2004 by Manchester University Press. Reproduced by permission of the publisher and author.—Wharton, Edith. From *The Ghost Stories of Edith Wharton.* Scribner, Simon & Schuster, 1973. Copyright © 1973 by William R. Tyler. Reproduced by permission of Scribner, an imprint of Simon & Schuster Macmillan and the Literary Estate of Edith Wharton and the Watkins/Loomis Agency.—Williams, Anne. From *Art of Darkness: A Poetics of Gothic.* University of Chicago Press, 1995. Copyright © 1995 by The University of Chicago. All rights reserved. Reproduced by permission of the publisher and the author.—Williamson, Paul. From an Introduction to *Gothic Sculpture 1140-1300.* Edited by Nikolaus Pevsner. Yale University Press, Pelican History of Art, 1995. Copyright © 1995 by Paul Williamson. Reproduced by permission.—Wisker, Gina. From "At Home All Was Blood and Feathers: The Werewolf in the Kitchen—Angela Carter and Horror," in *Creepers: British Horror and Fantasy in the Twentieth Century.* Edited by Clive Bloom. Pluto Press, 1993. Copyright © 1993 by Lumiere (Co-operative) Press Ltd. Reproduced by permission.—Wolfreys, Julian. From "'I Wants to Make Your Flesh Creep': Notes toward a Reading of the Comic-Gothic in Dickens," in *Victorian Gothic: Literary and Cultural Manifestations in the Nineteenth Century.* Edited by Ruth Robbins and Julian Wolfreys. Palgrave, 2000. Selection and editorial matter © Ruth Robbins and Julian Wolfreys, 2000. Preface and Chapter 3 © Julian Wolfreys, 2000. Chapter 10 © Ruth Robbins, 2000.

Chapters 1, 2, 4-9, 11, 12 © Palgrave Publishers Ltd, 2000. Reproduced with permission of Palgrave Macmillan.—Womack, Kenneth. From "'Withered, Wrinkled, and Loathsome of Visage': Reading the Ethics of the Soul and the Late-Victorian Gothic in *The Picture of Dorian Gray*," in **Victorian Gothic: Literary and Cultural Manifestations in the Nineteenth Century.** Edited by Ruth Robbins and Julian Wolfreys. Palgrave, 2000. Selection and editorial matter © Ruth Robbins and Julian Wolfreys, 2000. Preface and Chapter 3 © Julian Wolfreys, 2000. Chapter 10 © Ruth Robbins, 2000. Chapters 1, 2, 4-9, 11, 12 © Palgrave Publishers Ltd, 2000. Reproduced with permission of Palgrave Macmillan.—Wood, Martin J. From "New Life for an Old Tradition: Anne Rice and Vampire Literature," in **The Blood Is the Life: Vampires in Literature.** Edited by Leonard G. Heldreth and Mary Pharr. Bowling Green State University Popular Press, 1999. Copyright © 1999 Bowling Green State University Popular Press. Reproduced by permission.—Wood, Robin. From "An Introduction to the American Horror Film," in **American Nightmare: Essays on the Horror Film.** Edited by Robin Wood and Richard Lippe. Festival of Festivals, 1979. Copyright © Robin Wood, Richard Lippe, and Festival of Festivals. All rights reserved. Reproduced by permission of the publisher and the author.—Wright, Angela. From "European Disruptions of the Idealized Woman: Matthew Lewis's *The Monk* and the Marquis de Sade's *La Nouvelle Justine*," in **European Gothic: A Spirited Exchange, 1760-1960.** Edited by Avril Horner. Manchester University Press, Manchester, UK, 2002. Copyright © 2002 by Manchester University Press. Reproduced by permission of the publisher and author.

Photographs and Illustrations in Gothic Literature *were received from the following sources:*

A Description of Strawberry Hill, by Horace Walpole, frontispiece.—Abbotsford, home of Sir Walter Scott, photograph. © Bettmann/Corbis.—Ainsworth, William Harrison, photograph. © Getty Images.—Allston, Washington, photograph. The Library of Congress.—*American Gothic,* painting by Grant Wood, 1930, photograph. Photography © The Art Institute of Chicago. Reproduced by permission.—Atwood, Margaret, photograph by Christopher Felver. Copyright © Christopher Felver/Corbis.—Austen, Jane, engraving.—Baillie, Joanna, photograph. © Hulton-Deutsch/Corbis.—*Balshazzar's Feast,* painting by Washington Allston, ca. 1817-1843. © The Detroit Institute of Arts/Bridgeman Art Library.—Beckford, William, photograph. © Michael Nicholson/Corbis.—Bergman, Ingrid and Heywood Morse in the 1959 film adaptation of *Turn of the Screw* by Henry James, photograph. © Bettmann/Corbis.—Bierce, Ambrose, drawing by J. J. Newbegin, 1896.—Braddon, Mary Elizabeth, engraving. © Hulton Getty/Liaison Agency.—Brontë, Charlotte, illustration. International Portrait Gallery.—Brontë, Emily, painting by Bramwell Brontë.—Brown, Charles Brockden, print.—Bulwer-Lytton, Edward George, photograph. © Bettmann/Corbis.—Burke, Edmund, photograph. © Bettmann/Corbis.—Capote, Truman, photograph. © Hulton-Deutsch Collection/Corbis.—Carter, Angela, photograph. © Jerry Bauer. Reproduced by permission.—*Castle of Otranto,* by Horace Walpole, c. 1790, illustration.—*Castle of Wolfenbach; a German Story,* by Eliza Parsons, 1793, title page.—*Christine,* movie still, photograph. The Kobal Collection. Reproduced by permission.—Collins, William Wilkie, photograph. The Library of Congress.—Cooper, Alice, performing on the *In Concert* television show on November 24, 1972, photograph. © Bettmann/Corbis.—Dickens, Charles, photograph. Hesketh Pearson.—Dinesen, Isak, photograph. Corbis-Bettmann.—*Dr. Jekyll and Mr. Hyde,* Spencer Tracy as Dr. Jekyll, photograph. © Bettmann/Corbis.—*Dracula,* Helen Chandler, as Mina Seward, with Bela Lugosi, as Count Dracula, photograph. The Kobal Collection. Reproduced by permission.—*Dracula's Guest,* written by Bram Stoker, title page.—du Maurier, Daphne, photograph. © Time Life Pictures/Getty Images.—Faulkner, William, photograph. © Bettmann/Corbis.—*Frankenstein,* by Mary Wollstonecraft Shelley, 1831, illustration. Mary Evans Picture Library. Reproduced by permission.—*Fall of the House of Usher,* by Edgar Allan Poe, illustration. © Bettmann/Corbis.—Gargoyle of 15th Century Spanish Building, photograph. © Manuel Bellver/Corbis.—Gilman, Charlotte Perkins, c. 1890, photograph.—Godwin, William, painting by James Northcote. From *Vindication of the Rights of Women,* by William Godwin, 1802.—*Great Expectations,* by Charles Dickens, illustration. © Corbis.—Hawthorne, Nathaniel, photograph.—Hoffmann, E. T. A., photograph. Mary Evans Picture Library. Reproduced by permission.—Hogg, James, photograph. © Rischgitz/Getty Images.—Irving, Washington, photograph. The National Portrait Gallery, Smithsonian Institution.—James, Henry, photograph.—*Jane Eyre,* Orson Welles as Edward Rochester, with Joan Fontaine as Jane Eyre, photograph. The Kobal Collection. Reproduced by permission.—King, Stephen, photograph. Corbis-Bettmann.—Le Fanu, Joseph Sheridan, photograph.—*Legend of Sleepy Hollow,* by Washington Irving, illustration. © Bettmann/Corbis.—Lewis, Matthew Gregory, photograph by H. W. Pickersgill.—*Varney the Vampire; or, The Feast of Blood,* title page. © Getty

Images.—Lovecraft, H. P., photograph.—Lugosi, Bela, photograph. © Bettmann/Corbis.—Maturin, Charles Robert, photograph. © The Granger Collection, New York.—Melville, Herman, photograph. The Library of Congress.—Morrison, Toni, photograph. Copyright © Nancy Kazerman/ ZUMA/Corbis.—Nave of Basilique de Saint-Denis, June 19, 1996, photograph. © Robert Holmes/ Corbis.—*Nightmare,* painting by Henri Fuseli, 1791. Mary Evans Picture Library. Reproduced by permission.—*Nosferatu,* Max Schreck (Count Orlok) standing on deck of ship, 1922, photograph. © Bettmann/Corbis.—O'Connor, Flannery, photograph. AP/Wide World Photos.—Oates, Joyce Carol, photograph. © Nancy Kaszerman/Corbis.—Peck, Gregory, photograph. The Kobal Collection. Reproduced by permission.—Poe, Edgar Allan, photograph.—Polidori, John William, painting by F. G. Gainsford, c. 1816, photograph. © The Granger Collection, New York.—*Psycho,* Norman Bates (Anthony Perkins) approaching the motel, photograph. © Underwood and Underwood/Corbis.—Reeve, Clara, photograph. © Getty Images.—Rice, Anne, photograph. © Mitchell Gerber/Corbis.—*Roettgen Pieta,* wood carving, c. 1300, photograph. © Erich Lessing/Art Resource, NY.—Schiller, Friedrich von, engraving. The German Information Center.—Scott, Sir Walter, photograph. The Library of Congress.—Shelley, Mary Wollstonecraft, illustration.—*Son of Frankenstein,* with Boris Karloff, Basil Rathbone, and Bela Lugosi, photograph. © Bettmann/Corbis.—Stevenson, Robert Louis, engraving. The Library of Congress.—Stoker, Bram, photograph. © Hulton-Deutsch Collection/Corbis.—*The Castle Spectre,* by Matthew Gregory Lewis, illustration. Mary Evans Picture Library. Reproduced by permission.—*The Fall of the House of Usher,* directed by Roger Corman, photograph. © A.I.P./The Kobal Collection. Reproduced by permission.—*The Haunting,* 1963, movie still. © MGM/The Kobal Collection. Reproduced by permission.—*The Island of Dr. Moreau,* poster. © A.I.P./The Kobal Collection. Reproduced by permission.—*The Italian; or, The Confessional of the Black Penitents,* by Ann Radcliffe, 1797 edition, title page.—*The Mysteries of Udolpho,* frontispieces by Ann Radcliffe.—*The Narrative of Arthur Gordon Pym,* written by Edgar Allan Poe, title page. Special Collections Library, University of Michigan. Reproduced by permission.—*The Old English Baron: A Gothic Story,* by Clara Reeve, 1778, illustration.—*The Recess; or, A Tale of Other Times,* by Sophia Lee, 1786, title page.—*The Shining,* directed by Stanley Kubrick, 1980, photograph. © Warner Bros./The Kobal Collection.—*The Sicilian Romance; or, The Apparition of the Cliffs, an Opera,* by Henry Siddons, 1794, title page.—*The Table of the Seven Deadly Sins,* painting by Hieronymous Bosch, c. 1480-1490, Northern Renaissance, photograph. © Archivo Iconografico, S.A./Corbis.—*The Temptation of Ambrosio,* from Matthew Gregory Lewis's *The Monk,* illustration.—*The Woman in White,* by Wilkie Collins, title page. Special Collections Library, University of Michigan. Reproduced by permission.—*Things as They Are; or, The Adventures of Caleb Williams,* by William Godwin, title page.—*Twin Peaks,* scene from the television series by David Lynch, 1990, photograph. © Corbis Sygma.—Veidt, Conrad and Lil Dagover in the 1920 silent horror film *The Cabinet of Dr. Caligari,* photograph. © John Springer/Corbis.—von Goethe, Johann Wolfgang, photograph. © Bettmann/ Corbis.—Waddy, F., satirical caricature in "Once a Week," 1873. Mary Evans Picture Library. Reproduced by permission.—Walpole, Horace, photograph. © Bettmann/Corbis.—Wharton, Edith, 1905, photograph. The Library of Congress.—*Wieland; or, The Transformation,* by Charles Brockden Brown, Philadelphia, David McKay, Publisher, 1881, title page.—Wilde, Oscar, photograph. The Library of Congress.—*Wuthering Heights,* by Emily Brontë, movie poster, photograph. © Cinema-Photo/Corbis.

1081

- Suger of Saint Denis is born in Saint Denis, France.

1127

- Abbot Suger of Saint Denis begins redesigning the Abbey Church of Saint-Denis in France.

1151

- Abbot Suger of Saint Denis dies on 13 January in St. Denis, France.

C. 1163

- Construction of the current Cathedral of Notre Dame de Paris in France.

C. 1175

- Construction of the current Canterbury Cathedral in England.

C. 1194

- Construction of the current Cathedral of Notre Dame at Chartres (also known as Chartres Cathedral) in France.

C. 1211

- Construction of the current Cathedral of Notre Dame de Rheims (also known as Rheims Cathedral) in France.

1220

- Construction of the Cathedral of Amiens in France.
- Master Elias of Dereham begins designing the Salisbury Cathedral in England.

1245

- Construction of the current Westminster Abbey in London, England.

C. 1329

- Andrea Pisano begins his bronze sculptures for the Baptisery in Florence, Italy.

1485

- Hieronymus Bosch completes the painting *Tabletop of the Seven Deadly Sins.*

C. 1600-01

- William Shakespeare's *Hamlet* is staged.

C. 1606

- William Shakespeare's *Macbeth* is staged.

1717

- Horace Walpole is born on 24 September in London, England.

1727

■ Daniel Defoe's *An Essay on the History and Reality of Apparitions* is published.

1729

● Edmund Burke is born on 12 January in Dublin, Ireland.

● Clara Reeve is born on 23 January in Ipswich, Suffolk, England.

1742

■ Batty and Thomas Langley's *Ancient Architecture Restored and Improved* is published.

1749

● Johann Wolfgang von Goethe is born on 28 August in Frankfurt, Germany.

1750

● Sophia Lee is born in London, England.

■ Horace Walpole and Richard Bentley begin designing Strawberry Hill, Walpole's residence in Twickenham, England.

1753

■ Tobias Smollett's *The Adventures of Ferdinand Count Fathom* is published.

1756

● William Godwin is born on 3 March in Wisbeach, England.

1757

● William Blake is born on 28 November in London, England.

■ Edmund Burke's *A Philosophical Enquiry into the Origin of Our Ideas of the Sublime and Beautiful* is published.

1759

● Johann Christoph Friedrich von Schiller is born on 10 November in Marbach, Germany.

1760

● William Beckford is born on 29 September in London, England.

1762

● James Boaden is born on 23 May at White Haven in Cumberland, England.

● Joanna Baillie is born on 11 September in Bothwell, Lanarkshire, Scotland.

1764

● Ann Radcliffe is born on 9 July in London, England.

■ Horace Walpole's *The Castle of Otranto* is published.

1770

● James Hogg is born in Ettrick, Selkirkshire, Scotland.

1771

● Charles Brockden Brown is born on 17 January in Philadelphia, Pennsylvania.

● Sir Walter Scott is born on 15 August in Edinburgh, Scotland.

1772

● Samuel Taylor Coleridge is born on 21 October in Ottery St. Mary, Devonshire, England.

1773

■ John Aikin and Anna Laetitia (Aikin) Barbauld's *Miscellaneous Pieces in Prose, by J. and A. L. Aikin* is published.

1775

● Matthew Gregory Lewis is born on 9 July in London, England.

● Jane Austen is born on 16 December in Steventon, Hampshire, England.

1776

● Ernst Theodor Wilhelm (later E. T. A.) Hoffmann is born on 24 January in Königsberg, Germany.

1777

■ Clara Reeve's *The Champion of Virtue. A Gothic Story* is published.

1778

■ Clara Reeve's *The Champion of Virtue* is published as *The Old English Baron.*

1779

● Washington Allston is born on 5 November in South Carolina.

1780

● Charles Robert Maturin is born on 25 September in Dublin, Ireland.

1781

■ Henry Fuseli completes the painting *The Nightmare.*

1783

● Washington Irving is born on 3 April in New York City.

■ Sophia Lee's *The Recess; or, A Tale of Other Times* is published.

1786

■ The unauthorized translation of William Beckford's *Vathek* is published as *An Arabian Tale.*

1787

● Lewis Nockalls Cottingham is born on 24 October at Laxfield, Suffolk, England.

■ William Beckford's *Vathek* is published.

1788

● George Gordon Noel, Lord Byron is born on 22 January in London, England.

1789

■ James Cobb's *The Haunted Tower* is produced.

■ George Colman the Younger's *The Battle of Hexham* is produced.

1790

■ Johann Wolfgang von Goethe's *Faust: Ein Fragment* is published.

■ Ann Radcliffe's *A Sicilian Romance* is published.

1791

■ Ann Radcliffe's *The Romance of the Forest* is published.

1792

● Percy Bysshe Shelley is born on 4 August in Field Place, Sussex, England.

■ Mary Wollstonecraft's *A Vindication of the Rights of Woman: with Strictures on Political and Moral Subjects* is published.

1793

■ Mrs. Eliza Parsons's *Castle of Wolfenbach; A German Story* is published.

1794

■ James Boaden's *Fontainville Forest* is produced.

■ J. C. Cross's *The Apparition* is produced.

■ William Godwin's *Things As They Are; or, The Adventures of Caleb Williams* is published.

■ Ann Radcliffe's *The Mysteries of Udolpho, A Romance; Interspersed with some pieces of Poetry* is published.

■ Henry Siddons's *The Sicilian Romance; or, The Apparition of the Cliff* is produced.

1795

● John William Polidori is born on 7 September in England.

1796

■ Marquis von Grosse's *Genius (Horrid Mysteries)* is published.

■ Matthew Gregory Lewis's *The Monk: A Romance* is published.

1797

● Horace Walpole dies on 2 March in London, England.

● Edmund Burke dies on 9 July in Beaconsfield, Buckinghamshire, England.

● Mary Wollstonecraft Godwin (later Shelley) is born on 30 August in London, England.

■ Matthew Gregory Lewis's *The Castle Spectre: A Drama* is produced.

1798

- Regina Maria Roche's *Children of the Abbey* is published.

- The first volume of Joanna Baillie's *A Series of Plays: In Which it is Attempted to Delineate the Stronger Passions of the Mind—Each Passion Being the Subject of a Tragedy and a Comedy* is published.

- Charles Brockden Brown's *Wieland; or, The Transformation* is published.

1799

- Charles Brockden Brown's *Edgar Huntly; or, Memoirs of a Sleep-Walker* and the first volume of *Arthur Mervyn; or, Memoirs of the Year 1793* are published.

1800

- Washington Allston completes the painting *Tragic Figure in Chains.*

- The second volume of Charles Brockden Brown's *Arthur Mervyn; or, Memoirs of the Year 1793* is published.

1802

- The second volume of Joanna Baillie's *A Series of Plays: In Which it is Attempted to Delineate the Stronger Passions of the Mind—Each Passion Being the Subject of a Tragedy and a Comedy* is published.

1803

- Edward Bulwer-Lytton (Edward George Earle Lytton Bulwer) is born on 25 May in London, England.

- Thomas Lovell Beddoes is born on 30 June in Clifton, Shropshire, England.

- Alexander Jackson Davis is born on 24 July in New York City.

1804

- Nathaniel Hawthorne is born on 4 July in Salem, Massachusetts.

1805

- William Harrison Ainsworth is born on 4 February in Manchester, England.

- Friedrich von Schiller dies on 9 May in Weimar, Germany.

1806

- Charlotte Dacre's *Zofloya; or, The Moor* is published.

1807

- Clara Reeve dies on 3 December in Ipswich, Suffolk, England.

1808

- Johann Wolfgang von Goethe's *Faust—Der Tragödie erster Teil* (*Faust: Part One*) is published.

1809

- Edgar Allan Poe is born on 19 January in Boston, Massachusetts.

1810

- Charles Brockden Brown dies on 22 February in Philadelphia, Pennsylvania.

- Percy Bysshe Shelley's *Zastrozzi, A Romance* is published.

1811

- Percy Bysshe Shelley's *St. Irvyne; or, The Rosicrucian: A Romance* is published.

1812

- Charles Dickens is born on 7 February in Portsmouth, Hampshire, England.

- The third volume of Joanna Baillie's *A Series of Plays: In Which it is Attempted to Delineate the Stronger Passions of the Mind—Each Passion Being the Subject of a Tragedy and a Comedy* is published.

- George Gordon, Lord Byron's *Childe Harold's Pilgrimage: A Romaunt* is published.

1813

- George Gordon, Lord Byron's *The Giaour: A Fragment of a Turkish Tale* is published.

1814

- Joseph Sheridan Le Fanu is born on 28 August in Dublin, Ireland.

- Sir Walter Scott's *Waverly; or, 'Tis Sixty Years Since* is published.

1816

- Charlotte Brontë is born on 21 April in Thornton, Yorkshire, England.

- George Gordon, Lord Byron's *Childe Harold's Pilgrimage: Canto the Third* is published.

- Samuel Taylor Coleridge's *Christabel: Kubla Khan, a Vision; The Pains of Sleep* is published.

- Jane Scott's *The Old Oak Chest* is produced.

1817

- Jane Austen dies on 18 July in Winchester, Hampshire, England.

- Washington Allston begins the painting *Belshazzar's Feast*.

- George Gordon, Lord Byron's *Manfred, A Dramatic Poem* is published.

- E. T. A. Hoffmann's "Der Sandmann" ("The Sandman") is published.

1818

- Matthew Gregory Lewis dies on 16 May during a voyage across the Atlantic Ocean from Jamaica to England.

- Emily Brontë is born on 30 July in Thornton, Yorkshire, England.

- Jane Austen's *Northanger Abbey and Persuasion* is published.

- Mary Wollstonecraft Shelley's *Frankenstein; or, The Modern Prometheus* is published.

1819

- Herman Melville is born on 1 August in New York City.

- Percy Bysshe Shelley's *The Cenci* is produced.

- Washington Irving's *The Sketch Book of Geoffrey Crayon, Gent.* is published.

- John William Polidori's *The Vampyre; a Tale* is published.

1820

- John Keats's *Lamia, Isabella, The Eve of St. Agnes, and Other Poems* is published.

- Charles Robert Maturin's *Melmoth the Wanderer* is published.

1821

- John William Polidori commits suicide on 27 August in London, England.

- Thomas De Quincey's *Confessions of an English Opium Eater* is published.

1822

- E. T. A. Hoffmann dies on 25 June in Berlin, Germany.

- Percy Bysshe Shelley drowns on 8 July in the Gulf of Spezia near Lerici, Italy.

1823

- Ann Radcliffe dies on 7 February in England.

- Richard Brinsley Peake's *Presumption; or, The Fate of Frankenstein* is produced.

1824

- William Wilkie Collins is born on 8 January in London, England.

- Sophia Lee dies on 13 March in Clifton, England.

- Lord Byron dies on 19 April in Cephalonia, Greece.

- Charles Robert Maturin dies on 30 October in Dublin, Ireland.

- Catherine Gore's *The Bond, a Dramatic Poem* is produced.

- James Hogg's *The Private Memoirs and Confessions of a Justified Sinner* is published.

- Washington Irving's *Tales of a Traveller* is published.

1825

- James Fenimore Cooper's *Lionel Lincoln; or, The Leaguer of Boston* is published.

1826

- Edward Bulwer-Lytton's *Glenallan* is published.

1827

- William Blake dies on 12 August in London, England.

- Thomas Moore's *The Epicurean. A Tale* is published.

1830

● Christina Rossetti is born on 5 December in London, England.

1832

● Johann Wolfgang von Goethe dies on 22 March.

● Sir Walter Scott dies on 21 September in Abbotsford, Scotland.

▨ Architect Alexander Jackson Davis completes Glen Ellen, the Baltimore, Maryland residence of Robert Gilmor III.

1834

● Samuel Taylor Coleridge dies on 25 July in England.

1835

● James Hogg dies on 21 November in Scotland.

1836

● William Godwin dies on 7 April in London, England.

▨ Thomas Cole completes the painting *Ruined Tower*.

1837

▨ Charles Dickens's *Posthumous Papers of the Pickwick Club* is published under the pseudonym Boz.

▨ Nathaniel Hawthorne's *Twice Told Tales* is published.

1838

▨ Charles Dickens's *Oliver Twist* is published.

▨ Edgar Allan Poe's *The Narrative of Arthur Gordon Pym* is published.

1839

● James Boaden dies on 16 February in England.

1840

▨ Edgar Allan Poe's *Tales of the Grotesque and Arabesque* is published.

1842

▨ Edward Bulwer-Lytton's *Zanoni* is published.

● Ambrose Bierce is born on 24 June in Horse Cave Creek, Meigs County, Ohio.

1843

● Henry James is born on 15 April in New York City.

● Washington Allston dies on 9 July in Cambridge, Massachusetts.

▨ A. W. N. Pugin's *Apology for the Revival of Christian Architecture in England* is published.

1844

● William Beckford dies on 2 May in England.

1845

▨ Frederick Douglass's *Narrative of the Life of Frederick Douglass, an American Slave* is published.

▨ Edgar Allan Poe's *Tales by Edgar A. Poe* and *The Raven and Other Poems* are published.

1846

▨ Edward Bulwer-Lytton's *Lucretia; or, The Children of Night* is published.

▨ Fyodor Dostoevsky's *Dvoinik: Prikliucheniia gospodina Goliadkina* (*The Double: A Poem of St. Petersburg*) is published.

1847

● L. N. Cottingham dies on 13 October in London, England.

● Bram Stoker is born on 8 November in Clontarf, Ireland.

▨ Charlotte Brontë's *Jane Eyre. An Autobiography* is published under the pseudonym Currer Bell.

▨ Emily Brontë's *Wuthering Heights* is published under the pseudonym Ellis Bell.

▨ *Varney the Vampire; or, The Feast of Blood*, written by either Thomas Peckett Prest or James Malcolm Rymer, is published.

1848

● Emily Brontë dies on 19 December in Haworth, Yorkshire, England.

▨ Charles Dickens's *The Haunted Man, and The Ghost's Bargain* is published.

1849

- Thomas Lovell Beddoes commits suicide on 26 January in Basel, Switzerland.

- Edgar Allan Poe dies on 7 October in Baltimore, Maryland.

1850

- Robert Louis Stevenson is born on 13 November in Edinburgh, Scotland.

- Nathaniel Hawthorne's *The Scarlet Letter: A Romance* is published.

1851

- Mary Wollstonecraft Shelley dies on 1 February in Bournemouth, England.

- Joanna Baillie dies on 23 February in Hampstead, England.

- Nathaniel Hawthorne's *The House of the Seven Gables, a Romance* is published.

- Herman Melville's *Moby-Dick; or, The Whale* is published.

1852

- Harriet Beecher Stowe's *Uncle Tom's Cabin; or, Life among the Lowly* is published.

1853

- Charlotte Brontë's *Villette* is published under the pseudonym Currer Bell.

- Charles Dickens's *Bleak House* is published.

C. 1854

- Oscar Wilde is born on 16 October in Dublin, Ireland.

1855

- Charlotte Brontë dies on 31 March in Haworth, Yorkshire, England.

1856

- Sigismund Solomon Freud (later Sigmund Freud) is born on 6 May in Freiberg, Moravia, Czechoslovakia.

- Herman Melville's *The Piazza Tales* is published.

1857

- Wilkie Collins's *The Dead Secret* is published.

- Charles Dickens's *Little Dorrit* is published.

- G. W. M. Reynolds's *Wagner the Wehr-wolf* is published.

1859

- Washington Irving dies on 28 November in Irvington, New York.

1860

- Charlotte Perkins Gilman is born on 3 July in Hartford, Connecticut.

- Wilkie Collins's *The Woman in White* is published.

- Nathaniel Hawthorne's *The Marble Faun; or, The Romance of Monte Beni* is published.

1861

- Harriet Jacobs's *Incidents in the Life of a Slave Girl, Written by Herself* is published under the pseudonym Linda Brent.

1862

- Edith Wharton is born on 24 January in New York City.

- Edward Bulwer-Lytton's *A Strange Story* is published.

1864

- Nathaniel Hawthorne dies on 19 May in Plymouth, New Hampshire.

- Joseph Sheridan Le Fanu's *Uncle Silas: A Tale of Bartram-Haugh* is published.

1870

- Charles Dickens dies on 9 June in Rochester, Kent, England.

1872

- Joseph Sheridan Le Fanu's *In a Glass Darkly* is published.

1873

- Edward Bulwer-Lytton dies on 18 January in Torquay, Devonshire, England.

- Joseph Sheridan Le Fanu dies on 10 February in Dublin, Ireland.

1882

- William Harrison Ainsworth dies on 3 January.

- Bela Lugosi is born Béla Ferenc Dezsö Blask¢ on 20 October in Lugos, Hungary.

1885

- Karen Christentze Dinesen, who later wrote under the pseudonym Isak Dinesen, is born on 17 April near Copenhagen, Denmark.

1886

- Guy de Maupassant's "La Horla" ("The Horla") is published *Le Gil Blas.*

- Robert Louis Stevenson's *The Strange Case of Dr. Jekyll and Mr. Hyde* is published.

1887

- William Henry Pratt (later Boris Karloff) is born on 23 November in London, England.

1888

- Friedrich Wilhelm Plumpe (later F. W. Murnau) is born on 28 December in Bielefeld, Westphalia, Germany.

1889

- Wilkie Collins dies on 23 September in London, England.

1890

- Howard Phillips Lovecraft is born on 20 August in Providence, Rhode Island.

- Oscar Wilde's *The Picture of Dorian Gray* is published.

1891

- Herman Melville dies on 28 September in New York City.

- Oscar Wilde's *Lord Arthur Savile's Crime, and Other Stories* is published.

1892

- Alexander Jackson Davis dies on 14 January in West Orange, New Jersey.

- Charlotte Perkins Gilman's "The Yellow Wallpaper" is published.

1894

- Robert Louis Stevenson dies on 3 December in Apia, Samoa.

- Christina Rossetti dies on 29 December in London, England.

- Arthur Machen's *The Great God Pan and The Inmost Light* is published.

1896

- H. G. Wells's *The Island of Doctor Moreau: A Possibility* is published.

1897

- William Faulkner is born on 25 September in New Albany, Mississippi.

- Bram Stoker's *Dracula* is published.

1898

- Henry James's *The Two Magics: The Turn of the Screw, Covering End* is published.

1899

- Elizabeth Bowen is born on 7 June in Dublin, Ireland.

- Alfred Hitchcock is born on 13 August in London, England.

1900

- Oscar Wilde dies on 30 November in Paris, France.

1904

- Arthur Machen's "The Garden of Avallaunius" is published.

1906

- Algernon Blackwood's *The Empty House and Other Ghosts* is published.

1907

- Daphne du Maurier is born on 12 May in London, England.

- George Sylvester Viereck's *The House of the Vampire* is published.

1908

- *Dr. Jekyll and Mr. Hyde,* produced by the Selig Polyscope Company, is released.

1909

- *Dr. Jekyll and Mr. Hyde,* produced by the Nordisk Company, is released.

1910

- Gaston Leroux's *Le Fantôme de L'Opéra* (*The Phantom of the Opera*) is published.
- *Frankenstein,* directed by J. Searle Dawley, is released.

1911

- Edith Wharton's *Ethan Frome* is published.

1912

- Bram Stoker dies on 20 April in London, England.

1914

- Ambrose Bierce disappears c. 1 January in Mexico and is presumed dead.

1916

- Henry James dies on 28 February in London, England.

1919

- Shirley Jackson is born on 14 December in San Francisco, California.
- Sigmund Freud's "Das Unheimlich" ("The Uncanny") is published.

1920

- Ray Bradbury is born on 22 August in Waukegan, Illinois.
- *Der Golem, wie er in die Welt kam* (*The Golem: How He Came into the World,* directed by Carl Boese and Paul Wegener, is released.
- *Das Kabinett des Doktor Caligari* (*The Cabinet of Dr. Caligari*), directed by Robert Wiene, is released.

1922

- *Nosferatu, eine Symphonie des Grauens,* directed by F. W. Murnau, is released.

1924

- *Das Wachsfigurenkabinett* (*Waxworks*), directed by Paul Leni and Leo Birinsky, is released.

1925

- Edward Gorey is born on 22 February in Chicago, Illinois.
- (Mary) Flannery O'Connor is born on 25 March in Savannah, Georgia.

1927

- Algernon Blackwood's *The Dance of Death, and Other Tales* is published.

1929

- Ursula K. Le Guin is born on 21 October in Berkeley, California.

1930

- William Faulkner's *As I Lay Dying* and "A Rose for Emily" are published.

1931

- Chloe Ardelia Wofford (later Toni Morrison) is born on 18 February in Lorain, Ohio.
- F. W. Murnau dies on 11 March in Santa Barbara, California.
- *Dracula,* directed by Tod Browning and starring Bela Lugosi in the title role, is released.
- *Frankenstein,* directed by James Whale and starring Boris Karloff as the monster, is released.
- *M,* directed by Fritz Lang, is released.
- William Faulkner's *Sanctuary* is published.

1932

- *Murders in the Rue Morgue,* directed by Robert Florey, is released.
- *White Zombie,* directed by Victor Halperin, is released.
- William Faulkner's *Light in August* is published.

1933

▓ *King Kong,* directed by Merian C. Cooper, is released.

▓ *The Invisible Man,* directed by James Whale, is released.

▓ *Island of Lost Souls,* directed by Erle C. Kenton, is released.

1934

▓ Isak Dinesen's *Seven Gothic Tales* is published.

1935

● Charlotte Perkins Gilman commits suicide on 17 August in Pasadena, California.

▓ *Bride of Frankenstein,* directed by James Whale, is released.

1936

▓ Walter de la Mare's *Ghost Stories* is published.

▓ William Faulkner's *Absalom, Absalom!* is published.

▓ H. P. Lovecraft's "At the Mountains of Madness" is published.

1937

● H. P. Lovecraft dies on 15 March in Providence, Rhode Island.

● Edith Wharton dies on 11 August in St. Brice-sous-Foret, France.

▓ Edith Wharton's *Ghosts* is published.

1938

● Joyce Carol Oates is born on 16 June in Lockport, New York.

▓ Daphne du Maurier's *Rebecca* is published.

1939

● Sigmund Freud dies on 23 September in London, England.

● Margaret Atwood is born on 18 November in Ottawa, Ontario, Canada.

▓ *Son of Frankenstein,* directed by Rowland V. Lee, is released.

1940

● Angela Carter is born on 7 May in London, England.

▓ *Rebecca,* directed by Alfred Hitchcock, is released.

1941

● Howard Allen O'Brien (later Anne Rice) is born on 4 October in New Orleans, Louisiana.

1943

▓ *I Walked with a Zombie, The Leopard Man,* and *The Seventh Victim,* all produced by Val Lewton, are released.

1945

▓ *The Body Snatcher,* directed by Robert Wise, is released.

▓ Elizabeth Bowen's *The Demon Lover, and Other Stories* is published.

▓ H. P. Lovecraft's *Supernatural Horror in Literature* is published.

1947

● Stephen King is born on 21 September in Portland, Maine.

1949

▓ Shirley Jackson's *The Lottery; or, The Adventures of James Harris* is published.

1952

● Clive Barker is born on 5 October in Liverpool, England.

1955

▓ Flannery O'Connor's *A Good Man Is Hard to Find* is published.

1956

● Bela Lugosi dies on 16 August in Los Angeles, California.

▓ *Invasion of the Body Snatchers,* directed by Don Siegel, is released.

1957

▦ *The Curse of Frankenstein,* directed by Terence Fisher, is released.

1959

▦ Shirley Jackson's *The Haunting of Hill House* is published.

▦ *The Mummy,* directed by Terence Fisher, is released.

▦ *The Twilight Zone* is first televised.

1960

▦ *The Fall of the House of Usher,* directed by Roger Corman, is released.

▦ *Psycho,* directed by Alfred Hitchcock, is released.

1962

⊛ William Faulkner dies on 6 July in Byhalia, Mississippi.

⊛ Isak Dinesen dies on 7 September in Rungsted, Denmark.

1963

▦ Sylvia Plath's *The Bell Jar* is published.

▦ *The Birds,* directed by Alfred Hitchcock, is released.

▦ *The Haunting,* directed by Robert Wise, is released.

1964

⊛ Flannery O'Connor dies on 3 August in Milledgeville, Georgia.

▦ *The Addams Family* is first televised.

▦ *The Munsters* is first televised.

1965

⊛ Shirley Jackson dies on 8 August in North Bennington, Vermont.

1966

▦ Frank Zappa and The Mothers of Invention's *Freak Out!* is released.

1968

▦ Margaret Atwood's *The Animals in That Country* is published.

▦ *Night of the Living Dead,* directed by George A. Romero, is released.

▦ *Rosemary's Baby,* directed by Roman Polanski, is released.

1969

⊛ Boris Karloff dies on 2 February at Midhurst in Sussex, England.

▦ Led Zeppelin's first two self-titled albums are released.

1970

▦ Black Sabbath's self-titled debut album is released.

▦ Toni Morrison's *The Bluest Eye* is published.

▦ *Night Gallery* is first televised.

1971

▦ Richard Matheson's *Hell House* is published.

▦ Alice Cooper's *Killer* is released.

▦ Black Sabbath's *Paranoid* is released.

1972

▦ Margaret Atwood's *Surfacing* is published.

▦ Angela Carter's *The Infernal Desire Machines of Doctor Hoffman* is published.

▦ Alice Cooper's *School's Out* is released.

1973

⊛ Elizabeth Bowen dies on 22 February in London, England.

▦ *The Exorcist,* directed by William Friedkin, is released.

1974

▦ Angela Carter's *Fireworks: Nine Profane Pieces* is published.

▦ *The Texas Chainsaw Massacre,* directed by Tobe Hooper, is released.

▦ *Young Frankenstein,* directed by Mel Brooks, is released.

1975

- Stephen King's *'Salem's Lot* is published.
- *They Came from Within*, directed by David Cronenberg, is released.

1976

- Margaret Atwood's *Lady Oracle* is published.
- *Carrie*, directed by Brian De Palma, is released.
- *The Omen*, directed by Richard Donner, is released.
- Anne Rice's *Interview with the Vampire* is published.

1977

- Stephen King's *The Shining* is published.
- Joyce Carol Oates's *Night Side: Eighteen Tales* is published.

1978

- *Dawn of the Dead*, directed by George A. Romero, is released.

1979

- Bauhaus's 12-inch single "Bela Lugosi's Dead" is released.
- Angela Carter's *The Bloody Chamber and Other Stories* is published.
- Joy Division's *Unknown Pleasures* is released.
- *'Salem's Lot*, directed by Tobe Hooper, is televised.

1980

- Alfred Hitchcock dies on 29 April in Los Angeles, California.
- Joyce Carol Oates's *Bellefleur* is published.
- *The Shining*, directed by Stanley Kubrick, is released.

1981

- *Stephen King's Danse Macabre* is published.
- Siouxsie and the Banshees's *Juju* is released.

1982

- Joyce Carol Oates's *A Bloodsmoor Romance* is published.

1983

- Stephen King's *Pet Sematary* is published.
- New Order's *Power, Corruption, and Lies* is released.

1984

- Joyce Carol Oates's *Mysteries of Winterthurn* is published.

1986

- Clive Barker's *The Hellbound Heart* is published.
- Siouxsie and the Banshees's *Tinderbox* is released.
- Andrew Lloyd Webber's *The Phantom of the Opera* is produced.

1987

- Toni Morrison's *Beloved* is published.
- The Smiths's *Louder than Bombs* is released.

1988

- Toni Morrison is awarded the Pulitzer Prize for Fiction for *Beloved.*

1989

- Daphne du Maurier dies on 19 April in Cornwall, England.
- *Pet Sematary*, directed by Mary Lambert, is released.

1990

- *Twin Peaks* is first televised.

1992

- Angela Carter dies on 16 February in London, England.
- *Bram Stoker's Dracula*, directed by Francis Ford Coppola, is released.

1993

- Margaret Atwood's *The Robber Bride* is published.

1994

- Joyce Carol Oates's *Haunted: Tales of the Grotesque* is published.
- *Mary Shelley's Frankenstein,* directed by Kenneth Branagh, is released.

1996

- Margaret Atwood's *Alias Grace* is published.

2000

- Edward Gorey dies on 15 April in Cape Cod, Massachusetts.
- Margaret Atwood's *The Blind Assassin* is published.

JOSEPH SHERIDAN LE FANU

(1814 - 1873)

(Also wrote under the pseudonyms Charles de Cresserons and Reverend Francis Purcell) Irish novelist, short story writer, poet, journalist, and editor.

Le Fanu is a major figure among Victorian-era authors of Gothic and supernatural fiction. Critics praise his short stories and novels for their suggestive and detailed descriptions of physical settings, powerful evocation of foreboding and dread, and convincing use of supernatural elements. In addition to Le Fanu's mastery of these Gothic conventions in his fiction, his works are also admired for their insightful characterizations and skilled use of narrative technique. Scholars have observed that Le Fanu's subtle examinations of the psychological life of his characters distinguish his works from those of earlier Gothic writers.

BIOGRAPHICAL INFORMATION

Born in Dublin, Le Fanu was the second of three children of a Protestant clergyman. He began writing poetry as a teenager and was privately educated by tutors until entering Trinity College, Dublin, in 1833. There Le Fanu studied law, although he never practiced; instead he launched a joint career in journalism and literature. He contributed regularly to the *Dublin University Magazine* and gained recognition for his short stories and his ballads "Phaudrig Crohoore" and "Shamus O'Brien." Between 1838 and 1840 Le Fanu wrote short stories and poetry under the pseudonym Reverend Francis Purcell; these works were posthumously collected as *The Purcell Papers* (1880). In 1839 Le Fanu bought three Dublin periodicals and combined them to form the *Evening Mail,* a conservative publication in which many of his early works appeared. During this period he published two historical novels, *The Cock and Anchor* (1845) and *The Fortunes of Colonel Torlogh O'Brien* (1847), as well as his first collection of short stories, *Ghost Stories and Tales of Mystery* (1851). These early works were virtually ignored by both critics and the reading public. Le Fanu married Susanna Bennett in 1844, and they became a prominent couple in Dublin social and cultural circles. Le Fanu was considered a brilliant conversationalist and was a popular member of society until his wife's death in 1858. His anguish caused him to withdraw from his companions, who labeled him the "Invisible Prince." During this time Le Fanu produced the four novels for which he is best known: *The House by the Churchyard* (1863), *Wylder's Hand* (1864), *Uncle Silas* (1864), and *Guy Deverell* (1865). In addition, he became the editor of the *Dublin University Magazine* in 1859, and, in 1861, assumed its proprietorship as well. Le Fanu continued managing and editing the publication until a few months before his death in 1873.

MAJOR WORKS

In his earliest short stories, primarily those collected in *Ghost Stories and Tales of Mystery* and *The Purcell Papers*, Le Fanu only occasionally displayed the inventive use of the supernatural and psychological character studies that distinguish his most esteemed works. The five longer stories in the later collection *In a Glass Darkly* (1872) are widely acknowledged as his best work in the genre. In these stories Le Fanu combined many of the themes and techniques of traditional Gothic literature with those of modern psychological fiction. Le Fanu used the recurring character Dr. Martin Hesselius, a German physician specializing in mental disorders, to introduce each narrative as a case history illustrating both supernatural and psychological phenomena. This technique allowed Le Fanu to successfully link the stories and to explore the psychology of his characters. For example, in "Green Tea" Hesselius reports the case of Reverend Jennings, whose habit of drinking strong green tea causes him to see a small, black, talking monkey that torments him with its blasphemous chatter until he ultimately commits suicide. Critics have also expressed high praise for "Carmilla," in which Hesselius suggests a connection between the bloodlust of a female vampire and lesbian sexual desires. In these and others works of the supernatural, Le Fanu rarely depended on the stock devices of Gothic literature—such as isolated castles, forlorn landscapes, and maniacal villains—to further his eerie plots. Rather than relying on these clichéd tropes of prior fiction, he generally opted for subtlety and mystery, and routinely left incidents in his stories unexplained for the purpose of heightening suspense. Additionally, unlike much earlier horror fiction, there are no actual ghosts in Le Fanu's supernatural works; instead his characters are frequently haunted by phantasms that are solely the creations of their imaginations. Lastly, his stories generally feature a first person mode of narration designed to convey an individual's progressively developing experience of terror. This narrative technique, coupled with Le Fanu's realistic settings, skillfully imbued with a sense of menace, are thought to lend credibility to his supernatural stories and contribute to their dramatic impact.

Of Le Fanu's fourteen novels, *The House by the Churchyard*, *Wylder's Hand*, *Uncle Silas* and *Guy De-* *verell* are generally considered his finest. These works are characterized by the taut construction and psychological insight that inform the stories of *In a Glass Darkly*. While not a work of supernatural or even classically Gothic fiction, *The House by the Churchyard* is pervaded with a sense of chilling gloom, and is thought to represent an intermediate stage between Le Fanu's earlier historical novels and his later tales of mystery. The work also marks his first attempt at psychological analysis of character. *Wylder's Hand* is regarded as the most uncomplicated of Le Fanu's mysteries, and is sometimes referred to as his masterpiece. Featuring fewer characters than his previous novels, the work concentrates on establishing a fully realized psychological portrait of Wylder. The title figure of *Uncle Silas*, perhaps Le Fanu's best-known work, is an ominous figure who subtly calls upon the tradition of the murderous Gothic villain. Praised for its clear narrative and lucid structure, this novel is often regarded as the first psychological thriller. In it, Le Fanu deftly manipulates levels of suspense, gradually elevating the reader's anticipation and sense of horror as the brutal Silas intimidates his increasingly frightened niece and ward, Maud. *Guy Deverell*, the last of Le Fanu's critically acclaimed novels, is likewise noted for its mysterious atmosphere and finely delineated, realistic characterizations.

CRITICAL RECEPTION

During his lifetime, Le Fanu's works were moderately successful, although they received scant critical attention. With the appearance of *Uncle Silas*, however, some reviewers complained that Le Fanu had exceeded the boundaries of Gothic mystery writing and charged him with sensationalism. Following Le Fanu's death, his reputation suffered a gradual decline as readers and critics lost interest in his realistic and psychological mode of Gothic narrative. In the 1920s, however, the prominent ghost-story writer M. R. James (see Further Reading) drew attention to Le Fanu by writing introductions to several reissued volumes of his out-of-print works. V. S. Pritchett (see Further Reading) and Elizabeth Bowen (see Further Reading) later wrote essays championing Le Fanu as one of Gothic literature's foremost figures. After the reassessments of Le Fanu made by these and other late twentieth-century scholars, interest in Le Fanu grew, with commentators identifying him as a significant transitional figure in the Gothic tradition whose use of psychological horror is considered a key contribution to the genre. Additionally, several of Le Fanu's major works, including the novel *Uncle Silas* and the short story "Carmilla," have also been singled out for reappraisal. While he is not generally well-known today as a novelist, Le Fanu continues to be noted as an innovative and masterful writer of psychological horror stories and as a pivotal figure in the history of supernatural fiction.

PRINCIPAL WORKS

"Phaudrig Crohoore" (ballad) 1837; published in the journal *Dublin University Magazine*

The Cock and Anchor, Being a Chronicle of Old Dublin City. 3 vols. [as Charles de Cresserons] (novel) 1845; also published as *The Cock and Anchor*, 1895

The Fortunes of Colonel Torlogh O'Brien; A Tale of the Wars of King James [as Charles de Cresserons] (novel) 1847

"Shamus O'Brien" (ballad) 1850; published in the journal *Dublin University Magazine*

Ghost Stories and Tales of Mystery (short stories) 1851

The House by the Churchyard. 3 vols. (novel) 1863

Uncle Silas: A Tale of Bartram-Haugh. 3 vols. (novel) 1864

Wylder's Hand. 3 vols. [as Charles de Cresserons] (novel) 1864

Guy Deverell. 3 vols. (novel) 1865

All in the Dark. 2 vols. (novel) 1866

The Tenants of Malory: A Novel. 3 vols. (novel) 1867

Haunted Lives: A Novel. 3 vols. (novel) 1868

A Lost Name: A Novel. 3 vols. (novel) 1868

Checkmate. 3 vols. (novel) 1871

Chronicles of Golden Friars. 3 vols. (novel) 1871

The Rose and the Key. 3 vols. (novel) 1871

*In a Glass Darkly. 3 vols. (short stories) 1872

Willing to Die. 3 vols. (novel) 1873

The Purcell Papers, with a Memoir by Alfred Perceval Graves. 3 vols. (short stories) 1880

The Watcher and Other Weird Stories (short stories) 1894

The Poems of Joseph Sheridan Le Fanu [edited by A. P. Graves] (poetry) 1896

* This collection includes the short stories "Green Tea" (first published in the journal *All the Year Round*, October, 1869) and "Carmilla" (first published in the journal *Dark Blue*, December 1871 to March 1872).

JOSEPH SHERIDAN LE FANU (STORY DATE DECEMBER 1871-MARCH 1872)

SOURCE: Le Fanu, Joseph Sheridan. "Carmilla." In *Carmilla and 12 Other Classic Tales of Mystery*, pp. 288-97. New York: Penguin, 1996.

The following excerpt is from chapter 4 of "Carmilla," a short story first published serially in the journal Dark Blue *from December 1871 to March 1872.*

Her Habits—A Saunter

I told you that I was charmed with her in most particulars.

There were some that did not please me so well.

She was above the middle height of women. I shall begin by describing her. She was slender, and wonderfully graceful. Except that her movements were languid—*very* languid—indeed, there was nothing in her appearance to indicate an invalid. Her complexion was rich and brilliant; her features were small and beautifully formed; her eyes large, dark, and lustrous; her hair was quite wonderful, I never saw hair so magnificently thick and long when it was down about her shoulders; I have often placed my hands under it, and laughed with wonder at its weight. It was exquisitely fine and soft, and in colour a rich very dark brown, with something of gold. I loved to let it down, tumbling with its own weight, as, in her room, she lay back in her chair talking in her sweet low voice, I used to fold and braid it, and spread it out and play with it. Heavens! If I had but known all!

I said there were particulars which did not please me. I have told you that her confidence won me the first night I saw her; but I found that she exercised with respect to herself, her mother, her history, everything in fact connected to her life, plans, and people, an ever-wakeful reserve. I dare say I was unreasonable, perhaps I was wrong; I dare say I ought to have respected the solemn injunction laid upon my father by the stately lady in black velvet. But curiosity is a restless and unscrupulous passion, and no one girl can endure, with patience, that hers should be baffled by another. What harm could it do anyone to tell me what I so ardently desired to know? Had she no trust in my good sense or honour? Why would she not believe me when I assured her, so solemnly, that I would not divulge one syllable of what she told me to any mortal breathing?

There was a coldness, it seemed to me, beyond her years, in her smiling melancholy persistent refusal to afford me the least ray of light.

I cannot say we quarreled upon this point, for she would not quarrel upon any. It was, of course, very unfair of me to press her, very ill-bred, but I really could not help it; and I might just as well have let it alone.

What she did tell me amounted, in my unconscionable estimation—to nothing.

It was all summed up in three very vague disclosures:

First.—Her name was Carmilla.

Second.—Her family was very ancient and noble.

Third.—Her home lay in the direction of the west.

She would not tell me the name of her family, nor their armorial bearings, nor the name of their estate, nor even that of the country they lived in.

You are not to suppose that I worried her incessantly on these subjects. I watched opportunity, and rather insinuated than urged my inquiries. Once or twice, indeed, I did attack her more directly. But no matter what my tactics, utter failure was invariably the result. Reproaches and caresses were all lost upon her. But I must add this, that her evasion was conducted with so pretty a melancholy and deprecation, with so many, and even passionate declarations of her liking for me, and trust in my honour, and with so many promises that I should at last know all, that I could not find it in my heart long to be offended with her.

She used to place her pretty arms about my neck, draw me to her, and laying her cheek to mine, murmur with her lips near my ear, "Dearest, your little heart is wounded; think me not cruel because I obey the irresistible law of my strength and weakness; if your dear heart is wounded, my wild heart bleeds with yours. In the rapture of my enormous humiliation I live in your warm life, and you shall die—die, sweetly die—into mine. I cannot help it; as I draw near to you, you, in your turn, will draw near to others, and learn the rapture of that cruelty, which yet is love; so, for a while, seek to know no more of me and mine, but trust me with all your loving spirit."

And when she had spoken such a rhapsody, she would press me more closely in her trembling embrace, and her lips in soft kisses gently glow upon my cheek.

Her agitations and her language were unintelligible to me.

From these foolish embraces, which were not of very frequent occurrence, I must allow, I used to wish to extricate myself; but my energies seemed to fail me. Her murmured words sounded like a lullaby in my ear, and soothed my resistance into a trance, from which I only seemed to recover myself when she withdrew her arms.

In these mysterious moods I did not like her. I experienced a strange tumultuous excitement that was pleasurable, ever and anon, mingled with a vague sense of fear and disgust. I had no distinct thoughts about her while such scenes lasted, but I was conscious of a love growing into adoration, and also of abhorrence. This I know is paradox, but I can make no other attempt to explain the feeling.

I now write, after an interval of more than ten years, with a trembling hand, with a confused and horrible recollection of certain occurrences and situations, in the ordeal through which I was unconsciously passing; though with a vivid and very sharp remembrance of the main current of my story. But, I suspect, in all lives there are certain emotional scenes, those in which our passions have been most wildly and terribly roused, that are of all others the most vaguely and dimly remembered.

Sometimes after an hour of apathy, my strange and beautiful companion would take my hand and hold it with a fond pressure, renewed again and again; blushing softly, gazing in my face with languid and burning eyes, and breathing so fast that her dress rose and fell with the tumultuous respiration. It was like the ardour of a lover; it embarrassed me; it was hateful and yet overpowering; and with gloating eyes she drew me to her, and her hot lips travelled along my cheek in kisses; and she would whisper, almost in sobs, "You are mine, you *shall* be mine, and you and I are one for ever." Then she has thrown herself back in her chair, with her small hands over her eyes, leaving me trembling.

"Are we related," I used to ask; "what can you mean by all this? I remind you perhaps of some one whom you love; but you must not, I hate it; I don't know you—I don't know myself when you look so and talk so."

She used to sigh at my vehemence, then turn away and drop my hand.

Respecting these very extraordinary manifestations I strove in vain to form any satisfactory theory—I could not refer them to affectation or trick. It was unmistakably the momentary breaking out of suppressed instinct and emotion. Was she, notwithstanding her mother's volunteered denial, subject to brief visitations of insanity; or was there here a disguise and a romance? I had read in old story books of such things. What if a boyish lover had found his way into the house, and sought to prosecute his suit in masquerade, with the assistance of a clever old adventuress? But there were many things against this hypothesis, highly interesting as it was to my vanity.

I could boast of no little attentions such as masculine gallantry delights to offer. Between these passionate moments there were long intervals of common-place, of gaiety, of brooding melancholy, during which, except that I detected her eyes so full of melancholy fire, following me, at times I might have been as nothing to her. Except in these brief periods of mysterious excitement her ways were girlish; and there was always a languor about her, quite incompatible with a masculine system in a state of health.

In some respects her habits were odd. Perhaps not so singular in the opinion of a town lady like you, as they appeared to us rustic people. She used to come down very late, generally not till one o'clock, then she would take a cup of chocolate, but eat nothing; we then went out for a walk, which was a mere saunter, and she seemed, almost immediately, exhausted, and either returned to the schloss or sat on one of the benches that were placed here and there, among the trees. This was a bodily languor in which her mind did not sympathise. She was always an animated talker, and very intelligent.

She sometimes alluded for a moment to her own home, or mentioned an adventure or situation, or an early recollection, which indicated a people of strange manners, and described customs of which we knew nothing. I gathered from these chance hints that her native country was much more remote than I had at first fancied.

GENERAL COMMENTARY

T. W. ROLLESTON (REVIEW DATE 26 FEBRUARY 1887)

SOURCE: Rolleston, T. W. "Joseph Sheridan Le Fanu." *Irish Fireside* 1, no. 9 (26 February 1887): 133.

In the following excerpt, Rolleston offers a laudatory estimation of Le Fanu's skill as an author of sensation novels, noting particularly The House by the Churchyard.

Le Fanu was a poet as well as a novelist, and he was a poet *as* a novelist. Unfortunately his powers, though great, were limited, or rather he chose to exercise them too much in one particular groove. In taking up a novel of Le Fanu's we enter a region of mystery and terror, the region whose secrets such writers as Wilkie Collins, the late Hugh Conway, and too many others, have devoted themselves to bringing to light. But Le Fanu is incomparably superior to any of these. Where, in the best of them, do we find his wit, his learning, his sense of beauty, his passion, his mastery of language, his creative power? His characters in his best books are real human beings, in whom we can take interest apart from the tale in which they figure. . . .

Of all [Le Fanu's] works *The House by the Churchyard* seems to us to exhibit the richest and most varied power. For intensity of excitement nothing can match *Uncle Silas*. And yet in *Uncle Silas* one feels that Le Fanu has adopted a métier, and narrowed the sphere of his art. He defended this novel in express terms against the charge of sensationalism, and it certainly contains much that the usual sensational novel does not aim at. But on the whole it must be confessed that it and most of the author's other productions aim at working on the nerves, not on the spirit of the reader. This, however, cannot be said of *The House by the Churchyard*. It is true that in the latter the main interest is of a sinister kind, centering upon the fortunes of a criminal, and linked with circumstances of physical horror. But though such is the motive of the story, and such it must appear in any bare narration of the plot, yet there is so much beauty and dignity in some of the characters, so much pathos and noble passion, so much healthy humour and mirth, and vivid description of simple things and people, that the dark thread which runs through the whole fabric is rarely seen. The picture which this book gives of Irish society about the middle of the eighteenth century, is as brilliant an example as could well be found of the imaginative power which can revive a past epoch, and make it seem as real to us as our own. The plot is simple enough, although enveloped in mystery until near the end. . . .

Artists in general, writers of fiction. included, may be divided into two classes—those who make the main interest of their work centre on what is high, lovable, beautiful; and those who seek to impress us with revelations of the sinister, the malignant, the appalling. All great artists belong to the first order, nor is there any other way of being great than theirs. Le Fanu, on the whole, and

ABOUT THE AUTHOR

S. M. ELLIS ON LE FANU'S HORROR FICTION

[Le Fanu] at different times was a writer of ballads voicing the aspirations and romance of Irish national life; a journalist expressing High Tory views; an historical romance writer; a writer of squibs and satires; a fine poet; and a supreme author of ghost stories and novels of murder and mystery. In these last categories he is pre-eminent, and his success is almost entirely achieved by his art of *suggesting* evil presences and coming horrors. Very rarely is there an actual, visible ghost in his stories. His was not the old school of traditionary apparitions, in white or grey, with blue fire, clanking chain, and wailing cry. His spectres—far more terrible—are in the brain of the haunted. Demoniacal possession, and the resultant delusional apparition, or concrete crime—these are the bases of Le Fanu's finest stories. For the actual details of a murder it is true he had rather a morbid partiality, and spared no particulars about the wounds and blood and the aspect of the mangled or strangled corpse. Like Ainsworth, he was distinctly macaberesque, and both seem to have had a sort of flair for scenes of human torture and physical pain. There is a description in *Torlogh O'Brien* of the death of a man by the strappado which makes painful reading, so particular are the details of the agony. But, after all, this is merely realism, and realism is not unknown or unprofitable to romance writers of to-day. However realistic Le Fanu may be, there is over all his scenes of horror a softening veil of romance and mystery; and if Death is all too prominent in his books—why so it is, unhappily, in real life, and Le Fanu's chief exemplar is but a reminder of that inexorable enemy from whom no poor mortal may escape at the last.

SOURCE: Ellis, S. M. "Joseph Sheridan Le Fanu." *The Bookman* 51, no. 301 (October 1916): 15-21.

judging him by his most powerful and impassioned work, belongs to the second order. But in this order he stands high, he stands among the highest; and he stands there, in spite of a too diffuse and erratic manner of conducting his plots, mainly by virtue of his splendour of style and imagination. And he has traits of the higher school which ennoble his work, and make the ineffaceable impression which it leaves in our memory something better than a haunting horror.

VICTOR SAGE (ESSAY DATE 2004)

SOURCE: Sage, Victor. "Gothic and Romance: Retribution and Reconciliation." In *Le Fanu's Gothic: The Rhetoric of Darkness*, pp. 29-40. New York: Palgrave Macmillan, 2004.

In the following essay, Sage illustrates how Le Fanu departs from the typical Gothic formula in his historical romances.

When we come to the two historical romances which Le Fanu wrote in the 1840s, the rhetorical situation is somewhat different from that of *The Purcell Papers.* The evidentiary mode—the home of dark epiphany—has to go, and plot—the plot of History—must take its place. It was not really possible in the 1840s to write a historical romance that had a 'national' character, without responding to the work of Scott.[1] To emulate Scott, you had to find a way of doing the opposite of what Le Fanu had done so brilliantly in *The Purcell Papers*: you had to imply that two or more different traditions were one. The whole sweep of *Waverley*, the panorama created by its rhetorical fiction of 'centrality', suggests that if you look at history from a certain vantage-point, it all makes sense and leads into the present. And that meant introducing some kind of fictional *détente*, some notion of negotiation, even perhaps of mutual recognition, between hostile, or traditionally opposed, parties, within the parameters of a single language or, at least, a single text. The most striking example of this structure is the way the Jacobite cause is finally dismissed as outmoded by the modern political state in *Redgauntlet*, which is done by giving the violence and the romanticism of Jacobite conspiracy enough room and textual presence to allow it to become an anachronism and give way ('historically', i.e. by the choice of the characters) to the 'modern' (Hanoverian) political state.

But in these romances, although he adopts the overview method, Le Fanu reads Scott as romantic, not realist.[2] And he adopts a number of conventions to produce textual unity, which keep on breaking down and getting threatened. He adopts a sentimental register, which is broken into by the grotesque; and he adopts a historical discourse which exists in tension with very un-Scott-like outbreaks of the Gothic and the uncanny.

This latter point can be illustrated quite succinctly. *The Fortunes of Torlough O'Brien* (1847) recycles several of the stories from *The Purcell Papers,* but in each case, their Gothic or uncanny elements have been removed. For example, Turlogh O'Brien in Chapters 50 and 51, disguised as a pedlar, is captured by the Protestant forces and his enemy, Garrett. This incident is recycled from the short story 'An Adventure of Hardress Fitzgerald' from *The Purcell Papers.* There, it took place with the background of the (first, I take it) siege of Limerick. In the romance, *Torlough O'Brien,* it is transferred to just before the battle of Aghrim (Aughrim), three years later. In each case, the plot is the same: a resentful soldier betrays his Protestant masters, and the prisoner, Fitzgerald in the story (or O'Brien, in the romance) is given a weapon with which he kills his jailor and escapes. Here is the Gothic epiphany of the story, which violates the decorum of the Scott model:

> As I arose and shook the weapon and the bloody cloth from my hand, the moon, which he had foretold I should never see rise, shone bright and broad into the room, and disclosed, with ghastly distinctness, the mangled features of the dead soldier; the mouth, full of clotting blood and broken teeth, lay open; the eye, close by whose lid the fatal wound had been inflicted, was not, as might have been expected, bathed in blood, but had started forth nearly from the socket, and gave to the face, by its fearful unlikeness to the other glazing orb, a leer more hideous and unearthly than fancy ever saw.[3]

This is a moment of revenancy: the 'other world' shows through, here, in a flash of imagination (i.e. 'superstition') beyond mere 'fancy'; so that for the reader the 'leer' is asserted and denied in the same phrase. This is the chiaroscuro effect: attention is paid to the lighting of the scene. The corpse of Captain Oliver is resurrected here for a moment, in a pocket of the uncanny that is most undecorous from the Scott point of view: it exists in tension with the boy's own adventure story of Hardress Fitzgerald.[4]

But the epiphany also harnesses a political point: Captain Oliver is a (power-mad, vengeful) Protestant Williamite and the narrative pursues the adventure of a dauntless Catholic rebel. This incident is recycled in *The Fortunes of Torlough O'Brien.* But in the romance, Torlough O'Brien merely gets back his charger from the rascally Garrett and rides to Aughrim to join Sarsfield's cavalry unit, an engagement in which he is wounded. In the romance version, the Gothic effect—a moment that defies narrative extension—is subdued to sentimental and heroic plot-convention.[5]

Rewriting like this is evidently a response to the dominance of a certain rhetorical mode in the historical romance. There is a struggle to retain and yet occlude, and alter, the language of the grotesque; and the uncanny is also more interestingly evident in a number of places. These examples amount to a much more ambiguous and interestingly personal inflection of a tension between the the legalistic framing devices of the 'old Gothic' (already fully developed and updated by Le Fanu, in a strikingly effective fashion, as we have seen) and the quite different conventions of historical overview in Scott's new historical romance.

The Cock and Anchor *(1845): Gothic instabilities*

PLOT VERSUS RHETORIC

The plot of this novel is reconciliatory, crossing the divide between Catholic and Protestant; but the divisions in Irish culture which associate themselves with the overcoded epiphanies of a demonic rhetoric in *The Purcell Papers* are portrayed as fully established in the social system, and seem to have a more powerful and pervasive position in the immediately post-civil War society, in the anti-Whig argument of this first novel, *The Cock and Anchor.* The roots of Le Fanu's Gothic are close to satire.[6]

Here again the plot is a sentimental crossing of the boundaries between Catholic and Protestant traditions. We are now in the early eighteenth century, about 1710. Edmond O'Connor, the handsome young Milesian, and soldier in exile, has fallen in love with the daughter of the unpleasant Whig baronet, Sir Richard Ashwoode (i.e. wood that is, or has become, unsound). O'Connor has returned to Ireland from the Continent, to ask for Mary Ashwoode's hand. His love is returned by Mary, but Sir Richard Ashwoode, is determined, for economic reasons, that his daughter, Mary, should marry the ancient, foppish Whig peer, Lord Aspenly (even more unsound wood). O'Connor's friend, Mr Audley appeals on his behalf, to Sir Richard, offering a dowry, but is waved aside. Another friend, an old soldier, Major O'Leary, then intervenes and fights a duel with Lord Aspenly, who afterwards rejects the marriage. After a paroxysm of fury, Sir Richard dies. Meanwhile, his son and heir, Mary's brother, Sir Henry, is also deeply in in the hands of moneylenders.

O'Connor happens by chance to save his life, which he repays with rank treachery by acting as an agent for his father against O'Connor's interests in the marriage. Reduced by gambling debts to desperation, his own cynical marriage plans having fallen through, Sir Henry falls victim to a plot to ensnare him and forges a cheque in the name of a dastardly villain, Nicholas Blarden, the penalty for which is death. Sir Henry has publicly and savagely beaten Blarden at Smock Alley theatre for daring to approach his sister, and Blarden has sworn revenge; now, he is in Blarden's hands and Blarden's revenge on him is to have Mary in marriage, having hired a rascally clergyman to perform the ceremony, and take over Morley Court, where she is being kept a prisoner. In a long sequence of pastiche-Gothic suspense, Mary (the imprisoned heiress) escapes with her resourceful maid, Flora Guy, and they manage to travel to safety at her uncle, Old Oliver Trench's estate in the country at Ardgillagh. Sir Henry is hanged. O'Connor finally returns and finds Mary, and but too late. She has fallen ill and died.

RHETORIC

We first see O'Connor at the ramshackle inn which gives to the novel its title. This wooden structure (like the Carbrie in **Torlough O'Brien**) acts as a site of 'irregularity', of picturesque, a rambling building vaguely reminiscent of ecclesiastical architecture in the medieval Catholic tradition:

> The front of the building, facing the street, rested upon a row of massive wooden blocks, set endwise, at intervals of some six or eight feet, and running parallel at about the same distance, to the wall of the lower story of the house, thus forming a kind of rude cloister or open corridor, running the whole length of the building.

> The spaces between these rude pillars were, by a light frame-work of timber, converted into a succession of arches; and by an application of the same ornamental process, the ceiling of this extended porch was made to carry a clumsy but not unpicturesque imitation of groining. Upon this open-work of timber . . . rested the second story of the building; protruding beyond which again, and supported upon projected beams whose projecting ends were carved into the semblance of heads hideous as the fantastic monsters of heraldry, arose the third story, presenting a series of tall and fancifully-shaped gables, decorated, like the rest of the building, with an abundance of grotesque timber-work.[7]

This stretch of picturesque is a mini-allegory: a political set-piece. 'Cloisters', 'groining', 'fantastic monsters' and 'grotesque timber-work' all suggest the anti-utilitarian past, an earlier tradition of

(Catholic) cathedral-building in stone. This building is a part of this book's subdued, but insistent allegory about the unsound forests—the rottenness of the 'present' (i.e. 1710; 1845 is a discreetly silent layer here), Whig-dominated, house—of Ireland, to which it acts as a counterpoint.[8] It has been left behind, 'narrowing the street with a most aristocratic indifference to the comforts of the pedestrian public' (4) and the luxury and fancy of its charming old woodwork may suggest a lost tradition of benign patrician rule: sound aristocracy and religious tolerance—which opposes itself to the brutal and ruinous combination of commercial exploitation and penal law which claim to be 'modern'.

It is in this inn that the Jacobite plot is first developed; we witness an encounter between Edmond O'Connor and a stranger, Captain O'Hanlon, who turns out to be an old friend of O'Connor's father. O'Hanlon gives two speeches in O'Connor's room, the first of which is addressed to the spirit of his deceased old friend and comrade-in-arms, Richard O'Connor:

> 'Nevertheless—over-ridden, and despised, and scattered as we are, mercenaries and beggars abroad, and landless at home—still something whispers in my ear that there will come at last a retribution, and such a one as will make this perjured, corrupt, and robbing ascendancy a warning and a wonder to all after times. Is it a common thing, think you, that all the gentlemen, all the chivalry of a whole country—the natural leaders and protectors of the people—should be stripped of their birthright, ay, even of the poor privilege of seeing in this their native country, strangers possessing the inheritances which are in *all* right their own; cast abroad upon the world; soldiers of fortune, selling their blood for a bare subsistence; many of them dying of want; and all because for honour and conscience' sake they refused to break the oath which bound them to a ruined prince. Is it a slight thing, think you, to visit with pains and penalties such as these, men guilty of no crimes beyond those of fidelity and honour!'[9]

This ominous speech suggests the more retributive context of this romance, in this early eighteenth-century period. After the Civil War of the 1690s and the Williamite settlement, Ireland is now a betrayed house, the flower of whose Catholic aristocracy, or even middle class, have been driven from their land by the new interest, a cold-hearted company of rulers emblemised, and, briefly, led, by Lord Wharton. It turns out that O'Hanlon was one of the highwaymen who set about young O'Connor, on the road to the inn, mistaking his identity for that of a Whig messenger:

I took you for one who we were informed would pass that way, and about the same hour—one who carried letters from a pretended friend—one whom I have long suspected, a half-faced, cold-hearted friend, carried letters, I say, from such a one to the castle here; to that malignant, perjured reprobate and apostate, the so-called Lord Wharton—as meet an ornament for a gibbet as ever yet made feast for the ravens.[10]

Catholic reviewers objected to the way this plot is handled, and the bloodthirstiness of one of the conspirators, a Catholic priest, when they capture O'Connor who has strayed innocently into the grounds of Finiskea House in Phoenix Park, a house they are occupying, and threaten to execute him as a spy.[11] But it is not only Captain O'Hanlon's prejudice, as a Catholic exile, that represents Wharton as corrupt. Later in the novel, there is an interesting scene inside Dublin Castle, in which the text dramatises a conversation between Swift, Addison and Wharton. The text allows us to witness the way in which a patter of double-talk and blackmail is operating at the top of the social system. Swift is casually blackmailed by Wharton:

> He paused, but Swift remained silent. The lord lieutenant well knew that an English preferment was the nearest object of the young churchman's ambition.
>
> He therefore continued—
>
> 'On my soul, we want you in England—this is no stage for you. By——— you cannot hope to serve either yourself or your friends in this place.'
>
> 'Very few thrive here but scoundrels, my lord,' rejoined Swift.
>
> 'Even so,' replied Wharton with perfect equanimity—'it is a nation of scoundrels—dissent on the one side and popery on the other. The upper order harpies, and the lower a mere prey—and all equally liars, rogues, rebels, slaves, and robbers. By——— some fine day the devil will carry off the island bodily. For very safety you must get out of it. By——— he'll have it.'[12]

We catch a glimpse of the Gothic irony about 'superstition' here, and the retributive plot rears its head briefly. In his cynical frankness, Wharton jokes in the language of 'superstition', describing with ironical accuracy the culture he has himself created. It is the Devil's work. Wharton has Swift in his power here, and the process of corruption and cynicism in Ireland, in which the good and heroic are preyed upon by the merely manipulative, is portrayed as beginning at the top of the political system. Wharton is described ironically as 'a steady and uncompromising Whig, upon whom, throughout a long and active life, the stain

of inconsistency had never rested . . .'.[13] By contrast, when a country prebendary at a gathering Dublin castle looks upon Swift's face, he finds a 'countenance, full, as it seemed, of a scornful, merciless energy and decision, something told him that he looked upon one born to lead and command the people . . .' (I, 267).[14]

The text suggests that noble and natural (i.e. patrician) leaders, everywhere in this Whig-dominated Ireland, both Catholic and Protestant, are in thrall to mercenary and manipulative interests. What price now the old oak of the 'Cock and Anchor' which has lasted so long? The Williamite Settlement led to a drastic reduction in the numbers of old estates that were in Catholic hands. The bitter conditions created by the penal code partly explain this romance's tone and its code of 'unsound timber'. The novel's most recent editor, Jan Jedrejewski, sees the Wharton scene in Dublin Castle as a rather weak piece of historical realism, judging it by the standards of Scott, because Le Fanu had simply based it on a pamphlet by Swift.[15] But Joseph Spence argues, rightly, I think, that this scene is crucial to the intellectual structure of the novel because Le Fanu's anti-Whig polemic does not commit itself to being anti-Hanoverian. Le Fanu is careful not to praise, blame, or even mention, Wharton's successor, Ormonde, when he could have done. Seen in this light, the novel's 'even-handedness' is in tension with its rhetorical energy, a conflict which follows on from the ironical connection between 'superstition' and the theme of Williamite guilt in **The Purcell Papers**. This tension associates itself in the text with undercurrents of the Gothic—the grotesque and uncanny.

These are strange times, the text argues, which generate an exotic undergrowth of shabby blackmailers, grotesque money-lenders, and rascally parasitic lawyers, low types who creep into the lowest rungs of professions to leech off foolish or desperate Whig aristocrats and their wastrel offspring. The villain of the novel, Nicholas Blarden, is a kind of Gothic echo of Wharton's joke about the devil ('old Nick', as his friends refer to him) who drives the second-half of this plot in his relentless squeezing of young Sir Henry Ashwoode and pursuit of his sister, Mary. Old Sir Richard, likewise, has his creepy shadow, Mr Craven, who is a mixture of stereotypes:

> The bell pealed and the knocker thundered, and in a moment a servant entered, and announced Mr Craven—a spare built man, of low stature, wearing his own long, grizzled hair instead of a wig—having a florid complexion, hooked nose, beetle brows, and long-cut, Jewish, black eyes, set

close under the bridge of his nose—who stepped with a velvet tread into the room. An unvarying smile sate upon his lips, and about his whole air and manner there was a certain indescribable sanctimoniousness, which was rather enhanced by the puritan plainness of his attire.[16]

The demonising rhetoric of this figure is made up of two Dickensian stereotypes: the old-fashioned theatrical figure of the Puritan hypocrite, and the almost immemorial figure of the Jewish usurer. 'Craven' means coward, principally, but it also connotes 'pleading' (cf. Miles Garrett's 'I crave your pardon' in *Torlough O'Brien*) and Mr Craven is a lawyer, a professional pleader. It is implied that his 'lowness' is a combination of low church, low class, and low race. This anti-puritan, anti-Semitic caricature is the beginning of a long line of figures associated with the Whiggification of society in Le Fanu's later romances. Indeed this anti-Whig novel is really a template for many of those later texts, whose anti-Semitism reaches its apotheosis in *The Tenants of Malory*.[17]

I have no space here to scrutinise the nuances of the rhetoric, constantly shading into darkness, the grotesque and the uncanny, in which a number of minor characters (servants and hangers-on) are encased in this text.[18] But there is also another concealed Gothic story which deserves comment, because it simply looks an excrescence at first sight. In a characteristically roundabout and backhanded way, it again sets Catholic 'credulity' (superstition) against Whig rationalism. This is the curious rewrite of the 'Locked Room Mystery' in II, v, which is inset into Sir Richard Ashwoode's death. The retributive Gothic is mediated through the 'superstitious' witness, the Italian, forger and hanger-on, Parucci. Whole passages here are recycled from *The Purcell Papers*. Parucci pushes open the door of the baronet's dressing-room and encounters 'A candle, wasted to the very socket . . .' but still burning on the table beside the 'huge hearse-like bed . . .' (II, 53). Parucci seems to have heard Sir Richard speaking, in the next room, and he asks himself who could possibly have been with the baronet:

> 'What made him speak; nothing was with him—pshaw, nothing could come to him here—no, no, nothing.'

> As he thus spoke, the wind swept vehemently upon the windows with a sound as if some great thing had rushed against them, and was pressing for admission; and the gust blew out the candle; the blast died away in an lengthened wail, and then again came howling and rushing up to the windows, as if the very prince of the powers of

the air himself were thundering at the casement; then again the blue dazzling lightning glared into the room and gave place to deeper darkness.

> Pah! that lightning smells like brimstone. Sangue d'un dua, I hear something in the room.

> Yielding to his terrors, Parrucci stumbled to the door opening upon the great lobby, and with cold and trembling fingers drawing the bolt, sprang to the stairs and shouted for assistance in a tone which speedily assembled half the household in the chamber of death.[19]

This is a flash of Gothic. This wind was used to very good effect later by M. R. James. The undermining of the witness's full credibility yields the required ambiguity between natural and supernatural explanations. But this is not just a detached 'formal' property of the Gothic genre here, incongrously and perhaps wilfully thrust into a historical romance about the Williamite Settlement. There is a retributive logic: Parucci is a conventional materialist—hence his expressions of contempt—but here the irrational has taken him back to his Catholic roots and stimulated his imagination, and the supernatural ambiguities of the shorter fiction are left for the reader to respond to as an equilibrium of competing explanations.[20]

Coda: readerly darkness: The Fortunes of Torlough O'Brien *(1847)*

PLOT

We must go back to the summer of 1689. [In *The Fortunes of Torlough O'Brien*] King James II has left the throne of England and removed himself to France, and the Prince of Orange has entered London and occupied the throne of England. Ireland is in a state of anarchy, under the violently discriminatory rule of James's deputy, the Earl of Tyrconnel, who (in the eyes of many) has set about creating a Catholic state. The Irish Parliament has been disbanded. The countryside is full of 'rapparees', armed bandits who tend to be discharged soldiers from James's armies.

Old Sir Hugh Willoughby, a Protestant peer and the current occupant, when the novel opens in 1689, of Glindarragh Castle, a large rambling fortified house in County Limerick, is accused on a charge of treason, trumped up by his cousin, Miles Garrett of Lisnamoe. The time-serving Garrett who is a justice of the peace, is an apostate from Protestantism to Catholicism and his main concern in life is simple: to acquire Glindarragh for himself. He tries what he thinks of as the honourable way—by asking for the hand of Grace Willoughby, Sir Hugh's beautiful daughter, but the old man violently rejects him. Garrett, however, has acquired influence with Tyrconnel himself: it appears that Old Sir Hugh's wife, Lady Willoughby, who is now half-imprisoned in obscurity somewhere in Dublin, has had an affair with Tyrconnel, a fact which allows Garrett to blackmail him into accepting the charge of treason, despite its evident flimsiness.

Garrett calls on 'motley thousands' (97) of rapparees who besiege Glindarragh, on the pretext of seeking some allegedly stolen cattle. There is a pitched battle just before which, during the initial parlay, Garrett makes sure the name of King James is audibly insulted by the hot-tempered and outraged Willoughby, thus providing the charge of treason. Eventually, the castle is taken and Willoughby and his daughter are at the mercy of Garrett and his rapparees.

Grace Willoughby has already been rescued once from the clutches of a particularly ugly and grotesque rapparee, called Desmond Hogan, by an unknown and handsome dragoon, who is recognised by her old nurse as Torlogh Dhuv, or 'Dark Torlough', a scion of the ancient O'Brien family, who are the real owners of Glindarragh castle. The ancient Gaelic prophecy says that when the one with the shamrock mark on his brow is seen on Glindarragh Bridge, then the O'Briens will return to Glindarragh. It seems that the O'Briens were driven out at the dissolution of the monasteries and that the Willoughby family was subsequently given the castle by the 'old queen', Elizabeth.

Just at the moment of Garrett's triumph, Torlogh O'Brien appears with a troop of dragoons and takes over from him. O'Brien thus, for the first time, enters what is arguably his own property. He quarters his men at the castle and takes personal charge of Garrett's prisoners, escorting them himself to Dublin for the trial. It is plain that the honourable and kindly O'Brien has no sympathy for Garrett and every sympathy for Willoughby and his daughter, despite the fact that they are, technically, his enemies.[21]

James II enters Dublin, and we catch a glimpse of his Privy Council tetchily discussing Willoughby's case. In Dublin, thanks to the machinations of Garrett and his associates, who manipulate one of the key witnesses into betraying Willoughby, the trial goes against the old man. O'Brien, having declared himself to Grace Willoughby and been accepted, helps her to plead secretly with James himself for her father's life, but the King rejects her plea and her father is thrown into jail to await execution.

However, Garrett discovers that the Glindarragh estate has been set up in such a way that it will revert, not to the state, but to another party on Sir Hugh's death. It is imperative therefore that he not be hanged, while they search for the deed and destroy it. So Sir Hugh obtains a temporary reprieve, which is reported with teasing irony.

Meanwhile O'Brien has been obliged to rejoin his unit. He fights with Sarsfield's cavalry all the way through from Boyne Water to the battle of Aughrim where he is wounded, and we find him lying in the vaults of St Mary's Abbey towards the end of the book, very weak, but protected from the incursions of Protestant Williamite soldiery by a ragged crew of rapparees.

Garrett, who has in the meantime characteristically turned coat and become a Williamite, and is an officer in the Protestant forces, has been overtaken by history and fails in his project. Glindarragh is eventually reclaimed by O'Brien with Grace Willoughby as his bride and the old man carries on in residence, as the current but temporary owner. Garrett is finally killed by Ned Ryan, one of his neighbouring rapparees, in a skirmish after a cattle raid. The villain is thrown into a ravine, and his corpse is found by children picking 'frahans' (whortleberries).

RHETORIC

I am deliberately simplifying the plot in the above summary to reveal its main lines. It is clear that this plot is again reconciliatory, and that the story is sympathetic, in the manner of earlier writers of Irish romance, Lady Morgan and Charles Maturin, to 'the O's and the Mac's', the ancient Catholic (but also pagan) nobility of Ireland who were the original owners of the land. Willoughby, the doughty old Whig peer (a rather rare character in Le Fanu: a good (i.e. a high-toned) Whig, and O'Brien, the Milesian who resembles a 'Moorish prince', come to recognise one another because they share a common trait: honour. They are both true Irishmen, whatever their religious persuasions, family histories, and ancestral claims to the same piece of property.

This sentimental convention is, in a sense, a class recognition. Garrett, the ambitious villain, is a hypocrite opportunist who is born 'low'. He is typical of the 'New Interest'. There is a range of minor characters who occupy the place of other stereotypes hovering between the fictional and the historical. Another 'low' character, Old Tisdal, the respectable tenant of Glindarragh's manor farm at Drumgunniol, and follower of Sir Hugh, who betrays him and testifies against him, is a highwayman turned Puritan, whose pious exterior masks his murderous past. This again, though not simple hypocrisy, is an important version of 'lowness' which Le Fanu will exploit in the villains, and sometimes, in a twist of expectations, the sympathetic characters, of his later romances.[22]

THE NEW FRAME: THE MAGIC MIRROR

The Prologue of this text is a rhetorical feat, which goes some way towards providing Le Fanu with a solution to the conflict between the Gothic (i.e. the indirect and retributory) use of 'attestation' he has invented for the short story in **The Purcell Papers,** and the pressure of the historical romance towards panorama and overview, which implies a 'central' narrative voice, a more stable, or at least a more visible, relationship between implied author and reader:

> In the summer of the year 1686, at about ten o'clock at night, two scenes were passing, very different in all the accidents of place, plot, and personage; and which although enacted, the one in London, and the other near it, yet exercised an influence upon the events and persons of our Irish story, so important and so permanent, that we must needs lift the curtain from before the magic mirror, which every author, in virtue of his craft, is privileged to consult, and disclose for a minute the scenery and forms which flit across its mystic surface.[23]

At first sight, this device is simply mechanical: it is evidently a dramatic way of providing a 'backstory' for the novel's plot, whose main action begins in 1689. But it has certain oddities about it, which are in excess of this function. What is a *curtain* doing in front of the 'mirror'? The reader is metaphorically in the dark: a member of the audience at a fairground show, or perhaps a fantasmagoria.[24] And the author? A mixture of Gypsy Rose Lee, Hecate from *Macbeth,* and the Master of Ceremonies at a peepshow. Narration is a kind of prophecy about the past. We stare into the essence of the scene, and we watch while its 'forms'—characters shorn of names and all but the accidental properties of their clothing, bearing, and environment—act out a proleptic dumbshow of the novel's narrative.

But we are not just metaphorically in the dark. This process plainly teases the reader with their very distance from the images in front of them; our (modern) position of almost total ignorance and helplessness is mocked by the insistent intimacy of this partial realisation. How for example can we (even the early-nineteenth-century reader) identify whether these 'forms' are 'fictions' or representations of historical characters?

> In the chamber into which we are looking, there burns a large lamp, which sheds through its stained-glass sphere a soft, rose-coloured light on all the objects which surround it; and eight wax lights, flaring and flickering in the evening breeze which floats lightly in at the open windows, tend an additional distinctiveness to the forms that occupy the room.

> These are four in number: two lean over a table, which stands near the window, and seem to be closely examining a map, which nearly covers the board over which they stoop—the one sharp-featured, sallow, somewhat slovenly in his attire, his short cloak hanging from his shoulder, and his high-crowned hat (then an obsolete fashion) dangling in his hand, leans over the outspread plan, and with eager gestures and rapid enunciation, and yet with a strange mixture of deference, appears to harangue his listening companion. *He* is a strong, square-built man, somewhat perhaps, beyond the middle age, gravely and handsomely dressed—his huge perriwig swings forward and rests his chin upon his jewelled hand, and fixes upon the chart before him a countenance bold and massive, in which the strong lines of sense and sensuality are strikingly combined.[25]

We are placed in the position of one who must deduce from the signs the meaning of this scene. The 'chart'—as in a stage play—indicates planning, if not conspiracy. But the text tells us nothing directly. Our sensory targets are confined to the visual sign—the sound has effectively been turned off. The figures are seen from a distance, and with an uncertainty that represents our own ignorance in advance—the first form 'appears to harangue' the second, for example—of its actual appearance.

The first of these figures is a fiction: it is the villain of this novel, Miles Garrett, whose clothes and manners betray his lowly origins and his country fashions. The second figure is the brother of Richard Talbot, Earl of Tyrconnell, and is a historical figure. (The emphasis on 'He' may convey a clue to an Irish reader of the 1840s, but it is a rhetorical gamble, which looks more like teasing to me.) It might be supposed that the next chapter would begin by explaining all this. But no such revelation follows. How do I know this? Because after 144 pages, or twenty chapters, the author suddenly adds a series of 'casual' afterthoughts:

> . . . this was the very individual whom Sir Hugh had that day pointed out to his daughter as the "lay priest", and brother to the Earl of Tyrconnell, while the procession was passing beneath the

windows of the Carbrie; let us add too, that this is the identical person whom we described in the earliest chapter of this book as leaning over a certain map, in company with Miles Garrett, upon a soft summer's night in the year 1686, in a rich saloon in London.[26]

The fictional Garrett then, in the magic-mirror image, is setting up the first stage of his plan to gain Glindarragh castle—hence the map. The rest of the first magic-mirror scene is an equally unknowable mixture of fictional plot and historical fact:

> Pacing to and fro, and sometimes pausing half abstractedly at this table, looking for a moment at the outspread paper, and betraying the absence, and, perhaps, the agitation of his mind by his wandering gaze and the restless drumming of his knuckles on the table; then turning again to resume his rapid walk across the floor, and stealing occasionally a hurried and uneasy look towards a figure who sits alone upon a sofa in the obscurest part of the chamber, is seen a man of commanding stature and lofty mien, though somewhat tending to corpulence, richly dressed in a suit of dark velvet, sparkling with jewels, his neckcloth and ruffles fluttering with splendid point, having in his countenance a certain character of haughty command, according well with the high pretensions of his garb.

We are plunged again into the activity of deduction or guesswork. This must be 'Lying Dick Talbot', the Earl of Tyrconnel himself, a historical figure of great importance. The implication is that he is aware of the conspiracy which his brother is entering into with Miles Garrett, but is too distracted to find it of interest.

That is because of his apparently guilty interest in the fourth 'form':

> Another figure remains to be described, it is that toward which the regards of him we have just examined are so often turned: the form is that of a female, seated, as we have said, upon a sofa, and wrapped in a close travelling cloak, the hood of which falls over her face, so that, excepting she is tall, and possesses hands and feet of singular beauty and slimness, we can pronounce nothing whatever of her *personnel*—she is evidently weeping, her dress shows the vibration of every sob, and the convulsive clasping of her small hands, and the measured beating of her tiny foot upon the floor, betoken her inward anguish.[27]

This is Lady Willoughby, a fictional character, whose affair with Tyrconnell has become known to Garrett, who in his turn intends to use this knowledge as a means of convicting her husband, Sir Hugh Willoughby, of treason and thus gaining the object of his desire, the possession of Glindarragh castle in Limerick, the Willoughby seat.

Again, I infer this from having read the novel. I could not actually 'deduce' it from what is in front of me, so completely is it reduced to the bare 'forms' and 'figures' of the magic mirror's images. It intrigues me, of course; but the mirror reveals a drama I am explicitly forbidden at this stage to enter, and, indeed, for much of the novel to come. To read at this point is to enter the space of darkness. And yet the author—the showman-prophet—teases me mercilessly with my own efforts to infer meaning from the text in front of me, which he is in the act of creating:

> Lo! there must have been some sudden sound at the door! They all start and look toward it—the lean gentleman, in the shabby suit, clutches his map; his brawny companion advances a pace; the tall aristocrat arrests his walk, and stands fixed and breathless; while the lady shrinks further back, and draws her hood more closely over her face.
>
> Their objects, then, must be secret.
>
> It is, however, a false alarm, they resume their respective postures and occupations—and so leaving them, we wave the wand which conjured up the scene, and in a moment all is shivered, clouded, and gone.[28]

The frustration of that hackneyed old picturesque opening device of 'the hypothetical observer' becomes explicit here, as the narrator turns the parodic screw on the melodrama of the early Victorian reader's expectations, fed on a diet of Ainsworth, Reynolds, Dickens, Eugène Sue, and Sir Walter Scott.

What is interesting are the expressionistic lengths to which Le Fanu is prepared to go and what he is prepared to risk to gain his effect of readerly 'darkness'. The frame is an assimilation of reading—and specifically, the state of expectation—to the early cinema, and the darkness that descends between each scene. No sooner is the mirror 'wiped', than a second scene appears, just as obscure as the first. This time the reference-points are more obviously 'Gothic'; we seem to be in an undercroft or even burial vault of some kind:

> . . . it represents the dim vistas of a vaulted chamber, spanned with low, broad arches of stone, springing from the stone floor. Two blazing links, circled with a lurid halo from the heavy damps which hang there, in thin perpetual fog, shed a dusky, flickering glare upon the stained and dripping roof, and through the dim and manifold perspective of arches, until it spends itself in vapoury darkness.
>
> (3)

One thinks here of the numerous underground scenes (often Catholic—*Rookwood*, or *Guy*

Fawkes, for example) in Harrison Ainsworth's novels, much read at this time; and of the Jacobite climax to Scott's *The Black Dwarf,* which takes place in an underground chapel. But here we are treading the line of the frame, not the text proper: there is little clue as to what is happening. In fact, the rhetoric works hard to deny us information, undermining the reader's position of privilege once again, so that the 'fitful glow' of the turpentine torches acts as a metaphor for our state of knowledge as much as it 'illuminates' the characters before us:

> A group of some seven or eight figures stands in the fitful glow of this ruddy illumination—gentlemen of wealth and worship, it would seem, by the richness of their garb: some are wrapt in their cloaks, some are booted, and all wear their broadleafed, low-crowned hats. Strong lines and deep shadows mark many a furrowed and earnest face. This is no funereal meeting, as the place would seem to indicate—no trappings of mourning are visible, and the subject of their conversation, though deep and weighty, is too earnest and energizing for a theme of sorrow; neither is there, in the faces or gestures of the assembly, a single indication of excitement or enthusiasm. The countenances, the attitudes, the movements of the group, all betoken caution, deliberation, and intense anxiety. From time to time are seen, singly, or in couples, or in groups of three, other forms in the shadowy distance, as richly dressed, gliding like ghosts through the cloistered avenues, and holding with themselves, or one another anxious debate.[29]

All we are allowed to know from the text is that this is the summer of 1686. One year, that is, after the failure of the Monmouth rebellion. We are somewhere near London. I infer from the atmosphere that this is the beginning of the real rebellion against James II by leading Protestants who had grown tired of watching the transformation of England into a catholic state, a move which eventually led to the invitation to the Prince of Orange to invade their country and which was to lead to civil war in Ireland. There is a touch of irony about the odd use of 'wealth and worship' in the above (does 'worship' here refer to religion, or 'adulation based on', or even 'of', material prosperity? This is precisely the ambiguity of the demonic Vanderhausen, from 'Schalken the Painter') which suggests that the leading interests here might well be 'the New Interest' of the Whigs. This is no romantic, Jacobite conspiracy, for a lost kingdom; but a serious, worldly, and above all feasible affair.

The scene is suddenly animated:

> And now, a tall and singularly handsome man, in gorgeous military uniform, turning from an elder personage in a velvet cloak, to whom he has been deferentially listening, moves a pace or two toward the detached parties, who walk slowly up and down, as we have described, and raising his plumed hat, he beckons them forward; and so they come, and must with the rest; whereupon the elder gentleman, in the velvet cloak, draws forth a letter, and with a brief word or two of preface, as would seem, reads it for the rest, pausing from time to time to offer and receive remarks. This over, he says something further, whereupon he and all the rest raise their hats for a moment, and then he shows the letter to one of the company nearest himself, who takes it, looks to the end, and then to the beginning, and so passes it on to another, and so from hand to hand it goes, until again it first reaches him who first produced it; and then, with the same solemn and earnest looks and air, they, one by one, take leave, shake hands, and glide away, until the old gentleman in the cloak, and one other remain. Then he in the cloak holds the corner of the momentous letter to the flaring link, and now it floats to the ground in flame, and now all that remains of the mysterious paper, is a light black film, coursed all over by a thousand nimble sparkles.[30]

I am obliged to guess here. Among these shades of the obscure and dead, I take the leading conspirators to be the young Duke of Marlborough, second-in-command of James's army and a known plotter, and Anthony Ashley Cooper, the Earl of Shaftesbury, who had already been imprisoned in the tower for fomenting the Monmouth rebellion. This fateful letter is a draft of the invitation to William, Prince of Orange, son-in-law to King James, to invade the country and oust James from the throne. Either that, or it is James's reply. But Le Fanu would then have had to have moved it forward by two years because that did not occur until 1688, so I assume that this scene in the summer of 1686 perhaps represents the solemn undertaking to invite, rather than William's acceptance. Hence, everyone is given the opportunity to comment, finally, on the wording, and then health is wished to the enterprise and loyalty and respect are expressed towards the Protestant Prince, the arrangement is checked, sealed by handshakes, and this copy of the letter destroyed.

The nature of the image and what it represents is interesting. The Gothic vault is a fiction: the condensation of a set of underground political actions into a set of 'forms', not an attempt to portray realistically those actions. The reader's attempts to identify are kept at bay by the technique of (what we would call in modern jargon) defamiliarisation.

This is worthy of Pinewood Studies or Hollywood. Le Fanu shows he would have probably written for the movies if he had lived in the twentieth century. The Reader of the 1840s is invited to think of this as a version of the Fantasmagoria—a kind of magic-lanthern show of resurrected apparitions. Le Fanu has appropriated this literal phenomenon for its metaphorical value in alluding to the process of reading. The conceit sets the reader outside the text, and is an elaborately new form of framing and distancing, while ostensibly whipping up, the reader's responses. It establishes the dark space we enter when we read—the space of ignorance and 'superstition' and secrecy, which is there to be manipulated and preyed upon by the fictional text.[31] Le Fanu continues to insert, in other words, even in the leisurely overview of the romance genre, his estrangement of the reader from the text.

And, I think secondly, through the metaphor of 'forms' or 'figures', normally a temporary rhetorical device, he re-introduces a chiaroscuro effect into the frame of the fiction itself. This replaces, or shifts into a different form his earlier rhetoric of 'attestation'. It clearly assimilates the reading process to that of drama: and yields a space between the reader and the text, a kind of 'stage' on which the text performs itself, a non-mimetic plane, on which a complete mingling can take place between the discourses of history and fiction.

Notes

1. See Ian Duncan, *Modern Romance and Transformations of the Novel: The Gothic, Scott, Dickens* (Cambridge, 1992). See also on Scott's successors, A. Sanders, *The Victorian Historical Novel, 1840-1880* (London, 1978), 14-31.

2. For equivocations between realist and romantic readings of Scott, see Duncan, op. cit., 62. And see note 12, for bibliography. For the evidence Le Fanu thought of Scott as a romantic writer, see the Preface to *Uncle Silas*, ed. V. Sage (Harmondsworth, 2000), 3-4, and the commentary on this in relation to other Victorian readings of Scott in the Introduction, ix-xiii.

3. Le Fanu, *The Purcell Papers*, III, 217.

4. See his insistence on 'lowering' Maturin's effects in their correspondence, Ratchford and McCarthy, eds, op. cit., passim.

5. Le Fanu, *The Fortunes of Colonel Torlough O'Brien*, Dublin, 1847, 217.

6. In this case, Swift's own. See *The Cock and Anchor*, Ulster editions and Monographs 9, (Gerrard's Cross) 2001, ed. J. Jedrzewski, whose view of the novel is that Le Fanu was writing 'against himself' in this novel. See Intro., xviii.

7. Le Fanu, *The Cock and Anchor* (Dublin, 1845), 2-3.

8. This politicising of the 'picturesque' is an important theme which Purcell has established at the outset of *The Purcell Papers*, in his comments on the analogy

between the ancient forests of Ireland, and the depleted condition of the genealogical trees of great Catholic families. Later, the notion of 'waste' is made into a sub-plot in *Uncle Silas*; in his desperate need for money Silas begins to burn his patrimony, the 'grand old timber' on the estate for charcoal. The bitter conditions created by the penal code at this time in Ireland partly explain the tone of this romance and its code of 'unsound timber':

> 'The social and economic effects of the penal code must have been very considerable. Family life was disrupted in many ways: Catholic fathers were estranged from Protestant heirs; bitter disputes were caused by the activities of 'discoverers' within the family. As the Catholic class diminished in numbers and influence, they were more and more cut off from the social life of the countryside. Uncertainty of tenure discouraged investment in land improvement and led to the cutting of timber for immediate profit.'

A New History of Ireland, Oxford, 1986, Vol. IV, eds T.W. Moody and W.E. Vaughan, Chapter I, 20.

9. Le Fanu, op. cit., I, 20-1.

10. Le Fanu, ibid., I, 22-3.

11. See Jedrzejewski, Appendix, 476-8.

12. Le Fanu, op. cit., I, 271.

13. Le Fanu, ibid., I, 263.

14. Le Fanu, ibid., I, 267.

15. Jedrzewjski, op. cit., Introduction, xvi-xvii., and 416, note 4. Spence, op. cit., 314. For other aspects of the novel's analysis and its connection to the Gothic of Maturin, see also Spence, 348-9.

16. Le Fanu, op. cit., I, 202.

17. See Paul Hopkins, 'An Unknown Annotated Copy of *The Tenants of Malory*: J. Sheridan Le Fanu Regrets Some Anti-Semitic Expressions', *Long Room*, 30 (1985), 32-5.

18. Two examples I would briefly point to, however. Gordon Chancey, Blarden's lawyer has a dangerously languid nature and sleepy, glittering eyes. These eyes will become those of 'Carmilla', fifty years later. The other example is Black Martha, the demonic female servant of Old Mr Audley. She is the first example in Le Fanu of the 'unconscious hypocrite', whose compulsive, but totally concealed, interior, insists on emerging, in a splendid, purely theatrical soliloquy towards the end of the book. See below for further commentary on this. For a political analysis of this incident, see Spence, op. cit., 348. When Jedrzejewski, calls Le Fanu's characters 'puppets', he is disappointed, using Scott's rounded historical realism as an evaluative criterion, but if seen as a kind of combination of Gothic and political satire, these characters are comic as well as violent and threatening. Their artifice is that of the stage, but shifted into the novel.

19. Le Fanu, op. cit., II, 55-6.

20. The textual presentation of the incident and its equivalent effects in *The Purcell Papers* anticipate Le Fanu's very clear statement to Bentley about how he conceived of a rhetoric of 'explanation' in his texts. See Walter C. Edens, op. cit., 238: 'The 3rd Vol. [*The*

Haunted Baronet] is a story in equilibrium—between the natural and the *super*-natural. The supernatural phenomena being explainable on natural theories—and people left to choose what solution they please.'

21. Le Fanu is using the biography of Patrick Sarsfield in this novel for 'reconciliatory' purposes. See Piers Wauchope, *Patrick Sarsfield and the Williamite War* (Dublin, 1992). See the incidents at Birr castle (Offaly) reported in this book, which Le Fanu seems to have used as a model for the fictional Glindarragh castle plot, and the generous and just behaviour of O'Brien to his enemies, 50-3, 124, 170,186, and 242.

22. Paul Dangerfield in *The House by the Churchyard* straddles both low and high and is a fake gentleman, with a murderous past. Likewise, Walter Longcluse, in *Checkmate* is another mask for another personality in a past of bloodshed and murder. Both these are Gothic versions of the Double, who begin with Tisdall, the Ainsworthian ex-highwayman who conceals his past under a mask of pious puritanism. But Bryerly in *Uncle Silas*, and, to a lesser extent, Mr Dawe, in *The Rose and The Key* are inverted 'low' characters.

23. Le Fanu, op. cit., 1.

24. For the relation between this early form of cinema and the Gothic, see Terry Castle, 'The Spectralising of the Other in *The Myseries of Udolpho*', in *The New Eighteenth Century*, eds Felicity Nussbaum and Laura Brown (New York and London, 1987), 231-54. For a more extended account, see also the more detailed and extended background in 'Phantasmagoria and the Metaphorics of Modern Reverie' in *The Female Thermometer: Eighteenth Century Culture and the Invention of the Uncanny*, 140-67. For some further, more recent comment, see Thomas Ruffles, *Life after Death in the Cinema*, unpublished PhD thesis, University of East Anglia, 2001.

25. Le Fanu, ibid., 2.

26. Le Fanu, ibid., 144.

27. Le Fanu, ibid., 3.

28. Le Fanu, ibid., 3.

29. Le Fanu, ibid., 3-4.

30. Le Fanu, ibid., 4.

31. Cf Terry Castle's description of the ambiguities of the fantasmagoria as a badge of the Enlightenment:

> It was never a simple mechanistic model of the mind's workings. Technically speaking, of course, the image did fit nicely with post-Lockeian notions of mental experience; nineteenth century empiricists frequently figured the mind as a kind of magic-lantern, capable of projecting the image-traces of past sensation onto the internal 'screen' or backcloth of the memory. But the word phantasmagoria, like the magic lantern itself, inevitably carried with it powerful atavistic associations with magic and the supernatural. To invoke the supposedly mechanistic analogy was *subliminally* to import the language of the uncanny into the realm of mental function. The mind became a phantom-zone—given over, at least potentially, to spectral presences and haunting obsessions. A new kind of daemonic possession became possible.
>
> (Castle, (1995) op. cit., 144 (my italics))

Le Fanu is using the fantasmagoria here in the opposite way, not 'subliminally', but as a conscious and elaborate rhetorical analogy with the craft of the novelist, which allows him to exploit the ambiguities of 'superstition' which Castle describes so beautifully here, for his own (quasi-political) purposes. He frames his novel explicitly as a phantasmagoria in language, which immediately introduces another layer of representation.

TITLE COMMENTARY

"Carmilla"

CAROL A. SENF (ESSAY DATE 1987)

SOURCE: Senf, Carol A. "Women and Power in 'Carmilla.'" *Gothic* New Series 2 (1987): 25-33.

In the following essay, Senf considers the characterization of women as both victims and victimizers in "Carmilla."

Although Joseph Sheridan LeFanu (1814-1873) wrote eighteen books and numerous short stories, he is remembered today primarily as a writer of Gothic tales, such as **Uncle Silas** and "**Carmilla**." In "**Carmilla**," the most overtly supernatural of these Gothic tales, the title character is actually a centuries old vampire, who—unlike Charlotte Brontë's Bertha Mason or George Eliot's Bulstrode, characters who resemble the vampire—literally returns from the grave and sustains her unnatural existence by drinking human blood. Despite the presence of the supernatural in "**Carmilla**," however, LeFanu uses the vampire motif primarily to focus on the condition of women's lives during the time that he wrote. Revealing that women are neither the angels often portrayed in sentimental Victorian fiction, household management manuals, and periodical literature nor the devils of either Gothic novels or sensation novels, "**Carmilla**" demonstrates that women's lives are complex and varied. Sometimes victims of outright exploitation, women are also powerful victimizers as well.

A survey of LeFanu's works reveals a number of the sweet and passive women so common to nineteenth-century popular fiction. For example, his first novel, **The Cock and Anchor**, includes a young woman whose father is willing to sacrifice her to save himself from debt and whose brother will give her in marriage to a monster to avoid social and financial embarrassment. Even more extreme is Maud Ruthyn (in **Uncle Silas**) whose uncle is willing to murder her for her inheritance. Often LeFanu—as he does in "**Carmilla**," **Uncle**

Silas, *Loved and Lost*, and *Willing to Die*—uses young unmarried women as narrators. As W. J. McCormack observes in *Sheridan LeFanu and Victorian Ireland*, "the hysterical and untrustworthy" narrator of *Willing to Die*, LeFanu's last novel, "is the culmination of a series of female narrators, beginning with the inexperienced and . . . sexless Maud Ruthyn and including Edith Aubrey of *Loved and Lost* and the naive victim of lesbianism and vampirism in '*Carmilla*'" (243).

In fact, there are so many victimized women in LeFanu's work that Michael Begnal observes that LeFanu's women are tragic figures because they "perceive the inequities which exist in their own situations and in the society around them yet they are powerless to effect any significant change" (72). Similarly William Veeder also focuses on LeFanu's women characters:

Although men as well as women suffer from repression in "Carmilla," LeFanu chooses female protagonists because he agrees with clear-sighted Victorians that woman in particular is stunted emotionally. "Carmilla" is part of that High Victorian self-examination which called into question literary and social conventions and the moral orthodoxies underlying them.

(198)

The problem with both of these views is that, in seeing women only as victims, they ignore both the literary evidence—the powerful Carmilla and some of LeFanu's other competent women (including Miss Darkwell in *All in the Dark*, Laura Challys Gray in *Haunted Lives,* and Ethel Ware of *Willing to Die*)—and the facts of historical reality.

The feminist historian Gerda Lerner addresses this historical reality in her essay, "New Approaches to the Study of Women in American History." Although Lerner's observations about power refer specifically to the United States, they are applicable to all nations and all cultures:

Women have for centuries been excluded from positions of power, both political and economic, yet as members of families, as daughters and wives, they often were closer to actual power than many a man. If women were among the exploiters, if some women were dissatisfied with their limited opportunities, most women were adjusted to their position in society and resisted efforts at changing it.

(351)

In addition, the unique facts of Victorian history are addressed by Judith Newton who, using manuals and periodical literature as background for her reading of women's fiction in *Women,*

Power, and Subversion, demonstrates that some women in the nineteenth century had a great deal of power:

The debate over the "woman question," in addition to its mass production of theories about women's "mission," "kingdom," or "sphere," gave an emphasis to the subject of women's power, and in particular to their influence, which was historically unprecedented. One has only to take manuals addressed to genteel women in the late eighteenth century and lay them alongside those written for middle-class women some sixty to seventy years later to see a deepening tension over women's power begin to manifest itself.

(2)

As Newton suggests, the woman question was on many minds during the nineteenth century. Therefore, LeFanu, who was both a writer of fiction and a working journalist, could hardly have ignored the question of women's power and influence.

Besides the general nineteenth-century interest in women's issues, there may be personal reasons for LeFanu's preoccupation with the power of his women characters. The first is an unhappy marriage. Although LeFanu's wife was reputedly a quiet and inoffensive woman, McCormack notes that the marital difficulties about which LeFanu wrote in his diary affected the entire family and adds that LeFanu's mother-in-law, undoubtedly aware of these troubles, made the following bitter observation when she recorded her daughter's death in the family prayer-book:

My darling Susy died at No. 18 Merrion Square Wednesday 28 April 1858 suddenly. She was laid with her beloved father and two brothers in the vault at Mount Jerome near Dublin beloved and bitterly lamented by those who *knew* her loving and attractive nature.

(134-35)

Whatever the reason for their marital unhappiness, LeFanu apparently felt like the victimized party. In addition to a feeling of victimization that may have led him to identify with oppressed groups, he was extremely close to his mother; and that relationship may be the most important reason for his sympathetic identification with women. McCormack notes that both Joseph and his brother were attached to their mother and that she was Joseph's only confidante until her death in 1861 (121). In addition, Nelson Browne's study indicates that LeFanu's mother was an extremely complex woman and cites as proof the *Memoir* of T. P. LeFanu, which contains a bibliography of her works (11). Because she was a social activist and a woman of some power both within the family and outside it, LeFanu's mother may have been a source of his interest in the power that women have.

"Carmilla appears to divide women into two separate groups—the powerless and the potentially powerful. The powerless group includes young peasant women who are simply food for Carmilla; Laura's two governesses, gentlewomen apparently down on their luck; and Laura who, although descended from an aristocratic family, is forced to live in comparative retirement for financial reasons. All are victims or potential victims. Powerful women include Carmilla, the aristocratic seducer, and Carmilla's mother, who appears to be even more powerful than Carmilla herself.

That women are often victims is easily seen in Laura, the naive young narrator. A typical Victorian heroine, Laura is presented as an "everywoman" figure. For example, she is nameless for the first part of the story, and the reader never does learn her last name. She is interested in the subjects that were expected to be the center of a young woman's life—parties and the opportunities they represented for meeting eligible young men. Furthermore, even though she mentions in the first paragraph that her father is English and later that her mother is from an old Hungarian family,[1] these specific details do little to individualize her; and additional information, such as her pride in her rationalistic education (she mentions, for example, that she was "studiously kept in ignorance of ghost stories, of fairy tales" [399]), serves only to reinforce her typicality. Indeed the only thing that makes Laura unique is her perverse relationship with Carmilla; and that relationship will leave her drained and ultimately dead.

The relationship begins when Laura is a small child—too young to recognize either the sexual overtones of the vampire's embrace or the fact that such an embrace is ultimately deadly. Nonetheless, Laura is terrified by Carmilla's first visit, and she becomes more frightened when her father (the source of power and authority in her world) laughs at her fears. Two decades later the memory remains strong:

> I remember my father coming up and standing at the bedside, and talking cheerfully, and asking the nurse a number of questions, and laughing very heartily at one of the answers; and patting me on the shoulder, and kissing me, and telling me not to be frightened, that it was nothing but a dream and could not hurt me.

> But I was not comforted, for I knew the visit of the strange woman was *not* a dream; and I was *awfully* frightened.
>
> (400, LeFanu's italics)

Such patronizing treatment of a six-year-old child is perhaps understandable, but the same kind of condescension is more disturbing when she is a grown woman, for it reveals her father's inability to see her as a person. In fact, continuing to laugh off her questions when she asks what the doctor had revealed about her illness (caused by Carmilla's repeated nocturnal visits), her father fails to give her information that might enable her to protect herself: "'Nothing; you must not plague me with questions,' he answered, with more irritation than I ever remember him to have displayed before" (440). This refusal to divulge the doctor's suspicions may be the result of his rationalism or a misguided desire to protect her, but it leaves the ignorant Laura vulnerable to another attack. Lonely and ignorant, she is ready prey for Carmilla.

Furthermore, by constructing a partial genealogy of Laura's family, one that includes only the female line, LeFanu suggests that other women have been similarly victimized. Laura reveals that her mother was from an old Hungarian family and that the picture of the Countess Mircalla (the real name, of which Carmilla is an anagram) of Karnstein came from her mother's family. In addition, LeFanu suggests that Laura's mother may also have been a victim of vampire attack, for Laura hears her voice in a dream—"Your mother warns you to beware of the assassin" (432)—right before she awakes to discover a blood-drenched Carmilla at the foot of her bed; and Laura's father tells the general that his wife was "*maternally* descended from the Karnsteins" (442-43, my italics), a family now extinct. That Carmilla is a distant ancestor of Laura's mother, another woman who may have succumbed to vampire attack, leads the reader to infer that Laura is simply the last in a long line of victims.

The genealogy of victims seems to extend beyond Laura's mother, however, for even the powerful Carmilla reveals enigmatically that she had been almost assassinated (the word links her to the warning Laura receives), wounded in the breast after her first ball; and she seems to be surrounded by women who control her. Laura mentions, for example, that Carmilla's mother "threw on her daughter a glance which . . . was not quite so affectionate as one might have anticipated from the beginning of the scene" (407); and Laura's governess later describes a third woman . . . who was gazing all the time from the carriage window, nodding and grinning derisively toward the ladies, with gleaming eyes and large white eyeballs, and her teeth set as if in fury" (409). These references suggest that others may hold the same kind of power over Carmilla that she holds over Laura.

During the day Carmilla woos Laura with words and actions, behavior that the lonely girl describes as being "like the ardor of a lover":

> . . . it embarassed me; it was hateful and yet overpowering; and with gloating eyes she drew me to her, and her hot lips traveled along my cheek in kisses; and she would whisper, almost in sobs, "You are mine, you *shall* be mine, and you and I are one forever."
>
> (461)

Carmilla's nightly visits are less subtle than her daytime seduction. Nonetheless her power over Laura remains indirect:

> Sometimes there came a sensation as if a hand was drawn softly along my cheek and neck. Sometimes it was as if warm lips kissed me, and longer and more lovingly as they reached my throat, but there the caress fixed itself.
>
> (432)

In fact, this "attack," which is Carmilla's most overt show of power over Laura, is described in terms of love instead of aggression.

Although Carmilla's power over Laura is quite subtle, the relationship between vampire and victim reveals a great deal about the power and powerlessness of women. While the vampire does have the power of life and death over its apparently helpless victim, the vampire is itself subject to a number of constraints. For example, it is able to move only at night and (apparently LeFanu's invention) it has to use anagrams of its original name. On the other hand, the seemingly weak Laura has a significant kind of power—that of telling other women about their condition. Although the prologue suggests that she tells her story to Dr. Hesselius, she actually tells it to another woman, "a town lady" (416). Even though it is too late for Laura—the prologue reveals that she has died—it may not be too late for the woman to whom she writes. Thus, writing is a way of demonstrating a new kind of power to manipulate people and events.[2] There are sinister undertones as well, however, if one thinks about the way that vampires are created: Laura is both Carmilla's victim and someone who—more likely than not—will become a vampire in her turn. Even Carmilla had been a victim of vampire attack when she too was young and innocent.

In using the vampire motif to focus on certain aspects of women's lives, LeFanu follows a familiar pattern. The vampire, which had been a staple of English literature since the beginning of the nineteenth century, had been used metaphorically by other Romantic writers. James Twitchell's *The Living Dead* observes that writers used the vampire "to express various human relationships, relationships that the artist himself had with family, with friends, with lovers, and even with art itself" (4). A dead body that drinks the blood of its human victims to sustain its existence, the vampire is a metaphor in **"Carmilla"** for certain aspects of women's lives. Both vampires and women are parasitic creatures the one only by nature, the other by economic necessity. Both are dead, the one literally, the other legally. Both are defined primarily by their physiology rather than by their intelligence or emotions. Finally, however, both have a latent power to influence the lives of others. (In addition, unlike their demonic counterparts, women gained more overt power as the century progressed, with the passage of the Married Women's Property Acts in the 1870s and 1880s, the opening of Girton College, and the entry of women into the professions.)

As a vampire, Carmilla is a literal parasite, one that the reader sees standing at the foot of Laura's bed drinking the blood of her sleeping victim. However, LeFanu links this biological parasitism and the economic dependence that was virtually mandated for women during most of LeFanu's lifetime, for Carmilla is the idle guest of her victims' families in addition to being a literal bloodsucker. For example, her mother establishes this relationship on at least two separate occasions, when she asks Laura's father and the general to take charge of her daughter. Although this kind of traditional feminine behavior might be justified in Carmilla who is—after all—a creature from the past Laura apparently has no plans for a life outside her father's home either even though she is aware of her family's financial situation:

> A small income, in that part of the world, goes a great way. Eight or nine hundred a year does wonders. Scantily enough ours would have answered among wealthy people at home . . . But, in this lonely and primitive place, where everything is marvelously cheap, I really don't see how ever so much more money would at all materially add to our comforts, or even luxuries.
>
> (397)

Laura makes no mention of what she plans to do after her father's death, and one must wonder whether she has been adequately provided for.

Besides being parasites, vampires and women can be described as dead. Carmilla has been literally dead for centuries, but Laura lives a kind of half-life because she has no intellectual or spiritual life of her own. Her conversation is full of the cliches and platitudes of her day, of sentimental beliefs in romantic love, of obligations to family and friends, and of the excitement of parties.

Finally both vampires and women are defined primarily by their physiology. A vampire is a creature motivated exclusively by its need for blood; and the reader sees Carmilla as this kind of vampire. However, as a woman, she is also repeatedly described as beautifully languid, apparently passive in almost all ways. Having learned that such useless and ornamental behavior is desirable for women, Laura's father, the general, and Laura herself see this languor as attractive. Laura in fact describes Carmilla as "the prettiest creature I ever saw" and as "absolutely beautiful" (409). Since the other characters rarely question Carmilla about either her past or her family, Le Fanu suggests that it is enough for women to be physically attractive. After all, what are they to do except attend the kind of masked ball that General Spielsdorf describes so they can attract suitable husbands?

Acting as a surrogate mother, Carmilla seems to be teaching Laura to be exactly like her (that the relationship begins when the motherless Laura is a child is further indication of Carmilla's motherly role), for Laura becomes more and more languid as Carmilla's visits increase. A great deal of critical energy has been devoted to the lesbianism in "**Carmilla**" and also to LeFanu's supposed homosexuality,[3] but it is equally likely that he uses the relationship between vampire and victim, mother and child to reveal how women learn to become languid and ornamental parasites. Isolated and vulnerable, women are trained (as LeFanu suggests, by other women—mothers and surrogate mothers) to be beautiful and passive.

As LeFanu shrewdly reveals, however, some women ultimately learn to use this very passivity to gain power over others while still others—such as Carmilla's mother—learn to manipulate others directly. Carmilla, in fact, is much more aware of the manner in which women can use their passivity to manipulate others. She may not have control over her own mother, but she knows that women can manipulate others; and she is able to wrap Laura and her father and General Spielsdorf around her little finger. Furthermore, she confesses to Laura that romantic love, an emotion that many Victorians believed could be used to soften the most aggressive man and a virtue associated with women, could be used to gain power over others:

> You will think me cruel, very selfish, but love is always selfish; the more ardent the more selfish. How jealous I am you cannot know, you must come with me, loving, to death; or else hate me, and still come with me, and *hating* me through death and after.
>
> (426, LeFanu's italics)

Thus LeFanu reveals that women—even those who appear weak or delicate—may have the power to manipulate others. What these women are *not* trained to do is to understand themselves and the world around them, much less to attempt to change that world.

However, LeFanu reveals that the men in the story who attempt to change their world through violence are equally ineffectual.[4] The fact that their violent destruction of Carmilla seems not to work may be LeFanu's way of saying that a problem that has evolved over centuries can not be eradicated in an instant. Although Laura's narrative relates Carmilla's destruction in graphic detail, she concludes with the acknowledgement that Carmilla "returns to memory with ambiguous alternations . . . and often from a reverie I have started fancying I heard the light step of Carmilla at the drawing-room door" (465). Carmilla and everything that she stands for (a leisured and pampered feudal existence that depends on the subtle exploitation of others) thus continue to exist; and Laura's dreamy remembrance of Carmilla recognizes this fact. (That the preface points to Laura's death also suggests that she is finally destroyed by these forces and perhaps that she has switched from victim to victimizer.)

Nina Auerbach observes in *Woman and the Demon* that Carmilla resembles the Victorian ideal for good women, "Dickens' motherly angels . . . except that this angel proceeds to bite the child sharply in the breast" and adds that the "conceit of the Good Angel of the race has turned literal and become demonic, for Carmilla . . . has a vampire's power to survive generations, her cannabalistic loves keeping her face intact" (106-7).

Woman and the Demon focuses on powerful images of women in Victorian fiction, but it doesn't probe the real social reasons for this fear and awe. At the time LeFanu was writing, however, many women were insisting on greater power for themselves; and the issue of greater rights and responsibilities for women was constantly before the public eye. Others—including writers in the Gothic tradition and the group known as the sensation novelists—drew people's attention to the power that women already had.

Newton's preface reminds feminist critics of the necessity of exploring women's power as well as their oppression:

> For our experience of the magnitude and the complexity of the forces against us in the present seems to be prompting still another alteration in our reading of the past: a renewed sense . . . that it is women's power as well as their oppression which we must explore. . . .
>
> (xx)

Because "**Carmilla**" reveals that there are many methods of acquiring power, some of them both more legitimate and more humane than others and shows that women can be victimizers as well as victims, it serves as a healthy alternative view to an occasionally simplistic feminist approach to both history and literature. Women prior to the twentieth century were not simply passive victims of masculine oppression Indeed, some women were extremely powerful; and some of them used their power against other women. Recognizing the reality, Joseph Sheridan LeFanu uses a Gothic motif to paint a balanced picture of women's lives in "**Carmilla**."

Notes

1. Veeder also notes this fact, observing that "Laura is unnamed for forty pages, is never given a last name, and is not located specifically in time because she is everyperson—all men and women in every era who overdevelop the conscious" (199). However, Laura is an everywoman, not an everyperson. Her father's careful protection of her, her secluded life, her innocence of the world are all more characteristic of women during the nineteenth century than of men.

2. In *The Rape of Clarissa: Writing, Sexuality and Class Struggle in Samuel Richardson,* Terry Eagleton focuses on writing as a manifestation of female powerlessness:

   > The letter in *Clarissa,* then, is the site of a constant power struggle. For Clarissa herself, writing, like sexuality, is a private, always violable space, a secret enterprise fraught with deadly risk. In an oppressive society, writing is the sole free self-disclosure available to women, but it is precisely this which threatens to surrender them into that society's power. The Harlowes wrest writing materials from Clarissa in what she explicitly terms an 'act of violence.'
   >
   > (49)

   However, writing can also be an act of power, of telling the truth. In "Carmilla," Laura shares her experience with another woman and provides that woman with the power of shared experience.

3. Among the studies that focus on perverse love in "Carmilla" are Veeder, Begnal, and Twitchell. For example, Twitchell compares "Carmilla" and *Christabel,* calling

both stories of "a lesbian entanglement, a story of the sterile love of homosexuality expressed through the analogy of vampirism" (129). Begnal argues:

> LeFanu's purpose is not to attack . . . homosexuality, but rather to comment on the self-destruction of a total submission to sexuality. Just as Carmilla will drain the life's blood from her prey, so too will lust destroy the moral and physical lives of its victims.
>
> (44)

4. Waller is wrong to argue that Laura survives because of the men in the story:

   > . . . the old men of this rural world—doctor, father, General, scholar, Baron, priest—destroy the . . . female creature who has threatened their young women; through their alliance of social, religious, and scientific authority, these men reaffirm the power and the validity of a patriarchal ruling class that can only see female sexuality as an abberation.
   >
   > (53)

If anything, "Carmilla" suggests that women gain power over men.

Works Cited

Auerbach, Nina. *Woman and the Demon: The Life of a Victorian Myth.* Cambridge: Harvard UP, 1982.

Begnal, Michael. *Joseph Sheridan LeFanu.* Lewisburg, PA: Bucknell UP, 1971.

Browne, Nelson. *Sheridan LeFanu.* London: Arthur Barker, 1951.

Eagleton, Terry. *The Rape of Clarissa: Writing, Sexuality and Class Struggle in Samuel Richardson.* Minneapolis: U of Minnesota P, 1982.

LeFanu, Joseph Sheridan. "Carmilla." *Seven Masterpieces of Gothic Horror.* Ed. Robert Donald Spector. New York: Bantam, 1963. 397-465.

Lerner, Gerda. "New Approaches to the Study of Women in American History." *Liberating Women's History: Theoretical and Critical Essays.* Ed. Bernice A. Carroll. Urbana: U of Illinois P, 1976. 349-56.

McCormack, W. J. *Sheridan LeFanu and Victorian Ireland.* Oxford: Clarendon Press, 1980.

Newton, Judith. *Women, Power, and Subversion.* Athens: U of Georgia P, 1981.

Twitchell, James B. *The Living Dead: A Study of the Vampire in Romantic Literature.* Durham, NC: Duke UP, 1981.

Veeder, William. "*Carmilla*: The Arts of Repression." *Texas Studies in Literature and Language* 22 (1980): 197-223.

Waller, Gregory A. *The Living and the Undead: From Stoker's Dracula to Romero's Dawn of the Dead.* Urbana: U of Illinois P, 1986.

ROBERT F. GEARY (ESSAY DATE 1999)

SOURCE: Geary, Robert F. "Carmilla and the Gothic Legacy: Victorian Transformations of Supernatural Horror." In *The Blood Is the Life: Vampires in Literature,*

ABOUT THE AUTHOR

EDNA KENTON ON LE FANU'S LEGACY

Surely the unmitigated famelessness of Sheridan Le Fanu can be ranked among the outstanding curiosities of literature. One of the literal "best sellers" of the 1860-1880's, he has disappeared even from cursory addenda to Victorian literary history. Author of some of the really remarkable ghost stories of our literature, he is remembered today only by the "occultists"—the people, by the way, who really recognize a really ghostly tale. You will find his "Green Tea", his "Carmilla" and his "The Room in the Dragon Volonte" referred to still in occult literature. . . . Curious are the fates of little books and little writers—most curious of all sometimes when they are called great. Le Fanu was not a great writer, but he wrote a few great ghost stories. And even as the "sensation" author of *Uncle Silas, The House by the Churchyard, Checkmate* and *Wylder's Hand,* to mention no others of a list of famous fifty years ago, his unqualified passing within a half-century's short span is hardly comprehensible. . . .

For Le Fanu, better than most of his lurid school, could "write"; more than others of his school, with the exception of Bulwer-Lytton, he was "occult"; his backgrounds were distinguished, they were thick with medieval lore and his pages were whimsical as well as lurid.

SOURCE: Kenton, Edna. "A Forgotten Creator of Ghosts: Joseph Sheridan Le Fanu, Possible Inspirer of the Brontës." *The Bookman* 69, no. 5 (July 1929): 528-34.

edited by Leonard G. Heldreth and Mary Pharr, pp. 19-29. Bowling Green, Ohio: Bowling Green University Popular Press, 1999.

In the following essay, Geary declares that "'Carmilla' . . . stands as a paradigm of the transformation of the incoherent numinous elements of the faded Gothic into the enduring form of the modern supernatural horror story."

In recent years the Gothic novel and its rich legacy of supernatural horror tales—including, most prominently, vampire stories—have received serious and overdue attention. Such attention, however, has not been evenly bestowed upon all facets of the Gothic. Of the cluster of elements and emphases which F. R. Hart has called "the Gothic tendency"—antiquarian or otherwise remote settings, a preference for sublimity over didacticism, supernatural incidents, and a concentration on the darker aspects of the psyche (137)—the last of these, the psychological element, has attracted the most intense and sophisticated study. We have, as a result, come to understand how the Gothic novel and elements derived from it served important functions in literary explorations of the irrational and, until the twentieth century, of the hidden or repressed portions of the psyche.

Nowhere else has this psychological emphasis been more pronounced than in treatments of such classic vampire chillers as J. Sheridan Le Fanu's **"Carmilla"** (1872) and Bram Stoker's *Dracula* (1897). In **"Carmilla,"** for instance, the sinister lesbian eroticism is (considering the times) startlingly explicit. But if **"Carmilla"** and other vampire tales are more than half-disguised explorations of forbidden sexual themes, then their place in the Gothic tradition must be examined, especially the decisive and successful changes authors such as Le Fanu wrought upon the legacy of the defunct Gothic supernatural. Such an explanation can clarify not only the lineage of the vampire story but also its kinship to other Victorian and twentieth-century tales of supernatural dread. For this purpose, Le Fanu's **"Carmilla,"** the first really successful vampire story, is ideal; for it stands as a paradigm of the transformation of the incoherent numinous elements of the faded Gothic into the enduring form of the modern supernatural horror story.

Then, as now, the appeal of the Gothic and its progeny—always popular literary forms—resided largely in the lure of the supernatural, the chill of numinous dread—the very element often most embarrassing to modern critics, as it was to Mrs. Radcliffe. Yet to understand fully the Gothic novel and its successors—its rise, considerable diversity, decline, and especially its transformation in the last century into the modern ghost story—requires turning to the creaking "machinery" of ghosts, dreams, omens, and apparitions as well as to their cultural contexts. Though sometimes psychologized, sometimes simply explained away, the supernatural deserves treatment on its own terms to understand the complex phenomenon called the Gothic.

By the third decade of the nineteenth century, the life of the Gothic novel as a significant literary subgenre attracting writers of talent had ended. Indeed, its life of some fifty years had never been healthy: Gothic formulas had quickly become sensationalized clichés. Moreover, the form had failed to achieve what Horace Walpole sought from the outset—the coherent union of the marvelous and the probable.

Throughout its history, the supernatural elements of the Gothic had remained intractable. Escaping from the earlier providential context, the numinous elements could create terror but could not find a new coherence. Hence the absurdities of the supernatural interventions in *Otranto;* hence the strained didacticism of Mrs. Reeve's attempts to restore a providential framework to the Gothic; hence the irrelevant supernatural atmospherics in Mrs. Radcliffe and the quasi-pornographic diabolism of M. G. Lewis. Later serious experiments with the form by Godwin and Mary Shelley made the supernatural elements into veiled symbols in narratives concerned largely with the loss of traditional beliefs. Subsequent writers would return to the Richardsonian type of domestic novel, using Gothic elements only as traces within narrative contexts in which the supernatural had no significant role. In mainstream fiction, only an occasional haunting double, a mad wife in the attic, or the local color of a peasant witch in some historical romance would remain of the Gothic specters.

But the element of supernatural terror in fiction survived the eclipse of the Gothic novel. Transformed eventually into the supernatural horror story, shorn of its pseudo-medieval trappings, it found what the Gothic novel never provided—a coherent context for the supernatural in a credible contemporary setting. As such, the ghost story—including the vampire tale—endured as a hardy minor form practiced by writers of considerable craftsmanship. Sheridan Le Fanu, Lord Lytton, and Robert Louis Stevenson, for example, were able to develop strategies for integrating supernatural terror into a probable, contemporary setting without the embarrassments, evasions, and hesitations which plagued the Gothic novel in an earlier age. But how was this transformation of the Gothic legacy accomplished?

That "the roots of the modern horror story" are found in the Gothic novel is a commonplace of anthologies of supernatural terror (Parry 10). Nor are the historical stages of the development obscure. Edith Birkhead and Robert Mayo decades ago linked the classic nineteenth-century ghost story to the Gothic novel by way of the miniature Gothic romances and Gothic fragments in magazines, lurid chapbooks, and "Penny Dreadfuls" (*Terror* ch. 10; "Gothic Short Story"). So while the succession of events needs no explanation, the background and the nature of the transformations by which the ghost story became a coherent and lasting minor form remain obscure. What made the debased offspring of the Gothic novel, initially the plaything of hacks, attractive to accomplished writers? And what alterations did authors develop to give the supernatural tale a coherence lacking in its original Gothic models? These questions concerning the background of the supernatural story and its relation to larger cultural forces are less often addressed. Here the usual histories turn vague or worse.

The trouble begins with the common descriptions of the Gothic novel itself as, for instance, a "welcome escape from the straight-jacket of Augustan rationalism" (Parry 11) or (in Montague Summers's still-cited words) a "revolt against the heavy materialism, the dullness and drab actuality of Hanoverian days" (Haining 13). With such popular stereotypes about the eighteenth century still afloat, no wonder it is difficult to see the very different contexts within which the supernatural operates in the Gothic novel and in the Victorian ghost tale. Nor do such clichés make it easier to grasp why the Gothic novel degenerated into cheap shockers only to have the supernatural element revive in the successful minor form of the ghost story.

Such confusion lessens once the whole eighteenth century ceases to be typed as an age of frigid rationalism. The Augustan period was, instead, marked, first, by an aversion alike to the "enthusiastic" excesses of the Dissenters and to the supposed mystifications of the Catholics and, second, by a consequent stress on the commonly held points of morality over the controversial aspects of doctrine. The supernatural was not absent but was confined to a matrix of providential beliefs. What can be called a rational, consensus approach to religion was valued because, in part, it was seen as a barrier both to sectarian strife and atheism. As long as such a consensus held, the supernatural was unlikely to be used as a source of terror. (Recall how Imlac, speaking for Dr. Johnson in the thirty-first chapter of *Rasselas,* places Pekuah's fear of ghosts within an orthodox, hence unthreatening, religious context.)

When, later in the century, genuinely secular, rationalistic currents (of the sort we associate with Hume, Gibbon, and the French Enlightenment) weakened this context, the numinous emerged in the terrors of Gothic fiction. But at no time was the Gothic supernatural used as part of a counter-attack against a thoroughly secular, rationalistic mentality which would deny the very existence of the other-worldly. Hence the uncertainty, awkwardness, and occasional incoherence surrounding numinous manifestations in Gothic novels. The older Christian framework, though loosened by secular trends, still inhibited the Gothic supernatural; yet that framework was itself uncomfortable with the supernatural. Thus the impasse of the Gothic novel, which could neither live with the supernatural nor avoid absorption into other forms without it.

But in the three or four decades after Mrs. Radcliffe's major works, this cultural context had altered significantly. The earlier Augustan compromise treating the supernatural as Providence had long faded beyond the point where it could exercise even an inhibiting force. By the middle decades of the nineteenth century, many perceived the dominant intellectual trends as denying altogether the supernatural. The specter of a chilling, purposeless materialism confronted many whose view of humanity and the world no longer was dictated by Christian doctrines. Whether it be Dickens protesting the tyranny of an educational system based on dead facts without imagination or Tennyson contemplating the possibility of a "Nature, red in tooth and claw," Victorian intellectuals clearly were apprehensive about what was replacing the ebbing Sea of Faith. One need not multiply examples. The point here is that in this climate ghostly supernatural entities were for many no longer embarrassing reminders of dangerous superstitions; instead, the specters and weird events, now thoroughly detached from a Christian context, served as a refuge, if only a clandestine one, from the dominant materialistic scientism. The supernatural or "spiritualism" (the supernatural without the theology) could offer some assurance of an "other" world, especially to those for whom Christianity no longer held force but who feared the soulless materialism of the new age.

In this altered climate, the very sort of supernatural manifestations which the proper Mrs. Radcliffe felt obliged to explain away were, fifty years later, of avid interest to perfectly respectable people. Catherine Crowe's two volume compilation of supposedly genuine supernatural happenings, *The Night-Side of Nature* (1848), found more than enough eager response to inspire her to produce further, equally popular collections. Authors (or "collectors") of supernatural tales no longer needed to feel shame as purveyors of backward superstitions; they could instead proclaim themselves champions of a higher enlightenment against the narrow, partial view of reality offered by an intolerant science. Wrote Mrs. Crowe, with the confidence of someone challenging a dominant system of beliefs whose inadequacies were becoming apparent: "The contemptuous scepticism of the last age is yielding to a more humble spirit of enquiry; and there is a large class of persons amongst the most enlightened of the present who are now beginning to believe that much which they have been taught to reject as fable, has been, in reality, ill-understood truth" (8-9).

In this atmosphere the supernatural tale could develop without crippling hesitations the very elements of the weird, the eerie, the numinously terrifying which in the Gothic had only imperfectly escaped the context of orthodox providentialism. With appropriate alterations of narrative strategies, the ghost story became a vehicle not only for entertainment but also for expression of the uneasy fluctuations of belief on the part of the cognitive minority no longer content with the Christian supernatural yet appalled by the new scientism whose presuppositions they sought to reject or soften. Thus a central motif in much Victorian supernatural fiction is that the enlightened world of science, despite its contrary claims, offers an incomplete picture of reality: there is another realm—perhaps higher, certainly more encompassing, maybe more terrifying, but not restricted to the prevailing confines of what passes for truth. With this as a guiding motif, the ghost story succeeded where the Gothic had not in developing a coherent rationale for the use of the supernatural. The paradox is that supernatural fiction succeeded because the dominant intellectual attitudes were more secular, more thoroughly and therefore more oppressively materialistic, than in the eighteenth century.

To illustrate these changes, as well as the underlying continuities, let us examine several short supernatural narratives, one pre-Gothic, one Gothic, and one post-Gothic. A brief account of providential intervention from Henry Fielding's tract of 1752, *Examples of the Interposition of Providence in the Detection and Punishment of Murder*, will show the older containment of the supernatural within a theological framework. For the release of the numinous from that framework let us look to Anne Letitia Barbauld's Gothic fragment "Sir Bertrand" of 1773. Le Fanu's **"Carmilla"** can in this context represent the Victorian ghost story, not simply the sub-class of vampire narratives.

These examples, from three different cultural contexts, can suggest the nature of the literary transformations involved in the emergence of the classic ghost story out of the confused Gothic experiment.

A collection of nearly three dozen *exempla* (most borrowed from similar seventeenth-century works), Fielding's tract is a didactic effort with a specific aim—to check the increase of murders committed by people of the lower classes infected, in his view, by the fashionable "neglect (I wish I could say contempt) of religion" (*Miscellaneous Writings* 3: 115). While the accumulated tales do have a certain fascination, their purpose is not to entertain but to demonstrate, over and over, the truth of the old maxim "murder will out," by preternatural if not by natural means. In these brief pieces suspense is at a minimum: they build not to some shocking manifestation of the supernatural but to the seemingly inevitable execution of the felon who had appeared secure from punishment. One typical example—like most, short enough to be given in full—will make the pattern clear:

> A traveler was found murdered near Itzhow in Denmark; and because the murderer was unknown, the magistrates caused the hand of the slain to be cut off, and hung up by a string to the top of a room in the town prison. Ten years after, the murderer came into that room, having been taken up for some very slight offence, and the hand immediately began to drop blood upon the table that stood beneath it. The gaoler on that, accused the prisoner with the murder, who struck with the apparent judgment of God, in the discovery of it, confessed the fact, and submitted to the punishment so justly due to his crime.
>
> (Example 6; *Misc. Writings,* 3: 124)

In contrast, say, to the bleeding portrait in Walpole's *Otranto,* the blood-dripping hand here does not function to arouse interest or terror; rather, so embedded is it in the providentialist context that it seems an almost matter-of-fact detail, though a crucial one, in the events leading to what is the real focus of the little narrative, the inexorable "punishment so justly due to his crime."

Very different is Mrs. Barbauld's Gothic nightmare vision, "Sir Bertrand." This piece, which drew Walpole's praise, is all numinous atmospherics. The "fragment" is less the opening of a story (as some editors believe) than a dreamlike ritual approach to some numinous center. As the knight is drawn, trembling yet spellbound, toward the place of some unspecified yet fearful otherness, readers are treated to an exercise in mounting fascination and terror designed not to teach but stimulate specifically the emotion of numinous dread. Sir Bertrand, lost at night on the "dreary moors," is drawn by "the sullen toll of a distant bell" to a crumbling mansion. A mysterious flame and then a "dead cold hand" lead him through black passageways and vaults, until, after passing a menacing spectral figure, he reaches a coffin. From it a lady beckons to him. Terrified but courageous, the knight springs past the animated statues to embrace her. In so doing, it seems, he breaks some spell holding her in thrall, for, upon recovering from a trance, he finds himself being feasted by servants of the lady who calls him her savior (Haining 44-48).

Whether Mrs. Barbauld intended for these paragraphs to remain alone, we cannot but conjecture. Certainly the piece had gone too far to be worked into the providentialist pattern of a knight preternaturally charged to bring some foul deed to light. But as it stands, "Sir Bertrand" presents in miniature much of the artistic attraction and difficulty of the Gothic form. As a self-contained *tour de force,* it reminds us of the attraction such atmospherics in themselves had for writers and recalls the difficulty they encountered trying to fit such dark sublimities into credible narrative settings. In isolating the experience of numinous fascination and terror, "Sir Bertrand" testifies to the importance of the Gothic "machinery" so often dismissed as claptrap. For in the very machinery itself—"hidden," as Judith Wilt has said, in plain sight on the surface—lay much of the Gothic's appeal for generating quasi-religious dread not softened by a reassuring theological overlay (32). But having released the numinous from a weakening providential context, the Gothicists were uncertain what to do with it. In the novels the supernatural is nostalgic, or unreal, occasionally cheaply sensational—always awkward, never genuinely coherent.

Short pieces like "Sir Bertrand" seemingly had the potential for creating unearthly dread without encountering many of the realistic novel's problems with complex characterization, sustained plots, and detailed settings. But the innumerable short Gothic tales in magazines and chapbooks between 1790 and 1820 did not develop into an enduring mode. Most were mere abbreviated versions of full Gothic romances, with no reworking of the form to suit the shortened length. The rest were Gothic fragments, with "no exposition, no resolution." Such brief Gothic fiction set a "precedent" but did not create a real "model" for the short story of supernatural terror (Mayo 450-51, 454).

No single Victorian tale of supernatural horror captures every element of that subgenre. But Sheridan Le Fanu's **"Carmilla"** comes as close as one might wish to being a model of the differences between the new context and earlier uses. This story of a mysterious guest who preys on the unsuspecting daughter of an English civil servant, now widowed and retired in Austria, might appear but a simple continuation of the providential *exempla* and short Gothic tales, with only the difference of heightened suspense and improved narrative technique in fitting plot and character to length. But these differences, however important, are themselves grounded in more subtle transformations.

The Victorian horror tale escapes much of the confusion and embarrassment besetting the Gothic supernatural by insinuating a new context for the numinous, a context anti-materialistic and anti-profane yet one without any developed explanatory framework, theological or otherwise. This, in turn, enables the writer to discard the clumsy Gothic distancing devices of cardboard medieval settings and characters for a contemporary scene and sharply drawn figures. The shock to which the story advances, in spite of the obtuse scepticism of the characters, is, therefore, more than a device for suspense; it is the culmination of the story's underlying theme—the triumphant and horrific demonstration of the other reality denied by the prevailing culture, a demonstration appealing to those dismayed by the grimness of scientific materialism yet uprooted from the older orthodoxy which had tamed and rationalized the supernatural. At last the supernatural tale had found a rationale uniting thematics and structure.

This pattern of the insinuation of some frightening other reality into the ordinary, disbelieving world dominates **"Carmilla"** as it does so many celebrated tales of supernatural horror from the last century, controlling not just plot but narrative viewpoint, setting, and characterization as well. In Sheridan Le Fanu's classic vampire tale, a cozy rationalism constitutes the cultural norm to be undermined in the story and in the reader by the emergence of unnatural forces at once darkly sexual and terrifyingly preternatural. In contrast to Walpole's preface offering *Otranto* as an ancient manuscript, perhaps the work of monkish superstition, here the device of giving the story as a "case study" from the papers of Dr. Hesselius has the effect not of distancing the strange events but

of expanding the limited, materialistic outlook of science to include what the Doctor—symbol of the desired new fusion of rational and religious beliefs—considers "some of the profoundest arcana of our existence" (274). Similarly, though the setting in an isolated Austrian *schloss* seems simply another version of the Gothic castle, the effect changes as the narrator—the chatty, sensible daughter of an Englishman retired from the Austrian service—begins discoursing on how "marvelously cheap" (275; ch. 1) everything is in this picturesque place. The characters clearly are contemporaries; hence, the distance diminishes.

Even more contemporary are the father and daughter's "enlightened" attitudes which deny anything pointed to in the old, dark tales of the peasants. The daughter takes pride in having been "one of those happy children who are studiously kept in ignorance of ghost stories, of fairy tales, and all such lore as makes us cover our heads when the door creaks suddenly" (276-77; ch. 1). But this attitude turns out to be not enlightened sense but a form of the "conceited incredulity" which their friend, General Spielsdorf, curses in a mysterious letter at the story's opening. It is the family's portion of smug rationality which blinds them to the danger of the young woman, Carmilla, who arrives ominously to become their uninvited guest. When young peasant women in the area begin dying mysteriously and stories circulate of a vampire, the father proclaims that everything "is strictly referable to natural causes," mass delusion arising from unfortunate "superstitions." Ironically, his rational complacencies draw vehement support from Carmilla herself, who cuts off his pious reassurance that "We are in God's hands" by scornfully insisting "creator! Nature! . . . Nature. All things spring from nature" (296-97; ch. 4). Such purblind rationalism suits her purpose well, hiding from the family the clues to the horror which is draining their daughter's life.

Their rescue comes only when the General, who has recently lost his own daughter to the same languid guest, appears at the *schloss* in pursuit of the vampire. Rebuking the father's rational scepticism as "prejudices and illusions," the General recounts the ordeal by which he was "forced by extraordinary evidence to credit that which ran counter, diametrically, to all my theories" (317; ch. 10). With the General's revelation, the story's initial ethos has been overturned: what seemed at first "reason" is shown to be dogmatic denial of evidence; and what had passed for superstition or obsession now stands as a sensible willingness to admit realities outside the rationalistic paradigm. Only the acceptance of this enlarged yet humbled version of reason, one willing to admit ancient human testimony and the experience of the preternatural, saves the narrator from death or, worse, living death. To deny the dark realm is to become its victim.

The controlling motif here is not providential justice; it is the existence and the power of the supernatural forcing itself into a disbelieving world, leading at last to some fearful epiphany. In this motif such stories found what the Gothic sought unsuccessfully—a fusion of the probable and the marvelous. The formula proved enduring in large part because it avoided the Gothic embarrassment over the supernatural without presupposing a belief in any religious orthodoxy. Furthermore, the formula and its underlying rationale made the experience of numinous dread the logical climax of the story. Thus without the paralyzing fear of being thought either superstitious or sensationalistic, writers could scare audiences starved for the numinous in an incompletely secularized (or profaned) culture.

This hunger for the numinous the vampire has satisfied better than any other figure from the Victorian horror stories precisely because his (or her) combination of all-consuming eroticism and supernatural terror makes the creature a nearly perfect dramatic embodiment of the darkly numinous—fascinating yet dreadful, deeply attractive yet utterly terrifying. Rudolf Otto's classic description of the numinous experience has obvious affinities with the dreadful lure a Carmilla or a Dracula exerts on the intended victim: "The daemonic-divine object may appear to the mind an object of horror and dread, but . . . it . . . no less . . . allures with a potent charm, and the creature, who trembles before it . . . has always at the same time the impulse to turn to it, nay even to make it somehow his own" (31). But while this distinctive erotic/supernatural mixture endows the creatures with a rich power (over victims and audiences), we must recall that the vampire thrives in literature only in opposition to the dominant but incomplete and unsatisfying climate of rationalism first manifest in the last century. For it was in reaction to this rationalism that the tale of supernatural horror gained a confidence that generated coherent and successful narrative strategies. Within the tales themselves an analogous point about the power and inadequacy of the prevailing scientist materialism finds frequent assertion: in the words of Van Helsing from the most famous of all vampire novels:

"for in this enlightened age, when men believe not even what they see, the doubting of wise men would be his [Dracula's] greatest strength" (339; ch. 24). Indeed it is this very "doubting of the wise," this culturally dominant rationalism, that separates the failed Gothic from the successful Victorian and modern tales of supernatural horror which have made the vampire "probably the most enduring and prolific mythic figure we have" (Twitchell ix).

Works Cited

Barbauld, Anne Letitia. "Sir Bertrand: A Fragment." 1773. Rpt. in Haining 44-48.

Birkhead, Edith. *The Tale of Terror: A Study of the Gothic Romance.* 1921. New York: Russell & Russell, 1963.

Crowe, Catherine. *The Night-Side of Nature.* 1848. Wellingborough, England: Aquarian Press, 1986.

Fielding, Henry. *Examples of the Interposition of Providence in the Detection and Punishment of Murder. Complete Works.* Ed. William Ernest Henley. Vol. 16. New York: Croscup & Sterling, 1902.

Haining, Peter, ed. *Gothic Tales of Terror I: Classic Horror Stories from Great Britain.* Baltimore: Penguin, 1973.

———. Introduction. Haining 11-18.

Hart, Francis R. "Limits of the Gothic: The Scottish Example." *Studies in Eighteenth-Century Culture.* Ed. Harold Pagliaro. Vol. 3. Cleveland: Case Western Reserve, 1973. 137-59.

Le Fanu, Joseph Sheridan. "Carmilla." 1872. *Best Ghost Stories of J. S. Le Fanu.* Ed. E. F. Bleiler. New York: Dover, 1974.

Mayo, Robert D. "The Gothic Short Stories in the Magazines." *MLR* 37 (1942): 448-54.

Otto, Rudolf. *The Idea of the Holy.* 1917. Trans. J. W. Harvey. New York: Oxford Galaxy Books, 1958.

Parry, Michael. "Introduction: An Age of Horror." *Reign of Terror: Great Victorian Horror Stories.* 1976. New York: Barnes & Noble, 1980. 9-25.

Stoker, Bram. *Dracula.* 1897. New York: Bantam Classics, 1981.

Twitchell, James B. *The Living Dead: A Study of the Vampire in Romantic Literature.* Durham: Duke UP, 1981.

Wilt, Judith. "*Frankenstein* as Mystery Play." *The Endurance of* Frankenstein: *Essays on Mary Shelley's Novel.* Ed. George Levine and U. C. Knoepflmacher. Berkeley: U of CAP, 1979. 31-48.

FURTHER READING

Biography

McCormack, W. J. *Sheridan Le Fanu and Victorian Ireland.* Oxford: Clarendon Press, 1980, 310 p.

An extensively detailed biography of Le Fanu.

Criticism

Achilles, Jochen. "Fantasy as Psychological Necessity: Sheridan Le Fanu's Fiction." In *Gothick Origins and Innova-*

tions, edited by Allan Lloyd Smith and Victor Sage, pp. 150-68. Atlanta, Ga. and Amsterdam: Rodopi, 1994.

Elucidates Le Fanu's use of Gothic motifs to produce psychological effects in his supernatural novels and short fiction.

Andriano, Joseph. "'Our Dual Existence': Loving and Dying in Le Fanu's 'Carmilla.'" In *Our Ladies of Darkness: Feminine Daemonology in Male Gothic Fiction*, pp. 98-105. University Park: Pennsylvania State University Press, 1993.

Argues that the vampire in "Carmilla" is not a symbol of sterile lesbianism, but rather an iconic representation of death.

Barclay, Glen St. John. "Vampires and Ladies: Sheridan Le Fanu." In his *Anatomy of Horror: The Masters of Occult Fiction*, pp. 22-38. New York: St. Martin's Press, 1978.

Concentrates on motifs of vampirism and lesbianism in Le Fanu's short stories.

Bayer-Berenbaum, Linda. "*Uncle Silas*, by J. S. Le Fanu." In *The Gothic Imagination: Expansion in Literature and Art*, pp. 107-19. London: Associated University Presses, 1982.

Discusses the style of Le Fanu's major novel within the context of Gothic literature and architecture.

Begnal, Michael H. *Joseph Sheridan Le Fanu*. Lewisburg, Pa.: Bucknell University Press, 1971, 87 p.

Survey of Le Fanu's fiction that considers his place within the Victorian and nineteenth-century Gothic literary traditions.

Benson, E. F. "Sheridan Le Fanu." *Spectator* 146, no. 5356 (21 February 1931): 263-64.

Appraises the tales collected as In a Glass Darkly, focusing on Le Fanu's method of creating atmosphere and building suspense.

Bleiler, E. F. Introduction to *Best Ghost Stories of J. S. Le Fanu*, edited by E. F. Bleiler, pp. v-xi. New York: Dover, 1964.

Surveys Le Fanu's use of the supernatural in his fiction.

Bowen, Elizabeth. Introduction to *Uncle Silas: A Tale of Bartram-Haugh*, pp. 7-23. London: The Cresset Press, 1947.

Analyzes in detail the style, plot, characters, and setting of Uncle Silas.

Briggs, Julia. "Ancestral Voices, The Ghost Story from Lucian to Le Fanu." In *Night Visitors: The Rise and Fall of the English Ghost Story*, pp. 25-51. London: Faber, 1977.

Favorably locates Le Fanu in the context of other ghost story writers of the 1860s and 1870s. Argues that Le Fanu's works are distinguished by his "intuitive understanding and vivid portrayal of fear, guilt, and anxiety."

Browne, Nelson. *Sheridan Le Fanu*. London: Barker, 1951, 135 p.

Book-length critical survey of Le Fanu's fiction and poetry.

Brownell, David. "Wicked Dreams: The World of Sheridan Le Fanu." *Armchair Detective* 9, no. 3 (June 1976): 191-97.

Considers the overall effectiveness of Le Fanu's mystery and supernatural fiction.

Ellis, S. M. "Joseph Sheridan Le Fanu." In his *Wilkie Collins, Le Fanu, and Others*. 1931. Reprint edition, pp. 140-91. Freeport, N.Y.: Books for Libraries Press, 1968.

Biographical and critical study. Includes a bibliography of Le Fanu's works.

Gates, Barbara. "Blue Devils and Green Tea." *Studies in Short Fiction* 24 (1987): 15-23.

Concentrates on the theme of suicide in Le Fanu's short stories.

Howes, Marjorie. "Misalliance and Anglo-Irish Tradition in Le Fanu's *Uncle Silas*." *Nineteenth-Century Literature* 47, no. 2 (September 1992): 164-86.

Stresses the Anglo-Irish political context of Le Fanu's novel Uncle Silas, while studying the work's representation of female sexuality.

James, M. R. Prologue and Epilogue of *Madam Crowl's Ghost, and Other Tales of Mystery*, by Joseph Sheridan Le Fanu, edited by M. R. James, pp. vii-viii, 265-77. London: G. Bell and Sons, 1923.

Considers Le Fanu among the "first rank" of ghost story writers and appraises the strengths and weaknesses of his work.

Mangum, Teresa. "Sheridan Le Fanu's Ungovernable Governess." *Studies in the Novel* 29, no. 2 (summer 1997): 214-37.

Probes Sheridan's characterization of aggressive, sexually ambiguous, and perverse governesses in his novels Uncle Silas and A Lost Name, as well as in his Gothic short fiction.

Melada, Ivan. *Sheridan Le Fanu*. Boston: Twayne Publishers, 1987, 142 p.

Biographical and critical overview of Le Fanu's life and works.

Michelis, Angelica. "'Dirty Mama': Horror, Vampires, and the Maternal in Late Nineteenth-Century Gothic Fiction." *Critical Survey* 15, no. 3 (September 2003): 5-22.

Examines Le Fanu's symbolic treatment of mother and vampire in his short story "Carmilla," and its connection to anxiety and the theories of Sigmund Freud and Melanie Klein.

Milbank, Alison. "Doubting Castle: The Gothic Mode of Questioning." In *The Critical Spirit and the Will to Believe: Essays in Nineteenth-Century Literature and Religion*, edited by David Jasper and T. R. Wright, pp. 104-19. New York: St. Martin's Press, 1989.

Discusses the theme of religious doubt in Le Fanu's novels and short stories.

Nalęcz-Wojtczak, Jolanta. "*Uncle Silas*: A Link between the Gothic Romance and the Detective Novel in England." *Studia Anglica Posnaniensia: An International Review of English Studies* 12 (1980): 157-67.

Characterizes Uncle Silas as a transitional work in the tradition of the English novel that occupies a pivotal place between the eighteenth-century Gothic romance and late nineteenth-century mystery and detective novels.

——. "Joseph Sheridan Le Fanu and the New Dimensions of the English Ghost Story." In *Literary Interrelations: Ireland, England and the World*, edited by Wolfgang Zach and Heinz Kosok, pp. 193-98. Tübingen, Germany: Gunter Narr Verlag, 1987.

Explores the ways in which Le Fanu's interest in Irish folklore, Swedenborgian ideas, and psychology brought expanded possibilities to the English ghost story tradition.

Orel, Harold. "'Rigid Adherence to Facts': Le Fanu's *In a Glass Darkly.*" *Eire-Ireland: A Journal of Irish Studies* 20, no. 4 (winter 1985): 65-88.

Focuses on Le Fanu's device of presenting the supernatural stories of In a Glass Darkly as factual accounts.

Penzoldt, Peter. "Joseph Sheridan Le Fanu (1814-1873)." In *The Supernatural in Fiction*, pp. 67-91. London: Peter Nevill, 1952.

Discusses Le Fanu's importance to the history and development of the Gothic novel.

Pritchett, V. S. "An Irish Ghost." In *The Living Novel & Later Appreciations.* Revised edition, pp. 121-28. New York: Random House, 1964.

Praises the style and narrative technique of Le Fanu's short stories and contends that because he had primarily a "talent for brevity" Le Fanu never achieved the same level of success in his novels as he did in his short stories.

Scott, Ken. "Le Fanu's 'The Room in the Dragon Volant.'" *Lock Haven Review*, no. 10 (1968): 25-32.

Treats themes of love and death in "The Room in the Dragon Volant."

Shroyer, Frederick. Introduction to *Uncle Silas: A Tale of Bartram-Haugh*, by Joseph Sheridan Le Fanu, pp. v-xviii. New York: Dover, 1966.

Presents a general overview of Uncle Silas, outlining the elements that contribute to the novel's atmosphere of terror and claiming the work to be one of the best Gothic novels ever written.

Signorotti, Elizabeth. "Repossessing the Body: Transgressive Desire in 'Carmilla' and *Dracula.*" *Criticism* 38, no. 4 (fall 1996): 607-32.

Interprets Bram Stoker's Dracula as a patriarchal response to Le Fanu's rendering of an empowered female vampire in "Carmilla."

Stoddart, Helen. "'The Precautions of Nervous People Are Infectious': Sheridan Le Fanu's Symptomatic Gothic." *Modern Language Review* 86, no. 1 (January 1991): 19-34.

Assesses the paranoia motif of "Green Tea" and "Carmilla" in terms of Freudian psychoanalysis.

Sullivan, Jack. "'Green Tea': The Archetypal Ghost Story" and "Beginnings: Sheridan Le Fanu." In his *Elegant Nightmares: The English Ghost Story from Le Fanu to Blackwood*, pp. 1-68. Athens: Ohio University Press, 1980.

Detailed examination of Le Fanu's short fiction that explores his development as a writer while analyzing individual stories, including "Green Tea" and "Carmilla."

Sullivan, Kevin. "Sheridan Le Fanu: The Purcell Papers, 1838-40." *Irish University Review* 2, no. 1 (spring 1972): 5-19.

Explores themes of terror and humor in The Purcell Papers.

Sweeney, St. John. "Sheridan Le Fanu, the Irish Poe." *Journal of Irish Literature* 15, no. 1 (January 1986): 3-32.

Considers the prose style and plot structures of Le Fanu's short stories, concluding that Le Fanu was not simply the Irish version of Edgar Allan Poe.

Veeder, William. "Carmilla: The Arts of Repression." *Texas Studies in Literature and Language* 22, no. 2 (summer 1980): 197-223.

Studies the theme of emotional repression in "Carmilla," considering the work as "part of the High Victorian self-examination which called into question literary and social conventions and the moral orthodoxies underlying them."

Wagenknecht, Edward. "Sheridan Le Fanu." In *Seven Masters of Supernatural Fiction*, pp. 3-21. Westwood, Conn.: Greenwood Press, 1991.

Interpretive essay focusing on Le Fanu's supernatural novels and stories. Also features several plot summaries and commentary by additional critics.

OTHER SOURCES FROM GALE:

Additional coverage of Le Fanu's life and career is contained in the following sources published by Thomson Gale: *Dictionary of Literary Biography*, Vols. 21, 70, 159, 178; *DISCovering Authors Modules: Popular Fiction* and *Genre Authors*; *DISCovering Authors 3.0*; *Literature Resource Center*; *Nineteenth-Century Literature Criticism*, Vols. 9, 58; *Reference Guide to English Literature*, Ed. 2; *Reference Guide to Short Fiction*, Ed. 2; *St. James Guide to Crime & Mystery Writers*, Vol. 4; *St. James Guide to Horror, Ghost & Gothic Writers*; *Short Story Criticism*, Vol. 14; and *Supernatural Fiction Writers*, Vol. 1.

MATTHEW GREGORY LEWIS

(1775 - 1818)

English novelist, playwright, diarist, prose writer, and poet.

L̲ewis is best known as the author of *The Monk* (1796), a notorious eighteenth-century novel of horror that is considered one of the greatest examples of English Gothic fiction. Unlike Horace Walpole and Ann Radcliffe, his predecessors in the Gothic school who created genteel novels of suspense, Lewis emphasized the graphic and the sensational. *The Monk*'s blend of overt sexuality and terror created a scandal in England, and its author, branded licentious and perverse, came to be known solely as "Monk" Lewis. While the lurid elements of Lewis's work are still controversial, modern critics acknowledge his talent as an innovative writer of prose and verse who contributed to the Gothic literary tradition as well as the development of the English Romantic movement.

BIOGRAPHICAL INFORMATION

Lewis was born into a wealthy and socially prominent London family. His mother and father separated while he was young, and his attempts to remain on good terms with both parents created an emotional strain that endured throughout his life. Some biographers contend, in fact, that this stress resulted in an emotional immaturity that manifested itself in Lewis's work. Although Lewis displayed a talent for writing at an early age and was encouraged to write by his mother, his father urged him to pursue a diplomatic career instead. After graduation from Oxford in 1794, Lewis became an attaché to the British Embassy in Holland, an assignment he despised. To ease his boredom, Lewis wrote *The Monk* during a ten week period. The notoriety that accompanied *The Monk*'s publication in 1796 made Lewis a financially successful, if infamous, author. Led by Samuel Taylor Coleridge, contemporary critics labeled Lewis's tale of Ambrosio, the wayward monk, immoral and obscene. Lewis had recently been elected to the House of Commons, and *The Monk* proved so controversial that, in order to retain his position, he was required to issue an expurgated edition. Shortly thereafter, Lewis left politics and began writing drama. In the years before his death, Lewis spent most of his time on the Jamaican estates he had inherited, which were maintained by slaves. By all accounts, Lewis was a compassionate man who advocated the abolition of slavery and retained his plantations solely at the request of his slaves, who feared the financial responsibility of freedom. During his final trip to Jamaica, Lewis tried desperately to improve the living conditions of his slaves. Despite his efforts, he was able to implement little change and, despondent, decided to return home. By the time Lewis boarded a ship for England, he had already developed yellow fever. He died several days later. His crew prepared to bury him at sea, but as they lowered the casket, its shroud caught in the wind and the coffin sailed slowly back to Jamaica.

MAJOR WORKS

The Monk's protagonist, Ambrosio, who is a monk as well as a foundling of mysterious past and parentage, has risen to the position of abbot of the Capuchins, becoming a well-respected figure in medieval Madrid, revered by the populace. At the monastery, a young novitiate named Rosario approaches Ambrosio and reveals that he is actually a woman named Matilda de Villanges, whose love for Ambrosio has led her to disguise herself in order to be nearer to him. The two consummate a sexual relationship, though Ambrosio later feels remorse and disgust for his actions. After his interlude with Matilda, while visiting the nearby convent of St. Clare, Ambrosio discovers that Agnes, a nun, desires to elope with her lover, Don Raymond de las Cisternas. The monk discloses this information to Mother St. Agatha, prioress of the convent, who punishes Agnes by imprisoning her in a dungeon beneath the convent. Later, Ambrosio travels to the house of the ailing Donna Elvira Dalfa and there falls in love with her young daughter, Antonia. With the aid of Matilda and her knowledge of black magic, the monk summons a demon so that he might violate the girl. Ambrosio returns to Donna Elvira's house, kills her, and abducts Antonia, now unconscious through the action of a magical potion. In the meantime, Agnes's brother, Lorenzo, accuses Mother St. Agatha of murdering his sister and wins a warrant for her arrest. An angry mob forms in response to the accusation, and the crowd razes the convent, murdering the prioress and many innocent nuns. Amid the chaos, Lorenzo enters the convent grounds in search of his sister. When he finds her she is close to death and clutching the decaying body of her dead child. Hearing the screams of a young girl nearby, Lorenzo discovers Antonia's ravished and stabbed body and observes her attacker, Ambrosio, as he flees; later he notifies the Inquisition of Ambrosio's crimes. Ordered to be burned at the stake, Ambrosio, at the urgings of Matilda, makes a pact with Satan, exchanging his soul for freedom. The devil appears and saves him from the flames of the Inquisition, only to reveal that in killing Donna Elvira and raping Antonia, he has mur-

dered his own mother and committed incest with his sister. The story ends as the monk's forfeit soul is cast into hell.

Scholars observe that the thematic character of *The Monk* departs somewhat from that of the traditional Gothic novel. While it favors the evocation of grotesque horror rather than the rendering of a sentimental theme of justice based upon divine Providence, Lewis's novel nevertheless presents a critique of human vice and explores the conflict between religion and human sexuality. This conflict is dramatized in the character of Ambrosio through the juxtaposition of the monk's pride and destructive sexual appetite with the innocent virtue of Antonia and the forthrightness of Lorenzo. Many commentators note, however, that the dullness of the novel's virtuous characters fails to match the depth and complexity of Ambrosio and Matilda, and instead locate evidence of the novel's primary theme in the psychological exploration of its fallen protagonist and his accomplice. Likewise, many have observed that Matilda's strong will and intelligence make her far more compelling than her counterpart Antonia, despite her manipulative behavior and demonic nature. Others have commented on Lewis's attempts to establish an unsettling parallel between the violence of the riotous mob in his novel and that of the French Revolution, or on his deft integration of legends and folk tales, such as those of the Bleeding Nun and the Wandering Jew, in order to illicit terror and add universal appeal to his story.

Of Lewis's plays, the best known is *The Castle Spectre* (1797), a Gothic production that met the current demand for melodrama, spectacle, and two-dimensional characterization. Although it helped establish Lewis as one of the era's most popular playwrights, *The Castle Spectre* is largely overlooked by modern critics. In 1801, Lewis published *Tales of Wonder*, a collection of poems dealing with the supernatural that also includes works by Sir Walter Scott and Robert Southey. Lewis also composed poetry that he included in his plays and later published, as well as two novels that never enjoyed the success or notoriety of *The Monk*. He ceased writing fiction in 1812, when his father died and left him a great deal of money. Lewis's posthumously-published *Journal of a West India Proprietor, Kept during a Residence in the Island of Jamaica* (1834) recounts his voyages to Jamaica, inspections of the plantations, and plans for change. Written in lively prose, the *Journal* reveals Lewis as a sensitive and perceptive observer of the natural world. Though it is seldom read today, critics who have studied the work consider it one of Lewis's greatest achievements.

CRITICAL RECEPTION

With the exception of the *Journal*, Lewis's works were ignored from the time of his death until the twentieth century, when critics began to recognize Lewis's influence on the Romantic movement. When it was first published, *The Monk* created a considerable stir and earned Lewis instant fame, even infamy, as its author. Labeled obscene by a cast of critics, including Coleridge—who acknowledged that despite its immorality the novel was the "offspring of no common genius"—it was nevertheless extremely popular, and went through five editions before the end of the century. The controversy that the first edition sparked prompted Lewis to expurgate certain passages from these later printings, though scholars now agree that his changes were largely superficial. Early critics emphasized the lewdness and irreligion of the work, especially of a scene in which Antonia reads an edited version of the Bible given to her by her mother, and maintained that *The Monk* was a product of the revolutionary atmosphere of the late eighteenth century. In the twentieth century critics reevaluated the influence of the work on the writers of the Romantic movement. Modern scholars have since observed that *The Monk* represents a successful synthesis of the techniques and materials used by Gothic horror writers, leading many to take a renewed interest in the work. Recent critics have applied the tools of psychological criticism to *The Monk*, examining its sexual imagery and applying biographical information about Lewis's childhood development and psyche to understanding the novel. Later studies have probed the conflict between sexuality and religion and the juxtaposition of violence and passion within the novel. Angela Wright traces parallels between *The Monk* and the Marquis de Sade's novel *Justine*, noting that the two works influenced one another in significant ways, including in their narrative technique and portrayal of heroines. Montague Summers asserted that Lewis "introduced new and essential features both by his prose works, his verse and his dramas into the Gothic novel, upon which he exercised so tremendous, one might almost say so illimitable, an influence" and declared that "the vast imaginative force derived from Lewis which energized and inspired numerical novels and impelled the incidence of romance in particular

directions, . . . [can] very clearly be related to and are in effect resultant from the genius, often morbid and wayward, yet ever vital and compelling, of Matthew Gregory Lewis."

PRINCIPAL WORKS

The Monk: A Romance. 3 vols. (novel) 1796

Village Virtues: A Dramatic Satire. In Two Parts (play) 1796

The Castle Spectre: A Drama. In Five Acts (play) 1797

The Twins; or, Is It He, or His Brother? A Farce in Two Acts (play) 1799

The East Indian: A Comedy. In Five Acts (play) 1800

Adelmorn, the Outlaw: A Romantic Drama, in Three Acts (play) 1801

Tales of Wonder; Written and Collected by M. G. Lewis. 2 vols. [with Sir Walter Scott and Robert Southey] (poetry) 1801

Alfonso, King of Castile: A Tragedy, in Five Acts (play) 1802

The Captive: A Scene in a Private Mad-House (play) 1803

Rugantino; or, The Bravo of Venice. A Grand Romantic Melo-Drama, in Two Acts (play) 1805

Adelgitha; or, The Fruits of a Single Error. A Tragedy, in Five Acts (play) 1806

The Wood Daemon; or, The Clock Has Struck. A Grand Romantic Melo-Drama, in Two Acts (play) 1807

Romantic Tales. 4 vols. (poetry and prose) 1808

Twelve Ballads, the Words and Music by M. G. Lewis (poetry) 1808

Venoni, or, The Novice of St. Mark's: A Drama, in Three Acts (play) 1809

Timour the Tartar: A Grand Romantic Melo-Drama, in Two Acts (play) 1811

Poems (poetry) 1812

The Harper's Daughter; or, Love and Ambition: A Tragedy (play) 1813

The Isle of Devils. A Historical Tale, Founded on an Anecdote in the Annals of Portugal (poem) 1827

Journal of a West India Proprietor, Kept during a Residence in the Island of Jamaica (diary) 1834

MATTHEW GREGORY LEWIS (POEM DATE 1796)

SOURCE: Lewis, Matthew Gregory. "Preface." In *The Monk: A Romance*. 1796. Third edition, pp. iii-v. London: J. Bell, 1797.

In the following poem, a preface to his well-known novel first published in 1796, Lewis addresses his work, minimizing both its merit and his own talent.

Imitation of Horace, Ep. 20.—B. 1.

Methinks, Oh! vain ill-judging book,
I see thee cast a wishful look,
Where reputations won and lost are
In famous row called Paternoster.
Incensed to find your precious olio
Buried in unexplored port-folio,
You scorn the prudent lock and key,
And pant well bound and gilt to see
Your volume in the window set
Of Stockdale, Hookham, or Debrett.

Go then, and pass that dangerous bourn
Whence never book can back return:
And when you find, condemned, despised
Neglected, blamed, and criticised,
Abuse from all who read you fall,
(If haply you be read at all)
Sorely will you your folly sigh at,
And wish for me, and home, and quiet.

Assuming now a conjuror's office, I
Thus on your future fortune prophesy:—
Soon as your novelty is o'er,
And you are young and new no more,
In some dark dirty corner thrown,
Mouldy with damps, with cobwebs strown,
Your leaves shall be the book-worm's prey;
Or sent to chandler-shop away,
And doomed to suffer public scandal,
Shall line the trunk, or wrap the candle!

But should you meet with approbation,
And some one find an inclination
To ask, by natural transition,
Respecting me and my condition;
That I am one, the enquirer teach,
Nor very poor, nor very rich;
Of passions strong, of hasty nature,
Of graceless form and dwarfish stature;
By few approved, and few approving;
Extreme in hating and in loving;
Abhorring all whom I dislike,
Adoring who my fancy strike;
In forming judgments never long,
And for the most part judging wrong;
In friendship firm, but still believing
Others are treacherous and deceiving,
And thinking in the present æra
That friendship is a pure chimæra:
More passionate no creature living,
Proud, obstinate, and unforgiving;

But yet for those who kindness show,
Ready through fire and smoke to go.

Again, should it be asked your page,
"Pray, what may be the author's age?"
Your faults, no doubt, will make it clear,
I scarce have seen my twentieth year,
Which passed, kind Reader, on my word,
While England's throne held George the Third.

Now then your venturous course pursue:
Go, my delight!—Dear book, adieu!

MATTHEW GREGORY LEWIS (ESSAY DATE 1798)

SOURCE: Lewis, Matthew Gregory. "To the Reader." In *The Castle Spectre: A Drama. In Five Acts*, pp. 100-03. London: J. Bell, 1798.

In the following essay, Lewis addresses readers of The Castle Spectre, *informing them of the inspirations for his narrative and characters, and defending his work against negative criticism.*

Many erroneous assertions have been made respecting this Drama; some, that the language was originally extremely licentious; others, that the sentiments were violently democratic; and others again, that if Mr. Sheridan had not advised me to content myself with a single Spectre, I meant to have exhibited a whole regiment of Ghosts. To disprove these reports I have deviated from the usual mode of publishing Plays, as performed, and have printed mine almost verbatim, as originally written. Whether it merited the above accusations, the reader has now had an opportunity of judging for himself. I must just mention that the last line of the Piece is altered, and that in the Second Scene of the Fifth Act, *The Friar* was made to stick in the door-way, whereas he now makes his exit without difficulty.

Other charges, however, have been brought against me on better grounds, and I must request the reader's patience while I say a few words respecting them. To originality of character I make no pretence. Persecuted heroines and conscience-stung villains certainly have made their courtesies and bows to a British audience long before the appearance of "*The Castle Spectre;*" the *Friar* and *Alice* are copies, but very faint ones, from *Juliet's Nurse,* and Sheridan's *Father Paul,* and *Percy* is a mighty pretty-behaved young gentleman with nearly no character at all. I shall not so readily give up my claim to novelty, when I mention my misanthropic *Negro:* He has been compared to *Zanga;* but Young's Hero differs widely from what I meant in *Hassan. Zanga's* hatred is confined to one object; to destroy the happiness of that object is his sole aim, and his vengeance is no sooner accomplished, than he repents its gratification. *Hassan* is a man of violent passions, and warm feelings, whose bosom is filled with the milk of human kindness, but that milk is soured by despair; whose nature was susceptible of the tenderest affections, but who feels that all the chains of his affections are broken for ever. He has lost every thing, even hope; he has no single object against which he can direct his vengeance, and he directs it at large against mankind. He hates all the world, hates even himself; for he feels that in that world there is no one that loves him.

> "Lorsque l'on peut souffrir, sure que ses douleurs
> "D'aucun mortel ne font jamais couler les pleurs,
> "On se desinteresse à la fin de soi-même;
> "On cesse de s'aimer, si quelqu'un ne nous
>   aime!"

But though Hassan's heart is changed by disappointment and misfortune, that heart once was feeling and kind; nor could he hate with such inveteracy, if he had not loved with extreme affection. In my opinion this character is not *Zanga's*; but this I must leave to the public decision. I may, however, boldly, and without vanity, assert, that *Motley* is quite new to the Stage. In other plays the Fool has always been a sharp knave, quick in repartee, and full of whim, fancy, and entertainment; whereas *my* Fool (but I own I did not mean to make him so) is a dull, flat, good sort of plain matter of fact fellow, as in the course of the performance Mr. Bannister discovered to his great sorrow.

That *Osmond* is attended by *negroes* is an anachronism, I allow; but from the great applause which Mr. Dowton constantly received in *Hassan* (a character which he played extremely well), I am inclined to think that the audience was not greatly offended at the impropriety. For my own part, I by no means repent the introduction of my *Africans:* I thought it would give a pleasing variety to the characters and dresses, if I made my servants black; and could I have produced the same effect by making my heroine blue, blue I should have made her.

In the *Friar's* defence, when he most ungallantly leaves *Angela* in the cavern to shift for herself, I can only plead the necessity of the case. Stay where he was he could not; go he must at any rate: I trundled him off in the best way that I could; and, for the sake of the public, I heartily wish that way had been better. With regard to his not meeting *Osmond* in his flight, a little imagination will soon conquer that difficulty: It may be supposed, that as he lost his way in coming, he lost it again in going; or, that he concealed himself till *the Earl* had passed him; or, that he tumbled down and broke his neck; or, that he. . . . did any thing else you like better. I leave this matter entirely to the reader's fancy.

Against *my Spectre* many objections have been urged: one of them I think rather curious. She ought not to appear, because the belief in Ghosts no longer exists! In my opinion, this is the very reason why she *may* be produced without danger; for there is now no fear of increasing the influence of superstition, or strengthening the prejudices of the weak-minded. I confess I cannot see any reason why Apparitions may not be as well permitted to stalk in a tragedy, as Fairies be suffered to fly in a pantomime, or Heathen Gods and Goddesses to cut capers in a grand ballet; and I should rather imagine that *Oberon* and *Bacchus* now find as little credit to the full as the *Cock-lane Ghost,* or the Spectre of *Mrs. Veal.*

Never was any poor soul so ill-used as *Evelina's*, previous to her presenting herself before the audience. The Friends to whom I read my Drama, the Managers to whom I presented it, the Actors who were to perform in it—all combined to persecute my *Spectre,* and requested me to confine my Ghost to the Green-Room. Aware that without her my catastrophe would closely resemble that of the *Grecian Daughter*, I persisted in retaining her. The event justified my obstinacy: **The Spectre** was as well treated before the curtain as she had been ill-used behind it; and as she continues to make her appearance nightly with increased applause, I think myself under great obligations both to her and her representative.

But though I am conscious that it is very imperfect, I shall not so far offend my own feelings, or insult the judgment of the public, which has given it a very favourable reception, as to say that I think my Play very bad. Had such been my opinion, instead of producing it on the stage, or committing it to the press, I should have put it behind the fire, or, throwing it into the *Thames*, made a present of it to the British *Scombri*. Still its success on the stage (great enough to content even an author) does not prevent my being very doubtful as to its reception in the closet, when divested of its beautiful music, splendid scenery, and, above all, of the acting, excellent throughout. Without detracting from the merits of the other performers (to all of whom I think myself much indebted for their respective exertions), I must here be permitted to return particular thanks to Mrs. Jordan, whose manner of sustaining her character exceeded my most sanguine hopes, and in whose hands my heroine acquired an importance for which she was entirely indebted to the talents of the actress.

GENERAL COMMENTARY

MONTAGUE SUMMERS (ESSAY DATE 1938)

SOURCE: Summers, Montague. "Matthew Gregory Lewis." In *The Gothic Quest: A History of the Gothic Novel.* 1938. Reprint edition, pp. 202-38. New York: Russell & Russell, 1964.

In the following excerpt from his influential study of Gothic literature first published in 1938, Summers surveys Lewis's fictional and dramatic works and asserts that Lewis had tremendous influence upon other authors who wrote in the Gothic tradition.

He was a child, and a spoiled child, but a child of high imagination. . . . He had the finest ear for the rhythm of verse I ever heard—finer than Byron's. . . . He was one of the kindest and best creatures that ever lived.

SIR WALTER SCOTT

Lewis was a good man.

I would give many a Sugar Cane
Monk Lewis were alive again!

BYRON

"Names, madam! names! Whoever heard of such names as mine?—names, madam, that have ever been my horror, my abomination . . . think ma'am, think of my two—*two* ugly names! *Matthew*! *Gregory*! Heavens, madam! not content with permitting my helpless infancy to be outraged by the name of *Matthew,* you, without a murmur, permitted the additional infliction of *Gregory*! Twofold barbarity ma'am; I repeat, two-fold barbarity!" Thus Lewis delighted in quizzing his mother, who used to become earnest and explanatory, "Why, really my dear, Matthew being the name of your father, and Gregory the name of ———" "Barbarity, ma'am, *two*-fold barbarity!" and so well did he use to act his imaginary grievance that Mrs. Lewis never perceived the joke, nay, more she often expressed her surprise that a sensible young man, like her son, could make so much of a trifle. All the while, perhaps his vehement expostulations had a grain of truth in their fret and fume for Lewis, indeed, felt a particular aversion to his own Christian names, and frequently avowed a decided preference for his sobriquet "Monk."

Matthew Gregory Lewis was born in London, July 9th, 1775, being the eldest son of Matthew Lewis and Frances Maria, the third daughter of Sir Thomas Sewell, K. G., Master of the Rolls, 1764-84. The Lewises, who were an ancient house, not only possessed extensive West Indian property, as did the Sewells, but also a fine estate in the immediate neighbourhood of the Sewell seat, Ottershaw Park, Surrey. Hence an acquaintance sprung up between the two families and this at length ripened into the closer relationship of marriage. At this time Matthew Lewis occupied the position of Deputy-Secretary at War, in which office he was ever held to have acquitted himself with the strictest probity and honour. Of a tall and commanding person, stately, and in his manners formal even to coldness, his was a nature more like to be respected than loved. Nor can it be denied that he was ill-matched when on February 22nd, 1773, he led Fanny Sewell to the altar. She married when very young, and her artless simplicity of character was scarcely improved by a secluded girlhood, without companionship or regular culture. Her beauty, indeed, was very remarkable, and upon her introduction to London life the lovely bride was warmly, it may even be too warmly admired by the votaries of foppery and fashion. None the less, there was also a grave and serious, even a devout side to her character, which further exhibited itself hereditarily in her elder son and his absorption with the supernatural. For example, one of her favourite works for more studious reading was Joseph Glanvil's *Saducismus Triumphatus,*[1] and this she happened to possess in the first complete edition, 8vo, 1681, with Faithorne's two plates, the frontispiece depicting King Saul and the Witch of Endor and the panelled illustration of several apparitions,[2] the Dæmon of Tedworth; *"the villainous feats of that rampant hagg* Margaret Agar *of* Brewham"; the Somersetshire witch, Julian Cox; and other visions and sorceries. Over these engravings the young Mat used to pore with fearful interest,

For in the wax of a soft infant's memory
Things horrible sink deep and sternly settle.

It is significant, too, that a considerable portion of Lewis' childhood was passed at Stanstead Hall, Essex, a very ancient mansion, the family seat of a near relation on his father's side. A certain wing of the Hall had long been disused and closed, owing, it was said, to ghostly hauntings. There was, in particular, one magnificent apartment, the "Cedar Room," which the domestics expressly stipulated no one should be required to enter after dusk. The huge and strangely carved folding-doors gave on to a large landing, and in after years Lewis often recalled how when he was taken to bed at night and the moon shone palely

Illustration from *The Castle Spectre.*

through the painted oriel upon the sombre portals, with a quick glance of terror over his shoulder he hastened his steps, clinging closer to his companion's hand lest the leaves should fly apart and there stalk forth some grisly phantom of the dark, some bleeding apparition or carious skeleton. He added that to these dim memories he actually ascribed some of the most striking episodes in his famous play, *The Castle Spectre.*

In the *Life, Letters and Literary Remains of Edward Bulwer, Lord Lytton,*[3] by his Son, we are told that at Knebworth "two wings that contained apartments known by the name of 'The Haunted Chambers,' together with the whole character of the house, in itself a romance, powerfully and permanently influenced Lord Lytton's whole charcater. There were mysterious trap-doors and hiding-places, and in particular a kind of oubliette called 'Hell-hole.' As a child Lord Lytton was immensely impressed by the house, and himself in a letter recalled these early memories in vivid phrase: "I remember especially a long narrow gallery adjoining the great drawing-room (and hung with faded and grim portraits) which terminated in rooms that were called 'haunted.' . . . How

could I help writing romances when I had walked, trembling at my own footsteps, through that long gallery, with its ghostly portraits, mused in those tapestried chambers, and peeped, with bristling hair, into the shadowy abysses of Hell-hole?"[4]

. . . . .

The summer vacation of 1791 Matthew Lewis spent in Paris. He did not meet his mother as she had already returned to London, but in a letter dated September 7th, he speaks of a farce, *The Epistolary Intrigue,* which he has written, and the script of which he submits for her opinion. He has also commenced a novel, and composed a number of verses. This earliest essay of fiction, which was to be in the form of letters, rejoiced in the farcical mock-sentimental title *The Effusions of Sensibility; or, Letters from Lady Honoria Harrowheart to Miss Sophonisba Simper,* "a Pathetic Novel in the Modern Taste, being the first literary attempt of a Young Lady of tender feelings." The only portion which was ever printed occupies some nine and twenty pages (241-270) of the Second Volume of *The Life and Correspondence of M. G. Lewis,* 1839. It is extremely amusing and often very witty, amply sufficing to show that

Lewis had a keen sense of humour. The first letter which describes the Lady Honoria's departure for Portman Square from the antique towers and verdant bowers of Dunderhead Castle, the sensation she caused at the Duchess of Dingleton's ball, and the jealousy of Lady Mountain Mapletree, is written in a most mirthful vein and the adroit parody of such conventional openings is indeed a remarkable achievement for a boy of sixteen. Whether the author could have completely sustained the burlesque is another matter, a question it were unjust to inquire. Although he spoke of finishing it before his return to England, he does not appear to have carried the design beyond the second volume.

His farce, **The Epistolary Intrigue,** which he had written with the chief character Caroline intended for Mrs. Jordan, was refused by two managers, Lewis of Drury Lane, and Harris of Covent Garden, and he expresses himself in a letter to his mother as greatly mortified. None the less, not to be lightly discouraged, he set to work upon and in the same year had ready a comedy, **The East Indian,** which, however, was not to be produced until the spring of 1799. He also translated a play which he called *Felix.* This was never printed and cannot certainly be identified, but it may well be *Les Deux Amis*[5] (1770) of Beaumarchais. In writing to his mother from Oxford he promises that he will bring this with him when he comes down, so that it may be sent to Lewis of the Lane, but he adds: "I have begun something which I hope, and am indeed certain, will, hereafter, produce you a little money; though it will be some time before it is completed from the length of it, and the frequent interruption, and necessity of concealment, I am obliged to use in writing it. It is a romance, in the style of the 'Castle of Otranto.' . . . I have not yet quite finished the first volume." This romance, if completed, was never published, but Lewis subsequently founded upon these chapters the famous **Castle Spectre.**

It will not escape remark that young Lewis commenced author, translated plays, wrote a farce, composed a comedy, and employed himself upon a novel with the object of earning money for his mother. She seems at this time to have shown herself hysterical and exacting, but he never reproaches her for so frequent demands upon his purse;[6] at the most he remarks in an Oxford letter that if he enjoyed a fixed income he would gladly act as her banker, but since he had not as yet been made any settled allowance by his father, to him he was obliged to apply to meet her requirements, and this was a humiliating and disagreeable task, since he hated encroaching on a bounty which had never failed and never shown itself less than most liberal and kind. Accordingly he could but endeavour to furnish these extra subsidies from the profits of his pen. The point is important. Not only does it show Lewis in a most amiable and unselfish light, but it also reveals the motive which made him turn so early to literature. He was no dilettante, no coxcombical undergraduate with the sophomore's eternal itch for scribbling, but a worker, a practical writer whose output meant, if not bread and butter, at any rate the complement of strawberry jam, and that not for himself but for the mother whom he loved so tenderly and so well.

Matthew Gregory was intended by his father for the diplomatic service, and since for this career a knowledge of German was not merely useful but well-nigh essential, he proceeded to Weimar in the summer of 1792 in order to acquire the language of the country. After a tedious journey, and much suffering from sea-sickness during the crossing from Harwich to Helvoet, Lewis arrived at the capital of Saxe-Weimar-Eisenach on July 27th, 1792. Here the English Ambassador, to whom he carried personal letters of introduction, was Sir Brooke Boothby, Bart., himself a poet, and well known as a friend of the Edgeworths and the Lichfield literary circle. Weimar, although a small town, was at that period, the reign of Duke Karl-August, one of the most illustrious in Europe, owing to the presence at the ducal court of Goethe,[7] who had in the previous year been appointed Director of the State Theatre; Schiller[8]; Johann Gottfried Herder, first preacher in the town church; the romantic Wieland; and many other literary and artistic figures of great fame. Indeed, within three days of his arrival Lewis writes to his mother that he has been introduced not only to the original Iphigenia, the fair court-singer, Corona Elisabeth Wihelmina Schröter, but even to "M. de Goethe, the celebrated author of Werter," adding the jest "so you must not be surprised if I should shoot myself one of these fine mornings." Of *Werther* three translations had already appeared in England[9]; the first, a version through the medium of the French, in 1779, when it proved a huge success, new editions appearing at intervals until 1795; the second, this time from the author's text, in 1786; and the third in 1789. With one, perhaps with all of these, Lewis was familiar. He determined to read the original too. Eager and enthusiastic in his very first letter, July 30th, he says "I am now knocking my brains against German, as hard as ever I can. . . . As to my own nonsense, I write and write, and yet do not find I have got a bit further." The fact was that he could not conclude the second volume of the romance 'in the style of the *Castle of Otranto*' which had so long occupied his thoughts. As he himself declared, "an infernal dying man" clogged his pen, and finish him off he could not. "He has talked for half a volume already," is the plaint of the poor author. This moribund but verbose gentleman was to make his appearance as the "pale and emaciated" Reginald in **The Castle Spectre,** who certainly refuses to expire and is exceedingly loquacious.

That Matthew Gregory's residence in Weimar at a most impressionable age should have had a lasting influence upon his whole life, should have moulded his taste, directed his interests, and formed his literary style is a thing neither to be wondered at nor regretted. His enthusiasm directly inspired Scott, Shelley, Byron, and Coleridge, although the latter was ungenerous enough to gird at the very poetry to which he owed not a little of his own stimulation.[10] How vitally German Romanticism energized our literature and what it lent us need not be emphasized at this point, since these correspondences are amply discussed in another chapter, but undervalued and underrated—nay, even jeered and fleered—as the work of Lewis has been, the fact remains that his mystery and terror and his German sensationalism (I do not burke the phrase) for many years permeated English romance, and they have even to-day left us a legacy in the pages of many applauded and popularly approved writers, who with all their striving and pains do not possess a spark of that genius, which dark, fantastic and wayward as it may have shown, was undoubtedly his. . . .

At the end of April, 1794, had appeared Mrs. Radcliffe's *The Mysteries of Udolpho,* which Lewis commenced reading before he set out on his journey and finished immediately after his arrival at the Hague. It is, he cries, "in my opinion, one of the most interesting books ever published." It is significant, however, that he regarded the first nine chapters, as comparatively insipid, and yet these very passages with their exquisite descriptions of mountain scenery are among the finest of Mrs. Radcliffe's work. His imagination, however, was set afire by the lone Castle amid the far Appenines, those awful halls of dread where the dark Montoni was lord of life and death. Once more inspired to continue his own romance "in the style of *The Castle of Otranto,*" he set to work to

extricate the dying man from his difficulties, but finding himself unable to carry the story further, he was soon obliged yet again to lay it on one side.[11]

Not to be baffled, he wisely determined to begin altogether anew, on an entirely fresh track and this time things went smoothly, for on September 23rd. he triumphantly asks his mother: "What do you think of my having written, in the space of ten weeks, a romance of between three and four hundred pages octavo? I have even written out half of it fair. It is called **The Monk,** and I am myself so much pleased with it that, if the booksellers will not buy it, I shall publish it myself." Two months after, his last letter from the Hague, November 22nd, tells Mrs. Lewis that he will not send her the manuscript of **The Monk** since he prefers to hand it to her himself when they meet in London. "For my own part, I have not written a line excepting the Farce, and **The Monk,** which is a work of some length, and will make an octavo volume of 420 pages. There is a great deal of poetry inserted," and so as a *bonne bouche* he encloses a copy of the "Inscription in an Hermitage" which occurs in Chapter II. (In the printed text of **The Monk** there are some few trifling variants.) As Lewis signed his octosyllabic Preface, Imitation of Horace, Epistles, Book I, Ep. 20, "Hague, Oct. 28th, 1794," we may assume that he then completed his fair copy, and his pages were ready for the press.

Lewis' father now recalled him to England, and in December Matthew Gregory was back in London. He spent the Christmas of 1794 at Devonshire-place.

Very soon he set about finding a publisher for his romance, nor did he experience much difficulty in the quest. In March, 1796,[12] **The Monk** was first published, in three volumes, duodecimo, by John Bell, 148 Oxford Street, at nine shillings. It was re-issued in April[13] at half a guinea, whilst in October of the same year appeared a second edition, so designated on the title-page. The third, fourth, and fifth editions, all severally distinguished on their titles, followed in 1797, 1798, and 1800. In the fourth and fifth editions the title was changed to **Ambrosio, or The Monk.** Bell's advertisement, however, on the last leaf of **The Castle Spectre,** published, octavo, early in 1798, runs: "*In a few Days will be published,* By Joseph Bell, No. 148, Oxford Street, The Fourth Edition, *With considerable Additions and Alterations,* Of **The Monk, A Romance, In Three Volumes.** By M. G.

Lewis, Esq. M. P. Author Of *The Castle Spectre,* Etc. *Price* 10s. 6d."

. . . . .

It might seem difficult to decide whether it was Ann Radcliffe or Matthew Gregory Lewis who exerted the more powerful effect upon the temper and shaping of the Gothic Novel as it went its varied course, and since actually the influence of the former was far greater than that of the author of *The Monk,* it may appear a paradox to say that none the less it was the latter upon whom contemporary writers of fiction the more closely modelled certain prominent aspects of their work. The reason for this lies in the very practical consideration that the romances of Lewis were found to be far easier to copy, although we may add that the prentice pens showed themselves apter to reproduce and even to exaggerate his faults rather than to exhibit a tithe of his vigour and power, fastening upon his weakness and unable to reach after his strength.

The followers of both Mrs. Radcliffe and Lewis are legion, and very often the imitation is not only confined to theme, characters, incidents, all of which are repeated again and again in a hundred chapters with exemplary fidelity, but there are also very distinct verbal echoes to be heard, dialogue at second-hand which merely differs from the original by a bombast word inserted here and there, or a phrase dropped out for the worse.

In all essentials, it must be emphasized, Mrs. Radcliffe and Lewis differ very widely from one another. They have certain romantic subject-matter in common, but so entirely opposite are their several methods of approach and treatment that although casually they may appear at some points to contact this similarity is extremely superficial and proves but a deceptive glamour of resembling. Both employ picturesque properties, convents, castles, the Holy Office. Such a figure as the austere and stately Abbess of San Stephano in *The Italian,* although altogether improbable and exceptional, is barely possible; such a figure as Lewis' domina of S. Clare, Mother St. Agatha, is altogether chimerical, fantastic, and absurd. Lewis recked nothing of Mrs. Radcliffe's suspense, her sensibility, her landscape pictures which are not the least lovely passages of her genius. Indeed, he pronounced these uncommonly dull, and fervently wished that they had been left out, and something substituted in their room.[14] Certes, *The Mysteries of Udolpho* influenced him, but not so much as he thought and liked to make himself believe. Mrs. Radcliffe shrank from the dark diablerie of Lewis; his matricides, incests, rapes,

extremely shocked her; never did she admit his mouldering cerements and atomies; his Paphian encounters would have cruddled her very ink. Her terrors were spiritual, and for that reason her influence has most clearly shown itself in the writings of those authors whose natural reserve and a certain delicacy of talent would not have tolerated the high colouring and eroticism of *The Monk.* By his very violence, his impassioned realism, Lewis is widely separated from Mrs. Radcliffe and her school. It is the more pity that these two great writers have been so frequently and so erroneously confounded, and their work all lumped together as if they had exhibited precisely the same characteristics, developed the same style, and elaborated the same sensationalism. It is true that in their own day many minor novelists with a curious lack of perception repeatedly endeavoured to combine *Udolpho* and *The Monk* in their pages, to make one peerless heroine of Emily and Antonia, to bring an Ambrosio Montoni upon the scene, but these attempts were fore-doomed to failure; the pieces do not fit; there are awkward creaking joints, and untenoned mortises, discrepancy, contradictions even and incongruity both in the narrative and the springs of action.

The expert cook would have disdained to serve up so ill dressed an olio. The shrewder intelligencies were more quick to model their story either upon Mrs. Radcliffe or upon Lewis alone without commixture.

The novels which directly derive from *The Monk* are in themselves so numerous a company that rather than set down a large quota of parallel passages from a dozen writers it will be best to examine here in some detail two or three of the more important as a sample of the stuff. Other novels will be more conveniently noticed under their respective authors.

Charlotte Dacre, "better known as Rosa Matilda," was a professed disciple of *The Monk,* and her *Zofloya; or The Moor, A Romance of the Fifteenth Century,* 3 vols., 1806,[15] shows that she had learned her lesson well.

. . . . .

In Germany "the arch-priest of ultra-German romanticism," as he has been called, Ernst Theodor Wilhelm Hoffmann (1776-1822),[16] amply showed the influence of Lewis in one of his most powerfully fantastic tales, *Die Elixiere des Teufels* (1816),[17] of which an English translation appeared 2 vols., 1824, as *The Devil's Elixir.* For example, the first chapter of *The Monk* commences: "Scarcely had the abbey bell tolled for five minutes, and already was the church of the Capuchins thronged with auditors."

When a stranger makes inquiry concerning the crowds the answer is returned: "Can you possibly be ignorant that Ambrosio, Abbot of this monastery, pronounces sermon in this church every Thursday?" In Hoffmann's novel Medardus is a Capuchin,[18] and his sermons are crowded in similar fashion, a fact which ministers inordinately to his vanity. Thus: "An hour before the bells for assembling, the most aristocratic and cultured portion of the town's inhabitants crowded into the monastery church, no very large building, to hear the sermon of Brother Medardus."[19] A number of other passages might be instanced especially since in *The Monk* the painting of the Madonna which Ambrosio so admired is drawn from Matilda, so in *Die Elixiere, des Teufels* Medardus hears the confession of an unknown lady who acknowledges a forbidden yearning, and suddenly cries: "Thou thyself, Medardus, art the consecrated being whom I so unspeakably love!" The Capuchin is racked with concupiscence. "An impulse, till now never known, almost raged in my bosom. A passionate desire to behold her features—to press her to my heart—to perish at once in delight and despair—wholly took possession of me!" In agony he flies to kneel before the altar of S. Rosalia, which is crowned by a picture of the Saint. "In this picture which had never particularly struck me before, I now at once recognized the likeness of my beloved! Even her dress resembled the foreign habit of the unknown!"[20] It may be further remarked that in *The Monk* Antonia "Knelt before a statue of St. Rosolia [sic] her patroness, and sang a 'Midnight Hymn.'"

The adventures of *Die Elixiere des Teufels* differ considerably, of course, from those of *The Monk* in many ways, but generally it may be remarked that Monk Medardus corresponds to Ambrosio, Euphemia to Matilda, and Aurelia to Antonia.

It has been said by J. T. Bealby that *Die Elixiere des Teufels* can "scarcely be read without shuddering," and he further describes it as a "dark maze of human emotion and human weakness—a mingling of poetry, sentimentality, rollicking humour, wild remorse, stern gloom, blind delusion, dark insanity, over all which is thrown a veil steeped in the fantastic and the horrible."[21]

. . . . .

The Castle Spectre is the most famous and the most typical specimen of all Gothic melodramas. It must not indeed be judged from a purely literary point of view, for there are then very many quite palpable faults at which it is easy enough to smile with critical disdain. It has not, for example, the poetry and extraordinary power of Maturin's *Bertram,* but little imagination can be required to appreciate how upon the stage Lewis' scenes proved supremely effective. Personally, of all dramas, this "crusted grizzly skeleton melodrama" as my old friend Chance Newton who knew and loved it used to call **The Castle Spectre,** is the one I should most like to see, but unhappily the last revival in London was, more than half a century ago, at the Gaiety Theatre, for two matinée performances on May 5th and 12th, 1880, when John Hollingshead was giving "Palmy Day Neglected Dramas."[22] . . .

The scene is Conway Castle, now in possession of the villainous Earl Osmond, a usurper, who has caused his brother, Earl Reginald, and his brother's wife, to be murdered some sixteen years before. Unknown to his master, however, Kenric, major-domo of the Castle and Osmond's trusted accomplice, a character curiously compounded of greed, cruelty, pity and remorse, aided Earl Reginald, whom he has immured in a dungeon of the Castle, a secret prison of which he alone has the key. The rightful heiress of Conway, a mere babe, was scarcely saved from Osmond's wrath, but at length at Kenric's prayers she was concealed in a villager's cottage, where she grew to be the lovely Angela. She was wooed, and gave her heart to the peasant Edwy, who is none other than Percy, Earl of Northumberland. Osmond, knowing this and fearing that if she were to wed so powerful a supporter his guilt would be discovered, reclaims her from her rustic guardian, and, enraptured by her charms, designs himself to marry her, giving out that she has been discovered to be the daughter of Sir Malcolm Mowbray, long since deceased. Angela rejects his suit with scorn, whilst Earl Percy who has penetrated to the Castle to bear her thence, is recognized and held in confinement by Osmond. By a stratagem he escapes, and gathers his forces. Meanwhile Osmond compels Angela to keep her chamber, the Cedar Room, until the morrow when he threatens to espouse her by force. Here Kenric visits her and tells her that Earl Reginald, her father, still lives. They are surprised by Osmond who overhears the tale. Angela, however, is encouraged by a vision of her mother. Father Philip, who is her friend, contrives her escape from the Cedar Room by a subterranean passage, which leads them out through the vaults where she meets her father. Osmond and his minions burst in upon them, but at this very moment with a frantic gesture is about to cut down Reginald, the Spectre suddenly rises between them, and as he staggers back distraught, Angela stabs him with her poniard. He is borne away about to breathe his last, soothed by the forgiveness of his long injured and suffering brother.

I am very well aware that this bald outline can only give a poor idea of the effectiveness of the play, but even in the reading it does not require much visualization to see how skilfully the incidents have been managed and how admirably adapted they are to impress an audience. I would not seem to labour this point repeatedly, but it is distressing to read such ineptitudes as "we cannot to-day esteem Lewis any other than a mediocre dramatist intent upon the cheapest of effects."[23]

In various footnotes to the printed play,[24] and in a little appendix addressed "To The Reader," Lewis quite candidly draws attention to several hints he has adopted and in some cases improved. Thus in Act II, Scene I, the animated portrait of *The Castle of Otranto* suggested a striking bit of business; the escape of Earl Percy comes from a German play whose main incident was a similar escape of Ludwig, a Landgrave of Thuringia. When he wrote Motley's song, Lewis remembered Burgoyne's "Historical Romance" *Richard Cœur de Lion*.[25] The circumstance of Father Philip concealing himself in the bed and thus frightening Alice is from *The Mysteries of Udolpho*, where Emily and old Dorothée are alarmed when they visit at midnight the lone chamber where the Marchioness de Villeroi died.[26] In the Romance it brings forward a terrific scene. In the Play it is intended to produce an effect entirely ludicrous.[27]

Earl Reginald concealed in a secret vault may be a variation of the theme of *A Sicilian Romance*, where the Marquis of Mazzini imprisons his first wife in a subterranean abode belonging to the southern buildings of the castle of Mazzini, and gives out that she is dead. Lewis admired Marsollier's play *Camille, ou le Souterrain*[28] (1791) founded upon this very situation which is derived from the *Adèle et Theodore* (1782) of Madame de Genlis.

The Castle Spectre was most harshly criticized by those who were jealous of the young author's genius and success. Genest, who is always very severe on Lewis, is bound to allow that "Osmond, Father Philip, and Alice are very good characters—but the great run which this piece had, is a striking proof that success is a very uncertain criterion of merit."[29] It was said that Father Philip was copied from Sheridan's Father Paul; that Hassan was closely modelled on Zanga. In fact, that Os-

---

ABOUT THE AUTHOR

LORD BYRON ON "MONK" LEWIS

Lewis was a good man, a clever man, but a bore, a damned bore, one may say. My only revenge or consolation used to be, setting him by the ears with some vivacious person who hated Bores, especially M^e. de Stael, or Hobhouse, for example. But I liked Lewis: he was a Jewel of a Man had he been better set. I don't mean *personally*, but less *tiresome*; for he was tedious, as well as contradictory, to every thing and every body.

Being short-sighted, when we used to ride out together near the Brenta in the twilight in Summer, he made me go *before* to pilot him. I am absent at times, especially towards evening; and the consequence of this pilotage was some narrow escapes to the Monk on horseback. Once I led him *into* a ditch, over which I had passed as usual forgetting to warn my convoy. Once I led him nearly into the river, instead of *on* the *moveable* bridge which *in*commodes passengers; and twice did we both run against the diligence, which, being heavy and slow, did communicate less damage than it received in its leaders, who were *terrassé*'d by the charge. Thrice did I lose him in the gray of the Gloaming, and was obliged to bring to to his distant signals of distance and distress. All the time he went on talking without intermission, for he was a man of many words.

Poor fellow, he died, a martyr to his new riches, of a second visit to Jamaica—

"I'll give the lands of Deloraine
Dark Musgrave were alive again!"

that is

I would give many a Sugar Cane
Monk Lewis were alive again!

SOURCE: Byron, George Gordon, Lord. "A journal entry of October 15, 1821." In *The Works of Lord Byron: Letters and Journals*, Vol. V, edited by Rowland E. Prothero, 1821. Reprint edition, p. 418. New York: Octagon Books, 1966.

Percy who has gained admittance with his followers drives back the assassins, and when Osmond

mond should be attended by negroes was an anachronism and yet Lewis was bold enough to protest "I by no means regret the introduction of my *Africans*." He comically added that black servants gave a pleasing variety to the characters, "and could I have produced the same effect by making my heroine blue, blue I should have made her." Against the Spectre ridiculous objections were urged. "She ought not to appear because the belief in Ghosts no longer exists." It was bruited abroad that if Sheridan had not advised the author to content himself with a single Spectre, his purpose was "to have exhibited a whole regiment of Ghosts." The managers, the actors, the friends to whom the play was read, all begged Lewis to confine the Ghost to the Green-room. He persisted, and "*The Spectre* was as well treated before the curtain as she had been ill-used behind it." The two apparition scenes were greeted with tumultuous applause. Lewis quite candidly and very properly adds that if he with mock-modesty declared he thought *The Castle Spectre* very bad, what would such an avowal be save to insult the judgement of the public "which has given it a very favourable reception. . . . Still its success on the stage (great enough to content even an author) does not prevent my being very doubtful as to its reception in the closet, when divested of its beautiful music, splendid scenery, and above all, of the acting, excellent throughout."[30] None the less, *The Castle Spectre* was greeted with avidity by the reading public, and ran through no less than seven editions in 1798, whilst an eighth edition appeared in 1799, and a tenth edition in 1803.[31] The prolific Miss Sarah Wilkinson was not ill-advised when she turned the popular *The Castle Spectre* into a prose romance (1820).

. . . . .

In 1804 Lewis published with J. F. Hughes of Wigmore Street what is perhaps the most popular of his lesser works, *The Bravo of Venice,* "a Romance, Translated from the German" of Zschokke's *Abœllino, der grosse Bandit* (1794). The brief dedication to the Earl of Moira[32] is dated from Inverary Castle, October 27th, 1804. The fifth edition of *The Bravo of Venice* appeared in 1807. This tale is also the first number[33] of *The Romancist and Novelist's Library*, 1839, and there were constant reprints until the end of the century. In some of the later editions the form of the story is slightly altered, but although some minor details are perhaps more closely knit and the pace correspondingly quickened, the narrative can hardly be considered in every respect improved.

Lewis has pretty freely adapted from Zschokke as the fancy took him, and not without much profit to his pages. It cannot be needful to do more than remind ourselves very briefly of the theme of so famous a story. The riddling intrigue turns upon the disguise of the Neapolitan Count Rosalvo, who presents himself in Venice as Count Flodoardo, desirous of serving the Republic. He also fills the rôle of the mysterious and terrible Abellino, a monster of ugliness and ferocity, in which character he is able to penetrate the haunts of the banditti who are terrorizing Venice, and to unmask the conspirators who are plotting her downfall. As Flodoardo he wins the love of the Doge's fair niece, Rosabella of Corfu; she clings to him even when she believes Flodoardo to be the murderous Bandit; as Rosalvo he weds her and is acclaimed the saviour of the City.

Additions were also made by Lewis who in the Advertisement writes: "I have taken some liberties with the original—Every thing that relates to Monaldeschi (a personage who does not exist in the German romance), and the whole of the concluding chapter (with the exception of a very few sentences) have been added by myself."

The Critical Review, Series the Third, Vol. V, No. 3, July, 1805, devoted an article of several pages (pp. 252-6) to a detailed examination of *The Bravo of Venice*, although the writer confessed he was so inured as now to be able "to turn over the leaves of a Germanico-terrific Romance with an untrembling hand." He allowed that "The history of the *Bravo of Venice* is interesting, the language glows with animation, and the *denouement* is rapid and surprising." "Novels have commonly been divided into the pathetic, the sentimental and the humorous; but the writers of the German school have introduced a new class, which may be called the *electric*. Every chapter contains a shock; and the reader not only stares, but starts, at the close of every paragraph; so that we cannot think the wit of a brother-critic farfetched, when he compared that shelf in his library, on which the *Tales of Wonder,* the Venetian Bravo, and other similar productions were piled, to a galvanic battery.

Mr. Lewis possesses a fertile imagination and considerable genius: we would therefore advise him to quit the beaten track of imitation. "'*Ohe! jam satis est*!' We have had enough of ghastly visages, crawling worms, death's heads and crossbones. When we first visited Mrs. Salmon's waxwork, Mother Shipton's sudden kick startled us, and we were terrified at the monster who darts from the corner cupboard to devour Andromeda; but we can now visit this scene of wonders without terror or alarm, and if we affect surprise, it is merely in compliment to the woman, who exhibits them, that she may not be disappointed of her grin."

This is something more than severe, even a little ill-natured, for I do not think any reader could disentangle the thread of *The Bravo of Venice,* and he is certainly not to be envied whose interest is not held fast until the very end of this fascinating romance. Naturally when once we know the secret we peruse these chapters a second time with interest and with keenest admiration of the workmanship, but we cannot reasonably expect the same thrill.

· · · · ·

In the winter of 1804 there occurred an unhappy difference between Lewis and his father, which caused the former, at least, great pain and anxiety. The facts may be briefly told. The elder Mr. Lewis had commenced an acquaintance and maintained no very proper intimacy with a lady of fashion and ton, Mrs. R———, who after being a constant visitor to Devonshire Place, presently not only became an inmate of the house but was recognized as mistress of the establishment, where her son Frederick also made his home. Mr. Lewis' two daughters were now married, but Matthew could not help expressing his displeasure, not so much perhaps in words as by actions at seeing another woman installed in his mother's room. Mr. Lewis took pepper in the nose upon his son's eminently correct attitude, and with great severity informed him that he was no longer welcome under the paternal roof. It is true that Matthew occasionally visited the house, but only to be subjected to extreme mortification and open slights. At one period the father most wickedly and dishonourably curtailed his son's income by one half, contrary to his solemn promise and pledge. However the injustice, one is pleased to know, was not of long continuance, for Mr. Lewis soon came to a sense of his own gross misbehaviour in this regard, and Matthew's allowance was restored to the proper figure, as had been expressly engaged. A complete reconciliation between father and son, owing to the elder man's obstinacy and sullen brooding temper, could not be effected for some years.

Matthew certainly had need of literary success to support him under these domestic trials. In 1806 he published, 8vo, a tragedy *Adelgitha; or The Fruits of a Single Error,* which ran into no less than three editions during the one year, and reached a fifth edition in 1817. The play, which

had thus already won its way into popular favour, was not produced until Thursday, April 30th, 1807, when it was given at Drury Lane with Mrs. Powell in the title-rôle; Henry Siddons, Robert Guiscard, Prince of Apulia; Elliston, Lothair; Raymond, Michael Ducas; and Mrs. H. Siddons, Imma. The scene, Otranto. The year, 1080.

Lewis himself quite frankly acknowledged that the quasi-historical background of Guiscard and Michael of Byzantium is a flam. He had constructed his plot, sketched his characters, and then last of all fitted them into a striking framework, allowing stage pictures of "a Gothic room," "a splendidly illuminated Gothic hall," wherein an ancient minstrel strikes his harp, a grove terminated by a cloister which gives scope for that procession of nuns Lewis so loved to present.

Adelgitha, who is the wife of Guiscard, when very young had been seduced by George of Clermont, the fruit of the amour being Lothair, whom she represents to her husband as an orphan. Michael Ducas, Emperor of Byzantium, driven into exile by rebels, seeks the shelter of Guiscard's court, and here Lothair, who has risen to high honour by his valour and virtues, falls in love with the Princess Imma. Whilst Guiscard is absent waging war on behalf of Ducas, this latter attempts to win Adelgitha, and when she rejects his disloyal suit with scorn, he threatens to expose her secret which has become known to him. Immediately after Guiscard's return she resolves to acquaint him with the whole, relating her story as having happened to another. A very powerful and well-written scene follows in which Guiscard shows himself implacable and relentless in his anger against the unnamed deliquent. Adelgitha now implores Michael Ducas to return the letters which he holds and which prove her first unchastity. Mockingly he refuses, whereupon in a tumult of passion she drives a dagger to his heart. Lothair, who by the treachery of the dead emperor, is already suspect of being Adelgitha's lover, is accused of the murder, but as he is led to execution she avows the whole. After a struggle of agony her husband out of his tender love forgives, whereupon exclaiming:

> I'm happy! Guiscard, Guiscard! thus I thank thee
> And next *reward* thee thus!

she embraces him for the last time, and stabs herself.

Adelgitha is a very fine tragedy, and fully deserved the favour with which it was received by crowded houses. The music was composed by Michael Kelly.

. . . . .

During half a century and more, criticism of Lewis, such as it is, obvious and facile to the last degree, for the most part hardly seems to have gone beyond **The Monk**, and hence it has been necessary to consider both the romances and the ballads, and the plays at some length, since consciously or unwittingly he introduced new and essential features both by his prose works, his verse and his dramas into the Gothic novel, upon which he exercised so tremendous, one might almost say so illimitable, an influence. It is, I think, more useful for the purpose of our survey specifically to indicate (as indeed I have already done) the vast imaginative force derived from Lewis which energized and inspired numerical novels and impelled the incidence of romance in particular directions, rather than at this one point by summarizing to present what must necessarily become a vague, undefined, and in many respects incomplete and inadequate analysis of both those prominent characteristics and the many undercurrents of supernatural suggestion, which eddying fainter and fainter, it may be, through channels now brackish, now fair, until almost lost or sublimated in the chaotic spate of modern fiction, can none the less very clearly be related to and are in effect resultant from the genius, often morbid and wayward, yet ever vital and compelling, of Matthew Gregory Lewis.

Notes

1. "*Saducismus Triumphatus:* Or, Full and Plain Evidence Concerning Witches And Apparitions. . . . By *Joseph Glanvil* late Chaplain in Ordinary to his Majesty, and Fellow of the Royal Society. With a Letter of Dr. *Henry More* on the same Subject." The more usual spelling (of later editions) is *Sadducismus Triumphatus*. The earliest draft, *Philosophical considerations touching Witches and Witchcraft*, was published 1666. Dr. E. A. Baker, *History of the English Novel*, Vol. V (1934), p. 208, describes *Saducismus Triumphatus* as a "chamber of horrors," which this fine work most certainly is not. Nor do I conceive that a rather flippant and wholly unapt label would have been very acceptable to the great and profoundly philosophical divine who was the author.

2. "King Saul and the Witch of Endor" was reproduced in my *History of Witchcraft and Demonology*, 1926, p. 178. The panelled illustration of several apparitions was reproduced as the frontispiece to my *Geography of Witchcraft*, 1927.

3. Two volumes, 1883. Vol. I, chapter iv, pp. 32-8.

4. Unfortunately the haunted rooms were pulled down in 1812, when, after the death of Richard Warburton Lytton, December, 1810, Mrs. Bulwer (now Bulwer-Lytton) settled at Knebworth, but resolved to demolish three sides of the great quadrangle and confine the house to the fourth side. The haunted rooms, however, are minutely described in a little story by Miss James, entitled *Jenny Spinner; or, The Ghost of Knebworth House*, which was never published, but of which a few copies only were printed and preserved at Knebworth.

5. Used by the elder Colman in his *The Man of Business*, produced at Covent Garden, January 29th, 1774; and translated by C. H. as *The Two Friends, or, The Liverpool Merchant*, 8vo, 1800.

6. Many of Mrs. Lewis' difficulties were due to a number of persons who imposed upon her, and whose avidity she satisfied when in fact unable to supply their wants, had such even been genuine and well founded. See *The Life and Correspondence of M. G. Lewis*, 1839, Vol. I, p. 67.

7. Goethe had been invited to Weimar, where he took up his residence, November 7th, 1775, by the Duke. He died here March 22nd, 1832.

8. Actually Schiller had been appointed to a Professorship at Jena in 1789, which he resigned in 1799.

9. T. M. Carré, *Goethe en Angleterre* (1920), Chapter I; also *Bibliographie de Goethe en Angleterre*, Chapter I. Further, see the article by A. E. Turner in the *Modern Language Review*, Vol. XVI (July-October), 1921, pp. 364-70.

10. Coleridge, *Biographia Literaria*, 2 vols., London, 1817; Vol. II, p. 28.

11. In his fuliginous book with the fierce title *La Carne, La Morte e il Diavolo nella letteratura romantica!* (discreetly and appropriately translated, be it noted, into English as *The Romantic Agony*) Signor Mario Praz, amongst other errors in reference to Lewis, confuses *The Monk* with the first unfinished romance (see p. 60 of *The Romantic Agony*, English translation by Angus Davidson, 1933). I might hesitate, however, to suggest that Signor Praz is at fault, since Mr. Wyndham Lewis, in *Men Without Art*, p. 175, in reference to *The Romantic Agony*, spoke of "This gigantic pile of satanic bric-a-brac, so industriously assembled, under my directions by Professor Praz." This was repeated by Mr. Stephen Spender, *The Destructive Element*, p. 206. But Signor Praz wrote hotly to *The Times Literary Supplement*, August 8th, 1935, "to point out" that Mr. Wyndham Lewis' words were "grossly misleading." He added: "I am afraid I must disclaim the honour of being ranked as his disciple, sorry as I am to deprive him of this satisfaction." *Actum est de* Mr. Wyndham Lewis! After all it does not in the least matter who is responsible for such disjointed gimcrack as *The Romantic Agony*.

    The Sosii were celebrated booksellers in Rome. Lewis aptly has "Stockdale, Hookham, or Debrett."

12. *Monthly Magazine or British Register*, March, 1796. The List of new publications. In *The Life and Correspondence of M. G. Lewis*, 1839, Vol. I, p. 151, there is a bad blunder in regard to *The Monk*: "The first and greatest era in the literary life of Lewis was the publication of 'Ambrosio, or The Monk,' which event took place in the summer of 1795." Several writers have repeated the error that 1795 is the date of the first edition of *The Monk*. Thus Elton, *A Survey of English Literature, 1780-1830*, 1912, Vol. I, p. 215. Railo, *The Haunted Castle*, 1927, p. 89. Rudolf Schneider, *Der Mönch in der englischen Dichtung bis auf Lewis's "Monk," 1795*, 1927, p. 168. Herr Brauchli, *Der englische Schauerroman um*

1800, 1928, pp. 200, 235, 254. Miss J. M. S. Tompkins, *The Popular Novel in England, 1770-1800*, 1932, p. 278. E. A. Baker, *The History of the English Novel*, Vol. V (1934), p. 205. Both Baker, who is responsible for an edition of *The Monk* (1907), and Railo fall into a further mistake when they assert that the original title of Lewis' romance was *Ambrosio, or The Monk*.

13. *Monthly Magazine or British Register*, April, 1796. I have generally used the copy of *The Monk* which belonged to Francis Douce (1757-1834), and which is preserved in the Bodleian Library, Shelfmark, Douce: L. 307. This contains some interesting contemporary notes and cuttings.

14. Lewis in a letter from The Hague to his mother, May 18th, 1794. *Life and Correspondence of M. G. Lewis*, Vol. I, p. 123.

15. Longman, Hurst, Rees, and Orme, June, 1806, 13s. 6d. There is a reprint in the volume of *Zofloya* with an Introduction by the present writer, 1927.

16. *E. T. A. Hoffmann's Leben und Nachlass*, "von J. G. Hitzig, herausg. von Micheline Hoffmann, geb. Rorer," 5 vols., Stuttgart, 1839. See also *Erinnerungen aus meinem Leben*, von Z. Funck [G. Kunz], Leipzig, 1836.

17. The first volume was completed in less than a month. The second volume (after a considerable interval) was finished before the end of 1815. The work is, as Hoffmann himself avowed, something disjointed.

18. It should be said that in 1812 Hoffmann paid a visit to the Kapuziner-Kloster at Bamberg, and was extremely impressed by what he saw and by the conversation of a venerable friar, Father Cyrillus. See *Erinnerungen*, p. 60, *sqq*.

19. *The Devil's Elixir*. From the German of E. T. A. Hoffmann. Blackwood and Cadell, 1824, Vol. I, p. 78.

20. *Ibid.*, pp. 87, 89. S. Rosalia "born of the royal blood of Charlemagne," is the especial patroness of Palermo. Major feast, September 4th. I suppose the name was suggested to Lewis by a certain picturesqueness and beauty. The Saint was not, however, a martyr, as Hoffmann (p. 89) represents.

21. E. T. W. Hoffmann, *Weird Tales*. A new translation by J. T. Bealby. 2 vols., Nimmo, 1885. Vol. I, Biographical Notice, p. xlviii.

22. J. D. Beveridge acted Earl Osmond; J. B. Johnstone, Earl Reginald; Crawford, Percy; J. L. Shine, Father Philip; W. Elton, Motley; T. Squire, Kenric; Miss Louise Willes, Angela; Mrs. Leigh, Alice; and Miss Hobbes, the Spectre. See John Hollingshead's *Footlights*, 8vo, 1883; also Clement Scott and Cecil Howard, *Edward Leman Blanchard*, 2 vols., 1891; Vol. II, p. 501, n. 5.

23. J. R. A. Nicoll, *A History of Late Eighteenth Century Drama*, 1927, p. 100. This writer with rather heavy wit talks of the Spectre as "an exceedingly solid ghost."

24. 8vo, Printed for J. Bell, 1798; pp. 28, 41, 58, 69, and 100-3.

25. From the French of M. J. Sedaine. Produced at Drury Lane, October 24th, 1786. The original music by Grétry was arranged by Thomas Linley. This work proved exceedingly popular. Another adaptation from Sedaine, *Richard Cœur de Lion*, by Leonard Macnally, produced at Covent Garden, October 16th, 1786, was not so successful.

26. 1794; Vol. IV, chapter lv.

27. Note by Lewis. *The Castle Spectre*, 8vo, 1798, p. 58.

28. *Life and Correspondence of M. G. Lewis*, Vol. II, pp. 60-1.

29. *Some Account of the English Stage*, 1832, Vol. VII, pp. 332-3.

30. *The Castle Spectre*, 8vo, 1798, p. 103.

31. It was continually reprinted throughout the nineteenth century and appears in very many collections; for example, Cumberland's *British Theatre*, Vol. XV, 1827, "Printed from the Acting Copy"; Dicks Standard Plays, No. 35.

32. Francis Rawdon Hastings, first Marquis of Hastings and second Earl of Moira, 1754-1826.

33. Price 2d. J. Clements, 21 and 22 Little Pulteney Street, Regent Street.

TITLE COMMENTARY

The Monk

SAMUEL TAYLOR COLERIDGE (REVIEW DATE FEBRUARY 1797)

SOURCE: Coleridge, Samuel Taylor. "A review of *The Monk*." *The Critical Review* 19 (February 1797): 194-200.

In the following excerpt from a review of The Monk, *Coleridge acknowledges Lewis's genius but objects to what he perceives as* The Monk's *indecency, immorality, and irreligious air.*

[Cheaply] as we estimate romances in general, we acknowledge, [*The Monk: a Romance*], the offspring of no common genius. . . . Ambrosio, a monk, surnamed the Man of Holiness, proud of his own undeviating rectitude, and severe to the faults of others, is successfully assailed by the tempter of mankind, and seduced to the perpetration of rape and murder, and finally precipitated into a contract in which he consigns his soul to everlasting perdition.

The larger part of the three volumes is occupied by the underplot, which, however, is skilfully and closely connected with the main story, and is subservient to its development. The tale of the bleeding nun is truly terrific; and we could not easily recollect a bolder or more happy conception than that of the burning cross on the forehead of the wandering Jew. . . . But the character of Matilda, the chief agent in the seduction of Antonio, appears to us to be the author's master-piece. It is, indeed, exquisitely imagined, and as exquisitely supported. The whole work is distinguished by the variety and impressiveness of its incidents; and the author every-where discovers an imagination rich, powerful, and fervid. Such are the excellencies;—the errors and defects are more numerous, and (we are sorry to add) of greater importance.

All events are levelled into one common mass, and become almost equally probable, where the order of nature may be changed whenever the author's purposes demand it. No address is requisite to the accomplishment of any design; and no pleasure therefore can be received from the perception of *difficulty surmounted.* The writer may make us wonder, but be cannot surprise us. For the same reasons a romance is incapable of exemplifying a moral truth. . . . As far, therefore, as the story is concerned, the praise which a romance can claim, is simply that of having given pleasure during its perusal; and so many are the calamities of life, that he who has done this, has not written uselessly. The children of sickness and of solitude shall thank him.—To this praise, however, our author has not entitled himself. The sufferings which he describes are so frightful and intolerable, that we break with abruptness from the delusion, and indignantly suspect the man of a species of brutality, who could find a pleasure in wantonly imagining them; and the abominations which he pourtrays with no hurrying pencil, are such as the observation of character by no means demanded, such as 'no observation of character can justify, because no good man would willingly suffer them to pass, however transiently, through his own mind.' The merit of a novelist is in proportion (not simply to the effect, but) to the *pleasurable* effect which he produces. Situations of torment, and images of naked horror, are easily conceived; and a writer in whose works they abound, deserves our gratitude almost equally with him who should drag us by way of sport through a military hospital, or force us to sit at the dissecting-table of a natural philosopher. . . . Figures that shock the imagination, and narratives that mangle the feelings, rarely discover *genius,* and always betray a low and vulgar taste. Nor has our author indicated less ignorance of the human heart in the management of the principal character. The wisdom and goodness of providence have ordered that the tendency of vicious actions to deprave the heart of the perpetrator, should diminish in proportion to the greatness of his temptations. Now, in addition to constitutional warmth and irresistible opportunity, the monk is impelled to incontinence by friendship, by compassion, by gratitude, by all that is amiable, and all that is estimable; yet in a few weeks after his first frailty, the man who had been described as possessing much general humanity, a keen and vigorous understanding with habits of the most exalted piety, degenerates into an uglier fiend than the gloomy imagination of Danté would have ventured to picture. Again, the monk is described as feeling and acting under the influence of an appetite which could not co-exist with his other emotions. The romance-writer possesses an unlimited power over situations; but he must scrupulously make his characters act in congruity with them. Let him work *physical* wonders only, and we will be content to *dream* with him for a while; but the first *moral* miracle which he attempts, he disgusts and awakens us. Thus our judgment remains unoffended, when, announced by thunders and earthquakes, the spirit appears to Ambrosio involved in blue fires that increase the cold of the cavern; and we acquiesce in the power of the silver myrtle which made gates and doors fly open at its touch, and charmed every eye into sleep. But when a mortal, fresh from the impression of that terrible appearance, and in the act of evincing for the first time the witching force of this myrtle is represented as being at the same moment agitated by so fleeting an appetite as that of lust, our own feelings convince us that this is not improbable, but impossible; not preternatural, but contrary to nature. The extent of the powers that may exist, we can never ascertain; and therefore we feel no great difficulty in yielding a temporary belief to any, the strangest, situation of *things.* But that situation once conceived, how beings like ourselves would feel and act in it, our own feelings sufficiently instruct us; and we instantly reject the clumsy fiction that does not harmonise with them. These are the two *principal* mistakes in judgment, which the author has fallen into; but we cannot wholly pass over the frequent incongruity of his style with his subjects. It is gaudy where it should have been severely simple; and too often the mind is offended by phrases the most trite and colloquial, when it demands and had expected a sterness and solemnity of diction.

A more grievous fault remains,—a fault for which no literary excellence can atone,—a fault which all other excellence does but aggravate, as adding subtlety to a poison by the elegance of its preparation. Mildness of censure would here be criminally misplaced, and silence would make us accomplices. Not without reluctance then, but in full conviction that we are performing a duty, we declare it to be our opinion, that **The Monk** is a romance, which if a parent saw in the hands of a son or daughter, he might reasonably turn pale.

The temptations of Ambrosio are described with a libidinous minuteness, which, we sincerely hope, will receive its best and only adequate censure from the offended conscience of the author himself. The shameless harlotry of Matilda, and the trembling innocence of Antonia, are seized with equal avidity, as vehicles of the most voluptuous images; and though the tale is indeed a tale of horror, yet the most painful impression which the work left on our minds was that of great acquirements and splendid genius employed to furnish a *mormo* for children, a poison for youth, and a provocative for the debauchee. Tales of enchantments and witchcraft can never be *useful*: our author has contrived to make them *pernicious*, by blending, with an irreverent negligence, all that is most awfully true in religion with all that is most ridiculously absurd in superstition. He takes frequent occasion, indeed, to manifest his sovereign contempt for the latter, both in his own person, and (most incongruously) in that of his principal characters; and that his respect for the *former* is not excessive, we are forced to conclude from the treatment which its inspired writings receive from him. . . .

If it be possible that the author of these blasphemies is a Christian, should he not have reflected that the only passage in the scriptures [Ezekiel, Chap. xxiii], which could give a *shadow* of plausiblity to the *weakest* of these expressions, is represented as being spoken by the Almighty himself? But if he be an infidel, he has acted consistently enough with that character, in his endeavours first to inflame the fleshly appetites, and then to pour contempt on the only book which would be adequate to the task of recalming them. We believe it not absolutely impossible that a mind may be so deeply depraved by the habit of reading lewd and voluptuous tales, as to use even the Bible in conjuring up the spirit of uncleanness. The most innocent expressions might become the first link in the chain of association, when a man's soul had been so poisoned; and we believe it not absolutely impossible that he might extract pollution from the word of purity and, in a literal sense, *turn the grace of God into wantonness.*

We have been induced to pay particular attention to this work from the unusual success which it has experienced. It certainly possesses much real merit, in addition to its meretricious attractions. Nor must it be forgotten that the author is a man of rank and fortune.—Yes! the author of **The Monk** signs himself a LEGISLATOR!—We stare and tremble.

The poetry interspersed through the volumes is, in general, far above mediocrity.

A FRIEND TO GENIUS (REVIEW DATE APRIL 1797)

SOURCE: A Friend to Genius. "An Apology for *The Monk.*" *The Monthly Mirror* 3 (April 1797): 210-15.

In the following essay, the psuedonymous critic maintains that The Monk *advocates virtue, rather than—as many reviewers have contended—vice.*

It is with no inconsiderable pain that I have remarked the numerous attacks which have been made by the host of critics on the ingenious author of **The Monk,** for the supposed vicious tendency of that excellent romance. The author is universally allowed to be endowed with nature's best gift, genius, and in the work before us is generally acknowledged to discover throughout an imagination, rich, powerful, and fervid. This able writer is, however, attacked on a point which, I am sure, must make him feel little satisfaction in the applause which his genius commands. It is asserted by almost all the critics who have sat in judgment on this admirable performance, that its *tendency* is to deprave the heart, to vitiate the understanding, and to enlist the passions in the cause of vice. Differing as I do with these censors, as to this and other objections, I wish, through the medium of your impartial publication, to rescue his production from this undeserved obloquy. I have not the pleasure of Mr. Lewis's acquaintance, and I know not how this apology may be received on his part, but the defence of genius is the common cause of all men of the least pretensions to literature; and every person who can enjoy works of taste, has the right of rescuing them from unmerited attacks. I should, as little as the critics, wish to be the apologist of vice, or the defender of lasciviousness; but justice requires that error, and error of such magnitude, as it regards Mr. Lewis's character, should be detected and exposed.

The error of the principal objection to this romance, viz. that of its vicious *tendency,* appears to me entirely to arise from inaccuracy of observation of the author's work, of the human heart, and of the meaning of the word tendency. It is not a temporary effect, produced upon the imagination or the passions, by particular passages, which can fairly be cited as the tendency of the work; we must examine what are the probable general results from the whole, and not judge from these partial and fleeting effects.

In this view, I maintain, this beautiful romance is well calculated to support the cause of virtue, and to teach her lessons to man. I am not old enough to have my heart steeled against the effects of the strongest of the human passions, nor young enough to riot in lascivious description, or wanton in the regions of obscene imagery. I can feel as disgusted as the critics with such defects; but I entreat these *grey bearded* gentleman to consider again whether there are any such images in the work before us. The lessons of virtue which I see in the Monk, are striking and impressive. In the character of Ambrosio we see a man delineated of strong passions, which have been for a long period subdued by as strong resolution; of a natural disposition to virtue, but, like all other men, with some portion of vice, which has been fostered by the situation into which his fate had thrown him; he is haughty, vindictive, and austere. The greatest error of which he is guilty, is too great a confidence in his own virtue, too great a reliance on his own hatred of vice. We are taught by his conduct that this unbounded confidence, by blinding the mind as to the real consequences which result, lays the foundation for vice, and opens an easy road to great excesses. We have again a very forcible illustration in Ambrosio, a man of the strongest understanding and the highest powers of reason, of the danger of receding even in the least from the path of virtue, or giving way in the slightest degree to the insidious approaches of vice. *C'est te premier pas qui coute,* is a truth long established, and is well illustrated in the present instance. We see and feel strongly this danger, and the lesson is the more forcible, in proportion to the strength of understanding which is shown in the Monk. We learn that when once a man ventures into the pool of vice, that he plunges deeper and deeper till he is completely overwhelmed. These are striking and impressive lessons.

There are many other moral lessons which are inculcated by the work in the strongest manner; the tendency, therefore, i. e. the general effect likely to result, is favourable to the cause of virtue and morality. We are however told, that "the temptations of Ambrosio are described with a libidinous minuteness, which leaves the painful impression of great acquirements and splendid genius, employed to furnish poison for youth, and a provocative for the debauchee." [*Critical Review,* for February, 1797.] If this were the case, I must give up my author in part, though still the tendency of the whole would be good. But I deny the fact. I request that the character and circumstances of Ambrosio may be seriously considered. To a man of strong understanding, austerity of manners, and great self command, strong temptations must be offered. If the author had made the Monk sink under a slight temptation, he would have offended against the laws of probability, and shocked the reason of his readers. I ask if it be possible to describe such temptations as were calculated to seduce such a man, with greater delicacy and decorum than our author has done: and I will take for example the strongest instances—the conclusion of chapter 2. vol. I p. 253 of vol. 2. and his attack on Antonia in p. 36 and 37 of vol. 3. The answer, I am persuaded, must be—No! Highly coloured as these passages are, I maintain that no heart but one already depraved, could rise from them, if the preceding part of the work had been perused, with the least impurity. The mind that could draw food for vicious appetites from this work, must have made no little progress in the paths of profligacy and debauchery; so strong are the entrenchments erected before the heart, by the *general tendency,* of the work.

The previous part is calculated to prevent all the evil which may arise from warmth of description, by the interest we take in observing the gradual progress of vice in Ambrosio's bosom, and the hatred we of course must feel for this insidious adversary. The work can be read only by three descriptions of persons; either those whose minds, by habitual vice, are prepared to turn every the least hint to the purposes of food for their depraved appetites, or as incitements to their dormant desires, which require stimulants; or those who are wavering between vice and virtue, whose minds may be led to either, by interesting their passions strongly for one or the other; or else, young, innocent, and undepraved persons. The first deserve not notice: purity itself would be poison to their hearts, and the modestest allusion would excite depraved ideas. The passions of the second will be, I contend, excited more strongly to virtue than to vice by **The Monk,** because the horrors consequent on his vicious conduct are so strongly pourtrayed, as to destroy the momentary effect, if any were produced, of the passages which are rather warm in description. The last, from the very supposition of their being yet innocent and unpolluted, and in consequence ignorant, can not have improper ideas excited, or their passions roused to vice; as, in the first place, they will not be able to understand as much as our *knowing* critics, nor can the confused notions of felicity which may be excited destroy the purity of their minds,

49

or the effect of the moral lessons inculcated. The writer of this paper felt not a single loose idea excited by the warmest passages, so perfectly had he imbibed the moral lessons which the author has so forcibly brought forward.

The critics themselves seem aware of this tendency of the work, and therefore endeavour to deprive the author of the defence, by roundly asserting that "a romance is incapable of exemplifying moral truth; and that he who could rise superior to all earthly temptation, and whom the strength of the spiritual world alone would be adequate to overwhelm, might reasonably be proud, and would fall with glory" As applied to *The Monk,* there are two errors in this assertion. The reader of this romance has no reason to imagine, till the greater part of the mischief has been done, that any but earthly temptations are used against the hero. The fall of Ambrosio is precisely that which would happen to any man of a similar character, assailed as he was by the fascinating arts of a woman, skilled in exciting the strongest passions, and endowed with the most attractive charms. We see the gradual progress she makes in undermining his virtue by merely human means. His feelings, his gratitude, and finally the strong desires of human nature are all combined to ensure his fall. But still the temptations appear to be no more than human. We see where a man of truly virtuous principles would have commenced resistance; we observe and lament his first deviation from the path of virtue; and cannot withhold our wishes that he may remain firm when the first disposition to yield manifests itself. Matilda appears to be merely a woman, though a woman of the greatest charms, and of an extraordinary character; but still there is nothing improbable or unnatural in the means of temptation, nothing that a man of a strong mind and pure virtue would not have resisted. The lesson therefore is taught and deeply imbibed before the discovery of supernatural agency is made, and that discovery does not and cannot eradicate the morality before inculcated.

Nor is it true in general that moral truth cannot be conveyed in romance. The general sense of mankind is against the critics in this assertion. From the earliest ages fiction, and incredible fiction, has been thought a proper vehicle for moral instruction, from the fables of Æsop, to the tales, allegories, and visions of modern days. The religion itself which these gentlemen profess inculcates the notion that Lucifer is the author of all our vicious propensities, and that he is the continual seducer of man. An allegorical representa-

tion of this being visibly interfering is no more therefore than adopting popular belief, and turning it to the purposes of instruction. It is no more improbable, on the notion of this great tempter, that a man should yield to his agency, when he himself assumes the human figure, than when he is supposed, as he is, to inhabit the bodies of all the vicious, and supply the crafty and artful with the means of operating on inferior minds. We do not the less blame Eve, because we are told that she yielded to the temptation of the serpent.

As to the minor objections made to the conduct of parts of the story, and defects of style and description, I feel not myself called on to defend, my object not being to establish the literary but moral excellence of the work. The only remaining objection which I shall attempt to answer is that "our author has contrived to make his romance pernicious, by blending, with an irreverent negligence, all that is most awfully true in religion, with all that is most ridiculously absurd in superstition. He takes frequent occasion, indeed, to manifest his sovereign contempt for the latter, both in his own person and in that of his principal characters; and that his respect for the former is not excessive we are forced to conclude from the treatment which its inspired writers receive from him."

In support of this observation we have a garbled passage quoted by the critics, in which the author has noticed with too much warmth, we must confess, some of the passages of the bible, which are undoubtedly improper for the eye of a young female. It is not fair to quote this passage without adding the eulogiums which the author has passed on the morality of the sacred writings, both in that passage and others in the work, Whether the author be or be not a Christian, is not the inquiry, but whether there be any foundation for the observation made on the indecency of some parts of our religious code; this the critics are obliged to allow is the case in one instance, viz. Ezekiel chap. 23. There are also other examples which must be in the eye of every man who has react these writings with attention. The indiscriminate perusal of such passages as occur, in which every thing is called by its vulgar name, in which the most luxuriant images are described, as in Solomon's Song, must certainly be improper for young females. So fully aware were the Jews of this truth, that they prohibited the reading of Solomon's Song, till a certain age, when the passions are in subjection. The warmth of expression is too great, but we may pardon this, since we see a desire of preventing the mischievous effects of even the most generally excellent productions.—The author, so far from deserving to be stigmatized as an enemy to Christianity, appears to me to be acting as one of its best friends, when he endeavours to prevent the mischief which may ensue from mixing what may be improper for young minds, with the rest of a work so generally excellent in its morality, so pure in its doctrines. The mischief which might be produced would be the greater, because of the reverence with which young persons are generally, taught to regard the sacred writings. The impressions of such images as are blamed, would be the more deeply engraven on the mind, as they believe that nothing can be learned there but purity and innocence. I should have thought that these critics might have overlooked an error into which they themselves have fallen to a still greater excess: for they cannot allow the moral tendency of the romance to plead the pardon of two or three passages, which appear to them to be too luxuriant, and too replete with wanton imagery.

I have thus, Sir, endeavoured to shew that the attacks made on Mr. Lewis are unfounded, and that when the critic stares and trembles to find the author of **The Monk** a legislator, his horror is not reasonable; and that with propriety we may apply to those men who can drink vice at the fountain of the Monk, the expression of this very critic: "The most innocent expressions may become the first link in the chain of association, when a man's soul has been poisoned and depraved by the habit of reading lewd and voluptuous tales; and we believe it not absolutely impossible that he might extract pollution from the word of purity, and turn the grace of God into wantonness."

I hope I have succeeded in showing, that "the author has not endeavoured to inflame the fleshly appetites, and then to pour contempt on the only book which would be adequate to the task of reclaiming them." If I have not failed in this object, I shall feel a satisfaction in having employed a leisure horror in a task so delightful as rescuing from disgrace, in my opinion unmerited, a man of such talents, taste, and brilliancy of imagination, as the author of **The Monk**. I hope this attempt will not be displeasing to him who is the most concerned, nor fail of its effect on the public mind. My motives are, however, pure; I know I am as great an enemy to licentiousness as the critics them selves, and I trust I have shewn thyself

A FRIEND TO GENIUS.

THE MONTHLY REVIEW (REVIEW DATE AUGUST 1797)

SOURCE: A review of *The Monk. The Monthly Review* 23 (August 1797): 451.

In the following review, the critic discusses the literary sources for The Monk *and adds that obscenity "pervades and deforms the whole organization of this novel."*

[**The Monk**] has a double plot. The outline of the monk Ambrosio's story was suggested by that of the *Santon Barsisa,* in the Guardian: the form of temptation is borrowed from the *Devil in Love* of Cazotte; and the catastrophe is taken from *the Sorcerer.* The adventures of Raymond and Agnes are less obviously imitations; yet the forest-scene near Strasburgh brings to mind an incident in Smollet's Ferdinand Count Fathom: the bleeding Nun is described by the author as a popular tale of the Germans; and the convent-prison resembles the inflictions of Mrs. Radcliffe. This may be called plagiarism; yet it deserves some praise. The great art of writing consists in selecting what is most stimulant from the works of our predecessors, and in uniting the gathered beauties in a new whole, more interesting than the tributary models. This is the essential process of the imagination, and excellence is no otherwise attained. All invention is but new combination. To invent well is to combine the impressive.

Of the poetry, we have been best pleased with *the Water-Ring,* and with *Alonzo the brave and the fair Imogene,* the latter of which is written in a manner much resembling and little inferior to the Lenardo and Blandine of Bürger. A vein of obscenity, however, pervades and deforms the whole organization of this novel, which must ever blast, in a moral view, the *fair* fame that, in point of ability, it would have gained for the author; and which renders the work totally unfit for general circulation.

MARK M. HENNELLY, JR. (ESSAY DATE 1987)

SOURCE: Hennelly, Jr., Mark M. "*The Monk*'s Gothic Bosh and Bosch's Gothic Monks." *Comparative Literature Studies* 24, no. 2 (1987): 146-64.

In the following essay, Hennelly interprets the artistic significance and utility of the "Gothic machinery" in The Monk *by comparing Lewis's use of these devices to that of painter Hieronymus Bosch, noting similarities between the two and commenting on the possible sources for their works.*

Oh! wonder-working Lewis! monk, or bard,
Who fain wouldst make Parnassus a churchyard!
Lo! wreaths of yew, not laurel, bind thy brow,
Thy muse a sprite, Apollo's sexton thou!

Whether on ancient tombs thou tak'st thy stand,
By gibb'ring spectres hailed, thy kindred band;
Or tracest chaste descriptions on thy page,
To please the females of our modest age;
All hail, M.P.! from whose infernal brain
Thin-sheeted phantoms glide, a grisly train,
At whose command 'grim women' throng in
 crowds,
And kings of fire, of water, and of clouds,
With 'small gray men,' 'wild yagers,' and what
 not,
To crown with honour thee and Walter Scott;
Again all hail! if tales like thine may please,
St. Luke alone can vanquish the disease,
Even Satan's self with thee might dread to dwell,
And in thy skull discern a deeper hell.

Lord Byron, *English Bards and Scotch Reviewers,*
1809 (117, ll. 265-82)

Following the lead of Byron's early lampoon of **The Monk** (1896), criticism has remained generally unkind to what it considers the novel's Gothic bosh or absurd machinery. In fact, Nina da Vinci Nichols's recent appraisal concludes that the "mechanical grotesqueries" (200) in **The Monk** "hold no symbolic value, evoke no mystery, intimate no hidden identity" (204), and thus the novel clearly does "not integrate [its machinery] with the theme" (187).[1] And yet Lewis's preoccupation with voyeurism and penetrating prefabricated veils of repression and hyprocrisy suggests that the "gibb'ring spectres" lurking in his Gothic machine may have a significant, if ambivalent, tale to tell. And this tale begins in the novel's introit or first chapter, which offers a series of suggestive vignettes that unfold like some surreal triptych in the Madrid Cathedral.

The "crowds" that Byron derides initially flock to the Cathedral, betraying secular and especially sexual rather than spiritual motives, since they treat the service as if it were a "play" performance and since "the women came to show themselves, the men to see the women" (35).[2] This lonely crowd also confuses the "true devotion" of religious love with the indoctrinated idolatry of violent power and with fear because "superstition reigns with despotic sway . . . in Madrid" (35). And the crowd's overriding "curiosity" to see the celebrated Monk Ambrosio reflects the obsessive sin of the "prying eye" (109) whose exposed voyeurism more particularly reveals the related concerns of Byron's "deeper hell" and da Vinci Nichols's "hidden identity." For instance, Antonia's natural "features were hidden" so scrupulously "by a thick veil," and "her bosom was [so] carefully veiled" that Lorenzo is artificially aroused and begs to be allowed "to remove the gauze" from her face (37-39). Since Lorenzo is "our hero"

(55), the reader presumably is also guilty of complicity in his voyeurism and his compulsion to strip Antonia, although, ambiguously, Antonia's false modesty needs to be stripped away to reveal her natural self. Similarly, when Agnes "took the veil" to become a nun, she symbolizes her unnatural "seclusion from the world" and reinforces her mother's crime of "immuring so charming a girl within the walls of a cloister" (51).[3]

Next, Lorenzo's portentous dream in "the gothic obscurity of the church" reveals the shared extent of his own and Ambrosio's ambivalent desires as his marriage ceremony with Antonia, conducted by the Monk, is abortively interrupted by a savage ravisher. Thus, "half-hoping, half-fearing," Lorenzo passively watches as his Nemesis enacts the dreamer's about-to-be sanctified lust and prefigures Ambrosio's own later rape of Antonia, his unknown sister. At the same time, the schizoid vertical polarities of the Cathedral collapse, and the ravisher falls through the floor to the fiery vaults foretold in Ambrosio's sermon, while, naked, Antonia ascends through the "vaulted roof" toward a heavenly choir (52-54). Not having learned the severity of his own repressed and then projected desires, Lorenzo indulges in yet more voyeurism when minutes later he and Don Christoval agree to return to the Cathedral that night and secretly spy on the young nuns who must "take off their veils" before confession. "The gaze of such impure eyes" is ultimately punished when Lorenzo finds himself leering at *his* own unveiled sister, who is secretly receiving a love letter. At this point, Don Christoval cries, "What, your sister? Diavolo! Then somebody, I suppose, will have to pay for our peeping" (55-56), thus previewing the ambiguous value of symbolic stripteases of both body and soul throughout the novel.

The point of recounting these episodes from Chapter One is not only to remark that such a preoccupation with cloistered innocence, repressed sexuality, violent rebellion, and an enforced ambiguity between sacred and profane values recurs throughout **The Monk,** but also to emphasize that, contrary to prevalent criticism, the novel offers an integrated or at least repeated coordination of its Gothic machinery, especially the sense of place or space, and its Gothic visions. But for a fuller understanding of this coordination, we must ask why Lewis chose a *Madrid* cathedral and its adjoining "burial ground common" (228) to both the Capuchin monastery and the convent of St. Clare as the primary symbolic machines for transmitting his Gothic visions.

Perhaps it was because Spanish Gothic cathedrals, partially due to the prevalent Moorish influence, are uniquely known for "their *rejas* or wrought iron screens," which seem to be part of the same tradition as the Hispanic love of cloaks and fans (Sitwell 139), all of which promote an atmosphere of veiled, partial concealment. It is certainly also true that, as with the Church of San Lorenzo opening Ann Radcliffe's *The Italian* (itself clearly a critical response to **The Monk**), the Latin flavoring here helps season the novel's exposé of repressed fiery passion. Moreover, Spain is the native home of the Inquisition so dear to Lewis and other Gothicists; in fact, in *Melmoth the Wanderer* "all Spain is but one great monastery" (143) policed by the Inquisition. And yet in 1796, there was no Gothic cathedral in Madrid, only the Jesuit church of San Isidro el Real, which John Harvey describes as "a grim monument of the severest classicism" whose presence "startlingly suggests the portals of a prison" (198-201). But, of course, Lewis may simply have appropriated this relevant suggestion of repression and then altered it to suit his own Gothic specifications.

There may, however, be yet another possible reason for his choice of Madrid, one revealed in G. B. Street's chatty 1914 account of *Gothic Architecture in Spain*, namely, that although there are really "no old churches," still "there is one great attraction to me in Madrid, and only one— the Picture Gallery" (1:279), or Museo del Prado, the famous home of the more enigmatic canvases of Hieronymous Bosch, which Philip II brought to Madrid from the Netherlands around 1560. Philip hung twelve in his palace and treasury and twelve in his hunting lodge at El Prado. In 1574 the nine most significant were secretly "hidden away in his monastery stronghold, the Escorial" (Fraenger 8). Since that time, the name of Bosch and the Madrid repositories have become nearly synonymous. And the bizarre Gothic machinery in these works seems so close to the symbolic machinery in Lewis's novel that a survey of Bosch and the relevance of what Carl Justi calls "the most important of his works" (48)—his paintings of *The Table of Wisdom* (c. 1475-85), *The Hay Wain* (c. 1485-90), *The Garden of Earthly Delights* (c. 1485-1505), and *The Temptation of Saint Anthony* (c. 1505-16)—should place **The Monk**'s Gothic bosh in the proper clarifying context of Bosch's Gothic monks.[4] Of course, unless fresh evidence is uncovered, it will always remain debatable whether or not Lewis actually studied Bosch's canvases and exorcised their eerie spirit in **The Monk**. It does seem clear, however, that the haunting cor-respondences between the work of the painter and the novelist at the least reveal them to be "kindred spirits."

Bosch spent his entire life in his birthplace (which also gave him his name), the Dutch city of 's-Hertogenbosch, close to what is now the border of Belgium. This is significant because, besides Lewis's journeys to the continent in 1791 and 1792, which may well have introduced him to the art and architecture of Madrid, he spent much of 1794 at The Hague in the Netherlands serving as a staff member of the British embassy, but also writing **The Monk** (Irwin 18-22). And this locale too would have provided him with access to other examples of Bosch's art which were collected in the Low Countries at sites like The Hague, Rotterdam, and Brussels. Significantly, Bosch's visual perspective itself had been nurtured by the great Gothic Cathedral of St. John in his native town, and the curious gargoyles sitting on its roof buttresses perhaps turn up even more transmogrified in his own monastic and satanic grotesques (Gibson 14-16). In fact, like Lewis, Bosch too is often regarded as merely a *faiseur de diables*, and both were probably influenced by the notorious *Malleus Maleficarum*, or *Witches' Hammer* (1494), which schematically outlines the relationship between Satan and succubi, like Matilda, who use their sexual charms to debase and then damn ascetics. Thus, and again prefiguring Lewis, Bosch's work repeatedly excoriates the veiled evils of monastic life, particularly the lust of monks and the hypocritical virginity of nuns, perhaps recalling Saint Paul's second letter to Timothy in which he decries the doomed city of man as a Vanity Fair where clerics are "lovers of pleasures more than lovers of God; having the form of godliness, but denying the power thereof. . . . For of this sort are they which creep into houses, and lead captive silly women laden with sins, led away with divers lusts" (II Tim. 3:4-4, Fraenger 20).

It is further relevant that in 1947 Wilhelm Fraenger published a revolutionary study of Bosch's work that drastically revises the older view of him as primarily a painter of devotional altar pieces, but sees him rather as a practising member of the Adamites or Brethren of the Free Spirits, who allegedly indulged in religious rituals of free love, reflecting their desire to return to a state of prelapsarian innocence.[5] Thus Fraenger's Bosch emerges as a kind of complex Fra Lippo Lippi whose work manifestly preaches a gospel of the spirit while latently promoting the enjoyment of the flesh. In Fraenger's own words, Bosch "freed medieval art from its subjection to the church

Hieronymous Bosch's *Tabletop of the Seven Deadly Sins,* c. 1480-1490.

and, in the phantom world that he made his own creative domain, distorted the fear of God, which the church kept under control, into a terrifying pandemonium of lust." Thus he dramatizes "a new religious will to life, which clashed with the tradition of the church" and offered "the road to salvation of a religious doctrine of love, a mystery of eroticism" (15). Although art historians disagree on the validity of such a thesis, there can be little doubt that Fraenger honestly confronts the central paradox of Bosch's art, which seems simultaneously to scourge and sanctify sensual pleasures. And this, of course, is also the central paradox of ***The Monk.*** Equally relevant is Fraenger's attention to Bosch's manipulation of his onlooker's voyeuristic tendencies as his paintings stereoscopically focus on both sensual degradation and sexual innocence by setting "a trap for the viewer's eye" (42) at almost every point on its visual quest through the optical mine fields Bosch's canvases become.

What Fraenger at one point calls Bosch's "pupillary magic" (270) is perhaps nowhere more evidently relevant to ***The Monk*** than in *The Table of Wisdom,* once known as *The Seven Deadly Sins.*

On this forboding tabletop, Bosch presents a central sphere whose outer circumference displays a sevenfold pageantry illustrating each sin and whose inner circumference recreates Christ's emergence from His sarcophagus within the image of the Eye of God itself, which is captioned, "Beware, Beware, God sees." Flanking this central circle in each corner of the table hang smaller spheres limning the four last things: Death, Judgment, Heaven, and Hell. As with each of Bosch's pertinent works, we can only mention a fraction of the relevant detail here, but the provocative conversion of the Beatific Vision into a Divine Voyeur commands the viewer's own attention in much the same way as human voyeurism captivates and involves the reader of ***The Monk.*** In fact, the bottom scroll warns us of God's ubiquitous, veiled presence: "I will hide my face from them, I will see what their end shall be" (Deut. 32:20). What God sees, of course, is a reflection of the viewer's own collective experiences in the cartoonish allegories of the *Seven Deadly Sins,* which, like ***The Monk,*** feature follies from every rank of life including hypocritical monks and nuns. Thus the outer macrocosm of the earth and the inner microcosm of the eye coincide here, just as the image of the mirror, repeatedly associated with the sin of *Superbia,* may remind us not only that Lewis's own "passion for mirrors" (Irwin 26) is reflected in the magic glass exposing the bathing Antonia to Ambrosio, but also that Pride personified in Ambrosio controls each of its satellite pecadillos like Beatrice's lust, Baptiste's thieving avarice, Donna Rodolpha's envy of Agnes, Mother Agatha's raging anger, the parody of sloth in the "soporific draught" (321) which symbolizes the embowered Antonia as "the prey of ennui" (305), and even Flora's comically gluttonous feasting on fowl on Friday (314-15).

More particularly, the tableau of Death reminds us of the psychomachia staged during Ambrosio's execution vigil since dire Death and his satanic familiar seem at least as potent as the dour friars and nuns in the picture. This kind of doubling ironically implies that even the Church itself must invoke such spiritual horrors to frighten the departing soul to heaven, if the induced despair doesn't first precipitate the sinner, like Ambrosio, to hell. As Agnes cries apropos of the Draconian nuns who guard her, "they think themselves holy, while they torture me like fiends! . . . 'tis they who threaten me with eternal perdition!" (356). Moreover, in the vignette of Hell itself, which illustrates the particular punishment of each Deadly Sin, the burning towers stoked by demons recall the flaming convent torched by the demonic crowd in *The Monk,* and the nude female whose genitals are appropriately covered by a verminous toad is paradoxically reminiscent of the imprisoned and "half naked" (355) Agnes "who felt the bloated toad . . . dragging his loathsome length along my bosom" (395). The implication here is that, although Agnes's concupiscence may be less noxious in the viewer's eyes than that of Bosch's fleshly sinner, still her punishment identically fits her crime since she admits "I violated my vows of chastity," which Ambrosio rephrases as "you have defiled the sacred habit by your impurity" (71, 70).

Next, *The Hay Wain* triptych at the Escorial (another version survives in the Museo del Prado) presents two outer wings illustrating the Wayfarer or earthly Pilgrim travelling, much like Raymond, through a treacherous terrain of stylized robbers, executions, and sensual peasants, each of which, in different ways, anticipates the sensuous saraband depicted on the inner panels. Here an allegorical procession, praising folly like the Cathedral crowd in *The Monk,* quite literally "worships" *hay* or meaningless mercenary goods (Gibson 70,

73) and is flanked by smaller panels of Paradise and Hell, just as the images of "the garden and cemetery" (335) dominate monastic life in the novel. In fact, the eye's pilgrimage through these three panels and their visual snares traces a kind of typically Gothic *W* pattern as it sinks through Paradise, ascends to the crest of the wagon, and then plummets again through the topography of Hell. In this sense, it is significant that both Paradise and Hell are similarly structured according to analogous vertical levels, suggesting that the fall of innocence is as naturally inherent to both conditions as the repeated intrusion of the serpent. Both innocence and experience, according to Lewis's contemporary Blake, are "the Two Contrary States of the Human Soul" (Blake 171). Thus, as our eye descends through the planes of Paradise, it is as if we are psychonauts exploring the rough underbelly of embowered innocence. Adam and Eve first appear gracefully unclothed; then Eve cautiously veils herself with a figleaf during the temptation, and finally both are shamefully veiled upon being driven from the Garden. In Hell, although the figleaf is replaced first by the emblematic toad and then by the coiling serpent, the viewer's sense of the dialectic between innocence and experience is much the same, only darkened because of the infernal chromatic scale. Together both panels remind us that *The Monk* similarly moves from the monastery garden to Ambrosio's concluding inferno in a valley landscaped like Jehosaphat.

In the central panel, the symbolic bower of bliss crowning the hay wagon is complete with both a resident angel and serpentine demon, but the attitudes of the lovers suggest that the latter has won the day as they are about to "make hay." This kind of visual pun, so dear to Bosch, implies that here Luxuria, or Queen Lust, dominates the other Deadly Sins emblemized in the procession, as the seductress Matilda seems to dominate so much of the central action in *The Monk.* In fact, when Ambrosio is stung as he "stopped to pluck one of the roses" for Matilda in the monastery garden, his hand "swelled to an extraordinary size." The consequent sexual implications of his fall and the repeated poison-passion analogy suggest not only that "concealed among the roses" (92) of every innocent garden is a serpent, even if it is only the serpent of mutability, but also that the fall can always be a prelude to "extraordinary" self-development. Furthermore, the swarthy devils and burning towers in Hell and the secular prelates and worldly monks and nuns at the Hay festival suggest the *mise en scène* of Lorenzo's dream, besides the religious *danse macabre* of "grotesque attitudes" in the Procession of St. Clare, which precedes the burning of the convent (336). More generally, though, the sense of *déja vù* one feels when examining these uncanny panels is due to their strange Gothic intermixture of tones, which ineffably blends the blessed and bestial into a kind of consecrated cartoon like **The Monk.** In this sense, both viewer and reader feel much as Agnes does upon awakening in her crypt: "my senses were so bewildered, and my brain so dizzy, that I strove in vain to arrange the strange images which floated in wild confusion before me" (384).

At any rate, the paradoxes of the garden that Lewis and Bosch similarly dramatize are the primary focus of the triptych of *The Garden of Earthly Delights*, which flanks the central panel of the Earthly Paradise again with side panels of Eden and Hell. As in **The Monk,** the painting's visual challenge involves its questioning ambivalence toward love and sensual fulfillment. That is, does the canvas, like a traditional allegory of the Bower of Bliss, warn us, with Keats that we "dwell with Beauty—Beauty that must die?" This *Et in Arcadia Ego* motif was popularly rendered during the Renaissance in ivory miniatures exposing entwined lovers or an inviting nude female, behind whom lurks a decomposing grim reaper (Gibson 87-88) whose *memento mori* punishes the initial voyeurism much as the veiled, rotten corpse of the Bleeding Nun rebukes Raymond's fascination with Agnes (170). On the other hand, does the painting suggest that sensual fulfillment leads to Hell only if, like Lorenzo, one is guiltily programmed by orthodoxy to view pleasure as precipitating a sinful fall from the graceful innoncence of Paradise? The canvas's provocative marriage of heaven and hell seems to support both readings, and in this sense it closely resembles **The Monk.**

More specifically, it again prefigures the "voluptuous tranquility" of the "abbey-garden" (73-74) where Matilda first visually tempts Ambrosio with the "beauteous orb" of her "half exposed" breast (87). And the ocular geometry of the central pool of nude female bathers surrounded by the frenzied cavalcade of male voyeurs makes us wonder whether Bosch means to pluck out our eye or to glorify its gifts.[6] As Walter S. Gibson contends, Bosch's Earthly Paradise probably owes much of its landscaping to the *Romance of the Rose* (83-87), and Lewis's version is clearly in the same romance tradition: "Fountains, springing from the basons [*sic*] of white marble, cooled the air with perpetual showers, and the walls were entirely covered by jessamine, vines, and honeysuckles. . . . a gentle breeze breathed the fragrance of orange-blossoms along the alleys, and the nightingale poured forth her melodious murmur from the shelter of an artificial wilderness" (73). Lewis even includes a "hermitage" or "rustic grotto" nestled in "the bosom of this little grove" where Matilda and Ambrosio hold their trysts and where similarly, in the lower right foreground of Bosch's *hortus conclusus*, a hirsute Adam and Eve peep out from their cover. Fraenger again finds such a grotto to be of central importance to the Adamite cult which saw "Adam as the Christlike bearer of revelation, the underground cave as Paradise, and ritual nakedness associated with markedly religious love, which was regarded as innocent and above all sensuality, and was usually called 'angelic love'" (19).

We must remember, however, that the Hell panel restages this scenario like some monstrous immorality play, where the reign of Queen Lust becomes a reign of terror. The romance motif of "the music of the flesh" (Gibson 98) is here particularly punished, and the naked figure crucified on the serpent-entwined harp reminds us that Matilda beguiles Ambrosio's senses with her harp-playing, which suggestively "proves her a perfect mistress of the instrument" (95). Again and by now almost predictably, crumbling, burning towers overlay Bosch's topsy-turvy Gehenna structured partially like a Gothic monastery and Inquisition chamber, where the prisoners are judging their hypocritical judges and where a monkish confessor sodomistically ruts with his penitent and simultaneously reads about unpardonable sins from his confession manual. At the same time, a lascivious sow in a nun's habit, recalling Matilda's religious disguise, clutches a naked prelate and urges him to consign his estate to the priory as well as his soul to the pit. This quantitative approach to religion recalls Jacintha's comic concern with simony when she "purchased as many pardons from the pope as would buy off Cain's punishment" (313). Finally, the Prince of Darkness himself is here reminiscent of the winged Satan and his eagle familiars which alternately punish Ambrosio (420), since Lucifer is depicted as an insatiable bird of prey with a chamber pot, who engorges himself on one victim as he vents others into even lower depths of the infernal sewer from which peeps a parody of our first parents in their paradisal cave in the center panel. Thus love quite literally "pitches his mansion in the place of excrement," and yet the combined effect of all three panels is closer to Crazy Jane's major argument to her bishop (in Yeats's poem, not Lewis's own popular "**Crazy Jane Ballad**"):

'Fair and foul are near of kin,
And fair needs foul,' I cried!

. . . . .

'For nothing can be sole or whole
That has not been rent.'

(254-55, ll. 7-8, 17-18)

Finally, Fraenger reminds us that "Bosch's favorite theme [is] the temptation of St. Anthony" (305). And the painter's renditions of this theme are very relevant to our understanding of the temptations of Ambrosio in **The Monk**, who clearly identifies with the sense-plagued saint: "St Anthony had withstood all seductions to lust, then why should not he? Besides, St. Anthony was tempted by the devil . . ." (103). Thus, much more than their common Franciscan order link Bosch's and Lewis's frairs, not the least of which being that *Antonia* (Ambrosio's sister) is the feminine form of Anthony. Fraenger's masterful analysis of Bosch's late treatment of his other-worldly recluse, which hangs in the Prado, is especially perceptive in contrasting St. Anthony's external visual serenity with what the landscape reveals as tumultuous internal visions rivaling Ambrosio's: "the images generated by his unconscious instinctual drives usually represent masked and disguised sexuality" (307). These drives are especially personified in that "unknown brother" who peeps at Bosch's meditative monk from the pool before him like the dark paraclete in Lorenzo's dream: "With its cry of 'In vain!' this unexpectedly emerging self seeks to unmask the saint's ascetic effort as worthless self-deception and hopeless effort, since neither mortification of the flesh nor contemplative sublimation has been able to overcome his inborn nature" (308).

Much more famous and pertinent, however, is *The Temptation of Saint Anthony* triptych (c. 1485-1505), now in Lisbon, which grotesquely revises the hagiographical legends recounting Anthony's attack by demons while he was praying near a desert sepulchre, their second attack when they toss him skyward and allow him to fall battered back to earth, and his final test by the Devil Queen whose apparent compassion veils her carnal temptations. Thus, as Lewis's Ambrosio presents his reader with a kind of visual ambrosia, so too Bosch's Anthony fascinates our voyeuristic curiosities and is perhaps even a symbolic self-portrait of his creator (Justi 55). In Fraenger's words, Bosch "has called upon the four elements, plunging them into spooky tumult in which sexuality intertwines with the trefoil of idolatry, magic, and

sodomy and serves above all to excite the roving eye" (346). And relevantly it was during Bosch's life that the Humanists began to question the real value of Anthony's brand of cloistered and solipsistic innocence (Gibson 152), as Lewis later does with Ambrosio's "total exclusion from the world" which prevents him from knowing "in what consists the difference of man and woman" (44) and which repressively precludes even "the opportunity to be guilty" (47)—at least until such repression spawns instinctual rebellion.

More particularly, Anthony's vertical double exposure in the upper and lower sections of the right panel clarifies the similar trajectory of Ambrosio's fall, suggesting that the self-denying ascetic who overreaches human limits ultimately disembodies himself to less than human proportions as his pride goes before his fall. Furthermore, the burning monastery in the central panel is again relevant to the inferno which engulfs the convent and suggests the metaphoric context of the disease of *ergotism* or St. Anthony's fire, one of whose symptoms is satanic hallucinations (Gibson 145). The Black Mass offered next to the obelisk recalls Matilda's and Ambrosio's devil worship. But more significantly, at the center of the main panel is the parodic willow hag with her spectral infant and ghastly paramour, dubbed the "virgin" and noble "young man" (Fraenger 391), who seem disturbing prototypes of the cadaverous Agnes, her dead child, and the diseased Raymond. Finally, in the right panel, when the Devil Queen tries to veil her nudity with assumed modesty, Anthony's consequent resistance to this enforced voyeurism only drives his averted glance to the devil's obscene banquet being prepared in the lower left foreground, which seems to offer the anchorite only more fascinating sexual and satanic indelicacies, just as Ambrosio is driven from the affected modesty of Matilda to the artificially conditioned modesty of Antonia and finally to the black magic of Satan. In sum, whether or not Bosch's Anthony is indicted as Fraenger argues, his temptations, like Ambrosio's, appear self-conceived, and his demons and their familiars seem to be as much mentors as tormentors.

Thus, like the ambiguous vertical extremes in Lorenzo's dream, Bosch's ambivalent presentation of Anthony's descent helps prepare us for Lewis's ultimate presentation of Ambrosio's climactic rise and fall in the last paragraph of **The Monk** (419-20): "The daemon continued to soar aloft, till reaching a dreadful height, he released the sufferer. Headlong fell the monk through the airy waste; the sharp point of a rock received him; and he rolled from precipice to precipice, till, bruised and mangled, he rested on the river's banks." Subsequently, for "six miserable days did the villain languish. On the seventh a storm arose: . . . the waves overflowed their banks; they reached the spot where Ambrosio lay, and when they abated, carried with them into the river the corse of the despairing monk." These prolonged final moments of Ambrosio broadcast several significantly mixed extratextual and textual allusions which finally enlarge Lewis's indictment of voyeurism into the Gothic dialectical vision of the human condition, which Byron's Manfred summarizes as "Half dust, half deity, alike unfit / To sink or soar" (393, I, ii, 40-41).[7]

For example, besides its rather remarkable resemblance to Bosch's depiction of St. Anthony's satanically controlled descent, Ambrosio's fall recalls Adam's fall from grace and Lucifer's from heaven in *Paradise Lost,* and "his broken and dislocated limbs" suggest the consequent self-division which St. Anthony, Adam, and Satan all, at least symbolically, suffer. His wracked limbs may even conjure associations with Christ's crucifixion, and certainly the Abbot's early promise and sanctity render him as a figure of Christ before he devolves into an Antichrist. Furthermore, the seven day ordeal implies a chaotic parody of Creation (much as when "Universal Darkness buries All" at the end of Pope's *The Dunciad,* 584, IV, 655), although the cleansing river and storm may also refer to Noah's purging and purifying final flood. But then again the wrathful environment here also connotes the apocalyptic *Dies Irae* traditionally associated with the Valley of Jehosaphat. Moreover, the plague of insects which drink Ambrosio's blood as "they fastened upon his sores, darted their strings into his body, and covered him with their multitudes" seems at first glance almost a parasitic parody of his own violation of Antonia, and thus his punishment befits his crime. It also, however, represents one of several reversals of the legends of St. Ambrose documented in Jacobus de Voragine's medieval collection of the lives of the saints, *The Golden Legend,* which certainly influenced Bosch. Voragine describes not only how Ambrose was destined for greatness when, as a child, a swarm of bees flew into his mouth and then soared away toward heaven, but also how he affected paganism and whoremongering to avoid the honor of election to a bishop, how he prophesied his sister would one day kiss him earnestly when he attained an episcopacy, and how he was especially versed in exorcising demons (24-33)—all of which

legends seem parodied in Ambrosio's insect attack, sin of incest, and demonic idolatry.

Besides such paradoxically mixed allusions to sacred writings, there are other profane, classical allusions to the various tortures of Tartarus, especially the frustrations of Tantalus and Sisyphus since, though "a burning thirst tormented" Ambrosio, he "strove in vain to drag himself towards" the nearby river. The classical motif is rendered more relevant when "the eagles of the rock tore his flesh piecemeal, and dug out his eyeballs with their crooked beaks," since these predators seem to be grotesque exaggerations of the "tame linnet" which, while Ambrosio watched, "nibbled" Antonia's breast "in wanton play" as she "strove in vain to shake off the bird from its delightful harbour" (269). On the other hand, of course, their persecution recalls the plight of Prometheus and suggests the titanic scope of Ambrosio's rebellion against God. Finally, his symbolic blinding directly implies Oedipus's sin of incest, besides providing a final chastisement of his voyeurism.

Moreover, placed as it is at the very end of the novel, like Melmoth the Wanderer's fall from the sea cliff, Ambrosio's unrepentant tragic downfall radically rejects (rather than reinforces) the sense of Providential order and renewal which the Duke of Medina's political "prudence and moderation" (378) and the social contracts of the final marriages seem to establish. Thus, like Fortinbras at the end of *Hamlet,* Medina apparently insures that "order and tranquility once more prevailed through Madrid" (377), and yet the reader's actual response to the novel's political and social sense of retributive justice may share more with Elvira's earlier conclusions: "in a world so base, so perfidious and depraved, her heart swelled with the bitterness of apprehension" (277). As Lewis himself once observed in a letter to his mother, "in my opinion, the acuteness of *pleasure* in this world bears no proportion to the acuteness of pain" (Peck 222). Again, then, Ambrosio resembles Bosch's ambiguous monk because his diabolic punishment cannot be easily judged and, in fact, casts serious doubts on any facile, reductive reading of the novel as Lewis's self-indulgence in Gothic machinery.

In this context, when Ambrosio languishes "execrating his existence" after his fall, his possibly sympathetic *Angst* repeats the earlier existential agonies of Antonia and Agnes, just as the splintered selves of Bosch's Anthony are personified throughout the unspeakable practices fragmenting his canvases. Agnes's recalled notes from the underground (390-97) in her "subterraneous dwelling" partially reinforce this ultimate tone of Gothic existentialism,[8] which outlasts the questionable nature of her marital bliss. They also tend to duplicate Bosch's painted notes from his underground charnel and carnal houses. Thus Agnes is nearly "driven by despair to madness" when she finds herself "in silence and fortitude" forced to "drag on a miserable existence" in the subterranean torture chamber which also "terminated my sweet babe's short and painful existence." In fact, so memorable is this solitary confinement that her subsequent and almost absurd "sudden transition from misery to bliss" seems illusory; and her earlier captivity, like Ambrosio's final moments, becomes an existential paradigm of the prevalent human condition in the novel: "So lately a captive, oppressed with chains, perishing with hunger, suffering every inconvenience of cold and want, hidden from the light, excluded from society, hopeless, neglected, and, as I feared, forgotten." Consequently, her long-awaited marriage to Raymond (like the union of Bosch's Willow Hag and Noble Young Man) and Lorenzo's to Virginia hardly provide a happily-ever-after romance closure. Rather, they are like Theodore and Isabella's warped wedding at the end of *The Castle of Otranto* when, after the mayhem of Walpole's Gothic excess, the sober ceremony simply provides the bereaved Theodore with a receptive ear for his lamenting the loss of Matilda, that is, "the society of one, with whom he could for ever indulge the melancholy that had taken possession of his soul" (106). Here, too, the nuptials are suitably somber since Lorenzo's feeling for Virginia "partook not of the ardent character which had marked his affections for Antonia" (399). And like Bosch's black humor, Lewis's sense of absurdity, which Walpole sadly lacks, makes Agnes's marriage more sardonic than somber since she ominously suggests to Raymond that her premarital sexuality shall be replaced with complete marital chastity: "the more culpable have been the errors of your mistress, the more exemplary shall be the conduct of your wife" (398). Thus the veil prematurely removed would now seem to become a chastity belt locked forever, thereby perpetuating the repressive value systems which have plagued everyone in the novel.

In sum, just as hints of St. Anthony's damnation darken the tone of Bosch's canvases, so too the Gothic machinery of Ambrosio's climactic damnation casts a retrospective pall over *The Monk*'s several ambivalent soliloquies in a Spanish cloister. It reminds us of Ambroisio's tongue-in-cheek remark that the "sepulchre seems to me to be Love's bower" (366) and of Medina's more cynical echo from *As You Like It*: "men have died, and worms have ate them, but not for love" (381). It even reminds us of the profound sense of Gothic ruin which the many "objects of mortality" (367) and "images of corruption" (368), like "graves, and tombs, and skeletons" (366), instill in the novel. Ultimately, it may remind us that whether we take pride in, or feel pity for, Ambrosio's capital punishment, our response entraps us in bogs of moral ambiguity as deep and sticky as those in Bosch's work, since if we self-righteously exult in the Monk's torture, we grow like the sadistic Prioress or ironically like the brutal mob whose "barbarous vengeance" wrongfully punishes her. On the other hand, if we forgive Ambrosio as Agnes forgives Mother St. Agatha (395), our kindness seems a form of wilfull blindness, and our pardon may almost criminally betray an inner weakness. Thus neither a sense of retributive justice, nor a sense of forgiveness seems entirely defensible here. Even though the Inquisitorial ministers of God pardon the Abbot's unpardonable sin, his preemptive despair makes a mockery of that pardon and of his own opportunistic faith. And when we consider that Satan thus appears to have "triumphed" (418) in his battle with God over Ambrosio's soul, or at least that God must depend on Satan as His Executioner, the novel's assault on Divine Providence and Omnipotence seems equally disturbing.

As a matter of fact, the counterpointing energies in Lewis's Gothic romance, as in Bosch's Gothic art, create an honest doubt and healthy skepticism that are ultimately more redemptive than the warped value systems both artists condemn. Lord Holland meant gently to lament such iconoclasm in Lewis some years after his friend's death, but actually reveals the strength of Lewis's (and Bosch's) appeal: "his mind was vitiated with a mystical, though irreligious, philosophy; his taste in reading, writing, and thinking, corrupted by paradox; and his conversation disfigured by captious perverseness in controversy" (Peck 176). Thus, like Bosch's work, *The Monk* accommodates both God and ghosts, recalling Shelley's rather dismayed description of the way Lewis and Byron equated both forms of Gothic machinery, while he himself believed only in unholy spirits. While "Apollo's Sexton" (Byron's name for Lewis) rationally may have disbelieved in either, imaginatively the "many mysteries of his trade" in *The Monk* demanded both. In Shelley's words, "We talk of

Ghosts. Neither Lord Byron nor M. G. L. seems to believe in them; and they both agree, in the very face of reason, that none could believe in ghosts without believing in God. I do not think that all persons who profess to discredit these visitations, really discredit them; or, if they do in the daylight, are not admonished, by the approach of loneliness and midnight, to think more respectfully of the world of shadows" (Shelley 147).

But Shelley slights Lewis's uncompromising intellectual integrity, for his Gothic vision, like Bosch's, insists upon our remaining open to conflicting solutions to the human dilemma. Although both raise our eyebrows, these kindred spirits also open our eyes to the radical tolerance of "the innocent eye" or dialectical condition of "alert suspense" that their brother Gothicist,⁹ Sir Herbert Read, ultimately advocates: "For in the end I have put all in doubt / God, man; earth, heaven: I live on in alert suspense. / I believe in my unbelief" ("The Golden Disc," 242, ll. 91-93). Or as Lewis confessed to his mother after finishing *The Monk,* "I prefer knowing the whole, or nothing; for I have an admirable talent for tormenting myself, and the truth can never be worse, tha[n] what I imagine when left to myself" (Peck 216).

Notes

1. Several other critical responses have also addressed the problem of formal unity and the relevance of Gothic machinery in *The Monk.* Brooks and Grudin find an historical and philosophical unity in the novel, but for different reasons. The former believes "the novel can in fact be read as one of the first and most lucid contextualizations of life in a world where reason has lost its prestige, yet the Godhead has lost its otherness; where the Sacred has been reacknowledged but atomized, and its ethical imperatives psychologized" (249). The latter, on the other hand, sees *The Monk* reflecting "pre-enlightenment" rather than post-enlightenment ideas: "Unwilling to rely solely on the shopworn machinery of castles, armor and crypts, [Lewis] created a Gothic atmosphere with a fidelity that Walpole and Radcliffe never achieved. His novel recreates a world that is theologically as well as physically archaic" (144). Other relevant studies argue sporadically that Lewis's manipulation of reader response helps to coordinate his otherwise disparate material. For instance, Lydenberg's pertinent treatment of narrative "ambivalence" in *The Monk* finds that "Lewis' repeated ironic undercutting of the trappings of Gothic fiction, which he nevertheless persists in employing to maximum effect, reveals the same tentativeness which leads him to affect a flippancy and indifference towards all literary activity" (65). Kiely feels that "it is almost as though Lewis had played an unfair trick on the reader by endowing his Gothic stereotypes with life at unexpected and fatal moments" (114). And lastly Punter insists that, "above all," Lewis "wants the reader to see essentially private faults exposed mercilessly on a more or less public

stage, and he wants to mock his confused reactions. For Lewis, at all points, tries to be more cynical than his audience, and to dominate it by means of this cynicism" (92).

2. All future page references to *The Monk* are from the Evergreen edition and are included in the text.

3. For an excellent general discussion of the Gothic imagery of veils and surfaces, see Sedgwick.

4. The interested reader should consult Justi's entire discussion of "The Works of Hieronymous Bosch in Spain."

5. I am using Putnam's edition of Fraenger because it is a "complete edition" (506) of Fraenger's work on Bosch, including revisions of his seminal 1947 study and his later analyses of individual paintings. This Putnam edition also provides large illustrative plates and numerous helpful close-ups of detail from all of the paintings discussed in this essay. For a judicious evaluation of Fraenger's controlling hypothesis and its place in Bosch studies, see Patrik Reuterswärd's Postscript (499-506).

6. See MacAndrew for a discussion of this garden as "a distortion of the devices of the Sentimental novel" (92-93).

7. For other brief treatments of Ambrosio's final "downfall," see Gose (37-38), Fogle (43-44), Kiely (117), and Hallie (78-79).

8. Brooks also implies an existential reading of the novel (262-63). For an account of the relationships between Gothicism and Existentialism, see Hennelly's discussion of "Gothic Existentialism" with special reference to *Melmoth the Wanderer* (particularly 666-71).

9. *The Innocent Eye* is the relevant title of Read's autobiography. For an example of Read's interest in Gothicism, see his Introduction to Wilhelm Worringer's architectural study, *Form in Gothic,* where he not only defends Gothic machinery, but also finds in it a dialectical temper close to his own: "Gothic art must no longer be the romantic predilection of the traveller and archaeologist: it takes its place as the highest and most accurate expression of a great phase in the history of European culture." Consequently, Worringer's analysis of Gothic architectural psychology "necessarily makes demands on the reader: it exacts a close attention and a 'willing suspension' of prejudice" (xii).

Works Cited

Blake, William. *Engraved and Etched Writings. William Blake's Writings.* Ed. G. E. Bentley, Jr. 2 vols. Oxford: Clarendon Press, 1978. Vol. 2.

Brooks, Peter. "Virtue and Terror: *The Monk.*" *English Literary History* 40 (1973): 249-63.

Byron, George Gordon Lord. *Byron: Poetical Works.* Ed. Frederick Page. London: Oxford Univ. Press, 1970.

da Vinci Nichols, Nina. "Place and Eros in Radcliffe, Lewis, and Brontë." *The Female Gothic.* Ed. Juliann E. Fleenor. Montreal and London: Eden Press, 1983. 187-206.

de Voragine, Jacobus. *The Golden Legend.* Trans. Granger Ryan and Helmut Ripperger. New York: Longmans, Green and Co., 1941.

Fogle, Richard Harter. "The Passions of Ambrosio." *The Classic British Novel.* Ed. Howard M. Harper, Jr. and Charles Edge. Athens: Univ. of Georgia Press, 1972. 36-50.

Fraenger, Wilhelm. *Hieronymous Bosch*. Trans. Helen Sebba. New York: G.P. Putnam's Sons, 1983.

Gibson, Walter S. *Hieronymous Bosch*. New York and Washington: Praeger, 1973.

Gose, Elliott B. *Imagination Indulged: The Irrational in the Nineteenth-Century Novel*. Montreal: McGill-Queen's Univ. Press, 1972. 27-40.

Grudin, Peter. "*The Monk*: Matilda and the Rhetoric of Deceit." *Journal of Narrative Technique* 5 (1975): 136-146.

Hallie, Philip P. *The Paradox of Cruelty*. Middleton, Conn.: Wesleyan Univ. Press, 1969. 63-84 *passim*.

Harvey, John. *The Cathedrals of Spain*. New York: Hastings House, 1957.

Hannelly, Mark M., Jr. "Gothic Existentialism in *Melmoth the Wanderer*." *Studies in English Literature* 21 (1981): 665-79.

Irwin, Joseph James. *M. G. "Monk" Lewis*. Boston: Twayne, 1976.

Justi, Carl. "The Works of Hieronymous Bosch in Spain." *Bosch in Perspective*. Ed. James Snyder. Englewood Cliffs, New Jersey: Prentice-Hall, 1973.

Kiely, Robert. *The Romantic Novel in England*. Cambridge: Harvard Univ. Press, 1972. 98-117.

Lewis, Matthew Gregory. *The Monk*. Ed. Louis F. Peck. Intro. John Berryman. New York: Evergreen Book, 1959.

Lydenburg, Robin. "Ghostly Rhetoric: Ambivalence in M.G. Lewis' *The Monk*." *Ariel* 10 (1979): 65-78.

MacAndrew, Elizabeth. *The Gothic Tradition in Fiction*. New York: Columbia Univ. Press, 1979. 86-93.

Maturin, Charles Robert. *Melmoth the Wanderer*. Intro. William F. Axton. Lincoln: Univ. Nebraska Press, Bison Book, 1961.

Peck, Louis. *A Life of Matthew G. Lewis*. Cambridge: Harvard Univ. Press, 1961.

Pope, Alexander. *Poetical Works*. Ed. Herbert Davis. London: Oxford Univ. Press, 1966.

Punter, David. *The Literature of Terror: A History of Gothic Fiction from 1765 to the present day*. London and New York: Longman, 1980. 60-97 *passim*.

Read, Herbert. *Collected Poems*. New York: Horizon Press, 1966.

——. *The Innocent Eye*. New York: Holt, 1947.

——. Trans., ed., and intro. *Form in Gothic*. By Wilhelm Worringer. rev. ed. New York: Schocken Books, 1957.

Sedgwick, Eve Kosofsky. "The Character in the Veil: Imagery of the Surface in the Gothic Novel." *PMLA* 96 (1981): 255-70.

Shelley, Percy Bysshe. *The Complete Works of Percy Bysshe Shelley*. Ed. Roger Ingpen and Walter E. Peck. 10 vols. London: Ernest Benn and New York: Gordian Press, 1965. Vol. 6.

Sitwell, Sacheverell. *Gothic Europe*. New York: Holt, 1969.

Street, George Edmund. *Some Account of Gothic Architecture in Spain*. Ed. Georgiana Goddard King. 2 vols. New York and London: Benjamin Blom, 1914. Vol. 1.

Walpole, Horace. *The Castle of Otranto. Three Gothic Novels*. ed. E. F. Bleiler. New York: Dover, 1966. 1-106.

Yeats, William Butler. *The Collected Poems of W. B. Yeats*. New York: Macmillan, 1956.

ANGELA WRIGHT (ESSAY DATE 2002)

SOURCE: Wright, Angela. "European Disruptions of the Idealized Woman: Matthew Lewis's *The Monk* and the Marquis de Sade's *La Nouvelle Justine*." In *European Gothic: A Spirited Exchange, 1760-1960*, edited by Avril Horner, pp. 39-54. Manchester: Manchester University Press, 2002.

In the following essay, Wright traces parallels between The Monk *and the Marquis de Sade's novel* Justine *and maintains that the two works influenced one another in significant ways, including in their narrative technique and portrayal of heroines.*

Matthew Gregory Lewis and the Marquis de Sade are, in their own rights, well-researched authors. Lewis is rightfully accorded a prominent position in critical surveys of the English Gothic novel due to his notorious production **The Monk** (Miles 1993; Kilgour 1995; Botting 1996; Punter 1996); the Marquis de Sade has also recently been afforded a great deal of critical and biographical attention (Lever 1991; Schaeffer 1999). What is less well documented, however, is the mutually influential relationship under which both authors' work flourished.

The tracing of Matthew Lewis's numerous 'borrowed' sources in **The Monk** began swiftly after the novel's publication. In 1797, for example, an article in the *Monthly Review* took pleasure in identifying in **The Monk** a number of plot motifs taken from, amongst other sources, Smollett's *Ferdinand Count Fathom*, Cazotte's *Le Diable amoureux* (1772), and numerous German romances. The review, however, was surprisingly favourable of these 'borrowings'. It argued:

> This may be called plagiarism, yet it deserves some praise. The great art of writing consists in selecting what is most stimulant from the works of our predecessors, and in uniting the gathered beauties in a new whole, more interesting than the tributary models. This is the essential process of the imagination, and excellence is no otherwise attained. All invention is but new combination. To invent well is to combine the impressive.
>
> (Anon. 1797b: 451, n. 23)

Such accusations of lightly veiled plagiarism, coupled with the extensive documentation of Lewis's familiarity with and translations of German terror literature, have haunted the publication history of **The Monk** to such an extent that we are now inclined to read it as a Barthesian tis-

ABOUT THE AUTHOR

JOSEPH JAMES IRWIN ON LEWIS'S MASTERY OF HORROR AND TERROR

The Gothic novel has been reborn in the last half of the twentieth century, but it did not really need rediscovery, since M. G. Lewis's *Monk* has been almost continuously in print since its first publication in 1796. The new Gothic novel owes a debt to it and to its nineteen-year-old author, Matthew Gregory Lewis, better known by his nickname "Monk," for the new novel can hardly be written without some imitation, conscious or unconscious, of the old one. Monk brought terror literature to a high state of accomplishment in the approximately fifteen years in which he flourished as a writer. Although he did not try to write another novel, he worked on terror plays and terror poems in which he perfected three genre techniques that have become so traditional that they are almost the only methods used to present the pleasurable thrills of horror and of terror. Although the dominance of *The Monk* has obscured Lewis's other literary works, he wrote not only terror plays, such as his very popular *Castle Spectre,* but also legitimate tragedies and comedies, some of which were acted before enthusiastic audiences in spite of the unkind remarks of his critics and which are examples of the dramatic taste of the late eighteenth- and early nineteenth-century British theater. Despite such drama, Lewis was at his best in the horrific and the spectacular.

SOURCE: Irwin, Joseph James. "Writer and Humanitarian." In *M. G. "Monk" Lewis,* pp. 11-34. Boston: Twayne, 1976.

sue of other stories, rather than search for coherency of themes. This chapter, however, will begin by tracing the mutual influences which the texts of de Sade and Lewis shared, and conclude by charting the reciprocity of themes and ideas between Lewis and de Sade.

Matthew Lewis published **The Monk** in 1796, subsequent to some time spent in Paris. While he was in Paris in the summer of 1791, he acquired and read the second edition of the Marquis de Sade's novel *Justine, ou les malheurs de la vertu,* published in that same year. The reading of *Justine* undoubtedly influenced Lewis's subsequent novelistic creation, for **The Monk** sent the English Gothic novel in a radical new direction, on account of the terrors to which its pious female characters are subjected. **The Monk,** indeed, bears far more comparison with de Sade's libertine novels than with the English Gothic novel form because, as many critics have noted, it is a novel that focuses entirely upon the revelatory aspect of narrative. In this way, it clearly maps on to de Sade's project of '*tout révéler*', or 'the revelation of all'. Having acknowledged that de Sade's creation *Justine* was undoubtedly a source of inspiration for Lewis, the latter part of this chapter will chart how, in return, Lewis's novel appears to have influenced de Sade's third and final reprise of the story of *Justine.* Significantly, Lewis's **The Monk** was translated into French for the first time in 1797 under the simple title of **Le Moine.**[1] The publication date of this first translation is significant, for 1797 also marked the year in which, after a lapse of six years, de Sade revised the notorious *Justine, ou les malheurs de la vertu,* into a third and final edition entitled *La Nouvelle Justine.* Crucially, Lewis's novel lies between the second and third editions of de Sade's creation, and, I would argue, provided a stimulus for de Sade's comprehensive thematic revisions.

The first edition of de Sade's novel, *Les Infortunes de la vertu,* was written during his imprisonment in the Bastille between 1787 and 1788. *Les Infortunes* recounts the story of a pious and innocent girl named Justine, who, upon the death of her parents, is thrown out onto the streets from the convent where she has been living. She has an older sister called Juliette who is licentious by nature and who resolves to maintain herself by prostitution; to the fervently religious Justine, however, this is a fate worse than death. She resolves to earn her living through honesty and charity, but in the cruel world that de Sade depicts, she soon discovers that honesty and virtue are worthless commodities. Her starkly depicted naivety make her a victim of constant rape and torture from the figureheads of the institutions in which she places her faith.

This first edition of de Sade's novel was a modest two hundred pages in length and was described by its author as a '*conte philosophique*' or 'philosophical tale'. De Sade never published *Les Infortunes* and it did not see the light of day until 1930, when it was edited by Maurice Heine. De Sade's second edition, *Justine, ou les malheurs de la vertu*, published in 1791, retained the first-person narrative of the previous edition but redoubled the narrative of the heroine's distresses, and embodied much more salacious detail. It is this second edition of the novel that Lewis would have bought and read in Paris. Both Maurice Heine and Béatrice Didier have described the evolution between these first two versions as the progression from a simple tale to that of a romantic Gothic novel due to the subsequent additions of underground cells, macabre moments and reveries (Didier 1976: 106). In addition, Heine has drawn parallels between the trope of the 'explained supernatural' in Ann Radcliffe's novels, and de Sade's frequent and abrupt alternations between Gothic scenarios and their rational explanations (Heine 1973: III 36).

Such Gothic additions to de Sade's novel clearly influenced some of the scenarios in Lewis's novel. For example, the sepulchral location of Antonia's rape by Ambrosio in **The Monk** bears a strong resemblance to the underground seraglio in the Sainte-Marie-des-Bois monastery where Justine is raped and tortured. Besides locational and atmospheric resemblances, there are also clear thematic parallels between *Justine, ou les malheurs de la vertu*, **The Monk,** and de Sade's subsequent *La Nouvelle Justine*. One of the most striking themes which is shared by both authors lies in the brutal collation of their novelistic heroines with idolized versions of the Madonna. It was through this key coupling of their heroines with the Madonna that Lewis and de Sade launched a critique of the privileging of such iconography in religion.

In *Ways of Seeing,* John Berger has famously commented on the portrayal of women as visions that: 'Women watch themselves being looked at . . . The surveyor of woman in herself is male: the surveyed female. Thus she turns herself into an object—and most particularly an object of vision: a sight . . .' (1972: 47). According to Berger, then, there is little or no distinction between this 'sight', conjured by the female to flatter the male, and becoming an 'object of vision'. The word 'vision' is of vital importance in the way that the heroines of both **The Monk** and the various versions of *Justine* are portrayed. At the beginning of their novels, Lewis and de Sade both establish a discourse of spectacle in which both characters and readers are compelled to participate.

Lewis's novel **The Monk** signals its participation in this complicitous spectatorial discourse on the very first page, where an audience is gathered at the Church of the Capuchins to hear the eponymous monk Ambrosio preach:

Scarcely had the Abbey-Bell tolled for five minutes, and already was the Church of the Capuchins thronged with Auditors. Do not encourage the idea that the Crowd was assembled from motives of piety or thirst of information . . . The Women came to show themselves, the Men to see the Women: Some were attracted by curiosity to hear an Orator so celebrated; Some came because they had no better means of employing their time till the play began; Some, from being assured that it would be impossible to find places in the Church; and one half of Madrid was brought thither by expecting to see the other half.

(Lewis 1980: 7)

By establishing at the very beginning of this novel unstable connections between female beauty, male desire and religion, the novel immediately establishes the themes that it wishes to undermine. The narrator's stark honesty at the beginning of the novel provides a sharp contrast to the characters' own lack of motivational awareness. It also, however, forces the reader into a passive position where there is no mystery to be worked out. Everything is on display in **The Monk**: sexual desire, hypocrisy and naivety are all presented to us, forcing us into a spectatorial position.

Such a revelatory beginning to **The Monk** bears comparison with de Sade's second edition of *Justine* in 1791. In *Justine, ou les malheurs de la vertu*, Justine as first-person narrator is coaxed by her otherwise silent auditors at one point in the narrative to continue her revelation of all the horrors that have been forced upon her. Her delicacy makes her pause and consider the effects of the story on her audience. However, the audience, being comprised of her libertine sister Juliette and her lover de Corville, urges her to recount all:

Mais comment abuser de votre patience pour vous raconter ces nouvelles horreurs? N'ai-je pas déjà trop souillé votre imagination par d'infâmes récits? Dois-je en hasarder de nouveaux?

Oui, . . . dit Monsieur de Corville, oui, nous exigeons de vous tous ces détails, vous les gagez avec une décence qui en émousse toute l'horreur;

(de Sade 1986: III 240)

(But how can I abuse your patience by relating these new horrors? Have I not already more than soiled your imagination with infamous recitations? Dare I hazard additional ones?

'Yes, . . .' Monsieur de Corville put in, 'yes, we insist upon these details, you veil them with a decency that removes their edge of horror;'

(Seaver and Wainhouse 1991: 670)[2]

Every tiny detail of libertinism, horror and misfortune must be recounted in this novel, and contrary to de Corville's justifications, Justine's narrative does not gloss over the horror of the repeated violations. Although the first-person narrator, Justine, has reservations about revealing all, in contrast to Lewis's later anonymous narrator, the reader of both tales is none the less compelled to adopt the same prurient role, having duly been warned by the narrators of the horrors that await. In relation to The Monk, David Punter has demonstrated how Lewis 'tries constantly to challenge his audience, to upset its security, to give the reader a moment of doubt about whether he may not himself be guilty of the complicated faults attributed to Ambrosio' (Punter 1996: I 79), and Punter's argument here is equally applicable to de Sade's *Justine*.

If de Sade's and Lewis's narrative techniques are both brutally revelatory, then their portrayal of their heroines are similarly so. Berger's use of the term 'vision' is of vital importance in the way that the heroines of both The Monk and the various versions of Justine are characterized. At the beginning of their novels, Lewis and de Sade both immediately create very pictorial images of their heroines. These images establish the heroines as modest, virginal, religiously devout and naive. Such textual characterizations are knowingly situated within an eighteenth-century literary tradition which equated feminine beauty and distress. In *Les Malheurs de la vertu,* for example, there is a moment when Justine describes the effect that her distress has on the monk Antonin:

> La violence de mes mouvements avait fait disparaître les voiles qui couvraient mon sein; il était nu, mes cheveux y flottaient en désordre, il était inondé de mes larmes; j'inspire des désirs à ce malhonnête homme
>
> (de Sade 1986: III 291)

> (The violence of my movements had disturbed what veiled my breast, it was naked, my dishevelled hair fell in cascades upon it, it was wetted thoroughly by my tears; I quicken desires in the dishonest man)
>
> (Seaver and Wainhouse 1991: 720)

Here, Justine's self-depiction creates a tableau of distressed beauty which is, however, knowingly eroticized, revealing the tale's French literary heritage. For example, in Diderot's earlier novel *La Religieuse* (1780), the heroine Suzanne Simonin is similarly aware of the effect that she has on her male persecutors.[3] This earlier heroine does, however, admit to some possible complicity on her own part, stating: 'Je suis une femme, peut-être un peu coquette, que sais-je?' (Diderot 1961:

178) or 'Perhaps I am slightly flirtatious, who knows? I am a woman' (my translation). Diderot's Suzanne appears in many ways to be the French literary precursor to de Sade's Justine in her knowing admission of the desire she inspires in her persecutors. As such, she provides literary inspiration for both de Sade's and Lewis's critique of religion in her persecution by monks, and also in her confused couplings of her own beauty and distress with the desire that they inspire.

Such equations of beauty and distress inform, in turn, the construction of the English Gothic novel. The opening chapter of Ann Radcliffe's 1791 *The Romance of the Forest* (Radcliffe 1992) contains a similar scene. Here, through the focalization of a Monsieur La Motte, the heroine Adeline's features are described as having 'gained from distress an expression of captivating sweetness' and her clothes are described as having been 'thrown open at the bosom, upon which part of the hair had fallen in disorder' (Radcliffe 1992: 7). However, the crucial difference lies between the knowing eroticization provided by the female first-person narrators in the French novels, and the male-focalized third-person narratives that create these tableaux in the English Gothic novels.[4]

Our introduction to one of the principal female victims of The Monk, Antonia, confirms the spectatorial role into which Lewis's narrator forces us. When Antonia's veil is dislodged as she passes in the Church, we discover 'a neck which for symmetry and beauty might have vied with the Medicean Venus' (Lewis 1980: 9). What is more, through the focalization of the hero Lorenzo, she is also compared to an 'Hamadryad'. This choice of comparison is particularly telling and ironic: in Greek mythology, the Hamadryad is a tree nymph who dies when the tree dies. Inextricably bound in a symbiotic relationship, there is no autonomous existence for this creature. Desire is ineffably linked to the dual commodities of beauty and virginity in The Monk. Antonia is awarded attributes by her several admirers which can only be associated with purity. Therefore, once she is raped towards the end of the novel, she must die. Stripped of her perfect virginity, her most precious commodity in the eyes of the male, Antonia becomes as nothing.

Later in the novel, when Antonia has been fatally raped by the Monk Ambrosio, who claims that he has been seduced into violently raping her because of her perfect virginal beauty, she becomes simply a mirror who reflects his crimes. Ambrosio reproaches Antonia for his crime as follows:

What seduced me into crimes, whose bare remembrance makes me shudder? Fatal witch! Was it not thy beauty? Have you not plunged my soul into infamy? Have you not made me a perjured Hypocrite, a Ravisher, an Assassin! Nay, at this moment, does not that angel look bid me despair of God's forgiveness? Oh! When I stand before his judgement throne, that look will suffice to damn me! You will tell my Judge, that you were happy, till I saw you; that you were innocent, till I polluted you!

(Lewis 1980: 385)

Once Antonia's virginal integrity is shattered, her fragmented image mirrors Ambrosio's crime alone. The reproaches with which he loads her here are reminiscent of the blame that both Diderot's Suzanne and de Sade's second Justine inflict upon themselves. In all three cases, it is not the male authority figure to blame, but the female's irresistible beauty. Antonia's 'angel look' reminds Ambrosio of his irrecoverable sin, and shame and remorse subsume his previous identity as the pious, confident and irreproachable monk.

Antonia cannot survive the loss of her innocence in the textual space that this novel offers her precisely because of the unreality of her construction. In the eyes of the male characters, she is attributed solely the properties of virginal beauty, and, when this is taken from her, she mirrors only what passion has led Ambrosio to. Her death is a direct indictment of her textual establishment as an icon of modesty in the eyes of the male characters. Maggie Kilgour has commented that in the cases of both Ambrosio and Lorenzo, 'the attainment of sexual fantasies produces disgust, while the enlightened attempt to demystify only produces a deeper darkness' (1995: 160). This 'deeper darkness', as Robert Miles has suggested, is a consequence of the 'taboo territory' that their desire inhabits (1993: 27). This 'taboo territory' lies in the sublimation of their sexual fantasies within artistic representations of women.

Thus far, Lewis's novel has not really destabilized the connections between femininity, modesty and religion. If anything, it has reinforced them with the brutal death of Antonia. However, bearing in mind Teresa de Lauretis's point that 'to perform the terms of the production of woman as text, as image, is to resist identification with that image' (1984: 36), we will now turn our attention to the second female image in *The Monk,* offered by the demon lover Matilda. Matilda is important in this novel precisely because she seduces Ambrosio through his own constructions of the idealized female. By this, I refer to his key idealization of femininity as being necessarily equated with the Virgin Mary. When he has preached a particularly pious sermon, the monk Ambrosio returns to his cell to worship a portrait of the Madonna that hangs there. He congratulates himself on being above fleshly temptation:

'I must accustom my eyes to Objects of temptation, and expose myself to the seduction of luxury and desire. Should I meet in that world which I am constrained to enter some lovely Female, lovely . . . as you Madona . . . !'

As he said this, He fixed his eyes upon a picture of the Virgin, which was suspended opposite to him: This for two years had been the Object of his increasing wonder and adoration. He paused, and gazed upon it in delight.

'What beauty in that countenance!' He continued after a silence of some minutes; 'How graceful is the turn of that head! What sweetness, yet what majesty in her divine eyes! . . . Oh, if such a creature existed, and existed but for me! . . .

Fool that I am! Whither do I suffer my admiration of this picture to hurry me? Away, impure ideas! Let me remember, that Woman is for ever lost to me. Never was mortal formed so perfect as this picture . . . What charms me, when ideal and considered as a superior being, would disgust me, become Woman and tainted with all the failings of Mortality.

(Lewis 1980: 41)

Ambrosio's use of the words 'charm' and 'disgust', in reference to the Virgin and Woman, indicate his differing perceptions of the iconized Madonna and the reality of Womanhood. Women to him are tainted and impure: their presence threatens to taint him. It is gradually revealed to Ambrosio, however, that the image of the Madonna that hangs in his room, a painting that he venerates, is in fact a portrait of Matilda. Matilda herself, hitherto disguised as a novice, effects this shattering revelation. Matilda's declaration of love for Ambrosio occurs in parallel with her revelation of her true gender to him: she controls Ambrosio's responses and interests, just as she has controlled his desire for this portrait of the alleged Madonna. Equally, the gender-switch which she effects also disrupts Ambrosio's 'normative', heterosexual, desire for the portrait.

When Matilda, having nursed the dying Ambrosio back to health, gradually reveals her true identity as the woman portrayed in the portrait, Ambrosio's confusion over the idolized Madonna and the sexualized female is complete, and he falls prey to her desire. Ambrosio and Matilda embark upon a passionate sexual relationship where the monk's lust is given full vent upon her willing body. Their sexual relationship also involves their collusion in order to conceal it from the rest of

Illustration from *The Monk.*

the monastery. However, when Matilda begins to dominate their machinations, and coldly to plan their hypocrisy, Ambrosio begins to become disillusioned with her:

> Left to himself He could not reflect without surprize on the sudden change in Matilda's character and sentiments. But a few days had past, since She appeared the mildest and softest of her sex, devoted to his will, and looking up to him as a superior Being. But now she assumed a sort of courage and manliness in her manners but ill calculated to please him . . . what she gained in the opinion of the Man, She lost with interest in the affection of the Lover.
>
> (Lewis 1980: 231-232)

In order to remain sexually appealing to Ambrosio, Matilda should remain 'submissive' and, consequently, in his eyes, feminine. Ambrosio desires a reinforcement of the distinctions between male and female: he looks for someone to affirm his ideal of himself as a 'superior being' and confirm his elevated status in society. Matilda initially secures Ambrosio to herself by her very self-positioning as gentle and submissive. In order to continue to remain in his favour, such posturing should be maintained, but Matilda discards it

once she has secured Ambrosio. It is only when Matilda discards submission that she, as the double of the Madonna portrait, no longer satisfies.

This thematic enjambment is fully explored by Julia Kristeva in her essay 'Stabat Mater' where she questions the supremacy of images of the Madonna in Western culture. She locates Mary and the Lady as: 'the focal point of men's desires and aspirations. Moreover, because they were unique and thus excluded all other women, both the Lady and the Virgin embodied an absolute authority the more attractive as it appeared removed from paternal sternness' (1986: 170). When Matilda transgresses the boundary of ideal, feminine behaviour and becomes masterful, she no longer doubles the Madonna portrait and consequently no longer mirrors Ambrosio's desires. She ceases to represent his image of an ideal love, and is thus replaced with Antonia, another virginal object. None the less, it is Matilda who is responsible in this novel for destabilizing the equation of woman and modesty, and, as such, she occupies an important space. By portraying Ambrosio's fatal passion as being so linked to his love of the Madonna, Lewis also effectively critiques the location of the Virgin Mary as an icon in Western culture.

This critique offered by Lewis seems to be supported by a significant addition that he made to the ending of the second edition of the novel. Following the outraged reception of the first edition of The Monk in 1796, Lewis added an extra passage to the ending of the second, third and fourth editions of the novel.[5] In the first edition, the villainous monk Ambrosio is dashed to pieces and left to rot at the foot of a mountain by Lucifer, as a suitable punishment for his various crimes. The second edition kept that conclusion, but added a more moral note as the final closure to the tale:

> Haughty Lady, why shrunk you back when yon poor frail one drew near? Was the air infected by her errors? Was your purity soiled by her passing breath? Ah! Lady, smooth that insulting brow: stifle the reproach just bursting from your scornful lip: wound not a soul, that bleeds already! She has suffered, suffers still. Her air is gay, but her heart is broken: her dress sparkles, but her bosom groans.
>
> Lady, to look with mercy on the conduct of others, is a virtue no less than to look with severity on your own.
>
> (Lewis 1796: III 314-315)

Recent editors of **The Monk** have chosen largely to ignore this addition, only acknowledging its existence in a note upon the text. However, if we take into consideration the themes that we have just been exploring, it appears to offer a thematically tighter conclusion. By dwelling on the external appearances of two seemingly diametrically opposed female characters, named only 'Haughty Lady' and 'yon poor frail one', the author himself has cast two nameless women into stereotypical positions. However, Lewis has at the same time undermined this by his appeal for our compassion, and for external appearances to be mistrusted.

In this novel, a critique of the masculine tendency to veil the reality of the female presence is offered on several levels. One of these levels is the equation of the female form with artistic, religious representations of it. As Jerry Hogle has argued, 'all passionate desire in this book is really aroused, intensified, and answered by images more than objects or bodies, by signifiers more often than by signifieds or referents.' (1997: 1) The 'Haughty Lady' of this second edition, contrasted with the 'poor frail one' does not need a specific identity. Rather, she appears to signify the idealized versions of the Madonna, offered throughout this novel in various images, portraits and representations of women. She is also specifically contrasted with the 'poor frail one' who may represent the wronged heroines of this novel, wronged because of their unwitting similarities to the Virgin Mary.

In all, **The Monk** offers three core models of femininity that are both indebted to previous literary representations and intended to disrupt them. The first, Antonia, is a clear embodiment of previous literary representations drawn from, amongst others, Diderot, de Sade and Radcliffe. The second model, Agnes, who like Diderot's Suzanne is a nun who cannot disentangle herself from her orders, provides a remarkable representation of what happens when the flesh-and-blood reality of motherhood is neglected. The tale of her illegitimate baby, left to die on her chest as a 'suitable' punishment by her convent for fornication, is grotesquely realized. Finally, although Matilda is, as the *Monthly Review* noted in 1797, remarkably similar to Jacques Cazotte's devil Biondetta in *The Devil in Love,* she remains none the less a remarkable and unique indictment of the roles played by male desire in the previous models. Her ability to gender-switch, to posture submission when required, and her mimicry of the Madonna all undermine previous literary constructions of femininity. The character of Matilda incorporates Suzanne Simonin's knowledge of her effect on

men and parodies the earlier Justine's naivety in Lewis's endeavour to untangle the links between femininity, desire and the Madonna.

In his critical work 'Idée sur les romans', first published in 1800 as a preface to *Les Crimes de l'amour,* the Marquis de Sade praised Lewis's **The Monk** for being superior, in every respect, to the brilliantly imaginative novels of Ann Radcliffe. Paradoxically, however, it was also in this same work that de Sade famously disclaimed his authorship of *Justine,* an assertion which he persisted in repeating throughout his life. In this essay, he protested, 'I have never written any such immoral works, and I never shall' (1970: 63, my translation). Given that de Sade had only recently published his third edition of his Justine tale, *La Nouvelle Justine,* his critical and literary personae appear to be clearly at odds with each other. De Sade the public author, who writes with such authority in 'Idée sur les romans' on Richardson, Lewis and Radcliffe, clearly wanted to dissociate himself from his own literary efforts. Perhaps such vehement denial was due to the fact that Alexandre-Louis de Villeterque identified the Justine novels as de Sade's and subsequently calumniated them in the *Journal des arts, des sciences et de littérature* (de Villeterque 1800). However, de Sade's very obvious admiration of Matthew Lewis in his own critical essay does appear to undermine his self-distancing from the immoral works of *Justine.*

La Nouvelle Justine, ou les malheurs de la vertu, suivi de l'histoire de Juliette, sa soeur was a work of ten volumes, with a hundred obscene engravings. It was supposedly printed 'in Holland' in 1797, although it was actually typeset in Paris by de Sade's publisher Nicolas Massé. However, Jean-Jacques Pauvert, one of the co-editors of de Sade's complete works, has raised justifiable questions about the date, 1797, and the order of publication of *La Nouvelle Justine* and *L'Histoire de Juliette.* He argues that the third *Justine* followed an earlier 1796 version of *Juliette* in August 1800 (de Sade 1986: VIII 18). This third reprisal of the story tripled the length of the second edition, and added yet more persecution and torture.

Given Pauvert's correction of the dates of *La Nouvelle Justine,* it appears highly probable that some of the much-admired Matthew Lewis's methods of inscribing virtue in distress had an impact on de Sade's revisions. In this third edition, for the first time the character Justine is denied the first-person narrative voice and the entire story is told in the third person. It is equally as important to note that this third version of the novel is not a Gothic novel. As Didier has noted, with this third Justine we witness an 'explosion' of the Gothic novel (1976: 106). Whereas in the previous two editions we had some sympathy for the unfortunate heroine, here, instead, the third-person narrator makes us entirely complicit in his mockery of Justine. Like the narrative voice at the beginning of *The Monk* which urges us not to encourage the idea that piety attracts people to church, de Sade's narrator in this final edition mocks the ineffectual piety of Justine. At one point, for example, he castigates religion for promoting self-interest (1986: 100); later he relentlessly pursues Justine for crying when her religious consolation is revealed to be illogical by the Comte du Bressac, stating that tears are 'la ressource du faible, en se voyant ravir la chimère qui le consolait', or 'the resource of a weak person, when they have their last source of consolation torn away' (1986: 141, my translation). In this final, more picaresque edition, de Sade finally achieved exactly the disruption of the idolized feminine form which he wished.[6] What his libertine characters pursue with such violence are females who idolize the Madonna with such force that they are unwittingly seen to dress like her, and shown to act with a concomitant naivety that is breathtaking.

Why was de Sade so haunted by this tale that he revised it twice over the space of ten years? As with Lewis's novel, some of the answers lie in the portrayal of virtue in distress, and with the essential linkage of that virtue to religious piety. The narrator himself justifies this assumption on the very second page of this third edition, where he states that 'Il est essentiel que les sots cessent d'encenser cette ridicule idole de la vertu, qui ne les a jusqu'ici payés que d'ingratitude' (1986: IV 26). 'It is essential that fools stop worshipping this ridiculous idol of virtue, which until now has only repaid them with ingratitude' (my translation). What is interesting here is the deliberate confusion about the subject of de Sade's attack. Virtue as a concept is what he most wishes to denigrate for his readers; but equally, one could conclude that the 'ridiculous idol of virtue' could be his character Justine, made famous through the previous two editions of the novel, and clearly associated with both purity and religion. In all three editions, Justine's beauty is compared to that of Raphael's beautiful virgins. Like Lewis, then, de Sade makes implicit connections between Justine, virginity and painting. However, in contrast, his project is clearly stated at the very beginning of the tale. He wishes to use the character Justine to teach moralists a violent lesson about idolizing virtue. The subsequent linking of this virtue to specifically Catholic institutions such as monasteries display a disgust with the artifices and ornaments of the Catholic Church. De Sade's atheistic castigation of the ritualistic worship of artifices in the Catholic Church is remarkably similar to Lewis's Anglican-Protestant condemnation of the sensuality of this worship.

The trajectory of the unfortunate adventures of Justine involves successive encounters with different institutions. The foremost of these institutions in each edition is a monastery called Sainte-Marie-des-Bois where Justine goes to confess and be comforted by the monks. Justine's naivety, coupled with her religious fervour, makes her a desirable prey for the libertine monks who run this monastery, and want to admit her to their seraglio. A very detailed passage in the third edition, *La Nouvelle Justine*, describes Justine's confession:

> Justine, éblouie par les illusions de son ardente piété, n'entend rien, ne voit rien, et se prosterne; . . .
>
> Justine, immobile, fermement persuadée que tout ce qu'on lui fait n'a d'autre but que de la conduire pas à pas vers la perfection céleste, souffre tout avec une indicible résignation; pas une plainte . . . pas un mouvement ne lui échappe; son esprit était tellement élevé vers les choses célestes, que le bourreau l'eût déchirée sans qu'elle eût seulement osé s'en plaindre.
>
> (de Sade, 1986: IV 249-250)

> (Overcome by the illusions of her boundless piety, Justine hears nothing, sees nothing and kneels down; . . . motionless, certain that everything that she is subjected to has no other aim than to lead her step by step to celestial perfection, Justine suffers everything with an ineffable resignation; not one complaint passes her lips . . . not one movement comes from her; so much was her spirit transported on to a higher plane that her tormentor might have ripped her to pieces without her once even daring to protest.)
>
> (my translation)

This description situates Justine firmly on the side of innocence and piety, whilst simultaneously destroying this picture of innocence by describing the libertine monks' desecration of her. Thus fixed in her adoration of the Virgin Mary, Justine becomes blind to the immediate danger posed by the monks who lasciviously watch her devotions and undress her. De Sade firmly makes the point in this edition of the novel that it is precisely Justine's obsession with the Virgin Mary, her fervent piety, which delivers her so easily to the cruelties of the monks of Sainte-Marie-des-Bois. Justine adopts the posture of the Virgin Mary, and the posturing incites the monks' violent desires. What the monks wish to attain, apart from sexual gratification, is the violent destruction of this virginal image by reminding Justine of her all too mortal qualities. Her innocence here appears to owe more to Lewis's portrayal of Antonia (who is shrouded in both a 'bandage of ignorance' as well as a 'veil of innocence' (1980: 264)) than to the more wordly wise characterizations of Justine in the two previous versions of de Sade's own text.

Both Matthew Lewis and the Marquis de Sade embarked upon disrupting the collation of the venerated Madonna and women. They both used fairly brutal methods to destabilize these connections in their texts. Lewis portrayed one lascivious monk who falls prey to a lustful demon who deliberately postures herself as the Madonna. De Sade's relentless destabilization comes through the successive and ever-more-brutal revision of a rape scene in a monastery where the heroine becomes so lost in her devotions to the Madonna that she forgets the real dangers which surround her. In de Sade's *La Nouvelle Justine* we, as readers, are brutally taught of the follies of Justine's posturing by being forced to laugh at both her innocence and devotion. Lewis's **The Monk** conveys its message in slightly different terms—one of these terms, as I have argued, lies in the addition of the 'Haughty Lady' to the subsequent editions, the other term is by teaching Ambrosio through damnation that the ideal and the real, such as the Madonna, doubled by Matilda and Antonia, must remain forever separate. In the words of Angela Carter: 'Even if it is the dream made flesh, the real, once it becomes real, can be no more than real' (Carter 1982: 201).

Notes

1. Anon. 1797a. Although this four-volume edition is translated anonymously, it has been identified, and is widely acknowledged on library catalogues, as having been translated by four different translators: namely, Jacques-Marie Deschamps, Jean-Baptiste Després, Pierre Vincent Benoist and Pierre Bernard Lamare.

2. Where available, I have used authoritative translations of de Sade's works. However, in the case of *La Nouvelle Justine* and 'Idée sur les romans', where no translations have been available, I have used my own. These instances are marked in the body of the text.

3. As Peter France has documented, Diderot in fact wrote *La Religieuse* in 1760. However, it was published in the *Correspondance littéraire* in 1780, though a teasing set of letters, which describe the circumstances of composition, had been made public in 1770 (France 1983: 37). The *Monthly Magazine* noted in December 1797 the translation of *La Religieuse*: 'Two novels have been translated from the French of Diderot, with considerable vivacity, "The Nun" and "James the Fatalist": in each of these works are some masterly delineations of character, but the pen of Diderot is not remarkable for its chastity' (Anon. 1797c: 518).

4. For a fuller exploration of the similarities and differences between *The Romance of the Forest* and de Sade's second *Justine*, see Clery 1994. Clery discusses the similar plot motifs of both novels, but demonstrates the two novels' entirely different philosophical approaches.

5. Lewis, of course, reserved the most significant changes to the text for the fourth edition of the novel, *Ambrosio, or The Monk: A Romance* (1798). However, the crucial addition to the ending is present from the second edition. The British Library carries an annotated copy of the third edition owned by Lewis where he wrote in the vital changes to be made. The copy makes for interesting reading not only because of the corrections, but also because of the bitter asides that Lewis has scribbled in. For example, a scribbled footnote to his 'Imitation of Horace' epigraph 'And when you find, condemned, despised, / Neglected, blamed, and criticised.' bitterly records of the novel's reception 'Neglected it has not been, but criticised enough of all conscience' (BL: C.28. b 4-6: iv).

6. I would justify my use of the term 'picaresque' for this final edition of the novel because the overarching am of the novel, thanks to the editorial inventions, is to satirize virtue, and its embodiment in the naive character of Justine, whose travels take her from master to master.

References

Anon. (1797a) *Le Moine, traduit de l'anglais*, 4 vols, Paris, Maradan.

Anon. (1797b) *Monthly Review*, 23.

Anon. (1797c) *Monthly Magazine*, December.

Berger, J. (1972) *Ways of Seeing*, Harmondsworth, Penguin.

Botting, F. (1996) *Gothic*, London, Routledge.

Carter, A. (1982) *The Infernal Desire Machines of Doctor Hoffman*, Harmondsworth, Penguin [1972].

Cazotte, J. (1772) *Le Diable amoureux. Nouvelle espagnole*, Naples and Paris, n.p.

Clery, E. J. (1994) 'Ann Radcliffe and D. A. F. de Sade: thoughts on heroinism', *Women's Writing*, 1:2.

Diderot, D. (1961) *La Religieuse*, Paris, Armand Colin [1780].

Didier, B. (1976) *Sade: Une écriture du désir*, Paris, Denoel/Gonthier.

France, P. (1983) *Diderot*, Oxford, Oxford University Press.

Heine, M. (1973) 'Le Marquis de Sade et le roman noir', in A. Le Brun and J.-J. Pauvert (eds) *Oeuvres complètes du Marquis de Sade*, 16 vols, Paris, Société Nouvelle des Editions Pauvert.

LEWIS

Hogle, J. 'The Ghost of the Counterfeit—and the Closet—in *The Monk*', in *Romanticism on the Net* 8 (November 1997) <http://users.ox.ac.uk/~scat0385/ghost.html>.

Kilgour, M. (1995) *The Rise of the Gothic Novel*, London, Routledge.

Kristeva, J. (1986) 'Stabat Mater', trans. L. Roudiez, in T. Moi (ed.) *The Kristeva Reader*, Oxford, Blackwell.

de Lauretis, T. (1984) *Alice Doesn't: Feminism, Semiotics, Cinema*, Bloomington, Indiana University Press.

Lever, M. (1991) *Donatien Alphonse François, Marquis de Sade*, Paris, Fayard.

Lewis, M. G. (1796) *The Monk; a Romance*, 2nd edn, 3 vols. London, J. Bell.

———. (1797) *The Monk; a Romance*, 3rd edn, annotated copy: BL c.175. 113. 3 vols, London, J. Bell.

———. (1798) *Ambrosio, or The Monk; A Romance*, London, J. Bell.

———. (1980) *The Monk; a Romance* ed. H. Anderson, Oxford, Oxford University Press [1796].

Miles, R. (1993) *Gothic Writing: A Genealogy*, London, Routledge.

Punter, D. (1996) *The Literature of Terror*, 2nd edn, 2 vols, London and New York, Longman.

Radcliffe, A. (1992) *The Romance of the Forest: Interspersed with Some Pieces of Poetry*, ed. C. Chard, Oxford, Oxford University Press [1791].

de Sade, D. A. F. (1970) 'Idée sur les romans', Paris, Ducros.

———. (1986) *Oeuvres complètes du Marquis de Sade*, eds A. Le Brun and J.-J.

Pauvert, 16 vols, Paris, Société Nouvelle des Editions Pauvert [1800].

———. (1991) *Three Complete Novels and Other Writings*, trans. R. Seaver and A. Wainhouse, London, Arrow.

Schaeffer, N. (1999) *The Marquis de Sade: A Life*, London, Hamish Hamilton.

de Villeterque, A.-L. (1800) *Journal des arts, des sciences et delittérature*, 22 October.

FURTHER READING

Bibliography

Frank, Frederick S. "*The Monk*: A Bicentenary Bibliography." *Romanticism on the Net* 8 (November 1997): <http://users.ox.ac.uk/~scat0385/monkbiblio.html>.

Frank states: "[d]esigned to be consulted sequentially, the bibliography conducts a census of contemporary and historical criticism appearing in books, monographs, scholarly journals, and doctoral dissertations, with the eleven individual sections containing complete and compendious data except for Section VII, 'Eighteenth- and Nineteenth-Century Editions of *The Monk*' and Section IX, 'Chapbooks, Shilling Shocker Condensations, and Plagiarized Abridgements of *The Monk*,' which are selectively compiled and annotated."

Biography

Peck, Louis F. *A Life of Matthew G. Lewis*. Cambridge, Mass.: Harvard University Press, 1961, 331 p.

Comprehensive biography of Lewis.

Criticism

Birkhead, Edith. "The Novel of Terror: Lewis and Maturin." In *The Tale of Terror: A Study of the Gothic Romance*, pp. 63-93. New York: E. P. Dutton & Company Publishers, 1921.

A chapter from what is considered one of the first significant studies of the Gothic movement, in which Birkhead centers on the terrifying, evocative, and melodramatic elements of Lewis's works.

Blakemore, Steven. "Matthew Lewis's Black Mass: Sexual, Religious Inversion in *The Monk*." *Studies in the Novel* 30, no. 4 (winter 1998): 521-39.

Argues that in The Monk Lewis subverts traditional religious and gender roles.

Gose, Eliot B., Jr. "The Monk." In *Imagination Indulged: The Irrational in the Nineteenth-Century Novel*, pp. 27-40. Montreal, Quebec and Kingston, Ontario: McGill-Queen's University Press, 1972.

Undertakes a psychoanalytic survey of The Monk, noting its "unresolved tensions" of "sexual conflict, violated taboos, and self-destructive impulses."

Grudin, Peter. "*The Monk*: Matilda and the Rhetoric of Deceit." *The Journal of Narrative Technique* 5, no. 2 (May 1975): 136-46.

Assesses the "formal coherence" of The Monk, claiming that evidence for its structural unity exists in an interpretation of Matilda as a demonic being.

Hogle, Jerrold E. "The Ghost of the Counterfeit—and the Closet—in *The Monk*." *Romanticism On the Net* 8 (November 1997): <http://users.ox.ac.uk/~scat0385/ghost.html>.

Maintains that "Lewis' daemonic novel has the shocking force in our culture that it still does, not because of the sexual license or the use of German sources in it so fervently attacked at the time, but because it enacts and thus partially exposes a particular cultural agenda of both its time and today that underlies and motivates what I call 'the ghost of the counterfeit' in the rise of the Gothic during the later eighteenth century."

Jones, Wendy. "Stories of Desire in The Monk." *ELH* 57, no. 1 (spring 1990): 129-50.

Illustrates how the narrative structure of The Monk and its social and political stance are related and declares that Lewis offers in his novel "a defense of the concept of individual desire and of the right to articulate that desire in both speech and action."

Kauhl, Gudrun. "On the Release from Monkish Fetters: Matthew Lewis Reconsidered." *Dutch Quarterly Review* 19, no. 4 (1989): 264-80.

Examines the motif of transgression as both a psychological and a political fact in The Monk.

Lydenberg, Robin. "Ghostly Rhetoric: Ambivalence in M. G. Lewis' *The Monk*." *Ariel: A Review of International English Literature* 10, no. 2 (April 1979): 65-79.

> Investigates "Lewis's ambivalence toward his authorial responsibility" as moral judge in *The Monk*.

Mulman, Lisa Naomi. "Sexuality on the Surface: Catholicism and the Erotic Object in Lewis's *The Monk*." *Bucknell Review* 42, no. 1 (1998): 98-110.

> Focuses on "Lewis's use of . . . objects (precisely the veil, mirror, lamp, rosary, face) as sites of religious, aesthetic, and social anxiety rather than substitutive or fetishized sexual desire."

Sedgwick, Eve Kosofsky. "The Character in the Veil: Imagery of the Surface in the Gothic Novel." *PMLA: Publications of the Modern Language Association of America* 96, no. 2 (March 1981): 255-70.

> Studies works by Ann Radcliffe and Lewis's *The Monk* "to show that an analysis of the thematic attention to surfaces changes the traditional view of the Gothic contribution to characterization and figuration in fiction."

OTHER SOURCES FROM GALE:

Additional coverage of Lewis's life and career is contained in the following sources published by Thomson Gale: *Dictionary of Literary Biography*, Vols. 39, 158, 178; *Literary Movements for Students*, Vol. 1; *Literature Resource Center*; *Nineteenth-Century Literature Criticism*, Vols. 11, 62; *Reference Guide to English Literature*, Ed. 2; *St. James Guide to Horror, Ghost & Gothic Writers*; and *Supernatural Fiction Writers*.

CHARLES ROBERT MATURIN

(1780 - 1824)

(Also wrote under the pseudonym Dennis Jasper Murphy) Irish novelist and playwright.

Maturin is remembered primarily for his novel *Melmoth the Wanderer* (1820), which is considered among the finest examples of Gothic fiction in the English language. By virtue of its complicated revenge plot, seemingly supernatural phenomena, and use of landscape to create an atmosphere of horror and suspense, *Melmoth the Wanderer* is strongly reminiscent of the Gothic novels of Ann Radcliffe and Matthew Gregory Lewis. Critics distinguish it from the works of these earlier writers, however, by its attention to the psychology of despair and the torments of religious doubt. More popular in France than in England or Ireland, *Melmoth the Wanderer* exercised a great influence on nineteenth-century French writers. Maturin's most notable French admirer, Honoré de Balzac, was so impressed with the novel that he wrote a sequel to it entitled *Melmoth reconcilié.*

BIOGRAPHICAL INFORMATION

Maturin was born in Dublin, where he spent most of his life. He graduated from Trinity College in 1800 and in 1803 was ordained a minister of the Church of England. After a brief apprentice-

ship as curate of the county parish of Loughrea, Galway, where he became familiar with the Irish peasantry that he later wrote about in such novels as *The Wild Irish Boy* (1808) and *The Milesian Chief* (1812), Maturin went to St. Peter's Church in Dublin, where he served as curate for the rest of his life. Although Maturin greatly preferred the fashionable St. Peter's to the rural parish in Loughrea, he found it impossible to support his wife and family on his meager salary. In order to supplement his income, he embarked on a literary career. Fearful of jeopardizing his chances for advancement within the Church, Maturin published his first three novels, *Fatal Revenge; or, The Family of Montorio* (1807), *The Wild Irish Boy,* and *The Milesian Chief,* under the pseudonym of Dennis Jasper Murphy.

MAJOR WORKS

While critics consider Lewis's influence evident in the abundance of horrible details in *Fatal Revenge,* they attribute the rational denouement of the story to Radcliffe's influence. Critics consistently complain that Maturin's attempt to "explain away" the miraculous events of the story results in a disproportion between cause and effect that gives the novel, in the words of the critic Niilo Idman (see Further Reading), an "air of charlatanism." Nevertheless, *Fatal Revenge* is considered superior to *The Wild Irish Boy* and *The*

Milesian Chief, which are seldom included in critical discussions of Maturin's works. In 1814, Maturin sent Sir Walter Scott the manuscript of his first drama, *Bertram; or, The Castle of St. Aldobrand* (1816), a play that unites the Byronic hero and the Gothic villain in a single character. Scott was so impressed with the play that he referred Maturin to Lord Byron, who belonged to the committee that selected plays for production at London's Drury Lane Theater. Through Byron's influence, Drury Lane produced *Bertram* in 1816. Although the play's immediate success prompted Maturin to drop the pseudonym he had used for his first three novels and identify himself, his newfound literary recognition ultimately proved a disaster. Convinced that *Bertram* was the beginning of a brilliant dramatic career, he recklessly spent his profits and plunged deeply into debt. His subsequent plays, *Manuel* (1817) and *Fredolfo* (1819), were dismal failures, and to add to his difficulties, *Bertram*'s irreverent sentiments were imputed by ecclesial officials to Maturin himself, and he lost any chance of being promoted within the Church.

Maturin resumed his career as a novelist with *Women; or, Pour et contre* (1818), for which he temporarily abandoned the Gothic idiom. A satire on the religious views of a narrow middle-class Calvinist sect, *Women* reflects Maturin's opposition to religious fanaticism and is today considered an insightful analysis of Evangelicalism. Maturin returned to the Gothic form in the novel that is viewed as his masterpiece, *Melmoth the Wanderer.* Based on the Wandering Jew and Faust legends, *Melmoth the Wanderer* tells the story of a seventeenth-century scholar who sells his soul to the devil in exchange for a prolonged life. The novel's structure is complex, consisting of five interlocking tales. In Maturin's novel *The Albigenses* (1824), an historical romance modeled on the works of Scott, he treats the theme of religious fanaticism.

CRITICAL RECEPTION

With the exception of *Bertram,* none of Maturin's works was a critical or popular success during his lifetime. Nineteenth-century critics generally considered Maturin a talented but injudicious writer, whose novels and plays were marred by excesses of horror. Critical reaction to *Melmoth the Wanderer* in the nineteenth century was mixed: while some reviewers denounced Maturin's presentation of the diabolical Melmoth as impious, others praised the novel for its graphic descriptions of horror and suffering. Later nineteenth-century commentators frequently attributed Maturin's lack of critical acclaim to the diminishing popularity of Gothic fiction. Critics writing around the turn of the twentieth century applauded Melmoth's emotional intensity, and modern commentators support this opinion. Twentieth- and twenty-first-century critics have focused largely on *Melmoth the Wanderer,* and some critics have asserted that Maturin's reputation as a Gothic novelist has overshadowed his importance as a proponent of Irish regional literature. Some commentators argue that the impact of *Melmoth the Wanderer* derives primarily from Maturin's examination of human responses to terror and oppression. Douglas Grant (see Further Reading) terms Maturin a "brilliant psychologist of the perverse" whose interest in extreme emotional states anticipated the psychological novels of Fyodor Dostoevsky and Franz Kafka. In addition to its investigation of human psychology, *Melmoth the Wanderer* is also lauded for its analysis of the spiritual consequences of religious fanaticism. William F. Axton (see Further Reading), for example, distinguishes *Melmoth the Wanderer* from earlier Gothic novels because of its "compelling statement of the grand theme of perverted faith." Today Maturin is generally regarded as the unjustly forgotten author of one of the finest Gothic novels in English. *Melmoth the Wanderer* is said to have influenced the work of such diverse writers as Balzac, Charles Baudelaire, Alexander Pushkin, Nathaniel Hawthorne, Edgar Allan Poe, and Oscar Wilde. The breadth of the novel's appeal attests to its enduring interest.

PRINCIPAL WORKS

Fatal Revenge; or, The Family of Montorio. 3 vols. [as Dennis Jasper Murphy] (novel) 1807

The Wild Irish Boy [as Dennis Jasper Murphy] (novel) 1808

The Milesian Chief: A Romance. 4 vols. [as Dennis Jasper Murphy] (novel) 1812

Bertram; or, The Castle of St. Aldobrand (play) 1816

Manuel (play) 1817

Women: or, Pour et contre (novel) 1818

Fredolfo: A Tragedy (play) 1819

Melmoth the Wanderer. 4 vols. (novel) 1820

The Albigenses (novel) 1824

CHARLES ROBERT MATURIN (STORY DATE 1825)

SOURCE: Maturin, Charles Robert. "Leixlip Castle." In *Gothic Tales of Terror, Volume One: Classic Horror Stories from Great Britain,* edited by Peter Haining. 1972. Reprint edition, pp. 271-85. Baltimore, Md.: Penguin Books, Inc., 1973.

The following excerpt is from a short story first published in the collection The Literary Souvenir or Cabinet of Poetry and Romance *in 1825. The first portion of the excerpt contains Maturin's brief commentary on the story, and the last portion comprises the story's conclusion.*

The incidents of the following tale are not merely *founded* on fact, they are facts themselves, which occurred at no very distant period in my own family. The marriage of the parties, their sudden and mysterious separation, and their total alienation from each other until the last period of their mortal existence, are all *facts.* I cannot vouch for the truth of the supernatural solution given to all these mysteries; but I must still consider the story as a fine specimen of Gothic horrors, and can never forget the impression it made on me when I heard it related for the first time among many other thrilling traditions of the same description.

—C.R.M.

. . . . .

Lady Maxwell survived Sir Richard forty years, living to the great age of ninety-six; and, according to a promise, previously given, disclosed to a descendent with whom she had lived, the following extraordinary circumstances.

She said that on the night of the 31st of October, about seventy-five years before, at the instigation of her ill-advising attendant, she had washed one of her garments in a place where four streams met, and peformed other unhallowed ceremonies under the direction of the Collogue, in the expectation that her future husband would appear to her in her chamber at twelve o'clock that night. The critical moment arrived, but with it no lover-like form. A vision of indescribable horror approached her bed, and flinging at her an iron weapon of a shape and construction unknown to her, bade her 'recognize her future husband by *that.*' The terrors of this visit soon deprived her of her senses; but on her recovery, she persisted, as has been said, in keeping the fearful pledge of the reality of the vision, which, on examination, appeared to be incrusted with blood. It remained concealed in the inmost drawer of her cabinet till the morning of the separation. On that morning, Sir Richard Maxwell rose before daylight to join a hunting party—he wanted a knife for some accidental purpose, and, missing his own, called to Lady Maxwell, who was still in bed, to lend him one. The lady, who was half asleep, answered, that in such a drawer of her cabinet he would find one. He went, however, to another, and the next moment she was fully awakened by seeing her husband present the terrible weapon to her throat, and threaten her with instant death unless she disclosed how she came by it. She supplicated for life, and then, in an agony of horror and contrition, told the tale of that eventful night. He gazed at her for a moment with a countenance which rage, hatred, and despair converted, as she avowed, into a living likeness of the demon-visage she had once beheld (so singularly was the fated resemblance fulfilled), and then exclaiming, 'You won me by the devil's aid, but you shall not keep me long,' left her—to meet no more in this world. Her husband's secret was not unknown to the lady, though the means by which she became possessed of it were wholly unwarrantable. Her curiosity had been strongly excited by her husband's aversion to his countrymen, and it was so stimulated by the arrival of a Scottish gentleman in the neighbourhood some time before, who professed himself formerly acquainted with Sir Richard, and spoke mysteriously of the causes that drove him from his country—that she contrived to procure an interview with him under a feigned name, and obtained from him the knowledge of circumstances which embittered her after-life to its latest hour. His story was this:

Sir Richard Maxwell was at deadly feud with a younger brother; a family feast was proposed to reconcile them, and as the use of knives and forks was then unknown in the Highlands, the company met armed with their dirks for the purpose of carving. They drank deeply; the feast, instead of harmonizing, began to inflame their spirits; the topics of old strife were renewed; hands, that at first touched their weapons in defiance, drew them at last in fury, and in the fray, Sir Richard mortally wounded his brother. His life was with difficulty saved from the vengeance of the clan, and he was hurried towards the seacoast, near which the house stood, and concealed there till a vessel could be procured to convey him to Ireland. He embarked *on the night of the 31st of October,* and while he was traversing the deck in unutterable agony of spirit, his hand accidentally touched the dirk which he had unconsciously worn ever since the fatal night. He drew it, and, praying 'that the guilt of his brother's blood might be as far from his soul, as he could fling that weapon from his body,' sent it with all his strength into the air. This instrument he found secreted in the lady's cabinet, and whether he really believed her to have become possessed of it by supernatural means, or whether he feared his wife was a secret witness of his crime, has not been ascertained, but the result was what I have stated.

The reparation took place on the discovery:— for the rest,

> I know not how the truth may be,
> I tell the Tale as 'twas told to me.

GENERAL COMMENTARY

ROBERT LOUGY (ESSAY DATE 1975)

SOURCE: Lougy, Robert. "The Later Years, 1820-1824." In *Charles Robert Maturin*, pp. 64-87. Lewisburg, Penn.: Bucknell University Press, 1975.

In the following essay, Lougy surveys the events that took place during Maturin's final years, and analyzes the works that he composed during this period.

Even at the time of *Fredolfo*'s failure, and as early as September 1818, Maturin was already thinking about—if not actually engaged in writing—a new drama and also a romance. The drama, however, was never published and was not produced until six years after Maturin's death. The manuscript of this drama, entitled *Osmyn the Renegade* (also known as *The Siege of Salerno*), had been given to Edmund Kean for his perusal, and he had for unknown reasons refused to return it. Between the years of 1821-1822, it disappeared in London and was not recovered until late in 1825 by William, Maturin's eldest son. It was almost five more years before the play was successfully produced in Dublin. Mrs. Maturin realized 300 pounds from the production, but it was never published and only brief excerpts, quoted by Alaric Watts, have ever appeared in print.

The romance on which Maturin was working was *Melmoth the Wanderer.* He had received from Constable an advance of 500 pounds for *Melmoth* sometime in 1819 and was thus fairly solvent at the time of *Fredolfo*'s failure. In August, 1820, *Melmoth* was published, and it remains today the one work for which Maturin is best known. Balzac attested to Maturin's genius and to the greatness of his most famous work by placing Melmoth alongside of Moliere's Don Juan, Goethe's Faust, and Byron's Manfred as one of the four supreme allegorical figures in modern European literature. After reading *Melmoth*, one feels that it was a work that was always within Maturin, waiting for the proper conjunction of time and circumstances

to appear. He drew, of course, upon other literary sources, especially Marlowe's Dr. Faustus and Milton's Lucifer; yet *Melmoth* remains wholly Maturin's—his genius and style are indelibly marked throughout it. Using the legend of the Wandering Jew and the legend of Faust, he creates a unique work of art sharing only the broadest and most general similarities with its sources.

Although thematically related to some of Maturin's own writings as well as to the writings of others (for example, Lewis' *The Monk* and Godwin's *St. Leon*), *Melmoth* finally denies comparison and demands that we cope with it on its own terms. And like the fourth book of *Gulliver's Travels*, most of de Sade, and the writings of Celine, the terms established by *Melmoth* are neither easy nor pleasant to recognize or accept. There is no evidence to suggest that Maturin was even remotely insane while writing *Melmoth*; on the contrary, his letters during this period are perfectly lucid and coherent, and his last novel, *The Albigenses*, is certainly not the work of an obsessed or demented mind. Yet, one has the feeling that Maturin, in writing *Melmoth*, calls forth a reality that is so powerful, yet so grotesque, so cruel, and so foreign to Maturin's daily existence, that the dividing line between genius and madness is throughout it very thin. (Indeed, a contemporary account of him during the time he was writing this novel suggests that he was virtually obsessed by his creation.) And Maturin himself frequently alluded to his own creativity in terms of witchcraft—of how he wanted his reader to "sit down by my magic Cauldron, mix my dark ingredients, see the bubbles work, and the spirits rise." The danger, of course, in evoking spirits is that one can never be certain whether he can control them or of the price they will demand from him. The dangers would appear to be multiplied when one calls upon the spirits in their own territory, as Maturin seems to have done in *Melmoth.*

For to write such a novel is to probe those areas of knowledge, both "the visions of another world" and the darkest recesses of the human psyche, which strain the endurance of the mind, and to cross, perhaps irrevocably, forbidden boundaries. The writer then becomes isolated from the world around him, having used the incantatory power of the word to bring forth a reality that borders on the irrational and the insane. He is at once the possessor of secrets he will share with those readers who dare to sit down by his "magic Cauldron" and also possessed by those demons whose presence his art will reveal.

It is possible that Maturin, too, perceived in himself latent traces of insanity or, at least, interests that went beyond what most would call normal, and that he alluded to them in *Melmoth.* In his preface to the 1820 edition, Maturin states that "the original from which the Wife of Walberg is imperfectly sketched is a living woman, and long may she live." The "living woman" is almost certainly Maturin's own wife and the Wife of Walberg is Ines, from **"The Tale of Guzman's Family."** The tale itself is one of the mildest in *Melmoth,* and the role of Melmoth himself is minimal. The story revolves around Guzman, a wealthy merchant of Seville, whose sister had long ago incurred his wrath by eloping with a German Protestant musician named Walberg. When Guzman thinks that he is about to die, he invites his sister and her family to Seville and establishes them in luxury and wealth, although he refuses to see them. Walberg invites his parents to come from Germany to live with them and for a time, all live happily and comfortably. But when Guzman dies, it is discovered that he has left all of his money to the Church, and so the Walbergs are left penniless. In the midst of poverty and despair, the son sells his blood to a surgeon, the daughter is almost tempted into prostitution, and Walberg becomes virtually insane with worry. During this time, he is visited by Melmoth, but like the others whom Melmoth seeks out, Walberg refuses the terms Melmoth demands in order to help him. Finally the original will, in which Guzman bequeathed all of his money to his sister, is discovered, but not before Walberg almost commits murder. Eventually he recovers from his sickness and the family returns to Germany to live prosperously.

The tale is important for the background and history it gives us of Melmoth, but also for the emotional intensity with which Maturin once again deals with poverty. Like *Manuel,* this part of *Melmoth* is written with such vividness and force of feeling that Maturin's own life shines forth from every page. There are many instances within this story of strong correspondences to Maturin's own experiences—Walberg's feelings of guilt for his inability to provide for his family, his pressing anxieties of how he will get food for them, his squandering of the little money they did have, and his fears of going insane from worry. Most fascinating, however, is the relationship drawn between Walberg and his father. During those times when he himself did not know where the next meal was coming from, Maturin must have, in spite of himself, harbored strong resentment towards his father, who, in his financial ruin, had pulled down his son and his son's family with him. The guilt that this feeling undoubtedly gave rise to seems to be artistically expiated by Maturin in this tale. During one scene in which the family is seated at the dinner table, with barely enough to eat, Walberg grabs some food from his father's hand and gives it to his children, and later, when "the sufferings of his children seemed to inspire him with a kind of wild resentment," Walberg actually raises his arm against his father, "the deaf old man, who was sluggishly devouring his sordid meal." After Walberg recovers from his sickness and finds his father by his side, he is stricken with remorse and begs him for forgiveness. Thus we see Maturin externalizing the agony of his own sufferings, venting his hostilities toward his father, and yet simultaneously expiating his guilt and creating for his tale an ending that he must have hoped would find a parallel in his own life.

But as fascinating as the autobiographical implications of the tale make it, it is but a small part of the novel. *Melmoth* is composed of five tales, the second of which, **"The Spaniard's Tale,"** contains within it the last three tales. In turn, all five tales are contained within a larger frame-story centering around John Melmoth, a descendant of Melmoth the Wanderer. While taking care of a sick uncle during the year 1818, John Melmoth comes across a portrait inscribed "John Melmoth, anno 1646." He is told that the man in the portrait is a distant ancestor who, according to legend, is still alive. John later comes across an old manuscript whose contents form the basis of the first tale, **"The Tale of Stanton."** The next day, John, while observing a shipwreck on the rocks near the coast, hears a horrible laugh from a man also watching the disaster and recognizes him as the man in the portrait. Frightened, John tries to ascend some rocks, loses his footing, and falls into the water. He awakens in his uncle's house to discover that he has been rescued by the sole survivor of the shipwreck, a Spaniard by the name of Alonzo Moncada. Upon learning John Melmoth's name, Alonzo becomes extremely agitated, and then he tells John the **"Tale of the Spaniard."** This tale forms all but the few final pages of the novel and contains within itself the **"Tale of the Indians," "The Tale of Guzman's Family,"** and **"The Lover's Tale."**

Melmoth's structure is tightly organized and possesses an almost geometrical symmetry. The organizational pattern, appropriately described by one critic as resembling a child's set of toy boxes that fit into one another, serves several purposes.

First of all, it provides Maturin with a means of maintaining a tight aesthetic control over his material; and, given the nature of the world he creates in *Melmoth*—one filled with cruelty, insanity, torture, and death—such control is imperative. In some respects, *Melmoth* resembles a nightmare contained within a structure that, in its formal preciseness, serves to bring order out of chaos and a strange and haunting beauty out of subjects that are in themselves anything but beautiful. Secondly, the organization makes it possible for Maturin to explore his themes through the techniques of analogy and juxtaposition. For example, Maturin explores the nature of religious persecution in the **"Tale of the Spaniard"** and the **"Tale of the Indians,"** the nature of love in the **"Tale of the Indians"** and **"The Lover's Tale,"** and the different aspects of cruelty and insanity in **"The Tale of Stanton,"** the **"Tale of the Spaniard,"** and the **"Tale of the Indians."** Melmoth's presence in all of the tales creates a continuity by establishing a larger plot structure that links the tales together and by suggesting those common bonds of humanity that exist among characters otherwise separated by both chronology and nationality.

Melmoth's history and character are revealed throughout the novel by persons who have met or heard of him and also by Melmoth's own brief visitations. It is in the **"Tale of the Indians"** that Melmoth, through his relationship with Immalee, takes on an independent character and importance of his own. Not only does Maturin's technique of gradually revealing Melmoth increase the fear and mystery that surround him, but it is also appropriate that we meet Melmoth in this fashion, since for much of the novel he is primarily an observer, a man who periodically visits persons whom he believes might be willing to exchange their destiny for his own. Not until **"The Lover's Tale,"** the last tale in the novel, do we fully discover the nature of Melmoth's destiny. An Irishman, Melmoth had become attracted to astrology and the occult sciences during a trip to Poland and had been "promised . . . the knowledge and power of the future world—on conditions that are unutterable." Like Faust, Melmoth agreed to give up his soul to diabolic powers in exchange for profound and prophetic knowledge; and he can be released from this pact only if, in the course of 150 years, he can find someone willing to trade places with him. But although his search lasts the full 150 years and takes him to the darkest and most horrible regions of suffering humanity, he is unsuccessful in his quest: "I have traversed the world in the search, and no one, to gain the world, would lose his own soul."

Melmoth is never the immediate cause of suffering—those persons he encounters have suffered not at the hands of some superhuman power, but at the hands of other human beings. In this respect, Melmoth comes to represent those dark truths that men tend to bestow upon a demonic or diabolic world in order to mitigate their own sense of guilt or inadequacy. He is at once apart from and privy to the innermost secrets and hidden deeds of all men; he is a man who has the power to range the earth and to probe the fears and anxieties of other, yet is incapable of gaining power over them or of learning the secrets of his own heart.

What distinguishes Melmoth from Maturin's previous characters is the ambivalence of his emotions and the complex relationship that develops between Melmoth and Immalee. Although at first he views her as a means to escape his destiny he soon falls in love with her; as a consequence, his existence becomes more tormented, yet more beautiful. Immalee, having been raised on an island and knowing only beauty and peace, is an Eve surrounded by depravity, a figure of innocence and beauty in the midst of corruption and evil. By initiating her into the evils of this world, Melmoth buries his own heart deeper in cynicism and despair and thus cuts himself off from the possibilities of redemptive love. Maturin's depiction of the way in which Immalee's innocence and simple faith work upon Melmoth contains some of his very best writing, as he allows Melmoth to rediscover emotions long buried within him. For one brief moment, when he pleads with Immalee to stay, salvation is within his reach, but the moment of reawakening eludes him, and the full implications of it escape that intellect for which he sold his soul.

Immalee does not stay and the secret remains hidden. Love, for Maturin, is redemptive in that it opens the heart to emotions that bring man closer to his fellow beings and to God. Immalee says to Melmoth that "he who is without a God must be without a heart," and the converse of this is also true. He whose heart is closed to love is also separated from God. Like Faust, Melmoth is always within reach of God's salvation, for God's mercy and forgiveness are infinite and require only faith on man's part to be bestowed. His pact with the Devil does not remove Melmoth from God's grace, but his own cynicism and hardness of heart do.

Thus his damnation results not from the diabolic powers without, but from within, and in this lies the tragedy of his fate.

For Maturin, most men worship not the Christian God of love and compassion, "the God of smiles and happiness," but a harsh and sadistic deity, "the God of groans and blood." Employing religion as a mask behind which he may enact his basest desires, man perverts the meaning of the worship he engages in and creates a religion of hate and violence. Again in **Melmoth** Maturin explores the ways in which sadism and masochism arise from man's imposition of a system of unnatural and narrow constraints; the Inquisition is a symbol of the institutionalization of such cruelty. Early in their relationship, Melmoth shows Immalee two representative religions—in one flagellation and asceticism are practiced, and in the other torture and persecution. For Maturin, these two expressions of "religion" are inextricably related. The antithesis of Christianity in this novel is represented not by Melmoth, but by a parricide and lay-brother among the ex-Jesuits. His particular theology represents Maturin's final expression of anger and sorrow at what has become of the religion embodied by the Sermon on the Mount: "Mine is the best theology—the theology of utter hostility to all beings whose sufferings may mitigate mine."

Melmoth the Wanderer must be read as a religious work. H. P. Lovecraft in his *Supernatural Horror in Literature*, although critical of **Melmoth**'s structure, nevertheless recognizes its religious quality, "a pulse of power undiscoverable in any previous work of this kind—a kinship to the essential truth of human nature, and understanding of the profoundest sources of actual cosmic fear, and a white heat of sympathetic passion on the writer's part. . . ." In **Melmoth,** "Fear is taken out of the realm of the conventional and exalted into a hideous cloud over mankind's very destiny." Dante's Hell has been brought above ground and we see it through the eyes of its inhabitants rather than through the eyes of an observer. At the end, as we hear of Melmoth being pulled down to Hell by demons, the ultimate consequences of cynicism and despair are brought home to bear. In order to present this vision, Maturin had to himself descend more deeply into the Hell within, into the depths of cruelty and horror, and must have been both frightened and fascinated by that curiosity that drove him to write, for example, of two lovers being starved to death in an underground dungeon, or of a man dreaming of being burned alive during an *auto-da-fé.* And although

there may be signs of an abnormal imagination in **Melmoth,** such as led reviewers to speak of Maturin as a genius either mad or diabolic, if we try to dismiss such writing too easily, we are reminded, as Maturin wants us to be, of the normal world in which we live, a world in which *autos-da-fé,* wars, Dachau and Auschwitz do exist, a world presided over by normal kings, queens, politicians, and generals. And we are perhaps forced to reconsider our definitions of madness.

Maturin, however far his mind might have traveled into "the dark regions of romance," faced a more immediate and mundane world of unpaid bills and pressing creditors. In 1821, after having lived three years on the 500 pounds he received as an advance for **Melmoth,** he was once again without money, "distrained for taxes," and "under ejectment for rent." It was considerably longer than he anticipated before he published his next, and last, romance, **The Albigenses.** In the meantime, a long blank-verse poem entitled *The Universe* appeared in 1821 with Maturin listed as its author and dedicated to Coleridge "by his sincere admirer, the Author." The poem's authorship became a matter of immediate dispute when a Mr. James Wills claimed that he had written the poem and had been persuaded by Maturin, who had been advanced £500 for a poem he could not finish, to allow him to publish it under his name. It is possible that Maturin had asked Wills to finish the poem—or perhaps even to write all of it—but it is extremely unlikely that he had been advanced such a large sum of money. Whatever the true facts of the controversy are, the poem is at best mediocre and provides no evidence whatsoever of the presence of Maturin's particular genius and talents within it.

The reception of **Melmoth** seems to have driven Maturin into a deeper seclusion and consequently little is known of his public life during his last years. He had succeeded in alienating himself from his Church superiors even before **Melmoth,** had offended the Evangelicals in **Women: or Pour et Contre,** had angered the Catholics in **Melmoth,** and did not even enjoy that compensation of wealth that often accompanies notoriety. His financial situation was worse than it had ever been, and most of his energies were devoted to trying to eke out an existence for himself and his family.

It was not until 1824, the year of his death, that Maturin's last novel, **The Albigenses,** was published. Although it is the longest of Maturin's works, consisting of four volumes and nearly 1500 pages, it was conceived of by him as but the first part of a trilogy "illustrative of European feelings and manners in ancient times, in middle, and in modern." Much has been said of the influence of Scott and the popularity of his historical novels in Maturin's choice of subjects for his last novel. There can be no doubt that Maturin was indebted to Scott and in *The Albigenses* often rendered him through imitation the highest form of honor. But at the same time, it is quite consistent with Maturin's interests that he should have chosen to write a novel focusing on the Middle Ages and, more particularly, on the persecution of the Albigenses. Religious fanaticism, in its many guises, had always fascinated him and the Middle Ages presented him with a rich and often bizarre combination of human experience—of piety existing alongside of superstition, asceticism vying with sensuality, bravery bearing the banner of oppression, and courtly love imposing upon man an unnatural nobility of restraint.

There is, however, a certain ambivalence on Maturin's part towards the material of his last novel. The reason for this ambivalence is that the romantic bent in Maturin—seen in his obvious fondness and sympathy for certain aspects of the feudal ages—is always struggling against an essentially conservative strain within him. On one hand, Maturin is attracted to the age he is describing—to its richness of spirit, to the high ideals it professed, even if it left them too often unpracticed, and to the potential it offered for individual heroism and noble action. This attraction is only partially explained by the fact that Maturin was contemporary with the rise of romanticism and its interest in the literature and culture of other ages. More important in Maturin's case is the temperamental affinities he had with whatever partook of the aristocratic, an affinity seen in the legends Maturin used to tell of his own family's noble origins.

But if Maturin was politically and emotionally attracted to certain aspects of the Middle Ages, his philosophical and theological view of man prevented him from writing a conventional romance of history extolling the nobility of the age. Maturin might show affinities with the romantic temperament in his belief in nature's salutary powers and in its capacity to provide man with a glimpse of his Creator; but he does not share the romantic's belief in the innate goodness of man or in man's unlimited potential for social and ethical improvement. Goodness and even nobility are possible, although rare, but are constantly endangered by the forces of chance and mutability as well as by man's own propensity toward the base

and the ignoble. For Maturin man's struggle toward the noble and the good is fraught with additional danger by the fact that such a struggle often represses those human desires that if denied for long will ultimately turn against man and destroy him.

His idealization of the age, however, does come through in his depiction of women in *The Albigenses*. In *Women* and *Melmoth*, Zaira, Eva, and Immalee stand among the most memorable of his characters; in *The Albigenses*, on the other hand, Maturin creates two women who, in their conventionality of thought and action, closely resemble those typical romantic heroines he earlier satirized in a review of Radcliffe's novels. In the case of Genevieve, the granddaughter of the aged leader of the Albigenses, Maturin apparently envisioned every possible trial and tribulation that a heroine could face and then created circumstances whereby she could experience them all. She is sent into exile for rendering aid to a wounded knight she eventually marries, saves a group of women from being assaulted, is almost seduced by the Bishop of Toulouse, saves the life of Queen Ingelberg, and soon must use this fact to protect herself from the dishonourable advances of the Queen's son, the Dauphin of France. As if this were not enough adventure for a girl not yet twenty years old, she also meets and talks with Eloise, the immortal lover of Abelard. Isabelle, the other heroine, has fewer adventures—she falls in love with and marries a young knight whose destiny it is to kill the last survivor of the Courtenaye family: Isabelle herself. But through the aid of what is perhaps Maturin's strangest combination of protagonists, a Catholic monk and a sorceress, this disaster is averted and toward the end of the novel, a double wedding takes place.

If *The Albigenses* consisted only of the perils and plights of its two heroes and two heroines, it would be in no way distinguished from the many historical romances tha were flooding the market in Maturin's time, most of them trying to capitalize on Scott's success. Fortunately there is much more than that. First of all, Maturin provides us with a vast and sweeping panoramic view of the historical and religious background. He is also quite successful in capturing the essence of the age's most important figures. Both Simon de Montfort and the Bishop of Toulouse come across larger than life—in their energy and strength, in their enjoyment of the power they wielded, in their mutual hatred of the Albigenses, and in the struggle waged between them to gain recognition as the Champion of the Church. Because Maturin draws them with such vividness, he forces the reader to share his ambivalent attitude toward them. Even though we recognize their cruelty, their boundless egotism, and the discrepancy between their actions and the religion they are professedly defending, we are begrudgingly forced to give them at least our qualified admiration.

If Maturin's historical interests and his romantic impulses are responsible for his creation of those larger-than-life characters, there is another recurrent impulse in Maturin that checks his admiration for the Middle Ages. He is aware that even his most heroic figures were driven, in part, by unheroic needs and desires; like **Women** and, to a lesser extent, **Melmoth, The Albigenses** is a study of religious fanaticism. For Maturin, fanaticism under any guise separates man from himself and from his fellowmen; religious fanaticism, however, is especially dangerous because it deadens one to the feelings of sympathy and compassion and because the energy and enthusiasm of religious fervor are often turned, through violence, hatred, and rigid moral certainty, against religion itself. If Maturin had angered the Evangelicals in **Women,** the Catholics in **Melmoth,** in this novel he succeeded in antagonizing them both. But we have to believe Maturin (in spite of his fantasizing about the sexual and sadistic propensities of Catholic priests) when he maintains that he was not criticizing religion, but rather the perversion of religion by those "who . . . painted heaven to their imaginations and their hearers as a place whose joys would be exalted by their consciousness of the interminable sufferings of their persecutors and enemies."

The fact remains, however, that Maturin became progressively more alienated—at least in his fiction—from all organized religion, namely because he felt that any religion that tries to impose its will or creed upon others is in danger of transforming what should be an order of joy and love into an order of suffering and hatred. It is not simply coincidental that the two religious leaders who most clearly represent Maturin's ideal of the religious man, Pierre, the leader of the Albigenses, and the Monk of Montcalm, both antagonize the power structures of their respective churches. Maturin's ultimate distrust of all formal religion is further seen in the fact that the novel's true moral center is found in a scene reminiscent of Voltaire—a writer with whom Maturin shared more than he would have admitted—and involves a shepherd totally isolated from the outside world of chivalry, politics, and religious wars. Professing to a very simple and almost pagan religion, the shepherd is harshly chastized by visitors for his backwardness and informed of the ways of the civilized world beyond, where religion is such an important issue that it "had been the cause of wars that had desolated the fairest provinces of France; that it had marshalled armies with princes and pontiffs at their head; and already cost the lives of thirty thousand men, sacrificed by their own countrymen. . . ." But the shepherd, preferring his own ways, decided to remain uncivilized and "as the first light of dawn gleamed through the crevice, he unbarred his door, and silently motioned his guests to depart."

There are many strengths in **The Albigenses**— Maturin's imaginative recreating of the crusade of the Catholic Church against the Albigenses, his characterization of those men on both sides who play crucial roles in the campaign, and his probing of those emotions and often unacknowledged desires that were concealed beneath the banners of religion and chivalry—but in spite of this, Maturin's genius, that force we feel on virtually every page of **Melmoth,** is only sporadically present. This novel is finally weakened by the fact that Maturin is always so evidently in control of it. He knew too well those talents he possessed for creating an exciting tale and for peopling it with tormented characters; and in **The Albigenses** these skills appear, but in a tired and imitative fashion, lacking the imaginative force and capacity to court the unknown and horrible possessed by **Melmoth.**

It is, of course, impossible to foresee what Maturin would have written had he lived to complete his trilogy, but he seems to lack both the energy and the desire to bring his project to a conclusion, and Maturin lived on after **Melmoth** in poverty and isolation, fulfilling in life the debilitating and oppressive fate of those poverty-ridden and tormented characters about whom he wrote with such apprehension. On October 30, 1824 Charles Robert Maturin died at the age of forty-four. As his health faded in the last months of his life, he became even more isolated and consequently very little is known of this time. It was apparently a time of great depression for him, compounded by the anxieties of poverty and by illness exacerbated by long hours of work and little sleep during his composition of **The Albigenses.** Shortly after Maturin's death, his wife wrote to Scott:

> You no doubt by this time are acquainted with the death of my dear departed husband; he has left me with four children, the youngest of whom is only five years old, totally unprovided for—he laboured with incessant assiduity for his family even after it had pleased the Almighty to deprive him of health—his sufferings with regard to

pecuniary circumstances preyed on a constitution naturally delicate, till at last it put a period to his existence—

Scott had planned to visit Maturin in the summer of 1825, but Maturin died before he could meet the man who had for twelve years advised, consoled and encouraged him, and on several occasions had provided the only money that stood between Maturin and starvation.

After Maturin's death, two rumors circulated, both of which are false. The first was that Maturin's eldest son, William, had burned all of his father's manuscripts because of the shame he felt in his father's connection with the stage. William's letters to Scott after his father's death completely refute this rumor and suggest that he made every effort to have his father's literary remains either produced on stage or published. The second rumor—that Maturin had consciously precipitated his own death through a mistake in his medicines—is the sort of story that Maturin's eccentric habits and behavior would encourage, but it too, as Idman suggests, is unfounded. James Clarence Mangan, who knew Maturin during those final years, recalls seeing him shortly after he had officiated at a funeral:

> His long pale, melancholy, Don Quixote, out-of-the-world face would have inclined you to believe that Dante, Bajazet, and the Cid had risen together from their sepulchres, and clubbed their features for the production of an effect. But. . . . The great Irishman, like Hamlet, had that within him which passed show, . . . He bore the 'thunder-scars' about him, but they were graven, not on his brow, but on his heart.

The comparison of Maturin to Hamlet need not be examined, but Mangan's allusions to Dante and Don Quixote are relevant in considering Maturin's life and art. The romantic poets had explored that "deep and romantic chasm," that "savage place" Coleridge writes of in "Kubla Khan," but had pulled up short, except for the later books of *Don Juan*, in their description of what they found. The gothic novelists had, on the other hand, written of the emotions of fear and terror, but had relied heavily on external machinery and on a topography of horror often used for its own sake. Maturin's contribution to British literature is found in his ability to synthesize these two traditions, taking the literary medium provided by the gothic novel, but using it to examine more deeply those aspects of human experience embodied in those figures, such as Faust and the Wandering Jew, that had captured the romantic imagination. Yet Maturin is cut off from those romantics who preceded him by a strong Calvinis-

tic vein that finally prevented him, in spite of his own romantic leanings, from seeking redemption, or even solace from love, be it of Man, nature, or God. Few of the love relationships that he depicts are successful and even fewer of his novels end happily.

In one respect **Melmoth** is Maturin's attempt to find a basis for hope and belief; and in so far as none of the persons confronted by Melmoth is willing to sell his soul for worldly happiness, Maturin's world differs from Dante's Hell in the all-important fact that hope has not been abandoned. Immalee is the embodiment of Melmoth's antithesis: in her joy, beauty, and innocence we see Man as he once was and as Maturin would like to be; but she too is fated to die in an Inquisition dungeon, isolated and estranged from all but God.

Because Maturin's world is in many ways monstrous and cruel, his influence was felt most strongly not among the Victorian novelists, but among the French romantics, who found in Edgar Allan Poe and Maturin kindred investigators of that monstrous landscape Baudelaire was to traverse in *Les Fleurs du Mal*. Some of the later nineteenth-century British writers, such as Rossetti and Oscar Wilde, were to speak highly of Maturin, and one can see in *The Picture of Dorian Gray* why Wilde might have been attracted to the writings of his fellow countryman. In fact, during Wilde's final days of exile in Paris, after his release from prison, he assumed the name of "Sebastian Melmoth."

If Maturin's works evoke in their probing of the diabolic an image of Dante's *Inferno*, his own life in some respects painfully reminds one of Don Quixote. There was a certain naiveté and innocence about Maturin that worked against him in his quest for success, and he was unable to understand how his literature could possibly offend his superiors in the church. He maintained an unrealistic expectation that wise and rational men would and could keep separate the content of a novel from the moral character of the man who wrote it. To the very end of his painful life, he kept the hope, against all reason, that some person or event would intervene to alleviate his distress. One can only wish that Maturin had had his own Sancho Panza, someone who was as familiar with the realities of this world as Maturin was with the realities of the other world.

But Maturin is neither English, Italian, nor Spanish; he is Irish, and his work must finally be judged in terms of the Irish tradition. He has, of course, no place in that tradition if one excludes from his study all writers except the "Irish-speaking Irish." Maturin is an Anglo-Irishman who wrote in English primarily for an English audience; and although according to Thomas Flanagan's *The Irish Novelists, 1800-1850*, he and Lefanu are outside the mainstream of even this tradition because they "turned to tales whose somber and uncanny atmosphere seeks to transcend the immediacies of social fact," it is difficult to speak of Maturin as other than an Irish novelist, if only by virtue of the problems he shared in common with other Irish writers of his time. He faced the problems of trying to define Ireland as he saw it for a people who viewed it for the most part as an alien culture. Throughout his writings, and especially in **The Wild Irish Boy** and **The Milesian Chief**, he wrestles not only with the problem of Ireland's identity but also tries to educate his reading audience in Ireland's history, her traditions, her strengths, and her weaknesses. Maturin's love for Ireland shapes what he wrote and is manifest in the characters he created, from his aged chiefs to his blind and prophetic bards, in the Irish myths, music, and poetry that he spoke of, and in his descriptions of Ireland's lanscape and cities. He was, however, as firmly rooted in the present political and economic realities of Ireland as he was steeped in Irish folklore and history. As an Irish Protestant with Tory political leanings, he did not believe that Ireland could exist independently of England, but he writes, not as a political theorist or pamphleteer, but as a novelist, and his writings provide us not with answers, but with the articulation of problems. In the problems he writes of and in the conflict between his heart and head where the question of Ireland is concerned, we can see his sense of personal estrangement as an Irishman, and this estrangement is reflected in many of his major Irish characters who are drawn by the past but must find their role in the present.

Maturin was the author of six novels and three published plays; yet he is remembered today, if at all, only for **Melmoth the Wanderer.** It is unlikely that there will be a resurgence of interest in Maturin in the near future, even though at least two of his novels, **The Milesian Chief** and **Women: or Pour et Contre**, definitely do not deserve the obscurity they have suffered. But it is fitting that history has chosen to remember Maturin for that strange and foreboding Wanderer, for in Melmoth Maturin created, with fear and fascination, a figure who embodies in his isolation, his wanderings, and his descent into the recesses of the human heart, those haunted and darkened passages of his own genius. Through the magic of the written word, he evoked demons from within the human mind, and they, in turn, retaliated upon their summoner by isolating and estranging him from that world into which they were called. Of Maturin, James Clarence Mangan wrote:

> He—in his own dark way—understood many people; but nobody understood him in *any* way. And therefore it was that he, this man of the highest genius, Charles Robert Maturin, lived unappreciated—and died unsympathized with, uncared for, unenquired after—and not only forgotten, because he had never been thought about.

We may hope that his insights are not proved by history to be as prophetic as they are sensitive.

Selected Bibliography

The Principal Works of Charles Robert Maturin
(Dates refer to the first editions, unless otherwise noted)

DRAMA:

Bertram; or the Castle of St. Aldobrand. London: John Murray, 1816.

Manuel. London: John Murray, 1817.

Fredolfo. London: Constable and Co., 1819.

FICTION:

The Family of Montorio; or the Fatal Revenge. 3 vols. London: Longman, Hurst, Rees, and Orme, 1807.

The Wild Irish Boy. 3 vols. London: Longman, Hurst, Rees, and Orme, 1808.

The Milesian Chief. 4 vols. London: Henry Colburn, 1812.

Women; or Pour et Contre. 3 vols. Edinburgh: Constable and Co., 1818.

Melmoth the Wanderer. 4 vols. Edinburgh: Constable and Co., 1820. There is also a recent edition of this novel, edited and introduced by William F. Axton, Lincoln: Univ. of Nebraska, 1961.

The Albigenses. 4 vols. London: Hurst, Robinson and Co., 1824.

LETTERS:

The Correspondence of Sir Walter Scott and Charles Robert Maturin, ed. and intro. by Fannie E. Ratchford and Wm. H. McCarthy, Jr., Austin: Univ. of Texas, 1937.

Secondary Studies

Melmoth the Wanderer. vol. 1. London: Richard Bentley and Son, 1892. This particular edition, in addition to containing as its frontispiece the famous Brocas portrait of Maturin, also possesses some valuable biographical and bibliographical information: 1) "Memoirs of Charles Robert Maturin"; 2) "Separate

Notices of Each Book"; 3) "A Note on Charles Robert Maturin"; 4) "A List of Works by Charles Robert Maturin, With Translations and Adaptations by Other Authors."

Axton, William F. "Introduction," *Melmoth the Wanderer.* Lincoln: University of Nebraska, 1961.

Hume, Robert D. "Gothic Versus Romantic: A Revaluation of the Gothic Novel," *PMLA,* 84 (1969), 282-290.

Idman, Nilo. *Charles Robert Maturin: His Life and Works.* London: Constable and Co., 1923. A pioneering study containing a valuable bibliography.

Lovecraft, H. P. *Supernatural Horror in Literature.* New York: Ben Abramson, 1945.

Railo, Eino. *The Haunted Castle: A Study of the Elements of English Romanticism.* London: George Routledge and Sons, 1927.

Scholten, Willem. *Charles Robert Maturin: The Terror-Novelist.* Amsterdam: H. J. Paris, 1933.

Varma, Devendra P. *The Gothic Flame.* New York: Russel and Russel, 1957.

TITLE COMMENTARY

Melmoth the Wanderer

CHRIS BALDICK (ESSAY DATE 1989)

SOURCE: Baldick, Chris. Introduction to *Melmoth the Wanderer,* by Charles Robert Maturin, pp. vii-ix. New York: Oxford University Press, 1989.

In the following essay, Baldick discusses Maturin's place in the Gothic tradition and examines several themes in Melmoth the Wanderer.

Upon his release from prison in 1897, Oscar Wilde travelled to France under an assumed name carefully contrived to announce him as both martyred saint and blasted sinner: it was 'Sebastian Melmoth'. For, as Wilde well knew, the name of Melmoth still echoed in France, as it did no longer in Ireland or England, with the notoriety of high Romantic despair and damnation; it was the badge of the eternal outcast, of his grandiose self-hatred, and of his withering scorn for heaven and earth. It was, still more appropriately, something of an heirloom, because the author of **Melmoth the Wanderer** had been the uncle by marriage of Wilde's mother. Having helped a few years earlier to prepare a biographical introduction to an edition of his great-uncle's novel, Wilde knew the history and reputation of the Revd Charles Robert Maturin, Anglican curate of St Peter's in Dublin, novelist, playwright, eccentric, and failure: Ma-

turin had died in poverty in 1824, his literary efforts frowned upon by his ecclesiastical superiors in Dublin, slighted by most of the critics in Edinburgh, and laughed off the stage in London. In Paris, however, his reputation had flourished posthumously. Balzac, his most prominent admirer, had placed the figure of Melmoth the Wanderer alongside Goethe's Faust and Byron's Manfred as one of the great outcasts of modern literature, and he had even written a satirical sequel, *Melmoth réconcilié* (1835). Baudelaire had later acclaimed Melmoth as the outstanding model of the sneering melodramatic villain and had planned a new translation of **Melmoth the Wanderer** to replace the incomplete French version of 1821. In the French pantheon of sensational modern authors, Maturin had been given an honourable niche only a little below that of Edgar Allan Poe.

This exaltation Maturin owed almost entirely to the unusually fascinating power of his fifth novel, **Melmoth the Wanderer,** which appeared in 1820. His first, **Fatal Revenge** (1807), won a few admirers (including Walter Scott) for its treatment of Gothic intrigues, but the others—**The Wild Irish Boy** (1808), **The Milesian Chief** (1812), **Women** (1818), and **The Albigenses** (1824)—made little impression. Only once did Maturin, assisted and encouraged by Scott and Byron, achieve unmistakable literary success, with the sudden and spectacular triumph of his tragedy **Bertram** in 1816. Even this was a mixed blessing, though. Already financially burdened by his father's unfair dismissal from a lucrative Post Office position in 1809, Maturin had later stood surety for another relative who went bankrupt, thus soaking up in advance much of the fortune which **Bertram** earned. To add to his troubles, Samuel Taylor Coleridge, whose own work had been passed over by the Drury Lane theatre in favour of **Bertram,** launched a spiteful attack upon what he saw as subversive, even atheistic sentiments in Maturin's play. Since Maturin had now to abandon his pseudonym of Dennis Jasper Murphy in order to secure the rewards of his dramatic success, his chances of preferment in the Church of Ireland were compromised beyond repair. The humble stipend of a curate could not meet the expenses of his growing family (there were four children to feed by the time he finished **Melmoth**), so it was by writing that he would have to sustain it. **Bertram,** however, was followed by the failure of his next tragedy, **Manuel** (1817), after which his last drama, **Fredolfo** (1819), flopped disastrously in a hubbub of giggles and catcalls: the sight of a character killing his defeated adversary with a sword proffered in surrender drove the London audience into an indignant rage. Evidently out of touch with English notions of fair play, Maturin returned in *Melmoth* to the safer ground of mediterranean Catholic treachery—in other words, to the Gothic mode of fiction with which his literary career had begun.

Gothic fiction had flourished in England since the early 1790s, led by Ann Radcliffe and Matthew 'Monk' Lewis after the model had been established by Horace Walpole in *The Castle of Otranto* (1764), but by the time that *Melmoth the Wanderer* was written, the genre could be seen to be declining in its impact. This was the result partly of a flood of predictable imitations of Radcliffe's *The Mysteries of Udolpho* (1794) in which the Gothic formula became ridiculously repetitive and earned Jane Austen's affectionate mockery in *Northanger Abbey* (1818); and partly of a new vogue for regional and historical novels, which absorbed some elements of Gothic while eclipsing Radcliffe's followers in popularity: the pioneers here were the Anglo-Irish novelist Maria Edgeworth and Maturin's own literary mentor and pen-friend Walter Scott (although Maturin's nationalistic romance *The Milesian Chief* actually antedated the publication in 1814 of Scott's landmark novel *Waverley*). Part of Maturin's achievement in *Melmoth the Wanderer*, then, was to have breathed some belated vitality—albeit of a strangely nervous and galvanic sort—into what seemed an exhausted convention. I hope to define in the next few pages the nature and the novelty of that resuscitation, but first it will be worth clarifying the relation of *Melmoth* to its Gothic forerunners, since this book has always been read against the background of the thirty-year reign of 'Terror-novelists'.

There are two kinds of account given of Maturin's place in Gothic fiction, both of them potentially misleading. The first, adopted in several standard literary histories, speaks of *Melmoth the Wanderer* as the last—and possibly the greatest—of the Gothic novels in the line from Walpole through Radcliffe and Lewis; the final mad fling of a decadent fad for dungeons and ghosts. But of course *Melmoth* was not really the last of anything; Gothic fiction lingered on in James Hogg's *Private Memoirs and Confessions of a Justified Sinner* (1824) and soon revived in the work of Poe; it has remained defiantly undead as a significant presence in Western literature ever since. Nor is it very helpful to see *Melmoth* as a direct or linear outgrowth of the Radcliffe school

FROM THE AUTHOR

AN EXCERPT FROM MATURIN'S PREFACE TO *MELMOTH THE WANDERER*

The hint of this Romance (or Tale) was taken from a passage in one of my Sermons, which (as it is to be presumed very few have read) I shall here take the liberty to quote. The passage is this.

'At this moment is there one of us present, however we may have departed from the Lord, disobeyed his will, and disregarded his word—is there one of us who would, at this moment, accept all that man could bestow, or earth afford, to resign the hope of his salvation?—No, there is not one—not such a fool on earth, were the enemy of mankind to traverse it with the offer!'

This passage suggested the idea of *Melmoth the Wanderer*. The Reader will find that idea developed in the following pages, with what power or success *he* is to decide.

The 'Spaniard's Tale' has been censured by a friend to whom I read it, as containing too much attempt at the revivification of the horrors of Radcliffe-Romance, of the persecutions of convents, and the terrors of the Inquisition.

I defended myself, by trying to point out to my friend, that I had made the misery of conventual life depend less on the startling adventures one meets with in romances, than on that irritating series of petty torments which constitutes the misery of life in general, and which, amid the tideless stagnation of monastic existence, solitude gives its inmates leisure to invent, and power combined with malignity, the full disposition to practise. I trust this defence will operate more on the conviction of the Reader, than it did on that of my friend.

DUBLIN,
31st August 1820

SOURCE: Maturin, Charles Robert. "Preface." In *Melmoth the Wanderer*. 1820. Reprint edition, pp. 5-6. New York: Oxford University Press, 1998.

alone. The alternative account of Maturin's place in Gothic fiction, indeed, emphasizes his independence from 'the horrors of Radcliffe-Romance', citing his preface to **Melmoth** and claiming him as a precursor of Dostoevsky and Kafka, as a psychological novelist rather than a retailer of ghoulish gimmicks. There is no need, however, to counterpose the psychological and the Gothic in this way, as Maturin's modern admirers have often done, nor to deny **Melmoth**'s evident resort to Radcliffean effects: its crumbling parchments, its subterranean passages, its crucial scene of a wedding sealed by a dead hand.

A more discriminating account of the varieties of Gothic fiction, such as that offered in David Punter's survey *The Literature of Terror,* is able to reconcile these contending versions of **Melmoth**'s Gothic status, in the first place by reminding us that although Gothic fiction may be most easily recognized by its paraphernalia of props and settings, its distinctive animating principle is a psychological interest in states of trepidation, dread, panic, revulsion, claustrophobia, and paranoia. The most helpful contribution such an approach can make is to bring into view another cycle of novels whose concerns overlap with those of the most celebrated Gothic works, and share important qualities with **Melmoth the Wanderer.** this group includes, alongside the well-known *Frankenstein* (1818) of Mary Shelley, two novels by her father William Godwin—*Caleb Williams* (1794) and *St Leon* (1799)—together with Hogg's *Justified Sinner.* Our improved map now includes two linked groups of novels, each concerned with extreme states of mental disturbance. The first mainstream group could be called 'full-dress' Gothic, since it decks out its essential psychological tremors in a uniform costume of lurid effects and trappings; the second unorthodox group carries a much lighter cargo of chains and cowls, so that its similar obsessions with persecution and delusion stand out more clearly. Novels in this second group tend to rely less on the evocation of atmosphere from a monastic or castellar setting than on a fabulous principle of transgression, usually involving the Faustian acquisition of forbidden knowledge.

Melmoth the Wanderer belongs with this Godwinian line of novels, with which it shares some unusual features in its construction. Whereas the romances of Radcliffe had palliated their apparent terrors with the reassuring presence of a pious and rational omniscient narrator, the narratives of *Caleb Williams* and *Frankenstein,* like the second part of Hogg's *Justified Sinner,* give us the intensity of first-person testimony, leading us back through 'flashback' recollections and embedded

tales-within-tales to a realm of inward disturbance not commonly accessible to the more placid conventions of third-person narration. It seems from the subsequent history of Gothic fiction that the myth of transgression calls forth (if it does not absolutely require) a distinctive narrative strategy which wraps its central horror in protective or transitional layers of secondary and tertiary report: the 'concentric' accounts of explorer, experimenter, and monster in *Frankenstein,* the third-hand stories which reach us through Nelly and Lockwood in *Wuthering Heights,* the recollection of benighted yarn-spinning that constitutes Conrad's *Heart of Darkness,* the elaborately indirect reconstruction of Sutpen's outrages in Faulkner's *Absalom, Absalom!*—all these justly celebrated cases of narrative involution construct an imaginative topography of conventional surface and criminal depth which imparts a special resonance to the mythic crime while unsettling or corroding the moral certainties by which it might be condemned. Maturin's novel falls—inadvertently as much as consciously—under this law of Gothic design, although his execution of the embedded narrative pattern remains freakishly irregular even by these standards.

The reader should be forewarned that the design by which Maturin connects the various stories-within-stories in this novel is a preposterously convoluted contrivance, to the despair of his earliest critics, and to the embarrassment of his later admirers. It has neither the symmetry of *Frankenstein* nor the careful organization of *Wuthering Heights.* Fortunately, though, the essential logic of the plotting is still clear enough to follow, provided that one is willing not just to suspend disbelief but to throw it to the winds. The story leads us back twice from the early nineteenth century to the late seventeenth; first, through an introductory episode in which the young heir John Melmoth reads an account of the traveller Stanton, who encounters Melmoth the Wanderer in Spain in 1677 and later in London; then at much greater length through Monçada, a shipwrecked Spaniard, who not only tells young Melmoth of his own recent experiences at the hands of the Spanish Inquisition but also repeats to him the accounts of the Wanderer collected by an ancient Jew, Adonijah. The principal story relayed by and from Adonijah is the '**Tale of the Indians**', set on an oriental island and in Spain between 1680 and 1684; it allows Melmoth the Wanderer a much more visible role than before, and concerns his attempted seduction of the innocent young castaway Immalee (who reverts to the name of Isidora when restored to her Spanish family). Further embedded in this tale are two more stories set slightly earlier in the seventeenth century: another Spanish incident, the '**Tale of Guzman's Family'**—more exactly, the tale of his sister, who marries the impoverished Protestant Walberg; and '**The Lovers' Tale'**, a miniature historical romance concerning an aristocratic Shropshire family divided by the aftermath of civil war. As if this was were not complicated enough, '**The Lovers' Tale'** contains within it the testimony of a clergyman who knew Melmoth the Wanderer before he made his satanic bargain to prolong his life by 150 years. The whole creaky and lopsided structure of the novel is finally allowed to collapse: Monçada breaks off before exhausting Adonijah's compendium of tales, as Melmoth the Wanderer appears in person in the present day (that is, 1816), his time at last expiring.

Even if we put aside the multiple improbabilities of all this, we are still left with a strangely overwrought narrative structure. For example, the Shropshire clergyman's relation of Melmoth's early life in '**The Lovers' Tale'** forms part of an account spoken by Melmoth himself to Immalee's father, within a story relayed by an unknown source to Adonijah, which is in turn transcribed and later recalled by Monçada, who repeats this fifth-hand information to young John Melmoth; or so we gather, at one further remove, from the impersonal narrator of the novel. Despite the Radcliffean device of the crumbling or illegible manuscript to which Maturin resorts so often, the story is seen to pass unimpaired through these several layers of report and recall, down to the last detail of dialogue and gesture. It seems as if Melmoth's seventeenth-century escapades have the status of an indelible stain, like original sin itself according to the Calvinist doctrine to which Maturin subscribed. For a novel ostensibly concerned with its protagonist's inability to pass on his burden of guilt and horror to another, **Melmoth** is unusual in that it allows (and in fact demands) that burden to be passed on repeatedly from hand to hand as narration: Adonijah, for instance, is actually obliged, as penance for his crimes of curiosity, to transmit the legend of Melmoth to a younger scribe. This novel is secretly as much about transmission as it is about transgression, but its very structure assumes a principle of transmissibility which its theology denies. A noticeable symptom of this is that the layers of narration which one might expect to be marked by distinct narrative voices are in fact tonally continuous, so that the reader will often forget (as

Maturin himself seems to do) just who is speaking at any given point, and just how many pairs of inverted commas are hung around each incident.

The structural oddities observed above tend to run into serious collisions with the doctrinal aims of this novel; but before examining the inconsistencies and contradictions which thus arise, we should grasp Maturin's religious purpose in its context.

Modern approaches to Gothic novels too often take the first short cut to the incestuous and murderous undercurrents of these stories without pausing to consider the important concerns which are visible on the surface; the chief victim of this neglect being the Gothic preoccupation with religious delusions and bigotry. A significant part of the Gothic novel's appeal to its first readers, after all, was that its claustrophobic evocation of scheming, idolatrous Spaniards and Italians allowed Protestant readers in Britain to congratulate themselves on their liberty and their pious rectitude. As one character exclaims in Radcliffe's *Romance of the Forest* (1791), 'O exquisite misery! 'tis now only I perceive all the horrors of confinement—'tis now only that I understand the value of liberty!' Protestant cultures often seem to favour dramas of persecution and captivity as their adoptive myths of origin, but Maturin was more than usually predisposed to follow this paranoiac inclination of his faith. He was descended from a refugee Huguenot minister who fled France after the Edict of Nantes (which had guaranteed the Protestants some freedom of worship) was revoked by Louis XIV in 1685—the same period to which **Melmoth** repeatedly returns. This removal from one predominantly Catholic country to another eventually placed Charles Robert Maturin in the service of that Protestant Ascendancy in Ireland which nervously guarded its privileges from the dispossessed Catholic majority in the years between the 1798 uprising and the launching of Daniel O'Connell's Catholic Emancipation movement in 1824. In that same year Maturin published, shortly before his death, a series of sermons on the errors of Catholicism, sermons which were said to have packed his church with eager listeners.

To attack Catholicism was not for Maturin, as it was for Lewis in his prurient Gothic novel *The Monk* (1796), an antiquarian fancydress frolic. It was a very serious duty of his vocation, to which he was earnestly committed. When he writes in **Melmoth** of the sinister power which Catholic priests have over the lives of Spanish families, we can guess that his 'Spain' is partly a nightmarish extension of the anxieties he feels about the enduring priestly influence in Catholic Ireland, where the novel begins and ends.

Maturin at first designed this novel, he explains in his Preface, as an extended moral fable illustrating an argument in one of his sermons, to the effect that even the most despairing sinner would never 'accept all that man could bestow, or earth afford, to resign the hope of his salvation'. Our overriding fear of eternal damnation (so the argument runs) will always deter us from selling our souls to the devil, even for the most lavish bribes. When Maturin sets this argument to work within the framework of Gothic fiction, however, it becomes warped almost beyond recognition. To begin with, the central device through which he attempts to illustrate his point—the character of the Wanderer himself—is a glaring anomaly: Melmoth *has* done exactly what Maturin claims nobody would do, and his subsequent regrets do little to repair the inconsistency. Maturin tries to adjust the terms of his argument by making Melmoth interested only in the purest souls, which he then fails to tempt. As Poe complained in the introductory letter of his *Poems* (1831), any self-respecting devil would have consigned two thousand souls to perdition in the time Melmoth takes to put his infernal question to only two of his intended victims. From the perfunctory fashion in which several of the supposedly crucial temptations and refusals are skimmed over in this novel, it seems that Maturin's interest in his original plan had subsided in favour of other concerns.

What appears to have happened in the doctrinal foundations of *Melmoth*'s design is that the original sermon on bargains with the devil was usurped by another sermon, this time about bargains with God. The new sermon which takes over the theological direction of the story came from Maturin's stock repertoire of anti-Papist polemics. Its argument is summarized twice by Monçada: 'But Oh! *how false is a treaty made with God, which we ratify with our own blood*, when he has declared there is but one sacrifice he will accept, even that of the Lamb slain from the foundation of the world!' Later, Monçada reinforces the point, asking rhetorically

> if men were taught to look to the *one great Sacrifice*, would they be so ready to believe that their own, or those of others, could ever be accepted as a commutation for it? You are surprised, Sir, at these sentiments from a Catholic . . .

And so we should be, since the doctrine expressed here is one of the cardinal principles of Protestantism: Christ, through his unique sacrifice,

being the sole intermediary between man and God. (The ventriloquism by which Catholics often find themselves speaking in Lutheran tongues is a minor Gothic convention inherited from Radcliffe's *The Italian* (1797).) As Maturin extends this sermon, he contrasts the doctrine of the one great Sacrifice with the alleged Catholic belief that God can be hoodwinked into granting salvation to those who put themselves or others through penances, mortifications, and ritual observances. Extrapolated to the point of absurdity, the false doctrine of salvation through torture is voiced by the sadistic parricide who conducts Monçada through the vaults of the monastery, and who has been taught by the monks that his sins are remitted with every punishment he inflicts upon the Church's enemies: 'But your guilt is my exculpation, your sufferings are my triumph. I need not repent, I need not believe; if you suffer, I am saved.'

Maturin thus characterizes Catholicism, along with Hinduism and Judaism, as a religion of suffering, in the central chapter XVI where Melmoth shows Immalee the faiths of the world through a telescope. True biblical Christianity, on the other hand, is represented as a religion of love and tolerance. Accordingly Maturin himself has to make some gestures towards condemning sectarian intolerance, in the episode of the crazed preachers in Stanton's madhouse, and in the reconciliations of '**The Lovers' Tale**'; but the temptation to take clumsy swipes at Papists, Hindus, and Jews frequently gets the better of him. For example, the opening episode of the novel appears to maintain some even-handedness in its caricatures of desiccated Protestant miserliness in the dying uncle and of incoherent Catholic superstition in his attendant crones. But as the novel unfolds, attention to Protestant failings slips almost out of view while the image of the Catholic witch is heavily reinforced in later characters—notably the mothers of Monçada and Immalee, who both stand as types of 'the mother of witchcrafts and spiritual seduction': the Church itself. Maturin tends to cast mothers as greedy persecutors of their innocent offspring, the image of the blood-soaked son recurring with obsessive insistence in *Melmoth*.

The most significant maternal betrayal is enacted by Monçada's mother in the hope of expiating her sin of fornication through the sacrifice of her own son to the monastic discipline. Her motive here illustrates Maturin's doctrinal point, while the magnificent bejewelled dress in which she prostrates herself before Monçada and secures his monastic vows serves as an allegory of Catholicism's false humility, and above all of its artificiality. Throughout the novel Maturin sustains a thematic contrast between the internal repentance of true faith and the external observances of false superstition; a contrast which is often reduced further to the opposition between Nature and Artifice, especially in the description of monastic life. When Maturin sets up such contrasts, he often allows the dualism of his Calvinist ideology to freeze the novel's action into awkwardly static tableaux. The most protracted and unsatisfactory exercise in this vein is the attempted seduction of Immalee by Melmoth, in which Maturin evidently tries to recapture something of the encounters between Satan and Eve in *Paradise Lost*. In these chapters the 'unimaginable purity' of Immalee can only be a source of irritation to the modern reader, and even Melmoth's outbursts of self-loathing disappoint in their repetitiveness. There are some grand flourishes of bombast here ('amid thunder I wed thee—bride of perdition!'), but the allegorical postures in which Innocence and Experience signal to one another in these episodes lack convincing energy.

One thing rescues this portion of the novel from mediocrity, and that is the ironic catechism by which Melmoth introduces Immalee to the cruelty of the world beyond her island idyll. Although Maturin obliges his villain to expound (much to his surprise) a number of unimpeachable Protestant doctrines, it is the subversive blasphemies that resound most convincingly—as Maturin seems to have recognized when he appended a disclaimer to the Wanderer's antimonarchist diatribes. The novel comes alive most forcefully when the fixities of Maturin's thematic contrasts begin to dissolve amid the inconsistencies of his narrative structure. When, for example, Melmoth defends the Protestant view of the Bible against the Catholic Church, and we recall that this uncharacteristic behaviour is being related to us in a Jewish text transmitted by a Catholic, something more is involved than mere clumsiness or forgetfulness: an inadvertent dissolution of distinctions is taking place in which the same voice can utter sacrilegious sarcasms and pious platitudes almost in the same breath, erasing the clear line that was expected to lie between them in an 'improving' work of fiction. The whispered execrations of the dying monk in Monçada's monastery, like the confession of the parricide, shocked the novel's first critics, partly because the disorderly nature of the narrative provided no stable means by which these utterances could be isolated; their corrosion spreads uncontrollably through the novel.

These multiple contradictions between doctrinal piety and structural instability in **Melmoth** seem to radiate from the ambiguous figure of the Wanderer. As we have noticed, he invalidates the very dogma he is invented to illustrate, and he confounds heresy with orthodoxy in his wayward and sarcastic tirades. The problem seems to be that Maturin has overloaded the character with several functions working at cross-purposes. As many readers have observed, Melmoth is not just a Faust, he is a Mephistopheles at the same time; more exactly, he is a Faust whose punishment is to become a Mephistophelean tempter. This doubling of roles is ambitious enough, but Maturin's recklessness piles further responsibilities upon his villain's shoulders: in his visits to the innocent Immalee, the Wanderer has to act the role of Milton's Satan in Eden while also doubling up as the archangel Raphael who justifies the ways of God to Eve and warns her against the archtempter. We could say that Immalee's absolute innocence—a device intended to expose the self-thwarting nature of Melmoth's malignity—tempts Maturin into what is literally a daredevil narrative venture in which the sermons and the blasphemies become dangerously entangled. As Baudelaire remarked in his 1855 essay 'Of the Essence of Laughter', Melmoth the Wanderer is a living contradiction. It is precisely the alarming contradictions of his status that bring him, and the novel, to life.

A further peculiarity of the Wanderer is that while we may loosely refer to him as the novel's central character, his position is most often a marginal one: like the Irish landlords of his day, Melmoth is an absentee villain. Unlike Marlowe's Dr Faustus (Maturin would not have known Goethe's version), Melmoth is, of course, invisible to us as readers, but he is often invisible or unrecognizable even to the characters of the story. A Faust of rumour, his is an existence made up largely of report, reputation, and expectant surmise. He often functions as an offstage whisper, and the fear of his imminent arrival tends to be more powerful than his actual presence upon this melodramatic stage. The strongest parts of the novel, indeed, are those in which Melmoth himself is absent: Monçada's adventures in the monastery (some of them plagiarized from Diderot's novel *La Religieuse* (1796)) have a force and tension which is unforgettable partly because we forget Melmoth's existence amid the panic, his role as advocate of Despair having been dispersed more convincingly among the inhabitants of the monastery.

Melmoth's direct presence, corrosive as it is, is not necessary to that dissolution of stable identities which so enlivens the best parts of the novel. In the delirious claustrophobia of Monçada's tale, unmatched in any Gothic work in English before Poe, we have a fascinating study of those 'extraordinary vicissitudes of the human mind' in which emotions normally regarded as opposites begin to bleed into one another. From his dissection of Catholic hypocrisy as a blend of extreme libertinism and extreme austerity, Maturin proceeds to show monastic religion as a double-edged sword of ecstasy and despair, and exposes the secret complicity of laughter with guilt. Monçada discovers in himself contradictory mixtures of courage and pusillanimity, of curiosity and aversion; a revelation which culminates in the profound unease with which he recognizes that the conspiracy against him has been joined by his own strongest feelings: 'where the whole world is against us, we begin to take its part against ourselves, to avoid the withering sensation of being alone on our own side.'

Similar possibilities of self-betrayal are raised earlier in a very revealing description by Melmoth of a demented preacher whose yells disturb Stanton in the madhouse:

> Half the day he imagines himself in a pulpit, denouncing damnation against Papists, Arminians, and even Sublapsarians . . . He foams, he writhes, he gnashes his teeth; you would imagine him in the hell he was painting, and that the fire and brimstone he is so lavish of, were actually exhaling from his jaws. At night his *creed retaliates on him*; he believes himself one of the reprobates he has been all day denouncing, and curses God for the very decree he has all day been glorifying Him for.

It is tempting to take this as Maturin's confession, his acknowledgement that this novel is all the time mocking its own religious tenets with some species of nocturnal sabotage. Certainly he was alert to the treacherous subversions of what we now call the unconscious: 'Oh, Sir,' Monçada confides to young Melmoth, 'there are some *criminals of the imagination,* whom if we could plunge into the *oubliettes* of its magnificent but lightly-based fabric, its lord would reign more happy.'

A final remark should be made on one unexpected feature of this novel's psychological concerns. This is the recurrent theme of monotony which Maturin introduces and defends in his Preface, where he contrasts the startling adventures of Radcliffe-Romance with his own more credible portrayal of 'that irritating series of petty torments which constitutes the misery of life in general'. The events of the novel turn out after all to be more incredibly startling than anything in Radcliffe, but Maturin's indication of an interest in petty torments, in stagnation and boredom as the basis of curiosity and despair, is borne out in many of *Melmoth*'s stories. Maturin repeatedly dwells on a curious dialectic in which the monotonous becomes intense, while intensity becomes monotonous. He seems at times to be seeking the sources of Gothic horror in a realm usually assumed to be very remote from it: that of domestic realism, where the pressure of petty circumstances acts more powerfully than any devil as a temptation to crime. This 'realist' picture of life is visible even in some of the most macabre Gothic episodes, like that of the lovers whose hunger drives them to cannibalism; but the most remarkable of these fusions between realism and Gothicism occurs in the '**Tale of Guzman's Family**'.

The Guzman or Walberg Story is often dismissed as unimportant padding, but some more perceptive critics have identified it as a central clue to the obsessions which drive this novel. Deeply embedded in the heart of *Melmoth*'s lopsided structure, the tale of Guzman's heirs concentrates many of Maturin's own fears of impending poverty, and some of his presumed resentments against his family's financial claims upon him. It is money, after all, that sets this story in motion, from John Melmoth's first arrival at his rich uncle's deathbed to the fatal inheritance which ruins the Mortimers in '**The Lovers' Tale**'. More particularly, it is family wealth which repeatedly brings disaster to the novel's leading characters: Stanton, Monçada, Immalee, and Elinor are all in their various ways imprisoned by their own mercenary relatives, in an arrangement which marries the inheritance plot of realist fiction to the confinement plot of the Gothic novel. The disturbing feature of the Guzman tale is that it locates its Gothic obsessions—parricide, filicide, vampirism—so firmly within the bosom of the family institution itself, grafted as it is by legacies on to the root of all evil. *Melmoth the Wanderer* is, at its best, a 'gripping' novel, its furious intensity betraying a compulsion which possessed Maturin as he composed it: the grip, that is, of urgent financial necessity which, as the Preface admits, 'compels' him to write.

There is some aptness in the fact that the sequel which Maturin seems to have planned came to be written instead by Balzac, the great forerunner of realism in European fiction. For there is in this dungeon of a book something like a realist novel trying to escape. Intermittently it hints that the most powerful 'enemy of mankind' is not the devil but poverty and inherited property; but it never manages to break out of its Gothic bastille. We may, so to speak, hear it tapping feebly on the walls, but its protest is overwhelmed by the howling blasphemies of its neighbours, Maturin's more desperate criminals of the imagination.

RICHARD HASLAM (ESSAY DATE 1994)

SOURCE: Haslam, Richard. "Maturin and the 'Calvinist Sublime.'" In *Gothick Origins and Innovations,* edited by Lloyd Smith and Victor Sage, pp. 44-56. Atlanta, Ga. and Amsterdam: Rodopi, 1994.

In the following essay, Haslam studies the effects of Calvinist religious doctrine and nineteenth-century Irish society on Maturin, as evidenced in his use of the "Gothic sublime" in Melmoth the Wanderer.

Have pity upon me, have pity upon me, O ye my friends; for the hand of God hath touched me. Why do ye persecute me as God, and are not satisfied with my flesh? Oh that my words were now written! Oh that they were printed in a book! That they were graven with an iron pen and lead in the rock for ever!

(Job 19:21-24)

Job's request that his words be printed in a book is of course answered self-reflexively in the *Book of Job* itself, but his lament and his yearning echo also through the labyrinthine narrative of **Melmoth the Wanderer,** that celebrated gothic extravaganza published in 1820 and penned by Charles Robert Maturin (1780-1824), a Church of Ireland clergyman.[1]

I wish first to examine what I call the 'Calvinist sublime' at work in Maturin's novel and how it produces distinctively gothic effects, and then to consider how the trajectory of this Calvinist sublime is inflected by Maturin's historical situation in nineteenth-century Ireland and specifically by his involvement in religious polemics.

The first of the so-called 'five points' of Calvinist doctrine asserted the predestined election to Heaven or reprobation to Hell of every individual, not conditional on belief. Calvin usually silenced queries and fears about the workings of predestination by an appeal to the aggressive question of St Paul in *Romans* 9: 20-21: 'O man, who art thou that repliest against God? Shall the thing formed say to Him that formed it, Why hast thou made

me thus? Hath not the potter power over the clay, of the same lump, to make one vessel unto honour, and another unto dishonour?' But such was the controversy generated by the doctrine of predestination outlined in Book III of his *Institutes of the Christian Religion*[2] that Calvin was forced to produce a separate work justifying his interpretation: in *Concerning the Eternal Predestination of God* (1552), Calvin mobilises St Augustine to support his denial of the claim that those who believe are chosen; rather, they are chosen in order to believe—election comes before faith. The cause of this arrangement is 'just though unknown'.[3] Calvin defensively states that 'if those who attribute the hardening of men to His eternal counsel invest God with the character of a tyrant, we are certainly not the author of this opinion' (p. 60).

But the perception of God as an inscrutable tyrant, whimsically determining at the dawn of time that some should be elect, the rest reprobate, was nonetheless a possible and rebarbative by-product of Calvin's system. In attempting to justify the wiles of God to men, Calvin asserts that God is 'the cause of all happenings, yet not the author of evil', a paradox that unleashes intolerable moral and intentional contradictions within his system, and places an unbearable burden on those adherents who brood upon it too intensely (pp. 168-170). William Bouwsma, in his biography of Calvin, claims that the *Sermons on Job* (1563) support the hypothesis that Calvin believed there to be a kind of satisfaction owed by creature to Creator that is neither moral nor possible. 'He saw guilt in creatureliness itself, guilt shared even by human beings created in God's image before the Fall, guilt towards the Father even on the part of his good children, guilt in *existing*'.[4]

Two centuries after Calvin, the *Book of Job* acted as a stimulus to aesthetic as well as theological reflection. According to Paul Fry, 'not only Schiller but the entire eighteenth century makes *Job* the Ur-text of the sublime . . .'.[5] Forty years before Schiller's essay 'On the Sublime' (1797-1800), Edmund Burke in his *Philosophical Enquiry into the Origin of our Ideas of the Sublime and Beautiful* (1757) also drew upon the *Book of Job* in order to substantiate his innovative claim that a mode of terror was an essential component of the sublime sentiment.[6] Burke is significantly reluctant, however, to confront directly the central drama of Job: the spectacle of a swaggering, bullying, self-justifying God who, through his instrument 'the Satan', humiliates and tortures his innocent creature. Instead, in the section entitled

'Power', Burke claims that, while such divine attributes as wisdom, justice and goodness are evident to reason, the imagination is struck principally by the apprehension of divine power:

> But whilst we contemplate so vast an object, under the arm, as it were, of almighty power, and invested upon every side with omnipresence, we shrink into the minuteness of our own nature, and are, in a manner, annihilated before him. And though a consideration of his other attributes may relieve in some measure our apprehensions; yet no conviction of the justice with which it is exercised, nor the mercy with which it is tempered, can wholly remove the terror that naturally arises from a force which nothing can withstand.
>
> (p. 68)

In using the term Calvinist *sublime,* I refer both to Burke's terminology and to the Freudian concept of 'sublimation': the Calvinist sublime is a theologized aesthetics in which elements of the Calvinist system are sublimated out of a creed and into an artistic programme. A Calvinist sublime, however, can only function when some degree of religious doubt is at work. If, as a sincere Calvinist, one believes completely in the creed's more terrifying aspects then the conditions for a Calvinist sublime will be absent, for as Burke observes in his *Enquiry,* 'when danger or pain press too nearly, they are incapable of giving delight, and are simply terrible; but at certain distances, and with certain modifications, they may be, and they are delightful, as we see in everyday experience' (p. 40). Burke's sublime is a *mode* of terror, operating only if there is an aesthetic remove between event or object and perceiver. Unalloyed belief or pure terror disperse the Calvinist sublime; only when the parasite of doubt excavates an internal space can it coalesce.

The contribution of Burke's ideas on the sublime to the formation of gothic fiction was attested by Ann Radcliffe in her posthumously published essay, 'On the Supernatural in Poetry' (1826),[7] and has been substantiated by critics like David Punter, in his absorbing 1980 survey *The Literature of Terror,*[8] but what of the intersections between Calvinism and the Gothic? Joel Porte's 1974 essay 'In the Hands of an Angry God'[9] locates in William Godwin's *Caleb Williams* (1794), Mary Shelley's *Frankenstein* (1817) and *The Lost Man* (1826), and Charles Brockden Brown's *Wieland* (1798) the agency of an 'internalized Calvinism' (p. 54), a representation of terror that is fundamentally theological. Victor Sage, in *Horror Fiction in the Protestant Tradition* (1989),[10] asserts the relevance of Calvinism, contending that 'the cause and the effect of the horror experience

in English culture is a form of 'theological uncertainty', an anxiety which is recognisable at many different levels of consciousness' (p. xvii); along with earlier critics such as Irene Bostrom and Sister Mary Muriel Tarr,[11] Sage relates the rise and dominance of literary Gothic to the growth from the 1770s onwards of the campaign for Catholic Emancipation. The Emancipation Act was passed in 1829, but Sage suggests that the continuance of the horror novel 'is equally, if not more strongly, related to the subsequent struggles, doctrinal and political, which flared up between Catholic and Protestant throughout the course of the nineteenth century and well into the twentieth' (pp. 28-29). Maturin died before the passing of the Emancipation Act, but his novels and sermons are patently bound up with the religious controversies that smouldered and then flared up in Ireland in the wake of the 1801 Act of Union. The Calvinist sublime in Maturin's fiction is refracted through this historical prism. In the year 1813, Maturin wrote to his literary mentor Walter Scott, 'I am a High Calvinist in my religious opinions, and therefore viewed with jealousy by Unitarian Brethren and Arminian Masters';[12] by 1824, in his *Five Sermons on the Errors of the Roman Catholic Church,*[13] Maturin was referring to Calvinism as one of the 'melancholy aberrations of the human spirit' (p. 13). This suggests that Maturin's first novel, *Fatal Revenge; or, The Family of Montorio* (1807), was composed when the novelist was—as it were—a card-carrying Calvinist, while the more renowned *Melmoth the Wanderer* (1820) was composed in the period when Maturin was—at least officially—removing himself from hardline Calvinism. The aesthetic distance thereby gained may be one of the reasons for the greater achievement of *Melmoth.*

James Boulger, in his study *The Calvinist Temper in English Poetry* (1980),[14] has identified the following tenets as crucial to the formation of what he terms a 'Calvinist aesthetics': the sensation of terror; anxiety in the face of an arbitrary and inscrutable divine power; resentment against a god whose motives and actions seem those of an enemy; helplessness; a state of sin-consciousness unrelieved by any sustained sense of assurance; the ceaseless search for signs of election or reprobation within the self and the outside world; and detailed analysis of one's state of mind, heart and soul in written journals or letters. These tenets are presented in crude form in Maturin's *Fatal Revenge* and in more sophisticated guise in

Melmoth. Thus when describing Ippolito, one of the two unfortunate brothers in *Fatal Revenge,* the narrator declares:

> The anguish of terror that cannot name its object, and of guilt that cannot ascertain its danger, gathered over his mind. A sensation of rare and excruciating influence; the sensation of all our measures being anticipated; our progress measured and ruined; the exact reach of our boundary calculated and shadowed out; the inmost recesses of our mind violated and laid waste; and Omniscience engaged on the side of our enemies to destroy us, overcame him.
>
> (II, pp. 297-298)

The narrator revealingly employs scripture to evoke Ippolito's despair, his 'sense of invisible and universal persecution':

> His distraction almost applied to the stupendous frame of the Psalmist, when he exclaimed, 'Whither shall I go from thy presence?' Of the latter clause he felt the truth too forcibly, 'If I go down to *Hell,* thou art there also.
>
> (II, p. 282)

In *Melmoth the Wanderer,* Maturin develops these allusions to the inscrutable operations of an arbitrary Calvinist machine. Alonzo, protagonist of the 'Tale of the Spaniard', having been terrorised by his family and their spiritual 'Director' into joining a monastic community, laments:

> . . . I felt my destiny was fixed—I had no wish to avert or arrest it—I was like one who sees an enormous engine (whose operation is to crush him to atoms) put in motion, and, stupefied with horror, gazes on it with a calmness that might be mistaken for that of one who was coolly analyzing the complications of its machinery, and calculating the resistless crush of its blow.
>
> (p. 91)

Later, imprisoned in total darkness in a convent dungeon, Alonzo tries to occupy his mind by attempting to keep time, in order to measure the hours of his confinement. Assailed by doubts that he might be counting sixty-second periods faster than the clock, he 'wished to be the clock, that I might have no feeling, no motive for hurrying on the approach of time' (pp. 146-147). Released eventually from confinement, Alonzo reads of his brother's escape plan and prepares to flee from the convent:

> After reading these lines, I appeared to myself like a piece of mechanism wound up to perform certain functions, in which its co-operation was irresistible . . . the shortness of time left me no opportunity for deliberation, it left me also none for choice. I was like a clock whose hands are pushed forward and I struck the hours I was impelled to strike.
>
> (p. 180)

Such horological conceits, which keep pace with the claustrophobic conviction that time is fast running out, culminate near the end of the novel in the apocalyptic dream of Melmoth the Wanderer, in which he sees a vast 'dial-plate', a clock with one hand, which is nearing 'the appointed period of 150 years'; as Melmoth plummets into a burning ocean

> . . . his last despairing reverted glance was fixed on the clock of eternity—the upraised black arm seemed to push forward the hand—it arrived at its period—he fell—he sunk—he blazed—he shrieked! The burning waves boomed over his sinking head, and the clock of eternity rung out its awful chime—'Room for the soul of the Wanderer!'— and the waves of the burning ocean answered, as they lashed the adamantine rock—'There is room for more!'
>
> (p. 539)

Claude Fierobe has observed that because Melmoth is represented as having chosen his destiny, a choice which his victims later rejected, we cannot speak of predestination in the strict sense of the term (p. 575). We might also recall the claim of the sinister Fr. Schemoli in *Fatal Revenge* that 'the first movement is voluntary, all that follow are consequential and inevitable' (II, p. 240). But, despite such technical exemptions, the grain of both novels is in the direction of a metaphysics of predestination, of the 'omnipotence of fate' (*Fatal Revenge,* III, p. 110). The very structure of the novel, with its narratives incarcerated one within another, recapitulates this thematic determinism.

However, the sequence most relevant to the evocation of a Calvinist sublime is the tale which stands outside that 'Chinese box' of narratives nested in 'The Tale of the Spaniard', namely the mutilated manuscript discovered by young John Melmoth that tells of the experiences of the Englishman Stanton. Deceived into entering, and now incarcerated within, a madhouse outside London, Stanton is another of Maturin's victims of involuntary confinement; next door to his cell is a puritanical weaver, who had been driven mad by a single sermon from the celebrated Hugh Peters, and was sent to the mad-house 'as full of election and reprobation as he could hold—and fuller'. The mad weaver 'regularly repeated over the *five points* while day-light lasted, and imagined himself preaching in a conventicle with distinguished success; towards twilight his visions were more gloomy, and at midnight his blasphemies became more horrible': these ravings reveal an occluded, sanguine sexuality seething beneath the purified rites of the conventicle:

Sister Ruth, why doth thou uncover thy bosom to discover my frailty? . . . Dip all thy garments in blood, and let me weave thee fresh when thou art stained—when shall thy saints tread the winepress of thy wrath? Blood! blood! the saints call for it, earth gapes to swallow it, hell thirsts for it!—Sister Ruth, I pray thee, conceal thy bosom, and be not as the vain women of this generation. . . . Sister Ruth, tempt me not with that calf's head, it is all streaming with blood—drop it, I beseech thee, sister, it is unmeet in woman's hand, though the brethren drink of it. . . .

(pp. 50-51)

Stanton is tempted by Melmoth, who offers him release from the madhouse, on the terms of an 'incommunicable condition', which is ultimately communicated at the close of the novel: the condition is that Stanton exchange his fate for that of Melmoth, at the price of his soul. Stanton eventually rejects this proposal, but not before Melmoth brings home to him the full horror that confronts Stanton in the madhouse:

'Listen', said the tempter, pausing, 'listen to the wretch who is raving near you, and whose blasphemies might make a demon start. He was once an eminent puritanical preacher. Half the day he imagines himself in a pulpit, denouncing damnation against Papists, Arminians, and even Sublapsarians (he being a Supra-lapsarian himself). He foams, he writhes, he gnashes his teeth; you would imagine him in the hell he was painting, and that the fire and the brimstone he is so lavish of, were actually exhaling from his jaws. At night his creed retaliates on him; he believes himself one of the reprobates he has been all day denouncing, and curses God for the very decree he has all day been glorifying him for. . . . He grapples with the iron posts of his bed, and says he is rooting out the cross from the very foundations of Calvary; and it is remarkable, that in proportion as his morning exercises are intense, vivid, and eloquent, his nightly blasphemies are outrageous and horrible.—Hark! Now he believes himself a demon; listen to his diabolical eloquence of horror!' Stanton listened, and shuddered.

(pp. 57-58)

This resonant passage encapsulates what I mean by the term 'Calvinist sublime': in a process which Jungian psychology would term 'enantiodromia', Maturin's Calvinism retaliates on him and in response is aesthetically sublimated into the 'diabolical eloquence of horror'. William Haller, in *The Rise of Puritanism* claims that 'it was of the very essence of Puritan self-discipline that whatsoever thoughts and actions the old Adam within has most desire to keep hidden, the very worst abominations of the heart, one must when retired to one's chamber at night draw forth into the light of conscience. To set them down in writing, albeit in secret 'character', was a great help in

this. They were the devil incarnate in men and could drag him down to hell'.[15] This account of purging one's deepest abominations of heart through nocturnal writing in secret character might serve as a metaphor of Maturin's novel-writing, which was done principally at night.[16]

Paralleling this cryptographic Calvinism, however, is a recurrent fascination with the Roman Catholic church, which Maturin throughout his gothic novels depicts (in a manner strangely akin to his representation of the Calvinist sublime) as a vast system for subjugation. According to J. M. Roberts, in his *The Mythology of the Secret Societies*,[17] the common assertion underlying belief in such diverse secret societies as the Freemasons, the Jesuits, the Carbonari, or the Comintern, is that 'there is an occult force operating behind the seemingly real outward forms of political life. No discovery, no penetration of the veils of secrecy can ever be assumed to have revealed the full truth about the hidden directors who are, in extreme statements, said to preside over societies which appear to be in conflict with one another' (p. 150). We can see Maturin articulating this kind of conspiratorial paranoia in **Melmoth,** when the parricide monk harangues Alonzo:

'And you dreamt', he cried, 'in your temerity, you dreamt of setting the vigilance of a convent at defiance? Two boys, one the fool of fear, and the other of temerity, were fit antagonists for that stupendous system, whose roots are in the bowels of the earth, and whose head is among the stars,—you escape from a convent! you defy a power that has defied sovereigns! A power whose influence is unlimited, indefinable, and unknown, even to those who exercise it, as there are mansions so vast, that their inmates, to their last hour, have never visited all the apartments; a power whose operation is like its motto,—one and indivisible. The soul of the Vatican breathes in the humblest convent in Spain,—and you, an insect perched on a wheel of this vast machine, imagined you were able to arrest its progress, while its rotation was hurrying on to crush you to atoms.

(pp. 219-220)[18]

In his second novel, **The Wild Irish Boy,** Maturin had claimed that Evangelical students at Trinity College found 'the system of Calvin' to be 'amazingly splendid and awful', because 'a youthful mind in its first pursuit of religion neither inquires for evidence nor wishes conviction; it demands something that may fill to the utmost its capacity of the marvellous, something under which its faculties may succumb in mute acquiescence' (I, pp. 122-23). It is clear that in Catholicism as well as Calvinism Maturin sought this 'capacity of the marvellous'; for Maturin, Catholicism was the matrix of the malign Inquisition, the Jesuit cabal, and especially of every form of superstition. During the composition of *Melmoth*, Maturin wrote to Walter Scott thus:

> I am writing at present a poetical Romance, a wild thing that has a Chance of pleasing more than Regular performances . . . tales of superstition were always my favourites, I have in fact been always more conversant with the visions of another world, than the realities of this, and in my Romance I have determined to display all by diabolical resources, out-Herod all the Herods of the German school, and get the possession of the Magic lamp with all its slaves from the Conjurer Lewis himself.[19]

However, Maturin's obsession with Catholicism cannot be explained solely by the artistic possibilities and psychological satisfaction it afforded him. As already noted, his novels appeared in the period between the Act of Union and Catholic Emancipation and they are vehicles of propaganda as well as of entertainment. Maturin's gothic Spain of sinister priests and superstitious populace is also a veiled commentary on Ireland, while his Spanish Catholic heroes often utter rather unorthodox sentiments. Victor Sage notes that the Spaniard Alonzo is a 'Lutheran puppet' (p. 34) and Chris Baldick observes that 'the ventriloquism by which Catholics often find themselves speaking in Lutheran tongues is a minor Gothic convention inherited from Radcliffe's *The Italian* (1797)'.[20]

However, the different nature of pro- or anti-Emancipation pamphleteering in England and Ireland was conditioned by the simple fact that in the former country Catholics were a minority and in the latter a majority. Desmond Bowen, in *The Protestant Crusade in Ireland, 1800-1870*, locates a crucial turning point as the 24th of October, 1822, when the Church of Ireland Archbishop of Dublin, William Magee, attacked both Presbyterians and Catholics and, in effect, announced a 'Second Reformation'.[21] His address launched a furious pamphlet war and Maturin's 1824 *Five Sermons on the Errors of the Roman Catholic Church* can be seen as a strategic intervention and possibly as a bid for promotion. Maturin's stance, however, clearly antedates Magee's intervention, since it had already been articulated in less hyperbolic terms five years earlier in his *Sermons* (1819). The Catholicism against which Maturin inveighs in his sermons is less the 'stupendous system' of *Melmoth* and more the oppressor of spirit, gaoler of the soul, and traducer of the Bible: in a 'Charity Sermon' Maturin combines a charitable appeal for funds with an espousal of proselytizing, and while playing on the political fears of his Protestant

congregation, introduces the concept of religion as an ideological weapon:

> Your money cannot satiate the rage of the drunkard,—your money cannot make the indolent work,—your money cannot convince of his folly the giddy wretch who listens to the frantic and wicked lies of the demagogue,—your money cannot bribe to peace those fierce and horrid passions which have defaced the order of society, and made the aristocracy of this country tremble in their down and ermine. Money can never do this; but what money never can do, *religion* can.
>
> (*Sermons*, pp. 238-39)

In his *Five Sermons*, published five years later, Maturin is forced to concede that in Ireland, 'this unhappy country', 'political causes, perhaps, operate more powerfully than religious ones' (pp. 151-52), but he nonetheless apostrophises the Catholic community:

> Roman Catholics of Ireland hear me! Ye call on the rulers of the land for emancipation—emancipate yourselves from the yoke that has pressed on your intellect and your consciences for centuries. Whatever be the civil restraints ye complain of, I do not judge; but remember this, that the restraints ye voluntarily bear are a thousand times more deadly than any earthly despot could possibly lay on man. The shackles of political restraint when once broken, leave no marks; but the iron of priestcraft 'entereth the soul.'
>
> (pp. 123-24)

Nonetheless, the obsessive representation of Catholicism in Maturin's novels indicates a 'cathexis' in excess of any merely proselytizing agenda. An index of the complexity of his theologized aesthetics and his aestheticized theology can be found in *Women* (1818), the novel which preceded *Melmoth*: when his heroine Zaira encounters an old woman at a Dublin dissenter meeting-house, she 'revived in Zaira's memory the idea of the old nun in the convent near Paris. There was the same sterility, vacancy, and uniformity in their characters. A person unacquainted with religious distinctions would scarce have known one from the other; yet, in one respect, they were antipodes to one another—Catholicism and Calvinism placed an immeasurable distance between them' (III, p. 303). This is the daylight Maturin, repudiating Catholicism and Calvinism; yet, in his midnight-writing, the two creeds are—like Alonzo and the parricide monk—in a relationship that happens 'to unite very opposite characters in the same adventure . . . an union inevitable and *inseparable*', a *'union of antipodes'* (*Melmoth*, pp. 187, 202). There are, however, aesthetic if not theological benefits to be gained from the fusing of convent and conventicle: Zaira, the elegant and cosmopolitan actress who arrives in Dublin from Italy, is ultimately revealed to be both the daughter of a dissolute Protestant Ascendancy landlord and a Catholic peasant girl whom he had seduced, and the mother of a daughter who has been raised as an evangelical Methodist. Zaira's family ties link a number of Ireland's major denominations; presumably this triggers her self-created theology, which blends various religious systems. According to the narrator, Zaira's theology 'was more inquisitive, daring, and autocrative than Catholicism; more full of exterior forms, self infliction and 'voluntary humility' than the reformed religion; its speculative part verged very much towards Calvinism; its outward towards popery—for her imagination dictated even in religion, and it was gratified by combining the ambitious and exclusive theory of Calvin (which may be said to establish a kind of religious aristocracy,) with the meretricious and attractive exterior of Catholicism'.[22]

Thus Maturin's intense and memorable gothic fiction is a function of an aesthetic rapprochement between conflicting elements which, as his sermons indicate, he was not able to reproduce in the religious or political dimensions. The Calvinist sublime at work in his gothic novels is given a particular inflection by the forces of religious and political controversy operating at his particular historical moment.

The gothic fiction of another Irishman, Joseph Sheridan Le Fanu (1814-1873), also exhibits the characteristics of a Calvinist sublime, but because Le Fanu wrote at a later historical moment, the expression of this Calvinist sublime is subtly modulated. The same process occurs in writers like William Godwin, James Hogg, Charles Brockden Brown, Poe and Hawthorne, where the relevant cultural differences might allow us to speak of English, Scottish and American Calvinist sublimes, each inflected by their distinct historical moments.

Clearly, I do not have the space to substantiate my claim that these authors (and twentieth-century writers such as Thomas Pynchon) also explore the contours of the Calvinist sublime. But I would like to conclude with mention of a novel published 102 years after **Melmoth the Wanderer**. In the 'Oxen of the Sun' chapter of *Ulysses*, Joyce parodies the successive phases of English Literature; in the following extract, in which Malachi (Buck) Mulligan is entertaining medical students with accounts of a recent murder, a revelation is made (about the visiting Englishman Haines) that humorously encapsulates some of the ideas about Irish history and the Gothic that I've been pursuing:

> But Malachias' tale began to freeze them with horror. He conjured up the scene before them. The secret panel beside the chimney slid back and in the recess appeared . . . Haines! Which of us did not feel his flesh creep? He had a portfolio full of Celtic literature in one hand, in the other a phial marked Poison. Surprise, horror, loathing were depicted on all faces while he eyed them with a ghastly grin. 'I anticipated some such reception', he began with an eldritch laugh, 'for which, it seems, history is to blame'.[23]

Notes

1. *Melmoth the Wanderer* (London: 1820; 1968).

2. Jean Calvin, 1536-1559, *A Compend of the Institutes of the Christian Religion* (London: 1965), 1st ed. 1536, final ed. 1559.

3. *Concerning the Eternal Predestination of God* (London: 1961; 1st ed. 1552;) p. 156; see also pp. 62-68.

4. William Bouwsma, *Jean Calvin: A Sixteenth Century Portrait* (Oxford: 1988), p. 42.

5. Paul Fry, 'The Possession of the Sublime', *Studies in Romanticism* XXVI, no.2 (1987), pp. 187-220.

6. Edmund Burke, 1757, *A Philosophical Enquiry into the Origin of our Ideas of the Sublime and Beautiful* (London: 1958).

7. Ann Radcliffe, 'On the Supernatural in Poetry', *New Monthly Magazine* VII (1826), pp. 149-50.

8. David Punter, *The Literature of Terror* (London: 1980), pp. 44-45, 85-86.

9. Joel Porte, 'In the Hands of an Angry God', in *The Gothic Imagination: Essays in Dark Romanticism*, ed. G. R. Thompson (Washington: 1974), pp. 42-64.

10. Victor Sage, *Horror Fiction in the Protestant Tradition* (London: 1989).

11. Irene Bostrom, 'The Novel and Catholic Emancipation', *Studies in Romanticism* 11 (1963), pp. 155-76; Sister Mary Muriel Tarr, *Catholicism in Gothic Fiction in England (1762-1820)*, (New York: 1946; 1979).

12. Cited in Claude Fierobe, *Charles Robert Maturin (1780-1824): L'Homme et L'Oeuvre* (Lille: 1974), p. 577.

13. *Five Sermons on the Errors of the Roman Catholic Church* (London: 1824).

14. James Boulger, *The Calvinist Temper in English Poetry* (The Hague: 1980).

15. William Haller, *The Rise of Puritanism* (New York: 1938), p. 100; cited Boulger, p. 55.

16. See Fierobe, p. 155.

17. J. M. Roberts, *The Mythology of the Secret Societies* (London: 1972).

18. In Maturin's last novel, *The Albigenses*, the cynical Bishop invokes a similar rhetoric:

> 'The vast system of which I am no feeble engine, hastens to the consummation of its working—the conquest of the world. That

old and mighty Rome, of whom pedants prate, subdued but the meaner part of man—his body; but our Rome enslaves the mind—that mind, which, once enslaved, leaves nothing for opposition or for defeat . . . for ours is the power that not only binds the spirit but makes it clasp its chain; ours are the powers of the world to come; all that is potent in life, all that is mysterious in futurity, the fears the hopes the hearts of mankind, all are ours . . .'

(III, pp. 203-204)

19. In his *Sermons*, Maturin makes the following confession:

'The very first sounds almost that attract the ears of childhood are tales of another life—foolishly are they called tales of superstition; for, however disguised by the vulgarity of the narration, and the distortion of fiction, they tell him of those whom he is hastening from the threshold of life to join, the inhabitants of the invisible world, with whom he must soon be forever.'

(p. 358, cited in Peter Mills Henderson, *A Nut Between Two Blades: The Novels of Charles Maturin* (New York: 1980) p. 16)

20. Chris Baldick, 'Introduction' to *Melmoth the Wanderer* (Oxford: 1989), pp. vii-xxiv, p. xiv.

21. Desmond Bowen, *The Protestant Crusade in Ireland, 1800-1870* (Dublin: 1978), pp. 83-123.

22. *Women*, III, p. 235. A bleaker picture of Maturin's predicament is afforded in a letter written by Sir Charles Morgan, a few weeks before Maturin died:

'Poor Maturin is ill, severely ill; we (the Drs.) have sent him into the country, I fear, to die. Not content with drawing "the saints" down upon him, he has attacked the "papishes" and is now in the condition somewhat of a nut between the blades of a nutcracker.'

(cited in Niilo Idman, *Charles Robert Maturin: His Life and Works* (London: 1923), p. 308)

23. James Joyce, *Ulysses*, 1922 (New York: 1961), p. 412.

Other works cited:

Charles Maturin, *Fatal Revenge; or, The Family of Montorio*, 3 vols (London: 1807).

———. *The Wild Irish Boy*, 3 vols, New York (1808; 1979).

———. *Women; or, Pour et Contre*, 3 vols, New York (1818; 1979).

———. *Sermons*, London (1819).

———. *The Albigenses* London (1824).

CATHERINE LANONE (ESSAY DATE 2002)

SOURCE: Lanone, Catherine. "Verging on the Gothic: Melmoth's Journey to France." In *European Gothic: A Spirited Exchange, 1760-1960*, edited by Avril Horner, pp. 71-83. Manchester: Manchester University Press, 2002.

In the following essay, Lanone analyzes the influence of French culture, politics, and literature on Melmoth the Wanderer *and Maturin's influence on French writers such as Charles Baudelaire and Honoré de Balzac.*

Often considered to be the last true Gothic novel,[1] *Melmoth* was translated into French as early as 1821, first by Mme E. F. Bégin under the title *L'Homme du mystère, ou histoire de Melmoth le voyageur,* then by J. Cohen under the title *Melmoth ou l'homme errant.* But the text was cut and altered; only in 1965 was a full translation given by Jacqueline Marc-Chadourne. Jean-Jacques Pauvert chose to publish this with André Breton's famous 1954 preface, which praised its influence on French literature. Not surprisingly, the leader of Surrealism considered all the hallucinatory desires, the dark castles and visions found in Gothic novels as a potent 'drug'; indeed, Breton compared the visual impact of *The Castle of Otranto* to the cinematic thrill caused in 1929 by Bunuel's eerie image of the razor cutting through the eye in *Un chien andalou.* But Breton seems to find *Melmoth* particularly compelling, describing it as a great meteorite flashing through the frame of the Gothic window, an endless shower of ashes mysteriously suspended for a brief moment ('On doit attendre jusqu'à 1820 pour qu'un nouveau météore se détache du cadre rituel de la fenêtre ogivale, suspendant son interminable pluie de cendres' (Breton 1996: 15)). I wish to pursue here the motif of the shower of ashes, and discuss the way *Melmoth,* itself influenced by Diderot's *La Religieuse* (Lévy 1995: 579), crossed the Channel to spark fresh inspiration in France at the precise moment when the great Gothic fires of damnation were yielding to the ashen precision of realism in both countries.

For Annie Le Brun, nineteenth-century French literature defines itself in terms of its relationship with the Gothic—especially with *Melmoth the Wanderer*—whether this influence is acknowledged or not (Le Brun 1982). At a time when France was still scarred by the violence of the Revolution and of Napoleonic wars, and a new bourgeois order was emerging, the sheer darkness of *Melmoth* was bound to trigger fear and fascination, especially since the novel glosses over the circumstances which lead Melmoth to surrender his soul; it focuses on the aftermath, the long quest for someone who might sell a soul and free the tempter. Maturin becomes 'a practitioner of psychopathological taxonomy' (Punter 1996: 128), but the taxonomy is curiously unstable, as cruel religious institutions (Sage 1988) and everyday evil outdo the arch villain, whose death eventually fails to provide secure catharsis.

ABOUT THE AUTHOR

AN EXCERPT FROM AN EARLY REVIEW OF
MELMOTH THE WANDERER

We do not envy those who are incapacitated by extreme delicacy of taste, or, we should rather perhaps say, by extreme indulgence in the habits of strict criticism, from enjoying such works as those of Mr. Maturin. They are all, prose and verse, full of faults so numerous, that it would be quite fatiguing—so obvious, that it would be quite useless to point them out. . . . The author, in a very great proportion of every work he has written, has been contented with copying the worst faults of his predecessors and contemporaries, in the commonest walks of fictitious writing. In his best passages there is always a mixture of extravagance—in the whole of his works there is not, perhaps, to be found one page of perfectly natural thought, or perfectly elegant language. And yet, where is the lover of imaginative excitement, that ever laid down one of his books unfinished—or the man of candour and discrimination, who ever denied, after reading through any one of them, that Maturin is gifted with a genius as fervently powerful as it is distinctly original—that there is ever and anon a truth of true poetry diffused over the thickest chaos of his absurdities—and that he walks almost without a rival, dead or living, in many of the darkest, but, at the same time, the most majestic circles of romance?

Mr. Maturin is, without question, one of the most genuine masters of the dark romance. He can make the most practised reader tremble as effectually as Mrs. Radcliffe, and what is better, he can make him think as deeply as Mr. Godwin. We cannot carry the commendation sought for by this species of exertion much higher than we do when we say, that in our opinion, a little more reflection and labour are all Mr. Maturin wants, in order to enable him to attain a permanent eminence.

SOURCE: "Melmoth the Wanderer, &c." *Blackwood's Edinburgh Magazine* 8, no. 44 (November 1820): 161-68.

Thus *Melmoth the Wanderer* darkly conveys the disturbing forces plaguing society, and depicts potential disruption and the violence inherent in humanity. Baldick defines the Gothic as a 'sickening descent into disintegration' (Baldick 1992: xix). In this case, we have several descents into degradation and abjection; the pattern of claustrophobic enclosure occurs both symbolically—through poverty and lack of love—and literally—in the cells of the Inquisition or the subterranean labyrinth of convents. This core of darkness was bound to appeal to Romantics and Surrealists, who were fascinated by the apparition of Melmoth on a lonely rock towering above the stormy sea, or by the play on nightmares and dreams—those dreams which magically take Immalee back to her island every night.

Indeed, the text builds claustrophobic boundaries which it challenges, through the figure of the ubiquitous eponymous character whom no walls can stop; who appears quietly at the bottom of a hidden cell in Spain or in the middle of a wild, luscious island; who appears unchanged from one century to the next. Just as we share the sense of entrapment which shatters all secondary characters, we are fascinated by the dreamlike, bewildering erasure of all spatial boundaries as the powerful protagonist switches effortlessly from tale to tale.

The most subversive element in *Melmoth the Wanderer* may well be the structure of the text itself. Balzac especially was fascinated by Maturin's daring energy, calling him, in the Preface to *La Peau de chagrin,* the most original writer in contemporary Britain. Indeed, *Melmoth* plays obsessively with textual boundaries, embedding narrative layers to create a fractal set of Chinese boxes. Centuries go by while the focus switches from one sorry plight to another, weaving an ironic rosary of evil, as Monçada warns his listener: 'have patience, and you will find that we are all beads strung on the same string' (Maturin 2000: 332).

Thus the novel metatextually exposes its own devices, foregrounding gaps rather than excusing them, the way in which the Gothic text seeks both to establish and challenge boundaries, subverting systematic claustration into an exploration of emptiness, discovering a dark, giddy void at the heart of life. The novel delights in its literally amazing structure. The traditional witness account, which is faithfully reported, is mocked by the totally illogical discovery of an old Jew's cabinet of curiosities, in which Monçada must sit by skeletons and copy the wondrous tales of Melmoth, including the tediously slow courtship of

Immalee, though no possible explanation can ever be found for such a text. The oral repetition of the written copy of the mysterious illogical text (which paradoxically allows a straight heterodiegetic approach to the Wanderer's own love story) creates a dizzy narrative structure. Victor Sage points out 'the relentless fragmentation of the process of transmission' (Sage 2000: xviii). Rosemary Jackson also emphasizes the way in which *Melmoth* deconstructs the very notion of representation, equivocating over interpretation, interrogations and evasions: 'Its relentlessly fragmented structure permits the reader little security. One scene spirals and merges into another, each tale breaking off to lead to another tale, equally truncated, incomplete' (Jackson 1988: 104). The tainted palimpsest expands yet shrinks, the tales which are read, copied, told and retold or burnt, weave a cancerous texture, as if the text were eroded by an uncertain disease.

Thematically the reader must enter this deterritorialized, wandering text in order to share, not the story of the wanderer, but his bitter, inconclusive experience, along a dark line of flight which leads nowhere. As the narratives function as screens, we follow descent after descent towards anger and despair, but the object of temptation, the lure of the pact with the devil, is supposedly barred from language, only to reappear repeatedly elsewhere, sometimes through slips of the tongue. In Deleuzian terms, what we have here is a rhizome, a subterranean set of ramifications connecting at random. Melmoth's doomed, weary quest is shared by the reader who shifts from story to story at the very moment when satisfactory closure is denied. Baited, the reader follows the narrator, from one gloomy place of horror to the next, trapped by the slippery, treacherous narrative pact. And yet the end tantalizingly escapes the reader's grasp, as Monçada and young Melmoth play detectives by the sea.

Because of its unusual structure and bitter darkness, *Melmoth the Wanderer* aroused a fascination which was to last for more than a century in France. Whereas Melmoth's son by Immalee dies mysteriously, perhaps strangled by his father, Melmoth's textual 'hideous progeny'—to borrow Mary Shelley's expression—may well be found across the Channel, especially among the poets of darkness. One instantly thinks of Lautréamont or the Surrealists who redeemed the Gothic in a new era of doubt and darkening political prospects, but the most significant figure may well be Baudelaire—that advocate of modernity enamoured with satanic rebellion, who chose as poetical

objects skeletons, prostitutes and the depth of the abyss. Indeed, in his critical writings Baudelaire repeatedly refers to Maturin as a key influence, though he was no poet. He uses him to define his subversive aesthetic perspective, claiming that the dominant mode of modern art must be infernal: 'Je veux dire que l'art moderne a une tendance essentiellement démoniaque'[2] (Baudelaire 1990: 770). Lumping together Beethoven, Byron, Maturin and Poe, Baudelaire celebrates literary correspondences, the deep dark unison illuminating the clouds lurking within the human soul. We too may trace in his 'flowers of evil' the withered blossoms plucked by the Wanderer, which mar the exotic purity of Immalee's island. Balancing Christianity with erotic blasphemy, *Les Fleurs du mal* (1861)[3] display dark beds as deep as tombs, perfume flasks containing the decaying body of lost love, journeys beyond Eros towards Thanatos. Indeed, the long poem entitled 'The Voyage' roams from place to place, attempting to answer the haunting question, 'but what have you seen?', yet the world shrinks, a mere oasis of horror in a wearisome desert. In the end, the speaker yearns to dive into the unknown, no matter whether it be heaven or hell, so long as he finds something new. Rather than Baudelaire's beloved Poe, whom he translated,[4] the key influence here is Maturin's Melmoth, hopelessly wandering on the margins of the human world. Indeed, Baudelaire turned him into the epitome of the romantic outcast:

> Let us remember Melmoth, this admirable emblem. His unbearable suffering comes from the disproportion between his marvellous skills, which he acquired instantly through the pact with the Devil, and the surroundings where he is doomed to live as a creature of God. And none of those whom he wishes to seduce consents to buy back from him, at the same price, his own dreadful privileged condition . . . The man who would be God has thus soon fallen, by virtue of an uncontrollable moral law, lower than his own real nature. This is a soul selling itself bit by bit.
> (Baudelaire 1976: 438)[5]

Presumably each narrative episode of *Melmoth* corresponds to the itemized decay of the unredeemed soul. Here the praise of Melmoth is connected with the 'sulphurous dawn' of drugs, as the modern way of selling one's soul to the devil, but elsewhere Baudelaire shows that he is not simply fascinated by doom and eternal wandering, by the quest for a victim, but by Melmoth's laughter, which he defines in his 'Essay on the essence of laughter'[6] as 'a laughter which never sleeps, like a sickness which goes its own way and obeys some providential order'. For him, Melmoth is a contradiction in terms, 'a living contradiction', whose icy laughter tears one's entrails: 'And thus Melmoth's laughter is the highest expression of pride, and perpetually fulfils its task, by tearing and burning the lips of the irremediably laughing man' (Baudelaire 1990: 250) (my translation). Laughter is the true sign of hubris, the true curse. Melmoth is of course in many ways a satirist, and Punter praises his 'supremely self-conscious wit' (Punter 1996: 126), while Lévy points out that such laughter comes from an inner split, as when Melmoth both seduces Immalee and wishes to protect her from himself; laughter becomes the seam between good and evil, self and other, at the very edge of pain, enjoyment and defiance. Such devilish laughter echoes in Baudelaire's prose poem 'The Flawed Glass Maker' (1862), in which the poet's persona, exhilarated by his own madness, drops a flowerpot on a maker of window glass—shattering all his panes—on the grounds that he should make magic glass, pink panes that prove that life is beautiful, rather than ordinary glass.

While Baudelaire's fascination with *Melmoth* is fairly obvious, it is perhaps more surprising to find Balzac among the early worshippers of the novel. While the Gothic implies darkness and mad desire, Balzac's fiction establishes the realm of realism and explores nineteenth-century society throughout the 'Human Comedy'. Though Hugo's romantic melodramatic tastes may be automatically deemed to descend from the Gothic, Balzac's achievement seems at first sight to have little, if anything, to do with the Gothic. Yet if Balzac set the bulk of his work within the boundaries of realism, his early writings show very different aspirations. Balzac chose as his early pen names the pompous British title 'Lord R'hoone' and then the more European-sounding 'Horace de St Aubin', which presumably echoes both Horace Walpole and Ann Radcliffe's *Mysteries of Udolpho*. In so doing, Balzac was obviously paying lip service to the tastes of fashionable friends such as Nodier. But there was more to this than a mere fad. For perhaps the Gothic was the inevitable threshold of 'The Human Comedy': French realism was actually built on the very ruins of the Gothic, and Balzac had to exorcise the shadowy ghost of Melmoth before he could find his own voice.

Indeed, among what Balzac later called his literary 'rubbish',[7] the first significant text is unquestionably *Le Centenaire ou les deux Beringheld*, published in 1822, and re-issued in 1837 with little alteration under the title *Le Sorcier ou les deux Beringheld* (Balzac 1990). Clearly, though he openly criticized his early work, Balzac considered it worth publishing again. Unfortunately there is little magic in the Sorcerer's tale, and the frightful figure of the 'centenaire', the ageless old man who supposedly dominates the story, fails to arouse horror or even terror. The text is a clumsy attempt to rival the man he considered to be the greatest of English writers; indeed, Lévy points out that Balzac considered Maturin to be as important as Byron, Hoffmann or Goethe (Lévy 1995: 600). Certainly, *The Sorcerer* is so redolent of *Melmoth* that critics such as Breton and Barbéris (1965) dismiss the book as mere plagiarism. The text imitates the split between generations, and tries to spice it up by having the icy ancestor beget his own descendant, replacing an impotent father. Balzac also uses some of Immalee's love speeches (actually, he even drew upon them in writing his own love letters!). The Spanish Inquisition is replaced by Napoleon's campaign in Egypt. Balzac's wanderer retains Melmoth's fiery burning eyes, but he is extremely old throughout the novel, and he is preternaturally tall, clearly borrowing a few features from *Frankenstein*'s monster. Indeed, no longer content with attempting to steal souls, he abducts desperate maidens to steal the fluid of life so that he can regenerate himself. If Gothic castles bore Balzac and he considers their inhabitants degenerate, he nevertheless attempts tackling the subterranean maze at the end, only to complicate it with scientific apparatus (strangely enough, the wanderer has also proved to be a mysterious doctor who appears throughout the book). Misreading both *Melmoth* and *Frankenstein*, Balzac's work also botches the technique of embedded narrations, proudly announcing, for instance, Beringheld's memoirs, only to shift to a heterodiegetic flashback delivered by an intrusive if obsequious narrator who claims he is summing it all up for our own sake. Whilst we might retrospectively wish to dignify this work by describing it as pastiche, the book was probably meant to be taken seriously at the time of publication. It is Balzac's first piece of real writing, and might perhaps best lie forgotten, were it not for the fact that its very flaws suggest a desire to modernize the plot, and thus stage the action on the impossible boundary between a remote Gothic scenario and bourgeois society. The economy of restraint bars the powers of darkness, but they are not so easily subdued.

Melmoth réconcilié is Balzac's sequel to Maturin's novel, and it becomes extremely interesting as it attempts to lead us out of the Gothic into the world of proper bourgeois writing. But the parody seems to mock its own purpose. Perhaps

Balzac was not simply yielding to fashion when he wrote *Le Centenaire,* since the fascination with **Melmoth** appears again in 1828, by which time Balzac had bought Cohen's 1821 translation, and was hoping to print a second edition. *Melmoth réconcilié* was first published in 1835, and Balzac gives as an afterthought a short summary of **Melmoth** in a postscript, for those who may not know the book and who thus cannot understand his own tale. Balzac adds that though it may have seemed reasonable to Maturin not to send his protagonist to Paris, the demon must needs have found on his own the path to a city where the odds for accepting the bargain must be about a thousand to one. Amusingly enough, as Le Yaouanc points out,[8] Balzac's Melmoth reaches Paris in 1821, precisely when the translation of the book appeared (Balzac 1979: 1400).

Melmoth réconcilié is usually seen as a metaphysical tale, in which Balzac asserts potential redemption.[9] Instead of vanishing near the home of his ancestors, Melmoth dies in peace; after having found a victim at last, he confesses his crimes and spreads the divine light of revelation among the people surrounding his death bed. In writing the novel, Balzac borrows a few features from the original **Melmoth,** such as the burning eyes, the grim laugh and the absolute knowledge of his victims' circumstances, as well as the heavenly music which is followed by a ghastly vision. A few new fantastic effects are introduced, as when Melmoth displays his power by replacing the rainy evening street by the spectacle of a bright summer's day, or creates double vision at the theatre where, instead of a comedy with a quick-change artist, the victim witnesses the comedy of his own life as his mistress cuckolds him, the very mistress who now sits and laughs beside him, and for whom he sells his soul. The process of wandering from place to place and story to story is condensed into a bifocal show.[10] What is shrinking here, however, is the very nature of the world beyond boundaries offered by the supernatural traveller and his Faustian pact. The abnormal rule which triggers an abnormal unquenchable thirst for rebellion is no longer cruel religion but money. Melmoth has fallen into a materialistic world: the cell is bound by the iron bars of a cashier's window, Paris becomes the hellish city of temptation: 'cette ville aux tentations, cette succursale de l'Enfer' (Balzac 1979: 346), and it is through mediocre orgies that the mediocre cashier learns to yearn for the divine, panting for the unknown with a soul parched by debauchery. For Castanier no longer attempts to spread evil, he is only a demon in the making, weak and mean, helpless and powerless. He ends up in the stock exchange, buying the soul of a bankrupt investor, and in a single evening the hellish alliance is exchanged so many times that it loses all value. Thus, the narrator cynically concludes, the enormous power unleashed by Maturin was lost.

Though fantastic, the story is neither a failure nor truly Gothic; instead, it is a Gothic recantation. What Balzac is staging is not so much devalued desire or the triumph of money, as the devaluation of Gothic clichés. It is no surprise that the story should focus on Castanier rather than Melmoth, and that he should be a mere cashier forging a letter to steal money from a London bank. Borrowing from England can only be a simulacrum. For the pact is the coin which shifts from hand to hand, losing its value. What Balzac is coming to terms with here, with savage irony, is his own failure to transpose the Gothic to modern Paris, and adapt it to modern society. In a society which has given up honour for money, or in Barthes's words a noble name for a financial figure, the wild darkness of absolute desire can only be commodified, and thus hollowed out. Gothic images shrink into worthless clichés, coins which are worn out as they slip from hand to hand. Hence the mirror image, when Melmoth's name first appears as he signs his name backwards, from right to left. Hence also the first portrait we have, which deliberately mingles myth and cliché, from the unbearable eyes to topical puritanical clothes, so that the apparition is simply cut out as an Englishman: '[everything], including the shape of his clothes, bespoke an Englishman. He reeked of Englishness' (Balzac 1979: 350) (my translation). The tale ends with the ludicrous babble of some German 'Demon-expert' and the jokes of 'a devil of' a clerk; but this is not a completely irrelevant ending. The repetition of '*fiat*' and '*fiat lux*' actually emphasizes the arbitrary nature of the dénouement, in which the writer's '*fiat*' dismisses the darkness of Gothic clichés.

Before discarding the circulation of Gothic clichés as sterile imitation, though, Balzac wrote a fascinating novel in which he seems to step beyond the boundaries of both realism and the Gothic and to reach a unique balance. In *The Wild Ass's Skin,* which was the literary event of 1831, Balzac does not seek to imitate **Melmoth,** but he does rediscover the pact with evil, and rewrites it as a metaphor for desire and the passing of time. We no longer have a tale spanning centuries to arouse despair but, by a metonymic inversion, a life which is reduced to a shrinking piece of shagreen. The echoing French title *La Peau de chagrin* refers to shagreen or leather, but also sounds like the skin of sorrow, stressing the horror of nightmarish imprisonment beyond the boundaries of ordinary human life. The protagonist, the fair angelic Raphaël, meets his tempter in the guise of an old antique dealer, a gaunt Mephistophelian seer. The antique shop mixes the realistic delight for lists of objects with the darker intricacies of the Gothic maze, in an 'ocean of furnishings, inventions, fashions, works of art and relics' (Balzac 1977: 37). In the gilded rooms packed with trinkets, the windows grow dark, the fantasmagoric portraits quiver and dance, objects shift shapes in a 'weird witches' sabbath worthy of the fantasies glimpsed by Dr Faust' (Balzac 1977: 42). As in **Melmoth the Wanderer,** a portrait appears, this time an icon of youth and beauty painted by Raphaël's namesake. Raphaël's Christ is the antithesis of the deadly talisman, the magic skin which materializes the paradoxical double find of transgression: it grants all wishes, thus allowing its owner to step beyond the bounds of human life, but it consumes itself, as each wish shrinks the limits of the owner's life. Like Melmoth, the owner can but wander through the liminal space of death-in-life. Granting utmost power and utter helplessness, the talisman with its uncanny shimmer and supple solidity glitters like a comet, an image which foreshadows the shortness of Raphaël's life. Once again, the comet suggests fire and ashes, endless wandering but also regular, inevitable repetition and return. When Raphaël cries out that he would like the skin to grant his wishes, the antique dealer quickly replies that he has signed the pact, though nothing has been written.

Dismissing conventions, Balzac then switches to the growing awareness and horror of the victim of the pact, a theme which is extremely similar in spirit, though not in detail, to the core of **Melmoth.** Satisfied boundless desire is contrasted with the obsessive mapping of the ever-shrinking boundary of the skin, the ever-dwindling red line signalling loss of life and energy. This time, Balzac gets all the uncanny effects right. Raphaël seeks a way out, not by looking for another victim but by begging science to save him, yet neither chemistry nor an hydraulic press can manage to stretch the skin. Science pales before uncanny reality; and the horrified Raphaël becomes a wanderer fleeing his beloved Pauline, for each desire burns away his life. Like Melmoth he is the shunned traveller whose presence is unbearable. When he attempts to take the waters, he is challenged to a duel as he refuses to leave, an episode which echoes the

death of Immalee's brother. He then retreats to the middle of nowhere in the centre of France, Auvergne, a place which is clearly for Balzac beyond the boundaries of the civilized world, and which he describes fancifully, depicting sheer drops of lava. More than Balzac's unsteady geography, it is the abject appearance of Raphael's body which fascinates, the shrunken bloodless figure burnt by the hellish prospect of impending demise. Like Melmoth, Raphaël ultimately returns home, not to the place of his ancestors, but to his apartment in Paris where Pauline finds him. When she suddenly understands the situation and attempts to commit suicide to end all possibility of pleasure, Raphaël forgets all his resolutions to avoid desire and throws himself upon her. In this orgasmic 'embrace' he bites her breast, a dénouement which must be connected with the tale of the betrayed lovers who were starved below the convent in **Melmoth.**

The awkward epilogue gives us another key to Balzac's own version of the Gothic within this tale. While Pauline is turned into the spirit of Nature, and thus descends from Immalee's virgin island, Foedora, the other woman who first doomed Raphaël to attempt suicide, is suddenly identified as Society. The peremptory allegorical conclusion might puzzle the reader who remembers the vibrant erotic and voyeuristic scene in which Raphaël ventured into the countess's 'Gothic boudoir' and her bedroom to watch her go to bed. But it also adds a realistic element to the Gothic theme of a desire which burns unto death, for the pact with the Devil has been replaced by social hubris: one now loses one's soul by contracting debts and rashly adoring cold-hearted women, by following a new religion which obscures the pure Pauline. As such, *La Peau de chagrin* constitutes the true threshold of Balzac's 'Human Comedy'. Exposing in a nutshell the erotic economy of the modern world—and the modern text—the talisman creates a gloomy Gothic spell which is doomed to shrink and vanish, as dark textual enchantment yields to the cooler 'lost illusions' of the bulk of the work. Yet even in the ironic 'Human Comedy', some of the power of the dissections of the Parisian vanity fair may well come from unconscious Gothic reminiscences, as the arch deceiver and tempter Vautrin wanders from book to book, with the significant nickname of 'Trompe la Mort' . . .

Thus Maturin becomes a soothsayer, disseminating in France the ashes and sparks of his words, to use a Shelleyan image. Melmoth journeys to France not only to inform Baudelairian darkness or Surrealistic fantasies, but also to signify how a life can be corroded by barren capitalism as well as instinct and desire. Graham Robb considers that *The Wild Ass's Skin* is 'an astonishing exercise in psychic autobiography' (Robb 1995: 179), foreshadowing Balzac's theory of energy, abstinence and excess, which led to his own early death: 'The pattern of Balzac's life is laid out, as if in a premonitory dream' (Robb 1995: 179). The evil pact ultimately concerns writing itself, just as it did, perhaps, for Maturin. According to Michel Butor, the artist must choose to sacrifice his own share of heaven in order to bring revelation to men: 'such is the way Balzac interprets Faust and rewrites **Melmoth**' (Butor 1998: 123). As Sage points out, allusions to painting in **Melmoth the Wanderer** already question the mimetic connection between life and art, in 'that extraordinary anticipation of decadence which so attracts the French' (Sage 2000: xxiii). No wonder that Oscar Wilde, whose *Portrait of Dorian Gray* owes much to his great-uncle Maturin and Balzac's piece of shagreen, should have chosen to live in Paris under the fateful name of Sebastian Melmoth. Thus by crossing the Channel, **Melmoth** ceased to be a religious novel and turned into a metaphor for the curse of the artist. In Balzac's words, desire burns yet power destroys.

Notes

1. 'In literary histories, *Melmoth the Wanderer* (1820) often marks the end of the Gothic romance proper, as a genre' (Sage 2000: vii).

2. This is taken from an essay on Théodore de Banville which was first published in 1861.

3. Though a first collection appeared in 1857, and poems were added in 1868, the 1861 edition is usually considered to be the most significant one.

4. In 1852, Baudelaire read Poe avidly, convinced he had found a kindred spirit; he felt tremendous admiration for his conception of poetry. He had already completed a short translation in 1848, and between 1852 and 1865 he translated Poe's major works, including among other things *The Raven, The Black Cat, The Murders in the Rue Morgue, The Narrative of Arthur Gordon Pym, Eureka, The Philosophy of Composition,* and *Tales of the Grotesque and the Arabesque*. One should pay particular attention to *Histoires extraordinaires*, which was published in 1856, and *Nouvelles histoires extraordinaires*, which was published in 1857. The prefaces Baudelaire wrote show intellectual osmosis, to the point of sometimes plagiarizing Poe's *Poetic Principle*. Lemaître explains that towards the end of his life Baudelaire also wished to translate *Melmoth*, since he found the existing version deeply unsatisfactory (Baudelaire 1990: 249).

5. Translation mine. This appeared in 1860 as part of Baudelaire's preface to his long commentary (which included long extracts which he had translated) on De Quincey's *Confessions of an English Opium Eater.*

6. *De l'essence du rire* was first published in 1855 in *Le Portefeuille.*

7. The expression appears in a letter which Balzac addressed to his mother on 30 October 1835. When prefacing a recent edition of *The Sorcerer,* René Guise was so struck by the term that he checked the manuscript letter, assuming one should read 'oeuvres' (works) instead of 'ordures' (rubbish). But the hypothesis was proved wrong as the word 'ordures' appeared beyond all doubt.

8. Moïse Le Yaouanc is one of the editors of the famous 1979 'Pléiade edition', along with P.G. Castex, T. Bodin, P. Citron, M. Fargeaud, H. Gauthier and R. Guise.

9. The religious implications of Melmoth's failure to find a victim are discussed by Fowler; for her the righteous steadiness of the potential victims is crucial: 'Balzac's wry suggestion notwithstanding, it is not that Melmoth is remarkably stupid in selecting his targets . . . Like Satan, Melmoth fails to part his victims from God not because he is weak, but because they are strong' (Fowler 1986: 527-528). Balzac's deliberate shift is particularly revealing.

10. Interestingly enough, Sage draws attention to theatricality in *Melmoth*: 'For the Wanderer, moving across history and geography is like moving through the auditorium of a theatre' (Sage 2000: xx).

References

Baldick, C. (ed.) (1992) *The Oxford Book of Gothic Tales,* Oxford, Oxford University Press.

de Balzac, H. (1979) *La Comédie humaine,* coll. Pléiade, Paris, Gallimard.

———. (1990) *Le Sorcier ou les deux Beringheld* [1837], Preface by René Guise, Paris, José Corti.

———. (1977) *The Wild Ass's Skin,* trans. H.J. Hunt, Harmondsworth, Penguin.

Barbéris, P. (1965) *Aux sources de Balzac: les romans de jeunesse,* Paris, Les Bibliophiles de l'originale.

Baudelaire, C. (1976) *Oeuvres complètes,* ed. C. Pichois, coll. Pléiade, Paris, Gallimard.

———. (1990) *Curiosités esthétiques, L'Art romantique, et autres oeuvres critiques,* ed. H. Lemaître, Paris, Bordas.

Breton, A. (1996) *Preface,* in C.R. Maturin, *L'Homme errant,* Paris, Phébus [1965], pp. xi-xx.

Le Brun, A. (1982) *Les Châteaux de la subversion,* Paris, Jean-Jacques Pauvert.

Butor, M. (1990) *La Comédie humaine,* coll. Pléiade, Paris, Gallimard.

———. (1998) *Le Marchand et le génie,* Paris, Edition de la différence.

Fowler, K. (1986) 'Hieroglyphics in Fire: *Melmoth the Wanderer*', *Studies in Romanticism,* 25, pp. 133-147.

Jackson, R. (1988) *The Literature of Subversion,* London, Routledge [1981].

Lévy, M. (1995) *Le Roman gothique anglais 1764-1824,* Paris, Albin Michel [1967].

Maturin, C.R. (2000) *Melmoth the Wanderer,* ed. V. Sage, Harmondsworth, Penguin Classics [1820].

Punter, D. (1996) *The Literature of Terror,* Vol. 1, Harlow, Longman.

Robb, G. (1995) *Balzac*, London, Macmillan [1994].

Sage, V. (1988) *Horror Fiction in the Protestant Tradition*, London, Macmillan.

———. (2000) *Preface*, in C. R. Maturin, *Melmoth the Wanderer*, Harmondsworth, Penguin Classics.

FURTHER READING

Criticism

Axton, William F. Introduction to *Melmoth the Wanderer*, by Charles Robert Maturin, pp. vii-xviii. Lincoln: University of Nebraska Press, 1961.

Asserts that Maturin's primary intent in Melmoth *is to expose the corruption engendered by religious authoritarianism, and declares that* Melmoth *is "the highest artistic achievement" of the Gothic genre because in it "the Gothic mummery of the horror novel was brought to serve the uses of a profoundly tragic religious parable."*

Birkhead, Edith. "The Novel of Terror: Lewis and Maturin." In *The Tale of Terror: A Study of the Gothic Romance*, pp. 63-93. London: Constable & Company Ltd., 1921.

Regarded as an important twentieth-century study of the Gothic novel. Focuses on Maturin's Fatal Revenge *and* Melmoth the Wanderer, *noting Maturin's indebtedness to earlier Gothic novelists, but distinguishing him from his predecessors "by the powerful eloquence of his style and his ability to analyse emotion." Birkhead is one of the first twentieth-century critics to comment on the psychological insight displayed in* Melmoth.

Conger, Syndy M. "An Analysis of *Melmoth the Wanderer* and Its German Sources." In *Romantic Reassessment: Matthew G. Lewis, Charles Robert Maturin and the Germans, an Interpretative Study of the Influence of German Literature on Two Gothic Novels*, edited by James Hogg, pp. 160-255. Salzburg Studies in English Literature, edited by Erwin A. Stürzl, no. 67. Salzburg: Universität Salzburg, 1977.

Discusses the nature and extent of Maturin's reliance on German sources for his presentation of Melmoth as part Faust, part Mephistopheles, and part Wandering Jew. According to Conger, "no Gothic novelist before Maturin had ever attempted such a portrait of villainy; and it was German legendary figures which helped him to do so successfully."

Dansky, Richard. "The Wanderer and the Scribbler: Maturin, Scott, and *Melmoth the Wanderer*." *Studies in Weird Fiction* 21 (summer 1997): 10-16.

Investigates the possible influence of Maturin's correspondence, particularly with Sir Walter Scott, as well as Maturin's financial arrangements with his publisher, on the composition of Melmoth the Wanderer.

Dawson, Leven M. "*Melmoth the Wanderer*: Paradox and the Gothic Novel." *SEL: Studies in English Literature, 1500-1900* 8, no. 4 (autumn 1968): 621-32.

Asserts that the paradoxical enjoyment of fear and the eroticism of terror are fundamental elements of the Gothic novel and that Melmoth the Wanderer *is the most characteristic example of the use of paradox in Gothic fiction. Dawson demonstrates how the Gothic novelists' exploitation of paradox foreshadowed the Romantics' efforts to unify experience by a resolution of opposites and disparities.*

Grant, Douglas. Introduction to *Melmoth the Wanderer: A Tale*, by Charles Robert Maturin. Edited by Douglas Grant. London and New York: Oxford University Press, 1968, 560 p.

Surveys the impact of Melmoth the Wanderer *and assesses Maturin's literary talent.*

Hennelly, Jr., Mark M. "*Melmoth the Wanderer* and Gothic Existentialism." *SEL: Studies in English Literature, 1500-1900* 21, no. 4 (autumn 1981): 665-79.

Analyzes Melmoth the Wanderer's *"preoccupation with five particular but overlapping existential themes: absurdity, isolation, failure of communication, loss of freedom, and the lack of responsible commitment."*

Howells, Coral Ann. "C. R. Maturin, *Melmoth the Wanderer*." In *Love, Mystery, and Misery: Feeling in Gothic Fiction*, pp. 131-58. London and Atlantic Highlands, N.J.: The Athlone Press, 1978.

Argues that the impact of Melmoth the Wanderer *derives from Maturin's examination of human responses to terror and oppression. According to Howells, Maturin transforms suffering "into a literary aesthetic, so that in his hands it becomes nothing less than the raw material for psychological enquiry." She also maintains that* Melmoth the Wanderer *must be read as Maturin's commentary on the paradoxical nature of the human condition, in which the individual is both victim and tormentor.*

Idman, Niilo. *Charles Robert Maturin, His Life and Works*. London: Constable & Co., Ltd., 1923, 326 p.

Book-length study of Maturin that focuses on the Romantic aspects of his works.

Kiely, Robert. "*Melmoth the Wanderer*: Charles Robert Maturin." In *The Romantic Novel in England*, pp. 189-207. Cambridge, Mass.: Harvard University Press, 1972.

Distinguishes Melmoth the Wanderer *from earlier Gothic novels because of its depiction of the repressive practices of the Roman Catholic church and authoritarian political systems, and views the novel as important primarily for its explorations into "the dark side of the human mind." Maintains that the separate tales in* Melmoth the Wanderer *are united by the theme of human misery and that Maturin's examination of the effects of pain on the human personality "illustrates a whole phase of romantic psychology and the creative process."*

Kramer, Dale. *Charles Robert Maturin*. New York: Twayne Publishers, 1973, 166 p.

Comprehensive study of Maturin's life and works.

Null, Jack. "Structure and Theme in *Melmoth the Wanderer*." *Papers on Language and Literature* 13 (1977): 136-47.

Argues that Melmoth the Wanderer *derives its psychological intensity from its complex structure, contending that the novel's fragmented structure reflects "organically the disorientation caused by the characters' loss of values."*

Piper, H. W. and A. Norman Jeffares. "Maturin the Innovator." *The Huntington Library Quarterly* 21, no. 3 (May 1958): 261-84.

Maintains that Maturin's reputation as a Gothic novelist has overshadowed his importance as a proponent of Irish regional literature. Piper and Jeffares contend that Maturin's novels are explorations of Irish culture in which he combined Irish nationalism with Wordsworthian

Romanticism to contrast English and Irish culture as well as "natural" and cosmopolitan character.

Roberts, Marie. "Maturin and the Rosicrucian Heresy." In *Gothic Immortals: The Fiction of the Brotherhood of the Rosy Cross*, pp. 121-55. London and New York: Routledge, 1990.

Declares that "[w]ith its echoes of Faust and the Wandering Jew, Melmoth *advances the Rosicrucian novel into the realms of theological controversy."*

OTHER SOURCES FROM GALE:

Additional coverage of Maturin's life and career is contained in the following sources published by Thomson Gale: *British Writers Supplement*, Vol. 8; *Dictionary of Literary Biography*, Vol. 178; *Literary Movements for Students*, Vol. 1; *Literature Resource Center*; *Nineteenth-Century Literature Criticism*, Vol. 6; *Reference Guide to English Literature*, Ed. 2; *St. James Guide to Horror, Ghost & Gothic Writers*; and *Supernatural Fiction Writers*.

HERMAN MELVILLE

(1819 - 1891)

American novelist, short story writer, and poet.

Melville, a major American literary figure of the nineteenth century, is best known as the author of *Moby-Dick; or, The Whale* (1851), a complex metaphysical novel that is considered a classic of world literature. Virtually unrecognized at the time of his death, Melville is now praised for his rich, rhythmical prose and complex symbolism. A master of both realistic and allegorical narrative, Melville was also an incisive social critic and philosopher who sought to understand the ambiguities of life and to define the individual's relation to society and the universe. Though Melville is not ordinarily categorized as a Gothic writer, his relationship to this literary tradition has nevertheless been identified by numerous contemporary scholars who point to the frequent adapted use of Gothic conventions in his works. Principally, critics have noted Melville's exploitation of isolated shipboard settings for the purposes of evoking psychological terror, his use of naïve narrators who witness mysterious, unexplainable events and relate the exploits of menacing antiheroes, and his literary depiction of a cosmic struggle of Manichean polarities in an ambiguous world devoid of the sense that good will ultimately triumph and vanquish evil. For modern critics, all of these devices are pivotal to *Moby-Dick*, while elements therein have also been studied in conjunction with his shorter works of prose fiction.

BIOGRAPHICAL INFORMATION

Born in New York City, Melville enjoyed a relatively comfortable childhood until his father's business failure and early death. Melville ended his formal education at age twelve to help support his family. He worked in the family fur business and as a bank clerk and taught at various schools until, in 1839, he sailed as a cabin boy aboard a merchant ship bound for Liverpool, England. This experience, shocking in its revelation of squalor and human cruelty, subsequently inspired his fourth novel, *Redburn: His First Voyage* (1849). Melville's later journey to the South Seas, begun aboard the whaling ship *Acushnet*, provided the background for his most highly regarded works. Finding conditions unbearable aboard the *Acushnet*, Melville deserted the ship in the Marquesas and spent several months in captivity among a tribe of cannibalistic Polynesians. He finally escaped aboard a passing whaling vessel. Again appalled by the conditions at sea, Melville joined in a mutiny and was briefly imprisoned in Tahiti. He then moved on to Hawaii and later returned to New York aboard a U.S. naval vessel. Melville had never contemplated a literary career, but with no prospects for a career on his return to the U.S., he was encouraged by family and friends to write about his remarkable journeys. His first novels, *Typee: A Peep at Polynesian Life* (1846) and its sequel, *Omoo: A Narrative of Adventures in the South Seas* (1847), are fictionalized versions of his experiences in the Pacific. Generally praised for their excitement, romance, and splendid descriptions of the South Seas region, these novels were immediately successful and made Melville famous as the "man who lived among the cannibals"—a reputation he was never able to overcome and that interfered with the appreciation of his later works. Melville's mature literary voice began to emerge in *Mardi: And a Voyage Thither* (1849). At the time he wrote this work he was growing restless with the adventure narrative and was increasingly drawn to philosophical and metaphysical questions in his novels. *Mardi* represents an important step in Melville's artistic development, yet its publication marked the beginning of the decline in his popularity. Discouraged by the novel's poor reception and in need of money, Melville temporarily returned to the travel narrative and produced *Redburn* and *White-Jacket; or, The World in a Man-of-War* (1850). Melville wrote *Moby-Dick* between 1850 and 1851. An early chapter of the novel appeared in the October 1, 1851 issue of *Harper's New Monthly Magazine* while the complete novel was published in London and New York in the ensuing weeks. Critics and the reading public on both sides of the Atlantic took little notice of the work. Emotionally exhausted following the publication of *Moby-Dick* and desperate for recognition, Melville immediately began writing *Pierre; or, The Ambiguities* (1852), a pessimistic novel that is considered the most autobiographical of his works. His popularity, already damaged by the publication of *Moby-Dick*, was nearly destroyed by *Pierre*, which was poorly received by a reading public that preferred the entertainment of *Typee* and *Omoo*. Melville continued writing prose through the 1850s, despite the critical and popular failure of *Pierre* and *Moby-Dick*. He published numerous short stories in periodicals and collected six of his best in *The Piazza Tales* (1856). *Billy Budd,* his final novel, was left in manuscript at his death in 1891 and was not published until 1924.

MAJOR WORKS

Melville's mature works of fiction are considered complex pieces that illustrate their author's incisive exploration of philosophical themes, use of allegorical symbolism, and mastery of complex narrative technique. Although *Mardi* begins as an adventure story, it quickly becomes a combination of philosophical allegory and satire; as such, it anticipates both *Moby-Dick* and *Pierre* in its levels of meaning, concern with metaphysical problems, and use of a questing hero. Like *Mardi*, *Moby-Dick* was initially conceived as a realistic narrative about sea life; but it took on epic proportions as Melville progressed in its composition. In the novel, the narrator, Ishmael, recounts his ill-fated voyage as a hand on board the whaling ship *Pequod*. Outfitted with an eclectic crew including South Sea islanders, North American Indians, blacks, and New England salts, the whaler leaves Nantucket on Christmas Day, bound on a commercial hunt for whales. As the trip progresses, however, Ahab, the ship's captain, exerts his will over the crew and converts the voyage into a quest to destroy his personal nemesis, a celebrated white whale known as Moby Dick. Ahab had lost a leg to the whale in a previous encounter, and his search is further fueled by his monomaniacal conviction that Moby Dick visibly personifies all earthly malignity and evil. The story concludes with a turbulent three-day struggle between the white whale and the *Pequod*'s crew. The whale has been variously interpreted as God, evil, good, and as a symbol of the ambiguity of nature. Considered by many of Melville's contemporaries as a sentimental romance, *Pierre; or, The Ambiguities* treats such themes as illegitimacy, incest, and, as its subtitle suggests, ambiguity. Detailing the story of an idealist who consistently undermines his own good intentions and ultimately commits suicide, *Pierre* is a deeply psychological work that explores the recesses of the human mind, in particular repressed sexual urges, and examines how good can be transformed into evil in unpredictable ways. Melville's six-story compilation *The Piazza Tales* includes "Benito Cereno," which is generally considered his finest short story, as well as several noted tales, including "Bartleby the Scrivener," concerning an alienated Wall Street law copyist, and "The Bell-Tower," a moral parable on the sin of hubris set in Renaissance Italy. In "Benito Cereno" Melville relates an ironic narrative of slave mutiny at sea. Featuring a naïve narrator who stumbles upon the remnants of a violent rebellion but fails to recognize the horrors that have occurred, "Benito Cereno" offers a fascinating thematic study of human depravity and moral relativism. Other late works by Melville include two novels, *The Confidence-Man: His Masquerade* (1857), an allegorical satire on mid nineteenth-century American life, and *Billy Budd,* a heavily symbolic work featuring an unreliable narrator, which focuses on the execution of a young sailor accused of fomenting a mutiny aboard an English warship.

CRITICAL RECEPTION

At the time of his death, Melville was almost unknown as a writer, and his accomplishments were not properly recognized for over a generation. Nineteenth-century critics of *Pierre,* for instance, often expressed confusion over the novel's metaphysical questioning and found its theme of incest offensive. In the contemporary period, however, *Pierre* has been noted as a predecessor of the modern psychological novel. Indeed, a tremendous revival of interest in Melville's work began in the 1920s, following the publication of the biography *Herman Melville: Mariner and Mystic,* written by Raymond T. Weaver (see Further Reading), and constitutes a dramatic reversal nearly unprecedented in American literary history. By the middle of the twentieth century *Moby-Dick* was considered one of America's greatest novels and widely acclaimed as a work of genius. Critics generally agree that in this work Melville parlayed the story of a sea captain's vengeful search for a legendary whale into a narrative suffused with profound speculation concerning the nature and interrelationship of the individual, society, God, and the cosmos. The novel is also highly acclaimed as a distinctly American book. By resolutely grounding his speculations in American thought, language, and experience, Melville elevated *Moby-Dick* to the status of a national epic. Although Melville's contemporaries gave it little notice, *Moby-Dick* was studied more intensively in the twentieth century than any other American novel and is now considered one of the greatest novels of all time. Additionally, Melville's late work *Billy Budd* has been widely examined in an effort to determine Melville's final views on such issues as justice, morality, and religion. Viewed as one of his finest novels, *Billy Budd* has been consistently praised for its philosophical insight, multifaceted narrative technique, and complex use of symbol and allegory.

Melville's fiction, particularly *Moby-Dick,* has been the subject of innumerable interpretations, and the body of Melville criticism, already immense, continues to grow. Among the multitude of scholarly approaches to these works has been a recent appreciation of Gothic features in Melville's novels and short prose fiction. Newton Arvin has investigated the influence of the Gothic novel and Gothic literary tropes on Melville, highlighting affinities among the imagery, symbolism, and modes of characterization employed by Melville in his stories and similar devices used by writers such as Anne Radcliffe, Matthew Gregory Lewis, Horace Walpole, and Edgar Allan Poe. Nalini V. Shetty has argued that Melville's "Benito Cereno" reveals the author's substantial adaptation of Gothic fictional techniques, suggesting that Melville transferred some of the standard devices used to a evoke a mood of preternatural terror to the shipboard setting and mysterious, twisting plot of this noted story. Similarly, Steven T. Ryan has identified Gothic formulaic elements in "Bartleby, the Scrivener" by comparing Melville's tale with Poe's Gothic classic "The Fall of the House of Usher." Ryan observes that Melville uses a literal and commonsensical narrator together with a mysterious figure in this work to create a sense of enclosure and impending catastrophe without relying on the outward trappings of medieval gloom and decay ordinarily found in traditional Gothic narrative. Critics have also studied *Moby-Dick* as it is informed by Gothic themes, conventions, and characterizations. Tony Magistrale has viewed the novel's revenge-obsessed Captain Ahab as an embodiment of the demonic Gothic villain, while Benjamin F. Fisher IV has demonstrated Melville's use of the seagoing *Pequod* as a surrogate for the archetypal "haunted castle" setting of Gothic fiction. Other commentators have elucidated such Gothic motifs as isolation, insanity, and the pervasive presence of an unseen evil in Melville's *Moby-Dick* and his other works.

PRINCIPAL WORKS

Typee: A Peep at Polynesian Life. 2 vols. (novel) 1846

Omoo: A Narrative of Adventure in the South Seas (novel) 1847

Mardi: And a Voyage Thither. 2 vols. (novel) 1849

Redburn: His First Voyage (novel) 1849

White Jacket; or, The World in a Man-of-War (novel) 1850

Moby-Dick; or, The Whale (novel) 1851

Pierre; or, The Ambiguities (novel) 1852

Israel Potter: His Fifty Years of Exile (novel) 1855

The Piazza Tales (short stories) 1856

PRIMARY SOURCES

HERMAN MELVILLE (STORY DATE 1856)

SOURCE: Melville, Herman. "The Bell Tower." In *The Piazza Tales and Other Prose Pieces: 1839-1860*, by Herman Melville, pp. 174-87. Evanston and Chicago, Ill.: Northwestern University Press and The Newberry Library, 1987.

The following excerpt comprises the conclusion of the short story "The Bell Tower," first published in The Piazza Tales *in 1856.*

It was thought that on the day preceding the fatality, his visitors having left him, Bannadonna had unpacked the belfry image, adjusted it, and placed it in the retreat provided,—a sort of sentry-box in one corner of the belfry; in short, throughout the night, and for some part of the ensuing morning, he had been engaged in arranging every thing connected with the domino: the issuing from the sentry-box each sixty minutes; sliding along a grooved way, like a railway; advancing to the clock-bell, with uplifted manacles; striking it at one of the twelve junctions of the four-and-twenty hands: then wheeling, circling the bell, and retiring to its post, there to bide for another sixty minutes, when the same process was to be repeated; the bell, by a cunning mechanism, meantime turning on its vertical axis, so as to present, to the descending mace, the clasped hands of the next two figures, when it would strike two, three, and so on, to the end. The musical metal in this time-bell being so managed in the fusion, by some art perishing with its originator, that each of the clasps of the four-and-twenty hands should give forth its own peculiar resonance when parted.

But on the magic metal, the magic and metallic stranger never struck but that one stroke, drove but that one nail, severed but that one clasp, by which Bannadonna clung to his ambitious life.

For, after winding up the creature in the sentry-box, so that, for the present, skipping the intervening hours, it should not emerge till the hour of one, but should then infallibly emerge, and, after deftly oiling the grooves whereon it was to slide, it was surmised that the mechanician must then have hurried to the bell, to give his final touches to its sculpture. True artist, he here became absorbed; an absorption still further intensified, it may be, by his striving to abate that strange look of Una; which, though, before others, he had treated with such unconcern, might not, in secret, have been without its thorn.

And so, for the interval, he was oblivious of his creature; which, not oblivious of him, and true to its creation, and true to its heedful winding up, left its post precisely at the given moment; along its well-oiled route, slid noiselessly towards its mark; and aiming at the hand of Una, to ring one clangorous note, dully smote the intervening brain of Bannadonna, turned backwards to it; the manacled arms then instantly upspringing to their hovering poise. The falling body clogged the thing's return; so there it stood, still impending over Bannadonna, as if whispering some postmortem terror. The chisel lay dropped from the hand, but beside the hand; the oil-flask spilled across the iron track.

In his unhappy end, not unmindful of the rare genius of the mechanician, the republic decreed him a stately funeral. It was resolved that the great bell—the one whose casting had been jeopardized through the timidity of the ill-starred workman—should be rung upon the entrance of the bier into the cathedral. The most robust man of the country round was assigned the office of bell-ringer.

But as the pall-bearers entered the cathedral porch, nought but a broken and disastrous sound, like that of some lone Alpine land-slide, fell from the tower upon their ears. And then, all was hushed.

Glancing backwards, they saw the groined belfry crashed sideways in. It afterwards appeared that the powerful peasant who had the bell-rope in charge, wishing to test at once the full glory of the bell, had swayed down upon the rope with one concentrate jerk. The mass of quaking metal, too ponderous for its frame, and strangely feeble somewhere at its top, loosed from its fastening, tore sideways down, and tumbling in one sheer fall, three hundred feet to the soft sward below, buried itself inverted and half out of sight.

Upon its disinterment, the main fracture was found to have started from a small spot in the ear;

which, being scraped, revealed a defect, deceptively minute, in the casting; which defect must subsequently have been pasted over with some unknown compound.

The remolten metal soon reässumed its place in the tower's repaired superstructure. For one year the metallic choir of birds sang musically in its belfry-bough-work of sculptured blinds and traceries. But on the first anniversary of the tower's completion—at early dawn, before the concourse had surrounded it—an earthquake came; one loud crash was heard. The stone-pine, with all its bower of songsters, lay overthrown upon the plain.

So the blind slave obeyed its blinder lord; but, in obedience, slew him.

So the creator was killed by the creature. So the bell was too heavy for the tower. So that bell's main weakness was where man's blood had flawed it. And so pride went before the fall.[1]

Note

1. It was not deemed necessary to adhere to the peculiar notation of Italian time. Adherence to it would have impaired the familiar comprehension of the story. Kindred remarks might be offered touching an anachronism or two that occur.

GENERAL COMMENTARY

NEWTON ARVIN (ESSAY DATE MARCH 1949)

SOURCE: Arvin, Newton. "Melville and the Gothic Novel." *The New England Quarterly* 22, no. 1 (March 1949): 33-48.

In the following essay, Arvin delineates the various instances in which Melville's works are evocative of Gothic fiction by such authors as Ann Radcliffe, Horace Walpole, and E. T. A. Hoffmann.

I

There is a curious and rather unexpected passage in *Billy Budd* in which, alluding to Claggart's hatred of Billy, Melville remarks that the cause of this dark emotion was "in its very realism as much charged with that prime element of Radcliffean romance, *the mysterious,* as any that the ingenuity of the author of the *Mysteries of Udolpho* could devise."[1] *Billy Budd* and the *Mysteries of Udolpho!* Claggart and the melodramatic Montoni! Herman Melville and Mrs. Ann Radcliffe! Surely these are little better than laughable juxtapositions, and nothing could be idler or more pedantic than to look closely and seriously at the clue that Melville

ABOUT THE AUTHOR

JAY MACPHERSON ON MELVILLE'S "THE BELL TOWER" AND FRANKENSTEIN

Melville's "The Bell-Tower," 1855, an early moral fable about man and machine handled with Gothic suggestiveness is constructed out of a set of rather clearcut literary materials and takes in a number of interests that have proved durable since. Incidentally, it is the one piece of his fiction to remain in print during the next half-century.

Written somewhat under the influence of *Frankenstein,* which Melville bought in London ten years before, "The Bell-Tower" is perhaps the first story to show what *Frankenstein* is often wrongly supposed to show, namely the fate of a demonic creator destroyed by what he has created. Like *Frankenstein* it is a modern story in that no background scheme of divine judgment is necessary. The overreacher's crime is against man, not God. Like Frankenstein he fixes his sights on his intended achievement and fails to love his fellow, and he comes to his end through purely natural causes, though ones a little tidier than nature usually affords. This is the more striking because the main frame on which Melville builds his story is taken from the Bible, as is heavily emphasized by repeated reference.

SOURCE: MacPherson, Jay. "Waiting for Shiloh: Transgression and Fall in Melville's 'The Bell-Tower.'" In *Gothic Fictions: Prohibition/ Transgression,* edited by Kenneth W. Graham, pp. 245-58. New York: AMS Press, 1989.

dropped behind him in the passage I have just quoted. Such, at least, is bound to be one's first response to the suggestion that there is a certain strain of the Radcliffean, of the "Gothic," in Melville's own work—until, perhaps, one recalls how fond of Mrs. Radcliffe's books both Balzac and Stendhal were, and reflects that Melville would not be the first writer of great power to owe a certain debt to one of his small predecessors. The fact is, of course, that his mind was a very complex one; that he was tirelessly responsive to the imaginative currents of his age; and that he was indebted, as only writers of the first order can be, to a thousand books and authors who preceded him. In all that, the "influence" of the Gothic school is a slight and minor element; but every element in the sensibility of a writer like Melville has its interest and meaning for us.

There can be no doubt of his familiarity with the writers of the Tale of Terror school. He was probably familiar with them from an early date, no doubt from boyhood, though we have to guess at this. In any case, we know that Smollett's *Ferdinand Count Fathom,* with its one or two rather trumped-up scenes of what might be called premature Gothicism, was one of the books that, according to a passage in **Omoo,** oddly turned up in the possession of his amiable host Po-po, on the island of Moorea, and that he read with such delight.[2] Some years later, on his visit to England in 1849, Melville bought and brought home with him a quantity of books, among which were three or four of the favorite classics of the Gothic school: Horace Walpole's *Castle of Otranto,* Beckford's *Vathek,* Godwin's *Caleb Williams,* and Mrs. Shelley's *Frankenstein.*[3] How well Melville may have known the German writers of what is called the *Schauerroman* it is not easy to say, but in 1850 he is known to have borrowed from his friend Duyckinck the two volumes of Carlyle's *German Romance,* with its translations from such romantic and sometimes "Gothic" writers as Tieck and E. T. A. Hoffmann.[4] Still later, traveling in the Near East and finding himself followed about the bazaar in Constantinople by a suspicious-looking Greek, he remembered that "much of the fearful interest of Schiller's Ghost-Seer"—a once famous shuddertale—"hangs upon being followed in Venice by an Armenian."[5]

The singular passage in **Billy Budd** was not the only place where Melville alluded to the good Ann Radcliffe herself. There is another entry in the journal he kept of his trip to Palestine which is almost as noteworthy; he is speaking of the desolate, stricken landscape of the Holy Land, and remarks: "As the sight of haunted Haddon Hall suggested to Mrs Radcliffe her curdling romances, so I have little doubt, the diabolical landscape of Judea must have suggested to the Jewish prophets, their ghastly theology."[6] In some curious way, the imagery of Mrs. Radcliffe's books must have got itself intermingled with Melville's somber impressions of Palestine; an allusion to one of them occurs early in the first part of **Clarel,** the long metaphysical-descriptive poem he wrote on the basis of his travels in that country. He is describing the Church of the Holy Sepulchre in Jerusa-

lem. Those pilgrims, he says, who loiter near the sacred tomb at nightfall, and become aware of the lengthening shadows of the stone and the low mysterious sounds stealing from its vicinity,

> Shrink, much like Ludovico erst
> Within the haunted chamber . . .[7]

One wonders how many of **Clarel's** readers, in the seventies, would still have recognized in Ludovico the half-comic, half-heroic manservant at the Castle of Udolpho who assists the heroine, Emily St. Aubert, in escaping from that sinister pile, and who later, in the south of France, undertakes to spend the night in the haunted chambers of the Château-le-Blanc.

II

Of course there would have been a great deal in the Gothic writers to inspire risibility in Melville rather than serious emulation, and yet the fact is that there was also a strain of feeling and imagination in them, of romantic sensibility, of morbid fancy, even of "nerves," to which he was by no means unresponsive. There was, for example, that passion for "wild," "gloomy," and "sublime" landscapes which Mrs. Radcliffe and the others derived in part from the tradition of Baroque landscape-painting—from Salvator Rosa, especially, and from such painters as the poetic English landscapist, Richard Wilson—and which certainly contributed to form and educate Melville's manner of looking at the visible world.[8] Most readers of Mrs. Radcliffe will recall her habit of alluding to those painters; a narrow valley in the Pyrenees, for example, in *Udolpho,* characteristically strikes her as "such a scene as Salvator would have chosen . . . for his canvas."[9] In exactly the same manner, Melville, evoking in **Redburn** the spectacle of the dying sailor Jackson, brooding in the "infernal gloom" of his bunk, observes that he was a picture "worthy to be painted by the dark, moody hand of Salvator."[10]

His own landscapes are sometimes decidedly in the great Baroque tradition of Salvator Rosa—and of Ann Radcliffe. Even when it is a question of conjuring up a scene so far from Mrs. Radcliffe's romantic Pyrenees and Apennines as a wild ravine on the Marquesan island of Nukuhiva, the one in which Melville and Toby spend a wretched night before descending into the Valley of Typee, it seems as if Melville, on the spot, had gazed about him with eyes that had been trained in part by Mrs. Radcliffe:

> The sight that now greeted us was one that will ever be vividly impressed upon my mind. Five foaming streams, rushing through as many gorges,

and swelled and turbid by the recent rains, united together in one mad plunge of nearly eighty feet, and fell with wild uproar into a deep black pool scooped out of the gloomy-looking rocks that lay piled around, and thence in one collected body dashed down a narrow sloping channel which seemed to penetrate into the very bowels of the earth. Overhead, vast roots of trees hung down from the sides of the ravine, dripping with moisture, and trembling with the concussions produced by the fall. It was now sunset, and the feeble uncertain light that found its way into these caverns and woody depths heightened their strange appearance, and reminded us that in a short time we should find ourselves in utter darkness.[11]

In the particularly "painterly" quality of this piece of landscape-writing—in the dim uncertain lighting, the heavy shadows, the dark surface of the pool, the violence of the physical motions, and the rich accompaniment of awesome sounds—there is an inescapable reminiscence, in Polynesian terms, of some of Mrs. Radcliffe's fine, gloomy landscapes. Take, for example, that in which Emily St. Aubert finds herself when Montoni's banditti attempt to abduct her from the Castle of Udolpho:

> The sun had now been set some time; heavy clouds, whose lower skirts were tinged with sulphurous crimson, lingered in the west, and threw a reddish tint upon the pine forests, which sent forth a solemn sound as the breeze rolled over them. The hollow moan struck upon Emily's heart, and served to render more gloomy and terrific every object around her—the mountains, shaded in twilight—the gleaming torrent, hoarsely roaring—the black forests, and the deep glen, broken into rocky recesses, high overshadowed by cypress and sycamore, and winding into long obscurity.[12]

It is clear enough, from such a parallel, that Melville has insensibly transmuted the old Baroque or Gothic landscape into something genuinely his own, and the point would be equally clear if one turned to such passages as Pierre's dream of the ruinous and desolate scenery environing the Mount of Titans,[13] or the marvelous presentment, in the first sketch of "The Encantadas," of the blighted, nightmarish landscape of the Galápagos Islands.[14] It is, of course, Melville's own "painterly" powers that are really important in these passages, but it is impossible not to detect in them, nevertheless, the lingering vestiges of an older manner in fiction—the manner embodied in such scenes as that of the wild Adriatic seacoast in Mrs. Radcliffe's *The Italian*, or the frightful abysses into which the fiend dashes the guilty Am-

brosio in M. G. Lewis's *The Monk,* or the dreamlike horror of the bleak Arctic landscape in *Frankenstein.*

If we look in Melville's work for the great leading symbol of Gothic fiction, the Haunted Castle itself,[15] it is quite true that we shall not find it, at least not literally; there is of course, in Melville, no such grand and melancholy Gothic structure as that of Otranto or Udolpho or the Castle or R———sitten in Hoffmann's tale, *Das Majorat.* There is no House of Usher in his work nor even a House of the Seven Gables. Yet something of the poetic quality of the Haunted Castle—its strangeness, its antiquity, its dilapidation, its somber picturesqueness—may surely be felt, with all the differences, in Melville's description of the "Pequod" in **Moby Dick**, with its weather-stained hull, its venerable bows (which looked "bearded"), its spire-like masts, its worn and ancient decks, and its general grotesqueness and strangeness;[16] and perhaps one feels this quality still more strongly in Melville's drawing of the doomed Spanish vessel, the *San Dominick,* in **"Benito Cereno,"** suggesting as it does "a whitewashed monastery after a thunder-storm, seen perched upon some dun cliff among the Pyrenees."[17] One of Mrs. Radcliffe's beloved convents and monasteries comes immediately to mind, let us say the convent of San Stefano among the wild Abruzzi in *The Italian*; and certainly there is more than a touch of the Gothic in the *San Dominick*'s dilapidated tops, its castellated forecastle ("battered and mouldy" like "some ancient turret"), and the "faded grandeur" of its shield-like stern-piece, intricately carved with the arms of Castile and Leon.[18] And, of course, the emotional tone of **"Benito,"** its absorbing anxiety and half-pleasurable foreboding, is but a deeper and more serious version of Mrs. Radcliffe's "pleasing dread."[19]

Less interesting in every way is the image of the ruined tower, standing out like "the black mossed stump of some immeasurable pine," in the feeble Hawthornesque tale, **"The Bell-Tower"** (one of the **Piazza Tales**); yet this, too, is a dim echo of the towers, the turrets, the belfries in which the Gothic writers abound;[20] and when, in **Pierre,** the hero and his half-sister Isabel ensconce themselves in the city high up in the building that adjoins the Church of the Apostles, in chambers from which Pierre can gaze out at "the donjon form of the old gray tower" of the Church itself,[21] one is at any rate oddly reminded of the La Mottes and their protégée, the forlorn Adeline, in *The Romance of the Forest*, taking refuge amid the ruins of the Abbey of St. Clair, from the apartments of which they can contemplate the "almost demolished" eastern tower.[22] The tower is an obsessive symbol in Gothic fiction, but still more obsessive, and deeply characteristic, is the recurring, dreamlike symbolism of the subterranean—of ill-lighted, perplexing, labyrinthine corridors below ground, of obscure and gloomy vaults, of yawning dungeons; one finds it everywhere in Beckford, in Mrs. Radcliffe, in "Monk" Lewis; and such tales as "The Cask of Amontillado" and "The Pit and the Pendulum" suggest that this claustrophobic imagery had a quite special value for Poe. It is less characteristic in every way of Melville, but even in him there is a hint of it in the murky, stifling, vermin-infested forecastles of **Omoo**[23] and **Redburn;**[24] and for a moment or two, in the sketch called "**I and My Chimney,**" one finds oneself in the true underground realm of Mrs. Radcliffe and Poe. Very often, says the narrator of that sketch, he goes down into his cellar to survey the vast square base of his enormous chimney: "It has a druidical look, away down in the umbrageous cellar there, whose numerous vaulted passages, and far glens of gloom, resemble the dark, damp depths of primeval woods."[25] In Melville, as in Hoffmann and Poe, the Unconscious is powerfully symbolized in this imagery of the subterranean.

If not the Superconscious, then certainly the Inexpressible bodies itself forth for many of the romantics, and certainly for some of the Gothic writers, in the imagery of music and the musical instrument. One may well question whether Melville was so spontaneously sensitive to musical form as he certainly was to color, to line, and to the plastic in general. Yet he shared too fully the sensibility of romanticism not to be capable, at moments, of expressing himself almost in the vein of Novalis, of Hoffmann, of Shelley: "Now, music," he says in **Redburn,** "is a holy thing, and its instruments, however humble, are to be loved and revered. . . . Musical instruments should be like the silver tongs with which the high priests tended the Jewish altars—never to be touched by a hand profane."[26] Certainly musical instruments had been favorite emblems for Mrs. Radcliffe and her followers; stringed instruments especially, but wood-winds too and horns; and no cachet of the school is more individualizing than the *"picturesque* sounds,"[27] as Mrs. Radcliffe rather finely calls them, which her heroines so love to draw forth from some romantic instrument. Emily St. Aubert, in *Udolpho,* is representative, and Emily's pleasantest hours, we are told, were passed in a pavilion

to which she frequently retired "with a book to overcome, or a lute to indulge her melancholy."[28]

Isabel, in **Pierre,** is a not very remote descendant of Mrs. Radcliffe's Emilys and Adelines and Ellenas, and not least in her passionate penchant for music, especially the music she knows how to draw forth preternaturally, even without touching its strings, from her beloved guitar. This remarkable instrument, she tells Pierre, she had bought with some of her little earnings from a peddler; later, to her astonishment, she had found the name Isabel lettered in gilt on its interior surface, and when she learned that the instrument had come from the Glendinning mansion, she was at once intuitively certain that it had belonged to her mysterious mother. It is, in short, one of the delicate links in the ambiguous chain of circumstances which convinces Pierre that Isabel is in very truth his half-sister. But the poetic use of the symbol is subtler and less tangible than its use in the plot; the mystical melodies which Isabel, in Pierre's fascinated presence, evokes from her guitar are suggestive of the strangeness, the preternaturalness, the ambiguity of the relations that are at the same moment springing up between Pierre and her. "All the wonders that are unimaginable and unspeakable," as she herself says, "all these wonders are translated in the mysterious melodiousness of the guitar."[29] Indeed, it is while she bends over the speaking instrument, her long dark hair falling over its strings and glowing with a mystic radiance from the "scintillations" of the melody, that Pierre is first aware of the spell which is being cast over him—that spell from which he knows it is impossible for him ever to break.[30] Gothic as Isabel's guitar undoubtedly is, it serves a darker and more painful purpose than any of Mrs. Radcliffe's genuinely charming lutes.

In any case, there appears in this same novel a remarkable example of still another favorite Gothic device, the magic portrait. Paintings in general are highly characteristic symbols in romantic fiction—Balzac's *Chef-d'oeuvre inconnu* is a familiar example—and true to his romantic heritage Melville had already introduced two striking pictures in **Moby Dick,** the smoky and almost unintelligible painting hung up in the entry of the Spouter-Inn,[31] and the stormy seascape that hangs at the back of Father Mapple's pulpit in the Whaleman's Chapel.[32] The painting in **Pierre,** however, is not a landscape but a portrait, and it belongs in the line of all the mysterious, uncanny portraits that stem from the likeness of Prince Manfred's grandfather in *The Castle of Otranto*— the somber portrait which steps down out of its frame, at one juncture, and stalks gravely out of the room. Mrs. Radcliffe's portraits, mostly miniatures, are less preternatural than Walpole's, and Melville's imagination is more likely, here, to have been quickened by Hawthorne's various portraits—and perhaps also by the terribly strange portrait with the baleful eyes which, in Maturin's *Melmoth the Wanderer,* young John Melmoth burns to ashes at his dying uncle's injunction.[33]

The portrait in *Pierre,* as a matter of fact, is one of two pictures, two portraits of Pierre's deceased father, the elder Glendinning, one of which Pierre's mother approves of and allows to hang prominently in her drawing room; the other, however, she intensely dislikes and taboos, insisting that Pierre hang it safely out of her sight in a small closet that adjoins his bedroom. This latter picture represents Pierre's adored father as a carefree, irresponsible youth, seated negligently in an old-fashioned Malacca chair; and Pierre is much given to sitting before it and communing with it, for he at least imagines that it speaks to him and smiles at him in its suggestive, ambiguous way. He had learned, as a younger boy, of the circumstances under which it had been painted, and now, after the real action begins, his recollection of them sickeningly confirms the suspicions of his father's rectitude which Isabel's tale has implanted in his heart. From being the object of a kind of idolatry—a literal "father image," indeed—the portrait has turned to an object of loathing to Pierre, an emblem of the moral ambiguities that flicker and leer about him; and before he sets off for the city with Isabel, he destroys the chair-portrait by burning it. As he does so, and it writhes blackly in the flames, it stares at him tormentedly "in beseeching horror," quite as if it were a living thing.[34] It is perhaps not meaningless, psychologically, that both Pierre and Melville should so much have disliked to have their portraits painted or their pictures taken.[35]

III

Pierre, in any case, like some of Melville's other books, owes more than its symbols to his Gothic forerunners. The novel, from this somewhat pedantic point of view, represents an intertwining of three strands in Melville's literary heritage: Elizabethan tragedy, sentimentalism, and the Radcliffean novel that has so much in common with sentimentalism and that also expressed, in its own time, a kind of displaced Elizabethanism. The incest motive in *Pierre,* for example, might certainly have come to Melville from Webster or Ford, but it is still more reminiscent of the

sentimental, the Gothic, or in general the romantic school. In *White-Jacket,* Melville himself alludes to Walpole's incestuous tragedy, *The Mysterious Mother,* along with *Oedipus Tyrannus* and *The Cenci;*[36] and he may well have recalled how Mrs. Radcliffe had dallied with the theme in *The Romance of the Forest,* only to slip away from it unsullied, and how the less fastidious, or less timorous, Lewis had embraced it without coyness, restraint, or apology in *The Monk.* Needless to say, the fact that Melville turned to the theme of incest in *Pierre* has a far deeper meaning than any study of literary *Einflüsse* could possibly suggest; one speaks of these connections only for what they are, no more; and Melville—who, incredibly enough, seems actually to have fancied that *Pierre* was "calculated for popularity"[37]—may have thought that his novel would succeed as *The Monk* had done sixty years earlier, and partly for similar reasons.

At all events, Pierre's half-sister, the dark and doubtful Isabel, is a perfectly legitimate descendant, if not of Pierre's father, then certainly, as I have said, of a long line of betrayed and persecuted heroines or even heroes in Gothic fiction, from Walpole's Isabella in *The Castle of Otranto* (whose name is so close to her own), or Mrs. Radcliffe's Ellena, or M. G. Lewis's Antonia, to Charles Brockden Brown's Constantia Dudley. It is not only Isabel's dark beauty that links her with many of these, or her mysterious origins, but much more the fact that she is both innocent and victimized. The persecution of the helpless and the blameless, with its undertones of "romantic agony," of the fearfully attractive pair, sadism-masochism, is only too notoriously a pervasive theme in romantic literature generally, and full of meaning as it clearly was for Melville himself, there is nothing surprising in its appearing so continuously in his own work. It appears there essentially because the basis for it had been present in his own life and experience, and it would be pure pedantry to allege that there is anything peculiarly Gothic in the figure of the buffeted and put-upon Redburn or in that of White-Jacket, close as this latter allegedly comes to being flogged at the mast. Caleb Williams could have furnished a literary model for these unhappy youths, but it was not at all necessary that he should. Redburn and White-Jacket suffer from the commonplace and unromantic brutality of the everyday world; elsewhere in Melville there are victims of a more specifically romantic sort. Yillah, in *Mardi,* with her unearthly beauty and her mysterious provenance, is one of them; surely she is a sort of Polynesian and allegorical Ellena. Surely, too, the pathetic Benito Cereno, the so untragic Spanish sea-captain—with his morbid sensitiveness, his nervous anxieties, and his fainting spells—is a masculine and sea-going Isabella. And surely the innocent and ingenuous Billy Budd, victimized by the unreasoning hatred of Claggart, can count among his ancestors the handsome young Vivaldi in *The Italian,* who is so mercilessly hounded by his mother and his mother's confederate Schedoni, and perhaps also the upright and high-minded Caleb Williams, in his time too the object of so black and baseless a malignity.

It is not only Melville's victims who put us in mind, at least a little, of his Gothic predecessors; so too do the monsters who persecute them. Again it is true that Melville derived from experience itself his intense, appalled awareness of the evil in the heart of man, and of its baffling union, now and then, with a certain largeness and even heroism. But it is the most original, not the most imitative, writers who owe the deepest debt to their literary forerunners; and Melville cannot have been unaffected by the romantic writers, including the Gothic, in whose work he found so many embodiments of the type that is known as the Majestic Monster; the type that Schiller called the *Ungeheuer mit Majestät.*[38] Wickedness to the point of deviltry, associated nevertheless with a satanic grandeur and loftiness—the splendid ambiguity, indeed, that the romantics loved to see in Milton's Satan—had a deep and first-hand significance for Melville; he was disposed by native temper, as well perhaps as by chapters in his experience, to be impressed by such devilish but still somehow noble characters as Manfred in *Otranto,* or Schedoni in *The Italian,* or Ambrosio in *The Monk*—precursors as these were of Byron's Manfred, of Shelley's Count Cenci, of Balzac's Vautrin, and other personages in the work of far greater writers than Walpole or Mrs. Radcliffe.

It was certainly somewhere in the real world, if not on his Liverpool voyage,[39] that Melville encountered the misanthropic sailor, Jackson, with his eye of a starved tiger and his ferocious nihilism; but when we are told that "he was a Cain afloat; branded on his yellow brow with some inscrutable curse,"[40] we realize that an impression out of life itself has joined hands, and in a creative manner, with a literary inheritance. There is a touch of Schedoni in Jackson, as there is a touch of him in the wily, ingratiating, diabolical, yet somehow grandiose Negro slave, Babo, in "Benito," to whose masterfulness we cannot refuse a reluctant admiration; and combined in

very different proportions, elements of the same sort are discernible in the splendid figure of Paul Jones, in *Israel Potter,* "intrepid, unprincipled, reckless, predatory, with boundless ambition, civilized in externals but a savage at heart."[41] Nor have we left the tradition of the Majestic Monster wholly behind us when we arrive, late in Melville's career, at the baleful figure of Claggart, master-at-arms on the *Indomitable,* who wreaks so purposelessly the destruction of Billy Budd. Indeed, it is in the central passage which concerns Claggart that one comes upon the allusion with which this essay began, and the collocation seems not without meaning. At any rate, if there is no doubt of Claggart's monstrous wickedness, his "natural depravity," or the purity (so to say) of his malignity, neither is there any doubt of his not being a merely small and sordid villain. On the contrary, Claggart is physically tall, spare, and handsome, with a brow that hints of more than average intellect; a man of "superior capacity," who indeed is "dominated by intellectuality" and wholly free from "vices or small sins."[42] He is such a hero of pure evil as only a profoundly romantic imagination could envisage.

Profoundly romantic, in one of the largest senses of the word, Melville's imagination in fact was; and to say so is to say, especially for an English or American writer, that the Gothic or Radcliffean was almost certain to be a minor ingredient in its complex totality. Brockden Brown, our earliest novelist of any true genius, was a Gothic writer in the strictest sense, and the work of Poe and Hawthorne, of course, abounds in Gothic feeling and Gothic detail. This is far less true of Melville, for many reasons, one of which is simply that he was enough younger than any of them to have passed beyond the immediate reach of the Gothic magnetism. I need hardly add that the center of his mind, in any case, lay elsewhere, or that the effect upon him even of a minor master, such as Mrs. Radcliffe certainly was, could never have been a vital one. What is striking, indeed, is that that influence lingered so long as it did in this country, and that it preserved enough of its vitality to impart even the most delicate tincture to an imagination like Melville's. When one looks at his work with some of his own hints in mind, one observes that it did just that.

Notes

1. *Works* (London, 1922-1924), XIII, 43.

2. *Works,* II, 347.

3. Willard Thorp, editor, *Herman Melville: Representative Selections* (New York, 1938), xxviii, note. Mr. Merton M. Sealts, who is preparing a list of the books in Melville's personal library, tells me that there is no evidence of his having owned any of Mrs. Radcliffe's works. Only the first installment of Mr. Sealts' article, "Melville's Reading: A Check-List of Books Owned and Borrowed," has hitherto appeared in the *Harvard Library Bulletin*, II (Spring, 1948), 141-163.

4. *Herman Melville: Representative Selections*, xxviii, note. The volumes that Melville borrowed were probably the two volumes of Carlyle's *German Romance: Specimens of Its Chief Authors* (Boston, 1841).

5. Herman Melville, *Journal up the Straits . . .* (New York, 1935), 32. In *Der Geisterseher* the principal character, the Prince von———, visiting Venice incognito, is accosted at night in St. Mark's Square by a masked Armenian, who later appears in other guises and is in fact the Wandering Jew.

6. Melville, *Journal up the Straits*, 88.

7. *Works*, XIV, 18. There are even one or two other references to Mrs. Radcliffe elsewhere. See *Works*, XIII, 318 ("The Apple-Tree Table") and Merrell R. Davis, "Melville's Midwestern Lecture Tour, 1859," *Philological Quarterly*, XX (Jan., 1941), 51.

8. There is an interesting account of these artistic influences on Mrs. Radcliffe in Elizabeth Stockton Ullery, *Mrs. Ann Radcliffe as a Pioneer in the Use of Description in Fiction* (Northampton, 1933), an unpublished master's thesis in the Smith College Library.

9. Ann Radcliffe, *The Mysteries of Udolpho* (London, 1931), I, 30.

10. *Works*, V, 355.

11. *Works*, I, 59.

12. Ann Radcliffe, *The Mysteries of Udolpho*, II, 76.

13. *Works*, IX, 476-482.

14. *Works*, X, 181-187.

15. Interestingly treated in Eino Railo, *The Haunted Castle: A Study of the Elements of English Romanticism* (London, 1927).

16. *Works*, VII, 85-87.

17. *Works*, X, 68.

18. *Works*, X, 69-70.

19. Ann Radcliffe, *The Romance of the Forest* (London, 1904), 23.

20. *Works*, X, 253. Mediocre as it is, "The Bell-Tower" has a certain interest because of the "experimental automaton" which Melville introduces into it, and which recalls not only *Frankenstein* but such tales of Hoffmann as *Der Sandmann* and *Die Automate*.

21. *Works*, IX, 377.

22. Ann Radcliffe, *The Romance of the Forest*, 20. Towers occur several times in *Clarel*; the tower on Mount Olivet (Part I, XXXVI, "The Tower") and the "towers twain" on Mar Saba (Part III, XXI, "In Confidence") may be instanced. Nor should one forget, in *Moby Dick* (Chap. XCIX), the emblematic tower engraved on the doubloon that Ahab nails to the mainmast.

23. *Works*, II, 8, 46-49.

24. *Works*, V, 109-110.

25. *Works*, XIII, 283. There is an interesting discussion of the symbolism in this sketch in Merton M. Sealts, "Herman Melville's 'I and My Chimney,'" *American Literature*, XIII (June, 1941), 142-154.

26. *Works*, V, 321.

27. Ann Radcliffe, *The Mysteries of Udolpho*, I, 75.

28. *The Mysteries of Udolpho*, I, 126.

29. *Works*, IX, 177.

30. *Works*, IX, 211-214.

31. *Works*, VII, 13-14.

32. *Works*, VII, 48.

33. Charles Robert Maturin, *Melmoth the Wanderer* (London, 1892), I, 93-95.

34. *Works*, IX, 98-119, 273-277.

35. *Works*, IX, 352-357. See also a letter to Duyckinck in Meade Minnigerode, *Some Personal Letters of Herman Melville . . .* (New York, 1922), 72-73.

36. *Works*, VI, 474.

37. A phrase used by Melville in a letter to the English publisher, Bentley. See Harrison Hayford, "The Significance of Melville's 'Agatha' Letters," *English Literary History*, XII (Dec., 1946), 306.

38. Schiller used this phrase in the so-called *Unterdrückte Vorrede* to *Die Räuber*.

39. According to William H. Gilman, "Melville's Liverpool Trip," *Modern Language Notes*, LXI (Dec., 1946), 543-547, there was actually a sailor named Jackson on the *St. Lawrence*, the ship on which, in 1839, Melville signed up as a "boy" and made the trip to Liverpool, but the dramatic death of Jackson must have been pure invention, since (as Mr. Gilman has shown in his unpublished doctoral dissertation, "Melville's Early Life and *Redburn*," Yale, 1947) the whole crew of the *St. Lawrence* returned to New York alive and unscathed; and Jackson the imaginative creation may well have owed something to characters Melville had encountered elsewhere.

40. *Works*, V, 134.

41. *Works*, XI, 158. The adjectives quoted are used literally of the United States as a nation, but they are used in metaphorical relation to Paul Jones, whom they also characterize.

42. *Works*, XIII, 31-35, 43-47.

TITLE COMMENTARY

"Benito Cereno"

NALINI V. SHETTY (ESSAY DATE 1976)

SOURCE: Shetty, Nalini V. "Melville's Use of the Gothic Tradition." In *Studies in American Literature: Essays in Honour of William Mulder,* edited by Jagdish Chander and Narindar S. Pradhan, pp. 144-53. Delhi, India: Oxford University Press, 1976.

In the following essay, Shetty "define[s] Melville's use of the Gothic technique . . . in 'Benito Cereno,' and define[s] his extension of the Gothic form."

Literature abounds in images of the restless ghost who yearns for the burial of his corpse, the Wandering Jew who can find no place to rest his weary head, the magic potion which will keep one forever young and forever beautiful. The supernatural has always persisted in legends and ballads handed down from one generation to another. This taste for the supernatural worked its way back into literature and became an important vogue in the early eighteenth century. In the field of Gothic Romance, the names of Mrs Radcliffe, Horace Walpole, and 'Monk' Lewis are formidable. They bequeathed a remarkable collection of 'Properties' to a host of imitators—Gothic castles, underground vaults, ill-fitting doors with rusty hinges, trap doors, easily extinguished lamps, old pictures, tapestry—objects trivial and insignificant but fraught with terrible possibilities. But among the blue-blooded aristocracy of Gothic writers, for example, even the despised Mrs Radcliffe had a tendency to explain the supernatural by natural causes. This device of introducing apparently supernatural occurrences which are ultimately traced to natural causes became a predominant feature of the Gothic Romance in its career in the New World.

Literary conventions shift with a change in beliefs and myths and a consequent shift in our view of ourselves. By the time the Gothic trappings of Britain had been transplanted across the Atlantic, a considerable change in man's view of himself and his relation to the universe necessitated a corresponding change in the technique of the Gothic Romance. From Charles Brockden Brown, through Hawthorne and Poe down to the present day, the mechanical horrors of the Baroque genre have been used, but with a difference. The ability to take the stock trappings of Romanticism and to endow them with the genuine horror of tortured nerves has been, according to Mat-

thiessen, a peculiarly American combination from Philip Freneau's remarkable poem 'The House of Night' through Ambrose Bierce and William Faulkner.[1]

The American Gothic then is not identical with its European progenitor, but has undergone a subtle transformation. For example, the medieval setting had to be inevitably dropped. The attempt to create the atmosphere of brooding and unknown terror, which the original Gothic Romances had created through the haunted castle and appurtenances, remained. The stress, as in all true Gothic Romances, became essentially subjective, and the Gothic writer became primarily an explorer of private worlds. The Gothic writer usually presents the world of the hero as a microcosm, so that the hero's charting of the disorder of his inner life becomes parallel to the restoring of order in his microcosm. Characters are shown grappling with their universe, trying to read meanings into matter, but in so doing their own preoccupations tend to distort the meaning. This distortion of reality becomes the grotesque. The old Gothic props of the Radcliffean era serve as images, as 'objective correlatives' of the distraught psyche. Thus the haunted castle can become a symbol of authoritarianism, reflections in mirrors can serve to show us the doubleness of human nature. In the hands of a true artist, therefore, the mechanical horrors of the Gothic novel can be transformed into something really felt, so that the horror can become one of tortured nerves. It can be used to explore that mysterious borderland between fantasy and reality.

The thesis I propose is that Herman Melville was himself by no means unresponsive to the Gothic genre, and that he incorporated many of its techniques to convey his vision and version of the world. William Van O'Connor's insight is clear:

> Herman Melville . . . possessed a profound sense of the human mind as the carrier of long forgotten terrors and violences and he inclined to be contemptuous of writers who had little or no sense of man's living in the presence of roaring Niagaras.[2]

Professor Newton Arvin has an excellent study of 'Melville and the Gothic Novel', in which he points out that the novelist was familiar with the older tales of terror, including Walpole's *Castle of Otranto,* Beckford's *Vathek,* and Godwin's *Caleb Williams*[3] and also traces the influence of these original sources on Melville. I will briefly try to define Melville's use of the Gothic technique—the elements of intensity, terror and mystery found in **'Benito Cereno'**, and define his extension of the Gothic form.

Some of the devices which are the stock-in-trade of the Gothic writer are: the use of wild landscape to evoke terror; sudden shock techniques like moving portraits, trapdoors springing open, etc.; the haunted castle with subterraneous vaults and passages. Melville found that he could use the same technique in his fiction.

In **'Benito Cereno'**, where the setting is on board a ship, there is none of the terror of landscape, but Melville uses the shock technique effectively. For example, the beak of the ship remains covered until Captain Delano leaves the stalled vessel and returns with his crew. During the final fight, the cable of the *San Dominick* is cut. The fag end of the cable, in lashing out, whips away the canvas shroud which covers the beak and suddenly there is revealed, above the chalked words 'Follow your leader', a human skeleton.

There are no haunted castles in Melville, nor houses suggestive of terror such as the House of Usher, but how like these isolated buildings seem some of Melville's ships. Notable among these is the *Pequod* with its bearded chin. In **'Benito Cereno'**, the *San Dominick* is described as 'battered and mouldy, the castellated forecastle seemed some ancient turret, long ago taken by assault and then left to decay'. Instead of the vaults and haunted corridors of medieval castles, we have the ship's holds in **Omoo** and **Redburn**. But no hero racing down a subterranean vault with a moaning ghost at his heels has had a worse experience than Amasa Delano's claustrophobic experience in 'the narrow corridor dim as a tunnel, leading from the cabin to the stairs' with 'the Spaniard behind—his creature before'. Either way, to the terror-ridden mind of the American it seemed that violent death awaited him.

Besides these specific uses of Gothic devices, the overall effect of the story is also in the Gothic tradition. The tale begins matter-of-factly and continues so until the *San Dominick* appears in the distance. But as it approaches, it shows no colours and seems to be in desperate trouble. Nature also seems to help in evoking a sense of terror and brooding:

> With no small interest, Captain Delano continued to watch her—a proceeding not much facilitated by the vapors partly mantling the hull, through which the far matin light from her cabin streamed equivocally enough; much like the sun—by this time hemisphered on the rim of the horizon, and, apparently, in company with the strange ship entering the harbor—which, wimpled by the same low, creeping clouds, showed not unlike a Lima *intriguante*'s one sinister eye peering across the Plaza from the Indian loop-hole of her dusk *saya-y-manta*.

Captain Delano's mystification increases as he approaches the vessel. He thinks he sees a strange shipload of monks peering over the bulwarks in their dark cowls. Through the open portholes he can perceive other dark moving figures like Black Friars pacing their cloister. Melville emphasizes the strangeness and unreality of the situation as it exists. The costumes from afar are unusual, the ship is described as dreamlike, a 'shadowy tableau just emerged from the deep, which directly must receive back what it gave'.

On board, the Gothic elements of the story continue. There is the terrifying contrast of the tumult on the lower decks and the staid figures of the four sphynxlike grizzled negroes, sitting facing each other. They watch the proceedings carefully, while, as they pick junk into oakum, they chant a low monotonous chant. They appear to Delano like 'so many grey headed bagpipers playing a funeral march'.

The figure who brings the whole bizarre situation to a focus is that of Don Benito. His looks are distracted and he jerks out his speeches like a 'somnambulist suddenly interfered with'. Nothing can be more grotesque than this Spaniard with 'a certain precision in his attire curiously at variance with the unsightly disorder around, especially in the belittered Ghetto, forward of the mainmast, wholly occupied by the blacks'. Melville conveys to us the horror of this figure by comparing him to an 'invalid courtier tottering about London streets in the time of the plague'.

A wandering mind ridden by terror is a device used by the Gothic writers to the point of dullness. The imagined is often more important than the real in the medieval castle. On board the *San Dominick*, the dull-nerved Captain Delano has his first twitch of apprehension when he has to walk between the two files of grim hatchet polishers:

> Gingerly enough stepped good Captain Delano between them, and in the instant of leaving them behind, like one running the gauntlet, he felt an apprehensive twitch in the calves of his legs.

From then on, the cymballing of the hatchet polishers becomes a chorus to his own mounting fears:

> . . . passing from one suspicious thing to another, his mind revolved the strange questions put to him concerning his ship. By a curious coincidence

as each point was recalled, the black wizards of Ashantee would strike up with their hatchets as in ominous comment on the white stranger's thoughts . . . he began to feel a ghostly dread of Don Benito.

We see how Melville makes the tension depend in many cases, on how the sinister situation on the Spanish ship slowly comes to penetrate the consciousness of the trusting and obtuse Yankee captain. The *San Dominick* is the sinister microcosm whose riddle the good captain has to solve. All terror depends on the reader's ability to perceive more than Delano does; even while not fully understanding the situation aboard the vessel, the reader feels more perceptive than the captain. The knife blow on the cabin boy's head, the old sailor's knot, the shaving incident—all the various episodes provide a new type of Gothic horror. While these incidents add to the Gothic effect, they serve as clues offered to the captain to resolve the mystery in order to restore the normal order. The knot is offered for untying; the shaving scene gives the impression of a headsman with his victim; and when finally the canvas shroud is ripped off the beak of the ship to reveal the skeleton, the mental clarity of Delano parallels the final physical unmasking of the hideous plot. The constant view of the skeleton during the final fight is clearly a Gothic device, but it is more than that. Upon the water the skeleton casts a gigantic ribbed shadow, and one extended arm seems to beckon the whites to avenge the terrible murder, and in Captain Delano's mind the pieces of the jigsaw puzzle fall into place.

What I have tried to suggest in the foregoing discussion is that while Melville made free use of Gothic devices and techniques in his fiction, what distinguishes him from the run-of-the mill Gothic writer is that he uses these devices not merely to titillate the reader, but subordinates them to the technical requirements of his story.

Again, any discussion of similarity in theme between Melville and the Gothic writers is difficult because most of the Gothic themes found regular recurrence in other types of Romantic fiction. However, taking the short story '**Benito Cereno**', I will try to analyse how Melville uses a typical Gothic situation to advance two themes which are of major importance in the Melville canon. I refer to the mystery on board the *San Dominick* and to the ignorant and innocent visitor Amasa Delano, who is not so much instrumental in resolving the mystery as he is merely physically present at the resolution of the mystery. This kind of contrast between complete innocence and

desperate evil was a situation particularly favoured by the Gothic writers as it best carried the reader into the terror of Gothic regions. In '**Benito Cereno**', Melville goes beyond his European counterpart in that he uses the situation of an innocent man faced with evil, to give added dimension to the problem of evil in the world.

Amasa Delano, the captain of the American ship *Bachelor's Delight,* has his fictional counterpart in Henry James' Christopher Newman: Newman is the innocent American who has to face the guile of the Bellegardes. In Melville's Delano we have an innocence which has never faced evil. Confronted with the situation on board the *San Dominick*, Delano is like an untrained mountaineer scaling slippery heights: he is unable to grasp the footholds of clues offered to him, to climb out of the confusion and mystery surrounding him. Having never experienced evil, his mind registers cliche reactions to the various scenes which he witnesses on board the *San Dominick*. In the negro Babo he sees only a faithful slave, solicitous of his master's comfort and he observes:

> There is something in the negro which, in a peculiar way, fits him for avocations about one's person. Most negroes are natural valets and hair dressers; . . . when to this is added docility arising from the unaspiring contentment of a limited mind . . . one readily perceives why those hypochondriacs Johnson and Byron . . . took to their hearts, almost to the exclusion of the entire white race, their serving men, the negroes, Barber and Fletcher.

Far from realizing that Babo is the arch-villain of the piece, Delano dismisses all blacks as being 'too stupid' to plot against the whites, who 'were the shrewder race'. He feels, also, that Don Benito could not be in complicity with the blacks in plotting against him, because, 'who ever heard of a white so far renegade as to apostatize from his very species almost, by leaguing in against it with negroes?' Not till the final fight does Delano realize what a 'hive of subtlety' Babo has been: that his is the master mind which has hatched the plot against the whites on board the *San Dominick*, and later against Delano and his crew also. With the untying of the physical 'knot', Delano is forced to face the fact of evil and cunning on board the *San Dominick*. However, it is clear that even after this experience, Delano's mind has not dwelt on the problem of evil in the world, and he cannot understand the depression which siezes the Spaniard.

> "You are saved" cried Captain Delano, more and more astonished and pained; "You are saved: what has cast such a shadow upon you?"

The plot has been foiled, the Spaniard is saved and Delano feels that 'the past is passed'. But Don Benito's memory does not let him forget the horror that he has witnessed. He cannot accept evil as being only *one* face of the coin of existence, and draw the strength to live from the other side of the coin: the presence of good in the world. He sees corruption and evil as the only facts of life.

However, it must be noted that Don Benito is never pictured to us as an innocent man being confronted with his first experience of evil. If we were to play at equations, I would suggest, New Man: Delano = Don Benito: Bellegardes. Don Benito is the child of an ancient civilization which has seen good and evil, as the decrepit *San Dominick* has once seen pageantry and pomp on its decks. The battered and ancient *San Dominick* is a version of Don Benito's world, offered to us as the objective correlative of the Spanish culture and milieu. But even Don Benito quails when he looks into this abyss of evil on board the *San Dominick*—and his mind breaks before its awesome terror. Don Benito's will to live is broken long before Delano blunders in to affect the 'rescue'. And so, Don Benito, 'gathering his mantle about him as if it were a pall', prepares for death. It is implicit in the story that neither Delano who has never experienced evil, nor even Don Benito, is the well-adjusted man, since the latter sees only evil and fails to understand that experience of good and of evil are part of the human condition. It is suggested that while experience of evil is necessary, the ideal man would have to go beyond this experience, and his vision would have to accommodate the presence of both good and evil in the world. This emphasis on the dual nature of reality, and the preoccupation with the psychology of evil, runs through Melville's writing.

This preoccupation must be considered primarily in the nature of a corrective to the doctrine of Innocence proposed by the High Priests of Transcendentalism. While Emerson and his friends insisted on Man's Innocence, Hawthorne and Melville sagely proposed that there was something more to human nature than just that. Melville's Delano is the Innocent American who is horrified to discover the existence of evil on board the *San Dominick*. Melville, forcing Delano to face the fact of evil, seems to gently poke fun at the received doctrine that man is innocent, and at what appears to him, a naive attitude towards men and matters.

The basic situation—the mystery on board the *San Dominick*—also serves to underline another theme to which Melville devotes much attention in his fiction: the discrepancy between appearance and reality. For example, Captain Delano's assessment of the situation on board the *San Dominick* changes often. From the initial acceptance at face value of the hard luck story given to him when he boards the Spanish ship, he goes on to suspect that Don Benito may be plotting against him; and then finally when he leaves the *San Dominick*, he is made to realize that it is the negroes who are in piratical revolt against the whites, and that Don Benito has been a captive in the hands of the negroes. Besides the central situation which gives the lie to reality, there are a number of scenes, incidents, etc. which mislead Delano, and hinder him from striking at the heart of the matter. For example, through a process of tortuous reasoning Delano comes to the conclusion that Atufal has not really rebelled but is a 'pretended rebel', and is the 'punctual shadow' of Don Benito in order to trap Delano. When the scales drop from his eyes, Delano realizes that Atufal is indeed a 'pretended rebel' and a 'punctual shadow', but he is there to keep an eye on Don Benito, and to prevent him from communicating his plight to Delano. Similarly, Delano does not detect the tigerish nature of the mulatto steward Francesco who ushers them to the dining table with smiles and bows. In actuality he had been 'in all things, the creature and tool of the negro Babo, [and] . . . proposed . . . poisoning a dish for the generous Captain Amasa Delano', Again, there are the negresses who preferred to torture to death instead of simply killing the Spaniards, who also wanted to kill Don Benito, and sang and danced while the various acts of murder took place on board the *San Dominick*. These women appear to Delano as 'unsophisticated as leopardesses; loving as doves'. So, in a variety of scenes, Melville who made Ahab declare that 'all visible objects are but as pasteboard masks' which we have to strike through to reach the underlying truth, emphasizes that what appears on the surface is not all.

Herman Melville was too young to receive the direct force of the European Gothic writers with the same strength as his older contemporaries. But extrovert America had produced Gothic writers: Brown, Hawthorne, Poe—explorers of their own private hells, which excluded the optimism of the Transcendentalists. From them Melville drew the best elements of the Gothic genre without the medieval trappings and hackneyed forms. His own personal experience led him to feel the powerful enmity and evil present in the world and the elusive nature of reality. Part of the novelist's attempt to present this terror-ridden and baffling universe is done by the frequent use of Gothic techniques and themes—the persecution of the innocent, the use of desolated ships, etc. In the short story 'Benito Cereno', Melville presents Captain Delano's wrestling with the dark enigma of the *San Dominick* in terms of a Gothic horror story, and we once more have a glimpse of Melville's Gothic heart—present so often but frequently not recognized by the reader.

Notes

1. F. O. Matthiessen, *American Renaissance* (New York, 1941), pp. 201-2.

2. William Van O'Connor, '*The Grotesque; An American Genre' and Other Essays* (Carbondale, Ill., 1962), pp. 25-6.

3. Newton Arvin, 'Melville and the Gothic Novel', NEQ Vol. xxii (1949), p. 34.

"Bartleby the Scrivener"

STEVEN T. RYAN (ESSAY DATE 1978)

SOURCE: Ryan, Steven T. "The Gothic Formula of 'Bartleby.'" *Arizona Quarterly* 34 (1978): 311-16.

In the following essay, Ryan reveals how, in "Bartleby the Scrivener," Melville infuses the traditional Gothic formula with realism while still retaining "the character conflict, atmosphere, plot progression, and even the language of the Gothic thriller."

The most striking aspect of Melville's "Bartleby" is the story's amazingly contemporary quality. The story of the scrivener in form and philosophy appears as an eerie foreshadowing of our modern fabulations which balance between a surface reality and an epistemological terror. An ironic explanation for "Bartleby"'s modern flavor is that beneath Melville's original story form are the underpinnings of an old Gothic formula which also underlies the stories of many contemporary writers, like Joyce Carol Oates, Jerzy Kosinski, John Hawkes, and John Gardner. And like these present writers, Melville transforms the violence of Gothic destruction to a deeper fear of a quiet equilibrium. Melville, like these contemporary writers, is influenced by the Gothic genre.[1] Rather than writing standard tales of terror, Melville submerges the conventional devices so that the haunted house, the disembodied spirits, and the catastrophic climax are replaced by more believable images and events, but the story maintains the character conflict, atmosphere, plot progression, and even the language of the Gothic thriller.

The Gothic formula that "Bartleby" follows is typified by Edgar Allan Poe in "The Fall of the House of Usher." The formula requires a narrator who is an unabashed literalist. The story achieves credibility through the wariness of the narrator and also a tension is achieved between the commonsensical vision of the narrator (man of light) and the second character (man of darkness) who has moved into the realm of mystery. In "The Fall of the House of Usher," the reader is eased into the terrifying realm of Roderick Usher by riding with the worldly narrator to the mansion and observing Roderick Usher with the narrator's objectivity. Thus we are manipulated into the world of mystery through our trust in the narrator and strive with decreasing effectiveness to interpret the action, along with the narrator, in terms of material cause and effect relationships, such as interpreting the house's thick ambience as electrical phenomena.

Similarly in "Bartleby," we are introduced to the action by the lawyer, who is the practical American with faith in the rational world. Melville goes a step further than Poe and plays with the narrator's American characteristics of moderation and materialism. Still the lawyer, with his bust of Cicero and walled-in imagination, serves as a useful guide into the unknown. Along with the narrator, we grope for cause-effect explanations for Bartleby's behavior. We try to understand Bartleby according to his poverty, his failing eyesight, and his dead-letter experience. But we move along with the narrator from an "eminently safe" world to a terrifying world of uncertainty.

The antithesis of the narrator is the character that lives in a world beyond commonsensical security. This is the man of darkness who pulls the narrator (and thus the reader) beneath the surface of experience. As the messenger of darkness, this second character is clearly doomed. Roderick Usher is a typical romantic version of the sensitive young man. With his "cadaverousness of complexion," he is refined to a frightening level of fragility. His senses are so keen that he can listen only to certain musical chords. This sensitivity has placed him beyond the social security of human fellowship. Thus in the material world, he is doomed, but he is also capable of entering the realm beneath the surface reality. In the tension between the narrator and Roderick Usher, Usher clearly represents the more powerful force because the narrator must confront a world of boundless, terrifying potential. The narrator can return to safety only by backing away from this fiery force while admitting his own limited existence.

Bartleby, like Roderick Usher, is introduced with a quality of refinement which places him beyond the practical realm of the narrator—"Pallidly neat, pitiably respectable, incurably forlorn!" Bartleby, like Usher, is doomed by his sensitivity. He is isolated within his transcending vision, cut off from human fellowship because he sees and feels what we cannot see and feel. His "pallid haughtiness" separates him from the lawyer's world. The lawyer's material explanations and material solutions can neither explain nor help Bartleby. It is Bartleby who must show the lawyer a boundless world. And like Poe's narrator, the lawyer cannot really "see" what Bartleby sees except for a fleeting moment, and then he must also retreat to save himself, so he can continue his humble half-life.

The important aspect of the Gothic setting is not the creaking doors or even the Gothic architecture, but rather the human construct that becomes a trap. In Poe's story, Roderick Usher knows that he cannot escape his decaying family mansion, which expresses his cultural dream transformed into nightmare. The personality of this "mansion of gloom" becomes as important as the human personalities for it is a monster of human creation. With its "vacant and eye-like windows," it expresses the power of an indifferent physical universe. The gray walls, shielding with a vapor which is "dull, sluggish, . . . and leaden-hued," emphasize the cold neutral weight of decay and death. Matter shaped by man remains matter and obeys the natural laws which demand an indifferent downward pull of matter. Thus the civilized dream to shape and control nature becomes the Gothic nightmare to civilized constructs that imprison and destroy the life they are designed to protect.

Again as an American version of the ancient Gothic trap, Melville offers an office on Wall Street. The narrator does not realize that he is trapped within a construct as ominous as the decaying Usher mansion, but Bartleby does realize the threat and also realizes that he cannot escape the construct. Melville uses the office on Wall Street to demonstrate the nightmare reality of the optimistic American assumption that our capitalistic system can create a utopia. Melville allows the narrator to describe a setting as clearly destructive to human life as any Gothic mansion, while the narrator assumes he is presenting an ideally utilitarian setting. At one end is "the white wall of the interior of a spacious sky-light shaft, penetrating the building from top to bottom." For contrast, the windows in the opposite direction "commanded an unobstructed view of a lofty brick wall, black by age and everlasting shade; which wall required no spy-glass to bring out its lurking beauties, but, for the benefit of all near-sighted spectators, was pushed up to within ten feet of my window panes." The gap between the walls is described as resembling "a huge square cistern."

The narrator may see the American dream blossoming, but Bartleby sees the destructive power of dream transformed to nightmare. Bartleby, like Usher, knows that he cannot escape the construct. Until taken to the Tombs (another human construct revealing decay and death), Bartleby never leaves the office. Staring through the window at the black wall ten feet away, Bartleby understands the threat that was also present in the "vacant and eye-like windows" of the House of Usher—the manipulated physical matter will take its vengeance on man. The narrator cannot understand Bartleby's "dead-wall revery." When the narrator asks Bartleby why he will not return to writing, Bartleby responds, "Do you not see the reason for yourself?" Rather than looking at the vision revealed in the black wall, the narrator looks to Bartleby's eyes for a simple causal solution. The reader understands that the wall offers a vision, that through the human construct the evil mystery is revealed.

The important variation between Melville's setting and a standard Gothic setting like Poe's is that Wall Street is not physically crumbling. This variation parallels the significant variation in plots, for Melville will not offer the standard climactic thrill of the mansion collapsing into the tarn. The passivity of Melville's setting and plot places him closer to the modern Gothic vision which presents a greater threat in the quiet leveling of life than in a chaotic breakdown of life. Therefore, the black wall becomes more threatening because it suggests an invincible force that will eternally confine life. Similarly, Bartleby's quiet retreat into a fetal ball is as threatening an image of human decay as Roderick Usher howling in mad hysteria. Melville follows the important Gothic requirement that destruction and death are the necessary climax of the story. But the destruction offers the modern version of a civilized process that suffocates life while the process gains momentum. The death of both Bartleby and Roderick Usher is required by the powerful force of decayed life in the stories. The loss of these sensitive young men expresses the domination of matter over spirit. Bartleby is presented in one of his final passive stages through a clearly Gothic image of spiritual ruin: "like the last column of some ruined temple, he remained standing mute and solitary in the middle of the otherwise deserted room."

An appreciation for the effect Bartleby's destruction has on the narrator can be enhanced by an understanding of the Gothic language as well as the Gothic development of character, setting, and plot. Certain language used within the Gothic tradition developed profound connotation. Two words that carried a particular emotional significance were "gloom" and "melancholy." The words carried a heavy charge within the entire romantic movement, but this charge was particularly important in establishing atmosphere and communicating a deep sense of discovery in Gothic fiction. In "The Fall of the House of Usher" Poe describes the "melancholy House of Usher" and the narrator attempts to "alleviate the melancholy" of Roderick Usher. Approaching the mansion, "a sense of insufferable gloom pervaded" the narrator's spirit and an "irredeemable gloom hung over and pervaded all." By the excessive use of "melancholy" and "gloom" within such an obvious Gothic tale, Poe demonstrates their importance in creating the mood of the story, but also, like many self-consciously Gothic writers, he desensitizes the reader to the key words. However, the importance of their verbal charge could be saved for climactic moments such as Hawthorne describing Goodman Brown's "dying hour" as "gloom." Similarly Melville saves the words for a moment of insight when Bartleby manages to break through the narrator's hard Yankee skull: "For the first time in my life a feeling of over-powering stinging melancholy seized me. Before I had never experienced aught but a not unpleasing sadness. The bond of a common humanity now drew me irresistibly to gloom. A fraternal melancholy! For both I and Bartleby were sons of Adam."

One need not know the importance of "melancholy" and "gloom" in the Gothic tradition to see that this is an important moment of discovery, just as one need not see the underpinnings of a standard Gothic use of character, setting, and plot to understand Melville's story. However, by recognizing that the words expressed an emotional and intellectual profundity for Melville and his contemporaries, we begin to realize that even when a literary masterpiece transcends the standard literary form of any historical period, it may yet draw heavily from all the immediate resources available to the writer. Like the Gothic writers, Melville was striving to reveal a fathomless darkness beneath our materialistic security; thus he naturally adapted a Gothic formula.

Note

1. Two critical works which have demonstrated Melville's relationship to the traditional Gothic novel are Newton Arvin, "Melville and the Gothic Novel," *New England Quarterly*, 22 (1949), 33-48, and Heinz Kosok, *Die Bedeutung der Gothic Novel für das Erzählwerk Herman Melvilles* (Hamburg: Cram, de Gruyter & Co., 1963). Biographically, Melville's association with Hawthorne and his profound respect for Hawthorne's short stories are clear indications of the direct influence of Gothic fiction during the early 1850s, when "Bartleby" was written. My dissertation, entitled "Chaotic Slumber" (1976), examines the use of Gothic techniques in contemporary fiction.

Moby-Dick

TONY MAGISTRALE (ESSAY DATE 1988)

SOURCE: Magistrale, Tony. "'More Demon than Man': Melville's Ahab as Gothic Villain." In *Spectrum of the Fantastic: Selected Essays from the Sixth International Conference on the Fantastic in the Arts,* edited by Donald Palumbo, pp. 81-86. Westport, Conn.: Greenwood, 1988.

In the following essay, Magistrale discusses Captain Ahab in Moby-Dick *as an example of a quintessential Gothic protagonist, possessing both human and demonic qualities.*

Gothic literature reached its apex in England during the last decade of the eighteenth century, when the enlightenment's neoclassic lights were replaced by the brooding darkness of haunted castles and the supernatural. Gothicism emerged from an era surfeited with reason and the prosaic, anxious for something wildly different and bizarre. A reaction to the spirit of scientific rationalism that characterized the rest of the century, the Gothic school sought a return to the ambience of the Middle Ages: a renewed fascination with the mystical and the inexplicable as well as an intensified interest in the battle between good and evil. The Gothic environment of crumbling castles with their perilous crags and subterranean dungeons, of mysterious forests and seas, sinister monks and nuns, deformed humans, and demonic villains, anticipates and buttresses the Romantic movement of the nineteenth century. William Beckford's *Vathek* (1786), Horace Walpole's *The Castle of Otranto* (1764), Ann Radcliffe's *The Mysteries of Udolpho* (1794), Matthew Lewis's *The Monk* (1795), and Charles Maturin's *Melmoth the Wanderer* (1820) represent the best Gothic fiction because they transcend the horror story's conventions to focus on the supernatural, on the psychic, and on humankind's most morbid psychological states.

MELVILLE

English and German Gothicism reached the American literary consciousness most significantly in the nineteenth century. By then, standard Gothic apparatus had been absorbed by the larger Romantic movement. Consequently, the American progeny of the Gothic school—Ambrose Bierce, Charles Brockden Brown, Edgar Allan Poe, Nathaniel Hawthorne, and Herman Melville—concentrated on "refining" the Gothic by focussing on the more subtle and philosophical implications of the "horror story." Furthermore, since America was short on castles and monasteries, the form was adapted to an American psychic landscape: Traditional Gothic bonds with evil, haunted castles, and the reliance on supernatural terror were exploited and transformed to tell a more complicated story that often focused on the tragic imperfections inherent in American culture in particular or humankind in general.

Melville's canon ubiquitously evinces Gothic influences. The reasons for Melville's interest in this literary genre are diverse and complicated, but his fascination is certainly attributable in part to his own literary background as well as to the literary atmosphere of his century. Hawthorne, Melville's friend and metaphysical cohort, uses the Gothic formula everywhere in his fiction. Hawthorne was influenced not only by Mrs. Radcliffe and her contemporaries, but also by Poe and Brockden Brown. That Hawthorne shared his interest with the younger Melville is apparent. Melville's own reading indicates yet another connection to the Gothic. He had read Shakespeare (particularly the tragedies), Milton, and Dante thoroughly; Melville's own unique sense of evil and villainy owes much to these earlier writers. And he had drunk deeply from the polluted wells of eighteenth-century Gothic literature. Merton Sealts reports that Melville had read Walpole's *Otranto*, Beckford's *Vathek*, and even Mary Shelley's *Frankenstein* (1817) in addition to a number of lesser known but related Gothic texts.[1] Finally, Gothicism is centrally concerned with fallen humanity, often embracing and flaunting its sinful state. The genre's characteristic fascination with evil, fixation on rebellion from God and optimistic virtues, and emphasis on disorder, chaos, and ambiguity resonated with some darkly sympathetic chord in Melville's haunted psyche. The Gothic supplied Melville with a congenial tradition, a vehicle that enabled and encouraged him to give dramatic life to conflicting and often darkly pessimistic philosophical positions.

Perhaps nowhere in the canon does Melville use standard Gothic apparatus more successfully

EXCERPT FROM AN EARLY REVIEW OF *MOBY-DICK*

In this story Melville is as fantastically poetical as Coleridge in the "Ancient Mariner," and yet, while we swim spellbound over the golden rhythms of Coleridge feeling at every stroke their beautiful improbability, everything in *Moby-Dick* might have happened. The woe-struck captain, his eerie monomania, the half-devils of the crew, the relentless pursuit of the ever-elusive vindictive white whale, the storms and calms that succeed each other like the ups and downs of a mighty hexameter, all the weird scenery of the pursuit in moonlight and in daylight, all are so wonderfully fresh in their treatment that they supersede all doubt and impress one as absolutely true to the life. Even the recondite information about whales and sea-fisheries sprinkled plentifully over the pages does not interfere seriously with the intended effect; they are the paraphernalia of the journey. The author's extraordinary vocabulary, its wonderful coinages and vivid turnings and twistings of worn-out words, are comparable only to Chapman's translations of Homer. The language fairly shrieks under the intensity of his treatment, and the reader is under an excitement which is hardly controllable. The only wonder is that Melville is so little known and so poorly appreciated.

SOURCE: A review of *Moby-Dick; or, The White Whale. The Critic* 19, no. 582 (15 April 1893): 232.

than in his creation of Ahab in **Moby-Dick**. Ahab, like Pierre and Lewis's Father Ambrosio, is exalted far above common mortals. His prideful gaze is withering and imperious, not unlike the stares of Vathek or Radcliffe's Montoni. Ahab is developed as an embodiment of the fallen angel/demi-god who in the Christian myth was variously named Lucifer, Devil, Adversary, and Satan. Ahab is not Satan himself but is a human creature who possesses Satan's evil pride and energy. The madman Elijah warns Ishmael and Queequeg to fear for their souls, that a voyage with Ahab and his "shadowy figures" is certain to involve evil and destruction.

> "Yes," said I [Ishmael], "we have just signed the articles."
>
> "Anything down there about your souls?"
>
> "About what?"
>
> "Oh, perhaps you hav'n't got any," he said quickly.
>
> "No matter though, I know many chaps that hav'n't got any . . . He's got enough though, to make up for all deficiencies of that sort in other chaps," abruptly said the stranger, placing a nervous emphasis on the word *he*.[2]

The Biblical significance of Ahab's name also supports the demonic image: Ahab was an evil king of Israel who had done more to provoke the Lord to anger than all the kings before him.

But there is another side of Melville's captain that is not entirely wicked. Like Walpole's Manfred or Lewis's Ambrosio, "Ahab has his humanities" (p. 120). He thinks often of his bride and daughter, and his care of the pathetic Pip is significant. Despite his profound bond with evil, Ahab possesses an undeniable streak of sensitivity and melancholia that is found also in, and links him with, a number of earlier Gothic "villains."

Like the Biblical King Ahab, Captain Ahab lives in an ivory house, "the ivory *Pequod*," as it is often called, which is tricked out with trophies of whale bones and teeth from profitable voyages. The *Pequod* also possesses kinship to the Gothic haunted house, and Ahab is the captain who is lord over it. Its likeness to a haunted house is suggested in nearly every description of the *Pequod*: its weather-stained hull, its venerable bows, its spirelike masts, its worn and ancient decks, and its general atmosphere of grotesqueness and sombre picturesqueness.[3] It has much in common with the houses of Usher, Udolpho, or Otranto. The only Gothic apparatus that is missing is an incarcerated maiden. While it is possible to see Ishmael in the role of the passive maiden, and Ahab as his jailor,[4] this does a severe disservice to the complex psychosexual relationship often maintained between the Gothic villain and his captive. Perhaps it is more accurate to view Ahab's monomaniacal quest for Moby-Dick as a substitution for the Gothic villain's erotic fascination with his captive woman. Ahab is obsessed with the whale just as the Gothic characters of Lewis, Walpole, and Radcliffe are obsessed with perverse images of womanhood, bondage, and violation. Like his sexually frustrated Gothic forerunners, Ambrosio and Manfred, who are motivated by a warped attraction to the dark and malignant elements of eroticism, Ahab's quest for Moby-Dick is as self-destructive as it is passionate.

The male villain in Gothic fiction is often associated with evil forces, most specifically the devil. Vathek makes a pact with Satan in order to experience as many sensations as mortal life will afford. Gothic fascination with evil also entails a pervasive element of blasphemy. Ambrosio, a Catholic monk in *The Monk*, at one point violates, on top of an altar, a woman masquerading as a nun. Ahab is an "ungodly, god-like" man who is spiritually outside Christendom and exhibits a well of blasphemy and defiance. He rejects and scorns the gods, "cricket-players and pugilists" (p. 134) in his eyes, and he once spat in the holy goblet on the altar of the Catholic Church at Santa (p. 134). In the course of the whale voyage—a journey that ironically commences on Christmas Day—Ahab engages in three major blasphemous rituals. Each is a parody of a religious rite that casts Ahab in the role of high celebrant and incorporates the use of a harpoon. In the first of these rituals, "The Quarter-Deck," Ahab pours grog into the inverted ends of hollow harpoon heads and commands the harpooners to drink from the "murderous chalices" with this oath: "God hunt us all, if we do not hunt Moby-Dick to his death" (p. 225). When Starbuck suggests that perhaps Ahab's quest is blasphemous, the captain answers in a tone reminiscent of Ambrosio's or Manfred's enraged pride: "Talk not to me of blasphemy, man; I'd strike the sun if it insulted me. For could the sun do that, then could I do the other; since there is ever a sort of fair play herein, jealousy presiding over all creations" (p. 221). The demonical nature of Ahab's quest is again suggested in "The Forge" when Ahab baptizes a scorching harpoon in the name of the devil.

Finally, in "The Candles" Ahab hoists his "consecrated" harpoon while delivering a defiant speech that asserts his unconquerable individuality in the face of nature: "Oh, thou clear spirit, of thy fire thou madest me, and like a true child of fire, I breathe it back to thee . . . Yet blindfold, yet will I talk to thee. Light though thou be, thou leaping out of light, leaping out of thee!" (p. 642). Like Manfred on his mountain, Ahab speaks directly to the flashing lightning, calling it his ancestor: "There burn the flames! Oh, thou magnanimous! now I do glory in my genealogy. But thou art but my fiery father; my sweet mother, I know not" (pp. 642-43). Here Melville employs standard Gothic effects—tremendous fire, blackness, storm, and battering seas—to represent through pathetic fallacy the scene's high emotion, conflicting beliefs, and clash of personalities. Once more Ahab establishes his link to the male-dominated world of the Gothic by calling the flames his father while denying any knowledge of a mother.

Ahab's single name, like Manfred's, Ambrosio's, or Melmoth's, suggests a lonely and sinister independence from social ties. Ahab throws overboard, loses, or smashes several "social" objects on the voyage. Each act symbolizes the rejection of some aspect of humanity. In "The Pipe" Ahab realizes that he can no longer derive any pleasure from so leisurely an activity as smoking and throws his pipe into the sea. In "The Quadrant" Ahab dashes the valuable instrument to the deck and crushes it, shouting, "Cursed be all things that cast man's eyes aloft to that heaven, whose live vividness but scorches him" (p. 634). While the first scene suggests Ahab is alienated from simple human pleasures, the second indicates he has destroyed his ability to find and maintain his social bearings. The antisocial nature of the *Pequod*'s voyage under Ahab, in the grip of his obsession, is stressed in the ship's encounters with other whaling vessels.

> "Come aboard, come aboard!" cried the gay *Bachelor*'s commander, lifting a glass and a bottle in the air.
>
> "Hast seen the White Whale?" gritted Ahab in reply.
>
> "No; only heard of him; but don't believe in him at all," said the other good-humoredly. "Come aboard!"
>
> "Thou art too damn jolly. Sail on."
>
> (p. 627)

Not desirous simply of "avoiding company," Ahab disregards the values upon which society is built; his quest becomes not only a perversion of the aims of whaling, but also a fanatical violation of respect for other human beings.

Ahab's attitude mirrors the profoundly antisocial world of the eighteenth-century Gothic novel. The Gothic genre remains significant to literary history in large part because it foreshadows the destruction of the social order and stability that was characteristic of the rest of the eighteenth century. The last decade of this century—with its breakdown of social ties, social hierarchy, conventions, and institutions—belongs more to the "romantic" century to follow rather than to the "enlightened" period of reason and social purpose. It is the decade inaugurated by the French Revolution (1789), and that event's spirit of social disrup-

tion is most fully embodied in the brooding darkness of the Gothic novel. The captain of the *Pequod,* like the master of the Gothic castle, spends his time avoiding "social company" and tending to an assortment of perverted personal quests.

As Ahab's bonds with humanity slowly disintegrate in the course of the voyage, his links with the satanic grow proportionately stronger. His personal crew, those "shadows" that Ishmael and Queequeg see board the *Pequod,* resemble "mute supers from an old Gothic drama, indeed, from *Vathek.*"[5] The crew has a symbolic significance indicated in Ishmael's speculation that "Such a crew, so officered, seemed especially picked or packed by some infernal fatality to help Ahab to his revenge" (p. 251). The enigmatic Fedallah, the crew's leader, is developed as a satanic figure who, like the forces of evil in Gothic romances, is omnipresent but never clearly defined. Lurking mainly in the background but always weaving his intrigue, "that hair-turbaned Fedallah remained a muffled mystery to the last . . . He was such a creature as civilized, domestic people in the temperate zone only see in their dreams" (p. 307).

In depicting the end of Ahab's quest, Melville uses colossal effects similar to those employed in Gothic romances. Mrs. Radcliffe's castles inevitably vanish into forests or tarns or the reader's imagination at the conclusions of her novels. The end of *Moby-Dick,* like so many visual climaxes in Poe's tales or Walpole's *Otranto,* overwhelms the crew of the *Pequod* as well as the reader in a vortex of such intensity that it sucks down everything, including "a living part of heaven" (p. 723), with it.

The tale that Ishmael lives to tell, however, transcends the limited Gothic world of the late eighteenth century. The genre's scope is enlarged by Melville to include a tragic philosophical dimension: Ahab's quest is not simply to avenge his accident at the jaws of Moby-Dick, but to revenge a world-insult, the world-wound of existence dictating that human beings are fated to die from the moment of birth. Existential complexities lift *Moby-Dick* out of the Gothic cesspool; however, it is also through an adaptation of standard Gothic apparatus that the novel achieves the power and dimensionality of first-rate literature.

Notes

1. Merton M. Sealts, Jr., *Melville's Reading* (Milwaukee, Wis.: University of Wisconsin Press, 1968), pp. 40, 93, 103.

2. Herman Melville, *Moby-Dick* (1851; reprint, New York: Bobbs-Merrills Company, Inc., 1964), p. 133. All textual references are to this edition and are cited parenthetically.

3. Newton Arvin, "Melville and the Gothic Novel," *New England Quarterly* 22 (1949): 38.

4. In William Godwin's *Caleb Williams* (1795), a prototype of what may be called the novel of pursuit, the male protagonist occupies a role that in Gothic literature, Victorian melodrama, and American television drama usually belongs to a female. A victim equally of his insatiable curiosity and of his unrelenting pursuer, Caleb stumbles upon the knowledge that his employer, Falkland, is a murderer. Literally bound and gagged twice, Caleb is pursued and hounded by Falkland's agents until he maneuvers Falkland into confessing his guilt to the authorities. While it is absurd to compare Melville's Ishmael to Godwin's Caleb Williams on any significant level, Ishmael recognizes Ahab's power and, at several points in the narrative, feels the pressure of Ahab's will and voices his misgivings. Sealts notes that Melville had read *Caleb Williams*.

5. Lowry Nelson, Jr., "Ahab as Gothic Hero," in *Moby-Dick as Doubloon*, eds. Hershel Parker and Harrison Hayford (New York: W.W. Norton, 1970), p. 296.

Bibliography

Arvin, Newton. "Melville and the Gothic Novel." *New England Quarterly* 22 (1949): 33-48.

Beckford, William. *Vathek.* 1786; reprint, London: Oxford University Press, 1970.

Godwin, William. *Caleb Williams.* 1794; reprint, London, Oxford University Press, 1970.

Lewis, Matthew. *The Monk.* 1795; reprint, New York: Grove Press, 1952.

Maturin, Charles. *Melmoth the Wanderer.* 1820; reprint, Lincoln: University of Nebraska Press, 1961.

Melville, Herman. *Moby-Dick or the White Whale.* 1851; reprint, New York: Bobbs-Merrill Company, Inc., 1964.

Nelson, Lowry, Jr. "Ahab as Gothic Hero." In *Moby-Dick as Doubloon.* Hershel Parker and Harrison Hayford, eds. New York: W. W. Norton and Co., 1970.

Radcliffe, Ann. *The Italian.* London: T. Cadell and W. Davies, 1797.

———. *The Mysteries of Udolpho.* London: G. G. and J. Robinson, 1794.

Sealts, Merton M., Jr. *Melville's Reading.* Milwaukee, Wis.: University of Wisconsin Press, 1968.

Shelley, Mary. *Frankenstein.* 1817; reprint, Berkeley: University of California Press, 1984.

Walpole, Horace. *The Castle of Otranto.* 1764; reprint, New York: Dover, 1966.

BENJAMIN F. FISHER IV (ESSAY DATE 1994)

SOURCE: Fisher, Benjamin F., IV. "Gothic Possibilities in *Moby-Dick*." In *Gothick Origins and Innovations*, edited by Allan Lloyd Smith and Victor Sage, pp. 115-22. Atlanta, Ga. and Amersterdam: Rodopi, 1994.

In the following essay, Fisher illustrates Melville's handling of the "gothic castle" device in Moby-Dick, *arguing that the ship (the* Pequod) *and the sea serve as gothic castles in the novel, and function in the same manner, to provide a structure to fill with gloom, mystery, and intrigue.*

That Herman Melville turned now and again to the gothic mode is no startling news. Newton Arvin's essay, 'Melville and the Gothic Novel,' remains after more than forty years standard reading for anyone with greater than cursory interest in Melville studies, and his is by no means the sole probing at this vein of Melvillean artistry. And yet we might observe tendencies among critics, G. R. Thompson and Gordon Boudreau excepted, to shy away from the gothicism in *Moby-Dick*, although that book has been examined from many other angles—and bodes fair to continue to hold out lures for many, and heterogeneous, takers.[1] Melville's contemporaries, we might note, had been quick to detect his similarities and dissimilarities to predecessors in the gothic mode. Reviewing *Mardi*, in the *Athenaeum* for 24 March 1849, for example, Henry F. Chorley observed that Chapter 19 in Melville's book recalled the Imalee-Melmoth episode in Maturin's famous novel, *Melmoth the Wanderer*. The same Chorley, in his notice of *Moby-Dick*,[2] remarked that Chapter 42, 'The Whiteness of the Whale,' contained enough 'ghostly suggestions' to satisfy a Maturin or Lewis, although, ironically, an anonymous reviewer of *Moby-Dick* in the *Spirit of the Times*, complimented Melville, along with Dickens, for fresh methods in fiction—writing, in contrast to the slavish imitators of Mrs. Radcliffe.[3] Commentators on Melville's gothicism, however, find their quarry more often in *Pierre* or the short fiction, such as Edward Rose, in his study of Melville's interest in the incest in Walpole's gothic drama, *The Mysterious Mother*; the critics of 'The Bell-Tower'; or, most recently, Eugenia C. DeLamotte. Even Heinz Kosok, who painstakingly charted the gothic devices and character types employed by Melville, is rather more terse in treating *Moby-Dick* than we might wish.[4]

Here I wish chiefly to bring to bear upon *Moby-Dick* some of the ideas set forth by Norman N. Holland and Leona F. Sherman in their study, 'Gothic Possibilities.'[5] They offer valuable help in unlocking certain doors to the time-honored, or vilified, gothic property, the haunted castle. That edifice, they argue, may be customarily called a 'nighttime house,' as darkness is conducive to the creation of vague terrors in the protagonist (and reader alike). The weird noises that seem to be an inescapable part of gothic fiction or, for that matter, plays and verse, are also enhanced by such tenebrousness, giving rise to the sounds of what children often interpret as sexual violence. Gothic

Gregory Peck as Captain Ahab in John Huston's 1956 film adaptation of *Moby Dick*.

castles typically harbor some family secret, and in consequence the castles seem central in childish fantasies about an adulthood that can be discovered and possessed. There is usually some aspect of an idealized family past connected with these settings, although another, less pleasant, typicality of such castles is a connection with discomfort—often torture—and shame, which in turn are tied to feelings of powerlessness and desire. Fantasies of sexual penetration and of merging with an 'otherness' arise from these clusters of emotions. Gothic castles, therefore, are ambiguous locales, at once holding out attractions of nurturing and annihilation. Generally, the protagonist attempts to leave the castle environs, only to be irresistibly drawn back, just as, in other circumstances, one tends to long for home.

Parental figures flourish within these gothic castles, figures who in the main derive from the bad fathers and wicked stepmothers in fairy tales, although good parental types, who function as counters to their more lurid opponents, are also part and parcel of gothic fiction. Gothic villains tend to be older or more sexually experienced persons, demon-lovers, perhaps, who hold author-

ity over some more youthful or more naive protagonist. Possibilities for numerous ambiguities occur in the shadings of the environment and characters. The protagonist usually sustains feelings of anxiety or guilt for any covert wishes to do away with the villainous older character, who simultaneously attracts and repels her or him (Holland and Sherman remind us, by the way, that gothic novels enjoyed a long life of being written by women for women, witness the lasting popularity of Mrs. Radcliffe). Passive though the heroines or heroes may be, they manifest an undeniable resistance to their oppressors, thus offering yet another 'possibility'—that of passivity's leading to its own variety of power. Characters in gothic works may often discover that the situations they confront can affect their own senses of femaleness or maleness.

Ishmael, the teller of Melville's tale, is for much of his book as 'mysteriously alive to a dreadful feeling' as was his predecessor in the Melville canon, Redburn, during his. Like the biblical Ishmael, and like scores of other characters in gothic romance, Melville's creation is a wanderer who goes in search of identity and solidification of his personality. Given the mysteries that surround him, and his name (his chosen name, perhaps, as the opening sentence hints), we would expect to find no end of minuses in his personality. This wanderer goes beyond the shores of land, moreover, engaging in a fascinating, and yet often terrifying, aqua-gothic journey. His voyaging, however, is no mere physical hunt for actual whales, but is an attempt to shake the 'damp, drizzly November' in his soul, one which runs to visions of violence, suicide, and death. Therefore it is no oddity that his narrative is a conglomerate of one bit of gothicism after another, and that about those bits hover ambiguity piled upon ambiguity. Perhaps the Holland-Sherman approach may be put to use in throwing some light on Ishmael's story, which takes us from the traditional land-locked haunted castle onto the seas and the eerie 'haunted forecastle'—to use Kosok's term—of the *Pequod,* itself rife with hauntedness.

Ishmael's initial orientation toward suicide and death draws him toward Ahab and the great whales, of which Moby-Dick, a striking sport among his species, appears to be the most compelling and death-dealing. The old sea-captain has come to believe that in the notorious Moby-Dick is vested a cosmic harshness and evil. Because of his personal experience with this mysterious whale, he wishes to destroy—to bring death to the death-bringer, and thus to reassert his own potency, sexual and other. Ultimately, however, Ishmael more strongly resists this death-orientation as his experiences encourage him to perceive and accept the imperfectibilities in humankind. The strengthening of his credence in the worthwhileness of life leads him to forego the obsessive quest after ego-assertion that leads Ahab to doom in his final encounter with the white whale. Along the way to the closings with Moby-Dick, Ishmael attains a satisfaction in learning that mutuality becomes possible in human existence as we come to an understanding about extending ourselves to others, rather than trying to strive after what, as he comes to comprehend it, is revealed as a negative self-sufficiency.

Melville surpasses many of his predecessors in gothicism by presenting us with what amount to two 'haunted castles,' *The Pequod* and the sea. Each brings forth its mystifying noises to tantalize the ears of those who hear them. Mysteries of sexuality and power-plays are frequently associated with the strange sounds, just as they had been in the pair of miniaturized gothic castles, the inns where Ishmael and Queequeg lodged before embarking. Both the ship and the ocean are haunted by two

villains, as it is Ahab's intentness upon overcoming the whale that makes the latter so vital a presence in all thought and activity aboard *The Pequod* and in the surrounding waters. The ship, to be sure, more obviously descends from the foreboding castellated abbeys in the Appenines so familiar in the Walpole-Radcliffe heritage. The vessel is 'a rare old craft' (p. 164). Somewhat atypically, she is 'rather small if anything; with an old-fashioned claw-footed look.' Albeit small in dimension, *The Pequod* nonetheless manages to convey the sense of spaciousness—because of the dreaminess and mind-expansion that she engenders in Ishmael—associated with the vastnesses and shadowy obscurities that are described with a deliciousness in earlier Gothics, as if the beholders relished those features and the sensations they promoted. 'Long seasoned and weather-stained . . . , her old hull's complexion was darkened like a French grenadier's, who has alike fought in Egypt and Siberia. Her venerable bows looked bearded . . . Her ancient decks were worn and wrinkled.' Her 'original grotesqueness' is intensified by the ivory decorations with which Captain Peleg had adorned her to extravagance while he was chief mate (p. 165). Not only does this description mirror to some extent the appearance of Ahab, as he later appears to us; it recalls the hordes of other gothic villains whose nefarious activities in most un-American climes had bronzed them—colored them with the devil's mark, as it were. The subtle intermingling of male and female attributes here is but one of many throughout the novel. Gorgeous though she is, *The Pequod* carries about her further 'possibilities' in possessing something of the 'barbaric Ethiopian Emperor' and several suggestions of cannibalism. She is indeed a 'noble craft, but somehow a most melancholy!' This same combination of nobility with melancholy might with equal plausibility designate Ahab, or, for that matter, Ishmael himself after his long testing in whaling. The ocean also repeatedly brings close the borders of melancholy with nobility. In fact, although several important scenes fall credibly into representations of the 'nighttime house' mentioned by Holland and Sherman, the sea becomes a modification of gothicism in that its daytime guises mingle beauty and treachery, just as antecedent haunted castles did. Life or death may spring up from its unfathomed depths.

If we may for the nonce regard **Moby-Dick** as haunted by the twin presences of Ahab and the great whale, then we may perceive a kind of parenting being foregrounded here, as it had been in earlier Gothics, and as it still is in the racks and racks of drugstore and shopping-mall gothic paperbacks, according to the Holland-Sherman construct. Ahab, as derivative from the myth of the old-testament king, is, naturally, a patriarchal father-figure, one who seeks to dominate his crew and redirect his customary occupation for evil purposes. No wonder that he is abetted by the devil-creature, Fedallah, who worships fire, and whose physique hints of the snake. Moby-Dick is more ambiguous because of the varied masculine and feminine traits ascribed to him in his role of parent-figure against whom Ahab rebels. Like the paired gothic 'castles' sketched above, captain and his prey evince shifting traits of good and evil, appeal and appall, mystery and forthrightness, calm cunning and shocking violence.

Ahab appeals initially to Ishmael because the older man—who, like King Lear, in ascending importance, is a father, an old man, and a king—embodies much that Ishmael desires to be and feels in his early anxieties that he is not. Like many other gothic villains, who may owe much to the tragic protagonists in Renaissance drama, Ahab has potentially noble qualities. The captain's growing monomania, which leaves him in the end bereft of any mutuality with another human being and instead transforms him into a fiend imbued with more horrifying animalistic impulses than even Moby-Dick seems to possess, loses his allure for his nonetheless obedient crewman, whose healthy skepticism and sense of interdependence with others of his kind absolve him from the fate that befalls the others, who have wholly succumbed to Ahab's enchantment—which is negative, not positive, 'magic.' That Ahab should engage in the casting of spells, although they are in the vein of demogogic persuasion and not otherworldly in their origins, is no surprise. His fearsome eye and his Cain-like scar team with his overbearing personality to establish him as a thoroughgoing gothic villain, although the old captain is no simple derivative culled without forethought from Melville's models. Ahab's sexuality, never cast as the mere rampant lust of so many other evil gothic types, in its vagueness adds another element of interest to his character. Consistent with his being the master of a 'night-time house,' Ahab finally chooses darkness—of madness, isolation, and death—as he defiantly shouts: 'I turn my body from the sun' (Ch. 135).

The white whale, too, holds out temporary appeal to the wanderer because the voyage after self-realization encompasses aspects of sexuality, as well as maleness and femaleness, intellectuality and primitivism, life-giving and destructive inclinations: all embodied in him. He is what Eugenia DeLamotte labels 'the ever-receding object of desire and, as the prison wall "shoved near," . . . the ever-impinging source of terror.' Unlike Ahab, Ishmael finally comes to understand the whale as one more manifestation of an indifferent, if at times captivating, Nature, rather than as a diabolic and calculatingly cruel creature—or so one may interpret the whale's role in the book. Yet seeing and mulling the possibilities of gender-blendings in Moby-Dick's physical appearance and in his actions provide Ishmael with some greater, if not rationally clarified, comprehension of his own physio-psychal being than he had when his narrative commenced. Unlike Ahab, and the others in the crew—who have yielded altogether to their captain's evil spell—Ishmael travels down into the murkiness of the ocean in the vortex of Moby-Dick's annihilating whirlpool, but he returns to regions of light and life. He achieves a balancing, just as Ahab consciously eschews, between what Merlin Bowen, years ago, termed head and heart.[6]

The flight from the haunted castle, in hopes of eluding the consequences of mysteries and secrets sequestered there, also occurs, with certain modifications, in **Moby-Dick.** In the main, the flight is translated into psychological planes—although physical escapes are not forgotten—in terms of Starbuck's vain attempts to deter his captain from his mad quest. Were the crew to succeed in turning Ahab from his intentions, they would manage that feat by engaging in the ordinary business of whaling, or corporeally departing the ship if no further business were to be their occupation, or else mutinying (and thus cause something of a flight on Ahab's part). In the final encounter with Moby-Dick, when the distraught sailors who are set upon by their intended victim think hurriedly of the ship as a refuge, that ship proves to be no center of security as the great whale batters it to its destruction. So in Melville's handling of gothic possibilities, they can not return. Ishmael was among those who had departed the ship, in his case by the mere chance of Fedallah's death; and, although he does not literally return to what is no longer above the waves, he does achieve a kind of return as he lights on Queequeg's coffin, simultaneously a harbinger of death and life, and so much a part of the aura of *The Pequod,* another center for life and death. That coffin buoys him until *The Rachel* rescues him, and thus nurtures him as a kind of mother-refuge in contradistinction to the violent and death-dealing realm where phallic manias and animal unpredictability hold sway. Ishmael had gone to *The Pequod* in hopes of finding there a balm for his soul. The healing qualities in that balm came to him, ironically, only after he had received symbolic lashes from the whips that light on one's mentality as much as or more so than any actual stripes across the back. His being found by *The Rachel* suggests how Melville interjected another irony into the lost-child story of biblical origin. That is, Ishmael in fact is 'lost' in regard to his uninitiated self—but he has survived annihilation and been found because he developed another, more mature and stabilized selfhood. This wanderer returns to life because he has recognized the futility of trying to pierce the 'unreadable secret of the universe,' and in consequence becomes content to remain unheroic rather than to follow in the mindset of Ahab.

DeLamotte comments that in **Moby-Dick** Melville liberated gothic devices, 'allow[ing] them to float free of their old context' (p. 89). A problem that in its own manner 'haunts' the composer of studies such as this, is that as one pursues what at the outset seems a clearly, and succinctly, definable goal, he discovers that 'possibilities' ramify in all directions—excepting that of limitless time. Consequently, I conclude with hopes that my reading has called up, and will call up more, 'possibilities' under the surfaces of Melville's **Moby-Dick.**

Notes

1. Arvin's 'Melville and the Gothic Novel' first appeared in *New England Quarterly,* 22 (March 1949), pp. 33-48; rpt. *American Pantheon,* ed. Daniel Aaron and Sylvan Schendler (New York: Delacorte, 1966) pp. 106-122. Cf. Thompson's "Gothic Fiction of the Romantic Age: Context and Mode," the introduction to *Romantic Gothic Tales, 1790-1840* (New York: Harper & Row, 1979) pp. 35-43; Boudreau "Of Pale Ushers and Gothic Piles: Melville's Architectural Symbology," *ESQ: A Journal of the American Renaissance,* 18 (2 quar. 1972), pp. 67-82. I quote from *Moby-Dick,* ed. Harold Beaver (Harmondsworth and New York: Penguin Books, 1972).

2. *Athenaeum,* 25 October 1851.

3. 6 December 1851.

4. Kosok, *Die Bedeutung der Gothic Novel für das Erzähl-werk Herman Melvilles* (Hamburg: Cram, de Gruyter & Co., 1963). Pertinent bibliography on the topic may be found in my *The Gothic's Gothic: Study Aids to the Tradition of the Tale of Terror* (New York and London: Garland Publishing, Inc., 1988) pp. 232-38; Rose, '"The Queenly Personality": Walpole, Melville and Mother,' *Literature & Psychology,* 15 (Fall 1965), pp. 216-29; DeLamotte, *Perils of the Night: A Feminist Study of Nineteenth-Century Gothic* (New York, Oxford: Oxford University Press, 1990) pp. 48-49, 65-92. See also Allan Lloyd-Smith, *Uncanny American Fiction: Medusa's Face* (New York: St. Martin's, 1989) pp. 63-72.

5. 'Gothic Possibilities' was originally published in *New Literary History* 8 (Winter 1977), 278-94; rpt. *Gender and Reading: Essays on Readers, Texts, and Contexts,* ed. Elizabeth A. Flynn and Patrocinio P. Schweikart (Baltimore and London: The Johns Hopkins University Press, 1986).

6. *The Long Encounter: Self and Experience in the Writing of Herman Melville* (Chicago: University of Chicago Press, 1960) [esp. Ch. 3, 'Defiance: The Way of Tragic Heroism']; DeLamotte, p. 134.

Works Cited:

Arvin, Newton, 'Melville and the Gothic Novel', *New England Quarterly,* 22 (March 1949), pp. 33-48; rpt. *American Pantheon,* ed. Daniel Aaron and Sylvan Schendler (New York: Delacorte, 1966) pp. 106-22.

Boudreau 'Of Pale Ushers and Gothic Piles: Melville's Architectural Symbology,' *ESQ: A Journal of the American Renaissance,* 18 (2 quar. 1972), pp. 67-82

Bowen, Merlin, *The Long Encounter: Self and Experience in the Writing of Herman Melville* (Chicago: University of Chicago Press, 1960)

DeLamotte, Eugenia, *Perils of the Night: A Feminist Study of Nineteenth-Century Gothic* (New York, Oxford: Oxford University Press, 1990)

Fisher, Benjamin, *The Gothic's Gothic: Study Aids to the Tradition of the Tale of Terror* (New York and London: Garland Publishing, Inc., 1988)

Holland, Norman, & Sherman, Leona, 'Gothic Possibilities', originally published in *New Literary History* 8 (Winter 1977), 278-94; rpt. *Gender and Reading: Essays on Readers, Texts, and Contexts,* ed. Elizabeth A. Flynn and Patrocinio P. Schweikart (Baltimore and London: The Johns Hopkins University Press, 1986)

Kosok, Heinz, *Die Bedeutung der Gothic Novel für das Erzähl-werk Herman Melvilles* (Hamburg: Cram, de Gruyter & Co., 1963)

Lloyd-Smith, Allan. *Uncanny American Fiction: Medusa's Face* (New York: St. Martin's, 1989)

Rose, Edward, "The Queenly Personality': Walpole, Melville and Mother,' *Literature & Psychology,* 15 (Fall 1965), pp. 216-29

Thompson, G. R., 'Gothic Fiction of the Romantic Age: Context and Mode,' the introduction to *Romantic Gothic Tales, 1790-1840* (New York: Harper & Row, 1979) pp. 35-43

FURTHER READING

Biography

Weaver, Raymond M. *Melville: Mariner and Mystic.* New York: George H. Doran Co., 1921, 399 p.

The biography central to the Melville revival of the 1920s. This work was extremely influential in establishing Melville's reputation as an author of world importance.

Criticism

Braswell, William. *Melville's Religious Thought: An Essay in Interpretation.* New York: Octagon Books, 1973, 154 p.

Studies the background and influences central to Melville's religious disillusionment and analyzes the treatment of religious themes throughout his works.

Brodhead, Richard H. "The Uncommon Long Cable: *Moby Dick*." In *Hawthorne, Melville, and the Novel*, pp. 134-62. Chicago: University of Chicago Press, 1976.

Proposes that Moby-Dick *is founded on an opposition between two views concerning the nature of the world; namely, "a sense of reality as something inhuman that lies beyond the actual and apparent and a sense of it as something visible, tangible, and finally supportive of human scrutiny."*

Coviello, Peter. "The American in Charity: 'Benito Cereno' and Gothic Anti-Sentimentality." *Studies in American Fiction* 30, no. 2 (autumn 2002): 155-80.

Argues that in his story "Benito Cereno" Melville "pits gothic occlusion and opacity against sentimental modes of reading and response" particularly in terms of the work's naïve narrator and concerns with the politically volatile subject of race in mid-nineteenth-century America.

Hillway, Tyrus. *Herman Melville*. New York: Twayne, 1963, 176 p.

Book-length survey of Melville's life and works.

Hume, Beverly A. "The Despotic Victim: Gender and Imagination in *Pierre*." *American Transcendental Quarterly* 4, no. 1 (March 1990): 67-76.

Probes the conflicts inherent in Melville's writing of Gothic romance, both as a male author and as a revisionist of the genre.

———. "Of Krakens and Other Monsters: Melville's *Pierre*." *American Transcendental Quarterly* 6, no. 2 (June 1992): 92-108.

Considers Melville's rendering of "feminine monstrosities" in the novel Pierre.

Levin, Harry. "The Jonah Complex." In *The Power of Blackness: Hawthorne, Poe, Melville*, pp. 201-307. New York: Alfred A. Knopf, 1958.

Concentrates on darkness as a unifying theme in Moby-Dick.

Miles, Robert. "'Tranced Griefs': Melville's *Pierre* and the Origins of the Gothic." *ELH* 66, no. 1 (spring 1999): 157-77.

Comments on Melville's ironic use of English Gothic ideology and literary conventions in his novel Pierre.

Oates, Joyce Carol. "Melville and the Tragedy of Nihilism." In *The Edge of Impossibility: Tragic Forms in Literature*, pp. 59-83. New York: Vanguard Press, Inc., 1972.

Analysis of Melville's fiction that concentrates on the Manichean struggle between good and evil depicted in his works.

Smith, Henry Nash. "The Madness of Ahab." In *Democracy and the Novel: Popular Resistance to Classic American Writers*, pp. 35-55. New York: Oxford University Press, 1978.

Investigates the ways in which the insanity of Ahab in Moby-Dick *serves to qualify or elaborate his proposition that the universe is controlled by an evil power.*

Stern, Milton R., ed. *Discussions of* Moby-Dick. Boston: D. C. Heath and Co., 1960, 134 p.

A collection of essays on Moby-Dick *that includes discussion of contemporary reaction to the novel, the significance of Ahab's perception of evil, and other pertinent topics.*

Watters, R. E. "Isolatoes." *PMLA: Publications of the Modern Language Association of America* 50, no. 4 (December 1945): 1138-48.

Examines Melville's treatment of the theme of individual isolation in Moby-Dick and other works.

OTHER SOURCES FROM GALE:

Additional coverage of Melville's life and career is contained in the following sources published by Thomson Gale: *American Writers*; *American Writers Retrospective Supplement*, Vol. 1; *Authors and Artists for Young Adults*, Vol. 25; *Concise Dictionary of American Literary Biography, 1640-1865*; *Dictionary of Literary Biography*, Vols. 3, 74, 250, 254; *DISCovering Authors*; *DISCovering Authors: British*; *DISCovering Authors: Canadian*; *DISCovering Authors Modules: Most-studied Authors and Novelists*; *DISCovering Authors 3.0*; *Exploring Novels*; *Exploring Short Stories*; *Literature and Its Times*, Vols. 1, 2; *Literature Resource Center*; *Nineteenth-Century Literature Criticism*, Vols. 3, 12, 29, 45, 49, 91, 93, 123, 157; *Novels for Students*, Vols. 7, 9; *Reference Guide to American Literature*, Ed. 4; *Reference Guide to Short Fiction*, Ed. 2; *Short Stories for Students*, Vol. 3; *Short Story Criticism*, Vols. 1, 17, 46; *Something about the Author*, Vol. 59; *Twayne's United States Authors*; and *World Literature Criticism*.

TONI MORRISON

(1931 -)

(Born Chloe Ardelia Wofford) American novelist, essayist, playwright, critic, author of children's books, and editor.

In 1993, Morrison became the first African American to be awarded the Nobel Prize for Literature. Her fiction was noted for its "epic power" and "unerring ear for dialogue and richly expressive depictions of black America" by the Swedish Academy, while exploring the difficulties of maintaining a sense of black cultural identity in a white world. Especially through her female protagonists, her works consider the debilitating effects of racism and sexism and incorporate elements of supernatural lore and mythology. Many of Morrison's novels—particularly *The Bluest Eye* (1970) and *Beloved* (1987)—have become firmly established within the American literary canon, while simultaneously working to redefine and expand it.

BIOGRAPHICAL INFORMATION

Morrison was born Chloe Ardelia Wofford on February 18, 1931, in Lorain, Ohio, to Ramah Willis and George Wofford. She was the second of four children. Her father was originally from Georgia, and her mother's parents had moved to Lorain after losing their land in Alabama and working briefly in Kentucky. Morrison's father worked in a variety of trades, often holding more than one job at a time in order to support his family. To send money to Morrison during her school years, her mother also took a series of hard, often demeaning positions. Music and storytelling—including tales of the supernatural—were a valued part of family life, and children as well as adults were expected to participate. Morrison became an avid reader at a young age, consuming a wide range of literature, including Russian, French, and English novels. Morrison graduated from Howard University in 1953. She went on to earn a master's degree in English from Cornell University in 1955, and spent two years teaching at Texas Southern University in Houston. From 1957 to 1964 she served as an instructor at Howard. In 1958 she married Harold Morrison, a Jamaican architect, with whom she had two sons, Harold Ford and Slade Kevin. The marriage ended in divorce in 1964, and Morrison and her children returned briefly to her parents' home in Ohio. During this period she began to write, producing the story that would eventually become her first novel, *The Bluest Eye*. In 1966 she moved to Syracuse, New York, and took a job as an editor for a textbook subsidiary of Random House. She relocated again in 1968, this time to New York City, where she continued editing for Random House. She oversaw the publication of works by prominent black fiction writers such as Gayl Jones and Toni Cade Bambara, as well as the autobiographies of influential African Americans, including Angela Davis and Muhammad Ali. In 1987, Morrison left Random House to return to teaching and to concentrate on her writing. She has taught at numerous colleges and universities, among them the State University of New York, Bard College, Yale University, Harvard University, and Trinity College, Cambridge. Morrison currently serves on the faculty at Princeton University.

MAJOR WORKS

Although critics have noted certain Gothic elements in her first novel, *The Bluest Eye, Song of Solomon* (1977) was Morrison's first novel to explicitly incorporate mythical and supernatural elements into the narrative as a way for characters to transcend their everyday lives. The novel juxtaposes the pressures experienced by black families that feel forced to assimilate into mainstream culture with their unwillingness to abandon a distinctive African American heritage. *Tar Baby*, published in 1981 and set in the Caribbean, again uses myth and ghostly presences to mitigate the harshness of lives in which all relationships are adversarial—particularly in cultures where blacks are opposed to whites and women are opposed to men. In 1987 Morrison published *Beloved*, a novel based on the true story of a slave who murdered her child to spare the child from a life of slavery; the book won the Pulitzer Prize. In her exploration of slavery in *Beloved*, Morrison deals with her recurrent theme of family. The characters are deprived of all aspects of ancestry—mates, children, forebears and the sense of selfhood and dignity that they hold, and, most importantly, the ability to love. Also of central purpose to her theme is the importance of memory: the past is revealed in fragments, as if the characters' memories were too overwhelming to be presented at one time. The elements of the mythical and supernatural that have marked all of Morrison's works are prominent in *Beloved*, particularly in her characterization of the title character.

CRITICAL RECEPTION

According to critics, architecture figures heavily into Morrison's portrayal of the Gothic. Her first novel, *The Bluest Eye*, featured an American South version of the trademark Gothic castle in the form of the central character's home, a cavernous, run-down, one-room storefront. *Song of Solomon*, although set in urban Detroit, features a decaying mansion populated by a mournful old woman. The house in *Beloved*, known only by its address (in contrast to the plantation house "Sweet Home," which also appears in the novel), stands isolated and becomes haunted by a family's painful memories. Critics have also discussed at length Morrison's use of ghosts, often representing tragic histories or giving voice to the silenced. Katherine Piller Beutel likens these ghosts to the mythological figure Echo, a distinctly female voice. Critics have also underscored the psychological, and perhaps political, necessity of Morrison's ghosts, who speak of traumatic events that do not necessarily fit into a conventional historical narrative.

PRINCIPAL WORKS

The Bluest Eye (novel) 1970

Sula (novel) 1973

The Black Book [editor] (nonfiction) 1974

Song of Solomon (novel) 1977

Tar Baby (novel) 1981

Dreaming Emmett (play) 1986

Beloved (novel) 1987

Jazz (novel) 1992

Playing in the Dark: Whiteness and the Literary Imagination (criticism) 1992

Race-ing Justice, En-gendering Power: Essays on Anita Hill, Clarence Thomas, and the Construction of Social Reality [editor and author of introduction] (essays) 1992

Lecture and Speech of Acceptance upon the Award of the Nobel Prize for Literature (speech) 1994

The Dancing Mind: Speech Upon Acceptance of the National Book Foundation Medal for Distinguished Contribution to American Letters (speech) 1996

Paradise (novel) 1998

The Big Box [with Slade Morrison] (juvenilia) 1999

I See You, I See Myself: The Young Life of Jacob Lawrence [with Deba Foxley Leach, Suzanne Wright, and Deborah J. Leach] (juvenilia) 2001

The Book of Mean People [with Slade Morrison] (juvenilia) 2002

Love (novel) 2003

Who's Got Game?: The Ant or the Grasshopper? [with Slade Morrison] (juvenilia) 2003

TONI MORRISON (ESSAY DATE 1987)

SOURCE: Morrison, Toni. "Foreword." In *Beloved*. 1987. Reprint edition, pp. xv-xix. New York: Vintage Books, 2004.

In the following essay, her foreword to Beloved, *first published in 1987, Morrison recounts the personal experiences that inspired her to write* Beloved, *and provides insight into the essence of the "haunted house" in the novel and the characters that inhabit it.*

In 1983 I lost my job—or left it. One, the other, or both. In any case, I had been part-time for a while, coming into the publishing house one day a week to do the correspondence-telephoning-meetings that were part of the job; editing manuscripts at home.

Leaving was a good idea for two reasons. One, I had written four novels and it seemed clear to everyone that writing was my central work. The question of priorities—how can you edit and write at the same time—seemed to me both queer and predictable; it sounded like "How can you both teach and create?" "How can a painter or a sculptor or an actor do her work and guide others?" But to many this edit-write combination was conflicting.

The second reason was less ambiguous. The books I had edited were not earning scads of money, even when "scads" didn't mean what it means now. My list was to me spectacular: writers with outrageous talent (Toni Cade Bambara, June Jordan, Gayle Jones, Lucille Clifton, Henry Dumas, Leon Forrest); scholars with original ideas and hands-on research (William Hinton's *Shen Fan*, Ivan Van Sertima's *They Came Before Columbus*, Karen DeCrow's *Sexist Justice*, Chinweizu's *The West and the Rest of Us*); public figures eager to set the record straight (Angela Davis, Muhammad Ali, Huey Newton). And when there was a book that I thought needed doing, I found an author to write it. My enthusiasm, shared by some, was muted by others, reflecting the indifferent sales figures. I may be wrong about this, but even in the late seventies, acquiring authors who were certain sellers outranked editing manuscripts or supporting emerging or aging authors through their careers. Suffice it to say, I convinced myself that it was time for me to live like a grown-up writer: off royalties and writing only. I don't know what comic book that notion came from, but I grabbed it.

A few days after my last day at work, sitting in front of my house on the pier jutting out into the Hudson River, I began to feel an edginess instead of the calm I had expected. I ran through my index of problem areas and found nothing new or pressing. I couldn't fathom what was so unexpectedly troubling on a day that perfect, watching a river that serene. I had no agenda and couldn't hear the telephone if it rang. I heard my heart, though, stomping away in my chest like a colt. I went back to the house to examine this apprehension, even panic. I knew what fear felt like; this was different. Then it slapped me: I was happy, free in a way I had never been, ever. It was the oddest sensation. Not ecstasy, not satisfaction, not a surfeit of pleasure or accomplishment. It was a purer delight, a rogue anticipation with certainty. Enter ***Beloved.***

I think now it was the shock of liberation that drew my thoughts to what "free" could possibly mean to women. In the eighties, the debate was still roiling: equal pay, equal treatment, access to professions, schools . . . and choice without stigma. To marry or not. To have children or not. Inevitably these thoughts led me to the different history of black women in this country—a history in which marriage was discouraged, impossible, or illegal; in which birthing children was required, but "having" them, being responsible for them—being, in other words, their parent—was as out of the question as freedom. Assertions of parenthood under conditions peculiar to the logic of institutional enslavement were criminal.

The idea was riveting, but the canvas overwhelmed me. Summoning characters who could manifest the intellect and the ferocity such logic would provoke proved beyond my imagination until I remembered one of the books I had published back when I had a job. A newspaper clipping in ***The Black Book*** summarized the story of Margaret Garner, a young mother who, having escaped slavery, was arrested for killing one of her children (and trying to kill the others) rather than let them be returned to the owner's plantation. She became a cause célèbre in the fight against the Fugitive Slave laws, which mandated the return of escapees to their owners. Her sanity and lack of repentance caught the attention of Abolitionists as well as newspapers. She was certainly single-minded and, judging by her comments, she had the intellect, the ferocity, and the willingness to risk everything for what was to her the necessity of freedom.

The historical Margaret Garner is fascinating, but, to a novelist, confining. Too little imaginative space there for my purposes. So I would invent her thoughts, plumb them for a subtext that was historically true in essence, but not strictly factual in order to relate her history to contemporary issues about freedom, responsibility, and women's "place." The heroine would represent the unapologetic acceptance of shame and terror; assume the consequences of choosing infanticide; claim her own freedom. The terrain, slavery, was formidable and pathless. To invite readers (and myself) into the repellant landscape (hidden, but not completely; deliberately buried, but not forgotten) was to pitch a tent in a cemetery inhabited by highly vocal ghosts.

I sat on the porch, rocking in a swing, looking at giant stones piled up to take the river's occasional fist. Above the stones is a path through the lawn, but interrupted by an ironwood gazebo situated under a cluster of trees and in deep shade.

She walked out of the water, climbed the rocks, and leaned against the gazebo. Nice hat.

So she was there from the beginning, and except for me, everybody (the characters) knew it—a sentence that later became "The women in the house knew it." The figure most central to the story would have to be her, the murdered, not the murderer, the one who lost everything and had no say in any of it. She could not linger outside; she would have to enter the house. A real house, not a cabin. One with an address, one where former slaves lived on their own. There would be no lobby into this house, and there would be no "introduction" into it or into the novel. I wanted the reader to be kidnapped, thrown ruthlessly into an alien environment as the first step into a shared experience with the book's population—just as the characters were snatched from one place to another, from any place to any other, without preparation or defense.

It was important to name this house, but not the way "Sweet Home" or other plantations were named. There would be no adjectives suggesting coziness or grandeur or the laying claim to an instant, aristocratic past. Only numbers here to identify the house while simultaneously separating it from a street or city—marking its difference from the houses of other blacks in the neighborhood; allowing it a hint of the superiority, the pride, former slaves would take in having an address of their own. Yet a house that has, literally, a personality—which we call "haunted" when that personality is blatant.

In trying to make the slave experience intimate, I hoped the sense of things being both under control and out of control would be persuasive throughout; that the order and quietude of everyday life would be violently disrupted by the chaos of the needy dead; that the herculean effort to forget would be threatened by memory desperate to stay alive. To render enslavement as a personal experience, language must get out of the way.

I husband that moment on the pier, the deceptive river, the instant awareness of possibility, the loud heart kicking, the solitude, the danger. And the girl with the nice hat. Then the focus.

GENERAL COMMENTARY

KATHERINE PILLER BEUTEL (ESSAY DATE 1997-98)

SOURCE: Beutel, Katherine Piller. "Gothic Repetitions: Toni Morrison's Changing Use of Echo." *West Virginia University Philological Papers* 42-43 (1997-98): 82-7.

In the following essay, Beutel maintains that Morrison adapts the ancient myth of Echo to produce Gothic effects with ghostly characters in her works.

In responding to an interviewer's observation about her novels, Toni Morrison once claimed, "I am very happy to hear that my books haunt."[1] If her works are in fact haunting for most readers, in their disturbing and unforgettable characters and events, they also include haunting of a more ghostly sort. Ghosts, such as the horsemen of *Tar Baby* or the title character of *Beloved*, not only exist in her fictional world; they are also often as real, memorable, and central to the stories as "living" characters. They continue to feel pain and desire, for instance, and allow Morrison a means of "giving the dead voice, in remembering the forgotten."[2] The effect of these ghosts and of Morrison's ghostly themes is the effect of gothic literature—it is disquieting, unsettling, even subversive.

Morrison has never been afraid to allow the supernatural to slip into her fiction; even her 1977 novel *Song of Solomon,* while set in urban Detroit, includes many traditional gothic features, such as the decaying mansion occupied by the unnaturally aged Circe (described as a witch from the main character Milkman Dead's childhood), or the ghost of Milkman's grandfather, who appears regularly to mourn his wife to their daughter, Milkman's aunt Pilate, or even Milkman's search through the wilderness and dark of night for self, family, and home. Although the witchlike Circe and the ghost of Macon Dead bring the past into the lives of the characters, it is another haunting, which Milkman and reader encounter later in the story, that is one of the novel's most disturbing gothic elements. As Milkman joins the hunt in the woods near Shalimar, Virginia, he hears a sound like a woman crying. He learns the sound is an echo from Ryna's Gulch, according to local lore, the continuing sound of the mourning of his great-grandmother for the husband, Solomon, who left her to fly back to Africa. The central song we have been hearing throughout the novel, sung by Pilate and the children of Shalimar, the one that reveals Milkman's past to him, is thus Ryna's song: "Oh Solomon don't leave me here."[3] Ryna, who lives still as an echo in the woods, is echoed even beyond that in the song.

Although Morrison deals directly with an "Echo" only late in the story, it is central to the novel as a whole and acquires even wider significance when considered in light of the mythological figure of Echo.[4] The echo in **Song of Solomon** is the voice of female pain and longing, issuing from a rocky place, insuppressible, and thus a continuing reminder of Ryna's unfulfilled desire for the absent male. Echo's story in myth is also one of a female voice not silenced even by the death of the body. In Ovid's famous version of the tale, Echo, already condemned only to repeat the ends of others' speech, is spurned by Narcissus and pines away, becoming only a voice from woodland caves, repeating the mourning of Narcissus for himself.[5] In other versions of the myth, such as that related in a third-century romance by Longus, Echo survives as music, after being torn limb from limb by shepherds at Pan's instigation.[6] Thus the echoing singing in this novel also has roots in Echo's story.

As a disembodied voice (from beyond the grave in a sense) Echo fits well in a gothic setting.[7] Echoing, disembodied voices breaking out of forces (such as death) that ought to suppress them are reminders of an irrational "other side." They evoke creepy feelings of what Freud calls the "uncanny," that which "arouses dread and horror."[8] The decentering effect of voices without visible presence echoes classic gothic's subversive tendencies, putting rational notions of presence and absence or life and death into question. Thus the myth of Echo considered in light of a work's gothic inclinations can provide insights about the implications for gender and narrative of these disturbing bodiless and persistant voices.

As a distinctly female voice, Echo is like Morrison's Ryna, speaking the pain of what Morrison calls a "graveyard love" (128), a self-destructive

overly strong love, in this novel experienced by so many of the female characters for men who only leave them. In addition to Ryna, there is Hagar, Pilate's granddaughter, who is spurned by Milkman and dies after being left behind, in a parallel to Ryna and Solomon that even Milkman himself finally recognizes (332). The triumph of the novel is in fact this growth of a narcissistic male; Milkman is raised never to think beyond himself, and through a journey of discovery learns to lose the "cocoon" of self (277) and feel real love and concern for others. But this growth of Narcissus comes at the expense of Echo. As Ryna is sacrificed in Solomon's flight, Hagar is sacrificed for Milkman's growth and final "flight." Her voice may not live on in the same way Ryna's does, but even on her deathbed it is insuppressible; Pilate and Reba continually try to "Hush" her, yet she speaks of Milkman's rejection (315-16). At her funeral, Pilate and Reba sing an echoing refrain of "Mercy. Mercy. Mercy," and Pilate repeats the last line of a song, "My baby girl," again and again (317-19). The echoing of Milkman's voice then on the novel's final pages, as he yells across the valley to Guitar (described as the voice of the hills and rocks 337) emphasizes once again that Echo remains in song or repeated voice, while Solomon or Milkman leaps.

Morrison has maintained that the novel contains both strong and weak women, as does real life (McKay 145), but the role of Echo in this novel emphasizes a disturbing kind of feminine voice, a repetitive one that remains unfulfilled without the absent and longed-for male. If the Echo of myth is doomed to repeat, the recurring echoes of this text, the women doomed to love too much and their grieving voices, stress what seems to be inevitable repetition of a painful and victimized female role. Morrison does give us Pilate, a strong woman with a strong voice, who seems relatively in control of her destiny, but in general the haunting voices of this text emphasize pain and separation. Even Pilate echoes herself upon losing the object of her love, her granddaughter Hagar.

Echo's story (in its many variations), however, provides material for many different views of limitations upon and powers of feminine voice. In other novels, Morrison seems again drawn to Echo's story—to the pain but also the possibilities of this voice, deprived of body, repetitive, unfulfilled, but also strong and insuppressible and potentially productive and revisionary. Morrison shows haunting echoes in **Beloved**, for instance, as capable of bringing a healing, since they provide the opportunity for connection. Instead of the emphasis on separation we see in *Song of Solomon,* Morrison stresses the power of echo to connect past with present and individual with individual. And in her most recent novel, *Jazz,* Morrison confronts the notion of inevitable repetition by stressing the possibility of revision.

Beloved is Morrison's most explicitly Gothic novel, dominated by a haunted house, a haunted family and community even, and the flesh-and-blood ghost of Beloved herself. Some of this haunting is manifested again in echo—in the disembodied voices that float around the house at 124 Bluestone Road. This "conflagration"[9] of voices that Stamp Paid can hear from the road in the novel's second part consists of echoes of voices once suppressed, voices without body, floating around the gothic, cavelike house. Stamp identifies them as the "mumbling of the black and angry dead" (198), the indecipherable words of "the people of the broken necks, of fire cooked blood and black girls who had lost their ribbons" (181).

The voices from the house and even the voice that issues from the character Beloved—but seems at some points to encompass a collective memory of slave-ship experience—are echoes of the dead, illustrating the power of voice, especially feminine voice, to transcend body and time. The connection they provide between past and present allows the possibility for a beginning of healing, since the novel makes clear that the past cannot simply be shoved down and forgotten without disastrous results.

The healing connection provided by echo in this novel is not only between past and present but also among characters. The poetic sections of the novel's second part that give us the "unspeakable" (199) thoughts of Sethe and her daughters Denver and Beloved create a sort of merging among the three women since their voices become jumbled, echoing each other, losing much of their individuality. The chorus-like, poetic blending of the three voices that ends with the echoing refrain "You are mine, You are mine, You are mine" (215-17) sounds much like Pilate's refrain at Hagar's funeral in the earlier novel, but here in addition to the pain and love expressed there is also a merging of characters accomplished through echoes that cloud boundaries between them. The merging is both dangerous (Sethe nearly does not survive it) and necessary as a step in overcoming the pain of separation. Echo in the Narcissus myth is unable to accomplish the desired merging with her beloved, but the women locked in the house

do seem to achieve a connection, expressed through their blending voices, although it proves dangerous in the end.

Echoes that lead to community, a less overwhelming kind of connection, are ultimately the source of survival and salvation in *Beloved.* Denver, for instance, lives an isolated life dominated by silence (she is even deaf for two years), but an echo of her dead grandmother's voice speaks clearly to her, urging her to "go on out the yard" (244). When Denver does leave the yard to enter the community, she finds acceptance, work, and a future.

Echoing women's voices also come to Sethe's rescue. As the community women gather to exorcise Beloved from their midst, they are described as "Building voice upon voice" to get to "the right combination, the key, the code, the sound that broke the back of words" (261). The echoing among these women, the "Yes, yes, yes, oh yes. Hear me. Hear me. Do it, Maker, do it" (258) does drive Beloved from the house, opening the possibility for Sethe's survival.

The narrator's final echoing refrain, that this is "not a story to pass on" (274-75) shows some discomfort with the role of repetitive telling, but ultimately the gothic vision of the novel shows that echoes present powerful and necessary challenges to rationalist notions that would separate past from present or parent from child or one person's "story" from another's. The echoes of the angry dead that float around the haunted house and the echoes of the sixty million housed in Beloved's voice show the past that encroaches even when we do our best to forget it. But the echoes among characters, those that show a blending and merging of voice, show the interrelatedness of people, the fragility of independent identity, and the power of connection.

Set mainly in the vibrant city in the 1920s, *Jazz* seems on the surface much less gothic than *Beloved* or even *Song of Solomon,* but it too has hauntings, many of which are tied to Joe and Violet Trace's rural Southern past. Even the city is haunted, however, by "clarinets and lovemaking, fists and the voices of sorrowful women."[10] Joe has a "spooky love" (3) for Dorcas, like the dangerous loves of *Song of Solomon*'s Ryna and Hagar, and Violet attacks a corpse, proving, as Morrison's narrator tells us, that "underneath the good times and the easy money something evil ran the streets and nothing was safe—not even the dead" (9). Echoes that haunt in this novel, however, are more like Longus's Echo than Ovid's, music rather than disembodied voice per se.[11] "A colored man floats down out of the sky" in the song of his saxophone, for instance (8); Dorcas even hears a woman singing as she dies from Joe's gunshot (193). And in Joe's past in Virginia, he has listened to "the music the world makes, familiar to fishermen and shepherds, [and] woodsmen" (176). In this music, concentrated around a rock formation, Joe also hears a "word or two," a "scrap of a song" (177) mixed in and knows it comes from the cave where his presumed mother, a woman dubbed Wild, lives. Joe only has heard this woman from the rocks; to him she really is "powerless, invisible, wastefully daft. Everywhere and nowhere" (179), like a mythological Echo. Wild has apparently even lived with the character who most resembles Narcissus—Golden Gray, with his flowing golden hair and meticulously cared-for clothes. Joe's fruitless search for her, like Pan's "hot chase" of Echo's voice in Longus's story (127), can only be repeated, three times in Virginia and once again when the "object" of the search is actually Dorcas.

There is much repetition in the novel, but in Morrison's narrative technique we can see a clear development in her use of Echo. The self-conscious primary narrator is a personal, yet unnamed disembodied voice trying to copy the city and "speak its loud voice" (220). In its inability to do so, however, it opens up the possibility of revision—a possibility inherent in Echo's story but more fully realized in *Jazz* than in Morrison's previous novels. If Milkman and Hagar repeat the cycle of Solomon and Ryna in *Song of Solomon*, *Jazz* finally subverts the expected repetition, is subverted in the end when Joe, Violet, and Felice do not repeat the ending of the previous triangle.

While it might seem that Echo is stripped of the power to communicate, since she is "never around to speak first, never found not to reply" (Ovid 57), even in Ovid's tale, Echo's is a voice that can challenge authority by appearing to repeat while actually altering meaning. Echo does so by truncating sounds, turning Narcissus's "I'd die before I give myself to you," for instance, into the self-sacrificing "I give myself to you."[12] The narrator in *Jazz* sets up expectations of repetition by telling the whole story on the novel's first few pages and then implying that when Joe and Violet meet up with Dorcas's friend Felice, the only change will be in "who shot whom" (6). We expect to hear Joe, Violet, and Dorcas's story in more detail in the course of the novel, as we do, and we also expect a repeat in the second love triangle. But as the narrator admits, she was mistaken in thinking "That the past was an abused record with no choice but to repeat itself at the crack" (220). Unlike Violet's parrot, who can only repeat "I love you" even when pushed out of the apartment window—an image reminiscent of Echo's unrequited love—Joe and Violet can find a healthy love for each other again, surviving the threatened tragic ending to the second triangle. The narrator cannot fully echo the voice of the city; it has an independence impossible to repeat. But the narrator can create with what the city provides, taking an active role of revision and reshaping, rather than a passive one of simple repetition of pain. If the narrator is Echo, her relationship with this novel's Narcissus, Golden Gray, shows significant change, as she realizes that:

> Not hating him is not enough; liking, loving him is not useful. I have to alter things. I have to be a shadow wishing him well, like the smiles of the dead left over from their lives.
>
> (161)

As the narrator then pictures him gaining a "confident, enabling, serene power" from inside a well he stands next to, "a well dug quite clear from trees so twigs and leaves will not fall into the deep water" (161), it becomes obvious there is little mourning or painful desire on Echo's part, but rather a voice above and in control, making changes where necessary. Echo has grown stronger.

In a genre such as the gothic, that gives us "glimpses of the skeletons of dead desires,"[13] Echo's hauntings are especially effective. In overcoming silencing and speaking her desire, Echo is a figure standing for the voice gothic has historically provided its women writers and readers. But if that voice is only pain and desire, endlessly repeated, it gives a disturbing comment on feminine voice. Morrison's use of Echo in *Song of Solomon* does highlight the limitations dominating female voice in the myth, but in returning to echoes in later novels, Morrison plays more with the possibilities and powers of this disembodied, repeating feminine voice. And for a woman storyteller, a repeater of tales, this suggests an ever-growing confidence in the role of breaking silence.

Notes

1. Nellie Mcay, "An Interview with Toni Morrison," *Conversations with Toni Morrison,* ed. Danielle Taylor-Guthrie (Jackson: UP of Mississippi, 1994) 146.

2. Ashraf H.A. Rushdy, "Daughters Signifyin(g) History: The Example of Toni Morrison's *Beloved*," *AL* 64.3 (1992): 567-97. The function of Beloved as a ghost is

central to most critical discussion of that novel. See, for instance, Deborah Horvitz, "Nameless Ghosts: Possession and Dispossession in *Beloved*," *SAF* 17:157-67 and David Lawrence, "Fleshly Ghosts and Ghostly Flesh: The Word and the Body in *Beloved*," *SAF* 19:189-201. Critics have not, however, traced Morrison's recurring use of gothic elements in all of her fiction, focusing more on the grotesque than an overall gothic effect. This article looks at this gothic effect in three of Morrison's novels, especially through the device of disembodied and repetitive voice.

3. *Song of Solomon* (New York: Knopf, 1977) 301-03.

4. Studies of myth in *Song of Solomon,* for example, Cynthia Davis's "Self, Society and Myth in Toni Morrison's Fiction," *ConL* 23 (1982): 323-42, have made little mention of the Echo story, although most critics note the narcissism of the main character. No one has yet traced Morrison's developing uses of the Echo myth.

5. *The Metamorphoses,* trans. Charles Boer (Dallas: Spring, 1989) 58.

6. *The Story of Daphnis and Chloe,* ed. and trans. W. D. Lowe (Cambridge: Deighton Bell, 1908) 127.

7. For discussions of Echo related to writing and reading see, for instance, John Brenkman, "Narcissus in the Text," *GaR* 30 (1976): 293-327, John Hollander, *The Figure of Echo* (Berkeley: U of California P, 1981), and Susan C. Fishman, "Even as We Speak: Woman's Voice and the Myth of Echo," *Sexuality, the Female Gaze, and the Arts* (Selinsgrove: Susquehanna UP, 1992).

8. "The Uncanny," *On Creativity and the Unconscious* (New York: Harper, 1958) 122.

9. *Beloved* (New York: Knopf, 1987) 172.

10. (New York: Knopf, 1992) 7.

11. The novel's title itself makes the emphasis on music. For discussions of Morrison's "jazzy" narrative style, see Eusebio Rodrigues, "Experiencing *Jazz*," *MFS* 39 (1993): 733-53 and Alan J. Rice, "Jazzing It Up a Storm: The Execution and Meaning of Toni Morrison's Jazzy Prose Style," *J Am S* 28 (1994): 423-32.

12. Hollander discusses the tradition of Echo poetry that plays upon this power of communication in significantly truncated repetition (see esp. ch.III).

13. David Punter, *The Literature of Terror: A History of Gothic Fictions from 1765 to the Present Day* (New York: Longman, 1980) 409-10.

TITLE COMMENTARY

Beloved

LILIANE WEISSBERG (ESSAY DATE 1996)

SOURCE: Weissberg, Liliane. "Gothic Spaces: The Political Aspects of Toni Morrison's *Beloved*." In *Modern Gothic: A Reader,* edited and with an introduction by Victor Sage and Allan Lloyd Smith, pp. 104-20. Manchester: Manchester University Press, 1996.

In the following essay, Weissberg traces Morrison's utilization of the Gothic house as a structure of confinement in Beloved.

There is a blue house that sits on this river between two bridges. One is the George Washington that my bus has just crossed from the Manhattan side, and the other is the Tappan Zee that it's heading toward. My destination is that blue house, my objective is to tape a dialogue between myself and another black American writer, and I stepped on this bus seven years ago when I opened a slim volume entitled **The Bluest Eye**. Where does the first line of any novel—like any journey—actually begin?

> Gloria Naylor, 'A Conversation [with Toni Morrison]'

I

'Gothic' has its origin as an architectural term, applied to medieval buildings marked by pointed arches and vaults. Its first use dates to the early eighteenth century, when John Evelyn censored medieval buildings in favour of classical structures, those that 'were demolished by the Goths or Vandals, who introduced their own licentious style now called modern or Gothic'.[1] Modernity, thus invented with a backward glance, is defined as an architectural landscape built upon destruction, a vandalism against proper morals, taste, and the achievements of civilisation.

This invention of modernity as medieval destruction takes place at the time of the rise of the bourgeoisie. Housing structures changed. The term 'modern' was to accommodate concepts that excluded medieval vaults and arches, and which, indeed, relegated those features to a realm of exotic splendour. The word 'comfort', for example, was first applied to houses in the eighteenth century. The term shifted from the discourse of religious and legal studies to signify not simply satisfaction, but also to expand on the notion of convenience.[2] According to Witold Rybszynski, Walter Scott, a historicist dreamer of medieval times, was one of the first novelists to use the word in its newly acquired sense: 'Let it freeze without,' he wrote, 'we are comfortable within' (20). 'There is nothing like staying at home for real comfort', Jane Austen would soon write in *Emma*, as Rybszynski points out (101).

While Gothic architecture seemed to strive for an assimilation of the grandeur and vastness of nature and spirit, the bourgeois home, as invented in the eighteenth century, drew a clear line between the inside and the outside. Inside, one was able to find not only shelter but also thermal content; the inside provided protection against outside spaces filled with potentially hostile forces. In contrast to the bourgeois house, a medieval one offered fewer rooms; rooms were not yet designated for specific functions. The limited space did not acknowledge individual needs, and furniture was largely temporary. For the eighteenth-century bourgeois, the coldness and the emptiness of medieval spaces could signify discomfort only. With the separation of work and living quarters, rooms that allowed for privacy, the eighteenth-century bourgeois was, as an individual, able to construct an alternative life—the comfort of the 'inside'.

It was during the time of the redefinition of bourgeois private space that the medieval castle was rediscovered as a stage set for Gothic literature. Unlike the sheltering bourgeois home, but also unlike classical, symmetrical architecture, it does not represent the owner's control over its space. But the medieval castle clearly represents another class of owners as well. Compared to the bourgeois house, its aristocratic inhabitant was disowned of his authority over its structure even before a political movement would stress the difference in social positions, and the different avenues of the classes' development. In an aristocrat's house, the bourgeois owner would now suspect, anything could happen. Even ghosts could appear.

A Gothic building, as it survived in its representational form, and as it was represented in fiction, was simply unsuitable for the idea of home. Homes, however, were proper housing for the individuals of the eighteenth-century middle class. Not only comfort and privacy were promoted, but domesticity as well, which, in turn, became increasingly feminised. As work and living spaces separated, and work divided according to gender lines, the house became the woman's domain. 'Und drinnen waltet / Die züchtige Hausfrau', Friedrich Schiller was eager to explain what was already widely accepted as true.[3] In the Gothic novels of the eighteenth century, however, this power over the inside space, the authority of *walten,* was not given to women. Women rather suffered as the victims and captives of their male and often foreign persecutors. Ironically, this may have been a more precise account of the female social position and struggle for rights at that time than Schiller's idealisation, as the house's comforts were also established by a devaluation of women's work. Compared to the money that buys comfort, comfort's maintenance is a secondary task. As Clara Reeves and Ann Radcliffe, but also as many male authors, knew, not just the novel, but

precisely the Gothic novel became the fantasy space in which to explore women's roles and the feminine.[4]

The idea of modernity as related to bourgeois houses was not created by the backward glance, but by the idea of new acquisition and progress. Money, earned outside, bought comfort, and new objects contributed to the comfort and gave evidence of how a house could be put to the inhabitant's service. Privacy had to be protected, and the collection of objects, reified goods, provided such a protection as well. Instead of a person leaving the house, the world could symbolically enter. Because their presence itself would thus provide a usefulness of comfort, eighteenth-century collections encompassed objects of Gothic interiors as well, which, at the same time, seemed to have lost their meaning or sense of purpose in this context. The Gothic, once constructed, could be fragmented, imitated, fetishised. Indeed, Gothic elements were eclectically collected, and integrated into the new and more intimate space. The move to establish the uncanny was countered by the move to make it familiar in the bourgeois' own way: by economic appropriation.

II

The idea of the modern bourgeois home did not remain a European invention. It was imported to the American Colonies, and it has survived on either continent well into the twentieth century. A house as a home is, indeed, a recognisable commodity. It can be multiplied in the construction of neighborhood developments, or reduced to the outward simplicity of a child's drawing. In its deceptive simplicity, it can gain symbolic meaning and indicate the lifestyle of its dwellers. Introduced into a school primer, for example, a sketch of such a home would not only tell of the building's material and looks, but also of the individuals occupying it:

> Here is the house. It is green and white. It has a red door. It is very pretty. Here is the family. Mother, Father, Dick, and Jane live in the green-and-white house. They are very happy. See Jane. She has a red dress. She wants to play. Who will play with Jane?[5]

This house, built for the nuclear family, tells of the regular income of its adult inhabitants, their sense of order, and their acceptance of an American way of life as a celebration of middle-class values. The description is also generic enough to be recognised by young readers as a reference to their own home. Housing is translated into a familiar concept that would help to overcome the strangeness of the letters, and promote the learning of a new skill. This primer's modern house is both a lesson in reading, and a confirmation of values.

For those whose house does not resemble this picture, it is a lesson in acculturation. The description of Dick and Jane's house serves as the beginning of Toni Morrison's first novel, **The Bluest Eye.** Published in 1970, the novel turns to the 1940s to describe the life of Black families in the small town of Lorain, Ohio, struggling to come close to the bourgeois ideals that the primer promotes. These ideals, however, are defined by a society not only divided by class, but also by race. There is a jarring difference between the white-and-green house of the textbook, and the decaying storefront building on the southeast corner of Broadway and Thirty-fifth Street in which the Breedlove family lives. There is a jarring difference, too, between the ideal of beauty promoted by Greta Garbo or Ginger Rogers, and the looks of the little black girls who are compared with them (10). Drinking milk from her Shirley Temple cup, young Pecola Breedlove dreams of having blue eyes. The movie screen, the Shirley Temple cup, and Dick and Jane's house turn in Morrison's novel into facades that cover the social inequity, and translate the notion of home into a bourgeois concept that is part of a racially determined aesthetics. If you cannot change your looks, why try to change your house? We are told that the Breedloves accept their house and social standing because they admit to their ugliness (28).

The inside of the Breedlove's storefront residence resonates with an almost medieval one-room lifestyle:

> The plan of the living quarters was as unimaginative as a first-generation Greek landlord could contrive it to be. The large 'store' area was partitioned into two rooms by beaverboard planks that did not reach to the ceiling. There was a living room, which the family called the front room, and the bedroom, where all the living was done . . . In the center of the bedroom, for the even distribution of heat, stood a coal stove. Trunks, chairs, a small end table, and a cardboard 'wardrobe' closet were placed around the walls. The kitchen was in the back of this apartment, a separate room. There were no bath facilities. Only a toilet bowl, inaccessible to the eye, if not the ear, of the tenants.
>
> (25)

Clearly, this house does not offer any possibility of privacy. The distinction between inside and outside is, however, important nevertheless: to rent, or even to own, a house designates stability and social standing. To own or care for property

is, moreover, central to the bourgeois ideal. While the green-and-white house may never be within reach, burning down the house in which one lived, as Pecola's father, Cholly Breedlove, does, is not just arson, but a crime of larger proportions:

> Outdoors, we knew, was the real terror of life. The threat of being outdoors surfaced frequently in those days. Every possibility of excess was curtailed with it. If somebody are too much, he could end up outdoors. If somebody used too much coal, he could end up outdoors. People could gamble themselves outdoors, drink themselves outdoors . . . To be put outdoors by a landlord was one thing—unfortunate, but an aspect of life over which you had no control, since you could not control your income. But to be slack enough to put oneself outdoors, or heartless enough to put one's own kin outdoors—that was criminal. There is a difference between being put *out* and being put out*doors*. If you are put out, you go somewhere else; if you are outdoors, there is no place to go. The distinction was subtle but final. Outdoors was the end of something, an irrevocable, physical fact, defining and complementing our metaphysical condition.
>
> (11)

This transformation of a home by vandalism may have little to do with the modernity of the Gothic; the Breedlove's home is hardly a classical structure, nor is it replaced by a contemporary one. The ruin stands, confirming the difference between rich and poor, white and black, property owner and renter, and the act of drunken protest.

Only seemingly, race provides a dividing line that cuts through class distinctions. As the dominant model of beauty and the Breedlove's acceptance of their ugliness shows, the bourgeois ideals are defined for and by white people. Indeed, part of the Breedlove's tragedy is their acceptance of bourgeois values that leads to schizophrenia and self-annihilation. This is shown, quite poignantly, already in the comparison of houses.

Morrison's novel **Beloved** begins with the description of a house as well:

> 124 was spiteful. Full of a baby's venom. The women in the house knew it and so did the children. For years each put up with the spite in his own way, but by 1873 Sethe and her daughter Denver were its only victims. The grandmother, Baby Suggs, was dead, and the sons, Howard and Buglar, had run away by the time they were thirteen years old—as soon as merely looking in a mirror shattered it (that was the signal for Buglar); as soon as two tiny hand prints appeared in the cake (that was it for Howard).[6]

The house number, representing the building metonymically, acquires a life of its own. Each of the three sections of the novel begins, moreover, with a reference to 124 in which the house turns from being 'spiteful' to 'loud', and, finally, to 'quiet' (3, 169, 239). Morrison comments on the beginning of her novel as a conscious effort to start in *medias res*:

> Snatched just as the slaves were from one place to another, without preparation and without defense. No lobby, no door, no entrance—a gangplank, perhaps (but a very short one). And the house into which this snatching—this kidnapping—propels one, changes from spiteful to loud to quiet, as the sounds in the body of the ship itself may have changed. A few words have to be read before it is clear that 124 refers to a house (in most of the early drafts 'The women *in the house* knew it' was simply 'The Women knew it'. House was not mentioned for seventeen lines, and a few more have to be read to discover why it is spiteful, or rather the source of the spite.[7]

The reader is made to arrive at the house much as the protagonists do for whom 124 is, however, a dwelling of choice. '124' as a number constitutes an address, and therefore a desired property. But it contrasts sharply with Dick and Jane's house in the primer, too, reducing the description of a home to a series of ciphers that cannot, from the outset, refer to any comfort and intimacy. Preoccupied with the house's actions, the reader is not directed towards its looks. The 'posture of coziness' is,[8] indeed, suggested by another building's name in this novel, that of the Southern plantation 'Sweet Home'. The Garner family, owners of 'Sweet Home', insist that the members of their plantation live and work in a harmonious family setting, and that their slaves are treated as paid labourers. Indeed, the sweetness of their home seems to become their inhabitants' attributes: 'Mrs Garner put down her cooking spoon. Laughing a little, she touched Sethe on the head, saying, "You are one sweet child". And then no more' (26).

Sethe came to 'Sweet Home' as a young girl and she is the only female slave on the plantation. At 'Sweet Home', Sethe 'marries' Halle Suggs, and bears him two sons and a daughter. When Mr Garner dies, his brother, 'schoolteacher', and two nephews take over the plantation. Similar to the movies' false images in **The Bluest Eye,** the Garners' home reveals now the cruel character that it always had. Sethe realises her own role as a breeder and as an object without rights that would be available for the nephews' sexual assault. Trying to save her children from a similar fate, she sends them ahead to their freed grandmother Baby Suggs and flees herself, giving birth to her fourth child, Denver, during the escape. But the schoolteacher follows her, and finds her hiding place. Unwilling to send her children into slavery, Sethe decides to kill them, and indeed kills her older daughter, the 'crawling already?' child. While she is punished for her deed, she can also survive with her other three children and Baby Suggs in freedom and later move to 124. Halle, a traumatised witness of the nephews' sexual advances on Sethe, will never join her.

As the novel opens, 124 is already a house of women. Both sons have left. But it is the visit of Paul D., a freed 'Sweet Home' man, who provokes Sethe's memories of the past. These reflections centre again and again on the dead child. Perhaps it is also this child that turns 124 into a haunted house, which personifies this house, breaking the family further apart. This is 124's prehistory:

> Each one fled at once—the moment the house committed what was for him the one insult not to be borne or witnessed a second time. Within two months, in the dead of winter, leaving their grandmother, Baby Suggs; Sethe, their mother; and their little sister, Denver, all by themselves in the gray and white house on Bluestone Road. It didn't have a number then, because Cincinnati didn't stretch that far. In fact, Ohio had been calling itself a state only seventy years when first one brother and then the next stuffed quilt packing into his hat, snatched up his shoes, and crept away from the lively spite the house felt for them.
> (3-4)

124 continues to resist the move of the city to integrate houses into neighbourhoods and 'stretch out'. It thrives on its isolation, just as it is about to be geographically integrated into a community by receiving a number. Sethe, although in freedom, is shunned by her neighbours because of the murder of her child.

Combining references to the family history with American History, Morrison is able to give the house a life of its own. 124 is no green-and-white house, but one of the greyish color that corresponds to the Breedlove's storefront building. By being haunted by a child, and by acting like a child, 124 is both familiar and defamiliarised—an uncanny actor that rules over its inhabitants. With Paul D.'s arrival, there comes the hope that a semblance of family life could be restored, and that the ghost could be banned. But the past is not only resurrected by Paul D.'s arrival and in narratives. A new person appears, with the name Beloved:

> A fully dressed woman walked out of the water. She barely gained the dry bank of the stream before she sat down and leaned against a mulberry tree. All day and all night she sat there, her head resting on the trunk in a position abandoned

enough to crack the brim in her straw hat . . . It took her the whole of the next morning to lift herself from the ground and make her way through the woods past a giant temple of boxwood to the field and then the yard of the slate-gray house. Exhausted again, she sat down on the first handy place—a stump not far from the steps of 124 . . .

Women who drink champagne when there is nothing to celebrate can look like that: their straw hats with broken brims are often askew; they nod in public places; their shoes are undone. But their skin is not like that of the woman breathing near the steps of 124. She had new skin, lineless and smooth, including the knuckles of her hands.

(50)

The newness of Beloved's skin is as puzzling as her curious mixture of wisdom and ignorance. There is the rumour that a black girl had been kept imprisoned in one of the nearby houses, and Beloved acts indeed like a prisoner freed. Her body, as well as her behaviour, give rise, however, to the suspicion that it is not only the name that connects this Beloved to Sethe's dead daughter. Indeed, 'Beloved' is the only word written on the 'crawling already?' baby's tomb stone, the only word Sethe was able to buy by selling her body to the engraver; the word became thus the baby's name.

After Beloved enters Sethe's house, the baby ghost and the building seem to commence separate existences. Gaining physical presence, however, Beloved can both recall and provide a link to a past that Sethe previously tried to suppress. Beloved, pushing Paul D. aside in Sethe's affection, but finally being sent away by him, turns the novel less into an investigation about her identity, but about Sethe's and her family's history. 'She was my best thing' (272) Sethe says after Beloved leaves, stressing the bond between her and the young woman. This bond is reflected again in her relationship to Baby Suggs, her stepmother Nan, and her mother of whom she only knows that she arrived from Africa.

In a conversation with Gloria Naylor, Morrison cites two sources for her novel.[9] One was a newspaper clipping from 1851 that referred to Margaret Garner, a slave from Kentucky who escaped and killed one of her children; Garner stated when interviewed that she did not want her children to return to slavery. Morrison had come across her story while collecting material for **The Black Book,** a collection of writings on Black history and culture that she edited in 1974.[10] Next to the story of this 'serene young woman',[11] Morrison claims to have been struck by the photographs in James Van Der Zee's collection, *The Har-*

lem Book of the Dead, for which she wrote the foreword.[12] Van Der Zee's pictures feature dead loved ones in peculiar poses: a dead baby in the arms of its parents, or a fully dressed person in a coffin. To give the dead a semblance of life has an artistic tradition that extends the use of photography in the Black community.[13] Van der Zee, however, found a special variation for this genre. He worked not only with touch-ups, but also with double exposures. In addition to floating lines of scripture and poetry, many of his pictures also show angels and the Christ image. Photography, as the art of shadows, develops with Van der Zee in the art of religious ghosts, reminding the viewer of the comforting presence of the otherwise invisible divine. Van Der Zee's angels, as well as the Christ figure, are, moreover, white and 'conventional' images of Christian religion. Van Der Zee articulates implicitly already a confrontation of white and black reality and religion that Morrison will rewrite and rephrase in her own work.

One of the photographs shows an eighteen-year-old girl who was shot by her jealous lover, and who chose to help him escape rather than save her own life.[14] Morrison explains:

I had about fifteen or twenty questions that occurred to me with those two stories in terms of what it is that really compels a good woman to displace the self, her self. So what I started doing and thinking about for a year was to project the self not into the way we say 'yourself', but to put a space between those words, as though the self were really a *twin* or a thirst or a friend or something that sits right next to you and watches you, which is what I was talking about when I said 'the dead girl' . . . So I just imagined the life of a dead girl which was the girl that Margaret Garner killed, the baby girl that she killed.[15]

This space is also one of geographical distance. But the distance between Kentucky and Harlem, New York, parallels a temporal one. It is a distance of historical significance for Black people, that separates the plantation South from the abolitionist North. South to North is Sethe's route of escape, leading her from Kentucky's 'Sweet Home' to Cincinnati. It is not Van Der Zee's photograph but rather Margaret Garner's interview that renders a voice to the muted past. Garner's story is, first of all, a slave's history, framed by the newspaper text as the Breedlove's story is framed by quotations from the school primer, the words of which run together and form fragmented sentences, introducing every section of **The Bluest Eye.** *Beloved* reworks Garner's slave history in a collage of poetry, dreams, past and current stories, to reconstruct a memory that would lead beyond an individual's tale as a recovery of the Afro-American past. It is in this sense, that Samuels and Hudson-Weems called **Beloved** 'a ghost story about history' (135). In picturing the dead, Morrison constructs a language to make the past visible.

III

How is it possible, however, for a slave narrative and a Gothic tale to come together? Slave narratives, recorded since the late eighteenth century, were often dictated to white writers, and always edited and published by them. White editors vouched for their authenticity. Often very brief, these narratives are statements presenting a victim's point of view, a route of suffering that would lead from inhuman conditions to a better, if not always fully emancipated, way of life. Unlike confessions, these autobiographies do not describe a conversion due to an inner revelation. The slave's life and *Bildung* is entirely dependent on the economic conditions of his or her white surrounding, and his or her possibilities of protest and escape.

The genre of the document is based on the written word. Slave narratives strive to be documents. Though the slave's story is often told to the editor/writer rather than written, the narrative retains formulaic conventions that are familiar to the readers of literature. Part of the success of slave stories lies in the fact that they were recorded by white men for readers who came from a white tradition.[16] In her reworking of the slave narrative in **Beloved,** Morrison, in contrast, gives preference to the oral word. This is the tradition that she herself remembers as uniquely hers, but also as the tradition that the Black community can and should reclaim.[17]

According to Morrison, oral literature is open-ended, it asks for participation, and thrives on narratives of dreams, myths, and folkloric elements that can be traced back to African roots. This 'oral' literature may provide the voice of the slave that had been silenced in the slave narratives, turn Garner's story from a third-person into a first-person narrative. In changing perspectives, it may introduce an alternative tale that, as fiction, may bear more experiential truth.

For Morrison, this change focuses, above all, on the woman's voice. Although doubly silenced by the white Western tradition, black women emerge in Morrison's tale as persons of special strength. They are able to take action, and their government of the house finds its limitation not in black male power, but only in the white system. In a conversation with Rosemarie Lester, Morrison insists that black women, having always been mother and labourer at the same time, are better suited to feminist demands.[18] The ghost in **Beloved,** who is female, too, relates particularly well to the female members of the household. The novel proves that the supernatural is not truly alien, but that it takes the black women's side against white power. It represents Sethe's family and the historical past. In the novel, it also introduces with Sethe's story a history that may have been repressed by blacks, but that the white slaveholders and masters attempted to sever and obliterate.

For Walter Scott, history had been represented by the visual backdrop of British castles and Highland costumes; they provided a distance between the fictional world and that of his readers that provided the freedom and licence of the historicising effort. For novelists like Clara Reeve or Horace Walpole, the historicising was disrupted by supernatural elements that, introduced as accidental, established order by a denial of a continuum of events that would be shaped by their protagonists. Radcliffe's psychologising makes it clear to what extent the supernatural countered the historical. In Morrison, the supernatural is able to strengthen the position of the person who encounters it—the woman who encounters the female ghost. Fingerprints tell of the presence of unknown beings. Furniture moved or any other action taken by invisible powers echo the Gothic tradition. These signs and actions disrupt the continuum of events and disturb the sense of comfort. Sethe's sons, Howard and Buglar, know of this and flee. For the women who stay on, however, the supernatural is, far from being ahistorical, a reintroduction of history, the sign of memory that takes physical shape with the appearance of Beloved. The women in 124 seem to realise that the figures add up to the magic number seven; they accept the ghost because the house is really theirs: 'It's a feminine concept—things happening in a room, a house. That's where we live, in houses. Men don't live in those houses, they really don't.'[19] Living in a space that is feminised, women do not only become the bearers of children but also the bearer of history through their memory, or, as Morrison calls it, rememory. Sethe explains to her daughter Denver:

> I was talking about time. It's so hard for me to believe in it. Some things go. Pass on. Some things just stay. I used to think it was my rememory. You know. Some things you forget. Other things you never do. But it's not. Places, places are still there.

If a house burns down, it's gone, but the place—the picture of it—stays, and not just in my re-memory, but out there, in the world. What I remember is a picture floating around out there outside my head. I mean even if I don't think it, even if I die, the picture of what I did, or knew, or saw is still out there. Right in the place where it happened.

(35-6)

Elsewhere, Morrison writes that rememory designates 'a journey to a site to see what remains have been left behind and to reconstruct the world that these remains imply'.[20] Memory itself is understood as geographical space.

IV

One has only to compare recent novels by Stephen King with Toni Morrison's invocation of the supernatural to see a similarity of motifs; the dead come to life in both, and haunt the living. The ambiguity of the motif of a ghost's appearance cannot be denied. This may, on the one hand, prove the limitations of the study of motifs. On the other hand, however, it may also tell much about Morrison's craft and the attractiveness of her work for a wider audience of black as well as white readers. While Morrison insists on introducing Black voices, she has also been trained in British and American literature and wrote a master's thesis on Virginia Woolf and William Faulkner, the latter no stranger to the Gothic tradition. Introducing Beloved in *Beloved,* Morrison is, indeed, not only restoring Black history via Black folklore, but also reworking the white tradition of Gothic literature in writing the history of its ghosts. But Morrison's use of the Gothic does more than that. While treating slaves as invisible spirits, American plantation homes—like 'Sweet Home'—are described as Gothic settings that feature slaves as invisible Blacks. Ghosts, therefore, do not signify the limitations of a white man's power, but a social order that relies on their presence. Morrison's reframing is, therefore, a political one, and it has consequences not only for the contemporary Black novel, but also for a new evaluation of the British literature of the past.

In an essay on the place of the Afro-American experience within the literary canon, Morrison discusses white American literature and the Afro-American response. She argues for a rereading of texts by white authors to discover the 'unspeakable things unspoken', 'a search, in other words, for the ghost in the machine'.[21] In this essay, shattered mirrors or finger prints are not only signs of a Beloved, but also the signs of a different voice within American literature. This voice is, indeed, scarcely recorded yet, because it was deprived of the traditional letter, a claim to visibility that ghosts as well as oral literature cannot fulfill. Afro-American literature, moreover, is not simply housed within American literature, as the Breedlove family lives in the Greek landlord's house. Nor does it occupy a very separate realm, as Pecola's mother would suggest when she bars her daughter's entry into the kitchen of her white employers. Afro-American literature responds to the white tradition in and by subversion; by a renaming and retelling of the story.

In *Beloved,* examples for this renaming are given by individual protagonists. Stamp Paid, who helps Sethe in her escape, has given himself his name after he had to offer his wife to their white master. Baby Suggs rejects the name Jenny, stated on her slave bill, and calls herself by the name her husband had given her. Naming the house by its number only, 124, resonates with the renaming of geographical places elsewhere in Morrison's novels. In *Sula* (1973), for example, the black community calls their neighbourhood on the hill 'Bottom', and knows about the 'No Mercy Hospital' and the 'Not Doctor Street'.[22]

In her interviews, Morrison describes her work as 'village literature',[23] consciously turning back from the city to a community many Blacks experienced before moving 'North'.[24] Her 'village' is dependent on a linguistic community, and this linguistic understanding relies on references to the ancestral past, common experiences, as well as verbal action. While the act of renaming and naming is achieved by the Black author, the white and the black reader may read differently. Morrison quotes an early paragraph from *The Bluest Eye* that follows the excerpt from the primer:

> *The Bluest Eye* begins 'Quiet as it's kept, there were no marigolds in the fall of 1941.' The sentence, like the one that open each succeeding book, is simple, uncomplicated. Of all the sentences that begin all the books, only two of them have dependent clauses; the other three are simple sentences and two are stripped down to virtually subject, verb, modifier. Nothing fancy here. No words need looking up; they are ordinary, everyday words. Yet I hoped the simplicity was not simply-minded, but devious, even loaded. And that the process of selecting each word, for itself and its relationship to the others in the sentence, along with the rejection of others for their echoes, for what is determined and what is not determined, what is almost there and what must be gleaned, would not theatricalise itself, would not erect a proscenium—at least not a noticeable one.[25]

Morrison continues, however, to describe this beginning not just as a devious simplicity, but also as the indication of 'illicit gossip', 'whisper', 'oral language', 'comprehension as in-joke for some' (218-19) that defines for her Black literature. In her interviews, Morrison does not deny white critics the ability to read and interpret Black literature, in the same way as she herself insists on a reading of Faulkner or Emily Dickinson and an understanding of these authors' positions:

> If I could understand Emily Dickinson—you know, she wasn't writing for a *Black* audience or a *white* audience; she was writing whatever she wrote! I think if you do that, if you hone in on what you write, it will *be* universal . . . not the other way around![26]

On the one hand, Morrison accepts the idea of universal literature. On the other hand, Morrison suggests, white readers may realise the deviousness of her novel's first sentence, but not the whisper, smoothing over the differences to adjust to an ideal of universal literature. What Morrison is struggling with, and at times with contradictory statements, is the notion of a universal literature to be gained in the face of difference. The relationship of the 'universal' to 'difference', the peculiarity of a different voice that tries to subvert what it responds to, remains unclear. Africans have many words for yam, Morrison repeats in her interviews, seemingly exposing the universal as a simplifying and unifying measure of a white invention.[27] In an interview with Elsie Washington, Morrison insists that 'black' is no longer something one is born as, but a choice, a 'mindset'.[28]

White readers, in an act of bleaching purification, may indeed be tempted to read Morrison's reworking of a British tradition as a deafening act to prove that tradition's primacy. In the case of *Beloved*, Margaret Atwood may be such a reader in point. Her review of the book mentions neither the specificity of a Black novelistic tradition, nor does she refer to Morrison as a black woman author. Entitling her piece 'Haunted by their Nightmares', Atwood evaluates the novel with a simple account and counting that supersedes that of 124:

> *Beloved* is Toni Morrison's fifth novel, and another triumph. Indeed, Ms Morrison's versatility and technical and emotional range appear to know no bounds. If there were any doubts about her stature as a preeminent American novelist, of her own or any other generation, *Beloved* will put them to rest. In three words or less, it's a hair-raiser.[29]

And Atwood continues: 'The supernatural element is treated, not in an 'Amityville Horror', watch-me-make-your-flesh-creep mode, but with magnificent practicality, like the ghost of Catherine Earnshaw in *Wuthering Heights*' (143), and she finally applauds: 'Students of the supernatural will admire the way this twist is handled' (146).[30] Sometimes, it seems, the Gothic may offer the more familiar house.

Notes

I would like to thank Morgan & Morgan Press for permission to reproduce James Van Der Zee's photograph, published in *The Harlem Book of the Dead*.

1. J. Evelyn, 1702; quoted in 'Gothic', *Encyclopedia Britannica*, 11th edn (1910).

2. Witold Rybczinski, *Home: A Short History of an Idea* (New York: Viking Penguin, 1986), p. 20.

3. 'And the virtuous house wife rules inside.' Friedrich Schiller, 'Das Lied von der Glocke', stanza 8, 29-30.

4. In this context, I would like to refer to Nancy Armstrong and Leonard Tennenhouse's forthcoming study on American captivity tales and the 'origin' of the British novel. I believe that the Gothic novel in particular explores the captivity theme as a gendered one.

5. T. Morrison, *The Bluest Eye* (London: Chatto & Windus, 1979), p. 1.

6. T. Morrison, *Beloved* (New York: Knopf, 1987), p. 3.

7. T. Morrison, 'Unspeakable Things Unspoken: The Afro-American Presence in American Literature,' in Harold Bloom (ed.), *Toni Morrison* (ser.) *Modern Critical Views* (New York: Chelsea House, 1990), pp. 228-9.

8. Morrison, 'Unspeakable,' p. 228.

9. G. Naylor and T. Morrison: 'A Conversation', *The Southern Review* 21 (1985), pp. 583-5.

10. Published by Random House, Marylin Sanders Mobley points out rightly that a copy of the news article, entitled 'A Visit to the Slave Mother Who Killed Her Child', appears on p. 10 of Morrison's anthology; see Mobley, 'A Different Remembering: Memory, History and Meaning in Toni Morrison's *Beloved*', in Harold Bloom (ed.), *Toni Morrison* (ser.) *Modern Critical Views* (New York: Chelsea House, 1990), p. 190. Ironically, Wilfrid D. Samuels and Clenora Hudson-Weems insist that Garner's story was not included, but that Morrison 'saved' it for her novel; see Wilfrid D. Samuels and Clenora Hudson-Weems, *Toni Morrison* (Boston: Twayne, 1990), p. 95.

11. Morrison in Naylor, 'Conversation', p. 583.

12. J. Van Der Zee, Owen Dodson, and Camille Bishop, *The Harlem Book of the Dead* (Dobbs Ferry, NY: Morgan & Morgan, 1978).

13. See Stanley Burns, *Sleeping Beauty: Memorial Photography in America* (Altadena, CA: Twelvetrees Press, 1991).

14. Van Der Zee, *Harlem Book of the Dead*, p. 53; see illustration.

15. Morrison in Naylor, 'Conversation', p. 585.

16. This is, of course, played out in Morrison's citation of the school primer in *The Bluest Eye*, as Michael Awkward rightly observes. See his 'Roadblocks and Relatives: Critical Revision in Toni Morrison's *The Bluest Eye*', in Nelly McKey (ed.), *Critical Essays on Toni Morrison* (Boston: G. K. Hall, 1988), p. 59.

17. See Christina Davis, 'Interview with Toni Morrison', *Presence Africaine. New Bilingual Series* 145, 1 (1988), pp. 144-9.

18. R. K. Lester, 'An Interview with Toni Morrison, Hessian Radio Network, Frankfurt/M, West Germany', in Nellie Y. McKay (ed.), *Critical Essays on Toni Morrison* (Boston: G. K. Hall, 1988), pp. 48-9.

19. M. Watkins, 'Talk with Toni Morrison', *New York Times Book Review*, 11 September 1977 (New York: Arno Press, 1978), p. 50. In an interview with Robert B. Stepto, Morrison insists on 'a woman's strong sense of being in a room, a place, or in a house'; '"Intimate Things in a Place": A Conversation with Toni Morrison', in Michael S. Harper, and Robert B. Stepto (eds.), *Chant of Saints: A Gathering of Afro-American Literature, Art, and Scholarship* (Urbana: University of Illinois Press, 1979), p. 212. See also the interview with Rosemarie Lester in regard to girls' and boys' different relationship to architecture and space (p. 47), and Morrison's own rearranging of space to save her writing in the presence of her own sons: Jane Bakerman, '"The Seams Can't Show": An Interview with Toni Morrison', *Black American Literature Forum* 12, 2 (1978), p. 57.

20. Morrison, 'The Site of Memory,' in William Zinsser (ed.), *Inventing the Truth: The Art and Craft of Memoir* (Boston: Houghton Mifflin, 1987), p. 113. See also Ashraf H. A. Rushdy, '"Rememory": Primal Scenes and Constructions in Toni Morrison's Novels', *Contemporary Literature* 31, 3 (1990), pp. 300-23, and Susan Willis, 'Eruptions of Funk: Historicising Toni Morrison', *Black American Literature Forum* 16, 1 (1982), pp. 34-42. In an interview with Elizabeth Kastor, 'Toni Morrison's "Beloved" Country', *The Washington Post*, 5 October 1987, B 12, Morrison defines 'speculation' as the novelist's task; he/she does what the (professional) historian, concentrating on 'ages', 'issues', and 'great men' is unable to do. 'Rememory' is, quite obviously, such a speculation.

21. Morrison, 'Unspeakable', p. 210.

22. C. A. Davis discusses Morrison's use of names and naming in her essay 'Self, Society, and Myth in Toni Morrison's Fiction', in Harold Bloom (ed.), *Toni Morrison, Modern Critical Views* (New York: Chelsea House, 1990), pp. 7-8.

23. See, for example, Tom LeClair, 'An Interview with Toni Morrison', *Anything Can Happen: Interviews with Contemporary American Novelists* (Urbana: University of Illinois Press, 1983), p. 253; and Ntozake Shange with Steve Connon, 'Interview with Toni Morrison', *American Rag*, November 1978, p. 52. See also Morrison's essay 'Rootedness: The Ancestor as Foundation', in Mari Evans (ed.), *Black Women Writers (1950-1980): A Critical Evaluation* (Garden City, NY: Anchor Books, 1984), pp. 339-45.

24. See the discussion in Houston Baker, Jr, *Workings of the Spirit: The Poetics of Afro-American Women's Writing* (University of Chicago Press, 1991), p. 137, and Morri-son's essay 'City Limits, Village Values', in Michael C. Jaye and Ann Chalmers Watts (eds.), *Literature and the Urban Experience* (New Brunswick: Rutgers University Press, 1981), pp. 35-43.

25. Morrison, 'Unspeakable', p. 218.

26. J. Bakerman, 'The Seams Can't Show', p. 59.

27. See Tom LeClair, 'An Interview with Toni Morrison', p. 259; and Claudia Tate, 'Toni Morrison', in Claudia Tate (ed.), *Black Women Writers at Work* (New York: Continuum, 1983), pp. 123-4.

28. E. Washington, interview with Morrison, *Essence* (October 1987), p. 136.

29. M. Atwood, 'Haunted by Their Nightmares', in Harold Bloom (ed.), *Toni Morrison* (ser.) *Modern Critical Views* (New York: Chelsea House, 1990), p. 143; the review appeared first in the *New York Times Book Review*, 13 September 1987, 1, pp. 49-50.

30. See also Judith Thurman's description of *Beloved* as a 'ghost story,' in 'A House Divided', *The New Yorker*, 2 November 1987, 175, or Thomas R. Edwards, 'Ghost Story', *The New York Review of Books*, 5 November 1987, p. 18.

R. CLIFTON SPARGO (ESSAY DATE MARCH 2002)

SOURCE: Spargo, R. Clifton. "Trauma and the Specters of Enslavement in Morrison's *Beloved*." *Mosaic* 35, no. 1 (March 2002): 113-31.

In the following essay, Spargo considers how, in Beloved, *Morrison "uses the Gothic apparatus to invoke the specter of trauma" to produce a narrative that offers the therapeutic benefits of a protagonist's journey back inside, through, and ultimately outside of her traumatic past.*

In the literary world populated by ghosts that eventually became synonymous with the Gothic tradition, the plot of haunting figures its social concerns as metaphysical matters, even to the point where the dramatic spectacle of the ghost makes it hard to trace the social meaning of which it is a spectral emanation. The social relevance of the ghost seems especially obsolete when the haunting coincides with a narrative of fatalism, as if the one who experiences the ghost and the one who suffers history must alike submit to a symbolic social order overdetermined by the spirits of ancestry and cast too strongly in the die of the past. Toni Morrison's **Beloved,** through its turn to Gothic tradition, recovers an untold history of suffering, which seems both the product of such an overdetermined past and a criticism of our conventional historical narratives. As Valerie Smith has argued, Morrison's method of circling her story back upon itself marks a suspicion about the "limits of hegemonic, authoritarian systems of knowledge" (346). But it also marks, within the world of the story, the characters' inability to become adequate to a historical sense of themselves and thus to trace the social meanings behind their sufferings—a point made all too clearly when Paul D becomes frustrated with Sethe's inability to offer a linear, rational account of herself. Part of the problem, as Homi Bhabha has suggested, is that Sethe cannot construct herself by means of a teleological social narrative in which she would figure as an agent who chooses her own actions, and so, in Bhabha's view, we are forced to read the inwardness of the slave world from the outside—that is, through the ghostly returning memory of Sethe's infanticide (16-18). Like many readers of **Beloved**, Bhabha views this ghostly return as intimating a reclamation of Sethe's voice and a restoration of an interpersonal social reality eclipsed by the fatalism of slavery, so that history survives beyond the question of its overt visibility, if only in the "deepest resources of our amnesia, of our unconsciousness" (18).

Bhabha's use of psychoanalytic categories veers so close to the contemporary discourse of trauma as to make him complicitous—say, from the perspective of empiricist-minded critics who yield to the trauma all the status they would grant a ghost—with the trauma's most unreasonable tendencies. Lived as a resistance to an empirically conceived realism about persons, events, and, most significantly, time itself, trauma is a phenomenon that violently interrupts the present tense of consciousness, occurring for the first time only by being repeated. By virtue of this structure of repetition, trauma poses a challenge to historical knowledge, since it is always the symptomology of trauma that one confronts and never the event itself, much as it is always the lack of knowledge that perpetuates the traumatic effect. As an excess or afterlife of the event, trauma refers to an act not yet encountered—as it were, to a specter of the past. To the extent that it testifies, to borrow Cathy Caruth's phrase, to "a reality or truth that is otherwise not available" (4), the trauma depends by definition on the inadequacy of our knowledge in the present order. For this very reason, the trauma has come to function for many critics as a trope of access to more difficult histories, providing us with entry into a world inhabited by the victims of extraordinary social violences, those perspectives so often left out of rational, progressive narratives of history. Indeed, in this respect the trauma functions rather as a ghost of rationality, that which announces a history haunting the very possibility of history.

The problem, to recuperate Bhabha's conceit, may partly be conceived as a question of whether

FROM THE AUTHOR

AN EXCERPT FROM THE CONCLUSION OF BELOVED

It was not a story to pass on.

So they forgot her. Like an unpleasant dream during a troubling sleep. Occasionally, however, the rustle of a skirt hushes when they wake, and the knuckles brushing a cheek in sleep seem to belong to the sleeper. Sometimes the photograph of a close friend or relative—looked at too long—shifts, and something more familiar than the dear face itself moves there. They can touch it if they like, but don't, because they know things will never be the same if they do.

This is not a story to pass on.

Down by the stream in back of 124 her footprints come and go, come and go. They are so familiar. Should a child, an adult place his feet in them, they will fit. Take them out and they disappear again as though nobody ever walked there.

By and by all trace is gone, and what is forgotten is not only the footprints but the water too and what it is down there. The rest is weather. Not the breath of the disremembered and unaccounted for, but wind in the eaves, or spring ice thawing too quickly. Just weather. Certainly no clamor for a kiss.

Beloved.

SOURCE: Morrison, Toni. An excerpt from *Beloved*, pp. 323-24. New York: Vintage, 1987.

one stands inside or outside of traumatic history. In the case of **Beloved**, this is a question already pronounced by Morrison's revisionings of the Gothic and its rather fluid dualism, articulated, on the one hand, in the demand that we participate imaginatively in events beyond the scope or confidence of reason and, on the other, in a call for us to offer our resistances in the service of rationality and to demystify the story's supernatural logic. Much as therapists observe traumatic phenomena from the outside, we might argue that history arises not so much from traumatic consciousness as from those allegorical significances existing just beyond the characters' self-consciousness. In this view, the historically minded reader performs an act of intellectual intervention by restoring the sufferer of trauma to a more reasonable narrative. Yet such an intervention, modelled on the therapist's compassionate but critical listening, runs the risk of conceiving of history as finally in opposition to the private pathologies of history's victims. By contrast, Caruth espouses a reading of the trauma from within the structure of its symptomology, so that history speaks meaningfully through a content that we might not otherwise acknowledge, through the repetitions and pathology of the trauma. Strictly speaking, Caruth assigns trauma a meaning absent from Freud, who steadfastly insists upon an act of remembrance capable of dispelling the grip of the past on present consciousness. For Freud, as for the empirical historian, history must be built upon the possibility of an intervention, an intervention that develops as a reasonable and even compassionate opposition to the trauma.

It is upon the difficult premise of such an intervention in traumatic history that I focus in this essay. Although a number of critical readings of *Beloved,* such as Homi Bhabha's, cause us to focus our attention on the obliquity of a testimonial voice emerging in spite of violent repression, or (according to a reading through trauma) perhaps because of it, such readings speak impossibly from the inside of the trauma as a way of filling in history. This is to bypass the empiricist problem as also the therapist's concern, with its focus on the peculiar relation an indirect and incapable consciousness—which is to say, a traumatized one—bears to history. Among those who have brought the trauma to bear on questions of history, Dominick LaCapra has perhaps been most insistent on listening to trauma from the hitherside of the therapist's couch, privileging a rationality that remains outside the trauma. The therapist, as also the good student of history, should experience an "unsettlement" that is also "empathic," yet, as a lesson for history, the trauma will become meaningful, in LaCapra's account, only once it has been worked through (to use Freud's idiom); and so, in his own brief reading of *Beloved,* LaCapra gives heavy emphasis to the exorcism of Beloved's ghost as the moment in which community finds its place. If LaCapra's approach seems thoroughly reasonable, it may nevertheless be difficult to maintain such sensible interpretive strategies in

relation to the history offered in *Beloved.* This is so because Morrison has so closely configured the history she recovers with the evidence of the trauma itself. As *Beloved* opens toward abandoned history, Morrison demands that her readers encounter characters who inhabit history through the symptomology of trauma, apart from and before the acts of imaginative or rational intervention through which we might return them to a myth of American progress that we have made the equivalent of reason itself. *Beloved* is a novel especially hard on a history so conceived precisely because the benevolence of our reason and the possibility of intervention suppose a separation from—and by definition, an opposition to—the very phenomena upon which we would focus our attention. Just as there is a cynicism that may occur from outside the trauma in the name of reason—say, as the indifference to those people or events that do not fulfill the general progress of society—there is also a cynicism that may occur from inside suffering. Throughout the novel, we are made to wonder whether the symptoms of haunting necessarily contest history conceived as a narrative of subjects with the capacity to intervene in their own and others' histories. By figuring the recovery of history as an involuntary or traumatic phenomenon, and by suggesting that characters inhabit such a history at the expense of their own freedom, Morrison enacts a fundamental tension between the history of injustice that needs to be recorded and remembered and an ethics of corrective action that hovers, if only spectrally, over the imaginative moment of our witness.

We live in a land where the past is always erased and America is the innocent future in which immigrants can come and start over, where the slate is clean. The past is absent or it's romanticized. This culture doesn't encourage dwelling on, let alone coming to terms with, the truth about the past." This is Morrison from a 1988 interview (10-11), describing the myth of America as a land that cancels all debts in the name of freedom and its imagined privileges, yielding to the past only what it will give back to an understanding that cooperates with the freedoms of the future. Despite its etymology, we often give to *understanding* the very character of an action, that is, a modality of knowledge that intervenes in the past and so resolves the claims it makes on present consciousness. Having provided the condition for moral decisions and actions in the present, once our understanding makes the past serve a present course of thought and action, it puts to rest and, for all intents and purposes, contains the past from which it speaks. Such a view of understanding is evident in LaCapra's reading of the trauma. Much as the survivor begins to exercise "some measure of conscious control, critical distance, and perspective" with regard to extreme experiences and to work through loss by realistically positioning herself between the compelling past and the present in which she must be capable of acting, the historian, or secondary witness, will try to help a victim re-establish boundaries between the past and the present (*Writing* 90). It is the establishment of these boundaries—quite literally an intervention—that enables the subject to become cognizant of historical injustices without being merely determined by them. In the absence of intervention, the trauma might continue unabated, involving its survivors in the patterns of the precipitating violence, while also—and perhaps more importantly for our historical sense—exercising a mystifying influence on our social narratives of agency.

With his interventionist understanding of the trauma, LaCapra is highly dubious of any hermeneutics that promotes the excesses of traumatic experience as significations of the real itself, worrying that such a system of thought veers toward a negative sublime that may have affinities with theories of sacrificial violence and even with the Nazi belief in regenerative violence (*Representing* 100-10; *Writing* 92-95). Though he is suspicious of redemptive narratives in which the suffering of others becomes uplifting or central to the identity formation of a person or group, LaCapra nevertheless embraces the narrative progress entailed in the psychoanalytic process of working through loss. Endorsing a therapeutic ethic that would make the past accessible to present consciousness, he seeks to put to rest, as much as possible, the specter of injustice, which disturbs and limits both dialogic exchange and "ethically responsible agency" (*Writing* 90). What LaCapra wants to impress upon us is the capacity of a subjectivity that, having experienced a trauma, comes to inhabit its history rather than be inhabited by it. Many critics have proposed reading the ending of **Beloved** as an achievement on this order, with the communal exorcism denoting both an act of working through or moving beyond a traumatic relation to loss and, at the same time, an ethical intervention consistent with the therapeutic ethic. When Ella leads the communal charge to defeat the incarnate ghost, which is quite literally destroying Sethe's talent for surviving, the community finally comes to terms with the specter of

its own indifference and recuperates the pariah in its midst, as well as her daughter. If we are to read the novel's ending as truly recuperative or redemptive (and I have my doubts on this point), such an ethics would be anticipated earlier in the novel by the scene in which Baby Suggs preaches in the clearing:

> And O my people, out yonder, hear me, they do not love your neck unnoosed and straight. So love your neck; put a hand on it, grace it, stroke it and hold it up. And all your inside parts that they'd just as soon slop for hogs, you got to love them. The dark, dark liver—love it, love it, and the beat and beating heart, love that too. More than eyes or feet. More than lungs that have yet to draw free air. More than your life-holding womb and your life-giving private parts, hear me now, love your heart.
>
> (88-89)

Strictly speaking, this passage does not differ all that radically from a cynical remark that Baby Suggs makes at the start of the novel (though later in the chronological time of the story). Discouraging Sethe's plans to move out of a house haunted by a "baby's venom" (3), Baby Suggs declares, "Not a house in the country ain't packed to its rafters with some dead Negro's grief" (5). To the extent that the present is always a product of the past, there seems little one can do to alter the past and perhaps even less that falls to one's own agency apart from the determinations of cultural and social history. In each case, Baby Suggs accepts the rule of a hostile world enacting its traumatic injustices on the body parts of a community barely separated from the reality, never mind the memories, of slavery. As Baby Suggs advocates a care for self that might redeem some of the violences of the world, her counsel amounts to an ethics of self-intervention. According to the syntactical flow of this speech, the more overtly poetic turns of language ("love your neck unnoosed and straight" or "the beat and beating heart") involve rhetorical reversals of traumatic phenomena, which is to say that they are constituted as figurative redemptions of the violences of history. These traumatic references do not require the intervening understanding of a reader more perspicacious than the novel's represented audience. Morrison supposes that the ex-slaves who hear mention of the noose will remember those they have lost to the violence of the slaveholding culture and experience some anxiety about a fate of persecution awaiting each of them at any moment. When she refers them to their necks "unnoosed and straight," she sounds the note of traumatic fatalism, as if what has occurred to others also awaits them and cannot realistically be avoided. Yet the time of the figure suspends the universalized threat of the noose, imagining a valuation of self bracketed within the vulnerability to history, an opportunity to cease dwelling within the traumas of the past and to embrace freely the ephemeral joys of their own bodies. Although she does not demand from her audience a mythic confidence in American innocence, progress, or opportunity, Baby Suggs hypothesizes a future temporarily redeemed by their holding close to a present care for self and imagining the past as pure exteriority. Corresponding to this inversion of traumatic history, then, is the introverted movement of valuation persuading each member of her audience to appreciate what she or he still possesses, even if it is only those "inside parts" that—according to a social logic barely distinguishing the lives of blacks from animal existence—might as well be food for hogs.

As Baby Suggs testifies, however obliquely, to the traumatic hold of the past on the black community's present consciousness, her turns of phrase imply that she is, to employ LaCapra's words, "working over" the past and "possibly working it through" (*Writing* 89). This is imperfect redemption at best, as the parody of Pauline language in Baby Suggs's sermon suggests. Though Baby Suggs most likely is not meant to be privy to the allusion, she here revises a famous conceit from First Corinthians: "For as the body is one, and hath many members and also members of that one body, being many are one body, so also is Christ. For by one Spirit are we all baptized into one body" (12:12-13). The Pauline allegory erases individual distinctions under the rubric of communal faith, denying the affliction and individualism (and an affliction that is tantamount to individualism) of any particular part: "If the foot shall say, 'Because I am not the hand, I am not of the body'; is it therefore not of the body?" (12:15). The spiritual progression from part to whole is parodied and secularized when Baby Suggs converts the transcendent touch of grace into a physical caress no longer divinely abstract and no longer dependent upon the hands of another ("So love your neck; put a hand on it, grace it"). What is especially remarkable about the passage is the conversion of the excess of the spirit, which is like the excess of trauma, into an ethic of self-love. Working by way of a reduction from the claims of transcendence and communal universalism, Baby Suggs's sermon revises the corporate body, which stood for the community of faith in Paul, into a collection of unassembled corporeal parts, loved in their separateness and pain.

Though much of this language sustains the complexity that LaCapra attributes to the process of working through, Baby Suggs does not presume to imagine for any of the afflicted a final reincorporation into the communal whole. A note of traumatic ambiguity persists in any claim she makes for the present, with the act of self-valuation opening only vaguely toward the future, pushing only haltingly past the isolation of the trauma, and all the time preserving the idiom of the violent past. Thus, when she speaks of the "beat and beating heart," she refers to an existential condition founded on the interchangeability of the social violences done to the heart (the times the body has been *beat,* which are inscribed now on the heart) and the rhythm it lives from (a *beating* that cannot quite keep at bay the word's more violent connotation). Here is voiced, before the full advent of her cynicism, the fatalism of traumatic existence: knowing no other reality, the victim of violence accepts it as a given and seeks a redemption only from within violence. As she refers each of her listeners to his or her lungs "that have yet to draw free air," Baby Suggs imagines only a postponement of future injustice, an upholding of self against the imminence of violences still to come. She speaks as though lapsing from the idiom of working through into the language of trauma, offering at best a troubled testimony to her oppression. As Naomi Morgenstern observes, testimony in Morrison's novel always runs the risk of re-traumatizing the subject as it reproduces the past (see esp. 116-18). Since trauma remains the novel's language of historical witness, the fact that Baby Suggs never quite gets beyond trauma may intimate not only that therapeutic intervention is at its best an incomplete project but also that history might be lost if such an intervention were to be completed.

If I have begun to read **Beloved** as heir to a tradition of literary ghosts who come to seem figures for trauma, we should remind ourselves that the critical discourse on trauma often works in the other direction, reading from the trauma to the specter. Here, for instance, is LaCapra describing both the trauma and the superseding moment in which the ghosts of the psyche are laid to rest as if they were indeed quite real. In trauma, LaCapra says,

> words may be uttered but seem to repeat what was said then and function as speech acts wherein speech itself is *possessed or haunted by the past* and acts as a reenactment or an acting out. When the past becomes accessible to recall in memory, and when language functions to provide some measure of conscious control, critical distance, and perspec-

tive, one has begun the arduous process of working over and through the trauma in a fashion that may never bring the full transcendence of acting out (or *being haunted by revenants* and reliving the past in its shattered intensity) but which may enable processes of judgment and at least limited liability and ethically responsible agency. These processes are crucial for *laying ghosts to rest*, distancing oneself from *haunting revenants*, renewing an interest in life, and being able to engage memory in more critically tested senses.

(*Writing* 90, emph. mine)

I do not wish to accuse LaCapra of believing in ghosts; it is probably enough for some of his critics to say that he believes in trauma. Still, the reader cannot help noticing the logic whereby the one afflicted with trauma achieves distance from "haunting revenants," as if it were less likely that one could refute the unreality of trauma than make its reality remote enough to appear unreal. I put such weight on LaCapra's figurative language in this passage in order to draw attention to a strange literalism lurking there: one distances oneself from the trauma as from a ghost, which is to say, as from the reality of a ghost. Striking a largely pragmatic compromise with the disturbing reality of mind that threatens the real world of action, LaCapra's victim of trauma enacts a progression into reason that refutes the spectral reality that the trauma would otherwise re-enact endlessly in his life. There is a split here in the very meaning of the act. The necessary intervention of memory and language into the unconscious reign of the trauma assumes the capacity of the trauma not only to refer to a past act, but to act out the departed event all over again. Despite his figurative use of ghostly language, LaCapra hardly views the reign of the trauma as a fiction. Rather, the trauma's reality is so persuasive that it requires the work of memory, language, and rationality. The ghostly image connotes both a reluctantly superseded past and the progression beyond it, since, according to the Enlightenment social narrative upon which the Gothic is precariously founded, the ghost is necessarily a figure for a past quickly becoming obsolete.

If trauma can inspire LaCapra's turn to figurative excess, the trauma itself seems implicated in figurative logic. Since I am here focussed on the trauma's function in a work of fiction, we need to bear in mind that the progression from a testimonial text to the traumatic imaginings of the literary text resides in the latter's mediated, already interpreted, relation to the history from which it lives or of which it speaks. If one were trying to read the traumatic reality of African-American history as an unconscious force in Morrison's con-

sciousness determining her patterns of figuration, this distinction between the unconscious and mediated mechanics of the trauma might seem less necessary. But, as soon as one locates the trauma as a figure on the side of an authorial (or at least a textual) intention, the psychological phenomenality of trauma becomes a figure for storytelling itself. In Morrison's case, this means that she uses the Gothic apparatus to invoke the specter of trauma—first, as a motivational force explaining the characters' historical actions, and, second, as a figure for the act of a difficult transmission. As haunting performs the work of a figure, it poses a newness within language that hypothetically or temporarily alienates ordinary meaning and so forces a revision or reconsideration of the very possibilities of representation. Encountering the resistances of the trauma and the failures in understanding that it promotes, the reader remains always aware of what Morrison is trying to say about the history she dares to retell. By exploring the hard edges of a traumatic recalcitrance that is as much the author's reluctance to insert this recovered history into the myths of progress that inform American storytelling as it is an attempt to describe her characters' minds realistically, Morrison brings us to the brink of an unspoken history, which should return, if it is to return at all, only as a rupture of rationality, voice, and ordinarily conceived intentions. The novel emerges as an act of difficult listening, embodied, for example, in the person of Ella as she "listen[s] for the holes—the things the fugitives did not say; the questions they did not ask. Listened too for the unnamed, unmentioned people left behind" (92). To the extent that these "holes" are holes in both consciousness and relationship, the ex-slaves' forgettings function not only as an unconscious coping mechanism but, more surprisingly, as the space of an intention any storyteller who is also a listener—whether she be Ella or Morrison herself—forms against an unmentioned, unmentionable, or traumatically irreferential past.

Throughout ***Beloved***, Morrison develops characters who exist as too much or too little of themselves. And, if all of Morrison's characters in this novel never quite coincide in their own self-consciousness with the history they endure, it is also true that the lives they live inside history remain incommensurate with the novel's historical consciousness. By making her characters participate in structures of rhetorical excess that give their words and actions meaning beyond the immediate moment of their emplotted lives, Morrison develops a structure of reading in which our imaginative acts of identification are limited by the allegorical significances of excess and in which characters who stand for history stand at the same time for the limits of the realistic tradition of fiction with its rational account of history. Perhaps the most conspicuous example of this gap between the reality of a character's experience and a meaning existing outside self-consciousness occurs when Sethe takes account of the newspaper clipping describing her act of infanticide, knowing "that the words she did not understand hadn't any more power than she had to explain" (161). The failure here is not just in the white journalist's lack of empathy but also in the words themselves, which say both too little and too much about Sethe's act. When Paul D sees the photograph accompanying the article, he insists, "I been knowing her a long time. And I can tell you for sure: this ain't her mouth. May look like it, but it ain't" (158). Much like the holes through which Ella hears the unaccounted history of the fugitive slaves, the photograph offers a negative representation of the character Sethe, who becomes unreal in relation to the official history that would record her. Morrison exploits Paul D's obvious psychological defensiveness in order to make us reflect upon the gap between historical experience and history, between the reality of the trauma and the interpretations that make sense of it. Insofar as the novel develops its story through the phenomenality of the trauma, the psychological explanation, much like the historian's act of intervention, relies on a second interpretive sense of the trauma as explanatory trope.

Morrison's relation to the Gothic is to the point here, since viewed through the novelistic orthodoxy of empiricism, the persistent silliness of the Gothic plot arises in direct proportion to its rhetorical excess. It might well be said of the Gothic that it aims less to confront the psyche with the excesses of consciousness than to imagine the psyche as if it were already an excess in history. The most overt markings of psychological excess are of course ghosts, those figures through which the Gothic asks whether the spectral phenomenality of the past refers to an inability of the mind to become part of history or to the impossibility that history should become subject to the mind. In the first instance, the meaning of excess, even when it is not the actual source, would be subjective; in the latter, a sociality working against or to the detriment of subjectivity. In response to the dilemma of interpretation provoked by Gothic ghosts, the modern reader most often makes a choice to account for the excesses of plot through

the distortions of subjectivity and thus to promote the stability of our cultural narratives of rationality. Though the irrationality of the character who sees ghosts may appeal to a reader's imaginative bent for irrationality, the reader's ability to identify the flaws in the character's thinking and the patterns developing from his irrationality keeps the empirical world intact and releases the reader from any anxiety that history might persist without answer. I must emphasize here that in making the choice to explain away the excesses of the Gothic as a symptom of the character's irrationality, the reader chooses an option presented within the Gothic plot—but an option that, if chosen too soon or too absolutely, would ruin much of a story that has come to depend narratively on its fantastic mechanism.

Even when one can explain the extravagances of the Gothic plot as phenomena on the horizon of a subjective irrationality, the story itself seems to insist upon a literal return of a past that constructs Gothic excess, so that we are forced to ask what we ought to make of a past that lives anachronistically beyond its proper moment. As Derrida argues through his reading of *Hamlet* at the beginning of *Specters of Marx,* spectral plots demand that we investigate the manner in which present-tense ideology seeks historical foreclosure. The specters of the past—as, say, those that emerge in Marx's pronouncement at the beginning of the *Communist Manifesto* that "the specter of communism" haunts Europe—may become relevant precisely at the moment in which they have been put to rest for ideological reasons. As he suggests that the rules of empiricism tend to cooperate with the hegemony of the present social moment, Derrida criticizes those claims of presence belonging to any social order of justice, claims that omit reference to the injustices that the present social order both perpetrates and perpetuates. What the Gothic plot so well expresses is a conflict between social narratives endorsing the progresses obtained through empirical reason and those contrary patterns of thought through which the past remains unbound despite our rational attempts to foreclose it. Yet, since the Gothic specter remains an expression of the departed act and its obsolete era, any action owing to its influences might evoke a reactionary nostalgia for an outdated idealism or a fatalistic obligation to ancient constructs of identity. To adhere to the hurt of the past would be to fail the requirement of an empiricism rooted in the present and a progressive rationality oriented toward the future, and, if one is not simply to ignore the past and to adopt a purely presentist and ahistorical mode of knowledge, one must translate the hurt of the past in terms of present possibilities. The specter has a value proportionate to its commentary on the realities of the present, but it cannot maintain itself as a resistance to the present except perhaps through the deliberate archaism of a subject still under the spell of the past. As a reflection of partially eclipsed social paradigms, then, the Gothic figure of haunting enacts a disjuncture between past and present that brings with it a new requirement: to intervene in the social narratives governing our existence in the status quo. For Derrida, it is precisely because the specter is a figure for the unresolved past and the missed encounter that it can signify the future of an act not fully encountered.

According to liberal social theory and the rules of empirical investigation, in order for the trauma to be the product of injustice, we would first require proof that it occurred as a violation of a prior and just ordering of human relations in society. Moreover, as a result of the trauma's private mode of reference, even if we were able to ascertain that a trauma followed from an injustice, the subjectivity of the trauma might make the social occasion to which it witnesses seem merely the background of the traumatic data. Pre-empting just such a suspicion, Caruth perceives in the seemingly private character of trauma an emergent form of sociality, an aspect of history that unfolds from trauma and implicates each of us in one another's traumas (24). However one construes the potentially positive connotations of the trauma's legacy to history, since the trauma necessarily occurs in a subject or a group of people failing to recognize either the symptoms or the events behind them, it demands an event of secondary witness. Providing the very structure of the trauma's sociality, it is the secondary witness's reception, her act of listening for the event of injustice behind the symptoms, that should move us beyond the esoteric testimony of the trauma. In its spectral connotations, the trauma would not simply mystify the obsolescence of an injustice and obscure its causes. Rather, it might be introduced as that which intervenes between history as a departed act and history as that which impinges upon present memory and the ethical acts that follow from it. It is surely a deliberate irony of **Beloved** that not only must history return against the grain of desire and through a figure of haunting, but, once it returns, it must be defeated. This is the very ambiguity of the specter of an injustice or what Morrison elsewhere refers to as the "specter of enslavement," for, as long as she lives

within her trauma, Sethe is not only a witness to the past but also a pariah in the community. The ending of the novel poses what is at best a highly ambiguous resolution to a highly problematic historical truth, as the community's intervention in Sethe's and Denver's trauma requires an exorcism of a past that refutes the ironic witness of the trauma.

There is some evidence for reading the ending as a symbolic act of working through the past, and Ella's self-justified and self-promoting rationale for stirring the community's intervention offers the best expression of this ethic:

> When Ella heard 124 was occupied by something-or-other beating up on Sethe, it infuriated her. [. . .] Whatever Sethe had done, Ella didn't like the idea of past errors taking possession of the present. Sethe's crime was staggering and her pride outstripped even that; but she could not countenance the possibility of sin moving in on the house, *unleashed and sassy.* [. . .] As long as the ghost showed out from its ghostly place—shaking stuff, crying, smashing and such—Ella respected it. But if it took flesh and came in her world, well, *the shoe was on the other foot.* She didn't mind a little communication between the two worlds, *but this was an invasion.*
>
> (256-57, emph. mine)

What Ella objects to is an excess added to Gothic excess, as if Morrison were playing a meta-fictional joke on us: it is one thing to be haunted by ghosts, Ella says, representing the reader who makes allowances for the Gothic and believes in Morrison's ghosts, but to be beaten up by them, that is another. Ella interprets the ghost exactly as though it were a trauma needing to be worked through or (if we are truer to her tones) worked over, and like a highly empathetic therapist, she cannot stand the spectacle of the past "taking possession of the present." It is not clear to me what we are to make of the excessive clichés through which Ella gears herself up to fight Sethe's antagonist, unless they are supposed to demonstrate how far she is from seeing the ghost as the allegory for history that Morrison has made of it and how mistaken Ella may be in reducing the ghost to a traditionally conceived Gothic antagonist. As Ella conflates historical memory and Gothic oppression, Morrison shows us the fallacy of the therapeutic premise, whereby an injustice of the past can come to seem unjust mostly as a result of the havoc it creates in the lives of those who bother to recall it, perhaps with no choice but to remember. As was true of Baby Suggs's preaching in the clearing, the therapeutic ethic seems to collapse on itself—in that first instance by lapsing into the idiom of trauma, in the second by forging a distance from trauma that is achieved only through a clichéd language of melodramatic opposition. Falling into the clichéd phraseology of her characters, Morrison declares of Beloved, "They forgot her like a bad dream" (274). Against the grain of most critical readings of the communal intervention (see, for example: Harris 330-441; LaCapra, *Writing* 14; Rody 102-09), I hear in this ending the endurance of Morrison's suspicion of our cultural narratives of progress. As she presents this contrived resolution of the past, which is either a degenerative or melodramatic resolution of the plot of history, we seem to be in a world much like Shakespearean tragedy, where the ending declares only perfunctorily that history, even tragic history, shall be folded into the progress of society. To this very end, Morrison employs an anti-novelistic and meta-fictional refrain in the final pages, insisting that "this is not a story to pass on" (275) and superficially negating the act of transmission that occurs each time a reader receives this story. In negating her own story, it is as though Morrison has declared that her characters had to get on with their lives, that one can endure only so long in the full consciousness of traumatic history, but that, even so, the last thing we must do is read Sethe's survival as uplifting.

On the question of endings, it is interesting to consider Morrison's reading of *The Adventures of Huckleberry Finn* in her literary critical study **Playing in the Dark.** Effectively endorsing the critical tradition's disappointment with the novel's ending, Morrison finds fault with Twain for abandoning the escape plot and failing to deliver Jim into freedom at Huck's hands. The novel's deferment of Jim's freedom is essential to its complicity with American ideology, Morrison decides, and this is so "because freedom has no meaning to Huck or to the text without the specter of enslavement." The focus here is on Huck's lack of intervention, his failure to become ultimately implicated in Jim's story. There is a pretty overt reason for this: although *The Adventures of Huckleberry Finn* testifies to the "yearning of whites for forgiveness and love," it also requires that the blacks whom they would forgive be viewed as supplicants to the whites and that Jim respond "to the torment and humiliation" that he undergoes with "boundless love" (**Playing** 56-57). Thus the specter of enslavement of which Jim's story remains an emanation expresses a fundamental ambivalence of white America toward a history for which it would confess only a limited responsibility. However we read the mock escape to which Huck and Tom

subject Jim and the *deus ex machina* that releases Jim as a stipulation of the already deceased widow's will, it is evident that the novel's ending has lapsed into the traumatic idiom of slavery. Depicting Jim as altogether lacking the willfulness he showed in running away and Huck as failing to summon on Jim's behalf the resourcefulness with which he secured his own freedom, Twain refuses to give us the ending that Jim deserves and instead secures Jim's freedom as though it were consistent with the will of the slaveholding past. A specter of history casts itself over the agency of two characters who had seemed to denote the future of American idealism and freedom, indeed the emerging future of social mutuality. If there is a traumatic force at work here, Twain does not offer any subjective explanation of the trauma but rather employs it as a social allegory denoting the long reach of the past into the present, even past the point at which it had appeared to be defeated.

What is perhaps oddest about Morrison's assessment of Twain's novel is that the ending she would prefer would be perfectly consistent with American idealism. In delivering Jim to freedom, Huck would express the American belief in a freedom greater than all its contradictory evidences and become an exception to history with whom all readers could identify. As a true remnant of American idealism from a time in which our ugliest history was most conspicuous, Huck would embrace his responsibility and help us all to amend and work through the departed acts of the past. But, if Morrison seems to require a redemptive intervention from Twain and from his hero, her fictional rendering of a scenario that implicitly recalls Twain is much more complicated. In the scene from **Beloved** where Amy Denver intervenes to help Sethe make it through the night, Morrison revisits the specter of Huck's failed intervention, but she does so without providing the idealistic rendering she finds lacking in Twain. I close by focussing on the connotations of haunting in this central episode of **Beloved,** considering Amy's behaviour as a model of intervention that does not require the cancellation of traumatic history through a subjective return to the empirical rationalities of the status quo.

Any ethics that Morrison delineates through Amy's act of intervention exists in ironic tension with the possibilities of benevolent action, since Amy's story, narrated in two separate reminiscences, signifies a departure not only from the idealistic narrative of ethical action, but also from the very conception of justice arrived at through a person's (or character's) deliberated course of action. Moreover, since Amy's story is embedded in Denver's nostalgia for the story of her own birth, it is especially difficult to read the ethics of intervention that pertain to her actions apart from the question of idealism and the novel's larger questions about outsiders' interventions in the trauma of others. This story is part of the allegorical texture of the novel, and it is surely incumbent upon us to remember Amy in relation to the history that she symbolically stands against—not only thinking of Baby Suggs's having cynically contrasted the possibility of an escape from the traumatic past to all the available modes of memory, but also recalling that the haunting of Sethe has been the result of two catastrophic interventions. The first of these is the menacing intervention of the four white slaveholders who come apocalyptically to bring a fugitive slave to justice and thus incite the desperation that leads Sethe to murder her child. The concept of intervention in **Beloved** always carries this spectral history with it, and so, when Paul D strives generously to bring the reign of the ghost to an end, he brings the past to bear more fiercely on the present. For all his better intentions, Paul D reflects the biases of the predominant culture in his eagerness to participate in a forgetfulness conforming all experience to progress. What he occasions is the further degradation of Sethe before her history and a subjective response in her not unlike that of Twain's Jim, who not only permits his "persecutors to torment him," but responds to their torment with "boundless love" (Morrison, **Playing** 57). We may remind ourselves, when Sethe loves the source of her humiliation just as willingly as Jim does, that she is loving the spirit of her dead child, whereas Jim is only adoring the rights of authority; but, to the extent that each character's action is symptomatic of a traumatic history, it is also bound to the past in a manner that subordinates self-love to a spectral and obsolete mode of consciousness.

Having imagined Amy's story as a parable about intervening in an oppressive history, Morrison makes Amy stand not against but within the specters of indifference and neglect that characterize white society's perception of blacks. In the first telling of the story, Amy declares her intention to abandon Sethe ("I gotta go") and does so in unapologetically racist terms ("What you gonna do, just lay there and foal?" [33]). There is an odd humour at work here, as Morrison denotes Amy's emergent care but makes her character speak in an idiom of racism reminiscent of Huck's unre-

formed ideology, never letting us forget the point that Amy has a hard time perceiving her responsibility for Sethe and her history. Amy's callous reactions function a bit like the defensive reactions people have at horror movies, as they alternately whisper "Get out of there" and "Oh, she's so stupid." Indeed, when Amy says "You ain't got no business walking round these hills, miss" (78), she may refer to the fact that Sethe startled her, almost as if she were already one of the many ghosts populating black grief; or perhaps she only means to suggest that Sethe has put herself in harm's way. If her thought adopts the interpretive strategy of explaining Gothic phenomena as though they were purely subjective emanations, we see how easily such a course of explanation degenerates into an attitude of blaming the victim, since it must be either Sethe's irrationality or her moral guilt that functions as the principle of causation behind her suffering. When Amy observes the scars from Sethe's whipping, she concludes, "You must of did something" (80), unable quite to acknowledge her own implication in the fate of another.

Finally, however, it is through the idiom of haunting and the connotations of traumatic history that Morrison makes Amy an unwitting exception to the norms of indifference in Sethe's life and suggests the possibility of a non-benevolent ethical response to injustice in history. Having declared her departure and then remained, perhaps only out of curiosity, Amy expresses her ethical concern by way of a subtle defiance of the fatalistic narrative she has so far imposed on Sethe's life. Anticipating the future of Sethe's death suddenly, as if it were a trauma pertaining to herself, she continues to interrogate the dying pregnant woman at her side under the false name Sethe has given her:

"You ain't dead yet, Lu? Lu?"

"Not yet."

"Make you a bet. You make it through the night, you make it all the way."

(82)

Amy's ethical "bet" on Sethe's life rhymingly puns on the fatalism that Amy and Sethe have expressed in conceiving of her death as something "yet" to come, as though it were an inevitability demanding Hamletic resignation ("If it be now, 'tis not to come. If it be not to come, it will be now. If it be not now, yet it will come. The readiness is all" [5.2.158-60]). When we recall that in *Beyond the Pleasure Principle* Freud defined *anxiety* as the psychological condition that prevents trauma by preparing the self for what is awful and to come, it is hard to hear Amy's continued expression that Sethe will die by her side as anything less than the imagined future of a trauma: "Don't up and die on me in the night, you hear? I don't want to see your ugly black face hankering over me" (82). By way of this conversion of the trauma into that which refers not only to another's past, but to a future in which the suffering of another will be remembered, Amy unwittingly discovers an ethics of intervention that need not cancel the spectacle and hold of suffering to promote an act of responsibility. It goes to the heart of Morrison's critique of benevolence (a critique implicit, for example, in Mr. Garner's fairer treatment of his slaves) that Amy enacts her ethical care for another and promotes again the possibility of self-love in Sethe only through the anti-idealistic expression of her bigotry. *Beloved* asks us whether it is possible for memory to intimate an act not yet encountered, as it were, to glimpse a future of the self given over to ethical meanings not subordinated to a history of intentions. Amy's intervening action is literally a coming between Sethe and her fate and thus an expression of the paradox of responsibility. She fails to conceive of her actions and Sethe's fate as matters of necessity, and at the same time she fails to choose her actions as consistent with the rationale of an empirical cultural narrative. Her somewhat unwitting responsiveness interprets ethics as the encounter with the excess meanings of history, with the specters of injustice haunting the lives of others and by implication ourselves. Too often our conventions of narrative and the accompanying mores of empiricism underestimate the devastating trauma of injustice in order to overcome it. In more Gothic terms, we may inherit the past fatalistically or achieve separation from it by accounting for its pathologies through the aberrations of subjective motive and perspective. But for Morrison it is clear that to stand in history is to stand within range of all its specters, to allow history to take measure of us in our inability and still to require our response where none is yet imagined. To the extent that history's practitioners forget this premise, much of what counts as history may be merely an avoidance of the injustices of the past.

Works Cited

Bhabha, Homi K. *The Location of Culture.* New York: Routledge, 1994.

Caruth, Cathy. *Unclaimed Experience: Trauma, Narrative and History.* Baltimore: Johns Hopkins UP, 1996.

Derrida, Jacques. *Specters of Marx: The State of the Debt, the Work of Mourning, and the New International.* Trans. Peggy Kamuf. Intro. Bernard Magnus and Stephen Cullenberg. New York: Routledge 1994.

Freud, Sigmund. *Beyond the Pleasure Principle.* 1920. *The Standard Edition of the Complete Psychological Works of Sigmund Freud.* Trans. and ed. James Strachey. Vol. 18. London: Hogarth, 1955.

Harris, Trudier. "Escaping Slavery but Not Its Images." *Toni Morrison: Critical Perspectives Past and Present.* 1990. Ed. Henry Louis Gates Jr. and K.A. Appiah. New York: Amistad, 1993. 330-41.

LaCapra, Dominick. *Representing the Holocaust: History, Theory, Trauma.* Ithaca, NY: Cornell UP, 1994.

——. *Writing Trauma, Writing History.* Baltimore: Johns Hopkins UP, 2001.

Morgenstern, Naomi. "Mother's Milk and Sister's Blood: Trauma and the Neoslave Narrative." *differences: A Journal of Feminist Cultural Studies* 8.2 (1996): 101-26.

Morrison, Toni. *Beloved.* New York: Alfred A. Knopf, 1987.

——. "Living Memory" [an interview with Toni Morrison]. *City Limits* (31 March to 7 April 1988): 10-11.

——. *Playing in the Dark: Whiteness and the Literary Imagination.* New York: Random House, 1992.

Rody, Caroline. "Toni Morrison's *Beloved*: History, 'Rememory,' and a 'Clamor for a Kiss.'" *American Literary History* 7.1 (1995): 92-119.

Shakespeare, William. *Hamlet. The Norton Shakespeare.* Ed. Stephen Greenblatt et al. New York: W.W. Norton, 1997.

Smith, Valerie. "'Circling the Subject': History and Narrative in *Beloved.*" *Toni Morrison: Critical Perspectives Past and Present.* Ed. Henry Louis Gates Jr. and K. A. Appiah. New York: Amistad, 1993. 342-55.

Twain, Mark. *Mississippi Writings: The Adventures of Tom Sawyer; Life on the Mississippi; Adventures of Huckleberry Finn; Pudd'nhead Wilson.* Ed. Gary Cardwell. New York: Library of America, 1982.

FURTHER READING

Bibliographies

Middleton, David L. *Toni Morrison: An Annotated Bibliography.* New York: Garland Publishing, Inc., 1987, 186 p.

Includes considerable criticism on Morrison's first four novels, as well as other writings, interviews, and anthologies.

Mix, Debbie. "Toni Morrison: A Selected Bibliography." *Modern Fiction Studies* 39, nos. 3-4 (fall-winter 1993): 795-818.

Bibliography covering selected criticism on Morrison's novels.

Criticism

Britton, Wesley. "The Puritan Past and Black Gothic: The Haunting of Toni Morrison's *Beloved* in Light of Hawthorne's *The House of the Seven Gables.*" *Nathaniel Hawthorne Review* 21, no. 2 (fall 1995): 7-23.

Compares themes and techniques in Nathaniel Hawthorne's The House of the Seven Gables *and Morrison's* Beloved.

Corey, Susan. "Toward the Limits of Mystery: The Grotesque in Toni Morrison's *Beloved*." In *The Aesthetics of Toni Morrison: Speaking the Unspeakable,* edited by Marc C. Conner, pp. 31-48. Jackson: University Press of Mississippi, 2000.

Examines Morrison's disruption of familiar reality in Beloved.

Coundouriotis, Eleni. "Materialism, the Uncanny, and History in Toni Morrison and Salman Rushdie." *Lit: Literature Interpretation Theory* 8, no. 2 (1997): 207-25.

Examines the significance of the uncanny to Morrison's alternate presentation of history in Beloved *and* Sula.

Harris, Trudier. "*Beloved*: Woman, Thy Name Is Demon." In *Critical Essays on Toni Morrison's* Beloved, edited by Barbara Solomon, pp. 127-37. New York: G. K. Hall, 1998.

Explores Beloved's *basis in folk traditions.*

House, Elizabeth B. "Toni Morrison's Ghost: The Beloved Who Is Not Beloved." In *Critical Essays on Toni Morrison's* Beloved, edited by Barbara Solomon, pp. 117-26. New York: G. K. Hall, 1998.

Contends that the title character in Beloved *is not a supernatural being but a young woman who has experienced the horrors of slavery.*

Neubauer, Paul. "The Demon of Loss and Longing: The Function of the Ghost in Toni Morrison's *Beloved*." In *Demons: Mediators between This World and the Other: Essays on Demonic Beings from the Middle Ages to the Present,* edited by Ruth Petzoldt and Paul Neubauer, pp. 165-74. Frankfurt am Main, Germany: Peter Lang, 1998.

Assesses the reliance on African-American traditions of demonology in Beloved.

Nudelman, Franny. "Toward a Reader's History: 'Ghosts Might Enter Here.'" In *Hawthorne and Women: Engendering and Expanding the Hawthorne Tradition,* edited by John L. Idol and Melinda M. Ponder, pp. 278-85. Amherst: University of Massachusetts Press, 1999.

Compares the function of ghosts in Nathaniel Hawthorne's The Scarlet Letter *and* Beloved.

Redding, Arthur. "'Haints': American Ghosts, Ethnic Memory, and Contemporary Fiction." *Mosaic* 34, no. 4 (December 2001): 163-82.

Discusses Morrison's use of ghosts in light of American historical views of hauntings.

Stryz, Jan. "The Other Ghost in *Beloved*: The Specter of *The Scarlet Letter* (1991)." In *The New Romanticism: A Collection of Critical Essays,* edited by Eberhard Alsen, pp. 137-57. New York: Garland, 2000.

Positions Nathaniel Hawthorne's The Scarlet Letter *as a literary predecessor to* Beloved.

OTHER SOURCES FROM GALE:

Additional coverage of Morrison's life and career is contained in the following sources published by Thomson Gale: *African American Writers,* Eds. 1, 2; *American Writers: The Classics,* Vol. 1; *American Writers Supplement,* Vol. 3; *Authors and Artists for Young Adults,* Vols. 1, 22, 61; *Beacham's Encyclopedia of Popular Fiction: Biography and Resources,* Vol. 2; *Black Literature Criticism; Black Writers,* Eds. 2, 3; *Children's Literature Review,* Vol. 99; *Concise Dictionary of American Literary Biography, 1968-1988; Contemporary Authors,* Vols. 29-32R; *Contemporary Authors New Revision Series,* Vols. 27, 42, 67, 113, 124; *Contemporary Literary Criticism,* Vols. 4, 10, 22, 55, 81, 87, 173, 194; *Contemporary Novelists,* Ed. 7; *Contemporary Popular Writers; Dictionary of Literary Biography,* Vols. 6, 33, 143; *Dictionary of Literary Biography Yearbook,* 1981; *DISCovering Authors; DISCovering Authors: British; DISCovering Authors: Canadian; DISCovering Authors Modules: Most-studied Authors, Multicultural, Novelists,* and *Popular Fiction and Genre Authors; DISCovering Authors 3.0; Encyclopedia of World Literature in the 20th Century; Exploring Novels; Feminism in Literature: A Gale Critical Companion; Feminist Writers; Literary Movements for Students,* Vol. 2; *Literature and Its Times,* Vols. 2, 4; *Literature and Its Times Supplement,* Vol. 1; *Literature Resource Center; Major 20th-Century Writers,* Eds. 1, 2; *Major 21st-Century Writers; Modern American Women Writers; Novels for Students,* Vols. 1, 6, 8, 14; *Reference Guide to American Literature,* Ed. 4; *St. James Guide to Young Adult Writers; Short Stories for Students,* Vol. 5; *Something About the Author,* Vols. 57, 144; *Twayne's United States Authors;* and *20th Century Romance and Historical Writers.*

JOYCE CAROL OATES

(1938 -)

(Also wrote under the pseudonym Rosamond Smith) American novelist, short story writer, essayist, critic, playwright, author of children's books, nonfiction writer, and poet.

Considered one of the most prolific and versatile contemporary American writers, Oates has published, since the start of her award-winning literary career in 1963, more than twenty novels; hundreds of short stories in both collections and anthologies; nearly a dozen volumes of poetry; several books of nonfiction, literary criticism, and essays; and many theatrical dramas and screenplays. Writing in a dense, elliptical style that ranges from realistic and naturalistic to surrealistic, Oates concentrates on the spiritual, sexual, and intellectual malaise of modern American culture in her fiction, exposing the dark aspects of the human condition. Her tragic and violent plots abound with depictions of rape, incest, murder, mutilation, child abuse, and suicide, and her protagonists often suffer as a result of the conditions of their social milieu or their emotional weaknesses. Although her works in other genres address similar issues, most critics concur that her short fiction best conveys the urgency and emotional power of her principal themes. Among the dominant motifs in Oates's collected fiction is her evocation of a profoundly Gothic sensibility in American culture. Particularly in such works as her novels *Bellefleur* (1980), *A Bloodsmoor Romance* (1982), and *Mysteries of Winterthurn* (1984), and the short story collections *Night Side: Eighteen Tales* (1977) and *Haunted: Tales of the Grotesque* (1994), among several others, Oates draws upon the emotional extremes of human existence to produce what critics view as a modern and supremely Gothic vision of the history, culture, and collective psyche of the United States.

BIOGRAPHICAL INFORMATION

Born June 16, 1938, in Lockport, New York, the daughter of a tool-and-die designer and a homemaker, Oates was raised on her grandparents' farm in Erie County—later represented in much of her fiction as Eden County. A bookish, serious child, she first submitted a novel to a publisher at the age of fifteen. Oates attended Syracuse University on a scholarship and graduated Phi Beta Kappa in 1960; the following year she earned a master's degree at the University of Wisconsin and married Raymond Smith, a former English professor. From 1962 to 1968 the couple lived in Detroit, where Oates taught at the University of Detroit and published her first novels, short story collections, and poetry. She also witnessed the 1967 race riots, which inspired her National Book Award-winning novel *them* (1969). Shortly thereafter,

Oates accepted a teaching position at the University of Windsor, Ontario, staying until 1978, when she was named a writer-in-residence at Princeton University; she joined the faculty there as a professor in 1987. Despite the responsibilities of an academic career, Oates has actively pursued writing, publishing an average of two books a year in various genres since the publication of her first book, the short story collection *By the North Gate* (1963). Her early novels consistently earned nominations for the National Book Award, while her short fiction won several individual O. Henry Awards and the O. Henry Special Award for Continuing Achievement in both 1971 and 1986. A poet of some merit, and a regular contributor of essays and stories to scholarly journals, periodicals, and anthologies, Oates also is a respected literary critic whose work presents logical, sensitive analyses of a variety of topics. During the 1990s Oates gained additional recognition as a playwright for authoring many plays produced off-Broadway and at regional theaters, including *The Perfectionist* (1993), which was nominated by the American Theatre Critics Association for best new play in 1994. In subsequent years, Oates has continued her prolific output of novels, short stories, dramas, and criticism.

MAJOR WORKS

With her first novel, *With Shuddering Fall* (1964), Oates foreshadows her preoccupation with violence and darkness, describing a destructive romance between a teenage girl and a thirty-year-old stock car driver that ends with his death by accident. Oates's best known and critically acclaimed early novels form an informal trilogy exploring three distinct segments of American society: *A Garden of Earthly Delights* (1967) chronicles the life of a migrant worker's daughter in rural Eden County; *Expensive People* (1967) exposes the superficial world of suburbia; and *them* presents the violent, degrading milieu of an inner-city Detroit family. Oates's novels of the 1970s explore American people and cultural institutions, combining social analysis with vivid psychological portraits of frustrated characters ranging from a brilliant surgeon (*Wonderland*, 1971), a young attorney (*Do with Me What You Will*, 1973), and the widow of a murdered conservative politician (*The Assassins*, 1975), to religious zealots (*Son of the Morning*, 1978) and distinguished visiting poets and feminist scholars (*Unholy Loves*, 1979). Her short stories of this period, most notably in *Marriages and Infidelities* (1972), and *Where Have You Go-*

ing, Where Have You Been? (1974), considered by many to be her best work, concern themes of violence and abuse between the sexes. "Where Are You Going, Where Have You Been," among these, tells of the sexual awakening of a romantic girl by a mysterious man, Alfred Friend; this story is considered a masterpiece of the modern short form and was adapted for film. Two additional collections of short fiction from this period, *The Poisoned Kiss and Other Stories from the Portuguese* (1975) and *Night Side*, reflect Oates's developing interest in Gothic themes. Set in the late nineteenth century, the title piece of the latter collection takes the form of a Victorian ghost story and features a clash between the skeptical materialism of its narrator and the inexplicable qualities of the spirit.

During the early 1980s, Oates published several novels that exploit the conventions of nineteenth-century Gothic literature as they examine such sensitive issues as crimes against women, children, and the poor, and the influence of family history in shaping destiny. *Bellefleur* follows the prescribed formula of a Gothic multigenerational saga by depicting supernatural occurrences while tracing the lineage of an exploitative American family. *A Bloodsmoor Romance* displays such elements of Gothic romance as mysterious kidnappings and psychic phenomena as it details the lives of five maiden sisters in rural Pennsylvania during the late 1880s. In *Mysteries of Winterthurn* Oates explores the conventions of the nineteenth-century mystery novel. The protagonist of this work, Xavier Kilgarvan, is a brilliant young detective who models his career after that of Sir Arthur Conan Doyle's fictional sleuth, Sherlock Holmes. In the episodes that make up the novel, Kilgarvan investigates bizarre cases of murder and incest shrouded in supernatural mystery. Like these lengthier works, many of her subsequent shorter fiction, such as the stories of *Haunted: Tales of the Grotesque*, also rely on elements of Gothic horror, in many cases drawing inspiration from the writings of Edgar Allan Poe and Henry James. Other short stories by Oates, including "Demons" and "Family," probe the terrifying details of alienated and homicidal families.

Most of Oates's remaining fiction of the 1980s features more explicit violence than does her earlier fiction, which tends toward the depiction of psychological afflictions and obsessions. In *Marya* (1986) a successful academic searches for her alcoholic mother who had abused her as a child, and in *You Must Remember This* (1987) a former boxer commits incest with his niece during the McCarthyist 1950s. Oates's subsequent works continue to address relations between violence and such cultural realities of American society as racism (*Because It Is Bitter, and Because It Is My Heart*, 1990), affluence (*American Appetites*, 1989), alienation (*I Lock the Door upon Myself*, 1990), poverty (*The Rise of Life on Earth*, 1991), classism (*Heat*, 1992), sexual-political power dynamics (*Black Water*, 1992), feminism (*Foxfire*, 1993), success (*What I Lived For*, 1994), serial killers (*Zombie*, 1995), incest (*First Love: A Gothic Tale*, 1996), and familial implosion (*We Were the Mulvaneys*, 1996). In *My Heart Laid Bare* (1998) Oates returns to the Gothic family saga structure of *Bellefleur*, recounting the decline of an American family over two centuries in a story deeply concerned with the ongoing history of racial tensions in the United States. Additionally, Oates's series of mysteries published under the pseudonym of Rosamond Smith—*Lives of the Twins* (1988), *Soul/Mate* (1989), *Nemesis* (1990), *Snake Eyes* (1992), and *You Can't Catch Me* (1995)—concern the psychopathic exploits of aberrational academics and are noted for their use of Gothic motifs.

CRITICAL RECEPTION

Critics hold diverse opinions about Oates's work, particularly about her repeated use of graphic violence, which some have called a "distorted" vision of American life. Eva Manske (see Further Reading) has summarized the general view: "Some of her novels and stories are rather shrill in depicting the human situation, remain melodramatic renderings of everyday life, highly charged with unrelenting scenes of shocking, random violence, or madness and emotional distress that Oates chronicles as dominant elements of experience in the lives of her characters." Considering the often extreme content of her work, the mention of Oates's writing in conjunction with Gothic conventions has become a commonplace among contemporary critics. Several of her early novels, including realistic works such as *With Shuddering Fall* and *Wonderland* have been regarded for their grotesque depictions of both physical and psychological violence, and studied within Gothic literary contexts. Oates herself has suggested that Gothic concerns with the bizarre dimensions of human experience and extremes of brutality and psychological duress are essential components of contemporary life. She has also remarked that the term itself (when left uncapitalized) merely signifies "a work in which extremes of emotion are unleashed." According to this definition, Oates's entire oeuvre could be considered in terms of its generically "gothic" qualities. In particular, Oates's use and adaptation of the supernatural and psychological themes formally associated with the Gothic literary tradition have been most frequently discussed in conjunction with her novels *Bellefleur*, *A Bloodsmoor Romance*, and *Mysteries of Winterthurn*. These works draw heavily upon the preternatural atmosphere of dread and a collection of tropes and conventions evoked in the nineteenth-century Gothic novel. Other works discussed in Gothic contexts include the short story collection *Night Side*, which Greg Johnson has studied in terms of the link between the psychological and the unseen spiritual realm these stories draw upon in rendering the dark and inscrutable mysteries of the human psyche. Additionally, her novels penned under the pseudonym Rosamond Smith have been said to prominently feature the Gothic trope of the *doppelgänger*, or double, while her stories and novels set in Eden County are thought to strongly echo the "Southern Gothic" atmosphere found in the novels of William Faulkner and thus likewise explore a haunting landscape crafted in a peculiarly American idiom. While some critics have dismissed her Gothic fiction as whimsical, others have suggested that it invigorates this literary tradition, particularly feminist critics who often have likened Oates's ghosts to the cultural status of "invisible woman," as Cara Chell (see Further Reading) has pointed out. Overall, critical consensus has tended to characterize much of Oates's work as a powerful reinterpretation of a centuries-old literary tradition, one that adapts the Gothic sensibility into a contemporary mode by plunging readers into the often terrifying and hidden emotional recesses of modern American society.

PRINCIPAL WORKS

By the North Gate (short stories) 1963

With Shuddering Fall (novel) 1964

The Sweet Enemy (play) 1965

Upon the Sweeping Flood and Other Stories (short stories) 1966

Expensive People (novel) 1967

A Garden of Earthly Delights (novel) 1967

Women in Love and Other Poems (poetry) 1968

them (novel) 1969

OATES

The Wheel of Love and Other Stories (short stories) 1970

Wonderland (novel) 1971

Marriages and Infidelities (short stories) 1972

Angel Fire (poetry) 1973

Do with Me What You Will (novel) 1973

The Goddess and Other Women (short stories) 1974

Miracle Play (play) 1974

Where Are You Going, Where Have You Been?: Stories of Young America (short stories) 1974

The Assassins: A Book of Hours (novel) 1975

The Poisoned Kiss and Other Stories from the Portuguese (short stories) 1975

Childwold (novel) 1976

Triumph of the Spider Monkey: The First Person Confession of the Maniac Bobby Gotteson as Told to Joyce Carol Oates (novella) 1976

Night Side: Eighteen Tales (short stories) 1977

Son of the Morning (novel) 1978

Cybele (novel) 1979

Unholy Loves (novel) 1979

Bellefleur (novel) 1980

Angel of Light (novel) 1981

Contraries: Essays (nonfiction) 1981

A Sentimental Education (short stories) 1981

A Bloodsmoor Romance (novel) 1982

Invisible Woman: New and Selected Poems, 1970-1972 (poetry) 1982

Mysteries of Winterthurn (novel) 1984

Solstice (novel) 1985

Marya: A Life (novel) 1986

You Must Remember This (novel) 1987

Lives of the Twins [as Rosamond Smith] (novel) 1988

(Woman) Writer: Occasions and Opportunities (nonfiction) 1988

American Appetites (novel) 1989

Soul/Mate [as Rosamond Smith] (novel) 1989

The Time Traveler (poetry) 1989

Because It Is Bitter, and Because It Is My Heart (novel) 1990

I Lock the Door upon Myself (novel) 1990

Nemesis [as Rosamond Smith] (novel) 1990

I Stand Before You Naked (play) 1991

The Rise of Life on Earth (novel) 1991

Black Water (novel) 1992

Heat: And Other Stories (short stories) 1992

Snake Eyes [as Rosamond Smith] (novel) 1992

Foxfire: Confessions of a Girl Gang (novel) 1993

The Perfectionist (play) 1993

Haunted: Tales of the Grotesque (short stories) 1994

What I Lived For (novel) 1994

Will You Always Love Me? (short stories) 1995

You Can't Catch Me [as Rosamond Smith] (novel) 1995

Zombie (novel) 1995

Demon and Other Tales (short stories) 1996

First Love: A Gothic Tale (novel) 1996

Tenderness (novel) 1996

We Were the Mulvaneys (novel) 1996

Double Delight [as Rosamond Smith] (novel) 1997

Man Crazy (novel) 1997

My Heart Laid Bare (novel) 1998

Broke Heart Blues: A Novel (novel) 1999

The Collector of Hearts: New Tales of the Grotesque (short stories) 1999

Starr Bright Will Be with You Soon [as Rosamond Smith] (novel) 1999

Where I've Been, and Where I'm Going: Essays, Reviews, and Prose (essays and nonfiction) 1999

Blonde (novel) 2000

Faithless: Tales of Transgression (short stories) 2001

Middle Age: A Romance (novel) 2001

Beasts (novel) 2002

Big Mouth & Ugly Girl (novel) 2002

I'll Take You There (novel) 2002

Bad Girls (play) 2003

The Faith of a Writer: Life, Craft, Art (nonfiction) 2003

Freaky Green Eyes (novel) 2003

Small Avalanches and Other Stories (short stories) 2003

Tattooed Girl (novel) 2003

Where is Little Reynard? (juvenilia) 2003

I Am No One You Know (short stories) 2004

JOYCE CAROL OATES (STORY DATE 1996)

SOURCE: Oates, Joyce Carol. "The Temple." In *American Gothic Tales,* edited by Joyce Carol Oates, pp. 346-48. New York: Plume, 1996.

The following short story originally appeared in the collection Demon and Other Tales *in 1996.*

There, again, the vexing, mysterious sound!—a faint mewing cry followed by a muffled scratching, as of something being raked by nails, or claws. At first the woman believed the sound must be coming from somewhere inside the house, a small animal, perhaps a squirrel, trapped in the attic beneath the eaves, or in a remote corner of the earthen-floored cellar; after she searched the house thoroughly, she had to conclude that it emanated from somewhere outside, at the bottom of the old garden, perhaps. It was far more distinct at certain times than at others, depending upon the direction and velocity of the wind.

How like a baby's cry, terribly distressing to hear! and the scratching, which came in spasmodic, desperate flurries, was yet more distressing, evoking an obscure horror.

The woman believed she'd first begun hearing the sound at the time of the spring thaw in late March, when melting ice dripped in a continuous arhythmic delirium from chimneys, roofs, eaves, trees. With the coming of warm weather, her bedroom window open to the night, her sleep was increasingly disturbed.

She had no choice, then, did she?—she must trace the sound to its origin. She set about the task calmly enough one morning, stepping out into unexpectedly bright, warm sunshine, and making her way into the lush tangle of vegetation that had been her mother's garden of thirty years before. The mewing sound, the scratching—it seemed to be issuing from the very bottom of the garden, close by a stained concrete drainage ditch that marked the end of the property. As soon as she listened for it, however, it ceased.

How steady the woman's heartbeat, amid the quickening pulse of a May morning.

Out of the old garage, that had once been a stable, the woman got a shovel, a spade, a rake, these implements festooned in cobwebs and dust, and began to dig. It was awkward work and her soft hands ached after only minutes, so she returned to the garage to fetch gardening gloves—these too covered in cobwebs and dust, and stiffened with dirt. The mid-morning sun was ablaze so she located an old straw hat of her mother's: it fitted her head oddly, as if its band had been sweated through and dried, stiffened asymmetrically.

So she set again to work. First, she dug away sinewy weeds and vines, chicory, wild mustard, tall grasses, in the area out of which the cry had emanated; she managed to uncover the earth, which was rich with compost, very dark, moist. Almost beneath her feet, the plaintive mewing sounded! "Yes. Yes. I'm here," she whispered. She paused, very excited; she heard a brief flurry of scratching, then silence. "I'm here, now." She grunted as she pushed the shovel into the earth, urging it downward with her weight, her foot; it was a pity she'd so rarely used gardening implements, in all of her fifty years. She was a naturally graceful woman so out of her element here she felt ludicrous to herself, like a beast on its hind legs.

She dug. She spaded, and raked. She dug again, deepening and broadening the hole which was like a wound in the jungle-like vegetation. Chips and shards of aged brick, glass, stones were uncovered, striking the shovel. Beetles scurried away, their shells glinting darkly in the sunshine. Earthworms squirmed, some of them cut cruelly in two. For some time the woman worked in silence, hearing only her quickened heartbeat and a roaring pulse in her ears; then, distinctly, with the impact of a shout, there came the pleading cry again, so close she nearly dropped the shovel.

At last, covered in sweat, her hands shaking, the woman struck something solid. She dropped to her knees and groped in the moist dark earth and lifted something round and hollow—a human skull? But it was small, hardly half the size of an adult's skull.

"My God!" the woman whispered.

Squatting then above the jagged hole, turning the skull in her fingers. How light it was! The color of parchment, badly stained from the soil. She brushed bits of damp earth away, marveling at the subtle contours of the cranium. Not a hair remained. The delicate bone was cracked in several places and its texture minutely scarified, like a ceramic glaze. A few of the teeth were missing, but most appeared to be intact, though caked with dirt. The perfectly formed jaws, the slope of the cheekbones! The empty eye sockets, so round . . . The woman lifted the skull to stare into the sockets as if staring into mirror-eyes, eyes of an eerie transparency. A kind of knowledge passed between her and these eyes yet she did not know: was this a child's skull? had a child been buried here, it must have been decades ago, on her family's property? Unnamed, unmarked? Unacknowledged? Unknown?

For several fevered hours the woman dug deeper into the earth. She was panting in the overhead sun, which seemed to penetrate the straw hat as if it were made of gauze; her sturdy body was clammy with sweat. She discovered a number of scattered bones—a slender forearm, curving ribs, part of a hand, fingers—these too parchment-colored, child-sized. What small, graceful fingers! How they had scratched, clawed, for release! Following this morning, forever, the finger bones would be at peace.

By early afternoon, the woman gave up her digging. She could find no more of the skeleton than a dozen or so random bones.

She went up to the house, and returned quickly, eagerly, with a five-foot runner of antique velvet cloth, a deep wine color, in which to carry the skull and bones up to the house. For no one must see. No one must know. "*I am here, I will always be here*," the woman promised. "*I will never abandon you.*" She climbed to the second floor of the house, and in her bedroom at the rear she lay the velvet runner on a table beside her bed and beneath a bay window through whose diamond-shaped, leaded panes a reverent light would fall. Tenderly, meticulously, the woman arranged the skull and bones into the shape of a human being. Though most of the skeleton was missing, it would never seem to the woman's loving eye that this was so.

In this way the woman's bedroom became a secret temple. On the velvet cloth the skull and bones, unnamed, would be discovered after the woman's death, but that was a long way off.

GENERAL COMMENTARY

JAMES EGAN (ESSAY DATE 1990)

SOURCE: Egan, James. "'Romance of a Darksome Type': Versions of the Fantastic in the Novels of Joyce Carol Oates." *Studies in Weird Fiction* 7 (1990): 12-21.

In the following essay, Egan discusses Oates's combination of "the parodic, the visionary, and the apocalyptic, into a Gothic delineation of the American Dream" in Wonderland, Son of the Morning, Bellefleur, A Bloodsmoor Romance, *and* Mysteries of Winterthurn.

During the 1970s a critical consensus began to take shape about the fiction of Joyce Carol Oates, namely that her work was moving away from "external", realistic experiences toward the fantastic and visionary (Walker 27; Wagner xix). "Her writings," Mary Kathryn Grant has suggested, "presuppose a nightmare world which challenges the very limits of man's endurance and tries his spirit to the breaking point" (2). Increasingly, this "nightmare world" has assumed peculiarly Gothic qualities. Probably the best description of Oatesian Gothic has been offered by Greg Johnson: "Her work combines such traditionally Gothic elements as extreme personal isolation, violent physical and psychological conflict, settings and symbolic action used to convey painfully heightened psychological states, and a prose style of passionate, often melodramatic intensity" (16-17). The Gothic is prominent, concentrated and of particular importance to the thematic statement Oates makes in five novels: *Wonderland* (1971), *Son of the Morning* (1978), *Bellefleur* (1980), *A Bloodsmoor Romance* (1982), and *Mysteries of Winterthurn* (1984). An examination of these novels reveals that Oates has refined two forms of Gothicism, a contemporary and a somewhat antiquarian version, to the point where she can articulate an intricate cultural fable which integrates a wide range of thematic motifs, character types, and narrative patterns long associated with the Gothic tradition. That fable derives from her ironic perception of the American Dream and its workings. In short, Oates combines several discrete elements which recur in her writing, notably the parodic, the visionary, and the apocalyptic, into a Gothic delineation of the American Dream. As her Gothic mode evolves from *Wonderland* to *Mysteries of Winterthurn* another significant pattern develops: she moves from an indirect, allusive, and aesthetically remote high Gothic toward a direct, overt use of recognizable Gothic idioms found in popular literature for the past century.

Several parallels between the Gothic aesthetic and the general characteristics of Oates's fiction are readily apparent. Her vision of the world is typically dark, skeptical, and parodic, stressing "confrontations with mindless evil", frenetic quests which result in discoveries of inner "emptiness", "hidden, unlovely depths of passion", or the perilously thin line between civilized behavior and savagery (Creighton 27, 32, 40). Her first five novels have been described as "dramatizations of nightmares" (Grant 8). Consistently, Oates examines the shifting borders between the real and the illusory, the self and the Other. For more than a decade she has shown a recurring fascination with the "ways the personality may be invaded by mysterious and unpredictable moments of vision, insight or inspiration, and with the dislocations such invasions cause in the texture of everyday life" (Waller 82). In both her realistic and non-realistic fiction, Oates deals with a remarkably wide range of psychological horror, madness, obsession, and paranoia (Creighton 18). A discussion of the novels in question will illustrate their Gothic qualities.

In a 1980 interview with *The Paris Review* Oates was asked whether the fact that she had written about medicine, law, politics, religion, and spectator sports meant that she was consciously "filling out a 'program' of novels about American life" (370). Though Oates denied that she was deliberately developing such a scheme, American settings, characters, and themes manifest themselves prominently in all her long fiction, and as her vision of American culture and its value systems clarifies, the Gothic slant of her writing becomes more apparent. Written before Oates's Gothic aesthetic had fully asserted itself, *Wonderland* (1971) blends the realistic, grotesque, absurd, and macabre. *Wonderland* may be fairly described as "horrific" and a "shocker", yet Oates refrains from extremes of the fantastic in her subject matter and plot line. The novel's opening details the sort of sensational episode common in tabloids or even newspaper headlines: one day in December 1939 Jesse Harte returns from school to find that his father, having murdered the entire family, now waits for him in their chillingly quiet home. Jesse flees into the night as the sound of his father's shotgun blast fades behind him; though wounded, he has escaped death. After he has lived for awhile with his grandfather, doing heavy farmwork in a grimly naturalistic setting, the affluent Pedersen family adopts Jesse, who becomes a "project" for Dr. Karl Pedersen and strives to emulate his new "father" in all ways, eventually winding up in medical school. Oates presents realistically, almost minutely, the numbingly demanding duties of an intern in a large metropolitan hospital and the grinding pressures that beset Jesse as he evolves into a prominent brain surgeon.

The grotesque and the absurd, however, go hand-in-hand with his professional success. The entire Pedersen family is obscenely fat and obsessed with eating: Hildie and Friedrica, Jesse's siblings, are obese, neurotic child prodigies, and Mrs. Pedersen an obese alcoholic. Oates establishes grotesque gluttony as a metaphor of the various obsessions and compulsions which haunt Jesse throughout his life. She sets the Gothic tenor of

Wonderland by means of a motif Irving Malin associates with new American Gothic, the monstrous family, in this case headed by a narcissistic, "misery-giving" father and containing stunted siblings (58, 65). The Pedersen family tries in various ways to "suffocate" Jesse and "no solution to family strife" seems possible. As Malin argues, images of suffocation and endless strife characterize the new American Gothic version of the familial (9, 80-90). Problems more profound than gluttony set in when Jesse begins work as an intern at a Chicago hospital. At the point, *Wonderland* recalls Kafka's absurdist parable, "A Country Doctor". Jesse must confront the human wreckage, pain, and confusion of a brutal urban world: the horror of sick and beaten children; the gruesome sight of a woman who has aborted her fetus with a fruit juice glass; the endless wounds he must minister to. Like Kafka's country doctor, Jesse faces an impossible task, to heal the "wounds of life" which the order of things dictates cannot be healed. Jesse cannot stop the flow of blood any more than the country doctor can heal the inexplicable, worm-infested sore he has been summoned to cure.

Wonderland's parallels with Kafka's allegory also point to the Gothic subtexts which unify Jesse's journey through the nightmare world of American culture. Modern Gothic themes of violence, breakdown, and putrescence permeate the novel (Punter 3). Jesse narrowly escapes from a father who has collapsed, only to enter an environment where insanity reigns. The Pedersen family is a bizarre illusion, all of whose members have retreated into the neuroses that best sustain them. Despite Karl Pedersen's grandiose, patriarchal ambitions and tyrannical power, he and his family are degenerating, and the amount of psychological violence he can bring to bear on them cannot arrest the decline. Moreover, as Jesse interns he enters what amounts to an urban Gothic environment of dark hospital corridors, chaos, and various species of death, pressures which erode his sanity. His hospital setting contains various Gothic "paraphernalia of death", not only the grim devices of abortion (318), but the vast medical machines designed to save lives, machinery which seems at times to do the opposite (Hennessy 50). Yet *Wonderland*'s closest affinities with the Gothic tradition are classical; its echoes of Shelley's *Frankenstein*.[1] Early on, Karl Pedersen has a protective, almost messianic interest in Jesse, just as Victor Frankenstein had in the creature—the creature was Victor's "project", and Jesse becomes Pederson's. Like the creature, Jesse reads voraciously and tries earnestly to learn from the social world he inhabits. Ultimately, Pedersen disinherits and disowns Jesse, much as Victor disowned the creature. Yet in each case the legacy of the creator lives on: *Wonderland* abounds in macabre, perverse doctors and scientists, Dr. Perrault in particular, who all serve as ironic role models for Jesse as he tries to define his identity. Throughout the novel, Jesse's past haunts him, and he repeatedly tries to escape from it, as Victor did from his. No matter what Jesse does, though, he inevitably parrots Pedersen in thought, deed, even in word. Like the creature, Jesse is a double, a simultaneous embodiment and refutation of Pedersen's ideals.

Oates has, in effect, gothicized the American Dream, for the reader discovers in Jesse's life an inverted Horatio Alger parable in which Jesse acts much like a Gothic hero in his aggressive quest for power, success, and, in his role as brain surgeon, control over life and death (Day 17). The sins of Pedersen are revisited, in Gothic fashion, on Jesse, who lives an emotionally empty life in a mansion not unlike Pedersen's, torturing his daughters in some of the ways Pedersen had tortured his own children (MacAndrew 85). Zombie-like, Jesse acts out the false, horrific American Dream of "conquest, control, ownership" and the triumph over "mutability" (Friedman 177). As Jesse moves across the symbolic landscape of American culture he disappears into the Gothic darkness. The skeptical vision of Gothicism converts Jesse's search for success and freedom into the worship of a destructive bondage. Modern American culture often mythologizes the doctor as a secular savior. *Wonderland*'s Gothic vision offers a dark version of this mythology, for although Jesse the brain surgeon has the power to save life, by the novel's end he has become the psychological destroyer of his wife and daughters, as much the destroyer as his mad-doctor mentors were. Oates demythologizes the sacrosanct American healer of the body, the doctor. She does so with a sophisticated mixture of contemporary and classical Gothic motifs which are worked into the texture of a complex psychological novel. True, *Wonderland* qualifies as horrific in many ways, but Oates depends upon an erudite evocation of the Gothic rather than stereotypical devices of plot and character. Her extensive thematic reliance upon Shelley's *Frankenstein*, for example, is allegorical and indirect rather than literal, and the same might be said of her allusions to the fantastic works of Lewis Carroll and Franz Kafka. Her strategy of indirection

makes substantial demands of the reader, calling upon him to decipher patterns subtle enough to qualify as "high" Gothic. The reader must recognize the nuances of the Gothic tradition to feel comfortable with Oates's subtexts.

Published in 1978, shortly after Oates has "officially" experimented with Gothicism in two short story collections, the *Poisoned Kiss* (1975) and *Night-Side* (1977), *Son of the Morning* shows a more pronounced Gothic configuration than *Wonderland* did. Oates again draws upon recognizable features of contemporary American life, religious fundamentalism, electronic evangelism, and faith healing, treating many of the details of the evangelist Nathan Vickery's career realistically: Nathan's presence at a rural snake-handling ritual, his apprenticeship under the Reverend Marian Miles Beloff, and his final emergence as a Christian cult figure. Her primary concern in *Son of the Morning* appears to be exploring, through Vickery's behavior, the numinous (or what passes for it) and the relationship between divine and diabolic. As S. L. Varnado has demonstrated, a pronounced interest in the numinous, particularly in its "sense of absolute overpoweringness", the "mysterium" or form of the numinous experience and the paradoxical qualities of attraction and repulsion inherent in the numinous has long been a part of Gothic tradition (12-13). Put another way, "except for the fact that Gothicism rids itself of moral prohibitions, the Gothic vision clearly approximates religious affirmations" (Bayer-Berenbaum 13). Many similarities can be found between Christ's life and Vickery's. By the age of eight, Nathan has developed a "peculiar . . . precosity", almost a psychic intuition. Also at the age of eight, he has a conversation with his grandfather Thaddeus, a confirmed atheist, which parallels the young Christ's examination by the elders in the temple (117-26); like Christ, Nathan demonstrates to his elder a wisdom beyond the boy's years. From his adolescence on, moreover, Nathan experiences raptures, visions of Christ, and vivid, occasionally Dantean glimpses into the world of the damned (157). Throughout his life, Nathan's relationship with others seems remote, as though his comprehension of the human condition suffers because he is partly other, not completely human; the situation echoes the mysteries of Christ's divine-human nature. Nathan's intuitive insight, his power as a faith healer (which seems to grow as the book progresses), and his acute sensitivity to the workings of a world beyond the material suggest the Gothic qualities of the novel as well.[2] Whether or not Vickery's behavior and powers fully qualify him as a Gothic being, he surely does fit the prototype of a Gothic hero: active, seeking power, and in this case godhood (Day 17). Eventually, Vickery comes to believe that he is Christ, and in a public ceremony on Good Friday mutilates himself as an act of "humility" by cutting out his eye (236).

The mutilation signals a change in the tenor and direct of *Son of the Morning* as Oates begins to illustrate the relationships between the divine and the diabolic. Significantly she entitles the section of the novel where Nathan begins to appear demonic "Last Things", an apocalyptic phrase which calls to mind the reign of Antichrist before the end of time. In some respects, the mutilated Nathan's attitude resembles that of Satan, the biblical "Son of the Morning". After the blinding, for example, he considers himself above sin (257) and inclines to a regressive gospel of hate (323-24). Nathan revels in the public consciousness of him as an "avatar of Christ" (299), displaying some extraordinary powers which imply that he may, in fact, be the supernatural being his disciples perceive him to be. In one instance, Nathan disarms a follower who attacks him with a hunting knife. To witnesses, Nathan's fingers appear badly slashed, yet neither cuts nor blood can be found on his hands (313). Another time, an attacker delivers a vicious blow to his forehead with a crowbar, but his head is only bruised, not crushed (354).[3] Nathan's career as an avatar culminates in his most powerful experience of the Other:

> He saw that the hole before him *was* a mouth, and that the writhing dancing molecules of flesh were being sucked into it, and ground to nothing . . . but really he heard nothing and saw nothing, for You had swallowed the entire world. He knew his ministry was over, his life was over, that everything had come to pass as it was ordained, but he knew also—for even then You allowed him the realization of certain truths—that his terror had just begun.
>
> (362-633)

An ontological horror of a God consumes Nathan, a great vortex fully as terrifying as the scenes of hell he had witnessed earlier in the novel (157, 226). Or perhaps Satan has chosen to claim his fallen avatar.

Nathan's vision of the God-thing represents the culmination of a series of modern Gothic motifs which parody not only the messianic faith healer but the concept of the divine he represents. Nathan's "incarnation" mocks the Christian version of the Incarnation: his mother was gang-raped and his father was never identified. As Nathan testifies for Christ early in his career, he learns the "trade" of preaching from the Mammon-like Beloff troupe, whose every action mimics religious conviction. Violence and spiritual rape predominate in the "Last Things" (Punter 3). Nathan's followers physically and emotionally attack him and he appears to be undergoing a nervous collapse after becoming convinced that he and Christ are one. Gothic doubling mocks Nathan's raptures: the demonic imitates the divine and worse, seems inseparable from it. *Son of the Morning* offers a Gothic-fantastic treatment of the numinous—ontologically dreadful, cold, and repellent, totally Other and unknowable. The story contains enough conflicting or confusing data about the numinous to prevent the reader from achieving harmony with it. We are left, instead, with the discomforting idea that the numinous cannot be deciphered, and that if it were, mankind would tremble in fear before the God-thing, an alien, formless horror. Oates concedes in Nathan's vision of the vortex that the numinous appears to be overpowering, but her treatment of "creature-consciousness", of being "dust and ashes" and the sense of "sheer self-depreciation" that the numinous allegedly brings about seems ominous (Varnado 12). If the "mysterium" or form of the numinous is something "absolutely and intensely positive", she again calls the phenomenon into question (Varnado 12).

Oates's treatment of the numinous in *Son of the Morning* may be read as another Gothic version of the American Dream, focused this time on a healer of the soul instead of the body. Ambiguity and parody riddle her portrait of this spiritual healer. Even if one were to argue that she affirms rather than doubts the numinous, Oates echoes a Gothic "contempt for the forms of institutionalized religion" (Bayer-Berenbaum 37). The reader recalls that Nathan's rise to power and spiritual control causes him to join forces with the Beloffs, and then to set up his own megalomanic cult; in both cases the "forms of institutionalized religion" are suspect. Nathan's gospel of hate parodies the American Dream's assumptions about the New Jerusalem's redemptive powers, and his Gothic vision of the Other undercuts the notion of visionary transcendence itself. As she had done in *Wonderland,* Oates again treats the Gothic idiom allusively and indirectly. To cite one instance, the novel's title recalls Milton's Satan in *Paradise Lost,* a character Nathan comes to resemble in the story's final section. The concept of the numinous itself, the experience of God and the validity of the experience, is intricate, not easily accessible.

Oates handles this complex concept in a complex way, presenting **Son of the Morning** as a psychological novel, though it admittedly features the familiar American character type of the preacher. She adds yet another level of complexity to an indirect, ambiguous tale by means of an ambivalent narrative point of view. The reader must struggle to identify the narrator, who eventually turns out to be Nathan taking a retrospective look at his life. **Son of the Morning** uses the Gothic, but not to reach a wide audience.

In 1980 Oates began what she considered a "cycle" of experimental "genre" novels with **Bellefleur** (Johnson 6). The "Afterword" to the paperback edition of **Mysteries of Winterthurn** (1985) suggests that her efforts have a particular intention, to "present America . . . through the prismatic lens of its most popular genres—the family saga and family memoir, the Gothic romance, the detective-mystery novel, and the horror novel" (Johnson 6-7).

In **Bellefleur** Oates does more than draw upon virtually the entire range of Gothic conventions, for she manages, by means of the elaborate, interlocking tales in this family history, to fashion a Gothic epic and to recreate America in miniature. She combines genres in such a way that the story of the Bellefleurs could be described as a "demonic history text" (Gross 2). Bellefleur Manor, "known locally as Bellefleur Castle" (3), epitomizes a classical Gothic setting: huge, antique, ornate, and sometimes baroque in design, with storm-damaged turrets, a vast, gloomy cellar, and a maze of rooms, some of them unused for decades. So singular is the Bellefleur "history of misfortune" that the family could be said to be laboring under the sort of curse traditional in classical Gothic literature. Supernatural powers abound and a variety of Gothic beings thrive in the castle's environment or manage to work themselves into the sprawling Bellefleur family. The Turquoise Room distinguishes itself as one of the most prominent locations in the manor, possessed of a strange odor no matter how thoroughly it may be aired or scrubbed, and in which guests encounter a number of "*foreign* presences" (199). After spending a night in the room to investigate its foreign quality, Samuel Bellefleur undergoes a profound psychological change, so profound that his father acknowledges that "what stared coldly at him out of Samuel's eyes was no longer exactly his son" (202). Hepatica Bellefleur discovers an equally haunting presence in the form of her husband, a peculiarly dark man with "cruel red-rimmed eyes", who "gives off a fetid, meaty odor" (281), and

sports "tufts of hair . . . on the backs of his hands and high on his cheeks" (281). "No matter how improbable, how incredible it might seem" (281), Hepatica has married a black bear, a were-thing who certainly appeared human when she first met him. Veronica fares no better after falling in love with the mysterious count Ragnar Norst, whose courtship leaves her alternately rapturous and lethargic. Norst prefers that they meet in the evening, often in clandestine or deserted places (369). Veronica's brother, Aaron, suspicious of Norst, meets with a drowning accident—those who find his body discover a corpse that has been "bled white" (368). Veronica grows progressively more listless and pale until, after an attack of "pneumonia", she awakens, strangely transformed into a woman who now shares the Count's antipathy toward the living. Veronica, it seems, has succumbed to the charms of a vampire. Each of these vignettes represents a variation on the Gothic theme of metamorphosis and accentuates the narrative complexity of **Bellefleur**: Oates has incorporated into the novel three classical Gothic subgenres, the haunting, the werewolf fable, and the vampire tale. As David Punter points out, this technique of assimilation typifies a sophisticated Gothic narrative structure, and Bellefleur Castle has many such stories to tell (403).

Both the manor and the family, moreover, give off the odor of cultural and psychic decay which permeates modern Gothic literature. Once a wellspring of vitality, the robust marriage of Leah and Gideon gradually disintegrates. Gideon's passion turns to hatred and he engineers the apocalyptic climax of the novel by crashing his airplane into the castle and leveling it. Before her fiery death, Leah's relentless scheming finally succeeds in securing the release from prison of the aged Jean-Pierre Bellefleur II, imprisoned for most of his life on a murder charge. Seemingly senile and disoriented, Jean-Pierre recollects himself enough to address a migrant labor problem affecting the Bellefleur farming enterprises by murdering the leaders of the migrants' union. Nor are aesthetic or religious escapes from the family possible. Vernon, the only poetically inclined Bellefleur, is drowned in the Nautauga river by a drunken crowd of mill workers who fail to appreciate his efforts to incite poetic rapture in them (324). Jedediah, long an exile from the castle because of a burning mystical wish to experience God, finally realizes his desire, though in a bizarre form. Pleading with God to show His face, Jedediah suffers excruciating diarrhetic spasms (440) lasting more than a day. Suicide, murderous rampages, and spiritual degradation serve as modern expressions of the ancestral curse: Oates extends the Gothic motif of the collapsing self to the entire family (Day 78).

Moreover, she organizes the saga of the Bellefleurs around several specifically Gothic themes, notably sexual transgressions (Punter 19, 410-12). On a symbolically stormy night, a strange creature, rat-sized and skeletal, appears at the castle door. The creature turns out to be a large cat, eventually named Mahalaleel, who possesses uncanny powers and develops a strong affection for Leah; in fact, Mahalaleel sleeps in Gideon and Leah's bed—between them. Soon after the cat's arrival, Leah becomes pregnant and undergoes a fantastic physical change, growing to Gideon's height and experiencing a distortion of her facial features so that her "mouth and the flared nostrils and the eyes [seemed] visibly enlarged, as if a somewhat ill-fitting mask had been forced upon her" (55). She gives birth to a "monstrous" child, a hermaphrodite. The episode suggests that Leah has been impregnated by a demon and produced a semi-human child who proves preternaturally precocious—once the unnecessary male organs have been tidily snipped off with a scissors. Leah's inclination to the sexually perverse includes her fascination with Nightshade, a dwarf discovered by Gideon on a hunting trip. Like Mahalaleel, Nightshade dotes on Leah, taking on the role of her devoted servant and confidant; as Gideon's affections stray, the dwarf grows physically larger and more appealing. Again the narrative implies an eccentric sexual relationship, for this is the same Leah who, before she married, kept a huge pet spider named Love which intimidated her suitors (130). Sexual aberrations and "crimes caused by a distortion of natural drives" are not the only Gothic transgressions favored by the Bellefleurs (MacAndrew 88). The assumption that Gothic literature's most prevalent theme may be the revisiting of the sins of the fathers finds ample illustration in the novel. The "sins of the fathers" appears to be a synonym for the family curse, and as Leah's sexual peculiarities and occult child suggest, Oates allows mothers to share equally with fathers. The fate of Vernon indicates that he, too, has suffered for his fathers' errors—the mill workers vengefully drown him in part because he belongs to a family which has financially tyrannized them and their ancestors. In a bizarrely ironic way, the overbearing aristocratic pretensions of the Bellefleurs may even have accounted for the fate of Veronica: had an "aristocratic" mien not prevailed among the Bellefleurs, Count Norst would perhaps have bypassed them. In these and a multitude of other ways, the Bellefleur past wreaks havoc on the present. Fate seems to have decreed that the castle must fall, as inevitably as the House of Usher did.

Oates's creation of a sophisticated, multi-generational family saga allows her to comment on broader patterns in American culture while she recounts the family history. As the novel progresses, Leah grows obsessed with restoring Jean-Pierre's vast empire to its former glory; at the point where Gideon destroys the manor, she has barely over a thousand acres of the original property left to acquire. Leah's empire-building signals the crass indulgence of the most materialistic aspects of the American Dream, the crude desires for power in the form of wealth and the manipulation of others. This rage to live out the Bellefleur fantasy of empire puts her at the mercy of the foreboding ironies of the Gothic universe—indeed, as the novel's plot indicates, her capitalistic quest has dissolved into a Gothically circular journey to nowhere (Day 18). Leah's urge to consolidate and Gideon's passion to acquire and ruin people and possessions alike have led each to a cultural horror, the emptiness of the Dream. Both qualify as Gothic villains, overreachers blind to the probability that by dreaming out the deadly Dream they are compounding the Bellefleur curse invoked by the grasping ruthlessness of their forefathers. Like other Gothic overreachers, they deny fate, deny the basic and necessarily limiting conditions of their existence in a doomed attempt to recreate an earthly American paradise in the wilderness. *Bellefleur* cautions that the alluring wilderness conceals the dark and ominous, demons and specters eager for self-deluded victims. Oates's saga broadens her cultural critique of the American Dream by showing that the twentieth century shares an ancient Gothic malaise of the spirit.

As suggested earlier, Oates recounts in *Bellefleur* a designedly "popular" Gothic parable. Whether in the novels of Louisa May Alcott, Thornton Wilder, or John Steinbeck, or in the contemporary weekly television series, the family saga has long enjoyed an enthusiastic audience. Fanciers of the Gothic, moreover, would surely find Oates's tales of shape-shifters, supernatural possession, were-creatures, and vampires, along with the Gothic penchant for melodramatic exaggeration, visible and familiar from their many reincarnations in twentieth-century popular literature and film. As a possible final concession to the workings of popular idioms, Oates presents less psychological intricacy and a more fixed narrative point of view than she had utilized in *Wonderland* and *Son of the Morning.*

An Author's Note to *Bellefleur* claims that in the novel "the implausible is granted an authority and honored with a complexity usually reserved for realistic fiction", calling attention to Oates's creation of a sophisticated Gothic idiom. Having refined the idiom in *Bellefleur,* she provides variations on selected themes in *A Bloodsmoor Romance* (1982) and *Mysteries of Winterthurn* (1984), her most recent Gothic tales. As the narrator of *Bloodsmoor,* who designates herself the historian of the Zinn family, points out, her efforts may be construed as "allegorical" and "exemplary" (520), and *Bloodsmoor* could fairly be called a "romance of the darksome and Gothic type" as well (68). Oates establishes and interrelates several narrative worlds in the novel, the world of pastoral romance, the genteel, drawing-room world of manners, and the Gothic world. She organizes *Bloodsmoor* around a favorite motif, initiation, in this case with a Gothic twist: all the Zinn daughters enter the Gothic universe through various access routes and their experiences collectively constitute an allegorical fable about that universe. Malvinia, the most haughty and tempestuous of the lot, leaves home for a scandalous career as an actress, becoming the mistress and protégé of the renowned rake, Orlando Vandenhoffen. Malvinia indulges herself in the subtle Gothic decadence of the Gilded Age: dissolute parties, fashionable skepticism, and indulgent promiscuity. Malvinia's environment might easily pass for elegant instead of decadent if not for her regular, unsettling sexual experiences with what she considers the "Mark of the Beast". Frequently her paramours discover a ferociously aggressive female, one who bites, kicks, curses, and even yanks at the "masculine organ of regeneration" of Mark Twain, her most celebrated lover. Malvinia and the narrator see her sexuality as a type of demonic possession in which "The Beast [forces] himself into her slender, writhing body—fitting her arms and limbs, and torso, and the nether regions of her being, like a powerful hand thrusting itself into a snug and slightly resistant lady's glove" (463). The Beast parodies Malvinia's attempts at "love declarations, kisses, caresses, and other amorous indulgences" (454) with a Gothic expression of doubling, drawing out a hidden personality, an unorthodox self. Deirdre, adopted by John Quincy and Prudence Zinn at an early age, encounters more explicit and menacing forms of the supernatural. Occult presences surround Deirdre from her childhood on, and at times seem to control her. She takes the inevitable path to womanhood by becoming a famous medium, but her preternatural gifts prove perilous. At one of Deirdre's séances, a Professor Bey, participating in a rationalist inquiry into the proceedings, is invaded by an alien, hostile force. Not long after, Deirdre's own contact spirits overwhelm her, plunging her into the chaotic darkness of the Spirit World (499).

Octavia, the most conventional and tranquil of the sisters, opts for what she assumes will be a traditional marriage to Mr. Lucius Rumford, a wealthy widower of what prove to be decidedly eccentric sexual habits. Soon after the marriage, Rumford puts a hood over Octavia's head before performing the "*unitary act*" (386). With the passage of time, his conjugal demands grow "gradually more exacting, and more challenging of definition" (425), until they culminate in a most unusual request: he asks Octavia to put a noose around his neck and pull with all the force she can muster. The hooded wife obliges and proceeds to strangle her husband. The Rumford marriage, a Gothically mocking venture into the sexually bizarre, into rape, violence, and death, results in an equally disturbing offspring, Godfrey. An impish, unpredictable child bristling with a dark energy, Godfrey resents Sarah, his infant sister. One day Octavia awakens to a "vertiginous sense of horror, as of suffocation" (433) and rushes to Sarah's room, to find Godfrey standing near the crib of his dead sister. Octavia has perhaps witnessed the revisiting of the sins of the fathers, the disruption of her ordered world by a demonically inspired being from the Gothic universe. Constance Philippa Zinn starts early on a journey into that universe, and exotic transformations mark her passing. When her husband enters the boudoir on their wedding night, he finds a dressmaker's dummy occupying Constance Philippa's place in bed. His bride has disappeared, and she does not reappear until the final chapter, where another fantastic transformation reveals itself. Constance Philippa has adopted the name Philippe Fox, and for good reason: "Mr. Fox was assuredly a male, in every particular: the growth, and expansion, and forcible protuberance, of the inner female organ, being now nearly complete, and having attained a length of some five or six inches in repose" (596). A Gothic metamorphosis has occurred and a new identity has emerged, the true Constance Philippa. Samantha, long her father's devoted laboratory assistant, reckons with the Gothic universe in ways no less sensational than those of her sisters. John Quincy Zinn proves to be one of his age's most distinguished inventors, whose credits include a time machine and the electric chair and whose dreams late in life include a *"perpetual-motion machine"* which he expects to apply to the "phenomenon of *atom-expansion* or *detonation"* (607). Samantha's exposure to her father's eccentric habits, her marriage to the mysterious Nahurn, and her fascination with the process of invention suggest that she may evolve into the haunted wizard John Quincy Zinn finally became. Samantha, however, repudiates her father's apocalyptic zeal for the destruction of the human race, turning her energies to such mundane matters as the inventions of a *"self-filling pen"* and a *"baby-mobile"* (672). Her choice of more humane inventions implies that she has seen the implications of John Quincy Zinn's absorption by the Gothic universe.

The final chapters of **Bloodsmoor** clarify the ultimate significance of the Gothic initiations of the Zinn girls. Generally, Oates diminishes the traumatic effects of terror evoked by the Gothic universe, for each of the Zinns has not only survived her initiation but has seemingly gained from it. Confronting the reversals, deteriorations, violence, and lack of purpose in the Gothic universe has helped each to find her true self, accept it, and then maintain it in an America reluctant to take females seriously. In fact, entering the Gothic universe has, metaphorically, sophisticated all five and given them some distance from the corrosive influence of the patriarchal utopianism characteristic of the American Dream in the nineteenth century, a utopianism which renders femininity inferior and subordinate. As an "exemplary" fable, Bloodsmoor proposes that only when the Gothic universe which coexists with the materialistic, destructively genteel America of the nineteenth century has been reckoned with, can the nation meet the Modern Age as the Zinn sisters did. Oates implies that the Gothic world can be finally redemptive and not destructive by allowing each of the girls to find true love, in several cases a love abandoned since youth because of the unrealistic demands of gentility. Eileen Bender's claim that **Bloodsmoor** may be seen as a "work of feminist resistance" (132) can be supported by the novel's Gothic initiation rites, which all suggest the competence, creativity, resilience, honesty, and good judgment of the nineteenth-century American woman, despite the societal limitations designed for her. In **Bloodsmoor** women generally lead the way into the Gothic universe, whereas in the stock Gothic novel an aggressive male usually does, and they surmount daunting obstacles or find effective ways to mitigate the Gothic's dark power, proving the Dream's stereotypical perception of women wrong.

To popularize her Gothic romance, Oates not only draws upon the appeal of the supernatural in many ways, particularly in the character of John Quincy Zinn, a more overt and recognizable Frankenstein-figure than Jesse Pederson was in **Wonderland**, but she capitalizes upon American Gothic narrative's tendency to provide an "alternative history of the American experience" (Grass 3). In this case, she draws a series of ironic parallels between **Bloodsmoor** and a well-known nineteenth-century family history and female conduct book, Louisa May Alcott's *Little Women* (1868). Alcott's women were the essence of accepted, conventional behavior, and they had no contact whatever with the Gothic universe. Oates seems determined to achieve her own sort of popularity by writing an often lurid, dire, sensational exposé of the Alcott fable, offering in its place a "true history" of what the nineteenth century had denied and counting on her readers to recognize a send-up of an entrenched, easily detected myth about the lives of women. The Gothic serves to entice the reader with its enduringly popular melodramatic intrigue and "scandal".

Mysteries of Winterthurn revolves around the exploits of a detective figure, Xavier Kilgarvan, matching him against the caprices of the Gothic world and recording his attempts to win the love of Perdita, a distant cousin. "The Virgin in the Rose-Bower", Xavier's first case, exposes him to a classical Gothic situation, haunted Glen Mawr Manor and a supernatural murder. Mrs. Abigail Whimbrel, spending a night in the manor's Honeymoon Room, is attacked by vampiric cherubs who seem to inhabit the elaborate mural covering most of one wall. For their primary victim, however, the creatures select Abigail's infant son, eating away "part of the throat and torso, and much of the back of the tender head" (55). The mysterious assaults continue (the next victims are lambs who appear to have been attacked from the air), prompting Xavier to test his skills in a state of affairs for which the authorities have no explanation. The ominous Miss Georgina Kilgarvan, his cousin, strikes him as a prime suspect, but verifiable evidence remains elusive. However, Xavier's own analytical methods and the attitudes which underlie them may be his greatest drawbacks. While investigating the Honeymoon Room, he sees blood dripping from the mural, but soon recovers sufficiently to "observe, in a more composed tone, that the ceiling must be leaking" (103). Even when the demons swoop down on Xavier himself, he refuses to concede the reality of the supernatural. After his climactic discovery of a group of mummified infant corpses in the attic above the Honeymoon Room, he swoons, with the result that his future recollections of seeing Georgina hovering over the bodies cannot be proven to his own satisfaction. Nevertheless, Xavier's failures must not be dismissed as total—at least he meets in the manor the enchanting, beautiful Perdita, who seems very much a part of the preternatural environment, so much so that Xavier perceives a ghostly phantasm of her in his bedroom (92). When the tale ends, however, both the cherubs and Perdita remain mysteries to the young detective.

An older and wiser Xavier tries to solve another local crime, the gruesome ritual murders committed on an allegedly bewitched piece of ground, the Devil's Half-Acre. He methodically reviews the clues, utilizing the latest refinements in the art of criminology, and believes he has found the culprit, the foppish Valentine Westergaard. Now a veritable Sherlock Holmes, Xavier musters sufficient evidence for a trial, but with disastrous results. Westergaard claims that the ghost of a warlock, Elias Fenwick, commandeered him into bringing five sacrificial victims to the Half-Acre. The jury frees Westergaard and indicts Colin, Xavier's brother, as Fenwick's accessory, a situation for which Xavier's mother holds him accountable. Once again, Xavier fails to penetrate what may well have been the supernatural and, though he still loves Perdita, she appears to be further out of reach than ever.

Perdita, however, becomes a major figure in Xavier's last case, "The Bloodstained Bridal Gown", because her husband, the Reverend Harmon Bunting, has been the victim of a gory axe murder. Perdita claims she was raped by the killer, who wiped her own blood on her bridal gown as a way of claiming her for the devil. Summoned from New York to search out the infamous events in the Grace Episcopal rectory, Xavier brings to bear on the matter his highly polished skills, to no avail. Frustrated by false leads and faulty evidence, he turns to drink and dissolution, finally conceding the case. Ironically, concession has its rewards: Xavier eventually wins the hand of the widowed Perdita, vowing never to trade the satisfactions of a husband and father for the "accursèd art of crime detection" (482).[4]

Xavier's consistent failure to resolve mysterious crimes and the romantic reward that accompanies his failure constitutes yet another allegorical statement about the Gothic world. Clearly Xavier does not resemble the sort of detective-hero described by William Patrick Day, the type of character ideally suited to resolve the "genre's tendency toward absolute instability", who can survive in the Gothic world because he can "reconcile the qualities of the male protagonist with those of the Gothic heroine" (Day 50, 55). Xavier's shortcomings amount to a defense of the fantastic and mysterious, his initiations into the supernatural, the violent, and the bizarre validating the power and sacrosanct status of the dark world. Perdita came from that world, the metaphorical haunted manor, and before Xavier can win her he must concede that some knowledge should remain off limits; that the Gothic universe cannot be deciphered by blatantly analytical schemes; and that recognizing the perimeters imposed by the Gothic stands as a necessary condition of his emotional and psychological initiation. **Mysteries of Winterthurn** sacralizes the Gothic by preserving its aura of ambiguity, its Otherness. The process of sacralization constitutes yet another Oatesian indictment of fallacies in the American Dream, this time a metaphorical indictment. Xavier has become a renowned investigator, but at the same time his mindset has become reductively materialistic and his methods little more than Yankee ingenuity, clever tinkering. His materialistic approaches to problems of detection connote the arrogant, aggressive materialism inherent in the Dream itself, a materialism capable of comprehending only the literal and immediate, the very opposites of the elusive, symbolic Gothic. When Xavier confronts the Gothic universe, Oates encourages the reader to arrive at an alternative view of the dream, a view distinct from "pietistic . . . idealization" (Gross 89).

Oates makes the adventures of Xavier Kilgarvan recognizable and accessible by means of the genre of the detective tale and the subject matter of Xavier's investigations. From Dupin and Sherlock Holmes to Mike Hammer and the Continental Op, detective figures have become conspicuous, accepted archetypes of popular literature. Xavier's investigation of the vampiric cherubs allows Oates to link his actions with yet another popular genre, the horror story. She also works the sensational subject matter of the Gothic tradition into his investigation of witchcraft, ritual-cult murders, and, as Cara Chell argues, the possible love-triangle slaying of Perdita's husband (20). In

Winterthurn, then, Oates combines the popular genres of mystery, horror, and sensational romance with a linear narrative structure and psychological clarity to make her novel readable as a thriller.

In the novels we have examined, a broad range of Gothic themes and devices appear, from metamorphosis, to multiplication of the personality, to the transformation of time and space. Oates proves herself adept at evoking versions of the dualism central to both classical and contemporary Gothic, illustrating as well the Gothic premise that many closed worlds lie within the open and familiar. Particularly effective are her Gothic renditions of "alien [personalities] within the conscious self" (Creighton 138). In **Wonderland** and **Son of the Morning** Oates relies primarily upon modern Gothic motifs, while in **Bellefleur, Bloodsmoor,** and **Winterthurn** she adapts classical Gothic to her thematic needs. Each novel develops intricate narrative worlds which interact, with sophisticated effects. **Wonderland** juxtaposes literal and metaphysical Gothic, **Bellefleur** the cultural epic and the family history, and **Bloodsmoor** the utopian fable and the sensational exposé. Her sustained exploration of Gothicism in the context of American culture and mythology links the novels under consideration. The Gothic acts as a device for monstrous parody in **Son of the Morning,** as the crux of an initiation ritual which helps to define the feminine self in *Bloodsmoor,* and as a sacralized form of purification in **Winterthurn. Bellefleur** represents Oates's most ambitious and thorough effort to Gothicize the American Dream and to relate American culture to the fantastic worlds which surround or lie embedded in it. In **Bellefleur** she connects her perception of the Dream as pathology to suitably Gothic images of decay, violence, and the monstrous. Of course, the Gothic vision of Joyce Carol Oates continues to evolve and its final statement cannot yet be determined. However, it is fair to say that she wishes to employ both high and popular literary mediums to achieve her goals. **Bellefleur, Bloodsmoor,** and **Winterthurn** all display her familiarity with the genres, themes, and underlying assumptions of popular literature. In these three novels she has, in effect, translated the allusive, metaphorical, and metaphysically intricate Gothic idiom of **Wonderland** and **Son of the Morning** into a more direct and familiar way of evoking the powerful, durable impression that Gothic melodrama, horror, sensationalism, and violence have traditionally made on the popular imagination.

Notes

1. Cf. Bender, who notes that "*Wonderland* thus is another Oatesian *Frankenstein*" (55). She does not, however, develop the parallels with Shelley's novel in any detail.

2. Cf. Johnson 143, 153-54; Dean 140-43. Both Johnson and Dean point to parallels between Vickery and Christ but do not discuss Oates's treatment of the Gothic numinous.

3. Cf. Dean, who notes that Nathan is "unkillable" (141).

4. Cf. Bender, who points out that when Oates's "doomed detectives give up their search for rational solutions, they open the way for loving resolution" (177).

Works Cited

Bayer-Berenbaum, Linda. *The Gothic Imagination: Expansion in Gothic Literature and Art.* London: Associated University Press, 1982.

Bender, Eileen Tyser. *Joyce Carol Oates: Artist in Residence.* Bloomington: Indiana University Press, 1987.

Chell, Cara. "Untricking the Eye: Joyce Carol Oates and the Feminist Ghost Story." *Arizona Quarterly* 41 (1985): 5-23.

Creighton, Joanne V. *Joyce Carol Oates.* Boston: Twayne, 1979.

Day, William Patrick. *In the Circles of Fear and Desire: A Study of Gothic Fantasy.* Chicago: University of Chicago Press, 1985.

Dean, Sharon L. "Faith and Art: Joyce Carol Oates's *Son of the Morning.*" *Critique* 28 (1987): 135-47.

Friedman, Ellen G. *Joyce Carol Oates.* New York: Ungar, 1980.

Grant, Mary Kathryn. *The Tragic Vision of Joyce Carol Oates.* Durham, NC: Duke University Press, 1978.

Gross, Louis S. *Redefining the American Gothic: From* Wieland *to* Day of the Dead. Ann Arbor, MI: UMI Research Press, 1989.

Hennessy, Brendan. *The Gothic Novel.* London: Longman, 1980.

Johnson, Greg. *Understanding Joyce Carol Oates.* Columbia: University of South Carolina Press, 1987.

MacAndrew, Elizabeth. *The Gothic Tradition in Fiction.* New York: Columbia University Press, 1979.

Malin, Irving. *New American Gothic.* Carbondale: Southern Illinois University Press, 1962.

Oates, Joyce Carol. *Bellefleur.* New York: E. P. Dutton, 1980.

———. *A Bloodsmoor Romance.* New York: E. P. Dutton, 1982.

———. *Contraries: Essays.* New York: Oxford University Press, 1981.

———. "Daisy." *Night-Side: Eighteen Tales.* New York: Vanguard, 1977. 221-43.

———. Interview. *Writers at Work: The* Paris Review *Interviews.* Fifth Series. Ed. George Plimpton. New York: Penguin, 1981. 361-84.

———. *Mysteries of Winterthurn.* New York: E. P. Dutton, 1984.

———. *Son of the Morning.* New York: Vanguard, 1978.

———. *Wonderland.* New York: Vanguard, 1971.

Punter, David. *The Literature of Terror: A History of Gothic Fictions from 1765 to the Present Day.* London: Longman, 1980.

Varnado, S. L. *Haunted Presence: The Numinous in Gothic Fiction.* Tuscaloosa: University of Alabama Press, 1987.

Wagner, Linda W., ed. *Critical Essays on Joyce Carol Oates.* Boston: G. K. Hall, 1979.

Waller, G. F. *Dreaming America: Obsession and Transcendence in the Fiction of Joyce Carol Oates.* Baton Rouge: Louisiana State University Press, 1979.

TITLE COMMENTARY

Night-Side

GREG JOHNSON (ESSAY DATE 1994)

SOURCE: Johnson, Greg. "The Power of Allusion, the Uses of Gothic: Experiments in Form and Genre." In *Joyce Carol Oates: A Study of the Short Fiction,* pp. 68-93. New York: Twayne, 1994.

In the following excerpt, Johnson examines Oates's treatment of the Gothic in her works, particularly in the 1977 short story collection, Night-Side.

Night-Side

The attempt to define and evaluate literary Gothicism has created an ongoing controversy among critics and scholars, primarily because the term "Gothic" has achieved the kind of connotative vagueness—rather like that other free-floating term "Romantic"—that inspires its use in a startling variety of contexts. In 1969, Oates observed that "Gothicism, whatever it is, is not a literary tradition so much as a fairly realistic assessment of modern life,"[1] and in 1980 she added that "gothic with a small-letter 'g'" simply connotes "a work in which extremes of emotion are unleashed."[2] Both comments were in response to critical evaluations throughout her career that have associated her work with the Gothic tradition. In the early 1980s, of course, she published three postmodernist Gothic works—*Bellefleur* (1980), *A Bloodsmoor Romance* (1982), and *Mysteries of Winterthurn* (1984)—as part of a projected quintet of novels that view America through "the prismatic lens" of genre fiction (*WW*, 373); yet Oates's work had been labeled "Gothic" long before she began concocting these blatantly nonrealistic experiments. Such early novels as

With Shuddering Fall (1964), *Expensive People* (1968) and *Wonderland* also contained extremes of violence, psychological malaise, and grotesque characterization, and were written in a prose style of passionate, often melodramatic intensity. In the view of some critics, these elements aligned Oates with the Southern Gothic tradition of Faulkner, O'Connor, and Carson McCullers, but the dynamic, hallucinatory power of her best work also recalls the complex explorations of Dostoyevsky, the nightmare visions of Poe and Kafka, and even the fantastic world of Lewis Carroll—whose work Oates has often cited as a major influence.

Although most contemporary fiction described as "gothic"—the uncapitalized spelling having grown more common as the term's connotations have become more far-ranging—has eliminated the supernatural elements that characterized the generative eighteenth-century British Gothics of Horace Walpole and Ann Radcliffe, the themes of alienation and psychological breakdown have been notable in American literature from the beginning. As Irving Malin observes, Gothicism "is in the mainstream of American fiction" because it evokes the condition of psychological extremity at the heart of our literary tradition.[3] In his more recent study of Gothic fantasy, William Patrick Day describes the modernist permutations of the genre in a way strikingly applicable to Oates's work: "The isolation of the Gothic and modernist protagonist is enforced, not only by the failure of communal and traditional value systems, but by the breakdown of conventional concepts of causality and the idea of wholeness of personality and characters. The doubled and divided characters of the Gothic fantasy reflect the break-down of conventional notions of what constitutes a self. This same disintegration appears, more realistically, in the modernist fascination with states of consciousness."[4] In her pseudonymous Rosamond Smith novels—*Lives of the Twins* (1987), *Soul/Mate* (1989), *Nemesis* (1990), and *Snake Eyes* (1992)—Oates has examined "doubled and divided" characters by focusing on the phenomenon of twins, a particular fascination she has explored in her short stories ("**Heat**" and "**Twins**," for example) as well, but the more general "break-down of conventional notions of what constitutes a self" is a major theme throughout her work. Furthermore, as Oates asserts in her essay "**Wonderlands**," Gothic fiction represents "dimensions of the psyche given a luridly tangible form, in which unacknowledged (or rigorously suppressed) wishes are granted freedom. Impulse rises at once to the level of action. . . . Frequently in Gothic fiction the innocent are not only victimized but are co-opted by the wicked: the wonderland is a marvelous place where *we* are *they*—our shadow selves given both substance and potency" (**WW**, 83). Furthermore, in the preface to **Bellefleur** she argues that "if Gothicism has the power to move us (and it certainly has the power to fascinate the novelist) it is only because its roots are in psychological realism" (**WW**, 371).

For Oates, therefore, the Gothic mode provides an opportunity not to evade the social responsibility and philosophical inquiry traditionally associated with serious fiction; rather, its psychological focus and its liberating aesthetic conventions simply provide an alternative, vibrant, and highly dramatic means of expressing Oates's typical themes. Above all, the Gothic enables Oates to probe beyond conventional perceptions of reality, an ambition clearly visible also in one of her finest early novels, **Wonderland**. Itself based upon the Lewis Carroll books that most influenced Oates as a child, impressing her with their "wonderful blend of illogic and humor and horror and justice" (Phillips, "Art of Fiction," 75), the novel takes as its epigraph a passage from another postmodernist Gothicist, Jorge Luis Borges, which states a primary theme of Oates's short fiction as well: "We . . . have dreamt the world. We have dreamt it as firm, mysterious, visible, ubiquitous in space and durable in time; but in its architecture we have allowed tenuous and eternal crevices of unreason which tell us it is false."[5]

Virtually all her short-story volumes show some influence of the Gothic tradition, whether in the Faulknerian "Southern Gothic" vein of the early Eden county stories depicting rural isolation and madness; or in the sometimes hallucinatory psychological intensity of **"Where Are You Going, Where Have You Been?,"** **"The Metamorphosis,"** and **"The Dead"**; or in certain postmodernist experimental tales of the 1980s collected in **Raven's Wing** (1986), **The Assignation** (1988), and **Heat** (1991). In **The Assignation,** one of her two collections of "miniature narratives," such tales as **"Blue-Bearded Lover"** and **"The Others"** recall nineteenth-century Gothic fiction, while others convey the kind of hothouse psychological intensity, the precarious balance between sanity and madness, traditionally associated with the genre. With their brief, truncated scenes and their poetic intensity, they have a brutal, sometimes horrific impact, laying bare with deft economy and unflinching directness the anxieties, longings, and obsessions lying just beneath the surface of "ordinary" life.

Several of Oates's collections, however, are even more notable in their use of the Gothic mode in portraying human consciousness as an ongoing journey fraught with bewildering visions, inexplicable detours, unnameable terrors. Even before *Night-Side* (1977), Oates published *The Poisoned Kiss* (1975), her collection of mostly nonrealistic tales that, according to her, seemed to spring from an alter ego named "Fernandes." As Oates noted in the Afterword to the volume, "The only way I could accept these stories was to think of them as a literary adventure, or a cerebral/Gothic commentary on my own writing, or as the expression of a part of my personality that had been stifled" (*PK,* 188). Although this instance of literary "possession" by a foreign personality, who set all his stories in Portugal (which Oates had never visited), inspired Oates to read voluminously in parapsychology, mysticism, and the occult, she never fully comprehended the experience; eventually, "Fernandes" retreated, and his stories came to an end (*PK,* 189).

The Poisoned Kiss remains an anomaly in Oates's oeuvre, an experiment in fiction (and in consciousness) that, while lacking the psychological power and wealth of detail that characterize her strongest fiction, nonetheless provides a fascinating gloss on her ongoing exploration of psychological states. *Night-Side,* however, fully exploits the Gothic mode, occasionally including the traditional staples of supernatural events and exotic settings, but most often focusing upon extreme psychological aberration and isolation, which in turn force her characters to confront riddling and often profound philosophical questions. These stories tend, moreover, to point outward, toward political and social realities, even when they seem most concerned with states of consciousness and make use of fantastic elements. For Oates, as Eva Manske observes, "Gothic elements and fantasies have the larger function of expanding the thematic range and suggestiveness in conveying the atmosphere of public and private American life in the past and today."[6]

Night-Side certainly encompasses thematic concerns discussed extensively in other chapters: "**The Giant Woman,**" for example, is set in Eden County, "**The Widows**" and "**The Snowstorm**" focus intensely on female experience, "**Daisy**" and "**Further Confessions**" are highly allusive, and "**Bloodstains**" has allegorical elements, including a Hawthornean birthmark. As a unified collection,

however, *Night-Side* is located at the border between visible reality and another dimension—exciting but fearful, yielding expansive visions and nightmares—at which Oates's characters suffer a reassessment of their concept of self and their relationship to others, to the world, and to their previously held views of their own purpose and destiny. Often this reassessment pushes them to extremes of insanity or repression; a handful of stronger characters returns from the Gothic world, as do Oates's readers, with a heightened apprehension of a complex reality that is both beautiful and bizarre. Once again, Oates's comments on traditional Gothic fiction describe her own: "Here, suddenly, is a mysterious door in a wall, and here is the golden key that will unlock it, one has only to summon forth one's courage and enter. Whatever awaits will not only be strange and unexpected, it will, in a way impossible to explain, *make sense*; and it will be *ours*—as 'reality' never is" (*WW,* 79-80).

Oates suggests the nature of her enterprise in the book's subtitle: "Eighteen Tales." Like the later *Haunted: Tales of the Grotesque, Night-Side* inhabits a realm of storytelling with its own distinct conventions. Unlike the realistic, carefully plotted short story, the tale allows the narrative freedom of brisk pacing, improbable events, and idiosyncratic characters and settings. This freedom does not, however, preclude literary seriousness; as Poe remarked in the preface to his own volume of Gothic tales, *Tales of the Grotesque and Arabesque* (1840), artistic adaptations of established conventions are "the results of matured purpose and very careful elaboration."[7] Although some of the tales in *Night-Side* could, in another context, be read as typically Oatesian psychological realism—"**The Widows**" would fit smoothly into *Marriages and Infidelities,* for instance—there are others involving the paranormal, the dream state, and other nontraditional approaches to perception and knowledge, and these manage an eerie penetration into their more realistic companion-pieces such as "**The Widows,**" "**The Translation,**" and "**The Snowstorm.**" The result is a collection that, as a whole, brings even "ordinary" experiences—such as being temporarily stranded in a blizzard—into a psychological realm that, like the metaphorical storm itself, blurs the distinction between the familiar, daylight world of ordinary consciousness and a visionary landscape where repressed horrors may spring into vibrant life.

In both "**The Sacrifice**" and "**Bloodstains,**" for instance, a professional man's carefully constructed daytime self is revealed as alien and meaningless, while **"Famine Country"** and **"Daisy"** probe the border between sanity and insanity, focusing on the clash between two incompatible ways of viewing and knowing the world. These may be, as Oates has termed it, "gothic with a small-letter 'g'," yet the realms of experience they explore are so unstable and delusive that they plunge the reader not into the reassuring familiarity of realism but into the unpredictability of nightmares.

The tales that make the most explicit use of Gothic conventions are **"Night-Side,"** which opens the book, and **"A Theory of Knowledge,"** which concludes it. By enclosing the collection within these Gothic borders, Oates again suggests the sensibility that will, in differing ways, infiltrate and control the entire volume. The title piece, set in the 1880s and narrated by Jarvis Williams, a Harvard professor, focuses on his and a Boston colleague's investigation into a Quincy woman who holds séances and regularly makes contact with the spiritual realm. Although Williams is skeptical of the woman's psychic ability, his colleague Perry Moore is an even more "hardened" disbeliever, "a hearty materialist"[8] and "an empiricist who accepts nothing on faith" (*NS*, 8). Written in an ornate late-Victorian style, featuring a series of séances with the usual trappings—moving furniture, sudden drafts, an array of spirit voices gabbling in various languages—**"Night-Side"** begins as a typical ghost story. There are several turns of the screw, however, that mark the tale as distinctly Oatesian in its focus upon philosophical inquiry and psychological revelation. The narrator's intellectual complacency, his comfortable disbelief in a spiritual realm, is shattered when the medium makes contact with a ghost from Perry Moore's past: a spirit named Brandon, apparently a former male lover who committed suicide when Dr. Moore rejected him. (Earlier the narrator had mentioned that Moore's "failure to marry, or his refusal, is one of Boston's perennial mysteries" [*NS*, 8].) Brandon appeals plaintively to Dr. Moore, and the seemingly authentic voice of his dead lover brings Moore to a vehement repudiation of his former skepticism. He tells Williams excitedly, "There *are* spirits! . . . His entire life up to the present time has been misspent! . . . [and] most important of all—there is no death!" (*NS*, 14).

Williams, striving to hold a middle ground between his rationalist principles and his open-minded stance toward the paranormal, visits America's most famous living philosopher, William James, to discuss "the inexplicable phenomenon of consciousness" (*NS*, 18). James, whom Oates quotes often and admiringly in her essays, states what seems closest to Oates's own position regarding the seemingly nonrational possibilities of consciousness: "we inhabit not only our ego-consciousness but a wide field of psychological experience (most clearly represented by the phenomenon of memory, which no one can adequately explain) over which we have no control. . . . It is quite possible that there is an element of some indeterminate kind: oceanic, timeless, and living, against which the individual being constructs temporary barriers as part of an ongoing process of unique, particularized survival" (*NS*, 19). Parenthetically Williams remarks he is "too timid to ask Professor James whether it might be the case that we do not inevitably own these aspects of the personality—that such phenomena belong as much to the objective world as to our subjective selves" (*NS*, 19)—a qualification that suggests Oates's frequently stated antiromantic skepticism toward egocentric methods of interpreting reality. When James describes to Williams a philosophically acceptable view of "the 'other side' of the personality" (*NS*, 20) that might account for psychic ability and Williams decides James is merely describing insanity, Oates turns the screw once again by allowing James to "read" Williams's mind.

Thus the tale, in typical Oates fashion, investigates the mysteries of consciousness from several viewpoints—philosophical, psychological, and supernatural—but neither Oates nor the narrator can settle upon a single, consistent view of Moore's experience. When Moore dies of a stroke, having written a rambling essay on his new spiritualist beliefs that causes Williams to conclude that his friend had "gone insane" (*NS*, 22), Williams finds himself drawn back to the pure rationalism of Spinoza: "Away from the phantasmal, the vaporous, the unclear; toward lines, planes, and solids" (*NS*, 26). Tormented by dreams in which Moore appeals to him, hearing rumors that Moore has become a spiritual presence at local séances, Williams recoils in fear from the notion that death ushers human beings into "a hideous dreamlike state, a perpetual groping, blundering—far worse than extinction—incomprehensible" (*NS*, 29), and escapes back into ordinary life with his wife and children, who represent to him "the dayside of the world" (*NS*, 29).

For Professor Reuben Weber in **"A Theory of Knowledge,"** such escape is unavailable. At age seventy-seven, retired and living with his daughter in an old farmhouse in rural New York, he spends his days writing in his journal, going through his notes, meditating on his past, yet still hoping to organize a lifetime of philosophical thought into his masterwork, *A Theory of Knowledge*. Weber's sense of betrayal—by time, by his former colleagues—consumes him; his attachment to the small, underfed boy who visits from an impoverished neighboring family represents Weber's desperate attempt to alleviate his own childlike fear and vulnerability. When Weber rescues the boy late one night from severely abusive treatment by his family, Oates implies the entire incident may be only one of Weber's dreams, a projection in which he valiantly "saves" an unacknowledged version of his own wounded selfhood.

Like Perry Moore and other intellectually prideful characters throughout Oates's work, Weber cannot acknowledge his own defeat by natural processes, cannot relinquish his own self-image as a "disciplined philosopher" far superior to Emerson, a "scatterbrain" (*NS*, 360), or the "superficial" William James (*NS*, 354). Oates has remarked that she based Weber's character on that of American philosopher Charles Sanders Peirce, and that the story is "a poetic attempt to dramatize the contradictions inherent in philosophizing—in abstracting from the world of sense experience and personal history" (Sjoberg, 117). "A Theory of Knowledge" derives both its pathos and its ironic force from its characterization of old Weber, unable to dress himself or clearly to distinguish past from present (as when he suggests to his daughter that the neighbor boy might enjoy playing with Weber's grandsons, forgetting his grandsons are now fully grown). Weber nonetheless, in sudden spurts of rage and longing, thrusts his egocentric will against his own increasing mental befuddlement and approaching death. He recalls that he "had spent the greater part of his life trying to cut through obscurity, murkiness," yet his experience, like that of other characters in *Night-Side*, finally focuses upon the "perplexing, humiliating tricks of the mind" (*NS*, 352). His story turns upon the ironic contrast between two theories of knowledge: the grand but elusive philosophical design Weber still hopes to construct and the tale in which he appears, which dramatizes Oates's own, far less optimistic "theory."

Although "**Night-Side**" and "**A Theory of Knowledge**" are both set in the nineteenth century and include the ghostly apparitions and nocturnal adventures common to Gothic fiction, other tales in *Night-Side*, though employing contemporary settings and less eccentric characterizations, nonetheless explore psychological states—especially the delusive nature of consciousness, memory, and knowledge—with an eerie intensity and sense of mystery that allies them to the volume's more traditionally Gothic tales. "**The Sacrifice**," for instance, features yet another aging intellectual in Dr. Reaume, a renowned psychiatrist who "had guided his life perfectly" (*NS*, 262). His encounter with a troubled woman complaining of terrifying nightmares and hallucinations, like Weber's fascination with the little boy, feeds into his need to "save" other people. Similarly, Oates suggests he may be only dreaming the sequence in which, like the woman in Oates's later story, "**Naked**," he ventures outside his own neighborhood and is attacked by a group of black children, to whom he gives the ludicrous response: "don't you need me, can't I be of service to you . . . ?" (*NS*, 288).

Even though Dr. Reaume has spent a lifetime congratulating himself on his eminent sanity and his ability to transcend the psychological snarls his patients suffer, his complacency is itself revealed as a delusion; his very name, of course, suggests that his identity is only a "dream." Unlike Weber, Dr. Reaume has managed to produce a crowning achievement, "an immense encyclopedic work with the simple title *Psychologies*" (*NS*, 283). Again Oates critiques the intellectual hubris that attempts to transcend nature, to produce systematic explanations—whether philosophical, psychological, or religious—of an inexplicably complex reality. As she notes in the essay "**Against Nature**," this reality "eludes us even as it prepares to swallow us up, books and all" (*WW*, 67). This is a notion men like Weber and Reaume—in their egocentric need to create an essentially "fictional" reality, a phantasm, of which they can be the sole lord and master—are unwilling or unable to confront.

This basic pattern of an intelligent, accomplished protagonist, finding his or her assumptions about the world and the self abruptly rendered meaningless or absurd, recurs throughout *Night-Side*. In "Bloodstains," Lawrence Pryor's failure to recognize his wife one day from a distance, on the street, begins to haunt him, becoming "a dream he had dreamed while awake" (*NS*, 171) and forcing him into an uncertain new apprehension of his life as a physician, a husband, and a father. The controlling images of bloodstains—a dark-red birthmark he sees on the back of a stranger's neck, his wife's gloves soiled "with something that looks like rust or blood" (*NS*, 174), his daughter's bloodstained panties she has hidden in a drawer—strike him as clues to reality he has never quite perceived before. His very eyes feel like "crusts of blood," "wounds where his eyes once had been" (*NS*, 183). Like many of Oates's characters facing an important transition in their lives—Jesse Pedersen in *Wonderland,* for example, staring down at the locks from a bridge in Lockport, New York—Lawrence looks out into a river and sees the turbulent, flowing water as embodying a reality in ceaseless flux, one in which his own ephemeral, temporary identity has relatively little meaning.

Similarly, in "**The Snowstorm,**" a college counselor named Claire is accustomed to helping students in their crises of identity, but when she is trapped on campus in a blizzard, alone and vulnerable, she confronts her own sterility and fear of passion, the same limitation that afflicted earlier characters such as Sister Irene in "**In the Region of Ice**" and Pauline in "**Bodies.**" A cool, self-contained woman who has endured several romantic involvements while "her intelligence had stood apart from her, pitying her, scornful of her, waiting for the emotional madness to pass" (*NS*, 106-107), Claire, like Lawrence, glimpses a "dream-woman" in the distance, except in her case the woman is herself: "How strange it was that she should feel herself merge into that dream-woman, giving life to her, pumping life through her exhausted limbs!" (*NS*, 109). Unlike Sister Irene, Claire does seem to accept her turmoil as a stage of personal growth and yearns to merge with the dream-woman in order to bring to life a long-repressed element of personality; the conclusion of "**The Snowstorm**" suggests that, even though she will cling to her individuality, she may also be prepared to make a tentative move toward an intimate relationship that need not represent "madness."

Throughout *Night-Side,* Oates explores the extreme psychological risk of confronting the "other," whether in a supernatural form, as in the title story, or in haunting visions of an alien and unacknowledged self. Of course the theme of the doppelgänger, the dark alter ego, is present throughout Oates's work, from that brooding early parable of identity, *Wonderland,* to the later Rosamond Smith novels, but it pervades this collection more thoroughly than any other. Virtually every story, regardless of its style or technical strategy, considers the theme on some level. In the highly experimental "**The Dungeon,**" the artist, named "Farrell Van Buren," is merely a sardonic mask for "little gentle Daryl," who feels entrapped in the "dungeon" of his own self-absorption (*NS*, 144). A gay man who yearns to reveal his sexuality to a female friend, he nonetheless fears rejection so deeply (and, it would appear, justifiably) that his self-imprisonment is only reinforced, leading him into fantasies of grotesque and even murderous retaliation.

In the darkly comic "**Famine Country,**" a college-age boy, Ronnie, is released from an institution after a drug overdose that killed his girlfriend and almost killed him, and tries to become reintegrated into his family, who are presented as a parody of American banality; his mother is well-meaning but simple-minded, his father is coarse and self-important. Enmeshed in a pseudomystical pursuit of God, his mind damaged by drug abuse, Ronnie tells his baffled parents: "God enveloped me and gave me new life, and I don't know who you people are. . . . I try to be polite but it's a strain and then when you spy on me and try to make me eat—it's hopeless" (*NS*, 161). The only resolution for Ronnie's aggrieved mother is to bury the dead turtle that has washed up on their beachfront property, a creature Ronnie interpreted as the "**Turtle-God**" appearing magically from a primordial dreamscape of mud and slime. Her gesture is a symbolic act of determined repression—not only of Ronnie's madness by her sanity, but of the truth-seeking generation of the 1960s and 1970s by the stolid incomprehension of the more conventional 1940s and 1950s; yet it hardly suggests any possibility of bridging the extreme stances of each generation. America is dramatized here as a "famine country" that lies spiritually impoverished between two equally destructive and irreconcilable positions.

A less hopeless polarity is dramatized through Beatrice and Moira of "**The Widows,**" who are brought together after their husbands' deaths and have their first meeting at 3:00 A.M. Yet they long to escape the nocturnal realm into which their sudden solitude has plunged them. Like Sheila and Monica in Oates's novel *Solstice* (1985), Beatrice and Moira are physical and temperamental opposites—Beatrice dark and introverted, Moira blond and gregarious—and through their groping conversations, reminiscences, and self-assessments Oates implies a temporary symbiotic union and ultimately a regeneration of self for each woman.

Like Beatrice, the poet and widower Francis Bonham in "**Daisy**" reflects that "the physical being was untrustworthy, an inferior Siamese twin stuck to the soul, a clownish Doppelganger" (*NS*, 224), but another double is his daughter Daisy, a mentally unstable girl whose name means "the

Day's Eye" but whose hallucinations and violent tantrums suggest she is "The Night's Eye as well" (*NS*, 230). Based loosely on the relationship between James Joyce and his schizophrenic daughter Lucia, "**Daisy**," according to Oates, "deals in a surrealist manner with . . . the relationship between sanity and insanity" (Sjoberg, 117), and may also be read as an allegory for the artist's riddling relationship to the multidimensional world he attempts, and inevitably fails, to control through his art. Like many of the stories in *Night-Side*, "**Daisy**" is notable for its length and ambition: these traits reveal Oates's interest at this stage of her career "in developing stories that are really miniature novellas: stories that deal with a person's entire life, greatly condensed and focused" (Sjoberg, 117).

Perhaps the collection's most original handling of its predominant theme, "**The Translation**" also condenses its protagonist's life experience and again focuses on a painful and unexpected self-recognition. Oliver, a magazine editor and "cultural emissary" visiting Central Europe (*NS*, 119), becomes instantly infatuated with Alisa, a young music teacher. Unsuccessful in love and suffering a midlife crisis, Oliver depends on his mysterious young translator, Liebert, to convey his interest and admiration, and when Liebert translates Alisa's answers to his eager queries Oliver is charmed by her intelligence and her ability to live a cultured life within the moral complexities of the Soviet regime. Oliver, in his emotional and sexual excitement, views himself as Alisa's potential rescuer, and like many of Oates's characters glimpses in a mirror a new, emerging selfhood, though "the mirror looked smoky, webbed as if with a spider's web; his own face hovered there" (*NS*, 118).

He has actually become entangled, of course, in the web of his own American naïveté and egotism, for Liebert (Oates slyly gives the translator a name that approximates the German for "lover") is actually a con man who has invented Alisa's "cultured" personality. When he gets a sum of money from Oliver under a false pretext and disappears, Oliver is left with a new translator who convey's Alisa's actual dialogue, revealing she is simple-minded and interested primarily in Oliver's financial status and his love life. An intriguing reworking of Henry James's "international theme," "**The Translation**" presents Oliver as a hapless American enmeshed in the deceit and sophistication of old Europe, and is typically Oatesian in conveying both irony and compassion toward both points of view: Oliver, in his passion-

ate but misguided longing for love and a meaningful life; Liebert and Alisa, in their wily but self-serving ability to live "in the interstices of the political state" (*NS*, 124). Also characteristic is Oates's focus upon the beautiful but delusive possibilities of language. Liebert's false translations are, after all, quite artful, a form of fiction, and Oliver attributes an almost supernatural power to Liebert, who appears "as if he could read Oliver's thoughts" (*NS*, 116) and who seems to translate "magically. Surely it was magic" (*NS*, 123).

In the broadest sense, "translation" might be viewed as the controlling theme of *Night-Side* as a whole: how to unify the psyche, how to plunge into its turbulent, darker realms and translate, or integrate, these aspects of personality into the rational, contained "day-side" of the self? Most of Oates's characters remain trapped at one extreme or another: the near-madness of psychological grotesques on the one hand (Daryl in "**The Dungeon**," Ronnie in "**Famine Country**") and the stiff, sterile repression of people entrapped in their fearful lack of self-knowledge on the other (Dr. Reaume in "**The Sacrifice**," Weber in "**A Theory of Knowledge**"). Relationships of various kinds—between lovers, between parents and children, even between nations—wind through the stories as a kind of elaborate dance between the two realms, which at times seem mutually exclusive but more often are mysteriously intermingled and confused. Even though these "tales," like those collected in the later *Haunted: Tales of the Grotesque,* are more explicit than Oates's other stories in exploring this theme, they are integral to her larger endeavor in fiction, which is to probe relentlessly the complex mysteries of human personality and identity.

Notes

1. Quoted in "Writing as a Natural Reaction," *Time,* 10 October 1969, 108.

2. Tom Vitale, "Joyce Carol Oates Reads from *Angel of Light* & Interview," taped interview produced by a Moveable Feast (Columbia, Mo.: American Audio Prose Library, 1981).

3. Irving Malin, *New American Gothic* (Carbondale: Southern Illinois University Press, 1962), 4.

4. William Patrick Day, *In the Circles of Fear and Desire: A Study of Gothic Fantasy* (Chicago: University of Chicago Press, 1985), 168.

5. Epigraph to Oates's *Wonderland* (New York: Vanguard, 1971), 13.

6. Eva Manske, "The Nightmare of Reality: Gothic Fantasies and Psychological Realism in the Fiction of Joyce Carol Oates." *Restant* 20, no. 1 (1992): 132.

7. Edgar Allan Poe, preface to *Tales of the Grotesque and Arabesque*, reprinted in *Edgar Allan Poe: Poetry and Tales* (New York: Library of America, 1984), 130.

8. *Night-Side* (New York: Vanguard, 1977), 2; hereafter cited in text as *NS*.

Abbreviations

PK: Joyce Carol Oates, *The Poisoned Kiss* (New York: Vanguard, 1975).

Sjoberg: Leif Sjoberg, "An Interview with Joyce Carol Oates," in *Conversations with Joyce Carol Oates*, ed. Lee Milazzo (Jackson: University Press of Mississippi, 1989).

WW: Joyce Carol Oates, *(Woman) Writer: Occasions and Opportunities* (New York: E. P. Dutton, 1988).

FURTHER READING

Bibliography

Lercangée, Francine. *Joyce Carol Oates: An Annotated Bibliography.* New York: Garland Publishing, 1986, 272 p.

Complete, well-annotated bibliography of works by and about Oates, through 1986.

Biography

Johnson, Greg. *Invisible Writer: A Biography of Joyce Carol Oates.* New York: Dutton, 1998, 492 p.

Biography of Oates which describes how Oates's upbringing, her career stopovers in Detroit and Princeton are mythologized in her fiction.

Criticism

Bender, Eileen-Teper. *Joyce Carol Oates: Artist in Residence.* Bloomington: Indiana University Press, 1987, 207 p.

Explores the thematic and narrative experimentalism of Oates's novels.

Chell, Cara. "Un-Tricking the Eye: Joyce Carol Oates and the Feminist Ghost Story." *Arizona Quarterly* 41 (1985): 5-23.

Characterizes Mysteries of Winterthurn *as a novel informed by contemporary feminism that parodies many of the Gothic literary conventions of the nineteenth century.*

Coale, Samuel Chase. "Joyce Carol Oates: Contending Spirits." In *In Hawthorne's Shadow: American Romance from Melville to Mailer*, pp. 161-79. Lexington: University Press of Kentucky, 1985.

Concentrates on the Manichean vision of American society depicted in Bellefleur.

Creighton, Joanne V. *Joyce Carol Oates.* Boston: Twayne, 1979, 173 p.

Evaluates the formal and thematic materials employed by Oates in her novels of the 1960s and 1970s, particularly highlighting her departures from the tradition of American literary realism.

———. *Joyce Carol Oates: Novels of the Middle Years.* New York: Twayne, 1992, 142 p.

Continued analysis of Oates's fiction and its relationship to American romanticism.

Goodman, Charlotte. "Women and Madness in the Fiction of Joyce Carol Oates." *Women and Literature* 5, no. 2 (1977): 17-28.

Surveys Gothic themes associated with psychologically disturbed female characters in Oates's novels and short stories.

Hoeveler, Diane Long. "Postgothic Fiction: Joyce Carol Oates Turns the Screw on Henry James." *Studies in Short Fiction* 35, no. 4 (fall 1998): 355-71.

Focuses on Oates's imaginative reinterpretations of Henry James's Gothic tale The Turn of the Screw *in which she informs her versions of the story with a postmodern sensibility concerning the relationship between fiction and reality.*

Jeannotte, M. Sharon. "The Horror Within: The Short Stories of Joyce Carol Oates." *Sphinx* 2, no. 4 (1977): 25-36.

Considers Oates's moral and psychological juxtaposition of protagonists and antagonists in her short fiction.

Manske, Eva. "The Nightmare of Reality: Gothic Fantasies and Psychological Realism in the Fiction of Joyce Carol Oates." In *Neo-Realism in Contemporary American Fiction*, edited by Kristiaan Versluys, pp. 131-43. Atlanta, Ga. and Amsterdam: Rodopi, 1992.

Argues that Oates's fictional works represent her blending of psychological realism concentrated on the extremes of human emotion with the conventions of Gothic horror.

Nodelman, Perry. "The Sense of Unending: Joyce Carol Oates's *Bellefleur* as an Experiment in Feminine Storytelling." In *Breaking the Sequence: Women's Experimental Fiction*, edited by Ellen Friedman and Miriam Fuchs, pp. 250-64. Princeton, N.J.: Princeton University Press, 1989.

Elucidates Bellefleur *as a novel of feminist narrative experimentalism.*

Oates, Joyce Carol. "Wonderlands." *Georgia Review* 38 (1984): 487-506.

Introduces the Gothic theme of victimization in her novel Wonderlands.

Waller, G. F. *Dreaming America: Obsession and Transcendence in the Fiction of Joyce Carol Oates.* Baton Rouge: Louisiana State University Press, 1979, 224 p.

Centers on the Gothic themes central to the American experience depicted in Oates's fiction.

OTHER SOURCES FROM GALE:

Additional coverage of Oates's life and career is contained in the following sources published by Thomson Gale: *American Writers Supplement*, Vol. 2; *Authors and Artists for Young Adults*, Vols. 15, 52; *Authors in the News*, Vol. 1; *Beacham's Encyclopedia of Popular Fiction: Biography and Resources*, Vol. 2; *Beacham's Guide to Literature for Young Adults*, Vol. 11; *Bestsellers*, Vol. 89:2; *Concise Dictionary of American Literary Biography, 1968-1988*; *Contemporary Authors*, Vols. 5-8R; *Contemporary Authors New Revision Series*, Vols. 25, 45, 74, 113, 129; *Contemporary Literary Criticism*, Vols. 1, 2, 3, 6, 9, 11, 15, 19, 33, 52, 108, 134; *Contemporary Novelists*, Ed. 7; *Contemporary Poets*, Ed. 7; *Contemporary Popular Writers*; *Contemporary Women Poets*; *Dictionary of Literary Biography*, Vols. 2, 5, 130; *Dictionary of Literary Biography Yearbook, 1981*; *DISCovering Authors*; *DISCovering Authors: British*; *DISCovering Authors: Canadian*; *DISCovering Authors Modules: Most-*

studied *Authors, Novelists,* and *Popular Fiction and Genre Authors; DISCovering Authors 3.0; Encyclopedia of World Literature in the 20th Century,* Ed. 3; *Exploring Short Stories; Feminism in Literature: A Gale Critical Companion; Feminist Writers; Literature and Its Times,* Vol. 4; *Literature Resource Center; Major 20th-Century Writers,* Eds. 1, 2; *Major 21st-Century Writers;* *Modern American Women Writers; Novels for Students,* Vol. 8; *Reference Guide to American Literature,* Ed. 4; *St. James Guide to Horror, Ghost & Gothic Writers; Short Stories for Students,* Vols. 1, 8, 17; *Short Story Criticism,* Vols. 6, 70; *Supernatural Fiction Writers,* Vol. 2; *Twayne's United States Authors;* and *World Literature Criticism.*

EDGAR ALLAN POE

(1809 - 1849)

American short story writer, poet, novelist, essayist, editor, and critic.

Poe's stature as a major figure in world literature is primarily based on his highly acclaimed short stories, poems, and critical theories, which established an influential rationale for the short form in both poetry and fiction. Regarded in literary histories and handbooks as the architect of the modern short story, Poe was also the principal forerunner of the "art for art's sake" movement in nineteenth-century European literature. Whereas earlier critics predominantly concerned themselves with moral or ideological generalities, Poe focused his criticism on the specifics of style and construction that contributed to a work's effectiveness or failure. In his own work, he demonstrated what has been assessed as a brilliant command of language and technique as well as an inspired and original imagination. Poe's poetry and short stories greatly influenced the French Symbolists of the late nineteenth century, who in turn altered the direction of modern literature. It is this philosophical and artistic transaction that accounts for much of Poe's importance in literary history.

BIOGRAPHICAL INFORMATION

Poe's father and mother were professional actors who at the time of his birth were members of a repertory company in Boston. Before Poe was three years old both of his parents died, and he was raised in the home of John Allan, a prosperous exporter from Richmond, Virginia, who never legally adopted his foster son. As a boy, Poe attended the best schools available, and was admitted to the University of Virginia at Charlottesville in 1825. He distinguished himself academically but was forced to leave after less than a year because of bad debts and inadequate financial support from Allan. Poe's relationship with Allan disintegrated upon his return to Richmond in 1827, and soon after Poe left for Boston, where he enlisted in the army and also published his first poetry collection, *Tamerlane, and Other Poems* (1827). The volume went unnoticed by readers and reviewers, and a second collection, *Al Aaraaf, Tamerlane, and Minor Poems,* received only slightly more attention when it appeared in 1829. That same year Poe was honorably discharged from the army, having attained the rank of regimental sergeant major, and was then admitted to the United States Military Academy at West Point. However, because Allan would neither provide his foster son with sufficient funds to maintain himself as a cadet nor give the consent necessary to resign from the Academy, Poe gained a dismissal by ignoring his duties and violating regulations. He subsequently went to New York City, where *Poems,* his third collection of verse, was published in 1831, and then moved to Baltimore, where he lived at the home of his aunt, Mrs. Maria Clemm.

Over the next few years Poe's first short stories appeared in the *Philadelphia Saturday Courier* and his "MS. Found in a Bottle" (1832) won a cash prize for best story in the *Baltimore Saturday Visiter*. Nevertheless, Poe was still not earning enough to live independently, nor did Allan's death in 1834 provide him with a legacy. The following year, however, his financial problems were temporarily alleviated when he accepted an editorship at *The Southern Literary Messenger* in Richmond, bringing with him his aunt and his twelve-year-old cousin Virginia, whom he married in 1836. *The Southern Literary Messenger* was the first of several journals Poe would direct over the next ten years and through which he rose to prominence as a leading man of letters in America. Poe made himself known not only as a superlative author of poetry and fiction, but also as a literary critic whose level of imagination and insight had hitherto been un-approached in American literature. While Poe's writings gained attention in the late 1830s and early 1840s, the profits from his work remained meager, and he supported himself by editing *Burton's Gentleman's Magazine* and *Graham's Magazine* in Philadelphia and the *Broadway Journal* in New York City. After his wife's death from tuberculosis in 1847, Poe became involved in a number of romantic affairs. It was while he prepared for his second marriage that Poe, for reasons unknown, arrived in Baltimore in late September of 1849. On October 3, he was discovered in a state of semi-consciousness; he died four days later without regaining the necessary lucidity to explain what had happened during the last days of his life.

MAJOR WORKS

Poe's most conspicuous contribution to world literature derives from the analytical method he practiced both as a creative author and as a critic of the works of his contemporaries. His theory of literary creation is noted for two central points: first, a work must create a unity of effect on the reader to be considered successful; second, the production of this single effect should not be left to the hazards of accident or inspiration, but should to the minutest detail of style and subject be the result of rational deliberation on the part of the author. In poetry, this single effect must arouse the reader's sense of beauty, an ideal that Poe closely associated with sadness, strangeness, and loss; in prose, the effect should be one revelatory of some truth, as in "tales of ratiocination" or works evoking "terror, or passion, or horror."

Aside from a common theoretical basis, there is a psychological intensity that is characteristic of Poe's writings, especially the tales of horror that comprise his best and best-known works. These stories—which include "The Black Cat" (1843) "The Cask of Amontillado" (1846) and "The Tell-Tale Heart" (1843)—are often told by a first-person narrator, and through this voice Poe probes the workings of a character's psyche. This technique foreshadows the psychological explorations of Fyodor Dostoevsky and the school of psychological realism. In his Gothic tales, Poe also employed an essentially symbolic, almost allegorical method which gives such works as "The Fall of the House of Usher" (1839), "The Masque of the Red Death" (1842), and "Ligeia" (1838) an enigmatic quality that accounts for their enduring interest and also links them with the symbolical works of Nathaniel Hawthorne and Herman Melville. The influence of Poe's tales may be seen in the work of later writers, including Ambrose Bierce and H. P. Lovecraft, who belong to a distinct tradition of horror literature initiated by Poe. Just as Poe influenced many succeeding authors and is regarded as an ancestor of such major literary movements as Symbolism and Surrealism, he was also influenced by earlier literary figures and movements. In his use of the demonic and the grotesque, Poe evidenced the impact of the stories of E. T. A. Hoffman and the Gothic novels of Ann Radcliffe, while the despair and melancholy in much of his writing reflects an affinity with the Romantic movement of the early nineteenth century. It was Poe's particular genius that in his work he gave consummate artistic form both to his personal obsessions and those of previous literary generations, at the same time creating new forms which provided a means of expression for future artists.

A tale of sickness, madness, incest, and the danger of unrestrained creativity, "The Fall of the House of Usher" is among Poe's most popular and critically examined horror stories. The ancient, decaying House of Usher, filled with tattered furniture and tapestries and set in a gloomy, desolate locale is a rich symbolic representation of its sickly twin inhabitants, Roderick and Madeline Usher. Besides its use of classical Gothic imagery and gruesome events—including escape from live burial—the story has a psychological element and ambiguous symbolism that have given rise to many critical readings. Poe used the term "arabesque" to describe the ornate, descriptive prose in this and other stories in his collection. "The Fall of the House of Usher" is also considered representative of Poe's idea of "art for art's sake," whereby the mood of the narrative, created through skillful use of language, overpowers any social, political, or moral teaching.

The story is also one of several of Poe's which utilize as a central character the Decadent Aristocrat. This mad, often artistic noble heir took the place of the traditional Gothic villain in tales portraying the sublime hostility of existence itself rather than the evil embodied by individuals. In addition to "The Fall of the House of Usher," such characters appear in his stories "Metzengerstein" (1840), "Berenice" (1840), "Ligeia" (1838), "The Oval Portrait" (1842), and "The Masque of the Red Death" (1842). Central to the setting in many of these stories is a large, ominous castle, likened by critic Maurice Lévy to the medieval fortresses that appear in the writing of Radcliffe, Charles Robert Maturin, and Horace Walpole. Interior architectural elements, such as the moving tapestry in "Metzengerstein," serve almost as characters in these tales.

A second group of Poe's tales center, in obsessive detail, on the horror and misery wrought by a guilty conscience. These include "The Black Cat," "The Tell-Tale Heart," and the doppelgänger story "William Wilson" (1840). "The Black Cat" is narrated by a once-kind man who has fallen into alcoholism. One day, in a rage, he hangs his cat and is forever haunted by the image. Upon attempting to kill the cat's replacement, he instead kills his wife. It appears his deeds will go unpunished until he is given away by the screaming animal, who is sitting on his dead wife's head. "The Tell-Tale Heart" features a similarly mad narrator forever tormented by the heartbeat of a man he has murdered. While not widely acclaimed during his lifetime, it has become one of Poe's most famous stories. While the stories "Hop-Frog: Or, the Eight Chained Orang-Outangs" (1849), "The Pit and the Pendulum" (1843), and "The Cask of Amontillado" do not take a guilty conscience as their starting point, they share the same paranoid intensity demonstrated in these tales.

Poe first gained widespread acclaim for his poem "The Raven" (1845), which exhibits elements of the tales in both groups identified above. Set at the stroke of midnight in an otherwise empty chamber, the narrator hears a tapping at his door. The narrator, tormented by the ominous raven revealed to be the source of the noise, is not wracked with guilt, however. Rather, he mourns the loss of his love, Lenore, while the raven serves as a despicable and terrifying reminder of her death.

Poe completed only one novel, and it was written in the Gothic tradition. Poe's *The Narrative of Arthur Gordon Pym* (1838), the story of an ill-fated sea voyage, has captured the attention of generations of readers with its action-packed plot, imaginative use of symbol and myth, depiction of cannibalism, and numerous unusual occurrences. Critics studying the imagery of *Pym* have frequently cited Freudian and Jungian analyses, with the voyage identified as a seminal symbol of a journey inward into consciousness, or denoting a return to the womb.

CRITICAL RECEPTION

While most of his works were not conspicuously acclaimed during his lifetime, Poe has come to be viewed as one of the most important American authors in the Gothic tradition. While even today some critics deride the author's style as amateurish and overwrought, Pamela J. Shelden (see Further Reading) argues that Poe turned hackneyed styles to new and advantageous use. Likewise, Maurice Lévy regards the author as steeped in the tradition of Radcliffe, Walpole and Maturin, yet wholly original. Poe's stories and poems have become some of the most widely read in English-language literature.

"The Fall of the House of Usher" has been lauded by scholars as a prime example of the Gothic short story. Over the years, there have been many interpretations of the story, and much recent scholarship has viewed the tale as a fictional representation of many of Poe's own literary and social theories. For example, Stephen Dougherty sets the tale in the context of racism and fears of miscegenation in nineteenth-century society and also examines the potential influence of French theorist Michel Foucault's political ideas on the work. In general, "Usher" is acknowledged as one of Poe's most cerebral tales, with little or no action to carry the plot. Because of this, the story has lent itself to numerous interpretations, eliciting a large amount of scholarship that continues to explore the text from a variety of perspectives.

Poe's *The Narrative of Arthur Gordon Pym* underwent a remarkable transformation in reputation during the twentieth century. When it was first published and for the remainder of the nineteenth century, the novel was ignored completely, dismissed as a literary hoax, or deemed just another of Poe's fantastic tales. In the second half of the twentieth century, however, *Pym* emerged as the most frequently discussed of all of Poe's works. Critics have studied Poe's handling of language and Gothic imagery and explored Poe's use of narrative structure to produce special effects in the novel. Leslie Fiedler notes that many of the literary conventions used by Poe, and for which he was widely censured, were intended to offer ironic commentary on slavery and other accepted nineteenth-century practices and challenge the notion of innocence in the Western world. A. A. Markley traces Gothic authors who may have influenced *Pym*, such as William Godwin, and credits Poe with building on this tradition.

Today, Poe is recognized as one of the foremost progenitors of modern literature, and of the Gothic style in particular. In contrast to earlier critics who viewed writer and works as one, criticism of the past twenty-five years has developed a view of Poe as a detached artist who was more concerned with displaying his virtuosity than with expressing his soul, and who maintained an ironic rather than an autobiographical relationship to his work. His writing is viewed as highly revelatory of the darkest elements of human nature. Poe's tales "are a concatenation of cause and effect," observes D. H. Lawrence. "His best pieces, however, are not tales. They are more. They are ghastly stories of the human soul in its disruptive throes."

PRINCIPAL WORKS

Tamerlane and Other Poems. By a Bostonian (poetry) 1827

Al Aaraaf, Tamerlane, and Minor Poems (poetry) 1829

Poems. By Edgar Allan Poe. Second Edition. (poetry) 1831

"MS. Found in a Bottle" (short story) 1832; published in the journal *Baltimore Saturday Visiter*

"Ligeia" (short story) 1838; published in the journal *American Museum*

The Narrative of Arthur Gordon Pym, of Nantucket, North America: Comprising the Details of a Mutiny, Famine, and Shipwreck, During a Voyage to the South Seas; Resulting in Various Extraordinary Adventures and Discoveries in the Eighty-fourth Parallel of Southern Latitude [published anonymously] (novel) 1838

"The Fall of the House of Usher" (short story) 1839; published in the journal *Burton's*

Tales of the Grotesque and Arabesque. 2 vols. (short stories) 1840

"The Murders in the Rue Morgue" (short story) 1841; published in the journal *Graham's Magazine*

"The Masque of the Red Death" (short story) 1842; published in the journal *Graham's Magazine*

"The Mystery of Marie Rogêt" (short story) 1842; published in the journal *Snowden's*

"The Oval Portrait" (short story) 1842; published in the journal *Graham's Magazine*

"The Black Cat" (short story) 1843; published in the journal *Saturday Evening Post*

"The Pit and the Pendulum" (short story) 1843; published in the journal *The Gift*

"The Tell-Tale Heart" (short story) 1843; published in the journal *Pioneer*

"The Oblong Box" (short story) 1844; published in the journal *Godey's Lady's Book*

"The Premature Burial" (short story) 1844; published in the journal *Philadelphia Dollar Newspaper*

"The Imp of the Perverse" (short story) 1845; published in the journal *Graham's Magazine*

The Raven, and Other Poems (poetry) 1845

†*Tales by Edgar A. Poe* (short stories) 1845

"The Cask of Amontillado" (short story) 1846; published in the journal *Godey's Lady's Book*

Eureka: A Prose Poem (essay) 1848

"Hop-Frog: Or, the Eight Chained Orang-Outangs" (short story) 1849; published in the journal *Boston Flag of Our Union*

"Von Kempelen and His Discovery" (short story) 1849; published in the journal *Boston Flag of Our Union*

---

* This collection includes, among other stories, "Metzengerstein," "Berenice," "William Wilson," and "The Facts in the Case of M. Valdemar."

† This collection includes, among other stories, "The Purloined Letter," "The Gold-Bug," and "The Man of the Crowd."

PRIMARY SOURCES

EDGAR ALLAN POE (STORY DATE 1836)

SOURCE: Poe, Edgar Allan. "Shadow—A Parable." In *Great Tales of Terror from Europe and America: Gothic Stories of Horror and Romance, 1765-1840*, edited by Peter Haining. 1972. Reprint edition, pp. 503-06. Harmondsworth, Middlesex, England: Penguin Books Ltd., 1973.

The following short story was first published in The Southern Literary Messenger *in 1836.*

'Yea! though I walk through the Valley of the Shadow.'

Psalm of David

Ye who read are still among the living; but I who write shall have long since gone my way into the region of shadows. For indeed strange things shall happen, and secret things be known, and many centuries shall pass away, ere these memorials be seen of men. And, when seen, there will be some to disbelieve, and some to doubt, and yet a few who will find much to ponder upon in the characters here graven with a stylus of iron.

The year had been a year of terror, and of feelings more intense than terror for which there is no name upon the earth. For many prodigies and signs had taken place; and far and wide, over sea and land, the black wings of the Pestilence were spread abroad. To those, nevertheless, cunning in the stars, it was not unknown that the heavens wore an aspect of ill; and to me, the Greek Oinos, among others, it was evident that now had arrived the alternation of that seven hundred and ninety-fourth year when, at the entrance of Aries, the planet Jupiter is conjoined with the red ring of the terrible Saturnus. The peculiar spirit of the skies, if I mistake not greatly, made itself manifest, not only in the physical orb of the earth, but in the souls, imaginations, and meditations of mankind.

Over some flasks of the red Chian wine, within the walls of a noble hall, in a dim city called Ptolemais, we sat, at night, a company of seven. And to our chamber there was no entrance save by a lofty door of brass: and the door was fashioned by the artisan Corinnos, and, being of rare workmanship, was fastened from within. Black draperies, likewise, in the gloomy room, shut out from our view the moon, the lurid stars, and the peopleless streets—but the boding and the memory of Evil, they would not be so excluded. There were things around us and about of which I can render no distinct account—things material and spiritual—heaviness in the atmosphere—a sense of suffocation—anxiety—and, above all, that terrible state of existence which the nervous experience when the senses are keenly living and awake, and meanwhile the powers of thought lie dormant. A dead weight hung upon us. It hung upon our limbs—upon the household furniture—upon the goblets from which we drank; and all things were depressed, and borne down thereby—all things save only the flames of the seven iron lamps which illumined our revel. Uprearing themselves in tall slender lines of light, they thus remained burning all pallid and motionless; and in the mirror which their lustre formed upon the round table of ebony at which we sat, each of us there assembled beheld the pallor of his own countenance, and the unquiet glare in the downcast eyes of his companions. Yet we laughed and were merry in our proper way—which was hysterical; and sang the songs of Anacreon—which are madness; and drank deeply—although the purple wine reminded us of blood. For there was yet another tenant of our chamber in the person of young Zoilus. Dead, and at full length he lay, enshrouded;—the genius and the demon of the scene. Alas! he bore no portion in our mirth, save that his countenance, distorted with the plague, and his eyes in which Death had but half extinguished the fire of the pestilence, seemed to take such interest in our merriment as the dead may haply take in the merriment of those who are to die. But, although I, Oinos, felt that the eyes of the departed were upon me, still I forced myself not to perceive the bitterness of their expression, and, gazing down steadily into the depths of the ebony mirror, sang with a loud and sonorous voice the songs of the son of Teios. But gradually my songs they ceased, and their echoes, rolling afar off among the sable draperies of the chamber, became weak, and undistinguishable, and so faded away. And lo! from among those sable draperies where the sounds of the song departed, there came forth a dark and undefined shadow—a shadow such as the moon, when low in heaven, might fashion from the figure of a man: but it was the shadow neither of man nor of God, nor of any familiar thing. And quivering awhile among the draperies of the room, it at length rested in full view upon the surface of the door of brass. But the shadow was vague, and formless, and indefinite, and was as the shadow neither of man nor God—neither God of Greece, nor God of Chaldea, nor any Egyptian God. And the shadow rested upon the brazen doorway, and under the arch of the entablature of the door, and moved not, nor spoke any word, but there became stationary and remained. And the door whereupon the shadow rested was if I remember aright, over against the feet of the young Zoilus enshrouded. But we, the seven there assembled, dared not steadily behold it, but cast down our eyes, and gazed continually into the depths of the mirror of ebony. And at length I, Oinos, speaking some low words, demanded of the shadow its dwelling and its appellation. And the shadow answered, 'I am Shadow, and my dwelling is near to the catacombs of Ptolemais, and hard by those dim plains of Helusion which border upon the foul Charonian canal.' And then did we, the seven, start from our seats in horror, and stand trembling, and shuddering, and aghast: for the tones in the voice of the shadow were not the tones of any one being, but of a multitude of beings, and, varying in their cadences from syllable to syllable, fell duskily upon our ears in the well-remembered and familiar accents of many thousand departed friends.

EDGAR ALLAN POE (STORY DATE 1842)

SOURCE: Poe, Edgar Allan. "The Oval Portrait." In *Great Ghost Stories: 34 Classic Tales of the Supernatural,* compiled by Robin Brockman, pp. 55-7. New York: Gramercy Books, 2002.

The following short story was first published in Graham's Magazine *in 1842.*

The château into which my valet had ventured to make forcible entrance, rather than permit me, in my desperately wounded condition, to pass a night in the open air, was one of those piles of commingled gloom and grandeur which have so long frowned among the Apennines, not less in fact than in the fancy of Mrs Radcliffe. To all appearance it had been temporarily and very lately abandoned. We established ourselves in one of the smallest and least sumptuously furnished apartments. It lay in a remote turret of the building. Its decorations were rich, yet tattered and antique. Its walls were hung with tapestry and bedecked with manifold and multiform armorial trophies, together with an unusually great number of very spirited modern paintings in frames of rich golden arabesque. In these paintings, which depended from the walls not only in their main surfaces, but in very many nooks which the bizarre architecture of the château rendered necessary—in these paintings my incipient delirium, perhaps, had caused me to take deep interest; so that I bade Pedro to close the heavy shutters of the room—since it was already night,—to light the tongues of a tall candelabrum which stood by the head of my bed, and to throw open far and wide the fringed curtains of black velvet which enveloped the bed itself. I wished all this done that I might resign myself, if not to sleep, at least alternately to the contemplation of these pictures, and the perusal of a small volume which had been found upon the pillow, and which purported to criticise and describe them.

Long, long I read—and devoutly, devoutly I gazed. Rapidly and gloriously the hours flew by and the deep midnight came. The position of the candelabrum displeased me, and outreaching my hand with difficulty, rather than disturb my slumbering valet, I placed it so as to throw its rays more fully upon the book.

But the action produced an effect altogether unanticipated. The rays of the numerous candles (for there were many) now fell within a niche of the room which had hitherto been thrown into deep shade by one of the bedposts. I thus saw in vivid light a picture all unnoticed before. It was the portrait of a young girl just ripening into womanhood. I glanced at the painting hurriedly, and then closed my eyes. Why I did this was not at first apparent even to my own perception. But while my lids remained thus shut, I ran over in my mind my reason for so shutting them. It was an impulsive movement to gain time for thought—to make sure that my vision had not deceived me—to calm and subdue my fancy for a more sober and more certain gaze. In a very few moments I again looked fixedly at the painting.

That I now saw aright I could not and would not doubt; for the first flashing of the candles upon that canvas had seemed to dissipate the dreamy stupor which was stealing over my senses, and to startle me at once into waking life.

The portrait, I have already said, was that of a young girl. It was a mere head and shoulders, done in what is technically termed a *vignette* manner; much in the style of the favorite heads of Sully. The arms, the bosom, and even the ends of the radiant hair melted imperceptibly into the vague yet deep shadow which formed the background of the whole. The frame was oval, richly gilded and filigreed in *Moresque.* As a thing of art nothing could be more admirable than the painting itself. But it could have been neither the execution of the work, nor the immortal beauty of the countenance which had so suddenly and so vehemently moved me. Least of all, could it have been that my fancy, shaken from its half slumber, had mistaken the head for that of a living person. I saw at once that the peculiarities of the design, of the *vignetting,* and of the frame, must have instantly dispelled such idea—must have prevented even its momentary entertainment. Thinking earnestly upon these points, I remained, for an hour perhaps, half sitting, half reclining, with my vision riveted upon the portrait. At length, satisfied with the true secret of its effect, I fell back within the bed. I had found the spell of the picture in an absolute *life-likeliness* of expression, which, at first startling, finally confounded, subdued, and appalled me. With deep and reverent awe I replaced the candelabrum in its former position. The cause of my deep agitation being thus shut from view, I sought eagerly the volume which discussed the paintings and their histories. Turning to the number which designated the oval portrait, I there read the vague and quaint words which follow:

"She was a maiden of rarest beauty, and not more lovely than full of glee. And evil was the hour when she saw, and loved, and wedded the painter. He, passionate, studious, austere, and having already a bride in his Art: she a maiden of rarest beauty, and not more lovely than full of glee; all light and smiles, and frolicsome as the young fawn; loving and cherishing all things; hating only the Art which was her rival; dreading only the pallet and brushes and other untoward instruments which deprived her of the countenance of her lover. It was thus a terrible thing for this lady to hear the painter speak of his desire to portray even his young bride. But she was humble and obedient, and sat meekly for many weeks in the dark high turret-chamber where the light dripped upon the pale canvas only from overhead. But he, the painter, took glory in his work, which went on from hour to hour, and from day to day. And he was a passionate, and wild, and moody man, who became lost in reveries; so that he *would* not see that the light which fell so ghastly in that lone turret withered the health and the spirits of his bride, who pined visibly to all but him. Yet she smiled on and still on, uncomplainingly, because she saw that the painter (who had high renown) took a fervid and burning pleasure in his task, and wrought day and night to depict her who so loved him, yet who grew daily more dispirited and weak. And in sooth some who beheld the portrait spoke of its resemblance in low words, as of a mighty marvel, and a proof not less of the power of the painter than of his deep love for her whom he depicted so surpassingly well. But at length, as the labor drew nearer to its conclusion, there were admitted none into the turret; for the painter had grown wild with the ardor of his work, and turned his eyes from the canvas rarely, even to regard the countenance of his wife. And he *would* not see that the tints which he spread upon the canvas were drawn from the cheeks of her who sat beside him. And when many weeks had passed, and but little remained to do, save one brush upon the mouth and one tint upon the eye, the spirit of the lady again flickered up as the flame within the socket of the lamp. And then the brush was given, and then the tint was placed; and, for one moment, the painter stood entranced before the work which he had wrought; but in the next, while he yet gazed, he grew tremulous and very pallid, and aghast, and crying with a loud voice, 'This is indeed *Life* itself!' turned suddenly to regard his beloved:—*She was dead!*"

MAURICE LÉVY (ESSAY DATE 1968)

SOURCE: Lévy, Maurice. "Poe and the Gothic Tradition." *ESQ: A Journal of the American Renaissance* 18, no. 66 (1972): 19-29.

In the following essay, translated by Richard Henry Haswell and first published in French in Caliban *in 1968, Lévy assesses Poe's works within the context of the Gothic tradition.*

Since the appearance of Marie Bonaparte's study, only the daring speak of Poe without evoking his dipsomania, opiomania, cyclothymia, paraphrenia, and sado-necrophilia, all so obviously characterizing the major part of his work. Today how does one dare to see in Poe's architectural structures anything but mother-figures, or in the inextricable maze of the island of Tsalal where Pym got lost, anything but a fantasy of the maternal body from an intestinal point of view? The "shadows" and "doubles" and the Devil must be symbols of the castrating father-figure and **"The Oval Portrait"** must illustrate the sado-masochistic, partly necrophilistic theme of the Life-in-Death mother-figure.

But, at the risk of appearing profane, I feel that these themes, however attractive, codify too rigorously the most intimate impulses of the poet, and make *too much sense* in stories which also contain, I believe, on the very principle of the "bizarre," the "grotesque," and the "extravagant," something of the completely unmotivated and something—of *tradition*. Before Poe wrote, other authors had described tottering buildings, castles in ruins or on the point of collapse, or dark passages twisting in the bowels of the earth. At the time he was writing, the Gothic novel had formed an integral part of the Anglo-American literary patrimony for many years. In 1809, the year of Poe's birth, the genre that Walpole had created was still very much alive. And the young man landing in England in 1815, if he was old enough to be interested, no doubt would have noticed books with strange titles having to do only with "Haunted Castles," "Ruined Priories," "Italians," and "Monks" in the windows of the bookstores. He probably did not return to America before 1820, the year *Melmoth* was published.

Is it too daring to imagine the young pensioner of the "Manor House School" at Stoke Newington reading under his coat, in the manner of so many of his contemporaries, some really scary Radcliffean imitation? Or later the student at the brand-new university at Charlottesville feverishly turning the pages of *The Castle of Otranto* or *The Monk*, borrowed from the nearest circulating library? For the Gothic novel had extended its domain to New England. William Lane, whose Minerva Press, more than any other publishing house, had been responsible for the outpouring of "horrors" that had inundated the nation, had had a correspondent at New York since the end of the eighteenth century. During these years, Louis-Alexis Hocquet de Caritat, an exile from Champagne who owned on Broadway the most important lending library in town, offered to his innumerable clientele, alongside the insipidities of certain post-Richardson novels, the substantial pleasures of the terror that Walpole, Radcliffe, and Lewis so generously dispensed.

An observer of the epoch tells us that "the Library of Mr. *Caritat* was charming. Its shelves could scarcely sustain the weight of *Female Frailty, The Posthumous Daughter,* and *The Cavern of Woe*; they required the aid of the carpenter to support the burden of *The Cottage on the Moor, The House of Tynian,* and *The Castles of Athlin and Dunbayne*; or they groaned under the multiplied editions of *The Devil in Love, More Ghosts!* and *Rinaldo Rinaldini*."[1] One would have recognized there several of the more representative titles from the "Frantic School."[2] But an examination of the "Catalogue of Novels" published by this enterprising bookseller is more informative; in 1804 nearly 200 titles out of the 1,500 recorded represent the growing vogue of the transatlantic Gothic novel.[3] The disillusioned protests of the critics were unavailing.[4] Charles Brockden Brown, in the preface to *Edgar Huntly*, denounced in vain the puerile methods, the "Gothic castles and their chimeras," of the fiction of the day.[5] Far from confining itself to the ports and the larger towns, the "evil" little by little conquered the country. With his return to the United States after a prolonged absence, Royall Tyler, the author of a small forgotten novel, affirmed in 1797 that each rural village had its "social library" and that milkmaids and hired hands in the most remote areas trembled so much at the reading of the novels of Radcliffe that they did not dare go to bed alone.[6] When Poe began writing his tales, the duodecimos of Lane for a long time had found their place on the shelves of the descendants of the pilgrim fathers, to the neglect, said Tyler, of the family Bunyan.

That Poe had heard of them, that he himself had applied them, is occasionally acknowledged in his own works. **"The Oval Portrait"** is placed under the avowed patronage of Mrs. Radcliffe from the very first page.[7] In the "Letter to B———"

he mentions *Melmoth*, moreover, in respectful terms and in order to say that the Wandering Jew did not strike him as a satanic figure (**Works**, VII, xxxviii). In *The Southern Literary Messenger* in 1835, he gave a laudatory account of *The Heroine*, an amusing parody of the Gothic novel which Eaton Stannard Barrett had published in England in 1813 and which had just appeared in America. Without doubt the review was an occasion for Poe to relive the scenes and episodes of *The Romance of the Forest, The Mysteries of Udolpho,* or *The Children of the Abbey* by Regina-Maria Roche. Elsewhere he speaks of Godwin, and he mentions *Vathek*; and if Beckford's novel, much less *Caleb Williams*, does not truly belong to the genre created by Walpole, at least these references testify to his taste for what one could call more generically the "roman noir."[8] A closer reading of Poe's tales, in fact, makes inevitable the recognition of the presence of a certain number of "obsessive motifs," as well as certain characters and techniques of writing which are all, to differing degrees, connected with the Gothic tradition. My purpose here is to assemble these motifs and to juxtapose them with those affined motifs that characterize the countless descendants of *The Castle of Otranto*, allowing the reader to decide for himself the fitness and the merits of this approach.

I

The most obvious point of departure is the close resemblance of the huge, gloomy, and menacing Gothic castles which rise on the horizon of **"The Oval Portrait," "Ligeia,"** and **"The Fall of the House of Usher"** to the medieval fortresses that form the obligatory setting for the fictional adventures in Walpole, Lewis, Radcliffe, and Maturin. The château to which the wounded hero of **"The Oval Portrait"** is led by his servant is "one of those piles of commingled gloom and grandeur which have so long frowned among the Apennines, not less in fact than in the fancy of Mrs. Radcliffe" (**Works**, IV, 245). It is the castle of Udolpho that we are here explicitly invited to recall, with its turrets, battlements, and ruined ramparts, standing "silent, solitary, and sublime" in the heart of the Apennines. Moreover, the protagonist establishes himself in "a remote turret of the building." One thinks of the "Western Tower," the "Southern Tower," and the "Eastern Tower" dear to the Gothic imagination. It is also amusing to recall the "Southwest Tower" which perplexed M. Dabaud in the delightful pastiche by Bellin de la Liborlière, in *La Nuit Anglaise* (1799), because as a reader of "romans noirs" he could not remember any tower situated between cardinal points.[9] The apartment where Poe's character proposes to pass the night has the "antique and dilapidated" appearance of those which Mrs. Radcliffe's heroines harmlessly explore. Like the apartment of Signora Laurentini that Emily visits in *The Mysteries of Udolpho,* also accompanied by a servant, Poe's is also "abandoned." All human presence has vanished and the hero is alone face to face with the unexpected. In particular, as in Radcliffe's scene, the mysteriousness condenses around the portrait of a woman, whose strange gaze fascinates the hero.[10] The motif of the *isolated* turret and the *closed-off* apartment recurs in **"Ligeia."** It will be remembered that the hero, following the death of his first wife, buys an abbey—the setting of so many Gothic adventures—isolated in one of the wildest portions of England:

> The gloomy and dreary grandeur of the building, the almost savage, aspect of the domain, the many melancholy and time-honored memories connected with both, had much in unison with the feelings of utter abandonment which had driven me into that remote and unsocial region of the country.
>
> (*Works,* II, 258)

There, "although the external abbey, with its verdant decay hanging about it, suffered but little alteration," he furnishes the interior, just as La Motte in *The Romance of the Forest* (1791) or Saint-Aubespine in *Saint-Botolph's Priory* (1806) establish themselves in abbeys by making the interior comfortable and leaving the exterior ruins intact to preserve their "picturesque beauty." The entire drama of **"Ligeia"** takes place in a room that he decorates in a "semi-Gothic, semi-Druidical" style which was already old in the history of taste (**Works,** II, 259). Were it not for the slightly bizarre nature of the decorative elements imagined by the author of "The Philosophy of Furniture," the reader could truly believe himself introduced to a room dreamed up by one or another of the Gothic novelists. At this point we may note that in order to exercise freely Poe's imagination needs an interior space bounded by the tottering walls of a dwelling belonging to the past, a Gothic dwelling. The fears and the anguish of Poe, as those of Radcliffe, are always concretely lodged.

This of course appears best in **"The Fall of the House of Usher."** Here the architectural element not only plays a basic role in the plot but extends to the attitudes and behavior of the characters. With the first lines of the tale, the narrator, who discovers in the twilight "the bleak walls—the vacant eye-like windows" of the "melancholy" house of Usher, takes his place in the long line of heroes and heroines seized by gloomy presentiments and unreasonable fears at the threshold of the castle. He experiences "an utter depression of the soul," "an iciness . . . of the heart": "I know not how it was—but, with the first glimpse of the building, a sense of insufferable gloom pervaded my spirit." One recalls the fears of so many Gothic heroines—frail in spite of their intrepidity—whose souls falter the moment they are about to cross the threshold of those nightmarish dwellings, or of Piranesi prisons, or of tombs that give them the impression that they are going to be buried alive: "She viewed [the castle] with horror," the author of *The Ruins of Rigonda* (1808) had already written, "and as the massy but almost crumbling gates closed behind her, she heaved a sigh, and seemed as it were to have entered her tomb."[11] Monsieur Harcourt, in *The Romance of the Castle* (1800), exclaims to himself as he enters the castle of Llangwellein, "When I entered the portals of this Gothic structure, a dread (surely prophetic), chilled my veins, pressed upon my heart, and scarcely allowed me to breathe."[12] One also recalls Ellena who, in *The Italian* (1797), on entering the convent of San Stephano, is seized with sinister presentiments, or Rosalie, in *Sicilian Mysteries* (1812), who views the ramparts and the turrets of the fortress where she is led with a feeling of horror: "Its remote situation, its dilapidated state, struck the dreadful suspicion on her heart that *she was brought there to suffer.*"[13] A statement of all of the agonies of the threshold which torment the heart of Gothic heroines would be endless; I add only those of Cherubina, who embodies all of the virtues of the perfect "Heroine" so dear to Poe's heart.[14] At the moment of crossing the threshold of the solemn castle of Monckton, she also, the intrepid, warlike, virile Cherubina, feels her courage fail:

> While she surveyed its roofless walls, overtopt with briony, grass and nettles, and admired the Gothic points of the windows, where mantling ivy had supplied the place of glass, long suffering and murder came to her thoughts.[15]

The threshold of the castle—as much in Poe as in Radcliffe or the other followers of Walpole—establishes the boundary of a magic space, a sphere of the fantastic. To enter into the house of Usher as into the castle of Otranto or of Udolpho is to plunge into the irrational, to descend to the most primordial strata of the Self where the logic which presides over the elaboration of our conscious thoughts holds no sway: "To enter within a castle," Jean Roudaut has admirably written, "is to become a character in a dream; it is to be given

Illustration from "The Fall of the House of Usher."

over, completely whole and aware, to forces free of all logical or moral construct; it is to be put in a place where time ceases to be measurable and actions extend as far as desires."[16] This explains the sense of total estrangement which Poe's narrator experiences when he finds himself inside the house of Usher. To enter a residence is not only to enter someone else's home, but partly to enter *into* someone else. The further he penetrates this "mansion of gloom" and the further he familiarizes himself with the high vaulted chambers and the interminable corridors and the damp cellars, the more profoundly he penetrates the mystery which hovers around the personality of Roderick.

The house of Usher is an ancestral castle, Gothic, handed down from father to son through innumerable generations, a castle which strengthens the feeling of blood and is identified in a significant manner with the family. It should not be forgotten that the word *house* refers at the same time to a family line as well as to a family residence:

> The original title of the estate [was merged with] the quaint and equivocal appellation of the "House of Usher"—an appellation which seemed

to include, in the minds of the peasantry who used it, both the family and the family mansion.
>
> (***Works***, III, 275)

Just as in the title, for instance, of *The House of Tynian* (1795)—one of the most Gothic of novels that I am familiar with—it is simultaneously a matter of the Tynians and of their castle.

In fact there exist subtle and intangible ties between Roderick Usher and his *house*. It exerts on him "an influence which some peculiarities in the mere form and substance of his family mansion, had, by dint of long sufferance, he said, obtained over his spirit—an effect which the *physique* of the gray walls and turrets, and of the dim tarn into which they all looked down, had, at length, brought about upon the *morale* of his existence" (***Works,*** III, 281). This influence is so heavy, these correspondences between man and his home so profound, that the mysterious and apparently incurable sickness of Roderick can be seen as the symptom of some interior fault, of which the long fissure that marks the façade of the castle is only the visible sign. When the hero, the last descendant of the Ushers, arrives at the final stage of his drama, the castle, now unnecessary, collapses upon him; the flowing and tumultuous waters of the dream close in upon the dreamer.

In this connection it is impossible not to remember the direct ties which link the hero of *The Castle of Otranto* to his castle. In the first of the Gothic romances, the one that served from 1764 as model and norm for the literature of fantasy, the same secret correspondences can be discovered. Manfred himself is the last scion, or at least he believes he is, of the house of Otranto. The entire drama is played behind the walls of the old residence, where he lures the young woman whom he lusts after, sequesters those who oppose his ambitious projects, and threatens with death the young man who dares dispute his title. The castle of Otranto is a symbol of his will to power, the spatial projection of his destiny into an architectural form. The Prince is also directly connected with the threat which causes the growth of the giant to weigh upon the building that it secretly inhabits. When the Prince is forced to renounce the world and to shut himself in a convent, the castle of Otranto dissolves:

> A clap of thunder at that instant shook the castle to its foundations; the earth rocked, and the clank of more than mortal armour was heard behind. Frederic and Jerome thought the last day was at hand. The latter, forcing Theodore along with them, rushed into the court. The moment The-

odore appeared, the walls of the castle behind Manfred were thrown down with a mighty force.[17]

Is it not remarkable that in both the novel of Walpole and in the tale of Poe the decadence of a "house," of a family "gloriously ancient," leads ultimately to the collapse of the ancestral dwelling which had sheltered it?

II

Every Gothic residence worthy of that epithet not only proudly raises its crenellated towers toward the sky but also enroots itself in "Mother Earth" with deep underground passages, galleries that form an inextricable labyrinth at the most profound depths. It is customary for the heroes who have these incredible adventures to creep through subterranean mazes and to wander in narrow bowels which cross and recross, changing level and always burying themselves more deeply into the dense, solid darkness. The vocation of the Gothic heroes is essentially that of *losing their way*. To mention only one example, let us accompany Matilda for a moment in her peregrinations. She is one of those intrepid young women who pass an appreciable part of their lives underground.

> When she reached the bottom, she found herself in a narrow vaulted way, along which she proceeded for a considerable distance; when by the light of her lamp, she perceived she had got into a spacious cavern, out of which branched a number of narrow passages, made by nature or art out of the solid rock. She entered into one, which, winding round, she found, after walking about an hour, that it had brought her to the same place, from whence she had set out. She then took another, which proved to be that she had first come along, as it brought her to the foot of the staircase she had descended from the great hall. She returned back along the same passage till she again got into the same large cavern.
>
> She now entered one on the opposite side, which, appearing to be something wider than the others, she thought might lead, possibly, to some road out. She proceeded along it, for some time, when she was again bewildered by a number of narrow paths, not knowing which to take. She ventured upon one, however, which led her to another cavern, neither so lofty, or so large, as that she had just passed through. As she was crossing it, to enter an opening on the opposite side, she stumbled over something. On holding her lamp down to it, she perceived that it was the skeleton of a human body. In her horror and surprise, she dropped the lamp from her hand, and was in total darkness, the light being extinguished by the fall.[18]

Sometimes the narrow passages become so shrunken and obstructed that the characters must advance on hands and knees. Then, to the perplexity caused by the inextricable maze of subterranean tunnels is added the suffocating feeling of having to remain a prisoner of the earth forever; images of the claustrophobic universe of the grave complete the labyrinthine dream and make it more terrible. For instance in *Melmoth,* when Monçada felt the oneiric shrinkings which suddenly interrupt his subterranean progression, he remembers the story he had read of an explorer who suddenly *swelled* up in a gallery of the Egyptian pyramids, obstructed the passage, and died miserably, trampled by his companions.[19] In its extreme, this obsession with a narrow and constricting place is expressed by the dream of premature burial—no need to recall its obsessive character in Poe—the nightmare in which we picture ourselves *alive* in the grave. It appears, for example, in *The Restless Matron* (1799), *The Monk* (1796), *Count Eugenio; or, Fatal Errors* (1807) and in many other tales where the young heroine, under the effects of a powerful drug that someone has administered to her, is thought to be dead and is buried.

There is little need to emphasize the essential role, in the tales of Poe, played by images of the labyrinth—or, to speak in the terms of Gaston Bachelard, of the "prison dynamique." Only the most important examples need be cited: the school where William Wilson is pensioned, all filled with complex passages that give the boy the illusion of infinity; the subterranean walk of the narrator of **"The Cask of Amontillado"** and his victim; the aquatic maze formed by the endless meandering of the stream that Ellison floats on in his approach to the domain of Arnheim; the hold of the ship Pym is shut up in where he attempts to force a way between casks and barrels; or later, on the island of Tsalal, the tortuous road through labyrinths so complex that Poe must draw them.[20] Is it necessary to attribute these oneiric ambulations to an analistic exploration of the maternal body? According to Marie Bonaparte, the wells, pits, and cells that the subterranean passages lead to symbolize the maternal cloaca, which blocks or directs "the movement, in the bowels, of the faeces to which the child, in its anal sexual theories, likens itself."[21] I do not have the authority to deny or confirm such a hypothesis. All that I can say is that it must similarly explain many episodes from many Gothic novels, wherein the dream of the labyrinth had already, some thirty or forty years earlier than Poe, been popularized through the process of literary composition.

One could make an analogous remark about Marie Bonaparte's interpretation of "**The Man of the Crowd.**" She quite justifiably evokes, in connection with this indefatigable walker who ceaselessly travels the streets of London, the figure of the Wandering Jew, that great "déambulateur mythique" whose origins are lost in the night of time. But in her eyes he embodies nothing less than the formidable Father-figure since he derives from the *patriarchal* tribes which murdered the divine Son (p. 424). I will not further contest this point. But permit me to add that the character of the Wandering Jew was also, at the time Poe wrote his tale, an obligatory character in a certain category of novels that runs from *The Monk* through Godwin's *Saint-Leon* and Shelley's *Saint-Irvyne* to Maturin's *Melmoth*. Poe did not invent this figure of *homo viator*; he drew it from the ancient well of universal literature a short time after the Gothic novel had brought it again into favor with the Anglo-American public. The figure of the Wandering Jew is one of the great images; one of the "images primordiales" that has illustrated the human adventure from the time that men felt like putting it into fable. At the time Poe wrote, it had also become almost a literary cliché.

One could say the same about the appearances of the Devil that spread fear occasionally in Poe's tales. The Devil may also embody the figure of the castrating Father, particularly in "**Never Bet the Devil your Head.**" But however attractive the interpretation psychoanalysis may propose for this tale, it would seem to neglect the *traditional* nature of this most popular of fantasy characters. Several decades earlier he had already caused the fall of Ambrosio, Victoria, Berenice, Jaqueline d'Olzenburg, Melmoth, and countless other weak beings—young ladies in hoop skirts and gentlemen in lace frills—all cast down into the abyss in expiation of some ambitious bent of the soul.[22] The dream of falling is also, in itself, a dream as old as man, by means of which the dreamer enjoys descending into the deepest part of himself and pretends to be prisoner in the most archaic levels of his Self; but it is also a dream that Lewis, Charlotte Dacre, George Walker, Edward Montagu, Shelley, Maturin, and many others whose names have not survived, had just presented again to the tastes of the day, a dream which, thanks to them, formed part of the Anglo-American literary patrimony in Poe's day, a dream which served as a vehicle for anguish and disquietude in a specific and, from certain points of view, inevitable form.

III

So far we have pointed out, in particular, structural analogies between the tales of Poe and the Gothic tradition: the frequent recourse to a medieval setting in order to circumscribe the action and the sphere of fantasy, the descent into subterranean passages and tombs, and the use of certain of the most redoubtable characters typically haunting the architectural spaces of Walpole's genre. But more specific reminiscences of themes and devices belonging to the most characteristic manner of the Frantic School occur as well in certain of Poe's *Tales of the Grotesque and Arabesque.* The "**Pit and the Pendulum**" is one of these. The narrator, it will be recalled, falls into the hands of the Inquisition and, after a dubious trial, is incarcerated in one of their sinister prisons and subjected to intolerable tortures, moral as well as physical. Doubtless the Fathers of the Inquisition represent, as Marie Bonaparte says, "the infinitely multiplied Father, a sort of royal 'we'" (p. 587). But it is appropriate to remember the role that the Inquisitors and their prison play in *The Italian, The Monk, Melmoth,* and in countless and often anonymous descendants of the masterpieces of the genre.

The Gothic buildings are only the spatial representation of Catholicism, which at that time still remained for the Anglican conscience the symbol of all abuses and of the most refined mental cruelties. It would be impossible to list the dusty remains of all the minor imitations of Lewis and Radcliffe in which the hero is sometime confined in a filthy cell, from which only a natural event such as earthquake or tidal wave, or some quirk of exterior forces, liberates him. In *Sicilian Mysteries* (1812), *The Ruins of Rigonda* (1808), *Gonzalo di Baldivia* (1817), *Cesario Rosalba* (1819), and *The Abbess* (1799), to consider only these titles, the prisons of the Inquisition are not only places of solitary confinement but also torture chambers. After the tribunal scene, which always unfolds, as in "**The Pit and the Pendulum,**" in a vast chamber with walls draped in black, the victim is led through a maze of dim passageways to secret subterranean places where he makes out in the half-light ropes, pulleys, chains, and steel wheels, whose function he is not long in discovering.[23] He is stripped, his joints are dislocated, his flesh torn—the blood flows.[24] Sometimes he is stretched out under the burning sun while drops of ice water from a caldron fall one by one on his head.[25] It is difficult to say if it is more terrible to feel the steel of the tongs probe palpitating flesh or to see the inexorable approach of the honed edge of a pendulum; in any case Poe's "sadism" had many antecedents in the English literature of the beginning of the century.

Furthermore, it will be remembered that in **"The Pit and the Pendulum"** the walls of the hero's cell are wretchedly painted "in all the hideous and repulsive devices to which the charnel superstition of the monks has given rise. The figures of fiends in aspects of menace, with skeleton forms, and other more really fearful images, overspread and disfigured the walls" (**Works**, V, 76-77). In the mind of the Inquisitors these horrifying daubs are thought to add even more terrible tortures of the spirit to the physical suffering of the victim. Now Poe did not invent this detail. Is it possible that he found it in some popular work on the horrors of the Inquisition? In any case, it is certain that the device was used by many Gothic novelists eager to spare nothing in order to arouse terror. In W. H. Ireland's *The Abbess,* for example, the hero is awakened in the night by a horrifying cry and sees frightening forms come to life on the wall of his cell:

> Horrid objects struck his sight. He started from his miserable couch; he, for a moment, yielded to the impulse of fear. He approached the wall, on which the most dreadful images that human fancy could invent, were portrayed, to terrify the wretched inhabitants of this earthly cell. One demon of gigantic stature seemed to roll his eyes upon the Comte. Hissing serpents appeared to dart forth their blood-dripping tongues, whose points were armed with points of fire. Ghastly forms were represented in the background, and skeletons intwined with poisonous adders, and among chapless skulls, from whose eyeless sockets were issuing long wreathing worms, the speckled toad, and the death-dealing scorpion seemed to dwell.[26]

The same device occurs in *Melmoth* in the scene where Monçada is aroused from sleep by the glowing flames which suddenly invade his cell:

> I awoke one night, and saw my cell in flames; I started up in horror but shrunk back on perceiving myself surrounded by demons, who, clothed in fire, were breathing forth clouds of it around me. Desperate with horror, I rushed against the wall, and found what I touched was cold. My recollection returned, and I comprehended that these were hideous figures scrawled in phosphorus, to terrify me.[27]

It seems to me that here Poe is incontestably following a precise literary tradition. Although the "pit" and the "pendulum" can have precise significances on a psychoanalytic level, the general atmosphere of the tale, the secret and malevolent presence of the Inquisitors and their frightening designs, put the American writer directly in debt to British fiction of the beginning of the century. **"The Pit and the Pendulum"** is the most perfect, the most horrifying, and the best written of Gothic tales imitative of *The Italian* and *The Monk.*

IV

To complete this account, the frequent use that Poe makes of two motifs especially popular with Gothic novelists must be discussed. Long before the American thought of writing, the motifs of the portrait and of the animated tapestry formed part of the tested techniques of horror in literature. The "oval portrait" to which the artist has in some way transferred the life of the model is not the first of the genre. In *The Castle of Otranto* Walpole had made use of a picture which depicted a character in such a lively manner that it leaves the frame and signals Manfred to follow it.[28] And one cannot avoid thinking of the eyes of the portrait of Melmoth which in Maturin's novel follow the narrator wherever he goes.[29] It would be wearisome to provide an exhaustive list of all the portraits in Gothic novels which not only spread panic among credulous servants but seriously sway the equilibrium of the most intrepid hero. To note in *Edmund of the Forest* (1797), *The Castle of Ollada* (1794), *Netley Abbey* (1795), *The Spirit of Turretville* (1800), *The Castle of Caithness* (1802), *Reginald; or, the House of Mirandola* (1799), *The Spirit of the Castle* (1802), and in many other publications today fallen into well-deserved oblivion, that the instances of this device admit the same basic grounds of creating the effect of terror sought by their authors will suffice for a more exact estimate of Poe's originality, which resides less in the choice of subject than in the manner in which he treats it.

Finally, **"Metzengerstein"** illustrates, in two ways, the Gothic tradition which we are reviewing. First, the central motif of the tale is that of the animated tapestry. Here again it is not a matter of reducing the literary worth of Poe but, on the contrary, of making his art more obvious, if one recalls in connection with this scene (one of the most astonishing of the story), all the hangings and tapestries which, from the first novels of Charlotte Smith to *The Fatal Revenge; or, The House of Montorio* by Maturin, suddenly terrify the heroine by seeming to become alive. Of course, in *The Horrors of Oakendale Abbey, Clermont,* and *The Romance of the Castle,* as in the majority of the narratives belonging to the subclass where the supernatural is rationally explained, it is a current of air which seems suddenly to give life to the demons, dragons, and monsters depicted on the cloth.[30] Let us say that in his preference for the irrational the author of **"Metzengerstein"** exploited to the limit a device that some Radcliffean romance had provided him the germ for. The idea was attractive to him, for **"Ligeia"** contains impressive drapery, so arranged in the bizarre nuptial chamber designed by the hero that a shrewdly directed current of air keeps it perpetually moving. As the narrator reports in **"Ligeia"**:

> But in the draping of the apartment lay, alas! the chief phantasy of all. The lofty walls, gigantic in height—even unproportionably so—were hung from summit to foot, in vast folds, with a heavy and massive-looking tapestry—tapestry of a material which was found alike as a carpet on the floor, as a covering for the ottomans and the ebony bed, as a canopy for the bed, and as the gorgeous volutes of the curtains which partially shaded the window. The material was the richest cloth of gold. It was spotted all over, at irregular intervals, with arabesque figures, about a foot in diameter, and wrought upon the cloth in patterns of the most jetty black. But these figures partook of the true character of the arabesque only when regarded from a single point of view. By a contrivance now common, and indeed traceable to a very remote period of antiquity, they were made changeable in aspect. To one entering the room, they bore the appearance of simple monstrosities; but upon a farther advance, this appearance gradually departed; and step by step, as the visitor moved his station in the chamber, he saw himself surrounded by an endless succession of the ghastly forms which belong to the superstition of the Norman, or arise in the guilty slumbers of the monk. The phantasmagoric effect was vastly heightened by the artificial introduction of a strong continual current of wind behind the draperies—giving a hideous and uneasy animation to the whole.
>
> (**Works**, II, 260-261)

One might say that the narrator tries to recreate for his second wife the atmosphere and the setting where former heroines enjoyed being terrified, keeping in mind, however, that this statement makes several Baroque variations upon a Gothic theme.

But to return to **"Metzengerstein,"** the second element which makes it nearly a perfect Gothic story is the obscure prophecy that the entire plot turns upon. Announced from the first page, it is verified at the end: "A lofty name shall have a fearful fall when, as the rider over his horse, the mortality of Metzengerstein shall triumph over the immortality of Berlifitzing" (**Works,** II, 186). Now if there is one traditional motif of the Gothic novel, it is the prophecy formulated in the first pages that prepares for and justifies subsequent supernatural intervention. *The Castle of Otranto* itself opens with an ancient oracle proclaiming

that "the Castle and Lordship of Otranto should pass from the present family, whenever the real owner should be grown too large to inhabit it."[31] The meaning of these mysterious words is soon understood when one learns during the course of the narrative about the existence of a giant ceaselessly growing and threatening the dissolution of the dwelling that shelters it. Just as Walpole's drama resolves itself when this strange prediction comes true, **"Metzengerstein"** cannot continue beyond the sphere of fantasy strictly demarcated by the sybilline words with which it opens. Recall that analogous dramatic situations occur in dozens of minor novels, *The Cavern of Death* (1794), *The Traditions* (1795), *The Haunted Priory* (1796), and *Mort Castle* (1800) being only the most eloquent examples. Robert Evans introduces into his *The Dream; or, Noble Cambrians* (1801) a long note explaining the role that the prophecy should play in this class of fiction.[32]

Of course there is an element of extravagance in making Poe an American disciple of Radcliffe, Lewis, and Maturin. The least of his tales obviously contains more art than the most brilliant "Gothic" story, and the interior spaces that he explores are immeasurably more authentically those of the soul. But one must still acknowledge that there are situations and themes in the groundwork of his art and of his oneiric peregrinations which the numerous followers of Walpole had exploited before him. Poe infinitely surpasses the literary devices and recipes for terror which Radcliffe, Lewis, and their imitators had developed thirty years earlier. Poe surpasses them, but he utilizes them. Without abandoning the images of the Gothic castle, the subterranean passages, the labyrinth, and the prisons of the Inquisition, he gives these locations the new dimensions of prisons projected by anguish in dream. A psychoanalysis of Poe is incomplete that rests on the discoveries of Freud rather than on those of Jung and Gaston Bachelard. It should make obvious in Poe's work the great "images primordiales" of the dream of depths, the structures of the vertical imagination which the Gothic novelists had rediscovered at the end of the eighteenth century.[33] In this way the correspondences that we have outlined will explain themselves less perhaps by a direct and lucid description than by a return to the same archetypes.

Notes

[This essay was first] published as "Edgar Poe et la tradition 'gothique,'" *Caliban: Annales de la Faculté des Lettres de Toulouse*, 4 (1968), 35-51.

1. John Davis, *Travels of Four Years and a Half in the U.S.A.* (London, 1803), pp. 186-187.

2. [In his exhaustive study of the English Gothic novel, Lévy traces the phrase "l'école frénétique" to Charles Nodier, and states that it especially well applies "to the multiplying horrors and frenzied episodes" characteristic of the minor novels which descend from the works of Walpole, Radcliffe, and Lewis; *Le Roman "Gothique" Anglais: 1764-1824* (Toulouse, 1968), p. 383. Lévy also notes Wordsworth's reference to "frantic novels" in the "Preface" to *Lyrical Ballads*, p. 646.—Translator.]

3. G. G. Raddin, *An Early New York Library of Fiction* (New York, 1940).

4. As for example the following, which appeared in *The Portfolio*: "Horrible description predominates. The authors go out of the walks of nature to find some dreadful incident. Appalling noises must be created. Ghosts must be manufactured by the dozens. A door is good for nothing, in the opinion of a romance writer, unless it creak. The value of a room is much enhanced by a few dismal groans. A chest full of human bones is twice as valuable as a casket of diamonds. Every grove must have its quiet disturbed by the devil, in some shape or other. Not a bit of tapestry but must conceal a corpse; not an oak can grow without sheltering banditti." Cited by F. L. Pattee in the introduction to his edition of Charles Brockden Brown's *Wieland; or, the Transformation* (New York, 1958), p. xxvii.

5. *Edgar Huntly*, ed. David Lee Clark (New York, 1928), p. xxiii.

6. *The Algerine Captive* (New Hampshire, 1797), cited in *Prefaces to Three Eighteenth-Century Novels*, ed. Claude E. Jones, The Augustan Reprint Society (Los Angeles, 1957), pp. viii-ix.

7. *The Complete Works of Edgar Allan Poe*, ed. James A. Harrison, reprint of the New York 1902 edition (New York, 1965), IV, 245. Hereafter cited as *Works*.

8. See "The Philosophy of Composition," *Works*, XIV, 193; "Landor's Cottage," VI, 264.

9. "I assure you I know well the West Tower of *L'Abbaye de Grasville*, the South Tower of the castle of *Mazzini*, the East Tower of the castle of Udolpho, the North Tower of the castle of *Blanguy*, but the Southwest Tower, father, that is new," *La Nuit Anglaise* (Paris, 1799), I, 116-117 [my translation—Translator].

10. *The Mysteries of Udolpho*, Everyman edition (London, 1931), II, 204.

11. *The Ruins of Rigonda; or, the Homicidal Father* (London: Chapple, 1808), II, 128.

12. (London: Minerva Press, 1800), II, 55.

13. *The Italian*, Ballantyne's Novelist's Library (Edinburgh, 1824), X, 560; *Sicilian Mysteries; or, the Fortress Dei Vechii* (London: H. Colburn, 1812), II, 56.

14. Poe wrote: "Cherubina! Who has not heard of Cherubina? Who has not heard of that most spiritual, that most ill-treated, that most accomplished of women, of that most consummate, most sublimated, most fantastic, most unappreciated and most inappreciable of heroines? Exquisite and delicate creation of a mind overflowing with fun-frolic, farce, wit, humor, song, sentiment, and sense, what mortal is there so dead to everything graceful and glorious as not to have devoured thy adventures? Who is there so unfortunate as not to have taken thee by the hand? Who so lost as not to have enjoyed thy companionship? Who so much of a log, as not to have laughed until he has wept for very laughter in the perusal of thine incomparable, inimitable and inestimable eccentricities?" *The Southern Literary Messenger*, 2 (1835), 41.

15. Eaton S. Barrett, *The Heroine*, ed. M. Sadleir (London, 1927), p. 244.

16. "Les Demeures dans le Roman Noir," *Critique*, nos. 147-148 (1959), p. 725 [my translation—Translator].

17. *The Castle of Otranto*, ed. W. S. Lewis, Oxford English Novels (Oxford, 1964), p. 108.

18. *Matilda Montfort* (London: Spenser, 1809), II, 90-91.

19. *Melmoth* (London, 1892), II, 34-35.

20. See "William Wilson": "From each room to every other there were sure to be found three or four steps either in ascent or descent. Then the lateral branches were innumerable—inconceivable—and so returning in upon themselves, that our most exact ideas in regard to the whole mansion were not very far different from those with which we pondered upon infinity" (*Works*, III, 303). See "Amontillado," *Works*, VI, 169-172; "The Domain of Arnheim," VI, 191; "Pym," III, 30-33, 221-225.

21. *The Life and Works of Edgar Allan Poe: A Psycho-Analytic Interpretation*, tr. John Rodker (London, 1949), pp. 341-342.

22. Protagonists respectively of *The Monk* (1796) by Lewis, *Zofloya; or the Moor* (1806) by Charlotte Dacre, *The Three Spaniards* (London, 1800) by George Walker, *Jaqueline of Olzenburg; or, Final Retribution* (London, 1800), and *Melmoth the Wanderer* (London, 1820) by Maturin.

23. Cf. for example the descriptions in *Sicilian Mysteries*, V, 148; *The Ruins of Rigonda*, III, 87; *Gonzalo di Baldivia; or, a Widow's Vow* by Ann of Swansea (London: Minerva Press, 1817), I, 141; *Cesario Rosalba; or, the Oath of Vengeance* (London: Minerva Press, 1819), V, 263; etc.

24. Cf. W. H. Ireland, *The Abbess* (London: Earle & Hemet, 1834), III, 145; *Sicilian Mysteries*, V, 149; George Brewer, *The Witch of Ravensworth* (London: J. F. Hughes, 1808), II, 154; *The Castle of Villa-Flora* (London: Minerva Press, 1819), III, 152; etc.

25. *Gonzalo di Baldivia*, I, 141-142.

26. *The Abbess*, II, 196.

27. *Melmoth*, I, 258.

28. *The Castle of Otranto*, p. 24.

29. I, 20, 94. Remember that Maturin's novel gave Wilde the idea for *The Portrait of Dorian Gray*.

30. "The ragged tapestry represented still more horrible figures, all of which waved in lifelike movements as the air (admitted by the door) fanned the loose hanging on which they were represented," *The Horrors of Oakendale Castle* (New York: J. Harrison, 1799), p. 13. "Nor could she prevent herself from starting as the tapestry, which represented a number of grotesque and frightful figures, agitated by the wind that whistled through the crevices, every now and then

swelled from the walls," R. M. Roche, *Clermont* (London: Minerva Press, 1798), I, 113. The heroine is frightened by "the pallid figures on the tapestry now and then moved by the wind, admitted through various crevices of this dreary chamber. They had really a terrific appearance, and might well be mistaken for the ghosts of the heroes they represented," *The Romance of the Castle,* II, 71.

31. *The Castle of Otranto,* pp. 15-16.

32. (London: Minerva Press, 1801), I, 54-55.

33. [For Lévy's application of Jung and of Bachelard (especially Bachelard's concept of "verticalité") to Gothicism in general, see *Le Roman "Gothique" Anglais,* particularly pp. 601-643—Translator.]

CLARK GRIFFITH (ESSAY DATE 1972)

SOURCE: Griffith, Clark. "Poe and the Gothic." In *Papers on Poe: Essays in Honor of John Ward Ostrom,* edited by Richard P. Veler and Richard Beale Davis, pp. 21-7. Springfield, Ohio: Chantry Music Press at Wittenberg University, 1972.

In the following essay, Griffith studies Poe's impact on the treatment of madness in the Gothic tradition, asserting that Poe "was concerned with shifting . . . the locus of the terrifying."

Despite the emphasis in his criticism upon a need for novelty, Poe's tales of terror are clearly indebted to some literary forebears. From Gothic fiction of the English eighteenth century, Poe took the *imagery* of terror: the blighted, oppressive countryside; the machinery of the Inquisition; in particular, the haunted castle, swaddled in its own atmosphere of morbidity and decay. From the nineteenth-century Gothicized tales in *Blackwood's Magazine,* which he both ridiculed and admired, he took the *form* of terror: a first-person narrator, lingering typically over a single, frightening episode, and bringing matters to a climax in which he has grown deaf to every sound except the noise of his unique sensations. So close are the resemblances that one passes from Anne Radcliffe's architecture to the effusions of a *Blackwood's* speaker, convinced that Poe's effects often result from his combining the murky details of the one with the inveterate, uninterrupted talkativeness of the other. Yet I wish to argue that even as Poe borrowed, he also made a significant contribution. Imperfectly at first, but then with greater assurance, he was concerned with shifting what I shall call the locus of the terrifying. This change in stance is one measure of his originality as a practicioner in the Gothic mode. And to watch him make it is to find special meaning in his famous declaration that the terror of which he wrote came not from Germany but from the soul.

As the basis for contrast, let us glance briefly at Emily St. Aubert, before the Castle of Udolpho. Confronting it for the first time, she can only see the castle as a real and utterly objective fact. For Emily is a true child of the *Essay Concerning the Human Understanding.* It would please her to suppose that she has somehow been transported into "one of those frightful fictions in which the wild genius of the poet delights." But aware that there is nothing in the mind not first in the senses, she recognizes that she has no grounds for distrusting her perceptions; hence she must scorn as "delusion" and "superstition" the notion that the source of her agitation is anywhere except in the world around her. In Emily's case, therefore (as throughout Mrs. Radcliffe and the eighteenth-century Gothic generally), the direction of the horrifying is from without to within: from setting to self. Terror comes in consequence of what no less an authority than Horace Walpole had called the "extraordinary position," as it impinges upon "mere men and women" to alarm and dismay them.[1]

The situation seems identical in the early portions of "**MS. Found in a Bottle**" (1833). The storm at sea, which overtakes Poe's narrator, or the engulfing waves that "surpass . . . anything [he] had imagined possible": both appear to be examples of the received, physical ordeal, such as Walpole and Mrs. Radcliffe had devised. Halfway through "**MS.**," however, a change in emphasis occurs. Now, for the first time, the narrator speaks of strange "conceptions" which are arising from inside his mind. They consist of "feelings" and "sensations" to which no name can be given; nevertheless, they cause him to spell out the word "Discovery" as he beholds—in any case, apparently beholds—an entire new order of experience. At this point, I suggest, Poe has commenced to modify the traditional Gothic relationship. If terror is to be the effect of inner conceptions, it is no longer necessary to regard his narrator as a "mere man," beset and beleaguered by appalling circumstances. Instead, one can as readily think of him as Creative Man, and of the circumstances themselves as the products of his terrible creativity. At least potentially, the locus of the terrifying has passed from the spectacle into the spectator.

Admittedly, though, the change remains no more than implied and potential in "**MS. Found in a Bottle.**" It breaks down ultimately, because the scenery in the tale still seems too much founded upon the eighteenth-century convention of the "outer wonder." What Poe needed, if he intended to psychologize the Gothic, was nothing so spacious or openly exotic as the South Indian Ocean. He required the smaller, less public *mise-en-scène*, one which could more plausibly be transfigured by his narrators, and, above all, one which would dramatize the processes of transfiguration in action. He is best off, in short, when he returns to the dark, secluded interiors of eighteenth-century fiction, but portrays them in such a way that the interiors are made suggestive of the human mind itself. And this of course is the technique he has perfected two years later, with the publication in 1835 of "**Berenice**," his first example of a genuinely new Gothic.

Sitting within his ancestral mansion, Poe's Egaeus turns out to be both projector and voice, the source of a strange predicament as well as its spokesman. He has spent a lifetime gazing for "long unwearied hours" at objects which he half-suspects are trivial and without purpose—and watching while, gradually and inexplicably, they acquire some momentous significance. The story makes it clear, however, that the details present this heightened aspect only to Egaeus's "mind's eye"; whatever the meaning they come to possess, it is due solely to his fierce concentration upon them. Obviously, then, there has ceased to be any distance, or difference, between the terror and the terrified. Egaeus's realities are the realities of his own making; his world resembles a mirror in a madhouse, wherein distortions and phantasms appear, but only as the reflections of a particular sort of observer. And nowhere is this fact more evident than in his obsession with the teeth of Berenice:

> The teeth!—the teeth! they were here, and there, and everywhere, and visibly and palpably before me; long, narrow, and excessively white, with the pale lips writhing about them. . . .

At first glance, we are likely to be struck by the sheer, intense *physicalness* of these dreadful molars. Superficially, in fact, they may well seem of a kind with the highly tangible horrors which *The Monk* presents. Yet they function in quite another way. M. G. Lewis's ghoulish occurrences were rooted in a thoroughly Lockean landscape. The putrefying head, in the convent vaults at St. Clare, had to exist independently of Agnes de Medina, first to accost Agnes's senses and then to register on her appalled sensibility. By contrast, the teeth in Poe have no meaningful existence outside a sensibility; as Egaeus acknowledges, *"tous ses dients étaient des idées."* What the teeth might be like apart from Egaeus, or whether, for that matter, they even have an identity except in his vision of them: these are issues of no real moment.

So successfully has Poe internalized the Gothic that the old "outer wonders" of the eighteenth century now disappear into the stream of consciousness. They have become the conditions and consequences (if one likes, the "objective correlatives") of a psychic state.

The strategy of "**Berenice**" is one that with the slightest variations Poe would continue to utilize for the rest of his life. Barring the allegorical "**Masque of the Red Death**" and the fact-bound *Pym* (with its return to a glamorous out-of-doors), I know of none of the horror tales in which the perceiving mind does not seem much more nearly the originator of the terrifying than it is a mere passive witness. Moreover, I am convinced that to read them as though they were notes composed from within is often to clarify and enrich the stories. For example, the real key to the somewhat baffling "**Fall of the House of Usher**" (1839) appears to me to lie in the way it opens by re-enacting an episode out of Mrs. Radcliffe, but repeats the event for a totally different purpose.

Like Emily St. Aubert, Poe's speaker also rides up, at the end of a long day's journey, before an apparently haunted castle. He too feels it to be a massive and brooding presence in the foreground. And then, in an effort to dispel the alarm with which it quickly envelopes him, he decides to examine the place from a different perspective. But when he reins in his horse and proceeds to the new location, nothing happens. Where Emily could always look forward to being physically delivered from peril, the physical change in Poe only means that his narrator seems menaced anew. The "ghastly tree stems" and "vacant eye-like windows" continue to glare back at him with the same old ominousness.

Of course nothing happens. The truth about the speaker in "**Usher**" is that he has all along been engaged in a kind of symbolic homecoming. When at length he crosses the causeway and goes indoors, he finds himself among rooms and furnishings that are oddly familiar, because he has arrived at nothing less than the depths of his own being. Thereafter, it is not his talkativeness—his descriptive abilities, in the usual sense—that summon up Roderick and Madeline. The Ushers are products of the narrator's psyche; for they and their behavior become the embodiments of his trance, or they appear as the *personae* in his dream vision, or perhaps their incestuous relationship is a working out of his own, dark, tabooed, and otherwise inexpressible desires. Thus every subsequent event in "**Usher**" is prepared for by an opening tableau in which the power to terrorize could not be blotted from the landscape, because it had actually been brought into the landscape by the mind of the narrator. The organic unity, of which Poe makes so much, is a unity between the single creating self at the center of the story, and those shapes and forms which radiate outward as the marks of his continuous creative act. To me at least, no other interpretation of the tale can justify the amount of attention paid its narrator, or is so true to the form and manner of his narration.[2]

Poe's tinkerings with tradition are probably less eccentric and ultra-personal than, at first look, they appear to be. Behind them, after all, one discerns nothing more remarkable than a particular manifestation of the Romantic Movement. If the terrors of the eighteenth century were accountable in terms of Locke's *Essay*, then what is terror for Poe except an adjunct to the thirteenth chapter of the *Biographia Literaria?* That is, the horrifying now looms up out of a world in which the imagination "dissolves, diffuses, dissipates, in order to recreate" and wherein imaginative tendencies are "essentially *vital*, even as all objects (*as* objects) are essentially fixed and dead."

Granted that they represent extreme cases, Poe's narrators have to be understood as figures who are deeply involved in just the activity that Coleridge describes. Until their inner lives impinge upon the outer, the outer, if it is consequential at all, remains a dull and prosaic affair. It gains its extraordinary qualities, as we have seen, through the transforming and the transfiguring capacities of an imaginative self. To cite a last example, we are told by the speaker in "**Ligeia**" (1838) of how the *décor* in Lady Rowena's bedchamber "partook of the true character of the Arabesque only when regarded from a single point of view." As we read, however, it is to find that the single point of view has nothing to do with physical positioning. Rather, it seems expressive of the narrator's personality, an extension of his inward state. One concludes therefore that it is akin to Coleridge's "secondary imagination." In Poe's hands this faculty has become more nearly an instrument of the appalling than it is a strictly aesthetic principle. Nevertheless, it still operates as the means of discovering relevance, pattern, even a certain sort of beauty and ideality in objects which, left to themselves, would be "essentially fixed and dead."

Small wonder, consequently, that Poe's fiction is better unified but, at the same time, darker and much gloomier than the eighteenth-century Gothic had been. With their stress upon horror as an objective phenomenon, the earlier Gothic writers could introduce a whole range of tones and effects. As they evoked terror from the outside, so they were likewise free to suspend and withdraw it from without. Having opened what amounted to a trapdoor onto the world of menace, they found it possible to snap the door shut again, and so to conduct their characters back into a world of happy endings: of order, security and (typically) the celebration of marriage vows. The waking nightmare succeeded by the nuptials! It is the regular drift of events from *The Castle of Otranto* to *The Monk* and on into *Blackwood's*.[3]

But Poe possessed no such latitude. Since the stimulus for terror comes from within, there can, in the tale he tells, be no real survivors, no remissions of the terrible, no protagonists who, by pluck or by luck, either earn or are at least vouchsafed the right to turn backward through the trapdoor. Self-afflicted and self-victimized (so to speak, their own executioners), Poe's characters must perform a persistently downward journey, sinking further and further into voluble wonderment at themselves, until they arrive at one of those shattering silences with which their narratives customarily end. And yet, even as they descend, they are granted a kind of glory which no hero of the earlier Gothic could ever have matched. We may feel that the next step for Poe's narrators will be the tomb or the lunatic asylum. During a single, transcendent moment, however, they have had the privilege of calling up out of their very beings a totally new order of reality. They are Romantic heroes without peer, for they have been the masters, because the creators, of all that they survey.

And small wonder, finally, that *their* creator was fascinated by what he called "the power of words." Once he had got hold of his true theme, it was never enough for Poe simply to set a scene, describe an action, use words to provoke a shudder or two; that was the business of those attuned to the terrors of Germany. The test of language in his work lay in its ability to delve deeply within and bring to light the most hidden crannies of a suffering, yet oddly prolific self. Thus the descriptive devices of his Gothic predecessors re-emerge as Poe's metaphors of mind; their rhetorical flourishes are turned by him into a rhetoric of revelation. Out of the magic of words, Poe brings forth the symbolic countryside, self-contained and self-sustaining, utterly devoid of connections with the world as it is, yet recognizable still in the terms of its own special topography. And behind the countryside, he shows us the figure of the owner. This is the soul of man, cloaked in the works which it has made, and rendered thereby into a visible and articulate entity.

Notes

1. Walpole's formula appears in his preface to the second edition of *The Castle of Otranto*. It was still being echoed, forty years later, by an anonymous contributor to *Blackwood's*, who asserted that the occasions for horror come "from the cases . . . or circumstances of life." Before Poe, the real issue among Gothic writers was not whether fear was externally motivated (that was taken for granted), but whether "outer wonders" had to be natural and plausible (as in Mrs. Radcliffe) or could legitimately be supernatural visitations (as in Walpole and, sometimes, M. G. Lewis).

2. Though the opening of "Usher" seems closest to *The Mysteries of Udolpho*, it will also bear comparison with the preface to *The Castle of Otranto*. In a striking reversal of Walpole's formula, Poe's speaker transfers the quality of *mereness* away from himself and attaches it to the landscape. The prospect "out there," he feels, is a "mere" house, a domain with "simple features"; it ought not to alarm as it does. My position is, of course, that he is quite apart from the narrator's purview, the landscape might very well be "mere" and "simple"; without at all knowing it, he is an exceedingly complex fellow. And more and more of late, he is being restored to what seems to me his proper place in the story. See Richard Wilbur's "Introduction" to *Poe: Complete Poems* (New York, 1959) and James M. Cox, "Edgar Poe: Style as Pose," *VQR*, XLIV (Winter 1968), 67-89.

3. If the lurid high point of *The Monk* is Ambrosio's transformation from saint to devil, we should not miss another major movement in the book. In our last glimpse of Agnes and Raymond, they are a wedded couple, to whom all future vicissitudes will "seem as zephyrs which breathe over summer seas." Presumably, Raymond has earned this bliss by securing a decent Christian burial for the Bleeding Nun, while Agnes's entitlement to happiness derives from her simply having endured the outrages of the past.

TITLE COMMENTARY

The Narrative of Arthur Gordon Pym

LESLIE FIEDLER (ESSAY DATE 1960)

SOURCE: Fiedler, Leslie. "The Blackness of Darkness: E. A. Poe and the Development of the Gothic." In *Love and Death in the American Novel*. 1960. Reprint, pp. 370-82. New York: Anchor Books, 1992.

In the following essay, Fiedler offers a biographical interpretation of The Narrative of Arthur Gordon Pym.

In his harried career as a journalist, book-reviewer, short-story writer, poet, and critic, Edgar Allan Poe tried twice to write a full-length novel, reworking each time chronicles of American exploration on sea and land. Both *The Narrative of A. Gordon Pym* (1837-38) and *The Journal of Julius Rodman* (1840) strike us as improbable books for Poe to have attempted, concerned as they are with the American scene and the great outdoors. The former is based upon accounts of pioneering expeditions to the South Seas, and especially a South Polar expedition projected by an acquaintance of Poe called J. N. Reynolds; while the second borrows heavily from the journals of Lewis and Clark, purporting to describe a trip across the Rockies which had preceded theirs. Both long fictions are, superficially at least, full-fledged "Westerns" from the pen of an author none of whose more notable short stories (except the insufferably commercial **"The Gold Bug"**) involve either native problems or a native setting.

There is little doubt that Poe was trying to cash in on contemporary interest in the remote and the unexplored, exploited, on the one hand, by such popular histories as Washington Irving's *Astoria* or *Adventures of Captain Bonneville*, and, on the other, by the Indian novels of James Fenimore Cooper. In the course of a review of the latter's *Wyandotté*, written in 1843, Poe reflects on the Leatherstocking Tales and remarks a little ruefully:

> . . . we mean to suggest that this theme—life in the Wilderness—is one of intrinsic and universal interest, appealing to the heart of man in all phases; a theme, like that of life upon the ocean, so unfailingly omniprevalent in its power of arresting and absorbing attention, that while success or popularity is, with such a subject, expected as a matter of course, a failure might be properly regarded as conclusive evidence of imbecility on the part of the author. . . .

He goes on to add, however, that "the two theses in question," that is, the wilderness and life upon the ocean, are subjects to be avoided by the "man of genius . . . more interested in fame than popularity," for they belong to the lesser of the "two great classes of fiction," the "popular division" at whose head Cooper stands. Of this category, Poe remarks that "the author is lost or forgotten; or remembered, if at all, with something very nearly akin to contempt." He considers his own fiction in general part of the other great class, which includes the work of "Mr. Brockden Brown, Mr. John Neal, Mr. Simms, Mr. Hawthorne," of whom it can be said that "even when the works perish, the man survives."

Yet in **Gordon Pym** and **Julius Rodman,** Poe tried his hand at the two popular themes, attempting, for the first time perhaps, to treat the sort of legendary material which had appeared in Leatherstocking Tales with the scrupulous documentation of Irving's nonfictional accounts. The kind of book at which Poe aimed Melville was to produce with eminent success, beginning less than a decade later with the best-selling *Typee* (1846) and *Omoo* (1847), and raising the genre to unexpected power in *Moby Dick*. Poe is considerably less successful, failing completely in the case of the unfinished **Julius Rodman** to lend fictional life to borrowed documents; and achieving in **Gordon Pym** a work so hopelessly unpopular (in America at least!), that only within the last very few years has a major attempt to redeem it been undertaken. Poe himself, some time after its appearance, was willing to write off **Gordon Pym** as a "silly book"; and certainly from the first he had considered it, or pretended to consider it, a shameless bid for popular success—the sort of "Tale in a couple of volumes," which his friend Paulding had assured him would win him the mass audience that had snubbed his collections of short stories.

The whole apparatus which surrounds the anonymous final form of **Gordon Pym** is apologetic: an involved attempt on Poe's part to convince himself that his primary purpose in publishing the tale was to perpetrate a hoax on the reader. But this is an almost compulsive aspect of Poe's art in general, arising from a dark necessity, which dogged not only him among American writers, of remaining in ignorance about his own deepest aims and drives. Just so Cooper was obligated to believe that he was mocking his wife's literary taste before he could become an author, while Melville eternally persuaded himself that he was on the verge of producing a best-seller, and Twain pretended he was a writer of books for boys.

The apologetic and playful preface to **Pym** has for us now chiefly biographical interest, illuminating the author but not the work. Whatever Poe's ostensible or concealed motives, he created in his only complete longer fiction not a trivial hoax but the archetypal American story, which would be recast in *Moby Dick* and *Huckleberry Finn*. Why, then, did Poe's book not achieve either the immediate acclaim accorded the latter or the slowly growing reputation won by the former? All the attributes of the highbrow Western are present in his novel: the rejection of the family and of the world of women, the secret evasion from home and the turning to the open sea. Only a bevy of black squaws and a few female corpses ("scattered about . . . in the last and most loathsome state of putrefaction") intrude into the world of pure male companionship which Poe imagines; and they provide no competition to the alliance of Pym either with his boyhood friend and Anglo-

Saxon compeer, Augustus Barnard, or with his dusky demon, the "hybrid line-manager," Dirk Peters.

Rioting and shipwreck and rescue at sea do not break the rhythm of the flight that bears Pym farther and farther from civilization toward a primitive isolation, symbolized by the uncharted island and the lost valley, the derelict ship, and the small boat adrift at sea. Even Rip Van Winkle's initiatory draught, the alcoholic pledge to escape and forgetfulness, is represented in **Pym.** Buried in a coffin-like refuge in the black hull of a riot-torn ship, Gordon Pym finds at hand a bottle to console him; and later he and his companions fish up out of the flooded hold a flask of Madeira!

There are totemic beasts to spare in the pages of Poe's Western: a great white bear dramatically slaughtered, as well as legendary and exotic animals, compounded surrealistically out of incongruous familiar forms, and even stranger tabooed birds, who float lifelessly on a tepid and milky sea. And through it all, the outcast wanderer—equally in love with death and distance—seeks some absolute Elsewhere, though more in woe than wonder. Poe's realm of refuge and escape seems finally a place of death rather than one of love: the idyllic American dream turned nightmare as it is dreamed in its author's uneasy sleep. If the West means archetypically some ultimate innocence, there is no West in Poe's book at all—only an illusory hope that draws men toward inevitable disenchantment and betrayal. It is not merely that a gothic horror balances the quest for innocence in **Gordon Pym**; such a balance is the standard pattern of all highbrow Westerns: of *Moby Dick*, in which the sinister figure of Fedallah confronts the beneficent one of Queequeg; and even of *Huckleberry Finn*, in which the threat of Pap's ignorant spite and the shadow of slavery define by contrast the pure peace of Jackson's Island and the raft. Only in Poe's novel, however, is the dark counterpoint permitted to drown out the *cantus firmus* of hopeful joy or to mar a final harmonic resolution.

Huckleberry Finn closes on a note of high euphoria, sustained by rescue and redemption and promises of new beginnings, which quite conceal from the ordinary reader the tragic implications of the conclusion; while *Moby Dick* ends with the promise of adoption, the symbolic salvation of the orphaned Ishmael by the crushing, motherly *Rachel*. Only at the close of **Gordon Pym** is the Great Mother identified with total destruction, a death without resurrection, a sterile, white womb from which there is no exit. "And now we rushed

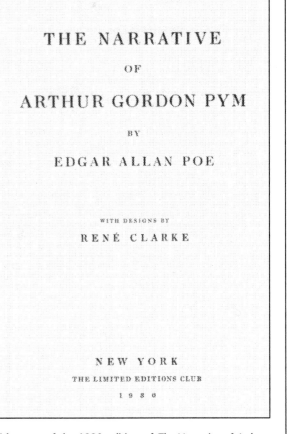

Title page of the 1930 edition of *The Narrative of Arthur Gordon Pym.*

into the embraces of the cataract, where a chasm threw itself open to receive us. But there arose in our pathway a shrouded human figure, very far larger in its proportions than any dweller among men. And the hue of the skin of the figure was of the perfect whiteness of snow." The white whale and the *Rachel* have been fused into a single symbol, the Great Mother as *vagina dentata*; and though Poe's preface has already assured us that Pym somehow escaped to write his story, we know this for a mere device to explain how such a first-person narrative could have been written at all—a gimmick and a lie. In the tone and feeling of the text, which alone have the right to ask an act of faith, there is every assurance that Pym and Peters died.

The book is finally an anti-Western disguised as the form it utterly travesties; and this fact the great public, which will not in such matters be fooled, perceived—and perceiving, rejected the work. From the beginning, a perceptive reader of **Gordon Pym** is aware that every current sentimental platitude, every cliché of the fable of the holy marriage of males is being ironically exposed.

Man's best friend, the dog, turns into a slavering monster ready to tear his master's throat to appease his hunger and thirst; a presumably loyal crew, led by the kind of standard black cook who plays the grinning and subservient comedian even in *Moby Dick,* mutinies; a bird flies through the pure blue air to drop "with a sullen splash" at the feet of a half-famished group of sailors "a portion of clotted and liverlike substance," a chunk of decayed human flesh; an approaching ship, hailed as a source of rescue, turns out to be a vessel loaded only with human carrion, from which issues "a smell, a stench, such as the whole world has no name for." Even the friendly bottle, traditional symbol of innocent male companionship, induces not joy but the D.T.'s, "an indescribable state of weakness and horror . . . a violent ague."

Most disconcerting of the parodies in *Pym* is that of the theme of resurrection itself, which later carries so much symbolic weight in both *Moby Dick* and *Huckleberry Finn.* Like Ishmael or Huck, Gordon Pym is presumably slain only to rise again, immersed and entombed only to be reborn—in his case, not once but over and over. Out of the coffin in the hold and out of a swoon that seems death itself, he is brought to life, but only to face mutiny and a new threat of destruction; and he emerges in the disguise of a ghost: his face coated with white chalk and blotched with blood, his clothes stuffed to resemble the bloated stomach of a swollen corpse. The threat of murder once again avoided, he is the victim of shipwreck; and almost dead once more (his life meagerly sustained by drinking the blood of a murdered shipmate), he is rescued by a passing ship, only to fall victim to a last catastrophe which leaves him buried alive just as in the beginning. A "living inhumation," Poe calls the state of life-in-death, to which his long circle brings him back; and he lingers almost sensuously over the details: "The blackness of darkness . . . the terrific oppression of the lungs, the stifling fumes from the damp earth . . . the allotted portion of *the dead.* . . ." But even from this plight, Pym is rescued, this time by his blood-stained, demonic mate, Dirk Peters; and the two together approach the ultimate plunge into a white polar chasm, from which there is no reason to believe either can emerge. Indeed, it is precisely such an end which the pariah poet-sailor has prayed for, has loved in anticipation: "death or captivity among barbarian hordes . . . a lifetime dragged out in sorrow and tears, upon some grey and desolate rock." The guilt of Pym and of his creator demands of experience not the consolation of love but the delicious punishment of a living death, not the gift of Queequeg but of Fedallah.

Since Pym lusts for Gehenna rather than Eden, the companions he chooses on his quest embody not fertility or patient endurance but impotence and terror. Augustus Barnard, his first specter bridegroom, dies horribly, rots away visibly on a parody before-the-fact of Huck's raft: "His arm was completely black from the wrist to the shoulder, and his feet were like ice. . . . He was frightfully emaciated; so much so that . . . *he now did not weigh more than forty or fifty* [pounds] *at the farthest.* His eyes were . . . scarcely perceptible, and the skin of his cheeks hung so loosely as to prevent his masticating any food . . . without great difficulty." His painful death is not even sacrificial, merely another device to produce a shudder, especially at the point where his entire leg comes off in the hand of the man who is attempting to heave his rotten corpse into the sea!

Augustus' impromptu grave-digger is his successor; for it is Dirk Peters who tosses the first good companion over the side, to the sharks who gather with gnashing teeth. But Peters is, as we have already noticed, a very ogre: such a monster, one of Poe's critics describes him, as children draw to scare themselves, a nightmare out of our racial beginnings. In him, the qualities of Queequeg and Fedallah and Captain Ahab are oddly combined; a savior and a beloved primitive, he is also a murderer, a consumer of human flesh, a demi-devil, a madman. He is, in fact, as Marie Bonaparte suggests, the accursed hero who has destroyed the Father, taking on himself the guilt of the artist who only writes or dreams such horror. He protects the artist-surrogate of the plot with almost maternal tenderness, fights his battles like a big brother; and like a lover, holds him safe and warm when the defeated wanderer seeks his bloody embrace, impotent and whimpering. Yet the sought-for embrace is a rape and a betrayal, a prelude to certain death.

The climax of the relationship of Pym and Peters comes at the moment when the two are trapped on the Island of Tsalal, where all their companions have been killed by an artificial landslide contrived by the bloodthirsty black aborigines. The two survivors are trying to find their way out of a cleft in the earth that has providentially sheltered them; and Pym is suspended in fright on a sheer cliff wall.

> For one moment my fingers clutched compulsively upon their hold, while, with the movement, the faintest possible idea of escape wandered, like a shadow, through my mind—in the next my

whole soul was pervaded with a *longing to fall*; a desire, a yearning, a passion utterly uncontrollable. I let go at once my grasp upon the peg, and, turning half round from the precipice, remained tottering for an instant against its naked face. But now there came a spinning of the brain; a shrill-sounding and phantom voice screamed within my ears; a dusky, fiendish and filmy figure stood immediately beneath me; and, sighing, I sank down with a bursting heart, and plunged within its arms.

The "dusky, fiendish . . . figure" is, of course, Peters, the half-breed; and the studied ambiguity of the passage, in which the language of horror becomes that of eroticism, the dying plunge becomes a climactic embrace, makes it clear that the *longing to fall* and the desire for the dark spouse are one, a single perverseness. Peters is not made an angelic representative of instinct and nature even at this critical instant; he remains still a fiend, even in the act of becoming a savior. And the reader is left to wonder what so dark and orgasmic a salvation can possibly mean except the exchange of one death for an even more damnable other. Poe presents us not with the standard resolution of the American's ambiguity toward the life of impulse: an opposition of good savage and evil savage, as in Cooper's confrontation of Pawnee and Sioux, or Mark Twain's contrast of benevolent Negro and malevolent Indian. Though the son of an Upsaroka mother preserves Pym from the menace of the black hordes of Too-Wit ("Seizing a club from one of the savages who has fallen, he dashed out the brains of the three who remained . . ."), Poe is not finally intent on playing the same symbolic game as Twain in reverse. He is rather portraying a world in which the primitive may save or destroy, but remains always brutal and amoral, from any Christian point of view—diabolic.

Poe espouses, that is to say, the view of instinctual life which is the common property of those writers whom he regards as "men of genius," the view of Brockden Brown and Hawthorne; and he quite consciously rejects the sentimentalizing of the savage which he finds in popularizers like Cooper. Poe is quite at home with that distinctively American strain of the gothic, in which the aristocratic villains of the European tale of terror are replaced by skulking primitives, and the natural rather than the sophisticated is felt as a primal threat. Indeed, Poe's aristocratic pretensions make it impossible for him to adopt such an attitude without the equivocations and soul-searching demanded of such liberal gothicists as the young Brockden Brown. His fictional world needs no good Indians because he believes in none; and try as he will, he cannot keep quite distinct the mutinous black cook, whom he calls a "perfect demon," from the "dusky, fiendish" figure of Dirk Peters. *Theoretically,* the tale of **Gordon Pym** projects through its Negroes the fear of black rebellion and of the white man's perverse lust for the Negro, while symbolizing in the red man an innocent and admirable yearning for the manly violence of the frontier; but in the working out of the plot, the two are confused. Certainly, Pym has prepared himself for the encounter with Peters by reading the journals of Lewis and Clark in his coffin-refuge in the hold; but Peters refuses to become a harmless embodiment of the West, remaining to the end an ogre, his great, bare teeth displayed like fangs.

It is true that the half-breed line-manager offers protection against the shipboard mutineers and the vicious natives of Tsalal; but his sheltering embrace is identified with the mortal hug of the grizzly bear, whose skin he wears to cover his bald pate. The figure of the black man blends ambiguously with that of the slave, while that of the red man blurs into that of the wild beast! The West, at any rate, was always for Poe only half real, a literary experience rather than a part of his life; but the South moved him at the deepest personal level. Insofar as **Gordon Pym** is finally a social document as well as a fantasy, its subject is slavery; and its scene, however disguised, is the section of America which was to destroy itself defending that institution. Poe's novel is surely the first which uses gothicism to express a peculiarly American dilemma identifying the symbolic blackness of terror with the blackness of the Negro and the white guilts he embodies. It is, indeed, to be expected that our first eminent Southern author discover that the proper subject for American gothic is the black man, from whose shadow we have not yet emerged.

Though the movement of **Gordon Pym** seems to bear us away from America, once Nantucket and New Bedford have been left behind, and to carry us through remoter and remoter seas toward the exotic Antarctic, it ends in a region quite unlike the actual polar regions. Heading toward an expected world of ice and snow, Pym finds instead a place of tepid waters and luxuriant growth; seeking a white world, he discovers, beside and within it, a black one. What has gone wrong? It is necessary for Poe to believe, in that blessed ignorance which frees forbidden fancies, that Pym's fictional voyage is bearing him toward the polar region, just as it was necessary for him to believe the whole story a delicious hoax; but we, as latter-day readers, need not be the victims of either delusion. For all the carefully worked-up details about penguins, *biche de mer,* galapagos tortoises (bait for the audience which was later to subscribe to the *National Geographic*), Poe follows the footsteps not of Captain Cook but of his own first voyage in the arms of his mother, undertaken before his memory began, from New England to the South. In his deepest imagination, any flight from the North bears the voyager not toward but away from the snow—not to the South Pole, but to the American South.

Certainly, it grows not colder, but warmer and warmer, as Pym aboard the last ship to rescue him, the *Jane Gay,* pushes closer and closer to the Pole. "We had now advanced to the southward more than eight degrees farther than any previous navigators. We found . . . that the temperature of the air, and latterly of the water, became milder." Whatever pseudo-scientific explanations Poe may have believed would sustain this improbable notion of a luke-warm Antarctica, certain *symbolic* necessities were of more importance; he is being, in fact, carried back to Ole Virginny—as the color of the natives he meets on the Island of Tsalal (latitude 83° 20', longitude 43° 5' W.) clearly indicates. They are brawny, muscular, and jet black, with "thick and woolen hair," "thick and clumsy lips," these "wretches," whom Pym describes, after they have destroyed all the white men but him and Peters, as "the most wicked, hypocritical, vindictive, blood thirsty, and altogether fiendish race of men upon the face of the globe." Poe very carefully does not ever call them Negroes, though he bestows on them those marks which, in a review of two books on abolition, he listed as the special stigmata by which God distinguished the race that were to become slaves. He "blackened the negro's skin and crisped his hair into wool." At any rate, where an informed reader might have expected some kind of Indian, Poe could only imagine plantation hands in masquerade; and he sets them in a world distinguished not only by blackness and warmth, but by a certain disturbing sexuality quite proper to Southern stereotypes of Negro life. That sexuality can only be expressed obliquely by Poe, who was so squeamish about matters of this kind that the much franker Baudelaire was driven to remark, "*Dans l'oeuvre d'Edgar Poe, il n'y a jamais d'amour.*" The phallicism of the island he, therefore, suggests not in human terms but by a reference to the islanders' chief crop, the *biche de mer*—a kind of sea-cucumber of which, Poe informs us, the

authorities say that it "renews the exhausted system of the immoderate voluptuary."

The inhabitants of Tsalal are not, of course, the burlesque Negroes, those black "rascals" or "scamps," named pompously "Jupiter" or "Pompey," who lend a minstrel-show note to Poe's lighter tales. Woolly-pated and bow-legged, these characters play the role of mischievous, cowardly, stupid and faithful dependents, good always for a laugh when they say "soldiers" for "shoulders" or "clause" for "cause." No more are the black savages of **Gordon Pym** like the ideal colored servants sketched by Poe in his review of *Slavery in the United States* by J. K. Paulding, the author whose suggestion led to Poe's writing his encoded Southern tale. The "degree of loyal devotion on the part of the slave to which the white man's heart is a stranger," Poe insists, is far "stronger than they would be under like circumstances between individuals of the white race"; and, indeed, such "loyal devotion" ranks high in "the class of feelings 'by which the heart is made better' . . ." It is precisely such loyalty which the actions of the natives in Poe's novel belie, since it is his hidden doubts on this score which they embody. The dark hordes of Too-Wit project the image of what the Southerner privately fears the Negro may be; just as the idealized body-servant of Poe's review projects the image of what the anti-abolitionist publicly claims he is. But the two images are complementary halves of a single view based on wish and terror: the subdued dependent bent to the sick-bed in love and the resentful victim abiding in patience a day of vengeance. It is the darker half, however, which is true to Poe's memories of his boyhood and youth in the Allan household; while the lighter belongs only to certain patriarchal legends, to which he learned to subscribe during his days on *The Southern Literary Messenger.* In the single reference to the Negro in his correspondence, Poe complains to his stepfather (the date is 1827): "You suffer me to be subjected to the whim & caprice, not only of your white family, but to the complete authority of the blacks."

At the climax of **Gordon Pym,** Poe dreams himself once more, though a grown man, subject to that nightmare authority; and the book projects his personal resentment and fear, as well as the guilty terror of a whole society in the face of those whom they can never quite believe they have the right to enslave. In Tsalal, blackness is no longer the livery of subjection but a sign of menace; so utterly black, that even the teeth concealed by their pendulous lips are black, the Antarctic savages inhabit a black land in which the vegetation and the animals, water itself are all subdued to the same dismal color. The voyage of Pym has transported him improbably into the black belt, a black belt transformed from the level of sociology to that of myth, in whose midst the reigning Caucasian is overwhelmed by a sense of isolation and peril. Not even the glimmer of white teeth bared in a heartening smile cuts the gloom of this exclusive and excluding dark world, whose ultimate darkness is revealed in that final chasm in which Pym and Peters are trapped after the treacherous destruction of their white shipmates. "We alone had escaped from the tempest of that overwhelming destruction. We were the sole living white men upon the island." At this point, the darkness of "Nigger-town" merges at last into the darkness of the womb which is also a tomb, an intestinal chamber from which there is apparently no way of being born again into a realm of light.

How has Pym arrived here, in this place where whiteness itself is taboo, where even the flicker of a handkerchief, the flash of sunlight on taut sails, a little flour in the bottom of a pan stir terror, and doom the white man who feels at home in a world full of such pale symbols? Pym has sought a polar whiteness and has discovered instead a realm of the domination of black. It was (as Marie Bonaparte and other analytical critics have made clear) his mother whom Poe was pursuing in his disguise as Pym: that lost, pale mother, white with the whiteness of milk and the pallor of disease; and the imaginary voyage is a long regression to childhood. But hostilely guarding the last access to the White Goddess, stands the black killer, Too-Wit. In the ultimate reaches of his boyhood, where he had confidently looked for some image of maternal comfort and security, Poe-Pym finds *both* the white chasm and cascade and the black womb sealed off by black warriors. Surely, the latter fantasies represent memories of the black mammy and the black milk brother, who has sucked at the same black breast.

Writing from the conscious level of his mind and addressing a public largely Southern, Poe dealt with the effect of these quasimaternal and fraternal bonds sanguinely enough. Those very feelings, he argued, "'by which the heart is made better' . . . have their rise in the relation between the infant and his nurse. They are cultivated between him and his fostering brother. . . . They are fostered by the habit of affording protection and favors to the younger offspring of the same nurse. . . ." But the buried mind of Poe does not believe what the rationalizing intelligence propounds; in dreams (and in the fiction which is close to those dreams), the foster-brother arises to destroy and crush, to block the way to the lost, pale mother who preceded the Negro nurse. And even the good foster-brother, whom Poe split off from his dark imago in Peters, he cannot finally feel as benign; for him the black man and the "blackness of darkness" are one. That they remain one in much distinguished American fiction after his time is probably not due to the direct influence of Poe. He rather prophetically anticipates than initiates a long line of American books, in which certain gothic writers exploit the fear and guilt which the comic Negro of popular art attempts to laugh out of existence.

A. A. MARKLEY (ESSAY DATE SPRING 2003)

SOURCE: Markley, A. A. "The Godwinian Confessional Narrative and Psychological Terror in *Arthur Gordon Pym.*" *The Edgar Allan Poe Review* 4, no. 1 (spring 2003): 4-16.

In the following essay, Markley traces how works by William Godwin—and by other Gothic writers who used Godwin's "confessional" style—influenced The Narrative of Arthur Gordon Pym.

The Narrative of Arthur Gordon Pym has enjoyed a surge of critical attention in recent years, much of which has been concerned with charting and analyzing the scores of source materials that Poe wove into the fabric of his complex and unusual novel.[1] Many scholars, such as Bruce Weiner, have recognized *Pym's* relationship to the widely popular genre of Gothic fiction, noting its particular correlation with the "explained" or "rational" mode of Gothic popularized by Ann Radcliffe, whose suspenseful page-turners ultimately provide a reasonable explanation for every supernatural or oddly coincidental occurrence in the plot.[2] *Pym's* strong debt to Daniel Defoe, particularly to *Robinson Crusoe* (1719) has also long been acknowledged; clearly Defoe is a critical source of influence not only in terms of subject matter, but in Poe's manner of developing a first person narrative voice.[3]

It was William Godwin, however, who first married the first person confessional narrative to elements of Gothic suspense in his novels of the 1790s and afterwards. Godwin's literary influence is much forgotten today, despite the wide appeal of his novels during his lifetime and despite the school of followers he inspired with his peculiar blend of terror and confessional narrative—figures such as Lord Byron, Mary Shelley, Edward Bulwer-

Lytton, William Ainsworth, and, perhaps most importantly in terms of his own influence on Poe, Charles Brockden Brown.[4] Burton Pollin has acknowledged the relationship between the theme and atmosphere of Poe's works and Godwin's and has cataloged both the nineteenth-century references that likewise acknowledge this connection and the seventeen times in Poe's own writings, largely in his reviews, in which Poe himself praises specific aspects of Godwin's fiction.[5]

In his review of Godwin's *Lives of the Necromancers*, for example, Poe writes

> The name of the author of *Caleb Williams* and of *St. Leon* is . . . a guarantee for . . . excellence. There is about all the writing of Godwin one peculiarity which we are not sure that we have ever seen pointed out for observation . . . an air of mature thought—of deliberate premeditation. . . . No English writer . . . with the single exception of Coleridge, has a fuller appreciation of the value of *words*; and none is more nicely discriminative between closely-approximating meanings.[6]

In a later review, Poe compares *Caleb Williams* with Ainsworth's *Jack Sheppard* (1839): "In both novels the hero escapes repeatedly from prison. In the work of Ainsworth the escapes are merely narrated. In that of Godwin they are *discussed*. With the latter we become at once absorbed in those details which so manifestly absorb his own soul. We read with the most breathless attention. We close the book with real regret."[7]

In a final example, in criticizing Charles Dickens' *Barnaby Rudge* (1841), Poe favors the works of Godwin and his disciple Bulwer-Lytton, calling them "the best constructors of plot in English literature."[8]

A passionate radical devoted to the idea of social reform in England, Godwin published in 1793 a mammoth work of political philosophy, *Enquiry Concerning Political Justice*, which idealistically looked forward to the dissolution of government in a society founded entirely on sincerity and rational thinking. Realizing, however, that both the cost and the approach of *Political Justice* precluded its wide dissemination amongst a mass audience of readers, Godwin turned next to the novel as a vehicle for expressing his political views to a wider readership. The result was perhaps the most influential British novel of this period, *Things As They Are, or, The Adventures of Caleb Williams*, published in 1794, and followed by dozens of reprints in England, America, and France in the years to follow.[9]

In setting out to illustrate the evils of Britain's political and class systems, Godwin developed a new sub-genre of the confessional narrative. One of the novel's most recognizable features lies in Godwin's particular manner of characterizing his first person narrator; in this case a narrator in torment, driven to tell the story of a disastrous life brought about by his own errors in judgment. The narrator, Caleb Williams, is secretary to a wealthy landowner named Falkland, an aristocrat who values his sense of personal honor above all other aspects of his life. By listening to neighborhood gossip and snooping around Falkland's possessions, Caleb gradually begins to piece together a crime in Falkland's past—the murder of a neighbor and the framing of two innocent tenant farmers for the crime. When Falkland discovers that Caleb knows his secret, he sets about ruining the young man's reputation, has him thrown into jail for alleged theft, and, when Caleb escapes, has him dogged from town to town, making sure that no one harbors Caleb or listens to his tale.

The political intention of the novel is clear in its deft illustration of the power that the aristocrat held over the reputation of those of the lower classes, merely by relying on the authority of his class status. But from a literary perspective, the deeper interest in the novel lies in Godwin's creation of Caleb as a narrator. Godwin drew heavily on his predecessors in developing his own brand of first-person narrative. Defoe's narrators, such as the titular heroes of *Moll Flanders* (1722), *Colonel Jack* (1722), and *Roxana* (1724) had shocked readers in the earlier eighteenth century with their frank confessions of lurid lives of crime. Godwin specifically turned to *Moll Flanders* and *Colonel Jack* in creating the voice of a character caught in the predicament of having to survive amongst the worst excesses of the British class system as a social outcast. These novels also inspired Godwin to depict the life and point of view of the criminal world from the inside. His particularly memorable depiction of the "gentleman-thief," Captain Raymond, brings home the point that nobility can exist even in those driven to crime. Moreover, the insider's point of view allowed him an opportunity to depict the brutality of contemporary British prisons and the blatant inequities of the judicial system.

Godwin also turned to Samuel Richardson in developing his first person narrator; in his epistolary format in *Pamela* (1740-41), *Clarissa* (1747-48), and *Sir Charles Grandison* (1753-54), Richardson achieved new levels of emotional veracity and psychological depth. Pamela's struggles with the relentless advances and irrational anger of her employer, Mr. B., provided a particular model for the troubled love/hate relationship between servant and master in the case of Caleb and Falkland.

Drawing on such influences and focused by a strong drive towards social reform, Godwin managed to create in Caleb Williams a startlingly realistic personality—a slippery narrator fully in control of his story, and yet one whose confessions and rants of terror and profound remorse evoke strong emotional responses in the reader. Pamela Clemit has pointed out that Godwin's use of first person is central to his political purpose: "the inbuilt unreliability of [the] first-person account throws the burden of interpretation and decision on the reader, soliciting his or her active participation," and thus fostering Godwin's ideal of private judgment in which each individual is obligated "to seek out objective truths in the moral and political realm."[10]

Godwin continued to write first person confessional novels for the rest of his career. Punctuated by periods in which he experimented with the essay, biography, history, and drama, and alongside a 25-year career as a publisher and author of children's books, Godwin published five more novels, most of which, unlike Caleb Williams, are given a particular historical setting which deeply informs the novels' political bent. The most fantastic of these in Gothic terms, St. Leon (1799), tells the story of a man who struggles with the unexpectedly unpleasant results of having been given the gifts of the elixir of life and the philosopher's stone against the back-drop of the Protestant Reformation in sixteenth-century continental Europe. The narrator of Fleetwood (1805) indicates Godwin's new interest in exploring the abnormal psyche in the tale of an aberrantly egocentric man whose inability to trust his wife nearly leads him to destroy her. Delving even deeper into abnormal psychology, Mandeville (1817) explores the descent of a troubled narrator into madness in an England torn apart by Civil War. These latter two novels in which the reader must weigh more and more evidence that his narrator is actually mad may well have influenced Poe's explorations of abnormal psychology in such tales as "The Tell-tale Heart," "The Black Cat" and "William Wilson."

Clearly Poe shared with Godwin a fascination with anatomizing the mind of a character by allowing that character to tell his own tale. His work in this vein was not, however, always in the serious mode; in his "How to Write a Blackwood Article," Poe humorously satirizes the dilemma of the author who attempts to achieve Gothic suspense with the use of a first person narrator. In this tale, Psyche Zenobia's first hand account of her tragic and bizarre decapitation on the town clock makes light of a central paradox of the genre and calls attention to the basic unreliability of the narrator who tells his or her own tale.[11]

Arthur Gordon Pym calls up the tradition of the Godwinian novel at nearly every turn—beginning with its very title. Critics have noted the similarity between the name of the narrator, "Arthur Gordon Pym" and the author, "Edgar Allan Poe." Similarly, "Caleb Williams" as a name raises questions concerning the relationship between narrator and author: "Williams" of course recalling Godwin's own first name, and "Caleb" alluding to a spy who worked for Moses in the Old Testament—thus Caleb can be interpreted as "William's spy."[12] Pym's opening words likewise recall the Godwinian tradition; Godwin's narrators inevitably open their tales by discussing their upbringing and education, usually in order to reveal aspects of their early life and early personal qualities that ultimately led to disaster. This convention has a twofold purpose; in addition to providing important background information for the reader to factor into his or her judgment of the narrator's actions as they unfold, beginning the character's story in such a way can also be seen as a bid for veracity, contributing to a distancing of the narrator from the author of the work.

Poe takes such a bid a step farther in actually having his narrator refer to Poe himself as editor in the Preface, and in closing the novel with the final "Note," presumably by the editor, Poe. Pym's expression of anxiety about his ability to write a viable novel, and about the credibility of his adventures are clearly a further attempt to fool the audience into thinking him to be real. In going to such lengths to establish the veracity of his narrator's existence, Poe seems to have followed the example of another gothic novelist who drew much from Godwin, Scottish author James Hogg. In his 1824 Private Memoirs and Confessions of a Justified Sinner, Hogg similarly took pains to distance himself from the text by having his narrator refer to "James Hogg" as an editor of the text; indeed "James Hogg" even appears as a character in the narrative towards the end of the tale. Hogg even went so far as to publish a letter in Blackwood's Edinburgh Magazine announcing particular discoveries relating to the events of the novel prior to the novel's publication, later incorporating this letter into the fabric of his novel as well.

Very much in the spirit of Godwin's narrators, Pym immediately displays a tendency towards what Godwin called "precipitation," or acting hastily and rashly, and without regard for possible consequences. Oddly, Pym's response to his near-death experience in the *Ariel* at the beginning of Chapter 1, and the sensational tales of mutiny, shipwreck, and cannibalism that he hears from his friend Augustus, lead him only to long the more to go to sea. One may think of Robert Walton, the narrator of Mary Shelley's *Frankenstein* (1818), the most famous of the products of the "Godwinian school," who as an ambitious sea captain experiences only a renewed passion for adventure from reading such sea tales as Coleridge's *The Rime of the Ancient Mariner*—the kind of sea tale that would make most readers hope never to set foot on a deck.

In addition to a tendency towards precipitative behavior, Godwinian narrators generally have a healthy regard for their own attributes, despite the remorse they unanimously express for their many past sins. Pym's self-assurance, particularly as he expresses it while attempting to survive on the wreck of the *Grampus*—"I suffered less than any of us, being much less reduced in frame, and retaining my powers of mind in a surprising degree, while the rest were completely prostrated in intellect, and seemed to be brought to a species of second childhood"[13]—bears a striking similarity to confident statements made by Godwinian narrators, who often confess to finding themselves physically attractive. Upon drinking his elixir of life and recapturing his youth, for example, Reginald St. Leon remarks, "I knew not how to take away my eyes from the mirror before me."[14] Similarly, Casimir Fleetwood, when relating his marriage to a much younger woman, avows, "My person was pleasing, and my demeanour graceful; circumstances which had acquired me in Paris the appellation of *the handsome Englishman*."[15]

As a common convention of Gothic fiction, imprisonment, or the fear of imprisonment in running from the law, plays an important role in many of Godwin's novels. Pym's period of imprisonment as a stowaway in the hold of the *Grampus* and Poe's exploration of the psychological effects of being deprived of light, fresh air, clean water, and adequate nourishment strongly parallels Caleb Williams' vividly depicted incarceration in jail as well as St. Leon's 12-year imprisonment by the Spanish Inquisition. One of Godwin's chief purposes in his political novels was to expose the indecencies of the prison system in contemporary Britain. Carefully researching the state of the prisons of the day, Godwin adds footnotes to the text of *Caleb Williams* during the episode of Caleb's incarceration in order to make it clear that his details relating to the state of prison cells and buildings and to the care of inmates are entirely factual. In Poe's novel, Pym's period of confinement seems also to function on a deeper level, and one much more psychological in nature—representing perhaps a gestational period, or Pym's passing through a period of death in the coffin-like box to a symbolic rebirth.

Pym's dog "Tiger" plays an interesting role in this episode. Having been twice rescued from death by Tiger in the past, Pym is delighted to find that Augustus has secreted the dog on board. Poe, however, puts a chilling twist on the love between man and beast when the measure of Pym's desperation in the hold can be assessed by Tiger's turning feral from want of food and water. Interestingly, Godwin, too, portrays the intense loyalty dogs to his narrators in at least two novels; in *Fleetwood*, the narrator's faithful pet follows him all the way from Wales to Oxford when the narrator enrolls in the university. In *St. Leon*, a dog described much like Pym's "Tiger" suffers for his great love for the narrator. Like Tiger, who in the mutiny of the *Grampus* saves his master yet again by killing a mutineer, St. Leon's dog performs similar feats of heroism, at one point pulling a drowning boy from a river. In each of these texts, a far-fetched episode demonstrating the pure love of a dog for his master seems to be a useful tool for intensifying the emotional experience of the novel and for making the narrator a more sympathetic personality.

The plot devices of imprisonment and escape allowed Godwin reliable means by which to develop high suspense in his novels. *Arthur Gordon Pym* is so loaded with suspense and adventure as to seem almost a parody of the Gothic genre. One way in which Godwin characteristically intensifies suspense is by creating situations in which a character's worst fear is realized immediately upon his expressing it. In putting together his theory concerning Falkland's past crime, Caleb repeatedly commits actions while hoping Falkland will not see or hear him. Inevitably, Falkland appears immediately, as if summoned supernaturally to the scene by Caleb's very anxiety. Poe seems almost to be making fun of this kind of heavy-handed device when, despite Augustus's careful plans to disguise Pym and to spirit him onto the *Grampus* after dark, Pym finds himself nevertheless face to face with his grandfather, the person he least wishes to meet. Pym proceeds to befuddle the poor old man in a humorous deflation of the suspense of the episode.

The element of disguise in this episode likewise parallels a common Godwinian situation. Caleb Williams often experiments with aspects of disguise in his desperate attempts to flee his relentless pursuers. At one point he rubs ash on his face and dresses in the rags of the poor in order to pass as a Jew in metropolitan London; at another point he quickly lays on an Irish brogue to confuse his captors when he is apprehended trying to escape the country. St. Leon similarly affects an array of disguises to elude pursuers throughout his narrative; ultimately his attainment of the elixir of life, which restores him permanently to a state of youth 32 years younger, proves to be the ultimate, fool-proof disguise. The issue of disguise in Godwin is, obviously, closely tied to the narrator's exploration of his own identity and his assertion of self through his narrative. Of course, the situation also allows for rich theoretical readings when one steps back from the narrative and considers the role of the writer in playing with his own sense of self and his role as author in creating a startlingly realistic first-person narrator. David Ketterer, for one, has discussed deception as a theme and a technique in this novel, focusing on the ways in which *Pym* continually challenges the reliability of our perceptions of reality.[16]

Certainly the richest episode of disguise in *Pym* is that in which Pym disguises himself to impersonate the dead body of his shipmate Hartmann Rogers, to terrify the mutineers and to help his friends stage a counter take-over. Pym's detailed description of the corpse and his various attempts to approximate its horrible aspect in his own appearance take the Godwinian narrator's exploration of self to a new and much darker level of confrontation with death and physical corruption. The disarming nature of this passage brings to mind similarly bizarre episodes in which Godwin experiments with this tactic particularly as a means of exploring aspects of the aberrant personality. The best examples are found in *Fleetwood*. As a young student in school, the narrator Fleetwood participates in a complex scheme by which he and his friends aim to humiliate one of their overachieving colleagues by creating a life-size puppet to impersonate a schoolmaster. The visually impaired over-achiever is perfectly fooled by the puppet, and the violent harangues of this pseudo-schoolmaster actually drive the boy to suicide in a prank gone horribly wrong. Later in the novel, Fleetwood deals with his rage at the presumed infidelity of his wife by dressing up two wax dummies in their clothing, using the dummies to act out a mock wedding feast, and then tearing the dummies to shreds in a terrifyingly psychotic fit of rage. It is interesting to note that as in *Pym*, what the author is exploring here is the power of outward appearance as the signifier of identity and ultimately as a means of attacking and even destroying others. In *Frankenstein*, Mary Shelley would explore this idea even further in demonstrating that when appearance is blindly accepted as a valid signifier of character, great violence can be the result.

One of the most intriguing elements of Poe's novel is the relationship between Pym and his friend Augustus, his companion throughout the first half of the novel. The references to the closeness of these young men's relationship, the fact of their sharing a bed and "lying close," strongly prefigure the relationship between Melville's Ishmael and Queequeg of *Moby-Dick* (1851). While scholars have noted that Augustus' age and the date of his death tie him closely to the figure of Poe's brother Henry,[17] the reader may also sense a subtle homoeroticism implicit in the attachment between these two characters. Judith Sutherland has identified aspects of the doppelgänger in their relationship, an old folk motif that offers a complex symbolic means of exploring identity and otherness, two aspects of the same personality, or the dangerously potent attraction and hatred between two characters who mirror each other in powerful ways; Poe's **"William Wilson"** is certainly one of the finest examples of the use of this motif in modern literature.[18] Clearly Poe is doing much more with Augustus than offering a portrait of his dead brother, as the two characters balance each other in intriguing ways. A drunken Augustus nearly leads a sober Pym to his death in the novel's first episode; later Augustus' life amongst the crew of the *Grampus* neatly balances Pym's pseudo-death in the ship's hold; this balance of active and passive "doubles" may remind the reader of the similar situation in which Victor Frankenstein falls into a nine-month state of near-delirium and confinement in bed while his newly created creature makes his first foray into the world.

But Poe, interestingly, strikes off from the doppelgänger aspects of Pym's relationship with Augustus nearly as soon as he develops it. Pym's reemergence from the ship's hold in the impersonation of a corpse, unsettles the balance of the doubles and knocks Augustus from his status as a major player in the novel. Augustus loses his place as Pym's older brother figure and caretaker and gradually becomes more and more ill, until he dies at the novel's exact center. His near immediate decomposition and the falling apart of his body when the others throw it into the sea to be devoured by the circling sharks, symbolize his decomposition as a key player.[19] Perhaps the oddest aspect of this scene is Pym's relatively rational response to Augustus' grisly end.

Pym's psychological movement away from his fraternal attachment to and his idolization of Augustus in the novel's earliest chapters charts an important aspect of his growth as a character. By the time of Augustus' death, he has been utterly superseded by the figure of the half-breed Dirk Peters, whose initially appalling physical qualities are gradually mollified in the reader's memory, as his behavior makes him seem more and more to be the most rational and capable actor in the tale. Interestingly, this process of mollification begins for the reader in Peters' humane treatment of Augustus during and after the mutiny on the *Grampus*; Peters' odd affection for Augustus is acknowledged by his grumbling fellow mutineers. How does one of the most dangerous, frightening, and unattractive characters in the novel become central both to the narrative and to the narrator's own life and mind? Again one might think of Melville's Ishmael and Queequeg. Perhaps the answer lies in such a character's ability to challenge the narrator's preconceptions about otherness and difference.

Godwin's use of subtle elements of homoeroticism is an aspect of many of his novels. Caleb Williams' intense love-hate relationship with his patron and tormenter Falkland and the ways in which these characters "double" each other have been fruitfully explored in this light.[20] His psychotic narrators, Fleetwood and Mandeville, each develop an intense hatred for a perceived rival that from a psychoanalytic perspective can only be interpreted as having a sexual basis; each frequently comments on the beauty and attractiveness of his particular nemesis. Both of these situations perfectly illustrate Eve Sedgwick's theory of homosocial desire, in which intense desire between men is channeled into hateful competition; one of the texts with which Sedgwick most persuasively illustrates this aspect of desire is Hogg's *Private Memoirs and Confessions of a Justified Sinner*.[21] Godwin's *Cloudesley* (1830) is

perhaps his most thorough treatment of the power of attraction between men and the inherent dangers therein. In this novel the young hero, Julian, continually expresses a desire for an intense male bond—first directed towards his friend Francesco Perfetti, and later towards the infinitely charming bandit known as St. Elmo—friendships described as having the mix of fraternal love and hero-worship characterized by Pym's early relationship with Augustus.

Another figure in *Cloudesley* that offers a strong parallel to Dirk Peters is Julian's dark and brooding guardian Borromeo, whose misanthropy is ultimately recuperated by the example of the noble Julian. Borromeo is actually a recasting of an earlier misanthrope, Bethlem Gabor, one of the most memorable figures in *St. Leon*, whose response to the violent loss of his family drives him to imprison and torment St. Leon because of St. Leon's attempts to contribute to the benefit of his fellow man.[22] In both of these cases, a wrathful, dangerous, and physically intimidating character is gradually softened by his contact with the hero of the novel; the evolution of Peters as a character clearly follows the same trajectory. It is important to note the clear relationship of these brooding characters to the Byronic hero, Byron himself having been deeply influenced by Godwin's work.[23]

Reading *Arthur Gordon Pym* as a product of the Godwin school places several of the novel's characteristics into sharp focus. Its near-parody of Gothic conventions and relentless suspense not only reveals Poe at his best as a master of this genre, but shows him working out aspects of these conventions that would turn up again and again throughout the body of his later work. More importantly, Poe is undeniably successful here in developing the veracity of a peculiar and challenging first-person narrator, and in exploring that narrator's psyche with incredible complexity in Pym's descriptions of his adventures, in symbolic episodes of death and rebirth, and in his relationships with other characters. In *Arthur Gordon Pym*, Poe seems to have set himself the goal of employing every convention he could glean from both Gothic fiction and the popular genre of the sea narrative—often abruptly moving away from one and on to another as soon as he has developed it. The sheer number of terrifying incidents and suspenseful episodes packed into this short work indeed suggest not merely an attempt to meet the conventions of any particular genre, but rather an effort to surpass them all.

As Burton Pollin aptly points out, Poe seems to have had little interest in the strain of social criticism running throughout Godwin's fiction, choosing instead to imitate Godwin's development of atmosphere, his unpredictable but carefully modulated plots, and his intensely realistic depictions of peculiar, often aberrant personalities.[24] Despite this major difference between Godwin's and Poe's approach, a close reading of *Arthur Gordon Pym* alongside Godwin's novels makes quite clear the particular aspects of Godwin's style and approach that Poe valued so highly. On the basis of *Arthur Gordon Pym* alone, Poe must be regarded as a major figure in the "school of Godwin," which managed by the mid-nineteenth century to take the first-person narrative to a startlingly new level of emotional intensity and psychological realism.

Notes

1. See, for example, Burton R. Pollin, ed. *The Imaginary Voyages: The Narrative of Arthur Gordon Pym, The Unparalleled Adventure of One Hans Pfaall, The Journal of Julius Rodman*, vol. 1 of *Collected Writings of Edgar Allan Poe* (Boston: Twayne, 1981; rpt. NY: Gordian P., 1994), and Pollin's "Poe's Life Reflected through the Sources of *Pym*," *Poe's Pym: Critical Explorations*, ed. Richard Kopley (Durham, NC: Duke UP, 1992), 95-103. See also Richard Kopley's edition of the novel, *The Narrative of Arthur Gordon Pym of Nantucket* (NY: Penguin, 1999), and Ronald C. Harvey's discussion of studies of Poe's sources in *The Critical History of Edgar Allan Poe's The Narrative of Arthur Gordon Pym: "A Dialogue with Unreason"* (NY: Garland, 1998), 110-12.

2. Bruce Weiner, "Novels, Tales, and Problems of Form in *The Narrative of Arthur Gordon Pym*," in Kopley, *Critical Explorations*, 49-50. See also Leslie Fiedler, *Love and Death in the American Novel* (NY: Stein and Day, 1960; rpt. NY: Dell, 1966), 392-400.

3. Burton Pollin, "Poe and Daniel Defoe: A Significant Relationship." *Topic* 16 (1976): 3-23.

4. For a discussion of Brockden Brown and Mary Shelley as disciples of Godwin, see Pamela Clemit, *The Godwinian Novel: The Rational Fictions of Godwin, Brockden Brown, Mary Shelley* (Oxford: Oxford UP, 1993).

5. Burton Pollin, "Poe and Godwin," *Nineteenth-Century Fiction* 19 (1965): 237-53; rpt. in *Discoveries in Poe* (Notre Dame: U. of Notre Dame P., 1970), 107-27. The majority of these references can be found in Pollin, *Godwin Criticism: A Synoptic Bibliography* (Toronto: U. of Toronto P., 1967), 554. See also Pollin's "Primitivism in *Imogen*," *Bulletin of the New York Public Library* 67 (1963): 186-90, for a discussion of analogies between Godwin's early novel *Imogen* (1784) and "The Fall of the House of Usher."

6. *Southern Literary Messenger* VIII (December 1835): 92-4; cited in Pollin, "Poe and Godwin," 240-1.

7. "Review of *Guy Fawkes: or the Gunpowder Treason. An Historical Romance*," *Graham's Magazine* X (November 1841): 214-22; cited in Pollin, "Poe and Godwin," 243.

8. "Chapter of Suggestions," *Opal* XIV (1845): 188-9; rpt. in Burton R. Pollin, ed., *Collected Writings of Poe: The Brevities: Pinakidia, Marginalia, Fifty Suggestions, and Other Works*, vol. II (NY: Gordian, 1985), 468-70; cited in Pollin, "Poe and Godwin," 250.

9. Godwin himself made revisions to the novel for new editions in 1796, 1797, 1816, and 1831.

10. Clemit, 6.

11. See Jonathan Auerbach's discussion of this tale as a satiric comment on the act of narration in *The Romance of Failure: First-Person Fictions of Poe, Hawthorne, and James* (Oxford: Oxford UP, 1989), 3-8.

12. Burton R. Pollin, "The Significance of Names in the Fiction of William Godwin." *Revue des Langues Vivantes* 37 (1971): 391.

13. Pollin, ed., *Collected Writings*, I:130.

14. William Godwin, *St. Leon: A Tale of the Sixteenth Century*, ed. Pamela Clemit, *Collected Novels and Memoirs of William Godwin*, vol. IV (London: Pickering and Chatto, 1992), IV:283.

15. William Godwin, *Fleetwood, or, The New Man of Feeling*, ed. Pamela Clemit, *Collected Novels and Memoirs of William Godwin*, vol. V (London: Pickering and Chatto, 1992), 189.

16. David Ketterer, *The Rationale of Deception in Poe* (Baton Rouge: Louisiana State UP, 1979), as discussed by Harvey, *Critical History*, 116.

17. See Marie Bonaparte, *The Life and Works of Edgar Allan Poe: A Psycho-Analytic Interpretation*. Trans. John Rodker. (London: Imago, 1949; rpt. NY: Humanities P., 1971), and Kopley, *Arthur Gordon Pym*, 224, n. 5., and 231, n. 3.

18. Judith Sutherland, *The Problematic Fictions of Poe, James, and Hawthorne*. (Columbia: U. of Missouri P., 1984), 33.

19. See J. Gerald Kennedy's thorough discussion of this aspect of the novel in "*Pym* Pourri: Decomposing the Textual Body," in Kopley, *Critical Explorations*, 169-71.

20. See Robert J. Corber, "Representing the 'Unspeakable': William Godwin and the Politics of Homophobia," *Journal of the History of Sexuality* 1 (1990): 85-101; and Alex Gold, Jr., "It's Only Love: The Politics of Passion in Godwin's *Caleb Williams*," *Texas Studies in Language and Literature* 19 (1977): 135-60.

21. Eve Kosofsky Sedgwick, "Murder Incorporated: *Confessions of a Justified Sinner*," in *Between Men: English Literature and Male Homosocial Desire* (NY: Columbia UP, 1985), 97-117.

22. For a thorough analysis of Godwin's Bethlem Gabor, see Gary Kelly, "History and Fiction: Bethlem Gabor in Godwin's *St. Leon*," *ELN* 14 (1976): 117-20.

23. For Godwin's influence on Byron, see William St. Clair, *The Godwins and the Shelleys: A Biography of a Family* (Baltimore: Johns Hopkins UP, 1989), 339-40.

24. Pollin, "Poe and Godwin," 253.

"The Fall of the House of Usher"

STEPHEN DOUGHERTY (ESSAY DATE WINTER 2001)

SOURCE: Dougherty, Stephen. "Foucault in the House of Usher: Some Historical Permutations in Poe's Gothic." *Papers on Language and Literature* 37, no. 1 (winter 2001): 3-24.

In the following essay, Dougherty examines the gothicism of "The Fall of the House of Usher" within the context of the racism and fear of miscegenation in nineteenth-century society.

"[I]n the nineteenth century," writes Reginald Horsman, "the Americans were to share in the discovery that the secret of Saxon success lay not in the institutions but in the blood" (24). This "discovery" was of monumental and devastating importance, and by the middle of the century the sign of blood seemed to be everywhere. Americans and Europeans were entering a new era of blood—of blood spilled as never before in genocides around the globe, of blood seeping inexorably into the sacred and profane imagination of race and the nation, and of blood horrors turned into a staple of mass entertainment.

This era of blood was the era of the bourgeoisie's entrenchment. In *Juice of Life* Piero Camporesi tells us, "At least up until the eighteenth century, blood was still dubbed the 'father of all the humors.' Life and salvation were closely tied up with its quality and purity" (14). Camporesi implicitly suggests a diminished rather than an augmented concern with blood in the modern world. But, if anything, this concern was heightened by its modified signification in the nineteenth century. After the collapse of the traditional theory of humors with the rise of scientific medicine in the eighteenth century, blood lost some of its old associations, but it gained some important new ones. Blood came to represent not the character of the individual, but the purity of the race or nation. The idea of purity—or impurity—of blood became the vessel of many bourgeois fears about confrontation with indigenous and colonized peoples, national identity, historical destiny, and the dream of progress. The race or nation whose mission—and manifest destiny—was to lead humanity into a better world could hardly dilute the very essence of its identity by "mixing" its blood. The most cherished precept of this era could be summed up in the words that John C. Calhoun spoke on the U. S. Senate floor in the aftermath of the Mexican-American War: ". . .

Ours is a government of the white man. . . . [I]n the whole history of man . . . there is no instance whatever of any civilized colored race, of any shade, being found equal . . ." (my emphasis; qtd. in Fredrickson 136).

Though the proud boast was meant to naturalize white colonialism and imperialism, which were already well into one of their most expansive phases in U. S. history, Calhoun's words belie a profound insecurity regarding the popular imagination of the white American destiny. The great fear was miscegenation, a mixing of bloodlines which, as historians and ethnologists of the era were becoming convinced, was the central factor in the decline of great civilizations. "Whenever in the history of the world the inferior races have been conquered and mixed in with the Caucasian," Josiah Nott appealed to fellow Americans, and to southern compatriots especially, "the latter have sunk into barbarism" (qtd. in Horsman 130). This fear was most routinely projected onto the Other who constituted the enemy internal to the body politic—the African. In 1839, the same year that **"The Fall of the House of Usher"** was published in *Burton's Gentleman's Magazine*, the revered New England theologian Horace Bushnell predicted that if the slaves were ever freed they would die off by the end of the century. As George Frederickson emphasizes in his valuable reading of the period in *The Black Image in the White Mind*, Bushnell's prediction represented an early transposition onto the slaves of the brutally callous view that had already made Native American genocide seem acceptable and natural to the whites: "'vices which taint the blood and cut down life' might well 'penetrate the whole stock, and begin to hurry them off, in a process of premature extinction; as we know to be the case with another barbarous people, [the Indians] now fast yielding to the infection of death'" (qtd. in Frederickson 155). Bushnell imagined this extinction to be a "glorious" possibility for the white man; and indeed Frederickson refers to this vision of black annihilation as Bushnell's "happy theme" (155). But if this theme is a positive one, then Bushnell's happiness was inextricably bound up with an equally potent fear of his own race's extinction, precipitated by a dystopic future of miscegenation in the North—the inevitable result of emancipation.

The fear of miscegenation, or tainted blood, belied deeper fears of disease and death. Insisting that degeneracy sets in when a nation does not secure its "leading ethnical principal," ethnologist J. Aitken Meigs urged that Americans "provide intelligently for the amelioration of that disease . . . whose deadly influences threaten, sooner or later, like the Lianes of a tropical forest, to suffocate the national tree over which they are silently spreading" (qtd. in Fredrickson 133). In this associative strategy that links together the tropical—embodied in the African—with disease that threatens the life-blood of the nation, the fear of miscegenation is exposed as the dread of a historical destiny gone awry. But even more importantly, it is exposed as the dread of destiny itself—of the inevitable decline and fall of civilizations, and, more viscerally, of the individual death that awaits us all. Whites read in the visage of blacks a figuration of their own mortality. It was not only the fear of death, a white rhetoric of denial, which was likewise an implicit claim to immortality, that they projected onto the Other, however; it was also death itself: "It is a shame that *you* shall die, that *your* race shall be exterminated." In Horace Bushnell's curiously telling expression, blacks, like Native Americans, were *infected* with death. They were the carriers of death whose continued presence within the legitimate white population endangered the bodily integrity and the sacred life-force of the nation. In their own threatened blood, the whites perceived the liquid medium by which they too could become infected with death and cheated of the great destiny promised them in the providential rhetoric of U.S. nationhood.

It is within the matrix of this collective racial/biological nightmare scenario that I will discuss **"The Fall of the House of Usher,"** justly the most famous of all Poe's Gothic horrors. For it is only within the context of this nightmare that one can explain adequately why **"Usher"** occupies such a seminal place in the nineteenth-century development of the Gothic genre. "If there is one work that announces the true arrival of the Gothic tale, its convincing emergence from cruder beginnings," writes Chris Baldick, "it is . . . **'The Fall of the House of Usher'"** (xviii). With painstaking attention to economy of expression and unity of effect, Baldick suggests, Poe managed to create a story that would become an *ur*-type for the Gothic up to the present day"—a remarkably crystalized pattern . . . for the future evolution of Gothic fiction" (xviii). Indeed, the pattern has been revisited and reworked by countless Gothic stylists since Poe. Nathaniel Hawthorne, George Washington Cable, Arthur Conan Doyle, Charlotte Perkins Gilman, Ambrose Bierce, H. P. Lovecraft, William Faulkner, Eudora Welty, Angela Carter, Joyce Carol

ABOUT THE AUTHOR

H. P. LOVECRAFT ON POE'S LITERARY INNOVATIONS

Before Poe the bulk of weird writers had worked largely in the dark; without an understanding of the psychological basis of the horror appeal, and hampered by more or less of conformity to certain empty literary conventions such as the happy ending, virtue rewarded, and in general a hollow moral didacticism, acceptance of popular standards and values, and striving of the author to obtrude his own emotions into the story and take sides with the partisans of the majority's artificial ideas. Poe, on the other hand, perceived the essential impersonality of the real artist; and knew that the function of creative fiction is merely to express and interpret events and sensations as they are, regardless of how they tend or what they prove—good or evil, attractive or repulsive, stimulating or depressing, with the author always acting as a vivid and detached chronicler rather than as a teacher, sympathizer, or vendor of opinion. He saw clearly that all phases of life and thought are equally eligible as subject matter for the artist, and being inclined by temperament to strangeness and gloom, decided to be the interpreter of those powerful feelings and frequent happenings which attend pain rather than pleasure, decay rather than growth, terror rather than tranquility, and which are fundamentally either adverse or indifferent to the tastes and traditional outward sentiments of mankind, and to the health, sanity, and normal expansive welfare of the species.

SOURCE: Lovecraft, H. P. "Edgar Allan Poe." In *Supernatural Horror in Literature*. 1945. Reprint edition, with a new introduction by E. F. Bleiler, pp. 52-9. New York: Dover, 1973.

Oates, Isabel Allende, and others would all write fictions that effectively pay homage to Poe's **"Usher."**

Ultimately, however, as Baldick explains, the importance of **"Usher"** in the history of Gothic has as much to do with its new, or newly amplified, theme as with its technical innovations:

> [Poe's] new formula involved not only the stripping down of a cumbersome conventional machinery to its essential elements but an accompanying clarification and highlighting of a theme long familiar to Gothic writing and to the surrounding culture of Romantic sensationalism, although hitherto left hovering in the shadows: that of the decline and extinction of the old family line. Perfectly harmonizing the terminal involution of the Usher family with the final crumbling of its mansion—of "house" as dynasty with house as habitation—Poe ensured that whereas before him the keynote of Gothic fiction had been cruelty, after him it would be decadence.
>
> (xviii)

Baldick's proposal of a gothic trajectory that moves from cruelty to decadence may be schematic—certainly Gothic literature exhibited a mixture of cruelty and decadence from its inception—but it is also provocative. What I am interested in is its resonance with Foucault's model for the transformation of the way in which sovereign power has been wielded since the classical age. With this resonance in mind we may follow Baldick's cue and map the Gothic's generic development onto a broader historical tableau in the following manner. The Gothic of cruelty, the Gothic of late eighteenth- and early nineteenth-century tales, with titles such as "The Vindictive Monk," "The Maniac's Fate," "The Poisoner of Montremos," and "The Parricide Punished," belong to a residually feudal European world where, as Foucault writes, "[t]he sovereign exercised his right of life only by exercising his right to kill, or by refraining from killing" (*History* 36). This was a Gothic that reflected a mode of power "exercised mainly as a means of deduction . . . a subtraction mechanism, a right to appropriate a portion of the wealth . . . goods and services, labor and blood, levied on the subjects. Power in this instance was essentially a right of seizure: of things, time, bodies, and ultimately life itself" (136). The Gothic of cruelty is obsessed with filiation and patrimonial inheritance, and it is inhabited by powerful, easily enraged, lascivious aristocrats whose perverted desires bring them into mortal conflict with men and women of lesser class origins. In its representation of perverts in power and fair maidens in distress, the Gothic of cruelty is motivated by a potent and revolutionary image of the end of aristocracy and the termination of a whole class structure (brought down by an excess of sexual desire). Of course,

this class structure was already in its death throes, or in a state of rigor mortis, even as these texts were being written.

If the Gothic of decadence represents a departure, or a mutation, as Baldick suggests, it is because it belongs to a modern, democratic world where the mechanisms of power are no longer exercised upon the social body from the outside, but are instead internal to it. This is a Gothic that reflects and reproduces the fears of a newly hegemonic bourgeoisie—fears that are no longer about dying at the hands of omnipotent perverts, but about the conditions of life and living, and how *these things* may become perverted and degenerated through the improper valorization of the body and through the botched management of the body's forces and pleasures. The Gothic that Baldick claims Poe more or less inaugurates is, in other words, a Gothic that focuses on what Foucault calls "the species body, the body imbued with the mechanics of life and serving as the basis of the biological processes . . ." (139). What Poe can help us to establish is that which is simultaneously gestured towards and occluded in the crucial final chapters of Foucault's *History of Sexuality*: the component part of this species body is the individual bourgeois body as it is in the process of becoming "whitened" in the first half of the nineteenth century.

It is a great deal to lay at his doorstep, but there is something compelling about interpreting Poe as the first "New World" gothicist—that is, the first writer to give the Gothic a uniquely American, as opposed to Old World, European spin, even as he put the terms of this Americanness in brackets so as to question its legitimacy. But I also mean something both more sweeping and less generic than what this claim usually implies. For Poe might well be the first full-fledged gothicist of the modern political world: the world of democratic nation-states in the ascendant, of nationalist ideological systems in the process of consolidation, and of national peoples becoming population groups. Such an interpretation further situates Poe as the seminal gothicist of this new life-form of which the nation-state is merely the comprehensive political expression: the population group or species body whose organic well-being is regulated by discursive strategies that separate out what properly belongs to the social body and what pathologically threatens its purity, order, and smooth functioning.

The House of Usher

As I will argue, **"Usher"** is a horror story about the racialized conditions of production of the new species body. Yet what one notices foremost about **"Usher"** is the emphasis on class and aristocracy. At the beginning of the tale, class affiliation is the primary means of marking division and establishing identity, and the story's focus is on filiation and estate patrimony—the conservation of power and wealth. The narrator's introductory observations invoke a class-bound notion of both family and "race":

> I had learned . . . the very remarkable fact, that the stem of the Usher race, all time-honored as it was, had put forth, at no period, any enduring branch; in other words, that the entire family lay in the direct line of descent, and had always, with very trifling and very temporary variation, so lain. It was this deficiency, I considered, while running over in thought the perfect keeping of the character of the premises with the accredited character of the people, and while speculating upon the possible influence which the one, in the long lapse of centuries, might have exercised upon the other—it was this deficiency, perhaps, of collateral issue, and the consequent undeviating transmission, from sire to son, of the patrimony with the name, which had, at length, so identified the two as to merge the original title of the estate in the quaint and equivocal appellation of the **'House of Usher'**. . . .
>
> (399)

Here, the isolate "Usher race" is merely another name for the ancient and inbred family lineage, defined and delimited by the estate with which it has become so intimately identified. What is transmitted undeviatingly is the patrimony. In this context, the Ushers' "deficiency" is linked to a shortage of new wealth; and their lack of "collateral issue" suggests their failure to enhance the family's fortunes by securing alliances with other aristocratic families.

But as the tale progresses, it becomes clear that the Ushers are deficient in other ways, too. Roderick's sister, Madeline Usher, suffers from a disease that "had long baffled the skill of her physicians. A settled apathy, a gradual wasting away of the person, and frequent although transient affections of a partially cataleptical character, were the unusual diagnosis" (404). Roderick Usher, too, suffers from a debilitating illness that manifests itself most clearly in a hyper-responsiveness to external stimuli: ". . . the most insipid food was alone endurable; he could only wear garments of certain texture; the odors of all flowers were oppressive; his eyes were tortured by even a faint light; and there were but peculiar sounds, and these from

stringed instruments, which did not inspire him with horror" (403). It is telling that Usher refers to his disease—a neurasthenia widely construed in the Victorian era as the sign of an advanced biological and intellectual development[1]—as the "family evil." For it suggests that the patrimony at issue in **"Usher"** is really disease itself, and that the deficiency in question is above all a matter of the "bloodline."

Later in the story, Usher will frame an incipient theory of hereditary influence based on his nightmarish obsession with the family evil:

> The belief, however, was connected . . . with the gray stones of the home of his forefathers. Its evidence . . . [was] in the gradual yet certain condensation of an atmosphere of their own about the waters and the walls. The result was discoverable, he added, in that silent, yet importunate and terrible influence which for centuries had moulded the destinies of his family, and which made *him* what I now saw him—what he was.
>
> (408)

The revelation of Usher's superstition signals an intensified emphasis on the eerie vitality of the house and on its status as an objective correlative for the family history. But this revelation also signals an historical shift in what the family history is a record of. It goes from being a record of transmitted patrimony—the house as estate passed on from sire to son—to being a record of transmitted genetic information. In the passage above, in other words, the house emerges as the very embodiment of Roderick Usher's biological destiny. Extrapolating from **"Usher"** to the cultural history of the nineteenth century, we can read in this shift the translation of an essentially aristocratic concern with genealogy and inheritance into the bourgeois obsession with biological integrity and the dangers of heredity. Whereas the old nobility prided itself on its "blue blood," the bourgeoisie did something similar but in diametrically opposite terms. Foucault provocatively suggests that bourgeois families "wore and concealed a sort of reversed and somber escutcheon whose defamatory quarters were the diseases or defects of the group of relatives . . ." (*History* 124-25). In other words, the bourgeoisie terrorized itself with the spectres of its psycho-sexual perversions, nervous afflictions, shameful cretinism and senile dementia, as well as with imaginings of racial degeneration and the contamination of its blood.

Why would the bourgeoisie choose to terrorize itself in this manner? Given the psychical cost, the expected ends had to be either extremely important or entirely unconscious. As Jacques Donzelot has argued, the proliferation of these anxieties helped to constitute no less than the bourgeois family unit itself by affecting "a tactical constriction of its members" over and against an imagined external threat (45). The racialization of culture in the nineteenth century empowered the bourgeoisie by providing its members with a racial Other against which to constitute their own social identity. At the same time, however, it led to what Daniel Pick incisively describes as a "profound [sense of] political confusion and historical disorientation" (237). In *Faces of Degeneration*, Pick explores the development of degeneracy theory and its intertwining with historical narratives of the nineteenth century. Objecting to the rigidity and the reductiveness built into many contemporary social histories of degeneracy theory, Pick argues that "[t]he discourse of degeneration . . . was never simply 'instrumental'; it articulated fears beyond the merely strategic, fears of inundation, the subject overwhelmed at every level of mind and body by internal disorder and external attack" (44). The medical-scientific discourse inaugurated by Benedict Morel gave the world the degenerate, "a given individual whose physiognomic contours could be traced out and distinguished from the healthy" (Pick, 9). But the real danger of degeneracy had more to do with that which could *not* be seen, because its symptoms were yet illegible. As Pick observes, "degeneration also connoted invisibility and ubiquity—thus suggesting the inadequacy of traditional phrenology and physiognomy; it was a process which could usurp all boundaries of discernible identity, threatening the very overthrow of civilisation and progress" (9).

Poe registers this sense of historical disorientation and the fear of inundation in the apocalyptic finale of "Usher." He also registers it by subverting the purity of being associated with whiteness in what we might call the affirmative racist imagination. As it is for Melville in *Moby Dick*, whiteness in "Usher" is an ambivalent marker. It connotes civilization as well as its threatened destruction. Usher's finely sculpted features indicate his superior white European ancestry. But his whiteness is tainted with illness and with death. His pigmentation is described as "[a] cadaverousness of complexion" and as having a "ghastly pallor" (401). His purity of race, in other words, belies a condition of decrepitude, leaving the narrator "at once struck with an incoherence—an inconsistency" in the whole manner and bearing of his

boyhood friend (402). The physical features of Usher's ancestral House bear the mark of an analogous inconsistency:

> Minute fungi overspread the whole exterior, hanging in a fine tangled webwork from the eaves. Yet all this was apart from any extraordinary dilapidation. No portion of the masonry had fallen; and there appeared to be a wild inconsistency between its still perfect adaptation of parts, and the crumbling condition of the individual stones.
>
> (400)

What is at stake in this peculiar attention to the discrepancy between integral and disintegrative forces bears on the discrepancy the heart of degeneracy theory between appearance and "inner constitution," between what *appears* to be healthy and vigorous and what is in fact, or is feared to be, blighted with disease and ultimately doomed.

In his *Essay on the Inequality of the Races* (1853-55), the "father" of modern racism, the Frenchman Count Arthur de Gobineau, writes, "The word degenerate, when applied to a people, means . . . that this people has no longer the same intrinsic value as it had before, because it has no longer the same blood in its veins, continual adulterations having gradually affected the quality of the blood" (qtd. in Biddis 114). Although Gobineau was the greatest nineteenth-century popularizer of racial degeneracy theory, he was not its first proponent; nor was he the first to situate it in the context of an elaborate vision of human history. For as we have already seen, many antebellum Americans were convinced—before Gobineau—that the true health of a people and the causes of national success and/or failure were to be found not in their system of government, but in a collective "inner constitution" that had become implicitly racialized. In a sense, then, "Usher" stands as a textbook example of the terrifying ambivalence about progress, evolution, and history that supremacist ideologies inevitably generate. Roderick Usher appears to be racially pure; he is cultured, a fabulous musician, and a painter, "the accomplished heir of all the ages," as Harry Levin suggests (161). But he is also "hopeless" and "frail" (404), and as the narrator ironically puts it, "a bounden slave" to a terror lurking in his heart for which neither he nor Usher can find a definite object.

Moon, Veins, Blood

The *indefinite* object of Usher's terror has been most commonly interpreted as a culturally constant death anxiety—the fear of the universal "inexorability of extinction," as Gillian Brown writes (332). But if we turn our attention towards the interpolated poem, "The Haunted Palace," we find evidence of a more culturally and historically specific source for Usher's terror. In this wild and mournful interlude to the tale, whose "under or mystic current" (406) of meaning so powerfully impresses the narrator, Usher dreams nostalgically about an ancient ruler who sits at a glorious throne. This mythical lord lives only to seek his pleasure, while a "A troop of Echoes whose sweet duty / Was but to sing . . . / The wit and wisdom of their king" (407) reassure him of his innate superiority and of the legitimacy of his dominion. As numerous critics have suggested,[2] the poem is a microcosmic account of Usher's one great story, the decline and fall of his ancient family lineage.

Once, long ago, as Usher nostalgically recounts in his guitar-accompanied dirge, the Haunted Palace was "a fair and stately palace":

> Wanderers in that happy valley
>   Through two luminous windows saw
> Spirits moving musically
>   To a lute's well-tuned law,
> Round about a throne, where sitting
>   (Porphyrogene!)
> In state his glory well befitting,
>   The ruler of the realm was seen.

But then the ballad takes a frightful turn:

> . . . evil things, in robes of sorrow,
>   Assailed the monarch's high estate;
> (Ah, let us mourn, for never morrow,
>   Shall dawn upon him, desolate!)
> And, round about his home, the glory
>   That blushed and bloomed
> Is but a dim-remembered story
>   Of the old time entombed.

(407)

Harry Levin's claim that **"Usher"** ought to be situated in a regional context offers us a useful point of departure for interpreting these lines. According to Levin, Poe's tale is a nightmarish prophecy of the cultural and political defeat of American slave society, as well as a prefiguration of its literary aftermath: "Much that seems forced in William Faulkner's work becomes second nature when we think of him as Poe's inheritor," Levin writes, thinking of "Caddy and Quentin, those two doomed siblings of the house of Compson, or of Emily Grierson, that old maid who clings to the corpse of her lover" (161). The narrator's reference to Usher as "the master" (400) gives a certain legitimacy to Levin's claim. So, too, does Usher's fantastic account of the family fall in "The Haunted Palace." For if we interpret **"Usher"** (*pace* Levin) as a white colonial nightmare about the impending destruction of the southern slavocracy, then what transpires in "The Haunted Palace" begins to sound like a slave uprising. Certainly the experience of violent slave rebellion was fresh in the minds of Virginians like Poe, and southerners more broadly, throughout the 1830s.[3]

More significant, however, is the way in which "The Haunted Palace" transforms its nightmare articulation of endangerment. So far, in its overwrought imagery of lordship and rebellion, the poem seems to evoke mainly political insurrection; and in its invocation of class antagonism we may justly trace the contours of a distinctively southern paranoia in Usher's. Initially, then, the poem specifically figures the southern slaveowner's fear of an external assault upon property by an oppressed class—those dressed in "robes of sorrow" who finally rise up in rebellion against their lord and master. It is, after all, the monarch's estate that is assailed in "The Haunted Palace," and thus his sense of lordliness in ownership that is debased.

The social and political threat is profoundly transformed in the poem's final stanza, however, when the racist and more broadly nationalist content of Usher's paranoia makes a startling reappearance:

> And travellers now within that valley,
>   Through the red-litten windows, see
> Vast forms that move fantastically
>   To a discordant melody;
> While, like a rapid ghastly river,
>   Through the pale door,
> A hideous throng rush out forever,
>   And laugh—but smile no more.

(407)

What is striking about these lines is their resonance with contemporary accounts, especially among northern travellers in the South, of the grotesquery of Negro song and dance. One might compare them to the description of Topsy's performance in *Uncle Tom's Cabin*:

> The black, glassy eyes glittered with a kind of wicked drollery, and the thing struck up, in a clear and shrill voice, an odd Negro melody, to which she kept time with her hands and feet, spinning round, clapping her hands, knocking her knees together, in a wild, fantastic sort of time, and producing the native music of her race . . . as odd and unearthly as that of a steamwhistle.

(237)

In Stowe's novel the menace of the racial Other is safely contained (and to a certain degree, dissolved) within the context of a liberal political project and a pluralistic social ethos. But there are no such humanizing forces at work in Poe's writ-

Scene from Roger Corman's 1960 film adaptation of "The Fall of the House of Usher."

ing; and so the menace of blackness is intensified. In "The Haunted Palace" it ultimately assumes the formlessness of a fluid infection that circulates within the house of the monarch. Although the imagery recalls Stowe's, it also anticipates a story Poe would write three years after "Usher"—"The Masque of the Red Death." The "red-litten windows" look forward to the grotesquely illuminated rooms of Prince Prospero's imperial suite and to the "scarlet stains" that disfigure the doomed victims in that story (670). Likewise, the "Vast forms that move fantastically / To a discordant melody" evoke the victims of the Red Death, the dancing knights and ladies who, along with Prince Prospero, vainly "bid defiance to contagion" (671). In its anticipation of Poe's more elaborate treatment of the fear of blood contagion in "The Masque of the Red Death," this stanza effects a biologization of the perceived endangerment; it marks a qualitative shift in the terms of its representation from a matter of class struggle for property, prestige, and power to a matter of bodily integrity, and conversely, the onslaught of infection and disease.

What I am suggesting is that the collective fantasy of impending doom embodied in "The Haunted Palace," and by extension, in "Usher," is transposed from being strictly classist fantasy to being racist and nationalist fantasy. Consequently, it transcends the regional specificity that Levin attaches to it. In the new racist consciousness of the antebellum era, as we have seen, the enslaved African became an infectious agent threatening the sacred life-force of the nation; and blood served as the fluid medium for—and the bodily sign of—contamination. Interrogating fantasies of contamination in an early modern European context, Piero Camporesi writes, "It seems clear that the notion of fertility is intertwined with the sense of contamination . . . that the metaphors of generation and life belong to the impure fleshliness of copula, and to semen, the excrement of blood" (114). Camporesi suggests, in other words, that what is involved in the fantasy of blood contamination is a fear of ungoverned male desire and an unregulated apportionment of sperm. Such a fear ineluctably manifested itself in the nineteenth century as, on one side of the race equation, the fear of excessive, limitless reproduction of the "inferior races," and on the other side, that of the *failed* reproduction of the "superior race"—the extinction of a white family, the collapse of a white nation.

It is appropriate, then, that the specter of blood presides over the final scene of **"Usher."** Here the narrator describes his desperate escape from the ill-fated house:

> . . . from that mansion, I fled aghast. The storm was still abroad in all its wrath as I found myself crossing the old causeway. Suddenly there shot along the path a wild light, and I turned to see whence a gleam so unusual could have issued; for the vast house and its shadows were alone behind me. The radiance was that of the full, setting, and blood-red moon, which now shone vividly through that once barely-discernible fissure, of which I have before spoken. . . . While I gazed, this fissure rapidly widened—there came a fierce breath of the whirlwind—the entire orb of the satellite burst at once upon my sight. . . .
>
> (417)

Blood, in Poe's tale, is as much an avatar of death as it is an avatar of life, the (failed) transmission of the pure racial stock from one generation of Ushers to the next. With this powerfully imagistic finale, **"The Fall of the House of Usher"** stands revealed as what Camporesi calls an "antique lunar and bloody motholog[y]" (37). Poe mixes "moon, veins, [and] blood" in a narrative that is about fertility and contagion, and the endangered reproduction of the white race. In this light, Usher's nightmare vision in "The Haunted Palace" is intimately connected to his dark fascination with "the old African Satyrs and Ægipans" in the pages of Pomponius Mela, over which, as the narrator tells us, his companion "would sit dreaming for hours" (409). In the guise of the satyr, the African in **"Usher"** is explicitly associated with biological/sexual danger. He appears, in the instructively conspicuous phrase of Frantz Fanon, as "the biological-sexual-sensual-genital-nigger" who "represents the sexual instinct (in its raw state) . . . the incarnation of a genital potency beyond all morality and prohibitions" (Fanon 202, 177).[4] Thus the dangerously vital African satyr emerges on the border of the tale as the antinomy of the sick and exhausted Usher.

Eerie Mansion

In the background of our reading of **"Usher"** lies the famous (or infamous) Foucauldian shift from the classical to the modern world. If the trajectory of the reading gives the impression of an unproblematical endorsement of the notion of

the shift as a clean semantic break, via the changing force of racial discourse from lineage to typology, then at this point I want to muddy the waters. Poe, I have suggested, is a gothicist whose horror is steeped in certain modern political realities of the nineteenth century, foremost of which is the rise of a biologized, statist, or nationalist, racism. By way of example, we have charted the often subtle manifestations of biologized racism in **"Usher."** However, we cannot say that a story like **"Usher"** signals anything like the consolidation of a new order where race simply supplants class. For the obvious fact is that we have had to rescue the racial element in **"Usher"** out of the matrix of a fantasy whose manifest obsession is classist because Usher's incipient dreams of blood contamination are embedded in a story about fallen aristocracy. Yet this is precisely why **"Usher"** is so instructive: it contains within it the aristocratic etymology of modern racism. Poe's Gothic in **"Usher"** does not signal the *consolidation* of a new world; rather, it traverses in its unfolding narration one of the main discursive axes upon which the temporal shift from the classical to the modern world occurs—the class-race axis. What it reveals, then, is not so much a radical change in the meaning of race from that of the nobility's to that of the bourgeoisie's, but rather, as Ann Laura Stoler writes apropos of Foucault's preoccupations at one point in his thinking on race,[5] "the processes of recuperation [of racial discourse], of the distillation of earlier discursive imprints, remodeled in new forms" (68).

In emphasizing this point too forcefully, however, we can fall prey to the opposite danger: the conclusion that **"The Fall of the House of Usher"** is in essence merely an upper-class fantasy—an interpretation that would certainly be in keeping with the conventional notion of Poe as a writer wholly out of step with his democratic time and place. Benedict Anderson, for instance, argues that

> The dreams of racism actually have their origin in ideologies of class, . . . above all in claims to divinity among rulers and to "blue" or "white" blood and "breeding" among aristocracies. No surprise then that the putative sire of modern racism should be, not some petty-bourgeois nationalist, but Joseph Arthur, Comte de Gobineau.
>
> (149)

For Anderson, as for Foucault, modern racism has an aristocratic pedigree. But unlike Foucault, Anderson sees modern racism as continuous with the old race discourse of the nobility; it represents the legitimization of upper-class domination according to the new criteria of skin color. According to Anderson, the "official nationalism" for which racism was pressed into service in the nineteenth century was an upper-class political project. Stoler observes that, for Anderson, "[t]hese two racisms become one and the same, welded by a nineteenth-century 'conception of empire'. . . . By his account 'late colonial empires even served to shore up domestic aristocratic bastions, since they appeared to confirm on a global, modern stage antique conceptions of power and privilege'" (Stoler 30). The problem with such a theory, like the problem with reading "Usher" as purely classist fantasy, is that it reduces racism to a mere effect of an historically prior class discourse.

Foucault argues to the contrary that nationalism and racism were inextricably related *bourgeois* political projects. Since we have been taking our historical bearings from Foucault all along it is only natural to assume that this hypothesis is, in fact, valid. It is, after all, the coterminous rise of the bourgeoisie and nationalist ideology that we began this essay by tracking. If for Foucault it is the lingering traces of "earlier discursive imprints" upon nineteenth-century racism that really matter, it also true in his thinking that, as Stoler notes, the "racisms of the nobility and the bourgeoisie are distinct . . ." (30). There is, in other words, a process of historical rescription at work by which elements in an earlier discourse resurface and take on altered meaning as they are aligned with new elements, for the purpose of legitimizing new power structures.

What, finally, is the effect of Poe's exposure of this process of rescription in "Usher"? What is achieved is the Gothic threat of a destabalized reality, the first sign of which is the narrator's sense of strangeness as he enters the grand and dilapidated House:

> A servant in waiting took my horse, and I entered the Gothic archway of the hall. A valet, of stealthy step, thence conducted me, in silence, through many dark and intricate passages in my progress to the studio of his master. . . . While the objects around me—while the carvings of the ceilings, the sombre tapestry of the walls, the ebon blackness of the floors, and the phantasmagoric armorial trophies which rattled as I strode, were but matters to which, or such as which, I had been accustomed from my infancy—while I hesitated not to acknowledge how familiar was all this—I still wondered to find how unfamiliar were the fancies which ordinary images were stirring up.
>
> (401)

The House is not quite as Usher's boyhood friend had remembered it. For the narrator, the strangeness is that of returning as an adult to old childhood haunts. In the context of my reading,

however, this experience of the uncanny has broader resonances. It is especially telling that the "armorial trophies," the insignia of Usher's pedigree, have become "phantasmagoric." The trappings of nobility had become unmoored in the modern world from the signifying constellation in which they were formerly enmeshed, and their new strangeness in "Usher" is the consequence of their being in an acute state of flux. The old aristocratic world-system had dissolved—that is to say, the signs that constituted it remained behind—and the shape of the world that followed it would depend in part on how these signs were redeployed.

The shape of this new world *greatly* depended on how the meaning of race was reconstituted in the nineteenth century. If the House is indeed the embodiment of the dynasty, or the ancient "Usher race," what we witness in Poe's story is the eerie biologization of the House precisely insofar as the concept of race was biologized. The ancient edifice teems with fungi; it is overspread with "a pestilent and mystic vapor" (400); "ebon blackness" goes from being a decorative marker of wealth (as in the rich ebony flooring in the passage above) to a marker of biological danger. It is due to this process of biologization, moreover, that we may just as intimately identify the House with the last scion of the race—the morbidly diseased figure of Roderick Usher. Based on this identification, the "dark and intricate passages" of the House through which the narrator is silently conducted at the beginning of the tale assume something of the quality (especially after the "Haunted Palace" interlude) of what Foucault refers to in *The Order of Things* as the "profound, interior, and essential space" (231) of the human organism—and human identity—as it is bio-racially redefined in the modern era.

With its "vacant and eye-like windows" (398), the House of Usher offers a glimpse into the deep and impenetrable mystery of this newly conceived identity. But what Poe's tale underscores in its Gothicism is that the loathsome blackness Usher fears is just as much a "phantasmagoric conception" (405) as the radiant vision of whiteness he paints on canvas and which the narrator describes as being suffused with "a ghastly and inappropriate splendor" (406).

Ultimately, the paranoid delirium of modern, bourgeois identity is Poe's great subject. Of this delirium, Gilles Deleuze and Felix Guattari remark that it

> has something like two poles, racist and racial. . . . And between the two, ever so many

subtle, uncertain shiftings where the unconscious itself oscillates between its reactionary charge and its revolutionary potential. Even Schreber finds himself to be the Great Mongol when he breaks through the Aryan segregation. Whence the ambiguity in the texts of great authors, when they develop the theme of races, as rich in ambiguity as destiny itself.

(105)

If "Usher" is one such richly ambiguous text it is because it bodies forth in such a concentrated fashion the mutation of race thinking at a pivotal point in its history. Yet it also articulates incisively how white supremacist ideology could redound upon its manipulators. Just as the psychotic Doctor Schreber finds that he is the Great Mongol in his delirium, so, too, does Usher discover a secret affinity between himself and the old African Satyr he sits dreaming about. He finds himself at the precise ideological locus that the latter reputedly occupied: biologically exhausted, infected with death.

Notes

1. See Athena Vrettos's *Somatic Fictions: Imagining Illness in Victorian Culture* (Stanford: Stanford UP, 1995) 147-51.

2. See, for example, Daniel Hoffman's *Poe Poe Poe Poe Poe Poe Poe* (Garden City, NY: Doubleday, 1972), and Richard Wilbur's "The House of Poe" (*Poe: A Collection of Critical Essays*. Ed. Robert Regan. Englewood Cliffs, NJ: Prentice-Hall, 1967. 98-120).

3. One of the most detailed accounts of the history of American slave insurrections in the nineteenth century, from the "Gabriel plot" of 1800 to Nat Turner's rebellion and beyond, is in Winthrop Jordan's *White Over Black: American Attitudes Towards the Negro, 1550-1812*. (Chapel Hill: U of North Carolina P, 1968).

4. The African in "Usher" possesses a paradoxical ontology. He is conjured as the slave dressed in robes of sorrow who rises up against his master, and as the Satyr, the black phallus over which Usher sits dreaming for hours; on the other hand, these figures fail to materialize as such. The African Satyr and the marauding slave enter the story's frame merely as traces, diseased projections of Usher's unconscious. Though the story obsessively circulates around them, we catch only fleeting, veiled glimpses of them.

The status of the African body is further complicated by its redundant and asymmetrical relation with Usher's consumptive and incestuous twin sister. Although Madeline figures sensationally in the story's closing moments as the vengeful undead, returning all bloodied from her premature entombment in the house's subterranean depths to clasp her brother in one final embrace, her place in the tale is shadowy, mysterious, and fleeting. She appears but once, as if spoken into presence by Usher at the very moment he first reveals her existence and her diseased condition to the narrator in a fit of despair, only to vanish once again:

"Her decease," he said, with a bitterness which I can never forget, "would leave him (him the hopeless and the frail) the last of the ancient race of the Ushers." While he spoke, the lady Madeline . . . passed slowly through a remote portion of the apartment, and, without having noticed my presence, disappeared. I regarded her with an utter astonishment not unmingled with dread—and yet found it impossible to account for such feelings. A sensation of stupor oppressed me, as my eyes followed her retreating steps . . . I learned that the glimpse I had obtained of her person would thus probably be the last I should obtain—that the lady, at least while living, would be seen by me no more.

(404)

Like the African, Madeline, too, signifies both excessively, and not at all. Passively consumed by disease in life, confined and controlled by her "medical men" (409), speaking no words, seen in the tableau above but not seeing, her subjectivity is acknowledged and refused all in the same moment. Only in death does she return to Usher, figuring dread as loathsome, feminine excess.

5. Stoler investigates Foucault's 1976 College de France lecture series in considerable detail in the third chapter of *Race and the Education of Desire: Foucault's History of Sexuality and the Colonial Order of Things*.

Works Cited

Anderson, Benedict. *Imagined Communities*. London: Verso, 1983.

Baldick, Chris. Introduction. *The Oxford Book of Gothic Tales*. Ed. Chris Baldick. Oxford: Oxford UP, 1993. xi-xxiii.

Biddis, Michael D. *Father of Racist Ideology: The Social and Political Thought of Count Gobineau*. New York: Weybright and Talley, 1970.

Brown, Gillian. "The Poetics of Extinction." *The American Face of Edgar Allan Poe*. Ed. Shawn Rosenheim and Stephen Rachman. Baltimore: Johns Hopkins UP, 1995. 330-344.

Camporesi, Piero. *Juice of Life: The Symbolic and Magic Significance of Blood*. Trans. Robert R. Barr. New York: Continuum, 1995.

Deleuze, Gilles, and Felix Guattari. *Anti-Oedipus: Capitalism and Schizophrenia*. Trans. Robert Hurley et al. Minneapolis: U of Minnesota P, 1983.

Donzelot, Jacques. *The Policing of Families*. Trans. Robert Hurley. New York: Pantheon Books, 1979.

Fanon, Franz. *Black Skin, White Masks*. Trans. Charles Lam Markmann. New York: Grove, 1967.

Foucault, Michel. *The History of Sexuality* Vol. 1. Trans. Robert Hurley. New York: Vintage, 1980. 3 vols. 1980-1986.

———. *The Order of Things: An Archaeology of the Human Sciences*. New York: Vintage, 1973.

Fredrickson, George M. *The Black Image In The White Mind: The Debate on Afro-American Character and Destiny 1817-1914*. Hanover, NH: Wesleyan UP, 1971.

Horsman, Reginald. *Race and Manifest Destiny: The Origins of American Racial Anglo-Saxonism.* Cambridge: Harvard UP, 1981.

Levin, Harry. *The Power of Blackness.* New York: Knopf, 1958.

Pick, Daniel. *Faces of Degeneration: A European Disorder, c. 1848-c. 1918.* Cambridge: Cambridge UP, 1989.

Poe, Edgar Allan. "The Fall of the House of Usher" and "The Masque of the Red Death." *Collected Works of Edgar Allan Poe.* Vol. 2. Ed. Thomas Ollive Mabbot. Cambridge: Harvard UP, 1978. 3 vols. 1969-1978.

Stoler, Ann Laura. *Race and the Education of Desire: Foucault's History of Sexuality and the Colonial Order of Things.* Durham: Duke UP, 1995.

Stowe, Harriet Beecher. *Uncle Tom's Cabin.* New York: Bantam, 1981.

FURTHER READING

Bibliography

Dameron, J. Lasley, and Irby B. Cauthen Jr. *Edgar Allan Poe: A Bibliography of Criticism, 1827-1967.* A John Cook Wyllie Memorial Publication. Charlottesville: University Press of Virginia, 1974, 386 p.

Annotated guide to critical and biographical writings on Poe published prior to 1968.

Biography

Quinn, Arthur Hobson. *Edgar Allan Poe: A Critical Biography.* 1941. Reprint edition. Baltimore, Md.: The Johns Hopkins University Press, 1998, 804 p.

Definitive biography of Poe, originally published in 1941.

Criticism

Baudelaire, Charles. *Baudelaire on Poe: Critical Papers,* edited and translated by Lois Hyslop and Francis E. Hyslop, Jr. State College, Pa.: Bald Eagle Press, 1952, 175 p.

Incorporates biographical and critical studies by Baudelaire written at various times, including those in Edgar Poe: His Life and Works *(1852 and 1856).*

Bonaparte, Marie. *The Life and Works of Edgar Allan Poe: A Psycho-analytic Interpretation,* translated by John Rodker. London: Imago, 1949, 749 p.

Story-by-story analysis of psychosexual symbolism and motifs in Poe's tales.

Brennan, Matthew C. "Poe's Gothic Sublimity: Prose Style, Painting, and Mental Boundaries in 'The Fall of the House of Usher.'" *Journal of Evolutionary Psychology* 11, nos. 3-4 (August 1990): 353-59.

Proposes that Poe used an ambiguous prose style in "The Fall of the House of Usher" to convey the psychotic condition of Roderick Usher's mind. Brennan also draws a parallel between the abstract-expressionism of Roderick's painting and actual nineteenth century art.

Brill, Robert Densmore. "Edgar Allan Poe's Prescription for a Good Night's Sleep: 'The Premature Burial.'" *The Atlantic Literary Review* 3, no. 1 (January-March 2002): 126-47.

Closely examines "The Premature Burial."

Budick, E. Miller. "Poe's Gothic Idea: The Cosmic Geniture of Horror." *Essays in Literature* 3 (1976): 73-85.

Asserts that "Gothicism in Poe is the natural human response to the implications of idealism."

Butler, David W. "Usher's Hypochondriasis: Mental Alienation and Romantic Idealism in Poe's Gothic Tales." *American Literature* 48, no. 1 (March 1976): 1-12.

Traces the appearance of characters with the mental disorder hypochondriasis in several of Poe's tales and discusses its suitability in a Gothic setting.

Elbert, Monika. "Poe's Gothic Mother and the Incubation of Language." *Poe Studies: Dark Romanticism: History, Theory, Interpretation* 26, nos. 1-2 (June-December 1993): 22-33.

Examines the effect of the death of Poe's mother on his writing.

Engel, Leonard W. "Claustrophobia, the Gothic Enclosure and Poe." *Clues: A Journal of Detection* 10, no. 2 (fall-winter 1989): 107-17.

Discusses Poe's use of the Gothic in stories such as "MS. Found in a Bottle" and "The Premature Burial," which depict eventual escape from enclosure.

Fisher, Benjamin F. "Poe's 'Metzengerstein': Not a Hoax." *American Literature* 42, no. 4 (January 1971): 487-94.

Treats the short story "Metzengerstein" as an early example of Poe's Gothic fiction.

Frank, Frederick S. "The Gothic at Absolute Zero: Poe's *Narrative of Arthur Gordon Pym.*" *Extrapolation* 21 (1980): 21-30.

Analyzes Poe's use of Gothic motifs in the context of a sea-story adventure.

Garrison, Joseph M., Jr. "The Function of Terror in the Work of Edgar Allan Poe." *American Quarterly* 18, no. 2, part 1 (summer 1966): 136-50.

Attempts to reconcile the mixture of beauty and terror in Poe's work.

Ginsberg, Lesley. "Slavery and the Gothic Horror of Poe's 'The Black Cat.'" In *American Gothic: New Inventions in a National Narrative,* edited and with an introduction by Robert K. Martin, pp. 99-128. Iowa City: University of Iowa Press, 1998.

Studies Poe's treatment of slavery in "The Black Cat."

Griffith, Clark. "Poe's 'Ligeia' and the English Romantics." *University of Toronto Quarterly* 24, no. 1 (October 1954): 8-25.

Maintains that "Ligeia" is primarily a satire of Gothic fiction.

Haggerty, George E. "Poe's Gothic Gloom." In *Gothic Fiction/Gothic Form,* pp. 81-106. University Park: The Pennsylvania State University Press, 1989: 8-25.

Focusing on "The Fall of the House of Usher," examines Poe's fascination with the mechanics of Gothic literature.

Heller, Terry. "Poe's 'Ligeia' and the Pleasures of Terror." *Gothic* 2, no. 2 (1980): 39-49.

Examines the means by which Poe's tale evokes horror on the part of the reader and argues that the enjoyment of such a reaction is a legitimate literary end.

Holland-Toll, Linda J. "'Ligeia': The Facts in the Case." *Studies in Weird Fiction* 21 (summer 1997): 2-10.

Argues against reading Poe's tale from a rational point of view in which each event corresponds to a natural explanation.

Hustis, Harriet. "'Reading Encrypted but Persistent': The Gothic of Reading and Poe's 'The Fall of the House of Usher.'" *Studies in American Fiction* 27, no. 1 (spring 1999): 3-20.

Provides a brief history of an ongoing debate over Poe's classification as a writer within American and French traditions, and notes that "Poe's 'The Fall of the House of Usher' calls attention to the narrative space it occupies as Gothic text in order to question those parameters and the means by which critics arrive at such dimensions."

Lenz, William E. "Poe's *Arthur Gordon Pym* and the Narrative Techniques of Antarctic Gothic." *CEA Critic* 53, no. 3 (spring-summer 1991): 30-8.

Assesses Poe's use of sea narrative and Gothic fiction, and suggests that it was Poe who discovered the Antarctic as a locale particularly suited to Gothic works.

Mainville, Stephen. "Language and the Void: Gothic Landscapes in the Frontiers of Edgar Allan Poe." *Genre* 14, no. 3 (fall 1981): 347-62.

Examines Poe's handling of language in Pym *and the unfinished* Journal of Julius Rodman, *and focuses on his creation of Gothic landscapes.*

Mooney, Stephen L. "Poe's Gothic Wasteland." *Sewanee Review* 70 (1962): 261-83.

Discusses Poe's use of "ironic images of man in the nineteenth-century age of anxiety."

Nadal, Marita. "Beyond the Gothic Sublime: Poe's *Pym* or the Journey of Equivocal (E)motions." *Mississippi Quarterly* 53, no. 3 (summer 2000): 373-88.

Investigates Poe's use of horror, terror, and the sublime in The Narrative of Arthur Gordon Pym.

Ringe, Donald A. "Edgar Allan Poe." In *American Gothic: Imagination and Reason in Nineteenth-Century Fiction,* pp. 128-51. Lexington: University Press of Kentucky, 1982.

Provides an overview of Gothic themes in Poe's work.

Rowe, Stephen. "Poe's Use of Ritual Magic in His Tales of Metempsychosis." *The Edgar Allan Poe Review* 4, no. 2 (fall 2003): 41-52.

Investigates references to metempsychosis, or the transmigration of souls, in Poe's work.

Shelden, Pamela J. "'True Originality': Poe's Manipulation of the Gothic Tradition." *American Transcendental Quarterly,* no. 29 (winter 1976): 75-80.

Discusses how Poe "combines" Gothic conventions "to represent the terror which wells from psychic reality."

Stein, William Bysshe. "The Twin Motif in 'The Fall of the House of Usher.'" *Modern Language Notes* 75, no. 2 (February 1960): 109-11.

Examines structural details in "The Fall of the House of Usher."

Swann, Charles. "Poe and Maturin—A Possible Debt." *Notes and Queries* 37, no. 235 (December 1990): 424-25.

Notes similarities between the title character's description of the island of Tsalal in The Narrative of Arthur Gordon Pym *and a passage in Charles Robert Maturin's* Melmoth the Wanderer.

Thompson, G. R. "'Proper Evidences of Madness': American Gothic and the Interpretation of 'Ligeia.'" *ESQ: A Journal of the American Renaissance* 66 (1972): 30-49.

Assesses "Ligeia" in the context of its Gothic predecessors.

——. *Poe's Fiction: Romantic Irony in the Gothic Tales.* Madison: University of Wisconsin Press, 1973, 254 p.

Contends that in both his Gothic and his comic stories Poe employed a conscious irony derived from writers of the German Romantic movement.

——. "Locke, Kant, and Gothic Fiction: A Further Word on the Indeterminism of Poe's 'Usher.'" *Studies in Short Fiction* 26, no. 4 (fall 1989): 547-60.

Analyzes "The Fall of the House of Usher" as a work of Gothic fiction.

Timmerman, John H. "House of Mirrors: Edgar Allan Poe's 'The Fall of the House of Usher.'" *Papers on Language and Literature* 39, no. 3 (summer 2003): 227-44.

Evaluates the historical context and influence of Poe's cosmology in "The Fall of the House of Usher."

Tombleson, Gary E. "Poe's 'The Fall of the House of Usher' as Archetypal Gothic: Literary and Architectural Analogs of Cosmic Unity." *Nineteenth-Century Contexts* 12, no. 2 (1988): 83-106.

Argues that the architectural references in "The Fall of the House of Usher" render the story archetypically Gothic.

Voller, Jack G. "The Power of Terror: Burke and Kant in the House of Usher." *Poe Studies* 21, no. 3 (December 1988): 27-35.

Contends that "The Fall of the House of Usher" represents a rejection of the theories of the sublime offered by Edmund Burke and Immanuel Kant, and instead focuses on terrors and emotions that could not be easily explained within the context of the optimistic aesthetic proposed by Burke and Kant.

Voloshin, Beverly R. "Explanation in 'The Fall of the House of Usher.'" *Studies in Short Fiction* 23, no. 4 (fall 1986): 419-28.

Assesses "The Fall of the House of Usher" as a unique variation of the Gothic genre of short fiction that blends natural, preternatural, and supernatural elements to create an unusually haunting effect.

Woodberry, George E. *Edgar Allan Poe.* 1885. Reprint edition. New York: AMS Press, 168, 354 p.

One of the first full-length studies of Poe's life and career.

OTHER SOURCES FROM GALE:

Additional coverage of Poe's life and career is contained in the following sources published by Thomson Gale: *American Writers; American Writers: The Classics,* Vol. 1; *American Writers Retrospective Supplement,* Vol. 2; *Authors and Artists for Young Adults,* Vol. 14; *Beacham's Encyclopedia of Popular Fiction: Biography & Resources,* Vol. 3; *Beacham's Guide to Literature for Young Adults,* Vols. 5, 11; *Concise Dictionary of American Literary Biography, 1640-1865; Dictionary of Literary Biography,* Vols. 3, 59, 73, 74, 248, 254; *DISCovering Authors; DISCovering Authors: British; DISCovering Authors: Canadian; DISCovering Authors Modules: Most-studied Authors* and *Poets; DISCovering Authors 3.0; Exploring Poetry; Exploring Short Stories; Literary Movements for Students,* Vol. 1; *Literature and Its*

Times, Vol. 2; *Literature and Its Times Supplement*, Vol. 1; *Literature Resource Center*; *Mystery and Suspense Writers*; *Nineteenth-Century Literature Criticism*, Vols. 1, 16, 55, 78, 94, 97, 117; *Poetry Criticism*, Vols. 1, 54; *Poetry for Students*, Vols. 1, 3, 9; *Poets: American and British*; *Reference Guide to American Literature*, Ed. 4; *Reference Guide to Short Fiction*, Ed. 2; *St. James Guide to Crime & Mystery Writers*, Vol. 4; *St. James Guide to Horror, Ghost & Gothic Writers*; *St. James Guide to Science Fiction Writers*, Ed. 4; *Science Fiction Writers*, Eds. 1, 2; *Short Stories for Students*, Vols. 2, 4, 7, 8, 16; *Short Story Criticism*, Vols. 1, 22, 34, 35, 54; *Something about the Author*, Vol. 23; *Supernatural Fiction Writers*; *Twayne's United States Authors*; *World Literature Criticism*; *World Poets*; and *Writers for Young Adults*.

ANN RADCLIFFE

(1764 - 1823)

(Born Ann Ward) English novelist, poet, and journal writer.

Considered one of the most important writers of the English Gothic tradition, Radcliffe transformed the Gothic novel from a mere vehicle for the depiction of terror into an instrument for exploring the psychology of fear and suspense. Her emphasis on emotion, perception, and the relationship between atmosphere and sensibility helped pave the way for the Romantic movement in England. Radcliffe's best-known novel, *The Mysteries of Udolpho* (1794), ranks as one of the chief exemplars of the Gothic genre.

BIOGRAPHICAL INFORMATION

Radcliffe was born in London. A shy child afflicted with asthma, she read widely. Though she was given private instruction in the classics, literature, painting, and drawing, Radcliffe received little encouragement from her parents to continue her studies. As a young woman, Radcliffe associated with the "bluestockings" Lady Mary Wortley Montagu and Hester Lynch Piozzi, who, biographers believe, provided her with inspiration and intellectual stimulation. In 1787 she married William Radcliffe, later the editor of the *English Chronicle*, who recognized her talent and encouraged her to begin writing novels.

Although Radcliffe was the most popular English novelist of her generation, she managed to avoid publicity almost entirely. In fact, when Christina Rossetti attempted to write a biography of Radcliffe in 1883, she was forced to abandon the project because of the lack of available information. For unknown reasons Radcliffe withdrew entirely from public life in 1817 at the peak of her fame. Her absence triggered a series of rumors, the most widespread being that she had suffered a nervous breakdown brought on by the terrors described in her own works. Sir Walter Scott speculated that she stopped writing because she abhorred the manner in which her imitators had cheapened and sentimentalized the Gothic novel. Obituaries appeared in newspapers on the supposition that Radcliffe had died. Also in circulation were legends that Radcliffe had died in an insane asylum and that her ghost returned to haunt her imitators.

MAJOR WORKS

Radcliffe's first novel, *The Castles of Athlin and Dunbayne: A Highland Story* (1789), made a negligible impression upon readers and reviewers alike. A historical romance set in Scotland, the novel abounds in the picturesque description and dark atmosphere that was to become Radcliffe's trademark. Yet it was criticized for its abundance of anachronisms, especially imposing upon feudal heroines a distinctively nineteenth-century sensibility. *A Sicilian Romance* (1790), Radcliffe's next work, established her reputation as the preeminent Gothic novelist. Here the distinctive features of Radcliffe's style emerge more fully: the use of landscape to create a mood of terror, mystery, and suspense, intricacy of plot, a lyrical prose style, and a focus on individual psychology. *The Romance of the Forest* (1791), and *The Mysteries of Udolpho,* her first signed work, strengthened her popularity and made her a best-selling author in England, the United States, and Europe. *The Mysteries of Udolpho* contains all of the classic Gothic elements, including a haunted castle, a troubled heroine, a mysterious and menacing male figure, and hidden secrets of the past. The most prominent theme in *Udolpho* is the triumph of virtue over villainy: a characteristic of all the novels by Radcliffe, who was a devout Christian. Montoni, who squanders his fortunes and turns to illegal and deadly means to win them back, is eventually imprisoned, while Emily, though she endures many trying adventures, maintains her moral principles and eventually finds happiness. Related to this theme is the importance of balance and moderation, which Emily's father teaches her. It is when Emily allows herself to go to emotional extremes, becoming imbalanced, that she suffers most. Also present in the story is Emily's search for truth and need to uncover the secrets at Udolpho and the Villeroi chateau. Another theme is the inescapable past. Many of the characters are haunted by their past, as Emily is; although the mysteries of Udolpho are eventually resolved, there is still a sense of an inescapable haunting that follows the characters. *A Journey Made in the Summer of 1794 through Holland and the Western Frontier of Germany* (1795) details Radcliffe's first trip outside of England. *The Italian; or, The Confessional of the Black Penitents* (1797), a Gothic mystery which is considered by some to be Radcliffe's best novel, traces the machinations of the monk Schedoni, who became a prototypical Gothic hero—brooding, mysterious, and fascinating.

CRITICAL RECEPTION

Critics have speculated on the various influences upon Radcliffe's style, noting the similarities between her landscapes and the paintings of the Neapolitan painter and poet Salvator Rosa and the French landscape painter Claude Lorrain. Crit-

ics also note that her linking of terror and beauty corresponds with Edmund Burke's philosophy of the sublime and that her poetry resembles that of William Collins, James Thomson, Thomas Gray, and James Macpherson. In addition, Radcliffe's motif of the heroine in distress indicates a knowledge of sentimental novelists such as Charlotte Smith, although her works most often appear to be modeled upon the works of Horace Walpole. The primary distinguishing feature of Radcliffe's style is her explained endings. After elaborately setting up a mystery, planting the seeds of supernatural agency, and piquing the reader's curiosity, Radcliffe invariably resolves her plots in a rational and orderly way, providing reasoned explanations for seemingly supernatural events. Whether they praise or criticize her for this practice, critics cite this as Radcliffe's distinctive contribution to the development of the English novel.

The Mysteries of Udolpho was both an extremely popular and critically acclaimed novel when it was first published and for many years after. Readers enjoyed Radcliffe's gift for description and her deftness at building dramatic tension throughout the story. She was acknowledged by critics of her time as the queen of the Gothic novel, and she was also considered a pioneer of the Romantic movement. With her popularity, however, also came a wide array of imitators who shamelessly—and often poorly—copied her style, plots, and characters. It was because of these lesser writers that Radcliffe's works often suffered by association. Her work was sometimes satirized, too, most famously in Jane Austen's 1818 novel, *Northanger Abbey.*

Overall, early critical response to Radcliffe's works was mixed: while Samuel Taylor Coleridge attacked her explained endings for their inadequacy in satisfying the expectations of the reader, Sir Walter Scott called her "the first poetess of romantic fiction" for her natural descriptions. Other contemporary critics assessed her explanations as tedious, her dialogue as wooden, and her characters as flat, while some praised her brilliant rhetorical style, her examination of fear, and her affirmation of moral order at the conclusion of each novel. Thomas Noon Talfourd (see Further Reading) attributed Radcliffe's anticlimactic endings to her obedience to the conventions of the Gothic novel. He proposed that Radcliffe determined that the conventions of romance did not allow for supernatural agency, and that she therefore felt bound to explain it away. Virginia Woolf (see Further Reading) disputed Talfourd by asserting that Radcliffe's novels were remarkably free from convention. At the turn of the century, Walter Raleigh (see Further Reading) enlarged the popular understanding of Radcliffe by noting her role as a predecessor of the Romantic movement in England. Wylie Sypher's Marxist analysis (see Further Reading) delineated the novels' simultaneously bourgeois and anti-bourgeois tendencies, which he considered hypocritical. On the whole, Radcliffe's works received very little critical attention until the late 1950s, when Devendra P. Varma's overview of her novels again spurred curiosity about her work. The 1960s and 1970s reflected this surge of renewed interest. Critics have pursued new approaches to defining the role of description in Radcliffe's works; the extent and intent of her preoccupation with the realm of irrational behavior have been debated extensively, and recent critics have analyzed *Udolpho* from feminist and psychological standpoints and offer scholarly considerations of Emily's character. *Udolpho* has also been considered in terms of its sensual subtext and Emily's growing sense of her sexuality. In this new light, the novel has gained greater appreciation among modern literary commentators. Such writers as William Wordsworth, Coleridge, Percy Bysshe Shelley, John Keats, Anne and Emily Brontë, Matthew Gregory Lewis, Robert Louis Stevenson, and Lord Byron (who used Schedoni as the model for the Byronic hero), admired Radcliffe's exploration of extreme emotional states and adapted her techniques in their own works. Most critics now view Radcliffe as a key figure in the Gothic tradition who freed the collective English literary imagination from conventional and rational constraints and ushered in English Romanticism.

PRINCIPAL WORKS

The Castles of Athlin and Dunbayne: A Highland Story [published anonymously] (novel) 1789

A Sicilian Romance. 2 vols. [published anonymously] (novel) 1790

The Romance of the Forest: Interspersed with Some Pieces of Poetry. 3 vols. [published anonymously] (novel) 1791

The Mysteries of Udolpho, A Romance; Interspersed with Some Pieces of Poetry. 4 vols. (novel) 1794

A Journey Made in the Summer of 1794, through Holland and the Western Frontier of Germany, with a Return Down the Rhine; To Which Are Added Observations during a Tour to the Lakes of Lancashire, Westmoreland, and Cumberland (travel essays) 1795

The Italian; or, The Confessional of the Black Penitents. A Romance. 3 vols. (novel) 1797

Gaston de Blondeville; or, The Court of Henry III. Keeping Festival in Ardenne, A Romance. St. Alban's Abbey, A Metrical Tale; With Some Poetical Pieces. To Which Is Prefixed a Memoir of the Author (novel and poetry) 1826

PRIMARY SOURCES

ANN RADCLIFFE (NOVEL DATE 1794)

SOURCE: Radcliffe, Ann. "The Haunted Chamber." In *Gothic Tales of Terror, Volume One: Classic Horror Stories from Great Britain,* edited by Peter Haining. 1972. Reprint edition, pp. 49-67. Baltimore, Md.: Penguin Books Inc., 1973.

The following excerpt is from an episode of Radcliffe's novel The Mysteries of Udolpho, *first published in 1794.*

The Provençal Tale

There lived, in the province of Bretagne, a noble baron, famous for his magnificence and courtly hospitalities. His castle was graced with ladies of exquisite beauty, and thronged with illustrious knights; for the honour he paid to feats of chivalry invited the brave of distant countries to enter his lists, and his court was more splendid than those of many princes. Eight minstrels were retained in his service, who used to sing to their harps romantic fictions taken from the Arabians, or adventures of chivalry that befell knights during the crusades, or the martial deeds of the baron, their lord; while he, surrounded by his knights and ladies, banqueted in the great hall of the castle, where the costly tapestry that adorned the walls with pictured exploits of his ancestors, the casements of painted glass enriched with armorial bearings, the gorgeous banners that waved along the roof, the sumptuous canopies, the profusion of gold and silver that glittered on the sideboards, the numerous dishes that covered the tables, the number and gay liveries of the attendants, with the chivalric and splendid attire of the guests, united to form a scene of magnificence such as we may not hope to see in these degenerate days.

Of the baron the following adventure is related:—One night, having retired late from the banquet to his chamber, and dismissed his attendants, he was surprised by the appearance of a stranger of a noble air, but of a sorrowful and dejected countenance. Believing that this person had been secreted in the apartment, since it appeared impossible he could have lately passed the ante-room unobserved by the pages in waiting, who would have prevented this intrusion on their lord, the baron, calling loudly for his people, drew his sword, which he had not yet taken from his side, and stood upon his defence. The stranger, slowly advancing, told him that there was nothing to fear; that he came with no hostile intent, but to communicate to him a terrible secret, which it was necessary for him to know.

The baron, appeased by the courteous manner of the stranger, after surveying him for some time in silence, returned his sword into the scabbard, and desired him to explain the means by which he had obtained access to the chamber, and the purpose of this extraordinary visit.

Without answering either of these inquiries, the stranger said that he could not then explain himself, but that, if the baron would follow him to the edge of the forest, at a short distance from the castle walls, he would there convince him that he had something of importance to disclose.

This proposal again alarmed the baron, who would scarcely believe that the stranger meant to draw him to so solitary a spot at this hour of the night without harbouring a design against his life, and he refused to go; observing at the same time, that if the stranger's purpose was an honourable one, he would not persist in refusing to reveal the occasion of his visit in the apartment where they stood.

While he spoke this, he viewed the stranger still more attentively than before, but observed no change in his countenance, nor any symptom that might intimate a consciousness of evil design. He was habited like a knight, was of a tall and majestic stature, and of dignified and courteous manners. Still, however, he refused to communicate the substance of his errand in any place but that he had mentioned; and at the same time gave hints concerning the secret he would disclose, that awakened a degree of solemn curiosity in the baron, which at length induced him to consent to the stranger on certain conditions.

'Sir knight,' said he, 'I will attend you to the forest, and will take with me only four of my people, who shall witness our conference.'

To this, however, the knight objected.

'What I would disclose,' said he with solemnity, 'is to you alone. There are only three living persons to whom the circumstance is known: it is of more consequence to you and your house than I shall now explain. In future years you will look back to this night with satisfaction or repentance, accordingly as you now determine. As you would hereafter prosper, follow me; I pledge you the honour of a knight that no evil shall befall you. If you are contented to dare futurity, remain in your chamber, and I will depart as I came.'

'Sir knight,' replied the baron; 'how is it possible that my future peace can depend upon my present determination?'

'That is not now to be told,' said the stranger; 'I have explained myself to the utmost. It is late: if you follow me it must be quickly; you will do well to consider the alternative.'

The baron mused, and, as he looked upon the knight, he perceived his countenance assume a singular solemnity.

(Here Ludovico thought he heard a noise, and he threw a glance round the chamber, and then held up the lamp to assist his observation; but not perceiving anything to confirm his alarm, he took up the book again, and pursued the story.)

The baron paced his apartment for some time in silence, impressed by the words of the stranger, whose extraordinary request he feared to grant, and feared also to refuse. At length he said, 'Sir knight, you are utterly unknown to me; tell me, yourself, is it reasonable that I should trust myself alone with a stranger, at this hour, in the solitary forest? Tell me, at least, who you are, and who assisted to secrete you in this chamber.'

The knight frowned at these words, and was a moment silent; then, with a countenance somewhat stern, he said, 'I am an English knight; I am called Sir Bevys of Lancaster, and my deeds are not unknown at the holy city, whence I was returning to my native land, when I was benighted in the forest.'

'You name is not unknown to fame,' said the baron; 'I have heard of it.' (The knight looked haughtily.) 'But why, since my castle is known to entertain all true knights, did not your herald announce you? Why did you not appear at the banquet, where your presence would have been welcomed, instead of hiding yourself in my castle, and stealing to my chamber at mid-night?'

The stranger frowned, and turned away in silence; but the baron repeated the questions.

'I come not,' said the knight, 'to answer inquiries, but to reveal facts. If you would know more, follow me; and again I pledge the honour of a knight that you shall return in safety. Be quick in your determination—I must be gone.'

After some farther hesitation, the baron determined to follow the stranger, and to see the result of his extraordinary request; he therefore again drew forth his sword, and, taking up a lamp, bade the knight lead on. The latter obeyed; and opening the door of the chamber, they passed into the ante-room, where the baron, surprised to find all his pages asleep, stopped, and with hasty violence was going to reprimand them for their carelessness, when the knight waved his hand, and looked so expressively at the baron, that the latter restrained his resentment, and passed on.

The knight, having descended a staircase, opened a secret door, which the baron had believed was only known to himself; and proceeding through several narrow and winding passages, came at length to a small gate that opened beyond the walls of the castle. Perceiving that these secret passages were so well known to a stranger, the baron felt inclined to turn back from an adventure that appeared to partake of treachery as well as danger. Then, considering that he was armed, and observing the courteous and noble air of his conductor, his courage returned, he blushed that it had failed him for a moment, and he resolved to trace the mystery to its source.

He now found himself on the healthy platform, before the great gates of his castle, where, on looking up, he perceived lights glimmering in the different casements of the guests, who were retiring to sleep; and while he shivered in the blast, and looked on the dark and desolate scene around him, he thought of the comforts of his warm chamber, rendered cheerful by the blaze of wood, and felt, for a moment, the full contrast of his present situation.

(Here Ludovico paused a moment, and, looking at his own fire, gave it a brightening stir.)

The wind was strong, and the baron watched his lamp with anxiety, expecting every moment, to see it extinguished; but though the flame wavered, it did not expire, and he still followed the stranger, who often sighed as he went, but did not speak.

When they reached the borders of the forest, the knight turned and raised his head, as if he meant to address the baron, but then closing his lips, in silence he walked on.

As they entered beneath the dark and spreading boughs, the baron, affected by the solemnity of the scene, hesitated whether to proceed, and demanded how much farther they were to go. The knight replied only by a gesture, and the baron, with hesitating steps and a suspicious eye, followed through an obscure and intricate path, till, having proceeded a considerable way, he again demanded whither they were going, and refused to proceed unless he was informed.

As he said this, he looked at his own sword and at the knight alternately, who shook his head, and whose dejected countenance disarmed the baron, for a moment, of suspicion.

'A little farther is the place whither I would lead you,' said the stranger; 'no evil shall befall you—I have sworn it on the honour of a knight.'

The baron, reassured, again followed in silence, and they soon arrived at a deep recess of the forest, where the dark and lofty chestnuts entirely excluded the sky, and which was so overgrown with underwood that they proceeded with difficulty. The knight sighed deeply as he passed, and sometimes paused; and having at length reached a spot where the trees crowded into a knot, he turned, and with a terrific look, pointing to the ground, the baron saw there the body of a man, stretched at its length, and weltering in blood; a ghastly wound was on the forehead, and death appeared already to have contracted the features.

The baron, on perceiving the spectacle, started in horror, looked at the knight for explanation, and was then going to raise the body, and examine if there were any remains of life; but the stranger, waving his hand, fixed upon him a look so earnest and mournful, as not only much surprised him, but made him desist.

But what were the baron's emotions when, on holding the lamp near the features of the corpse, he discovered the exact resemblance of the stranger his conductor, to whom he now looked up in astonishment and inquiry! As he gazed he perceived the countenance of the knight change and begin to fade, till his whole form gradually vanished from his astonished sense! While the baron stood, fixed to the spot, a voice was heard to utter these words:

(Ludovico started, and laid down the book for he thought he heard a voice in the chamber, and he looked towards the bed, where, however, he saw only the dark curtain and the pall. He listened, scarcely daring to draw his breath, but heard only the distant roaring of the sea in the storm, and the blast that rushed by the casements; when, concluding that he had been deceived by its sigh-ings, he took up his book to finish his story.)

While the baron stood, fixed to the spot, a voice was heard to utter these words:

'The body of Sir Bevys of Lancaster, a noble knight of England, lies before you. He was this night waylaid and murdered, as he journeyed from the holy city towards his native land. Respect the honour of knighthood, and the law of human-ity; inter the body in christian ground, and cause his murderers to be punished. As ye observe or neglect this, shall peace and happiness, or war and misery, light upon you and your house for ever!'

The baron, when he recovered from the awe and astonishment into which this adventure had thrown him, returned to his castle, whither he caused the body of Sir Bevys to be removed; and on the following day it was interred, with the ho-nours of knighthood, in the chapel of the castle, attended by all the noble knights and ladies who graced the court of Baron de Brunne.

Ludovico, having finished this story, laid aside the book, for he felt drowsy; and after putting more wood on the fire, and taking another glass of wine, he reposed himself in the armchair on the hearth. In his dream he still beheld the chamber where the rally was, and once or twice started from imperfect slumbers, imagining he saw a man's face looking over the high back of his armchair. This idea had so strongly impressed him, that, when he raised his eyes, he almost expected to meet other eyes fixed upon his own; and he quitted his seat, and looked behind the chair before he felt perfectly convinced that no person was there.

Thus closed the hour.

The count, who had slept little during the night, rose early, and, anxious to speak with Lu-dovico, went to the north apartment; but the outer door having been fastened on the preceding night, he was obliged to knock loudly for admit-tance. Neither the knocking nor his voice was heard: he renewed his calls more loudly than before; after which a total silence ensued; and the count, finding all his efforts to be heard inef-fectual, at length began to fear that some accident had befallen Ludovico, whom terror of an imagi-nary being might have deprived of his senses. He therefore left the door with an intention of sum-moning his servants to force it open, some of whom he now heard moving in the lower part of the château.

To the count's inquiries whether they had seen or heard anything of Ludovico, they replied, in affright, that not one of them had ventured on the north side of the château since the preceding night.

'He sleeps soundly, then,' said the count, 'and is at such a distance from the outer door, which is fastened, that to gain admittance to the chambers it will be necessary to force it. Bring an instru-ment, and follow me.'

The servants stood mute and dejected, and it was not till nearly all the household were as-sembled, that the count's orders were obeyed. In the meantime, Dorothee was telling of a door that opened from a gallery leading from the great staircase into the last ante-room of the saloon, and this being much nearer to the bedchamber, it appeared probable that Ludovico might be easily awakened by an attempt to open it. Thither, therefore, the count went; but his voice was as ineffectual at this door as it had proved at the remoter one; and now, seriously interested for Lu-dovico, he was himself going to strike upon the door with the instrument, when he observed its singular beauty, and withheld the blow. It ap-peared on the first glance to be of ebony, so dark and close was its grain, and so high its polish; but it proved to be only of larch wood, of the growth of Provence, then famous for its forests of larch. The beauty of its polished hue, and of its delicate carvings, determined the count to spare this door, and he returned to that leading from the back staircase, which being at length forced, he entered the first ante-room, followed by Henri and a few of the most courageous of his servants, the rest waiting the event of the inquiry on the stairs and landing-place.

All was silence in the chambers through which the count passed, and, having reached the saloon, he called loudly upon Ludovico; after which, still receiving no answer, he threw open the door of the bedroom, and entered.

The profound stillness within confirmed his apprehensions for Ludovico, for not even the breathings of a person in sleep were heard; and his uncertainty was not soon terminated, since the shutters being all closed, the chamber was too dark for any object to be distinguished in it.

The count bade a servant open them, who, as he crossed the room to do so, stumbled over something, and fell to the floor, when his cry oc-casioned such a panic among the few of his fellows who had ventured thus far, that they instantly fled, and the count and Henri were left to finish the adventure.

Henri then sprang across the room, and, opening a window-shutter, they perceived that the man had fallen over a chair near the hearth, in which Ludovico had been sitting;—for he sat there no longer, nor could anywhere be seen by the imperfect light that was admitted into the apartment. The count, seriously alarmed, now opened other shutters, that he might be enabled to examine farther; and Ludovico not yet appearing, he stood for a moment suspended in astonishment, and scarcely trusting his senses, till his eyes glancing on the bed, he advanced to examine whether he was there asleep. No person, however, was in it; and he proceeded to the Oriel, where everything remained as on the preceding night; but Ludovico was nowhere to be found.

The count now checked his amazement, considering that Ludovico might have left the chambers during the night, overcome by the terrors which their lonely desolation and the recollected reports concerning them had inspired. Yet, if this had been the fact, the man would naturally have sought society, and his fellow-servants had all declared they had not seen him; the door of the outer room also had been found fastened, with the key on the inside; it was impossible, therefore, for him to have passed through that; and all the outer doors of this suite were found, on examination, to be bolted and locked, with the keys also within them. The count, being then compelled to believe that the lad had escaped through the casements, next examined them; but such as opened wide enough to admit the body of a man were found to be carefully secured either by iron bars or by shutters, and no vestige appeared of any person having attempted to pass them; neither was it probable that Ludovico would have incurred the risk of breaking his neck by leaping from a window, when he might have walked safely through a door.

The count's amazement did not admit of words; but he returned once more to examine the bedroom, where was no appearance of disorder, except that occasioned by the late overthrow of the chair, near which had stood a small table; and on this Ludovico's sword, his lamp, the book he had been reading, and the remains of his flask of wine, still remained. At the foot of the table, too, was the basket, with some fragments of provision and wood.

Henri and the servant now uttered their astonishment without reserve, and though the count said little, there was a seriousness in his manner that expressed much. It appeared that Ludovico must have quitted these rooms by some concealed passage, for the count could not believe that any supernatural means had occasioned this event; yet, if there was any such passage, it seemed inexplicable why he should retreat through it; and it was equally surprising, that not even the smallest vestige should appear by which his progress could be traced. In the rooms, everything remained as much in order as if he had just walked out by the common way.

The count himself assisted in lifting the arras with which the bedchamber, saloon, and one of the ante-rooms were hung, that he might discover if any door had been concealed behind it; but after a laborious search, none was found; and he at length quitted the apartments, having secured the door of the last antechamber the key of which he took his own possession. He then gave orders that strict search should be made for Ludovico, not only in the château, but in the neighbourhood, and retiring with Henri to his closet, they remained there in conversation for a considerable time; and whatever was the subject of it, Henri from this hour lost much of his vivacity; and his manners were particularly grave and reserved, whenever the topic, which now agitated the count's family with wonder and alarm, was introduced.[1]

Note

1. The château had been inhabited before the count came into its possession. He was not aware that the apparently outward walls contained a series of passages and staircases, which led to unknown vaults underground, and, therefore, he never thought of looking for a door in those parts of the chamber which he supposed to be next to the air. In these was a communication with the room. The château (for we are not here in Udolpho) was on the sea-shore in Languedoc; its vaults had become the store-house of pirates, who did their best to keep up the supernatural delusions that hindered people from searching the premises; and these pirates had carried Ludovico away.

ANN RADCLIFFE (ESSAY DATE 1826)

SOURCE: Radcliffe, Ann. "On the Supernatural in Poetry." *New Monthly Magazine* 16 (1826): 145-52.

In the following excerpt from a fictional conversation between two travelers, Radcliffe presents a distinction between horror and terror.

[Said W———:] "Terror and horror are so far opposite, that the first expands the soul, and

ABOUT THE AUTHOR

SIR WALTER SCOTT ON RADCLIFFE'S TALENT

Mrs. Radcliffe's powers, both of language and description, have been justly estimated very highly. They bear, at the same time, considerable marks of that warm, and somewhat exuberant imagination, which dictated her works. Some artists are distinguished by precision and correctness of outline, others by the force and vividness of their colouring; and it is to the latter class that this author belongs. The landscapes of Mrs. Radcliffe are far from equal in accuracy and truth to those of her contemporary, Mrs. Charlotte Smith, whose sketches are so very graphical, that an artist would find little difficulty in actually painting from them. Those of Mrs. Radcliffe, on the contrary, while they would supply the most noble and vigorous ideas, for producing a general effect, would leave the task of tracing a distinct and accurate outline to the imagination of the painter. As her story is usually enveloped in mystery, so there is, as it were, a haze over her landscapes, softening indeed the whole, and adding interest and dignity to particular parts, and thereby producing every effect which the author desired, but without communicating any absolutely precise or individual image to the reader. . . .

It may be true, that Mrs. Radcliffe rather walks in fairy-land than in the region of realities, and that she has neither displayed the command of the human passions, nor the insight into the human heart, nor the observation of life and manners, which recommend other authors in the same line. But she has taken the lead in a line of composition, appealing to those powerful and general sources of interest, a latent sense of supernatural awe, and curiosity concerning whatever is hidden and mysterious; and if she has been ever nearly approached in this walk, which we should hesitate to affirm, it is at least certain, that she has never been excelled or even equalled.

SOURCE: Scott, Sir Walter. "Ann Radcliffe." In *Sir Walter Scott on Novelists and Novels*. 1824. Reprint edition, edited by Ioan Williams, pp. 102-19. London: Routledge & Kegan Paul, 1968.

awakens the faculties to a high degree of life; the other contracts, freezes, and nearly annihilates them. I apprehend, that neither Shakespeare nor Milton by their fictions, nor Mr. Burke by his reasoning, anywhere looked to positive horror as a source of the sublime, though they all agree that terror is a very high one; and where lies the great difference between horror and terror, but in the uncertainty and obscurity, that accompany the [latter] . . . , respecting the dreaded evil?" . . .

"How can any thing be indistinct and not confused?" said Mr. S———. . . .

[Replied W———: "Obscurity,] or indistinctness, is only a negative, which leaves the imagination to act upon the few hints that truth reveals to it; confusion is a thing as positive as distinctness, though not necessarily so palpable; and it may, by mingling and confounding one image with another, absolutely counteract the imagination, instead of exciting it. Obscurity leaves something for the imagination to exaggerate; confusion, by blurring one image into another, leaves only a chaos in which the mind can find nothing to be magnificent, nothing to nourish its fears or doubts, or to act upon in any way; yet confusion and obscurity are terms used indiscriminately by those, who would prove, that Shakspeare and Milton were wrong when they employed obscurity as a cause of the sublime, that Mr. Burke was equally mistaken in his reasoning upon the subject, and that mankind have been equally in error, as to the nature of their own feelings, when they were acted upon by the illusions of those great masters of the imagination, at whose so potent bidding, the passions have been awakened from their sleep, and by whose magic a crowded Theatre has been changed to a lonely shore, to a witch's cave, to an enchanted island, to a murderer's castle, to the ramparts of an usurper, to the battle, to the midnight carousal of the camp or the tavern, to every various scene of the living world."

GENERAL COMMENTARY

DAVID S. MIALL (ESSAY DATE 2000)

SOURCE: Miall, David S. "The Preceptor as Fiend: Radcliffe's Psychology of the Gothic." In *Jane Austen and Mary Shelley and Their Sisters*, edited by Laura Dabundo, pp. 31-43. Lanham, Md.: University Press of America, Inc., 2000.

In the following essay, Miall considers Radcliffe's treatment of women's education in her works.

From the perspective of the 1990s, we might regard the Britain of the 1790s as marked by a pervasive neurosis of the social order. Nowhere is this more evident than in the position assigned to women, who were subjected to a range of legal and social disabilities. Although these disabilities were not new to the 1790s, they acquired a special intensity in the aftermath of the French Revolution and the reaction against all things Jacobin. One notable turning point was the eruption of hysteria following the publication of the first edition of William Godwin's *Memoirs* of Mary Wollstonecraft in 1797, which helped ensure that Wollstonecraft's *Vindication of the Rights of Women* (1792) would quickly lose the regard it had initially enjoyed and would soon fall into obscurity. Another instance is the publication of the Gothic novels of Ann Radcliffe, from **The Castles of Athlin and Dunbayne** (1789) to **The Italian** (1797). The extraordinary popular success that the novels enjoyed, together with the rash of third-rate imitations that immediately ensued, suggests that the novels fulfilled an urgent social need.

Despite different aims, the writings of both Wollstonecraft and Radcliffe share one obvious preoccupation, concern with the education of women. Both react, although differently, to the contemporary emphasis in fashionable education on feminine accomplishments and the cult of sensibility. The teacher's role in Radcliffe's novels, however, surpasses that of parent or tutor. Suspense or terror, supernatural intimations, the use of the sublime, and the persecution by powerful men also support pedagogical issues; in this respect the novels point to another principle underlying the neurosis of the 1790s. There was enforced upon most women by the prevailing culture—that "perpetual babyism" of which Mary Hays complained (97). To be more precise, the Radcliffean Gothic is constructed from a psychological machinery that enacts the predicament of the abandoned child, for whom the only resolution available is the temporary one of wish fulfillment. The novels' significance, and their attraction for their first readers, perhaps lies in that they capture the borderline status of women, neither child nor adult, and portray, albeit in disguised and symbolic form, the attendant disabilities to which their middle-class female readers were themselves victim.

Radcliffe probably did not consciously design her novels to explore such issues; on the contrary, their paradoxes of plot and character suggest conflicted, unconscious materials. No record indicates that Radcliffe received any formal educa-tion, although her novels show familiarity with English literature of the eighteenth century, Shakespeare and Milton, and a wide range of travel literature.

Radcliffe as a girl is likely to have been exposed to educational issues discussed within the Wedg-wood circle, which also conducted experiments in education involving children of both sexes. The later publication of her novels coincided with an intensification of the debate on female education, which peaked in the 1790s.[1] Her novels make apparent that Radcliffe studied some of the central issues with increasing seriousness and depth of understanding, particularly the place of sensibility and the moral education of women. But the failures of the educational model that Radcliffe came to know, above all its failure to ensure the maturity of women and meaningful social roles, are reflected in the Gothic form intrinsic to Rad-cliffe's fiction. Thus I interpret the novels as stud-ies in the psychopathology of childhood. Although Radcliffe hoped for an education for women that would secure their virtue and sensitivity, her novels actually hold up to society a distort-ing mirror in which the preceptors of women ap-pear fiendish and predatory.

That Radcliffe was concerned with education is apparent in all her novels from the first, **The Castles Athlin and Dunbayne,** the opening pages of which consider the heroine's education. Rad-cliffe's reading of Rousseau's *Emile* is manifest in **The Romance of the Forest,** in which the character of La Luc is modeled on Rousseau's Savoyard vicar. The most elaborate treatment of female education appears in the early chapters of **Udolpho,** where Radcliffe dwells at some length on St. Aubert's upbringing of Emily and his valedictory precepts to her before his death. Radcliffe's views on educa-tion cannot be identified with those of St. Aubert, however, but they do correspond significantly with contemporary discussions by such writers as Thomas Gisborne and Hannah More. Her hand-ling of the issues, however, suggests a profound, if unconscious, distrust of the ideological implica-tions of current practices in female education, which she is likely to have encountered with the Wedgwood circle and perhaps even in her own experience.

Radcliffe was related maternally to a wide and influential world. Her uncle was Thomas Bentley, who became the partner of Josiah Wedgwood the potter in 1769, and appears to have been keenly interested in education. Wedgwood's first surviv-ing letter to Bentley, in 1762, refers to "an excel-lent piece upon *female education,* which I once had the pleasure of reading in MS." and which Bentley is urged to publish (i:2). As a child, she stayed with Bentley at his Chelsea house: the longest period appears to have been autumn, 1771, to spring, 1772, when Ann was aged seven.

Apart from Bentley's direct influence, Ann would also have become aware of contemporary educational practice in the example of Wedgwood's daughter (Susannah [1765-1817]), who was one year younger than Ann and who, upon marrying Dr. Robert Darwin in 1796, became the mother of Charles Darwin. Susannah stayed either with Bentley or at a nearby school in Chelsea called Blacklands between October, 1775, and April, 1778. She seems to have received the standard education for a girl. Wedgwood speaks in one letter of her improvements "as well in her general carriage, & behavior, as in her Music, Drawing & c." (ii:302-03).

Female education when Radcliffe was growing up placed its primary focus on accomplishments. Many critics noted that these were merely utilitarian and subverted any genuine educational achievement. In a diary entry of 1784, for example, Mrs. Thrale (later Piozzi) writes that the female student's "Mother only loads her with Allurements, as a Rustic lays Bird Lime on Twigs, to decoy & catch the unwary Traveller"—that is, a husband (*i*: 590-91). Yet these same accomplishments constitute almost all that we first see of an Emily or an Ellena, to whom Valancourt or Vivaldi respond in textbook manner by falling immediately and irrevocably in love. Radcliffe's heroines, in fact, keep themselves occupied very much as contemporary guides recommended. Gisborne's *Enquiry* (1797) suggests improving reading (citing poets that Radcliffe particularly prized, such as Milton, Thomson, Gray, Mason, and Cowper), including poems that instill a sense of the sublime in nature; and he urges the performance of regular acts of charity to poor neighbors (223). Ellena, in **The Italian,** supports herself by selling fine work anonymously through the local convent, somewhat after the manner of Mrs. Cooper's shop in London, noticed by Priscilla Wakefield, which discreetly sold goods made by ladies in deprived circumstances (115).

But in themselves accomplishments are insufficient, as Radcliffe's novels imply. Numerous parents in the 1790s enabled their sons and daughters to ape the manners of the upper classes by attending boarding schools, but as Catherine Macaulay warned, such a polite exterior "is liable to change into a determined rudeness whenever motives of caprice or vanity intervene" (172)—a change that occurs only too readily in the case of a Madame Cheron. The touchstone of Emily's virtue, as with Valancourt, is unswerving sensibility, whether to poetry or to nature. Radcliffe thus accepts the prototype, which so many boarding schools were designed to reproduce, in endowing her heroines with all the fashionable accomplishments; but she shows its limitations at the same time, a stance that ennobles her heroines but weakens their credibility as protagonists.

The physical ideal of womanhood that evolved toward the end of the eighteenth century was equally damaging. Increasing restrictions on body shape and clothing meant, in Lawrence Stone's account, "extreme slimness, a pale complexion and slow languid movements, all of which were deliberately inculcated in the most expensive boarding schools" (*Family* 445). Weakness of body and mind seems to have given women greater sexual attractiveness by increasing the scope for male control. As Fanny Burney's Mr. Lovel in *Evelina* says, "I have an insuperable aversion to strength, either of body or mind, in a female" (361). Radcliffe's heroines, who are capable of little physical exertion and often faint, seem close to this anorexic paradigm. The achievement of this ideal formed the "hidden curriculum" of their schooling. Female education in Radcliffe's period was not primarily about singing or embroidery, it was the enforcement of an anemic, passive, and compliant disposition to prolong women's childhood state constantly on the edge of adolescence. Thus, in **Athlin and Dunbayne,** Mary's indisposition makes her more attractive to Alleyn since it gives her "an interesting languor, more enchanting than the vivacity of blooming health" (110). In her later novels Radcliffe achieves similar effects through the emotional suffering of her heroines, which renders the countenance "more interesting" (**Udolpho** 161).

Besides the heroines' illnesses, their childlike qualities contribute directly to their attractiveness. This is stated most blatantly in **Romance of the Forest** when Theodore reflects that Adeline's charms are best described by the lines of a poem: "Oh! have you seen, bath'd in the morning dew, / The budding rose its infant bloom display; / When first its virgin tints unfold to view" (**Forest** 172). Wollstonecraft bitterly complains about this view, speaking of women "hanging their heads surcharged with the dew of sensibility" (149). Adeline is also said to be amiable, beautiful, and possessing a simplicity of manners (29); she has a love of virtue that makes it difficult for her to dissemble (160). She has just those virtues, in fact, that More advocates in her *Strictures* (1799) while complaining about women's passion for dress and ornament: "Modesty, simplicity, humility, economy, prudence, liberality, charity are almost inseparably, and not very remotely, connected with an habitual victory over personal vanity and a turn to personal expense" (i:336). Such a heroine is simultaneously strong and weak; she has the finest, best-honed moral sense yet is liable to faint at every critical moment (although the frequency of fainting fits steadily diminishes across Radcliffe's novels).[2] The source of this paradox emerges with the role of moral instruction in Radcliffe's fiction, that is, the use of the precept.

In *Udolpho* the most important education received by the heroine is largely in the form of precepts; yet Radcliffe manages this ambiguously. Emily's father appears to subscribe to a model of female education similar to More's, although his precepts may not be intended at face value. Valancourt's elder brother is described "haranguing on the virtues of mildness and moderation:" (117), which seems to caricature St. Aubert's advice to Emily. Madame Cheron frequently talks in precepts: "she failed not to inculcate the duties of humility and gratitude" (121). More disturbingly, however, Montoni also speaks in maxims, referring to "friends who assisted in rescuing you from the romantic illusions of sentiment . . . they are only the snares of childhood, and should be vanquished the moment you escape from the nursery" (196)—an even more brutal version of St. Aubert's advice to Emily. Also, Cheron's precepts, based as she claims on "a little plain sense" (204) or "only common sense" (205), are shown actually to involve an acceptance of and complicity in the world of Montoni. Thus, common sense is invoked to disguise patriarchal tyranny. Not coincidentally, then, while Montoni attempts to gain control over Emily's property, he talks to her in precepts: "you should learn and practise the virtues, which are indispensable to a woman—sincerity, uniformity of conduct and obedience" (270).[3] Compliance and self-control are demanded by the preceptor in contrast to the method of the teacher, who emphasizes development in the pupil's own interests—a role rarely found in Radcliffe's fiction (except perhaps Madame de Menon in *A Sicilian Romance*).

Therefore, precepts may be the primary agents of the patriarchal perspective, like Polonius's toward his children; preceptors invariably stand against sensibility. Feeling must be controlled by the patriarchal force of reason since feeling is an agent of discovery and would enable its possessor to challenge the preceptor's authority. Thus although Radcliffe seems on the one hand to applaud the precepts of a St. Aubert, on the other hand the tenor of her novels points not only to the inadequacy of such precepts, but also suggests that those who wield them are agents of repression or terror. In educating Emily, St. Aubert strives "to teach her to reject the first impulse of her feelings, and to look, with cool examination, upon the disappointments he sometimes threw in her way" (*Udolpho* 5). But as Robert Kiely notes, "the incongruity between human behavior and moral principles which increases as the book progresses is strangely prefigured in Emily's philosophical father" (71), who fails to abide by his own precepts. While he speaks to Emily of controlling her feelings by reason or mind on the day of her mother's funeral (20-21)—surely a highly premature injunction—he himself is unable in 20 years to overcome his grief at the death of his sister, the poisoned Marchioness de Villerois (660). This prevents his letting Emily know that he even had such a sister, and his silence borders on the culpable, since her knowledge of this piece of family history might have alerted her to the danger of Montoni's guardianship. Whether Radcliffe expected readers to infer that is not clear; her plot lacks internal consistency. The surface structure of her fiction, with its notorious explanations of the supernatural, supports the principles of reason and a rational control over sensibility, and St. Aubert is rendered a mouthpiece for precepts from contemporary treatises on female education. Yet these same principles are repeatedly subverted by Radcliffe's focus on extreme states of feeling. By placing her heroines at the borders of perception and rationality, she enables their aroused sensibilities to acquire knowledge essential for survival.

Radcliffe's handling of sensibility is thus equivocal at a critical juncture of cultural change. More, for example, in her early poem to Mrs. Boscawen "**Sensibility**," written in 1782, gives her subject high praise: "Unprompted moral! sudden sense of right!" (i:34). In the *Strictures* of 1799, however, several pages warn of the dangers of sensibility, and she withdraws her earlier trust in its moral powers. Women of sensibility, she declares, "are apt to employ the wrong instrument to accomplish the right end. They employ the passions to do the work of the judgment" (i:380). Richard Edgeworth, who brought up his first son on principles of freedom and sensibility inspired by Rousseau, later moved away from sensibility. When considering female education with his coauthor Maria Edgeworth he advises, "we must cultivate the reasoning powers at the same time that we repress the enthusiasm of *fine feeling*" (i:380). Radcliffe occupies both sides of this debate. She accepts the high valuation placed on women's moral judgment in shaping society through the men they influence (a role on which More and others insisted). For example, Adeline, Emily, and Ellena decide to reject immediate marriage with their suitors at a critical moment, thus becoming moral guides to the men. At the same time, Radcliffe values the impulses of sensibility in ways that More and Edgeworth reprobated. Anticipating the Edgeworths, she makes St. Aubert warn Emily, in terms very similar to ones used by More or the others, "do not indulge in the pride of fine feelings, the romantic error of amiable minds" (*Udolpho* 80). Yet such rational caution has serious limitations.

Contemporary education manuals emphasize keeping females occupied, hence the ceaseless cultivation of accomplishments such as embroidery, etching, drawing, or ribbon work. A woman should carefully avoid reverie, as More stresses. "she, who early imposes on herself a habit of strict attention to whatever she is engaged in, begins to wage early war with wandering thoughts, useless reveries, and that disqualifying train of busy, but unprofitable imaginations . . . "(i:336). But Radcliffe likely would have disagreed with these prescriptions. Although Emily, for instance, feels some guilt when she notices that she has dropped her needlework and fallen into a reverie or has lingered in communion with the falling dusk and the sounds of nature, this is when her sensibilities, thus activated, register the signals that contribute in the long run to her safety. For Emily—and Ellena after her—reverie provides a training in anticipatory reflection on her plight; it becomes soon enough a more urgent interpreting of various critical events and the intellectual study of the logic of different possibilities. To imagine a particular outcome is to gain some control over its actuality. Radcliffe heroines spend an increasing amount of time doing this, as the ratio of action to cogitation decreases over the course of her novels. Reverie strengthens, not weakens, the preparedness of the Radcliffe heroine.

Thus to debate the priority of reason or sensibility in Radcliffe is perhaps fallacious. The novels demonstrate the convergence of these faculties, that sensibility itself is a form of reason. "Despite its elaborate assertions of the need to dominate feeling by reason," as Spacks observes, "*The Mysteries of Udolpho* dramatizes the power of feeling to guide people accurately" (174). Hence,

Radcliffe presents an insight that Coleridge or Wordsworth shortly offers more explicitly: for example, Coleridge claims in 1803 that his philosophy is "to make the Reason spread Light over our Feelings, to make our Feelings diffuse vital Warmth thro' our Reason" (*Notebooks* i:1623). Thus feelings, far from coming under the control of reason, increasingly guide the heroine's behavior. Conger, noting this, points to Ellena's sudden suspicion of Spalatro's food in *The Italian* (216): "Here is one of Radcliffe's most successful fictional demonstrations of the finely tuned sensibility in action, and one that presents that sensibility unequivocally as an instinctive survival skill" (*135*). Radcliffe also extends the heroine's clairvoyance to premonitory dreams, such as Adeline's, which lead her to her murdered father's manuscript (*Forest* 108-110), a device in which Radcliffe improves upon a predecessor's strategy (Clara Reeve's *Old English Baron* [1778]).

Despite these significant accomplishments, however, the Radcliffe heroine oddly fails to mature either socially or psychologically. Although she survives her ordeals in order to marry and, presumably, bear children, she seems quite untouched by the succession of terrifying experiences she has had to endure. *Udolpho,* in the words of Macdonald (1989), is "a novel of education in which her heroine starts out with nothing to learn, a novel of maturation in which her heroine ends up as innocent, and as infantile, as she began"(203; also Kiely 78, Howells 9). This analysis applies to the heroines of all the novels. Radcliffe's vision, then, cannot encompass maturation.

At the same time, the Gothic heroine is a survivor, as Punter has suggested (11). Representative of some aspect of actual female experience, she survives amidst the social disruptions and gender politics of the late eighteenth century, but only at the cost of considerable psychological injury. She is the plaything of a Gothic machinery that involves removal of parents, extreme social isolation, prolonged incarcerations, and states of excessive terror, all of which symbolize a predicament that in reality is too threatening to be adequately comprehended.

The repetitive nature of Radcliffe's plots, not only within each novel but from one novel to the next, points to a version of the repetition compulsion which, as Freud pointed out, lies at the root of the uncanny (xvii:238). Endlessly replicating situations of terror, the novels point to a primary source in the experience of women of Radcliffe's generation, the repeated failure to master a trauma. The remarkable success of the Gothic genre she created shows that the representation of woman's predicament in her novels met an urgent cultural need, not just in the 1790s, but in the several decades and numerous imitators that followed.

Although critics have noted that Radcliffe's Gothic fictions occupy a borderland poised between natural and supernatural, the suspense this causes mainly serves plot machinery. Their evocation of a more important psychological borderland generates their genuine emotional power, that between childhood and adulthood. Punter's point that readers of Gothic fiction are free to indulge in regressive visions does not fully account for the experience of women writers such as Radcliffe and their first female readers.[4] Our regressive vision was their historic reality. In this sense, the infantilism imposed on women during the Romantic period perpetuates the psychodrama of early childhood, manifest in the plot of such a novel as **The Italian** as uncanny appearances and connections, meaningful coincidences (portrayed as providence), and the omnipotence of the prevailing powers of church and class. The reader's emotions, in short, reproduce the response to the oppressors that controlled women's lives.

Above all, the hallucinatory symptoms that occur in terror reflect as in a distorting mirror the ethical framework of 1790s patriarchy, with its extravagant and psychotic ethical demands on women. In this world, even the suspicion of a single ethical slip by a woman precipitates a fall into the abyss of ruin; a scale of retribution both disproportionate to the degree of guilt incurred and radically different from that under which men operated.[5] This primitive and savage ethical order imposed upon women suggests one source for the atavism of the Gothic novel, the fear of pollution springing from women's sexuality. As Paul Ricoeur comments on the fear of defilement: "When [man] first wished to express the order in the world, he began by expressing it in the language of retribution" (30). Working out this problematic, Gothic fiction partly desexualizes its heroine by pushing her back across the borders of adolescence, at the same time visiting upon her massive and not entirely explicable sufferings. These serve to increase her sensibilities, sometimes to hallucinatory intensity, but this supplies the heroine's strength as well as her liability. As Emily reflects, "when the mind has once begun to yield to the weakness of superstition, trifles impress it with the force of conviction" (**Udolpho** 634-35). Yet much of the behavior that preserves her at Udol-

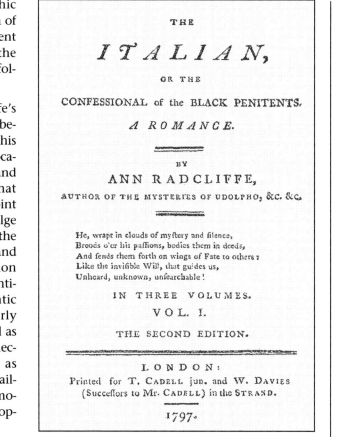

Title page of *The Italian; or, The Confessional of the Black Penitents*, 1797.

pho derives from just such conviction based upon apparent trifles—a few words, gestures, remote sounds.

But the heroine's hallucinatory perceptions are not merely fantasy, even though they are often factually mistaken at the banal level of plot. A hallucination intimates repressed unconscious thoughts. As Freud remarks in speaking of "conversion hysteria," a hallucination reproduces in disguised form the actual experience when the repression occurred (xx:111). In this way Radcliffe disguises experiences that properly belong to childhood animism, in which no events are unexplained or random; every strange sight or sound holds a meaning with felt personal significance, even though this significance may be obscure or inexplicable. Just so does a Radcliffe heroine respond with hallucinatory intensity to the sights and sounds around her. Although the animism is later withdrawn in the bathos of explanation (Macdonald 199), the intimated meaning often remains in force and fails to dispel the atmosphere of threat or providence surrounding the heroine. For example, the improbable coincidences on which a Radcliffe plot depends are never adequately explained.[6] Such animism belongs normally only to childhood, but it is likely to be reawakened later in life during crises, such as separation or bereavement. Radcliffe seems to replay such a crisis in the plot of each of her novels, given that her heroines find themselves bereft of one or, usually, both parents, leaving the heroine exposed to vengeful or providential powers beyond her understanding or control. The plot, in other words, replays the regression to animism, in which nothing is meaningless. As Freud says, animism is the "most consistent and exhaustive" and "truly complete" explanation of the universe (xiii:77).

Another dimension of such animism is that the internalizing of the preceptor's voice, which psychoanalytically produces the superego or conscience, is incomplete. Thus the threatening behavior of a Montalt, a Montoni, or a Schedoni echoes the paternal language of the late eighteenth century toward Radcliffe's generation. These men are indeed the "monstrous and phantastic" parental images of which Melanie Klein speaks (250), but in Radcliffe they are not merely outgrowths of the inner aggressive impulses to which Klein attributes them; they correspond to the actual forces that shaped the lives of women and sought to confine them to a state of perpetual adolescence. The Gothic thus embodies the chronic paranoia imposed upon women, easy to ridicule or disregard, as the high culture of the period did only too readily, but representing a genuine persecution nonetheless.

Radcliffe's novels thereby reproduce the kind of persecution often seen in modern clinical reports of hallucinations, especially those of children (Cain 205, Pilowsky 10). At the same time, her heroine's stories invariably replicate the precipitants for hallucinations—being orphaned, isolated, and set adrift in conditions of sensory deprivation (imprisoned in a castle or a convent); in addition, the novels follow a wish-fulfillment pattern, repeated across all the novels, of ultimate rescue by a hero of similar adolescent attributes, following successive failures at deliverance. As the problems faced by women outside the novel are insoluble, neither is development possible for the fictional heroines; they have virtually nothing to learn that would be of use, and they contribute nothing to the society to which they supposedly return after their persecutions cease (and it should be noted that the social structures that facilitated their persecutions remain intact, whether class, religion, or gender). Protagonists such as Ellena

and Vivaldi are thus given only the most elementary and contingent of concerns, arising from their love and the various predicaments that follow from it. This is in striking contrast to a Montoni or Schedoni, whose concerns relate to a complex social system of rewards, privileges, and duties. While their concerns are ended only by their deaths, the concerns of Ellena and Vivaldi, by contrast, end with marriage. Hence, the aptness of the refrain that sounds through the last chapter of *The Italian,* "O! giorno felice!" signifying the story's end. With their elementary problems resolved, Ellena and Vivaldi's story has nothing to sustain it beyond a single day. This final freeze frame betrays the stasis in which the women Radcliffe portrays are trapped. Another century must elapse before such Gothic congealment would begin to loosen its regressive grip.

Notes

1. Miller lists the number of publications devoted to the "character, duties and education of women" in Britain: in the decade beginning 1760 there were 16, in 1770, 23; 1780, 25; 1790, 41; 1800, 35; 1810, 13 (492-98).

2. Someone faints on average after every 11 pages in *Athlin* (converting the page sizes of the Arno reprint to those of the Oxford editions), 18 pages in *Sicilian,* 40 pages in *Forest,* 48 pages in *Udolpho,* and 52 pages in *The Italian.*

3. Anne Mellor's recent discussion of the sublime in *Udolpho* touches on this question: "Radcliffe's point is clear: the deepest terror aroused by the masculine sublime originates in the exercise of patriarchal authority within the home" (93).

4. Punter refers to our pleasure in "being able to peer backwards through our own personal history, because all psychotic states are simply perpetuations of landscapes which we have all inhabited at some stage in our early infancy" (8).

5. Even Radcliffe's preoccupation with the incarceration of her heroines seems less a mere fantasy in light of how often wives were forcibly and legally confined by their husbands (Stone, *Road* 164-69).

6. Perhaps the most absurd examples are from *Forest,* where the fleeing La Mottes and Adeline end up at the Abbey of St. Clair, which just happens to be owned by Adeline's uncle, and when Peter and Adeline flee to his village in the Savoy, Adeline just happens to end up living with La Luc, the father of her lover Theodore, but all the novels depend in some degree on such coincidences.

Works Cited

Burney, Fanny. *Evelina.* Ed. Edward A. Bloom. Oxford: Oxford University Press, 1982.

Cain, Albert C. "The Impact of Parental Suicide on Children." *The Child and Death.* Ed. Olle Jane Z. Sahler. St. Louis: Mosby, 1978.

Coleridge, Samuel Taylor. *The Notebooks of Samuel Taylor Coleridge.* Ed. Kathleen Coburn. London: Routledge, 1957-.

Conger, Syndy. "Sensibility Restored: Radcliffe's Answer to Lewis's *The Monk.*" *Gothic Fictions: Prohibition/ Transgression.* Ed. Kenneth W. Graham. New York: AMS Press, 1989.

Edgeworth, Richard and Maria. *Practical Education.* 1798. London: Hunter, 1815.

Freud, Sigmund. *The Standard Edition of the Complete Works of Sigmund Freud,* Trans. James Strachey. London: Hogarth Press, 1955-74.

Gisborne, Thomas. *Enquiry Into the Duties of the Female Set.* London: Cadell, 1797.

Hay, Mary. *Appeal to the Men of Great Britain in Behalf of Women.* London: Johnson, 1798.

Howells, Coral Ann. *Love, Mystery, and Misery.* London: Athlone Press, 1978.

Kiely, Robert. *The Romantic Novel in England.* Cambridge: Harvard University Press, 1972.

Klein, Melanie. *Love, Guilt and Reparation and Other Works, 1921-1945.* London: Hogarth Press, 1975.

Macdonald, D. L "Bathos and Repetition: The Uncanny in Radcliffe." *Journal of Narrative Technique* 19:2 (1989), 197-204.

Macaulay, Catherine. *Letters on Education: With Observations on Religious and Metaphysical Subjects.* London: Dilly, 1790.

Mellor, Anne. *Romanticism and Gender.* New York: Routledge, 1993.

Miller, Peter J. Appendix B. "The Education of the English Lady, 1770-1820." Diss. University of Alberta, 1969.

More, Hannah. *Strictures on the Modern System of Female Education. The Complete Works of Hannah More.* New York: Harper, 1835.

Piowsky, Daniel. "Problems in Determining the Presence of Hallucinations in Children." *Hallucinations in Children.* Ed. Daniel Pilowsky and William Chambers. Washington: American Psychiatry Press, 1986.

Piozzi, Hester Lynch. *Thraliana: The Diary of Mrs. Hester Lynch Thrale.* Ed. Katherine C. Balderston. Oxford: Oxford University Press, 1951.

Punter, David. "Narrative and Psychology in Gothic Fiction." *Gothic Fictions: Prohibition/Transgression.* Ed. Kenneth W. Graham. New York AMS Press, 1989. 1-27.

Radcliffe, Ann. *The Castles of Athlin and Dunbayne.* 1821; rpt. New York Arno: Press, 1972.

———. *The Italian.* Ed. Frederick Garber. Oxford: Oxford University Press, 1981.

———. *The Mysteries of Udolpho.* Ed. Bonamy Dobrée. Oxford: Oxford University Press, 1980.

———. *The Romance of the Forest.* Ed. Chloe Chard. Oxford: Oxford University Press, 1986.

Ricoeur, Paul. *The Symbolism of Evil.* Trans. Emerson Buchanan. Boston: Beacon Press, 1969.

Spacks, Patricia Meyer. *Desire and Truth: Functions of Plot in Eighteenth-Century English Novels.* Chicago: Chicago University Press, 1990.

Stone, Lawrence. *The Family, Sex and Marriage in England 1500-1800.* New York Harper, 1977.

———. *Road to Divorce: England 1530-1987.* Oxford: Oxford University Press, 1990.

Wakefield, Priscilla. *Reflections on the Present Condition of the Female Sex; with Suggestions for Its Improvement.* London: Johnson, 1798.

Wedgewood, Josiah. *Letters of Josiah Wedgewood: 1762-1795.* 3 Vols. Ed. Katherine Eufemia Farrer. 1903; rpt. Manchester: Morton, 1973.

Wollstonecraft, Mary. *A Vindication of the Rights of Women.* 2nd ed. Ed. Carol H. Poston. New York: Norton, 1988.

TITLE COMMENTARY

The Mysteries of Udolpho

SAMUEL TAYLOR COLERIDGE (REVIEW DATE AUGUST 1794)

SOURCE: Coleridge, Samuel Taylor. A review of *Mysteries of Udolpho,* by Ann Radcliffe. *Critical Review* (August 1794): 361-72.

In the following excerpt from a review of The Mysteries of Udolpho, *Coleridge faults the work as a substandard effort, compared to Radcliffe's earlier literary achievements.*

[**The Mysteries of Udolpho** does not] require the name of its author to ascertain that it comes from the same hand [that produced **The Romance of the Forest**]. The same powers of description are displayed, the same predilection is discovered for the wonderful and the gloomy—the same mysterious terrors are continually exciting in the mind the idea of a supernatural appearance, keeping us, as it were, upon the very edge and confines of the world of spirits, and yet are ingeniously explained by familiar causes; curiosity is kept upon the stretch from page to page, and from volume to volume, and the secret, which the reader thinks himself every instant on the point of penetrating, flies like a phantom before him, and eludes his eagerness till the very last moment of protracted expectation. This art of escaping the guesses of the reader has been improved and brought to perfection along with the reader's sagacity. . . . In this contest of curiosity on one side, and invention on the other, Mrs. Radcliffe has certainly the advantage. She delights in concealing her plan with the most artificial contrivance, and seems to amuse herself with saying, at every turn and doubling of the story, 'Now you think you have me, but I shall take care to disappoint you.' This method is, however, liable to the following inconvenience, that in the search of what is new, an

ABOUT THE AUTHOR

EDITH BIRKHEAD ON RADCLIFFE AND THE GOTHIC

The enthusiasm which greeted Walpole's enchanted castle and Miss Reeve's carefully manipulated ghost, indicated an eager desire for a new type of fiction in which the known and familiar were superseded by the strange and supernatural. To meet this end Mrs. Radcliffe suddenly came forward with her attractive store of mysteries, and it was probably her timely appearance that saved the Gothic tale from an early death. The vogue of the novel of terror, though undoubtedly stimulated by German influence, was mainly due to her popularity and success. The writers of the first half of the nineteenth century abound in references to her works, and she thus still enjoys a shadowy, ghost-like celebrity. Many who have never had the curiosity to explore the labyrinths of the underground passages, with which her castles are invariably honeycombed, or who have never shuddered with apprehension before the "black veil," know of their existence through *Northanger Abbey,* and have probably also read how Thackeray at school amused himself and his friends by drawing illustrations of Mrs. Radcliffe's novels.

SOURCE: Birkhead, Edith. "'The Novel of Suspense': Mrs. Radcliffe." In *The Tale of Terror: A Study of the Gothic Romance,* pp. 38-62. London: Constable & Company, Ltd., 1921.

author is apt to forget what is natural; and, in rejecting the more obvious conclusions, to take those which are less satisfactory. The trite and the extravagant are the Scylla and Charybdis of writers who deal in fiction. With regard to the work before us, while we acknowledge the extraordinary powers of Mrs. Radcliffe, some readers will be inclined to doubt whether they have been exerted in the present work with equal effect as in the *Romance of the Forest.* Four volumes cannot depend entirely on terrific incidents and intricacy of story. They require character, unity of design, a delineation of the scenes of real life, and the variety of well supported contrast. *The Mysteries of Udolpho* are indeed relieved by much elegant description and picturesque scenery; but in the descriptions there is too much of sameness: the pine and the larch tree wave, and the full moon pours its lustre through almost every chapter. Curiosity is raised oftener than it is gratified; or rather, it is raised so high that no adequate gratification can be given it; the interest is completely dissolved when once the adventure is finished, and the reader, when he is got to the end of the work, looks about in vain for the spell which had bound him so strongly to it. There are other little defects, which impartiality obliges us to notice. The manners do not sufficiently correspond with the aera the author has chosen. . . . The character of Annette, a talkative waiting-maid, is much worn, and that of the aunt, madame Cheron, is too low and selfish to excite any degree of interest, or justify the dangers her niece exposes herself to for her sake. We must likewise observe, that the adventures do not sufficiently point to one centre. . . .

These volumes are interspersed with many pieces of poetry, some beautiful, all pleasing, but rather monotonous. . . . [Poetical] beauties have not a fair chance of being attended to, amidst the stronger interest inspired by such a series of adventures. The love of poetry is a taste; curiosity is a kind of appetite, and hurries headlong on, impatient for its complete gratification. . . .

If, in consequence of the criticisms impartiality has obliged us to make upon this novel, the author should feel disposed to ask us, Who will write a better? we boldly answer her, *Yourself;* when no longer disposed to sacrifice excellence to quantity, and lengthen out a story for the sake of filling an additional volume.

WILLIAM ENFIELD (REVIEW DATE NOVEMBER 1794)

SOURCE: Enfield, William. Review of *The Mysteries of Udolpho,* by Ann Radcliffe. *The Monthly Review* (November 1794): 278-83.

In the following review, Enfield offers a highly favorable assessment of The Mysteries of Udolpho.

If the merit of fictitious narratives may be estimated by their power of pleasing, Mrs. Radcliffe's romances will be entitled to rank highly in the scale of literary excellence. There are, we believe, few readers of novels who have not been delighted with her *Romance of the Forest;* and we incur little risque in predicting that the *Mysteries of Udolpho* will be perused with equal pleasure.

The works of this ingenious writer not only possess, in common with many other productions of the same class, the agreeable qualities of correctness of sentiment and elegance of style, but are also distinguished by a rich vein of invention, which supplies an endless variety of incidents to fill the imagination of the reader; by an admirable ingenuity of contrivance to awaken his curiosity, and to bind him in the chains of suspense; and by a vigour of conception and a delicacy of feeling which are capable of producing the strongest sympathetic emotions, whether of pity or terror. Both these passions are excited in the present romance, but chiefly the latter; and we admire the enchanting power with which the author at her pleasure seizes and detains them. We are no less pleased with the proofs of sound judgment, which appear in the selection of proper circumstances to produce a distinct and full exhibition, before the reader's fancy, both of persons and events; and, still more, in the care which has been taken to preserve his mind in one uniform tone of sentiment, by presenting to it a long continued train of scenes and incidents, which harmonize with each other.

Through the whole of the first volume, the emotions which the writer intends to excite are entirely of the tender kind. Emily, the heroine of the tale, early becomes familiar with sorrow, through the death of her parents; yet not before the reader is made acquainted with their characters and manners, and has accompanied them through a number of interesting circumstances, sufficient to dispose him to the exercise of tender sympathy. At the same time, her heart receives, by slow and imperceptible degrees, the soft impressions of love; and the reader is permitted, without the introduction of any dissonant feelings, to enjoy the luxury of observing the rise and progress of this passion, and of sympathising with the lovers in every diversity of sentiment, which an uncommon vicissitude of events could produce; till, at last, Emily is separated from her Valancourt, to experience a sad variety of woe. With the interesting narrative of this volume, are frequently interwoven descriptions of nature in the rich and beautiful country of the South of France, which are perfectly in unison with the story; at the same time that they display, in a favourable light, the writer's powers of fancy and of language, and afford no small addition to the reader's gratification. We should have great pleasure, would our limits permit, in giving to our readers some specimens of these descriptions.

Something of the marvellous is introduced in the first volume, sufficient to throw an interesting air of *mystery* over the story; and the reader feels the pleasing agitation of uncertainty concerning several circumstances, of which the writer has had the address not to give a glance of explanation till toward the close of the work. In the remaining volumes, however, her genius is employed to raise up forms which chill the soul with horror; and tales are told that are no less fitted to "quell each trembling heart with grateful terror," than those with which, "by night,

"The village matron round the blazing hearth
Suspends her infant audience."

Without introducing into her narrative any thing really supernatural, Mrs. Radcliffe has contrived to produce as powerful an effect as if the invisible world had been obedient to her magic spell; and the reader experiences in perfection the strange luxury of artificial terror, without being obliged for a moment to hoodwink his reason, or to yield to the weakness of superstitious credulity. We shall not forestall his pleasure by detailing the particulars: but we will not hesitate to say, in general, that, within the limits of nature and probability, a story so well contrived to hold curiosity in pleasing suspense, and at the same time to agitate the soul with strong emotions of sympathetic terror, has seldom been produced.

Another part of the merit of this novel must not be overlooked. The characters are drawn with uncommon distinctness, propriety, and boldness. Emily, the principal female character, being naturally possessed of delicate sensibility and warm affection, is early warned by her father against indulging the pride of fine feelings,—(the romantic error of amiable minds,)—and is taught that the strength of fortitude is more valuable than the grace of sensibility. Hence she acquires a habit of self command, which gives a mild dignity to her manners, and a steady firmness to her conduct. She is patient under authority, without tameness or cunning. Desirous, in the first place, of her own approbation, she is equally unaffected by the praise and the censure of fools. In love, she is tender and ardent without weakness, and constant notwithstanding every inducement, from interest or terror, to abandon the object of her affection. Good sense effectually fortifies her against superstitious fear; and a noble integrity and sublime piety support her in the midst of terrors and dangers. In the character and fortunes of Emily's aunt, Madame Cheron, to whom her sufferings are solely owing, is exhibited an example of the mischief which silly pride brings on itself and others. Dazzled with shew, she wants the sense both to discern merit and to detect imposture: supercilious in her condescension, and ostentatious in her pity, she inflicts cruel wounds without intention; she admires and despises by turns, and equally without reason: she neither bears injuries with meekness nor resents them with dignity; and her exasperated pride vents itself in feeble lamentation, and prevents her from using the necessary means for her safety, till at length it exposes her to cruel insults, and precipitates her destruction.—Montoni, her second husband, is an Italian of strong talents, but of an abandoned character and desperate fortune: he is unprincipled, dauntless, and enterprising; reserved through pride and discontent, deep craft conceals all his plans: wild and various in his passions, yet capable of making them all bend to his interest, he is the cause of cruel wretchedness and infinite terror to those who are under his power. Some gleams of comic humour play through the gloom of the story, in the character and conversation of the faithful servant Annette, who has an insuperable propensity to credulity, and an irresistible impulse to communication: but whose *naïveté*, simple honesty, and affection, render her character interesting. Several other portraits are drawn with equal strength; for which we must refer to the volumes.

The numerous mysteries of the plot are fully disclosed in the conclusion, and the reader is perfectly satisfied at finding villainy punished, and steady virtue and persevering affection rewarded. If there be any part of the story which lies open to material objection, it is that which makes Valancourt, Emily's lover, fall into disgraceful indiscretions during her absence, and into a temporary alienation of affection. This, in a young man of noble principles and exalted sentiments, after such a long intimacy, and such a series of incidents tending to give permanency to his passion and stability to his character, we must think *unnatural*. The performance would in our opinion have been more perfect, as well as more pleasing, if Du Pont, Emily's unsuccessful admirer, had never appeared; and if Valancourt had been, as Emily expected, her deliverer from the Castle of Udolpho. The story, we apprehend, might have been easily brought to its present termination on this supposition.

The embellishments of the work are highly finished. The descriptions are rich, glowing, and varied: they discover a vigorous imagination, and an uncommon command of language; and many of them would furnish admirable subjects for the

pencil of the painter. If the reader, in the eagerness of curiosity, should be tempted to pass over any of them for the sake of proceeding more rapidly with the story, he will do both himself and the author injustice. They recur, however, too frequently; and, consequently, a similarity of expression is often perceptible. Several of the pieces of poetry are elegant performances, but they would have appeared with more advantage as a separate publication.

Our readers may form some judgment of the writer's descriptive and poetical talents from the following specimen; the scene of which is at Venice:

'In the cool of the evening the party embarked in Montoni's gondola, and rowed out upon the sea. The red glow of sun-set still touched the waves, and lingered in the west, where the melancholy gleam seemed slowly expiring, while the dark blue of the upper æther began to twinkle with stars. Emily sat, given up to pensive and sweet emotions. The smoothness of the water, over which she glided, its reflected images—a new heaven and trembling stars below the waves, with shadowy outlines of towers and porticos, conspired with the stillness of the hour, interrupted only by the passing wave, or the notes of distant music, to raise those emotions to enthusiasm. As she listened to the measured sound of the oars, and to the remote warblings that came in the breeze, her softened mind returned to the memory of St. Aubert and to Valancourt, and tears stole to her eyes. The rays of the moon, strengthening as the shadows deepened, soon after threw a silvery gleam upon her countenance, which was partly shaded by a thin black veil, and touched it with inimitable softness. Hers was the *contour* of a Madona, with the sensibility of a Magdalen; and the pensive uplifted eye, with the tear that glittered on her cheek, confirmed the expression of the character.

'The last strain of distant music now died in air, for the gondola was far upon the waves, and the party determined to have music of their own. The Count Morano, who sat next to Emily, and who had been observing her for some time in silence, snatched up a lute, and struck the chords with the finger of harmony herself, while his voice, a fine tenor, accompanied them in a rondeau full of tender sadness. To him, indeed, might have been applied that beautiful exhortation of an English poet, had it then existed:

—"Strike up, my master,
But touch the strings with a religious softness!
Teach sounds to languish through the night's
    dull ear
Till Melancholy starts from off her couch,
And Carelessness grows concert to attention!"
With such powers of expression the Count sang
    the following

RONDEAU.

'Soft as yon silver ray, that sleeps
Upon the ocean's trembling tide;
Soft as the air, that lightly sweeps
Yon sail, that swells in stately pride;
'Soft as the surge's stealing note,
That dies along the distant shores,
Or warbled strain, that sinks remote—
So soft the sigh my bosom pours!
'True as the wave to Cynthia's ray,
True as the vessel to the breeze,
True as the soul to music's sway,
Or music to Venetian seas;
'Soft as yon silver beams that sleep
Upon the ocean's trembling breast;
So soft, so true, fond Love shall weep,
So soft, so true, with *thee* shall rest.'

After the remarks which we have already made, we need scarcely add our recommendation of these interesting volumes to general readers.

KENNETH W. GRAHAM (ESSAY DATE 1989)

SOURCE: Graham, Kenneth W. "Emily's Demon-Lover: The Gothic Revolution and *The Mysteries of Udolpho*." In *Gothic Fictions: Prohibition/Transgression*, edited by Kenneth W. Graham, pp. 163-71. New York: AMS Press, 1989.

In the following essay, Graham discusses the narrative pace of The Mysteries of Udolpho *and how it works to build suspense and evoke the revolutionary spirit of Gothic fiction in a storyline that contains very little actual action.*

In a metaphor that Ann Radcliffe probably and perhaps rightly would have found lacking in taste, Robert Scholes compares the act of fiction with the act of sex:

For what connects fiction . . . with sex is the fundamental orgastic rhythm of tumescence and detumescence, of tension and resolution, of intensification to the point of climax and consummation. In the sophisticated forms of fiction, as in the sophisticated practice of sex, much of the art consists of delaying climax within the framework of desire in order to prolong the pleasurable act itself.[1]

Although the quotation is taken from a discussion of John Fowles' *The Magus*, it shows a startling aptness to Mrs. Radcliffe's fictional method which is to draw out a situation longer than seems possible by delaying the climax. The amplitude of her accomplishment becomes apparent when one measures the majesty of the three to four bulky volumes that comprise each of her novels against the modest paragraph that could contain a just summary of her plot. That so much impends in Ann Radcliffe's fictions and so little happens is surely evidence of an astonishing degree of narrative sophistication.

It is precisely in the attenuation of threatening situations that Mrs. Radcliffe's chief success and chief fascination as a writer of Gothic romances lie. Her employment of suspense entraps her readers in a mounting rhythm of excitement and irresolution as terror succeeds terror, while the climax, a total and satisfying release from tension, is continually promised and continually postponed. Because the terrors themselves derive intensity from vague threatenings of moral dissolution, a sexual metaphor for the rhythm of tension and intermission seems an appropriate one. Thus her narrative method, approximating that described by Scholes, operates through delaying climax within a framework of both fear and desire.

That she employed such a method, and repeated it in most of her romances, suggests that Mrs. Radcliffe was addressing her narratives to a human psychology more complex than those of the reductionist theories current in eighteenth-century Britain from Locke's *tabula rasa*[2] to Hartley's materialist associationism. To direct, as I think she does, a significant overtone of her narratives at pre-rational levels of human consciousness is to commit something of a revolutionary act. While it may appear absurd (and, indeed, ill-bred) to argue an affinity between the refined Mrs. Radcliffe and the *sans-culottes* who stormed the Bastille, it is fruitful to consider the Marquis de Sade's observation that the Gothic novel was an inevitable result of the revolutionary shocks that all Europe was feeling during these revolutionary times.[3] For Sade, what links the Gothic novel to the revolution is its willingness to extend the boundaries that convention ascribes to the concept of human nature, its willingness to call for the aid of hell to present the whole truth of human depravity. Those impending calamities on which Mrs. Radcliffe's narratives focus such lingering attention are the product of an imagination prepared to acknowledge the diabolical. When Dr. Johnson dismissed the poems of Ossian with the declaration: "Sir, a man might write such stuff for ever, if he would *abandon* his mind to it,"[4] he was voicing a traditional ethical distrust of the unregulated imagination, a fear of the monsters the abandoned mind might spawn. Ann Radcliffe's are the novels of a respectable woman. They manifest an apparent capitulation to all the restraints, decorums and tyrannies of late eighteenth-century conventionalities in erotic and ethical matters. Yet she overcame many restrictions with subtle audacity: her narratives insinuate the dissolution of the very conventionalities they uphold. They continually anticipate perils, contemplate imminent assaults on the social order in the crimes of murder, incest and rape, and thus extend an imaginative validity to evil in its most vicious forms. To recall Dr. Johnson's warnings in *Rambler* No. 4 against the romance for its "wild strain of imagination," its heating the mind "with incredibilities," its creation of men "splendidly wicked" whose "resemblance ought no more to be preserved, than the art of murdering without pain,"[5] and to note how her romances return repeatedly to situations in which moral values seem threatened by splendidly wicked men is to perceive how wholeheartedly Ann Radcliffe had embraced a revolutionary aesthetic.

The Mysteries of Udolpho is vitally revolutionary in a manner that the marquis would approve and Dr. Johnson might well protest. The momentum of the account builds towards a situation rich in imaginative possibility that Mrs. Radcliffe hastens to establish and labours to prolong: the maiden is in perilous proximity to the villain in the castle and the hero is locked out. It is one of those situations that we have come to recognize as typically, even archetypally, Gothic. The castle, its centrality underlined in the very title of Mrs. Radcliffe's romance, is prison-like in its function of keeping people in and out. But it is more intricate than a prison or bastion: it is described as "a strange, rambling place."[6] Emily is "perplexed by the numerous turnings"; "she feared to open one of the many doors that offered"; she "began to fear that she might . . . lose herself in the intricacies of the castle" (I 262). Such passages show Radcliffe's Gothic castle to be a kind of labyrinth and a labyrinth is, of course, a place of peril and misdirection where a monster lurks and where the maiden may be held in bondage. Versions of the labyrinth that resound through Cretan legend, Sleeping Beauty's wall of thorns and Brünhilde's wall of fire point to contrasting interpretations: it is a place of sterility from which the hero's rescue of his bride betokens a return of fruitfulness to the wasteland, or it is a place of fearful virility in which the demon-lover has entrapped the enthralled maiden. In the Gothic novel the second emphasis predominates: the monster in the labyrinth is Manfred in his castle, looking to beget an heir to Otranto upon the frightened Isabella; it is Ambrosio in the catacombs, holding Antonia in thrall to his lust; and, of course, it is Montoni, whose ominous presence forms the forefront of Emily's anxious apprehensions. The allure of the Gothic situation lies chiefly in the vulnerability of the maiden to the dark designs and unpredictable violence of the Gothic villain.

The Montoni that emerges from Mrs. Radcliffe's narrative is a potentially-explosive force of obscure purposes who smoulders in the shadows of his castle like a monster in its labyrinth. She makes him alien to the novel's system of values. He is cruel, unresponsive to domesticity and indifferent to the picturesque, yet he is handsome: his eyes are somber and sparkling and his features "manly and expressive." Radcliffe underlines his sexual attractiveness with repeated references to his terrible energies, desperate temper and vigorous passion. Each turn of the page threatens to reveal a feudal noble of barely-bridled sensuality, *l'homme fatal*, the enslaver of woman, a perilously absorbing mixture of Don Juan and Bluebeard.

As is usual with Radcliffe, the illusion is more potent than the reality. Viewed objectively, Montoni's life forms a pattern of unfulfillment. He gambles in casinos but loses. He is ambitious to be a military leader but becomes only a robber captain, one whose capture is perfunctory when the narrative has no further use for him. Despite his displays of passion and energy, he lacks sexual drive. He marries Mme. Charon to obtain her money; yet he does not see through her pretensions of wealth, nor does he make sure of what fortune she has before he marries her. Since Mme. Charon has neither wit nor beauty with which to beguile him, his lack of judgment in these matters is astonishing. After marriage he grumbles, blusters and threatens in order to obtain her property. He does not succeed and after Mme. Charon's death he has to make Emily the target of blusterings and threatenings, with similar unsuccess. To sustain the role given him, Ann Radcliffe made Montoni surprisingly impotent.

When we seek the source of the lasting impression of Montoni as the smouldering, passionate demon-lover, we discover the figure to be almost wholly the creation of Emily, the chaste, pure maiden. At an early meeting "Emily felt admiration, but . . . it was mixed with a degree of fear she know not exactly wherefore" (I 23). When through marriage Montoni becomes head of her family, Emily watches him eagerly, trying to fathom from his gloomy features the thoughts concealed beneath. "Emily observed these written characters of his thought with deep interest and not without some degree of awe, when she considered that she was entirely in his power" (I 195). We might assume this last reflection to be accompanied by a *frisson* of anxious apprehension. Emily's mind dwells on Montoni, creates of him a figure of Burkean sublimity that both attracts and repels her. He frightens and fascinates her because he undermines her notions of patriarchy and domesticity. Her father had been a man of feeling; Montoni is a man of action and cruelty. His "stern manners" contrast with "the tenderness and affection to which she had been accustomed till she lost her parents" (I 239). He disorients her and threatens her conditionings. Domesticity and filial affection become disturbingly intermingled in her mind with vague shadowings of slavery and incest. She is agitated by his presence: ". . . Montoni is coming himself to seek me! In the present state of his mind, his purpose must be desperate" (II 100). Montoni represents a vital disorder foreign to Emily's values and she exaggerates his power and makes of him an erotic fantasy based on terror.[7] Consciously Emily fears and deplores Montoni, yet his presence lingers in her mind as if her spirit is reaching out after him, longing for the unspeakable fulfillment that he represents.

Emily's irrational attraction to Montoni reflects one facet of Mrs. Radcliffe's awareness of the potency of that central Gothic situation that brings together maiden, villain and castle over which her narrative lingers with such unconscionable sophistication. As Mrs. Radcliffe seems to have been aware, the ambivalence of Emily's love-hate attitude to her demon-lover reflects the ambivalence of her century towards the unregulated imagination. Mrs. Radcliffe may have held the belief with Dr. Johnson that "he that thinks reasonably must think morally"[8] but her works manifest a stronger interest in the statement's corollary about the irrational and the immoral. In the inclination of her narratives to contemplate human kinship with mystery and human fascination with evil, Mrs. Radcliffe seems to reveal an attitude that has more in common with the Marquis de Sade than with Dr. Johnson. Sade's own attraction to the Gothic novel is connected to a similar willingness to suspend ethical concerns in order to contemplate the perils of the maiden perplexed in a Gothic labyrinth where each turning may carry her into the clutches of the monster. Such willingness means for Sade a shadowing forth of his own revolutionary credo that the unnatural is natural. What is revolutionary about the Gothic novel in general and **The Mysteries of Udolpho** in particular is an assumed license to contemplate levels of human thought and behaviour hitherto almost ignored in literature of the eighteenth century. In Emily's disconcerted mind are opposed versions of reality. One is a comforting world of pastoral domesticity and sensibility centered on two almost interchangeable male figures, her father St. Aubert and her lover Valancourt. They inhabit the providential and ordered world that begins the novel

On the pleasant banks of the Garonne . . . stood . . . that chateau of Monsieur St. Aubert. From its windows were seen the pastoral landscapes of Guienne and Gascony, stretching along the river, gay with luxuriant woods and vines, and plantations of olives.

(I 1)

and ends it:

Oh! how joyful it is to tell of happiness such as that of Valancourt and Emily; to relate that . . . they were at length restored to each other—to the beloved landscape of their native country—to the securest felicity of this life . . . while the bowers of La Vallée became once more the retreat of goodness, wisdom, and domestic blessedness!

(II, 344)

The other world flourishes in the secret inner spaces of Emily's nervous apprehensions; it is the disordered and labyrinthine world of barely-controlled passion and energy centred on the male figure of Montoni. The demonic world looms in the body of the narative. Ann Radcliffe is careful to emphasize that this world is an aberration, yet her narrative lingers there. Her imagination abides unjustifiably long in conditions of ambivalence, where, at least aesthetically, the rational is not superior to the irrational, the moral to the immoral, the providential to the demonic. When considering the Gothic in a revolutionary perspective, it is easy to underestimate Ann Radcliffe's achievement. Compared to the projections of fragmented psychologies in Godwin's *Caleb Williams* and the audacious portrayals of living evil in works of Beckford and Lewis, Radcliffe's hintings and suggestings may appear unduly hesitant. In the tension between conventional sanctities and the desire to transgress limits, the sanctities are explicitly dominant and the woman wailing for her demon lover remains well beneath the levels of Emily's consciousness. That woman's existence is never acknowledged yet her presence is felt as Emily is haunted by apprehensions both supernatural and sexual. Ann Radcliffe's art lies in the careful balancing of the explicit and the implicit that permits her to be revolutionary without ceasing to be conventional. Triumphantly, her art leaves the unspeakable unspoken.

Notes

1. Robert Scholes, "The Orgastic Fiction of John Fowles". *The Hollins Critic*, VI, 5 (December, 1969), 1.

2. Indeed, Locke's *tabula rasa* theory, by cutting man off from his unconscious, gave impetus to a general rejection of the total psyche in eighteenth-century psychological theory.

3. ". . . il devenait le fruit indispensable des secousses révolutionnaires dont l'Europe entière se ressentait." Marquis de Sade, "Idée sur les Romans" in *Les Crimes de L'Amour, Oevres Complètes,* vol. 10 (Paris: Au Cercle du Livre Précieux, 1966), p. 15.

4. *Boswell's Life of Johnson,* ed. George Birkbeck Hill, 6 vols. (New York: Harper & Brothers, n.d.), IV, 211.

5. Samuel Johnson, *The Rambler,* No. 4 in *Selected Writings,* ed. R.T. Davies (Evanston: Northwestern University Press, 1965), 76-79.

6. Ann Radcliffe, *The Mysteries of Udolpho,* 2 vols. (London: J.M. Dent, 1931; rpt. 1962), I, 234. Subsequent citations from the novel will be taken from this edition and page references enclosed within parentheses and inserted in the text.

7. Edmund Burke, *A Philosophical Enquiry into the Origin of Our Ideas on the Sublime and Beautiful,* ed. J.T. Boulton (Notre Dame: University of Notre Dame Press, 1968), pp. 86, 65.

8. Samuel Johnson, "Preface to Shakespeare," *Johnson on Shakespeare,* ed. Arthur Sherbo (New Haven: Yale University Press, 1968), vol VII of the Yale Edition of the Works of Samuel Johnson, p. 71.

ANNE WILLIAMS (ESSAY DATE 1995)

SOURCE: Williams, Anne. "The Eighteenth-Century Psyche: *The Mysteries of Udolpho.*" In *Art of Darkness: A Poetics of Gothic,* pp. 159-72. Chicago: University of Chicago Press, 1995.

In the following essay, Williams argues that in The Mysteries of Udolpho *"Radcliffe's romance conventions, which generate the Female Gothic tradition, embody the myth of Psyche and an alternative to Oedipus."*

"O! do not go in there, ma'amselle," said Annette, "you will only lose yourself further."

"Bring the light forward," said Emily, "we may possibly find our way through these rooms."

Annette stood at the door, in an attitude of hesitation, with the light held up to show the chamber, but the feeble rays spread through not half of it. "Why do you hesitate?" said Emily, "let me see whither this room leads."

The Mysteries of Udolpho (p. 232)

This exchange occurs early in Emily's sojourn at Udolpho. Like Psyche exposed upon the rock, Emily, an orphan and a dependent, must go with her aunt, now married to Montoni, to his mysterious castle in the Apennines. Her servant Annette, credulous and fanciful, plays the role of Psyche's sisters, feeding her mind with imaginary fears. But unlike them, Annette discourages the transgression of boundaries. For the moment, she persuades Emily to seek the relative safety of her chamber: a room with a door that may be locked from the outside, but not from within. A few pages later, however, Emily will again take her lamp, again seek out the mysterious chamber, and finally lift the infamous black veil.

If Emily embodies an eighteenth-century version of Psyche, however, this paradigmatic Female Gothic heroine is also, momentarily, barely distinguishable from Bluebeard's wife. Driven by curiosity, each chooses to gaze upon the forbidden. Each confronts the heart of patriarchal darkness. But as Radcliffe's own distinction between "horror" and "terror" suggests, there is a difference between a dead body, such as the wife finds, and the waxwork representation of a corpse, however "realistic." Furthermore, the wife violates an explicit, a conscious, rule laid down by her husband, whereas Emily's explorations of her culture's implicit rules constitute a "feminine" rather than a "masculine" mode of subversion: a desire to comprehend the other rather than to mount an implacable rebellion against it. And in contrast to the experience of the fairy-tale heroine, Emily's curiousity discloses a "reality" that is shocking only at first sight. When she takes the lamp and enters the shadowy chamber, she is enacting a process of "enlightenment" that may remind us of Keats's figure for life itself: "a mansion of many apartments." The wife's experience, like the tale of Bluebeard, implies that the human psyche is regulated by an order of the forbidden and the permitted. Such a self is Oedipal, following the pattern described by Freud; it is grounded on a forbidden "other." The *other* psyche, however, resembles the mythical Psyche as we have seen her: a self that is a "precipitate of lost ego-cathexes," built up, like sandstone, from the slow layering of accumulated perceptions. The patriarchal imagination conceives of Bluebeard's wife as the embodiment of a categorically "female" curiosity; Emily St. Aubert is more complex. Though, like all Female Gothic heroines, she sometimes feels compelled to explore dark corridors, and sometimes discovers frightening secrets, she is a part of *all* that she has felt, not only curiosity but love and fear, the sublime and the beautiful. In some sense, Emily's psyche is coextensive with the world of her perceptions.

Thus the Female Gothic narrative confirms Anne Mellor's observation that "feminine" Romanticism explores the possibilities of female Reason.[1] I shall argue that Radcliffe's romance conventions, which generate the Female Gothic tradition, embody the myth of Psyche and an alternative to Oedipus. I do not mean to suggest that Ann Radcliffe or any other producer of Female Gothic deliberately imitated the Psyche myth. Nothing so simple. Anna Barbauld, in her "Prefaces, Biographical and Critical" to her edition of British novelists, did mention the tale of Psyche among the antecedents of the modern romance.[2] Certainly, the mass-market female formula of the 1960s imitated a set of conventions in place with the publication of *Jane Eyre,* which was undoubtedly a conscious model for many of these authors.[3] *Jane Eyre* itself bears more than a passing resemblance to the myth of Psyche (as does *Wuthering Heights*).[4] But it is really far more interesting—and more appropriate, given the implications of the myth—that there should not have been any direct influence in the usual sense. Perhaps this tradition of authorial mothers and daughters even implies an alternative to Bloom's Oedipal theory of literary influence: a model not founded on conflict but on accretion.

Julian Jaynes speculates that the appearance of writing as a cultural force was directly related to the birth of consciousness as we know it. This consciousness—although Jaynes does not make the connection—is patriarchal consciousness, preoccupied with law, authority, hierarchy, and intent upon organizing the world according to these principles.[5] We have examined some of the relations between Gothic conventions and the disruptions of the patriarchal Symbolic hypothesized as *l'écriture féminine.* Why should such female revisions not extend to the plot as well? As Robert May argues in *Sex and Fantasy* (1980), clinical evidence suggests that the characteristic structure of fantasies may be related to gender; he discovered in his subjects the male's tendency to the (tragic) pattern of "Pride" while female fantasies follow the (comic) pattern of "Caring."[6]

The possible relation of Psyche and *soma* is outside the scope of this book.[7] Given the presence of the Female Gothic plot, however, I would speculate that when "the middle-class woman began to write" for a female audience that as consumers had power to encourage certain narratives, the Psyche plot—the story of the female self making her way in an essentially patriarchal social order—reemerged. This story admits (in both senses of the word) the power of the female and the maternal. It shows such a self growing up in a world organized by the same basic assumptions about male and female that control the world of Oedipus, but such knowledge would derive from a

daughter's experience. Psyche and Emily St. Aubert share similar weak (though *not* helpless) positions in a world where cultural authority belongs to the male. A genuinely new paradigm of human development could occur only in a conceptual universe where the mother was not associated exclusively with nature/matter, and the father with culture/spirit, or where "male" and "female" were not basic categories; but such a world is purely hypothetical, though explored in the realm of a daughter of Gothic, "science fiction."[8] But it is not coincidental that this Gothic heroine's plot turns out to create a new discourse of the *human* psyche as well, for it posits a new relation of matter and spirit, of the mind to the mother.

If those Female Gothic heroines born in the eighteenth century are all versions of Psyche, they are a distinctly "post-Enlightenment" edition. In view of M. H. Abrams's thesis about the difference between the neoclassical and Romantic theories of art (the mirror and the lamp), it is appropriate that this heroine should reappear toward the end of the eighteenth century. *The Mysteries of Udolpho*—Radcliffe's most female-centered Female Gothic—is extraordinarily attentive to the "female" dimensions of experience and extraordinarily concerned with "reality." If we read it as a version of Psyche, we may begin to understand the function of several of Radcliffe's idiosyncratic conventions: her super-sensitive heroine so inclined to poetry, song, and sketching, her leisurely narrative pace, her ceaseless attention to natural description, and her insistence on explaining the ghosts. And as the "lamp stage" of feminine fiction, Radcliffe is closer to the myth's version of the male "other" than are the post-Brontë fusion of hero and villain.

The Mysteries of Udolpho is long—672 pages in the Oxford World Classics edition. The heroine Emily loses both her parents early: her mother dies at the end of chapter 1, her father dies in chapter 7. Before his untimely death, however, St. Aubert voices his approval of a very attractive young man named Valancourt. But Emily goes to live with her vulgar and ostentatious aunt and now guardian, Madame Cheron, a widow who disapproves of Valancourt. So Emily and Valancourt are separated. Madame Cheron remarries, and her husband, the mysterious Italian Montoni, takes the two of them to Udolpho, his ruined fortress in the Apennines. There Montoni tries to force her marriage to Count Morano and tricks Emily into signing a paper that will give him control of her property. He also separates her from her aunt, causing Emily to fear that he has murdered her. In exploring the castle Emily discovers all kinds of threatening, frightening, and unintelligible clues which lead her to much terrified speculation about the fate of Laurentini di Udolpho, a mysterious woman who had once lived here. She hears strange music several times. She learns that a young man is imprisoned in the castle, a youth whom she increasingly expects to be Valancourt, but when they finally meet, she discovers that he is a man named Du Pont. Eventually her aunt dies, and Emily manages to escape with her maid Annette and her betrothed.

The party make their way back to the South of France, to Château-le-Blanc, where they are welcomed by the de Villefort family (who have inherited it from Emily's uncle by marriage, the Marquis de Villeroi). The Château has a secret chamber that is reputedly haunted, but the mysterious noises in the secret room turn out to be caused by the operation of pirates. Meanwhile Emily hears that Valancourt has pursued a disgraceful career in Paris, gambling and becoming involved with a "well-known Parisian Countess."[9] Emily is forced to confront the reality that the Valancourt who returns to her "is not the Valancourt I have been accustomed to love" (p. 516). He is "ruined," financially and morally, but feels intense remorse and confesses his shortcomings to Emily. Du Pont proposes to her, but she refuses. Temporarily withdrawing to the neighboring convent, she learns the story of "Sister Agnes"—who turns out to be Laurentini di Udolpho, who had been in love with the Marquis de Villeroi and thus murdered his wife, Emily's aunt (her father's other sister). She had yielded to her passions and ruined her own and many other lives. Eventually, all the mysteries are solved. Emily is reconciled with Valancourt, who has turned away from his wild career. Because his family is pleased with the marriage, they give the couple considerable property. Emily also inherits Udolpho, but gives it away, and they live happily ever after in Emily's childhood home of La Vallée.

This narrative has the same structure as the Psyche myth. Emily is Psyche, alone in the world, who early meets and then is separated from her beloved. There are two Valancourts, just as there are two Eroses, a "before" and "after," for each is missing from the middle of the story and reappears having been transformed by a process of experience apart from the heroine. This "other" is no sooner recognized by the heroine as lovable than he disappears. Like Psyche, Emily is impelled forward by forces beyond her control; her trials involve confronting the demands of cruel circumstances both natural and cultural. In the course of the action, Emily is separated from her parents, her home, her country, and her suitor Valancourt. Even when she is reunited with him, she must struggle with the fear that he has been corrupted by the wickedness of Paris, transformed into another Valancourt than the one she had loved. In the darkness of Udolpho she is even separated from herself, by being made to doubt her own reason, and in moments of crisis, by losing consciousness altogether. (Emily faints ten times during the course of the narrative.)

Radcliffe's version both depersonifies some aspects of the myth and psychologizes others. The female principle is personified in the tale of Psyche as Aphrodite, who represents the individual mother, Mother Nature, and all that is associated with the culturally female, including irrational passions such as jealousy and anger. In *Udolpho*, the dangers of the female are split into various aspects of Emily's experience: into natural dangers such as storms and perilous mountains; into human mortality; into embodiments of disruptive passion such as Laurentini di Udolpho, who murders her lover's wife and then goes mad; and into Emily's own tendency to collapse into excessive "sensibility," which Radcliffe explicitly defines as a kind of pride and hence a temptation. As her father warns her on his deathbed, "Do not indulge in the pride of fine feeling, the romantic error of amiable minds":

> Those, who really possess sensibility, ought early to be taught, that it is a dangerous quality, which is continually extracting the excess of misery, or delight, from every surrounding cirmcumstance. And, since, in our passage through this world, painful circumstances occur more frequently than pleasing ones, and since our sense of evil is, I fear, more acute than our sense of good, we become the victims of our feelings, unless we can in some degree command them.
>
> (pp. 79-80)

According to St. Aubert, "Happiness arises in a state of peace, not of tumult" (p. 80). But before Emily finally sees "the prospect of rational happiness" (p. 672), she must experience again and again and again that regulating or tempering of the sensibility that her father warned her about. Psychologically, Emily's task is to escape the *dangers* of sensibility, of feeling that threatens to engulf or overwhelm the mind, just as the dungeons and dark rooms of Udolpho threaten to swallow her up. The conventions of Female Gothic, like those of the male tradition, express a point of view about reality that derives from its assumptions about "the female." I would argue that "rational happiness" is possible for the heroine within this world precisely because that coming to terms with the "female" (including nature, unbearable sensibility, madness) which is the process of self-formation *is* a process rather than an abrupt event or conquest. Emily's happy marriage to Valancourt, which brings with it wealth and a return to the happy home of her childhood, is that "access," the place within the Symbolic that the myth figures as Psyche's access to Olympus.

What Emily bears within her during her journey of trials are the principles inculcated by her father's education, the seeds of "rational happiness." If Emily has a task analogous to Psyche's of sorting the seeds, it is her repeated need to distinguish the real from the imaginary, to see the truth behind the various ambiguous signals of nature and imagination. Like Psyche as well, Emily

Frontispieces from the four volumes of the 1799 edition of *The Mysteries of Udolpho.*

is placed in situations that seem to be literally a matter of life and death. Her adventures provide her with a metaphorical exploration of the nature and culture around her, by constantly threatening her survival in each realm. Sometimes she fears for her life, the end of her existence in nature. And she fears the loss of her chastity (the "fate *worse* than death"), which would be equally fatal to her social identity.

For this Enlightenment Psyche is implicitly in quest of "reason."[10] Not only is reason an ideal taught Emily by her father and an explicit theme in the novel; "reason" is overdetermined throughout its structure and conventions. Like the myth of Psyche, Radcliffe's Female Gothic turns upon the relation between apprehension as "fear" and apprehension as "learning." According to the *OED,* "reason" is derived from the Latin word meaning "to think, to reckon." It is "a fact or circumstance forming, or alleged to form, a ground or motive leading, or sufficient to lead, a person to reject or adopt some course of action, procedure, belief." All of these appear in some dimension of Radcliffe's Female Gothic formula, where the plot enacts the transformation of apprehension from fear into learning, of anxiety about the unknown into a recognition of realities.

The first of these modes of reason, the power to distinguish real from apparent—appears in Emily's continuing need to make valid discriminations, to "realize" the validity of her perceptions, a theme reminiscent of Psyche's first task. The two realms of nature and culture that the heroine explores are confusing and ambiguous. In the shadowy Gothic world, things are frequently not as they seem. Both nature, represented by the landscape, and culture, represented by the castle, have dual aspects. Nature may be sublime or beautiful, nurturing or destructive. Emily's sensitivity to natural scenery (which remains part of the Gothic formula) is thus a function of literary theme as well as a familiar symptom of eighteenth-century taste. The howling storm may intensify the heroine's terrors, or nature may afford peace: "The deep repose of the scene . . . soothed and gradually elevated [Emily's] mind to that sublime complacency, which renders the vexations of this world so insignificant and mean in our eyes" (p. 114). This sensitivity to nature also contributes to the plot, since it makes the heroine especially vulnerable; she is, in a sense, the ideal Wordsworthian reader, who "builds up greatest things / From least suggestions," who "need[s] not extraordinary calls to rouse [her]" (*The Prelude* 14:101-2, 103-4).

But in contrast to the traditional male heroic narrative, Radcliffe's plot confronts the heroine with a universe where one must not only *know* good from bad, but must also learn to perceive the often ambiguous distinctions between them— and further to perceive that one's survival and salvation depends upon *not* depending upon appearances. (Radcliffe's mode of suspense as a dramatization of this principle could be an essay in itself.) Thus it also follows that the natural location of any particular house in Female Gothic narrative signifies its suitability for comic resolution. Emily's childhood home to which she returns with Valancourt is situated in a beautiful landscape and is named "La Vallée" (which may remind us of Dr. Johnson's Edenic happy valley in *Rasselas*). Udolpho, hostile and brooding, was built in the midst of mountains. It is thematically appropriate that after Emily has escaped Udolpho and learned most of its secrets, she inherits the castle and then gives it away, for it is "foreign" to her in more ways than one.

In **Udolpho**, as in subsequent Female Gothic plots, the heroine's problem of distinguishing the good from the bad is most crucially centered in her relationship with the male "other." In describing the Female Gothic plot, I have treated the hero who emerged in Brontë's *Jane Eyre* as the norm: the ambiguously threatening and attractive Mr. Rochester whose "kindliness" becomes apparent only at the end of the story, an aspect of its resolution. For psychological reasons, this convention is undoubtedly potent, and is indeed, true to its mythic origins. But in Radcliffe—as in Emily Brontë—the "hero" and the "villain" appear as separate characters, for in some versions of Female Gothic, the Beast and Prince Charming need not occupy the same body.[11] In part 1 [of *The Art of Darkness*] I suggested that the romance mode represents the highly "poetic" realm on the border of the Symbolic, and that its conventions frequently expose the relation of cognition and *rec*ognition. Thus romance characters may intimate expressions of the pre-Symbolic, and thus by definition the "unreal." Psychoanalysts have long contended that the preponderance of Wicked Stepmothers in folktales manifests the infant's experience of "good" and "bad" mother, the one who gratifies her wishes and the one who does not. As Bettelheim points out, this Wicked Stepmother is frequently associated with food; she may, as in "Snow White," offer poisoned food, or food may simply be lacking, as in "Hansel and Gretel." *Really* Wicked Stepmothers are cannibals, like the witch in the latter story.[12]

A Gingerbread House inhabited by a hungry witch might be seen as the infantile, food-centered version of that omnipresent archetype of the male imagination: the *femme fatale,* whose superficial sexual allure also shelters danger and death. Praz's term, the *homme fatal,* coined to account for the Byronic hero and the Gothic villain, is a simple reversal of the female archetype. These characters, like their female counterpart, primarily address "natural" threats to the human psyche, the affinity of sex and death. I have suggested, however, that the male "other" in Female Gothic represents both nature *and* culture to the female self always already defined as "other" by that culture.

As we have seen in Male Gothic, the symptoms of "natural" otherness tend to be "abject" in Kristeva's sense; the gross materiality of blood, corpses, decay. But abjection also has its moral dimension. Kristeva aligns the abject with "what does not respect borders, position, rules," including such characters as "the traitor, the liar, the criminal with a good conscience" (*Powers*, p. 4). Thus in either Gothic tradition, hero/villains tend to be outcasts, priests who have broken their vows to God, bandits, pirates, and outlaws of every kind. From this perspective, Satan is the archetype of the abject, being cast down from heaven into hell, a realm created to manifest his moral condition. Furthermore, according to the logic of the Symbolic, his otherworld is figured by the "feminine"; Milton's hell, that "universe of death," concretely embodies "the line of evil." And Satan himself is "feminized" by his fall, carrying with him "signs of remorse and passion" for his fellow fallen angels, feelings which fuel his continuing desire to subvert the Law of the Father.

But in the looking-glass world of Female Gothic, the culturally feminine, the "natural" may not be so neatly categorized as "other" and "evil." *Some* aspects of "the feminine" are felt as good; the mother-child relation, what May calls "the pattern of caring," is nonhierarchical, which is not to say that the two parties involved in a particular relationship have equal power; Demeter as mother/goddess has more power than Persephone; Eros as a god has inherently more power than the human Psyche; and so on. What is striking, however, is that this power is used not to control and to punish, but to succor and to protect.

By the time Radcliffe began to publish in the 1790s, the "man of feeling" was a familiar character in popular fiction. Though one might tend to assume that in terms of gender codes he is a "feminized male," it is more useful to seem him as a "masculinized female": that is, a projection of female definitions of the self into the realm of masculine endeavor. This hero is attractive (and reassuring) because he shares feminine ways of seeing the world. The heroine is reassured that he will be a good husband because he is of her "kind." The marker of such a character in Radcliffe (as in other writers of the time) is taste and sensitivity to nature. M. St. Aubert is saddened to see his status-conscious brother-in-law cut down the old elms that spoil the vista (according to certain preconceived notions of the picturesque). Valancourt is a reader of poetry and connoisseur of the sublime. Montoni, of course, is not.

And yet, merely by virtue of being male, any male, however sensitive, has access to a kind of power and identity that the female does not. In the myth of Psyche, this power is figured as "divinity," supernatural and immortal. In Radcliffe's "low mimetic" mode, power is represented by economic and social status: bourgeois aspect of *jouissance*. "Abject" others like Montoni or Ambrosio characteristically manipulate the heroine as "object"—of their lust, greed, or desire for power.

Heroes of "affect," like Valancourt—or Eros—may also cause her suffering. But rather than trying to control her, they cause suffering by their own absence, a separation adumbrating that between the heroine and the maternal principle. And furthermore, this hero may, like Valancourt, be troubling to the heroine by seeming to have traded in his "affection" for "abjection"—to have become a manipulator. (Hence the function of gambling, Montoni's favorite vice, and one that Valancourt takes up during his sojourn in Paris.) Each male type also has his characteristic mystery. The abject hero has Bluebeard-like secrets hidden in his house. (Montoni's vaguely adumbrated "business" has to do with political, military, and monetary schemes: hence his desire to control Emily and her fortune.) Emily's father, a hero of affect, hides the mysterious portrait of "a lady not [Emily's] mother." Valancourt's "sins" are also sins of affection: his liaison with the Parisian *comtesse*.[13]

The suitor/antagonist functions may be divided into different characters, but the characteristic ambivalence remains evident in their names. Emily's suitor and eventual husband is M. de la Valancourt (we never learn his first name). The first part sounds like the name of her home "La Vallée," while the second, "court," suggests both public and legal aspects of experience. In fact, in volume 1, as Mme Cheron is scolding Emily for her interest in Valancourt, she makes a "Freudian slip" that points to just such an identity:

> I did not think you capable of so much duplicity, niece; when you pleaded this excuse for remaining here, I foolishly believed it to be a just one, nor expected to have found with you so agreeable a companion as this M. de la Val———, I forget his name.
>
> (p. 110)

"Montoni," the Italian villain, has a name that suggests "mountains" in his own language. Emily's second suitor is most appropriately named "Du Pont," for he bridges the gap between mountain and valley for Emily. In proposing marriage he both reassures her that Valancourt is not unique in finding her lovable and provides information exonerating Valancourt, thus clearing the way for the happy conclusion. Like all Female Gothic heroes—though less dramatically than later ones— Valancourt undergoes a transformation in the eyes of the heroine. Before he and Emily can live happily ever after, she must see that he is not the *roué* corrupted by Paris—a kind of cultural beast—but rather the ideal husband.

The night before Emily departs unwillingly but dutifully for the distant castle of Udolpho, she sleeps badly. Radcliffe writes, "Her unquiet mind had, during the night, presented her with *terrific images* and *obscure circumstances* concerning her affection and her future life" (p. 161; my emphasis). This statement occurs in chapter 1 of volume 2, the part of the novel that explores Udolpho, a place of "real" terror and "actual" darkness (though for the reader they offer *virtual* terror and darkness). The subsequent narrative "realizes" her nightmare; that is, the imagined is experienced in literal, concrete terms.[14]

Emily's trials test the principles of her education. Much of the suspense involves her uncertainty as to whether "first impressions" *can* be trusted, and this suspense is resolved when she learns, again and again, that they are *not* reliable. The music she hears at midnight *seems* to be of ghostly origin; the track of blood on the stairs of Udolpho *seems* to say that her aunt has been murdered; the terrible object behind the black veil *seems* to be a worm-eaten corpse. But none of these fearful impressions turns out to be accurate.

Since Emily's experiences affirm the value of reason, it is appropriate that her antagonists personify unreasonable passion. Montoni embodies pride and greed and power arbitrarily used. Laurentini di Udolpho, Radcliffe explicitly tells us, was *not* taught by a loving father to "strengthen her mind." She is to Emily as the demented Bertha Mason is to Jane Eyre, a dark double representing all that the heroine must reject—passion, madness, violence, extremity in everything. After having jealously poisoned her lover's wife, Laurentini becomes a nun, literally veiling or repressing passionate propensities—an alternative which Radcliffe rejects as an unacceptable alternative to "the real world." She is also implicitly rejecting her culture's definition of "the female," and not merely in being a "good girl" who conforms to patriarchal standards of proper behavior. She is not rewarded for being rational; instead, her reward is a direct result of her rationality.

Thus like Psyche's tasks which confront her with increasingly complex and difficult tests, *Udolpho* places Emily in a series of increasingly threatening situations. Early on, she faces slight mysteries such as the matter of the sonnet in the fishing house; later she experiences the far greater mysteries of Udolpho; the last test is the problem of Valancourt: dare she follow her heart and trust herself to this man she once loved? Through the series of tasks and tests, however, Emily like Psyche finally perceives an orderly world—one

that is "sensible," both because one may trust the senses to give accurate information about it and because it "makes sense." It is then thematically necessary that the ghosts always have a rational explanation.

Another sense of "reason" is equally manifest in the female plot: reason as "cause." The Female Gothic exemplifies (to a degree *creates*) what would later be called a "mystery" plot; it is propelled by our—and Emily's—desire to learn certain secrets. Emily does not know who left the sonnets in the fishing house; she does not know why her father wept over the portrait of the beautiful lady not her mother. She does not know why Montoni has chosen to imprison her in Udolpho or what he plans for her next. At the same time her anxiety is intensified by the problem of reading the signs correctly. Upon his deathbed her father requests that she retrieve some papers from a secret hiding place and burn them unread. Ever the dutiful daughter, Emily follows his instructions. But as she is about to burn them, "her eyes involuntarily settled on the writing of some loose sheets, which lay open; and she was unconscious that she was transgressing her father strict injunction, till a sentence of dreadful import awakened her attention and her memory altogether" (p. 103).

In short, the various forms of "reason" constitute an informing principle of the Female Gothic plot, even as they construct this faculty as one threatened by its "other"—dark passions, madness. Both the shape of the narrative and the nature of the characters are manifestations or transformations of the familiar meanings of the term: reason as motive, reason as power to discriminate real from imaginary, reason as sanity.

This overdetermination of "reason" in the female plot is perhaps surprising because Western culture has generally insisted that "reason" is not a feminine strength. During the Enlightenment, the age-old debate about what it was, exactly, that women *lacked,* focused on their supposed incapacity for this "highest" and most definitive human capacity.[15] But whereas patriarchal philosophy has often tended to conceive of "reason" as a metaphysical or transcendent entity, and thus removed from the "female" and material, the eighteenth-century Psyche tends to replace it in the "real world," a principle "realized" in the human experience and evident in conscious experience. Mellor's *Romanticism and Gender* documents the appearance of "female reason" in many different forms in the late eighteenth century. Though it may seem ironic that women were claiming "reason" for themselves in their writing as the male Romantics were discovering "feeling" in theirs, the Lacanian view of the Symbolic offers insight into this paradox. The user of language by definition gains access to the Symbolic, the Law of the Father. Perhaps the sheer novelty of the terrain would account for this feminine exploration of Reason's possibilities, even as the male writer would be turning to the other possibilities of an *écriture féminine*. But further, this empirical version of "reason" and the "other" against which it is defined roughly corresponds to what Freud would call "consciousness" a century later.

The plot of **Udolpho** (and the Female Gothic plot in general) is a narrative of disclosure and reparation: the fiction of "psychoanalysis." Like that of the Freudian analysand, the heroine's "hysterical misery" may be alleviated by exploring the dark corridors, opening the closed doors, lifting the black veil. She experiences the weight of the past as a reality that may be escaped only when its secrets are brought to light through this process of discovering connections between past and present, herself and others. This accounts in part for the great emphasis the Gothic plot places on the importance of the family tree. A diagram of Emily's family ties, or of Jane Eyre's, or of the Lintons and the Earnshaws in *Wuthering Heights* graphically illustrates the intricacy—yet the inevitability—of the sometimes apparently coincidental *denouement*. Thus family ties, like the heroine's aesthetic sensitivity, her spiritual affinity for landscape and for the feelings of others, her characteristic intuitiveness, manifest the theme as well as serving the plot.[16] The prevalence of coincidence and accident in the tradition, no mere awkward plotting, is a thematic assertion that human experience creates a web of intricate connections, partly known, partly hidden (though no less powerful). The past impinges upon the present in the form of family history, and happiness is possible only when those hidden ties are brought to light. In Radcliffe, the past functions in the narrative as the unconscious affects the ego, according to Freud. But the Female Gothic asserts that happiness is possible. As Radcliffe exclaims at the end of **Udolpho**: "O! . . . though the vicious can sometimes pour affliction upon the good, their power is transient and their punishment certain; and . . . innocence, though oppressed by injustice, shall, supported by patience, finally triumph over misfortune!" (p. 672). This is a summary of the Psyche plot and of the Female Plot of Gothic Fiction.

The implications of Female Gothic are as revolutionary as any Woolf discerned when "the middle-class woman began to write" during the eighteenth century. It claims "reason" for the female, it affirms the reality principle, and it claims that a young woman should not marry a man who does not offer her the prospect of "rational happiness." The Female Gothic plot validates the perspective of what Foucault calls "the deployment of sexuality"; although the heroine may be trapped within the ancient structures of the Oedipal complex, the walls built in "the deployment of alliance," she escapes them. And they were partly ruined anyway.

Ironically, it is "Male Gothic" that has usually been associated by critics with "revolution." The Marquis de Sade saw *The Monk* as a direct expression of the turmoil incited by the French Revolution; and as a whole, certainly, the Male Gothic's eroticized obsession with transgression, with violating taboos, might on the surface seem "revolutionary." But as Stephen King astutely remarks in *Danse Macabre*, his treatise on horror fiction, "The writer of horror fiction is neither more nor less than an agent of the status quo" (p. 51). In trying to define the appeal of monstrosity, he suggests that "it is a reaffimation of the order which we all crave as human beings. . . . It is not the physical or mental aberration in itself which horrifies us, but rather the lack of order which these aberrations seem to imply" (p. 50). Exactly. But I would point out that as is so often true, that category "we as human beings" in fact represents only the masculine gender.

A "revolution" does not merely cross forbidden boundaries; etymologically the word means to "turn around." If we remember this meaning, Female Gothic is the more revolutionary of the two traditions. In writing as "other" it does not simply break the rules, it creates a new game with different rules altogether.

Notes

1. Anne Mellor, *Romanticism and Gender* (New York: Routledge, 1993), especially pp. 40-64.

2. "The pastoral romance of Longus is also extant in the Greek language. It is esteemed elegant, but it would be impossible to chastise it into decency. The Latins, who had less invention, had no writings of this kind, except the *Golden Ass* of Apuleius may be reckoned such. In it is found the beautiful episode of Cupid and Psyche, which has been elegantly modernized by Fontenelle" ("On the Origins and Progress of Novel-Writing" [London, 1810], pp. 6-7). I want to thank Elizabeth Kraft for bringing this essay to my attention.

3. The heroine of Mary Stewart's *Nine Coaches Waiting* (published in 1956, but frequently reprinted during

the 1960s) is very conscious of her role as a latter-day Jane Eyre who shuns black bombazine in favor of Italian silk when it is available.

4. Victoria Schwartz, "'The Soul Made of Fire': *Jane Eyre* and the Legend of Eros and Psyche," *DAI* 49, no. 5: p. 1154A, Temple University, November 1988.

5. *The Origin of Consciousness,* especially pp. 176-254. The changes described by Gerda Lerner (*The Creation of Patriarchy* [New York: Oxford University Press, 1986]) and Riane Eisler (*The Chalice and the Blade* [San Francisco: Harper and Row, 1987]) are congruent with the process Jaynes describes. Lerner does not refer to Jaynes's hypothesis. Eisler discusses it briefly and rejects it (pp. 74-75). Her comments suggest to me, however, that she does not entirely grasp the argument.

6. Robert May, *Sex and Fantasy* (New York: W. W. Norton, 1980).

7. One might note, however, that Brooks's theory of plot (*Reading for the Plot* [New York: Knopf, 1984]) attempts to "plot" the interaction of body and mind, as does Freud's theory of the death drive in *Beyond the Pleasure Principle.*

8. Some female writers of science fiction have experimented with just such alternative sets of principles, such as Ursula K. LeGuin's *The Left Hand of Darkness.*

9. Ann Radcliffe, *The Mysteries of Udolpho,* Oxford World Classics (New York: Oxford University Press, 1980), p. 507. Further citations will be made in the text.

10. Mellor, *Romanticism and Gender,* pp. 40-64.

11. As Joanna Russ points out in her essay "Somebody's Trying to Kill Me and I Think It's My Husband" (*Journal of Popular Culture* 6 [1973]), the often attractive (and frequently blond) male often turns out to be a villain in mass-market Gothics of the 1960s. I have argued this point in regard to Emily Brontë in "Natural Supernaturalism in *Wuthering Heights,*" *Studies in Philology* 82, no. 1 (Winter 1985): pp. 104-27.

12. Bruno Bettelheim, *The Uses of Enchantment* (New York: Knopf, 1976), pp.159-66.

13. In Radcliffe's early female Gothic, these two types appear as separate characters. But observing them and their implicit thematic functions helps us to understand how brilliant was Charlotte Brontë's fusion of the two. To embody them in one, to show Rochester's transformation, is effective because it condenses the "problem of masculinity." Rochester appears to be a Montoni: he manipulates Jane (through her feelings, not her property—she has none, of course). His "sins" are sins of affiliation—the past mistresses. Even his Bluebeard-like secret—a living wife, not a dead one, locked away in the secret room—while a Montoni-like sin of property is still a very "feminine" error of illusion; he is deceived by those in power.

14. Thus *Udolpho* also supports the thesis in Margaret Homans's *Bearing the Word,* which argues that the language of women's narratives often tends to "concretize" or "realize" abstract figurations. Homans argues that this technique implies women's different relationship to the Symbolic in a patriarchal culture. (*Bearing the Word: Language and Female Experience in Nineteenth-Century Women's Writing* [Chicago: University of Chicago Press, 1986].)

15. See Eva Figes, *Patriarchal Attitudes: Women in Society* (1970; reprinted New York: Persea Books, 1978) for a brief, witty survey of this history.

16. The Female Gothic heroine's power of empathy is often dramatized metaphorically in the occasional appearance of paranormal or "psychic" phenomena, as when Jane Eyre hears Mr. Rochester calling her from a long journey's distance just as she is about to agree to marry St. John Rivers.

Bibliography

Abrams, M. H. *The Mirror and the Lamp: Romantic Theory and the Critical Tradition.* New York: Oxford University Press, 1953.

Barbauld, Anna. "On the Origins and Progress of Novel-Writing." London, 1810.

Bloom, Harold. *The Anxiety of Influence: A Theory of Poetry.* London: Oxford University Press, 1973.

Jaynes, Julian. *The Origin of Consciousness in the Breakdown of the Bicameral Mind.* 1976. Reprint, Boston: Houghton Mifflin, 1990.

Keats, John. *The Letters of John Keats.* Edited by E. Hyder Rollins. 2 vols. Cambridge: Harvard University Press, 1958.

———. *Complete Poetry.* Edited by Jack Stillinger. Cambridge and London: Harvard University Press, Belknap Press, 1982.

Kristeva, Julia. *Powers of Horror: An Essay on Abjection.* 1980. Translated by Leon S. Roudiez. New York: Columbia University Press, 1982.

May, Robert. *Sex and Fantasy: Patterns of Male and Female Development.* New York: W. W. Norton, 1980.

Wordsworth, William, and Samuel Taylor Coleridge. *Lyrical Ballads.* 1798. Edited by W. J. B. Owen. 2d ed. Oxford: Oxford University Press, 1969.

FURTHER READING

Criticism

Anderson, Howard. "Gothic Heroes." In *The English Hero, 1660-1800,* edited by Robert Folkenflik, pp. 205-21. Newark, Del. and London: University of Delaware Press and Associated University Press, 1982.

Analyzes the male characters in The Mysteries of Udolpho *and measures their complexity and traits versus the men in such works as Horace Walpole's* The Castle of Otranto, *Matthew G. Lewis's* The Monk, *and Radcliffe's* The Italian.

Castle, Terry. "The Spectralization of the Other in *The Mysteries of Udolpho.*" In *The New Eighteenth Century: Theory, Politics, English Literature,* edited by Felicity Nussbaum and Laura Brown, pp. 231-53. New York: Methuen, 1987.

Points out that although critics of The Mysteries of Udolpho *usually focus on the Gothic episodes of the novel that occur at the castle, the events in the other sections of the book also deserve attention for their fantastical undertones and preoccupation with death and the dead.*

————. Introduction to *The Mysteries of Udolpho*, by Ann Radcliffe, pp. vii-xxvi. New York: Oxford University Press, 1998.

While agreeing with other critical assessments that Radcliffe's work is erratic and seriously flawed, argues that The Mysteries of Udolpho *should not be dismissed completely because the novel has a definite emotional power that the unprejudiced reader can learn to appreciate.*

Durant, David. "Ann Radcliffe and the Conservative Gothic." *SEL: Studies in English Literature, 1500-1900* 22, no. 3 (summer 1982): 519-30.

Insists that Radcliffe is not a forerunner of the Romantic movement in England. Her reactionary nature in the novels, Durant points out, can be seen in the way she rejected the chaos she perceived in contemporary life and advocated a return to the pastoral simplicity symbolized by the family circle.

Epstein, Lynne. "Mrs. Radcliffe's Landscapes: The Influence of Three Landscape Painters on Her Nature Descriptions." *Hartford Studies in Literature* 1, no. 2 (1969): 107-20.

Explores the relationship between Radcliffe's depiction of landscape and her acquaintance with three seventeenth-century landscape painters: Salvator Rosa, Claude Lorrain, and Nicolas Poussin.

Fawcett, Mary Laughlin. "Udolpho's Primal Mystery." *SEL: Studies in English Literature, 1500-1900* 23, no. 3 (summer 1983): 481-94.

Explores the underlying sexual themes in The Mysteries of Udolpho, *and theorizes that Gothic novels can be seen not just as escapist literature but, when viewed psychoanalytically, as symbolic explorations into thoughts and desires that are suppressed within the mind.*

Flaxman, Rhoda L. "Radcliffe's Dual Modes of Vision." In *Fetter'd or Free? British Women Novelists, 1670-1815,* edited by Mary Anne Schofield and Cecilia Macheski, pp. 124-33. Athens: Ohio University Press, 1986.

Urges the recognition of Radcliffe's work as innovative for its time, emphasizing the author's descriptive skills and highlighting her particular techniques in painting a scene.

Howells, Coral Ann. "Ann Radcliffe, *The Mysteries of Udolpho*." In *Love, Mystery and Misery: Feeling in Gothic Fiction,* pp. 28-61. London: Athlone Press, 1978.

Analyzes the manner in which Radcliffe stimulates the imagination of her readers. According to Howell, Radcliffe uses her characters to reflect emotion and activate the reader's "pattern of emotional association." Concludes that Radcliffe always remains a separate presence in control of her narrative so that she can always be "manipulating her readers' responses."

————. "The Pleasure of the Woman's Text: Ann Radcliffe's Subtle Transgressions in *The Mysteries of Udolpho* and *The Italian.*" In *Gothic Fictions: Prohibition/Transgression,* edited by Kenneth W. Graham, pp. 151-61. New York: AMS Press, 1989.

Maintains that when the reader examines particular passages in The Mysteries of Udolpho *and* The Italian *that do not appear to fit well within the rest of the narratives, a pattern evolves involving transgressions and the appropriateness of women's feelings.*

Kiely, Robert. "*The Mysteries of Udolpho*: Ann Radcliffe." In *The Romantic Novel in England,* pp. 65-80. Cambridge, Mass.: Harvard University Press, 1972.

Compares Emily St. Aubert, the heroine of The Mysteries of Udolpho, *with earlier heroines of the English novel, and finds that Emily is unique because "both the moral and material aspects of her ordeal are subordinated to the struggle which takes place within her mind." Argues that the achievement of the novel is "the projection of the nonrational mentality into a total environment"; in this, Kiely asserts, Radcliffe "has succeeded in doing something new for the novel."*

MacKenzie, Scott. "Ann Radcliffe's Gothic Narrative and the Readers at Home." *Studies in the Novel* 31, no. 4 (winter 1999): 409-31.

Discusses Radcliffe's Gothic style and its effects on the eighteenth-century public mind.

Miles, Robert. *Ann Radcliffe: The Great Enchantress.* Manchester and New York: Manchester University Press, 1995, 201 p.

Book-length study of Radcliffe's life and works from a sociopolitical perspective, offering aesthetic and historical context.

Moers, Ellen. "Traveling Heroinism: Gothic for Heroines." In *Literary Women,* pp. 122-40. New York: Doubleday & Company, Inc., 1976.

Emphasizes "a locus of heroinism" in Radcliffe's Gothic fantasies, which later women "have turned to feminist purposes." Recognizes the theme of the dangers of sensibility in Radcliffe's work, and compares Radcliffe with Fanny Burney, noting similarities in their treatment of "the horrors of a woman's life."

Murray, E. B. *Ann Radcliffe.* New York: Twayne Publishers, 1972, 178 p.

Overview of Radcliffe's life and major works, and an evaluation of her literary legacy.

Raleigh, Sir Walter. "The Revival of Romance." In *The English Novel: Being a Short Sketch of Its History from the Earliest Time to the Appearance of "Waverly."* Fifth edition, pp. 216-52. New York: Charles Scribner's Sons, 1911.

Commends Radcliffe's handling of suspense, fine use of romance conventions, and effective manipulation of scenery and sensation. In exhibiting these characteristics in her prose, Raleigh maintains, Radcliffe "anticipated and guided the poetry of the Romantic revival."

Sypher, Wylie. "Social Ambiguity in a Gothic Novel." *Partisan Review* 12, no. 1 (1945): 50-60.

Detects beneath the surface of Radcliffe's work "a pattern of socioeconomic contradictions, paradoxes, ambivalences, and ambiguity that affords some criteria of the greater romantics and of British romanticism generally." The principal ambiguity in The Mysteries of Udolpho, *according to Sypher, lies between "aesthetic values and moral values."*

Talfourd, Thomas Noon. "Memoir of the Life and Writings of Mrs. Radcliffe." In *Gaston de Blondeville; or, The Court of Henry III,* Vol. I, by Ann Radcliffe, 1826. Reprint edition, pp. i.-cxxxii, New York: Arno Press, 1972.

First memoir ever written about Radcliffe; prefixed to the posthumously published Gaston de Blondeville. *Praises Radcliffe's literary innovations, her "daring economy" in employing "instruments of fear," and her excellent portrayal of scenery, but acknowledges her shortcomings in the area of characterization.*

Tompkins, J. M. S. "The Gothic Romance." In *The Popular Novel in England: 1770-1800*. 1932. Reprint edition, pp. 243-95. Lincoln: University of Nebraska Press, 1961.

States that Radcliffe's novels are "unashamedly romantic, with no didactic intent," and stresses that Radcliffe contributed to the development of the psychological novel in her analyses of fear, adding that many of her prose passages are unmatched in eighteenth-century fiction.

Tooley, Brenda. "Gothic Utopia: Heretical Sanctuary in Ann Radcliffe's *The Italian*." *Utopian Studies* 11, no. 2 (2000): 42-56.

Asserts that "Radcliffe's Gothic tale participates in a strategy whereby British Gothic writers situate their novels at a discreet distance (spatially and/or temporally) from current events while at the same time commenting upon political and familial questions sparked by the Revolutionary decade."

Woolf, Virginia. "Phases of Fiction." In *Granite and Rainbow: Essays*, pp. 93-145. London: Hogarth Press, 1958.

Essay originally published serially in The Bookman, *New York, in 1929. Considers descriptive writing to be Radcliffe's greatest talent, but argues that, because she is incapable of creating in her readers a mood which would make the mysteries believable, Radcliffe's books are ultimately "stale, forced, unappetizing."*

OTHER SOURCES FROM GALE:

Additional coverage of Radcliffe's life and career is contained in the following sources published by Thomson Gale: *Dictionary of Literary Biography*, Vols. 39, 178; *Literary Movements for Students*, Vol. 1; *Literature Resource Center*; *Nineteenth-Century Literature Criticism*, Vols. 6, 55, 106; *Reference Guide to English Literature*, Ed. 2; *St. James Guide to Horror, Ghost & Gothic Writers*; *Supernatural Fiction Writers*; and *World Literature and Its Times*, Vol. 3.

ANNE RICE

(1941 -)

(Born Howard Allen O'Brien; has also written under the pseudonyms Anne Rampling and A. N. Roquelaure) American novelist, short story writer, and screenwriter.

Anne Rice is the best-selling author of mainstream Gothic fiction that centers on the alluring subjects of vampirism, occult demonology, and the supernatural. Her debut novel, *Interview with the Vampire* (1976), attracted a large popular audience and established her as a foremost contemporary author of horror fiction. Subsequent installments in the "Vampire Chronicles" series, including *The Vampire Lestat* (1985) and *The Queen of the Damned* (1988), fortified her reputation as a highly imaginative writer of macabre fantasy. Rice's engaging novels are distinguished for their richly descriptive settings, provocative eroticism, and looming metaphysical concerns that reflect the precarious nature of religious faith and truth in the postmodern world. Her vampires, demons, and historical personages are typically dispossessed or alienated individuals who wrestle with existential questions of morality, religion, sex, and death. Though best known for her "Vampire Chronicles" and "Mayfair Witches" series, Rice has also published several successful historical novels, *The Feast of All Saints* (1980) and *Cry to Heaven* (1982), both of which feature exotic historical settings and social outcasts.

BIOGRAPHICAL INFORMATION

Rice was named Howard Allen after her postal worker father, Howard O'Brien, and mother, Katherine Allen O'Brien. As a child she disliked her first name so much that she changed it to Anne in grade school. The second of four sisters, Rice grew up in the blue-collar "Irish Channel" neighborhood of New Orleans. The Irish Channel borders the affluent Garden District of the city, and Rice has credited walking by the neighborhood's opulent homes, conscious of her status as an outsider, as an influence on her life and work. Rice attended a Catholic church as a child, but she eventually rejected organized religion in her teenage years. After her mother's death from health complications caused by alcoholism when Rice was fourteen, the family moved to Texas, where Rice met her high school sweetheart and husband, poet Stan Rice. They married in 1961 and shortly afterward moved to San Francisco, where their daughter, Michelle, was born. Rice initially attended Texas Women's University but transferred to San Francisco State University, where she earned a bachelor's degree in political science in 1964 and a Master of Arts in creative writing in 1971. She also took graduate classes at the University of California, Berkeley. When five-year-old Michelle died of leukemia in 1972, Rice and her husband began abusing alcohol as a means of escaping their grief, a destructive pattern that lasted several years. Rice found some measure of relief by writing *Interview with the Vampire* in only five weeks; the novel's child-vampire character, Claudia, resembles Michelle in age and appearance. Two works of historical fiction, *The Feast of All Saints* and *Cry to Heaven* followed during the early 1980s before Rice returned to the subject of vampires. Her popularity soared with the 1985 publication of the second book in the "Vampire Chronicles" series, *The Vampire Lestat*, followed by *The Queen of the Damned*, a Literary Guild main selection in 1988, *The Tale of the Body Thief* (1992), *Memnoch the Devil* (1995), and *The Vampire Armand* (1998). The popular "Mayfair Witches" series, comprised of *The Witching Hour* (1990), a Book-of-the-Month selection, *Lasher* (1993), and *Taltos* (1994), added to her popularity and incredible commercial success. Rice also adapted *Interview with the Vampire* into the screenplay for the 1994 film version of the novel that starred Tom Cruise and Brad Pitt. Rice returned to New Orleans in 1988, purchasing a mansion in the Garden District, which serves as the setting for her books about the Mayfair Witches. Following the death of her husband in 2002, Rice decided to discontinue writing about vampires, and announced to her fans in January, 2004, that she was selling her homes in New Orleans and moving to an anonymous suburban address. Rice's "Vampire Chronicles" novel series has been adapted as *Lestat*, a stage musical with music by Elton John, lyrics by Bernie Taupin, and book by Linda Woolverton.

MAJOR WORKS

Rice's fiction revolves around the experiences of outsiders and misfits in society, questions of atheism and agnosticism, and themes of power and submission. Often including supernatural characters and plotting, Rice's work is noted for its darkness, eroticism, and evocation of setting and historical detail. In *Interview with the Vampire*, a vampire named Louis relates his life story and adventures to a reporter who records their session. Recalling his transformation into a vampire in 1790 at age twenty-five, Louis describes his first kill and evolving relationships with Lestat, his maker, and Claudia, a child-vampire whom they created together. Unlike Claudia and Lestat who revel in murderous bloodshed, Louis is tormented by a moral dilemma—he believes it is wrong to kill, but he must kill to survive. An ensuing power struggle between Louis and Lestat results in Lestat's second death, for which Louis is imprisoned in the Theatre des Vampires, a coven of

vampires in Paris. After burning the Theatre and escaping with Armand, an older vampire who mentors him, Louis returns to New Orleans where he lives as an outcast. As in much Gothic fiction, underlying themes of homoeroticism and incest are prevalent throughout the novel. Rice also examines religious beliefs by comparing Louis, who tries and fails to construct his own moral framework, to his brother, a devout Roman Catholic. In the sequel, *The Vampire Lestat*, Lestat awakes from a moribund slumber in the year 1980, and becomes a leather clad rock star. Presented as an autobiographic account, the novel traces the origins and history of vampirism through ancient, medieval, and modern history. The story concludes as Lestat performs in San Francisco to an audience of vampires who prepare to kill him for revealing their secrets in his published autobiography and lyrics. A continuation of the previous novel, *The Queen of the Damned* involves Akasha, mother of all vampires, whose scheme to institute world peace involves exterminating most of the male population and founding an empire governed by women.

In *The Tale of the Body Thief* Lestat contemplates suicide and eventually agrees to exchange his body with a mortal to temporarily escape his relentless ennui. Lestat must relearn mortal habits and a desperate chase follows after his counterpart disappears with his immortal body. Rice grapples with a shift in her personal philosophy from atheism to uncertainty about God's existence in *Memnoch the Devil*, in which Lestat converses with God and the Devil and tours Hell before deciding whether to join forces with the Devil. In *The Vampire Armand*, the sixth installment of the "Vampire Chronicles," Rice resurrects the title character, who earlier succumbed to a lethal dose of sunlight. Armand recollects his apprenticeship to Marius De Romanus in sixteenth-century Venice and subsequent rise as head of a Parisian vampire clan. Rice's "Vampire Chronicles" series created a legion of devoted fans who enthusiastically purchased each new book and thronged The Anne Rice Collection, the author's New Orleans retail shop that sold everything from clothing and fragrances to dolls based on her fictional characters. While Rice's popularity showed no sign of waning, following the death of her husband in 2002 the author announced that she was done with vampires, citing a desire to write something different, to create characters who were not damned or condemned. *Blood Canticle* (2003) was the last volume in the "Vampire Chronicles" series.

The "Mayfair Witches" series features Rowan Mayfair, scion of a matrilineal old New Orleans family whose members possess supernatural gifts and have been shadowed through time by a mysterious entity named Lasher. These books are characterized by intricate plotting, cliffhanger endings, and frequent flashbacks that tell the story of the Mayfair family's entanglement with Lasher over hundreds of years. *The Mummy* (1989) takes place in London, where young Julie Stratford falls in love with the reanimated mummy of Pharaoh Ramses III, who possesses the secret elixir of life. Julie and Ramses travel to Egypt where Ramses revives a murderous Cleopatra. In *Servant of the Bones* (1996), the genie Azriel fights the attempts of a demented millionaire to commit genocide on the population of the Third World.

Rice combined her interest in history with her exploration of social exiles by writing two historical novels. *The Feast of All Saints* enters the world of the *gens de couleur,* the group of free mulattoes who lived in antebellum New Orleans. The story focuses on the experiences of siblings Marcel and Marie, whose distinctive golden skin prohibits their full acceptance within either black or white society. *Cry to Heaven* centers upon the life of an eighteenth-century Italian castrati, a male singer who is castrated as a boy to preserve his high voice. The protagonist, Tonio Treschi, attempts to fulfill his desire to become one of the greatest opera singers in Europe while plotting revenge on his brother for treacherously having him castrated and exiled. Both books focus on characters who, like Rice's vampires and witches, exist on the fringes of mainstream society without being accepted by it. Rice also explored her fascination with sadomasochism by writing a pseudonymous series of pornographic novels—*The Claiming of Sleeping Beauty* (1983), *Beauty's Punishment* (1984), and *Beauty's Release* (1985) as A. N. Roquelaure and *Exit to Eden* (1985) and *Belinda* (1986) as Anne Rampling.

CRITICAL RECEPTION

Most critics recognize Rice's remarkable talent for constructing page-turning plots, evoking a sense of place—particularly when writing about her native New Orleans—and creating whole new universes peopled by supernatural characters. She is widely praised for rejuvenating the hackneyed genre of vampire fiction with her intelligent, ambitious novels. Rice's novels are also noted for their appealing eroticism and have attracted the interest of readers who identify with the themes of alienation depicted in the underground culture of vampire society. Though some critics appreciate Rice's philosophical musings on immortality and incorporation of occult history in her novels, others find her writing verbose, implausible, and clichéd. Some dismiss her otherworldly subject matter and frequent erotic descriptions as unworthy of serious literary effort. Commentators studying Gothic elements of Rice's works have emphasized particularly how she transforms traditional vampire fiction by creating monsters with whom readers can sympathize, and even identify. Martin J. Wood has asserted that "Rice's works force a jarring revision of our understanding of vampire mythology and, finally, of ourselves." Critics have also examined Rice's contemporary treatment of traditionally Gothic themes and conventions—particularly her explorations of the darker side of society, psychology, and culture—and have noted how her works remain true to the tradition while expressing modern concerns and sensibilities. Edward J. Ingebretsen assesses Rice's exploration of religious issues, declaring that "[t]heological disputation . . . remains a traditionally gothic activity, and nowhere is it more in evidence than in Anne Rice's *Interview with the Vampire.*" Lynda and Robert Haas (see Further Reading) contend that "there is no contemporary writer with stronger ties to the Gothic tradition than Anne Rice."

PRINCIPAL WORKS

Interview with the Vampire (novel) 1976

The Feast of All Saints (novel) 1980

Cry to Heaven (novel) 1982

The Claiming of Sleeping Beauty [as A. N. Roquelaure] (novel) 1983

Beauty's Punishment [as A. N. Roquelaure] (novel) 1984

Beauty's Release: The Continued Erotic Adventures of Sleeping Beauty [as A. N. Roquelaure] (novel) 1985

Exit to Eden [as Anne Rampling] (novel) 1985

The Vampire Lestat (novel) 1985

Belinda [as Anne Rampling] (novel) 1986

The Queen of the Damned (novel) 1988

The Mummy; or, Ramses the Damned (novel) 1989

The Witching Hour (novel) 1990

The Tale of the Body Thief (novel) 1992

Lasher (novel) 1993

Interview with the Vampire [adaptor; from her novel] (screenplay) 1994

Taltos (novel) 1994

Memnoch the Devil (novel) 1995

Servant of the Bones (novel) 1996

Violin (novel) 1997

The Vampire Armand (novel) 1998

Vittorio the Vampire (novel) 1999

Merrick (novel) 2000

Blood and Gold (novel) 2001

Blackwood Farm (novel) 2002

Blood Canticle (novel) 2003

GENERAL COMMENTARY

MARTIN J. WOOD (ESSAY DATE 1999)

SOURCE: Wood, Martin J. "New Life for an Old Tradition: Anne Rice and Vampire Literature." In *The Blood Is the Life: Vampires in Literature*, edited by Leonard G. Heldreth and Mary Pharr, pp. 59-78. Bowling Green, Ohio: Bowling Green State University Popular Press, 1999.

In the following essay, Wood argues that "Rice's works force a jarring revision of our understanding of vampire mythology and, finally, of ourselves."

Most vampire fiction succeeds in thrilling its readers because humans find stories of evil and horror immensely attractive. Few monsters have seemed quite so evil or quite so horrible as vampires, and their very attractiveness has largely distracted us from some fairly silly aspects of their traditional myths. So long as authors have been able to conjure up the allure of vampirism they could ignore the apparent irrelevance of its mythology. But since 1976, Anne Rice has done much to challenge this notion of irrelevance. Her vampire novels, probably the most popular ever written, may also be the most disturbing because they force readers to confront the core truths of the myth itself. Especially with her first two or three novels in the vampire tradition, readers find themselves feeling an uneasy sympathy with monsters, enjoying their murderous assaults on human beings. Caught up in the stories yet mystified by their own uneasiness, readers frequently wonder whether something else is going on.

Those who look more deeply into Rice's early works may become even more unsettled. Beneath a seductive text that repeatedly portrays the attraction and compulsion of evil they sense a disturbing subtext. Sensuousness seems suddenly to become equated with death, pleasure with evil, erotic (especially homoerotic) behavior with possession, consumption, and destruction. Fortunately neither the text nor subtext ultimately encourages these equations; rather, I suggest, these arise as a result of a conditioned misreading, an unconscious use of inappropriate codes for translating the events of Rice's books into meaning. When appropriately translated, Rice's works force a jarring revision of our understanding of vampire mythology and, finally, of ourselves. In other words, the vampire myth is indeed relevant, but the literary and cultural codes by which it has been inscribed and transmitted—before Anne Rice—have become obsolete. Rice's vampire fiction succeeds not merely because it is thrilling and well written, but because it also translates mythic truth by means of new, powerful codes.

Such reinscription is not without precedent; indeed, the Gothic genre itself can be considered a response to the inadequacy of the code embodied in eighteenth-century fiction. Despite the popular appeal of romantic, sentimental, and moral fiction, many readers found value in the unreal work of Ann Radcliffe, Monk Lewis, and Mary Shelley. Years later they took time out from Dickens and Darwin to read *Dracula*. As Gabriel Ronay has said, Stoker's "unerring eye for the Victorian love of the horrific and the macabre" fastened on inchoate vampire mythology and produced "a vampire to suit popular tastes" (54). Similarly in the late twentieth century, in a secular, technological culture nearly devoid of spiritualism, Anne Rice has resurrected the vampire from its moldering texts, infusing an obsolete myth with new blood. Stripped of its silliness and illogical superstitions, the vampire myth emerging from her earlier books is vigorous, modern, and coherent. The stories themselves are frightening and their characters compelling. Like Stoker before her, Rice has changed the code. She has challenged the traditional portraits of vampires in several fundamental ways, producing a series of books that cannot properly be understood if read according to the old codes.

Rice has named her series *The Vampire Chronicles.* The first two, **Interview with the Vampire** and **The Vampire Lestat,** appeared in 1976 and 1985. They became extremely popular and commercially successful novels, propelling their author into a kind of cult stardom. And while it is their rewriting of vampire mythology that is most interesting, their market successes helped Rice's version of the myths become the most influential since Stoker's *Dracula*. Among the other volumes in the series are *The Queen of the Damned* (1988), *The Tale of the Body Thief* (1992), and *Memnoch the Devil* (1995). These and later *Chronicles* also achieved strong commercial success. However, they offer less innovation to the body of vampire literature. Indeed, *Memnoch the Devil* is hardly a vampire novel at all. The most significant challenges to the older narrative codes were established in *Interview with the Vampire* and *The Vampire Lestat*.

Characteristic elements of the obsolete codes include depictions of humans as heroes, the vampire as enemy; humans as comrades, the vampire as loner; virtue as a human trait, evil as inhuman; humans as Christian, vampires as Satanic. Rice's early vampire novels revise these depictions in several ways. First, she has changed the surface features of the myth, dispensing with ridiculous and often contradictory elements in favor of something more reasonable, more attuned to our time. Second, Rice has modernized the nature of the vampires; no longer simple or single-minded personifications of evil, her blood-drinkers are fully realized characters who sensibly confront the problems of their lives. Third, instead of locations emphasizing death and decay, she has set her stories in vital urban landscapes. And fourth, Rice has tampered with the code of the narration itself, bringing the vampire closer to readers both spatially and psychologically. As if these modifications in the fictional elements were not enough, Rice has also challenged her readers to change their own attitudes, to reread their own lives by a new code, a code of absolute sexual equality. Readers who fail to make this last translation will find themselves puzzled, perhaps disturbed, by what goes on in *The Vampire Chronicles*.

Traditional Features of the Myth

Numerous differences between Rice's vampires and those of the tradition illustrate how profoundly she has altered the myth. While her central vampires, Louis and Lestat, are aristocratic, undead, nocturnal, and thirsty for blood, they share few other traits with their literary predecessors. And when the ancient, more powerful vampires Maharet and Akasha finally exert their full strength in *The Queen of the Damned*, they contrast even more sharply with Dracula and his fictional descendants. None of Rice's vampires transform themselves into dust, fog, bats, wolves, or anything else. Their victims are seldom the

traditional female virgins; indeed, they often belong to the same sex as the vampire attacker. More significantly, victims in *The Vampire Chronicles* never become new vampires except by deliberate design. Here vampiric reproduction is always a conscious sharing of the spirit-charged blood. Fledgling creatures are often chosen from among physically beautiful and spiritually profound young humans, and as a result, Rice's vampires have none of the repulsive physical traits of the traditional undead.

Rice has changed their nature in other ways as well. Although vampires in folklore and previous literature needed to be invited into their victims' homes, no such restriction applies here—a suggestion, in the new code, that our complicity as victims is far more subtle than we had suspected. The new vampires show no fear of garlic, whitethorn, or the wild rose, respect neither priest nor church nor crucifix, can sleep in any ground they wish, cast reflections into mirrors, cross moving water at will, and survive nearly any calamity—not even a stake through the heart will kill them. And, until *Memnoch the Devil*, her vampires had no connection to Satan; indeed, their longing to discover their origins and spiritual purpose is one of the more familiar and appealing features of the vampires of the first several books.

Even Rice's plot lines contrast with, for example, Stoker's and Stephen King's; no gallant band of humans unites in struggle for the preservation of virgins and the social status quo. And while Stoker's chief vampire-hunter, Van Helsing, puts great store in the fact that Dracula and his kind cannot act in concert, Rice's vampires not only can but often do. It is especially ironic that in **The Queen of the Damned** the only gallant band is one made up of the ancient and venerable vampires united to save humanity from the mother-vampire Akasha.

In Rice's hands the vampire comes to represent the most important kind of myth, the kind whose truth intellectuals prefer not to acknowledge. Other myths, the Promethean for example, are accepted as valid human truth even in this technological society—and not only because Mary Shelley infused Prometheus with new life in 1818. We look at nuclear and toxic waste, thermonuclear weaponry, and recombinant DNA, and we feel in our bones the truth of a myth about stealing knowledge we are incompetent to handle. Science takes us to the frontiers, but once there we read the warning, "There be dragons here." Prometheus is serious business. In marked contrast, the vampire myth carries an aura of triviality. We are supposed to take seriously a myth about a cadaver that walks, drinks blood, turns into a bat, and endures for centuries, but runs in terror from a plastic crucifix?

And yet the myth has a history and a truth that insist upon its vitality generation after generation. This is evident not only in the great popularity enjoyed by vampire stories over the last two centuries and in the literal belief in vampires still prevalent in many parts of the world, but also in the deep cultural acknowledgment of vampirism in sources we would not ordinarily think to examine. The basic concept of a transfer of vitality from one creature to another is as old as humankind, and is celebrated in Romantic and post-Romantic art in a variety of forms (Twitchell). We see it in Poe's "The Oval Portrait" and in Wilde's *Dorian Gray,* or in any image of the old living off the vitality of the young, whether by means of organ transplants or by theft of intellectual property. Naturally, these images appear in our literature because they have significance in our lives. To the extent that Rice's alterations of the myth have given readers new reason to take it seriously, to reread their own lives in its light, she has performed a great service.

Traditional Characteristics of the Vampire

In revising the mythology to renew its significance, Rice has redeemed the vampires themselves. They are no longer the outside antagonist, the enemy whose destruction marks humanity's triumph and the end of the story. In each novel Rice's key vampire is the protagonist of the book,

surviving beyond the narrative and posing no threat to the human social fabric. These vampires are not antichrist nor even, obviously, antihuman. Their chief anxieties are their love for humans—not merely appetite but genuine love—and their fear of the potential boredom and meaninglessness of eternal life. And their enemies, almost without exception, are members of their own kind (or other supernatural antagonists like the Body Thief). They are, in other words, very much like individual human beings. Rice has in fact made a point of stating this comparison in interviews (Hoppenstand and Browne 4).

This second revision, making the new vampires more human than the old, can be illustrated with a comparison of their speeches. Each of the following excerpts is characteristic of the individual vampire's speech and attitude. The first vampire is J. Sheridan Le Fanu's Carmilla: "Think me not cruel because I obey the irresistible law of my strength and weakness; if your dear heart is wounded, my wild heart bleeds with yours. In the rapture of my enormous humiliation I live in your warm life, and you shall die—die, sweetly die—into mine" (92). Though beautifully done, the speech reveals Carmilla to be an old-style vampire. She is not human but something wild; her evident desire is very much motivated by physical appetite as she obeys an "irresistible law." The next speaker is Dracula himself, stirred by the sound of howling wolves outside his (of course) gloomy castle: "Listen to them—the children of the night. What music they make! . . . Ah, sir, you dwellers in the city cannot enter into the feelings of the hunter" (Stoker 18). Throughout the book Dracula is the hunter, humans the prey. Both Carmilla and Dracula characterize the old code that represents evil as something outside, not in the reader, but in something other.

Unfortunately for traditional vampire tales, readers of the later twentieth century know themselves to be their own worst enemy. Rice has noted this and rewritten the myth in a new code. Here is an excerpt from **Interview with the Vampire**; the speaker is Louis, on board ship as he sails for the old world:

> It seemed at moments, when I sat alone in the dark stateroom, that the sky had come down to meet the sea and that some great secret was to be revealed in that meeting, some great gulf miraculously closed forever. But who was to make this revelation when the sky and sea became indistinguishable and neither any longer was chaos? God? Or Satan? It struck me suddenly what consolation it would be to know Satan, to look upon his face, no matter how terrible that countenance was, to

know that I belonged to him totally, and thus put to rest forever the torment of this ignorance. To step through some veil that would forever separate me from all that I called human nature.

(146)

If these are the words of a monster, it is the kind of monster easily recognized by modern readers.

Louis contrasts sharply with Dracula, a predator whose comprehension of nature is confined to the physical struggle; Louis looks beyond nature's beauty to philosophy or metaphysics. This evidence of human motivation is underscored in an excerpt from *The Vampire Lestat,* spoken by Lestat himself as he described a game he often played in pursuit of an unsuspecting mortal:

> I'd fall in love with the being. I'd imagine friendship, conversation, intimacy that we could never have. In some magical and imaginary moment I would say: "But you see what I am," and this human being, in supreme spiritual understanding, would say, "Yes, I see. I understand." Nonsense, really. Very like the fairy tale where the princess gives her selfless love to the prince who is enchanted and he is himself again and the monster no more. Only in this dark fairy tale I would pass right into my mortal lover. We would become one being, and I would be flesh and blood again.

(337-38)

Instead of a ruthless monster driven by appetite, readers find a lonely, anguished creature yearning for understanding. Lestat's desire is quintessentially human. He and Louis not only represent more complex characterizations, but also reveal the more ambiguous world they inhabit, a world of indeterminacy where inscrutable forces pit biological survival against purely ethical behavior. It is also, clearly, the modern world of humankind.

It is useful to consider vampires' personalities because critics have suggested that the heart of a vampire story is the character of the vampire itself; when we know the character, we know the story. In *The Living and the Undead,* Gregory Waller has extended this notion to include the confrontations between these vampire characters and the humans around them, confrontations in which "the living as well as the undead can come to embody and enact our hidden fears and desires" (5). But such direct conflicts also illustrate the differences between humans and monsters, and Rice avoids stressing these distinctions. A second point of Waller's concerns in some sense another kind of confrontation; he emphasizes how each vampire story "participates in an ongoing series of narratives" including all previous vampire tales (6).

Rice has turned each of these confrontations on its head: she focuses not on vampires confronting mortals but vampire against vampire, and "participates" in the literary tradition only in the sense that a vampire "participates" in its victim's life: she takes what is vital, and leaves the dead husk behind. The result is a set of characters with a greater potential, when read according to the right code, to show us something about ourselves.

Thus Rice's Louis, for example, is not merely silly, scary, or irrelevant. Louis is a troubled vampire, depressed by evil in himself, disturbed by his need to murder innocents but unable to act otherwise. As Lestat notes early in his book, Louis is a romantic, and so his vampire life is a kind of torture to himself. Louis is more akin to Hamlet than Dracula. He loves mortals for their brevity, their fragility, their humanity, and when he thinks he shares none of this with them, not even their humanity, he despairs. He loses his passion, his interest in the beauty of life—or so he says. Lestat tries to convince him he is wrong. In other words these two vampires behave very much as would a pair of human friends. By portraying such characteristics Rice refuses to endorse a convenient morality that allows us to locate evil outside human will.

Traditional Settings for the Vampire Tale

Before Anne Rice, vampire fiction and film had been preoccupied with locations that emphasize isolation, gloom, decay, and death. Castles, dungeons, cemeteries, and crypts, especially in remote locations, have served as the home of the vampire from the very beginning. As a creature of the night the *revenant* needs darkness, but the other traditional features carry a built-in horrific element that saves the writer a lot of work. Indeed, well into this century Gothic literature merely adopted a thrilling and horrifying atmosphere, borrowing proven settings for its conventionally horrid creatures. This atmosphere emphasized the distances and differences between the monster and the humans. However frightened they might become during a vampire story, readers would know that vampires live far away in undesirable settings. Thus the readers need not take their fear seriously.

Clearly, mere atmosphere is not enough to evoke the truth of myth. All Gothic tales, and especially vampire stories, mingle fascination and repulsion, seduction and horror, sensuality and death in ways readers find hard to resist. Horrifying forms alone will not suffice; good Gothic literature involves a thorough transformation of both form and content. Writing about George Eliot's Maggie Tulliver, Nina Auerbach speaks of "the wide swings through time and space that constitute the rhythm of Gothic fiction." This rhythm can be felt without the familiar Gothic trappings that are, of course, missing from *Mill on the Floss*; Auerbach's point is that Eliot "evokes but does not inhabit" such a world in her book (234). The distinction is crucial. Clearly it is the successful evocation, not the mere inhabitation, that informs Gothicism's power and purpose. Traditionally (that is, before Anne Rice), vampire literature failed to transcend mere horror precisely because it inhabited horrific landscapes without evoking the appropriate human subliminal terrain.

Not even in the fiction of Stephen King is there a "vampire for these times," as Lestat puts it in *The Vampire Lestat* (228). Despite King's unmatched ability to tell a thrilling story, *'Salem's Lot* is finally not much more than Stoker's *Dracula* transported to Maine. The vampire serves Satan even in 1975 New England, despite the fact that few people there lose much sleep over the Evil One. King's vampire Barlow is profoundly wicked, allied with the Devil himself, threatening the citizens' immortal souls. The trouble is, few citizens today fear for their souls in quite the way their ancestors did. The symbols are nearly empty. In this barren fiction, monsters inhabit the Gothic landscape without evoking the mythic terrain. Thus, instead of a frightful truth, audiences settle for fright alone; instead of evoking the mythic landscape, monsters merely inhabit scary places.

Into this Gothic desert, then, come the vampires Louis and Lestat, Marius and Maharet, both to inhabit and to evoke. These vampires require no dungeons, and they stopped wearing capes and robes when such attire went out of human fashion. Their homes are comfortable, well-furnished places generously appointed with art and cultural artifacts gathered through the centuries. Significantly, soon after Lestat becomes a vampire in the decaying castle of the alchemist-turned vampire Magnus, he abandons the site that had served Magnus for centuries. By similarly rejecting the dusty settings of most vampire stories, Rice's comfortable, modern-day locations underscore the attractiveness of the real horror just as her use of genuine, nearby cities emphasizes its proximity. Furthermore, instead of featuring a remove to a distant horror followed by a safe return, both of Rice's first two books begin in modern San Francisco, return to the past for historical narration, gradually moving back toward the present, but bringing all of the horror with them. The movement in the third book is the same, though the narrative locus is not San Francisco but Miami; still the evil comes to the present, now stalking both coasts. As Auerbach noted in her discussion of the rhythms of Gothicism, "All Gothic journeys seem to take place in a time machine" (234), but only in Rice does the evil persist throughout all time and space.

Thus, while inviting readers to view the vampire not as a monster but as one of them, Rice also suggests they identify the vampire world as their own. The monster comes to be seen as any modern human who was offered a different path and took it. It is an attractive path, the one Faust took—and, at least until the world Lestat confronts in *Memnoch the Devil*, it is Faust's path minus the Devil. To live as a powerful human in the civilized world but without fear of death or damnation: who would not choose to join the vampires? It is this ultimately seductive view of evil that makes Rice's stories both relevant and true. The seduction is so powerful that the vampires' brutal acts seem little more than unsavory traits. And, in truth, their violence, their predation, their murder is human violence on a grand scale: we, too, kill that we might live, though our victims are less thrilling, less challenging, less sentient. And we kill so that we might live a paltry hundred years; vampires kill to live forever. According to the new code, vampires might be seen as a more admirable, more subtly evolved version of humans.

Traditional Narration in the Vampire Tale

One of the most distinctive and consistent features of horror literature in general and of vampire fiction in particular is its manner of narration. Instead of the third-person (limited or omniscient) narrative characteristic of standard fiction texts, horror stories more often employed documents such as letters, diaries, journals, discovered confessions, and so forth. The assembler of these documents—who was seldom the protagonist of the story itself—typically assumed a pose of naive surprise at the shocking story the fragments appeared to disclose. Consequently the narration became, in Victor Sage's words, "clumsy and labyrinthine" (127). In *Dracula* the narration seemed even more bizarre as the several protagonists themselves collected journals, letters, typewritten memoirs, and even phonograph dictations to help each other keep the story straight. The technique might have been intended to help prove that the story was really true, that no one made it up. But it had another effect as well. When a monster already removed from the reader spatially and psychologically becomes removed narratively as well, becomes a creature accessible only through several layers of narrative filtering, that monster more than ever becomes something outside the reader's experience. Like *Dracula*, "Carmilla" employs this distancing approach. Carmilla's victim relates her history ten years afterward, rendering it particular, remote, and less immediately threatening. For most readers, the realism is also tempered by the distancing that accompanies the tale. And as the technique became more predictable and formulaic, it added to the artificial, trivial aura already gathering around the genre.

Anne Rice's code changes all this. In her books, the narrative method helps forge the identification readers make with the vampires, reinforcing the sense that real evil is in the human self. As I noted earlier, portions of her stories take place in the present day, and not only are her monsters not loathsome; they are breathtakingly attractive. Indeed they are themselves the protagonists with whom the readers sympathize. And what is more, these vampires either narrate the stories themselves or, as with Louis in *Interview with the Vampire,* serve as the single consciousness through whom the third-person narrative is focalized.

Louis's narration provides an interesting study by itself. According to any narrative code familiar to readers, the title *Interview with the Vampire* indicates that they will read an interview, a question-and-answer session between an interlocutor and a subject. The subject represents someone readers seek to know more about; the interlocutor, serving as the narrator, is either familiar and known or else irrelevant. But in *Interview* the reader encounters a tale *about* an interview. The narrator is not the interviewer but someone else—some unnamed third person who refers to Louis only as "the vampire," to the interviewer only as "the boy." This account of an interview even includes brief interruptions that describe the actions of the vampire and the boy. Readers finish the book without having learned who could be narrating the story; it seems irrelevant. Then in *The Queen of the Damned* the boy-interviewer's name is revealed: Daniel Molloy. In this book Molloy receives royalties for *Interview with the Vampire;* evidently Rice herself does not exist in her own books except perhaps as a pseudonym used by her fictional narrators. Within the Rice-free world of the fiction, then, Daniel Molloy

has written *Interview* to recount his meeting with Louis, deciding for his own reasons to refer to himself as "the boy," not as "I."

The Vampire Lestat includes similar references to the previous book. This time, however, Lestat narrates the book himself, telling the entire story in the first person. Early in his version Lestat discovers *Interview with the Vampire,* a popular and often-read "novel" that turns out to be Louis's story masquerading as fiction. Once again Rice narrows the gap between the readers' world and the vampires' world; the world represented in *Lestat* includes the real-world artifact *Interview.* And the use of Lestat as narrator in his own book means that he is not only the protagonist but also "the author of an autobiography" (3), a storyteller in a world that looks increasingly like our own. And he claims to write partly in response to the earlier book. It is almost as though Lestat says, following Huck Finn's lead, "I am the vampire Lestat. You don't know about me without you have read a book called *Interview with the Vampire.* It is a true book mainly." But Lestat finds himself provoked by what he calls the "lies" he reads in *Interview.* He writes his own book to provoke a confrontation not between vampires and mortals but between himself and all other vampires.

The Queen of the Damned is even more of the same kind of self-referential fiction, of narrating within narrating. Here Lestat is once again the writer; near the end of the book he shows himself at the word processor composing that very book. But much of the story cannot truly be told by Lestat because it involves vampires other than himself: Maharet, Marius, Pandora, Khayman. His solution is deceptively simple:

> In other words, a lot was going on which I had to reconstruct later. And it is the reconstruction I offer you now. . . .
>
> And by the way, when these other characters think or say of me that I am beautiful or irresistible, etc., don't think I put these words in their heads. I didn't! It's what was told to me after, or what I drew out of their minds with infallible telepathic power; I wouldn't lie about that or anything else.
>
> (8)

True to his word, Lestat submerges his personality and appears to present the others' narrations in their own idiom. Only near the end does he regain overt control of the narration for good. But the sophisticated reader realizes immediately that Lestat always controls the narration; at best, he is faithfully reporting others' words, but readers have no way of judging how close his version is. And his assertion that he would not lie is of course useless. The twist in this narrative, then, is that human readers must trust a vampire narrator to convey to them not only his own thoughts and history, as he had in **The Vampire Lestat,** but also the thoughts of many other blood drinkers. And this Lestat they must trust is an egocentric vampire who confesses, "I hate not being the first person narrator all the way through!" (8). His narrative control follows much the same pattern in the next two books as well. Clearly the deck is stacked.

Thus, far from preventing the reader from sympathizing with the vampire, Rice's innovative method insists that readers not only like vampires and identify with them, but also trust them. This form of narration allows the reader no comfortable distancing and ensures that at least the narrating vampire must survive at the end of the story. The implied threat is therefore immediate. For example, in **Interview,** Louis is not only alive at the end, but has attacked and nearly killed the boy-interviewer (though readers discover in the third book that the boy has survived). Louis has tried, and failed, to demonstrate to the boy that humanity itself is worth the price of mortality. When the boy begs at the end to become a vampire, Louis is enraged at his failure to convey the agony of inhuman immortality. He has one tactic left: to attack the boy, to kill him or to drain him so near to death that the boy will cherish what brief existence humans have. Thus the underlying threat in Rice's novel, the myth's dark truth, is real and nearby: humans could, if tempted, sacrifice anything to avoid death. The boy is utterly seduced by the vampire's beauty and immortality, and the implication of the narrative device, underscored by readers' initial identification with the boy, is that any listener would be seduced as well, seduced by a horrible desire too strong to resist. And indeed, this is Molloy's eventual fate, as he becomes a vampire in **The Queen of the Damned.**

The point is also emphasized by the narrative method of **The Vampire Lestat.** Only a vampire himself could have narrated this tale, because Lestat's real quarrel is with his own kind, whose limitations he constantly assails throughout the book. Such limitations as their vulnerability to crosses and religious remedies turn out to be the fault of superstitious vampires too timid to realize that nothing can hurt them. And the vampire narrator can see, as humans cannot, that while some few vampires are morally weak, most are not. While a few do not adhere to strict codes of moral conduct, and will feed on the innocent and guilty alike, these are not typical. But these are the ones

humans normally hear of, and for good reason: to consider themselves prey to intelligent, ethical beings is unthinkable. As the magnificent vampire Marius says to Lestat:

> In this world the vampire is only a Dark God. He is a Child of Darkness. He can't be anything else. And if he wields any lovely power upon the minds of men, it is only because the human imagination is a secret place of primitive memories and unconfessed desires. The mind of each man is a Savage Garden, to use your phrase, in which all manner of creatures rise and fall, and anthems are sung and things imagined that must finally be condemned and disavowed.
>
> (**The Vampire Lestat** 465)

This is why the traditional undead will not fully operate as agents of evil for today's readers. The real danger to humans lies in glimpsing the true beauty of the vampire, thereby unwittingly acknowledging and surrendering to the genuine evil within themselves.

Rice's use of Lestat as a modern, attractive horror is complicated somewhat by the narrative difference between **Interview with the Vampire** and **The Vampire Lestat,** and by her changing focus in the later books of the *Chronicles.* In the first two novels Lestat is portrayed (by Louis) as a consummate hunter of humans, too beautiful for them to resist, but ultimately too coarse for Louis's own tastes. With the change of narrators from Louis to Lestat in the first and second books, he grows much more attractive. This change—from a brutal, sullen, and finally broken vampire in **Interview** to a creature much more vibrant and appealing in **The Vampire Lestat**—also reflects the human weakness of vanity. Here he is a conceited, self-indulgent sensualist, albeit with the beauty and cleverness to justify his cocky arrogance—in his own narrating, at least. His mortal prowess, exemplified by his battle with a pack of wolves, carries over into his vampiric existence to establish him as a formidable monster. If this is the shape of evil, a reader might respond, perhaps evil is not such a bad thing.

But in later books Lestat reveals tendencies toward gesture instead of substance, pose instead of achievement, sensation instead of comprehension, willfulness instead of strength of will. At times he seems little more than a caricature, a flat actor with a flair for seeming outrageous but with little integrity of character or coherence of self. In **The Queen of the Damned** he is often irrelevant or, despite incredible new powers of flight and telekinesis, truly weak—a mere boytoy for the mother-vampire Akasha. Then, by the fourth book, he has inexplicably become stupid enough to fall for the Body Thief's clumsy and obvious attempts at trickery. Even worse, he spends most of *Memnoch the Devil* as a totally passive observer, whimpering and cowering for hundreds of pages at a time, ultimately duped by—surprise!—the Devil himself.

As with his vanity, however, Lestat's occasional stupidity may serve to intensify readers' potential identification with evil. Having spent much of his narrative time in the earlier books yearning for a return to mortality, he gets his wish in *The Tale of the Body Thief.* Of course, once this is accomplished, he is miserable. And his misery is graphically illustrated in his vivid descriptions of the intolerable torments that afflict him. The trouble is, these torments are normal events of mortal life: the pain of cold, the discomfort of hunger, the misery of viral illness. Even the grand liar Lestat sees the falsehood of his romantic yearning for the return of mortality. But during his time in mortal form he commits forcible rape—arguably the most evil and selfish act Lestat has yet committed. What the reader sees, then, is human misery and human evil—familiar, immediate. In this way a sense of inescapable evil—curiously absent in the save-humanity, kill-only-the wicked ethic of *The Queen of the Damned*—is back in *The Tale of the Body Thief.* For today's world the horror, the evil of Dracula is too clearly located outside humankind, and if Akasha was also too conveniently distant, then Lestat in *The Tale of the Body Thief* restores the unwelcome but real proximity of evil to human nature.

Although his narrating agency continues in *Memnoch the Devil,* Lestat mostly retells the story told him by Memnoch, the antagonist formerly known as Satan. The same Lestat who could not resist the temptation offered by the Body Thief is no stronger with Memnoch, and agrees to accompany the Devil on a journey to Heaven and Hell in an attempt to understand (from Memnoch's perspective) the true history and theology of God and the Devil. But as a vampire and as a narrator, Lestat is nearly out of the picture. The question of his reliability remains, of course, but is virtually effaced by the problem of the Devil's reliability. The question of Lestat's evil, or of his potential for evoking the evil within human readers, has become irrelevant. All of these fascinating issues appear subsumed under the central problem of the nature of the Devil.

Indeed, it is difficult to understand how *Memnoch the Devil* advances Anne Rice's contribution to the tradition of vampire literature. Even though *The Queen of the Damned* and *The Tale of the Body Thief* broaden the supernatural pantheon to include spirits and entities more powerful in their own ways than the vampires themselves, the essential focus of each book remains the same as in the first two books. For these four *Chronicles* this focus is on the nature of the relationship between human and vampire—particularly between those on collision courses of nostalgia: the vampires who longed for their absent humanity, and the humans who longed for vampiric immortality. But this productive conflict is missing from *Memnoch the Devil.* In its place, amid many pages of numbing philosophy, is a nearly static tale of the Devil's struggle to convince God of his errors, and to assist human souls in achieving Heaven. In contrast to her bold departures from the traditions of vampire literature, Rice settles here for the stock features of the most conventional Catholic theology. To be sure, these stock features are offered with the Devil's spin on them, but it is hardly a stroke of boldness or innovation to make the Devil deceptive.

When Lestat pleads to the reader at the very end of *Memnoch the Devil,* "Let me pass now from fiction into legend" (354), it is unclear whether the greater hubris lies within Lestat or his author. What Rice seems to attempt with this novel is to present a profound theological ambiguity; what she has achieved, rather like Lestat, is the appearance of profundity without its substance. The ambiguity, though complicated by narrative and philosophical layering, is little more than this: either Lestat is telling the truth, or he is not. If is lying, there is no ambiguity. If he is telling the truth, then either the Devil is telling the truth or he is not. However, the story makes it very clear that the Devil has tricked Lestat into returning a sacred object—lost since the Crucifixion—into the eager hands of the Church, and that this will plunge the Church into great discord, beginning of course with the Jesuits (339).

Rice clearly had comparisons with the *Divine Comedy* in mind—no reader who has read both can miss the features in *Memnoch* that evoke Dante's great work—but in the end the book is to the *Divine Comedy* rather as Charlton Heston is to Moses. It is not clear that her eager biographer Ramsland advanced Rice's credit by boasting that Rice "wrote *Memnoch the Devil* in a month" (31). The novel is too superficial and predictable to be as truly profound as her earlier works. A reader may be disappointed finally to learn that the Devil has tricked Lestat, but the only truly surprising thing is that Rice would so wholly adhere to conventional theology. Of all the possible spiritual, philosophical, or religious systems Lestat could have explored, he seems to end where Dracula began. Readers have been there and done that. To appreciate the strongest and boldest features of Rice's challenges to the old codes of vampire mythology, one must return to her earlier vampire novels.

The New Code for the Readers

Anne Rice could hardly have written a serious vampire story, let alone an entire series of *Vampire Chronicles,* without paying close attention to the erotic elements inherent in the genre. One of the few constants in all of vampire literature, the erotic theme is conventionally understood to result from Victorian writers' and audiences' fascination with the horrifying spectre of sexuality run wild, of appetite transcending all limits—including death. No new understanding of this genre can be complete without an explanation of its erotic themes. But for Rice, in particular, it is especially important. In all of her works the sensuousness is obvious, palpable, luxuriant; every reader remarks it. Readers of the first two vampire novels may disagree over its significance, but two features stand out: no intercourse is even remotely suggested, and the erotic encounters often occur between two men (or male vampires). Thus readers' traditional understanding of how fiction works might prompt them to label the sensuous aura of Rice's vampire novels as homoerotic. But to do so is to misread new symbols according to an old code. Once again, to do Rice justice, readers need to learn the new code.

Perhaps the most impressive fact about the sexuality of Louis, Lestat, and their colleagues is its non-discriminatory nature. Where Dracula and most of his literary descendants relentlessly stalk victims of the opposite sex, Rice's vampires feel no such inclination. Their pleasure in the kill and the feeding is intensely erotic, but bears little physical resemblance to human sexuality. All notion of gender, even of genitalia, is obsolete. On one level this represents yet another way in which Rice is simply being sensible; in natural creatures sexual arousal serves the innate need to reproduce in order to ensure their species' survival. But Rice's vampires will survive forever as individuals merely by killing and feeding, and should they ever decide to reproduce, they create new vampires by allowing humans to feed upon them. For Rice's vampires, the kill is sexual, both in function and in sensation, though never in human physical form. But on another level there is an element of apotheosis in their eroticism. With the loss of functioning reproductive organs, Rice's vampires focus not on mere anatomy but on the total experience of proximity and contact, not on a single, limited orgasmic event but on an erotic process.

A single passage will serve to illustrate this non-genital eroticism. The episode is narrated by the vampire Louis, recalling in *Interview* his sensations as he attacked his first victim and "went into his neck":

> The sucking mesmerized me; the warm struggling of the man was soothing to the tension of my hands; and there came the beating of the drum again, which was the drumbeat of his heart—only this time it beat in perfect rhythm with the drumbeat of my own heart, the two resounding in every fiber of my being, until the heart began to grow slower and slower, so that each was a soft rumble that threatened to go on without end. I was drowsing, falling into weightlessness. . . .
>
> (27)

The passage is characteristically sensuous, non-genital, and homoerotic—at least according to the old code. But the reader who approaches the text without relying exclusively upon prior knowledge might well ask what relevance gender has for creatures who have no sexual reproduction.

It may prove helpful momentarily to consider Rice's vampires not as monsters of the tradition but simply as "Strangers," people on the outside, outcast, alien, monstrous. The Stranger is not the same as the human readers but is similar to them; if readers fear and despise the vampire immediately, it is because they don't know the creature or can't understand it. An analogy may readily be made to the way the dominant culture positions those who are sexually "Strangers"—particularly androgynous or homosexual people. Accordingly, as readers who fear the vampires take the time to become familiar with these Strangers, they stand to learn about the monsters inside themselves, and ultimately how their sexuality can partake of that monstrosity.

The term "Stranger" is deliberate; a motif of outcasts and strangers pervades Rice's work, and particularly *The Vampire Chronicles.* In her first book, Louis, the tortured, introspective vampire, is an outcast even from other blood drinkers. He and his family, Claudia and Lestat, are Strangers among their fellow vampires, who are themselves estranged from humankind. The outcast status continues to characterize Lestat and other vampires throughout the *Chronicles,* and appears to be embodied again in the Devil Memnoch. And this characterization continues to accompany scenes of sexuality without intercourse and its apparently homoerotic nature. Witness Lestat's love for Marius, Armand, and Louis, and his voraciously erotic appetite. Again, readers profit by translating such features through the new code, a feature of which is that the gender of a vampire's victim or lover is now utterly irrelevant. True, Dracula sexually preyed on women only, and readers understood this in terms of conventional sexuality. But Rice's vampires feel intensely erotic pleasure in the kill and the feeding without regard to gender. And it seems no great stretch to consider the androgyny and homoeroticism (or pan-eroticism) present in much recent vampire literature as evidence of Rice's profound influence.

Thus the code suggests we interpret a sensuously described encounter between a male human and a male vampire, or even between two male vampires, not as evidence of Rice's preoccupation with homosexuality but as an example of sex without gender. When the old understanding forces readers to choose between two gender-determined sexual types, they resort to labels like "homosexual." But in novels where none of the main characters, male or female, have functioning sexual organs, that label is slightly absurd. The new code helps readers see how maleness or femaleness might be understood not by physical apparatus or by what goes where during sex, but instead by a quality of personality, of selfhood, far more complex and difficult to define. Once such a code is adopted, we may read it as reflecting an appreciation of how male sexuality in the real world could benefit by assuming many characteristics traditionally associated with female sexuality. Like Rice's vampires, males might focus not on isolated anatomical mechanisms but on the total experience of proximity and contact. Like Rice's other Strangers, men can learn the empowerment of eschewing power.

The third book in *The Vampire Chronicles* portrays once more a world of vampiric Strangers or outsiders, a world imbued with their sensuousness, their erotic killings regardless of gender. But there is something new as well: a new creation myth, one in which the racial progenitors even have the archetypal initials A. and E., except the A. is not Adam but Akasha, the female. In this creation story the serpent figure is the stupid, unwitting spirit Amel, and only women are the truly active parties: Akasha's will sets in motion the creation of the vampire race, albeit unintentionally; the sisters Maharet and Mekare are the essential catalysts, and the important sacrificial victims; and all males, even Lestat, are powerless in an apocalyptic struggle among vampire women. The book suggests a powerful matriarchy among the vampires, counterpoised against the predominantly patriarchal order among humans. Furthermore, Akasha's aspirations to divinity and her desire to save the world provoke her to begin systematically murdering 99 percent of all human males.

Men, or at least men's propensities, are the mundanely sinister force in Akasha's view of the world. She envisions instead a world in which women are free and unafraid; even when provoked, such women "would shrink from the common violence that lurks in the heart of every man" (277). She intends to save a few men, keeping them, she says, "where the women may have them when they want them, and I assure you they shall not be used as women have been used by men" (334). Other ancient vampires also know of darkness in the male heart. When Maharet recalls a time when she was punished by being publicly raped, she remembers thinking that the appointed rapist would not be able to perform his duty because he sympathized with her; but she confesses, "I knew little of men then, of how the pleasures of the flesh can combine in them with hatred and anger; of how they can hurt as they perform the act which women perform, more often than not, for love" (313).

In this view males are clearly flawed creatures. But they are not flawed beyond redemption; in the end Akasha is not permitted to destroy the males of the world. In a supremely ironic scene Rice reveals the bankruptcy of Akasha's position; Akasha is arguing with Lestat that her plan is flawless, when suddenly she says to him, "I love you because you are so perfectly what is wrong with all things male. Aggressive, full of hate and recklessness, and endlessly eloquent excuses for violence—you are the essence of masculinity" (336). The irony is that Lestat has been arguing against violence, against her plan of wholesale slaughter; she is the one who has eloquently excused violence, who has been aggressive and hateful. Finally it is not men or maleness that Rice's books deplore, but an unthinking allegiance to a system where power determines everything, including sexuality—allegiance, in other words, to an outdated social code.

This is nowhere more clear than in *The Tale of the Body Thief,* the fourth book of the *Chronicles.* Here Lestat's reentry into the body of an ordinary mortal human male has scarcely been accomplished before he finds himself overwhelmed by this body's sexual impulses to the degree that he actually commits the rape of a mortal female. His subsequent resolve not to allow such impulses to be expressed unchecked is borne out in his relationship with the mortal nun Gretchen. If their sexual congress is a violation of Catholic law and doctrine, it is at least consensual and not some kind of celebration of traditionally male sexual power. Lestat's personal penchant for evil, a welcome reappearance in *The Tale of the Body Thief,* finds its true expression not in the kind of sexual rape he inflicts upon the young woman, but instead in the symbolic rape whereby he forces vampirism on his mortal friend David Talbot. This latter act, while clearly evil to human sensibilities, is neither particularly male nor particularly sexual. Nor, from a vampiric perspective, is it an oppressive act; rather, it frees Talbot from the prison of mortal flesh, and allows Lestat forever after to love his friend as an equal. Thus this novel, like the others before it, rejects the kind of male sexuality valorized in the old code, where oppressiveness was read as masculine energy, where the typically selfish male orgasm translated as total fulfillment. The new code suggests instead that love is what can happen between equals; as such it promotes its own energy, its own fulfillment.

Of course, the traditional vampire story supported the old code. In Hebrew mythology all humans as children of Eve are potential victims for Lilith, whose fury over Adam's rejection of her—because she would not consent to subservience under him—drives her to destroy and consume human beings. Men thus learned long ago to fear the woman who would not be subjugated. In all of her novels, Rice offers a revised view of human sexuality and portrays different ways of attempting to fulfill human needs. She argues against a view of sexuality that considers coitus the only vehicle and orgasm the only goal for erotic expression. This view of sexuality, while juvenile, has nonetheless been perpetuated in our culture, certainly in most pornography, but even in much if not most popular literature and film. It stresses sex as an activity characterized by a definite, brief event; it includes assumptions of dominance and submission as functions of gender; it is obsessed with anatomical structures; its focus is not sensuous but mechanistic. And one of its most potent symbols is the male vampire who puts the young virgin into a submissive swoon. Rice argues instead for a sexuality that is patient and respectful, that loves without debasement. We too can enjoy the benefits of a society free of arbitrary distinctions; we need merely try and understand those who are utterly Strangers to us—people of the other gender.

Rice has preempted us, in a way. Together with all her re-inscriptions of the essential codes of vampire narrative, together with her depiction of a concept of human relations not before attempted in horror fiction, she has stepped in one other way into unfamiliar territory, and has entered the consciousness of a sex opposite hers: virtually all her narrators and protagonists are men. In so doing she has done what we all must do: overcome the alienation, the strangeness, the monstrousness perceived in those who are different from ourselves, finally to locate the true horror not in the other but in the self. Then, and only then, can we hope to subdue it.

Works Cited

Auerbach, Nina. *Romantic Imprisonment: Women and Other Glorified Outcasts.* New York: Columbia UP, 1985.

Hoppenstand, Gary, and Ray B. Browne, eds. *The Gothic World of Anne Rice.* Bowling Green, OH: Bowling Green State University Popular P, 1996.

———. "Vampires, Witches, Mummies, and Other Charismatic Personalities: Exploring the Anne Rice Phenomenon." Hoppenstand and Browne 1-12.

Le Fanu, J. Sheridan. "Carmilla." 1872. *A Clutch of Vampires.* Ed. Raymond T. McNally. Greenwich, CT: New York Graphic Society, 1974.

Ramsland, Katherine. "The Lived World of Anne Rice's Novels." Hoppenstand and Browne 13-33.

Rice, Anne. *Interview with the Vampire.* New York: Knopf, 1976.

———. *Memnoch the Devil.* New York: Knopf, 1995.

———. *The Queen of the Damned.* New York: Knopf, 1988.

———. *The Tale of the Body Thief.* New York: Knopf, 1992.

———. *The Vampire Lestat.* New York: Knopf, 1985.

Ronay, Gabriel. *The Truth About Dracula.* New York: Stein and Day, 1972.

Sage, Victor. *Horror Fiction in the Protestant Tradition.* New York: St. Martin's, 1988.

Stoker, Bram. *Dracula.* 1897. Oxford: Oxford UP, 1983.

Twitchell, James B. *The Living Dead: A Study of the Vampire in Romantic Literature.* Durham, NC: Duke UP, 1981.

Waller, Gregory A. *The Living and the Undead.* Urbana: U of IL P, 1986.

EDWARD J. INGEBRETSEN (ESSAY DATE 1996)

SOURCE: Ingebretsen, Edward J. "Anne Rice: Raising Holy Hell, Harlequin Style." In *The Gothic World of Anne Rice*, edited by Gary Hoppenstand and Ray B. Browne, pp. 91-108. Bowling Green, Ohio: Bowling Green State University Popular Press, 1996.

In the following essay, Ingebretsen studies the theological debate that takes place in Interview with the Vampire.

> . . . the first maker of the Gods was fear.
>
> —William James, *The Varieties of Religious Experience*

> Our fiction is not merely a flight from the physical data of the actual world. . . . It is, bewilderingly and embarrassingly, a gothic fiction, non-realistic and negative, sadist and melodramatic—a literature of darkness and the grotesque.
>
> —Leslie Fiedler, *Love and Death in the American Novel*

> what can be imagined can be done
>
> —Anne Rice

The American gothic—like its Old World counterpart—remains a tradition almost obsessively concerned with the hazards of social memory. Fantasy genres, generally devalued and discredited, nonetheless have important work to do; they construct within approved parameters public memory, principally, one could argue, looking ahead and looking behind—formulaic terror on the one hand and formalized nostalgia on the other. Both extremes have been crucial modes of self-reflection in the New World since colonial times.

It is customary to talk about "subtext" and "submerged values" in the gothic tradition (by which, generally, are meant garden-variety Marxist, political ones).[1] However, it is less usual to consider this protean genre from a theologically nuanced perspective—that is, as a genre that questions metaphysical ideologies, in addition to whatever social commentary it may make. Perhaps it is easier to presume that writers of Christian allegory read life through the prescriptive focus of an a priori cosmology. John Bunyan's *The Pilgrim's Progress*, for instance, enacts metaphysics as politics while displacing social conflict into moralized emotions. At first glance it may be less easy to observe that same mystification at work in Robert Heinlein's *Stranger in a Strange Land*, or in Ray Bradbury's *Something Wicked This Way Comes*, or in Anne Rice's *Interview with the Vampire*. Yet all three are equally weighted with moralistic zeal—much of it post-puritanical, even post-Christian.[2]

Nonetheless, theology always had been the ghost rattling in the gothic literary basement. In *Horror Fiction in the Protestant Tradition* Victor Sage points out that the "rhetoric of the horror novel is demonstrably theological in character."[3] Joel Porte explains that in the tradition of Ann Radcliffe, the "proper business of the orthodox novel of Terror was to expand the soul religiously" ("In the Hands of an Angry God" 43).[4] Porte likewise argues for the importance of "Protestant—indeed Calvinist—religious motifs" in the genre of the novel of terror:

> Viewing Gothic mystery thus, as a substitute for discredited religious mystery, we may consent to recognize that . . . *le genre noir* represented for its producers and consumers alike a genuine expression of profound religious malaise.
>
> (43n)

Porte concludes as "surprising," how little "systematic consideration has been given to Gothic fiction as the expression of a fundamentally Protestant theological or religious disquietude" (43).

Elsewhere (in *Maps of Heaven, Maps of Hell: Religious Terror as Memory from the Puritans to Stephen King*) I extend Porte's observation that gothic texts derive their emotive power from a metaphysical discourse that is fiercely disallowed in public. I argue that the "terroristic literature" (Oral Coad's term) of an Anglophile literary tradition serves as a repository for religious imperatives suppressed by political expediency. A quick glance reflects the still-evident theologies shadowing political fantasies of chosenness, race, and nationalism. For example, Cotton Mather (of Salem infamy), in sermons and apocalyptic theologies, customarily employed a rhetoric of spiritual terror for the purpose of reforming civic order. Jonathan Edwards, likewise, caused civic hysteria through his use of paranoiac religious fantasies. From a more literary perspective, in his short fiction and novels Nathaniel Hawthorne's irony undercuts domestic as well as religious pieties, while Melville's Captain Ahab finds the "pasteboard masks" of illusory reality as formidable an adversary as the white whale. In this century H. P. Lovecraft's breathless apostasies invert this tradition of religious rhetoric, while contemporary markets for horror and sentiment keep raising these restless

FROM THE AUTHOR

RICE ON HER FEARS

I think all my writing has been part of a battle with my fears. When I write, I explore my worst fears and then take my protagonist right into awful situations that I myself am terrified by. And I think that the act of putting all that fear and terror and confusion into an orderly, plotted story has been very therapeutic for me. It definitely helps me to continue through life.

Obviously I'm obsessed with death. I'm not obsessed, *per se,* with pain and suffering. I actually try not to write about it, surprisingly enough. And so even though my books are supposed to be bloody and horrible, there is a shrinking from this. Or at least there's a terrible moral dilemma there. I mean, I have to write about pain, obviously— the pain that other people have suffered and pain I'd be afraid to suffer myself. I feel very driven to do it, and it clearly helps me. I only hope that it's in such a framework that it does not simply add to the horror of someone else.

SOURCE: Rice, Anne, with Mikal Gilmore. "The Devil and Anne Rice." *Rolling Stone* (13-27 July 1995): 92-4, 97-8.

ghosts. In a determinedly secular age, shadows still exist of a history of divine privilege.

The religious cosmology inspired by the Calvinists and typified in Edwards's classic sermon, "Sinners in the Hands of an Angry God," can be seen, then, to continue as paradigm of American intellectual history. It was abstracted, mystified, and secularized in Emerson and the nineteenth-century tradition of drawing-room poetry. Reappropriated in the fantasies of horrorists like Poe and H. P. Lovecraft, the confusing mix of entrapment, victimization, and expiation typical of this cosmology blended into an enduring and recognizable formula of "religious eroticism" (Germaine Greer qtd. in Russ 676). Such a process is at work in the early days of the horror revival (Friedkin's *The Exorcist*), and more recently, in the breathless

tabloid moralisms of Stephen King, Dean Koontz, and in the various gothics of Anne Rice.

Theological disputation, then, remains a traditionally gothic activity, and nowhere is it more in evidence than in Anne Rice's *Interview with the Vampire.* Dictating his life to a young man wielding a tape-recorder (*interview* is not quite the proper term for the one-way nature of the narration), the novel's main character, the vampire Louis, finds himself interleaving theodicies and proofs for the existence of God along with his autobiographical reflections. After much anguished speculation, Louis concludes that his own immortal existence is an ontological impossibility and, therefore, the greatest *proof* of God's absence. Louis recalls the time he wandered into the Cathedral of St. Louis in New Orleans, only to realize that he was the sole supernatural presence in the sacred building. Louis muses, ". . . neither heaven nor hell seemed more than a tormenting fancy. To know, to believe, in one or the other . . . that was perhaps the only salvation for which I could dream" (*Interview* 164). Louis's reflection confirms Maurice Levy's insight that "in some sense the fantastic is a compensation that man provides for himself, at the level of the imagination, for what he has lost at the level of faith" (qtd. in Porte 43). Louis himself says as much when he meets Armand, the powerful Parisian vampire: "after seeing what I have become . . . I can now accept the most fantastical truth of all: that there is no meaning to any of this!" (*Interview* 241).

In its theological self-reflexivity, then, Rice's *Interview* conforms to the theologized gothic identified by Sage, Porte, DeLamotte, and Levy. Yet more remains to be said. Among other problems there remains the difficulty of taxonomizing gothic texts in the first place. David H. Richter's analysis of the gothic mode leaves the way clear for some useful distinctions, particularly between the gothic genre and its hybrid offspring, the text of terror, with which David Punter sees the gothic as "primarily" concerned (*Literature of Terror*).

> By 1830, the original impulse of the Gothic was spent, though the tale of terror was to survive both as an influence upon mainstream realistic fiction through the Victorian era and beyond, and in its purest form as a minor subgenre of the novel in both high and popular art right up to the present. (Richter 149)

Richter is correct in distinguishing between the "original impulse of the Gothic" and the "tale of terror" that survived it. The "original impulse," as numerous critics observe, was a reaction to the conservativism of neoclassic literature; the "tale of terror" emerged from a tradition of sermons and broadsides, flourished for a time with the traditional genre, and then finally superseded it in its tabloid and sentimentalized versions. Nonetheless, while I don't share Richter's confidence that "we all know intuitively what the Gothic is" I do agree with him that "it is not one but at least three things" (150). The "Gothic flame," in Devendra Varma's expression, has kindled a number of diverse sparks—including, as Bette Roberts catalogs them, "Gothic science fiction, Gothic detective fiction, Gothic erotica, and other hybrids" (Roberts 18).

In her study of Anne Rice, Bette Roberts argues that Rice follows the "male Gothic" example of Matthew Lewis, noting that his ur-gothic *The Monk* is characterized by "physical horror," rather than by the interiorized drama proper to the Radcliffean tradition. The difference, Roberts writes, is the "distinction between the . . . psychological terror in the female Gothic novels and that of physical horror in those written by men" (16). Yet Rice is accomplished in both modes, as well as being conversant with several others. Although she is best known for her trilogy, *The Vampire Chronicles,* she has also written at least two historical novels and an assortment of other "erotics." In all of these, elements of the gothic—as well as the romance, historical novel, and sentimental tale of confession—mix and conjoin. Consequently, it is often difficult, critically, to place a specific text.[5]

In her gothic texts, for instance, Rice consciously rejects the anti-Catholicism conventionally associated with the genre. As she remarked in a *Playboy* interview with Digby Diehl, it was exposure to the vivid and marvelous lives of the Catholic hagiographic tradition that first interested her in genres of the supernatural. Nor are her unabashedly New World vampires ecclesiaphobic in the accustomed mode of vampires. Louis, good New Orleans Catholic, loves the baroque trappings of church equipage and liturgy: "I was a Catholic; I believed in saints. I lit tapers before their marble statues in churches; I knew their pictures, their symbols, their names" (*Interview* 7-8). Further, speaking to the young man in contemporary San Francisco, Louis mocks his superstition about vampires and crucifixes: "Nonsense . . . I can look on anything I like. And I rather like looking on crucifixes in particular" (22). Many of his meditations on the failure of religious belief, become, for Louis, meditations on aesthetic first principles rather than problems of metaphysical agency. In this respect Louis seems to speak for his creator; Rice herself observed that the Protestant vision renders the mysteries of life "more sterile" (Roberts 23).

Yet there is another aspect to Rice's eclectic Gothicism that must be considered, and which in some ways is more typical to the complexity of Rice's thought. *Interview with the Vampire* is not only gothic, it is a specifically Americanized version of the genre. First, it signals a departure from claustrophobic familial haunts, as Sage argues them, as well as from the troubled domestic sites customarily associated with the gothic.[6] Rice's fiction considers haunted spaces more broadly construed, perhaps reflecting Fiedler's seminal observation that in New World gothic, wild geographic spaces replace the darkened and deteriorating family castle.[7] Rice is at her best in illuminating the horror of empty metaphysical spaces. Second, the novel is in many respects an ironic exploration of the novel of sensibility, and as such it explores how a commodified flight from the body results in the production, as Joanna Russ describes it in another context, of a "strange fusion of prurience and exaltation" (676).[8] Finally, the form of the novel itself rehearses the captivity narrative—a theological trope rendered contemporary as Louis recounts the metaphysical implications of his seduction and vampiric conversion—first at the hands of the callous, cruel, and indifferent Lestat, and later, by the willful and charming Armand. Louis's anguished and highly moralized recollections of his serial "enslavements" recall a tradition of such confessionary texts, including *Narrative of the Captivity, Sufferings and Remarks of Mrs. Mary Rowlandson; My Life and Bondage* by Frederick Douglass, and others. Characteristic of these texts is a formula of captivity and spiritualized confession that puts deviance on display as moral uplift and theological lesson.[9]

With this history in mind, then, we can turn to Rice's revisions of the gothic and see how she employs its conventions to address a quite different "sensation or 'body' genre."[10] Rice blends the theological moralisms of the captivity with the gothic images of social entrapment in order to argue the genre from what DeLamotte suggests is its original perspective—that of a woman.[11] In addition she combines another staple of the vernacular theological tradition—the sermonizing spectacle of deviances, titillatingly confessed—with the romance genre's formula of sentimentalized sex. At stake here for Rice and her vampires (I use the metaphor advisedly), are the horrific implications of a creature as metaphysically ambiguous as the vampire—the gendered woman, especially as this hapless creature takes form trapped in the repressive representations of the Harlequin romance.

The complex parallels and intersections between the "imitation" that is gender and its enscription in the vampire metaphor rescue Rice's novel from formulaic banality (Butler 21). Louis's tale of his guilt-provoked seduction by Lestat reflects the ontological ambiguity he feels as a vampire and the gendering confusion he experiences in his subsequent relations with Lestat. On the one hand, Louis is the eldest son of a wealthy New Orleans family. At twenty-five, his father dead, Louis was "head of the family" when he meets Lestat (*Interview* 5). He is thus heir to the tradition of male privilege, representing not only the investment of the state but familial primogeniture as well. As agent of state and family in New Orleans, Louis is the visible sign of patriarchy, equally busy about disposing the lands of his estate and arranging for the futures of his sister and mother. (In the waning years of this privilege, that is; Louis's name ironically recalls the ineffectual Louis XVI, who historically, would have been beheaded two years after Louis's transformation as a vampire.)

Yet despite Louis's primogeniture and male birthright, he finds the situation reversed when it comes to telling the story of his turbulent relationship with Lestat—an affair which he couches in the language of romantic pursuit. Significantly, Louis suggests that it was greed for his family's plantation, Pointe Du Lac, that first attracts Lestat's attention to him. Reading between the lines of Louis's narrative, the reader understands that Lestat finds, wooes, and finally, seduces the passive Louis, thus assuming a kind of dowry-like control over the lands and properties of his estate. Thus, Louis's metaphysical anxiety, which takes up so much of his dialogue with himself, finds its more mundane parallel in the confusing, passive, often imitative role he finds himself in vis-à-vis Lestat, his "maker" and, in many respects, his master. Ontological ambiguity is, appropriately enough, mirrored forth in gender, and one suspects Rice of drawing from another tale for this motif—*Frankenstein*, by Mary Shelley. Like Shelley's creature, Louis is created as both copy of and supplement to an ostensibly superior being; further, both are defined and valued from the point of a commandeering, prior, male, and thus seemingly original gaze. Louis, Lestat's companion, in short, is gendered female.

Lestat's primary function as vampire, he says, is to be God-like, a master. Explaining this to Louis he says, "God kills, and so shall we . . . for no creatures under God are as we are, none so like Him as ourselves, dark angels" (*Interview* 89). Lestat, active, male, disposes as he will. Louis, however, cannot kill because he finds it aesthetically revolting. If Lestat is gendered by action and silence, in typical Harlequin fashion, Louis is gendered feminine in his passivity and his reliance upon words and feelings. In his passivity Louis acquires the feminine—as Roberts notes, the "moral equivalent of virtue" (Roberts 18). Lestat critiques Louis's ethics—as well as his aesthetic sensibilities—as nostalgia for an originary fantasy of being mortal. And yet origins, precisely—or lack of them—are what trouble Louis. Though gendered male as a mortal, as a vampire Louis finds himself stripped of male prerogative; he functions as similacrum, a copy and supplement of an unknown original. Even Lestat is a simulacrum, a copy without original, as Louis finds out to his dismay; whatever origins he has Louis cannot discover.

Doubly troubled by Lestat's apparent lack of origin and by the confusions of his own being, Louis says he "burned with the questions of my own divided nature" (*Interview* 80). Monique Wittig wittily reflects this more mundane aspect of the vampire's discontent in another way: "So what is this divided Being introduced into language through gender? It is an impossible Being, it is a Being that does not exist, an ontological joke" (66). Gender and vampirism are imperfect fits of a role that is always by definition a kind of "theatre," as Clover observes: a role that is always slipping, a role that passes only in dark shadows, and never takes too strongly to the light.[12] Louis remains anxious, even obsessed, about the adequacy of his "passing"; he finds his role as vampire equally a difficult fit, one that demands skills he lacks; the failure of his performance is always a concern to him.[13] Indeed, with good reason; Louis's inability to "pass"—as Armand says—is evident to all: "That you are flawed is obvious to [the other vampires]: you feel too much, you think too much" (*Interview* 254).

Lestat tells Louis that it is his "sensibility" that is the problem, not his vampirism. After hearing Louis proclaim his intention to leave him, Lestat responds dismissively: "I thought as much . . . and I thought as well that you would make a flowery announcement. Tell me what a monster I am; what a vulgar fiend" (*Interview* 80). Lestat's repudiation of Louis's "sensibility" is appropriate, or at least understandable; since throughout the narrative Louis is aestheticized (or, rather, he aesthetizes himself), delineating for himself an inner sphere of emotional fulfillment and need that Lestat says other vampires abhor: "We have no need of your sensitivity." Louis has only the power to feel, and to tell his feelings, which he does, at length. As one critic observes—chiefly about Louis I suspect—a Rice vampire "could talk an adder to death" (Adams 105).

Louis relies upon words to create and sustain his world. He needs the protection of literary mediation; he relies upon feelings to orient himself in the "savage garden" when, as Lestat charges, he should be engaged in making himself a space in it. As he details his turbulent relationship with Lestat to the boy, Louis laments, "You must understand I did not snub him because he did not appreciate his experience. I simply could not understand how such feelings could be wasted" (*Interview* 31). Louis is the quintessential man of feeling, two hundred years beyond his time. And Lestat? As Louis sighs, "Lestat understood nothing." But then, Lestat didn't have to "understand"—his function, as he reminded Louis, was to be a "killer." Louis's passivity and sensitivity accomplish what gender does: confirm and augment the totalizing image of the superior creature, the active male.

In essence, then, Louis's problem is one of gender, metaphysically as well as physically. Roberts argues, wrongly, I think, that Rice's vampires are "genderless" in nature (Roberts 20). Nor does the narrative offer the "gender-free perspective" suggested by one reviewer (qtd. in Roberts 33). To the contrary, Rice's vampires parodically reenact gender conventions and their customary politics. Nowhere is Rice's revision of these gender politics more evident than in the scenes surrounding the vampirization of Claudia, the orphan child. To forestall Louis's threat of leaving him, Lestat vampirizes a young child named Claudia, whose mother has died of plague and left her an orphan. Lestat presents her to Louis, knowing that his need to nurture will bind him to the child, and thus, make him forget about leaving Lestat. This dark parody of reproductory politics as a substitute for male love is only a prelude to what follows, as Lestat, Louis, and Claudia begin a bizarre enactment of the conventional family drama. Bound together by a mix of emotions—death and hatred, need and hunger—Louis describes the three in the romantic imagery of love or, alternately, in the archly sentimental language of domestic bliss. Rice's horror here, one might observe, is family values, seen through a glass, horrifically. Through Louis's eyes Rice chronicles the deathless horror of being trapped for all eternity in an unwanted, or unfulfilling, intimacy, trapped by economics and social need into the formal and horrific replication of an empty structure.

Finally, the question of gender and the possibilities of perversion it makes possible encourages a look at what is thought to be the novel's "homoeroticism." Since Ernest Jones's revisionist Freudianism, which conflated semen with blood in the psychic economy, the vampire theme has a history of identification with homoeroticism. Yet Jones's theory, explains Ellis Hanson, "has the unfortunate consequence of rendering every cocksucker a kind of blood sucker" (328).[14] Accordingly, Rice's novels have developed, at least in the straight press, a reductive gay appeal: "Gays took the book to heart for its homoeroticism . . . guys in capes sucking each other's blood" (Gates 76). Such a reading only reenacts a cultural homophobia; it reflects a taboo against deviant sexuality except when sexual expression is useful for consumption, erotic titillation, or policement along a normalizing "straight" axis. Sexual repression—a staple of the gothic and of a gothicized commodity culture, it might be noted—spectacularizes and moralizes the taboo. It thereby authorizes its expression and exploitation, rather than negating it.

In Rice's *Interview,* for instance, what appear at first to be descriptions (purple, if not quite torrid) of ecstatic union between two males, Lestat and Louis, become, rather, the traditional assaultative rhetoric of sex, coded male. Indeed, to reverse the equation Christopher Craft lays out, in Rice's *Interview* "an implicitly [heteroerotic] desire achieves representation as a monstrous [homosexuality]."[15] With some slight changes, Rice's novel—like many love-soaked tales of another, closely allied genre—"reveals the anxieties of women in a subordinate social position" (Roberts 17).

Anne Rice published *Interview with the Vampire* in 1976—a year that witnessed, as Ann Snitow notes, a "boom in romantic fiction market for women," one with a subsequent "growth of 400 percent" in the following years (259). Snitow refers specifically here to the genre of Harlequin-type romances, an eponymous genre whose sales now number in the "several hundred million a year" (259). In "Mass Market Romance" Snitow analyzes the Harlequin formula, arguing that it offers women sex—the "one adventure" permitted them in a late-capitalist social order. Of course, as Snitow lucidly explains, what begins as esteemed privilege becomes problematic, for when women try to fantasize about sex, the society offers them "taboos on most of its imaginable expressions except those that deal directly with arousing and satisfying men" (266). Harlequins, Snitow says, "fill a vacuum"; their "romances make bridges" (266) between the "contradictions" of a society's permitted myths and its feared nightmares.

But myths and nightmares can easily displace each other; often the lines blur, and the one completes or becomes the other. In this respect the "glamor and change" of fantasy and romance genres easily become recoded in the fears of metamorphosis and instability of another genre entirely. Much, therefore, is clarified in Rice's ostensible gothicism when considered from the perspective of "romantic fiction marketed for women" (Snitow 259). Both are genres of desire and fear, emotions formulaically elicited yet punitively proscribed.[16] Like Louis, the women of the Harlequin formula are allowed no recourse other than words and the socially necessary fiction of gender and its spurious prize—the anticipatory illusion of romance. Louis finds that having to pass as mortal is, necessarily, having to reestablish gender and its constraints; although he views them, now, from another perspective, as a waking confinement not unlike the coffin in which he rests.

Like so much of the gothic genre, Rice's novel is a first-person "confessional," and much of what Louis confesses is coded, as we have seen, feminine. Louis's subject is Lestat—his whimsy, capriciousness, his cruelty. Despite the title, Louis is not so much interviewed but just talks—his tone of mixed indignation and rage echoing the fury of Faulkner's Rosa Coldfield, who, as Quentin observes, is still obsessing about Sutpen's crude sexualizing appraisal of her. As Quentin reflects in *Absalom, Absalom!*: "It's because she wants it told" (10). Narrative is the only weapon she has.[17] Similarly, much of Louis's narrative is precisely his attempt to read (first) Lestat and then Armand—to know something more of their origins and their purpose and thus, in some fashion to escape the power of their degradation. Louis's narrative mixes fury and anger and guilt over his seduction, although the narrative derives its power from his retrospective understanding that initially he very much wanted what Lestat had to offer.

Snitow writes that "since all action in the [Harlequins] is described from the female point of view" the reader "identifies with the heroine's efforts to decode the erratic gestures of 'dark, tall and gravely handsome' men" (261). The semiotics of the male is the subject, and as Louis finds out, this is a hermeneutics of suspicion if there ever was one. Lestat is the center of Louis's emotional, often erotically detailed narrative. His first description of Lestat pays careful attention to specifics. Without a sound, says Louis, a "tall fair-skinned man with a mass of blond hair and a graceful, almost feline quality to his movements" entered his room (12), appearing in the manner, as Louis remarks offhandedly, of a "lover" (17). In the impassioned transformation scene Louis recalls that Lestat "put his right arm around me and pulled me close to his chest. Never had I been this close to him before, and in the dim light I could see the magnificent radiance of his eye" (18). Feminized, Louis feels the gaze. The young man who is taping Louis breaks into the narration here and comments, "It sounds as if it was like being in love." Louis's eyes "gleamed" and he responds, "That's correct. It is like love" (31). Of course. Those molded in the Harlequin school of romance know too well the vampiric thrall of love.

Says Snitow, "The books [of the Harlequin formula] are permeated by phallic worship. Male is good, male is exciting. . . . Cruelty, callousness, coldness, menace . . . are all equated with maleness and treated as a necessary part of the package" (261). Lestat is well socialized in male behaviors and conforms easily to Snitow's Harlequinized male, one who, in contradistinction to the woman, is "complete in isolation." Vampires, Lestat tells Louis, are "lone predators and seek for companionship no more than cats in the jungle" (*Interview* 84). What companionships exist will be slave relationships, as Lestat pointedly says, "one will be the slave of the other, the way you are of me" (84). Louis, about to object to this characterization, "realized [he'd] been his slave all along" (84). Indeed, his narrative continually references his slave-like dependency upon Lestat's energy and vampiric knowledge.

Snitow argues that novels following the Harlequin formula "have no plot in the usual sense. All tension and problems arise from the fact that the Harlequin world is inhabited by two species incapable of communicating with each other, male and female" (260). While the the two species in question (male and female) are, from one perspective, fictions represented and enforced by gender, their mutual fictiveness and incomprehensibility are close enough a fit to the melodrama of relations offered in *Interview*. Its hundreds of pages resembles Joanna Russ's description of the modern gothics: "Over-subtle emotions, a 'denseness' of interpersonal texture that is at its most complex, simply baffling, and at its simplest, bathetic" (Russ 681). One could indeed argue that Louis's need for metaphysical clarity—to which he constantly alludes—is in some ways a distraction from the more pressing confusions he experiences as Lestat's companion; historically, as Marx notes, the religious quest has served this purpose, as well as others.

Standing aboard ship en route to Europe, Louis, like Ahab, meditates upon the "great secret" that he had hoped to find revealed in the Old World:

> But who was to make this revelation when the sky and sea became indistinguishable and neither any longer was chaos? God? Or Satan? It struck me suddenly what consolation it would be to know Satan, to look upon his face, no matter how terrible that countenance was, to know that I belonged to him totally, and thus put to rest forever the torment of this ignorance.
>
> (*Interview* 164)

Good metaphysician, Louis finds his logic based upon a first principle of ignorance. Even in his relations with the Divine, Louis finds he must be passive, accepting—for lack of anything better—what minor consolations he could. Even at a level of metaphysics, then, Louis finds himself responding in gender-determined ways. It is Louis's great crisis that he cannot understand his own existence outside of a framework made possible by the belief in God; as the ontological copy, he has no existence outside that a priori originating (and authorizing) gaze. Yet his relationship with God is as phallic and as controlling, as cruel and emotionally anorexic as Lestat's. In the ironically named St. Louis Cathedral, morally outraged at himself, at his captivity and victimization by Lestat, distressed by the silence of God, Louis thrusts himself at the priest and cries, "Do you see what I am! Why, if God exists, does He suffer me to exist!" (*Interview* 148).

One might attribute Rice's blurring of the lines between gothic and Harlequin formulas to mere chance, or as a coincidental intersection of cultural tropes. But one can also view Rice's *Vampire Chronicles* as—at least in part—an elaborate and deft satire of the inherently vampiric nature of a commodity culture, especially one in which gender is chief fantasy as well as chief commodity. Victorian culture was "gender anxious" (Craft 219), agonizing over the fluidity of gender roles; and in the words of one of its greatest scholars, the vampire's blood exchange "stands for every conceivable union of men with women, men with men, women with women"—every "permutation, normal, subnormal, hypernormal, or supernatu-

ral."[18] Contemporary American culture has not left that anxiety in the dark, gothic repositories of Victorian history; indeed, that fear is still socially formative. The vampire is a reigning cultural metaphor encoding numerous, often contradictory, social emotions. Reflecting upon the themes of her *Chronicles*, Rice calls the vampire a "fathomless well of metaphor," adding that "once I was looking through the vampire's eyes . . . I was able to describe the world as I really saw it."[19] Rice's horror revisits an uncanny scene, one too familiar and routinely idealized (or essentialized) out of consciousness. The world Rice sees is ontologically odd, constructed of seemingly fixed gender roles—or, at least, roles with an apparent necessary political fixity. Whether as text, as vampire, or as the rote duties of a "gendrified" shopper, it's all done with mirrors, a kind of slavish imitation; and as Lestat observes with satisfaction, "that's how vampires increase . . . through slavery" (*Interview* 84).

Snitow writes that one of the culture's "most intense myths"—the "ideal of an individual who is brave and complete in isolation"—is "for men, only." Women, on the other hand, "are grounded, enmeshed in civilization, in social connection, in family, and in love. . . . Their one socially acceptable moment of transcendence is romance" (266). In "Compulsory Heterosexuality" Adrienne Rich makes a similar point: "heterosexual romance has been represented as the great female adventure, duty, and fulfillment" (242). The formula romance books, observes Snitow,

> fill a vacuum created by social conditions. When women try to picture excitement, the society offers them one vision, romance. When women try to imagine companionship, the society offers them one vision, male, sexual companionship. When women try to fantasize about success, mastery, the society offers them one vision, the power to attract a man.
>
> (266)

This observation suggests why Rice's *The Vampire Chronicles*, though ostensibly gothic, are horror rewritten in a Harlequin mode—and why, as Adrienne Rich observes in another context, they are horrific: "The ideology of heterosexual romance, beamed at [the woman] from childhood out of fairy tales, television, films, advertising, popular songs, wedding pageantry, is a tool ready to the procurer's hand" (237). Rice's Harlequin horrors are romance rather than horror; or better, they are the horror of romance in which, as Russ observes, "'Occupation: Housewife' is simultaneously avoided, glamorized, and vindicated" (675).

Christopher Craft suggests that the power of the vampire is its power of "subversion of the stable and lucid distinctions of gender" (218). Robin Wood observes that the power of the vampire mythology lies in its "privileged focus for any inquiry into the possibilities of liberation within Western civilization" (175). Vampires conventionally serve as icon of desire unfilled, and Rice's great achievement is to find another icon for that desire much closer to home. Her image is much more recognizable—yet for all that, one as horrific. The endless chain of unfilled desire, elicited yet voided in Harlequin fiction is comparable to the endless fear of fulfilled desire that so often is the subtext of gothic horror Vampires, in particular, are endlessly adaptable, as resurrectable as the gothic genre itself. Yet both "sensation" genres under discussion are noted for their conservatism. Writes Stephen King in *Danse Macabre*: "The writer of horror fiction is neither more nor less than an agent of the status quo" (51); the horror story, he writes, contains a "moral code so strong it would make a Puritan smile" (368). In Anne Rice's case, the moral seems equally clear.

It is customary to denigrate the gothic genre, to accuse it of being a kind of "book lite," zombie fodder for the unthinking (although heavily shopping) masses. It has even been called by critic Peter Parisi closet pornography, for "people ashamed to read pornography" (qtd. in Snitow, 267). But then, this sort of dismissal is consistent with, and similar to arguments made against other forms of cultural dissimulations called oddly enough, "diversions." Of course, the chief of these arguments in the extent to which violence is the pornography of choice in a culture that repudiates sex—except when it can be seamlessly inserted into cultural semiotics of consumption. Claudia, by accident of her youth, is less tied to mortal sensibilities than is her guardian, Louis. In her innocence of these constraints she speaks to the point of both horror and pornography: "I seduce [humans], draw them close to me, with an insatiable hunger, a constant never-ending search for something . . . something, I don't know what it is" (*Interview* 125). Desire is the thing; it is the nature of desire, always, to replicate itself, to become the copy of the copy—to remain in itself unknown, even unknowable, vampiric. Thus, as Parisi argues (in Snitow 267), if sex is the reason for Harlequin romance, similar things might be said for the moralization of other "sensibilist"

genres in which eros is fetishized, rather than enacted, either in violent representation or in romantic mystification.

Finally, as Carol Clover notes, "Abject terror . . . is gendered feminine, and the more concerned a given film with that condition—and it is the essence of modern horror—the more likely the femaleness of the victim" (117). The American tradition of gothic eroticizes this victimization; it draws attention to its constitutive place in a social metaphysics, in practical effect, derivatively Christian. That is, any problematic gendering—female, vampire, or homosexuality—is arraigned as transgressive and public, and thus available both for spectacle as well as policement.

Of course, critics of pornography argue that such systemic victimization is the essence of pornography, too. Yet pornography is another genre of fantasy, busy about doing culture's unspeakable business. Carol Clover writes, "Pornography . . . has to do with sex (the act) and horror with gender" (93). None of this is news to Rice, of course, who comes to gothic fiction with side interests in S& M soft porn, under the name of A. N. Roquelaure, published by E. P. Dutton, and two other erotic novels under the name Anne Rampling. Rice does it all. To return to an earlier question, then, Rice's first two vampire novels can indeed be considered gothic, though possibly for all the improper reasons. Her horrorification of the Harlequin formula of "travel, glamor, sex" disguises a deeper level in which the vampire's ontological crisis of existence reflects the greater horror of the Harlequin sentimentalized dead end—which itself derives from debased social metaphysics. Even Armand observes, perhaps with some irony, that Louis speaks for his age: "'You reflect your age differently. You reflect its broken heart'" (*Interview* 312). Rice's vampire novels are, in essence, parables of gender horror, in which the metaphor of vampire shows the extent to which gender is the great vampire, the "imitation," as Judith Butler argues, *"for which there is no original"* (21) (Butler's emphasis).

Perhaps this is why Louis torches the Theatre Des Vampires in Paris, realizing that only fire can effectively kill a vampire. In vampires and in genders, there are only copies without originals, and desire without basis or fulfillment. He understands then, the true horror of vampirism—eternal life without eternal rest, always hungry, never full. In this context I recall a popular country western song in which an abused and long-suffering wife, on Independence Day, burns down the house in which (presumably) she has been held by force of patriotic custom and law. In Rice's clever revaluation of domestic gothic, life in the afterlife of gendered mortality is not unlike a more mundane domesticity—as DeLamotte puts it, it is a "guise of transcendence" that "may be only a version of that old Gothic peril, domestic entrapment" (ix). *Interview with the Vampire* is, then, however disguised, yet one more book about a woman "who just can't seem to get out of the house" (DeLamotte 10). Whether a slave to love or a slave to terror, Hell is better than no hell, even for a vampire.

Notes

1. See Frank McConnell, "Rough Beast Slouching." McConnell writes, "The horror film is . . . a remarkable instance of submerged value, precisely because that value has come to consciousness and full articulation not through the development of critical intelligence but through the development of art itself" (110).

2. Bradbury, however, is a particular example of the close connection between terror and sentimental nostalgia. In *Trillion Year Spree*, Brian Aldiss writes, "Bradbury is of the house of Poe. The sickness of which [Bradbury] writes takes the form of glowing rosy-cheeked health" (248).

3. Sage writes, "Horror fiction gives the reader a unique insight into the way these factors [in the psychology of individual writers] operate, because the interaction between cultural homogeneity and political divergence is displayed in a peculiarly clear form in the language of these texts" (xvi). Differing from Freud, Sage argues that "the cause and the effect of the horror experience in English culture is a form of 'theological uncertainty,' an anxiety which is recognizable at many different levels of consciousness" (xvii).

4. See David Punter, *The Hidden Script*.

5. In the matter of religion, for example, while the earlier of Anne Rice's *Chronicles* most directly invoke the metaphysical inscrutabilities involved here her metaphysic (for lack of a better word) is considerably less moralistic—and considerably more "Catholic"—than Stephen King's *'Salem's Lot* (a tribute to Stoker's *Dracula*). These differences, alone, would provide an illuminating study.

6. See Sage, *Horror Fiction*; see also Eugenia DeLamotte's feminist reading of the genre, *Perils of the Night*.

7. See Fiedler, *Love and Death in the American Novel*.

8. See Russ: "No longer bodiless and yet within the code of romance—the result is a very strange fusion of prurience and exaltation, i.e., the confusion of values described by Firestone (sex = personal worth) [*The Dialectic of Sex*, 1970] combines with the 'religious' eroticism Greer [*The Female Eunuch*, 1970] notes in romance stories" (676).

9. See Marilla Battilana, *The Colonial Roots of American Fiction*.

10. Carol J. Clover, "Her Body, Himself: Gender in the Slasher Film" (93); Clover lists other "body" genres as "horror and pornography, in that order."

11. DeLamotte argues this perspective, saying that "women were (and are) the primary readers, protagonists, and creators of the genre" (8).

12. In "Her Body, Himself," Clover writes, "The idea that appearance and behavior do not necessarily indicate sex—indeed, can misindicate sex—is predicated on the understanding that sex is one thing and gender another; in practice, that sex is life, a less-than-interesting given, but that gender is theatre" (123).

13. Which is one reason, among others, Louis prefers the night. Indeed, when we hear Louis reflecting about "passing," it is always in the context of some potentially glamorous mortal setting, although at night—an evening at the theatre, restaurant, ball. Claudia, then, has additional troubles passing—either as vampire or as women, which is reflected in Louis's thinking about her: "Doll, doll." If he is a copy of a copy, she, more perversely, is even more derivative.

14. See Ernest Jones, *On the Nightmare* 119; Ellis Hanson, "Undead"; see also Sue-Ellen Chase, "Tracking the Vampire."

15. Craft argues that "the sexual threat that this novel first evokes, manipulates, sustains, but never finally represents is that Dracula will seduce, penetrate, drain another male" (218). *Dracula*, then, is another parable of gender-confusion.

16. See William Patrick Day, *In the Circles of Fear and Desire: A Study of Gothic Fantasy*.

17. Louis, who records his on a tape recorder for the reader, must, as the book's title explains, tell it all. Throughout the novel he finds himself unburdening to passing strangers, repeatedly confessing his captivity and freedom to anyone who will listen—first to Claudia, then to Lestat himself, then, later to a priest—and finally, as the novel makes clear, the narrator, and the reader. (Indeed, Louis attempts to "care for" the narrator. This reverses the customary gendering formula in fairy tale, in which the "bad girls" do all the talking while "good girls" are notable for their silence.)

18. Leonard Wolf, qtd. in "Fangs for Nothing," Tom Mathews with Lucille Beachy, *Newsweek* 30 Nov. 1992: 75.

19. Qtd. in "Fangs for Nothing," Mathews and Beachy, *Newsweek* 30 Nov. 1992: 74.

Works Cited

Adams, Phoebe-Lou. Rev. of *Interview with the Vampire*. *Atlantic Monthly* June 1976: 105.

Aldiss, Brian. *Trillion Year Spree: The History of Science Fiction*. New York: Avon, 1986.

Battilana, Marilla. *The Colonial Roots of American Fiction: Notes Toward a New Theory*. Florence, IT: Olschki, 1988.

Butler, Judith. "Imitation and Gender Insubordination." Fuss 13-31.

Chase, Sue-Ellen. "Tracking the Vampire." *Differences* 3.2 (1991): 1-21.

Clover, Carol J. "Her Body, Himself: Gender in the Slasher Film." *Fantasy and the Cinema.* Ed. James Donald. London: British Film Institute, 1989. 91-133.

Coad, Oral Sumner. "The Gothic Element in American Literature Before 1835." *Journal of English and German Philology* 25 (1925): 72-93.

Craft, Christopher. "'Kiss Me with Those Red Lips': Gender and Inversion in Bram Stoker's *Dracula.*" *Speaking of Gender.* Ed. Elaine Showalter. New York: Routledge, 1989. 216-42.

Day, William Patrick. *In the Circles of Fear and Desire: A Study of Gothic Fantasy.* Chicago: U of Chicago P, 1985.

DeLamotte, Eugenia. *Perils of the Night: A Feminist Study of the Nineteenth-Century Gothic.* New York: Oxford UP, 1990.

Diehl, Digby. "Playboy Interview: Anne Rice." *Playboy* Mar. 1993: 53-64.

Faulkner, William. *Absalom, Absalom!* New York: Modern Library, 1964.

Fiedler, Leslie. *Love and Death in the American Novel.* Rev. ed. New York: Dell, 1966.

Fuss, Diana. *Inside/Out: Lesbian Theories, Gay Theories.* New York: Routledge, 1991.

Gates, David. "Queen of the Spellbinders." *Newsweek* 5 Nov. 1990: 76.

Hanson, Ellis. "Undead." Fuss 324-41.

Ingebretsen, Edward, S. J., ed. *Maps of Heaven, Maps of Hell: Religious Terror as Memory from the Puritans to Stephen King.* New York: M. E. Sharpe, 1996.

James, William. *The Varieties of Religious Experience.* Ed. Martin Marty. New York: Penguin, 1982.

Jones, Ernest. *On the Nightmare.* New York: Liveright, 1951.

King, Stephen. *Danse Macabre.* New York: Berkley, 1982.

McConnell, Frank. "Rough Beast Slouching: A Note on Horror Movies." *Kenyon Review* 1 (1970): 109-20.

Porte, Joel. "In the Hands of an Angry God: Religious Terror in Gothic Fiction." *The Gothic Imagination: Essays in Dark Romanticism.* Ed. G. R. Thompson. Pullman: U of Washington P, 1974. 1-10.

Punter, David. *The Hidden Script: Writing and the Unconscious.* Boston: Routledge, 1985.

———. *The Literature of Terror: A History of Gothic Fictions from 1765 to the Present Day.* New York: Longmans, 1980.

Rice, Anne. *Interview with the Vampire.* New York: Ballantine, 1976.

Rich, Adrienne. "Compulsory Heterosexuality and Lesbian Existence." *The Lesbian and Gay Studies Reader.* Ed. Henry Abelove, Michele Aina Barali, and David M. Halperin. New York: Routledge, 1993. 227-54.

Richter, David H. "Gothic Fantasia: The Monsters and the Myths, a Review-Article." *Eighteenth Century* 28.2 (1987): 149-70.

Roberts, Bette B. *Anne Rice.* New York: Twayne, 1994.

Russ, Joanna. "Someone's Trying to Kill Me and I Think It's My Husband: The Modern Gothic." *Journal of Popular Culture* 6.4 (1973): 666-91.

Sage, Victor. *Horror Fiction in the Protestant Tradition.* New York: St. Martin's, 1988.

Snitow, Ann Barr. "Mass Market Romance: Pornography for Women Is Different." *Passion and Power: Sexuality in History.* Ed. Kathy Peiss and Christina Simmons. Philadelphia: Temple UP, 1989.

Varma, Devendra P. *The Gothic Flame.* New York: Russell, 1966.

Wittig, Monique. "The Mark of Gender." *The Poetics of Gender.* Ed. Nancy K. Miller. New York: Columbia UP, 1986. 62-73.

Wood, Robin. "Burying the Undead: The Use and Obsolescence of Count Dracula." *Mosaic* 16.1-2 (1983): 175-87.

FURTHER READING

Criticism

Doane, Janice Devon Hodges. "Undoing Feminism: From the Preoedipal to Postfeminism in Anne Rice's *Vampire Chronicles.*" *American Literary History* 2, no. 3 (fall 1990): 422-42.

Asserts that "Anne Rice's massively popular vampire books . . . provide a useful way of beginning to explore the difficulties of the feminist attempt to represent the mother through the language of the preoedipal."

Haas, Lynda and Robert Haas. "Living with(out) Boundaries: The Novels of Anne Rice." In *A Dark Night's Dreaming: Contemporary American Horror Fiction,* edited by Tony Magistrale and Michael A. Morrison, pp. 55-67. Columbia: University of South Carolina Press, 1996.

Contends that "there is no contemporary writer with stronger ties to the Gothic tradition than Anne Rice . . . Rice has consistently and successfully combined many of the Gothic conventions initiated by Horace Walpole . . . with her own unique style and with the concerns of postmodern philosophy."

Hoppenstand, Gary, and Ray B. Browne, eds. *The Gothic World of Anne Rice.* Bowling Green, Ohio: Bowling Green State University Popular Press, 1996, 261 p.

Comprehensive collection of essays studying Rice's works within the context of the Gothic tradition.

Kemppainen, Tatja. "Your Heart Bleeds for Me: Finding the Essential Human in Anne Rice's *Interview with the Vampire.*" *Moderna Språk* 94, no. 2 (2000): 122-36.

Compares Rice's treatment of the vampire in Interview with the Vampire *and Friedrich Wilhelm Nietzsche's treatment of the superman in* Also sprach Zarathustra, *and examines Rice's novel in terms of the theories of Sigmund Freud.*

Roberts, Bette B. *Anne Rice.* New York: Twayne, 1994, 173 p.

Book-length study of Rice's life and works.

Rout, Kathleen. "Who Do You Love? Anne Rice's Vampires and Their Moral Transition." *Journal of Popular Culture* 36, no. 3 (winter 2003): 473-79.

Maintains that "over the years" Rice's "moral neutrality toward a murderous but fascinating group of creatures has gradually evolved into a non-violent endorsement of global peace between vampires and human beings."

Tomc, Sandra. "Dieting and Damnation: Anne Rice's *Interview with the Vampire*." *English Studies in Canada* 22, no. 4 (December 1997): 441-60.

Surveys the cultural significance of female body image, androgyny, and self-abnegation in Interview with the Vampire.

Waxman, Barbara Frey. "Postexistentialism in the Neo-Gothic Mode: Anne Rice's *Interview with the Vampire*." *Mosaic* 25, no. 3 (summer 1992): 79-97.

Explores the confluence of existential philosophy, postmodernism, and Gothic fiction in Interview with the Vampire *and subsequent Rice novels.*

OTHER SOURCES FROM GALE:

Additional coverage of Rice's life and career is contained in the following sources published by Thomson Gale: *American Writers Supplement,* Vol. 7; *Authors and Artists for Young Adults,* Vols. 9, 53; *Beacham's Encyclopedia of Popular Fiction: Biography & Resources,* Vol. 3; *Bestsellers,* Vol. 89:2; *Contemporary Authors,* Vols. 65-68; *Contemporary Authors New Revision Series,* Vols. 12, 36, 53, 74, 100, 133; *Contemporary Literary Criticism,* Vols. 41, 128; *Contemporary Novelists,* Ed. 7; *Contemporary Popular Writers; Contemporary Southern Writers; Dictionary of Literary Biography,* Vol. 292; *DISCovering Authors Modules: Popular Fiction and Genre Authors; DISCovering Authors 3.0; Gay & Lesbian Literature,* Ed. 2; *Literature Resource Center; Major 20th-Century Writers,* Ed. 2; *Major 21st-Century Writers; St. James Guide to Horror, Ghost & Gothic Writers; St. James Guide to Young Adult Writers;* and *Supernatural Fiction Writers,* Vol. 2.

SIR WALTER SCOTT

(1771 - 1832)

(Also wrote under the pseudonym Jedediah Cleishbotham) Scottish novelist, poet, short story writer, biographer, historian, critic, and editor.

An immensely popular writer of both poetry and fiction during his lifetime, Scott exerted a profound influence on early nineteenth-century European literature. Modern scholars consider him both the inventor of the historical novel and the first best-selling novelist. As the anonymous and enormously prolific "Author of *Waverley*," Scott not only elevated the novel to a status equal to that of poetry but also influenced the way history has been written and understood by subsequent generations of historians and novelists. Despite the unprecedented success of his novels and poetry, Scott's literary reputation and popularity underwent one of the most pronounced reversals in the history of English literature following his death. Today his poetry is largely ignored, although his novels continue to attract the attention of literary historians. Among the many areas of continued scholarly interest in Scott's fiction, substantial notice has been paid to the Gothic qualities his novels and short stories. Even though Scott urged his readers to distinguish *Waverley; or, 'Tis Sixty Years Since* (1814) and the subsequent series of Waverley Novels from tales of Gothic horror, modern scholars have observed that these works nevertheless exhibit numerous affinities to the Gothic literary mode. Scott's fiction, which makes broad use of historical and frequently medieval settings, alludes to the mysterious workings of fate and the supernatural, and often depicts violent clashes between romantic and modern sensibilities, is routinely cited for its substantial exploitation of these and other Gothic themes and devices.

BIOGRAPHICAL INFORMATION

Scott was born in Edinburgh to middle-class parents, the fourth surviving child of Walter Scott and Anne Rutherford. At the age of two, he suffered an attack of polio that rendered him lame for the rest of his life. In spite of his illness, however, Scott led an active outdoor life during his childhood and developed an appreciation for the picturesque scenery that later figured so prominently in his writings. He enrolled in Edinburgh High School in 1778 and five years later entered the University of Edinburgh, studying history and law. In 1786, he was apprenticed to his father's legal firm and was called to the bar in 1792. While serving his apprenticeship, Scott traveled extensively in the Scottish Border country and Highlands, where he delighted in the natural settings and rural inhabitants. In 1800 he was able to combine his love for Scottish lore and literature with his ongoing excursions into the countryside as he started collecting and editing ballads for his *Minstrelsy of the Scottish Border* (1802-03). Although the work produced only modest sales when published, the collection enjoyed critical favor. The positive reception of the *Minstrelsy* and the encouragement of his friends prompted Scott to attempt an original work based on Scottish themes. His efforts resulted in *The Lay of the Last Minstrel* (1805). The success of this work when it appeared was immediate and substantial. Determined to earn a living through his writings, Scott gave up the law as a full-time profession and, beginning in 1808 with *Marmion*, published a series of highly popular and remunerative poems with Scottish backgrounds and themes, including what is perhaps his best-known long poem, *The Lady of the Lake* (1810). From this time, Scott's expenditures increased as quickly as his income, and many critics and biographers have tied his enormous output directly to a desire for material gain. Scott had purchased a farm in 1811 and, after renaming the property Abbotsford, began devoting huge sums of money to building, planting, and collecting relics from Scotland's past. Thus, though his income was large, his financial situation was often precarious. By the time *Rokeby* appeared in 1813, readers were also beginning to lose interest in his poetry. In addition, the triumph of the first two cantos of Lord Byron's *Childe Harold* in 1812 had convinced Scott that he could not compete with the younger poet. Anxious to retain his audience and large income, Scott decided to revise and complete a fragment of a novel that he had begun ten years before.

Waverley proved a popular sensation when published in 1814. Considered the first historical novel, *Waverley* quickly became the most successful work of its kind ever to appear, and brought huge profits to Scott and his publishers. Buoyed by his first venture as a novelist, Scott began writing at a rapid pace, and over the next seventeen years produced more than two dozen novels and tales in a series that has since become known as the Waverley Novels. He was able to maintain his prolific output not only because he never plotted his works ahead of time and seldom revised his manuscripts, but also because he maintained strenuous work habits even when gravely ill. Because at the time writing novels was perceived as less respectful than writing poetry, Scott had published *Waverley* anonymously. When the success of *Waverley* increased the public's appreciation for novelists, he nevertheless chose to retain his anonymity for many years, a practice his biographers have traced both to his love of secrecy and to his perception that the mystery surrounding the novels contributed to their sales. Many of the novels were published as "by the Author of *Waverley*," and he was often referred to simply as the "Great Unknown." Despite his policy of anonymous publication, numerous readers and critics knew of his authorship; he became the most popular writer in contemporary English literature and a highly respected and admired figure throughout Europe. In 1818 he accepted a baronetcy, becoming Sir Walter Scott. In 1826, disaster struck when a publishing house in which he was a silent partner failed. Instead of choosing to declare bankruptcy, Scott arranged to work off the debt through his writings. The remainder of his life was devoted to the increasingly difficult task of producing saleable works in a variety of genres. Beginning in 1830 he suffered a series of strokes as he labored to pay his creditors. A trip to the Mediterranean in 1831 to regain his health proved unsuccessful, and after experiencing further strokes and paralysis he died at Abbotsford in 1832.

MAJOR WORKS

A prolific writer of both poetry and prose, Scott enjoyed astounding popular success as a writer in both these genres during a literary career that roughly spanned the first three decades of the nineteenth century. Among his earliest poetic collections, the three-volume *Minstrelsy of the Scottish Border* contains numerous Scottish ballads that had never before appeared in print, as well as imitated ballads written by Scott and others. His *The Lay of the Last Minstrel* is an original poem set in medieval times that, in Scott's words, was "intended to illustrate the customs and manners which anciently prevailed on the borders of England and Scotland." The work launched his career as a poet, and was followed by several more narrative pieces crafted in the same spirit. Scott's first novel *Waverley; or, 'Tis Sixty Years Since*, features the tale of an Englishman who travels to the Scottish Highlands and becomes caught up in the Jacobite rebellion of 1745. *Waverley* spawned more than twenty similar works of historical fiction, collectively known as the Waverley Novels. In these stories, most of which describe the lives of ordinary individuals who become involved in great historical events, Scott presented in lavish detail the speech, manners, and customs of past ages. In studying these works, critics have often divided them into three groups. The first, the so-called "Scotch Novels," are stories that evoke the declining feudal culture of the Scottish Highlands prior to Scotland's absorption into Great Britain. They include *Guy Mannering* (1815), *The Antiquary* (1816), and *Old Mortality* (1816), as well as two novels set during the Jacobite uprising of 1715, *Rob Roy* (1818) and *The Heart of Midlothian* (1818), followed by *The Bride of Lammermoor* (1819), *The Legend of Montrose* (1819), and *Redgauntlet: A Tale of the Eighteenth Century* (1824). The second group features works concerned with medieval history in England and Europe, including such novels as *Ivanhoe* (1820), set during the reign of King John and depicting the figure of Locksley (better known as Robin Hood), *Quentin Durward* (1823) and *Anne of Geierstein; or, The Maiden of the Mist* (1829). Works placed in the third category are those focused on the Tudor-Stuart era in England, including *Kenilworth* (1821), which plays out among the intrigues of the Elizabethan court, *The Fortunes of Nigel* (1822), *Peveril of the Peak* (1822), and *Woodstock; or, the Cavalier* (1826), the last two set during the seventeenth-century English Civil War. Other novels by Scott particularly noted for their use of mystery, the uncanny, and other Gothic literary conventions include *The Black Dwarf* (1816), featuring a deformed, enigmatic hero who hides his identity until the end of the novel, *The Pirate* (1822), set in the remote Orkney islands in 1700 and detailing a struggle between two half-brothers, the pirate Cleveland and his rival Mordaunt, *St. Ronan's Well* (1824), also depicting a brutal rivalry between half-brothers but set in early nineteenth-century Scotland, and *Castle Dangerous* (1832), concerned with the excesses of the late medieval chivalric code.

While many of the Waverley Novels feature hints of the supernatural, Scott generally relegated his literary depiction of the inexplicable and otherworldly to his short fiction. Among these works, the collection *Chronicles of the Canongate* (1827) includes two darkly pessimistic short stories. The first of these, called "The Highland Widow," is a tale that dramatizes the passing of the old Scotch way of life in the death of a widow's son, apparently caused by the supernatural power of a fatal curse. In the second story, "The Two Drovers," a misunderstanding coupled with the strange and tragic workings of fate leads to the murder of an English cattleman by a Scottish drover, and eventually to the Highlander's execution for his crime. Another collection of short fiction, *The Keepsake for 1829* (1828) includes Scott's ghost story "The Tapestried Chamber; or, The Lady in the Sacque," and a tale of sorcery, "My Aunt Margaret's Mirror," featuring a magical mirror that

allows gazers to witness important events as they transpire miles away. Further evidence of Scott's interest in the supernatural is located in his critical writings, notably in his late study of folk superstitions entitled *Letters on Demonology and Witchcraft* (1830).

CRITICAL RECEPTION

The novelty of Scott's writing style and subject matter captivated his early audience; in fact, his writings created a vogue for Scottish culture and even led to an increase in tourism in Scotland. Many contemporary critics, however, have agreed that Scott's poetry and novels reveal glaring deficiencies, including careless construction, prolixity, and bad grammar. Yet most early reviewers acknowledged the superiority of his novels, arguing that their originality, vivid portrayal of history, and lively characters outweighed their faults. Scott's ability to bring Scottish and English history to life—to capture the language, costumes, and settings of the past—as well as his understanding of the effects of social change upon the lives of ordinary people, were entirely new contributions to English fiction. To many early Victorians, Scott was a heroic figure whose exemplary life and courageous struggle to pay his debts were reflected in the morally irreproachable qualities of his works. Yet certain critics, prominent among them Thomas Carlyle, felt that Scott's life should not be confused with his works, which were shallow, lacking in true passion, and written largely for material gain. As the nineteenth century progressed, the increasingly sophisticated design and self-conscious art of the novel as practiced by such writers as George Eliot and Henry James caused numerous commentators to deride the disorganized plots and intellectual superficiality of Scott's fiction. Although his admirers countered by praising his enduring appeal as a storyteller and the entertainment value of the Waverley Novels, by the turn of the century many critics maintained that Scott could no longer be considered a major English novelist. His readership as well as his critical stock had been declining since mid century, and while the second half of the twentieth century would show mounting scholarly interest in his works, Scott, a writer who in his own day had been compared with William Shakespeare, would eventually be described by W. E. K. Anderson as the "Great Unread."

Nevertheless, twentieth-century critics have emphasized Scott's important role in literary history. Scholars have traced his influence on the masterpieces of novelists as diverse as Charles Dickens, Gustave Flaubert, Honoré de Balzac, and William Makepeace Thackeray. Commentators have also explored Scott's significant contribution—through his invention and development of the historical novel—to the history of ideas, specifically with respect to the modern concept of historical perspective. Modern studies of the Waverley Novels have consistently stressed the superiority of the "Scotch Novels" over the rest, and critics have given particular attention to *The Heart of Midlothian*, often considered his finest novel. Scott's works have attracted increasing scholarly notice since the general proliferation of English literary scholarship that began in the 1950s, and recent commentators have explored such specific aspects of his novels as his passive heroes and his portrayal of the Middle Ages. Contemporary scholars studying the relationship of Scott's fiction to the Gothic tradition have found numerous points of contact, despite the writer's efforts to distance himself from this literary mode he frequently disparaged. Among them, Marilyn Orr (see Further Reading) has explored the generic conflict between romance and Gothic in *The Pirate* and *St. Ronan's Well*. Concentrating on motifs of doubling and repetition in these novels, Orr characterizes the former work as a romance that strives toward a synthetic unification of opposites, while assessing the latter as a thoroughly Gothic work symbolically focused on the subversion and dominance of the double. Fiona Robertson has concentrated on Scott's extensive use of such Gothic devices as deferral, detachment, and denial in his Waverley Novels, particularly in *The Pirate, Rob Roy*, and *Peveril of the Peak*, viewing these as works that foreground a sense of mystery, secrecy, and anxiety in a resoundingly Gothic manner. Other critics have traced the extensive use of Gothic motifs in Scott's collected fiction, particularly in his Waverley Novels. Such tropes as the delayed disclosure of a central narrative mystery, an evocation of dread and emotional anxiety caused by threats of violence or imprisonment, and a use of the uncanny and supernatural, often through reference to terrifying ghostly apparitions or in allusions to superstitious beliefs and nefarious secret societies, are common features throughout these works. Likewise, Scott's interest in fatalist themes, his medieval settings, romantic characterizations, and occasional use of the supernatural in both his novels and short fiction strongly recall the English Gothic mode in transition from the eighteenth to nineteenth centuries. And, while Scott's im-

mensely popular works have now largely become the concern of literary specialists, such studies have reaffirmed Scott's status as a crucial figure in the development of the English novel and a seminal influence on nineteenth-century European literature.

PRINCIPAL WORKS

The Eve of Saint John (poetry) 1800

Minstrelsy of the Scottish Border. 3 vols. [editor and contributor] (poetry) 1802-03

The Lay of the Last Minstrel (ballad) 1805

Ballads and Lyrical Pieces (poetry) 1807

Marmion: A Tale of Flodden Field (poetry) 1808

The Lady of the Lake (poetry) 1810

The Vision of Don Roderick (poetry) 1811

The Bridal of Triermain; or, the Vale of St. John (poetry) 1813

Rokeby: A Poem (poetry) 1813

Waverley; or, 'Tis Sixty Years Since. 3 vols. (novel) 1814

The Field of Waterloo (poetry) 1815

Guy Mannering; or, The Astrologer (novel) 1815

The Lord of the Isles (poetry) 1815

The Antiquary (novel) 1816

The Black Dwarf (novel) 1816

Old Mortality (novel) 1816

Harold the Dauntless (poetry) 1817

The Heart of Midlothian (novel) 1818

Rob Roy (novel) 1818

The Bride of Lammermoor (novel) 1819

The Legend of Montrose (novel) 1819

The Abbot (novel) 1820

Ivanhoe (novel) 1820

Miscellaneous Poems (poetry) 1820

The Monastery (novel) 1820

Kenilworth (novel) 1821

The Fortunes of Nigel (novel) 1822

Peveril of the Peak (novel) 1822

The Pirate (novel) 1822

Quentin Durward (novel) 1823

Redgauntlet: A Tale of the Eighteenth Century (novel) 1824

St. Ronan's Well (novel) 1824

†*Tales of the Crusaders* (novels) 1825

Woodstock; or, The Cavalier: A Tale of the Year Sixteen Hundred and Fifty-One (novel) 1826

‡*Chronicles of the Canongate* (short stories) 1827

‡*Chronicles of the Canongate. Second Series.* (novel) 1828

§*The Keepsake for 1829* (short stories) 1828

Anne of Geierstein; or, The Maiden of the Mist (novel) 1829

Waverley Novels. 48 vols. (novels) 1829-33

Letters on Demonology and Witchcraft (nonfiction) 1830

*Castle Dangerous (novel) 1832

**Count Robert of Paris* (novel) 1832

The Miscellaneous Works of Sir Walter Scott. 30 vols. (biographies, travel essays, history, and criticism) 1870-71

The Journal of Sir Walter Scott (journal) 1890

The Waverley Novels. 25 vols. (novels) 1892-94

The Complete Poetical Works of Sir Walter Scott. 5 vols. (poetry) 1894

The Letters of Sir Walter Scott. 12 vols. (letters) 1932-37

---

*   These works were written under the pseudonym Jedediah Cleishbotham and originally published in the four series of *Tales of My Landlord, Collected and Arranged by Jedediah Cleishbotham, Schoolmaster and Parish-Clerk of Gandercleugh.*

†   Comprised of the novels *The Betrothed* and *The Talisman.*

‡   The first series of this work consists of the short stories "The Highland Widow," "The Surgeon's Daughter," and "The Two Drovers." The second series contains the novel *St. Valentine's Day; or, The Fair Maid of Perth.*

§   This collection includes the short stories "My Aunt Margaret's Mirror," "The Tapestried Chamber; or, The Lady in the Sacque," and "The Laird's Jock."

PRIMARY SOURCES

SIR WALTER SCOTT (POEM DATE 1799)

SOURCE: Scott, Sir Walter. "The Erl-King's Daughter." In *An Apology for Tales of Terror*, pp. 73-6. Printed at the Mail Office: Kelso, 1799.

In the following poem, Scott offers a companion piece to his translation of Johann Wolfgang von Goethe's "Der Erlkonig" ("The Erl-King"), collected in the same volume.

O'ER hills and through forests Sir Oluf he wends,
To bid to his wedding relations and friends:
'Tis late, and arriving where sports the elf-band,
The Erl-King's proud daughter presents him her hand.

"Now welcome, Sir Oluf! Oh! welcome to me!
"Come, enter our circle my partner to be."
"Fair lady, nor can I dance with you, nor may:
"To-morrow I marry, to-night must away."

"Now listen, Sir Oluf! Oh! listen to me!
"Two spurs of fine steel will I give unto thee;
"A shirt too of satin receive as thy boon,
"Which my Queen-mother bleach'd in the light of the moon.

"Then yield thee, Sir Oluf! Oh! yield thee to me,
"And enter our circle my partner to be."
"Fair lady, nor can I dance with you, nor may:
"To-morrow I marry, to-night must away."

"Now listen, Sir Oluf! Oh! listen to me!
"An helmet of gold will I give unto thee."
"An helmet of gold would I willingly take,
"But I will not dance with you for Urgola's sake."

"And deigns not Sir Oluf my partner to be?
"Then curses and sickness I give unto thee;
"Then curses and sickness thy steps shall pursue:
"Now hence to thy lady, thou lover so true!"

Thus said she, and laid her charm'd hand on his heart;
Oh! never Sir Oluf had felt such a smart!
Swift spurr'd he his steed till he reach'd his own door,
And there stood his mother the castle before.

"Now riddle me, Oluf, and riddle me right,
"Why look'st thou, my dearest, so wan and so white?"
"How should I not, mother, look wan and look white?
"I have seen the Erl-King's cruel daughter to-night.

"She cursed me, her hand to my bosom she prest:
"Death followed the touch, and now tortures my breast:
"She cursed me, and said—To thy lady now ride!
"But ne'er shall my lips kiss the lips of my bride!"

"Now riddle me, Oluf, and what shall I say,
"When here comes the lady so fair and so gay?"
"Oh! say, I am gone for a while to the wood,
"To prove if my hounds and my courser be good."

Scarce dead was Sir Oluf, and scarce shone the day,
When in came the lady, so fair and so gay,
And in came her father, and in came each guest,
Whom the hapless Sir Oluf had bade to the feast.

They drank the red wine, and they ate the good
    cheer,
"Oh! where is Sir Oluf? Oh! where is my dear?"
"Sir Oluf is gone for a while to the wood,
"To prove if his hounds and his courser be
    good."

Then trembled the lady so fair and so gay:
She eyed the black curtain, she drew it away:
But soon from her bosom for ever life fled,
For there lay Sir Oluf, pale, breathless, and dead.

SIR WALTER SCOTT (STORY DATE 1828)

SOURCE: Scott, Sir Walter. "The Tapestried Chamber."
In *The Oxford Book of English Ghost Stories,* chosen by
Michael Cox and R. A. Gilbert, pp. 1-12. New York:
Oxford University Press, 1989.

*The following excerpt is from a short story first collected
in* The Keepsake of 1829, *published in late 1828.*

'My dear lord,' he at length said, 'what happened to me last night is of nature so peculiar and
so unpleasant, that I could hardly bring myself to
detail it even to your lordship, were it not that,
independent of my wish to gratify any request of
yours, I think that sincerity on my part may lead
to some explanation about a circumstance equally
painful and mysterious. To others, the communications I am about to make, might place me
in the light of a weak-minded, superstitious fool
who suffered his own imagination to delude and
bewilder him; but you have known me in childhood and youth, and will not suspect me of having adopted in manhood the feelings and frailties
from which my early years were free.' Here he
paused, and his friend replied:

'Do not doubt my perfect confidence in the
truth of your communication, however strange it
may be,' replied Lord Woodville; 'I know your
firmness of disposition too well, to suspect you
could be made the object of imposition, and am
aware that your honour and your friendship will
equally deter you from exaggerating whatever you
may have witnessed.'

'Well then,' said the general, 'I will proceed
with my story as well as I can, relying upon your
candour; and yet distinctly feeling that I would
rather face a battery than recall to my mind the
odious recollections of last night.'

He paused a second time, and then perceiving
that Lord Woodville remained silent and in an attitude of attention, he commenced, though not
without obvious reluctance, the history of his
night's adventures in the Tapestried Chamber.

'I undressed and went to bed, so soon as your
lordship left me yesterday evening; but the wood
in the chimney, which nearly fronted my bed,
blazed brightly and cheerfully, and, aided by a
hundred exciting recollections of my childhood
and youth which had been recalled by the unexpected pleasure of meeting your lordship, prevented me from falling immediately asleep. I
ought, however, to say, that these reflections were
all of a pleasant and agreeable kind, grounded on
a sense of having for a time exchanged the labour,
fatigues, and dangers of my profession, for the
enjoyments of a peaceful life, and the reunion of
those friendly and affectionate ties which I had
torn asunder at the rude summons of war.

'While such pleasing reflections were stealing
over my mind, and gradually lulling me to slumber, I was suddenly aroused by a sound like that
of the rustling of a silken gown, and the tapping
of a pair of high-heeled shoes, as if a woman were
walking in the apartment. Ere I could draw the
curtain to see what the matter was, the figure of a
little woman passed between the bed and the fire.
The back of this form was turned to me, and I
could observe, from the shoulders and neck, it
was that of an old woman, whose dress was an
old-fashioned gown which, I think, ladies call a
sacque; that is, a sort of robe, completely loose in
the body, but gathered into broad plaits upon the
neck and shoulders, which fall down to the
ground, and terminate in a species of train.

'I thought the intrusion singular enough, but
never harboured for a moment the idea that what
I saw was anything more than the mortal form of
some old woman about the establishment, who
had a fancy to dress like her grandmother, and
who, having perhaps (as your lordship mentioned
that you were rather straitened for room) been
dislodged from her chamber for my accommodation, had forgotten the circumstance, and returned
by twelve to her old haunt. Under this persuasion
I moved myself in bed and coughed a little, to
make the intruder sensible of my being in possession of the premises.—She turned slowly round,
but gracious heaven! my lord, what a countenance
did she display to me! There was no longer any
question what she was, or any thought of her being a living being. Upon a face which wore the
fixed features of a corpse, were imprinted the
traces of the vilest and most hideous passions
which had animated her while she lived. The body
of some atrocious criminal seemed to have been
given up from the grave, and the soul restored
from the penal fire, in order to form, for a space, a

union with the ancient accomplice of its guilt. I started up in bed, and sat upright, supporting myself on my palms, as I gazed on this horrible spectre. The hag made, as it seemed, a single and swift stride to the bed where I lay, and squatted herself down upon it, in precisely the same attitude which I had assumed in the extremity of horror, advancing her diabolical countenance within half a yard of mine, with a grin which seemed to intimate the malice and the derision of an incarnate fiend.'

Here General Browne stopped, and wiped from his brow the cold perspiration with which the recollection of his horrible vision had covered it.

'My lord,' he said, 'I am no coward. I have been in all the mortal dangers incidental to my profession, and I may truly boast that no man ever knew Richard Browne dishonour the sword he wears; but in these horrible circumstances, under the eyes, and as it seemed, almost in the grasp of an incarnation of an evil spirit, all firmness forsook me, all manhood melted from me like wax in the furnace, and I felt my hair individually bristle. The current of my life-blood ceased to flow, and I sank back in a swoon, as very a victim to panic terror as ever was a village girl or a child of ten years old. How long I lay in this condition I cannot pretend to guess.

'But I was roused by the castle clock striking one, so loud that it seemed as if it were in the very room. It was some time before I dared open my eyes, lest they should again encounter the horrible spectacle. When, however, I summoned courage to look up, she was no longer visible. My first idea was to pull my bell, wake the servants, and remove to a garret or a hay-loft, to be ensured against a second visitation. Nay, I will confess the truth, that my resolution was altered, not by the shame of exposing myself, but by the very fear that, as the bell-cord hung by the chimney, I might, in making my way to it, be again crossed by the fiendish hag, who, I figured to myself, might be still lurking about some corner of the apartment.

'I will not pretend to describe what hot and cold fever-fits tormented me for the rest of the night, through broken sleep, weary vigils, and that dubious state which forms the neutral ground between them. A hundred terrible objects appeared to haunt me; but there was the great difference betwixt the vision which I have described,

and those which followed, that I knew the last to be deceptions of my own fancy and over-excited nerves.

'Day at last appeared, and I rose from my bed ill in health, and humiliated in mind. I was ashamed of myself as a man and a soldier, and still more so, at feeling my own extreme desire to escape from the haunted apartment, which, however, conquered all other considerations; so that, huddling on my clothes with the most careless haste, I made my escape from your lordship's mansion, to seek in the open air some relief to my nervous system, shaken as it was by this horrible rencounter with a visitant, for such I must believe her, from the other world. Your lordship has now heard the cause of my discomposure, and of my sudden desire to leave your hospitable castle. In other places I trust we may often meet; but God protect me from ever spending a second night under that roof!'

Strange as the general's tale was, he spoke with such a deep air of conviction, that it cut short all the usual commentaries which are made on such stories. Lord Woodville never once asked him if he was sure he did not dream of the apparition, or suggested any of the possibilities by which it is fashionable to explain supernatural appearances, as wild vagaries of the fancy or deceptions of the optic nerves. On the contrary he seemed deeply impressed with the truth and reality of what he had heard; and, after a considerable pause, regretted, with much appearance of sincerity, that his early friend should in his house have suffered so severely.

'I am the more sorry for your pain, my dear Browne,' he continued, 'that it is the unhappy, though most unexpected, result of an experiment of my own! You must know, that for my father and grandfather's time, at least, the apartment which was assigned to you last night had been shut on account of reports that it was disturbed by supernatural sights and noises. When I came, a few weeks since, into possession of the estate, I thought the accommodation which the castle afforded for my friends was not extensive enough to permit the inhabitants of the invisible world to retain possession of a comfortable sleeping apartment. I therefore caused the Tapestried Chamber, as we call it, to be opened; and without destroying its air of antiquity, I had such new articles of furniture placed in it as became the modern times. Yet as the opinion that the room was haunted very strongly prevailed among the domestics, and was also known in the neighbourhood and to many of my friends, I feared some prejudice might be entertained by the first occupant of the Tapestried Chamber, which might tend to revive the evil report which it had laboured under, and so disappoint my purpose of rendering it a useful part of the house. I must confess, my dear Browne, that your arrival yesterday, agreeable to me for a thousand reasons besides, seemed the most favourable opportunity of removing the unpleasant rumours which attached to the room, since your courage was indubitable and your mind free of any preoccupation on the subject. I could not, therefore, have chosen a more fitting subject for my experiment.'

'Upon my life,' said General Browne, somewhat hastily, 'I am infinitely obliged to your lordship—very particularly indebted indeed. I am likely to remember for some time the consequences of the experiment, as your lordship is pleased to call it.'

'Nay, now you are unjust, my dear friend,' said Lord Woodville. 'You have only to reflect for a single moment, in order to be convinced that I could not augur the possibility of the pain to which you have been so unhappily exposed. I was yesterday morning a complete sceptic on the subject of supernatural appearances. Nay, I am sure that had I told you what was said about that room, those very reports would have induced you, by your own choice, to select it for your accommodation. It was my misfortune, perhaps my error, but really cannot be termed my fault, that you have been afflicted so strangely.'

'Strangely indeed!' said the general, resuming his good temper; 'and I acknowledge that I have no right to be offended with your lordship for treating me like what I used to think myself—a man of some firmness and courage.—But I see my post-horses are arrived, and I must not detain your lordship from your amusement.'

'Nay, my old friend,' said Lord Woodville, 'since you cannot stay with us another day, which, indeed, I can no longer urge, give me at least half an hour more. You used to love pictures, and I have a gallery of portraits, some of them by Vandyke, representing ancestry to whom this property and castle formerly belonged. I think that several of them will strike you as possessing merit.'

General Browne accepted the invitation, though somewhat unwillingly. It was evident he was not to breathe freely or at ease until he left Woodville Castle far behind him. He could not refuse his friend's invitation, however; and the

less so, that he was a little ashamed of the peevishness which he had displayed towards his well-meaning entertainer.

The general, therefore, followed Lord Woodville through several rooms, into a long gallery hung with pictures, which the latter pointed out to his guest, telling the names, and giving some account of the personages whose portraits presented themselves in progression. General Browne was but little interested in the details which these accounts conveyed to him. They were, indeed, of the kind which are usually found in the old family gallery. Here was a cavalier who had ruined the estate in the royal cause; there a fine lady who had reinstated it by contracting a match with a wealthy Roundhead. There hung a gallant who had been in danger for corresponding with the exiled Court of St Germain's; here one who had taken arms for William at the Revolution; and there a third that had thrown his weight alternately into the scale of Whig and Tory.

While Lord Woodville was cramming these words into his guest's ear, 'against the stomach of his sense', they gained the middle of the gallery, when he beheld General Browne suddenly start, and assume an attitude of the utmost surprise, not unmixed with fear, as his eyes were caught and suddenly riveted by a portrait of an old lady in a sacque, the fashionable dress of the end of the seventeenth century.

'There she is!' he exclaimed; 'there she is, in form and features, though inferior in demoniac expression to the accursed hag who visited me last night!'

'If that be the case,' said the young nobleman, 'there can remain no longer any doubt of the horrible reality of your apparition. That is the picture of a wretched ancestress of mine, of whose crimes a black and fearful catalogue is recorded in a family history in my charter-chest. The recital of them would be too horrible; it is enough to say, that in yon fatal apartment incest and unnatural murder were committed. I will restore it to the solitude to which the better judgement of those who preceded me had consigned it; and never shall any one, so long as I can prevent it, be exposed to a repetition of the supernatural horrors which could shake such courage as yours.'

Thus the friends, who had met with such glee, parted in a very different mood; Lord Woodville to command the Tapestried Chamber to be unmantled and the door built up; and General Browne to seek in some less beautiful country, and with some less dignified friend, forgetfulness of the painful night which he had passed in Woodville Castle.

TITLE COMMENTARY

The Waverley Novels

FIONA ROBERTSON (ESSAY DATE 1994)

SOURCE: Robertson, Fiona. "Secrecy, Silence, and Anxiety: Gothic Narratology and the Waverley Novels." In *Legitimate Histories: Scott, Gothic, and the Authorities of Fiction*, pp. 161-95. Oxford: Clarendon Press, 1994.

In the following excerpt, Robertson asserts that in the Waverley Novels "Scott's narrative techniques of deferral and denial have much in common with the Gothic, and are used with a complex alertness to their literary signification."

What is this secret sin; this untold tale,
That art cannot extract, nor penance cleanse?[1]

They dare not murder me,—they dare not incarcerate me;—they are answerable to the court to which I have appealed for my forthcoming,—they dare not be guilty of any violence.
(Monçada, *Melmoth the Wanderer*)[2]

When Edie Ochiltree is not sitting at his elbow Scott writes stories structured by loss, anxiety, and what is called in *Peveril of the Peak* 'the influence of undefinable apprehension'.[3] It would be easy, given the common critical association of Gothic, repression, and the unconscious, to make these stories into subtexts of the Waverley Novels, 'buried letters' of the type Mary Jacobus has proposed for the workings of Gothic in *Villette*.[4] This [essay proposes instead] to interpret individual Waverley Novels in some detail without presupposing any such aesthetic ranking or blurring the distinction between the claims that Scott uses Gothic devices to represent anxiety and that Gothic can in any way be equated with Scott's personal fears. [T]he argument aims first to establish that imitation, parody, and extension of Gothic conventions in the Waverley Novels help Scott to construct some of the non-authorial and even anti-authorial voices described in the previous chapter. The discussion of *The Pirate, Rob Roy,* and *Peveril of the Peak* in this [essay] focuses on the techniques (not lapses) of tone, narrative structure, description, and interior monologue by which Scott both raises and controls interpretations of the social world which sharply contradict the interpretations endorsed by his rational authorial voice. From this discussion two points emerge most strongly. One is that Scott's narrative techniques of deferral and denial have much in common with Gothic, and are used with a complex alertness to their literary signification. This is particularly true of the manipulation of secrets and narratorial secrecy, and it reinforces the argument that when looking for the impact made by Gothic on the Waverley Novels critics must attend to technique and tone as well as to events and settings. All Scott's plots depend upon the preservation then unravelling of secrets, although few go so far as *Kenilworth,* which can be read as an allegory of secrecy, as a cautionary tale about what happens when a man compromises with truth and plain-dealing, and when the secret (Amy) to which he rashly commits himself bursts out of his control. The second main point is that Scott, so often censured for a supposed shallowness in psychological representation, is much more versatile and resourceful as an analyst of states of mind than he first appears.

The first section of Chapter 2 [in *Legitimate Histories: Scott, Gothic, and the Authorities of Fiction*] analysed the methods developed in Gothic fiction to ritualize 'not secrets . . . but Secrecy', in Kermode's formulation. This process in Gothic is self-consciously literary, bolstered by close reference to other texts. The first epigraph to this [essay], the plea for explanation in Walpole's play about incest, *The Mysterious Mother* (1781), became a favourite point of reference in later Gothic fiction, used to suggest both the fearfulness and the inexpressibility of the secrets around which literary Gothic is plotted. A constant point of reference in Radcliffe's *The Romance of the Forest* and *The Italian,* the 'untold tale' of 'secret sin' hints at the forbidden subject of incest (between Montalt and Adeline, Schedoni and Ellena) with which both novels flirt, but which they finally evade.[5] More generally, novelists used the promise of the 'untold tale' both as a stimulus to readers' curiosity and as an acknowledgement of the limits of the fictional 'art' which could never hope to satisfy it. Although all narratives depend upon a degree of secrecy, Gothic novels are particularly dominated by the sense of 'secret sin', the unutterable or unnarratable source of mystery which must remain safely beyond the bounds of fiction.

The Waverley Novels, likewise, hint repeatedly at horrors which they do not enact, and build mysterious plots around the silence (willed or

ABOUT THE AUTHOR

WILLIAM HAZLITT ON SCOTT'S ACHIEVEMENTS AS A WRITER OF PROSE

The Author of *Waverley* has got rid of the tagging of rhymes, the eking out of syllables, the supplying of epithets, the colours of style, the grouping of his characters, and the regular march of events, and comes to the point at once, and strikes at the heart of his subject, without dismay and without disguise. His poetry was lady's waiting-maid, dressed out in cast-off finery: his prose is a beautiful, rustic nymph, that, like Dorothea in *Don Quixote* when she is surprised with dishevelled tresses bathing her naked feet in the brook, looks round her abashed at the admiration her charms have excited. The grand secret of the author's success in these latter productions is that he has completely got rid of the trammels of authorship; and torn off at one rent (as Lord Peter got rid of so many yards of lace in the "Tale of a Tub") all the ornaments of fine writing and worn-out sentimentality. All is fresh, as from the hand of nature: by going a century or two back and laying the scene in a remote and uncultivated district, all becomes new and startling in the present advanced period. Highland manners, characters, scenery, superstitions, northern dialect and costume, the wars, the religion, and politics of the sixteenth and seventeenth centuries, give a charming and wholesome relief to the fastidious refinement and "overlaboured lassitude" of modern readers, like the effect of plunging a nervous valetudinarian into a cold-bath.

SOURCE: Hazlitt, William. "Sir Walter Scott." *The New Monthly Magazine* 10, no. 40 (April 1824): 297-304.

enforced) of key characters. In order to do this they employ techniques of deferral and delay which owe much to the example of Gothic; and they also develop ways of suggesting forms of free-floating anxiety, best analysed by Alexander Welsh in his discussion of ***Rob Roy,*** which again have much in common with the construction of fear in

Radcliffean Gothic. Secret sins and unvoiced (what *Melmoth the Wanderer* terms 'unutterable') fears are traceable to many of the same narratorial ploys and habits of imaginative reference. A simple and striking instance may be found in the passage in ***The Fortunes of Nigel*** in which the Lady Hermione relates her life-story to Margaret Ramsay and delays its crisis by lingering over insignificant details:

> 'It is only,' said the Lady Hermione, 'because I linger like a criminal on the scaffold, and would fain protract the time that must inevitably bring on the final catastrophe. Yes, dearest Margaret, I rest and dwell on the events of that journey, marked as it was by fatigue and danger, though the road lay through the wildest and most desolate deserts and mountains, and though our companions, both men and women, were fierce and lawless themselves, and exposed to the most merciless retaliation from those with whom they were constantly engaged—yet would I rather dwell on these hazardous events than tell that which awaited me at Saint Jean de Luz.'[6]

The long sentence, elaborating on details of the journey, delays the moment when Hermione must instantiate Dalgarno's villainy. When, anticipating many other readers, Maria Edgeworth complained of Scott's tendency to 'huddle the cards together in such a shameless manner' at the end of his novels, she responded to a structural pattern characteristic of fictions based on secrets, seen here in miniature in Hermione's effort to expand on every detail except the one her listener wants to hear.[7]

There are close technical links, therefore, between narratorial delay (the 'huddled' structure), secrecy-driven plotting, and the suggestion, but not explication, of anxiety. By bringing these closer together in the following discussion I hope also to question one of the most common and most damaging of all complaints about Scott: that is, that he did not understand, or did not care to investigate, the workings of the mind in states of anger, obsession, neurosis, or desire. Lukács, as usual, pronounces decisively on the matter: 'Scott does not command the magnificent, profound psychological dialectics of character which distinguishes the novel of the last great period of bourgeois development.'[8] A belief in Scott's 'sunny' disposition may have been useful for writers who, like Carlyle, wished to attack the morbid tendencies of modern literature. For twentieth-century critics, however, accustomed to praise different (and equally conventional) methods of psychological examination in fiction, Scott has sometimes seemed embarrassingly inadequate. Even for Carlyle, the conviction that Scott was 'a genius *in extenso,* as we may say, not *in intenso'* limited his artistic standing.[9] Virginia Woolf, reappraising Scott at a time when his work was out of fashion among critics, had to conclude that he was 'not among the great observers of the intricacies of the heart'.[10] David Cecil agreed: 'Scott was no analyst.'[11] Scott himself made coy asides referring to this supposed deficiency. 'I like so little to analyze the complication of the causes which influence actions', he demurs (thinking of Fielding) in the first chapter of **The Antiquary**.[12] The aside in **The Antiquary** is clearly misleading, however. Scott does deal with the darker aspects of psychology, but in order to preserve the usefulness of his rational narrative persona he is obliged to find alternative, extra-narratorial ways of exploring them. If one leaves aside for a moment the complications introduced by fictional contexts, the technique can be seen quite clearly at work in Scott's private writings. When obliged to describe distressing experiences in his own life in his letters and **Journal** he uses a distinctive language of literary reference and suggestion, overstatement and cliché. A friend's disgrace leads him to reflect in the **Journal**:

> It is a mercy our thoughts are concealed from each other. O if at our social table we could see what passes in each bosom around we would seek dens and caverns to shun human society. To see the projector trembling for his falling speculations, the voluptuary ruing the event of his debauchery, the miser wearing out his soul for the loss of a guinea—all—all bent upon vain hopes and vainer regrets—we should not need to go to the hall of the Caliph Vathek to see men's hearts broiling under their black veils.[13]

In this passage, Scott progressively distances himself from the immediate cause of his abhorrence by making it increasingly figurative and literary. He first imagines other examples which elaborate his friend's disgrace but which also place it in a more general moral context. Here he is close to the practice of eighteenth-century moralists and ultimately to the evocative style of the pulpit. Then he uses literary precedent (*Vathek*) and exaggerated literary language ('hearts broiling under their black veils') as a form of protection by exaggeration. Elsewhere in his personal writings, Scott imagines the conflicts between abstracted qualities of the mind in strikingly literary ways, some of which resemble the common elements of his own novels. Trying to express his feelings about the suicide of his friend Huxley, for example, he writes in his **Journal** in December 1826:

> A thousand fearful images and dire suggestions glance along the mind when it is moody and discontented with itself. Command them to stand and shew themselves and you presently assert the power of reason over imagination. But if by any strange alterations in one's nervous system you lost for a moment the talisman which controuls these fiends? Would they not terrify into obedience with their mandates rather [than] we would dare longer to endure their presence?[14]

This passage, sparked by the experience of a vivid nightmare, echoes a passage from the fictional journal of Darsie Latimer in **Redgauntlet**, written eighteen months earlier. In turn, both passages recall Clarence's account of his dream in the first act of *Richard III* ('Methoughts I saw a thousand fearful wracks . . .').[15]

Scott uses comparable techniques of detachment followed by literary exaggeration at emotional crisis-points in his fiction. Faced simultaneously with emotional and linguistic collapse, characters search, like Scott in his **Journal**, for a 'talisman' by which to control the fiends of imagination. This talisman is as much linguistic as rational. Their passivity being strongly linked to an inability to speak effectively, they are reduced, like **Rob Roy**'s Frank Osbaldistone, to outbursts of childish passion rendered in self-consciously literary terms:

> Heaven knows, it was not apathy which loaded my frame and my tongue so much, that I could neither return Miss Vernon's half embrace, nor even answer her farewell. The word, though it rose to my tongue, seemed to choke in my throat like the fatal *guilty,* which the delinquent who makes it his plea knows must be followed by the doom of death. . . . I felt the tightening of the throat and breast, the *hysterica passio* of poor Lear; and, sitting down by the wayside, I shed a flood of the first and most bitter tears which had flowed from my eyes since childhood.[16]

Frank Osbaldistone's inability to grasp the reality of his youthful experiences is to some extent a special feature of his individual personality.[17] Even so, the way in which Frank describes his outburst of emotion, veering away from the uncomfortably personal to the safely literary (*King Lear*), has much in common with distinctive habits of Scott's narrative technique throughout the Waverley Novels. The intrusion of possibly incongruous literary references does not always work so abruptly to defuse moments of horror as does the sudden appearance of Fang and Snare in the climactic confrontation from *Melmoth the Wanderer* described in Chapter 2 [of *Legitimate Histories: Scott, Gothic, and the Authorities of Fiction*], but it works on the same principle of literary transgression.

Frank Osbaldistone's description of a baffling and complex paralysis—physical, emotional, and linguistic—holds true for the experiences of many characters in Scott's novels. Like many Gothic fictions, the Waverley Novels trace the consequences of the sins of curiosity, a movement out of the unaccountability of childhood not into adult power but into adult responsibility, often detached from power. Julia Mannering, the heroine of Scott's second novel, gives a memorable account of this process:

> I feel the terrors of a child, who has, in needless sport, put in motion some powerful piece of machinery; and, while he beholds wheels revolving, chains clashing, cylinders rolling around him, is equally astonished at the tremendous powers which his weak agency has called into action, and terrified for the consequences which he is compelled to await, without the possibility of averting them.[18]

Such a perception of the world is very close to that lack of control so vividly described by Maturin's Monçada in *Melmoth the Wanderer,* where human beings, in a kind of parody of the Newtonian universe, set machines moving which they are then unable to halt:

> Every thing passed before me as in a dream. I saw the pageant move on, without a thought of who was to be the victim. I returned to the convent—I felt my destiny was fixed—I had no wish to avert or arrest it—I was like one who sees an enormous engine (whose operation is to crush him to atoms) put in motion, and, stupefied with horror, gazes on it with a calmness that might be mistaken for that of one who was coolly analysing the complication of its machinery, and calculating the resistless crush of its blow.[19]

This sense of physical paralysis extends, as many critics after Alexander Welsh have noted, to a breakdown of control and a rhetoric of anxiety and persecution. The rationalist commitments of the Waverley Novels are continually undermined by the terms in which Scott's protagonists perceive and describe their experiences. 'Undefinable apprehension', 'acute anxiety', and 'irrational dread' beset one protagonist after another. Even the redoubtable Hereward the Varangian of *Count Robert of Paris,* left alone in a chamber which leads to the palace dungeons, responds in the unmistakable tones of Waverley-Novel anxiety: '"I have done nothing," he thought, "to merit being immured in one of these subterranean dens. . . ."'[20] As Nigel Oliphant complains, the hero is placed in a situation 'where every fair construction of [his] actions and motives is refused [him]'.[21] Alternatively, as Scott describes the situation of Harry Bertram, in terms which already move his experiences one step away from actuality, he is confused by 'the mysteries which ap-

peared to thicken around him, while he seemed alike to be persecuted and protected by secret enemies and friends'.[22]

The form of paralysis which is most rewardingly analysed in the context of Gothic, however, is the linguistic variety, recalling the many scenes in Gothic in which characters are implored to speak or to take decisive action to save loved ones (typified, perhaps, by Lorenzo's nightmare vision of Antonia's death near the beginning of *The Monk*). Scott's young heroes struggle for speech yet find themselves 'chocked', struggle to declare their love or honour yet are laughed at as children, seek action but find paralysis, 'enchantment', and imprisonment. Ironically, the Waverley Novels built their reputation upon speech. In the opening chapter of ***The Bride of Lammermoor,*** Dick Tinto complains that Peter Pattieson's characters 'make too much use of the *gob box* . . . there is nothing in whole pages but mere chat and dialogue'.[23] Yet despite the garrulousness of some characters many others undergo agonies of self-expression in which they are silent, inarticulate, and hesitant. The Waverley Novels repeatedly test the hero who cannot speak out, or who stifles his emotions, often in legal situations or crises which are described in the language of law. Two such narratives—***Rob Roy*** and ***Peveril of the Peak***—are analysed below. The focus of the first part of the chapter, however, is one of Scott's most complex analyses of secrecy and the ideological implications of secrecy-driven plotting—***The Pirate.*** It is chosen here partly because it is one of the Waverley Novels most frequently decreed to have been spoilt by inappropriate literary conventions, and partly because it seems to be such a clear endorsement of rational interpretations of life. David Brown is typical in linking the proliferation of supernatural and fantastic elements to a lack of basic historical understanding: 'With only a limited understanding of the period and setting concerned, Scott instinctively falls back on Gothic horrors, spurious romance, and antiquarian curiosities to sustain the novel for its four hundred pages.'[24] ***The Pirate,*** however, was the novel which irritated Coleridge into his marginal comments on the 'make-believe' supernatural in the Waverley Novels, already quoted in the Introduction. Throughout ***The Pirate*** Scott experiments with different literary forms with the apparent intention of sorting and ranking them, and it is not difficult to determine which form(s) win. Despite this, however, it is significant that Coleridge registers such tensions and difficulties in the novel. ***The Pirate*** seems to offer supporters of a pro-rationalist, anti-Gothic Scott their ideal text. Yet the contest actively foregrounds the complexity of the forces at work.

1. *The Pirate: 'The Interest of a Riddle'*

> I must remain the dreaded—the mystical—the Reimkennar—the controller of the elements, or I must be no more! I have no alternative, no middle station. . . . The parricide shall never also be denounced as the impostor!
>
> (Norna of the Fitful Head)[25]

In *The Pirate*, Scott takes up the social and literary challenges presented by piratical heroes from Byron's Conrad to Maturin's Bertram, firmly rejecting the charismatic misanthropy which they had substituted for heroism. Although some of this rejection stems from the ironic depiction of the pirate, Clement Cleveland, much is conducted on the level of plot. *The Pirate* is a deconstruction of mystery and its alliance with anti-social imagination. In spite of all Norna's misgivings, it systematically denounces the parricide as the impostor, the rebel against society as the victim of delusive visions.

In *The Pirate,* as in Gothic fiction, readers play a double role which makes them simultaneously detectives, actively piecing together evidence, and passive listeners, knowing that everything strange will eventually be explained. After a brief introduction to the geography and social conditions of Zetland at the end of the seventeenth century, *The Pirate* confronts its readers with a series of mysteries, which are presented as imaginatively compatible with its desolate and recess-riddled scenery. In the order in which they are introduced, these mysteries are: Basil Mertoun's misanthropic gloom, misogyny, and indifference towards his son Mordaunt;[26] the instinctive enmity between Mordaunt Mertoun and the pirate, Clement Cleveland; Mordaunt's sudden expulsion from the charmed circle of the Troil household; and the 'fatal secret' of Norna's alienation from society. When introducing the first of these, the strange isolation and misanthropy of Basil Mertoun, Scott acknowledges the special imaginative appeal of the principle of mystery itself. Deciding that none of Basil Mertoun's qualities equals in the eyes of the Zetlanders the mystery surrounding him, the narrator concludes: 'Above all, Mr Mertoun's secret seemed impenetrable, and his presence had all the interest of a riddle, which men love to read over and over, because they cannot find out the meaning of it.'[27] These are highly reader-conscious terms. They also anticipate the strong interest shown throughout *The Pirate* in riddles, 'wild' rhymes,

and mysterious withheld speech. Not only is the narrative itself a triumph of rational explanation over riddling mystery. The novel's restructuring of social and domestic life after the mysteries in which it begins also follows the principles established by clear and direct speech. Language triumphs over gesture. Open communication replaces rumour and incantation.

In the imagination of Mordaunt Mertoun, also, mystery is given a special prominence. He is seen meditating the secrets of the ocean, 'aided by the dim twilight, through which it was imperfectly seen for more than half the year'. Vividly the narrator describes the creatures thought to inhabit the 'bottomless depths and secret caves', the mermaid, kraken, and sea-snake, sometimes glimpsed by mariners through banks of fog.[28] Scott presents Zetland as a land enshrining secrets. And it is significant that the man who both casts dissension into the community of Zetland and eventually brings about its more lasting harmony—the pirate himself—is plucked from the sea by Mordaunt in contravention of all the islanders' convenient taboos about sea-rescue. Through this association Cleveland himself becomes a sort of kraken, rising from the secrets of the past.

The mysteries of *The Pirate* are capable of being solved at any moment by a few words uttered by two characters, Norna of the Fitful Head and Basil Mertoun, who have been lovers many years before and have had an illegitimate child. Norna believes this child to be Mordaunt, who is assumed by the Zetlanders to be Mertoun's only son, but it transpires that Mordaunt is Mertoun's second son, his child by a failed later marriage. Norna discovers too late that her son is in fact the pirate, Cleveland, whose schemes she has worked so hard to frustrate. One part of the mystery, then, is their youthful love-affair and the extreme distrust of women it has produced in Mertoun. The second is Norna's conviction that she is to blame for the death of her father, which leads to her self-imposed isolation and necromantic 'enthusiasm'. These mysteries are linked thematically by the moral and social question of the proper relationship between father and child.

When the novel opens, Norna and Mertoun are living as strangers to each other in a community ignorant of their secret but intrigued by their different styles of linguistic indirectness. The misanthropic Mertoun is nicknamed the 'Silent Man of Sumburgh'.[29] Norna, in her role as 'Sibyl', 'Pythoness', 'Reimkennar', speaks predominantly in riddles or in a form of inspired private language.

Her closest tie is with her dumb servant, Nick Strumpfer (or 'Pacolet', one of Scott's favourite nicknames for minor characters). In a rhetoric which recalls *Melmoth the Wanderer,* and all the traditions of Faustian overreaching which lie behind it, she repeatedly hints that the reason for her outcast speech is a pact made with the dark powers and 'a sacrifice which human tongue can never utter'.[30] The two interviews between these cryptic recluses are neatly designed as complementary exercises in linguistic indirection and revelation. In the first, Mertoun meets Norna at the ruinous church of St. Ninian, hoping to hear news of his missing son. Ignorant of Norna's true identity and failing to recognize in the mysterious sibyl his former beloved, Mertoun conjures her disdainfully to speak plainly, to 'Lay aside this useless affectation of mystery'.[31] Norna complies, but only by whispering words to him which are withheld from the reader:

> 'Hearken, then!' said the old woman. 'The word which I speak shall touch the nearest secret of thy life, and thrill thee through nerve and bone.'
>
> So saying, she whispered a word into Mertoun's ear, the effect of which seemed almost magical.[32]

In their second meeting, this time in the cathedral of St Magnus in Kirkwall, it is Mertoun's turn to break the silence by revealing that Cleveland, not Mordaunt, is Norna's son. His explanation breaks the spell of what Mertoun calls 'the legerdemain of lunacy—the mere quackery of insanity'.[33] Realizing the true limits of her power and knowledge, Norna resumes her name and her original place in society.

The Zetland community as a whole is beset by other silences and mysterious forms of speech or riddles. In the central chapter of the novel (chapter 21 out of forty-two), Magnus Troil asks his guests, and obliges his daughters, to take part in a traditional fortune-telling conducted through riddling rhymes, and in a later explanation of the mysteries of Norna's wonderful knowledge and power, the narrator demonstrates how the everyday instances of Norna's dealings with the supernatural powers depend upon pacts of silence. The islanders who provide her with information are ignorant of each other's actions, and, 'as her orders were generally given under injunctions of the strictest secrecy, men reciprocally wondered at occurrences, which had in fact been produced by their own agency, and that of their neighbours, and in which, had they communicated freely with each other, no shadow of the marvellous would have remained'.[34] As the love-story of *The Pirate* emphatically declares, only when characters com-

municate freely are they able to break the spells which surround them. *The Pirate* is torn between the recognition that sociability and speech are essential to happiness and stability, and a fascination with anti-social, secretive, and silent characters.

On the one hand, the narrative voice insistently denies the fanciful claims of the superstitious and romantic characters, repeatedly explaining, for example, that Norna's supernatural powers are merely delusions of her imagination, and can be explained by reference to the specific historical and cultural conditions of Zetland. It makes Norna's addiction to mysterious speech both comic and maddening, as in the scene soon after Mordaunt becomes an unwelcome guest at Burgh-Westra, when she tries to warn Mordaunt of 'the machinations of a villain',[35] without giving him enough information to be of practical use. To Norna's fanciful description of the adder who has crept into the eagle's nest, Mordaunt replies: 'You must speak more plainly, Norna . . . if you would have me understand or answer you. I am no guesser of riddles.'[36] The same sceptical narrative voice exposes the connections between superstition, madness, and imagination.[37] It insists that Norna's imagination has led to madness and alienation, and that the same fate threatens 'the high-minded and imaginative Minna', as a result of her 'unusual intensity of imagination'.[38] Minna is constitutionally inclined to the sublime scenery of 'solitary and melancholy grandeur' suited to her 'wild and poetical visions'.[39] When she falls into a nervous illness brought on by her consciousness of the secret (as she thinks it) that Cleveland has murdered Mordaunt, her plight is described in terms which closely echo Norna's description of the secret of her parricide. It is a 'horrible secret, which haunted her while awake, and was yet more tormenting during her broken and hurried slumbers'. The narrator underlines the point: 'There is no grief so dreadful as that which we dare not communicate.'[40] Minna is taken to Norna's strange outpost dwelling, a place described in terms which make literal the threat of division imperilling her, and defining Norna:

> This natural fosse, which seemed to have been the work of some convulsion of nature, was deep, dark, and irregular, narrower towards the bottom, which could not be distinctly seen, and widest at top, having the appearance as if that part of the cliff occupied by the building had been half rent away from the isthmus which it terminated,—an idea favoured by the angle at which it seemed to recede from the land, and lean towards the sea, with the building which crowned it.[41]

Norna's unnatural (though unintentional) crime against her father is repeated in the image of the rock torn away by natural convulsion, and leaning out towards the sea which (conventionally enough) is the source of passion and secrecy in the novel.

On the other hand, however, Scott shows that imagination and desire are stimulated by denial and silence, a recognition which, as I have suggested, is implicit in the organization of his own mystery-novel. He describes Mordaunt's distress when the Troil sisters withdraw their friendship:

> Mordaunt felt, as it were, assured upon the instant, that the regard of Minna was extinguished, but that it might be yet possible to recover that of the milder Brenda; and such is the waywardness of human fancy, that though he had never hitherto made any distinct difference betwixt these two beautiful and interesting girls, the favour of her, which seemed most absolutely withdrawn, became at the moment the most interesting in his eyes.[42]

The whole imaginative venture of *The Pirate* is based on the same association between what is withheld and what is desired. Scott's readers, like Mordaunt Mertoun, are to be shown that it is wrong to equate denial with desire.

At all its stages the story told in *The Pirate* constructs this lesson by contrasting the powers of communication and silence. Near the end of the first volume in the Magnum Opus edition, Minna and Brenda tentatively discuss the barriers to their free communication which have been created by their love for two men who are enemies. This scene is contrasted to the failures of communication between Mordaunt and Basil Mertoun, and between Mordaunt and Magnus Troil. Soon afterwards, Minna and Brenda take part in a fortune-telling scene in which Norna foretells in rhyme their future lives and loves. Finally, the romantic entanglements of the plot are explicable in terms of communication and silence. Minna and Cleveland never communicate directly enough to establish the differences between her ideals of an ancient sea-king and the reality of his life as a pirate. Mordaunt's imagination is stimulated by Minna's silence, and his emotions baffled by his father's silence, but his love is fixed by Brenda's speech. Only Brenda risks her family's displeasure to explain to Mordaunt the reasons for his fall from favour, and tries to help Minna by discussing her fears with Mordaunt. Minna, by contrast, is nearly driven mad because she must not communicate her own 'fatal secret'.[43] Brenda, the heroine of communication, and the sociable

Mordaunt, break out of the bond of secrecy and silence which holds other characters fatally entranced.

Even in their dreams, Minna and Brenda are contrasted in terms of speech and silence. Before they awake to discover Norna sitting by the hearth, singing, her voice has become interwoven with their dreams. Each dream is symbolic of one sister's situation. Minna dreams that she is alone in a desolate cavern by the seashore, and is beckoned by a mermaid who sings to her a prophetic song of 'calamity and woe'. Brenda dreams that she is sitting in a bower surrounded by her father and his friends. She tries to entertain them with her favourite lively song, but loses control of her voice, which assumes, 'in her own despite, the deep tones and wild and melancholy notes of Norna of Fitful-head'.[44] Brenda is the heroine of society and also its entertainer, its speaker and singer. Minna is silent while another sings. Brenda's dream is also expressive of her plight while forbidden by her father to communicate with Mordaunt, to assume cold words which are not her own. Since Norna is about to tell the story of her demonic pact and supposed parricide, it is also significant that it is her song which intrudes in each sister's dream. Norna is the mermaid tempting Minna from society, the voice she must resist. She is also the doleful voice against which Brenda must struggle to assert her own right of social, harmonious speech.

The drama of language, imagination, and desire conducted in *The Pirate* touches on some of the most prevalent concerns of Scott's fiction. Although all the Waverely Novels demonstrate Scott's interest in language as the primary medium of social interaction, and his commitment to finding a suitable language of fiction to achieve the same ends, most also contain one or more characters whose non-conforming speech, or whose refusal or inability to speak, is a threat. Some of these are characters whose language does not seem to obey the conventions of social speech (like the songs of Davie Gellatley in *Waverley* and Madge Wildfire in *The Heart of Midlothian*) although it is later discovered to be meaningful in its own way. Other characters harbour terrible secrets which they must eventually tell, such as Elspeth Mucklebackit in *The Antiquary* and Norna in *The Pirate*. A third, and especially threatening, group consists of mute or seemingly mute characters. It includes Norna's dumb dwarf Nick Strumpfer and the fake mute Fenella in *Peveril of the Peak,* supported in the introduction to the Magnum Opus by the tale of the servant girl 'Dumb Lizzie' from

Scott's own family history. This is the context of debate about society and language in which one should position **The Pirate**'s contrast between Minna and Brenda Troil, and between the characters in the novel who take to extremes the principles by which this contrast is governed (Norna being the correlative of Minna's guilty silence and Magnus Troil, or less flatteringly the gossip Bryce Snailsfoot, being the correlative of Brenda's social speech). Equally complex is Scott's evaluation of imagination in the context of secrecy or of what is tantalizingly withheld. The plots of the Waverley Novels usually punish anti-social and secretive characters who misuse imagination, like George Staunton in **The Heart of Midlothian** and Richard Middlemas in **"The Surgeon's Daughter,"** crushed to death by a ceremonial elephant which is a kind of grotesque symbol of his Indian fantasy-life. More sentimental images of the romantic imagination (usually feminized, although Scott's most savage portrayals of imagination also take female form), such as Minna Troil, prove problematic, however. Minna's renunciation of her dreams at the end of **The Pirate** is a particularly sour version of the conflict between 'romance' and 'real history' which, since Edward Waverley, Scott's imaginative characters had had to negotiate. Minna declares to Cleveland: 'The delusions which a solitary education and limited acquaintance with the modern world had spread around me, are gone and dissipated forever.'[45] Scott recognizes the harshness of this, however, and is anxious to reassure. 'Reader, she *was* happy', declares the narrator, making an unusually direct and decisive intervention.[46] In **The Pirate**, Scott restricts his characters' imaginative indulgences, exposing the dangers of allowing the world of private imagination to dominate the social, public world. Clearly there is much more at stake in the novel's creation of an alternative, extra-rational, highly charged world of the imagination than critics usually grant.

The Pirate, in conclusion, is a deconstruction of fictions based on mystery but also a powerful reinvention and redirection of Gothic plotting. It replaces silence with speech and secrecy with openness, but in doing so it continues rather than discredits Gothic aesthetics as typified by Radcliffe. As in Gothic, the genuine complications are to be found not in the explicit statements made by the narrative voice but in the imaginative activity prompted in the reader. Readers of **The Pirate** are engaged in solving mysteries while its hero is being taught that such fascinations are delusive. In a more subtle way, however, they are engaged in a fiction which accepts conventions—including novelistic ones—as a precondition of social interaction. The contrast with the 'unutterable' in *Melmoth the Wanderer* is instructive. In this novel, Maturin celebrates a private language, exemplified by Immalee-Isidora who learns social corruption as she learns a system of speech but who always retains a degree of linguistic as well as moral purity. Maturin shows language to be necessarily social but ideally also personal, and ultimately a private instrument of communication with God. In **The Pirate** Scott rejects a range of private, 'secret' languages and in the marriage of his hero and heroine enshrines the sociability of speech. To do so, however, he is forced to deploy all the authority of his narrating voice: 'Reader, she *was* happy.' Not all his novels choose to make so unequivocal an intervention.

Notes

1. Horace Walpole, *The Mysterious Mother: A Tragedy* (London, 1781), I. iii. 8.

2. *Melmoth*, ii. 31.

3. *WN* [*The Waverley Novels*] xxix. 186.

4. 'The Buried Letter: *Villette*' (1979), repr. in *Reading Woman: Essays in Feminist Criticism* (London, 1986), 41-61.

5. *Italian*, chs. 1, 4, 9; *Romance of Forest*, ch. 2.

6. *WN* xxvii. 50-1.

7. In a letter of Jan. 1824 about *St Ronan's Well*, quoted in *Letters*, viii. 142 n.

8. Lukács, *Historical Novel*, 34.

9. Carlyle, *Works*, xxix. 35.

10. Woolf, *Collected Essays*, 4 vols. (London, 1966-7), i. 142.

11. Cecil, *Scott*, 36.

12. *WN* v. 13. David Craig links this to Scott's supposed unwillingness to examine his own psychology, in *Scottish Literature and the Scottish People*, 311. Kurt Wittig notes that Scott does not pry into 'the dark abysses of its deepest passions', *The Scottish Tradition in Literature* (Edinburgh, 1958), 221.

13. *Journal*, 236-7. Scott was probably reacting to the Heber scandal, which he reports, *Journal*, 162.

14. *Journal*, 253 (Scott's attempt to deal with his thoughts of Huxley's suicide, which he describes in terms of macabre compulsion: see his nightmares about Huxley, pp. 247-8). For Scott's growing fear of madness and loss of control, see also pp. 615, 621, 632.

15. *WN* xxxvi. 47; *Richard III*, 1. iv. 24.

16. *WN* viii. 271-2.

17. The argument proposed by Millgate, *Making of the Novelist*, ch. 7.

18. *WN* iv. 18.

19. *Melmoth,* i. 233-4.

20. *WN* xlvi. 66.

21. *WN* xxvii. 243.

22. *WN* iv. 210.

23. *WN* xiii. 271: see Woolf on Scott's 'chatterboxes', *Collected Essays,* i. 42.

24. *Historical Imagination,* 187.

25. *WN* xxv. 221.

26. Not really a problem, according to Nassau Senior in his review of *The Pirate, Quarterly Review,* xxvi (Oct. 1821), 456, where he notes Mertoun's misanthropy and silence, 'which, at once, indicate, to a practised novel-reader, one of the numerous family of retired criminals, or injured lovers'.

27. *WN* xxiv. 8.

28. All quotations from *WN* xxiv. 25.

29. *WN* xxiv. 80.

30. *WN* xxiv. 175.

31. *WN* xxv. 94.

32. *WN* xxv. 95.

33. *WN* xxv. 355.

34. *WN* xxv. 212: the link is reinforced by the presence of Norna's dumb dwarf, 'Pacolet', xxv. 122-3.

35. *WN* xxiv. 177.

36. *WN* xxiv. 176.

37. *WN* xxv. 99, 225, 354-5: on Minna, xxiv. 333, xxv. 36, 66, 112, 130, 148, 371: contrast Brenda, xxiv. 353, xxv. 106, 370-1: Halcro's alternative opinion, xxiv. 228.

38. *WN* xxv. 371, xxiv. 333.

39. *WN* xxiv. 36, 40.

40. Both quotations from *WN* xxv. 98.

41. *WN* xxv. 118.

42. *WN* xxiv. 207-8.

43. *WN* xxv. 98-101 (100).

44. The dreams passage, *WN* xxiv. 331-2.

45. *WN* xxv. 365.

46. *WN* xxv. 371.

Bibliography

Brown, David, *Walter Scott and the Historical Imagination* (London, 1979).

Carlyle, Thomas, *The Works of Thomas Carlyle,* Centenary Edition, ed. H. D. Traill, 30 vols. (London, 1896-9).

Cecil, Lord David, *Sir Walter Scott,* The Raven Miscellany (London, 1933).

Lukács, Georg, *The Historical Novel* (1937), trans. Hannah and Stanley Mitchell (London, 1962).

Maturin, Charles Robert, *Melmoth the Wanderer: A Tale,* 4 vols. (Edinburgh, 1820). [Ed. and introd. Alethea Hayter (Harmondsworth, 1977).]

Millgate, Jane, *Walter Scott: The Making of the Novelist* (Edinburgh, 1984).

Radcliffe, Ann, *The Romance of the Forest: Interspersed with Some Pieces of Poetry,* 3 vols. (London, 1791). [Ed. and introd. Chloe Chard (Oxford, 1986).]

————, *The Italian; or, The Confessional of the Black Penitents: A Romance,* 3 vols. (London, 1797). [Ed. and introd. Frederick Garber (Oxford, 1968, 1981).]

Scott, Sir Walter, Bt., *Rob Roy,* 3 vols. (Edinburgh, 1818, for 1817).

————, *The Waverley Novels,* 48 vols. (Edinburgh, 1829-33).

————, *The Letters of Sir Walter Scott,* ed. H. J. C. Grierson *et al.,* 12 vols., Centenary Edition (London, 1932-7).

————, *The Journal of Sir Walter Scott,* ed. W. E. K. Anderson (Oxford, 1972).

Shakespeare, William, *The Riverside Shakespeare,* textual ed. G. Blakemore Evans, gen. introd. Harry Levin *et al.,* essay on stage history Charles H. Shattuck (Boston, Mass., 1974).

Woolf, Virginia, *Collected Essays,* 4 vols. (London, 1966-7).

ROBERT IGNATIUS LE TELLIER (ESSAY DATE 1995)

SOURCE: Le Tellier, Robert Ignatius. "Gothic Motifs in the Waverley Novels." In *Sir Walter Scott and the Gothic Novel,* pp. 125-49. New York: Edwin Mellen Press, 1995.

In the following excerpt, Le Tellier surveys the Gothic elements in the Waverley Novels.

VI. Gothic Motifs in the Waverley Novels

The Waverley Novels constitute a vast corpus of 22 novels written over a span of 18 years. The approach adopted here in endeavouring to investigate a particular type of influence and occurrence will initially be different from that used in looking at the poems, a much more contained group, and also the beginning of Scott's creative writing. The analogy of the overture will be recalled: the poems present in miniature, in artful compression, many of the themes and ideas worked out in immense detail in the novels. The nature and density of the influence obviously varies from work to work.

As in the exercise on the poems, the pioneer in this exploration who provides the foundation of scholarly enquiry after the texts themselves, is Freye who concentrates essentially on the poetry but devotes a small section to the supernatural occurrences in the novels,[1] and Hartland who also has a chapter on the novels,[2] while Parsons in his section on the prose provides the most detailed study available on the diverse types and strands of folklore found in Scott's fiction.[3]

ABOUT THE AUTHOR

MARIA EDGEWORTH, IN A LETTER TO SIR
WALTER SCOTT, 1814

We have this moment finished *Waverley.* It
was read aloud to this large family, and I wish
the author could have witnessed the impression it made—the strong hold it seized of the
feelings both of young and old—the admiration raised by the beautiful descriptions of
nature—by the new and bold delineations of
character—the perfect manner in which
every character is sustained in every change
of situation from first to last, without effort,
without the affectation of making the persons
speak in character—the ingenuity with which
each person introduced in the drama is made
useful and necessary to the end—the admirable art with which the story is constructed
and with which the author keeps his own
secrets till the proper moment when they
should be revealed, whilst in the mean time,
with the skill of Shakespeare, the mind is
prepared by unseen degrees for all the
changes of feeling and fortune, so that nothing, however extraordinary, shocks us as
improbable; and the interest is kept up to
the last moment. We were so possessed with
the belief that the whole story and every
character in it was real, that we could not
endure the occasional addresses from the
author to the reader. They are like Fielding;
but for that reason we cannot bear them, we
cannot bear that an author of such high powers, of such original genius, should for a moment stoop to imitation. This is the only thing
we dislike, these are the only passages we
wish omitted in the whole work; and let the
unqualified manner in which I say this, and
the very vehemence of my expression of this
disapprobation, be a sure pledge to the
author of the sincerity of all the admiration I
feel for his genius.

SOURCE: Edgeworth, Maria. An excerpt from a letter to Sir Walter Scott. In *The Life and Letters of
Maria Edgeworth,* Vol. I, edited by Augustus J.
C. Hare, pp. 239-44. New York: Houghton, Mifflin and Company, 1895.

1. MYSTERIES.

It is no accident that the enduring fame of
Mrs Radcliffe's most illustrious work, *The Mysteries
of Udolpho,* contains in the title so much of its
mystique, a mystique of faraway time and place.
This is rendered even more intangible by the
nexus of riddles and puzzles which complicate the
course of the action and make the unfolding of
the heroine's progress synonymous with a process
of clarification of unanswered questions and
unsolved enigmas that reach back into the remot-
est past. It will be remembered that the central
thread running through the plot of the verse
romances is invariably related to a concealed
identity, of De Wilton in *Marmion,* of James V in
The Lady of the Lake and of Redmund O'Neal in
Rokeby. Indeed, kidnapping, borrowing, disguising and imposture run through the poems, and
also through the novels, so providing a nexus of
recurrent ideas, helping to create "a single, though
not seamless, body of work mysteriously united
by a continuing return to a number of key images
and ideas".[4] Connected with this is a series of
figures which Wilt sees generated by a recurrent
sense of a type of original sin in civilization which
she identifies as "usurpation", violent and illegal
self-appropriation, which gives rise to types like
"the red-handed king, the reluctant soldier, the
corrupted priest" from real history, and other
types like "the spellbinding lady, the Protean
outlaw, the shape-shifting minstrel-author of *Waverley* himself" who emerges from the romance
world of the Gothic or pure fantasy. For Wilt the
central crisis of usurpation can eventually be
explained in terms of "the fragmentation and
virtual disappearance of the kingdom called Christendom which is part of the construction of state
and self." It is this which "causes him the greatest
unease of all, [and] is at the very root of the long
Waverleyan dream/history of the the loss that
gains. "The illegitimate actions on the part of
these various types of people enable a construction of those modern fictions of legitimacy, the
state and the self": the first is an appropriation, a
romance of property,[5] that justifies usurpation;
the second is the fixing of an identity, the ending
of uncertainty, disguise or imposture.

Thus central to the plot of so many of Scott's
works is a sustaining of mystery, a mystery invariably centred on a cloudy or lost origin, of heroes
and heroines whose parents are unknown. At the
end of the novel, the child recovers his family and
his legitimate property—so that state and self are
affirmed.[6] The matter is presented with clarity
already in 1815 in his second novel, *Guy Man-*

nering which presents a good example of this type of mystery. George Brown, lover of Julie, the daughter of Guy Mannering, after many adventures and setbacks, is at last able to marry Julie since it is proved that he is the son of Bertram the landowner and inheritor of Ellogowan Castle. Brown was kidnapped by gypsies when he was small in an act of vengeance on Bertram for the expulsion of the gypsies from his land.

At the very end of his literary career, Scott was to use this very same mystery as a principle of plot. Towards the end of *Castle Dangerous* (1832), one learns that the young man Augustine, presumed the son of a minstrel, is the heroine Augusta of Berkley, betrothed to the castellan, Sir John de Walton. She is in danger of being treated as a spy by Sir John before her identity is discovered, only to be captured by the enemy Sir James Douglas, and is then offered in exchange for the castle. Sir John's impossible position which would entail the loss of the all-important property is solved by the arrival of orders to surrender the castle, after which the lady is restored to her lover. State and identity, both of the Lady Augusta and of Sir John, are preserved. The novels between *Guy Mannering* and *Castle Dangerous* often conceal the nature of this mystery. It is, for example, only at the end of *The Black Dwarf* (1816) that one learns who the mysterious dwarf is, and from where he derives his authority over the other principal characters. He secretly and beneficently intervenes in the story to the advantage of his neighbours, saving Grace Armstrong from abduction by robbers, and restoring her to her lover Hobbie Elliot, and preventing the marriage of Isabella Vere with Sir Frederick Langley. Isabella's father, the Laird of Ellieslaw, has wrung her consent to the marriage for his own ends. The Dwarf is eventually revealed to be the rich Sir Edward Manley, a near kinsman of Isabella, a man embittered by deformity and his unhappy love for Isabella's mother, who has long been supposed dead. The revelation restores identity, clarity, a mystery in family history, and saves the integrity of Ellieslaw's self and property.

It is similarly only at the end of *A Legend of Montrose* (1819) that one recognizes in Annot Lyle, the long-lost daughter of Sir Duncan Campbell. He has believed her to be dead, lost in the capture of his castle and killed along with his other children by a group of Highland bandits known as "the Children of the Mist". The McAulays had saved her and adopted her at the time when they had launched a punitive expedition against the wild tribe.

The mystery of Annot's origin, the obscurity of her birth, prevent both Allen McAulay and the Earl of Menteith from pressing their suit. Only when the deathbed confession of the leader of the Children of the Mist reveals that Annot is the daughter of Sir Duncan Campbell does her marriage with Menteith become possible. The proof of her identity arrives opportunely to give a happy denouement to the story, confers on her not only a full perception of self, her status in society, but also restores her property, "the castle of her father" (ch. 23).

Mordaunt Morton in *The Pirate* (1822) learns from the mouth of Ulla Troil (Norna of the Fitful Head) that he is her son. But this is a false trail in a nexus of family secrets, and at the very end of the novel one learns that he is in fact the legitimate son of Basil Mertoun, and it is his rival, the disturbing buccaneer interloper Cleveland who is her son by an earlier illicit union with Basil. The truth about the family relationships leads to clarity about identity and origins, the dangerous stranger moving away and the legally sanctioned son affirming self and property in his marriage and the implied inheritance of two families.

Similar mysteries envelop Darsie Latimer in *Redgauntlet* (1824) who is really the head of his house, a fact hidden from him. He is kidnapped by his ruthless uncle, Herries of Birrensworth, a fanatical Jacobite, as part of a last-ditch attempt to restore the Stuarts, to secure the support of his followers. Only after many experiences based on the attempts of his friend Alan Fairford to rescue him, does Darsie learn who he really is—Sir Arthur Darsie Redgauntlet—and is he able to assume his rightful role and his responsibilities as head of his family.

There is similarly a mystery hanging over the parentage of Roland Graeme in *The Abbot* (1820) who is sent as a page to the imprisoned Mary Queen of Scots and becomes an active agent in devising her flight. The mystery of his birth is explained and he is found to be heir of the house of Avenel. He is pardoned by the Regent and able to marry Catherine Seyton in full possession of self and state.

The pattern is similar for the poor Scottish Crusader, Sir Kenneth or the Knight of the Leopard, in *The Talisman* (1825) who must live through trials and humiliations before a final combat with his enemy, the Marquis of Monserrat whom he defeats and wounds, and is revealed to be Prince David of Scotland. The obstacle which his supposed lowly birth presented to his union with Edith Plantagenet is thus removed.

The mystery pattern is thus at the heart of concepts of the self and one's role in society. The family and possession of identity, integrity, status, or property and its attendant public duties, is the ideal medium of expression. The pattern is usually a positive one, the revelation and secret disentangling of a network of disabling mysteries resulting in restoration or resumption of what was lost or usurped.

Sometimes though the outcome is reversed: the clarification of mysteries reveals crime and precipitates distress or loss. The medium is always that of the family though. In *The Heart of Midlothian* (1818) Effie Deans bears the illegitimate child of one Robertson who is really a young nobleman, George Staunton. Effie is accused of the murder of her child and her life is saved only because of the heroic action of her sister Jeanie, after which she is able to marry her lover and becomes Lady Staunton, in possession both of identity and property. Her illegitimate son was not murdered, but rather kidnapped by Madge Wildfire, the insane daughter of Margaret Murdockson (an old harridan who had charge of Effie during her confinement). The boy has grown up with banditti and when Staunton, now Sir George, in his efforts to recover his son, comes upon them unexpectedly, he is killed by his own son. A nexus of disruption, violence and crime has rent asunder family ties and social restraints leading to fatal loss of self and destruction of life itself.

This negative pattern is repeated in *St Ronan's Well* (1824) which is also realized entirely in terms of family relationships. The story centres around two half-brothers, sons of the late Earl of Etherington, who had married secretly abroad and then publicly at home. The younger brother, though unentitled, bears the title and is at bitter emnity with his half-brother, Francis Tyrrel. He has intervened in a love affair between Francis and Clara Mowbray, and has actually impersonated his brother at a midnight marriage with Clara who finds herself married to a man she hates. The brothers make a compact to leave Clara undisturbed and still bearing her maiden name, both of them undertaking never to return to Scotland. But Etherington, who is threatened with dispossession of the earldom by Francis, and tempted to believe that fortune will accrue if his marriage with Clara is acknowledged, returns to demand her hand in a more open manner and public celebration of the marriage. He puts pressure on her brother Mowbray who in turn menaces Clara with death

if she does not co-operate. Although the plotter is finally exposed, Clara's mind has been unhinged by the terror and pressures and she dies. The secret and general miasma of mystery has led to an unravelling of the structures of society, to chaos and eventually death itself.

Just how much the mystery motif, the search for true identity, is central to the establishment of self and state is illustrated most sustainedly and positively in *Ivanhoe* (1819) where the action is interlaced by decisive appearances of both the outlaw Robin Hood and the king himself, Richard Coeur-de-Lion, both in numbers of various disguises and personae. Richard intervenes to save Ivanhoe at the beginning and at the end of the novel, as does Robin Hood in the middle. Both represent poles of authority and rightness—one outside the law, the other the embodiment of the law. Both are active in a lawless society where the usurpation of power is endemic and sanctioned by the ambitions of Prince John during Richard's supposed imprisonment ("kidnapping") in Austria. Both intervene to restore order, symbolized in the the disclosure of their identities. The revelation of self is directly connected to the restoration of the state; clarification of mystery is associated with legitimacy, the foiling of usurpation, the ascendancy of law.

2. TERROR AND HORROR

The Gothic novels are famous for their evocation of terror, for an atmosphere of uncertainty and fear provoked by superstitious dread, emotional anxiety, the advent of the supernatural, whether real or imagined, and a confrontation with distress provoked by actual encounter with violence and pain. If the terrors of Mrs Radcliffe's heroines stop short of this actual encounter with the unspeakable, while using the potential and imminence of such a possibility to the full, then in Lewis, as later with Maturin, the potential becomes actual and the imminent made present. The darker side of Romanticism found its first release in the scenes of stress in the Gothic novel, initiating what Mario Praz came famously to call the "Romantic Agony".[7] This aspect of the Romantic experience was considered in terms of its aesthetic meaning in the discussion of sublimity. Mrs Radcliffe distinguished clearly between terror and horror,[8] although she remained always a practitioner of terror only, of a terror understood as a stimulus, an emotional response to overwhelming sensory perception, akin to fear. Lewis's depiction of the fate of Agnes in the vaults of the monastery in *The Monk* is a case in point: while the evocation of of these subterranean prisons is a source of mystery and terror, the actual description of Agnes's imprisonment, the detailed account of her anguish, her torment with the death and corruption of her baby, is pure horror. The mind is numbed, or recoils from the graphic nature of the experience. Scott's appropriation of this famous episode in **Marmion** underlines the aesthetic difference very pertinently: his account of the vaults in St Cuthbert's is full of the sublime evocation of terror, but avoids actually describing her fate; it is suggested in the terrifying screams of fear which can be heard as the inquisitional tribune leaves the place of trial.

The Gothic novel is justly famous for its evocation of fear and agony, and it is probable that the agonies of *The Monk* with their echoes of the German *Schauerroman*, contributed to fashioning a tendency in Scott to produce scenes of surprising fearfulness which use the principles of terror and horror. Several of the Waverley Novels depict scenes of great distress and suffering which are in the mainsteam of the Romantic Agony.

At the end of his first novel **Waverley**, there is an account of the execution of Fergus McIvor which illustrates the tendency, and also draws attention to the application of the aesthetics of fear. The scene opens with a static tableau that focuses on some frightening detail.

> The court was occupied by a squadron of dragoons and a battalion of infantry, drawn up in hollow square. Within their ranks was the sledge, or hurdle, on which the prisoners were to be drawn to the place of execution. . . . It was painted black, and drawn by a white horse. At one end of the vehicle sat the Executioner, a horrid-looking fellow . . . with the broad axe in his hand . . .
>
> (**Waverley** ch. 69)

The impression is visual and singles out hurdle, axe and headsman. When it continues, the emphasis is aural.

> The dead march was then heard, and its melancholy sounds were mingled with those of a muffled peal, tolled from the neighbouring cathedral. The sound of the military music died away as the procession moved on . . .

The last part moves away from the outer scene to focus on Waverley's reactions which reveal the classic symptom of terror, of a mind numbed with the perception of dread and grief.

> . . . the court yard was now totally empty, but Waverley still stood there as if stupified, his eyes fixed upon the dark pass where he had seen the last glimpse of his friend.

At no point is the actual execution depicted; the closest one comes is to placing the traitors'

heads on the walls, and even here the actual and inescapable confrontation with the agony is obviated.

> He dared hardly look back towards the Gothic battlements . . .
>
> 'They're no there,' said Alan Polwarth. . . . with the vulgar appetite for the horrible, [he] was master of each detail of the butchery—'the heads are ower the Scotch yate . . .'

The treatment of this scene has been more in the manner of Mrs Radcliffe than Lewis. Here is how the latter deals with Ambrosio's treatment by the Inquisition.

> Returned to his dungeon, the sufferings of Ambrosio's body were far more supportable than those of his mind. His dislocated limbs, the nails torn from his hands and feet, and his fingers mashed and broken by the pressure of the screws, were far surpassed in anguish by the agitation of his soul . . .
>
> (*Monk* III, 425)

The scene is horrific, but in its lurid yet impersonal details and broad description of human reactions, it has an unfocused quality which leaves its effects melodramatic and generalized. In **Old Mortality** (1816), Scott again conjures up scenes of terror. Initially, the impression is rather like that of the execution scene in **Waverley**. There is a procession which instils dread.

> Trumpets, drums, and kettle-drums, contended in noise with the shouts of a numerous rabble . . .
>
> (**Mortality** ch. 35)

The mood is suddenly changed by the undramatic appearance of grisly details.

> The next object was two heads borne upon pikes; and before each bloody head were carried the hands of the dismembered sufferers . . .

Morton's reaction is like Waverley's, weak with the apprehension of terror. However, what ensues is in a different league altogether: when Hartland asserts, "ajoutons cependant que les horreurs de Scott ne sont jamais si crues que celles de Lewis. Néanmoins il s'en souvient constamment",[9] he is right about Scott's subtler approach, but even Lewis does not produce the following effects. The opening part of the scene of Macbriar's torture is a classic instance of the inducement of terror: there is a definite effect on the spectator.

> A dark crimson curtain, which covered a sort of niche, or Gothic recess in the wall, rose at the signal, and displayed the public executioner, a tall, grim, and hideous man, having an oaken table before him, on which lay thumbscrews. . . . Morton who was unprepared for this ghastly apparition, started when the curtain rose . . .
>
> (Ibid. ch. 36)

But the scene is developed further, and the reader is trapped with Macbriar in an horrific and inescapable situation of agony and distress. The refinement of detail and psychological reaction produces a hair-raising effect, even in reading.

> The executioner . . . enclosed the leg . . . within the tight iron boot, or case, and then placed a wedge of the same metal between the knee and the edge of the machine, took a mallet in his hand, and stood waiting. . . . the second blow fell. The third and fourth succeeded; but at the fifth, when a larger wedge had been introduced, the prisoner set up a scream of agony. Morton, whose blood boiled within him at witnessing such cruelty, could bear no longer . . .

Other scenes of fear centre on torture and execution which run like a *Leitmotif* through the Waverley Novels. In *Ivanhoe* there is the grim spectacle of Front-de-Boeuf's torture chamber where Saracen slaves from Palestine become executioners and prepare the instruments of torture with which to begin the torment of Isaac of York to induce him to pay up a vast ransom. The scene is full of gloom and fear as the surroundings, the props, the intentions, elicit terror in the imminent prospect of the horror of torture (ch. 22).

Scenes of execution occur at various times. In *A Legend of Montrose,* among the traces of the brutality of the Highlanders is the cruel fate of the "Children of the Mist". Dalgetty observes the lugubrious testimonies of their repression as he approaches the Castle of the Marquis of Argyle, images of suffering and death ("Midway this space was erected a rude gibbet, on which hung five dead bodies . . ." ch. 12).

The executioner himself is described in *The Talisman* (ch. 17). As a character he also appears in *Anne of Geierstein,* surrounded by the appurtenances of his trade (ch. 14), as in *Old Mortality.* The horror of the actual execution is depicted in this novel. The matter-of-factness of the events reduce the horror of the description, but not the power of the detail.

> . . . somewhat behind the captive, appeared a tall man, attired in red . . . the sword was brandished, the blow was struck, and the victim's head rolled on the scaffold . . . while the headless corpse shot streams from the arteries, which were drunk up by the saw-dust that strewed the scaffold . . .
>
> (*Geierstein* ch. 16)

Closely related to these images of pain and death, and directly linked to the perception of horror, are the reiterated situations of imprisonment so common in the Waverley Novels. Again the idea is central to the Gothic experience where at some point the central protagonists find themselves entrapped, often incarcerated and menaced. Emily's central adventure in *Udolpho* entails a confinement, an inescapable loss of freedom in a distant wilderness of castle, mountain and forest. Ellena is Schedoni's prisoner in the sea cottage in Apulia in *The Italian,* while Agnes's immuring in the vaults of St Clare is a *locus classicus* of Gothic horror. Imprisonment is established as a dominant motif in **Waverley** where the hero's romantic attachment to a dangerous cause leads to arrest and imprisonment from which he must be rescued by his devoted Rose. In **Guy Mannering,** the rascal lawyer Glossin and the smuggler Hatteraick are finally seen in prison together where Glossin is murdered by Hatteraick who then takes his own life. The prison becomes the symbol of the nexus of crimes and villainy the two have perpetrated. The prison scene in **Old Mortality** has already been mentioned. The very title of **The Heart of Midlothian** is that of a prison; it opens with the storming of the prison and the lynching of Captain Porteous.

The purported infanticide of Effie means that she is imprisoned in the Talbooth as well until Jeanie Deans secures her pardon. In **A Legend of Montrose** Dalgetty experiences imprisonment in Argyle Castle, while the central episode of **Ivanhoe** depicts the mass imprisonment of Cedric and Rowena, the wounded Ivanhoe, Athelstane, Isaac of York and Rebecca. The dungeons and turrets of Torquilstone represent the locus of lawlessness, the collapse of civilized standards. Rebecca is later held captive on a charge of witchcraft until freed by Ivanhoe's victory on her behalf.

The Abbot is similarly centred on the imprisoned Mary Queen of Scots held at Lochlevan Castle, the archetypal tragic Romantic heroine held against her will by the harsh forces of an anti-romantic political reality. **Kenilworth** likewise is built around the *de facto* incarceration of the beautiful Amy Robsart, who has secretly married the Earl of Leicester. He is forced to conceal his marriage for fear of incurring the wrath of the jealous Queen Elizabeth. Amy is accordingly mewed up in Cumnor Place, an old country house near Oxford, where through evil misrepresentation and intrigue, she is done to death.

Imagery of capture and imprisonment also occur in **The Pirate,** where Magnus and his daughters are apprehended by the pirates before they themselves are taken prisoners by the frigate 'Halcyon'.

In *The Fortunes of Nigel* the young hero is led into bad ways and caused to break the law against duelling by his enemy Lord Dalgarno: he is imprisoned in the Tower from where he is rescued only by the efforts of his beloved, Margaret Ramsay. His imprisonment is part of the loss of his inheritance, reputation and name, the low-point of his disrupted fortunes which reflect a corruption in society, as embodied in the court. The same pattern and implication is traced in *Peveril of the Peak,* where Julian Peveril and his father fall foul of the Duke of Buckingham, and are accused of complicity in the Popish Plot. Only with the help of the mysterious Fenella is their case brought to the notice of the King who intervenes to save them, sharing a sense of obligation for the kindness shown in the past by the old cavalier, Sir Geoffrey Peveril.

Quentin Durward is full of images of violence and imprisonment. The reference to Louis XI's dreaded castle of Loches not only captures the Gothic flavour of the prison imagery, but serves as a representative symbol for all the prisons of the Waverley Novels. These are often prisons of the mind, as in *St Ronan's Well,* where the setting is contemporary and domestic, and yet the fate of Clara is a type of psychological enthrallment which is simply another form of imprisonment. Also in *Redgauntlet,* the prison idea is not literal: Darsie is kidnapped by his uncle and legally restrained by him (itself a type of deception with an injunction from a corrupt magistrate). The imprisonment is far more to do with the spirit, with the hold of the past as represented in an untenable ideology embodied by Herrie's Jacobite fanaticism.

The notions of prisons of the mind and emotions are further explored in the Crusader novel *The Betrothed,* where both the heroine Eveline Berenger and the old constable, Hugo de Lacy, idealistically sign away their freedom of action and choice in rash vows, which they feel obliged to honour in spite of changed circumstance and the pressures of time and age. Hugo's absence on Crusade and Eveline's growing love for the young Damian, as well as the machinations of Randal de Lacy, lead to a charge of high treason and actual imprisonment, which is cleared up by the rational behaviour of the old constable. In *The Talisman* Sir Kenneth's ignorance of his true identity, his victimization, detention and near execution before being rescued by Saladin, are all metaphysical extensions of a type of imprisonment of his true self.

Woodstock too presents a prison more of the mind than actually. Charles II's hiding in the old lodge is a kind of self-imposed imprisonment because of the opportunities for concealment offered by the place. Cromwell hopes that Charles will take advantage of this facility and be captured there, but the intrigue which follows, the simulated haunting of the mansion, foils the plan and shows the Puritan soldiers to be prisoners of superstition.

Scott's last novels are also full of the imagery of imprisonment. In *Anne of Geierstein* the Philipsons are seized by Archibald of Hagenbach, and only narrowly escape death by the uprising of the people and his condemnation and execution by the *Vehmgericht.* In *Count Robert of Paris* the hero and his wife are detained as hostages for the Crusaders when they cross to Asia, Robert is thrown into prison and must be rescued by the chivalrous Hereward. In *Castle Dangerous* Augusta de Berkley is captured by the Douglas and offered in exchange for the castle. The vulnerable, uncertain identity of all these characters is stressed by their victimization symbolized in imprisonment.

The terror and horror of abduction, kidnapping, torture, imprisonment and execution finds expression in other images of disruption and chaos, like the evocation of mass violence which is a hallmark of the Gothic novel, and shows a fundamental disruption in nature and the heart of man reflected in the chaos of uncontrolled and uncontrollable behaviour. In *The Monk,* the riot which develops outside the convent rapidly degenerates into mass confusion, in which elemental forces of destruction are unleashed, the outcome of which is the murder of the Abbess.

> . . . one of the Gates was forced open. The Rioters poured into the interior part of the Building. . . . The Flames rising from the burning piles caught part of the Building, which being old and dry, the conflagration spread rapidly from room to room. The Walls were soon shaken by the devouring element: . . . nothing was to be heard but shrieks and groans; The Convent was wrapped in flames, and the whole presented a scene of devastation and horror.
>
> (*Monk* III, 357-358)

Scott reflects this perception of the frightening potential for violence and chaos in the hearts of men most startlingly perhaps in the account of the Porteous Riots of 1736 in the opening episodes of *The Heart of Midlothian.* As in the torture scenes, Scott's handling of materials is sharper than Lewis's, more perceptive of detail and human motivation and reaction. The violence and chaos are as torrential though.

> A huge red glaring bonfire speedily arose close to the door of the prison . . . illuminating the ferocious and wild gestures of the rioters who surrounded the place, as well as the pale and anxious groups of those who, from windows in the vicinage, watched the progress of this alarming scene. . . . The flames roared and crackled . . . and a terrible shout soon announced that the door had kindled and was in the act of being destroyed. . . . the rioters rushed . . . over its yet smouldering remains. Thick showers of sparkles rose high in the air . . .
>
> (*Midlothian* ch. 6)

This type of scene is found throughout the Waverley Novels, but is related more to the human confusion of purpose that leads to conflict, often on a vast scale of confrontation, as already seen in *Marmion*. The description of the Battle of Prestonpans in *Waverley* is a decisive turning-point in the hero's life, and the cause for him to question his romantic espousement of a lost cause. The same occurs in *Rob Roy*, where Francis Osbaldistone becomes the unwilling witness of an encounter between clansmen and royal troops, the symbol of a dangerous and futile way of life.

It is in *Ivanhoe* though that such scenes of violence and chaos are considered in several variations. The tournament at Ashby-de-la-Zouche represents a controlled form of violence, but is symptomatic of a wasteful arrogance in the heart of man. The siege of Torquilstone is a great set-piece, and a sustained evocation of destructive chaos which culminates in the conflagration of the castle. During the siege the discussion between Ivanhoe and Rebecca represents a central point of reference to the place and meaning of anger and violence in human affairs. The theme is brought to a sustained consideration in *The Fair Maid of Perth*, filled with the imagery of violence and chaos which reaches its highpoint in the battle of the champions from the clans of Qulele and Chatten in the final episodes. The violence and carnage cause the hero Henry Smith to reconsider his life and attitudes to impulsiveness, anger and violence. The final defeat of Charles the Bold by the peaceable Swiss at the Battles of Granson and Morat in *Anne of Geierstein* signifies the choice of moderation over the glamorous but facile and destructive violence that is the heritage of original sin.

Closely connected with the terror and the horror of the mass violence are the instances of personal acts of anger and force in the Gothic novel. Crimes by individuals are recurrent. As always, the differences between Mrs Radcliffe and Lewis are instructive. The closest Mrs Radcliffe comes to depicting murder is Schedoni's sinister contemplation of the sleeping Ellena in *The Italian*. In *The Monk* though, the horrendous highpoint to the criminal career of Ambrosio is the murder of Elvira followed by the rape and murder of Antonia. The personal crime is a reflection of the disruption in the universe and the reality of evil.

The Waverley Novels do not present personal violence in quite this lividness, but nevertheless trace a series of frightening actions which violate the natural law and the standards of love. Some of the crimes of violence are fundamental to this movement of plot, like the succession of abductions and kidnappings, the recurrent imprisonments. But these more individual and isolated actions of violence are threaded throughout the novels as points of disruption, and often as moments of personal confrontation.

In *Guy Mannering* Bertram [=Brown] is wrongly suspected by Mannering of paying attentions to his wife, and is wounded by him in a duel and left for dead. The forcible expulsion of the gypsies from the Ellogowan estate, and the murder and suicide in prison of Glossin and Hatteraick respectively, continue the record of violent deeds. *Old Mortality* depicts the assassination of the Archbishop of St Andrew's, *Rob Roy* the murder of the spy Morris by Helen McGregor; Rashleigh is killed by Rob Roy after having betrayed his Jacobite associates. *The Heart of Midlothian* depicts the lynching of Captain Porteous as well as the parricide of George Staunton by the Whistler, his own son. In *The Bride of Lammermoor* Lucy murders her husband on their wedding night, while in *A Legend of Montrose* the wedding of Annot Lyle and Menteith is interrupted by Allan MacAulay, who stabs his rival. *Ivanhoe* is filled with images of violence and pain, with its multiple abductions, imprisonments, tournaments, all of which are highlighted in the final ironic comment on violence when Bois-Guilbert falls dead in combat with Ivanhoe, although untouched by his rival's lance.

Amy Robsart is murdered in *Kenilworth*; Lord Dalgarno is killed by robbers as he proceeds to Scotland in a last attempt to seize Nigel's property. *The Talisman* as well is filled with violence, an attempted assassination of Richard Coeur-de-Lion, and the combat between Conrad de Monserrat and Sir Kenneth. *The Fair Maid of Perth* similarly moves from one act of disruption to another, the attempted abduction of Catherine by Rothsay, the hacking off of Ramornay's hand by Henry Smith, the murder of Rothsay in the Castle of Falkland, the suicide of Conachar. It is the last word in Scott's consideration of the disruption and confusion endemic to the view of the world explored in dark Romanticism, and an integral part of the imagery used by Scott to explore his own universe more fully.

Associated in a minor way with these acts of criminality and violence are figures from the world of romance, who both add to the mystery of the plots and intensify the elements of terror and horror. These are those embodiments of the exotic and the lawless that haunt the pages of Romantic fiction, the gypsies and robbers, both groups used extensively in the German literature and the Gothic novel, which so influenced Scott, from Goethe's robber baron *Götz von Berlichingen* (1773) and Schiller's *Die Räuber* (1782) through the banditti of Mrs Radcliffe and Lewis. Mrs Radcliffe constantly heightens the sublime effect of her wild scenes by etching the landscape with figures of outlaws, discerned in the distance, menacing life and property, but safely at a remove.

> There was a singularity in their dress, and a certain ferocity in their air, that fixed her attention. She withdrew from the casement while they passed, but soon returned to observe them further. Their figures seemed so suited to the wildness of the surrounding objects, that, as they stood surveying the castle, she sketched them for banditti amid the mountain view of her picture . . .
>
> (*Udolpho* I, 280-281)

In *The Monk* the balladesque terrors of Raymond's tale set in the forests of Germany contains a skirmish with robbers.

Robbers (and their variants, banditti, smugglers and pirates) are always a symbol of extreme lawlessness and disruption. Robbers occur in *The Heart of Midlothian* and *The Fortunes of Nigel,* where they cause death to protagonists who have themselves engaged in criminal activity. The buccaneers of *The Pirate* represent an alien intrusion that a close and ordered society cannot contain. In *Guy Mannering,* the challenge to law and possession is symbolized in the kidnapping of Bertram by smugglers, while the exercise of just and prudent stewardship is stressed by the way the nomadic and lawless gypsies are treated. Meg Merrilies, one of Scott's most vivid creations, represents a world of folklore and mystery, a challenge to order and to crime alike, since it is her reaction to the reckless disregard for tradition embodied in the Laird of Ellangowan's expulsion of the gypsies from his illegally acquired estates, symptomatic of a violation of the deeper values of tradition and

justice. It is her action further which reveals the conspiracy of Glossin and Hatteraick to kidnap Harry Bertram again, and leads to the restoration of true identity and property.

In *Quentin Durward,* gypsies also make an ambiguous contribution, beyond the law, but an elemental force that if harnessed sympathetically, can put the hero in touch with untapped springs of folk wisdom and insight.

3. THE MARVELLOUS AND THE IMPROBABLE.

Mystery and terror are partially underpinned in the Waverley Novels by an undertow of unease, eeriness or premonition induced by the introduction of the supernatural or the superstitious. The debate about the nature of the marvellous, as to whether Walpole's or Lewis's direct presentation of a numinous world, or Mrs Radcliffe's technique of indirect presentation through sensory deception and rational explanation, is discussed by Scott in his *Lives of the Novelists.* It will be recalled that while professing to dislike the explained supernatural, the evidence of his poems shows a movement from numinous reality through mystification by explicable means to psychological impressionability. The Waverley Novels themselves occupy an ambiguous position since he includes episodes derived from Scottish and German folklore that have a numinous nature with other events that are disturbing but fixed in human behaviour.

This ambiguity of response is present from the outset in *Waverley,* where the clansman Vich Ian Vhor sees the Bodach Glas, the grey ancestral spirit that predicts the imminence of death. The spectre is real to its recipient, but rationally explicable to Waverley as a sociological/psychological phenomenon. No editorial intrusion tries to manipulate the reader in either direction.

> ". . . I . . . was astonished at the man's audacity in daring to dog me. I called to him but received no answer. I felt an anxious throbbing at my heart; and to ascertain what I dreaded I stood still. . . . By Heaven, Edward, turn where I would, the figure was instantly before my eyes at the same distance! I was then convinced it was the Bodach Glas. My hair bristled, and my knees shook. . . . I made the sign of the cross, drew my sword, and uttered, 'In the name of God, Evil Spirit, give place!' 'Vich Ian Vohr,' it said, in a voice that made my very blood curdle, 'beware tomorrow!' The words were no sooner spoken than it was gone. . . ." Edward had little doubt that this phantom was the operation of an exhausted frame and depressed spirits, working on the common belief to all Highlanders in such superstitions.
>
> (*Waverley* ch. 59)

The *Doppelgänger* motif borrowed from German literature, appears again without sceptical qualification in **Old Mortality,** where during Morton's long absence from England, there is a supposed apparition of him in his home areas, as if his inheritance were guarded by a manifestation of himself, an assertion of his living presence. In **A Legend of Montrose,** the *Doppelgänger* reappears and is rather more sinister, as it predicts to Allan the violence he will perpetrate on his rival.

The most famous example in Scott of the use of the direct supernatural, occurs in **The Monastery** in the person of the ghostly White Lady, a figure again derived from German legend of the elemental spirits of the water, the undine, which Scott had read about in Baron Friedrich de la Motte Fouqué's *Novelle* (1811). She is represented as a guardian figure of the Avenel family and provides a mystic tie between humans and creatures of the elements, and appears from time to time to give predictions and advice, and work acts of beneficence, like restoring Sir Percy Shafton to life after he has been fatally wounded, appearing and disappearing at will, a real spirit.

Another instance of apparently genuine ghostly manifestation is in **The Betrothed,** where Evelyn is visited by a lady with a bleeding finger who predicts the pattern of events to follow.

These examples of the genuinely marvellous are rare exceptions in the Waverley Novels, the heritage of all Scott's reading and researches into demonology and sorcery.

Instances of the use of the superstitious, explicable forms of folktale or the eerie, occur in characters like Meg Merrilies, whom Mannering comes across in the Gothic ruins of Ellogowan Castle. He finds her spinning a thread drawn from wool of three different colours, black, white and grey. She sings and spins a kind of spell, which is an evocation of the ancient connection between fate and spinning. The model for Scott has surely been the Three Norns of German mythology familiar from his wide reading in German superstition and in his correspondence with Jakob Grimm. Meg provides a connecting link with a kind of preternatural insight, prophetic forewarning throughout the action. Her presence, expanded in eerie effectiveness, is developed in **The Bride of Lammermoor** into the three old hags who embittered by old age, poverty or neglect, exert a baleful and gloomy influence of foreboding and disaster throughout the novel, like a type of superstitious chorus, "one of Scott's best contributions to demonology".[10]

Norna of the Fitful-Head in **The Pirate** also serves to represent dark, pagan forces of pre-Christian belief in her insights and rituals, intensifying the indigenous background and deepening the sense of fatefulness.

Integral to Scott's use of the eerie, the explained supernatural, the probable, so much Mrs Radcliffe's stock-in-trade, are thus conversations, recitals of legends and popular rumours which induce an atmosphere of tension, even alarm. Sometimes characters are disturbed without cause, but rendered uneasy by murmurs or intimations produced by the mist or the night. But as with the great Poetess of Romantic fiction, there is a preference for association of these effects with architectural images—empty, or uninhabited buildings, or newly ruined ones. Caves, crypts, secret passages, trap doors, sliding panels are the essential elements in the construction of intrigue. Fear inspired by apparently supernatural agents are really the result of trickery explained by the rules of Mrs Radcliffe. The conformity with her approach is very close.[11]

Ruins themselves seem to invite the manifestation of unusual or frightening events, the imagery of abandonment, remoteness and decay providing an objective correlative to the lonely, isolated and frightened/impressionable human consciousness. There is a good example in **Guy Mannering** where Bertram reaches a building in ruins, where he finds a wounded man watched over by a gypsy. He hides when the accomplices of the sufferer arrive, watching and listening to them from his hiding. When they leave to dispose of the body, he escapes. The scene is full of the remoteness, eeriness, terror and tension of the Gothic (ch. 27-28).

> Impelled by curiosity to reconnoitre the interior of this strange place before he entered, Brown gazed in at this aperture. A scene of greater desolation could not well be imagined. There was a fire upon the floor, the smoke of which . . . escaped by a hole broken in the arch above. The walls, seen by this smoky light, had the rude and waste appearance of a ruin of three centuries old at least . . .
>
> (*Mannering* ch. 27)

This basic experience of fear is used as a manifestation of the gullibility and impressionability of others, and put to thematic purposefulness in other instances. In **The Antiquary,** for example, Eddie Ochiltree and Lovel, hidden in the ruins of a church, frighten the Baronet and the scoundrel Dousterswivel by their groanings and shrill cries in order to foil their dishonest plans (ch. 21). Later the German is terrified anew in these ruins at midnight by his experiences (ch.

25). *The Black Dwarf* contains analogous passages: a church rather than the ruins provides the emotive setting, where the Dwarf mysteriously intervenes, hidden in the shadows, to interrupt the coerced marriage of Isabella (ch. 17). A similar scene is to be found in *The Pirate* where Kirkwall intervenes to stop the marriage of Cleveland and Mina (ch. 37).

Closely related to ruin and church, but of a decidedly melodramatic character, is the imagery of secret architecture, of passages and rooms that exist hidden behind the surface and provide a dimension of the clandestine, inevitably for the deception of others, be this for positive or negative reasons.

Dalgetty and Ronald in *A Legend of Montrose*, for example, are able to escape from Argyle Castle by means of a secret passage. A hidden mechanism opens the door and the passage leads to the apartments of the Marquis (ch. 13-14). Norna in *The Pirate* bolsters her reputation as a sorceress by the installation of sliding panels and doors in her house by which she and her deformed dwarf are able to exercise their trickery. The Hermit of Engeddi in *The Talisman* leads Sir Kenneth though secret passages to a magnificent chapel (ch. 4). Only later is the explanation given of the vision he experiences (ch. 8). The arc of tension and the explanation are the classic techniques of the Gothic novel. *Peveril of the Peak* is full of these *frisson*-inducing mysteries where the architectural motif is now a prison: Julian in prison is surprised to be addressed by a mystery voice (ch. 35). The following night the same voice speaks to him at length. Only at the end of the novel does one learn how the acrobatic Fenella was able to enter Julian's prison.

But it is in *Woodstock* where one finds what is probably the most developed instance of the explained supernatural with its concomitant architectural associations so much used by Walpole and Mrs Radcliffe. Doors close violently without apparent human agency; strange sounds are heard, distant subterranean thunder; beds are moved; doors resist being opened, then spring open introducing currents of air which extinguish candles; Everard hears a voice which gives him menacing advice: soon after he finds himself in danger of death; mysterious music is heard and a voice urging Everard to leave Woodstock. The minister Holdenough believes that he sees the ghost of a boyhood friend, first in a mirror, then gliding slowly towards the door (ch. 17). Later one sees the passages and secret appartments where Charles II has been hiding (ch. 22). Then it is

revealed that Dr Rochecliffe with his assistants has chased away the agents of the Commonwealth. The nature of this terrorizing has been by architectural-mechanical trickery, all of which is revealed in what must be the most extended instance of the explained supernatural in Romantic literature (ch. 34). Some of the effects could be by Mrs Radcliffe herself, as in this instance of mysterious music so much loved by the authoress.

> A wild strain of melody, beginning at a distance, and growing louder as it advanced, seemed to pass from room to room, from cabinet to gallery, from hall to bower, through the deserted and dishonoured ruins of the ancient residence of so many sovereigns; and, as it approached, no soldier gave alarm, nor did any of the numerous guests of any degrees, who spent an unpleasant and terrified night in that ancient mansion, seem to dare to announce to each other the inexplicable cause of apprehension.
>
> (*Woodstock* ch. 15)

The association is not only with Mrs Radcliffe but also with Karl Grosse whose novel *Der Genius* (1791-95) appeared in English as *Horrid Mysteries* (1796), and must have been known to Scott. Here the methods of terror and subjugation used by a sinister secret society hinge on just such a sustained and intricate use of mechanical trickery.[12]

The terrifying apparatus so plentiful in *Woodstock* reappears in *Anne of Geierstein*. Arthur on guard duty is mystified and thrilled when he sees the spectral form of Anne (ch. 10). Later he is in prison anticipating the advent of his assassins. Anne and a black figure appear again to relieve him of his bonds; the black form takes him out of prison by the ordinary passages (ch. 15). The older Philipson later feels his bed moving, descending by means of cords and pulleys into a subterranean vault where he is involved in the terrifying ceremonies of a secret society—the centre of a trial of the dread *Vehmgericht*, and barely escapes sentence of death (ch. 20).

In his last novel, *Castle Dangerous*, Scott again returns to the appurtenances and architectural ploys of the supernatural, as Ursula with Augusta escapes from her cell by opening a secret door which has access to a tortuous secret passage.

In his use of the marvellous and the improbable then, his incidents and imagery are methods of instilling terror and mystery; all are culled from his memories of the ballads of the Border, the ballads and tragedies of the *Schauerromantik*, and his own researches into the superstitions, beliefs and practices of Scotland and the Middle Ages. On this foundation he has added circumstances and ideas found already in the Gothic novel which he knew so well. In these instances, the imitation is almost self-conscious, a use of conventions and motifs in the ordering of plot and range of imagery. A subtler integrating of the deeper, disturbing implications of dark Romanticism though can be discerned in his adaptation of the Gothic mode itself, the projection of a view of the world. It is in this adaptation and revitalization of a whole vision that he carries the implications of the *roman noir* to new depths and insights.

Notes

1. Freye, 53-63.

2. Hartland, 57-72.

3. Parsons, 68-285.

4. Wilt, 19-20.

5. Welsh, 93-126.

6. Parsons, 264: "In the *strife* plot, the problem of worth and status is complicated by war rather than by parentage, as in the *identity* plot. . . . The dénouement brings peace after hostilities, the reward of pardon and marriage for the good man, and the punishment of death or disgrace for the bad."

7. M. Praz, *The Romantic Agony* (London, 1970).

8. "Terror and horror are so far opposite, that the first expands the soul, and awakens the faculties to a high degree of life; the other contracts, freezes and nearly annihilates them. . . . neither Shakespeare nor Milton by their fictions, nor Mr Burke by his reasoning anywhere looked to positive horror as a source of the sublime, though they all agree that terror is a very high one." Mrs Radcliffe's theory was published in the *New Monthly Magazine,* 8(1826). See Letellier, *Kindred Spirits,* 267 for a survey of Mrs Radcliffe's place in the late eighteenth- early nineteenth-century discussions of the aesthetics of the sublime.

9. Hartland, 63.

10. D. Cameron, "The Web of Destiny: The Structure of *The Bride of Lammermoor*" 185, observes that the taut structure, harmony and effect of this novel lies in "Scott's brilliant use of the supernatural as a device to suggest certain qualities of the historical context, to express the secret desires of the characters, and to control the pace of the narrative."

11. Hartland, 68.

12. Cf. Letellier, *Kindred Spirits,* 206-209.

Bibliography

I. Primary Texts

1. SIR WALTER SCOTT

a) Poetry

—*Collected Poetry and Plays.* (Oxford Standard Authors.) Oxford, 1904.

b) Novels

—Numerous complete editions exist, among them the first edition, *The Waverley Novels: New Edition* (Edinburgh: R. Cadell, 1830) and *The Centenary Edition* (Edinburgh: Adam and Charles Black, 1871). The Everyman Library contains one of the best collected editions. Fine popular editions include the Collins Library of Classics and the Nelson Classics. Other modern editions of individual novels are published by Penguin. No significant textual variations exist between these different editions. The new critical edition was launched by the Edinburgh University Press in 1993.

2. THE GOTHIC NOVELISTS

Beckford, W. *Vathek* [1786] in *Three Gothic Novels.* Ed. P.FAIRCLOUGH with an Introductory Essay by M.PRAZ. Harmondsworth, 1968.

Lewis, M. G. *The Monk: A Romance* [1796]. Ed. H.ANDERSON. London, 1973.

Maturin, C. R. *Melmoth the Wanderer: A Tale* [1820]. Ed. D.GRANT. London, 1972.

Radcliffe, A. *The Italian, or the Confessional of the Black Penitents* [1797]. Ed. F. GARBER. London, 1971.

———*The Mysteries of Udolpho* [1794]. (Everyman's Library 865-866.) Introduction R.AUSTIN FREEMAN. 2 vols. London, 1931, 1968.

———*The Romance of the Forest* [1791]. (The World's Classics.) Ed. C.CHARD. Oxford, 1986. Quotations from London first edition.

Reeve, C. *The Old English Baron: A Gothic Story* [1777]. Ed. J.TRAINER. London, 1967.

Shelley, M. *Frankenstein, or The Modern Prometheus* [1818] in *Three Gothic Novels.* Harmondsworth, 1968.

Walpole, H. *The Castle of Otranto: A Story* [1764] in *Three Gothic Novels.* Harmondsworth, 1968.

II. Secondary Texts

Freye, W. *The Influence of "Gothic" Literature on Sir Walter Scott.* Rostock, 1902.

Hartland, R. W. *Walter Scott et le roman 'Frénétique': Contribution à l'étude de leur fortune en France.* Paris, 1928.

Letellier, R. I. *Kindred Spirits: Interrelations and Affinities between the Romantic Novels of England and Germany (1790-1820).* (Salzburg Studies in English Literature 33:3.) Salzburg, 1982.

Parsons, C. *Witchcraft and Demonology in Scott's Fiction.* Edinburgh and London, 1964.

Praz, M. *The Romantic Agony.* Trans. A. Davidson. London, 1970.

Scott, W. *Journal (1825-1832).* Ed. J. G. TAIT and W. M. PARKER. London, 1950.

———. *Letters.* Ed. GRIERSON, H. J. C. et al. 12 vols. London, 1932- 7.

———. *The Prose Works of Sir Walter Scott, Bart..* 30 vols. Edinburgh, 1834-6.

Welsh, A. *The Hero of the Waverley Novels.* New Haven and London, 1963.

Wilt, J. *Secret Leaves: The Novels of Sir Walter Scott.* Chicago, 1985.

Criticism

Boatright, Mody C. "Scott's Theory and Practice Concerning the Use of the Supernatural in Prose Fiction in Relation to the Chronology of the *Waverley Novels.*" *PMLA: Publications of the Modern Language Association of America* 50, no. 1 (March 1935): 235-61.

Elucidates the critical principles Scott devised concerning the proper use of the supernatural in fiction, ideas and techniques that he believed would distinguish his novels from those of his Gothic precursors. Boatright then goes on to apply these principles to Scott's works in an attempt to verify the rough order of composition of his novels.

Chandler, Alice. "Origins of Medievalism: Scott." In *A Dream of Order: The Medieval Ideal in Nineteenth-Century English Literature*, pp. 12-51. London: Routledge & Kegan Paul, 1971.

Examines Scott's role in introducing medievalism into nineteenth-century English literature.

Hart, Francis R. *Scott's Novels: The Plotting of Historic Survival.* Charlottesville: University Press of Virginia, 1966, 371 p.

A detailed study of the Waverley Novels divided into four sections: "The Quixotic Tragedy of Jacobism," "Opposing Fanaticisms and the Search for Humanity," "The Historical Picturesque and the Survivals of Chivalry," and "The Falls and Survivals of Ancient Houses."

Hayden, John O., ed. *Walter Scott: The Critical Heritage.* New York: Barnes and Noble, 1970, 554 p.

Reprints selected nineteenth-century critical commentary on Scott and his works.

Hennelly, Mark M. "*Waverley* and Romanticism." *Nineteenth-Century Fiction* 28, no. 2 (September 1973): 194-209.

Analyzes Scott's use of myth, dialectic, and romantic literary conventions in Waverley.

Irvine, Robert P. "Scott's *The Black Dwarf*: The Gothic and the Female Author." *Studies in Romanticism* 38, no. 2 (summer 1999): 223-48.

Evaluates Scott's innovative blending of social-realistic and Gothic elements in his 1816 novel The Black Dwarf in conjunction with his appropriation of feminine authorial discourse in this work.

Jack, Ian. "The *Waverley* Romances." In *English Literature, 1815-1832*, pp. 185-212. Oxford: Oxford University Press, 1963.

A biographical and historical introduction to the Waverley Novels.

Lauber, John. *Sir Walter Scott.* New York: Twayne Publishers, 1966, 166 p.

A concise introduction to Scott and his writing featuring both biographical and critical material.

Orr, Marilyn. "Repetition, Reversal, and the Gothic: *The Pirate* and *St. Ronan's Well.*" *English Studies in Canada* 16, no. 2 (June 1990): 187-99.

Focuses on Scott's use of the Gothic device of the double to represent the opposition between "the rational beneficence of romance" and "the irrational malignancy of its Gothic alternative" in two of the Waverley Novels, The Pirate *and* St. Ronan's Well.

Parsons, Coleman O. *Witchcraft and Demonology in Scott's Fiction: With Chapters on the Supernatural in Scottish Literature.* Edinburgh: Oliver & Boyd, 1964, 363 p.

Discusses Scott's developing use of supernatural elements in his poetry and prose.

Wilt, Judith. "Transmutations: From Alchemy to History in *Quentin Durward* and *Anne of Geierstein.*" *European Romantic Review* 13, no. 3 (September 2002): 249-60.

Focuses on two novels set in Renaissance Burgundy; considers elements Scott portrayed through the lens of historical objectivity and those he rendered as Gothic and occult mysteries.

Woolf, Virginia. "Sir Walter Scott." In *Collected Essays,* pp. 134-43. London: The Hogarth Press, 1966.

Impressionistic assessment of Scott that concludes: "The emotions . . . in which Scott excels are not those of human beings pitted against other human beings, but of man pitted against Nature, of man in relation to fate."

OTHER SOURCES FROM GALE:

Additional coverage of Scott's life and career is contained in the following sources published by Thomson Gale: *Authors and Artists for Young Adults*, Vol. 22; *Beacham's Guide to Literature for Young Adults*, Vol. 2; *British Writers*, Vol. 4; *Concise Dictionary of British Literary Biography, 1789-1832*; *Dictionary of Literary Biography*, Vols. 93, 107, 116, 144, 159; *DISCovering Authors*; *DISCovering Authors: British*; *DISCovering Authors: Canadian*; *DISCovering Authors Modules: Most-studied Authors, Novelists,* and *Poets*; *Literature and Its Times*, Vol. 1; *Literature Resource Center*; *Nineteenth-Century Literature Criticism*, Vols. 15, 69, 110; *Poetry Criticism*, Vol. 13; *Reference Guide to English Literature*, Ed. 2; *Reference Guide to Short Fiction*, Ed. 2; *St. James Guide to Horror, Ghost & Gothic Writers*; *Short Stories for Students*, Vol. 10; *Short Story Criticism*, Vol. 32; *Supernatural Fiction Writers*, Vol. 1; *Twayne's English Authors*; *World Literature and Its Times*, Vol. 3; *World Literature Criticism*; and *Yesterday's Authors of Books for Children.*

MARY WOLLSTONECRAFT SHELLEY

(1797 - 1851)

(Born Mary Wollstonecraft Godwin) English novelist, editor, critic, short story and travel writer.

Shelley is best known for her novel *Frankenstein; or, The Modern Prometheus* (1818), which has transcended the Gothic and horror genres and is now recognized as a work of philosophical and psychological resonance. Critics agree that with the depiction of a seemingly godless universe where science and technology have gone awry, Shelley created a powerful metaphor for the modern age; indeed, the Frankenstein myth, which has been adapted to stage, film, and television, has pervaded modern culture. Shelley's achievement is considered remarkable, moreover, because she completed the book before her twentieth birthday. In addition to *Frankenstein*, Shelley's literary works include several novels that were moderately successful when published but are little-known today and an edition of poetry by her husband, the Romantic poet Percy Bysshe Shelley, which she issued with notes that are now regarded as indispensable. Her reputation rests, however, on what she once called her "hideous progeny," *Frankenstein*.

BIOGRAPHICAL INFORMATION

Shelley's personal life has sometimes overshadowed her literary work. She was the daughter of Mary Wollstonecraft, the early feminist and author of *A Vindication of the Rights of Woman*, and William Godwin, the political philosopher and novelist. Her parents' wedding, which occurred when Wollstonecraft was five months pregnant with Mary, was the marriage of two of the day's most noted freethinkers. While they both objected to the institution of matrimony, they agreed to marry to ensure their child's legitimacy. Ten days after Mary's birth, Wollstonecraft died from complications, leaving Godwin, an undemonstrative and self-absorbed intellectual, to care for both Mary and Fanny Imlay, Wollstonecraft's daughter from an earlier liaison. Mary's home life improved little with the arrival four years later of a stepmother and her two children. The new Mrs. Godwin, whom contemporaries described as petty and disagreeable, favored her own offspring over the daughters of the celebrated Wollstonecraft, and Mary was often solitary and unhappy. She was not formally educated, but absorbed the intellectual atmosphere created by her father and such visitors as Samuel Taylor Coleridge. She read a wide variety of books, notably those of her mother, whom she idolized. Young Mary's favorite retreat was Wollstonecraft's grave in the St. Pancras churchyard, where she went to read and write and eventually to meet her lover, Percy Shelley.

An admirer of Godwin, Percy Shelley visited the author's home and briefly met Mary when she was fourteen, but their attraction did not take hold until a subsequent meeting two years later. Shelley, twenty-two, was married, and his wife was expecting their second child, but he and Mary, like Godwin and Wollstonecraft, believed that ties of the heart superseded legal ones. In July 1814, one month before her seventeenth birthday, Mary eloped with Percy to the Continent, where, apart from two interludes in England, they spent the next few years traveling in Switzerland, Germany, and Italy. These years were characterized by financial difficulty and personal tragedy. Percy's father, Sir Timothy Shelley, a wealthy baronet, cut off his son's substantial allowance after his elopement. In 1816, Mary's half-sister Fanny committed suicide; just weeks later, Percy's wife, Harriet, drowned herself. Mary and Percy were married in London, in part because they hoped to gain custody of his two children by Harriet, but custody was denied. Three of their own children died in infancy, and Mary fell into a deep depression that was barely dispelled by the birth in 1819 of Percy Florence, her only surviving child. The Shelleys' marriage suffered, too, in the wake of their children's deaths, and Percy formed romantic attachments to other women. Despite these trying circumstances, both Mary and Percy maintained a schedule of rigorous study—including classical and European literature, Greek, Latin, and Italian language, music and art—and ambitious writing; during this period Mary completed *Frankenstein* and another novel, *Valperga* (1823). The two also enjoyed a coterie of stimulating friends, notably Lord Byron and Leigh Hunt. The Shelleys were settled near Lenci, Italy, on the Gulf of Spezzia in 1822 when Percy drowned during a storm while sailing to meet Leigh and Marianne Hunt. After one mournful year in Italy, Mary returned permanently to England with her son.

Shelley's life after Percy's death was marked by melancholy and hardship as she struggled to support herself and her child. Sir Timothy Shelley offered her a meager stipend, but ordered that she keep the Shelley name out of print; thus, all her works were published anonymously. In addition to producing four novels in the years after Percy's death, Mary contributed a series of biographical and critical sketches to *Chamber's Cabinet Cyclopedia*, as well as occasional short stories, which she considered potboilers, to the literary annuals of the day. The Shelleys' financial situation improved when Sir Timothy increased Percy Florence's allowance with his coming of age in 1840, which enabled mother and son to travel in Italy and Germany; their journeys are recounted in *Rambles in Germany and Italy in 1840, 1842, and 1843* (1844). Too ill in her last few years to complete her most cherished project, a biography of her husband, Shelley died at age fifty-four.

MAJOR WORKS

Although *Frankenstein* has consistently dominated critical discussions of Shelley's oeuvre, she also composed several other novels in addition to critical and biographical writings. Her five later novels attracted little notice, and critics generally agree that they share the faults of verbosity and awkward plotting. After *Frankenstein*, *The Last Man* (1826) is her best-known work. This novel, in which Shelley describes the destruction of the human race in the twenty-first century, is noted as an inventive depiction of the future and an early prototype of science fiction. *Valperga* and *The Fortunes of Perkin Warbeck* (1830) are historical novels that have received scant attention from literary critics, while *Lodore* (1835) and *Falkner* (1837), thought by many to be autobiographical, are often examined for clues to the lives of the Shelleys and their circle. Shelley's stories were collected and published posthumously, as was *Mathilda*, a novella that appeared for the first time in 1959. The story of a father and daughter's incestuous attraction, it has been viewed as a fictional treatment—or distortion—of Shelley's relationship with Godwin. The posthumously published verse dramas, *Proserpine and Midas* (1922), were written to complement one of Percy Shelley's works and have garnered mild praise for their poetry. Critics have also lauded Shelley's nonfiction: the readable, though now dated, travel volumes, the essays for *Chamber's Cabinet Cyclopedia*, which are considered vigorous and erudite, and her illuminating notes on her husband's poetry.

CRITICAL RECEPTION

Since Shelley's death, critics have devoted nearly all of their attention to *Frankenstein*. Early critics, generally with some dismay, usually classified the novel as belonging to the Gothic genre then practiced by such authors as Ann Radcliffe and Matthew Gregory "Monk" Lewis. While most early Victorian reviewers reviled what they considered the sensationalist and gruesome elements in *Frankenstein*, many praised the anonymous author's imagination and powers of description. In the later nineteenth century and throughout *Frankenstein* criticism, commentators have focused on Prometheanism in the novel, an aspect that Shelley herself highlighted in the book's subtitle. This line of inquiry, which continues to engage critics, likens Dr. Frankenstein to the Greek mythic figure who wreaks his own destruction through abuse of power. Percy Shelley treated the same mythic-philosophic theme in his poetry, most notably in *Prometheus Unbound,* and critics have searched for his influence on *Frankenstein,* particularly in the expression of Romantic ideals and attitudes. Scholars have also debated the value of the additional narratives that Percy encouraged Mary to write. While some have praised the novel's resulting three-part structure, others have argued that these additions detract from and merely pad the story. Nevertheless, most have valued the otherworldly Arctic scenes. Commentators have also frequently noted the influence of Shelley's father, tracing strains of Godwin's humanitarian social views; in addition, some critics have found direct thematic links to his fiction, particularly to his novel, *Caleb Williams.* Other literary allusions often noted in *Frankenstein* include those to John Milton's *Paradise Lost,* the source of the book's epigraph, as well as Johann Wolfgang von Goethe's *Faust* and Samuel Taylor Coleridge's "The Rime of the Ancient Mariner."

Frankenstein criticism has proliferated since the 1950s, encompassing a wide variety of themes and approaches. The monster, who is often the focus of commentary, has been interpreted as representing issues ranging from the alienation of modern humanity to the repression of women. Many commentators have viewed the monster as Dr. Frankenstein's double, an example of the *doppelgänger* archetype. In a similar vein, critics have discussed Dr. Frankenstein and the monster as embodying Sigmund Freud's theory of id and ego. Students of the Gothic, supernatural horror, and science fiction novel have adopted *Frankenstein* as a venerable forebear and have approached it from a historical slant. Alternately, Shelley's life has served as a starting point for those who perceive in the novel expressions of the author's feelings toward her parents, husband, children, and friends. Feminist critics, in particular, have found Shelley and *Frankenstein* a rich source for study, describing it, for example, as a manifestation of the author's ambivalent feelings toward motherhood.

PRINCIPAL WORKS

History of a Six Weeks' Tour through a part of France, Switzerland, Germany, and Holland, with Letters descriptive of a Sail around the Lake of Geneva, and of the Glaciers of Chamouni (nonfiction) 1817

Frankenstein; or, The Modern Prometheus. 3 vols. (novel) 1818; revised edition, 1831

Valperga: or, The Life and Adventures of Castruccio, Prince of Lucca. 3 vols. (novel) 1823

Posthumous Poems [editor] (poetry) 1824

The Last Man. 2 vols. (novel) 1826

The Fortunes of Perkin Warbeck. 3 vols. (novel) 1830

Lodore. 3 vols. (novel) 1835

Falkner. 3 vols. (novel) 1837

The Poetical Works of Percy Shelley [editor] (poetry) 1839

Rambles in Germany and Italy in 1840, 1842, and 1843 (travel essays) 1844

The Choice: A Poem on Shelley's Death (poetry) 1876

Tales and Stories by Mary Wollstonecraft Shelley (short stories) 1891

Proserpine and Midas [first publication] (plays) 1922

*Mathilda [edited by Elizabeth Nitchie] (novella) 1959

Collected Tales and Stories (short stories) 1976

The Journals of Mary Shelley (journals) 1987

The Letters of Mary Wollstonecraft Shelley. 3 vols. (letters) 1988

* Originally titled *The Fields of Fancy, Mathilda* is believed to have been written c. 1819.

PRIMARY SOURCES

MARY WOLLSTONECRAFT SHELLEY (ESSAY DATE MARCH 1824)

SOURCE: Shelley, Mary Wollstonecraft. "On Ghosts." In *London Magazine* 9 (March 1824): 253-56.

In the following essay, Shelley treats the subject of belief in ghosts, offering her own thoughts and creative writings, as well as anecdotes and excerpts from others' writings.

I look for ghosts—but none will force
Their way to me; 'tis falsely said
That there was ever intercourse
Between the living and the dead.

—Wordsworth

What a different earth do we inhabit from that on which our forefathers dwelt! The antediluvian world, strode over by mammoths, preyed upon by the megatherion, and peopled by the offspring of the Sons of God, is a better type of the earth of Homer, Herodotus, and Plato, than the hedged-in cornfields and measured hills of the present day. The globe was then encircled by a wall which paled in the bodies of men, whilst their feathered thoughts soared over the boundary; it had a brink, and in the deep profound which it overhung, men's imaginations, eagle-winged, dived and flew, and brought home strange tales to their believing auditors. Deep caverns harboured giants; cloud-like birds cast their shadows upon the plains; while far out at sea lay islands of bliss, the fair paradise of Atlantis or El Dorado sparkling with untold jewels. Where are they now? The Fortunate Isles have lost the glory that spread a halo round them; for who deems himself nearer to the golden age, because he touches at the Canaries on his voyage to India? Our only riddle is the rise of the Niger; the interior of New Holland, our only terra in. cognita; and our sole mare incognitum, the north-west passage. But these are tame wonders, lions in leash; we do not invest Mungo Park, or the Captain of the Hecla, with divine attributes; no one fancies that the waters of the unknown river bubble up from hell's fountains, no strange and weird power is supposed to guide the ice-berg, nor do we fable that a stray pick-pocket from Botany Bay has found the gardens of the Hesperides within the circuit of the Blue Mountains. What have we left to dream about? The clouds are no longer the charioted servants of the sun, nor does he any more bathe his glowing brow in the bath of Thetis; the rainbow has ceased to be the messenger of the Gods, and thunder longer their awful voice, warning man of that which is to come. We have the sun which has been weighed and measured, but not understood; we have the assemblage of the planets, the congregation of the stars, and the yet unshackled ministration of the winds:—such is the list of our ignorance. Nor is the empire of the imagination less bounded in its own proper creations, than in those which were bestowed on it by the poor blind eyes of our ancestors. What has become of enchantresses with their palaces of crystal and dungeons of palpable darkness? What of fairies and their wands? What of witches and their familiars? and, last, what of ghosts, with beckoning hands and fleeting shapes, which quelled the soldier's brave heart, and made the murderer disclose to the astonished noon the veiled work of midnight?

These which were realities to our fore-fathers, in our wiser age—

—Characterless are grated
    To dusty nothing.

Yet is it true that we do not believe in ghosts? There used to be several traditionary tales repeated, with their authorities, enough to stagger us when we consigned them to that place where that is which "is as though it had never been." But these are gone out of fashion. Brutus's dream has become a deception of his over-heated brain, Lord Lyttleton's vision is called a cheat; and one by one these inhabitants of deserted houses, moonlight glades, misty mountain tops, and midnight church-yards, have been ejected from their immemorial seats, and small thrill is felt when the dead majesty of Denmark blanches the cheek and unsettles the reason of his philosophic son. But do none of us believe in ghosts? If this question be read at noon-day, when—

Every little corner, nook, and hole,
    Is penetrated with the insolent light—

at such a time derision is seated on the features of my reader. But let it be twelve at night in a lone house; take up, I beseech you, the story of the Bleeding Nun; or of the Statue, to which the bridegroom gave the wedding ring, and she came in the dead of night to claim him, tall, and cold; or of the Grandsire, who with shadowy form and breathless lips stood over the couch and kissed the foreheads of his sleeping grandchildren, and thus doomed them to their fated death; and let all these details be assisted by solitude, flapping curtains, rushing wind, a long and dusky passage, an half open door—O, then truly, another answer may be given, and many will request leave to sleep upon it, before they decide whether there be such a thing as a ghost in the world, or out of the world, if that phraseology be more spiritual. What is the meaning of this feeling?

For my own part, I never saw a ghost except once in a dream. I feared it in my sleep; I awoke trembling, and lights and the speech of others could hardly dissipate my fear. Some years ago I lost a friend, and a few months afterwards visited the house where I had last seen him. It was deserted, and though in the midst of a city, its vast halls and spacious apartments occasioned the same sense of loneliness as if it had been situated on an uninhabited heath. I walked through the vacant chambers by twilight, and none save I awakened the echoes of their pavement. The far mountains (visible from the upper windows) had lost their tinge of sunset; the tranquil atmosphere grew leaden coloured as the golden stars appeared in the firmament; no wind ruffled the shrunk-up river which crawled lazily through the deepest channel of its wide and empty bed; the chimes of the Ave Maria had ceased, and the bell hung moveless in the open belfry: beauty invested a reposing world, and awe was inspired by beauty only. I walked through the rooms filled with sensations of the most poignant grief. He had been there; his living frame had been caged by those walls, his breath had mingled with that atmosphere, his step had been on those stones, I thought:—the earth is a tomb, the gaudy sky a vault, we but walking corpses. The wind rising in the east rushed through the open casements, making them shake;—methought, I heard, I felt—I know not what—but I trembled. To have seen him but for a moment, I would have knelt until the stones had been worn by the impress, so I told myself, and so I knew a moment after, but then I trembled, awe-struck and fearful. Wherefore? There is something beyond us of which we are ignorant. The sun drawing up the vaporous air makes a void, and the wind rushes in to fill it,—thus beyond our soul's ken there is an empty space; and our hopes and fears, in gentle gales or terrific whirlwinds, occupy the vacuum; and if it does no more, it bestows on the feeling heart a belief that influences do exist to watch and guard us, though they be impalpable to the coarser faculties.

I have heard that when Coleridge was asked if he believed in ghosts,—he replied that he had seen too many to put any trust in their reality; and the person of the most lively imagination that I ever knew echoed this reply. But these were not real ghosts (pardon, unbelievers, my mode of speech) that they saw; they were shadows, phantoms unreal; that while they appalled the senses, yet carried no other feeling to the mind of others than delusion, and were viewed as we might view an optical deception which we see to be true with our eyes, and know to be false with our understandings. I speak of other shapes. The returning bride, who claims the fidelity of her betrothed; the murdered man who shakes to remorse the murderer's heart; ghosts that lift the curtains at the foot of your bed as the clock chimes one; who rise all pale and ghastly from the churchyard and haunt their ancient abodes; who, spoken to, reply;

and whose cold unearthly touch makes the hair stand stark upon the head; the true old-fashioned, foretelling, flitting, gliding ghost,—who has seen such a one?

I have known two persons who at broad daylight have owned that they believed in ghosts, for that they had seen one. One of these was an Englishman, and the other an Italian. The former had lost a friend he dearly loved, who for awhile appeared to him nightly, gently stroking his cheek and spreading a serene calm over his mind. He did not fear the appearance, although he was somewhat awe-stricken as each night it glided into his chamber, and,

Ponsi del letto insula sponda manca.
[placed itself on the left side of the bed]

This visitation continued for several weeks, when by some accident he altered his residence, and then he saw it no more. Such a tale may easily be explained away;—but several years had passed, and he, a man of strong and virile intellect, said that "he had seen a ghost."

The Italian was a noble, a soldier, and by no means addicted to superstition: he had served in Napoleon's armies from early youth, and had been to Russia, had fought and bled, and been rewarded, and he unhesitatingly, and with deep relief, recounted his story.

This Chevalier, a young, and (somewhat a miraculous incident) a gallant Italian, was engaged in a duel with a brother officer, and wounded him in the arm. The subject of the duel was frivolous; and distressed therefore at its consequences he attended on his youthful adversary during his consequent illness, so that when the latter recovered they became firm and dear friends. They were quartered together at Milan, where the youth fell desperately in love with the wife of a musician, who disdained his passion, so that it preyed on his spirits and his health; he absented himself from all amusements, avoided all his brother officers, and his only consolation was to pour his love-sick plaints into the ear of the Chevalier, who strove in vain to inspire him either with indifference towards the fair disdainer, or to inculcate lessons of fortitude and heroism. As a last resource he urged him to ask leave of absence; and to seek, either in change of scene, or the amusement of hunting, some diversion to his passion. One evening the youth came to the Chevalier, and said, "Well, I have asked leave of absence, and am to have it early tomorrow morning, so lend me your fowling-piece and cartridges, for I shall go to hunt for a fortnight." The Chevalier gave him what he asked; among the shot there were a few bullets. "I will take these also," said the youth, "to secure myself against the attack of any wolf, for I mean to bury myself in the woods."

Although he had obtained that for which he came, the youth still lingered. He talked of the cruelty of his lady, lamented that she would not even permit him a hopeless attendance, but that she inexorably banished him from her sight, "so that," said he, "I have no hope but in oblivion." At length lie rose to depart. He took the Chevalier's hand and said, "You will see her to-morrow, you will speak to her, and hear her speak; tell her, I entreat you, that our conversation tonight has been concerning her, and that her name was the last that I spoke." "Yes, yes," cried the Chevalier, "I will say any thing you please; but you must not talk of her any more, you must forget her." The youth embraced his friend with warmth, but the latter saw nothing more in it than the effects of his affection, combined with his melancholy at absenting himself from his mistress, whose name, joined to a tender farewell, was the last sound that he uttered.

When the Chevalier was on guard that night, he heard the report of a gun. He was at first troubled and agitated by it, but afterwards thought no more of it, and when relieved from guard went to bed, although he passed a restless, sleepless night. Early in the morning some one knocked at his door. It was a soldier, who said that he had got the young officer's leave of absence, and had taken it to his house; a servant had admitted him, and he had gone up stairs, but the room door of the officer was locked, and no one answered to his knocking, but something oozed through from under the door that looked like blood. The Chevalier, agitated and frightened at this account, hurried to his friend's house, burst open the door, and found him stretched on the ground—he had blown out his brains, and the body lay a headless trunk, cold, and stiff.

The shock and grief which the Chevalier experienced in consequence of this catastrophe produced a fever which lasted for some days. When he got well, he obtained leave of absence, and went into the country to try to divert his mind. One evening at moonlight, he was returning home from a walk, and passed through a lane with a hedge on both sides, so high that he could not see over them. The night was balmy; the bushes gleamed with fireflies, brighter than the stars which the moon had veiled with her silver light. Suddenly he heard a rustling near him, and the figure of his friend issued from the hedge and

stood before him, mutilated as he had seen him after his death. This figure he saw several times, always in the same place. It was impalpable to the touch, motionless, except in its advance, and made no sign when it was addressed. Once the Chevalier took a friend with him to the spot. The same rustling was heard, the same shadow slept forth, his companion fled in horror, but the Chevalier staid, vainly endeavouring to discover what called his friend from his quiet tomb, and if any act of his might give repose to the restless shade.

Such are my two stories, and I record them the more willingly, since they occurred to men, and to individuals distinguished the one for courage and the other for sagacity. I will conclude my "modern instances," with a story told by M. G. Lewis, not probably so authentic as these, but perhaps more amusing. I relate it as nearly as possible in his own words.

> A gentleman journeying towards the house of a friend, who lived on the skirts of an extensive forest, in the east of Germany, lost his way. He wandered for some time among the trees, when he saw a light at a distance. On approaching it he was surprised to observe that it proceeded from the interior of a ruined monastery. Before he knocked at the gate he thought it proper to look through the window. He saw a number of cats assembled round a small grave, four of whom were at that moment letting down a coffin with a crown upon it. The gentleman startled at this unusual sight, and, imagining that he had arrived at the retreats of fiends or witches, mounted his horse and rode away with the utmost precipitation. He arrived at his friend's house at a late hour, who sate up waiting for him. On his arrival his friend questioned him as to the cause of the traces of agitation visible in his face. He began to recount his adventures after much hesitation, knowing that it was scarcely possible that his friend should give faith to his relation. No sooner had he mentioned the coffin with the crown upon it, than his friend's cat, who seemed to have been lying asleep before the fire, leaped up, crying out, 'Then I am king of the cats;' and then scrambled up the chimney, and was never seen more.

MARY WOLLSTONECRAFT SHELLEY (STORY DATE 1891)

SOURCE: Shelley, Mary Wollstonecraft. "The Transformation." In *Masterpieces of Terror and the Supernatural*, selected by Marvin Kaye, pp. 107-21. New York: Barnes & Noble, 1985.

The following excerpt is from a short story written in 1831, but first published in Tales and Stories by Mary Wollstonecraft Shelley *in 1891.*

"Forthwith this frame of mine was wrenched
    With a woful agony,

Which forced me to begin my tale;
    And then it left me free.

"Since then, at an uncertain hour,
    That agony returns:
And till my ghastly tale is told,
    This heart within me burns."
—Samuel Taylor Coleridge "The Ancient Mariner"

I have heard it said, that, when any strange, supernatural, and necromantic adventure has occurred to a human being, that being, however desirous he may be to conceal the same, feels at certain periods torn up as it were by an intellectual earthquake, and is forced to bare the inner depths of his spirit to another. I am a witness of the truth of this. I have dearly sworn to myself never to reveal to human ears the horrors to which I once, in excess of fiendly pride, delivered myself over. The holy man who heard my confession, and reconciled me to the Church, is dead. None knows that once—

Why should it not be thus? Why tell a tale of impious tempting of Providence, and soul-subduing humiliation? Why? answer me, ye who are wise in the secrets of human nature! I only know that so it is; and in spite of strong resolve,—of a pride that too much masters me—of shame, and even of fear, so to render myself odious to my species,—I must speak. . . .

The country people were all alive and flocking about; it became necessary that I should conceal myself; and yet I longed to address some one, or to hear others discourse, or in any way to gain intelligence of what was really going on. At length, entering the walks that were in immediate vicinity to the mansion, I found one dark enough to veil my excessive frightfulness; and yet others as well as I were loitering in its shade. I soon gathered all I wanted to know—all that first made my very heart die with horror, and then boil with indignation. Tomorrow Juliet was to be given to the penitent, reformed, beloved Guido—tomorrow my bride was to pledge her vows to a fiend from hell! And I did this!—my accursed pride—my demoniac violence and wicked self-idolatry had caused this act. For if I had acted as the wretch who had stolen my form had acted—if, with a mien at once yielding and dignified, I had presented myself to Torella, saying, I have done wrong, forgive me; I am unworthy of your angel-child, but permit me to claim her hereafter, when my altered conduct shall manifest that I abjure my vices, and endeavour to become in some sort worthy of her. I go to serve against the infidels; and when my zeal for religion and my true penitence for the past shall appear to you to

cancel my crimes, permit me again to call myself your son. Thus had he spoken; and the penitent was welcomed even as the prodigal son of Scripture: the fatted calf was killed for him; and he, still pursuing the same path, displayed such open-hearted regret for his follies, so humble a concession of all his rights, and so ardent a resolve to reacquire them by a life of contrition and virtue, that he quickly conquered the kind old man; and full pardon, and the gift of his lovely child, followed in swift succession.

Oh, had an angel from Paradise whispered to me to act thus! But now, what would be the innocent Juliet's fate? Would God permit the foul union—or, some prodigy destroying it, link the dishonoured name of Carega with the worst of crimes? To-morrow at dawn they were to be married: there was but one way to prevent this—to meet mine enemy, and to enforce the ratification of our agreement. I felt that this could only be done by a mortal struggle. I had no sword—if indeed my distorted arms could wield a soldier's weapon—but I had a dagger, and in that lay my hope. There was no time for pondering or balancing nicely the question: I might die in the attempt; but besides the burning jealousy and despair of my own heart, honour, mere humanity, demanded that I should fall rather than not destroy the machinations of the fiend.

The guests departed—the lights began to disappear; it was evident that the inhabitants of the villa were seeking repose. I hid myself among the trees—the garden grew desert—the gates were closed—I wandered round and came under a window—ah! well did I know the same!—a soft twilight glimmered in the room—the curtains were half withdrawn. It was the temple of innocence and beauty. Its magnificence was tempered, as it were, by the slight disarrangements occasioned by its being dwelt in, and all the objects scattered around displayed the taste of her who hallowed it by her presence. I saw her enter with a quick light step—I saw her approach the window—she drew back the curtain yet further, and looked out into the night. Its breezy freshness played among her ringlets, and wafted them from the transparent marble of her brow. She clasped her hands, she raised her eyes to heaven. I heard her voice. Guido! she softly murmured—mine own Guido! and then, as if overcome by the fulness of her own heart, she sank on her knees;— her upraised eyes—her graceful attitude—the beaming thankfulness that lighted up her face— oh, these are tame words! Heart of mine, thou imagest ever, though thou canst not portray, the celestial beauty of that child of light and love.

I heard a step—a quick firm step along the shady avenue. Soon I saw a cavalier, richly dressed, young and, methought, graceful to look on, advance. I hid myself yet closer. The youth approached; he paused beneath the window. She arose, and again looking out she saw him, and said—I cannot, no, at this distant time I cannot record her terms of soft silver tenderness; to me they were spoken, but they were replied to by him.

"I will not go," he cried: "here where you have been, where your memory glides like some heaven-visiting ghost, I will pass the long hours till we meet, never, my Juliet, again, day or night, to part. But do thou, my love, retire; the cold morn and fitful breeze will make thy cheek pale, and fill with languor thy love-lighted eyes. Ah, sweetest! could I press one kiss upon them, I could, methinks, repose."

And then he approached still nearer, and methought he was about to clamber into her chamber. I had hesitated, not to terrify her; now I was no longer master of myself. I rushed forward—I threw myself on him—I tore him away—I cried, "O loathsome and foul-shaped wretch!"

I need not repeat epithets, all tending, as it appeared, to rail at a person I at present feel some partiality for. A shriek rose from Juliet's lips. I neither heard nor saw—I *felt* only mine enemy, whose throat I grasped, and my dagger's hilt; he struggled, but could not escape. At length hoarsely he breathed these words: "Do!—strike home! destroy this body—you will still live: may your life be long and merry!"

The descending dagger was arrested at the word, and he, feeling my hold relax, extricated himself and drew his sword, while the uproar in the house, and flying of torches from one room to the other, showed that soon we should be separated. In the midst of my frenzy there was much calculation:—fall I might, and so that he did not survive, I cared not for the death-blow I might deal against myself. While still, therefore, he thought I paused, and while I saw the villainous resolve to take advantage of my hesitation, in the sudden thrust he made at me, I threw myself on his sword, and at the same moment plunged my dagger, with a true, desperate aim, in his side. We fell together, rolling over each other, and the tide of blood that flowed from the gaping wound of each mingled on the grass. More I know not—I fainted.

Again I return to life: weak almost to death, I found myself stretched upon a bed—Juliet was kneeling beside it. Strange! my first broken request was for a mirror. I was so wan and ghastly, that my poor girl hesitated, as she told me afterwards; but, by the mass! I thought myself a right proper youth when I saw the dear reflection of my own well-known features. I confess it is a weakness, but I avow it, I do entertain a considerable affection for the countenance and limbs I behold, whenever I look at a glass; and have more mirrors in my house, and consult them oftener, than any beauty in Genoa. Before you too much condemn me, permit me to say that no one better knows than I the value of his own body; no one, probably, except myself, ever having had it stolen from him.

Incoherently I at first talked of the dwarf and his crimes, and reproached Juliet for her too easy admission of his love. She thought me raving, as well she might; and yet it was some time before I could prevail on myself to admit that the Guido whose penitence had won her back for me was myself; and while I cursed bitterly the monstrous dwarf, and blest the well-directed blow that had deprived him of life, I suddenly checked myself when I heard her say, Amen! knowing that him whom she reviled was my very self. A little reflection taught me silence—a little practice enabled me to speak of that frightful night without any very excessive blunder. The wound I had given myself was no mockery of one—it was long before I recovered—and as the benevolent and generous Torella sat beside me, talking such wisdom as might win friends to repentance, and mine own dear Juliet hovered near me, administering to my wants, and cheering me by her smiles, the work of my bodily cure and mental reform went on together. I have never, indeed, wholly recovered my strength—my cheek is paler since—my person a little bent. Juliet sometimes ventures to allude bitterly to the malice that caused this change, but I kiss her on the moment, and tell her all is for the best. I am a fonder and more faithful husband, and true is this—but for that wound, never had I called her mine.

I did not revisit the sea-shore, nor seek for the fiend's treasure; yet, while I ponder on the past, I often think, and my confessor was not backward in favouring the idea, that it might be a good rather than an evil spirit, sent by my guardian angel, to show me the folly and misery of pride. So well at least did I learn this lesson, roughly taught as I was, that I am known now by all my friends and fellow-citizens by the name of Guido il Cortese.

DIANE LONG HOEVELER (ESSAY DATE 1997)

SOURCE: Hoeveler, Diane Long. "Mary Shelley and Gothic Feminism: The Case of 'The Mortal Immortal.'" In *Iconoclastic Departures: Mary Shelley after* Frankenstein: *Essays in Honor of the Bicentenary of Mary Shelley's Birth,* edited by Syndy M. Conger, Frederick S. Frank, and Gregory O'Dea, pp. 150-63. Madison, N.J.: Fairleigh Dickinson University Press, 1997.

In the following essay, Hoeveler discusses the "Gothic feminism"—characterized by women engaging in passive-aggressive, self-negating behavior—in Shelley's works, particularly in the short story "The Mortal Immortal."

During the month of May 1794, the most popular drama in London, playing nightly to packed houses at Covent Garden, was Henry Siddons's *The Sicilian Romance; or The Apparition of the Cliff,* loosely based on Ann Radcliffe's second novel, published in 1790. One of the more interesting changes in the play concerns the villain of the Siddons piece, who keeps his inconvenient wife chained to solid stone in a rocky cave in the forest, a place he visits only to feed her and blame her for inflicting wounds of guilt on his heart. Although the Gothic villain would later metamorphose into the Byronic hero consumed by unspeakable guilt over illicit sins, the villain of the Siddons drama is a bit more prosaic. He simply desires to marry a younger and more beautiful woman, one who will further improve his social and political status, because his first wife, the mother of his children, has become redundant. The young woman he desires, whom we would recognize as a future trophy wife, is pursued from castle to convent to cavern, aided by the hero, the villain's son-turned-outlaw. As the above synopsis makes obvious, female Gothic novels like Radcliffe's *Sicilian Romance* provided the subject matter, techniques, and melodramatic formulae that, first on the stage in England, later on the French stage, and much later in the Hollywood "women in jeopardy" films such as *The Silence of the Lambs,* have continued to promulgate the primal Gothic tradition of "good" or femininity triumphing over "evil" or masculinity.

The typical female Gothic novel presents a blameless female victim triumphing through a variety of passive-aggressive strategies over a male-created system of oppression and corruption. The melodrama that suffuses these works is explicable only if we understand that, as Paula Backscheider has recently demonstrated, a generally hyperbolic sentimentalism was saturating the British literary scene at the time, informing the Gothic melodramas that were such standard fare during the popular theater season.[1] But melodrama, as Peter Brooks has demonstrated, is also characterized by a series of moves or postures that made it particularly attractive to middle-class women. Specifically, Brooks lists as crucial to melodrama the tendency toward depicting intense, excessive representations of life that tend to strip away the facade of manners to reveal the primal conflicts at work, leading to moments of intense confrontation. These symbolic dramatizations rely on what Brooks lists as the standard features of melodrama: hyperbolic figures, lurid and grandiose events, masked relationships and disguised identities, abductions, slow-acting poisons, secret societies, and mysterious parentage. In short, melodrama is a version of the female Gothic, while the female Gothic provides the undergirding for feminism as an ideology bent on depicting women as the innocent victims of a corrupt and evil patriarchal system.

If husbands can routinely chain their wives to stone walls and feed them the way one feeds a forsaken pet that will not die, then what sort of action is required from women to protect and defend themselves against such abuse? Demure, docile behavior is hardly adequate protection against a lustful, raving patriarch gone berserk. According to Brooks, the Gothic novel can be understood as standing most clearly in reaction to desacralization and the pretensions of rationalism.[2] Like melodrama, the female Gothic text represents both the urge toward resacralization and the impossibility of conceiving sacralization other than in personal terms. For the Enlightenment mentality, there was no longer a clear transcendent value to which one could be reconciled. There was, rather, a social order to be purged, a set of ethical imperatives to be made clear. And who was in a better position to purge the new bourgeois world of all traces of aristocratic corruption than the female Gothic heroine? Such a woman—professionally virginal, innocent, and good—assumed virtual religious significance because, within the discourse system, so much was at stake. Making the world safe for the middle class was not without its perils. Gothic feminism was born when women realized that they had a formidable external enemy—the lustful, greedy patriarch—in addition to their own worst internal enemy—their consciousness of their own sexual difference, perceived as a weakness.

A dangerous species of thought for women developed at this time and in concert with the sentimentality of Samuel Richardson and the

ABOUT THE AUTHOR

MARILYN BUTLER ON SHELLEY'S LIFE AND ITS IMPACT ON *FRANKENSTEIN*

Among the tumultuous events of Mary Shelley's life from 17 to 19, its emotional stresses must have had subtle, powerful effects on the shaping of *Frankenstein,* her first and best novel. Her thwarted but longed-for dialogue over the years with her father (which she afterwards described in a letter as "an excessive & romantic attachment"[*]) was interrupted, to be replaced by a richer but almost equally problematic relationship with her lover Shelley. In the four and a half years from 1815 to mid-1819 she was to lose the first three of her four children. Her suffering over their deaths was complicated by her own sense of guilt, probably dating back to her first realization that her own birth had caused the death of her mother. Mary's capacity for guilt must have been further exercised by two pathetic and from her point of view reproachful suicides in the autumn of 1816: those of Fanny Imlay, Mary's half-sister, on 9 October, and of Harriet (Westbrook) Shelley, Percy's wife, in November-December.

Percy Shelley should have helped his young wife to cope, but he resembled her father in offering support that was intellectually superb, emotionally inadequate; unintentionally he even contributed to the death of her second daughter, another Clara, in September 1818, by ordering Mary to travel across Italy with the sick child in the Italian summer heat. After each bereavement, William Godwin wrote her letters which briskly recommended as little mourning as possible. To the extent that *Frankenstein* is a family drama, centred on parental nurture (or the lack of it), on the failure of communication and mutual support, and on the death of its gentlest, most vulnerable members, it reads like the imaginative reworking of experience.

[*]*Letters of Mary Wollstonecraft Shelley,* ed. Betty T. Bennett, 3 vols. (Baltimore: Johns Hopkins University Press, 1980, 1983, 1988), ii. 215.

SOURCE: Butler, Marilyn. Introduction to *Frankenstein; or the Modern Prometheus: The 1818 Text,* by Mary Wollstonecraft Shelley. Reprint edition, edited and with notes by Marilyn Butler, pp. ix-li. Oxford: Oxford University Press, 1998.

hyperbolic Gothic and melodramatic stage productions of the era. This ideology graphically educated its audience in the lessons of victimization.[3] According to this powerful and socially coded formula, victims earned their special status and rights through no action of their own but through their sufferings and persecutions at the hands of a patriarchal oppressor and tyrant. One would be rewarded not for anything one did but for what one passively suffered. According to this paradigm, women developed a type of behavior now recognized as passive aggression; they were almost willing victims not because they were masochists but because they expected a substantial return on their investment in suffering. Whereas Richardson's Clarissa found herself earning a crown in heaven for suffering rape by Lovelace, the women in female Gothic texts were interested in more earthly rewards. The lesson that Gothic feminism teaches is that the meek shall inherit the Gothic earth; the female Gothic heroine always triumphs in the end because melodramas are constructed to suit this version of poetic justice. The God we call Justice always intervenes and justice always rectifies, validates, and rewards suffering. Terrible events can occur, but the day of reckoning invariably arrives for Gothic villains. This ideology fostered a form of passivity in women, a fatalism that the mainstream feminist would be loathe to recognize today. Yet Gothic feminism undergirds the special pleading of contemporary women who see themselves even today as victims of an amorphous and transhistorical patriarchy. When the contemporary feminist theorist Naomi Wolf identifies what she calls "victim feminism"—characterized by a loathing of the female body and a reification of victimization as the only route to power—we can hardly be faulted for hearing the echo of Mary Shelley's literary visions.[4]

As the daughter of Mary Wollstonecraft and William Godwin, Mary Wollstonecraft Godwin Shelley was destined to be an overdetermined personality. A heavy intellectual burden rested on her slight shoulders, and for the most part she fulfilled that expectation not only by marrying extravagantly but by writing well. In fact, her union with Percy Shelley may have been her greatest literary performance—her real and imagined victimization on his account, first as wife, then as widow, being only slightly less painful than the sufferings experienced by her fictional heroines. And although her husband's presence haunts all of her works, the real heroes or hero-villains of Mary's life were always her parents, who also recur obsessively in various mutated forms in everything she wrote. Mary Wollstonecraft may have left us only two inadequately realized fictions and two vindications, but she also left us Mary Shelley, in many ways destined to complete and fulfill her mother's aborted philosophical and literary visions.[5] If Wollstonecraft failed to understand the full implications of her suggestions for women—that they effectively "masculinize" themselves and shun "feminine" values as weak and debilitating—her daughter understood all too well the consequences of such behavior for both men and women. Mary's major work, *Frankenstein* (1818), stands paradoxically as the Gothic embodiment of the critique of Gothic feminism. If Wollstonecraft could barely imagine a brave new world for women inhabited by sensitive Henrys, Mary Shelley puts her fictional women into that world and reveals that the sensitive male hero is a mad egotist intent on usurping feminine values and destroying all forms of life in his despotic quest for phallic mastery. Her other two works most clearly in the Gothic mode, *Mathilda* (1819) and the short story "**The Mortal Immortal**" (1833), also critique the female Gothic formulae as they had evolved by the time she was writing. For instance, *Mathilda* rewrites *Frankenstein,* turning the prior text inside out, revealing the incestuous core of the Gothic feminist fantasy as she experienced it. Everyone in Mary Shelley's corpus is a victim, but her female characters are the victims of victims and thus doubly pathetic and weak.

We do not think of Mary Shelley as a feminist by contemporary standards, nor did she think of herself as one. She once stated: "If I have never written to vindicate the rights of women, I have ever befriended women when oppressed—at every risk I have defended and supported victims to the social system. But I do not make a boast." But she understood all too well what her mother failed to grasp—that woman's protection was in her studied pose of difference and weakness. In fact, she went so far as to observe that "the sex of our [woman's] material mechanism makes us quite different creatures [from men]—better though weaker."[6] But Mary's notion of the social system—the legal, financial, class, religious, and educational superstructure that undergirded nineteenth-century British culture—was finally codified and symbolized by her in the patriarchal bourgeois family. Her fathers are not simply demigods of the family hearth, they are representatives of a larger, oppressive, patriarchal system. They inherit and bequeath wealth because they represent and embody

that lucre themselves, in their very persons.[7] The body of the male in Mary Shelley's fiction is always a commodity of worth, an object to be valued, reconstructed, reassembled, and salvaged, while the bodies of the women in her texts are always devalued, compromised, flawed, and inherently worthless.

At the core of all of Mary Shelley's works, however, is the residue of what Freud has labeled in "A Child Is Being Beaten" (1919) as variations on the beating fantasy that children generally experience between the ages of five and fifteen. In these repeated scenarios of desire and repression a girl will typically move through three psychological positions. In the first and third positions, her stance is sadistic and voyeuristic—"another child is being beaten and I am observing the act"—but in the second psychic position her posture is masochistic, erotic, and deeply repressed: "I am the child being beaten by my father." For the boy, the psychic transformation is less complex due to the elimination of one stage. For him, the first position, "I am loved (or beaten) by my father," is transformed into the conscious fantasy "I am being beaten by my mother." According to Freud, the roots of the phallic mother (the all-powerful mother in possession of the father's phallus) can be located precisely in this early fantasy,[8] but for Mary Shelley, the psychic terrain is complicated by the fact that she, as a woman writer, typically seeks to elide gender by assuming the position of a male protagonist. The basic beating fantasies we see throughout her works—the attacks the "creature" makes on various members of Victor Frankenstein's family, the incestuous attack on Mathilda by her father, the attack on the body of the idealized female icon in "**The Mortal Immortal**"—all represent variations on the beating fantasy, expressing the child's ambivalence and impotence when confronted with the power and mystery of the parental figures.

Why does incest hover so blatantly over Mary (not to mention Percy) Shelley's Gothic works in ways that do not occur quite so self-consciously in the works of other female Gothic writers? Why are her heroines always defined and self-identified as daughters first, wives second, mothers only briefly? Why would she send the text of *Mathilda,* a shockingly graphic (for its time) portrayal of a father's incestuous love for his daughter, to her own father? And why would she then be surprised when he failed to arrange for its publication?[9] Writing on the very margins of her unconscious obsessions, Mary Shelley played the role of dutiful daughter to the end, leaving the ashes of Percy in

Rome and having herself buried with her parents and son in England. In many ways, Percy was as ephemeral a presence in her life as she was in his. It would appear from a reading of their letters and journals that both of them were playacting at love with ideal objects of their own imaginary creation. Unfortunately, as Mary learned too late, the real loves in both their lives were their parents, both real and imagined.

"The Mortal Immortal: A Tale" (1833),[10] one of the many short stories Mary wrote for money in her later life, plays in its oxymoronic title with ambiguity and impossibility, suggesting that there may be a way to make mortals immortal, just as Mary desperately wanted to believe that there may be a way to equalize women with men. Note, however, that the fear and loathing of the female body that activated *Frankenstein* and *Mathilda* recur as dominant motifs in a majority of Mary's short stories, not simply in this one. *Frankenstein* punished every female body in that text, scarring and disfiguring all female attempts to rewrite the generative body as sacred and whole. It replaced the maternal womb with chemical and alchemical artifice, only to blast masculine attempts at procreation as futile and destructive. In *Mathilda*, the male principle once again would appear to be the only effectual parent; but, as in the earlier work, the father produces his progeny only to consume it, feeding on his daughter as a vampire feeds on victims in order to sustain a perverse form of death-in-life.

"The Mortal Immortal" situates the reader within the same psychic terrain, and, like the other works, it plays with variations of beating fantasies, with sometimes the male protagonist as victim, sometimes the female. But we begin this narrative initially within the frame of legendary discourse, this time of the Wandering Jew. We learn early in the text that the narrator defines himself in negative terms, in terms of what he is not. He tells us that he is not the Jew because he is infinitely younger, being only 323 years old ("TMI," 314). "The Mortal Immortal" actually reads as if it were inspired not by that particular old legend but by E. T. A. Hoffmann's "The Sandman" or "The Devil's Elixirs," the latter reviewed in *Blackwood's* in 1824 (16:55-67). Mary Shelley does not record in her journal having read "The Sandman" in either a French or Italian translation, and her knowledge of German was certainly not strong enough for her to have read it in the

original, but the tale was well-known in England by 1833, the year she wrote and published "The Mortal Immortal."[11]

Like the Hoffmann tale, "The Mortal Immortal" is told by a naive narrator attempting to decode the scientific experiments of a quasi crank and supposed quack, Cornelius Agrippa, the famous German alchemist whose assistant supposedly "raised the foul fiend during his master's absence, and was destroyed by him" ("TMI," 314). A deep fear of death and its association with the father's phallic power motivate Hoffmann's "Sandman," while they occur in more muted form in the Shelley tale. The invocation of the name of Cornelius Agrippa, the association of Agrippa and Satan, both of whom figured so prominently in *Frankenstein* as the inspiration of Victor's dabbling in reanimating the base metal of the human body, suggest that masculine, scientific, and phallic powers are as dangerous as they are crucial to the development of human civilization. Once again, the human body is the obsessive focus of this tale, as it was in the two earlier Gothic works by Mary Shelley. Now, however, the issues are not only clear but very clearly delineated: the female body is decayed and fraudulent; it is a pale and inadequate copy of the prior and superior male body. The tale is predicated on the decline of the body of the beauteous Bertha, whose fading is contrasted to the continuing phallic power of the immortal Winzy, her body rotting while his flourishes over the course of their marriage.

Mary Shelley constructs her tale over the body of Bertha, but before she gets to Bertha, the narrator, Winzy, introduces the reader to his own desperate state of mind. He is a man who has lived for 323 years and fears that he may indeed be immortal. He is a man who feels "the weight of never-ending time—the tedious passage of the still-succeeding hours" ("TMI," 314). Traditionally read as a slightly veiled autobiographical statement expressing Mary Shelley's own repugnance at having survived her husband, parents, and three of her children, the fear of time in this text actually expresses a fear of death, a terror about the nonexistence of an afterlife.[12] Life at least prolongs the uncertainty that there may indeed be an afterlife where one will be reunited with the souls of one's beloveds. Death will bring the final and unequivocal answer, and that is something that Mary Shelley was as unprepared to face in 1833 as she was in 1818.

Like a fairy tale, this short fiction begins with the poor. young assistant—"very much in love"—

working for the notorious "alchymist" Cornelius Agrippa, who keeps killing all of his assistants because of the inhuman demands he makes on them. One need not search far to see Winzy as the victim of a beating fantasy at the hands of this father substitute. Thwarted in his efforts to persuade his recently orphaned childhood sweetheart Bertha to live "beneath [his] paternal roof," Winzy suffers greatly when Bertha goes off to live with "the old lady of the near castle, rich, childless, and solitary" ("TMI," 315). Rather than have a child herself, this wealthy woman "buys" (or, as we might more euphemistically say, "adopts") a beautiful adult woman and then tries to barter her off to the highest bidder. Bertha is dramatic and self-dramatizing. She begins to dress in "silk," pose in her "marble palace" ("TMI," 315), and generally amuse herself by taunting and tormenting the frustrated Winzy. Bertha wants Winzy to prove his love by accepting the risky job of working for Agrippa: "'You pretend to love, and you fear to face the Devil for my sake!'" ("TMI," 315). Accepting a "purse of gold" from Agrippa makes Winzy feel "as if Satan himself tempted me" ("TMI," 315). Bertha wants to put her would-be lover through a test, and she can think of no better one than to subject him to the ultimate evil father, the ultimate beater. No simple coquette, Bertha specializes rather in psychic and emotional abuse of her lover, continually subjecting him to anxiety and jealousy: "Bertha fancied that love and security were enemies, and her pleasure was to divide them in my bosom" ("TMI," 316). Notice, however, that everything Bertha metes out to Winzy is later delivered to her. She plays the role of Gothic villainess and later Gothic victim in this work.

If Cornelius Agrippa as the masculine and phallic aspect of the narrator is identified with the fires of Satan, Bertha as the feminine principle is associated with water and the fountain, "a gently bubbling spring of pure living waters" ("TMI," 315). While ordered to work overtime stoking the furnaces of Agrippa, Winzy loses the favor of Bertha, who rejects him in favor of the rich suitor Albert Hoffer. Consumed with frustrated jealousy, Winzy decides to drink the magical elixir that Agrippa is preparing because he has been told that the brew is "'a philter to cure love; [if] you would not cease to love your Bertha—beware to drink!'" ("TMI," 317). But that is precisely what Winzy wants—he wants to be free of his attachment to the feminine, or to put it another way, Mary Shelley wants to be free of her tie to the female body.

Once again, her male narrator expresses Mary Shelley's own ambivalence and repugnance toward not only the female body but female sexuality and the chains of love. Listen to these revealing words from Winzy about his state of mind and motivations:

> False girl!—false and cruel! . . . Worthless, detested woman! I would not remain unrevenged—she should see Albert expire at her feet—she should die beneath my vengeance. She had smiled in disdain and triumph—she knew my wretchedness and her power. Yet what power had she?—the power of exciting my hate—my utter scorn—my—oh, all but indifference! Could I attain that—could I regard her with careless eyes, transferring my rejected love to one fairer and more true, that were indeed a victory!
>
> ("TMI," 317)

What power had she indeed? Questioning the source and the power of the female body stands as the central query of Mary Shelley's corpus. The answer she discovers suggests that the female body has only as much power as the male chooses to allot to it. But the focus in this passage is on the male response to the female body, running the gamut from hate to scorn to indifference. Notice the progression of emotions. Only when one reaches indifference is one free of the obsessive hold of the other on one's consciousness. Mary Shelley throughout her works strives to escape just exactly this—the corrosive effect of the passions on her heart and body, seeking the cool indifference, the frigidity, the stark embrace of reason that she represented in the climactic presentation of the Arctic Circle in *Frankenstein.*

Grabbing the elixir and drinking, Winzy declares his intention to be cured "of love—of torture!" He finds himself sinking instead into a "sleep of glory and bliss which bathed [his] soul in paradise during the remaining hours of that memorable night," only to awake and find his appearance "wonderfully improved" ("TMI," 317, 319). When he ventures out to Bertha's neighborhood, he finds himself the amorous object not only of Bertha but also of her rich old protectress, the "old high-born hag," "the old crone." The ugly old woman represents a standard feminine archetype, the double-faced goddess motif that Mary and Percy would have been familiar with through their readings in classical mythology. Blake (in "The Mental Traveller"), Keats (in "Lamia" and "La Belle Dame Sans Merci"), and Percy himself (in "Prince Athanase") had used the duplicitous female figure. The old hag in this text represents not simply what Bertha will become, a sort of humanized foreshadowing element, but also a version of the phallic mother as class avenger. Now conceiving a lecherous attraction to Winzy, the old hag aggressively pursues him, sending Bertha back to the castle with the peremptory command, "Back to your cage—hawks are abroad!" ("**TMI**," 319). Ironically, the only hawk is the old hag, seeking to feast on her prey, the masculine flesh of Winzy.

But Winzy is now free of the earlier "respect" he had for the old hag's "rank." Now he boldly runs after Bertha, only to discover that he is as much in love with her as ever: "I no longer loved—Oh! no, I adored—worshipped—idolized her!" ("**TMI**," 319). The two triangles operating here—Winzy/Bertha/old hag and Winzy/Bertha/false suitor—place the young lovers in the two varieties of oedipal rivalry that recur throughout Mary Shelley's fiction. The prior and more powerful association for her heroes and heroines is always the paternal and maternal home. The old hag represents the child-consciousness's (re)construction of the father and mother as one potent figure, all-powerful and all-consuming. This father/mother monad has been traditionally understood within psychoanalytical discourse as the phallic mother, the mother with the father's phallus, the fearful composite of maternity with power.[13] If Ann Radcliffe was finally able by the conclusion of her novels to kill the phallic mother, Mary Shelley is able to flee only temporarily from her. Rather, Bertha decides to reject the old hag's wealth and power and to run away to an alternate maternal abode: "'O Winzy!' she exclaimed, 'take me to your mother's cot.'" But not only does Bertha gain a new mother-figure, Winzy's father also "loved her" and "welcomed her heartily" ("**TMI**," 320). Winzy is not so much gaining a wife as Bertha is gaining new parents. Or, to put it another way, Winzy is not so much gaining a wife as a new sibling.

Five years of bliss pass quickly, and one day Winzy is called to the bed of the dying Cornelius, who finally explains that his elixir had been not simply "a cure for love" but a cure "for all things—the Elixir of Immortality" ("**TMI**," 321). Love is here presented as another form of disease, a weakening and debilitating condition that leaves one prey to the ravages of mortality. To be "cured of love" is to be made immortal, impregnable, godlike, because to be human is to embody all the opposite qualities ("**TMI**," 321). Love here is also presented as something that feminizes or weakens the masculine self, but the narrator is hardly a realistic presentation of a male character. His

consciousness, his sensibility is feminine. He loves; therefore, he is as vulnerable as Mary Shelley found herself. He seeks to escape the ravages to which the flesh is prone, the never-ending pregnancies that Mary endured for six years, the repeated processions to the cemetery to bury babies. Winzy is the idealized masculine component of Mary Shelley—her reason and her intellect—that she desperately wants to believe will provide a means of escape for her. If she can be like a man—free from the biological curse—she would be like a god, immortal, inhabiting a world of the mind.

But the feminine aspect of Mary Shelley lives in the figure of Bertha, the female body that rots and decays before the saddened eyes of Winzy. Years pass and Bertha is now fifty, while Winzy appears to be her son. The two are "universally shunned" ("**TMI**," 322) by their neighbors, largely because they embody the most pernicious incestuous dream of all—the tabooed love of a mother and son. Winzy has finally married the old crone, much to his dismay. Fleeing to a new country, the two decide to "wear masks," although Bertha's mask is infinitely less successful than Winzy's. Resorting to "rouge, youthful dress, and assumed juvenility of manner," Bertha is a parody of her former self. A desperate caricature of femininity, she has become a "mincing, simpering, jealous old woman." In other words, she has become another phallic mother, guarding her son Winzy with a "jealousy [that] never slept" ("**TMI**," 323). The female body—once so beautiful and perfect—has become a flawed and diseased artifice, a shell fitted over a mass of stinking corruption. The male body, in stark contrast, continues to exist as statuesque and youthful, a perfect emblem of the triumph of masculinity and masculine values over the feminine. The female body has become the target and object of the beating given to it by the ultimate Nobodaddy—life, time, and mortality.

The years pass until Bertha is finally bedridden and paralytic and Winzy functions as her nurse: "I nursed her as a mother might a child" ("**TMI**," 324). The wheel has come full circle. The mother is the child, while the husband/son has become a "mother." All gradations in the family romance have been tried in much the same way that Blake depicted them in "The Mental Traveller." Confined within the bourgeois domicile, the sexes feed on each other parasitically until they have consumed themselves in the process of playing all their gendered and ungendering roles to a limited audience. When Bertha finally dies, Winzy decides to escape the family romance. He lives alone in melancholy depression, contemplating suicide, until he decides to "put [his] immortality" to the test by journeying to the Arctic Circle. Like Victor Frankenstein, he decides to seek his destruction in the embrace of the "elements of air and water" ("TMI," 325). This desire to reconcile opposites, to bathe and immerse himself in mutually exclusive physical elements, represents Mary Shelley's attempt to depict the catastrophic merging of masculine and feminine elements in the human psyche. If men are associated with the realm of air, the intellect, reason, and the mind, then women are identified with water, the physical, and the body and its fluids. Winzy's seeking oblivion in the extremely gender-coded landscape of the Arctic Circle suggests that the apocalypse Mary Shelley imagined for herself and her characters involved an escape from all polarities, or rather a freezing and holding of the two elements in a static situation. We do not know what becomes of Winzy, just as we never know what becomes of the creature at the conclusion of *Frankenstein*.

But the dream of desire is the same at the end of all of Mary Shelley's texts: to escape the body and live in the realm of pure mind. Like her mother, Mary Shelley was a reluctant sensualist. She needed, philosophically, to embrace free love and open marriage, but her disappointments in her philandering husband could not be concealed. Claiming to support free love is easy as long as one does not have a husband who has a history of collecting pretty young things and bringing them home. Finally a deep revulsion toward the female body emerges as clearly in Mary Shelley's works as it does in Wollstonecraft's.

Gothic feminism for Mary Shelley entailed the realization that women would always be life's victims, not simply because social, political, economic, and religious conventions placed them in inferior and infanticizing postures, but because their own bodies cursed them to forever serve the wheel of physical corruption. Being a mother, bringing to life a child who would die, and perhaps would die soon, condemned women to serve a merciless god—the cycle of generation, birth, and death—in a way that men did not. The nightmare haunting Mary Shelley's life was not simply that she caused the death of her mother but that she recapitulated a reversed version of the same tragedy with three of her own children. She experienced her life as a sort of curse to herself and the ones she loved, and why? She understood that her life, her very physical being, fed on her mother's body parasitically, cannibalistically consuming it. Later she watched her children

wither, unable to be sustained by her. These recurring nightmares fed her fictions, but they also spoke to a deeper fear that has continually plagued women.

Gothic feminism seeks to escape the female body through a dream of turning weakness into strength. By pretending that one is weak or a passive victim, one camouflages oneself in a hostile terrain, diverting attention from one's real identity. Mary Shelley knew that on some level she was no victim; she knew her strength and intelligence were more than a match for anyone's. But she also sensed danger in that strength, or at least experienced it ambivalently, fearing that it caused the deaths of others. The grotesque freakishness of the creature in *Frankenstein*, made material in the description of "his" oddly assembled body and his continual rejection by everyone he seeks to love, trope Mary Shelley's own sense of herself and all women as diseased, aberrant, and freakish composites of the hopes and dreams of other people. Gothic feminism for Mary Shelley is embodied in the sense of herself and the female body as a void, an empty signifier, a lure into the cycle of painful birth and disappointing death. Railing against the female body—sometimes disguised as male and sometimes blatantly presented as female—is finally the only position that Mary Shelley can take. She can laud the bourgeois family, she can valorize community and what we now label "family values," but she ultimately cannot escape the mortality that gives the lie to everything she seeks to praise. She inhabits a female body, she bleeds and causes bleeding in others, and those unfortunate facts define for her and her fiction the Gothic feminist nightmare in its starkest terms.

Notes

1. See the suggestive discussion of "Gothic Drama and National Crisis" in Paula R. Backscheider, *Spectacular Politics: Theatrical Power and Mass Culture in Early Modern England* (Baltimore, Md.: Johns Hopkins University Press, 1993), 149-234.

2. For the best discussion of the stock tropes of melodrama, see Peter Brooks, *The Melodramatic Imagination* (New Haven: Yale University Press, 1976), 3, 16-17. Brooks acknowledges the importance on his thinking of Eric Bentley's "Melodrama" in *The Life of the Drama* (New York: Athenaeum, 1964), 195-218.

3. The best discussion of the development of sentimentality (also known as "sensibility") as a change in consciousness can be found in Jean Hagstrum's *Sex and Sensibility: Ideal and Erotic Love from Milton to Mozart* (Chicago: University of Chicago Press, 1980). On the same subject, also see the valuable collection of essays titled *Sensibility in Transformation: Creative Resistance to Sentiment from the Augustans to the Romantics*, ed. Syndy McMillen Conger (Totowa, N.J.: Fairleigh Dickinson University Press, 1990). On weakness

as a central component of sentimentality, see R. W. Brissenden, *Virtue in Distress: Studies in the Novel of Sentiment from Richardson to Sade* (New York: Barnes and Noble, 1974) and Janet Todd, *Sensibility: An Introduction* (London: Methuen, 1986).

4. Naomi Wolf, *Fire With Fire: The New Female Power and How It Will Change the 21st Century* (New York: Random House, 1993), 136-37.

5. The relationship, real and imagined, between Mary Shelley and her dead mother and flawed father is explored most revealingly in William St. Clair's *The Godwins and the Shelleys: The Biography of a Family* (New York: Norton, 1989). Sandra M. Gilbert and Susan Gubar's *Madwoman in the Attic: The Woman Writer and the Nineteenth-Century Literary Imagination* (New Haven: Yale University Press, 1979) discusses Mary Shelley's relationship with her mother and its influence on her works (213-47), as does Janet M. Todd's "Frankenstein's Daughter: Mary Shelley and Mary Wollstonecraft," *Women and Literature* 4 (1976): 18-27. On the influence of Godwin on her works, see Katherine Powers, *The Influence of William Godwin on the Novels of Mary Shelley* (New York: Arno, 1980), and on Mary's relationship with her father, see U. C. Knoepflmacher, "Thoughts on the Aggression of Daughters," in *The Endurance of* Frankenstein, ed. George Levine and U. C. Knoepflmacher (Berkeley and Los Angeles: University of California Press, 1979), 88-119. Several recent biographies of Mary Shelley explore the parental influence on her writings. In particular, see Anne K. Mellor, *Mary Shelley: Her Life, Her Fiction, Her Monsters* (London: Routledge, 1988); Emily Sunstein, *Mary Shelley: Romance and Reality* (Boston: Little, Brown, 1989); and Muriel Spark, *Mary Shelley* (1951; rprt., London: Constable, 1987).

6. The full text of Mary's well-known journal confession reads:

> With regard to "the good Cause"—the cause of the advancement of freedom & knowledge—of the Rights of Woman, & c.—I am not a person of opinions. . . . Some [people] have a passion for reforming the world:—others do not cling to particular opinions. That my parents and Shelley were of the former class, makes me respect it. . . . I was nursed and fed with a love of glory. To be something great and good was the precept given me by my Father: Shelley reiterated it. Alone & poor, I could only be something by joining a party—& there was much in me—the woman's love of looking up & being guided, & being willing to do anything if any one supported & brought me forward, which would have made me a good partizan—but Shelley died & I was alone. . . . If I have never written to vindicate the Rights of women, I have ever befriended women when oppressed.

> (21 October 1838)
> (*The Journals of Mary Shelley*, ed. Paula R. Feldman and Diana Scott-Kilvert [Oxford: Clarendon, 1987] 2:553-54)

The second Shelley quotation is taken from her letter of 11 June 1835 (*Selected Letters of Mary W. Shelley*, ed. Betty T. Bennett [Baltimore: Johns Hopkins University Press, 1995], 257).

7. Analyzing fathers and mothers in Mary Shelley's fiction has been a persistent focus in the literary criticism of her work. A useful overview of the critical history on this topic can be found in Jane Blumberg, *Mary Shelley's Early Novels: 'This Child of Imagination and Misery'* (Iowa City: University of Iowa Press, 1993). See also Marc A. Rubinstein, "'My Accursed Origin': The Search for the Mother in *Frankenstein*," *Studies in Romanticism* 15 (1976): 165-94; James B. Carson, "Bringing the Author Forward: *Frankenstein* through Mary Shelley's Letters," *Criticism* 30 (1988): 431-53; and Kate Ellis, "Mary Shelley's Embattled Garden," in *The Contested Castle: Gothic Novels and the Subversion of Domestic Ideology* (Urbana: University of Illinois Press, 1989), 181-206.

8. See Sigmund Freud, "'A Child is Being Beaten': A Contribution to the Study of the Origin of Sexual Perversions," in *The Standard Edition of the Complete Psychological Works of Sigmund Freud*, trans. and ed. James Strachey et al., 24 vols. (London: Hogarth Press, 1953-74), 17:175-204. The fullest attempt to apply the beating fantasy motif to female Gothic fiction can be found in Michelle Massé, *In the Name of Love: Women, Masochism, and the Gothic* (Ithaca: Cornell University Press, 1992). In particular, see her chapter "'A Woman Is Being Beaten' and Its Vicissitudes," 40-106.

9. Mary Shelley sent the manuscript of *Mathilda* to Godwin via their mutual friend Maria Gisborne in May 1820. After almost two years of fruitless inquiry, she finally concluded that Godwin would not help see the manuscript into publication, so she began trying to recover it. She never succeeded, and the novella was not published until Elizabeth Nitchie prepared an edition for press in 1959 (*Mathilda* [Chapel Hill: University of North Carolina Press, 1959]). Terence Harpold explores the incestuous core and motivation of *Mathilda* in his article "'Did you get Mathilda from Papa?': Seduction Fantasy and the Circulation of Mary Shelley's *Mathilda*," *Studies in Romanticism* 28 (1989): 49-67. Harpold concludes that the novel "represents a fantasy of seduction," and that the submission of the novel to Godwin "signals Mary's effort to engage him in the seduction fantasy, but to acknowledge the authority of his desire in the primal scene which determines her understanding of herself and her relations with each of her parents" (64).

10. All quotations from "The Mortal Immortal" are taken from text reprinted in *The Mary Shelley Reader*, ed. Betty Bennett and Charles E. Robinson (New York: Oxford University Press, 1990), 314-26, hereafter cited in the text as TMI. The first printing of "The Mortal Immortal" was in *The Keepsake* (1834), 71-87.

11. Although I have been unable to document Mary Shelley's reading of the Hoffmann tale through her own record of her readings in the journal, I believe she may at least have been familiar with the story's rough plotlines through the text's circulation in British literary circles by 1833. E. T. A. Hoffmann's "The Sandman" is itself a seminal literary source in psychoanalytic discourse systems. Freud developed his theory of the uncanny while reading the story, and it has inspired a number of French feminist meditations on "the phallic gaze," most notably Hélène Cixous's fruitful "Fiction and Its Phantoms: A Reading of Freud's 'The Uncanny,'" *New Literary History* 7 (1976): 525-48. An overview of the psychoanalytic history of the Hoffmann story can be found in Sarah Kofman, *Freud and Fiction*, trans. Sarah Wykes (Cambridge: Polity Press,

1991), while its status within the Romantic tradition is examined by Marianne Thalmann, *The Literary Sign Language of German Romanticism*, trans. Harold Basilius (Detroit: Wayne State University Press, 1972).

12. Like *Mathilda* and the other novels besides *Frankenstein*, the short stories of Mary Shelley are now the focus of critical interest. For a very different reading of the female body in this text, see Sonia Hofkosh, "Disfiguring Economies: Mary Shelley's Short Stories" in *The Other Mary Shelley: Beyond* Frankenstein, ed. Audrey A. Fisch, Anne K. Mellor, and Esther H. Schor (New York: Oxford University Press, 1993), 204-19.

13. For useful overviews and summaries of the theoretical and psychoanalytical background on the phallic mother, see Marcia Ian, *Remembering the Phallic Mother: Psychoanalysis, Modernism, and the Fetish* (Ithaca: Cornell University Press, 1993); and Dana Birksted-Breen, ed., *The Gender Conundrum: Contemporary Psychoanalytic Perspectives on Femininity and Masculinity* (New York: Routledge, 1993).

TITLE COMMENTARY

Frankenstein; or, The Modern Prometheus

PERCY BYSSHE SHELLEY (ESSAY DATE 1817)

SOURCE: Shelley, Percy Bysshe. "On *Frankenstein*." *The Athenaeum*, no. 263 (10 November 1832): 730.

Shelley wrote the following highly favorable review of Frankenstein *in 1817, but it was not published until 1832. Unlike most early reviewers, he emphasized the novel's moral aspects. He also traces similarities between Mary Shelley's narrative style and characterization and William Godwin's.*

The Novel of *Frankenstein; or, the Modern Prometheus*, is undoubtedly, as a mere story, one of the most original and complete productions of the day. We debate with ourselves in wonder, as we read it, what could have been the series of thoughts—what could have been the peculiar experiences that awakened them—which conduced, in the author's mind, to the astonishing combinations of motives and incidents, and the startling catastrophe, which compose this tale. There are, perhaps, some points of subordinate importance, which prove that it is the author's first attempt. But in this judgment, which requires a very nice discrimination, we may be mistaken; for it is conducted throughout with a firm and steady hand. The interest gradually accumulates and advances towards the conclusion with the accelerated rapidity of a rock rolled down a mountain. We are led breathless with suspense and sympathy, and the heaping up of incident on incident, and the working of passion out of passion. We cry "hold, hold! enough!"—but there is yet something to come; and, like the victim whose history it relates, we think we can bear no more, and yet more is to be borne. Pelion is heapen on Ossa, and Ossa on Olympus. We climb Alp after Alp, until the horizon is seen blank, vacant, and limitless; and the head turns giddy, and the ground seems to fail under our feet.

This novel rests its claim on being a source of powerful and profound emotion. The elementary feelings of the human mind are exposed to view; and those who are accustomed to reason deeply on their origin and tendency will, perhaps, be the only persons who can sympathize, to the full extent, in the interest of the actions which are their result. But, founded on nature as they are, there is perhaps no reader, who can endure anything beside a new love story, who will not feel a responsive string touched in his inmost soul. The sentiments are so affectionate and so innocent—the characters of the subordinate agents in this strange drama are clothed in the light of such a mild and gentle mind—the pictures of domestic manners are of the most simple and attaching character: the father's is irresistible and deep. Nor are the crimes and malevolence of the single Being, though indeed withering and tremendous, the offspring of any unaccountable propensity to evil, but flow irresistibly from certain causes fully adequate to their production. They are the children, as it were, of Necessity and Human Nature. In this the direct moral of the book consists; and it is perhaps the most important, and of the most universal application, of any moral that can be enforced by example. Treat a person ill, and he will become wicked. Requite affection with scorn;—let one being be selected, for whatever cause, as the refuse of his kind—divide him, a social being, from society, and you impose upon him the irresistible obligations—malevolence and selfishness. It is thus that, too often in society, those who are best qualified to be its benefactors and its ornaments, are branded by some accident with scorn, and changed, by neglect and solitude of heart, into a scourge and a curse.

The Being in *Frankenstein* is, no doubt, a tremendous creature. It was impossible that he should not have received among men that treatment which led to the consequences of his being a social nature. He was an abortion and an anomaly; and though his mind was such as its first impressions framed it, affectionate and full of moral sensibility, yet the circumstances of his existence are so monstrous and uncommon, that, when the consequences of them became developed in action, his original goodness was gradually turned into inextinguishable misanthropy and revenge. The scene between the Being and the blind De Lacey in the cottage, is one of the most profound and extraordinary instances of pathos that we ever recollect. It is impossible to read this dialogue,—and indeed many others of a somewhat similar character,—without feeling the heart suspend its pulsations with wonder, and the "tears stream down the cheeks." The encounter and argument between Frankenstein and the Being on the sea of ice, almost approaches, in effect, to the expostulations of Caleb Williams with Falkland. It reminds us, indeed, somewhat of the style and character of that admirable writer, to whom the author has dedicated his work, and whose productions he seems to have studied.

There is only one instance, however, in which we detect the least approach to imitation; and that is the conduct of the incident of Frankenstein's landing in Ireland. The general character of the tale, indeed, resembles nothing that ever preceded it. After the death of Elizabeth, the story, like a stream which grows at once more rapid and profound as it proceeds, assumes an irresistible solemnity, and the magnificent energy and swiftness of a tempest.

The churchyard scene, in which Frankenstein visits the tombs of his family, his quitting Geneva, and his journey through Tartary to the shores of the Frozen Ocean, resemble at once the terrible reanimation of a corpse and the supernatural career of a spirit. The scene in the cabin of Walton's ship—the more than mortal enthusiasm and grandeur of the Being's speech over the dead body of his victim—is an exhibition of intellectual and imaginative power, which we think the reader will acknowledge has seldom been surpassed.

SIR WALTER SCOTT (ESSAY DATE MARCH 1818)

SOURCE: Scott, Sir Walter. "Remarks on *Frankenstein*." *Blackwood's Edinburgh Magazine* 2, no. 12 (March 1818): 612.

In the following excerpt, Scott places Frankenstein *in the philosophical, rather than merely sensational, school of supernatural fiction, assessing it as a work of creative and poetic genius, despite its implausible plot.*

[*Frankenstein*] is a novel, or more properly a romantic fiction, of a nature so peculiar, that we ought to describe the species before attempting any account of the individual production. . . .

[The] class of marvellous romances admits of several subdivisions. In the earlier productions of imagination, the poet or tale-teller does not, in his own opinion, transgress the laws of credibility, when he introduces into his narration the witches, goblins, and magicians, in the existence of which he himself, as well as his hearers, is a firm believer. This good faith, however, passes away, and works turning upon the marvellous are written and read merely on account of the exercise which they afford to the imagination of those who, like the poet Collins, love to riot in the luxuriance of oriental fiction, to rove through the meanders of enchantment, to gaze on the magnificence of golden palaces, and to repose by the waterfalls of Elysian gardens. In this species of composition, the marvellous is itself the principal and most important object both to the author and reader. . . .

A more philosophical and refined use of the supernatural in works of fiction, is proper to that class in which the laws of nature are represented as altered, not for the purpose of pampering the imagination with wonders, but in order to shew the probable effect which the supposed miracles would produce on those who witnessed them. In this case, the pleasure ordinarily derived from the marvellous incidents is secondary to that which we extract from observing how mortals like ourselves would be affected,

> By scenes like these which, daring to depart
> From sober truth, are still to nature true.

Even in the description of his marvels, however, the author, who manages this style of composition with address, gives them an indirect importance with the reader, when he is able to describe, with nature and with truth, the effects which they are calculated to produce upon his dramatis persona. . . . But success in this point is still subordinate to the author's principal object, which is less to produce an effect by means of the marvels of the narrations, than to open new trains and channels of thought, by placing men in supposed situations of an extraordinary and preternatural character, and then describing the mode of feeling and conduct which they are most likely to adopt. . . .

In the class of fictitious narrations to which we allude, the author opens a sort of account-current with the reader; drawing upon him, in the first place, for credit to that degree of the marvellous which he proposes to employ; and becoming virtually bound, in consequence of this indulgence, that his personages shall conduct themselves, in the extraordinary circumstances in which they are placed, according to the rules of probability, and the nature of the human heart. In this view, the *probable* is far from being laid out of sight even amid the wildest freaks of imagination; on the contrary, we grant the extraordinary postulates which the author demands as the foundation of his narrative, only on condition of his deducing the consequences with logical precision.

We have only to add, that this class of fiction has been sometimes applied to the purposes of political satire, and sometimes to the general illustration of the powers and workings of the human mind. Swift, Bergerac, and others, have employed it for the former purpose, and a good illustration of the latter is the well known *Saint Leon* of William Godwin. In this latter work, assuming the possibility of the transmutation of metals and of the *elixir vito,* the author has deduced, in the course of his narrative, the probable consequences of the possession of such secrets upon the fortunes and mind of him who might enjoy them. *Frankenstein* is a novel upon the same plan with *Saint Leon*; it is said to be written by Mr Percy Bysshe Shelley, who, if we are rightly informed, is son-in-law to Mr Godwin; and it is inscribed to that ingenious author. . . .

[In *Frankenstein*] the author seems to us to disclose uncommon powers of poetic imagination. The feeling with which we perused the unexpected and fearful, yet, allowing the possibility of the event, very natural conclusion of Frankenstein's experiment, shook a little even our firm nerves; although such, and so numerous have been the expedients for exciting terror employed by the romantic writers of the age, that the reader may adopt Macbeth's words with a slight alteration:

> We have supp'd full with horrors:
> Direness, familiar to our "callous" thoughts,
> Cannot once startle us.

It is no slight merit in our eyes, that the tale, though wild in incident, is written in plain and forcible English, without exhibiting that mixture of hyperbolical Germanisms with which tales of wonder are usually told, as if it were necessary that the language should be as extravagant as the fiction. The ideas of the author are always clearly as well as forcibly expressed; and his descriptions of landscape have in them the choice requisites of truth, freshness, precision, and beauty. The self-education of the monster, considering the slender opportunities of acquiring knowledge he possessed, . . . [is] improbable and overstrained. That he should have not only learned to speak, but to read, and, for aught we know, to write—that he should have become acquainted with *Werter,* with

Plutarch's *Lives,* and with *Paradise Lost,* by listening through a hole in a wall, seems as unlikely as that he should have acquired, in the same way, the problems of Euclid, or the art of book-keeping by single and double entry. . . . We should also be disposed, in support of the principles with which we set out, to question whether the monster, how tall, agile, and strong however, could have perpetrated so much mischief undiscovered; or passed through so many countries without being secured, either on account of his crimes, or for the benefit of some such speculator as Mr Polito, who would have been happy to have added to his museum so curious a specimen of natural history. But as we have consented to admit the leading incident of the work, perhaps some of our readers may be of opinion, that to stickle upon lesser improbabilities, is to incur the censure bestowed by the Scottish proverb on those who start at straws after swallowing *windlings.*

The following lines, which occur in the second volume, mark, we think, that the author possesses the same facility in expressing himself in verse as in prose.

> We rest; a dream has power to poison sleep.
> We rise; one wand'ring thought pollutes the
> day.
> We feel, conceive, or reason; laugh, or weep,
> Embrace fond woe, or cast our cares away;
> It is the same; for, be it joy or sorrow,
> The path of its departure still is free.
> Man's yesterday may ne'er be like his morrow;
> Nought may endure but mutability!

Upon the whole, the work impresses us with a high idea of the author's original genius and happy power of expression. We shall be delighted to hear that he has aspired to the *paullo majora*; and, in the meantime, congratulate our readers upon a novel which excites new reflections and untried sources of emotion. If Gray's definition of Paradise, to lie on a couch, namely, and read new novels, come any thing near truth, no small praise is due to him, who, like the author of *Frankenstein,* has enlarged the sphere of that fascinating enjoyment.

HAROLD BLOOM (ESSAY DATE 1965)

SOURCE: Bloom, Harold. "*Frankenstein,* or the New Prometheus." *Partisan Review* 32 (1965): 611-18.

In the following essay, Bloom discusses the image of the double and the Promethean myth in Frankenstein.

The motion picture viewer who carries his obscure but still authentic taste for the sublime to

ABOUT THE AUTHOR

ELLEN MOERS ON MOTHERHOOD, THE FEMALE GOTHIC, AND *FRANKENSTEIN*

Mary Shelley was a unique case, in literature as in life. She brought birth to fiction not as realism but as Gothic fantasy, and thus contributed to Romanticism a myth of genuine originality. She invented a mad scientist who locks himself in his laboratory and secretly, guiltily, works at creating human life, only to find that he has made a monster.

It was on a dreary night of November, that I beheld the accomplishment of my toils. With an anxiety that almost amounted to agony, I collected the instruments of life around me, that I might infuse a spark of being into the lifeless thing that lay at my feet. . . . The rain pattered dismally against the panes, and my candle was nearly burnt out, when, by the glimmer of the half-extinguished light, I saw the dull yellow eye of the creature open; it breathed hard, and a convulsive motion agitated its limbs. . . . His yellow skin scarcely covered the work of muscles and arteries beneath; his hair was of a lustrous black, and flowing . . . ; but these luxuriances only formed a more horrid contrast with his watery eyes, that seemed almost of the same colour as the dun white sockets in which they were set, his shrivelled complexion and straight black lips.

That is very good horror, but what follows is more horrid still: Frankenstein, the scientist, runs away and abandons the newborn monster, who is and remains nameless. Here, I think, is where Mary Shelley's book is most interesting, most powerful, and most feminine: in the motif or revulsion against newborn life, and the drama of guilt, dread, and flight surrounding birth and its consequences. Most of the novel, roughly two of its three volumes, can be said to deal with the retribution visited upon monster and creator for deficient infant care. *Frankenstein* seems to be distinctly a woman's mythmaking on the subject of birth precisely because its emphasis is not upon what precedes birth, not upon birth itself, but upon what follows birth: the trauma of the afterbirth.

SOURCE: Moers, Ellen. "Female Gothic: The Monster's Mother." *The New York Review of Books* 21, No. 4 (21 March 1974): 24-8.

the neighborhood theater, there to see the latest in an unending series of *Frankensteins*, participates in a Romantic terror now nearly one hundred and fifty years old. The terror is a familiar and a pleasing one, and few figures in contemporary mythology are as universally loved as Frankenstein's once pathetic monster, now a star beaconing from the abode of television, comic strips and the sweatshirts of the young.

"Frankenstein," to most of us, is the name of a monster rather than of a monster's creator, for the common reader and the common viewer have worked together, in their apparent confusion, to create a myth soundly based on a central duality in Mary Shelley's novel.[1] As Richard Church and Muriel Spark were the first to record, the monster and his creator are the antithetical halves of a single being. Miss Spark states the antithesis too cleanly; for her, Victor Frankenstein represents the feelings, and his nameless creature the intellect. In her view, the monster has no emotion, and "what passes for emotion . . . are really intellectual passions arrived at through rational channels." Miss Spark carries this argument far enough to insist that the monster is asexual, and that he demands a bride from Frankenstein only for companionship, a conclusion evidently at variance with the novel's text.

The antithesis between the scientist and his creature in **Frankenstein** is a very complex one, and to be described more fully it must be placed in the larger context of Romantic literature and its characteristic mythology. The shadow or double of the self is a constant conceptual image in Blake and Shelley, and a frequent image, more random and descriptive, in the other major Romantics, especially in Byron. In **Frankenstein**, it is the dominant and recurrent image, and accounts for much of the latent power the novel possesses.

Mary Shelley's husband was a divided being, as man and as poet, just as his friend Byron was, though in Shelley the split was more radical. **Frankenstein, or The Modern Prometheus** is the full title of Mrs. Shelley's novel, and while Victor Frankenstein is *not* Shelley (Clerval is rather more like the poet), the Modern Prometheus is a very apt term for Shelley or for Byron. Prometheus best suits the uses of Romantic poetry, for no other mythic figure has in him the full range of Romantic moral sensibility, and the full Romantic capacity for creation and destruction.

No Romantic writer employed the Prometheus archetype without a full awareness of its equivocal potentialities. The Prometheus of the ancients had been for the most part a spiritually reprehensible figure, though frequently a sympathetic one, both in terms of his dramatic situation and in his close alliance with mankind against the gods. But this alliance had been ruinous for man, in most versions of the myth, and the Titan's benevolence toward humanity was hardly sufficient recompense for the alienation of man from heaven that he had brought about. Both sides of Titanism are evident in earlier Christian references to the story. The same Prometheus who is taken as an analogue of the crucified Christ is regarded also as a type of Lucifer, a son of light justly cast out by an offended heaven.

In the Romantic readings of Milton's *Paradise Lost* (and **Frankenstein** is implicitly one such reading), this double identity of Prometheus is a vital element. Blake, whose mythic revolutionary named Orc is another version of Prometheus, saw Milton's Satan as a Prometheus gone wrong, as desire restrained until it became only the shadow of desire, a diminished double of creative energy. Shelley went further in judging Milton's Satan as an imperfect Prometheus, inadequate because his mixture of heroic and base qualities engendered in the reader's mind a "pernicious casuistry" inimical to the spirit of art.

Blake, more systematic a poet than Shelley, worked out an antithesis between symbolic figures he named Spectre and Emanation, the shadow of desire and the total form of desire, respectively. A reader of **Frankenstein,** recalling the novel's extraordinary conclusion with its scenes of obsessional pursuit through the Arctic wastes, can recognize the same imagery applied to a similar symbolic situation in Blake's lyric on the strife of Spectre and Emanation:

> *My Spectre around me night and day*
> *Like a Wild beast guards my way.*
> *My Emanation far within*
> *Weeps incessantly for my Sin.*
>
> *A Fathomless and boundless deep,*
> *There we wander, there we weep;*
> *On the hungry craving wind*
> *My Spectre follows thee behind.*
>
> *He scents thy footsteps in the snow,*
> *Wheresoever thou dost go*
> *Thro' the wintry hail and rain . . .*

Frankenstein's monster, tempting his revengeful creator on through a world of ice, is another Emanation pursued by a Spectre, with the enormous difference that he is an Emanation flawed, a nightmare of actuality, rather than a dream of desire.

Though abhorred rather than loved, the monster is the total form of Frankenstein's creative power, and is *more imaginative* than his creator. The monster is at once more intellectual *and* more emotional than his maker, indeed he excels Frankenstein as much (and in the same ways) as Milton's Adam excels Milton's God in *Paradise Lost.* The greatest paradox, and most astonishing achievement, of Mary Shelley's novel is that the monster is *more human* than his creator. This nameless being, as much a Modern Adam as his creator is a Modern Prometheus, is more lovable than his creator and more hateful, more to be pitied and more to be feared, and above all more able to give the attentive reader that shock of added consciousness which compels a heightened realization of the self. For, like Blake's Spectre and Emanation, or Shelley's Alastor and Epipsyche, Frankenstein and his monster are the solipsistic and generous halves of the one self. Frankenstein is the mind and emotions turned in upon themselves, and his creature is the mind and emotions turned imaginatively outward, seeking a greater humanization through a confrontation of other selves.

I am suggesting that what makes **Frankenstein** an important book, though it is only a strong, flawed, frequently clumsy novel is that it vividly projects a version of the Romantic mythology of the self, found, among other places, in Blake's *Book of Urizen,* Shelley's *Prometheus Unbound* and Byron's *Manfred.* It lacks the sophistication and imaginative complexity of such works but precisely because of that **Frankenstein** affords a unique introduction to the archetypal world of the Romantics.

William Godwin, though a tendentious novelist, was a powerful one, and the prehistory of his daughter's novel begins in 1794 with his best work of fiction, *Caleb Williams.* Godwin summarized the climactic (and harrowing) final third of his novel as a pattern of flight and pursuit, "the fugitive in perpetual apprehension of being overwhelmed with the worst calamities, and the pursuer, by his ingenuity and resources, keeping his victim in a state of the most fearful alarm." Mary Shelley brilliantly reverses this pattern in the final sequence of her novel, and she also takes from *Caleb Williams* her destructive theme of the monster's war against what Caleb Williams from his prison cell calls "the whole machinery of human society." Muriel Spark, pointing to Shelley's equivocal Preface to his wife's novel, argues that **Frankenstein** can be read as a reaction "against the rational-humanism of Godwin and Shelley."

Certainly Shelley was worried lest the novel be taken as a warning against the inevitable moral consequences of an unchecked experimental Prometheanism and scientific materialism. The Preface insists that:

> The opinions which naturally spring from the character and situation of the hero are by no means to be conceived as existing always in my own conviction; nor is any inference justly to be drawn from the following pages as prejudicing any philosophical doctrine of whatever kind.

There are two paradoxes at the center of Mrs. Shelley's novel, and each illuminates a dilemma of the Promethean imagination. The first is that Frankenstein *was* successful: he *did* create Natural Man, not as he was, but as the meliorists saw him. Indeed, Frankenstein did better than this, since his creature was more imaginative even than himself. Frankenstein's tragedy stems, not from his Promethean excess, but from his own moral error, his failure to love. He *abhorred his creature,* became terrified of it, and fled his responsibilities.

The second paradox is the more ironic. This disaster either would not have happened, or would not have mattered anyway, if Frankenstein had been an esthetically successful maker; a beautiful "monster," or even a passable one, would not have been a monster. The creature himself bitterly observes:

> Shall I respect man when he contemns me? Let him live with me in the interchange of kindness; and, instead of injury, I would bestow every benefit upon him with tears of gratitude at his acceptance. But that cannot be; the human senses are insurmountable barriers to our union.

As the sensuous horror of his creature was no part of Victor Frankenstein's intention, it is worth noticing how this came about. It would not be unjust to characterize Victor Frankenstein, in his act of creation, as being momentarily a moral idiot. There is an indeliberate humor, to which readers since 1945 are doubtless more sensitive than earlier ones, in the contrast between the enormity of the scientist's discovery, and the mundane emotions of the discoverer. Finding that "the minuteness of the parts" slows him down, he resolves to make his creature "about eight feet in height, and proportionally large." As he works on, he allows himself to dream that "a new species would bless me as its creator and source; many happy and excellent natures would owe their being to me." Yet he knows his is a "workshop of filthy creation," and he fails the fundamental test of his own creativity. When the "dull yellow eye" of his creature opens, this creator falls from the

autonomy of a supreme artificer to the terror of a child of earth: "breathless horror and disgust filled my heart." He flees his responsibility, and sets in motion the events that will lead to his own Arctic immolation, a fit end for a being (rather like Lawrence's Gerald in *Women in Love*) who has never achieved a full sense of another's existence.

It is part of Mary Shelley's insight into her mythological theme that all the monster's victims are innocents. The monster not only refuses actively to slay his guilty creator; he *mourns* for him, though with the equivocal tribute of terming the scientist a "generous and self-devoted being." Frankenstein, the Modern Prometheus who has violated nature, receives his epitaph from the ruined second nature he has made, the God-abandoned, who consciously echoes the ruined Satan of *Paradise Lost,* and proclaims "Evil thenceforth became my good." It is imaginatively fitting that the greater and more interesting consciousness of the creature should survive his creator, for he alone in Mrs. Shelley's novel possesses character. Frankenstein, like Coleridge's Ancient Mariner, has no character in his own right; both figures win a claim to our attention only by their primordial crimes against original nature.

The monster is of course Mary Shelley's finest invention, and his narrative (Chapters XI through XVI) forms the highest achievement of the novel, more absorbing even than the magnificent and almost surrealistic pursuit of the climax. In an age so given to remarkable depictions of the dignity of natural man, an age including the shepherds and beggars of Wordsworth, Frankenstein's hapless creature stands out as a sublime embodiment of heroic pathos. Though Frankenstein lacks the moral imagination to understand him, the daemon's appeal is to what is most compassionate in us:

> "Oh, Frankenstein, be not equitable to every other, and trample upon me alone, to whom thy justice, and even thy clemency and affection, is most due. Remember, that I am thy creature; *I ought to be thy Adam; but I am rather the fallen angel, whom thou drivest from joy for no misdeed.* Everywhere I see bliss, from which I alone am irrevocably excluded. I was benevolent and good; misery made me a fiend. Make me happy, and I shall again be virtuous."

The passage I have italicized is the imaginative kernel of the novel, a reminder of the novel's epigraph:

> *Did I request thee, Maker, from my clay*
> *To mould me man? Did I solicit thee*
> *From darkness to promote me?*
> —*Paradise Lost,* Book X, 743-5

That desperate plangency of the fallen Adam becomes the characteristic accent of the daemon's lamentations, with the influence of Milton cunningly built into the novel's narrative by the happy device of Frankenstein's creature receiving his education through reading *Paradise Lost* "as a true history." Already doomed because his standards are human, which makes him an outcast even to himself, his Miltonic education completes his fatal growth in self-consciousness. His story, as told to his maker, follows a familiar Romantic pattern "of the progress of my intellect," as he puts it. His first pleasure after the dawn of consciousness comes through his wonder at seeing the moon rise. Caliban-like, he responds wonderfully to music, both natural and human, and his sensitivity to the natural world has the responsiveness of an incipient poet. His awakening to a first love for other beings, the inmates of the cottage he haunts, awakens him also to the great desolation of love rejected, when he attempts to reveal himself. His own duality of situation and character, caught between the states of Adam and Satan, Natural Man and his thwarted desire, is related by him directly to his reading of Milton's epic:

> It moved every feeling of wonder and awe that the picture of an omnipotent God warring with his creatures was capable of exciting. I often referred the several situations, as their similarity struck me, to my own. Like Adam, I was apparently united by no link to any other being in existence; but his state was far different from mine in every other respect. He had come forth from the hands of God a perfect creature, happy and prosperous, guarded by the especial care of his Creator; he was allowed to converse with, and acquire knowledge from, beings of a superior nature: but I was wretched, helpless, and alone. Many times I considered Satan as the fitter emblem of my condition; for often, like him, when I viewed the bliss of my protectors, the bitter gall of envy rose within me.

From a despair this profound, no release is possible. Driven forth into an existence upon which "the cold stars shone in mockery," the daemon declares "everlasting war against the species," and enters upon a fallen existence more terrible than the expelled Adam's. Echoing Milton, he asks the ironic question, "And now, with the world before me, whither should I bend my steps," to which the only possible answer is: toward his wretched Promethean creator.

If we stand back from Mary Shelley's novel, in order better to view its archetypal shape, we see it as the quest of a solitary and ravaged consciousness first for consolation, then for revenge, and finally for a self-destruction that will be apocalyp-

tic, that will bring down the creator with his creature. Though Mary Shelley may not have intended it, her novel's prime theme is a necessary counterpoise to Prometheanism, for Prometheanism exalts the increase in consciousness despite all costs Frankenstein breaks through the barrier that separates man from God and apparently becomes the giver of life, but all he actually can give is death-in-life. The profound dejection endemic in Mary Shelley's novel is fundamental to the Romantic mythology of the self, for all Romantic horrors are diseases of excessive consciousness, of the self unable to bear the self. Kierkegaard remarks that Satan's despair is absolute, because Satan as pure spirit is pure consciousness, and for Satan (and all men in his predicament) every increase in consciousness is an increase in despair. Frankenstein's desperate creature attains the state of pure spirit through his extraordinary situation, and is racked by a consciousness in which every thought is a fresh disease.

A Romantic poet fought against self-consciousness through the strength of what he called imagination, a more than rational energy by which thought could seek to heal itself. But Frankenstein's daemon, though he is in the archetypal situation of the Romantic Wanderer or Solitary, who sometimes was a poet, can win no release from his own story by telling it. His desperate desire for a mate is clearly an attempt to find a Shelleyan Epipsyche or Blakean Emanation for himself, a self within the self. But as he is the nightmare actualization of Frankenstein's desire, he is himself an emanation of Promethean yearnings, and his only double is his creator and denier.

When Coleridge's Ancient Mariner progressed from the purgatory of consciousness to his very minimal control of imagination, he failed to save himself. He remained in a cycle of remorse. But he at least became a salutary warning to others, and made of the Wedding Guest a wiser and a better man. Frankenstein's creature can help neither himself nor others, for he has no natural ground to which he can return. Romantic poets liked to return to the imagery of the ocean of life and immortality; in the eddying to and fro of the healing waters they could picture a hoped-for process of restoration, of a survival of consciousness despite all its agonies. Mary Shelley, with marvelous appropriateness, brings her Romantic novel to a demonic conclusion in a world of ice. The frozen sea is the inevitable emblem for both the wretched daemon and his obsessed creator, but the daemon is allowed a final image of reversed Prometheanism. There is a heroism fully earned in the being who cries farewell in a claim of sad triumph: "I shall ascend my funeral pyre triumphantly, and exult in the agony of the torturing flames." Mary Shelley could not have known how dark a prophecy this consummation of consciousness would prove to be for the two great Promethean poets who were at her side during the summer of 1816, when her novel was conceived. Byron, writing his own epitaph at Missolonghi in 1824, and perhaps thinking back to having stood at Shelley's funeral pyre two years before, found an image similar to the daemon's, to sum up an exhausted existence:

> The fire that on my bosom preys
> Is lone as some volcanic isle;
> No torch is kindled at its blaze—
> A funeral pile.

The fire of increased consciousness stolen from heaven ends as an isolated volcano, cut off from other selves by an estranging sea. "The light of that conflagration will fade away; my ashes will be swept into the sea by the winds," is the exultant cry of Frankenstein's creature. A blaze at which no torch is kindled is Byron's self-image, but he ends his death poem on another note, the hope for a soldier's grave, which he found. There is no Promethean release, but release is perhaps not the burden of the literature of Romantic aspiration. There is something both Godwinian and Shelleyan about the final utterance of Victor Frankenstein, which is properly made to Walton, the failed Promethean, whose ship has just turned back. Though chastened, the Modern Prometheus ends with a last word true, not to his accomplishment, but to his desire:

> "Farewell, Walton! Seek happiness in tranquility and avoid ambition, even if it be only the apparently innocent one of distinguishing yourself in science and discoveries. Yet why do I say this? I have myself been blasted in these hopes, yet another may succeed."

Shelley's Prometheus, crucified on his icy precipice, found his ultimate torment in a Fury's taunt: "And all best things are thus confused to ill." It seems a fitting summation for all the work done by Modern Prometheanism, and might have served as an alternate epigraph for Mary Shelley's disturbing novel.

Note

1. Mary Shelley, second wife of Percy Bysshe Shelley and daughter of William Godwin and Mary Wollstonecraft, was 19 when she wrote the original *Frankenstein*.

MARCIA TILLOTSON (ESSAY DATE 1983)

SOURCE: Tillotson, Marcia. "'A Forced Solitude': Mary Shelley and the Creation of Frankenstein's Monster." In *The Female Gothic*, edited by Julian E. Fleenor, pp. 167-75. Montreal, Quebec: Eden Press, 1983.

In the following essay, Tillotson analyzes how Shelley's personal experience with solitude or loneliness informed her thematic treatment of solitude and loneliness in Frankenstein.

The story of how Mary Shelley came to write *Frankenstein* usually begins where she herself began it, in Switzerland, in the summer of 1816, when Lord Byron proposed to her, Percy Bysshe Shelley, Claire Clairmont, and John Polidori, "We will each write a ghost story." Shortly thereafter, Shelley had her "waking dream": "I saw the pale student of unhallowed arts kneeling beside the thing he had put together. I saw the hideous phantasm of a man stretched out, and then, on the working of some powerful engine, show signs of life."[1]

This dream may explain how Shelley got the idea for her novel and for its hero, Victor Frankenstein. It does not, however, explain how the monster became the novel's second protagonist. For the plot that the dream suggests requires that only Frankenstein be sympathetic yet awesome, admirable yet pitiful: in trying to benefit mankind, he created a monster. Frankenstein's tragedy was sufficiently horrifying to be the basis for a tale of terror, and Shelley knew that: "Frightful must it be; for supremely frightful would be the effect of any human endeavour to mock the stupendous mechanism of the Creator of the world." The second tragedy, the monster's, does not seem to have been part of Shelley's original idea; at least her dream gives no hint that the monster's situation would be as pitiable as the scientist's, and as important to the novel.[2] The monster developed into a second hero because Shelley imagined his isolation and his resentment with special vividness.

It has often been pointed out that Shelley shared with the monster a loneliness that began with life itself.[3] If a child may see a parent's death as a deliberate desertion, then she had been abandoned by her mother at birth just as the monster was abandoned by Frankenstein: thus, Shelley had Frankenstein do to the monster what she, on some unconscious level, may have felt Mary Wollstonecraft had done to her. But this similarity between Shelley's life and the monster's helps to explain only Frankenstein's desertion of his "baby" on the night he gave it life, not the monster's subsequent behavior or his ability to justify himself. In other words, this similarity may help us understand why Shelley sympathized with the monster but not how she compelled her readers to do the same thing.

Why the novel has two protagonists, and why the monster is so unmonstrous, are questions that no one, from Shelley herself to Ellen Moers, has answered—or even asked. Calling *Frankenstein* a "birth myth" and attributing much of the novel's originality and power to its author's experience of motherhood, Moers does not deal with the monster's qualities.[4] Like Shelley's own comments on her novel, Moers' ideas help us to understand Frankenstein but not the monster. Moers' basic argument, however—that women writers used Gothic mechanisms to express feeling and beliefs and even facts about their existence that they could communicate in no other way—is as enlightening about the monster as it is about Frankenstein. For the experiences women drew on to create the Female Gothic were not all as profoundly affecting as childbirth. Less elemental experiences were still powerful or painful or terrifying enough to be transformed by a woman's imagination into Gothic fiction. From this more ordinary kind of Gothic source material—social neglect and unkindness, and the consequent feelings of exclusion—came the pitiable monster, the novel's second hero; at least, this is how I shall try to account for the monster and his ability to win our compassion. The question I cannot answer is whether Shelley was fully aware of what she was doing: did she deliberately use the monster's self-defense to protest against men's behavior toward women, or did she merely make the monster speak for her without knowing herself that the source of his rage was her own?

In any case, Shelley had been lonely all her life, but there is evidence that at the time she conceived of and began writing *Frankenstein,* she was subjected to a new and particularly painful isolation: she was excluded from the companionship of Percy Shelley and Lord Byron. A similar exclusion is, of course, the devastating experience that turns the monster into a murderer. For the monster was not innately evil, nor was he driven to crime by a vague and general loneliness. The agony that makes him kill is quite specifically the agony of a creature whose best hopes for himself and others cannot be realized or even communicated. This was how Shelley saw herself by the end of that summer in Geneva: her lover and his brilliant, fascinating friend ate, talked, drank,

Illustration from the 1831 edition of *Frankenstein.*

and sailed together, but she could not join their conversations or share their amusements.

Although she was by no means ugly, her problem, like the monster's, was her appearance: her strong mind was housed in a woman's body. With interests and aspirations resembling those of the men with whom she associated, she was isolated from them by her sex. Her exclusion may not have been as violent or as absolute as the monster's but it was as real. Leslie A. Marchand understood her situation when he told how, in Pisa during the winter of 1821-22, she and Teresa Guiccioli would walk or ride out to meet Byron, Percy Shelley, and their male companions as they were returning from their daily pistol-shooting excursions: ". . . it was for Mary, strongly attracted by the intellect and charm of Byron, almost the only opportunity to associate in this man's world, for which by temperament and intellectual proclivities she was eminently fitted."[5] Writing to Marianne Hunt from Pisa on 5 March 1822, Shelley complained about this exclusion: "Our good cavaliers flock together, and as they do not like *fetching a walk with the absurd womankind,* Jane [Mrs. Williams] and I are off together, and talk morality and pluck violets by the way."[6] Marchand contrasts Shelley's exclusion in Pisa to the closer association with the two poets that she had enjoyed five and a half years earlier in Geneva.

But the surviving information about how the two households passed their time during the summer when *Frankenstein* was begun indicates that she did not always share in the companionship of the two poets. Writing about that summer six years later, on 19 October 1822, three months after her husband's death, she attributed her onlooker's role to her own diffidence:

> I have seen so little of Albé [the Shelleys' name for Byron] since our residence in Switzerland, and, having seen him there every day, his voice—a peculiar one—is engraved on my memory with other sounds and objects from which it can never disunite itself. . . . [S]ince incapacity and timidity always prevented my mingling in the nightly conversations of Diodati, they were, as it were, entirely tête-à-tête between my Shelley and Albé.[7]

The important fact is not that if she was too shy to intrude her ideas, the men did not ask her for them. The important fact is that even this silent participation in the men's conversations did not last long.

The two poets lived near each other on Lake Geneva for three months, from 25 May 1816, when Byron arrived (the Shelley party had been there since 13 May), to 29 August, when the Shelley party returned to England.[8] With Percy Shelley were Mary, who was not yet his wife; Claire Clairmont, who was already Byron's mistress; Percy's and Mary's infant son, William; and a nursemaid. Byron was traveling with Dr. John Polidori and three servants. Soon after the two groups met a routine of afternoon sails and evening conversations began, in which the two poets, the two women, and the doctor all took part. On 3 or 4 June the Shelley party moved across the lake to Montalègre, where they had rented a house. They still saw Byron daily, and on 10 June he moved into the Villa Diodati, a ten-minute walk away. Byron probably suggested the ghost stories on 15 or 16 June, for on the 17th Polidori recorded in his diary that everyone but he had started writing.

The first interruption in the closeness of the group came when they had spent nearly a month together: on 22 June the poets began a sailing trip around Lake Geneva, leaving the women and Polidori behind. After their return on 1 July, the intimacy that all five had shared began to disintegrate. Polidori's foolish vanity had begun to annoy the poets even before their trip together, and when he sprained his ankle, they were both glad to go off without him. Then Madame de Staël, whom Byron had met in England in 1813, arrived at her house across the lake from Diodati, and early in July he began visiting her. Although he occasionally took Polidori there, Byron never brought any member of the Shelley party along. Finally, Clairmont began to be a problem. Byron let her copy the poetry he had been working on since the trip around the lake, but in mid-July he decided he could no longer tolerate her presence, so he got his fellow poet to keep her away from Diodati. Within a few days of this break, Percy, Mary, and Claire went on a tour of Chamonix. They were gone from 21 to 27 July. True, they stopped at Diodati the night they returned, and spent three hours with Byron before going home to see their baby. But the temporary separation did not bring Byron and Clairmont back together. By August her pregnancy as well as her personality were causing more difficulties; Byron agreed to support the child but became more and more determined to have nothing to do with its mother.

But whatever happened to the others, Mary Shelley's closeness to the two poets diminished as the summer of 1816 progressed. Her journal indicates that after 20 July she was no longer included in their sails on the lake, which they took almost daily and often twice a day. After 14 August, when "Monk" Lewis arrived to visit Byron, she never again went to Diodati, although her lover continued to go there most evenings. When Lewis was followed by John Cam Hobhouse and Scrope Davies on 26 August, Percy Shelley passed that evening at Diodati, and he dined, sailed, and talked with Byron and his friends the following day. In the two weeks between Lewis' arrival and the Shelley party's departure on 29 August, Byron occasionally spent an hour or so at Montalègre but he did not bring his guests along, and Mary Shelley never met them. Clairmont went to Diodati three times during this period, but only to copy Byron's poetry and not to participate in supper parties and conversations. Once Hobhouse and Davies were there, she did not go to Diodati at all. The company at Byron's house had become exclusively masculine.

Thus, as far as Mary Shelley was concerned, the last part of the summer at Geneva was very much like the winter at Pisa; she was cut off from the society "for which by temperament and intellectual proclivities she was eminently fitted." The first month or so in Switzerland, when she was included in the poets' pastimes, far from making up for the subsequent neglect, would only make her feel it more. Furthermore, Ernest J. Lovell, Jr., argues persuasively that she was seriously attracted to and fascinated by Byron, but was unconscious of the nature of her interest in him.[9] Uncomplicated by guilt, her pain at being excluded from his company would be all the stronger. Byron's dislike of dining with women, his disgust with Clairmont, and his desire to entertain his friends without introducing them to any embarrassingly free females left Shelley more and more out of things. She must have suffered from her isolation—or, more accurately, from her relegation to the company of Clairmont, whom Shelley called "the bane of my life since I was three years old."[10] Looking back nearly fifteen years later, when both her husband and Byron were dead, Shelley said that the period in Geneva had been the happiest in her life, and Lovell suggests that this was because Clairmont's infatuation with Byron had at last removed her from rivalry for Percy Shelley's attentions.[11] After the first month Byron's presence often meant not that Mary Shelley had her lover to herself but that she had Clairmont.

In order to see how likely it is that the monster's pain and anger express what Shelley went through during the last part of that summer on Lake Geneva, we must remember that she only began the novel in Switzerland. The longest sustained bout of writing took place later, back in England. Her journal shows that she wrote nearly every day from 18 October to 13 December 1816, that she worked irregularly in January and March 1817, and that she corrected and copied her finished manuscript between 10 April and 13 May. She had plenty of time to come to terms with her feelings of exclusion, to comprehend them and give them shape, so that she could draw on them to create first the motivation for the monster's violence and then the arguments with which he justifies himself and wins our compassion. Furthermore, from 6 to 9 December, while she was working daily on **Frankenstein,** she recorded in her journal that she was reading her mother's *Vindication of the Rights of Women.* The monster's assertion that his impulses were benevolent until Frankenstein's desertion and other people's cruelty drove him to crime resembles Wollstonecraft's argument that women's education turns potentially virtuous, sensible, and loving creatures into vain, foolish, selfish ones.

To see the similarity between the loneliness and frustration to which an intelligent, educated, serious-minded woman is subjected on account of her sex, we need only remember that both suffer because of the disparity between the nature of their minds and forms of their bodies. The monster regrets having the germs of an intelligence, for his "sorrow only increased with knowledge." He says, "I wished sometimes to shake off all thought and feelings; but I learned that there was but one means to overcome the sensation of pain, and that was death. . . ." The monster insists that he suffers because he has the capacities to think and feel, but cannot use them. He curses the creator who "had endowed me with perceptions and passions, and then cast me abroad an object for the scorn and horror of mankind." Having failed to win companionship by helping people, by learning their language, by asking for their understanding and good will, he turns to his creator. The monster explains that inside he is just like the people who despise him, with the same desires, the same affections: he sympathized with the cottagers he had watched and listened to, and he identified with the feelings in the books he had heard them read. But after developing all these ideas and emotions, he learned that there was no context in which he could express them. The world has no more use for a loving monster than it has for a thinking woman. So the monster asks Frankenstein to make him a mate, justifying this request by saying, "My vices are the children of a forced solitude that I abhor; and my virtues will necessarily arise when I live in communion with an equal."

Percy Shelley had offered Mary "communion with an equal" when she ran off with him in the summer of 1814.[12] She expected her lover to treat her as a companion and not just a mistress. Whatever William Godwin's deficiences as a father were, he had brought her up to read and think; she used his library, went with him to lectures and the theater, and met the literary men who came to the house. Certain facts about her education are disputed: some writers see her as neglected by her father, others as indulged by him.[13] But one fact emerges clearly: a great part of her childhood misery was caused by her claiming for herself the intellectual stimulation that the men around her took for granted.

Godwin's second wife, however, expected all the girls of the household, including Wollstonecraft's daughter, to sew and cook and clean, not to talk or read or write. There is a story that the girls hid behind a chair one night to hear Coleridge read "The Rime of the Ancient Mariner"; Mrs. Godwin discovered them and would have sent them to bed if Coleridge had not pleaded for them. If this apocryphal story is not true—it appears without any source in most lives of Mary Shelley[14]—it seems to have been invented to illustrate the conflict about Shelley's education, Mrs. Godwin believing that daughters should be trained to be wives and mothers, Godwin and his friends, admirers of Wollstonecraft, believing that if daughters were not to be brought up like sons—

sent away to school and prepared for professional careers—they should at least be allowed to exercise their understanding and expand their imagination.

Because of the influences of her father and her dead mother, Shelley did not accept the intellectual separation between women and men that was the rule in her society. She had always resisted domestic tasks while growing up, and she naturally expected more from her relation with her lover than to keep his house and bear his babies. In the summer of 1816, when Byron was around, she suddenly found herself treated like other women, as an inferior. By the end of August she was not even a silent auditor of the poets' conversations. She came closest to being with the two of them on 24 August, when she wrote in her journal: "Write. Shelley goes to Geneva. Read. Lord Byron and Shelley sit on the wall before dinner; after, I talk with Shelley, and then Lord Byron comes down and spends an hour here. Shelley and he go up [to Diodati] together." This laconic description lets us see not only the two men talking to each other outdoors but also the woman watching them hungrily, unable to hear what they are saying.

For a while that summer there had been none of the customary segregation of the sexes. The women were included in the men's talk about art and politics, science and religion. True, Byron seemed to have taken such segregation for granted when he first met the Shelley party in Geneva: after Clairmont introduced both of her traveling companions to Byron, he invited only Percy Shelley to dine with him and Polidori that night. However, the next day both women began to be included in the daily breakfasts and sailing parties, and the pattern of sexual segregation seemed to be broken. Clairmont knew how universal that pattern was, writing to Byron while on her way to Switzerland "that she had ten times rather be his male friend than his mistress." It was obvious to her that a male friend would enjoy an intellectual intimacy that a mistress, admitted only to physical intimacy, would never know. Polidori is a good example of the difference sex made. He was automatically included in that first dinner party with Percy Shelley although Byron already thought him a fool by the time they got to Geneva. At the end of August, without having improved in anyone's opinion, Polidori was still taking part in the gatherings at Diodati from which the women were excluded.[15]

We cannot know for certain that Shelley used the monster to express her own pain and resent-ment. But when a literary character is, against all expectations, as sympathetic and "real" as this monster, we recognize that the author was doing more than mechanically constructing a figure to meet the needs of her plot. The monster's terrifying solitude and frustrated rage, which make him the novel's second protagonist and Mary Shelley's most original and fascinating invention, must have had their source in her own strongest emotions. After all, she made his arguments so convincing that Percy Shelley found "the direct moral of the book" in the monster's defense of himself:

Nor are the crimes and malevolence of the single Being, though indeed withering and tremendous, the offspring of any unaccountable propensity to evil, but flow irresistibly from certain causes fully adequate to their production. They are the children, as it were, of Necessity and Human Nature. In this the direct moral of the book consists.[16]

Percy did more than accept the monster's ideas. Although Mary Shelley based the character of Frankenstein on Percy, the poet identified not with the scientist but with the monster. Applying the moral he had found, "Treat a person ill and he will become wicked," Percy came to this conclusion:

It is thus that too often in society those who are best qualified to be its benefactors and its ornaments are branded by some accident with scorn, and changed by neglect and solitude of heart into a scourge and a curse.[17]

While the monster cannot really be described as "best qualified" to benefit society, that is indeed how Percy Shelley saw himself.[18] That he found the impulse to identify with the monster so powerful is a sign of Mary Shelley's success in creating him.

If Shelley tried to make her novel a compaint to her husband about her treatment in Geneva, she failed when he saw himself as the victim rather than as the victimizer. In another way, however, she succeeded in using her novel to oppose the intellectual isolation of women. Except for Polidori, the others who were present when Byron made his suggestion put their ghost stories aside almost as soon as they began them. Shelley, unlike Clairmont, wanting to be a writer and not just the mistress or wife or daughter of a writer, went ahead to complete her novel, imitating her mother as well as her father and husband.[19] *Frankenstein* should not be seen as an aberration—the grotesque product of the morbid imagination of a woman not yet twenty—but as the first achievement of a professional writer. The publication, the good reviews, and the general success of *Franken-*

stein gave her something she wanted, something her husband never achieved in his lifetime. The daughter of Mary Wollstonecraft and William Godwin was only doing the natural thing when she wrote her tale. It was just as natural for her to continue writing: she wrote a travel book, two dramas, a long story, and a second novel before her husband's death, and as a widow she supported herself and her son by her writing. She never produced anything else as good or successful as *Frankenstein,* but she achieved a small amount of independence in what was, for her as it had been for her mother, the only profession open to women besides governess or schoolmistress.

Naturally diffident, serious, quiet, she was called by her husband, and she has since been called cold by modern students of her works and his.[20] She denied the charge: "A cold heart! Have I a cold heart? God knows! But none need envy the icy region this heart encircles; and at least the tears are hot which the emotions of this cold heart force me to shed." But the best refutation is in her first novel and its monster. That monster is finally a collection of ideas. He owes his origin at least as much to books as he does to the experiences Shelley shared with him—the loss of a mother and the experience of motherhood.[21] But the monster comes from nowhere but her own imagination. As an abstract conception, he may be related to Adam or Lucifer or the Noble Savage, but when he begins to move and speak, the compelling logic of his demand for understanding and pity proves that he expressed something that Shelley herself felt deeply. And what else could that be if it was not her experience of a similarly unjust, painful, and unremitting isolation?

Notes

1. Mary W. Shelley, *Frankenstein, or the Modern Prometheus,* ed. K. Joseph, Oxford English Novels (London: Oxford Univ. Press, 1971), Introduction, p. 9. All subsequent quotes are from this text.

2. Not until she wrote the introduction to her tale for its second edition, published in 1831, did Mary Shelley tell how the idea came to her after she had stayed up late listening to the two men, Percy Shelley and Lord Byron, talking about galvanism. In *The Mutiny Within* (New York: Braziller, 1967), James Rieger questions her story of the dream, arguing on the basis of an entry in Polidori's diary that she overheard him and not Byron discuss galvanism with Percy Shelley (pp. 243-44). If Shelley did indeed invent her dream, then we are more justified than ever in looking elsewhere for the origin of the novel. Rieger does just that, but he finds his answer not in Mary Shelley's mind but in Percy's: "His assistance at every point in the book's manufacture was so extensive that one hardly knows whether to regard him as editor or minor collaborator"

(Introduction, *Frankenstein,* by Mary Wollstonecraft Shelley [Indianapolis: Bobbs, Merrill, 1974], p. xviii). Once again, a man is given credit for a woman's achievement.

3. It has long been a critical commonplace to see the monster, Frankenstein, and Walton as expressions of Shelley's lifelong loneliness. See, for example, M.G. Lund, "Mary Godwin Shelley and the Monster," *University of Kansas City Review,* 28 (1962), 253-58; Elizabeth Nitchie, *Mary Shelley: Author of "Frankenstein"* (New Brunswick, N.J.: Rutgers Univ. Press, 1953), pp. 13-21; and Sylvia Norman, "Mary Wollstonecraft Shelley," *Shelley and His Circle, 1773-1822,* ed. Kenneth Neill Cameron, III (Cambridge, Mass.: Harvard Univ. Press, 1970), 399.

4. Ellen Moers, *Literary Women* (New York: Anchor Books, 1977), pp. 141-51.

5. Leslie A. Marchand, *Byron: A Biography* (New York: Knopf, 1957), III, 947-48.

6. Mary Shelley, *Letters of Mary Shelley,* ed. Frederick L. Jones (Norman, Oklahoma: Univ. of Oklahoma Press, 1944), I, 158; the italics are Shelley's.

7. Mary Shelley, *Mary Shelley's Journal,* ed. Frederick L. Jones (Norman, Oklahoma: Univ. of Oklahoma Press, 1947), p. 184.

8. My sources for the events of the summer of 1816 are Marchand, II, 620-36, 643-46; Richard Holmes, *Shelley: The Pursuit* (New York: Dutton, 1975), pp. 319-46; Newman Ivey White, *Shelley* (New York: Knopf, 1940), I, 438-64; John Buxton, *Byron and Shelley: The History of a Friendship* (London: Macmillan, 1968); and Mary Shelley, *Journal,* pp. 50-61. Her journal for the period 14 May 1815 to 20 July 1816 is missing. Polidori also kept a diary, but he made only sketchy entries from 25 May to 2 July 1816, and then wrote nothing at all until 5 September (*The Diary of John William Polidori,* ed. William Michael Rossetti [London: Elkin Mathews, 1911]). Clairmont's journal for this period has not survived. Thus, there is no daily record of the first two months of the Geneva summer, and the letters of the two Shelleys and Byron from that period are not very numerous or very helpful.

9. Ernest J. Lovell, Jr., "Byron and Mary Shelley," *Keats-Shelley Journal,* 2 (1953), 35-49.

10. W.E. Peck, *Shelley: His Life and Work* (Boston: Houghton, 1927), I, 401, quoting Mrs. Julian Marshal, *The Life and Letters of Mary Wollstonecraft Shelley* (1889), II, 312. Clairmont had come along when Mary and Percy ran off to France in July 1814, and continued to live with them until 13 May 1815, when they found a place for her away from them. She was, however, back with them early in 1816 (White, I, 383-85, 402-4, 434).

11. Lovell, pp. 38-39.

12. Percy's letter to Mary of 28 October 1814 shows how he talked to her about their relationship: "Your thoughts alone can waken mine to energy. My mind without yours is dead and cold as the dark midnight river when the moon is down. . . . How divinely sweet a task it is to imitate each others excellencies—and each moment to become wiser in this surpassing love. . . ." (*Letters of Percy Bysshe Shelley,* ed. Frederick L. Jones [Oxford: Clarendon Press, 1964], I 414). He justified his betrayal of his first wife by saying that she could not give him such companionship. On 5

October 1814 he wrote to Harriet Shelley: "I shall watch over your interests, mark the progress of your future life, be useful to you, be your protector, and consider myself as it were your parent; but as friends, as equals those who do not sympathize can never meet" (Shelley, *Letters*, I, 404).

13. Those who see Godwin as paying a great deal of attention to his daughter's education include Holmes (*Shelley*, p. 170) and Muriel Spark (*Child of Light* [Hadleigh, Essex: Tower Bridge, 1951], p. 17). Those who take the opposite view include Rieger (Introduction, *Frankenstein*, p. xiii) and Richard Church (*Mary Shelley* [New York: Viking, 1928], p. 32).

14. Nitchie, p. 29; Spark, p. 17; Church, p. 28. R. Glynn Grylls tells the story but calls it a legend in *Mary Shelley: A Biography* (1938; rpt., New York: Haskell, 1969), p. 17.

15. Holmes, pp. 325, 372, 324-344 passim; Marchand, II, pp. 619-51 passim.

16. Percy Bysshe Shelley, "Review of Mary Shelley's *Frankenstein*," *Shelley's Prose, or The Trumpet of a Prophecy*, ed. David Lee Clark (Albuquerque, N.M.: Univ. of New Mexico Press, 1954), p. 307. Apparently this review was never published in Percy's lifetime.

17. "Review of Mary Shelley's *Frankenstein*," pp. 307-08.

18. Holmes makes this point about Percy's view of *Frankenstein*, attributing "extraordinary premonition" to Mary because she exploited the theme of exile that would be so important in her husband's poetry several years later (pp. 333-34). Knowing that in Italy the poet saw himself as a social outcast because of his beliefs, Holmes does not recognize that in Switzerland Mary Shelley was an outcast because of her sex.

19. Byron published the fragment of his vampire story with *Mazeppa* in 1819. Polidori completed not only his own tale, *Ernestus Berchtold*, which he published in 1819, but also Byron's; Polidori's version of *The Vampyre* was published as the poet's in April 1819. Nothing is known about Percy Shelley's and Clairmont's attempts. In her introduction to the second edition of her tale Mary talked about how she had always thought of being an author: "It is not singular that, as the daughter of two persons of distinguished literary celebrity, I should very early in life have thought of writing. As a child I scribbled; and my favourite pastime, during the hours given me for recreation, was to 'write stories'" (*Frankenstein*, p. 5).

20. See Percy Shelley's description of his wife in *Epipsychidion*, 277-307. Among modern writers, Spark (pp. 120-21) and Moers (pp. 143-44) talk about Shelley's coldness, and Rieger says that "Shelley's spiritual dalliances slowly embittered his wife and froze a temperament that had always been cool" (Introduction, *Frankenstein*, p. xv). As Doris Langley Moore shows in *Lord Byron: Accounts Rendered* (London: Murray, 1974), pp. 487-95, Percy's dalliances were not always just spiritual, and Mary had a difficult life both with and without him.

21. The most stimulating and enlightening recent studies of the novel concentrate on the similarities between Mary Shelley and Frankenstein, and especially on the fact that both were mothers. See Moers, pp. 141-51, and Robert Kiely, *The Romantic Novel in England* (Cambridge, Mass.: Harvard Univ. Press, 1972), pp. 155-73.

FRED BOTTING (ESSAY DATE 2000)

SOURCE: Botting, Fred. "Reflections of Excess: Frankenstein, the French Revolution, and Monstrosity." In *Frankenstein: Complete, Authoritative Text with Biographical, Historical, and Cultural Contexts, Critical History, and Essays from Contemporary Critical Perspectives*, edited by Johanna M. Smith and Ross C. Murfin, pp. 435-49. Boston and New York: Bedford—St. Martin's Press, 1993.

In the following essay, Botting views the monster and monstrosity as a metaphor in Frankenstein *within a cultural, historical, and literary context.*

This essay examines the appearance and effect of monsters in British political positions immediately after the French Revolution and analyses some of their reverberations in *Frankenstein.* The project, however, is not one that simply tries to identify *Frankenstein*'s meaning in terms of British exchanges concerned with the French Revolution, it also regards *Frankenstein* as a novel that provides reflections on, as much as reflections of, revolutionary and counter-revolutionary texts. Focusing on the repeated appearances of the monster metaphor, the essay attempts to identify some of the implications of the monster's diverse and prolific animations within different political and literary positions.

At once necessary and terribly dangerous, the figure of the monster takes on a multitude of different forms and functions. Its effects are multiple also: it defines the limits of a position as a threat to the continued existence of that position. Constructed as a figure of transgression, an other that marks out the boundaries of discourse, the monster also begins to disclose internal contradictions within discursive frameworks. Produced by positions that cannot contain them, monsters activate an excessive force which continually poses a challenge to unity, singularity and stability, a threat that demands repeated attempts to reconstitute boundaries from within. The friction involved in this internal and external confrontation, however, engenders a proliferation of monsters, an excess that encourages interrogations and transformations which upset the stability and unity of yet more limits and distinctions. The excess marked by various forms of monstrosity can be described loosely, and perhaps monstrously, as a force of difference between opposed poles that questions the privileged status one pole attempts to sustain by disclosing its dependence on its other. Undermining the system which holds distinctions in place, the tension poses further questions and releases further movements of difference. Monsters are thus produced by and also reveal inherent instabilities: refusing to remain in a fixed space of exclusion or to be contained at the margins of any one position, they pose a permanently shifting challenge and produce the possibility of significant transformations. The excess that is constructed by various positions in order to define their limits also works upon and within them, inhabiting and undermining the fixity of their boundaries.

Frankenstein is not only about the manufacture of a monster. It is, as many critics have noted, a monster itself. Like the natural and unnatural inhuman human life created by Frankenstein out of pieces from various corpses, the novel is composed from an extensive literary corpus: direct citations of Romantic poetry, *Paradise Lost* and myths of Prometheus, references to many literary, philosophical and historical texts, events and figures, as well as traces of many others, all distinguish the novel as an "assemblage" of fragments, a disunified text that subverts the possibility and implications of textual and semantic coherence. Indeed, the phrase "my hideous progeny" (p. 25 in this volume) which the author's 1831 Introduction to the novel uses to describe both book and monster, not only equates the two, but draws the author into the scene of commentary and repetition by suggesting a parallel between the writer's and Frankenstein's projects, as well as injecting a note of difference. Unlike Frankenstein, who tries to subject his creation to his will, Mary Shelley makes no such tyrannical gesture: she bids her text-monster farewell and hopes it might "go forth and prosper" (p. 25). Ironically her creation obeys, engendering a multitude of monsters and mythical monstrosities on the stage, in cinemas and in books.

Many of these reappearances and reproductions of *Frankenstein* are conservatively recuperated in popular culture and mythology, especially in their silencing of the monster, as Chris Baldick argues in his book, *In Frankenstein's Shadow*. For Baldick (62), the "eloquent invisibility" of the monster ensures its more radical survival in the liberal confines of literary criticism. Yet, even in the profusion of literary meanings that give form and identity to the monster, strategies of limitation and exclusion still seem to function to contain the interrogative excess of monstrosity as it reflects on all institutions, literary criticism included.

Frankenstein, distinguished by Baldick from its reproductions by means of an opposition of literary tradition and popular culture, does not, however, respect such boundaries since, for many, it is hardly "literature" at all. Sensational Gothic

fiction or a clumsy Romantic novel (Bloom 613), a "minor work" (Norman 408) that is "not one of the living novels of the world" (Grylls 320), *Frankenstein* occupies an unstable place on the boundaries that separate "literature" and its values from second-rate fiction. It is a monstrous space, itself subject to the excessive effects of monstrosity. For Deleuze and Guattari (50) literature is also a kind of monster, an "assemblage." Composed of disjunctive parts and fragments, "literature" forms an amalgam of multiplicitous and heterogeneous positions, a form of writing that combines elements and upsets their autonomy, blurring and questioning the artificial distinctions that construct its meaning.

In this context of excess and transgression, it would be presumptuous indeed to adopt a position outside the play of those forces, a position that refuses to acknowledge its own investments, involvements and interests in the texts it reads. It would also be foolish since it would mark another attempt to restrict or recuperate the excessive and dangerous movements of difference that it analyses and is affected by, another Frankensteinian attempt at mastery perhaps. Instead, the theoretical position adopted here, a product of a different French revolution—the revolutions of structuralism and post-structuralism, forms something of a monster itself. As an amalgam or "assemblage" of disparate elements drawn from a number of French theorists, this paper is situated along lines of intersection and divergence between several theoretical positions. Partially formed in the diverse conjunctions of and differences between various theories, the project attempts, not to restrict or to confine, but to open up possibilities and inhabit a frictional position that both resists closure and produces, in its engagements with revolutions and monsters, questions concerning the differences and power relations involved in politics, literature, theory and reading itself.

Of the multiple and diverse theoretical utterances that have informed this paper, a few can be specified for their direct bearings upon this account of *Frankenstein* and the French Revolution. In the essays "Preface to Transgression" and "Language to Infinity," Michel Foucault considers the way that language displays its monstrous potential to both set and transgress limits and engender a dangerous profusion of self-reflection and doubling. There are certain similarities between Foucault's account of writing and Derrida's description of deconstruction, in "Signature Event Context," as a "double gesture, a double science, a double writing." The doubling effects of deconstruction demand a transgression of the limits imposed on writing by hierarchical binary oppositions: deconstruction must "put into practice a *reversal* of the classical opposition *and* a general *displacement* of the system" (Derrida 195). Double

gestures thus disturb the stability of oppositions by activating the differences between one pole and its other.

For Jacques Lacan, the construction of subjectivity in language also involves relations of doubling: identifying with its specular image in the mirror, identifying with the Other of language, the subject exists only in relations of difference and desire. Determined by the laws of the symbolic order, the subject is constructed by the effects of signification and is also subject to the shifts, the displacements of desire, within the system of differences that is language. Constituting the limits of subjectivity and meaning, the differences and desires at work in language also transgress and exceed those limits. In and between language and theory, then, a space of reflections appears in a fragmented, mirrored, doubled and interrogative form, a space from which meanings multiply. A similar position is disclosed by the monsters that appear in revolutionary controversies and in *Frankenstein*. From this space of reflections, this position of doubling and monstrosity, it becomes possible to generate different readings of Burke's *Reflections*, radical responses to it and *Frankenstein*'s monsters and doubles.

Burke's *Reflections on the Revolution in France* (1790) exemplifies the diffractions involved in processes of reflection: his text casts its rather partial light on events in France and reflects back on the situation in England and upon its own modes of representation. Monsters proliferate among these reflections. Already a conventional image of the enraged and riotous mob, monsters are also used to signify the French National Assembly's destructive capacity and the Constitution of Republican France (see Burke 279-80, 313). This written document is opposed to the unwritten "constitution" of 1688, which Burke sets up as the guardian of English liberty, tradition and good order. Indeed, everything in France is constructed as England's other: "out of nature," irrational, irreligious and illegitimate, the affairs of France form a "monstrous fiction" that displays the rightness of English "good order" as well as the obvious truth of Burke's case (Burke 124).

This is a most traditional deployment of monstrosity, one which, as Chris Baldick (10-11), following Foucault, observes, stages vice in order to vindicate virtue, presenting a cautionary tale that warns against the horrors of transgression. The "monstrous tragi-comic scene" performed in France describes a state of chaos, of revolving and uncontrollable extremes. In Burke's words, "the most opposite passions necessarily succeed, and sometimes mix with each other in the mind; alternate contempt and indignation; alternate laughter and tears; alternate scorn and horror" (Burke 92-93). Revolutionary France, moreover, exists as a monstrous fiction in several other senses. It is the invention of "literary caballers and intriguing philosophers," revolutionary alchemists whose evil imaginations conjure up and attempt to realize their own extreme and perverse ambitions (Burke 93). Exposing the deceptions of such conspirators in France and England, Burke attempts to forestall revolution in Britain, a revolution advocated publicly in the monstrous fictions of radicals, like Richard Price, that identify with the revolutionary slogans of France.

The monsters constructed in Burke's text as figures that affirm the presence and value of good order in England betray a certain anxiety. Instead of affirming good order they expound the need for, and thus lack of, good order. Burke's final metaphor is telling in this respect. His book, he humbly admits, comes from one who "when the equipoise of the vessel in which he sails, may be endangered by overloading it upon one side, is desirous of carrying the small weight of his reasons to that which may preserve its equipoise" (Burke 377). The ship of State in which he sails is already unstable, however, already under threat from forces which are beginning to exceed the bounds of liberal reason. To follow Stephen Blakemore's 1988 analysis of Burke's texts as writings deeply concerned about the maintenance of linguistic propriety and decorum within traditional orders of meaning, the ship might also be interpreted as a figure of conventional discourse upset by radical and revolutionary contestations and appropriations of meaning. These struggles raise the danger of the ship being cast adrift in chaotic seas of signification. In the name of good order, reason, nature, liberty and tradition, Burke's text becomes another monstrous fiction engaged in, and seriously affected by, the "revolution in sentiments, manners and moral opinions" that it sets out to control (Burke 175).

Furthermore, the project of preserving "equipoise" has the opposite effect. Instead of quelling resistance and dissent, the *Reflections* provoked a great many vigorous and diverse responses, responses that extended, rather than contained, the dangerous proliferation of monsters. In his reply to Burke in *The Rights of Man* (1792), Paine attacks the former's "marvellous and monstrous" method and goes on to criticize the system Burke defends, describing, in the process, the aristocracy as a monster (see Paine 202, 229). From radical per-

spectives, it is the social system that bears the responsibility for creating monsters. In her response to Burke in *A Vindication of the Rights of Men* (1790), Mary Wollstonecraft castigates the system of hereditary property for making monsters of humans: "man," she states, "has been changed into an artificial monster by the station in which he was born" (quoted in Butler 72-73). For William Godwin, writing a few years later, the "monstrous edifice" of government by courts and ministers "will always be found supported by all the various instruments for perverting the human character" (Godwin 439).

The system that defines its own limits in the construction of monsters thus has its terms challenged and reversed. Burke, a maker of monsters and a supporter of the system that creates them, is made monstrous himself. In this battle of meanings, the monster functions as a double-edged weapon and continues to reproduce at an enormous rate. The *New Annual Register* for 1794 stated that "the whole system of insurrection lay in the monstrous doctrine of the Rights of Man, and the Corresponding Society composed of the meanest and most despicable of people."[1] Later, the followers of Godwin and Wollstonecraft were described by the *Anti-Jacobin Review* as the "spawn of the monster."[2] As an awful threat that was still at large, disseminating among radical writings, the designation of monsters legitimates their exclusion or suppression as figures dangerously opposed to national unity.

The excessive threat of the French Revolution appears in its capacity to engender other revolutions. Indeed, the word "revolution," Ronald Paulson argues, underwent a significant change to mean an inversion, a half, or 180 degree, turn (Paulson 49-50). These turns initiate a momentum that shifts meanings from one pole to the other in a similar manner to the way that the monsters created by Burke challenged the authority of his order of meaning and appropriated and transformed his terms: monster-makers become monstrous in the very act of creating monsters or in the resistance of the monsters they create. In turn, systems of authority attempt to return defiant radicals to their monstrous place. Like the Revolution in France which, in the name of liberty, overthrew tyranny only to repeat tyrannical practices, the revolving momentum of monsters and monster-makers releases forces that exceed the determining limits of binary oppositions and raise the possibility of other positions.

Godwin, for example, rejects the need for any form of government other than rational and individual responsibility in the same text in which he rejects revolution as a useful means of establishing a free, benevolent and just society: "revolutions," he contends, "are the produce of passion, not sober and tranquil reason" (Godwin 252). But, unable to escape the violent and repressive logic of opposition that produces the polarizations of revolution in the name of some fixed and transcendent principle, Godwin's argument returns to bellicose binary distinctions: "truth will bring down all her forces, mankind will be her army, and oppression, injustice, monarchy and vice, will tumble into a common ruin" (Godwin 462). The sober and tranquil language of reason cedes to the passionately rhetorical mode of prophetic and apocalyptic vision. Truth constitutes the authority and promise of victory as well as the cause of conflict, the ultimate booty as well as the bugle that begins the battle. Passion returns within the discourse of divine reason and revolutions rotate still more.

The monster, a figure constructed to legitimate the exclusion or suppression of others, betrays their necessity and fecundity. Demarcating the limits of a position, monsters, at the same time, possess the power to interrogate and transgress all limits.

The excessive momentum of revolution and monster-making powerfully affects and is also transformed by *Frankenstein*. This focus on monstrosity and excess necessarily precludes detailed consideration of other readings of the novel's relation to the French Revolution by Ronald Paulson, Lee Sterrenburg and Chris Baldick. Offering many important insights into the relationship between *Frankenstein* and the French Revolution, these critics, particularly Paulson and Sterrenburg, seem to identify a unity too firmly in the conjunction of text, history and biography through recourse to the name of the author. Divided between Burkean conservatism and her family's radicalism, between love and political differences, it is the personal pole that is privileged in Paulson's and Sterrenburg's accounts. These readings are thus forced to contain or exclude the many excesses that surround *Frankenstein*'s production. The multiplicitous impact of the French Revolution, its polarization and dispersion of political positions, as well as the fascinating but complicated biographical archive surrounding Mary Shelley, all contribute to an overdetermined set of pretexts for the novel and its interpretations.

Frankenstein does not resolve these contradictions and intricate interconnections, but extends and entangles them. Echoes of British Revolutionary debates abound. Victor Frankenstein is educated at Ingolstadt, a town that is also the birthplace of the Illuminati, the secret society founded by Adam Weishaupt. The Illuminati, the Abbé Barruel argues in his conservative account of the French Revolution, were the conspirators responsible for revolutionary agitations. Frankenstein also embodies Burke's fear of revolutionary alchemists or Enlightenment philosophers whose dangerous experiments upset all order by releasing dark and chaotic forces of evil. The monster forms the hideous result, a revolutionary mob that cuts a wake of terror across Europe.

But the monster also speaks, not only to challenge his creator's authority and question unjust human practices, but to claim recognition and human kindness. His argument, that "misery made me a fiend" (p. 94), echoes the radical descriptions of monsters as socially produced creatures. In opposing Frankenstein, then, the resistance of the monster constructs a relationship that doubles the polemics of Burke and the radicals, and invites a reading in which Frankenstein can be seen, not as a dangerous radical philosopher, but as a pastiche, or even a parody, of paranoid Burkean fictions. *Frankenstein*'s heterogeneous assembly of political positions makes many identifications possible, but refuses to specify a single, recognizable and dominant viewpoint. This is the significant and divergent aspect of *Frankenstein*'s account of the French Revolution. Replaying and extending the structures of reversal that emerge in revolutionary polemics, the novel also represents their totalizing desires, their invocations of some transcendent unity, whether it be Burkean good order or Godwinian rational truth.

Robert Walton, the explorer whose letters begin the novel, sets out to discover the North Pole and the "wondrous power that attracts the needle" so that he "may regulate a thousand celestial observations" and "render their seeming eccentricities consistent for ever" (p. 28). The imagined unity of this world of "eternal light" excites Walton's aspirations. Victor Frankenstein, similarly, aspires to metaphysical knowledge and imagines he can attain the unity and presence of a singular and privileged pole of significance beyond the bounds of binary oppositions:

> Life and death appeared to me ideal bounds, which I should first break through, and pour a torrent of light into our dark world. A new species would bless me as its creator and source; many

happy and excellent natures would owe their being to me. No father could claim the gratitude of
his child so completely as I should deserve theirs.

(p. 58)

Transcending human constraints, the superhuman creator envisages a world beyond difference in which his "new species" exists only to
adore the master.

But the others—death, darkness, women, bodies—on which Frankenstein depends in order to
steal the secrets of nature and succeed in his illumination of life in full, are not effaced: "to
examine the causes of life," Frankenstein comments, "we must first have recourse to death" (p.
56). In conjunction with many of the others
Victor's project aimed to efface, like women, bodies, sexuality and darkness, death returns with a
vengeance in the dream that follows the animation of the monster. As he wakes from his disturbing sleep of dreams, the creator sees the horrible
form of his creation approaching him and he flees
from this inverted image of his aspirations.

Frankenstein has not achieved the fullness of
life and illumination that he projected: he has
revitalized the forces of otherness which he hoped
to efface. The creature he designed to be beautiful
is realized as an ugly and repulsive being. But then
how could anything have lived up to the exorbi-
tant ideals of the creator's imagination? Frankenstein's totalizing dream discovers its dependence
on systems of difference as the human creator
encounters the necessity of monstrosity when,
waking from his dream, he repeats the convulsive
physical agitations that announced the first stir-
rings of life in the monster. One turns into other;
dreams become nightmares: "dreams that had
been my food and pleasant rest for so long a space
were now become a hell to me; and the change
was so rapid, the overthrow so complete!" (p. 61).
This subjective upheaval is described in terms of a
revolution: it is Frankenstein's first revolution.

The momentum inaugurated by this overturn-
ing is not arrested, but rolls on through the course
of the novel in an excessive play of differences
that blurs all distinctions and questions all limits.
In the next encounter between Frankenstein and
monster, in the sublime setting of the Alps, more
reversals occur: forced to be a listener, the creator
is subjected to the monster's demands for a mate
that conclude the latter's story. The shift in their
relationship is declared, after Frankenstein has
destroyed the half-finished female creature, when
the monster exclaims: "you are my creator, but I
am your master;—obey!" (p. 146). Ironically, the
creator has just performed an act of resistance.

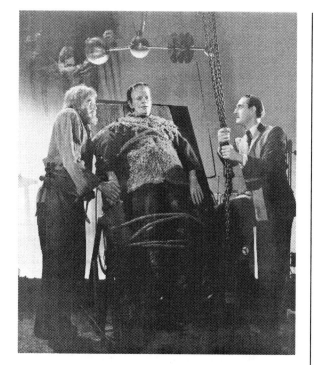

Scene from the 1939 film *Son of Frankenstein,* starring
Boris Karloff, Basil Rathbone, and Bela Lugosi.

The ensuing struggle involves both figures in
a tense dialectic in which they both try negatively
to affirm their lost authority: Frankenstein vows
to kill his creation, while the monster destroys
almost all the creator's friends and relations. The
subsequent confused and mutually sustaining
pursuit speeds the novel to an end in which the
life-giver attempts to persuade Walton to continue
his destructive quest but fails and dies, while the
creation announces his intention to kill himself
on a funeral pyre at the pole in the only act of
self-possession available to him. Fire amid ice,
light in darkness, with this promised extinction of
the first and last of a new species the novel ends
in an entangled assembly of opposites. The hopes
of discovering a world of "eternal light" that
began the novel have been overturned by the end,
as Walton, reluctantly and disappointedly returning home, gazes at the monster becoming "lost in
darkness and distance" (p. 189).

Yet the novel does not simply describe the collapse of one pole of significance into its other,
light into dark, life into death, creation into
destruction; it also questions the tensions between
oppositional limits and engenders different positions, positions that can criticize and subvert,
challenge and transform. From his position as a
voyeur on the De Lacey family, the monster learns
about the arbitrary system of differences called

language; he learns about gender differentiation and learns that humans have more than one identity, since signifiers have different effects. From this position, within and yet outside human orders, he is able to expose the inhumanity of human codes and values since they are the very things that define him as a monster.

An artificial yet natural man, alive yet composed of dead bodies, benevolent and destructive, the monster shifts along the margins of many distinctions. His shifting and excluded situation produces the critical faculty that engenders an excessive array of disturbing effects. For example, when the monster frames the Frankenstein family servant, Justine, for the murder of William Frankenstein, she is found guilty and sentenced to death despite her, and others', testimonies to her innocent character. The verdict, however, for the reader who is aware of the existence of the monster, reflects upon the inadequacy and injustice of judicial institutions. Furthermore, the behaviour of Justine's confessor extends the reflections of monstrosity since he forces her to confess a lie: "he threatened and menaced," Justine tells Elizabeth, "until I almost began to think I was the monster that he said I was" (p. 83). The confessor's actions reflect less on Justine than the clerical institutions that make her a monster.

The proliferation of monsters and the challenging and critical interrogations they provoke extend still further. Elizabeth, Frankenstein's adopted sister and fiancée, deeply upset by Justine's ordeal, learns that vice and injustice are not the "imaginary evils" she thought they were. In her words, "misery has come home, and men appear to me as monsters thirsting for each other's blood" (p. 88). A critique of masculinity as much as human inhumanity, Elizabeth echoes some of the monster's own sentiments and goes on to question the possibility of making any distinctions at all in a world in which the limits and authority of any order seem so arbitrary. She exclaims: "alas! Victor, when falsehood can look so like the truth, who can assure themselves of certain happiness? I feel as if I were walking on the edge of a precipice, towards which thousands are crowding, and endeavouring to plunge me into the abyss." Swept up by the monstrous momentum of interrogative doubt, no bonds are secure and no position is safe.

The uncontainable excess of monstrous otherness transgresses the limits set by any order as it operates along a position's lines of demarcation and resistance. Structurally too, *Frankenstein* opens itself up to the forces of critical reflection that operate in its own fraught bipolar momentum. As a set of broken frames, the narrative encloses the monster's story within Frankenstein's, the latter's being surrounded by Walton's letters, letters that are addressed to his sister on the edges of the text: the reader is at once moved inward to a presumed center, the monster's account of the De Lacey family, and outwards, to the absent addressee on the margins. But the story at the center fragments, dispersed by the rage of the monster, while the monster, neither wholly inside and contained by the structure, nor completely outside and excluded from it, appears at the end to confront Walton directly. Inside and outside, center and margin, have their distinctions subverted by a novel in which the different speakers and writers also occupy the positions of readers and listeners. But, in its refusal of a dominant, authorial overview, the novel does not necessarily equivocate or compromise between the poles it identifies and confuses. Walton's final situation, suspended uneasily between departure and return, success and failure, light and darkness, is divided in such a way that it perpetuates doubts and dilemmas and engenders further questions: the ship may be returning home, but his gaze still attempts to penetrate the darkness into which the monster disappears.

The direction of the monster's disappearance itself engenders doubled effects. Moving in an opposite direction to the middle-class reader to whom Walton is returning, the monster approaches another place on the fractured margins of the text, a position which contrasts with the comfortable and domestic situation in which the text's absent reader, Mrs Saville, is constructed. Dividing the marginal and uncertain identity of the reader, the movement of the monster turns that position into a critical space of reading. Reading thus becomes dangerous and excessive. A space of passive reception, it is also a space from which resistance and transformation can begin. Readers, indeed, become monsters. As one alarmed critic of the enormous popularity of Gothic novels wrote:

> The class of readers, for whom this kind of entertainment is provided, as if no longer capable of deriving pleasure from the gentle and tender sympathies of the heart, require to have their curiosity excited by artificial concealments, their astonishment kept awake by a perpetual succession of wonderful incidents, and their very blood congealed with chilling horrours.[3]

Upsetting the bounds of literary propriety with their insatiable appetites, readers of Gothic fiction eschew taste and decorum with their demands for more and more awful thrills.

Novels were constructed in a similar manner to readers—as monsters. In 1796, a brief review of Matthew Lewis's *The Monk* lamented the waste of the author's talents on the production of a text so irredeemably devoted to excess:

> Lust, murder, incest, and every atrocity that can disgrace human nature, brought together, without the apology of probability, or even possibility, for their introduction. To make amends, the moral is general and *very practical*; it is, 'not to deal in witchcraft and magic, because the devil will have you at last!' We are sorry to observe that good talents have been misapplied in the production of this monster.[4]

Patently exceeding the bounds of literary propriety and taste, *The Monk* displayed its monstrosity and reflected that of the readers of Gothic romances.

The origin for the threatening proliferation of those figures of excess—Gothic tales and their readers—was identified as Horace Walpole's *The Castle of Otranto*. One commentary noted how "Otranto Ghosts have propagated their species with unequalled fecundity. The spawn is in every novel shop."[5] Like the phrase "the spawn of the monster" that was used to describe the followers of Godwin and Wollstonecraft, the "new species" of fiction created by Horace Walpole's *The Castle of Otranto* reproduced at an alarming rate (Walpole 12). Frankenstein, too, imagines the creation of a "new species." But his own "hideous progeny" resists, subverts and exceeds his control. Like Burke who, Paulson argues, constructed the French Revolution as a Gothic novel, and like Walpole, Frankenstein cannot limit the effects of his monstrous creation. Indeed, the demand for greater thrills and more excessive pleasures subjected authors and the literary establishment to the desires of their readership in a similar manner to the way that radicals demanded liberty and equality from the systems that ruled them. More than passive consumers, readers begin to possess, in their function within the necessary and dangerous conditions of production, a certain power. Consuming, constructing and demanding, they form significant others, figures of difference crucial to the work of creation even as they exist beyond the determinations of authority.

Reading positions, glimpsed and activated among *Frankenstein*'s unstable frames, betray their monstrous power. Neither inside nor outside the novel, necessary yet unknown, absent addressees that produce powerful effects, readers can not be contained by the limits of a single text. Inhabiting and generating textual contradictions, readers can identify and recognize themselves in parts of the text as passive addressees, but they can also resist such constructions and produce readings that attempt to decide Walton's disturbing dilemma: they can privilege Frankenstein or the monster. Furthermore, as the monstrous and marginal space engenders a surplus of meanings that cannot be limited by the novel's broken frames, so reading positions might multiply and challenge the terms and patterns prescribed in textual representations to interrogate and reactivate issues of difference and power.

Not merely subjected to or positioned by the effects of writing, the construction of readers within the text allots a certain power and resistance to acts of reading and offers subject positions which can be refused, adopted or, even, transformed. Who knows? The writer, for sure, does not. The possibility of adopting different positions, always available in the frictions of textual oppositions and differences, is the partial and yet powerful prerogative of that figure of potential excess, the reader. Readers always might, like the monsters of Gothic fiction and the French Revolution, follow the exciting and unknown lines of excess that operate within the limits in which they are partially constructed, since reading always involves some differences and thus entails the possibility of monstrous literary and political transgressions.

Notes

1. Cited by Kramnick, "Introduction" to Godwin 40.

2. *The Anti-Jacobin Review,* V (1800): 427; quoted in Sterrenburg 147.

3. Review of *Count Roderic's Castle; or, Gothic Times, Analytical Review* 20 (1794): 489; cited by Napier vii.

4. Review of *The Monk, a Romance, The British Critic,* 7 June 1796: 677.

5. T. J. Matthias, *The Pursuits of Literature: A Satirical Poem in Four Dialogues,* London, 1797: 87, n. iii; cited by Napier viii.

Works Cited

Baldick, Chris. *In Frankenstein's Shadow,* Oxford: Clarendon, 1987.

Blakemore, Steven. *Burke and the Fall of Language,* Hanover: UP of New England, 1988.

Bloom, Harold. "*Frankenstein,* or the new Prometheus," *Partisan Review* 32 (1965): 611-18.

Bouchard, Donald F., ed. *Language, Counter-Memory, Practice.* Trans. Bouchard and Sherry Simon. Oxford: Basil Blackwell, 1977.

Burke, Edmund. *Reflections on the Revolution in France*. Ed. Conor Cruise O'Brien, Harmondsworth, UK: Penguin, 1968.

Butler, Marilyn, ed. *Burke, Paine, Godwin, and the Revolution Controversy*, Cambridge: Cambridge UP, 1984.

Deleuze, Giles, and Guattari, Felix. "Rhizome," *Ideology and Consciousness* 8 (1981): 49-71.

Derrida, Jacques. "Signature event context," *Glyph* 1 (1977): 172-97.

Foucault, Michel. "Language to infinity." Bouchard 53-67.

———. "Preface to transgression." Bouchard 29-52.

Godwin, William. *Enquiry Concerning Political Justice*. Ed. Isaac Kramnick, Harmondsworth, UK: Penguin, 1985.

Grylls, Rosalie Glynn. *Mary Shelley: A Biography*. London: Oxford UP, 1938.

Lacan, Jacques. "Desire and the Interpretation of Desire in *Hamlet*." *Yale French Studies* 55/56 (1977): 11-52.

———. *Ecrits*. Trans. Alan Sheridan. London: Tavistock, 1977.

———. "Seminar on 'The Purloined Letter.'" *Yale French Studies* 48 (1972): 38-72.

Napier, Elizabeth R. *The Failure of Gothic*, Oxford: Clarendon, 1987.

Norman, Sylva. "Mary Wollstonecraft Shelley." *Shelley and his Circle 1773-1822*. 8 vols. Ed. Kenneth Neill Cameron. London: Oxford UP, 3:397-422.

Paine, Thomas. *The Rights of Man*. 1791-92. *The Thomas Paine Reader*. Ed. Michael Foot and Isaac Kramnick. Harmondsworth: UK: Penguin, 1987. 201-364.

Paulson, Ronald. *Representations of Revolution 1789-1820*. New Haven: Yale UP, 1983.

Sterrenburg, Lee. "Mary Shelley's Monster: Politics and Psyche in *Frankenstein*." *The Endurance of Frankenstein*. Ed. George Levine and U. C. Knoepflmacher. Berkeley: U of California P, 1979. 143-71.

Walpole, Horace. *The Castle of Otranto*. 1764. Ed. W. S. Lewis, London: Oxford UP, 1964.

FURTHER READING

Bibliography

Frank, Frederick S. "Mary Shelley's *Frankenstein*: A Register of Research." *Bulletin of Bibliography* 40, no. 3 (September 1983): 163-88.

A bibliography of twentieth-century research on Frankenstein published through 1982.

Biographies

Mellor, Anne K. *Mary Shelley: Her Life, Her Fiction, Her Monsters*. New York and London: Routledge, 1988, 275 p.

Draws on unpublished material and Shelley's fiction to present an analysis of Shelley's life.

Seymour, Miranda. *Mary Shelley*. New York: Grove Press, 2000, 672 p.

Utilizes feminist scholarship to present a balanced picture of Shelley's life.

Sunstein, Emily W. *Mary Shelley: Romance and Reality*. Boston and Toronto, Ontario: Little, Brown, and Co., 1989, 478 p.

Defines Shelley as an exemplary Romantic, and seeks to provide an authoritative biography that dispels common myths surrounding Shelley's life and those of her contemporaries.

Williams, John. *Mary Shelley: A Literary Life*. London: Palgrave, 2000, 222 p.

Provides an overview of Shelley's life.

Criticism

Birkhead, Edith. "Later Developments of the Tale of Terror." In *The Tale of Terror: A Study of the Gothic Romance*. 1921. Reprint edition, pp. 157-84. Russell & Russell, Inc., 1963.

Chapter in what is considered one of the first significant studies of the Gothic tradition. Offers a thoughtful overview of Frankenstein, *and briefly considers* Valperga, The Last Man, *and some of Shelley's short stories.*

Botting, Fred, ed. *New Casebooks*: Frankenstein. London: Macmillan, 1995, 271 p.

Compilation of essays representing the different critical approaches commonly employed in analyses of Frankenstein.

Clery, E. J. "Mary Shelley." In *Women's Gothic: From Clara Reeve to Mary Shelley*, pp. 117-46. Horndon, Tavistock, Devon: Northcote House in Association with the British Council, 2000.

Studies Shelley within the tradition of Gothic literature written by women.

Clifford, Gay. "*Caleb Williams* and *Frankenstein*: First-Person Narratives and 'Things as They Are.'" *Genre* 10, no. 4 (winter 1977): 601-17.

Outlines the artistic and philosophical viewpoints of the first-person narratives in Caleb Williams *and* Frankenstein *and compares Shelley's narrative techniques with those of her father.*

Eberle-Sinatra, Michael, ed. *Mary Shelley's Fictions: From Frankenstein to Falkner*. New York: Macmillan—St. Martin's Press, 2000, 250 p.

Collection of essays on Shelley's works, arranged in sections titled "The Craft of Writing," "Gender," "The Contemporary Scene," and "The Parental Legacy."

Garbin, Lidia. "*The Fortunes of Perkin Warbeck*: Walter Scott in the Writings of Mary Shelley." *Romanticism On the Net* 6 (May 1997): <http://users.ox.ac.uk/~scat0385/warbeck.html>.

Argues "that we cannot understand Perkin Warbeck *unless we see that it stands in Scott's shadow and that Mary Shelley is deeply sympathetic to the tenor of Scott's works."*

Gilbert, Sandra M. and Susan Gubar. "Horror's Twin: Mary Shelley's Monstrous Eve." In *The Madwoman in the Attic: The Woman Writer and the Nineteenth-Century Literary Imagination*, pp. 213-47. New Haven, Conn.: Yale University Press, 1979.

Views Frankenstein *in terms of Shelley's relationship to the general patriarchy of literature as figured in John Milton's* Paradise Lost. *Noting that Shelley read Milton's* poem before writing her novel, Gilbert and Gubar assert that Shelley adopted the misogyny of Paradise Lost *into her own "pained ambivalence toward mothers."*

Goldberg, M. A. "Moral and Myth in Mrs. Shelley's *Frankenstein.*" *Keats-Shelley Journal* 8 (winter 1959): 27-38.

Investigation of the themes of isolation and knowledge in Frankenstein *that is considered one of the first comprehensive assessments of the novel and a milestone in* Frankenstein *scholarship.*

Hill-Miller, Katherine C. *"My Hideous Progeny": Mary Shelley, William Godwin, and the Father-Daughter Relationship.* Newark, Del.: University of Delaware Press, 1995, 249 p.

Devotes attention to Godwin's influence on Shelley, particularly as her literary predecessor.

Hoeveler, Diane Long. "Fantasy, Trauma, and Gothic Daughters: *Frankenstein* as Therapy." *Prism(s): Essays in Romanticism* 8 (2000): 7-28.

Argues that Frankenstein*'s "power resides . . . in its unconscious working out and through the author's own intense sense of victimization, and her increasingly desperate struggle for love and family."*

Hogle, Jerrold E. "*Frankenstein* as Neo-Gothic: From the Ghost of the Counterfeit to The Monster of Abjection." In *Romanticism, History, and the Possibilities of Genre,* edited by Tilottama Rajan and Julia Wright, pp. 176-210. Cambridge: Cambridge University Press, 1998.

*Contends that "*Frankenstein *turns out to be one major apogee of the Gothic's development from the Walpolean ghosts of older ghosts to the ghost-like representation and sequestering of the abject."*

Johnson, Barbara. "My Monster/My Self." *Diacritics* 12, no. 2 (summer 1982): 2-10.

A landmark essay in which Johnson presents Frankenstein *as a both a complex fictionalization of Shelley's autobiography and a commentary on the nature of female autobiography, contending that "*Frankenstein *can be read as the story of the experience of writing* Frankenstein.*"*

Kaplan, Morton, and Robert Kloss. "Fantasy of Paternity and the Doppelgänger: Mary Shelley's *Frankenstein.*" In *The Unspoken Motive: A Guide to Psychoanalytic Literary Criticism,* pp. 119-45. New York: Free Press, 1973.

Offers a classic psychoanalytic approach to Frankenstein, *employing Freudian paradigms and methods of dream analysis.*

Kiely, Robert. "*Frankenstein*: Mary Wollstonecraft Shelley." In *The Romantic Novel in England,* pp. 155-73. Cambridge, Mass.: Harvard University Press, 1972.

Examines and elaborates upon what he considers to be two dominant themes in Frankenstein: *"the monstrous consequences of egotism" and "the virtue of friendship."*

Knoepflmacher, U. C. "Thoughts on the Aggression of Daughters." In *Endurance of Frankenstein: Essays on Mary Shelley's Novel,* edited by George Levine, U. C. Knoepflmacher, and Peter Dale Scott, pp. 88-119. Berkeley: University of California Press, 1979.

*Contends that "*Frankenstein *is a novel of omnipresent fathers and absent mothers," a situation he relates explicitly to Shelley's own family history and the repressed anger at her father that appears to surface in the novel.*

Miyoshi, Masao. "The Logic of Passion: Romanticism." In *The Divided Self: A Perspective on the Literature of the Victorians,* pp. 47-106. New York: New York University Press, 1969.

Suggests that the characters Walton, Clerval, and the Monster in Frankenstein *serve to illuminate various aspects of Victor Frankenstein's personality. According to Miyoshi, Walton mirrors Frankenstein in his Faustian striving, while Clerval and the Monster represent the good and evil extremes, respectively, of the scientist's nature.*

Poovey, Mary. "My Hideous Progeny: Mary Shelley and the Feminization of Romanticism." *PMLA* 95, no. 3 (May 1980): 332-47.

Explores the pressures faced by Shelley, who was expected to be both an original writer and a conventional feminine model of propriety.

———. "'My Hideous Progeny': The Lady and the Monster." In *The Proper Lady and the Woman Writer: Ideology as Style in the Works of Mary Wollstonecraft, Mary Shelley, and Jane Austen,* pp. 114-42. Chicago: University of Chicago Press, 1984.

Depicts Shelley as torn between the desire for self-expression and the desire to conform.

Rauch, Alan. "The Monstrous Body of Knowledge in Mary Shelley's *Frankenstein.*" *Studies in Romanticism* 34, no. 2 (summer 1995): 227-53.

Reads Frankenstein *as "Shelley's critique of knowledge"—specifically of scientific knowledge as a discourse owned, shaped, and frequently misused by men.*

Rieger, James. Introduction to *Frankenstein; or, The Modern Prometheus: The 1818 Text,* by Mary Wollstonecraft Shelley, edited by James Rieger. 1974. Reprint edition, pp. xi-xxvii. Chicago: The University of Chicago Press, 1982.

Disputes the notion that Frankenstein *is either Gothic romance or early science fiction, and discusses it as an example of mythic fiction.*

Rubenstein, Marc A. "'My Accursed Origin': The Search for the Mother in *Frankenstein.*" *Studies in Romanticism* 15, no. 2 (spring 1976): 165-94.

Utilizes Shelley's biography and psychoanalytic methodology to analyze Frankenstein *as a struggle with "the problem of motherhood."*

Schoene-Harwood, Berthold. *Mary Shelley*: Frankenstein. New York: Columbia University Press, 2000, 208 p.

Surveys the major critical approaches to Frankenstein, *as well as film adaptations and other works that have been influenced by the novel.*

Shelley, Mary Wollstonecraft. "Appendix A." In *Frankenstein or the Modern Prometheus: The 1818 Text,* edited by James Rieger, pp. 222-29. Chicago: The University of Chicago Press, 1982.

Written in 1818. Shelley briefly recounts her biography, with an emphasis on her intellectual development and the events that led to the "waking dream" in which she first envisioned Victor Frankenstein and his creature.

Spivak, Gayatri Chakravorty. "*Frankenstein* and Devi's Pterodactyl." In *Empire and the Gothic: The Politics of Genre,* edited by Andrew Smith and William Hughes, pp. 56-68. New York and Basingstoke: Palgrave Macmillan, 2003.

Argues that focusing on Frankenstein "in terms of English cultural identity," reveals "that, although Frankenstein is ostensibly about the origin and evolution of man in society, it does not deploy the axiomatics of imperialism for crucial textual functions."

Thomas, Ronald R. "Demons and Disease in *Frankenstein*." In *Dreams of Authority: Freud and the Fictions of the Unconscious*, pp. 81-99. Ithaca, N.Y.: Cornell University Press, 1990.

Asserts that "Frankenstein is an extended, elaborate account of its author's remarkable dream," and contends that "[t]he gothic novel Mary Shelley called the 'transcript' of her dream may be read as a symptom—a text that expresses the desire for an adequate language to describe the mysterious forces that produced it."

Twitchell, James B. "*Frankenstein* and the Anatomy of Horror." *The Georgia Review* 37, no. 1 (spring 1983): 41-78.

Discusses Frankenstein and its popular culture legacy as part of an effort to define "horror" as a genre and discern the source of its audience appeal.

Veeder, William. *Mary Shelley and* Frankenstein: *The Fate of Androgyny*. Chicago: University of Chicago Press, 1986, 277 p.

Applies the concepts of "androgyny" and "bifurcation" to an examination of the presence of aggression in Shelley's work, considering in particular its relation to gender identity.

Walling, William A. *Mary Shelley*. New York: Twayne Publishers, 1972, 173 p.

Full-length study of Shelley's life and works.

Williams, John. "Translating Mary Shelley's *Valperga* into English: Historical Romance, Biography or Gothic Fiction?" In *European Gothic: A Spirited Exchange, 1760-1960*, edited by Avril Horner, pp. 147-60. Manchester: Manchester University Press, 2002.

Investigates the genre classification of Valperga by discussing its roots in the traditions of Gothic fiction, the historical novel, and the Victorian biography.

Yousef, Nancy. "The Monster in a Dark Room: Frankenstein, Feminism, and Philosophy." *Modern Language Quarterly* 63, no. 2 (June 2002): 197-226.

Maintains that "Frankenstein contends with ideals of autonomy and self-sufficiency not only by narrating the unnatural fashioning of a creature in an act of solitary conception but, perhaps more important, by narrating the unnatural development of the creature after it has been abandoned to its solitary fate."

Zimmerman, Lee. "Frankenstein, Invisibility, and Nameless Dread." *American Imago: Studies in Psychoanalysis and Culture* 60, no. 2 (summer 2003): 135-58.

Contends that Victor Frankenstein's claims to have lived a happy childhood with kind and indulgent parents are "idealized and defensive," and asserts that "just as the monster suffers from parentlessness, so too does Victor, who is his double. The monster's story of emotional abandonment is Victor's story."

OTHER SOURCES FROM GALE:

Additional coverage of Shelley's life and career is contained in the following sources published by Thomson Gale: *Authors and Artists for Young Adults*, Vol. 20; *Beacham's Encyclopedia of Popular Fiction: Biography & Resources*, Vol. 3; *Beacham's Guide to Literature for Young Adults*, Vol. 5; *British Writers*, Vol. 3; *British Writers: The Classics*, Vol. 2; *British Writers Supplement*, Vol. 3; *Concise Dictionary of British Literary Biography, 1789-1832*; *Dictionary of Literary Biography*, Vols. 110, 116, 159, 178; *DISCovering Authors; DISCovering Authors: British; DISCovering Authors: Canadian; DISCovering Authors Modules: Most-studied Authors* and *Novelists; DISCovering Authors 3.0; Exploring Novels; Feminism in Literature: A Gale Critical Companion; Literary Movements for Students*, Vols. 1, 2; *Literature Resource Center; Nineteenth-Century Literature Criticism*, Vols. 14, 59, 103; *Novels for Students*, Vol. 1; *Reference Guide to English Literature*, Ed. 2; *St. James Guide to Horror, Ghost & Gothic Writers; St. James Guide to Science Fiction Writers*, Ed. 4; *Science Fiction Writers*, Eds. 1, 2; *Something about the Author*, Vol. 29; *Twayne's English Authors; World Literature and Its Times*, Vol. 3; and *World Literature Criticism*.

ROBERT LOUIS STEVENSON

(1850 - 1894)

(Full name Robert Louis Balfour Stevenson) Scottish novelist, short story writer, poet, essayist, and playwright.

An inventive prose stylist, Stevenson is the versatile author of classic works in several genres. Renowned for his adventure novels *Treasure Island* (1883) and *Kidnapped: Being Memoirs of the Adventures of David Balfour in the Year 1751* (1886), and for his outstanding work of supernatural horror *The Strange Case of Dr. Jekyll and Mr. Hyde* (1886), Stevenson is additionally remembered as a travel writer and author of children's verse. Just as his famous stories of piracy and horror have placed him at the forefront of writers of romances, his unusual life and personality have made him one of literature's most intriguing individuals, to the extent that his biography has often overshadowed his literary reputation. Nevertheless, critics credit his continued esteem to the enduring appeal of his fiction, which features fast-paced action, intricate plots, and well-drawn characters. Stevenson is also admired for his fecund imagination and affinity for the psychology of children, as displayed most notably in his early "boys' novels" and his poetry collection *A Child's Garden of Verses* (1885). Although his present critical standing does not equal that accorded him by his contemporaries, his mass popularity continues, and his novels and stories are still considered seminal to the late nineteenth-century development of adventure, romance, and Gothic literature.

BIOGRAPHICAL INFORMATION

Stevenson was born in Edinburgh. A sickly, fragile child, he suffered from severe respiratory ailments that frequently interrupted his schooling. Although he wanted to be a writer, his father insisted that Stevenson be trained in a more secure profession. Thus he attended Edinburgh University between 1866 and 1871, studying engineering, although the subject held little appeal for him. Later, in a compromise with his father, he took a law degree in 1875, but never practiced. Motivated by his love for adventure and his desire to seek out a climate agreeable to his health, Stevenson traveled extensively throughout his life. His journeys to France in the 1870s provided much of the material for his early travel books, *An Inland Voyage* (1878) and *Travels with a Donkey in the Cévennes* (1879). In 1876, while in France, Stevenson met Mrs. Fanny Osbourne, an American woman eleven years his senior. When Osbourne returned to California two years later to arrange a divorce, Stevenson followed. The newly married couple stayed in America for almost a year and then returned to Europe with Lloyd Osbourne, Fanny's son. During the 1880s, despite his continuing poor health, Stevenson wrote many of his best-known works, including *Treasure Island*. Originally begun as a game for his stepson, the novel was published serially in a children's magazine under the title "The Sea-Cook" and became Stevenson's first popular and critical success. The works that followed, including *A Child's Garden of Verses, Dr. Jekyll and Mr. Hyde,* and *Kidnapped,* strengthened his growing reputation. In 1887, the Stevensons returned to the United States. From California, they sailed to Samoa, where they settled, Stevenson finding the climate congenial to his respiratory condition. His life on the island consisted of dabbling in local politics, managing his plantation, and writing several works, including collaborations with Lloyd Osbourne. He died unexpectedly at the age of forty-four from a cerebral hemorrhage.

MAJOR WORKS

Stevenson's short stories and novels for adults include the works most often cited by modern critics as his best: *The Merry Men and Other Tales and Fables* (1887), *Island Nights' Entertainments* (1893), *The Strange Case of Dr. Jekyll and Mr. Hyde, The Master of Ballantrae* (1889), and *Weir of Hermiston* (1896). Unlike his earlier works, these novels and stories examine moral dilemmas presented in an atmosphere imbued with mystery and horror. Modern commentators note certain recurring themes, such as those of the divided self and the nature of evil. Several of these pieces partake directly in the Gothic tradition, featuring elements of the horrific and supernatural. Reputedly based upon a nightmare brought on by fever and narcotic drugs, *Dr. Jekyll and Mr. Hyde* centers on the ill-fated attempt of the scientist Jekyll to dissociate the good and evil components of his being for the purposes of isolating and eliminating the latter. Compounding a drug to achieve this goal, Jekyll unwittingly transforms himself into the villainous Hyde upon drinking it. The metamorphoses begin to occur randomly, and ultimately Jekyll kills himself to stop Hyde's predations. The story has been variously interpreted as an allegory of the twofold nature of human beings, a moralizing tale about good and evil, and a satire concerned with the cultural forces that require individuals to suppress natural urges. Sometimes seen as a didactic Victorian cautionary tale about the dangers of abandoning oneself to base instincts, *Dr. Jekyll and Mr. Hyde* escapes sensationalism through its controlled narrative: gruesome events are described after the fact by

different observers. Aside from this extended work, Stevenson also wrote several other pieces of short fiction that explore Gothic and supernatural subjects. Originally published in 1885 and posthumously collected in Stevenson's *The Story of a Lie, and Other Tales* (1904), "The Body-Snatcher" is an account of supernatural retribution that befalls two medical students who rob graves and commit murder to obtain cadavers for dissection. One of Stevenson's most celebrated short stories, "Markheim" was first published in 1885 and was later featured in *The Merry Men and Other Tales and Fables*. Exhibiting the influence of writings by Edgar Allan Poe as well that of Fyodor Dostoevsky's *Crime and Punishment,* "Markheim" is a tale of psychological horror centered on its eponymous protagonist as he commits an evidently premeditated murder and then encounters a stranger, a devilish *doppelgänger,* who seems to know everything about him, including his crime. The major themes in "Markheim" are similar to those of *Dr. Jekyll and Mr. Hyde,* namely the struggle between good and evil—and freewill and predestination—within the human soul. In the story, this assay between the opposing forces of virtue and malevolence in the individual is expressed through the figure of the ambiguous double, the visitant, who most critics interpret to be the embodiment of Markheim's conscience.

Several more of Stevenson's works of short fiction follow in the Scottish literary tradition established by Sir Walter Scott, with many drawing upon the Gothic conventions of the uncanny and inexplicable used by Scott in his romances. These include "Thrawn Janet," a ghost story that exploits superstitious belief in witchcraft and demonic possession; "The Merry Men," a hallucinatory sea tale concerned with madness and conscience; and "The Pavilion on the Links" and "Black Andie's Tale of Tod Lapraik," adventure stories with detailed historical backgrounds. Other stories, such as "The Bottle Imp" and "The Isle of Voices," draw upon the folklore of the South Seas Islands. Collected in *Island Nights' Entertainments,* "The Bottle Imp" recounts the tale of a Hawaiian man who, while visiting San Francisco, buys a bottle containing a magical but malevolent creature that grants its possessor wishes. He soon learns, however, that the imp is evil and seeks to relieve himself of its curse. Another of Stevenson's most famous stories "The Beach of Falesá" (1892) is principally a work of literary realism concerned with British imperialism in the South Seas. The story's characteristic eeriness, however, has prompted some to comment on its subtle use of

Gothic conventions. For many of his remaining stories, including "Providence and the Guitar" (1878) and "The Story of a Lie" (1879), Stevenson drew on his own vagabond youth, wryly detailing the posing and fakery that can accompany a bohemian way of life in these pieces.

CRITICAL RECEPTION

After Stevenson's untimely death, his family issued editions of his letters and approved an official biography designed to sustain popular perception of Stevenson as a brave, talented, and somewhat fey invalid whose life and works were above reproach. Although several critics warned readers against this eulogistic approach to the writer, the content of Stevenson criticism did not change significantly until 1915, when Frank Swinnerton (see Further Reading) published his *R. L. Stevenson: A Critical Study.* Considered by modern critics the most important challenger to the Stevenson myth, Swinnerton rejected the uncritical adoration of early readers and inspired a change in the critical approach to Stevenson, which had previously focused on personal rather than literary subjects. Although critics are still fascinated by his life and reputation, they now respond to his work more often with serious analysis and acclaim. In the contemporary period, *Weir of Hermiston,* the novel that Stevenson was at work upon when he died, has come to be regarded by many as his best effort for its forceful style and for its psychologically and morally complex characters. Meanwhile *Treasure Island, Kidnapped* and *A Child's Garden of Verses* remain popular with young readers, and continue to be regarded as classics of children's literature.

Critical appreciation of Stevenson's status as an influential Gothic writer has largely focused on his novella *The Strange Case of Dr. Jekyll and Mr. Hyde.* The work itself was immensely popular with contemporary readers, although early critics' reactions varied widely. Almost all acknowledged Stevenson's skill as a writer of suspense, though many questioned the work's moral intent. Some viewed the story as a moral allegory on the nature of evil, while other commentators found Stevenson's own remarks illuminating, particularly his statement that the transformation of Jekyll into Hyde was meant to show that desires, when ignored, become perverted. Since the middle of the twentieth century, critics have continued to forward moral, thematic, and psychological interpretations of Stevenson's novella. Masao Miyoshi

has studied *Dr. Jekyll and Mr. Hyde* as a complex work that explores the paradoxical "double nature" of man, a favorite theme of both eighteenth-century Gothic and later romance authors who sought to depict the unresolved dualities inherent in all human beings. Joyce Carol Oates has assessed the novella as a characteristic work of Victorian Gothic, describing it as a moral parable, a cautionary tale concerned with the good and evil impulses that reside within us all. Matthew C. Brennan represents numerous contemporary critics who have taken a psychological and cultural approach to *Dr. Jekyll and Mr. Hyde* by emphasizing its use of such Gothic tropes as unconscious repression and the urge toward self-destruction. Linda Dryden (see Further Reading) has returned to the contemporary Victorian reception of Stevenson's novella, arguing that the story capitalized upon a peak in late nineteenth-century concern with such quintessentially Gothic themes as cultural degeneracy, criminal insanity, and atavism. Dryden has likewise linked the book's popular success to its artistic rendering of the particularly urban and imperial anxieties associated with life in *fin de siècle* London. While scholarly interest in Stevenson's novella endures, opinion remains divided over the overall value of the writer's oeuvre. Despite some critical neglect of his writings, however, his children's poetry, adventure stories, and adult romances persist in attracting readers who appreciate fine writing and exciting adventure, and his *Dr. Jekyll and Mr. Hyde* continues to be regarded as one of the outstanding examples of late-Victorian Gothic horror.

PRINCIPAL WORKS

The Pentland Rising: A Page of History, 1666 (essay) 1866

An Inland Voyage (travel sketches) 1878

"Providence and the Guitar" (short story) 1878; published in the journal *London*

"The Story of a Lie" (short story) 1879; published in the journal *New Quarterly Magazine*

Travels with a Donkey in the Cévennes (travel sketches) 1879

Virginibus Puerisque and Other Papers (essays) 1881

Deacon Brodie; or, The Double Life: A Melodrama Founded on Facts [with William Ernest Henley] (play) 1882

Familiar Studies of Men and Books (essays) 1882

*New Arabian Nights. 2 vols. (short stories) 1882

Treasure Island (novel) 1883

"The Body Snatcher" (short story) 1885; published in the journal Pall Mall Magazine

A Child's Garden of Verses (poetry) 1885

Macaire [with Henley; first publication] (play) 1885

More New Arabian Nights: The Dynamiter [with Fanny Stevenson] (short stories) 1885

Prince Otto (novel) 1885

Kidnapped: Being Memoirs of the Adventures of David Balfour in the Year 1751 (novel) 1886

The Strange Case of Dr. Jekyll and Mr. Hyde (novella) 1886

Memories and Portraits (essays) 1887

†The Merry Men and Other Tales and Fables (short stories) 1887

Underwoods (poetry) 1887

The Black Arrow: A Tale of the Two Roses (novel) 1888

The Master of Ballantrae: A Winter's Tale (novel) 1889

The Wrong Box [with Lloyd Osbourne] (novel) 1889

Admiral Guinea [with Henley] (play) 1890

Ballads (poetry) 1890

Beau Austin [with Henley] (play) 1890

Across the Plains, with Other Memories and Essays (essays) 1892

"The Beach of Falesá" (short story) 1892; published in the journal Illustrated London News

The Wrecker [with Osbourne] (novel) 1892

Catriona, a Sequel to "Kidnapped": Being Memoirs of the Further Adventures of David Balfour at Home and Abroad (novel) 1893; also published as David Balfour: Being Memoirs of His Adventures at Home and Abroad, 1893

‡Island Nights' Entertainments (short stories) 1893

The Ebb-Tide: A Trio and Quartette [with Osbourne] (novel) 1894

The Works of R. L. Stevenson. 28 vols. (novels, unfinished novels, short stones, travel sketches, poetry, essays, drama, and letters) 1894-98

Weir of Hermiston (unfinished novel) 1896

#St. Ive's: Being the Adventures of a French Prisoner in England (novel) 1897

Poems Hitherto Unpublished. 2 vols. (poetry) 1916; also published as New Poems and Variant Readings, 1918

*   This collection contains the short story "The Pavilion on the Links."

†   This collection contains the short stories "Markheim," "The Merry Men," and "Thrawn Janet."

‡   This collection contains the short stories "The Bottle Imp," "Black Andie's Tale of Tod Lapraik," and "The Isle of Voices."

This work was completed by A. T. Quiller-Couch.

PRIMARY SOURCES

ROBERT LOUIS STEVENSON (STORY DATE FEBRUARY-MARCH 1891)

SOURCE: Stevenson, Robert Louis. "The Bottle Imp." In *Masterpieces of Terror and the Supernatural,* selected by Marvin Kaye, pp. 46-70. New York: Barnes & Noble, 1985.

The following excerpt is from a story written around 1889 and first published in the New York Herald from February to March, 1891.

Now there was an old brutal Haole drinking with him, one that had been a boatswain of a whaler—a runaway, a digger in gold mines, a convict in prisons. He had a low mind and a foul mouth; he loved to drink and to see others drunken; and he pressed the glass upon Keawe. Soon there was no more money in the company.

"Here, you!" says the boatswain, "you are rich, you have been always saying. You have a bottle or some foolishness."

"Yes," says Keawe, "I am rich; I will go back and get some money from my wife, who keeps it."

"That's a bad idea, mate," said the boatswain. "Never you trust a petticoat with dollars. They're all as false as water; you keep an eye on her."

Now this word struck in Keawe's mind; for he was muddled with what he had been drinking.

"I should not wonder but she was false, indeed," thought he. "Why else should she be so cast down at my release? But I will show her I am not the man to be fooled. I will catch her in the act."

Accordingly, when they were back in town, Keawe bade the boatswain wait for him at the corner by the old calaboose, and went forward up the avenue alone to the door of his house. The night had come again; there was a light within, but never a sound; and Keawe crept about the corner, opened the back door softly, and looked in.

There was Kokua on the floor, the lamp at her side; before her was a milk-white bottle, with a round belly and a long neck; and as she viewed it, Kokua wrung her hands.

A long time Keawe stood and looked in the doorway. At first he was struck stupid; and then fear fell upon him that the bargain had been made amiss, and the bottle had come back to him as it came at San Francisco; and at that his knees were loosened, and the fumes of the wine departed from his head like mists off a river in the morning. And then he had another thought; and it was a strange one, that made his cheeks to burn.

"I must make sure of this," thought he.

So he closed the door, and went softly round the corner again, and then came noisily in, as though he were but now returned. And, lo! by the time he opened the front door no bottle was to be seen; and Kokua sat in a chair and started up like one awakened out of sleep.

"I have been drinking all day and making merry," said Keawe. "I have been with good companions, and now I only came back for money, and return to drink and carouse with them again."

Both his face and voice were as stern as judgment, but Kokua was too troubled to observe.

"You do well to use your own, my husband," said she, and her words trembled.

"Oh, I do well in all things," said Keawe, and he went straight to the chest and took out money. But he looked besides in the corner where they kept the bottle, and there was no bottle there.

At that the chest heaved upon the floor like a sea-billow, and the house spun about him like a wreath of smoke, for he saw she was lost now, and there was no escape. "It is what I feared," he thought. "It is she who has bought it."

And then he came to himself a little and rose up; but the sweat streamed on his face as thick as the rain and as cold as the well-water.

"Kokua," said he, "I said to you to-day what ill became me. Now I return to house with my jolly companions," and at that he laughed a little quietly. "I will take more pleasure in the cup if you forgive me."

She clasped his knees in a moment, she kissed his knees with flowing tears.

"Oh," she cried, "I ask but a kind word!"

"Let us never one think hardly of the other," said Keawe, and was gone out of the house.

Now, the money that Keawe had taken was only some of that store of centime pieces they had laid in at their arrival. It was very sure he had no mind to be drinking. His wife had given her soul for him, now he must give his for hers; no other thought was in the world with him.

At the corner, by the old calaboose, there was the boatswain waiting.

"My wife has the bottle," said Keawe, "and, unless you help me to recover it, there can be no more money and no more liquor to-night."

"You do not mean to say you are serious about that bottle?" cried the boatswain.

"There is the lamp," said Keawe. "Do I look as if I was jesting?"

"That is so," said the boatswain. "You look as serious as a ghost."

"Well, then," said Keawe, "here are two centimes; you just go to my wife in the house, and offer her these for the bottle, which (if I am not much mistaken) she will give you instantly. Bring it to me here, and I will buy it back from you for one; for that is the law with this bottle, that it still must be sold for a less sum. But whatever you do, never breathe a word to her that you have come from me."

"Mate, I wonder are you making a fool of me?" asked the boatswain.

"It will do you no harm if I am," returned Keawe.

"That is so, mate," said the boatswain.

"And if you doubt me," added Keawe, "you can try. As soon as you are clear of the house, wish to have your pocket full of money, or a bottle of the best rum, or what you please, and you will see the virtue of the thing."

"Very well, Kanaka," says the boatswain. "I will try; but if you are having your fun out of me, I will take my fun out of you with a belaying-pin."

So the whaler-man went off up the avenue; and Keawe stood and waited. It was near the same spot where Kokua had waited the night before; but Keawe was more resolved, and never faltered in his purpose; only his soul was bitter with despair.

It seemed a long time he had to wait before he heard a voice singing in the darkness of the avenue. He knew the voice to be the boatswain's; but it was strange how drunken it appeared upon a sudden.

Next the man himself came stumbling into the light of the lamp. He had the devil's bottle buttoned in his coat; another bottle was in his hand; and even as he came in view he raised it to his mouth and drank.

"You have it," said Keawe. "I see that."

"Hands off!" cried the boatswain, jumping back. "Take a step near me, and I'll smash your mouth. You thought you could make a catspaw of me, did you?"

"What do you mean?" cried Keawe.

"Mean?" cried the boatswain. "This is a pretty good bottle, this is; that's what I mean. How I got it for two centimes I can't make out; but I am sure you shan't have it for one."

"You mean you won't sell?" gasped Keawe.

"No, sir," cried the boatswain. "But I'll give you a drink of the rum, if you like."

"I tell you," said Keawe, "the man who has that bottle goes to hell."

"I reckon I'm going anyway," returned the sailor; "and this bottle's the best thing to go with I've struck yet. No, sir!" he cried again, "this is my bottle now, and you can go and fish for another."

"Can this be true?" Keawe cried. "For your own sake, I beseech you, sell it me!"

"I don't value any of your talk," replied the boatswain. "You thought I was a flat, now you see I'm not; and there's an end. If you won't have a swallow of the rum, I'll have one myself. Here's your health, and goodnight to you!"

So off he went down the avenue towards town, and there goes the bottle out of the story.

But Keawe ran to Kokua light as the wind; and great was their joy that night; and great, since then, has been the peace of all their days in the Bright House.

TITLE COMMENTARY

The Strange Case of Dr. Jekyll and Mr. Hyde

THE TIMES, LONDON (REVIEW DATE 25 JANUARY 1886)

SOURCE: A review of *The Strange Case of Dr Jekyll and Mr Hyde,* by Robert Louis Stevenson. *The Times,* London, no. 31665 (25 January 1886): 13.

In the following laudatory review of The Strange Case of Dr. Jekyll and Mr. Hyde, *the critic praises Steven-*

son's handling of his supernatural subject matter, comparing his work favorably with Edgar Allan Poe's.

Nothing Mr. Stevenson has written as yet has so strongly impressed us with the versatility of his very original genius as [*The Strange Case of Dr. Jekyll and Mr. Hyde,*] this sparsely-printed little shilling volume. From the business point of view we can only marvel in these practical days at the lavish waste of admirable material, and what strikes us as a disproportionate expenditure of brain-power, in relation to the tangible results. Of two things, one. Either the story was a flash of intuitive psychological research, dashed off in a burst of inspiration; or else it is the product of the most elaborate forethought, fitting together all the parts of an intricate and inscrutable puzzle. The proof is, that every connoisseur who reads the story once must certainly read it twice. He will read it the first time, passing from surprise to surprise, in a curiosity that keeps growing, because it is never satisfied. For the life of us, we cannot make out how such and such an incident can possibly be explained on grounds that are intelligible or in any way plausible. Yet all the time the seriousness of the tone assures us that explanations are forthcoming. In our impatience we are hurried towards the denouement, which accounts for everything upon strictly scientific grounds, though the science be the science of problematical futurity. Then, having drawn a sigh of relief at having found even a fantastically speculative issue from our embarrassments, we begin reflectively to call to mind how systematically the writer has been working towards it. Never for a moment, in the most startling situations, has he lost his grasp of the grand ground-facts of a wonderful and supernatural problem. Each apparently incredible or insignificant detail has been thoughtfully subordinated to his purpose. And if we say, after all, on a calm retrospect, that the strange case is absurdly and insanely improbable, Mr. Stevenson might answer in the words of Hamlet, that there are more things in heaven and in earth than are dreamed of in our philosophy. For we are still groping by doubtful lights on the dim limits of boundless investigation; and it is always possible that we may be on the brink of a new revelation as to the unforeseen resources of the medical art. And, at all events, the answer should suffice for the purposes of Mr. Stevenson's sensational *tour d'esprit.*

The *Strange Case of Dr. Jekyll* is sensational enough in all conscience, and yet we do not promise it the wide popularity of *Called Back.* The *brochure* that brought fame and profit to the late Mr. Fargus was pitched in a more commonplace key, and consequently appealed to more vulgar circles. But, for ourselves, we should many times sooner have the credit of *Dr. Jekyll,* which appeals irresistibly to the most cultivated minds, and must be appreciated by the most competent critics. Naturally, we compare it with the sombre masterpieces of Poe, and we may say at once that Mr. Stevenson has gone far deeper. Poe embroidered richly in the gloomy grandeur of his imagination upon themes that were but too material, and not very novel—on the sinister destiny overshadowing a doomed family, on a living and breathing man kept prisoner in a coffin or vault, on the wild whirling of a human waif in the boiling eddies of the Maelstrom—while Mr. Stevenson evolves the ideas of his story from the world that is unseen, enveloping everything in weird mystery, till at last it pleases him to give us the password. We are not going to tell his strange story, though we might well do so, and only excite the curiosity of our readers. We shall only say that we are shown the shrewdest of lawyers hopelessly puzzled by the inexplicable conduct of a familiar friend. All the antecedents of a life of virtue and honour seem to be belied by the discreditable intimacy that has been formed with one of the most callous and atrocious of criminals. A crime committed under the eyes of a witness goes unavenged, though the notorious criminal has been identified, for he disappears as absolutely as if the earth had swallowed him. He reappears in due time where we should least expect to see him, and for some miserable days he leads a charmed life, while he excites the superstitious terrors of all about him. Indeed, the strongest nerves are shaken by stress of sinister circumstances, as well they may be, for the worthy Dr. Jekyll—the benevolent physician— has likewise vanished amid events that are enveloped in impalpable mysteries; nor can any one surmise what has become of him. So with overwrought feelings and conflicting anticipations we are brought to the end, where all is accounted for, more or less credibly.

Nor is it the mere charm of the story, strange as it is, which fascinates and thrills us. Mr. Stevenson is known for a master of style, and never has he shown his resources more remarkably than on this occasion. We do not mean that the book is written in excellent English—that must be a matter of course; but he has weighed his words and turned his sentences so as to sustain and excite throughout the sense of mystery and of horror. The mere artful use of an "it" for a "he" may go far in that respect, and Mr. Stevenson has carefully chosen his language and missed no op-

ABOUT THE AUTHOR

JOHN ADDINGTON SYMONDS ON *DR. JEKYLL AND MR. HYDE*

At last I have read *Dr Jekyll.* It makes me wonder whether a man has the right so to scrutinise "the abysmal deeps of personality". It is indeed a dreadful book, most dreadful because of a certain moral callousness, a want of sympathy, a shutting out of hope. . . . As a piece of literary work, this seems to me the finest you have done. . . . But it has left such a deeply painful impression on my heart that I do not know how I am ever to turn to it again.

SOURCE: Symonds, John Addington. "Excerpt from a letter dated 3 March 1886." Quoted in *Selected Letters of Robert Louis Stevenson,* edited by Ernest Mehew, p. 310. New Haven, Conn.: Yale University Press, 1886.

portunity. And if his style is good, his motive is better, and shows a higher order of genius. Slight as is the story, and supremely sensational, we remember nothing better since George Eliot's "Romela" than this delineation of a feeble but kindly nature steadily and inevitably succumbing to the sinister influences of besetting weaknesses. With no formal preaching and without a touch of Pharisaism, he works out the essential power of Evil, which, with its malignant patience and unwearying perseverance, gains ground with each casual yielding to temptation, till the once well-meaning man may actually become a fiend, or at least wear the reflection of the fiend's image. But we have said enough to show our opinion of the book, which should be read as a finished study in the art of fantastic literature.

MASAO MIYOSHI (ESSAY DATE MARCH 1966)

SOURCE: Miyoshi, Masao. "Dr. Jekyll and the Emergence of Mr. Hyde." *College English* 27, no. 6 (March 1966): 470-80.

In the following essay, Miyoshi explores the biographical and Gothic literary influences on The Strange Case of Dr. Jekyll and Mr. Hyde.

We recall him with pleasure as a fine story teller, the author of those classics of juvenile literature, *Kidnapped* and *Treasure Island*. Probably very few who loved those books will have occasion to read him again, but even the scholars whose business he is neglect the novels these days. Robert Louis Stevenson: he is himself so much the biographer's novelist, the fascinating "life" to be read, that his work is almost incidental. Some, it is true, regard him as a superb craftsman of the novel, but they talk only of the Stevenson style, as though a good style were detachable, the manner from the matter, the art from the thought.

The *Strange Case of Dr. Jekyll and Mr. Hyde* is not exactly a nursery tale, and it is reasonable to expect that, of all the Stevenson stories, that would be the one to get an occasional nod in an article or in the classroom as having something more than entertainment quality, even as having something to do with ideas. Everyone is familiar with its two-men-in-one motif—the Barrymore version is now a film classic—but perhaps not unrelated to this popular status, the book is usually dismissed as crude science fiction or cruder moral allegory. Henry James certainly praised it, soon after it appeared: "the most serious of the author's tales," he said, "a really imaginative production," but then in the same essay called its theme "the relation of the baser parts of man to his nobler."[1] G. K. Chesterton, whose *Robert Louis Stevenson* continues as one of the few good critiques of the author, saw in the story a reassertion merely of a "strictly orthodox"[2] moral. And even the otherwise eloquent defender of Stevenson, Professor David Daiches, hands down the usual verdict: "as an allegory it does not stand up very well to detailed examination."[3] Are such views fair to the book, really? Should *Jekyll and Hyde* be remembered solely or primarily for its author's supposed invention of the dual-personality theme? Is the book too slight for any more conscientious critical effort? I would like to think that, the movies not-withstanding, *Dr. Jekyll and Mr. Hyde* may be read and studied as a story of ideas, that it will by this means yield insights into certain aspects of the late Victorian society that was its milieu, and that it will finally suggest something of the literary tradition which fathered it.

The book comprises ten chapters, the first eight written in the third person (mostly Mr. Utterson's point of view) and the last two in the form of letters, one from Dr. Lanyon and the other from Dr. Jekyll, to their lawyer friend Mr. Utterson. "Henry Jekyll's Full Statement of the Case," which constitutes the last chapter, is frequently cited as the "moral" the author attached to explain the story. But the statement is intrinsic to the work and must be read as such—as Henry Jekyll's statement, not as Robert Louis Stevenson's.

In approaching the work, it would be best to envision the world of the story—its men and landscape—before turning to the Jekyll-Hyde relationship itself. To begin with Mr. Utterson, who is evidently a highly respected citizen. The lawyer is always correctly professional and trustworthy, yet there is something furtive and suppressed about him. He is "austere with himself." He never smiles. He is "cold, scanty, and embarrassed in discourse" (Chap. 1).[4] He claims to like the theater, though he has not been to a play in twenty years. He makes no new friends and socializes only with men he has known well for a very long time. As for his renowned tolerance toward other people's misconduct, this looks suspiciously like the result not of charity but of indifference, though there is the subtlest suggestion of vicarious pleasure. Utterson, too, it turns out, has a past not quite innocent. When it occurs to him that blackmail may be at the root of Hyde's connection with Jekyll, he considers the possibility of a similar threat to himself: "And the lawyer, scared by the thought, brooded a while on his own past, groping in all the corners of memory, lest by chance some Jack-in-the-Box of an old iniquity should leap to light there" (Chap. 2). When his friend and client Sir Danvers Carew is murdered, the event stirs no deeper emotion in him than worry "lest the good name of another should be sucked down in the eddy of the scandal" (Chap. 5). And when his relative Mr. Enfield observes the unspoken rule of never asking questions—"the more it looks like Queer Street, the less I ask" (Chap. 1)—Utterson gives his unequivocal approval. Only his confrontation with Mr. Hyde's unpleasant face cracks the smooth varnish of his existence, making him feel "(what was rare with him) a nausea and distaste of life" (Chap. 2).

Dr. Hastie Lanyon is, by contrast, an apparently healthy and genial man. Yet he too is shielded from life by an imposing respectability. Estranged from Dr. Jekyll for ten years, Dr. Lanyon is a scientist of "practical usefulness" (Chap. 9), who sees Jekyll as a man gone wrong with his "scientific heresies" (Chap. 3). As it happens, when the great Dr. Lanyon confronts a phenomenon which his matter-of-fact science cannot explain, his life is "shaken to its roots" (Chap. 9). He says to Utterson, "I sometimes think if we knew all, we should be more glad to get away"

(Chap. 6). Too late he has learned the ghastly aspect of life, and, with undiminishing horror at it all, he shrivels and dies.[5]

The important men of the book, then, are all unmarried, barren of ideas, emotionally stifled, joyless. In the city at large the more prosperous business people fix up their homes and shops, yet there is something sleazy about the decor: the houses give an appearance of "coquetry," and the store fronts invite one like "rows of smiling saleswomen" (Chap. 1). The handsome houses in the back streets of Dr. Jekyll's neighborhood are rented out to all sorts—"map-engravers, architects, shady lawyers, and the agents of obscure enterprises" (Chap. 2). And everywhere the London fog is inescapable, even creeping under the doors and through the window jambs (Chap. 5). The setting is of a wasteland, but a wasteland hidden by the secure and relatively comfortable respectability of its inhabitants.

In this society of respectables Dr. Jekyll stands out as "the very pink of the proprieties" (Chap. 1). Although his studies, like those of Faust and Frankenstein before him, tend toward "the mystic and the transcendental" (Chap. 10), he still manages to maintain a considerable scientific reputation. And yet, despite Jekyll's social role—in fact, because of it—it is Jekyll, rather than Utterson or Lanyon, who brings forth Mr. Hyde.

It will be remembered that, for a period long before the emergence of Mr. Hyde, Dr. Jekyll was "committed to a profound duplicity of life": alongside his "imperious desire" for dignity and reputation, there was that "impatient gaiety of disposition" (Chap. 10). But for those in the Victorian wasteland, gaiety and respectability are not easily reconciled. Dr. Jekyll, in particular, sees the two as mutually exclusive: a respectable pleasure would be a contradiction in terms. The exacting nature of his ambitions was such that the most unremarkable pleasure resulted in shame. Meanwhile, his Faustian studies, which had already "shed such a strong light on this consciousness of the perennial war among my members" (Chap. 10), suggested to him a practical means of settling the whole question. (Dr. Jekyll, it should be understood, is incapable of expanding the mere self to the scale of the universe, nor can he hope to unify the antagonists within by a commitment to the betterment of all mankind, both of which Dr. Faust found feasible. Respectable society, of which Jekyll is a member in good standing, would repudiate such spurious modes of self-transcendence. Thus, whereas Faust was irrepressible by definition, Jekyll, the latter-day Faust, must at all costs hold his place as a reputable man and even rise in the establishment if he can.) And so, though pleasure had been suppressed for a long time by the dreary decency that was his life, Dr. Jekyll will enjoy it, after all, in the person of a totally new identity, Edward Hyde.

Hyde, once unleashed, arouses disgust in everyone. Dr. Jekyll's servant, for one, feels "kind of cold and thin" in his marrow after meeting Hyde for the first time (Chap. 8), and even the "Sawbones" has the urge to do away with him. To catch sight of Hyde is to be reminded of the hidden "*je*" in each of us, the "troglodytic" (Chap. 2) animal that only waits for the moment of release. In most societies men agree to curb the "*je*" and are not required to totally suppress it. But in Jekyll's world, the "*je*" must be ruthlessly suppressed—most unequivocally so by the man known as "the very pink of the proprieties," Dr. Henry Jekyll, the most thoroughgoing "*je*-killer" of them all.

Hyde, at once Jekyll's Mephistopheles and his (Frankenstein) monster, looks like the very incarnation of evil, but at the beginning he is in fact merely Jekyll's unrepressed spontaneous existence. Going about in the guise of Mr. Hyde, Dr. Jekyll discovers a new freshness and joy in his life. He feels "younger, lighter, happier in body" and is conscious of a "heady recklessness," of a "current of disordered sensual images running like a millrace in my fancy, a solution of the bonds of obligation, an unknown but not an innocent freedom of the soul" (Chap. 10). Not respectable certainly, and therefore utterly despicable by the standards of the Utterson-Enfield-Lanyon world.

But Hyde gradually shows himself dissatisfied with his role as mere "impatient gaiety," and scornful of the rights of others. His "every act and thought [were] centred on self" (Chap. 10). In fact, his pleasure comes to depend on his torturing others. At this point, the self and society are enemies to the death.

Soon after the episode in which Hyde tramples the child, the Jekyll-Hyde metamorphosis becomes involuntary: the doctor goes to bed Henry Jekyll and awakes as Edward Hyde. The hidden "*je*" released by the social "I" threatens now to overpower it. Yet he believes it is still within his ability to stop this emergence of Mr. Hyde. Resolving to forego the "leaping impulses and secret pleasures," he determines to live once again the life of an "elderly and discontented doctor" (Chap. 10). Of course, having once allowed his "*je*" the taste of freedom, he finds he cannot long suppress it. Soon Edward Hyde leaps out "roaring" (Chap. 10) from

Spencer Tracy as Dr. Jekyll in the 1941 film adaptation of
Dr. Jekyll and Mr. Hyde.

the cave of Henry Jekyll. When the brutal murder
of Sir Danvers Carew is disclosed, Jekyll's remorse
is intense, if short-lived, recalling the reaction of
countless Gothic villains after indulging their
sadism. Hyde is now a known criminal, hunted
down not only by Utterson (who calls himself
"Mr. Seek" [Chap. 2]) but also by the police, and
the doctor can no longer risk taking advantage of
the Hyde persona for his sojourns in the netherworld. The next time he goes out it is in the guise
of Dr. Henry Jekyll. No wonder, then, that the
metamorphosis should have become completely
involuntary and the magic drug virtually ineffectual. There are no longer any inner or outer
marks to distinguish the two. The merging, however, is in no sense a reconcilement of the Jekyll-
Hyde duality. Rather, it signals a return to the
starting point of Jekyll's whole experience. Only
the annihilation of one of the two selves "reconciles" them: at the end of the story the doctor
finally suppresses the *"je"* by murdering Hyde,
thereby, of course, becoming a "self-destroyer"
(Chap. 8), a suicide.

Chesterton is the first, I believe, to have
pointed out the autobiographical elements in ***Dr.
Jekyll and Mr. Hyde.*** He argues that Edinburgh,
not London, is the scene of the story, on the basis
that the black and white distinction of good and
evil, the horror of tainting respectability with the

disclosure of human failings, is Puritan, especially
Caledonian. Chesterton sees Jekyll's fastidiousness
as the trait of one who "knew the worst too
young; not necessarily in his own act or by his
own fault, but by the nature of a system which
saw no difference between the worst and the
moderately bad."[6] This notion is developed in
Malcolm Elwin's *The Strange Case of Robert Louis
Stevenson* (London, 1950), though the biographer
tends to read ***Jekyll and Hyde*** into the author's
life rather than Stevenson's life into the story. Elwin's view is that Stevenson, who was the only
child of very pious parents, suffered from their
Puritan restrictiveness from his earliest days.
Although he rebelled in adolescence against
middle-class morality, leaving home for a bohemian love-life in the Edinburgh slums, he was
soon suppressed by it again, this time at the hands
of his wife, the highly respectable Fanny Osborne
Stevenson. Since he required her services as his
amanuensis, it gradually developed that both his
work and his personal correspondence were
regimented and censored by her.

Unfortunately, Elwin's scanty documentation
makes it hard to determine the accuracy of his
view of the author's personal life.[7] However, we
do know that Stevenson had been long familiar
with the story of Deacon Brodie, an Edinburgh
cabinet maker by day and burglar by night, and as
early as 1865 he was at work on a drama based on
the man's life. (He later completed the work with
W. E. Henley, titling it, ***Deacon Brodie, or the
Double Life.***) Then, in 1883 he wrote "**The Travelling Companion,**" a ghastly horror story which
was rejected by his publisher and afterward
destroyed by the author. He called it a "carrion
tale" in a letter to Colvin in 1888, and elsewhere
explained his reasons for writing it: "I had long
been trying to write a story on this subject, to find
a body, a vehicle, for that strong sense of man's
double being which must at times come in upon
and overwhelm the mind of every thinking
creature. I had even written one, "**The Travelling
Companion**" . . . which I burned the other day
on the ground that it was not a work of genius,
and that ***Jekyll*** had supplanted it."[8] Two other
stories, "**Olalla**" and "**Markheim,**" both published in 1885, also fall into this category.

But biographical references alone will not
explain Stevenson's preoccupation with the theme
of man's double nature. As suggested earlier, Dr.
Jekyll bears a close family resemblance to the
Gothic romances of the late eighteenth century, a
resemblance in respect both to the theme of
double personality and their similar wide depar-

ture from the realism of the orthodox novel.[9] *The Castle of Otranto, Vathek, The Italian, Caleb Williams, The Monk,* and many other stories feature outrageous villains whose abrupt and inexplicable transformations from a state of uncontrollable passion to that of heartfelt remorse indicate the dual personality in almost as virulent a form as Jekyll's. Vathek is cursed by his mother—herself unflaggingly evil—as a "two-headed, four-legged monster."[10] And Caleb Williams likens human beings in general to "those twin-births that have two heads indeed, and four hands."[11] This characteristic theme of the romances suggests a central concern of modern writers to document the dualism by examining particularly the disjunct passion and reason which have remained, pretty much throughout the modern period, alien to each other like the two sealed and separate chambers of the Gothic personality.

The romance declined at the turn of the century, but the dualism that was its principal motif was taken up by all the major Romantic poets. Wordsworth and Coleridge tailored it to fit what they felt was the schism between the ineffable imagination and the demands of reason, and the same rift is apparent in countless poems of Byron, Shelley, and Keats (*Childe Harold, Alastor,* and *Lamia,* to name just a few). Not unexpectedly, the prose romances of this period, Mary Shelley's *Frankenstein* and James Hogg's *Justified Sinner,* embody the same Romantic paradox, and, what is more interesting for this discussion, the situation of the principal characters in these books strikingly anticipates that of the scientist-cum-devil in Stevenson's tale.

It might seem to make little sense to speak of Gothicism per se in connection with the greater part of the Victorian era, but we do find there countless instances of the "double" motif. Such poems as Tennyson's "The Two Voices" and "Supposed Confessions" and Browning's *Pauline* and *Sordello* embody the Romantic paradox, but with this difference: what had been for the earlier poets a problem with a transcendental dimension (the struggle between imagination and reason) was here brought down to earth and conceived as a problem of personal faith vs. social responsibility. For it is a commonplace of our understanding of the period that the Victorian writer wanted above all to "stay in touch." Comparing his situation with that of his immediate predecessors, he recognized that indulgence in a self-centered idealism was no longer viable in a society which ever more insistently urged total involvement in its occupations. The world was waiting to be improved

upon, and solved, and everyone, poets included, had to busy themselves and "make up their minds on as many matters as possible."[12] For the most part, they did make up their minds, though often at great cost, as may be seen in the crisis-marked personal histories of men like Newman, Mill, and Carlyle, as well as Tennyson and Browning.

In the Brontës' novels many commentators see a development of the Gothic romance tradition.[13] But if Heathcliff and Rochester seem unremittingly Gothic for a time, all passionate intensity, they are both, after all, "resolved" at the end, the one by death, the other by a civilizing union with Jane. The fact is, it was becoming more and more difficult for the artist to unite conflicting impulses through social commitment, as the older Victorians had. In Arnold as in Clough, there is scarcely a poem that does not reduce thematically to a long and perversely unsettled dialogue of the mind with itself, despite both poets' anxiety to put their talents to some social purpose. About the time of Dickens' *Our Mutual Friend,* probably the last major Victorian work which places a high value on the achievement of a stable personal identity, a species of resigned acceptance of ambiguity, apparent particularly in the poems of Rossetti and Thomson, became the rule. Thus, toward the end of the century the conflict was more often expressed as a psychological than a moral problem, a development that may be traced in such works as Hardy's *Tess* and *Jude the Obscure,* Wilde's *Dorian Gray,* Beerbohm's *The Happy Prince,* Conrad's *Lord Jim,* in many poems by Yeats, Dowson, and Johnson, and in, of course, *Jekyll and Hyde.*

Of all the enormous output of the 1890s it is the Stevenson work which, unluckily, has given us a convenient epithet ("Jekyll-and-Hyde") for the post-Freudian with an unhappy double self. Paradoxically, Stevenson was too successful, both in his story-idea and in what has come to be a silly name for it: by that silly name we have been diverted from reading what should have great interest for us. By far the largest part of that interest lies in the vision the book conjures of the late Victorian wasteland, truly a de-Hyde-rated land unfit to sustain a human being simultaneously in an honorable public life and a joyful private one.

Notes

1. "Robert Louis Stevenson," first published in the *Century Magazine,* April 1888, and reprinted in *Henry James and Robert Louis Stevenson: A Record of Friendship and Criticism,* ed. Janet Adam Smith (London, 1948), p. 155.

2. (New York, 1928), p. 53.

3. *Robert Louis Stevenson* (Norfolk, 1947), p. 13.

4. My references throughout are to the Vailima Edition, the seventh volume of which contains *Dr. Jekyll and Mr. Hyde*. The chapters are not numbered in this edition, but I have done so here for ease of reference.

5. Dr. Lanyon's fate bears a strong resemblance to Captain Brierly's in *Lord Jim*.

6. Chesterton, p. 53.

7. Professor Bradford Booth has informed me that his forthcoming edition of Stevenson's letters will correct Mr. Elwin's views on many matters. The work is not available to me at this writing, and in any case additional biographical data would add little to my reading of the story.

8. "A Chapter on Dreams," *Works*, XII, 247.

9. In this connection, Stevenson's essays on the nature of the romance and the novel—"A Gossip on Romance," "A Note on Realism," "A Humble Remonstrance," etc.—might profitably be compared with the pronouncements on the same subject, about a century earlier, by the romancers Horace Walpole, Clara Reeve, and Sir Walter Scott, and with Hawthorne's Preface to *The House of the Seven Gables*. So considered, the development of the romance is seen to parallel that of the orthodox realistic novel. While remaining clearly distinguishable throughout the greater part of the nineteenth century, the two merge in the last decade to form the new symbolic novel.

10. *Vathek*, 3rd ed. (London, 1816), p. 176.

11. *Caleb Williams* (London, 1831), p. 420.

12. Geoffrey Tillotson, *Thakeray the Novelist* (Cambridge, 1954), p. 60.

13. See, for example, "Charlotte Brontë's 'New' Gothic" by Robert E. Heilman in *From Jane Austen to Joseph Conrad*, ed. Robert C. Rathburn and Martin Steinmann, Jr. (Minnesota, 1958), pp. 118-132.

JOYCE CAROL OATES (ESSAY DATE 1990)

SOURCE: Oates, Joyce Carol. "Foreword." In *The Strange Case of Dr. Jekyll and Mr. Hyde*, by Robert Louis Stevenson, pp. ix-xviii. Lincoln: University of Nebraska Press, 1990.

In the following essay, Oates discusses The Strange Case of Dr. Jekyll and Mr. Hyde *and some of its literary precedents and descendents within the framework of Victorian morality.*

Like such mythopoetic figures as Frankenstein, Dracula, and, even, Alice ("in Wonderland"), Dr.-Jekyll-and-Mr.-Hyde has become, in the century following the publication of Robert Louis Stevenson's famous novella, what might be called an autonomous creation. That is, people who have never read the novella—people who do not in fact "read" at all—know by way of popular culture who Jekyll-Hyde is. (Though they are apt to speak of him, not altogether accurately, as two disparate beings: *Dr.* Jekyll, *Mr.* Hyde.) A character out of prose fiction, Jekyll-Hyde seems nonetheless autogenetic in the way that vampires and werewolves and (more benignly) fairies seem autogenetic: surely he has always existed in the collective imagination, or, like Jack the Ripper, in actual history? (As "Dracula" is both the specific creation of the novelist Bram Stoker and a nightmare figure out of middle European history.) It is ironic that, in being so effaced, Robert Louis Stevenson has become immortalized by way of his private fantasy—which came to him, by his own testimony, unbidden, in a dream.

The Strange Case of Dr. Jekyll and Mr. Hyde (1886) will strike contemporary readers as a characteristically Victorian moral parable, not nearly so sensational (nor so piously lurid) as Stoker's *Dracula*; in the tradition, perhaps, of Mary Shelley's *Frankenstein*, in which a horrific tale is conscientiously subordinated to the author's didactic intention. Though melodramatic in conception it is not melodramatic in execution since virtually all its scenes are narrated and summarized after the fact. There is no ironic ambiguity, no Wildean subtlety, in the doomed Dr. Jekyll's confession: he presents himself to the reader as a congenital "double dealer" who has nonetheless "an almost morbid sense of shame" and who, in typically Victorian middle-class fashion, must act to dissociate "himself" (i.e., his reputation as a highly regarded physician) from his baser instincts. He can no longer bear to suppress them and it is impossible to eradicate them. His discovery that "Man is not truly one, but two" is seen to be a scientific fact, not a cause for despair. (And, in time, it may be revealed that man is "a mere polity of multifarious, incongruous and independent denizens"—which is to say that the ego contains multitudes: multiple personalities inhabit us all. It cannot be incidental that Robert Louis Stevenson was himself a man enamoured of consciously playing roles and assuming personae: his friend Arthur Symons said of him that he was "never really himself except when he was in some fantastic disguise.")

Thus Dr. Jekyll's uncivilized self, to which he gives the symbolic name Hyde, is at once the consequence of a scientific experiment (as the creation of Frankenstein's monster was a scientific experiment) and a shameless indulgence of appetites that cannot be assimilated into the propriety of everyday Victorian life. There is a sense in which Hyde, for all his monstrosity, is but an addiction like alcohol, nicotine, drugs: "The moment I choose," Dr. Jekyll says, "I can be rid of him." Hyde must be hidden not simply because he is wicked but because Dr. Jekyll is a willfully good man—an example to others, like the much-admired lawyer Mr. Utterson who is "lean, long, dusty, dreary and yet somehow [improbably?] lovable." Had the Victorian ideal been less hypocritically ideal or had Dr. Jekyll been content with a less perfect public reputation his tragedy would not have occurred. (As Wilde's Basil Hallward says in *The Picture of Dorian Gray*: "We in our madness have separated the two [body and soul] and have invented a realism that is vulgar, and an ideality that is void." The key term here is surely "madness.")

Dr. Jekyll's initial experience, however, approaches ecstasy as if he were, indeed, discovering the Kingdom of God that lies within. The magic drug causes nausea and a grinding in the bones and a "horror of the spirit that cannot be exceeded at the hour of birth or death." Then:

> I came to myself as if out of a great sickness. There was something strange in my sensations, something indescribably new and, from its very novelty, incredibly sweet. I felt younger, lighter, happier in body; within I was conscious of a heady recklessness, a current of disordered sensual images running like a mill race in my fancy, a solution of the bonds of obligation, an unknown but not an innocent freedom of the soul. I knew myself, at the first breath of this new life, to be more wicked, tenfold more wicked, sold a slave to my original evil; and the thought, in that moment, braced and delighted in me like wine.

Unlike Frankenstein's monster, who is nearly twice the size of an average man, Jekyll's monster is dwarfed: "less robust and less developed" than the good self since Jekyll's rigorouly suppressed life has been the consequence of unrelenting "effort, virtue and control." (Stevenson's anatomy of the human psyche is as grim as Freud's—virtually all a "good" man's waking energies are required in beating back and denying the "badness" in him!) That Hyde's frenzied pleasures are even in part specifically sexual is never confirmed, given the Victorian cast of the narrative itself, but, to extrapolate from an incident recounted by an eyewitness, one is led to suspect they are: Hyde is observed running down a ten-year-old girl in the street and calmly trampling over her body. Much is made subsequently of the girl's "screaming"; and of the fact that money is paid to her family as recompense for her violation.

Viewed from without Hyde is detestable in the abstract: "I never saw a man I so disliked," Jekyll's friend Enfield says, "and yet I scarce know why. He must be deformed somewhere. . . ." Another witness testifies to his mysteriously intangible deformity "without any nameable malformation." But when Jekyll looks in the mirror he is conscious of no repugnance, "rather of a leap of welcome. This, too, was myself. It seemed natural and human." When Jekyll returns to himself after having been Hyde he is plunged into wonder rather than remorse at his "vicarious depravity." The creature summoned out of his soul and sent forth to do his pleasure is a being "inherently malign and villainous; his every act and thought centered on self; drinking pleasure with bestial avidity from any degree of torture to another; relentless like a man of stone." Yet Hyde is safely *other*—"It was Hyde, after all, and Hyde alone, that was guilty."

Oscar Wilde's equally didactic but far more suggestive and poetic *The Picture of Dorian Gray* (1890) makes the disturbing point that Dorian Gray, the *unblemished* paragon of evil, "is the type of which the age is searching for, and what it is afraid it has found." (Just as Wilde's Lord Henry defends insincerity "as a method by which we can multiply our personalities.") By contrast Jekyll's Hyde is a very nearly Bosch-like creature, proclaiming his wickedness to the naked eye as if, in Utterson's words, he is a "troglodyte . . . the mere radiance of a foul soul that thus transpires through, and transfigures, its clay continent." One is reminded of nineteenth-century theories of criminology advanced by C. S. Lombroso and Henry Maudsley, among others, who argued that outward physical defects and deformities are the visible signs of inward and invisible faults: the criminal is a type that can be easily identified by experts. Dr. Jekyll is the more reprehensible in his infatuation with Hyde in that, as a well-trained physician, he should have recognized at once the telltale symptoms of mental and moral degeneracy in his alter ego's very face.

By degrees, like any addict, Jekyll surrenders his autonomy. His ego ceases being "I" and splits into two distinct and eventually warring selves, which share memory as they share a common body. Only after Hyde commits murder does Jekyll make the effort to regain control; but by this time, of course, it is too late. What had been "Jekyll"—that precarious cuticle of a self, that field of tensions in perpetual opposition to desire—has irrevocably split. It is significant that the narrator of Jekyll's confession speaks of both Jekyll and Hyde as if from the outside. And with a passionate eloquence otherwise absent from Stevenson's prose:

> The powers of Hyde seemed to have grown with the sickliness of Jekyll. And certainly the hate that now divided them was equal on each side. With Jekyll, it

was a thing of vital instinct. He had now seen the full deformity of that creature that shared with him some of the phenomena of consciousness, and was co-heir with him to death: and beyond these links of community, which in themselves made the most poignant part of his distress, he thought of Hyde, for all his energy of life, as of something not only hellish but inorganic. This was the shocking thing; that the slime of the pit seemed to utter cries and voices; that the amorphous dust gesticulated and sinned; that what was dead, and had no shape, should usurp the offices of life. And this again, that that insurgent horror was knit to him closer than a wife, closer than an eye; lay caged in his flesh, where he heard it mutter and felt it struggle to be born; and at every hour of weakness, and in the confidence of slumber, prevailed against him, and deposed him out of life.

"Think of it," Jekyll had gloated at the start, "—I did not even exist!" And the purely metaphorical becomes literally true.

The Strange Case of Dr. Jekyll and Mr. Hyde, though stimulated by a dream, is not without its literary antecedents: among them Edgar Allan Poe's "William Wilson" (1839), in which, paradoxically, the "evil" self is the narrator and the "good" self, or conscience, the double; and Charles Dickens's uncompleted *The Mystery of Edwin Drood* (1870), in which the Choirmaster Jack Jasper, an opium addict, oscillates between "good" and "evil" impulses in his personality with an anguish so convincingly calibrated as to suggest that, had Dickens lived to complete the novel, it would have been one of his masterpieces—and would have made ***The Strange Case of Dr. Jekyll and Mr. Hyde*** redundant. Cautionary tales of malevolent, often diabolical doubles abound in folklore and oral tradition, and in Plato's *Symposium* it was whimsically suggested that each human being has a double to whom he was once *physically* attached—a bond of Eros that constituted in fact a third, and higher, sex in which male and female were conjoined.

The visionary starkness of ***The Strange Case of Dr. Jekyll and Mr. Hyde*** anticipates that of Freud in such late melancholy meditations as *Civilization and Its Discontents* (1929-30): there is a split in man's psyche between ego and instinct, between civilization and "nature," and the split can never be healed. Freud saw ethics as a reluctant concession of the individual to the group, veneer of a sort overlaid upon an unregenerate primordial self. The various stratagems of culture—including, not incidentally, the "sublimation" of raw aggression by way of art and science—are ultimately powerless to contain the discontent, which must erupt at certain periodic times, on a collective scale, as war. Stevenson's quintessentially Victo-

rian parable is unique in that the protagonist initiates his tragedy of doubleness out of a fully lucid sensibility—one might say a scientific sensibility. Dr. Jekyll knows what he is doing, and why he is doing it, though he cannot, of course, know how it will turn out. What is unquestioned throughout the narrative, by either Jekyll or his circle of friends, is mankind's fallen nature: sin is *original,* and *irremediable.* For Hyde, though hidden, will not remain so. And when Jekyll finally destroys him he must destroy Jekyll too.

MATTHEW C. BRENNAN (ESSAY DATE 1997)

SOURCE: Brennan, Matthew C. "Robert Louis Stevenson's *Dr. Jekyll and Mr. Hyde.*" In *The Gothic Psyche: Disintegration and Growth in Nineteenth-Century English Literature*, pp. 97-112. Columbia, S.C.: Camden House, 1997.

In the following essay, Brennan surveys critical reaction to The Strange Case of Dr. Jekyll and Mr. Hyde *and offers a psychological and cultural approach to the novella.*

Published in 1886—a decade before Freud's *Interpretation of Dreams*—Robert Louis Stevenson's ***The Strange Case of Dr. Jekyll and Mr. Hyde*** has long been read as a stunning example of the dual nature of the human personality. Frequently Stevenson's tale gets grouped with the literature of the double, which includes late-Victorian, early-modern works such as Joseph Conrad's "Secret Sharer" (1910) and Oscar Wilde's *The Picture of Dorian Gray* (1891) as well as earlier Gothic fiction—James Hogg's *Confessions of a Justified Sinner* (1824) and Edgar Allan Poe's "William Wilson" (1845). Stevenson himself wrote that he spent years searching for a story that could embody his "strong sense of man's double being."[1] A few commentators, such as Jeremy Hawthorn and Morton Prince, have narrowly viewed the physical splitting of Henry Jekyll into Edward Hyde as a literal case of multiple personality. But this interpretation stresses not the universality of the story but rather—given the rarity of such a mental disorder—the incredible unlikelihood that one of your friendly neighbors just might be Jack the Ripper. A more fitting and imaginative psychological view is Carl Jung's. He identifies Jekyll's transformation as a case of "dissociation," a neurotic splitting in the psyche that threatened many repressed Victorians and that results from an unresolved projection of the *shadow*, a term Jung uses for unconscious elements of the personality that are either unpleasant or undeveloped.[2] For while Stevenson could not have been fully aware of the implications for modern psychology that his novel uncannily reveals, like Jung he clearly understood that the transformation of the scientist into a dwarfish, repulsive shadow is really metaphorical. It is metaphorical of the relationship between the unconscious and conscious sides of the psyche; accordingly, it depicts what happens to the psyche when it fails to achieve balance or—to use Jung's term—*individuation* and instead risks the open mental boundaries and self-fragmentation of schizophrenia.

Significantly, like other novelists in the Gothic tradition who paid close attention to the workings of their unconscious and used this intuitive knowledge to construct their plots, Stevenson drew heavily on his dream life. Not surprisingly, then, many of his attitudes toward his own "double being" anticipate Jungian ideas about the unconscious. In the essay **"A Chapter on Dreams"** (*Across the Plains,* 1892), Stevenson speaks of his "double life" as a college student, when he had dreams not only "more vivid" "than any printed book," but a "dream life" that "he had no means of proving to be false." Indeed, he goes so far as to maintain that his "Brownies"—who populate and personify his unconscious—"do one-half" of his creative work while he sleeps. In fact, since his "conscience ego" [*sic*] is "bemired up to the ears in actuality," he may be "no story-teller at all." If that is true, Stevenson concludes, "the whole of my published fiction" is "the single-handed product of some Brownie, . . . some unseen collaborator." The prime example of Stevenson's literary appropriation of dreams is of course *Dr. Jekyll.* Just as Horace Walpole and Mary Shelley found inspiration for their Gothic novels in their own nightmares and reveries, so too did Stevenson finally find his story of humanity's dual nature in his own unconscious. After two days of racking his brains for a plot, he dreamed the essence of his novel, his so-called "Gothic gnome": first, "the scene at the window" when Richard Enfield and Gabriel Utterson pass by Jekyll's house and speak with him through an open window until they glimpse the start of a transformation; and next, "a scene afterwards split in two, in which Hyde, pursued for some crime" (the murder of Sir Danvers Carew), takes "the powder" and undergoes "the change in the presence of his pursuers" (who in the novel are reduced to Dr. Hastie Lanyon, the sole witness of Jekyll's transformation).[3]

Given the importance Stevenson places on dreams, the unconscious, and "man's double being," Jung's psychology proves a useful lens

FROM THE AUTHOR

STEVENSON ON HIS DEDICATION IN *DR. JEKYLL AND MR. HYDE*

Dearest Katharine, Here, on a very little book and accompanied with your lame verses, I have put your name. Our kindness is now getting well on in years; it must be nearly of age; and it gets more valuable to me with every time I see you. It is not possible to express any sentiment, and it is not necessary to try at least between us. You know very well that I love you dearly, and that I always will. I only wish the verses were better, but at least you like the story; and it is sent to you by the one that loves you—Jekyll and not Hyde.

R.L.S.

SOURCE: Stevenson, Robert Louis. An excerpt from a letter to Katharine de Mattos: 1 January 1886. In *Selected Letters of Robert Louis Stevenson,* edited by Ernest Mehew, p. 297. New Haven, Conn.: Yale University Press, 1886.

through which to interpret the novel. Because Jung's theory of individuation and dream analysis outlines a process of psychic growth, it illuminates how the Gothic psyche becomes decentered and ultimately self-disintegrates. As in *Dr. Jekyll,* the Gothic generally shows the importance of recognizing and integrating the unknown inner selves of the psyche; specifically, it dramatizes the psychological damage that results when the conscious personality denies its shadow, just as Jekyll denies his dark side, Hyde. The cautionary tale of *Dr. Jekyll,* then, clearly demonstrates the reader's need to assimilate the shadow into consciousness, and not only through its disastrous conclusion, in which Stevenson's hero destroys himself—and his doubled shadow—by rejecting it as other. The novel also manifests the need in other ways: through Jekyll's discovery of man's dual nature; through Jekyll's subsequent repression and deterioration and Hyde's simultaneous growth; and finally, through Hastie Lanyon's and Gabriel Utterson's contrasting responses to Jekyll's Hyde. Like Walton in *Frankenstein,* Utterson elicits the identification of the Gothic reader, who attends like Utterson to the cautionary tales of Jekyll and Lanyon and learns of the urgent need to understand what nightmares teach about "man's double being."

Jekyll's "Double Being"

Despite his eventual psychic disintegration, Henry Jekyll begins life auspiciously both professionally and personally; moreover, by scientifically pursuing the nature of his own double consciousness, he seems to entwine these often opposed sides of personality in a way that might have led to individuation, much as did Jung's own exploration of the unconscious, both his patients' and his own. Like Victor Frankenstein—a scientist whose work and character resemble Henry's—Dr. Jekyll was blessed by both nature and nurture: "I was born," he writes in his "Full Statement of the Case," in the 1800s "to a large fortune, endowed besides with excellent parts, inclined by nature to industry, fond of the respect of the wise and good among my fellowmen, and thus, as might have been supposed, with every guarantee of an honourable and distinguished future" (69). Like Victor's, Henry's ambition, training, and personal habits coincide to produce a major scientific discovery that extends the boundaries of human knowledge: whereas Frankenstein uncovers the origins of generation, thus bridging the boundary of life and death, Jekyll discovers the unconscious. Personally, Jekyll commits himself to duplicity, hiding his desires for pleasure—what he innocuously calls an "impatient gaiety" (69)—while adopting a persona crafted to advance him professionally, a head held high and "a more than commonly grave countenance" (69). These traits—arrogant ambition, moral righteousness, and awareness of his socially unacceptable desires—couple with his interest in transcendental medicine to help him find what no other scientist had seen: "that man is not truly one, but truly two"; furthermore, Jekyll recognizes that "of the two natures that contended in the field of [his] consciousness," he "could rightly be said to be either" one—the reputable, accomplished scientist or the profane, sensual primitive—"only because," he concludes, "I was radically both" (70).

Jekyll's ability to perceive and admit his duplicity, his public persona and private shadow, makes him unusually self-aware for a Victorian. He believes he "was in no sense a hypocrite" (70), and certainly before his experiment got out of hand he could be clearly distinguished from the typically repressed yet dutiful gentleman. Take, for instance, Enfield—"the well-known man about town" (6). When he encounters Hyde while walking home at 3:00 A.M., he loathes him "at first sight," comparing him to Satan. He reacts so negatively to Hyde partly because he has apparently just spent the night in taverns and brothels—a common, unacknowledged pastime of proper gentlemen, such as John Fowles's Charles Smithson in *The French Lieutenant's Woman*, who, though engaged to Ernestina Freeman, passes a wild night first getting drunk at his men's club and then picking up a prostitute. Consequently, to keep such carousing hidden in its place, the typical Victorian home served not only as a temple of domestic virtues, as Walter Houghton observes, but also, Irving Saposnik notes, as a screen "from the all-seeing eye of Mrs. Grundy." Caught away from home, the morally indignant Enfield covers up the exposure of his recent adventures by collaring Hyde after he tramples a little girl (8). And though Victorians like Enfield shrank from admitting their own duality, they faced duality daily in their city: one mid-century minister speaks of London as "at once the emporium of crime and the palladium of Christianity. . . . It is here that [virtue and vice] join issue in the most deadly proximity."[4]

Jekyll, then, proves extraordinarily courageous in facing his shadow. Like Jung, who explains in *Memories, Dreams, Reflections* that his reading of Faust awakened in him "the problem of opposites, of good and evil, of mind and matter, of light and darkness," Jekyll's experiments in transcendental medicine and reflections on his own dual nature evoke awareness of what Jung describes as "the dark side of his being, his sinister shadow," and his "own inner contradictions." "For most people," Joseph L. Henderson explains, "the dark or negative side of the personality remains unconscious,"[5] and to recognize it, Jung emphasizes in *Aion*, requires "considerable moral effort."[6] Unlike Jekyll, Enfield and Lanyon—two representative male Victorians—cannot bear to face their shadows, which they project onto Hyde. But facing the shadow is the first crucial step toward psychic integration.

In Jungian psychology, the first stage of the individuation process involves the experience of the shadow, whose sex usually matches that of the ego personality. The shadow is either symbolized by an inward figure, as in a Gothic dream like Stevenson's, or projected onto an actual figure met in the phenomenal world (*Psychology and Religion*, C.W. 11:75-79). Much as Mary Shelley represents the relations between Victor and his monster, Stevenson depicts Jekyll's experience with Hyde as both an inward image and an outward projection. On the one hand, Hyde is a "familiar" Jekyll "called out of [his] own soul" (76), "a brute that slept within" his nightmarish unconscious (86). On the other hand, he is a projection (74, 78) whose external existence as a real person is verified legally in Jekyll's will and socially by numerous people—the bank and the police as well as Jekyll's servants and even his friends and acquaintances such as Enfield, Lanyon, and Utterson. As either projection or dream image, Hyde embodies Jekyll's shadow—unpleasant, inferior traits, undeveloped or stunted functions, and contents of the personal unconscious that Jekyll has hidden and repressed; Hyde is the alter ego Jekyll had submerged in the unconscious while advancing his public career. However, in actively recognizing and retrieving his shadow from decades of repression, Jekyll stands on the threshold of overcoming his inferiority by assimilating Hyde into consciousness and thereby centering his imbalanced Self.

As Jekyll's shadow, Hyde represents more than just a buried capacity for evil; he manifests various weaknesses that Jekyll needs to recognize and correct as well as some positive qualities he has let atrophy. During an early transformation, Jekyll peers into a mirror—a common symbol of identity—and sees the smaller, younger, darker side of himself; though Hyde differs from Jekyll in appearance, when beholding the shadow Jekyll does not lose his identity. Rather, he deepens it, acknowledging that the "ugly idol in the glass" also lays claim to his psyche: "This, too," Jekyll confesses, "was myself" (73). Though Jekyll labels Hyde "pure evil," he recognizes that all humans "are commingled out of good and evil" (74), just as Jung writes that there is no doubt that humanity is "on the whole less good than" it "imagines" itself "or wants to be" (C.W. 11:76). However, at first, Hyde's worst sins amount merely to what Jekyll had been repressing: the desire for "gaiety." Jekyll recounts how while young he indulged "a certain gaiety of disposition," then later "concealed [his] pleasures" (69). Hyde initially indulges in "pleasures" that are simply "undignified" (76), perhaps less blamable than Enfield's unnamed nocturnal peccadilloes. In any case, this unleashed desire for pleasure compensates for "the dryness" and "self-denying toils" of the scientist's "life of study" (75, 82), and Hyde's self-centered intentions balance Jekyll's reputation as a self-sacrificing do-gooder (10).

Besides these negative aspects, Hyde, like Frankenstein's monster, also contains positive qualities—either undeveloped or lost—that Jekyll needs to assimilate to balance his personality. For one thing, when transformed as Hyde, Jekyll overcomes the "renunciation" and "restrictions of natural life" (82) demanded by his profession. He feels "natural" and "human" as Hyde (73), not only "younger, lighter" and "happier in body" (72) but also "livelier" in "spirit" (73). Hyde reconnects Jekyll to his primitive, sensual instincts and thus elicits eyewitness comparisons to "apes" (27, 88) and "a monkey" (52)—images of humanity's all but forgotten primordial roots that circulating ideas of Darwinian atavism surely brought to Stevenson's attention. As Jung puts it in *Psychology and Religion*, "We carry our past with us," namely "the primitive and inferior man with his desires and emotions." So if the shadow is inferior, it is not "obviously evil," for it includes primitive, childish traits that can "vitalize" an overly rational, conscious personality (C.W. 11:76-78).[7]

Accordingly, Jekyll needs to integrate Hyde into consciousness because what he represents compensates for Jekyll's overdeveloped scientific and moral persona. Jekyll grounds this side of himself on logos, which Jung describes as the male principle, comprising discrimination, cognition, detachment, and knowledge (C.W. 9.ii:14, 16; 13:41). Conversely, Jekyll's personality excludes eros, the feminine principle that encompasses human connectedness and relatedness. This imbalance inflates his ego and creates his vulnerability to divided consciousness, for while the noninflated ego retains the potential to align itself with the Self, the inflated ego appropriates the Self. According to Edward F. Edinger, inflation of the ego becomes apparent when someone "is transcending proper human limits." Clearly Jekyll's transcendental medicine, with its "high views," "exacting . . . aspirations" (69), and boundary-breaking experiments that no scientist can duplicate, feeds his inflation, just as Frankenstein's scientific ambitions to cross the boundary of life and death reveal his godlike inflation. Other symptoms of inflation that fit Jekyll are "too much arrogance," too much "altruism," and—especially in the guise of Hyde—too much selfishness.[8] Hyde, then, presents Jekyll with a chance to adjust his attitude toward the parts of his psyche that he has been neglecting: his senses, his instincts, and his natural desires.

Several critics have argued that what Jekyll represses and then lets out through Hyde is the desire for pleasure, sex in particular. Stevenson, however, insisted that "Hyde was not . . . a mere voluptuary" and that even if he were, "there is no harm in a voluptuary." Moreover, "the harm was in Jekyll"—not Hyde—and it was "because he was a hypocrite—not because he was fond of women." The almost complete absence of women in the novel does suggest that Jekyll has repressed his sexuality, even if Stevenson never indicates it.[9] More important, though, the lack of women in the novel underscores Jekyll's underdeveloped eros. While he manages to achieve consciousness of his shadow problem, he never so much as glimpses his deeper psychological problem—an undeveloped anima. In this way, Henry is like the Gothic protagonist Victor Frankenstein, who also distorts his rational, scientific faculties to the obsessive point of almost completely withdrawing from society and, as a result, allows his unresolved shadow problem with the Monster to deepen into an anima complex involving his dead mother, Caroline, the mother-substitute Justine, and his "more than sister"/fiancée, Elizabeth.

Barbara Hannah remarks on "the absence of any important feminine figures" in *Dr. Jekyll,* but perhaps she goes too far in asserting that the only anima figure is "Hyde's purely negative land-lady."[10] In fact, three females appear in Stevenson's narrative, and each signals Jekyll's detachment from the feminine principle. The little girl that Hyde tramples is running to get a doctor when their paths abruptly and violently intersect (8), a suggestion that Jekyll's anima is not only unripe but also in dire need of nurturing and healing. Later we learn of the old woman who lives in Hyde's Soho apartment building; her distaste for Hyde as well as her advanced age and infertility imply that Jekyll's anima is hopelessly barren (29-30). Though seemingly contradictory, both these images of the anima convey infertility. The most revealing anima figure, however, is the maid who witnesses Hyde's murder of Sir Danvers Carew. Before it happens, Stevenson describes her as romantically gazing out her window at the moon, a common symbol of the feminine and, through its circular shape, a sign of the wholeness of the Self. She notes the gentleness of the old man, whose stature as member of Parliament and inherent civility link him with the Wise Old Man archetype. When Hyde destroys him and the maid loses consciousness, it is as if Hyde were destroying Jekyll's last chance to consciously connect with his anima and to center his Self (26-27). So while Jekyll's intellectual detachment entails avoidance of sex, his lack of sex is really a symptom of a greater deficiency—an undeveloped eros, an anima undifferentiated in the unconscious. In reacting to Hyde's uncontrollable, murderous violence, Jekyll goes into seclusion. Thus Jekyll is

as far away as could be from the Sacred Marriage, which symbolizes the integration of logos and eros and constitutes individuation of the Self.[11] It is no surprise that during Jekyll's last days sequestered in the lab, the butler says he hears "*it* weeping," "weeping like a woman or a lost soul" (54, my emphasis). In the end of his Gothic nightmare, Jekyll not only loses the chance to eventually expand his identity to include the shadow and anima (the feminine or soul-image he loses); he even loses identity altogether, which becomes undifferentiated from the "it" (Id) of oceanic unconsciousness.

Jekyll's Self-Destructive Repression of Hyde

But before a man can face and attempt to absorb the anima, he must successfully assimilate the shadow, which Jekyll fails to do. To be sure, Jekyll bravely delves into his unconscious, acknowledging his dark side as an element of his dual identity. Jekyll's problem is that he fails to incorporate his shadow, and instead—after his initial delight in renewing long-repressed pleasures and instincts—he rejects Hyde as other. As Jung points out—to cite Anthony Storr—the acts of bringing "the repressed tendencies" into conscious awareness and of "confessing the less desirable aspects of personality which the shadow portrays [do] not rid us of them."[12] Indeed, rather than trying to integrate his shadow, Jekyll tries to get rid of it. First he turns his scientific efforts toward separating the dual elements of his psyche (71), and then, when Hyde turns from being merely merry to monstrous, he tries to repress him. And though initially Jekyll seems successful, he really only worsens his psychosis, intensifying the imbalance of his Gothic psyche.

Despite realizing that his "two natures" contend in the same "field" of "consciousness," Jekyll finds this consciousness an "agonised womb" and so wants to dissociate "these polar twins." He decides to house each in a "separate" identity (70-71). Accordingly, he furnishes Hyde with his own separate residence in Soho. Until the murder of Carew, Jekyll's separation seems to work, as he counters his dry life in the lab with Hyde's selfish pleasures, drawing vicarious amusement from them. Through his dual identities, Jekyll brags, he "could plod in the public eye with a load of genial respectability" and by drinking his potion could "doff at once the body of the noted professor," springing "headlong" as Hyde "into the sea of liberty" (75). This comment of Jekyll's describes his psychological state when Utterson finds him "quite at ease" after one of the "pleasant dinners" (23) the doctor gives just before the murder.

However, by separating his identity as Hyde from his identity as Jekyll, the scientist represses Hyde. In turn, this repression creates a growing psychic imbalance and makes Hyde monstrous. The less dignified Hyde's pleasures become, the more Jekyll divides himself from Hyde. Before the murder, Utterson tries to persuade Jekyll, his client as well as his friend, to confide in him about Hyde, but Jekyll insists that it is a "private matter" and refuses to speak of him (25). "Let it sleep," he commands Utterson, as if explicitly urging that they repress all thoughts of Hyde, burying him in the unconscious. After the murder, Jekyll rejects Hyde altogether: he tells Utterson that he is "done with him" and that "I cannot say I care what becomes of Hyde" (33). So divided from Hyde does Jekyll grow that Jekyll "stood at times aghast before the acts of Edward Hyde" and judged "Hyde alone" as "guilty" (76). Hence, having failed to assimilate the shadow, Jekyll begins to resemble Jung's "highly moral people, unaware of their other side, who develop particularly hellish moods" (*Psychology and Religion, C.W.* 11:76). Moreover, by clinging to his moral standing as "Dr. Jekyll," Jekyll refuses to accept Hyde as part of their shared consciousness, a repression that in turn makes Hyde a murderous monster. As Jung explains in *The Practice of Psychotherapy,* the psyche becomes divided and produces "monsters" when consciousness, like Jekyll's, refuses to accept the unconscious. Although "the unconscious is not a demoniacal monster," the shadow "becomes dangerous when our conscious attitude to it is hopelessly wrong," as Jekyll's surely is. Furthermore, Jung adds, "to the degree we repress" the shadow, "its danger increases" (*C.W.* 16:152).

After the murder, Hyde's danger to the terror-stricken Jekyll continuously increases. At this point, Jekyll loses confidence in himself, as he puts it to Utterson (34), and also loses his balance (79, 83) and control of his "original and better self" (79). In effect, his weakening ego begins to collapse into the unconscious. Lanyon diagnoses Jekyll as suffering from "a cerebral disease" (64), and indeed, as if growing psychotic, he loses the ability to distinguish between waking and sleeping—a characteristic common to both schizophrenics and chronic nightmare sufferers whose mental boundaries are thin, open, and permeable. For instance, Jekyll comes "home to [his] own house" "partly in a dream," and when he then slumbers, he is wrung by "nightmares" (86). Moreover, if he goes to sleep as Jekyll, "it was always as Hyde that [he] awakened" (86-87). Other manifestations of the Gothic experience of open boundaries include the fog in Soho that makes Hyde's neighborhood resemble "some city in a nightmare" (28-29) and Jekyll's constant shifting between first and third pronouns to refer to Hyde after the murder (81-85). These images of open boundaries signify that, as Hyde, Jekyll experiences the liminal. In Victor Turner's formulation, the liminal can be creative and regenerative if followed by a stage of reintegration with normal society or, psychologically, with normal consciousness—as it is for Walton in *Frankenstein.* The liminal liberates "human capacities" from social "constraints." However, it also involves danger and disorder and may be the scene of breakdown and destruction. Clearly, for Jekyll, the liminal results in no rebounding or re-membering, only in Gothic disintegration, for he is unable to respond positively to the liminal's duality.[13]

Progressively, then, Hyde the shadow grows bigger the longer he is repressed, and as Jekyll the ego weakens, Hyde's powers strengthen (87). Hyde even assumes the power to transform physically into Jekyll without warning and without pharmaceutical stimulus. This physical autonomy parallels how Jekyll's unconscious dominates his psyche and precipitates his breakdown. Because Jekyll's ego essentially coincides with his persona, as Jung explains in *Psychological Types,* "it can have no conscious relation to the unconscious processes," for in fact "it *is* these processes"; moreover, Jung points out, "anyone who is himself his outward role will infallibly succumb to the inner processes," a situation Jung calls enantiodromia, which literally means "running backwards" and refers to "the emergence of the unconscious opposite" (*C.W.* 6:470, 426). Even before the murder, Jekyll realizes, "That part of me which I had the power of projecting, had lately been much exercised and nourished; it had seemed to me of late as though the body of Edward Hyde had grown in stature . . . and I began to spy a danger that, if this were much prolonged, the balance of my nature might be permanently overthrown" (78-79). Indeed, at the close of this passage, Jekyll intuits that it is already too late, that his ego is sinking into the uroboric unconscious: "All things therefore seemed to point to this; that I was slowly losing hold of my original and better self, and becoming slowly incorporated with my second and worse" (79). He becomes "a creature eaten up" and is "solely occupied by one thought: the horror of my other self" (87). Finally, on the novel's last page, Jekyll's expectation is met, as he ends anticipating the permanent metamorphosis from his form into Hyde's, thereby completing his Gothic disintegration and his ego's collapse into the unconscious.

Lanyon's Disintegration and Utterson's Growth

Like Henry Jekyll, the Scottish doctor Hastie Lanyon—his fellow scientist and estranged friend—experiences a complete psychic, as well as physical, disintegration when faced with the shadow, Mr. Hyde. As Saposnik notes, "Lanyon is afraid to admit vital truths about himself," and when he encounters their symbolic representation in the form of Hyde, "he cannot struggle with their emergence." Saposnik brands Lanyon a "coward," perhaps because, unlike Jekyll, Lanyon cannot even acknowledge the shadow; and Masao Miyoshi, equally harsh with Lanyon, attacks him and the rest of Stevenson's men as "joyless."[14] But I think these critics overstate the flaws in Lanyon's character. If we can trust the omniscient narrator, Lanyon indeed possesses a "geniality" that rests "on genuine feeling" (14). Moreover, considering their strained relations, Lanyon's response to Jekyll's urgent cry for help is not less than generous when, without demanding an explanation, he retrieves a drawer of chemicals from Jekyll's lab, then waits for the "unnamed man" to appear on his doorstep at midnight. And even if his decision to witness Hyde's desperate drinking of the potion smacks of what Hyde calls greedy curiosity (67), to his credit Lanyon has humanely fulfilled Jekyll's opaque request. Rather, then, Lanyon's real flaw is that, like Jekyll, he has repressed part of his personality and developed a one-sided attachment to what is rational, empirical, and conventional. As a result, Lanyon is vulnerable to the sudden unexpected encounter with his shadow, which he has so rigidly repressed and rejected that his Gothic psyche divides, thus making the shadow an ego-consuming monstrosity.

While Lanyon has enjoyed considerable public success as a doctor, he has ignored and left undeveloped other sides of his imbalanced psyche. Like Jekyll, Lanyon is professionally accomplished: Utterson refers to "his crowding patients" and not only locates Lanyon's office in "that citadel of medicine" but precedes Lanyon's name with the epithet "great" (14). His success stems not from ingenious interdisciplinary experimentation that advances knowledge but from a logical, "narrow" adherence to what Jekyll labels "material views" (67). In Jekyll's opinion, Lanyon is an "ignorant" and "hide-bound pedant" (24); he is a kind of logi-cal positivist, like Stoker's Dr. John Seward, who accepts as truth only whatever can be proven empirically, only whatever is sensible and reasonable. Hence, just as Seward rejects Dr. Van Helsing's use of folklore, superstition, and ritual to diagnose and treat Lucy Westenra's "mental condition," Lanyon rejects Jekyll's research in transcendental medicine as "unscientific balderdash" (15). Having overdeveloped his logos—whose principles include cognition and knowledge—Lanyon remains ignorant of his own buried capacities to appreciate the mystical and the intuitive. A lifelong bachelor like Brontë's Lockwood, he also stays blind to the workings of his anima, and this blighted potential contributes to his inability to reconnect with his estranged friend Henry Jekyll. But, as I said of Jekyll, first the shadow must be faced and assimilated. Thus Stevenson symbolizes Lanyon's intolerant view of Jekyll's research, which is mystical and transcendental, in two ways: through the projection of Lanyon's unconscious prejudices and weaknesses onto Hyde, the product of Jekyll's experiment; and through Lanyon's disgust upon seeing Hyde. As Colin Manlove puts it, what Lanyon is "violently responding to is" the Hyde in himself.[15]

Lanyon's inability to deal with his unconscious—and its unpleasant, long-hidden contents—manifests itself both in his repeated repression of Jekyll/Hyde and in the lethal Gothic terror Hyde instills in him. Lanyon can bear to think of Jekyll neither in his conversation nor in his written narrative. When Utterson visits Lanyon after Jekyll has permanently shut himself up in the upstairs lab, Lanyon twice objects to the mention of his former friend. First he tells Utterson, "I wish to see or hear no more of Dr. Jekyll" since he is "quite done with that person" (40)—a telling echo of what Jekyll has previously told Utterson about Hyde (33). Next, more passionately and unreasonably, Lanyon insists, "If you cannot keep clear of [the] accursed topic [of Jekyll], then in God's name, go, for I cannot bear it" (40). Even in his written narrative—which he can control as he cannot control the dialogue with Utterson—Lanyon again twice strains to repress traces of Jekyll/Hyde: he "cannot bring," he says, his "mind to set on paper" what Jekyll told him, for "even in memory," he "cannot . . . dwell on it without a start of horror" (68). As Jung writes, "to the degree we repress" the shadow "its danger increases"; accordingly, the more Lanyon represses Hyde and what he represents as a complement to Lanyon's conscious, logocentric, scientific point of view, the sicker his soul—which means psyche—

becomes. Ultimately, Lanyon betrays the signs of psychic disintegration. Like the mind of a sufferer of nightmares or schizophrenia, his Gothic mind is "submerged in terror" (68). Having witnessed the melting and altering of Hyde's physical boundaries (67-68), Lanyon loses his own psychic integrity, his dissolving mental boundaries mirroring the open, permeable relation of Hyde to Jekyll once Jekyll loses control of his "better self." The haunting images of Jekyll's Gothic destruction even ruin Lanyon's sleep: the "deadliest terror sits by [him] at all hours of day and night," blurring the line between the conscious and the unconscious, a boundary that stays intact in healthy people. Consequently, he realizes he "must die" (68), and like Jekyll, he does, the ego nightmarishly swallowed into the unconscious.

Unlike his scientific friends Lanyon and Jekyll, Gabriel Utterson grows psychologically from the crisis with Edward Hyde, as Walton does from his encounter with Frankenstein and the Monster. Some critics attack Utterson as dishonest and hypocritical, joyless and repressed, and even regressively Oedipal and subversive toward his friends.[16] However, Utterson alone among the novel's characters is able to deepen his self-knowledge and—with obvious limits—use it to help others. It is Utterson's ignorance of Hyde—symbolically a part of his own unconscious—that first drives him on his quest to unmask Hyde and to save Henry Jekyll from Hyde's domination. After learning from Enfield of Hyde's savage stomping of the little girl and of his questionable use of Dr. Jekyll to acquit his liability for it, Utterson, like Stevenson, dreams of Hyde. This presence of Hyde as an image in Utterson's unconscious clearly indicates his role as shadow to Utterson's persona. As with Jekyll and Lanyon, the encounter with Hyde serves to provoke a self-examination in Utterson. But not only does Utterson dream of Hyde, he also remembers the dream and acts on it, thus initiating a process of assimilation that can lead to greater psychic awareness and wholeness. In the Gothic narrative, then, Utterson operates as a go-between with the reader, like Walton in *Frankenstein* and Lockwood in *Wuthering Heights*. Though Utterson is the centered consciousness of Stevenson's third-person narration and not (like Walton) a narrator himself, he nonetheless responds positively to the archetypal images of Jekyll's and Lanyon's cautionary tales; that is, he strives to draw them into consciousness, where they can strengthen his psyche. Like a Gothic reader and a Jungian analyst, Utter-

son attends to Jekyll's and Lanyon's stories and perceives in them what Jung calls "the substratum of" his "own nature."

Following his dream—an unconscious call to broaden his consciousness—Utterson attempts to understand the dream and decides to satisfy his curiosity to see Hyde, decides to "lighten the mystery" and to find "a reason" (16). He resolves to be "Mr. Seek" to compensate for "Mr. Hyde." Consequently, he stands watch waiting for Hyde once again to enter the side entrance to Jekyll's lab, as Enfield saw him do. When Utterson finally catches him, Utterson reacts as do all the others—the "sawbones" doctor, Enfield, Lanyon: he immediately recoils with disgust and identifies Hyde with Satan (18-20), thus projecting his shadow onto him. But unlike the others, Utterson does not repress Hyde to escape his nameless sense of this "foul soul" (20); instead, he passes a sleepless night of self-examination. His encounter with Hyde causes him to exhume from his unconscious the ghosts of his old sins, which humble him. Facing his own repressed shortcomings, Utterson withdraws his projected shadow and realizes that even Hyde must "hide" black secrets. In other words, Utterson knows everyone harbors a dark side, a realization like Jekyll's that all humans have dual natures. Moreover, Utterson understands that only when the dark side is exposed can one's vulnerability to it be outgrown. This intuitive epiphany leads Utterson to prod Jekyll into spending less time "indoors," a place that becomes synonymous with Jekyll's unhealthy solipsistic withdrawal into his unconscious self, Edward Hyde. It is as if Utterson were prodding Jekyll to acknowledge Hyde rather than repress him.

Because this Gothic tale ends abruptly with the discovery of Jekyll and Hyde's death, it remains indeterminate whether Utterson would have progressed toward fuller psychic integrity. From a Jungian point of view, one problem with prognosticating Utterson's psychic fate is that he does not tell his "own wholly personal story," and as Jung maintains in *Memories, Dreams, Reflections*, the patient's story is what is "crucial" to therapy. Moreover, there is no place in the novel where Utterson appears prepared for the second stage of individuation, which when successful results in the assimilation of anima images. In fact, if Jekyll appears remote from the realm of feminine influence, Utterson the avuncular bachelor is cut off from it completely. Still, unlike Jekyll, he maintains a desire to connect with others; most dramatically, when Poole, Jekyll's butler, is leading him to the lab to witness Jekyll's final disintegration, Utterson wishes "to see and touch his fellow-creatures" (46). It seems reasonable to conjecture that Utterson's attempts to balance the inner and outer worlds ensure his survival and sanity, even if they do not guarantee the psychic equilibrium ultimately earned by survivors of Dracula's Gothic nightmare—namely, Mina and Jonathan Harker. Still, several aspects of Utterson's personality point toward his readiness to begin the process of individuation. Besides his dream, he twice exhibits acute intuition. One instance accompanies the desire to connect with fellow creatures while approaching Jekyll's lab: "Struggle as he might," Stevenson reports, "there was borne in upon [Utterson's] mind a crushing anticipation of calamity" (46). Significantly, this intuition of Jekyll's suicidal destruction parallels Utterson's first meeting with Hyde. During his stakeout, Utterson hears footsteps, and "with a strong prevision of success" he withdraws "into the entry of the court," where seconds later, as he uncannily knew he would, he faces Mr. Hyde (17-18). This example indicates how alert Utterson is to the images of the unconscious and how well equipped he is to avoid the kind of psychic collapse suffered by Jekyll and Lanyon.

In addition to his openness to these promptings of the unconscious, Utterson seems well equipped for an encounter with the shadow by the natural tendencies of his personality. Stevenson stresses Utterson's "tolerance for others" and his readiness "to help" rather than judge them (5). Moreover, as Edwin Eigner and Barbara Hannah have remarked, the first doppelgänger we meet in the narrative is not that of Jekyll and Hyde but of Utterson and the "the well-known man about town," his distant relative Richard Enfield.[17] Though to others they appear to have nothing in common, so strong a bond unites these opposites that they consider their time together "the chief jewel of each week" (6). Fittingly, Utterson is with his social opposite Enfield when he last sees Jekyll and urges him to come outside before Utterson glimpses the start of a transformation. Indeed, repeatedly Utterson has tried to steer his friend from his regressive retreat into Hyde's control, though of course not fully realizing the true nature of Jekyll and Hyde's archetypal relation. Utterson's willingness to deal with Hyde—as Jekyll's shadow and by extension his own—climaxes with his courageous decision to break down the door to the lab and enter this space symbolic of the monstrous unconscious ("The Last Night"). Here his ability to face the shadow and expose it correlates with Jung's statement that it takes "considerable moral effort" to assimilate the shadow into the conscious personality. So if Jekyll and Lanyon fail to make the necessary moral effort and are thus destroyed, Utterson at the least has faced the shadow squarely, lightening its darkness by assimilating the bits of understanding cast upon it by his own experience and the experiences of Lanyon and Jekyll as recounted in their Gothic narratives.

Though Henry Jekyll faces his shadow, Edward Hyde, and so discovers the psyche's dual identities, he mistakenly attempts to maintain their separation. Consequently, instead of tempering the moral, analytic side of his conscious personality with the natural desires of the shadow, Jekyll stiffens the one identity while utterly rejecting the other. By repressing what Hyde represents, Jekyll not only strays from the path to individuation but worse makes Hyde into a murderous monster. After Hyde breaks all bounds and murders Sir Danvers Carew, Jekyll tells Utterson, "I have had a lesson" (33). Tragically, however, Jekyll either does not learn from it or, what is more likely, never understands it in the first place. Nevertheless, the lesson of Jekyll's cautionary tale is not lost on Stevenson's Gothic reader.

Barbara Hannah interprets Jekyll's failure to consciously integrate the shadow figure as expressing Stevenson's own psychological failure: "It was probably not possible at [the time of writing *Dr. Jekyll*] for Stevenson to realize . . . that this was essentially his own problem." If he had realized his "mistake," Hannah continues, he would have made a "serious attempt to find a solution" in the novel. But in conflating the character's psyche with the author's, Hannah overlooks the possibility that Stevenson intended not simply to write "a successful thriller" but instead to warn readers of the Gothic fate of ignoring "the war in the members."[18] In fact, in his essay "Lay Morals," Stevenson sounds like Jung in asserting the need to balance the various parts of the psyche—the only possible solution to Jekyll's Gothic problem. Stevenson states, "[The soul] demands that we should not live alternately with our opposing tendencies in continued see-saw of passion and disgust, but seek some path on which the tendencies shall no longer oppose, but serve each other to common end. . . . The soul demands unity of purpose, not the dismemberment of man" (2:179). While Stevenson plots the psychic dismemberment of man through Jekyll and Lanyon, he provides the solution Hannah calls for through Utterson, who learns—as the two scientists do not—the cautionary lesson of unifying "the thorough and primitive duality" of human consciousness (70).

Notes

1. See Albert J. Guerard, "Concepts of the Double," 8-9; and Robert Rogers, *A Psychoanalytic Study of the Double in Literature*, 93-94; Robert Louis Stevenson, *Across the Plains*, 227.

2. See Morton Prince, *Psychotherapy and Multiple Personality*, 197, 201; and Jeremy Hawthorn, *Multiple Personality and the Disintegration of Literary Character*, 62-63. Also see C. F. Keppler, *The Literature of the Second Self*, 8-9. Hawthorn stresses that a person's multiple personalities not only display "contradictory behavior patterns" but also have "different and mutually exclusive memories," 2. Significantly, Stevenson's Jekyll underscores that his "two natures had memory in common," 10:79. This and the following references in the text to *The Strange Case of Dr. Jekyll and Mr. Hyde* and to Stevenson's other works, unless otherwise noted, are from *The Works of Robert Louis Stevenson*. For Jung's comment, see *Man and His Symbols*, 7. Other brief links of Jung to *Dr. Jekyll* include those by Mark M. Hennelly Jr., "Stevenson's 'Silent Symbols' of the 'Fatal Cross Roads' in *Dr. Jekyll and Mr. Hyde*," 10; Erich Neumann, *The Origins and History of Consciousness*, 98; Harold Schechter, *The New Gods*, 38; Clifton Snider, *The Stuff That Dreams Are Made On*, 15. In her often insightful study *Striving towards Wholeness*, Barbara Hannah devotes an entire chapter to interpreting Stevenson's life and works from a Jungian viewpoint. However, as a practicing psychoanalyst, Hannah is more interested in speculating on ways his story reveals the state of his psyche than in close textual analysis.

3. Stevenson, "A Chapter on Dreams," in *Across the Plains*, 211, 225-28; he uses the phrase "Gothic gnome" in a letter to W. H. Low, *Works*, 30:278.

4. John Fowles, *The French Lieutenant's Woman*, 300-325; Walter E. Houghton, *The Victorian Frame of Mind 1830-1870*, 343; Irving Saposnik, *Robert Louis Stevenson*, 96, 90.

5. Carl G. Jung, *Memories, Dreams, Reflections*, 235; Joseph L. Henderson, "Ancient Myths and Modern Man," 118-20.

6. Jung, *The Collected Works of C. G. Jung*, 9.ii:8. Except where noted otherwise, all quotations of Jung's writings are from this source. Further citations appear parenthetically as *C.W.* and are followed by volume and page numbers.

7. See also *C.W.* 9.i:284-85; *C.W.* 9.ii:266-67. See Douglas Thorpe, "Calvin, Darwin, and the Double"; and Charles Blinderman, "Vampurella."

8. Edward F. Edinger, *Ego and Archetype*, 14-15.

9. Stevenson quoted by George S. Hellman, *The True Stevenson*, 129. See William Veeder's "Children of the Night," 139-48; Stephen Heath, "Psychopathia Sexualis."

10. Hannah, 55.

11. See *C.W.* 11:439. As Benjamin G. Lockerd Jr. notes, it is "out of the wholeness of the Sacred Marriage that the highest symbol of the Self can arise." See *The Sacred Marriage*, 185.

12. Anthony Storr, *The Essential Jung*, 87.

13. On the relations of mental boundaries to schizophrenia and bad dreams, see Ernest Hartmann, *The Nightmare*. Victor Turner, *From Ritual to Theatre*, 41, 44, 46, 84.

14. Saposnik, 93, 92; Masao Miyoshi, *The Divided Self*, 297.

15. Colin Manlove, "'Closer Than an Eye,'" 94.

16. See Daniel V. Fraustino, "The Not So Strange Case of Dr. Jekyll and Mr. Hyde," 207-8; Miyoshi, 297; William Patrick Day, *In the Circles of Fear and Desire*, 92; Veeder, 109.

17. Edwin Eigner, *Robert Louis Stevenson and the Romantic Tradition*, 145; Hannah, 52-54.

18. Hannah, 51; letter to John Addington Symonds, *Works* 30:292.

Works Consulted

Blinderman, Charles. "Vampurella: Darwin and Count Dracula." *Massachusetts Review* 21 (1980): 411-28.

Day, William Patrick. *In the Circles of Fear and Desire: A Study of Gothic Fantasy*. Chicago and London: University of Chicago Press, 1985.

Edinger, Edward F. *Ego and Archetype*. 1972. Reprinted, Baltimore: Penguin, 1973.

Eigner, Edwin. *Robert Louis Stevenson and the Romantic Tradition*. Princeton: Princeton University Press, 1966.

Fowles, John. *The French Lieutenant's Woman*. Boston and Toronto: Little, Brown, 1969.

Fraustino, Daniel V. "The Not So Strange Case of Dr. Jekyll and Mr. Hyde." *Journal of Evolutionary Psychology* 5 (1984): 205-9.

Freud, Sigmund. *The Interpretation of Dreams*. Edited and translated by James Strachey. New York: Avon, 1965.

Guerard, Albert J. "Concepts of the Double." In *Stories of the Double*, edited by Albert J. Guerard, 1-14. Philadelphia and New York: Lippincott, 1967.

Hannah, Barbara. *Striving towards Wholeness*. 2d ed. Boston: Sigo Press, 1988.

Hartmann, Ernest. *The Nightmare: The Psychology and Biology of Terrifying Dreams*. New York: Basic Books, 1984.

Hawthorn, Jeremy. *Multiple Personality and the Disintegration of Literary Character*. New York: St. Martin's, 1983.

Heath, Stephen. "Psychopathia Sexualis: Stevenson's *Strange Case*." *Critical Inquiry* 28 (1986): 93-108.

Hellman, George S. *The True Stevenson: A Study in Clarification*. Boston: Little, Brown, 1925.

Henderson, Joseph L. "Ancient Myths and Modern Man." In *Man and His Symbols*, edited by Carl G. Jung, 95-156. 1964. Reprinted, New York: Dell, 1968.

Houghton, Walter E. *The Victorian Frame of Mind 1830-1870*. New Haven and London: Yale University Press, 1957.

Jung, Carl G. *Collected Works of C. G. Jung*. Edited by Sir Herbert Read et al. Translated by R. F. C. Hull. Bollingen Series 20, 20 vols. Princeton: Princeton University Press, 1953-79.

————. *Memories, Dreams, Reflections.* Edited by Aniela Jaffé. Translated by Richard and Clara Winston. 2d ed. New York: Vintage, 1965.

————, ed. *Man and His Symbols.* 1964. Reprinted, New York: Dell, 1968.

Keppler, C. F. *The Literature of the Second Self.* Tucson: University of Arizona Press, 1972.

Lockerd, Benjamin G., Jr. *The Sacred Marriage: Psychic Integration in "The Faerie Queene."* Lewisburg, Pa.: Bucknell University Press, 1987.

Manlove, Colin. "'Closer Than an Eye': The Interconnections of Stevenson's *Dr. Jekyll and Mr. Hyde.*" *Studies in Scottish Literature* 23 (1988): 97-103.

Miyoshi, Masao. *The Divided Self: A Perspective on the Literature of the Victorians.* New York: New York University Press, 1969.

Neumann, Erich. *Depth Psychology and a New Ethic.* Translated by Eugene Rolfe. New York: Published for the C. G. Jung Foundation for Analytical Psychology by G. P. Putnam's, 1969.

————. *The Great Mother: An Analysis of the Archetype.* Translated by Ralph Manheim. 2d ed. Bollingen Series 47. Princeton: Princeton University Press, 1963.

————. *The Origins and History of Consciousness.* Translated by R. F. C. Hull. Bollingen Series 42. Princeton: Princeton University Press, 1954.

Prince, Morton. *Psychotherapy and Multiple Personality.* Edited by Nathan G. Hale Jr. Cambridge: Harvard University Press, 1975.

Rogers, Robert. *A Psychoanalytic Study of the Double in Literature.* Detroit: Wayne State University Press, 1970.

Saposnik, Irving. *Robert Louis Stevenson.* Boston: Twayne, 1974.

Schechter, Harold. *The New Gods: Psyche and Symbol in Popular Art.* Bowling Green, Ohio: Bowling Green State University Popular Press, 1980.

Snider, Clifton. *The Stuff That Dreams Are Made On: A Jungian Interpretation of Literature.* Wilmette, IL: Chiron Publications, 1991.

Stevenson, Robert Louis. *Across the Plains.* 1892. Reprinted, New York: Scribner's, 1914.

————. *The Strange Case of Dr. Jekyll and Mr. Hyde.* Vol. 10 of *The Works of Robert Louis Stevenson.* South Seas Edition. 32 vols. New York: Scribner's, 1925.

————. *The Works of Robert Louis Stevenson.* South Seas Edition. 32 vols. New York: Scribner's, 1925.

Storr, Anthony. Introduction to *The Essential Jung,* selected by Anthony Storr. Princeton: Princeton University Press, 1983.

Thorpe, Douglas. "Calvin, Darwin, and the Double: The Problem of Divided Nature in Hogg, MacDonald, and Stevenson." *Newsletter of Victorian Studies Association of Western Canada* 11, no. 1 (1985): 6-22.

Turner, Victor. *From Ritual to Theatre: The Human Seriousness of Play.* New York: Performing Arts Journal Publications, 1982.

Veeder, William. "Children of the Night: Stevenson and Patriarchy." In *Dr. Jekyll and Mr. Hyde after One Hundred Years,* edited by William Veeder and Gordon Hirsch, 107-60. Chicago and London: University of Chicago Press, 1988.

FURTHER READING

Bibliography

Swearingen, Roger G. *The Prose Writings of Robert Louis Stevenson: A Guide.* Hamden, Conn.: Archon Books, 1980, 217 p.

Full-length bibliography of primary and secondary sources.

Biographies

Bell, Ian. *Dreams of Exile: Robert Louis Stevenson, a Biography.* New York: Henry Holt, 1995, 296 p.

Full-length biography of Stevenson.

Calder, Jenni. *Robert Louis Stevenson: A Life Study.* Oxford: Oxford University Press, 1980, 362 p.

Biographical study focused on Stevenson's literary career and influences.

McLynn, Frank. *Robert Louis Stevenson: A Biography.* New York: Random House, 1994, 567 p.

Well-regarded and comprehensive biography of Stevenson.

Criticism

Block, Ed. "James Sully, Evolutionist Psychology, and Late Victorian Gothic Fiction." *Victorian Studies* 25, no. 4 (summer 1982): 443-67.

Analyzes Stevenson's novella The Strange Case of Dr. Jekyll and Mr. Hyde and short stories "The Merry Men" and "Olalla" with respect to late Victorian evolutionist psychology and its theories regarding psychological aberration.

Brantlinger, Patrick and Richard Boyle. "The Education of Edward Hyde: Stevenson's 'Gothic Gnome' and the Mass Readership of Late-Victorian England." In *Dr. Jekyll and Mr. Hyde after One Hundred Years,* edited by William Veeder and Gordon Hirsch, pp. 265-82. Chicago: University of Chicago Press, 1988.

Reads The Strange Case of Dr. Jekyll and Mr. Hyde "as an unconscious 'allegory' about the commercialization of literature and the emergence of a mass consumer society in the late-Victorian period."

Brantlinger, Patrick. "Imperial Gothic: Atavism and the Occult in the British Adventure Novel, 1880-1914." In *Rule of Darkness: British Literature and Imperialism, 1830-1914,* pp. 227-54. Ithaca, N.Y.: Cornell University Press, 1988.

Discusses The Strange Case of Dr. Jekyll and Mr. Hyde as an "imperial Gothic fantasy," equating Hyde's actions with the degenerate behavior of colonials who "go native."

Doane, Janice Devon Hodges. "Demonic Disturbances of Sexual Identity: The Strange Case of Dr. Jekyll and Mr/s Hyde." *Novel: A Forum on Fiction* 23 (1989): 63-74.

Relates the theme of the demonic "other" in Dr. Jekyll and Mr. Hyde to Victorian concerns about shifts in traditional gender roles.

Dryden, Linda. "'City of Dreadful Night': Stevenson's Gothic London." In *The Modern Gothic and Literary Doubles: Stevenson, Wilde and Wells,* pp. 74-108. Basingstoke, England: Palgrave Macmillan, 2003.

Studies the sources and expression of gothicism in Stevenson's works, particularly in The Strange Case of Dr. Jekyll and Mr. Hyde.

Egan, Joseph J. "The Relationship of Theme and Art in *The Strange Case of Dr. Jekyll and Mr. Hyde.*" *English Literature in Transition, 1880-1920* 10 (1967): 28-32.

Suggests that the artistic design and structure of Stevenson's story supports its central theme "that Dr. Jekyll himself is both good and evil."

Eigner, Edwin M. *Robert Louis Stevenson and Romantic Tradition.* Princeton, N.J.: Princeton University Press, 1966, 258 p.

Finds Stevenson's fiction "closely related to . . . the nineteenth century prose romance." Eigner defines that tradition, as well as Stevenson's place within it, through comparisons with other works.

Hennelly, Jr., Mark M. "Stevenson's 'Silent Symbols' of the 'Fatal Cross Roads' in *Dr. Jekyll and Mr. Hyde.*" *Gothic* 1, no. 1 (June 1979): 10-16.

Studies mythologized and Jungian symbols of the crossroads and the wasteland in Dr. Jekyll and Mr. Hyde.

Herdman, John. "The Double in Decline." In *The Double in Nineteenth-Century Fiction,* pp. 129-31. London: Macmillan, 1990.

Probes Stevenson's use of the doppelgänger *motif in "Markheim."*

Jolly, Roslyn. "South Sea Gothic: Pierre Loti and Robert Louis Stevenson." *English Literature in Transition, 1880-1920* 47, no. 1 (2004): 28-49.

Surveys Gothic elements derived from the juxtaposition of Polynesian supernaturalism and western rationalist materialism depicted in Stevenson's "The Beach of Falesá" and Loti's The Marriage of Loti.

Kempton, Kenneth Payton. "Plausibility." In *The Short Story,* pp. 172-88. Cambridge, Mass.: Harvard University Press.

Identifies the principal theme of Stevenson's "Markheim" as the "conquest of a man by his conscience" and studies the narrative elements of the short story.

Lawler, Donald. "Reframing Jekyll and Hyde: Robert Louis Stevenson and the Strange Case of Gothic Fiction." In *Dr. Jekyll and Mr. Hyde after One Hundred Years,* edited by William Veeder and Gordon Hirsch, pp. 247-61. Chicago: University of Chicago Press, 1988.

Describes The Strange Case of Dr. Jekyll and Mr. Hyde *as an early transitional work in the tradition of Gothic science fiction.*

MacAndrew, Elizabeth. "The Victorian Hall of Mirrors." In *The Gothic Tradition in Fiction,* pp. 151-329. New York: Columbia University Press, 1979.

Views Dr. Jekyll and Mr. Hyde *as exemplary of the late nineteenth-century integration of Gothic effects into social novels.*

Maixner, Paul. *Robert Louis Stevenson: The Critical Heritage.* London: Routledge & Kegan Paul, 1981, 532 p.

Collects significant early reviews and commentary on Stevenson's principal works.

Massie, Irving. "The Third Self: *Dracula, Jekyll and Hyde,* 'Lokis.'" In *The Gaping Pig: Literature and Metamorphosis,* pp. 98-114. Berkeley: University of California Press, 1976.

Argues that the action of Dr. Jekyll and Mr. Hyde *derives from the unity rather than duality of the central character, who in tampering with his own unified nature, incorporating both good and evil, allowed only evil to remain.*

McAlpin, Edwin A. "Sin and Consequences." In *Old and New Books as Life Teachers,* pp. 36-49. Garden City, N.Y.: Doubleday, Doran, and Co., 1928.

Asserts that Dr. Jekyll and Mr. Hyde *demonstrates that indulgence in sin will destroy the ability to distinguish between right and wrong.*

Menikoff, Barry. "Introduction: Fable, Fiction, and Modernism." In *Robert Louis Stevenson: Tales from the Prince of Storytellers,* by Robert Louis Stevenson, pp. 29-35. Evanston, Ill.: Northwestern University Press, 1993.

Characterizes "Markheim" as an allegorical representation of "the struggle of good and evil for the heart of man."

Meyers, Jeffrey. Introduction to *The Body Snatcher and Other Stories,* by Robert Louis Stevenson, edited by Jeffrey Meyers, pp. vii-xviii. New York: New American Library, 1988.

Surveys the themes, styles, and plots of Stevenson's short stories.

Miyoshi, Masao. "Masks in the Mirror: The Eighteen Nineties." In *The Divided Self: A Perspective on the Literature of the Victorians,* pp. 289-340. New York: New York University Press, 1969.

Includes discussion of The Strange Case of Dr. Jekyll and Mr. Hyde *and "Markheim" in examining the double or secret self in Victorian literature.*

Nabokov, Vladimir. "Robert Louis Stevenson: *The Strange Case of Dr. Jekyll and Mr. Hyde.*" In *Lectures on Literature,* edited by Fredson Bowers, pp. 179-204. New York: Harcourt, Brace, Jovanovich, 1988.

Analyzes the style and artistic intent of Dr. Jekyll and Mr. Hyde, *dismissing popular estimations of the novel as a mystery story while concentrating on its evocation of psychological terror.*

Orel, Harold. "Robert Louis Stevenson: Many Problems, Some Successes." In *The Victorian Short Story: Development and Triumph of a Literary Genre,* pp. 115-37. Cambridge: Cambridge University Press, 1986.

Examines "Markheim," "Olalla," and "Thrawn Janet" as representing some of Stevenson's most successful horror stories.

Parsons, Coleman O. "Stevenson's Use of Witchcraft in 'Thrawn Janet.'" *Studies in Philology* 43, no. 3 (July 1946): 551-71.

Appraises Stevenson's familiarity with and invention of witchcraft lore as illustrated in his story "Thrawn Janet."

Penzoldt, Peter. "The Ghost Story with a Moral—Dickens and Stevenson." In *The Supernatural in Fiction,* pp. 92-117. New York: Humanities Press, 1965.

Asserts that Stevenson and Charles Dickens were the only short story writers to create horror tales with moral messages.

Punter, David. "Gothic and Decadence." In *The Literature of Terror: A History of Gothic Fictions from 1765 to the Present Day,* pp. 239-67. London: Longmans, 1980.

Considers The Strange Case of Dr. Jekyll and Mr. Hyde *"one of the most potent of modern literary myths" to arise from the "decadent Gothic" literature of the 1890s.*

Saposnik, Irving S. *Robert Louis Stevenson.* Boston: Twayne Publishers, 1974, 164 p.

Critical introduction to Stevenson that includes thematic and structural analysis of Dr. Jekyll and Mr. Hyde *and the author's short fiction.*

Swinnerton, Frank. *R. L. Stevenson: A Critical Study.* New York: Mitchell Kennerly, 1915, 215 p.

One of the most important and frequently discussed works on Stevenson in the twentieth century. As the first major attack on Stevenson, it has had a significant impact on his reputation, and from the time of its publication, fewer critics have defined Stevenson as a major writer. Swinnerton avoided discussing Stevenson's personality and attempted to evaluate his work using objective critical methods.

Tymms, Ralph. "The Double in Post-Romantic Literature." In *Doubles in Literary Psychology,* pp. 72-118. Cambridge: Bowes & Bowes, 1949.

Elucidates the use of the doppelgänger, *or double, in* The Strange Case of Dr. Jekyll and Mr. Hyde.

Veeder, William, and Gordon Hirsch, eds. *Dr. Jekyll and Mr. Hyde after One Hundred Years.* Chicago: University of Chicago Press, 1988, 312 p.

Collection of essays with varying approaches to The Strange Case of Dr. Jekyll and Mr. Hyde *that offer analyses of the novella within biographical, cultural, and historical frameworks. Many of the essays examine the* work within the Gothic literary tradition, comparing it to other Gothic works, including Mary Shelley's *Franken-stein.*

OTHER SOURCES FROM GALE:

Additional coverage of Stevenson's life and career is contained in the following sources published by Thomson Gale: *Authors and Artists for Young Adults,* Vol. 24; *Beacham's Encyclopedia of Popular Fiction: Biography & Resources,* Vol. 3; *Beacham's Guide to Literature for Young Adults,* Vols. 1, 2, 4, 13; *British Writers,* Vol. 5; *British Writers: The Classics,* Vol. 1; *British Writers Retrospective Supplement,* Vol. 1; *Children's Literature Review,* Vols. 10, 11; *Concise Dictionary of British Literary Biography, 1890-1914; Dictionary of Literary Biography,* Vols. 18, 57, 141, 156, 174; *Dictionary of Literary Biography Documentary Series,* Vol. 13; *DISCovering Authors; DISCovering Authors: British; DISCovering Authors: Canadian; DISCovering Authors Modules: Most-studied Authors* and *Novelists; DISCovering Authors 3.0; Junior DISCovering Authors; Literature and Its Times,* Vols. 1, 3; *Literature Resource Center; Major Authors and Illustrators for Children and Young Adults,* Eds. 1, 2; *Nineteenth-Century Literature Criticism,* Vols. 5, 14, 63; *Novels for Students,* Vols. 11, 20; *Reference Guide to English Literature,* Ed. 2; *Reference Guide to Short Fiction,* Ed. 2; *St. James Guide to Horror, Ghost & Gothic Writers; St. James Guide to Young Adult Writers; Short Story Criticism,* Vols. 11, 51; *Something about the Author,* Vol. 100; *Supernatural Fiction Writers; Twayne's English Authors; World Literature and Its Times,* Vol. 4; *World Literature Criticism; Writers for Children; Writers for Young Adults;* and *Yesterday's Authors of Books for Children,* Vol. 2.

BRAM STOKER

(1847 - 1912)

(Full name Abraham Stoker) Irish novelist, short story writer, and essayist.

Stoker is best known as the author of *Dracula* (1897), one of the most famous horror stories of all time, and a work frequently cited as a culminating example of the late-Victorian Gothic novel. Stoker also wrote adventure novels and romances, several other works of horror, and numerous pieces of short fiction. These works, however, have been overshadowed by Stoker's most popular novel and have attracted relatively little critical attention. For most, Stoker is regarded as a one-book author, his sole memorable contribution being the creation of the Transylvanian count whose name has become synonymous with vampirism.

BIOGRAPHICAL INFORMATION

Born on November 8, 1847, in Dublin, Stoker was stricken with illness as a child that left him bedridden for the first seven years of his life. During this period, his mother reputedly told him stories of her own childhood during the cholera plague in the Irish town of Sligo, recounting instances of live interment and corpse burnings. At Trinity College, Stoker made up for his early invalidism by excelling in athletics as well as in

his studies. He graduated with honors in mathematics in 1870 and followed his father into the Irish civil service, where he worked for ten years. During this time Stoker also was an unpaid drama critic for the Dublin *Mail*, contributing glowing reviews, more unabashed praise than criticism, of Henry Irving's theatrical performances. The two men became friends and, in 1879, Stoker left his job to become Irving's manager. He also discharged various managerial, secretarial, and even directorial functions at the Lyceum Theatre. Despite his extensive duties, Stoker wrote a number of novels, including *Dracula*. Following Irving's death in 1905, Stoker was associated with the literary staff of the London *Telegraph*. In his final years, Stoker was afflicted with gout and Bright's disease. Some biographers also believe he contracted syphilis about the time he was writing *Dracula*, and that the advanced stages of the disease led to his death in 1912.

MAJOR WORKS

Stoker composed *Dracula* as an epistolary novel comprised of journal entries, letters, newspaper clippings, a ship's log, and phonograph recordings. The story begins with the journey of a young English solicitor, Jonathan Harker, sent to Transylvania to counsel a wealthy client, Count Dracula. During his two-month stay at Dracula's castle, Harker becomes disconcerted by Dracula's odd appearance, eccentricities, and predatory behavior. After some investigation, he discovers that Dracula sleeps in a coffin in a crypt beneath the castle during the day and spends his nights stealing babies from the nearby town. Harker manages to escape the castle and return to England where he is reunited with his fiancée Mina Murray. Strange events in London, including the arrival of a Russian schooner containing fifty boxes of earth, and the mysterious death of Mina's acquaintance Lucy Westenra, suggest that Dracula has followed Harker back to England. Harker engages the help of Lucy's former doctor, Van Helsing, when she reemerges as a vampire. Together with several assistants the men locate the undead Lucy and destroy her. When it becomes clear that Mina is the Count's next victim, Harker, Van Helsing, and the others extend their search for Dracula himself. Discovering that he has fled London, they track him down and kill him. As Dracula's body disintegrates, Mina is saved.

As is *Dracula,* Stoker's remaining novels and works of short fiction are primarily characterized by their macabre nature and focus on such themes as death, male rivalry, ambivalence toward women, and the morality of good and evil. Among them, "Dracula's Guest," originally intended as a prefatory chapter to *Dracula,* is one of Stoker's best-known stories. The tale opens with Jonathan Harker traveling to Dracula's castle, only to be stranded alone in the countryside when his frightened driver refuses to complete the trip. He takes refuge from a violent storm in a mausoleum in a nearby cemetery. As he rests, a beautiful female apparition rises from the tomb and approaches him. Suddenly, he is thrown to the ground and later wakes to find himself warmed and protected by a werewolf. In another story, "The Squaw," an American visiting Nuremberg drops a pebble from the top of a castle, killing a kitten. Its vengeful mother stalks the man, eventually causing his death. Of Stoker's other supernatural novels, *The Jewel of Seven Stars* (1903) is generally considered his best effort after *Dracula.* The work concerns an ambitious Egyptologist who attempts to reanimate the mummified remains of an ancient Egyptian queen. During the course of the novel the scientist, Trelawney, discovers that this mummy has been exerting a mysterious influence over his daughter Margaret, from which he eventually manages to free her. Probably Stoker's second most popular work of fiction, his late novel entitled *The Lair of the White Worm* (1911) is generally perceived by scholars as a lurid and somewhat incoherent pastiche of grotesque horror. Its story concentrates on the sinister figure of Lady Arabella March, whom the novel's protagonists eventually learn can transform herself into a repulsive worm of monstrous proportions. Although not well regarded by critics, the novel is sometimes discussed in terms of its bizarre, sexualized imagery and as a troubling indicator of Stoker's mental decline shortly before his death.

CRITICAL RECEPTION

Most Victorian readers interpreted *Dracula* as a straightforward horror novel. Some early reviewers noted the "unnecessary number of hideous incidents" which could "shock and disgust" readers. One critic even advised keeping the novel away from children and nervous adults. Later commentators began to take a more scholarly approach to the novel, exploring the theme of repressed sexuality within the story. Critics have asserted that the transformation of Dracula's female victims, Lucy and Mina, from chaste to sexually aggressive should be considered a commentary on attitudes toward female sexuality in Victorian society. Homoerotic elements in the relationship between Dracula and Harker have also been analyzed. Moreover, Dracula's drinking of blood in the novel has been regarded as a metaphor for sexual intercourse, and the stakes that kill Lucy and three other vampire women have been discussed as phallic symbols. Among contemporary critical approaches to *Dracula,* Clive Leatherdale has traced the origins of Stoker's Transylvanian count from the stories of eastern European folklore and history, and has examined the novelist's ambivalent and at times paradoxical rendering of the vampire as both victimizer and victim. Valerie Clemens (see Further Reading) has considered *Dracula* within the contexts of late nineteenth-century England, exploring Stoker's representation of rapid changes in Victorian science, technology, and culture in the work. Jerrold E. Hogle has suggested that Stoker's novel both exaggerates and intensifies the English Gothic literary conventions laid down by Horace Walpole in his supernatural romance *The Castle of Otranto,* arguing that *Dracula* offers a bourgeois, capitalist "counterfeit" of the social and symbolic structures originally depicted in the Gothic novel through its use of narrative simulacra. Joseph Valente has studied gender construction and social marginality in *Dracula,* particularly highlighting the idealized feminine and maternal virtues associated with Mina and the work's allegorized cultural and political contexts. Other critics have frequently evaluated *Dracula* from a Freudian psychosexual standpoint, and the novel has additionally been interpreted from folkloric, political, feminist, and religious points of view. Still other commentators have identified themes of parricide, infanticide, and gender reversal in the novel. In recent years, the diverse literary origins of *Dracula* have also been identified, with *Varney the Vampyre; or, The Feast of Blood*, John William Polidori's *The Vampyre*, Joseph Sheridan Le Fanu's "Carmilla," and Guy de Maupassant's "Le Horla" studied among its Gothic forerunners.

Though Stoker's other novels were favorably reviewed when they appeared, most are now considered dated by their stereotyped characters and romanticized Gothic plots; and except by aficionados of supernatural fiction they are rarely read today. Even the earliest reviews frequently decried the stiff characterization and tendency to melodrama which flaw Stoker's writing. Critics have universally praised, however, Stoker's beautifully precise place descriptions. Stoker's short stories, while sharing the faults of his novels, have fared better with modern readers. Meanwhile, *Dracula* has garnered much critical and popular attention since the time of its publication and through the years has spawned countless stories and novels by other authors, as well as numerous theatrical and cinematic adaptations. Indeed, *Dracula* has never gone out of print since its first publication. Many critics regard the novel as the best-known and most enduring Gothic vampire story ever published. Whether Stoker evoked a universal fear, or as some modern critics would have it, gave form to a universal fantasy, he created a powerful and lasting image that has become an indelible part of popular culture.

PRINCIPAL WORKS

The Duties of Clerks of Petty Session in Ireland (handbook) 1879

Under the Sunset (short stories) 1881

A Glimpse of America (essays) 1886

The Snake's Pass (novel) 1890

The Watter's Mou' (novel) 1894

Dracula (novel) 1897

The Mystery of the Sea: A Novel (novel) 1902

The Jewel of Seven Stars (novel) 1903

The Man (novel) 1905

Personal Reminiscences of Henry Irving (biography) 1906

The Lady of the Shroud (novel) 1909

Famous Imposters (essays) 1910

The Lair of the White Worm (novel) 1911

Dracula's Guest, and Other Weird Stories (short stories) 1914

The Bram Stoker Bedside Companion (short stories and novels) 1973

*   This collection contains the short stories "Dracula's Guest" and "The Squaw."

PRIMARY SOURCES

BRAM STOKER (STORY DATE 1914)

SOURCE: Stoker, Bram. "Dracula's Guest." In *Masterpieces of Terror and the Supernatural*, selected by Marvin Kaye, pp. 3-13. New York: Barnes & Noble, 1985.

The following short story, written in the 1890s, comprises an intended, but deleted, prefatory chapter to Dracula. *It was first published in 1914 in* Dracula's Guest, and Other Weird Stories.

When we started for our drive the sun was shining brightly on Munich, and the air was full of the joyousness of early summer. Just as we were about to depart, Herr Delbrück (the maître d'hôtel of the Quatre Saisons, where I was staying) came down, bareheaded, to the carriage and, after wishing me a pleasant drive, said to the coachman, still holding his hand on the handle of the carriage door:

"Remember you are back by nightfall. The sky looks bright but there is a shiver in the north wind that says there may be a sudden storm. But I am sure you will not be late." Here he smiled, and added, "for you know what night it is."

Johann answered with an emphatic, "Ja, mein Herr," and, touching his hat, drove off quickly. When we had cleared the town, I said, after signalling to him to stop:

"Tell me, Johann, what is to-night?"

He crossed himself, as he answered laconically: "Walpurgis nacht." Then he took out his watch, a great, old-fashioned German silver thing as big as a turnip, and looked at it, with his eyebrows gathered together and a little impatient shrug of his shoulders. I realised that this was his way of respectfully protesting against the unnecessary delay, and sank back in the carriage, merely motioning him to proceed. He started off rapidly, as if to make up for lost time. Every now and then the horses seemed to throw up their heads and sniffed the air suspiciously. On such occasions I often looked round in alarm. The road was pretty bleak, for we were traversing a sort of high, wind-swept plateau. As we drove, I saw a road that looked but little used, and which seemed to dip through a little, winding valley. It looked so invit-ing that, even at the risk of offending him, I called Johann to stop—and when he had pulled up, I told him I would like to drive down that road. He made all sorts of excuses, and frequently crossed himself as he spoke. This somewhat piqued my curiosity, so I asked him various questions. He answered fencingly, and repeatedly looked at his watch in protest. Finally I said:

"Well, Johann, I want to go down this road. I shall not ask you to come unless you like; but tell me why you do not like to go, that is all I ask." For answer he seemed to throw himself off the box, so quickly did he reach the ground. Then he stretched out his hands appealingly to me, and implored me not to go. There was just enough of English mixed with the German for me to under-stand the drift of his talk. He seemed always just about to tell me something—the very idea of which evidently frightened him; but each time he pulled himself up, saying, as he crossed himself: "Walpurgis nacht!"

I tried to argue with him, but it was difficult to argue with a man when I did not know his language. The advantage certainly rested with him, for although he began to speak in English, of a very crude and broken kind, he always got excited and broke into his native tongue—and every time he did so, he looked at his watch. Then the horses became restless and sniffed the air. At this he grew very pale, and, looking around in a frightened way, he suddenly jumped forward, took them by the bridles and led them on some twenty feet. I followed, and asked why he had done this. For answer he crossed himself, pointed to the spot we had left and drew his carriage in the direction of the other road, indicating a cross, and said, first in German, then in English: "Buried him—him what killed themselves."

I remembered the old custom of burying suicides at cross-roads: "Ah! I see, a suicide. How interesting!" But for the life of me I could not make out why the horses were frightened.

Whilst we were talking, we heard a sort of sound between a yelp and a bark. It was far away;

but the horses got very restless, and it took Jo-hann all his time to quiet them. He was pale, and said: "It sounds like a wolf—but yet there are no wolves here now."

"No?" I said, questioning him; "isn't it long since the wolves were so near the city?"

"Long, long," he answered, "in the spring and summer; but with the snow the wolves have been here not so long."

Whilst he was petting the horses and trying to quiet them, dark clouds drifted rapidly across the sky. The sunshine passed away, and a breath of cold wind seemed to drift past us. It was only a breath, however, and more in the nature of a warning than a fact, for the sun came out brightly again. Johann looked under his lifted hand at the horizon and said:

"The storm of snow, he comes before long time." Then he looked at his watch again, and, straightway holding his reins firmly—for the horses were still pawing the ground restlessly and shaking their heads—he climbed to his box as though the time had come for proceeding on our journey.

I felt a little obstinate and did not at once get into the carriage.

"Tell me," I said, "about this place where the road leads," and I pointed down.

Again he crossed himself and mumbled a prayer, before he answered: "It is unholy."

"What is unholy?" I enquired.

"The village."

"Then there is a village?"

"No, no. No one lives there hundreds of years." My curiosity was piqued: "But you said there was a village."

"There was."

"Where is it now?"

Whereupon he burst out into a long story in German and English, so mixed up that I could not quite understand exactly what he said, but roughly I gathered that long ago, hundreds of years, men had died there and been buried in their graves; and sounds were heard under the clay, and when the graves were opened, men and women were found rosy with life, and their mouths red with blood. And so, in haste to save their lives (aye, and their souls!—and here he crossed himself) those who were left fled away to other places, where the living lived, and the dead were dead and not—not something. He was evidently afraid to speak the last words. As he proceeded with his narration, he grew more and more excited. It seemed as if his imagination had got hold of him, and he ended in a perfect paroxysm of fear—white-faced, perspiring, trembling and looking round him, as if expecting that some dreadful presence would manifest itself there in the bright sunshine on the open plain. Finally, in an agony of desperation, he cried:

"Walpurgis nacht!" and pointed to the carriage for me to get in. All my English blood rose at this, and, standing back, I said:

"You are afraid, Johann—you are afraid. Go home; I shall return alone; the walk will do me good." The carriage door was open. I took from the seat my oak walking-stick—which I always carry on my holiday excursions—and closed the door, pointing back to Munich, and said, "Go home, Johann—Walpurgis nacht doesn't concern Englishmen."

The horses were now more restive than ever, and Johann was trying to hold them in, while excitedly imploring me not to do anything so foolish. I pitied the poor fellow, he was so deeply in earnest; but all the same I could not help laughing. His English was quite gone now. In his anxiety he had forgotten that his only means of making me understand was to talk my language, so he jabbered away in his native German. It began to be a little tedious. After giving the direction, "Home!" I turned to go down the cross-road into the valley.

With a despairing gesture, Johann turned his horses towards Munich. I leaned on my stick and looked after him. He went slowly along the road for a while: then there came over the crest of the hill a man tall and thin. I could see so much in the distance. When he drew near the horses, they began to jump and kick about, then to scream with terror. Johann could not hold them in; they bolted down the road, running away madly. I watched them out of sight, then looked for the stranger, but I found that he, too, was gone.

With a light heart I turned down the side road through the deepening valley to which Johann had objected. There was not the slightest reason, that I could see, for his objection; and I daresay I tramped for a couple of hours without thinking of time or distance, and certainly without seeing a person or a house. So far as the place was concerned, it was desolation itself. But I did not notice this particularly till, on turning a bend in the road, I came upon a scattered fringe of wood; then I recognised that I had been impressed unconsciously by the desolation of the region through which I had passed.

I sat down to rest myself, and began to look around. It struck me that it was considerably colder than it had been at the commencement of my walk—a sort of sighing sound seemed to be around me, with, now and then, high overhead, a sort of muffled roar. Looking upwards I noticed that great thick clouds were drifting rapidly across the sky from North to South at a great height. There were signs of coming storm in some lofty stratum of the air. I was a little chilly, and, thinking that it was the sitting still after the exercise of walking, I resumed my journey.

The ground I passed over was now much more picturesque. There were no striking objects that the eye might single out; but in all there was a charm of beauty. I took little heed of time and it was only when the deepening twilight forced itself upon me that I began to think of how I should find my way home. The brightness of the day had gone. The air was cold, and the drifting of clouds high overhead was more marked. They were accompanied by a sort of far-away rushing sound, through which seemed to come at intervals that mysterious cry which the driver had said came from a wolf. For a while I hesitated. I had said I would see the deserted village, so on I went, and presently came on a wide stretch of open country, shut in by hills all around. Their sides were covered with trees which spread down to the plain, dotting, in clumps, the gentler slopes and hollows which showed here and there. I followed with my eye the winding of the road, and saw that it curved close to one of the densest of these clumps and was lost behind it.

As I looked there came a cold shiver in the air, and the snow began to fall. I thought of the miles and miles of bleak country I had passed, and then hurried on to seek the shelter of the wood in front. Darker and darker grew the sky, and faster and heavier fell the snow, till the earth before and around me was a glistening white carpet the further edge of which was lost in misty vagueness. The road was here but crude, and when on the level its boundaries were not so marked, as when it passed through the cuttings; and in a little while I found that I must have strayed from it, for I missed underfoot the hard surface, and my feet sank deeper in the grass and moss. Then the wind grew stronger and blew with ever increasing force, till I was fain to run before it. The air became icy-cold, and in spite of my exercise I began to suffer. The snow was now falling so thickly and whirling around me in such rapid eddies that I could hardly keep my eyes open. Every now and then the heavens were torn asunder by vivid lightning, and in the flashes I could see ahead of me a great mass of trees, chiefly yew and cypress all heavily coated with snow.

I was soon amongst the shelter of the trees, and there, in comparative silence, I could hear the rush of the wind high overhead. Presently the blackness of the storm had become merged in the darkness of the night. By-and-by the storm seemed to be passing away: it now only came in fierce puffs or blasts. At such moments the weird sound of the wolf appeared to be echoed by many similar sounds around me.

Now and again, through the black mass of drifting cloud, came a straggling ray of moonlight, which lit up the expanse, and showed me that I was at the edge of a dense mass of cypress and yew trees. As the snow had ceased to fall, I walked out from the shelter and began to investigate more closely. It appeared to me that, amongst so many old foundations as I had passed, there might be still standing a house in which, though in ruins, I could find some sort of shelter for a while. As I skirted the edge of the copse, I found that a low wall encircled it, and following this I presently found an opening. Here the cypresses formed an alley leading up to a square mass of some kind of building. Just as I caught sight of this, however, the drifting clouds obscured the moon, and I passed up the path in darkness. The wind must have grown colder, for I felt myself shiver as I walked; but there was hope of shelter, and I groped my way blindly on.

I stopped, for there was a sudden stillness. The storm had passed; and, perhaps in sympathy with nature's silence, my heart seemed to cease to beat. But this was only momentarily; for suddenly the moonlight broke through the clouds, showing me that I was in a graveyard, and that the square object before me was a great massive tomb of marble, as white as the snow that lay on and all around it. With the moonlight there came a fierce sigh of the storm, which appeared to resume its course with a long, low howl, as of many dogs or wolves. I was awed and shocked, and felt the cold perceptibly grow upon me till it seemed to grip me by the heart. Then while the flood of moonlight still fell on the marble tomb, the storm gave further evidence of renewing, as though it was returning on its track. Impelled by some sort of fascination, I approached the sepulchre to see what it was, and why such a thing stood alone in

such a place. I walked around it, and read, over the Doric door, in German—

COUNTESS DOLINGEN OF GRATZ
IN STYRIA
SOUGHT AND FOUND DEATH.
1801.

On the top of the tomb, seemingly driven through the solid marble—for the structure was composed of a few vast blocks of stone—was a great iron spike or stake. On going to the back I saw, graven in great Russian letters:

"The dead travel fast."

There was something so weird and uncanny about the whole thing that it gave me a turn and made me feel quite faint. I began to wish, for the first time, that I had taken Johann's advice. Here a thought struck me, which came under almost mysterious circumstances and with a terrible shock. This was Walpurgis Night!

Walpurgis Night, when, according to the belief of millions of people, the devil was abroad—when the graves were opened and the dead came forth and walked. When all evil things of earth and air and water held revel. This very place the driver had specially shunned. This was the depopulated village of centuries ago. This was where the suicide lay; and this was the place where I was alone—unmanned, shivering with cold in a shroud of snow with a wild storm gathering again upon me! It took all my philosophy, all the religion I had been taught, all my courage, not to collapse in a paroxysm of fright.

And now a perfect tornado burst upon me. The ground shook as though thousands of horses thundered across it; and this time the storm bore on its icy wings, not snow, but great hailstones which drove with such violence that they might have come from the thongs of Balearic slingers—hailstones that beat down leaf and branch and made the shelter of the cypresses of no more avail than though their stems were standing-corn. At the first I had rushed to the nearest tree; but I was soon fain to leave it and seek the only spot that seemed to afford refuge, the deep Doric doorway of the marble tomb. There, crouching against the massive bronze-door, I gained a certain amount of protection from the beating of the hail-stones, for now they only drove against me as they ricochetted from the ground and the side of the marble.

As I leaned against the door, it moved slightly and opened inwards. The shelter of even a tomb was welcome in that pitiless tempest, and I was about to enter it when there came a flash of forked-lightning that lit up the whole expanse of the heavens. In the instant, as I am a living man, I saw, as my eyes were turned into the darkness of the tomb, a beautiful woman, with rounded cheeks and red lips, seemingly sleeping on a bier. As the thunder broke overhead, I was grasped as by the hand of a giant and hurled out into the storm. The whole thing was so sudden that, before I could realize the shock, moral as well as physical, I found the hailstones beating me down. At the same time I had a strange, dominating feeling that I was not alone. I looked towards the tomb. Just then there came another blinding flash, which seemed to strike the iron stake that surmounted the tomb and to pour through to the earth, blasting and crumbling the marble, as in a burst of flame. The dead woman rose for a moment of agony, while she was lapped in the flame, and her bitter scream of pain was drowned in the thundercrash. The last thing I heard was this mingling of dreadful sound, as again I was seized in the giant-grasp and dragged away, while the hailstones beat on me, and the air around seemed reverberant with the howling of wolves. The last sight that I remembered was a vague, white, moving mass, as if all the graves around me had sent out the phantoms of their sheeted-dead, and that they were closing in on me through the white cloudiness of the driving hail.

Gradually there came a sort of vague beginning of consciousness; then a sense of weariness that was dreadful. For a time I remembered nothing; but slowly my senses returned. My feet seemed positively racked with pain, yet I could not move them. They seemed to be numbed. There was an icy feeling at the back of my neck and all down my spine, and my ears, like my feet, were dead, yet in torment; but there was in my breast a sense of warmth which was, by comparison, delicious. It was as a nightmare—a physical nightmare, if one may use such an expression; for some heavy weight on my chest made it difficult for me to breathe.

This period of semi-lethargy seemed to remain a long time, and as it faded away I must have slept or swooned. Then came a sort of loathing, like the first stage of sea-sickness, and a wild desire to be free from something—I knew not what. A vast stillness enveloped me, as though all the world were asleep or dead—only broken by the low panting as of some animal close to me. I felt a warm rasping at my throat, then came a consciousness of the awful truth, which chilled me to the heart and sent the blood surging up through my brain. Some great animal was lying on me and now licking my throat. I feared to stir, for some instinct of prudence bade me lie still; but the brute seemed to realize that there was now some change in me, for it raised its head. Through my eyelashes I saw above me the two great flaming eyes of a gigantic wolf. Its sharp white teeth gleamed in the gaping red mouth, and I could feel its hot breath fierce and acrid upon me.

For another spell of time I remembered no more. Then I became conscious of a low growl, followed by a yelp, renewed again and again. Then, seemingly very far away, I heard a "Holloa! holloa!" as of many voices calling in unison. Cautiously I raised my head and looked in the direction whence the sound came; but the cemetery blocked my view. The wolf still continued to yelp in a strange way, and a red glare began to move round the grove of cypresses, as though following the sound. As the voices drew closer, the wolf yelped faster and louder. I feared to make either sound or motion. Nearer came the red glow, over the white pall which stretched into the darkness around me. Then all at once from beyond the trees there came at a trot a troop of horsemen bearing torches. The wolf rose from my breast and made for the cemetery. I saw one of the horsemen (soldiers by their caps and their long military cloaks) raise his carbine and take aim. A companion knocked up his arm, and I heard the ball whizz over my head. He had evidently taken my body for that of the wolf. Another sighted the animal as it slunk away, and a shot followed. Then, at a gallop, the troop rode forward—some towards me, others following the wolf as it disappeared amongst the snow-clad cypresses.

As they drew nearer I tried to move, but was powerless, although I could see and hear all that went on around me. Two or three of the soldiers jumped from their horses and knelt beside me. One of them raised my head, and placed his hand over my heart.

"Good news, comrades!" he cried. "His heart still beats!"

Then some brandy was poured down my throat; it put vigour into me, and I was able to open my eyes fully and look around. Lights and shadows were moving among the trees, and I heard men call to one another. They drew together, uttering frightened exclamations; and the lights flashed as the others came pouring out of the cemetery pell-mell, like men possessed. When the further ones came close to us, those who were around me asked them eagerly:

"Well, have you found him?"

The reply rang out hurriedly:

"No! no! Come away quick—quick! This is no place to stay, and on this of all nights!"

"What was it?" was the question, asked in all manner of keys. The answer came variously and all indefinitely as though the men were moved by some common impulse to speak, yet were restrained by some common fear from giving their thoughts.

"It—it—indeed!" gibbered one, whose wits had plainly given out for the moment.

"A wolf—and yet not a wolf!" another put in shudderingly.

"No use trying for him without the sacred bullet," a third remarked in a more ordinary manner.

"Serve us right for coming out on this night! Truly we have earned our thousand marks!" were the ejaculations of a fourth.

"There was blood on the broken marble," another said after a pause—"the lightning never brought that there. And for him—is he safe? Look at his throat! See, comrades, the wolf has been lying on him and keeping his blood warm."

The officer looked at my throat and replied:

"He is all right; the skin is not pierced. What does it all mean? We should never have found him but for the yelping of the wolf."

"What became of it?" asked the man who was holding up my head, and who seemed the least panic-stricken of the party, for his hands were steady and without tremor. On his sleeve was the chevron of a petty officer.

"It went to its home," answered the man, whose long face was pallid, and who actually shook with terror as he glanced around him fearfully. "There are graves enough there in which it may lie. Come, comrades—come quickly! Let us leave this cursed spot."

The officer raised me to a sitting posture, as he uttered a word of command; then several men placed me upon a horse. He sprang to the saddle behind me, took me in his arms, gave the word to advance; and, turning our faces away from the cypresses, we rode away in swift, military order.

As yet my tongue refused its office, and I was perforce silent. I must have fallen asleep; for the next thing I remembered was finding myself standing up, supported by a soldier on each side of me. It was almost broad daylight, and to the north a red streak of sunlight was reflected, like a path of blood, over the waste of snow. The officer was telling the men to say nothing of what they had seen, except that they found an English stranger, guarded by a large dog.

"Dog! that was no dog," cut in the man who had exhibited such fear. "I think I know a wolf when I see one."

The young officer answered calmly: "I said a dog."

"Dog!" reiterated the other ironically. It was evident that his courage was rising with the sun; and, pointing to me, he said, "Look at his throat. Is that the work of a dog, master?"

Instinctively I raised my hand to my throat, and as I touched it I cried out in pain. The men crowded round to look, some stooping down from their saddles; and again there came the calm voice of the young officer:

"A dog, as I said. If aught else were said we should only be laughed at."

I was then mounted behind a trooper, and we rode on into the suburbs of Munich. Here we came across a stray carriage, into which I was lifted, and it was driven off to the Quatre Saisons—the young officer accompanying me, whilst a trooper followed with his horse, and the others rode off to their barracks.

When we arrived, Herr Delbrück rushed so quickly down the steps to meet me, that it was apparent he had been watching within. Taking me by both hands he solicitously led me in. The officer saluted me and was turning to withdraw, when I recognized his purpose, and insisted that he should come to my rooms. Over a glass of wine I warmly thanked him and his brave comrades for saving me. He replied simply that he was more than glad, and that Herr Delbrück had at the first taken steps to make all the searching party pleased; at which ambiguous utterance the maître d'hotel smiled, while the officer pleaded duty and withdrew.

"But Herr Delbrück," I enquired, "how and why was it that the soldiers searched for me?"

He shrugged his shoulders, as if in depreciation of his own deed, as he replied:

"I was so fortunate as to obtain leave from the commander of the regiment in which I served, to ask for volunteers."

"But how did you know I was lost?" I asked.

"The driver came hither with the remains of his carriage, which had been upset when the horses ran away."

"But surely you would not send a search-party of soldiers merely on this account?"

"Oh, no!" he answered; "but even before the coachman arrived, I had this telegram from the Boyar whose guest you are," and he took from his pocket a telegram which he handed to me, and I read:

BISTRITZ.

"Be careful of my guest—his safety is most precious to me. Should aught happen to him, or if he be missed, spare nothing to find him and ensure his safety. He is English and therefore adventurous. There are often dangers from snow and wolves and night. Lose not a moment if you suspect harm to him. I answer your zeal with my fortune.—Dracula."

As I held the telegram in my hand, the room seemed to whirl around me; and, if the attentive maître d'hotel had not caught me, I think I should have fallen. There was something so strange in all this, something so weird and impossible to imagine, that there grew on me a sense of my being in some way the sport of opposite forces—the mere vague idea of which seemed in a way to paralyse me. I was certainly under some form of mysterious protection. From a distant country had come, in the very nick of time, a message that took me out of the danger of the snow-sleep and the jaws of the wolf.

TITLE COMMENTARY

Dracula

THE ATHENAEUM (REVIEW DATE 26 JUNE 1897)

SOURCE: A review of *Dracula*, by Bram Stoker. *The Athenaeum*, no. 3635 (26 June 1897): 235.

In the following review, the critic faults Stoker's sensationalism in Dracula while acknowledging his effective—if inconsistent—rendering of terror and mystery.

Stories and novels appear just now in plenty stamped with a more or less genuine air of belief in the visibility of supernatural agency. The strengthening of a bygone faith in the fantastic and magical view of things in lieu of the purely material is a feature of the hour, a reaction—artificial, perhaps, rather than natural—against late tendencies in thought. Mr. Stoker is the purveyor of so many strange wares that *Dracula* reads like a determined effort to go, as were, "one

better" than others in the same field. How far the author is himself a believer in the phenomena described is not for the reviewer to say. He can but attempt to gauge how far the general faith in witches, warlocks, and vampires—supposing it to exist in any general and appreciable measure—is likely to be stimulated by this story. The vampire idea is very ancient indeed, and there are in nature, no doubt, mysterious powers to account for the vague belief in such beings. Mr. Stoker's way of presenting his matter, and still more the matter itself, are of too direct and uncompromising a kind. They lack the essential note of awful remoteness and at the same time subtle affinity that separates while it links our humanity with unknown beings and possibilities hovering on the confines of the known world. *Dracula* is highly sensational, but it is wanting in the constructive art as well as in the higher literary sense. It reads at times like a mere series of grotesquely incredible events; but there are better moments that show more power, though even these are never productive of the tremor such subjects evoke under the hand of a master. An immense amount of energy, a certain degree of imaginative faculty, and many ingenious and gruesome details are there. At times Mr. Stoker almost succeeds in creating the sense of possibility in impossibility; at others he merely commands an array of crude statements of incredible actions. The early part goes best, for it promises to unfold the roots of mystery and fear lying deep in human nature; but the want of skill and fancy grows more and more conspicuous. The people who band themselves together to run the vampire to earth have no real individuality or being. The German man of science is particularly poor, and indulges, like a German, in much weak sentiment. Still Mr. Stoker has got together a number of "horrid details," and his object, assuming it to be ghastliness, is fairly well fulfilled. Isolated scenes and touches are probably quite uncanny enough to please those for whom they are designed.

THE SPECTATOR (REVIEW DATE 31 JULY 1897)

SOURCE: "Recent Novels." *The Spectator* (31 July 1897): 150-51.

In the following review, the critic asserts that the strength of Dracula lies in Stoker's vivid imagination.

Mr. Bram Stoker gives us the impression—we may be doing him an injustice—of having deliberately laid himself out in *Dracula* to eclipse all previous efforts in the domain of the horrible,—to "go one better" than Wilkie Collins (whose method of narration he has closely followed), Sheridan Le Fanu, and all the other professors of the flesh-creeping school. Count Dracula, who gives his name to the book, is a Transylvanian noble who purchases an estate in England, and in connection with the transfer of the property Jonathan Harker, a young solicitor, visits him in his ancestral castle. Jonathan Harker has a terrible time of it, for the Count—who is a vampire of immense age, cunning, and experience—keeps him as a prisoner for several weeks, and when the poor young man escapes from the gruesome charnel-house of his host, he nearly dies of brain-fever in a hospital at Buda-Pesth. The scene then shifts to England, where the Count arrives by sea in the shape of a dog-fiend, after destroying the entire crew, and resumes operations in various uncanny manifestations, selecting as his chief victim Miss Lucy Westenra, the fiancée of the Honourable Arthur Holmwood, heir-presumptive to Lord Godalming. The story then resolves itself into the history of the battle between Lucy's protectors, including two rejected suitors—an American and a "mad" doctor—and a wonderfully clever specialist from Amsterdam, against her unearthly persecutor. The clue is furnished by Jonathan Harker, whose betrothed, Mina Murray, is a bosom friend of Lucy's, and the fight is long and protracted. Lucy succumbs, and, worse still, is temporarily converted into a vampire. How she is released from this unpleasant position and restored to a peaceful post-mortem existence, how Mina is next assailed by the Count, how he is driven from England, and finally exterminated by the efforts of the league—for all these, and a great many more thrilling details, we must refer our readers to the pages of Mr. Stoker's clever but cadaverous romance. Its strength lies in the invention of incident, for the sentimental element is decidedly mawkish. Mr. Stoker has shown considerable ability in the use that he has made of all the available traditions of vampirology, but we think his story would have been all the more effective if he had chosen an earlier period. The up-to-dateness of the book—the phonograph diaries, typewriters, and so on—hardly fits in with the mediaval methods which ultimately secure the victory for Count Dracula's foes.

THE TIMES, LONDON (REVIEW DATE 23 AUGUST 1897)

SOURCE: "Recent Novels." *The Times*, London, no. 35289 (23 August 1897): 6.

In the following review, the critic relates the plot of Dracula, *asserts that it offers highly dramatic reading,*

and adds: "We would not, however, recommend it to nervous persons for evening reading."

Dracula cannot be described as a domestic novel, nor its annals as those of a quiet life. The circumstances described are from the first peculiar. A young solicitor sent for on business by a client in Transylvania goes through some unusual experiences. He finds himself shut up in a half ruined castle with a host who is only seen at night and three beautiful females who have the misfortune to be vampires. Their intentions, which can hardly be described as honourable, are to suck his blood, in order to sustain their own vitality. Count Dracula (the host) is also a vampire, but has grown tired of his compatriots, however young and beautiful, and has a great desire for what may literally be called fresh blood. He has therefore sent for the solicitor that through his means he may be introduced to London society. Without understanding the Count's views, Mr. Harker has good reason for having suspicions of his client. Wolves come at his command, and also fogs; he is also too clever by half at climbing. There is a splendid prospect from the castle terrace, which Mr. Harker would have enjoyed but for his conviction that he would never leave the place alive:—

> In the soft moonlight the distant hills became melted, and the shadows in the valleys and gorges of velvety blackness. The mere beauty seemed to cheer me; there was peace and comfort in every breath I drew. As I leaned from the window my eye was caught by something moving a storey below me, and somewhat to my left, where I imagined, from the lie of the rooms, that the windows of the Count's own room would look out. The window at which I stood was tall and deep, stone-mullioned, and, though weather-worn, was still complete, but it was evidently many a day since the casement had been there. I drew back behind the stonework and looked carefully out.
>
> What I saw was the Count's head coming out from the window. I did not see the face, but I knew the man by the neck and the movement of his back and arms. In any case, I could not mistake the hands, which I had had so many opportunities of studying. I was at first interested and somewhat amused, for it is wonderful how small a matter will int-rest and amuse a man when he is a prisoner. But my very feelings changed to repulsion and terror when I saw the whole man slowly emerge from the window and begin to crawl down the castle wall over that dreadful abyss, face down, with his cloak spreading out around him like great wings.

These scenes and situations, striking as they are, become commonplace compared with Count Dracula's goings on in London. As Falstaff was not only witty himself but the cause of wit in other people, so a vampire, it seems, compels those it has bitten (two little marks on the throat are its token, usually taken by the faculty for the scratches of a brooch) to become after death vampires also. Nothing can keep them away but garlic, which is, perhaps, why that comestible is so popular in certain countries. One may imagine, therefore, how the thing spread in London after the Count's arrival. The only chance of stopping it was to kill the Count before any of his victims died, and this was a difficult job, for, though several centuries old, he was very young and strong, and could become a dog or a bat at pleasure. However, it is undertaken by four reso- lute and highly-principled persons, and how it is managed forms the subject of the story, of which nobody can complain that it is deficient in dra- matic situations. We would not, however, recom- mend it to nervous persons for evening reading.

JERROLD E. HOGLE (ESSAY DATE 1998)

> SOURCE: Hogle, Jerrold E. "Stoker's Counterfeit Gothic: Dracula and Theatricality at the Dawn of Simulation." In *Bram Stoker: History, Psychoanalysis, and the Gothic,* edited by William Hughes and Andrew Smith, pp. 205-24. New York: Macmillan—St. Martin's, 1998.
>
> *In the following essay, Hogle illustrates how "Stoker builds on and intensifies the mixed 'counterfeit' founda- tions of Gothic fiction"* in Dracula.

Bram Stoker is now widely celebrated as a major contributor to Gothic fiction—and even to Gothic theatre and film—but the exact nature of his contribution needs to be better understood. I want to show here that Stoker draws us forcefully back to the most basic foundations of 'Gothic' fic- tion and theatre, especially in *Dracula,* while simultaneously offering a 'zone of horror' that vividly harbours a host of anxieties basic to Anglo- European, white middle-class culture at both the *fin de siècle* of Stoker's time and our own turn of the century. For me it forms no mere coincidence that 1897, the 'birth-year' of *Dracula,* was the 100th anniversary of the death-year of Horace Walpole, the first writer to subtitle a novel 'A Gothic Story'. Stoker intensifies the most funda- mental and lasting tendencies in the Walpolean Gothic, and does so, I would contend, nowhere more so than in *Dracula.* Even his alterations of the Gothic tradition, the ones most revealing of his own culture at his own historical moment, are arresting fulfilments of the principal 'technologies' (the modes of symbolisation) that emerge in the Gothic from the writings of Walpole through those of Radcliffe, Lewis, Polidori and Charlotte Brontë, to Stevenson's *The Strange Case of Dr Jekyll and Mr Hyde* (1886).

ABOUT THE AUTHOR

MONTAGUE SUMMERS ON THE ENDURING NATURE OF *DRACULA*

If we review *Dracula* from a purely literary point of approach it must be acknowledged that there is much careless writing and many pages could have been compressed and something revised with considerable profit. It is hardly possible to feel any great interest in the characters, they are labels rather than individuals. As I have said, there are passages of graphic beauty, passages of graphic hor- ror, but these again almost entirely occur within the first sixty pages. There are some capital incidents, for example the method by which Lord Godalming and his friend obtain admittance to No. 347 Piccadilly. Nor does this by any means stand alone.

However, when we have—quite fairly, I hope—thus criticized *Dracula,* the fact re- mains that it is a book of unwonted interest and fascination. Accordingly we are bound to acknowledge that the reason for the im- mense popularity of this romance—the rea- son why, in spite of obvious faults it is read and reread—lies in the choice of subject and for this the author deserves all praise.

SOURCE: Summers, Montague. "The Vampire in Literature." In *The Vampire: His Kith and Kin.* 1928. Reprint edition, pp. 271-340. New Hyde Park, N.Y.: University Books, 1960.

To some extent, we already know how fully these links can be made. Because of work on the Gothic from the Freudian Marxism of Leslie Fiedler (1966), David Punter (1980) and Franco Moretti (1988) up through the recent feminist and cultural studies of Nina Auerbach, Anne Williams, Maggie Kilgour and Judith Halberstam (all 1995) among others, we have come to understand how the rising middle class since the eighteenth century 'displaces the hidden violence of present social structures, conjures them up again as past, and falls promptly under their spell' by specifi- cally employing the Gothic mode in fiction, theatre, architecture and other forms.[1] We now realise that quandaries about class conflicts and economic changes, uneasiness over shifting family arrangements and sexual boundaries, and versions of the 'other' which establish racial and cultural distinctions when traditional economic divisions are being challenged, are projected (or *retro*jected) together into frightening 'Gothic' spectres and monsters, from Walpole's ancestral effigy-ghost to the vampire-aristocrat from Transylvania. These both contain the socially 'unmentionable', yet bring it forth to be seen in some of its horror, albeit displaced and disguised in a fashion that is both alluring and repulsive. In particular, much as Halberstam asserts, Stoker's Count performs the longest-lasting function of Gothic ghosts/monsters/'others'. He/it 'aggregates' the kinds of men or women, races, class-types and social or sexual behaviours that are regarded as most 'foreign and perverse' by the Anglo-European middle class; and he/it conflates these into one figure designed to be set against 'a hegemonic ideal', to define that reigning ideological construct, in fact, by being its negation and its dark unconscious.[2]

Dracula enacts this Gothic 'ghosting' so thoroughly, and aggregates so wide a range of culturally defined 'perversities' in the process, that he/it becomes, not just a Gothic 'other', but 'foreignness' incarnate and 'otherness itself'.[3] As some of the best readings of **Dracula** have shown, the vampire, being a corpse (an 'it') as well as an animate humanoid (apparently a 'he'), can embody a range of potentially oxymoronic significations. Thus Dracula condenses the invasion of life by death and vice versa, as well as a range of racial, cultural, sexual/heterosexual and gender tensions. Stoker's 'creature' is a mixture of so many culturally fashioned contraries that (s)he/it threatens the socio-economic distinctions of its author's culture with complete dissolution, a vampiric death that could suck the life from them in a perverse intercourse between numerous realms, all supposedly separate.

No wonder some recent analysts of **Dracula** choose to see this kind of 'monster' as a version of what Julia Kristeva has called 'the abject', or of the process of 'abjection'.[4] Like Kristeva's 'abject', the vampire is an utterly betwixt-and-between anomaly which includes its 'other' as a part of itself: it is living/dead, maternal/paternal, human/ animal. Such a condition echoes the most primal, and thus the most abject-ed, state in *Powers of Horror*: the moment of birth where the emerging infant is half-inside and half-outside the mother, partly dead and partly alive (arguably, 'un-dead'), in a liminal 'either/or' of which we retain dim somatic memories.[5] During the growth of the

'civilised' individual, this state and others like it must be 'thrown off' or 'thrown under' a different and more socially coherent realm, so that a seemingly independent body and subject can, with cultural support, emerge, though always with a pre-conscious longing and loathing for the 'root' heterogeneity so basic to it. The Gothic monster, such as Dracula, is a 'throwing' of this 'abject' into a supposedly alien figure which seems to take it all far away from 'us' into 'strange' class, racial, geographical, historical and largely non-human conditions. At the same time, this 'other' brings us face to face, and haunts us with what we in the Anglo-European West would most dissociate from ourselves, though it is at the deepest foundations *of* ourselves: the heterogeneous, even multi-gendered, physical, familial, racial, cultural and symbolic conditions into which and out of which we are actually born. Like Walpole's portrait-ghost, which is dead *and* alive, a painting *and* a person, Stoker's Dracula is an 'other' which contains and sequesters many later cultural anomalies, combining and scapegoating the anxieties they arouse in his day and ours, extending the symbolic method of abjecting many heterogeneities which Walpole first suggested within his 'Gothic Story'.[6]

But there are ways, it appears, in which **Dracula** does not seem to repeat the Gothic tradition at all. Jennifer Wicke has argued how much Stoker's book is produced out of the Western technologies of communication in the late 1890s. Its presentation of the tale through coded journal entries, letters, transcriptions of recordings, telegrams and newspaper articles or advertisements, while somewhat reflective of the 'Gothic' penchant for documents within documents, is far more dependent on near twentieth-century uses of shorthand, typewriting, phonograph records, photography, the telegraph and the mass-market circulation of journalism, all of which help to produce 'the mechanical replication of culture' in Stoker's time and ours.[7] One threat now embodied in the vampire-aristocrat, Wicke points out, since he/it is already a hollowed-out, living-dead version of a late medieval warlord, is its/his resemblance to the forms of mass culture which now depict it and try to contain it, *and* which it employs itself in its quest for blood. Both the vampire and the newest mechanical modes of reproduction and reception transform human beings into the merest husks or signs of their supposed selves in a process that increasingly generates 'evacuated social languages'—mere signifiers—as representations of people.[8] For Lucy Westenra, who is both transmogrified by Dracula and 'vamped' by the fictional press accounts of her activity, this is to be turned into a figure of continual consumption so much so that consuming, especially all-consuming, women seem more and more alike as the novel goes on. In that condition even a woman's potential 'unruliness of speech' is 'technologised' into wording, and thus into behaviour, that suits the 'print-language of hegemony' (the sanctioned discourses *about* women), whether a woman resists it (in the way Lucy attempts) or mostly submits to it (as Mina does).[9] The vampire, meanwhile, the more he/it learns the forms of modern British mass culture so as both to invade and circulate in England effectively, comes to embody the very mechanical and linguistic means of English imperialism over other cultures, *its* symbolic sucking of *their* lifeblood, the same means that Dracula's British observers use on him/it supposedly to subdue his/its/her foreign otherness.

This connection of the 'other' to increased mass-market simulation and hence to another 'unconscious' level in the culture, however, is also fundamentally Gothic. As E. J. Clery has demonstrated, the 'supernatural in *The Castle of Otranto* figures . . . a conflict between two versions of economic "personality"': landed property and the private family.[10] The Gothic, or really the early capitalist *imitation* of much older 'Gothic' structures, is haunted from its beginnings by what we also find in Count Dracula: the heterogeneity of incompatible tendencies in the Western middle-class self pulled backwards and forwards in conflicting economic and social directions, one of which turns the self into a marketable representation, the self as picture or sign, able to gain wide circulation like a coin or a middle-class novel. For Stoker thus to emphasise the modes of symbolic production in a more recent capitalist world where every represented being becomes alienated into the exchangeable figurations of itself is therefore for him to drive once more down to the Gothic's most basic underpinnings, its harkening back towards antiquated social orders *within* the advance of its symbols towards the 'free market' circulation and consumption of uprooted signifiers.

As I have argued elsewhere, the Walpolean 'Gothic' is constituted from the start by fakery in its use of fragmented and evacuated figures from the past—the 'counterfeit' nature of the picture or effigy that appears at the very heart of what haunts most 'Gothic Stories' in explicitly *figural* animations of the already dead.[11] The Gothic allows the at least partly middle-class reader and

author to feel the attraction of the lost and once 'magical' powers in the now emptied icons of the late Middle Ages and Renaissance. Yet, further, it permits the marketing of these symbols as false antiquities which give their new consumers the power to recirculate—and thus profit from—them without being strictly bound to their old meanings and contexts of social order. The moving signs of the distant past (such as Walpole's portrait-ghost or Count Dracula), however, are not simply counterfeits, but *ghosts* of counterfeits in the eighteenth-century Gothic and its progeny. Jean Baudrillard has helped us to view the Renaissance to which the Walpolean Gothic looks back as a time when signs—words, gestures, behaviours, modes of dress, ways of spending money, the rhetorical and theatrical presentations of the self—were generally conceived of *as* already counterfeit. Such signs were 'counterfeit' because they were both recollections of supposedly 'natural' links of birth and status to their signifiers in medieval times and highly mobile figures that could be moved from person to person as the rising beneficiaries of post-medieval urban mercantilism gained the capacity to wear clothes, spend money, use words and otherwise display relocated and fabricated marks of rank which were not 'naturally' theirs as they might have had to be in the 'Dark Ages'.[12]

The Renaissance fake, with all its nostalgia for '*bound* meaning' (Baudrillard's phrase), gives way in *The Castle of Otranto* to a simulacrum of it, available for 'freer' circulation aimed at social, political or economic effect, especially since the most hidden sin of Manfred's grandfather (the fakery behind the portrait) turns out to be his counterfeiting of a will which transferred Otranto from its founding aristocratic owners to his less upper-class, more entrepreneurial family. By taking that ghost of the counterfeit(er) and recasting it further, with some intervening Gothic (and other) influences, into a vampire-aristocrat who tries to master and is mastered by many simulacra of the mass market, Bram Stoker attains his great stature as a Gothic novelist in the way he extends the chief symbolic indicators of the cultural conflicts, aspirations and anxieties that lie at the highly unsettled foundations of Gothic novels and plays.

Dracula, like most 'Gothic Stories' from Walpole on, is a highly theatrical novel. Indeed, it combines aspects of the numerous French and English vampire melodramas staged from the 1820s onwards with Stoker's own sense of vampire theatre, the mass market and even of Henry Irving, the demanding egotist whom many consider as one of the models for the constantly role-playing Count Dracula.[13]

In the rest of this essay, I shall argue generally that Stoker builds on and intensifies the mixed 'counterfeit' foundations of Gothic fiction by working through, and being driven by, what Baudrillard has revealed as the half-hidden assumptions about signs in the West that come out of and displace the sense of the sign as counterfeit. *Dracula*, as it reproduces the Walpolean ghost of the counterfeit, plays out and points to two progressions: first, the turn from the assumptions that animate the counterfeit to those of the '*simulacrum*', the industrial age sense of the sign as a 'copy' struck off from a mechanically produced mould (itself a ghost of the counterfeit); and, later, the shift from that schema to the even more modern sign as primarily a '*simulation*' referring to other simulations, more and more a 'hyperreality' (for Baudrillard a 'code') without single moulds for originals, even at its moments of nostalgia for older forms of supposedly direct reference from sign to person or object.[14] What has always been 'ghosted' in the Gothic has been the terror of the historical passage into a bourgeois promoted, yet mechanised, order of sign-production and reproduction. In this order the longing for older sureties of reference, however ideological they really were, is conscripted into capitalistic exchanges of signs for signs and the consequent effort to represent a now more privatised 'inner' self in outward figures that are reproduced mechanically and circulated by their mechanisms through and beyond 'private' spaces.[15] Stoker's *Dracula* deals both indirectly and directly with this historical passage, its tensions and its anxieties, by contrasting them as quandaries at the heart of the Gothic. The chilling possibilities of Baudrillard's 'digital and programmatic sign' is faced incipiently by the Gothic ghost of the counterfeit as early as Walpole and is confronted far more directly in Stoker's vision of the vampiric simulacrum of the ghost of the counterfeit in a world of everincreasing simulation.[16]

This process appears in *Dracula* when Stoker has Mina set the stage into which Dracula enters when he/it first arrives on British shores. The scene is the resort town of Whitby, and Mina's Radcliffean journal-description of it keeps finding itself forced to admit the entirely simulated 'nature' in how the scene is viewed and rendered by its viewer:

> A great viaduct runs across, with high piers, *through which the view seems somehow further away than it really is. . . . The houses of the old town . . . are all red-roofed, and seem piled up one over the other anyhow, like the pictures we see of Nuremberg.* Right over the town is the ruin of Whitby Abbey, which was sacked by the Danes, *and which is the scene of part of 'Marmion,' where the girl was built up in the wall.* It is a most noble ruin, of immense size, and *full of beautiful and romantic bits; there is a legend that a white lady is seen in one of the windows.* Between it and the town there is another church, the parish one, round which is a big graveyard, all full of tombstones. . . . I shall come and sit here very often myself and work. *Indeed, I am writing now, with my book on my knee, and listening to the talk of three old men who are sitting beside me.*[17]

There could hardly be a more quintessentially 'Gothic' setting, the continual presentation of each portion of the scene being followed at once by indicators of its artificial existence in its framing by a painter's or tourist's representation, or in its having been written in a book. If a part of the scene is not framed within other parts by the reproduction of it, it is textualised by the allusions, literary or legendary, that it already seems to carry with it. The whole landscape then becomes most explicitly a text when the handwriting of it is mentioned directly and the act of writing is complicated by the further intertextual references provided by the old men telling stories about the place. All this is 'Gothic' counterfeiting *presented as such* within a series of layers that re-counterfeit it again and again. The once medieval and ruined Gothic abbey is recontextualised by more current (and marketable) reframings of it; these reframings themselves are reframed by tourist points of view; and these latter perspectives are coloured and reoriented by the texts of authors, legends or older folk. Ultimately, too, all these layers gain their places in this series of simulations by being admittedly written down yet again—and in 'shorthand' (p. 53), which has to be transcribed into what we now read, a document of rewriting included among many 'papers' and 'records . . . given from the standpoints and within the range of knowledge of those who made them' (p. xxxviii). Mina explicitly fashions all such transcriptions according to 'what I see lady journalists do' under a very prescribed code for 'interviewing and writing descriptions' (p. 54).

Even more to the point, the 'objects' being simulated at this juncture turn out to be mostly counterfeits of counterfeiting within themselves, particularly the tombstones in the graveyard. One of the old men whom Mina hears talking in the cemetery is the seemingly oracular Mr Swales, an apparently marginal character who, according to

William Veeder, 'indicts the hollowness of the patriarchal structures' of knowledge in the novel. Early in the narrative, for example, he reveals to Mina 'that the graves of the sailors in Whitby Churchyard are all empty, and thus that the tombstones' [inscribed] pieties are all hollow rhetoric'.[18] Even the stones that actually encrypt physical bodies are quite often simulacra of fakery by Swales' account, as in the case of the 1873 grave of 'George Canon', where the 'tomb' is inscribed as 'erected by his sorrowing mother to her dearly beloved son', even though this 'mother was a hell-cat that hated' her son and 'he committed suicide in order that she mightn't get an insurance she put on his life' (pp. 66-7).

All the surfaces of Whitby seen in this light become potentially opaque misrepresentations and signifiers of hollowed-out and uncertain pasts which can be reconstructed only with allusions to verbalised knowledge, much of it little more reliable than the tourist-oriented legend of the White Lady in the abbey. To be sure, Swales later tries to recant his claim that 'The whole thing be only lies' (p. 65) when he seeks to restore the conventional religious text of hope beyond the grave to soften his premonition that 'soon the Angel of Death will sound his trumpet for me' (p. 74). But what he gets in answer to his proleptic final reference is an extremely false Angel of Death by Christian standards. Swales dies of a broken neck at the hands of the too-white Dracula, who leaves the old sage frozen with 'a look of fear and horror on his face' (p. 87). He has seen 'Death with his dying eyes' (p. 87), though his grimace is also a reaction to the falsity of another lie: Dracula's simulation and *negation* of what the Angel of Death is supposed to be and do. Swales exposes the simulated nature of virtually all perceived 'reality'. The very origins, as well as English settings, of **Dracula** stem partly from simulations of earlier Gothic fictions, combined with accounts such as Emily Gerard's 'Transylvanian Superstitions', the contents of which are superimposed upon British locations that were already filled with simulacra of a counterfeited past.[19]

Dracula, consequently, as he enters this stage (which is such a palimpsest of signs), is, among other things, an anamorphosis towards multiple simulations of what was already a simulacrum of the Gothic ghost of the counterfeit. The Lord Ruthven-style vampire-aristocrat had become a 'stock villain' in the novels and theatres of England, France and Germany well before Stoker's Count.[20] As early as the 1830s, it was established as an industrial age 'mould' which for decades

was copied with only minimal variation. This now hackneyed simulacrum of the Polidorian counterfeit, a subject of satire by the 1870s and 1880s, is turned by Stoker into an almost endless *and* groundless set of simulations from the moment Dracula first appears to Jonathan Harker 'like a statue' all in black (p. 15).[21]

The opening of such a Gothic simulacrum to a past and future of simulation permeates this scene and much that surrounds it. Here Dracula harkens back to the second major ghost of a counterfeit in *The Castle of Otranto*, the 'black marble' effigy on the tomb of the castle's founder, which suddenly becomes enlarged, fragmented and hauntingly mobile.[22] Harker even goes on to renounce the very literary lineage behind Walpole's ghosts of mere figures when Dracula's departure at 'cock crow' makes the young lawyer view him as 'like the ghost of Hamlet's father' just after the Count has lamented that 'the glories of the great races [of past warrior-princes] are now as a tale that is told' in the more modern world (pp. 29-30). Only a little later, Harker discovers that this ghost of a ghost of a counterfeit and self-confessed and self-textualised remnant of old-style aristocrats can assume virtually any other visage at will, including Jonathan's own (pp. 44, 48). This is a multiplicity far beyond that of any previous figure in the Ruthven tradition. As Harker himself records in shorthand 'all that has happened', so he finds himself bringing the stock vampire-aristocrat 'up-to-date with a vengeance' (p. 36). Moreover, at the conclusion of the novel, the Count is found in his coffin looking 'just like a waxen image', and thus arguably like a Walpolean statue converted to a simulated live body in a wax museum of Stoker's own day (p. 376). Once the traditional penetration of the vampire is achieved, 'the whole body crumble[s] to dust' in an instant, not only because Dracula has been dead for centuries and his sins lead from dust to dust in Christian terms, but also because the 'ground' of all his/its simulations is no more than this non-existence all along, an ageold and now recreated 'dissolution' (p. 377). Stoker's Dracula in any embodiment, even in his most native and settled state, is never more than a synthetic image of other images, while any 'essence' sought behind the forms his body takes turns out to be no more than an absence or a constant passing away. All of this comes from an interplay of texts that Stoker read, rather than from any first-hand knowledge of Transylvania. There is no 'essential Dracula' in Stoker's work beyond a combination of second hand simulacra or stories. Stoker's Dracula at any level is always already a recollection of previous deaths in the process of changing from one form to another, since it has never come from anything other than an interaction of forms of the dead.

When **Dracula** takes already Gothic ghosts of counterfeits, and even their hackneyed simulacra, and turns them into simulations nearly always in the process of turning into or away from others, it is not simply because Stoker incorporates his awareness of the newest sign-making technologies into them, even if Wicke is right to notice him doing so. It is also because his refigurations of the Gothic ghost and the vampire-aristocrat all draw forth the increasingly visible tendency in post-Renaissance 'Gothic' counterfeits and simulacra to become sheer figures of other figures, one of the sources of a modern way of life based so entirely on simulations. Stoker does not just employ forms of mass communication, though they do provide his text with an ironically *un*real 'realism', an illusion of journalistic truth very much of his time; he also shows how such newer simulations and recast Gothic monsters have finally become forms of one another as they all suck some of the life out of the objects of their attentions. The reason for this convergence of symbolic modes is what both underlies and is made possible by the shift from the industrial simulacrum to modern simulation: the growing tendency in Western middle-class life to define the 'inner self' through the 'others' of artificially reproduced forms, many of which are emptied-out recastings of past figures (such as the Walpolean ghost or the conventional vampire-aristocrat when Stoker first encounters it). Dracula him/itself in Stoker's novel supremely incarnates this inevitably doomed quest. From the start, the vampire is grasping at the 'other' of English signifiers and accoutrements such as *Bradshaw's Guide* and 'Kodak views' of a Gothic house in London, all to keep incessantly renewing his/its anomalous, yet largely empty existence (pp. 22-3). As a result, he/it can be constructed as *the* 'other' into which Stoker's other characters can 'throw over' the anguished creation of the self in the pursuit of ever-circulating commodity-signifiers—a pursuit which they fear to acknowledge, but on the basis of which they strive to 'become'.

It is one thing to say that Dracula's 'otherness' from it/himself—seeking and feeding on simulation after simulation to keep the Count the anomaly that he/it is—can be made a symbolic repository for that same tendency in his/its observers and readers. It is quite another to understand how such a Gothic 'abjection' of this monster's and his audience's relation to signs can

also become the means by which Stoker, his other characters, and his readers 'throw off' many more contradictory conditions basic to themselves: the often repressed but very real crossings of the cultural boundaries established between species, races, ethnicities, classes, sexes, sexualities, stages of evolution, forms of expression, life and death, or even our own body as opposed to the body of the mother. How and why, in the figure of Dracula, can a forcing of the Gothic ghost of the counterfeit into a near-explosion of simulations of simulacra be so effective as an 'abject' site for so many varied, primordial yet 'thrown down' possibilities of being? What, indeed, *are* the effects of an abjection of all of these into a both horrifying and alluring Gothic performer of nearly endless simulations and no one foundation? Exactly how are this abjection and the reader's responses to it bound up with the theatricality that Stoker clearly brings to **Dracula**—the very Gothic theatricality of the spectre/actor as 'a figure in a picture'—and with the myriad technological and increasingly public forms of *narration* in which he finally frames his sometimes stagy scenes?

One answer lies in Stoker's rendition of Irving's philosophy of theatrical acting in *Personal Reminiscences of Henry Irving*. Granted, in line with his famous endorsement of semi-'realistic' over declamatory acting, Irving (as Stoker quotes him) advocates a performance that is 'a truthful picture' based on 'a definite conception of what [the actor] wants to convey', rooted in a truth that is 'supreme and eternal' and yet is grasped individually in 'the working of the mind . . . before the tongue gives it words'.[23] But this 'working' generally begins for Stoker's Irving in an actor's knowledge of existing simulacra, a 'study in recognisable material types and differentiated individual instances of the same type' (Vol. 2, p. 7). Behaviours adaptable for theatre are 'recognisable' mainly because there is one 'material' figure of each kind, as in printer's type, which many copies can repeat with some variations across particular 'instances' in an era of mechanical reproduction. Then, too, in this 'combining [of] things already created', the Irving-Stoker actor is really engaged in an 'accumulation of . . . effects' (supposedly Irving's words), which Stoker translates as a continual 'clothing of the player's own identity with the attributes of another', layer upon layer, under the assumption that the 'player's identity' is itself 'of [a] plastic nature', a malleable, synthetic formation already inclined towards continual *ref*ormation (Vol. 2, pp. 8-10). Platonic and organic metaphors for the basis of acting, while certainly recalled and attempted in this redaction of a dead celebrity's philosophy, are constantly pulled towards figures of simulacrum-repetition whose overtones oscillate between the mechanical replication of standardised forms and the sheer transmigration and translation of images without their having to be manufactured one by one from moulds. For Irving, Stoker concludes, the transition from words on the page to a staged enactment of them is determined most by the 'phantasmal image which is conveyed [to the actor] from the words of the poet' (Vol. 2, p. 24), words that are themselves phantasmal. The actor, then, achieves an effective 'figure in a picture' only if he or she, in a layering of simulacrum effects, can materially reproduce an *im*material but visualisable spectre prompted by different visible spectres of past writing. At his time and in the words he writes, theatricality for Stoker is irretrievably inhabited by the simulation of simulacra of older ghostly counterfeitings.

The more theatre in the 1890s turns out to be based on the simulation of simulacra, as is certainly the case in Stoker's vision of Henry Irving as well as **Dracula,** the more it resembles the simulacra of the Gothic ghost of the counterfeit. While this is partly because Stoker *thinks* quite 'Gothically' by this time in consequence of extensive reading and some writing in that mode, it is also because he faces a 'Gothicising' of theatre in the way he believes he must represent drama and its greatest actor for the middle and upper classes during this period. Stoker and his view of Irving keep being pulled into a rhetoric, very much within their pretensions to 'realism'; one which states that 'all art has the aim or object of seeming and not of being' (Vol. 2, p. 17) in the sense that all performances, including Stoker's in his biography of Irving, are the Walpolesque animations of 'phantasmal images' projected by mere ciphers and fleshed out by an 'accumulation' of simulacrum 'effects'.

Now we are beginning to see at least partial answers to some of our remaining questions. *Fin-de-siècle* theatricality, simulation and recast Gothic all become aspects of each other in and around **Dracula** because all three are especially pointed enactments of the Western progression in human self-projection from the use of the sign as counterfeit to the simulation of simulacra of counterfeits of the past.

Moreover, we have now arrived at evidence for how Stoker's life is bound up with such a Gothic interaction of modes at the time he wrote **Dracula.** What else but a rhetoric of simulation

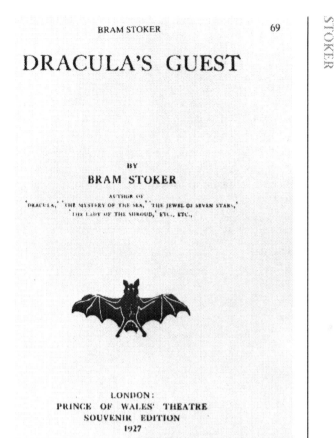

Title page of the 1927 edition of *Dracula's Guest.*

about acting could Bram Stoker use? He was, after all, the factotum of Irving, in charge of the advertising, promotion, theatre-refurbishing, inviting of reviewers, portrait-commissioning, finance and even ghost-writing of correspondence. This the 'business' of simulating the simulations in the theatre, out of which Irving's public image and drawing-power were to a great extent built.[24] Stoker's ghostly descriptions of theatricality, even when he tries to resist the simulation in them, are driven by the economics of widely circulating figures of figures underpinning and marketing the theatre and its top 'actor-managers'. As his narration of Irving's career proceeds, Stoker reveals that the money-raising and advertisements that supposedly furthered the Lyceum acting had become the prime movers of which the acting was now the effect: 'the more [Irving] had to spend [on production and its consequences] the harder he had to work to earn the wherewithal to do it' (Vol. 2, p. 313). Money rendered as a representation of, or entitlement to, theatre had become the exchangeable simulacrum which drove the theatre to pursue every available form of capital as a goal in itself. Stoker and Irving, in the former's increasingly Gothic account, became frantic seekers after properties, tours and financial backers, to the point of finally signing contracts that later came back to haunt them (Vol. 2, pp. 315-20). Dracula, as we have noted, though more obsessed with blood than money supply, is a deeply complicated extension of this craving. That is partly because this ever-unsatisfied, economically-driven, always newly simulated and thus frightening state of being is inseparable for Stoker from the condition of theatre, acting and the business of both in London at the end of the nineteenth century.

The greater terror in these ways of viewing the self by 1897, however, is the possibility that they and their increasingly groundless foundations may really be governing middle-class life *outside* the theatre. In other words, those living a middle-class existence are consciously or preconsciously driven to cast it symbolically away from themselves into what seems 'only' fictional, theatrical or 'other.' Stoker's awareness of these intertwined tendencies is quite apparent in the short nonfiction biographies he offers in **Famous Impostors** (1910). In this volume a series of fake constructions of identity down through history is presented as beginning no earlier than the late Middle Ages or the dawn of the Renaissance, the exact time-frame most simulated by 'Gothic' fictions later, and the era in which the sense of signs as largely 'counterfeit' arises.[25] During that period the imposture of the book's first case, that of Perkin Warbeck, a false pretender to royal succession, comes about, not as in John Ford's play or Mary Shelley's novel about him, but primarily because his 'family was of the better middle class' in the 'manufacturing and commercial' 'Low Countries [of] the fifteenth century'. Upon such a stage 'growing youths [came] in touch at many points with commerce, industry and war', fields of activity in which origins could be disguised and from which others might thus cast a 'susceptible' youth into the 'part' of a Plantagenet heir.[26] Somewhat earlier in late medieval times, too, the legend of the 'Wandering Jew', a precursor figure for Dracula, had its source for Stoker in the 'gossip of an Armenian lacquey' conveyed to a 'serving brother of the monastery' of the Middle Eastern Bishop who later published the story as fact (p. 10). The Wandering Jew was and remains an impostor in the sense of being no more than a 'marvellous [Eastern] story' (p. 111) from the start. Yet the legend grew, a much recounterfeited counterfeit, from the thirteenth though to the sixteenth centuries by Stoker's account, because these 'were the ages of Jew-baiting in the king-

doms of the West' (p. 113) when many evil qualities were attributed to Jews as scapegoats, of whom the Wanderer was an exaggerated composite conflating 'many old beliefs and fables'.

Imposture for Stoker is usually a veiling of questionable middle-class affiliations or longings behind the appropriated features and symbols of other classes *or* a layering of fables on top of fables, with no more than stories at the base. Into the latter fears and prejudices are projected by the observers who employ and recast these convenient 'others'. These processes as Stoker sees them, however bogus, are increasingly the means since the thirteenth century by which 'selves' and their 'others' have been fashioned by a great many bourgeois Europeans in both historical circumstances and in the crafting of fictions. All these different forms of imposture operate in and are cast upon Stoker's Dracula, who anamorphoses into an immense variety of simulations precisely as he/it continues to enact middle-class self-construction and exists as a site for what is 'thrown off' in that process to produce an illusion of coherent identity. Indeed, as Stoker says in revealing the legend of the Wandering Jew as groundless, 'It is the tendency' of such 'beliefs to group or nucleate themselves as though there were a conscious and intentional effort at self-protection' (p. 111), even when no single person or group makes the effort on their own. For Stoker there is a force in counterfeiting ideologies and collations of symbols that layers simulacra over earlier fabrications, thereby protecting the root imposture (the basic anomaly of a false truth) so that the 'baiting' (or othering) that is repeatedly directed at the often-recast construction is never seen for the falsehood and imposture that *it* is too.

At this point we can more clearly say why Gothic ghosts of counterfeiting, theatrical 'figures in a picture', are unusually effective places for abjections of 'thrown off' and anomalous conditions, particularly when they acquire as many simulations as Stoker's Dracula does and when these simulations harbour as many othered states of transition as Dracula is able to incarnate and mask. Such figures joining with and 'nucleating' others are driven by that very mechanism to cover and thus to 'protect' such multiple 'foundations' even as they work also to reveal them, albeit minimally, within that production of disguise after disguise. This layered concealment is even more active in Dracula's continual mutation of him/itself in many different visages and locations, since all these 'experiments' (p. 302), as Van Helsing calls them, are designed to prevent detection of the actual 'weaknesses' that he/it harbours in being so floating a signifier of perpetual dissolution. This cloaking of layering by layering itself is what allows Gothic simulations of simulacra to perform processes of abjection, to 'throw down' or 'throw under' features of themselves within the spectral veils upon veils out of which they are formed. They are thus especially apt locations into which their spectators and audience can 'throw off' the anomalies in themselves and their basic recollections, already complexes of dim memories and vague understandings recast in forms not their own. This personal incoherence, which includes the insecurities and ideological conflicts endemic to the European middle classes, can find few more suitable repositories for itself than a ghostly Gothic palimpsest. The manner of this figure's layered construction is similar to how the bourgeois sense of self has developed historically and individually, yet the same figure is able to conceal that development behind supposedly antiquated and alien surfaces. Indeed, the more distorting simulations there are, as in Dracula's case, the better the monster is for incarnating both cultural and human multiplicity and for covering it over as 'stranger than strange' at the same time. Finding anomalies at their own roots, the middle classes generate a greater and greater need to produce the self through multiple simulations they cannot control. Hence, they need a multi-levelled Dracula as an 'abject' both to take all those horrors into a 'darkness visible', and to make all of them seem alien and nearly invisible in many simulations of simulacra of Gothic ghosts of the counterfeit.

To be sure, this symbolic abjection throughout the Gothic becomes the object of relatively orthodox religious, scientific and paternalistic containment. Stoker is justly (in)famous for presenting the technological searching out, the academic verbalisation and the ritualistic (and phallic) staking of vampires, aggressive women and old-style aristocrats by the Anglo-American/Continental alliance instructed and led by Van Helsing. But, as with the 'causes' for abjecting simulations recounted above, the effects that Stoker produces with his counterfeit Gothic are never ones of simple castigation and repression. His achievement in *Dracula* is a supremely Gothic one for yet another reason: he uses the Gothic novel's endemic oscillation between theatricality and narrative to intensify its ideological hesitation between the conservative preservation of public social orders and the transgressive attraction in returns of the repressed. In Stoker's book, for

example, the much discussed feeding of Mina from Dracula's breast is presented twice, almost in succession. First there is its simulation in the diary of Dr Seward,

> His face was turned from us, but the instant we saw we all recognised the Count—in every way, even to the scar on his forehead. With his left hand he held both Mrs. Harker's hands, keeping them away with her arms at full tension; his right hand gripped her by the back of the neck, forcing her face down on his bosom.
>
> (p. 282)

And then there is Mina's own half-dreamy recollection (interpolated later in Seward's journal) of this 'nursing' form of intercourse which also resembles fellatio:

> 'You have aided in thwarting me; now you shall come to my call. When my brain says "Come!" to you, you shall cross land or sea to do my bidding; and to that end this!' With that he pulled open his shirt, and with his long sharp nails opened a vein in his breast. When the blood began to spurt out, he took my hands in one of his, holding them tight, and with the other seized my neck and pressed my mouth to the wound, so that I must either suffocate or swallow some of the—Oh, my God, my God! what have I done?'
>
> (p. 288)

Although these simulations of Mina's simulacrum narrative say much about the multiple interpretations of anything prompted by the different perspectives in *Dracula*, they also epitomise and strengthen the interaction of conflicting techniques and attitudes in the counterfeit Gothic. Seward's own account is both scientifically exact (and therefore rationally removed to some degree) and extremely theatrical, describing the precise arrangement of the figures in the scene as though the Doctor's words were a set of directions for theatrical 'blocking'. Mina's version is more the work of the narrative stenographer, the 'lady journalist', who sequentially recounts the words spoken and the actions performed—until the final shift when her description gives way to self-dramatising confession and abject religious repentance. In both cases, dispassionate narrative is pulled towards the theatricalising of the self and others, and distance is then only half-restored by the dramatised repulsion of a horror which cannot hide its own erotic interest in the spurting, even eating, of seminal fluids. If Seward's version tilts towards the descriptive dispassion of a stage manager, Mina's offers the immediate, almost pornographic involvement of the actress, yet only as she goes on to make a confession to the male transcriber of her words. Meanwhile, the repetition of the scene simultaneously increases its sensuous attraction and sado-masochistic horror on the one hand, and encourages greater judgemental distance from the 'act' on the other, even as the act is more and more physically described. Then, too, since each simulation of the scene is similar, but not exactly the same, and both views come coloured by emotions and cultural scripts, there is no single 'more original version', no 'primal' scene outside all perceivers, not even a master simulacrum at the base of these multiple renditions.

Bram Stoker in **Dracula** has forcefully carried the Gothic ghost of the counterfeit to its more modern extension in the haunting explosion of simulations, including media simulations, with no single source. After all, this metamorphic progression of ideologies is one in which the very middle-class author, his world of the theatre, the development of the Gothic, and the economy of England were all very much caught by 1897. At the same time, though, Stoker's exaggeration of long-standing Gothic tendencies intensifies and complicates the Gothic's placement (and pulling) of the reader between hegemonic social dominations felt as both necessary and confining, and the disguised visualisation of what hegemony abjects or 'throws off', felt as both desirable and horrifically repellent. Stoker's **Dracula** makes his many simulations of numerous abjected anomalies both objects of virulent, even excessively patriarchal repression *and* riveting allurements for desire, especially as desire moves from simulation to simulation much more than the public ideology of the bourgeois self generally allows. Even before Stoker advocated the censorship of sexually explicit language in a 1908 article and died in 1912 of what has since been revealed as a syphilis contracted through extramarital sex, his greatest Gothic novel narratively and dramatically placed both author and reader between the force of suppression, the denial of endless simulation in the face of it, and the half-tempting, half-horrifying force of constant self-transformation—the option half-secretly held out to middle-class longing by the movement across simulations on which desire now depends for self-definition.[27] To some degree, the Gothic has always been about this conflicted position, for characters *and* readers, partly because the Walpolean Gothic ghost of the counterfeit looks both backward to 'grounded' absolutes and forward to the sheer exchange of signifying commodities. Stoker, most vividly in **Dracula,** brings that oscillation between the possible foundations of bourgeois identity to the edge of the twentieth century—and then into it in his later works. He

does so first by extending the capacity of the Gothic fake for harbouring and concealing abjections and then by using it to make us both see and not see so many of the basic anomalies that we strive to deny, yet deeply desire, in our always theatrical quest for selfhood in a world of simulations.

Notes

1. David Punter, *The Literature of Terror* (1980), 2 vols (London: Longman, 1996) Vol. 2, p. 198.

2. Judith Halberstam, *Skin Shows: Gothic Horror and the Technology of Monsters* (Durham NC: Duke University Press, 1995) pp. 88, 101 and 89.

3. Ibid., pp. 105 and 88.

4. Julia Kristeva, *Powers of Horror: An Essay on Abjection* (New York: Columbia University Press, 1982); Halberstam, *Skin Shows,* p. 18; J.E. Hogle, 'The Struggle for a Dichotomy: Abjection. in Jekyll and his Interpreters', in W. Veeder and G. Hirsch, eds, *Dr Jekyll and Mr Hyde After One Hundred Years* (Chicago: University of Chicago Press, 1988) pp. 161-207; Anne Williams, *Art of Darkness: A Poetics of Gothic* (Chicago: University of Chicago Press, 1995) pp. 66-79 and 124-34.

5. Kristeva, *Powers of Horror,* p. 10.

6. Kathleen L. Spencer, 'Purity and Danger: *Dracula,* the Urban Gothic, and the Late Victorian Degeneracy Crisis', *ELH,* LIX (1992) 179-225, at pp. 209-14.

7. Jennifer Wicke, 'Vampiric Typewriting: *Dracula* and its Media', *ELH,* LIX (1992) 467-93, at p. 476.

8. Ibid., pp. 472 and 478.

9. Ibid., p. 488.

10. E. J. Clery, *The Rise of Supernatural Fiction, 1762-1800* (Cambridge: Cambridge University Press, 1995) p. 77.

11. Jerrold E. Hogle, 'The Ghost of the Counterfeit in the Genesis of the Gothic', in Allan Lloyd Smith and Victor Sage, eds, *Gothick Origins and Innovations* (Atlanta, GA: Rodopi, 1994) pp. 23-33; and 'Frankenstein as Neo-Gothic: From the Ghost of the Counterfeit to the Monster of Abjection', in Tilottama Rajan and Julia Wright, eds, *Reforming Genre in British Romanticism* (Cambridge: Cambridge University Press, 1997).

12. Jean Baudrillard, 'The Structural Law of Value and the Order of Simulacra', trans. Charles Levin, in John Fekete, ed., *The Structural Allegory: Reconstructive Encounters with the New French Thought* (Minneapolis: University of Minnesota Press, 1984) pp. 54-73 and 61-2.

13. See Roxana Stuart, *Stage Blood: Vampires of the 19th-Century Stage* (Bowling Green: Bowling Green State University Popular Press, 1994) pp. 190-3.

14. Baudrillard, 'The Structural Law of Value . . .', pp. 62-73.

15. Andrea Henderson, '"An Embarrassing Subject": Use Value and Exchange Value in Early Gothic Characterisation', in M.A. Favret and N. J. Watson, eds, *At the Limits of Romanticism: Essays in Cultural, Feminist, and Materialist Criticism* (Bloomington, IN: Indiana University Press, 1994) pp. 225-45.

16. Baudrillard, 'The Structural Law of Value . . .', p. 65.

17. Bram Stoker, *Dracula*, ed. Maud Ellmann (Oxford: Oxford University Press, 1996) pp. 62-3, italics mine. All subsequent references are to this edition, and are given in the text.

18. William Veeder, 'Foreword', to M. Carter, ed., *Dracula: The Vampire and the Critics* (Ann Arbor, MI: UMI Research Press, 1988) pp. ix-xviii and xii.

19. C. Leatherdale, *The Origins of Dracula* (London: William Kimber, 1987) pp. 237-9.

20. Stuart, *Stage Blood*, p. 106.

21. Such satires included Gilbert and Sullivan's *Ruddigore* (1887). Ibid., pp. 164-78.

22. Horace Walpole, *The Castle of Otranto: A Gothic Story*, ed. W.S. Lewis (Oxford: Oxford University Press, 1982) pp. 18-19.

23. Bram Stoker, *Personal Reminiscences of Henry Irving*, 2 vols (London: William Heinemann, 1906) Vol. 2, pp. 11-15. Subsequent references are to this edition, and appear in the text.

24. See Phyllis Roth, *Bram Stoker* (Boston: Twayne Publishers, 1982) pp. 6-16.

25. Baudrillard, 'The Structural Law of Value . . .', pp. 61-2.

26. Bram Stoker, *Famous Impostors* (London: Sidgwick and Jackson, 1910) pp. 6-7. Subsequent references are to this edition and appear in the text.

27. Daniel Farson, *The Man Who Wrote Dracula: A Biography of Bram Stoker* (London: Michael Joseph, 1975) pp. 207-15 and 233-5.

CLIVE LEATHERDALE (ESSAY DATE 2001)

SOURCE: Leatherdale, Clive. "The Making of the Count." In Dracula: *The Novel and the Legend: A Study of Bram Stoker's Gothic Masterpiece*. 1985. Third edition, pp. 105-17. Westcliff-on-Sea, Essex, United Kingdom: Desert Island Books, 2001.

In the following essay, from a chapter of a third edition of a book first published in 1985, Leatherdale considers Stoker's characterization of Count Dracula, noting Stoker's sources in history, folklore, and aristocratic society.

[Dracula's] face was a strong—a very strong—aquiline, with high bridge of the thin nose and peculiarly arched nostrils; with lofty domed forehead, and hair growing scantily round the temples, but profusely elsewhere. His eyebrows were very massive, almost meeting over the nose, and with bushy hair that seemed to curl in its own profusion. The mouth, so far as I could see it under the heavy moustache, was fixed and rather cruel looking, with peculiarly sharp white teeth; these protruded over the lips, whose remarkable ruddiness showed astonishing vitality in a man of his years. For the rest, his ears were pale and at the tops extremely pointed; the chin was broad and strong, and the cheeks firm though thin. The general effect was one of extraordinary pallor.

Jonathan Harker's Journal, *Dracula* 2:51-52.

ABOUT THE AUTHOR

AN EXCERPT FROM AN EARLY REVIEW OF *DRACULA*

Since Wilkie Collins left us we have had no tale of mystery so liberal in matter and so closely woven. But with the intricate plot, and the methods of the narrative, the resemblance to stories of the author of *The Woman in White* ceases; for the audacity and the horror of *Dracula* are Mr. Stoker's own. A summary of the book would shock and disgust; but we must own that, though here and there in the course of the tale we hurried over things with repulsion, we read nearly the whole with rapt attention. It is something of a triumph for the writer that neither the improbability, nor the unnecessary number of hideous incidents recounted of the man-vampire, are long foremost in the reader's mind, but that the interest of the danger, of the complications, of the pursuit of the villain, of human skill and courage pitted against inhuman wrong and superhuman strength, rises always to the top. Keep *Dracula* out of the way of nervous children, certainly; but a grown reader, unless he be of unserviceably delicate stuff, will both shudder and enjoy.

SOURCE: "Novel Notes: *Dracula*." *The Bookman* 12, no. 71 (August 1897): 129.

Before attention turns to some of the deeper themes of Stoker's most famous novel, it will be helpful to look more closely at the characters he created and the purposes they fulfil—beginning with Count Dracula himself. Stoker spared no effort to present his demonic vampire as dramatically as possible. Other, mortal, figures, he leaves under-sketched, relying on the reader's imagination to fill in the flesh on the bones he provides, but Dracula is painted with enormous attention to detail. After the first four chapters he is 'offstage' for most of the rest of the novel,[1] yet not for a moment is the reader allowed to forget the Count's awesome presence.

Visually, aside from his facial features (described above), Dracula is clean-shaven save for a long white moustache, and dressed without a single speck of colour about him anywhere. He is a tall, old man. He could not have been uncommonly tall, however, for Dracula makes off wearing Harker's clothes—which presumably fit satisfactorily—and Harker, himself, when later described by others invites no comment as to his size. Moreover, the accepted notion of Dracula's ever-present black cloak would seem to be an invention of the cinema. Only once is such a garment mentioned (3:75) and the more usual description 'clad in black from head to foot' (2:48) would hardly be appropriate to a single item of clothing.

Much has been made of the only surviving description of Vlad the Impaler:

> He was not very tall but very stocky and strong with a cold and terrible appearance, a strong and aquiline nose, swollen nostrils, a thin and reddish face, in which the very long eye lashes framed large wide-open green eyes; the bushy black eye brows made them appear threatening. His face and chin were shaven, but for a moustache. The swollen temples increased the bulk of his head. A bull's neck connected his head [to the body] from which black curly locks hung on his wide shouldered person.[2]

There is little enough here by way of similarity—other than standard physiognomic indicators of nature's villains—even if one overlooks the improbability of Stoker ever having heard of Vlad the Impaler. Even if he had, it is beyond the bounds of plausibility to suggest that Stoker somehow stumbled upon this description.

As a fictional character, Count Dracula is an alloy: he combines in his persona certain qualities taken from Irving and perhaps others of his acquaintance; the tradition of the literary vampire descended from Lord Ruthven and Sir Francis Varney; the great myths of Romantic literature from which Stoker liberally borrowed; the wealth of Continental folklore to plant the novel firmly back in its roots; as well as an original flourish by Stoker to turn his Count into a master magician—as we shall see.

Let's consider these components in turn, beginning with real-life inputs into the Count. Henry Irving is the most obvious. Consider this description of the great actor: 'a tall, spare man . . . a peculiarly striking face, long grey hair thrown carelessly back behind the ears, clean shaven features remarkable for their delicate refinement, united with the suggestion of virile force [and] rather aquiline nose'.[3] Against this, Stoker also noted Irving's 'fine' hands and

'sweetness' of face,[4] inappropriate surely for the embodiment of evil. Belford's biography of Stoker carries Irving's significance to implausible lengths, but that significance can be measured in different ways—Irving's supposed physical likeness to the Count, his psychological domination of Stoker, and his magnetic stage presence. Irving was well used to playing Mephistopheles and his kind, as forcefully as any actor ever had. Many have speculated that Stoker intended **Dracula** to enjoy success on the stage as well as on the page, with Irving in the title role. Certainly, the novel is awash with theatrical detail, and is easy to adapt so that characters might enter stage right and exit stage left. But Irving could never have been envisaged as the Count, for the simple reason that Dracula has such a tiny part, being virtually written out of the script after the first act (in Transylvania). Irving's ego would never have tolerated that!

Other critics have suggested Franz Liszt and Walt Whitman as likely models, based on little more than that in old age they both had long white hair. Henry Morton Stanley, the explorer, has been linked on account of his looking 'more like a dead man than a living one', according to Stoker, who then describes Dracula's icy hand as 'more like the hand of a dead than a living man'.[5] Richard Burton and Lord Tennyson both earned mention in Stoker's **Reminiscences** for their pointed canine teeth.

Being a literary vampire, Dracula conforms to the requirement of belonging to the ranks of nobility. He boasts of having a distinguished lineage, possessing in his veins the blood of Attila the Hun. In some respects, Dracula's behaviour is what one might expect of the conventional literary aristocrat. He exudes charm of manner; he is contemptuous of the common man; and he speaks several languages—German excellently, and more impressive English than the Dutch professor, Van Helsing. At intervals, Stoker puts in little touches, which increase Dracula's sense of refinement. The Count is seen wearing white kid gloves and a straw hat, and he carries a brush for his clothes and a brush and comb for his hair. But on other levels he does not act like a nobleman at all. He lacks the typical aristocrat's high standard of living and conspicuous over-indulgence. He does not eat or drink to excess, nor does he pursue women (as normally understood). His lifestyle does not revolve around fashionable clothes, the theatre, or hunting; he does not hold receptions or build stately homes. He actually chooses to live in a Gothic ruin. Not even his violent pastimes are undertaken purely for pleasure.[6] Most unusual of all, for a thriving aristocrat, is the absence of servants. Dracula is not averse to performing all the necessary menial tasks—driving the calèche, preparing meals, and even making beds—to prevent Harker, his guest, from deducing that he employs no domestic staff.

By way of character, Dracula conveys more than a vague presence of malice. Stoker endows him with a personality, of sorts. He has a mannerism of tugging his moustache during animated discourses on his family history—the only subject touched on in the book capable of making him pleasantly excitable (3:66). He exhibits a full range of powerful emotions: hate, passion, anger, disdain, baffled malignity, vanity. He is mentally bright, is fearless, remorseless, and cunning—not averse to executing a strategic retreat in the face of disadvantageous odds, as the handbooks on guerrilla warfare dictate. Stoker displays his ignorance of Vlad the Impaler when describing Dracula's pre-vampire life, for when speaking of his own past the Count naturally does not see himself as a merciless psychopath, but as a stern, principled statesman. And Van Helsing concedes: 'he was in life a most wonderful man. Soldier, statesman, and alchemist . . .' (23:413-14). In this, of course, Dracula resembles Mephistopheles in Goethe's *Faust*, whose portrayal by Irving left such a deep impression on Stoker. Overall, legal-minded Harker is so impressed by his host's great foresight and intellectual prowess that he utters the book's most memorable understatement: Dracula, if he had chosen, 'would have made a formidable solicitor' (3:71).

This intelligence and urbanity, while allowing Dracula to be firmly located within the tradition of the literary vampire, only partly accounts for his all-pervading menace. He also partakes of the characteristics of the folkoric vampire. Stoker is keen to highlight the animalistic quality of his master-vampire, taking full advantage of the folkloric connection between vampires and werewolves. Besides having pointed ears and protruding canine teeth, Dracula possesses coarse, broad hands with squat fingers—as werewolves are described. His palms, too, are hairy and the nails cut to a sharp point. His eyes glow red. The stench which clings to his places of rest, and which produces a feeling of nausea to those in proximity, is the stench of excrement, of all the ills of mortality, of death, of arrested decay—augmented, when his thirst has been slaked, by the sickly-sweet, acrid smell of blood. Even his persona is animalistic: anti-rational, childlike, instinctive.

His vitality is shown as feral, and his cunning is that of an animal that resorts to swift physical action to counter any errors of judgment.

Dracula enjoys the gymnastic abilities of reptiles, animals, and birds. He can climb face-foremost down a castle wall, gripping the vertical surface with toes and fingers—though he does not fear death should he fall, for he is immune to the natural laws of mortality. These wall-descending activities are described as lizard-like (3:75). Later, Dracula's agility is expressed as 'panther-like'; he has a 'snarl' on his face; and he shows 'lion-like disdain' (23:418-19). His empathy with the animal world is demonstrated by his control over lower forms of life: rats, bats and wolves.

Dracula is obedient to the vampire specifications of European folklore. Being undead, his flesh is icy to the touch; he casts no reflection in the mirror, and when standing in front of flames does not obstruct a view of them. He is unable to impose his presence on a victim at the time of first contact, unless his prey shows complicity in some form. This is evident in Harker's stepping over the threshold at Castle Dracula (2:48), and in the Count's later visits to Lucy and Renfield (21:383). Dracula possesses enormous physical strength and speed of movement; his eyes can induce hypnotic effects; and with selective victims he is capable of psychic transfer.

Dracula can direct the elements around him, such as creating a puff of wind. He can see in the dark and vaporise himself at will. He is able to change into a dog, wolf, or bat; he can dematerialise to be transported as mist; and he can take shape from phosphorescent specks riding on moonbeams—whose whirring motions weaken powers of resistance. He is restricted by the presence of running water, being unable to cross it except at the slack or flood of the tide, unless with manual assistance. He sleeps and wakes with the precision of clockwork—dawn and dusk being calculated to the second. While sleeping, Dracula appears to be dead, eyes open with no pulse or respiratory motion. All the while he is 'conscious' of activity around him, although searching hands cannot 'wake' him (4:100).

Crucially, although Dracula can theoretically be kept at bay by garlic and other pagan safeguards (though in practice these uniformly fail), he is essentially a vampire of the Christian mould. In other words he is a representative/client/manifestation of the devil (in London he aptly assumes the alias 'Count *de Ville*' (20:375). He must therefore be shown to be vulnerable to Christian icons and imagery. The crucifix—arch-symbol of the Christian faith—makes him recoil and cower, and the application of holy wafer sterilises his places of rest.[7]

But Stoker did not wish to restrict his vampire-king within the parameters prescribed by folklore. Dracula would have to be special, both in his attributes and in his manner of becoming a vampire. Several of Dracula's qualities differentiate him from more common varieties of his ilk, for example Stoker's insistence that Dracula can sleep only in consecrated earth: 'in soil barren of holy memories [he] cannot rest' (18:338). This requirement would seem to possess neither folkloric nor historic antecedent.[8] According to Orthodox superstition, the undead, if excommunicated, were unable to rest in hallowed soil. So what were Stoker's motives? Maybe he intended Dracula's 'sacrilege' to heighten the reader's sense of outrage. Stoker's innovation makes the Count's lairs harder to locate, for he is 'sleeping' deceitfully among God's true dead.

Another example of Dracula's uniqueness is his immunity to the rays of the sun. The vampire of superstition is the quintessential apparition of night; it being believed that sunlight could pass through, or harm, sensitive tissue. Dracula, however, cannot be destroyed by direct sunlight as film versions would have us believe. That would make him too vulnerable. Once he is strong and vigorous from the consumption of fresh blood, he is permitted in the novel to wander the streets of London quite naturally. Dracula's only handicap is that his vampire powers become neutralised during daylight, when he reverts, to all intents, to being a mere mortal. He must therefore take care that at the moment of sunrise he is in the place and form that he wishes to be for the coming day. Otherwise he must await the precise moment of noon or sunset to effect the desired transference (22:401).

Most important, Stoker could not allow his arch-fiend to have become a vampire by any of the standard procedures of folklore, for all imply falling victim in some manner. Count Dracula can be a victim of nobody and nothing. If he is a vampire, it must have been through his choice and his power. He was neither bitten whilst alive by another undead, nor was he sentenced to a vampiric punishment for any of the appropriate transgressions. In his human life, Count Dracula was an alchemist and magician. He had studied the secrets of the black arts and other aspects of devilry when enrolled as a student at the Scholomance (18:337; 23:414)—a mythical academy situated high in the Carpathian Mountains, overlooking the town of Sibiu (known in Saxon as Hermannstadt).[9] The patron of the academy is the devil himself, who instructs on the dark secrets of nature: thunder and lightning, the language of animals, magical spells. Those who studied natural phenomena were assumed to be capable of mastering them. Legend has it that the Scholomance would admit students ten at a time. Upon acquisition of the devilish insight, nine would return to their everyday lives, leaving the tenth to be taken up by the devil as group payment. He would be mounted on an *ismejeu* (dragon—a merging of Dracula's devil/dragon associations) and recruited as the devil's aide-de-camp.[10] Needless to say, Dracula was the tenth student, whose arcane wisdom is demonstrated by Stoker early in the novel. The Count inspects mysterious blue flames flickering in the forest, which, according to folklore, conceal treasure and gold.

Stoker does not permit Dracula's transition from man to vampire to be left to the reader's imagination. Such were the resources of Dracula's brain that, together with the magical powers gleaned from the Scholomance, his mental faculties survived physical death (23:414). But they did not survive intact. He paid the price of having much of his memory destroyed, and has to engage in the re-learning process almost in the manner of an infant. Van Helsing, the guru of Dracula's adversaries, is an exponent of the scientific method of 'experimentation'. He appreciates the Count's emerging mental powers because he, Van Helsing, also employs scientific method, reaching out to acquire knowledge slowly but surely, one step at a time. Van Helsing's fears are twofold: that Dracula has acquired immortality through forging a special, yet undisclosed relationship with the devil; and that he has centuries ahead of him to sharpen his cunning and his intellect. Dracula undergoes a dramatic shift in power during the course of the novel. At the outset he appears as a cautious old man, not yet sure of the powers at his command. Despite his longevity, he is in the position of a fledgling bird about to leave the nest and fly for the first time. He has not yet employed the full range of vampire powers which are about to be unleashed.

Count Dracula is physically dead. But if he is, as it were, living in death, then it might be asked whether he is more dead than alive, or more alive than dead. If he is really dead, then why does he never speak of life beyond the grave, or communicate its wonders or its terrors? The only time Dracula reflects on his past is when recalling his martial exploits during his pre-vampire existence. He has nothing to say about the four hundred years since he signed up with the devil. It would appear that his only aspect that is dead is his body, for his mind has never travelled beyond the experiences of this earth.

To reinforce Dracula's grasp of black magic, Stoker invests the Count's native Transylvania with suitably mysterious rocks and waters. It might easily be a lost world inhabited by dinosaurs, for it is a land

> full of strangeness of the geologic and chemical world. There are deep caverns and fissures that reach none know whither. There have been volcanoes, some of whose openings still send out waters of strange properties, and gases that kill or make to [sic] vivify. Doubtless there is something magnetic or electric in some of these combinations of occult forces which work for physical life in strange way [sic].
>
> (24:436)[11]

These gases are discovered at first hand by Van Helsing when he sniffs sulphurous fumes inside the chapel of Castle Dracula (27:499). Stoker's Transylvania, in other words is not only a land beyond the forest, it is also a land beyond scientific understanding—a netherworld—where the known laws of nature are suspended. It is a fitting haunt for an agent of diabolism.

Awareness of Dracula's vampire origins leads to the next, vital, question—his motives. He is no zombie-like automaton driven solely by a blind lust for blood. The relationship between Dracula and blood is much more subtle. For one thing, its consumption actually alters his appearance. Absorption of blood changes him from an old, into a younger, stronger man with dark, not white, hair. In just three days between 'meals' his hair reverts to showing white streaks (11:216).

Dracula is not out to bite the neck of every victim who comes his way. He does not patrol nightly in search of liquid nourishment. Rather, his is the addiction of the junkie or the alcoholic. Dracula will not die if no blood is available, any more than will the alcoholic if deprived of spirits. In each case just one substance supplies vigour, energy. It is not that Dracula *likes* drinking blood. He *needs* blood—not for life (with which he is blessed/cursed) but for power. It functions as a stimulant.

The only exception is when his taking of blood is tactical. Dracula's blood-banks are always female.[12] His szgany (gypsy) henchmen, who do his earthly bidding, do not go in fear of his teeth. Renfield, similarly, becomes a servant of Dracula,

not his blood supply. Still more illuminating is Dracula's trivial interest in Jonathan Harker, who serves as his estate agent and English language tutor, not his provider of nourishment. When Harker cuts himself shaving, Dracula only momentarily loses control of himself. This suggests that the sight of blood induces in him a love-hate ambivalence, not dissimilar to the reactions stimulated in the alcoholic by the prospect of liquor.

Dracula's strategic, as opposed to his biological, interest in blood is to ensnare female victims. These, in turn, will ensnare their menfolk, so that his vampire empire enlarges evermore through incestuous expansion. Here, Stoker, acknowledges the folkloric requirement that vampires always seek their nearest and dearest: 'The holiest love was the recruiting sergeant for their ghastly ranks' (22:408). Dracula is aware of how he can turn this to advantage: 'Your girls that you all love are mine already: and through them you and others shall yet be mine—my creatures, to do my bidding, and to be my jackals when I want to feed' (23:421).

In no instance does he destroy the lives of his victims for pleasure, but always in order to make use of them. As bloodlessness is not life-threatening to Dracula, his search must stem from a deeper, psychological drive. Dracula tells an unsuspecting Harker of his ambitions: 'I long to go through the crowded streets of your mighty London, to be in the midst of the whirl and rush of humanity, to share its life, its change, its death, and all that makes it what it is' (2:55).

This confession is revealing. In the Europe of the 1890s Dracula has become outdated.[13] Transylvania is depicted as a peasant land in decline, unfitting as the continued habitat for a proud descendant of Attila. Admittedly, it is Dracula's blood-sucking over the centuries which is partly responsible for the enfeeblement of his native land, for its depleted population flout his authority by immunising themselves with garlic and crosses. He feels cheated and deprived. No longer can he wage war against invading Turks: instead he is reduced to hunting defenceless children. In the meantime, Britain has become the hub of Western industrialism. By switching his arena and his methods of operation, Dracula sees new opportunities to be exploited.

His objective is therefore to establish a contemporary vampire empire in Britain. In this he will be aided by British laws and customs. The rational West will not suspect him. Its contempt for Eastern superstitions will leave him free; its democratic customs will enable him to flourish undetected; and its legal principle of presumption of innocence will work to his devious advantage. Jails cannot hold vampires. British society will unconsciously provide both his sheath and his armour, and 'the doubting of wise men would be his greatest strength' (24:438).

Notwithstanding, Dracula's motives contain a more personal element. When narrowly escaping ambush in London he reveals his burning grievance: 'My revenge has just begun! I spread it over centuries, and time is on my side' (23:421). Revenge? Revenge for what? Stoker seems to be harking back to the pages of Wilkinson, which stated that 'Dracula' was driven back to Wallachia and defeated by the Turks. If by the 1890s Count Dracula can no longer take revenge against the Turks, a fifteenth century superpower, he could at least direct it against the modern superpower. Britain must pay for the crimes of the Ottomans, perhaps by coming to symbolise the ingratitude and treachery of Christian Europe—though when the time comes for the Count to vent his anger the identity of his enemies is suitably vague (21:396).

This desire for revenge, however, is not totally persuasive. Like the Wandering Jew, Dracula is doomed to wander the earth for eternity unless his heart be pierced. The Count is bored. It is sport he craves. He toys with his adversaries, taunting them, almost defying them to pit their puny wits against him. Despite this range of motives, it is not Stoker's aim to elicit sympathy for Dracula, or reveal him a victim as much as a victimiser. Stoker portrays him as incarnate evil, without any redeeming features, someone deserving not the least vestige of sympathy.

Presumably, Stoker's intention was that the reader breathes a sigh of relief when Dracula meets his doom. But can we be so sure? Clearly his pursuers think they have destroyed Dracula, and continue to think so several years afterwards. But have they? This is how Mina describes that climactic moment:

> As I looked, the eyes [of Dracula] saw the sinking sun, and the look of hate in them turned to triumph. But, on the instant, came the sweep and the flash of Jonathan's great knife. I shrieked as I saw it sheer through the throat; whilst at the same moment Mr Morris's bowie knife plunged in the heart . . . the whole body crumbled into dust and passed from our sight . . . in that moment of dissolution there was in the face a look of peace such as I never could have imagined might have rested there.
>
> (27:509)

This might seem conclusive enough, until it is recalled that Van Helsing had earlier given precise instructions on how to be rid of the vampire. Folklore, too, insists on ritualistic observation of prescribed rites. These are not followed in the case of Dracula, who is despatched as if he were human, with cold steel. No wooden stake is used; his head is not detached from the body; and no corpse remains to be properly treated or devoured by flames. Initially it seems that Dracula's look of 'triumph' is premature, but could it be the attackers' sense of satisfaction that is misplaced? Stoker had already informed his readers that vampires have the power of dematerialisation and can transform themselves into specks of dust. Conceivably, then, the Count dematerialised just in time. Realising his narrow escape he prefers to lay low, until such time as Stoker resurrects him in a sequel.

Alternatively, Stoker might have felt uncomfortable at the homoerotic notion of Dracula being phallically 'staked' by men and—following the example of the female vampires—writhing and screeching in his orgasmic death-throes. This could have been avoided if Mina . . . had staked Dracula. But while retaining the heterosexual pattern, it would still have left Stoker the problem of depicting the male orgasm. Jonathan Harker . . . would also be denied his cherished revenge, and whatever Mina's other qualities the idea of her hammering a three-foot stake into Dracula would have stretched credibility. It would also, of course, have wrecked the sexual focus on the stake-phallus. One imagines that Stoker thought long and hard about who would destroy Dracula, and how, but never quite came up with a satisfactory answer.

Notes

1. The Count, in fact, has only two speaking parts once he arrives in England. Stoker's final decision to have Dracula 'on view' as little as possible appears, from his notes, to have been reached in a late draft. Earlier drafts show Dracula onstage more frequently.

2. Nicholas Modrussa, in Radu Florescu and Raymond T McNally, *Dracula: A Biography*, p.50.

3. Newspaper report from *New York Tribune*, November 1883, reprinted in Austin Brereton, *The Life of Henry Irving*, Vol 2, p.14.

4. *Reminiscences*, 1:234 and 1:88. For a detailed examination of all the inputs into Count Dracula see Elizabeth Miller, *Dracula: Sense & Nonsense*, Chapter 1.

5. *Reminiscences*, 1:370; Belford, p.238.

6. Franco Moretti, *Signs Taken for Wonders: Essays in the Sociology of Literary Forms*, pp.90-91.

7. Stoker's working notes show that Dracula was meant to register fear only when presented with relics older than himself.

8. Leonard Wolf, *A Dream of Dracula*, p.264.

9. Most of Stoker's information on the Scholomance came from Emily Gerard's 'Transylvanian Superstitions'.

10. Gerard, op. cit.

11. Here again, Stoker may have consulted the works of Emily Gerard, *The Land Beyond the Forest* and *The Waters of Hercules*.

12. A possible exception is Dracula's 'attacks' on the crew of the *Demeter*. Whether he merely kills them, or kills them for their blood, or they throw themselves overboard in terror, is not made clear.

13. See Thomas P Walsh, '*Dracula*: Logos and Myth', p.230.

Select Bibliography

Articles

Norman Adams, 'Bram Stoker', *Leopard* 2:8, 22 June 1976.

Stephen D Arata, 'The Occidental Tourist: *Dracula* and the Anxiety of Reverse Colonization', *Victorian Studies* 33:4, 1990.

Richard Astle, 'Dracula as Totemic Monster: Lacan, Freud, Oedipus and History', *Sub-Stance* 25, 1980.

C F Bentley, 'The Monster in the Bedroom: Sexual Symbolism in Bram Stoker's *Dracula*', *Literature and Psychology* 22, 1972.

Joseph S Bierman, 'Dracula: Prolonged Childhood Illness, and the Oral Triad', *American Imago* 29, 1972.

——, 'The Genesis and Dating of "Dracula" from Bram Stoker's Working Notes', *Notes and Queries* 24, Jan-Feb 1977.

Charles S Blinderman, 'Vampurella: Darwin and Count Dracula', *Massachusetts Review* 21, Summer 1980.

Wanda Bonewits, 'Dracula, the Black Christ', *Gnostica* 4:7, March-May 1975.

Thomas B Byers, 'Good Men and Monsters: The Defences of *Dracula*', *Literature and Psychology,* 31:4 1981

M M Carlson, 'What Stoker Saw: An Introduction to the History of the Literary Vampire', *Folkore Forum*, 10:2, 1977.

Christopher Craft, '"Kiss Me with Those Red Lips": Gender and Inversion in Bram Stoker's *Dracula*', *Representations*, 8 1984.

Bernard Davies, 'Mountain Greenery', The Dracula Journals, 1:1, Winter 1976-77.

Stephanie Demetrakopoulos, 'Feminism, Sex Role Exchanges, and Other Subliminal Fantasies in Bram Stoker's *Dracula*', *Frontiers: A Journal of Women's Studies*, 2:3, 1977.

Peter Denman, 'Le Fanu and Stoker: A Probable Connection', *Eire-Ireland (Irish American Cultural Institute)* 9, Autumn 1974.

Robert E Dowse and David Palmer, '"Dracula": the Book of Blood', *The Listener*, 7 March 1963.

James Drummond, 'Bram Stoker's Cruden Bay', *Scots Magazine*, April 1976.

——, 'Dracula's Castle', *The Scotsman*, 26 June 1976.

——, 'The Mistletoe and the Oak', *Scots Magazine*, October 1977.

——, 'The Scottish Play', *The Scottish Review*, 23 August 1981.

Paul Dukes, 'Dracula: Fact, Legend and Fiction', *History Today* 32, July 1982.

Ernest Fontana, 'Lombroso's Criminal Man and Stoker's *Dracula*', *Victorian Newsletter*, 66, 1984.

Christopher Frayling, 'Vampyres', *London Magazine*, 14:2, June-July 1974.

Carrol L Fry, 'Fictional Conventions and Sexuality in *Dracula*', *Victorian Newsletter* 42, 1972.

Jean Gattegno, 'Folie, Croyance et Fantastique dans "Dracula",' *Littérature* 8, December 1972.

Gail Griffin, '"Your girls that You all Love are Mine": *Dracula* and the Victorian Male Sexual Imagination', *International Journal of Women's Studies,* 3:5 1980.

Burton Hatlen, 'The Return of the Repressed/Oppressed in Bram Stoker's *Dracula*', *The Minnesota Review* 15, 1980.

Mark M Hennelly Jr, '*Dracula*: the Gnostic Quest and the Victorian Wasteland', *English Literature in Transition*, 20:1, 1977.

——, 'Twice Told Tales of Two Counts', *Wilkie Collins Society Journal* 2, 1982.

Gwyneth Hood, 'Sauron and Dracula', *Mythlore*, 52, 1987.

Eric Irvin, 'Dracula's Friends and Forerunners', *Quadrant*, 135, 1978.

Alan Johnson, 'Bent and Broken Necks: Signs of Design in Stoker's *Dracula*', *Victorian Newsletter*, 72, 1987.

——, '"Dual Life": The Status of Women in Stoker's *Dracula*', *Tennessee Studies in Literature*, 27, 1984.

E Randolph Johnson, 'The Victorian Vampire', *Baker St Journal* 18, December 1968.

Roger Johnson, 'The Bloofer Ladies', *The Dracula Journals* 1:4, Summer 1982.

R W Johnson, 'The Myth of the Twentieth Century', *New Society*, 9 December 1982.

Bacil F Kirtley, '*Dracula,* the Monastic Chronicles and Slavic Folklore', *Midwest Folklore* 6:3, 1956.

Royce MacGillivray, '"Dracula": Bram Stoker's Spoiled Masterpiece, *Queen's Quarterly* 79, 1972.

Lionel Milgrom, 'Vampires, Plants, and Crazy Kings', *New Scientist*, 26 April 1984.

Agnes Murgoci, 'The Evil Eye in Roumania, and its Antidotes', *Folklore* 34, 1923.

——, 'The Vampire in Roumania', *Folklore* 37, 1926.

Brian Murphy, 'The Nightmare of the Dark: the Gothic Legacy of Count Dracula', *Odyssey* 1, 1976.

Grigore Nandris, 'A Philological Analysis of *Dracula* and Rumanian Placenames and Masculine Personal Names in -a/-ea', *Slavonic and East European Review* 37, 1959.

———, 'The Historical Dracula: The Theme of His Legend in the Western and in the Eastern Literatures of Europe', *Comparative Literature Studies* 3:4, 1966.

Felix J Oinas, 'Heretics as Vampires and Demons in Russia', *Slavic and East European Journal* 22, Winter 1978.

Robert Phillips, 'The Agony and the Ecstasy: A Jungian Analysis of Two Vampire Novels, Meredith Ann Pierce's *The Darkangel* and Bram Stoker's *Dracula*', *West Virginia University Philological Papers*, 31, 1986.

Christopher Gist Raible, 'Dracula: Christian Heretic', *The Christian Century* 96, 31 January 1979.

Maurice Richardson, 'The Psychoanalysis of Ghost Stories', *Twentieth Century* 166, December 1956.

Phyllis A Roth, 'Suddenly Sexual Women in Bram Stoker's *Dracula*', *Literature and Psychology* 27, 1977.

Ronald Schleifer, 'The Trap of the Imagination; the Gothic Tradition, Fiction, and "The Turn of the Screw",' *Criticism* 22, Autumn 1980.

David Seed, 'The Narrative Method of *Dracula*', *Nineteenth Century Fiction*, 40:1 1985.

Carol A Senf, '*Dracula*: the Unseen face in the Mirror', *Journal of Narrative Technique*, 1979.

———, '"Dracula": Stoker's Response to the New Woman', *Victorian Studies* 26:1, Autumn 1982.

Seymour Shuster, 'Dracula and Surgically Induced Trauma in Children', *British Journal of Medical Psychology* 46, 1973.

Gerard Stein, '"Dracula" ou la Circulation du "Sans",' *Littérature* 8, December 1972.

John Allen Stevenson, 'A Vampire in the Mirror: The Sexuality of *Dracula*', *PMLA*, 103:2, 1988.

Bram Stoker, 'The Censorship of Fiction', *Nineteenth Century*, 64, September 1908.

Philip Temple, 'The Origins of Dracula', *The Times Literary Supplement*, 4 November 1983.

James Twitchell, 'The Vampire Myth', *American Imago* 37, 1980.

Geoffrey Wall, '"Different from Writing": *Dracula* in 1897', *Literature and History*, 10:1, 1984.

Thomas P Walsh, '*Dracula*: Logos and Myth', *Research Studies* 47:4, December 1979.

Richard Wasson, 'The Politics of Dracula', *English Language in Transition* 9:1, 1966.

Judith Weissman, 'Women and Vampires: *Dracula* as a Victorian Novel', *Midwest Quarterly*, 18:4, 1977.

Books

Lory Alder and Richard Dalby, *The Dervish of Windsor Castle: The Life of Arminius Vambery*, Bachman and Turner (London, 1979).

Paul Barber, *Vampires, Burial and Death*, Yale University Press (New Haven, 1988).

Glen St John Barclay, *Anatomy of Horror: Masters of Occult Fiction*, Weidenfeld & Nicolson (London, 1978).

Barbara Belford, *Bram Stoker: A Biography of the Author of Dracula*, Weidenfeld & Nicolson, (London, 1996).

Austin Brereton, *The Life of Henry Irving*, 2 Vols, Longmans, Green London, 1908).

Dom Calmet, *Dissertation on those Persons who Return to Earth Bodily, the Excommunicated, the Oupires or Vampires, roucalacas, & c*, reprinted as *Treatise on Vampires & Revenants, The Phantom World*, Desert Island Books (Westcliffon-Sea, 1993).

Margaret Carter (ed.), *Dracula: the Vampire and the Critics*, UMI Research Press (Ann Arbor, Michegan, 1988).

Basil Copper, *The Vampire: In Legend, Fact and Art*, Hale (London, 1973).

Richard Dalby, *Bram Stoker: A Bibliography of First Editions*, Dracula Press (London, 1983).

Carol M Davison (ed.), *Bram Stoker's Dracula: Sucking Through the Century 1897-1997*, Dundurn Press (Toronto, 1997).

Hamilton Deane and John Balderston, *Dracula: the Vampire Play in Three Acts*, Samuel French Inc. (New York, 1960).

Robert Eighteen-Bisang and J Gordon Melton, *Dracula: A Century of Editions, Adaptations and Translations*, Transylvania Society of Dracula (Santa Barbara, 1998).

Daniel Farson, *The Man Who Wrote Dracula: A Biography of Bram Stoker*, Michael Joseph (London, 1975).

Leslie Fielder, *Freaks: Myths and Images of the Secret Self*, Simon and Schuster (New York, 1978).

Radu Florescu and Raymond T McNally, *Dracula: A Bibliography*, Hale (London, 1973).

Christopher Frayling (ed.), *Vampyres: Lord Byron to Count Dracula*, Faber (London, 1991).

Nancy Garden, *Vampires*, Lippincott (London, 1973).

Michael Geare and Michael Corby, *Dracula's Diary*, Buchan and Enright (London, 1982).

Ken Gelder, *Reading the Vampire*, Routledge (London, 1994).

Donald F Glut, *The Dracula Book*, Scarecrow Press (New York, 1975).

Peter Haining (ed.), *The Dracula Scrapbook*, New English Library (London 1976).

———, *The Leprechaun's Kingdom*, Pictorial Presentations/Souvenir Press (London, 1979).

———, *Shades of Dracula: The Uncollected Stories of Bram Stoker*, William Kimber (London, 1982).

———, *The Un-Dead: The Legend of Bram Stoker and Dracula*, Constable (London, 1997).

William Hughes, *Beyond Dracula: Bram Stoker's Fiction and its Cultural Context*, Macmillan (London, 2000).

———, *Bram Stoker: A Bibliography*, Victorian Fiction Research Unit, University of Queensland (Queensland, Australia 1997).

Bernhardt J Hurwood, *Vampires*, Omnibus Press (London, 1981).

Laurence Irving, *Henry Irving: The Actor and his World,* Faber and Faber (London, 1951).

Rosemary Jackson, *Fantasy: The Literature of Subversion,* Methuen (London, 1981).

Clive Leatherdale (ed.), *Dracula Unearthed,* Desert Island Books (Westcliff-on-Sea, 1998).

———(ed.), *The Jewel of Seven Stars,* Desert Island Books (Westcliff-on-Sea, 1996).

———(ed.), *The Origins of Dracula: The Background to Bram Stoker's Gothic Masterpiece,* Desert Island Books (Westcliff-on-Sea, 1998).

Harry Ludlam, *A Biography of Bram Stoker: Creator of Dracula,* New English Library (London, 1977).

Elizabeth MacAndrew, *The Gothic Tradition in Fiction,* Columbia University Press (New York, 1979).

Andrew MacKenzie, *Dracula Country: Travels and Folk Beliefs in Romania,* Arthur Barker (London, 1977).

———, *Romanian Journey,* Hale (London, 1983).

Raymond T McNally and Radu Florescu, *In Search of Dracula,* Houghton Mifflin (Boston, 1994).

———, *The Essential Dracula,* Mayflower Books, (New York, 1979).

Raymond T McNally, *Dracula Was a Woman,* Hale (London, 1984).

Anthony Masters, *The Natural History of the Vampire,* Hart-Davis (London, 1972).

J Gordon Melton, *The Vampire Book: The Encyclopaedia of the Undead,* Visible Ink Press (Detroit, 1999).

Elizabeth Miller, *Dracula: Sense & Nonsense,* Desert Island Books, (Westcliff-on-Sea, 2000).

———(ed.), *Dracula: The Shade and the Shadow,* Desert Island Books (Westcliff-on-Sea, 1998).

———*Reflections on Dracula,* Transylvania Press, (Whiterock, BC, 1997).

Franco Moretti, *Signs Taken for Wonders: Essays in the Sociology of Literary Forms,* New Left Books/Verso (London, 1983).

Charles Osborne (ed.), *The Bram Stoker Bedside Companion,* Quartet (London, 1974).

Sean O'Sullivan, *The Folklore of Ireland,* Batsford (London, 1974).

Barrie Pattison, *The Seal of Dracula,* Lorimer Publishing (London, 1975).

David Pirie, *The Vampire Cinema,* Hamlyn (London, 1977).

John Polidori, *The Vampyre,* Gubblecote Press, (Tring, Herts, 1973).

Mario Praz, *The Romantic Agony,* Oxford University Press (London, 1933).

David Punter, *The Literature of Terror,* Longman (London, 1980).

John R Reed, *Victorian Conventions,* Ohio University Press (Ohio, 1975).

Martin V Riccardo, *Vampires Unearthed: the Complete Multi-Media Vampire and Dracula Bibliography,* Garland Publishing

Gabriel Ronay, *The Dracula Myth,* W H Allen (London, 1972).

Phyllis A Roth, *Bram Stoker,* Twayne Publishers, G K Hall (Boston, 1982).

Raymond Rudorff, *The Dracula Archives,* Sphere (London, 1973).

Carol Senf, *The Critical Response to Bram Stoker,* Greenwood Press (Westport, 1993).

Penelope Shuttle and Peter Redgrove, *The Wise Wound: Menstruation and Everywoman,* Gollancz (London, 1978).

David Skal, *Hollywood Gothic: The Tangled Web of Dracula from Novel to Stage to Screen,* Norton (London, 1990).

Jacob Sprenger and Heinrich Kramer, *Malleus Maleficarum* (translated by Montague Summers), Arrow (London, 1971).

Sylvia Starshine (ed.), *Dracula: or The Un-Dead,* Pumpkin Books (Nottingham, 1997).

Nicolai Stoicescu, *Vlad Tepes: Prince of Walachia,* Academy of the Socialist Republic of Romania (Bucharest, 1978).

Bram Stoker (in chronological order), *The Primrose Path,* Desert Island Books (Westcliff-on-Sea, 1999).

———, *The Duties of Clerks of Petty Sessions in Ireland,* Published by Authority (Dublin, 1879).

———, *Under the Sunset,* Sampson Low (London, 1881).

———, *A Glimpse of America,* Sampson Low (London, 1886).

———, *The Snake's Pass,* Sampson Low (London, 1890).

———, *The Watter's Mou',* Constable (Westminster, 1895).

———, *The Shoulder of Shasta,* Desert Island Books (Westcliff-on-Sea, 2000).

———, *Dracula (Unearthed),* Desert Island Books (Westcliff-on-Sea, 1998).

———, *Miss Betty,* Pearson (London, 1898).

———, *The Mystery of the Sea,* Heinemann (London, 1902).

———, *The Jewel of Seven Stars,* Desert Island Books (Westcliff-on-Sea, 1996).

———, *The Man,* Heinemann (London, 1905).

———, *Personal Reminiscences of Henry Irving,* 2 Vols, Heinemann (London, 1906).

———, *Lady Athlyne,* Heinemann (London, 1908).

———, *Snowbound: The Record of a Theatrical Touring Party,* Desert Island Books (Westcliff-on-Sea, 1908).

———, *The Lady of the Shroud,* Desert Island Books (Westcliff-on-Sea, 2001).

———, *Famous Impostors,* Sidgwick and Jackson (London, 1910).

———, *The Lair of the White Worm,* Rider (London, 1911).

———, *Dracula's Guest - and Other Weird Stories,* Routledge (London, 1914).

———, 'Bram Stoker's Original Foundation Notes & Data for his *Dracula*.' (unpublished), Rosenbach Museum & Library, Philadelphia. MS EL3 F.5874D.

George Stoker, *With 'The Unspeakables'; or Two Years' Campaigning in European and Asiatic Turkey,* Chapman & Hall (London, 1878).

Douglas Oliver Street, 'Bram Stoker's "Under the Sunset" with Introductory Biographical and Critical Material (unpublished PhD thesis), University of Nebraska-Lincoln (1977).

Montague Summers, *The Gothic Quest,* The Fortune Press (London).

——, *The Vampire: His Kith and Kin,* Kegan Paul (London, 1928).

——, *The Vampire in Europe,* Kegan Paul (London, 1929).

Thomas Ray Thornburg, 'The Quester and the Castle: the Gothic Novel as Myth, with Special Reference to Bram Stoker's Dracula' (unpublished PhD thesis), Ball State University (1970).

James B Twitchell, *The Living Dead: A Study of the Vampire in Romantic Literature,* Duke University Press (North Carolina, 1981).

——, *Dreadful Pleasures: An Anatomy of Modern Horror,* Oxford University Press (London, 1985).

Devendra P Varma, *The Gothic Flame,* Arthur Barker (London, 1957).

——, *Introduction to Varney the Vampire; or, the Feast of Blood,* Arno Press (New York, 1970).

Ornella Volta, *The Vampire,* Tandem Books (London, 1965).

Leonard Wolf, *The Annotated Dracula,* New English Library (London, 1975).

——, *Dracula: The Connoisseur's Guide,* Broadway Books (New York, 1997).

——, *A Dream of Dracula,* Little, Brown and Co (Boston, 1972).

Dudley Wright, *Vampires and Vampirism,* Rider (London, 1924).

Bram Stoker's Sources listed in his Working Notes

Rev Sabine Baring-Gould MA, *The Book of Were-Wolves: Being an Account of a Terrible Superstition,* Smith, Elder & Co (London, 1865).

——, *Curious Myths of the Middle Ages,* Rivingtons (London, 1877).

——, *Germany, Present and Past,* (2 vols), Kegan Paul, Trench (London, 1879).

Fletcher S Bassett (Lieutenant US Navy), *Legends and Superstitions of the Sea and of Sailors - in all Lands and at all Times,* Sampson Low (London, 1885).

Isabella L Bird, *The Golden Chersonese,* John Murray (London, 1883).

Charles Boner, *Transylvania: Its Products and its People,* Longmans, Green, Reader and Dyer (London, 1865).

Sir Thomas Browne, *Religio Medici.*

Andrew F Crosse, *Round About the Carpathians,* Blackwood (London, 1878).

Rushton M Dorman, *The Origin of Primitive Superstitions: And Their Development into the Worship of Spirits and the Doctrine of Spiritual Agency Among the Aborigines of America,* Lippincott & Co (London, 1881).

A Fellow of the Carpathian Society, *'Magyarland': Being the Narrative of our Travels Through the Highlands and Lowlands of Hungary,* (2 Vols), Sampson Low (London, 1881).

Emily Gerard, 'Transylvanian Superstitions' *The Nineteenth Century,* July 1885.

Major E C Johnson MAI, FRHistS, *On the Track of the Crescent: Erratic Notes from the Piraeus to Pesth,* Hurst and Blackett (London, 1885).

John Jones, *The Natural and the Supernatural: Or, Man—Physical, Apparitional and Spiritual,* H Balliere (London, 1861).

William Jones FSA, *Credulities Past and Present,* Chatto and Windus (London, 1880).

——, *History and Mystery of Precious Stones,* Richard Bentley & Son (London, 1880).

Rev W Henry Jones, and Lewis L Kropf, *The Folk-Tales of the Magyars,* Elliot Stock (London, 1889).

Henry Charles Lea, *Superstition and Force—Essays on: The Wager of Law, The Wager of Battle, The Ordeal, and Torture,* H C Lea (Philadelphia, 1878).

Rev Frederick George Lee DCL, Vicar of All Saints', Lambeth, *The Other World: Or, Glimpses of the Supernatural—Being Facts, Records and Traditions* (2 vols), Henry S King and Co (London, 1875).

Henry Lee FLS, FGS, FZS, Sometime Naturalist of the Brighton Aquarium, *Sea Fables Explained,* William Clowes and Sons (London, 1883).

——, *Sea Monsters Unmasked,* William Clowes and Sons (London, 1883).

Sarah Lee (sometimes classified under her former name, Mrs Bowdich), *Anecdotes of Habits and Instincts of Birds, Reptiles and Fishes,* Lindsay Blalmston (Philadelphia, 1853).

——, (see also *Anecdotes of Habits and Instincts of Animals,* Lindsay Blalmston, Philadelphia, 1853).

L F Alfred Maury (no titles given, but probably include the following), *Essai sur les Légendes Pieuses du Moyen-Age,* Chez Ladrange (Paris, 1843).

——, *La Magie et L'Astrologie dans L'Antiquité et au Moyen Age: ou, Étude sur les Superstitions Païennes qui sont Perpétuées jusqu'à jours,* Didier et Cie (Paris, 1860).

——, *Le Sommeil et Les Rêves: Études Psychologiques sur ces Phénomènes et les divers États qui s'y Rattachent,* Didier et Cie (Paris, 1865).

Herbert Mayo MD, *On the Truths contained in Popular Superstitions—with an Account of Mesmerism,* William Blackwood and Sons (London 1851).

Thomas Pettigrew FRS, FSA, *On Superstitions connected with the History and Practice of Medicine and Surgery,* John Churchill (London, 1844).

Rev Albert Réville DD, *The Devil: His Origin, Greatness and Decadence,* Williams and Norgate (London, 1871).

F C and J Rivington, *The Theory of Dreams,* (2 Vols), 62 St Paul's Churchyard (London, 1808).

F K Robinson, *A Whitby Glossary*, 1876.

Robert H Scott MA FRS, Secretary of the Meterological Office, *Fishery Barometer Manual*, HMSO (London, 1887).

William Wilkinson, Late British Consul Resident at Bukorest, *An Account of the Principalities of Wallachia and Moldavia: with various Political Observations Relating to Them*, Longman, Hurst (London 1820).

JOSEPH VALENTE (ESSAY DATE 2002)

SOURCE: Valente, Joseph. "Beyond Blood: Defeating the Inner Vampire." In *Dracula's Crypt: Bram Stoker, Irishness, and the Question of Blood*, pp. 121-43. Urbana and Chicago: University of Illinois Press, 2002.

In the following essay, Valente demonstrates how Stoker uses characters to comment on and illuminate political and cultural experiences from an Irish perspective in Dracula.

If Seward errs, and errs fatally, in ascribing Renfield's first startling transformation entirely to the civilizing female influence of Mina Harker, it is nonetheless true that the inmate and the helpmate possess a special bond in which the Victorian construction of her gender importantly factors. Just as Renfield would continue to enjoy unimpeachable membership in the general society of Little England were it not for his perceived disability—his intermittent mania and zoophagy—so 'Mina would continue to enjoy unqualified membership in the inner councils of Little England were it not for her perceived disability—her feminine delicacy or weakness. The personal rapport the two display stems in fact from their shared status as wards of Little England, figures of a certain social marginality, condescension, and confinement. Stoker dramatizes this parallel by way of tendentious narrative counterpoint. First, Seward abruptly curtails Mina's interview with Renfield—ignoring the hints that his patient telegraphs concerning her imminent peril—in order to "meet Van Helsing at the station" (*D* 207), where the two immediately conspire to exclude Mina from all future deliberations. In successive scenes, then, Renfield is effectively silenced on the subject of Dracula, and Mina is relegated *to* silence on the subject of Dracula.

All of this might be written off as mere coincidence had Stoker not elected to reinscribe the contiguity immediately in reverse order. Van Helsing and Seward convene a war room meeting at the end of which Mina is debarred, for the duration, from further access to the tactical plans of her intimates ("'you no more must question'"; 214). She is then told, like a child, "'to go to bed'" (214), where she records the entire incident in her diary. Even as she makes the entry, the men embark for their group interrogation of Renfield, on which occasion Seward will finally reject his appeal for relief and, once again, turn a deaf ear to his inklings of impending disaster for all. In simultaneous scenes, then, Renfield is locked away with his dangerous knowledge and Mina is imprisoned in her dangerous ignorance. And, what is more, as we learn from Mina's diary and Dracula's subsequent pronouncements, even as the men pursue their interrogation of Renfield, Dracula makes his *first* in a series of visits to a sleeping Mina to have her "veins appease [his] thirst" (251):

> I remember hearing . . . a lot of queer sounds, like praying on a very tumultuous scale, from Mr. Renfield's room, which is somewhere under this. And then there was silence over everything. . . . Not a thing seemed to be stirring, but all to be grim and fixed as death or fate; so that a thin streak of white mist, that crept with almost imperceptible slowness across the grass towards the house, seemed to have a sentience and a vitality of its own. . . . The mist was spreading, and was now close up to the house, so that I could see it lying thick against the wall, as though it were stealing up to the windows. The poor man was more loud than ever, and though I could not distinguish a word he said, I could in some way recognize in his tones some passionate entreaty on his part. Then there was the sound of a struggle, and I knew that the attendants were dealing with him. I was so frightened that I crept into bed. . . . I was not even a bit sleepy . . . but I must have fallen asleep. . . . The mist grew thicker and thicker. . . . The last conscious effort which imagination made was to show me a livid white face bending over me out of the mist.
>
> (226-28)

The upshot, then, of the men's disposition of their respective wards is that both find themselves abandoned to Dracula's abuse, and the climactic effects of this practice are likewise rendered emphatically in adjacent and complementary scenes. Hearing that an "accident" has befallen Renfield, the two physicians rush to his side, only to find him badly mutilated by the vampiric assault. As he languishes toward death, Renfield reveals that he has indeed seen Mina's "sweet face again" (207), with the disastrous consequences he had dimly bruited: "When Mrs. Harker came in to see me this afternoon she wasn't the same; it was like tea after the teapot had been watered. . . . It made me mad to know that he had been taking the life out of her" (245). Although the gravely ill Renfield reports fighting with his master on Mina's behalf—"'I didn't mean for him to take any more of her life'" (246)—the doctors abruptly forsake him, in clear violation of their Hippocratic oath, and barge off to the Harkers' bedroom, where they discover a matching spectacle of vampiric depredation.

This is yet another instance of the narrative syntax secreting implications at variance with and more telling than the narrative point of view controlled by the individual protagonists would seem to admit. Renfield and Mina are paired as inlets for the great spectral stranger because both, notwithstanding the wide differences in their present stations, have been alienated to some degree from their community and consigned to a shadowy corner of their world. It is within the terms of this social correlation, furthermore, that those wide differences acquire a special symbolic and thematic significance.

Renfield occupies a particularly abject and pathological social margin, which was attracting increasingly intense concern as the nineteenth century drew to a close: a species of masculine breakdown involving a cluster of nervous disorders classified and treated medically, but identified with a kind of moral incontinence.[1] In the case of Renfield, vampiric inhabitation serves as a Gothic trope of this emasculating malaise, indexing its subversion of both individual integrity and, given the male's presumptive social leadership, the collective sovereignty of the modern ethnos or nation. As discussed earlier, the prevailing code of "muscular" manliness took austere self-reliance and rigid self-containment as its defining norm, and so made the voluptuous self-surrender figured in vampiric seduction both a powerful temptation, as Harker and Van Helsing illustrate, and a synonym of male ruin. *Thus constituted in an allergic relation to otherness, the gender ideal of Victorian masculinity tends not only to encourage but also to encode the sort of defensive xenophobic racial mentality that Dracula both arouses and espouses.*

Renfield clearly accepts, even as he defaults upon, this masculine standard. He acts out his vampiric inhabitation, his failure of boundary maintenance, by orally incorporating an evolutionary chain of other creatures, in an attempt to enlarge his own vital capacity. In other words, his express allegiance to Dracula centers on an identification with his hypermasculine mastery, which Renfield tries to assert on his own behalf. By the same token, when he ultimately endeavors to break with Dracula, he struggles to couch his appeals and admonitions to Seward in the idiom of bourgeois manliness, of which his chivalric protectiveness toward Mina is perhaps the most assured exhibition. For that very reason, however, his communication with the men of Little England

does more to reinforce than to alter the existing social dynamic. He desperately wishes to demonstrate how akin to them he is, down to justifying their tribalistic code of values, which unfortunately mandates his own exclusion. His warnings can only confirm the vampire warriors in a mentality that (through the self-reflexive logic of the Gothic fantasy) is at the root of the villainy they confront.

Mina, by contrast, occupies a minoritized and yet *idealized* social margin, that of *properly* feminine fragility, dependency, non-self-sufficiency, heteronomy in sum, which came to attract increasingly intense cultural investments with the fin de siècle emergence of its antitype, the New Woman. Insofar as the traditional "womanly woman," which Mina consents to play at this juncture, exists primarily *to be protected* and thus to confer legitimacy and purpose upon an anxious British patriarchy, the infiltration of Mina's body and spirit by Dracula signifies utter catastrophe, the evisceration not just of her essential role within the hegemonic cultural script but of her essential role in underwriting the script itself. But insofar as that essential role is predicated upon women's socially mandated heteronomy, vampiric inhabitation is uncannily continuous with her interpellation to the enshrined "feminine" virtues of unselfishness, submissiveness, other-directedness. Indeed, the long-established, intuitively obvious identification of vampiric blood-sucking with maternal breast-suckling speaks precisely to this continuity.[2] For beyond the physical acts themselves, this identification, however parodic, points to a close psychosocial analogy between the doppelgänger transaction of vampirism and the dyadic pre-Oedipal engrossment of mother and child, each of which involves a mode of connectivity that tends to confound or dissolve the borders of selfhood so prized by patriarchal liberalism.

Since the maternal care and nurture crystallized in the act of nursing was deemed to be at once the highest and the most natural office of a woman, the gold standard of her womanliness, any supposed compromise of her ego boundaries would register less as a default on the phallic law of assured self-ownership than as compliance with a conflicting imperative promoted by that very same law as its necessary supplement: a sentimental adhesiveness or connectivity that ensures species survival in both its animal and social dimensions. More than an alternative ethics, this conventionally "feminine" supplement represents an ethics of alterity—an openness toward, respon-

Helen Chandler as Mina Seward, and Bela Lugosi as Count Dracula, in Tod Browning's 1931 film adaptation of *Dracula.*

siveness to, solicitude for, and self-sacrificing identification with *others*—that crucially informed the Victorian sense of the family home, women's domestic preserve, as a "haven in a heartless world." Constituted in a kind of rudimentary and limited xenophilia, normative femininity could serve Stoker as a model of the ethnic ideal of domestic colonialism that he wished to advance. We should not be surprised, therefore, to find him relying strongly upon this gender typology—not, as has often been assumed, to confine his women within traditional stereotypes (Mina's masculine intellect, after all, is repeatedly noted)—but rather to vindicate the ethical disposition traditionally associated with womanliness in general and maternity specifically.[3] Working from this conceptual base, Stoker develops and contextualizes Mina's vampiric inhabitation so that it can signify *beyond parodic catastrophe to redemptive possibility,* with Mina in the role of transformative agent.

To showcase the alembic potential of Mina's seemingly conventional ethos, Stoker revisits the dream logic of metalepsis with a (gendered) difference. As the phantasmatic racial/racist other,

Dracula personifies and elicits the violent abrogation of social connectivity already implicit in the blood consciousness of Little England; and, as a result, the men's tactics against the Count tend to facilitate his campaign of incorporation and recruitment. However, as a phantasmatic transfusion of blood identity, at once compulsory and desirable, the vampiric exchange itself, divorced from its telos of conversion, both objectifies and intensifies the sense of radical social communion already implicit in Mina Harker's extraordinarily maternal-being-in-the-world; and, as a result, her repeated vampings ultimately redound to the detriment and even the destruction of Dracula and his campaign.

Stoker underlines the significance of this process/project divide in the respective fates assigned his differently minded female protagonists. Lucy Westenra, who exhibited no particular maternal bent in life, is fully converted to *nosferatu.* In this condition, she reappears as an archetype of the evil mother: she waylays little children, feeds upon instead of feeding them, and then casts them callously aside. Mina Harker, by contrast, remains suspended *within* the dynamics of vampiric transfusion, neither incorporated in nor disentangled from Dracula. And in this condition, she extends to new breadths and depths an already capacious maternal sympathy, which moves her to comfort most of the other characters in their hour of need.

It is worthy of notice, moreover, that Mina's long record of motherly service bears a close and unbroken affiliation with vampirism from the start. Her first maternal display has her wandering into the night to retrieve the sleepwalking Lucy Westenra, her erstwhile student and charge, from the suicide seat to which Dracula has lured her for his nightly repast. In an arresting proleptic reversal of Lucy's performance as the "Bloofer Lady," Mina leads her friend home, like a lost child, taking special care to protect both "her health" and her "reputation" (88-89). Her second such display occurs in a Budapest hospital, where she *begins* her marriage by "attend[ing] to her husband" (101) as he suffers the effects of his doppelgänger encounter with Dracula. Almost a month later, she reports, "Jonathan wants looking after still. . . . Even now he sometimes starts out of his sleep in a sudden way and awakes all trembling until I can coax him back to his usual placidity" (141). For Mina, it would seem, the vampire is a wish-fulfilling nightmare, compelling her to satisfy her penchant for profound fellow feeling, which tends to seize upon each occasion of emotional attachment as a site of maternal care and concern.

The third conspicuous exercise of Mina's prompt motherly instinct involves comforting Arthur Holmwood in his "hysterical" grief over the ruination of his fiancée by Dracula. A full citation of this well-known episode is in order:

> He grew quite hysterical, and raising his open hands, beat his palms together in a perfect agony of grief. . . . I felt an infinite pity for him, and opened my arms unthinkingly. With a sob he layed his head on my shoulder, and cried like a wearied child, whilst he shook with emotion.
>
> We women have something of the mother in us that makes us rise above smaller matters when the mother-spirit is invoked; I felt this big, sorrowing man's head resting on me, as though it were that of the baby that some day may lie on my bosom, and I stroked his hair as though he were my own child. I never thought at the time how strange it all was.
>
> (203)

This passage has been rightly deemed crucial for making explicit the centrality of the maternal ideal to Mina's self-image, to the evolving social economy of Little England, and, by extension, to

Stoker's sexual politics. But it is equally crucial for our purposes because in the same stroke it unfolds a visual and conceptual rhyme between the mother-child dyad and the vampiric couple. Mina's reflexive accommodation of Arthur's importunate hunger for comfort ("opened my arms unthinkingly") recalls the unconscious gesture of permission or consent that is necessary for the vampire to press his suit. The bodily attitude of the pair, Arthur poised on her "shoulder," his face presumably turned toward her neck, evokes a classic vampire tableau, while Mina's simile displacing the action from her shoulder to her "bosom" nudges the reader to draw the bloodsucking/breast-suckling parallel. Finally, Mina's sense of being called outside of herself by the invocation of the "mother-spirit" extends the analogy to vampirism from one of physical posture and activity to one of spectral visitation and inhabitation. With all of this in mind, her reflection, "I never thought at the time how strange it all was," unwittingly references the scene's uncanny resemblance to and reversal of the parody of motherhood in vampirism.

A still stranger and more decisive reversal is in the offing. During the above interlude, a subtle turnabout of roles transpires. As the pressure of the man-child/vampire's demand for consolation subsides, the mother/host comes to be possessed *of* as well as *by* the active and spectral power, here troped as "mother-spirit." It is as if in not being held to the masculine law of disciplined self-enclosure, Mina is not only able to enjoy, in an intimate eroticized manner, responding to the solicitation of fellow feeling, but also able to *draw* abnormal emotional strength from being *drawn upon* in this way. As opposed to building herself up through acts of incorporation, the masculinized, colonial form of aggrandizement favored by Renfield and his master, she secures enhancement through an outpouring and divestment of the self, a strategy that requires her to remain within the moment, as it were, of interdependency and exchange. With Arthur finally becalmed, she evinces an immediate willingness to renew her maternal efforts on behalf of his comrade-in-mourning, Quincy Morris, whose inferred urgency of grief elicits from her an offer, a proposition, that is not simply bold and unexpected, but, for her time and class, forward to the point of impropriety:

> He bore his own troubles so bravely that my heart bled for him . . . so I said to him:—

"I wish I could comfort all who suffer from the heart. Will you let me be your friend, will you come to me for comfort if you need it?"

(204)

So hard upon her tête-à-tête with Arthur, so comprehensive in the avowed scope of its desire, Mina's gesture unmistakably evokes and inverts the motif of vampiric recruitment. She seeks out recipients for her "heart" blood instead of donors, dressing, in each case, the collateral wounds left by Dracula. In the very next scene she makes her critical visit to Renfield, taking *her* campaign of maternal consolation directly to the vampire's minions.

One more strand of this narrative warp needs to be traced, for it simultaneously marks and points beyond the last remaining limit to Mina's motherly largesse of spirit. Immediately prior to her encounter with Arthur, Mina ponders the fate of Dracula himself, now that her menfolk are so doggedly in pursuit: "I suppose one ought to pity anything so hunted as is the Count. That is just it: this Thing is not human—not even beast. To read Seward's account of poor Lucy's death, and what followed, is enough to dry up the springs of pity in one's heart" (202). Mina's rationale for denying Dracula her compassion (literally, "feeling-with") is in true Little England fashion inextricably racial and moral: his ontological foreignness—neither man nor beast—naturalizes a moral debasement that absolves her of an otherwise painful but necessary exercise of the sympathetic imagination. Still, Mina's evident discomfort in not reaching the highest standard of magnanimity that she can envisage might well account for her subsequent zeal to afford solace to virtually everyone else. More importantly, this moment of doubt leaves in her mind—and the reader's—the intuition of a regulative ethico-political ideal of *caritas,* comprising a finally unconstrained willingness to acknowledge one's imbrication with others through a generous emotional investment in them. It thereby lays the ground for a truly decisive turning point in the novel, when Mina fully assumes this seemingly impossible empathetic mandate.

After being vamped, Mina calls God's pity on herself, adducing a life of virtue as grounds for his consideration—"'What have I done to deserve such a fate, I who have tried to walk in meekness and righteousness all my days'" (252). But as with Job, to whom her biblically phrased sentiments allude, Mina's bitter fate enables her to reach new heights of meekness and righteousness, to extend her call for mercy to the great Reprobate who brought her to this pass.

"I want you to bear something in mind through all this dreadful time. I know that you must fight—that you must destroy even as you destroyed the false Lucy so that the true Lucy might live hereafter; but it is not a work of hate. The poor soul who has wrought this misery is the saddest case of all. Just think what will be his joy when he too is destroyed in his worser part that his better part may have spiritual immortality. You must be pitiful to him too, though it may not hold your hands from his destruction."

(268-69)

While her compassion cannot be allowed to preempt the spectacle of "destruction" compulsory to the genre, it does augur a change in its symbolic significance. Thus, when her husband reverts to form, ventilating his undiminished "hate" of Dracula in contemplation of his "spiritual immortality" in "burning hell" (269), Mina repeats her demand that he reconsider his asperity, reminding him of their own blood tie to the vampire tribe: "'Oh hush! oh hush! in the name of the good God. Don't say such things . . . or you will crush me with fear and horror. Just think, my dear—I have been thinking all this long, long day of it—that . . . perhaps . . . some day . . . I too may need such pity; and that some other like you—and with equal cause for anger—may deny it to me!'" (269). The "pity" Mina summons (in both senses) might be more accurately termed compassion, the same feeling-with that she expressly withheld earlier. While her grievance against Dracula has surely grown more serious in the interim, it has also germinated a certain identification with him. She overtly predicates her charitable sentiments toward her tormentor, those she would inculcate in her loved ones, on her coerced family resemblance to the vampire. *We* cannot utterly cast Dracula off, she declares in effect, because *I* am now of his party as well, so much so that I can envision my loving husband as "some other" who justifiably abhors me.

In presuming that her change of blood automatically spells a spiritual deterioration, Mina's *method of reasoning* remains faithful to the established Little England creed that moral properties reside in blood makeup, be it race (Harker's slovenly Orientals), class (Van Helsing's feckless servants), or the most common anthropological transcription of race, "species" (Dracula as hibernicized "brute"). But Mina's transitional *state of being,* between the living and the undead—plainly a temporal metaphor of "mixed" blood—defies any easy or absolute correlation between ethnic status and ethical stature. What is more, this transitional state affords Mina access to a privileged moral and political vantage in its own right: her multiple identifications allow her a more prismatic understanding and thus a finer strain of empathy than has been attained heretofore in the novel. Mina alone has a glimmer of the irrevocable linkage between the knight-errants of Little England and the nightstalkers of Transylvania, and this awareness, while a suspicious, identificatory effect of her enthrallment to Dracula,[4] paradoxically proves the means of individual, group, and even national deliverance from him.

The representational strategy underlying Mina's carefully circumscribed transcendence of the Little England mindset is vintage Stoker, a testament to his parvenu facility for sly, self-insulating criticism of the community whose approval he continued to demand on his own, Irish-inflected terms. Instead of directly challenging the racial essentialism that tended to cramp his own social prospects, Stoker makes it the epicenter of an internecine conflict, and he adapts, in the person of Mina, a broadly Christian rhetoric to celebrate the Utopian possibilities of ethnic hybridization. On both counts, he closely follows the script he first wrote for "The Dualitists." Just as the various counterpart relationships between Little England and the vampire kingdom rehearse the schismatic form of duality displayed by Harry Merford and Tommy Santon, so Mina's acceptance of the vampiric other in herself and her intimates transposes, in a distant but still recognizable key, the symbiotic duality of the Bubb twins. Moreover, just as the symbiotic blessedness of the Bubb twins is embellished with Irish resonances, which index the aptitude for social connectivity buried deep within the often divisive metrocolonial condition, so the enhancement and refinement of Mina's compassion unfolds under Irish colors. As noted earlier, Mina's birth surname encrypts a deeply hybrid Irish heritage—at once native and settler, Anglo and Celt, Catholic and Protestant—which her infiltration by a similarly hybrid, hibernicized vampire can be seen to have activated, augmenting her inherited potential for entertaining alterity. As Stoker knew, the Irish prided themselves on a communitarian *Weltanschauung* that distinguished them from the more atomized individualism dear to John Bull, and the English did not dispute them on this point, doubtless feeling that such other-directedness consorted well with the "essentially feminine" character of the Celtic race.[5]

The metaphor clinching this ethno-national association is precisely that of maternity. With her allegorically weighted name and her metropolitan marriage, Mina invokes a long, storied line of female personae of Ireland and personae of a feminized Ireland—the Shan Von Vacht, Cathleen Ni Houlihan, Hibernia, the Speirbhean or Sky Woman, and Erin, among others. As the Blessed Virgin Mary became the dominant personification of the national ideal, reflecting the increased political power of Catholic Irish-Ireland during the Victorian era, the entire array of female icons came to be consolidated under the figure of Mother Ireland, who provides a perfect allegorical "fit" for Mina's role in the novel. Insofar as Mina's ethics of profound connectivity, imaged in and intensified by her vampiric inhabitation, represents a distinctively feminine and maternal supplement to phallic self-containment, it articulates a cultural ideal with special pertinence to Ireland, one that coheres with that country's national symbolism and positively transvalues the half-embraced stereotype of its people as emotional, impulsive, sentimental, "essentially feminine." It is surely no accident that Mina has already been cast in the role of the Blessed Mother by the Catholic Van Helsing, nor that he does so in the process of announcing her fateful exclusion from the conferences of Little England: "'You must be our star and our hope, and we shall act all the more free that you are not in the danger, such as we are'" (214). These words endow Mina with the iconic attributes of "Mary, Star of the Sea," the merciful patron of voyagers, and they usher her off to bed where she will shortly be forced to "mother" that seaborn "Irish" voyager so in need of her "pity," Count Dracula.[6]

Ironically, however, the very elements coding Mina's ethics of alterity "Irish"—the intimate yet iconic experience of motherhood coupled with the sectarian yet universalizing discourse of Christianity—speak to interpersonal relations so fundamental and so sweeping that they automatically extend the pertinence of her sentiments beyond the metrocolonial problematic to all manner of social intercourse.

Mina's "sweeter counsels" of sympathy for the vampire do prevail over Jonathan's hatred, reducing the men to tears and effectively turning her personal insight into a collective decision.[7] She not only reconciles herself to the racialized taint of the vampiric contagion; she also convinces the men to accept her on these terms, which is to say, to accommodate a virulent strain of otherness at the heart of their community. At this moment, a conversion narrative suddenly irrupts within the conquest narrative of **Dracula,** and the implications of this modal shift for the novel's political fantasy are decisive, touching upon its central self-reflexive conceit. As we have seen, in violently dissociating themselves from Dracula qua racial other, the men of Little England only testify to their unconscious projection of Dracula qua specter of racism, and this fantasy dynamic takes narrative form in the symptomatic persistence with which their schemes to subdue the vampire seem rather to abet him. It thus stands to reason, as a matter of symbolic logic, that in suspending this unconscious complicity, Mina's acceptance of racialized otherness in herself and her persuasion of her menfolk to do likewise would mitigate or even reverse the self-defeating trajectory of Little England's campaign against vampirism. That is *exactly* what happens, as Stoker accentuates through a painstaking juxtaposition of events.

In the scene just *before* the "sweeter counsels" of Mina prevail, the men have their climactic London confrontation with Dracula, which provides perhaps the most egregious instance of their collective, unconsciously motivated ineptitude, Despite cornering Dracula in a classic ambush, with numbers on their side, with ample time for their strategic ace, Morris, to devise the perfect "plan of action," and despite possessing the concerted will to advance "with a single impulse," they nevertheless wind up empty-handed (266). As Dracula eludes their grasp, the experienced reader of thrillers is left, or rather asked, to wonder exactly what advantages, if not these, would finally permit this platoon of heroes to corral their diabolic counterpart.

In the scene immediately *after* the "sweeter counsels" of Mina prevail, the answer surfaces; Mina herself hits upon what proves to be the *single dispositive means* for hunting the vampire, as it were, to ground. Divining that her blood-suckling of Dracula has laid down an intimate, subliminal line of psychic contact with him, she tells Van Helsing, "'I want you to hypnotize me!'" (271), on the supposition that, being a channel for the vampire's mental impressions, she can serve as a homing device for his movements. With its play on the doppelgänger motif, this pre-Vulcan mindmeld is an ingenious plot contrivance typical of the Gothic adventure genre, which the last third of the novel, a protracted chase scene, otherwise plays out rather perfunctorily. But the stratagem also—and this is the chief part of its ingenuity—perfectly encapsulates Mina's transformative

significance in the novel, her incubation of a badly needed ethics/politics of connectivity.

Taken by itself, the men's violent confrontational tactics play into the vampire's hands insofar as he is but the phantasmal emanation of their own antisocial tendencies, their commitment to a metrocolonial ideology of domination and absorption. Their agonistic approach to Dracula only ratifies the depth of their identification. Mina's tactic of subterranean communication reverses this self-reflexive curve. Her secret sharing with the vampire, which registers a certain degree of identification, paradoxically breaks with, stands against, and finally defeats the egoistic agenda and racist ideology he advances.

As the active expression of radical self-absorption and aggrandizement, both individual (egoism) and collective (tribalism), the vampiric act seeks to impose unilateral mastery at a most intimate point of social intercourse, the exchange of bodily fluids, turning the participants into possessor and possessed, respectively. The mindmeld is, from Dracula's perspective, an extension of this violent erotic economy. He is the one who originally enjoins the psychic commerce as a device for monitoring and manipulating his newest "helpmeet" (252). Mina herself is under no illusions on this score: "'he may have used my knowledge for his ends'" (297). But in self-consciously embracing the interior alterity that the mindmeld entails, she effectively restores the reciprocal character of interpersonal exchange and thereby escapes being controlled by the vampire, which is to say by the ideology of expansive self-enclosure.

As Little England enters upon the "great hour" of its offensive into Transylvania, it is given to Van Helsing to translate this ethico-political allegory into the lexicon of Gothic narrative. Confirming that Dracula "'has so used [Mina's] mind'" for his own purposes, Van Helsing describes how and why he will be hoisted on his own petard—in a kind of mirror image of the vampire fighters' earlier contretemps. Dracula's selfish "child-brain" never foresaw that the mindmeld could bind him into a bilateral social relationship, one in which his authority and his desires were not final. He believes he can dispose of Mina as he will, but precisely because she has put herself at his disposal, suspending the collective fixation with mastery, he cannot do so after all.

> "He think, too, that as he cut himself off from
> knowing your mind, there can be no knowledge
> of him to you; there is where he fail! That terrible

baptism of blood which he give you makes you free to go to him in spirit, as you have yet done in your times of freedom. . . . And this power to good of you and others, you have won from your suffering at his hands. This is all the more precious that he know it not, and to guard himself have even cut himself off from his knowledge of our where. We, however, are not all selfish."

(297)

Like his doppelgänger, however, Van Helsing "only saw so far" (297). Assuming that he and his crew "are not all selfish," he overlooks how far their much celebrated norm of manhood, with its emphasis on assured self-possession, self-containment, and self-mastery, is constituted in an allergic relation to otherness, and so carries the seeds of a certain kind of "selfish"-ness within it. The power that Mina has "won" from her maternal "suffering" is the power to persuade her colleagues to relieve their anxious manliness with the unqualified compassion and other-directedness necessary to defeat the egoistic force of Dracula, that is, to effect a conversion that counters *in spirit* the "blood" conversion of vampirism. As a corollary to this conversion, the men once again allow Mina to be an active participant in the campaign rather than its mascot, abandoning the effort to aggrandize their collective male ego by reducing her to a passive and helpless type of the feminine.

With this narrative turn, it should be noted, Stoker bids to effect his own conversion in the racial and gender currencies of Irishness. He tropes the gender ambivalence of his Anglo-Celtic heritage into an alternative value structure. The hysterical heroism/heroic hysteria that has marked much of the vampire hunt begins to give way at this point to another "feminine" style of heroism, which entails confronting and conquering one's innermost xenophobia.

Van Helsing concludes his account of Mina's psychic telepathy by exhorting the others to "'follow'" Dracula "'even if we peril ourselves that we become like him'" (297). With its play on the meaning of the word *follow*, the last proviso has typically been taken to express Stoker's concern about the corrupting effects on otherwise high-minded British liberals of a violent struggle against a lawless colonial resistance.[8] Our analysis, to this point, however, frames Van Helsing's remarks as a belated and still subliminal recognition of the family resemblance that has always subsisted between the members of Little England and their vampiric double. The occasion of his words is significant in this regard, since his recognition is not just induced by but is virtually emergent in

his understanding of how the mindmeld operates. Moreover, in acknowledging, first, the possibility of their collective kinship to what has seemed an unspeakably alien figure and, second, the consequent need for the group to guard against its own vampiric aggressions, Van Helsing's address participates in the subtle but seismic shift facilitated by Mina in the symbolic stakes of the vampire hunt. Even as the action reported in the journal entries flattens into a conventional conquest adventure in an exotic locale, the introduction of the conversion narrative has leavened the symbolic register in which the action transpires. Instead of an intrusive spectral signifier of some outward racial caste (the Irish) or condition (degeneracy), a focus appropriate to more conventional imperialist romance, the vampire becomes a literalized or embodied signifier of an inward racial attitude.

* * *

One problem facing Stoker was how to map this inward turn, with its localized psychic terrain, onto the broader geopolitical landscape allegorized in the novel. His ingenious stratagem was to coordinate the successes enjoyed by the Little Englanders in their crusade with their increasing willingness to "turn Irish" in their means and manner of pursuing it. That is to say, in one of the more sweeping Gothic symmetries in the novel, Stoker counterbalances the colonial mimicry of Dracula, his strategic simulation of English metropolitan ways of being, with the *reverse* mimicry of the Little England crew, its adoption of presumptively Irish methods of combating him. And just as, owing to the impacted political conditions of "the union," the Irish Dracula poses or passes as what he in some sense already is (a Briton), so the members of Little England come to embrace—on duress at first and gradually by design—an otherness proper to or at least indissociable from their "true" ethno-national selves.

From the outset of the novel, some of the most potent defensive measures undertaken against the vampire derive from the liturgical rites of the Roman Catholic church, which in the Britain of Stoker's day were far less prominently associated with the historic sectarian enemies, France and Spain, than with the restive Irish people-nation.[9] The first such instance sees Jonathan Harker outwardly expressing his discomfort at the receipt of a crucifix that, "as an English churchman, I have been taught to regard . . . as in some measure idolatrous" (13). During the mirror scene, however, he comes to regard the crucifix as his salvation from the advances of Dracula (31).

In the second instance, Van Helsing seals the grave of the undead Lucy with the Eucharist, for which he claims a papal dispensation. Van Helsing does speak elsewhere of the need to rely upon superstitious traditions in the war on vampirism, but being a Catholic, he certainly does not regard the Sacrament in this light. Nor are the occult uses of the Eucharist greeted with more than momentary shock by his Protestant cohorts, who shortly find themselves escorting the Host and holding their own crucifixes aloft in an effort to drive Dracula from the body of Mina (247). In this validation of beliefs and observances typically associated with the backward, "idolatrous" peasantry of Ireland, there is an understated inversion of the single most pivotal event in Anglo/Irish history. Instead of a Protestant Dutchman, William III, being called across the water to save England from the perils of Catholicism and, by the time of the Boyne, from its Irish exponents, Stoker gives us a Catholic Dutchman called across the water to save England, and William's namesake, *with* the sacred objects of Catholicism and, by extension, the sectarian markers of Irishness.

One of the more prominent aspects of Irish Catholicism eschewed in Anglican culture was marialotry, a zealous, some would say excessive devotion to the Blessed Virgin, which left a deep imprint, in turn, upon nationalist symbology of Irish-Ireland. As noted above, with the growingly Catholic leadership of both the Home Rule and Republican movements, Mary was often conflated with the ancient goddesses Hibernia, Erin, and Cathleen as figures of "the sovereignty," hortatory symbols of an independent Ireland whose honor and dignity her sons were enlisted to avenge. So when Van Helsing proclaims the hypermaternal Mina "'our star and our hope'" in "'danger,'" exalting her as an avatar of Our Lady, Star of the Sea, he implicitly organizes her champions in a symbolic economy that unmistakably recalls contemporary Irish Catholic Fenianism. After Mina's surprising plea on behalf of Dracula and her ensuing entry into telepathy with him, events that catalyze the group's more conscious accommodation of otherness, Van Helsing progresses from mirroring the iconography of advanced Irish nationalism to echoing its philosophy. His quoted comment that Mina has "won" power over Dracula "'from [her] suffering at his hands'" articulates the cardinal principle underlying the Fenian-identified ethos of blood sacrifice and anticipates Terence MacSwiney's celebrated formula: victory comes to those who endure suffering rather than those who inflict it.[10] Blood

sacrifice is, of course, a policy of the dispossessed. It aims to make a virtue out of necessitousness, if you will, out of an absence of resources beyond the fully committed bodies of those involved. The avowal of this ethos by Little England, Van Helsing's express belief that Mina's suffering of a "blood sacrifice" may itself prove the key to victory, amounts to a marked structural identification with the disempowered yet dangerous element of Irish patriotism that Dracula has often been taken to allegorize.

A certain topical allusion, highly provocative for Stoker's contemporary audience, not only underlines this cross-ethnic/cross-class identification but also calls attention to the self-consciousness with which Little England assumes it. In his journal, Seward calls the vampire fighters' entire strategy of pursuing Dracula into Transylvania their "Plan of Campaign" (*ED* 383), and since he uses the uppercase letters that turn this colloquial expression into a proper name, he can only be read as affiliating their effort with *the* Plan of Campaign, a scheme undertaken between 1886 and 1890 for the Irish tenantry to secure the right of collective bargaining through systematic rent strikes and boycotting.[11] At the primary level, Seward's use of the term as a corporate self-description identifies the struggle of the Little Englanders against Dracula with a moral force resistance movement undertaken by their ethnic and class antipodes. There is, as usual in **Dracula,** a vertiginous exactitude to this arrangement. The change in Little England's moral and political objective, allegorically considered, from defeating the vampire without (the racial other) to defeating the vampire within (the racialist predisposition) forms a precise corrective reversal of the form of projection demanded of the metrocolonial subject, the displacement of the otherness within onto some external threat. Hence, the change in moral and political objective is not merely accentuated or even supplemented, but literally realized and to a degree explained by the transmutation of metropolitan Anglo mandarins into barbarous Irish aliens.

But the gesture enacted in Seward's journal entry carries still greater evidentiary force and political resonance. In the Plan of Campaign, Seward hits on more than an event in Irish history with which *Little* England might identify, he hits on a conspicuous site in the history of *liberal* England's identification with the Irish tenantry during the so-called Union of Hearts, which covered roughly the same period. What made the Plan of Campaign such a salient political movement was less its direct effects on landlord-lessee relations, which were negligible, than its indirect effects on the way certain more advanced, progressive constituencies of English liberalism came, in despite of the party leadership, to view the plight of the Irish, that is, its capacity to mobilize in historical fact the sort of sympathetic imagination that Mina Harker mobilizes in Gothic fiction. Initiated by Stoker's cousin John Dillon, among others, the plan of Campaign was designed to bait the largely Ascendancy landlords into staging ruthless evictions that would hopefully be witnessed by English visitors invited to Ireland for that purpose.[12]

One such prominent visitor was a Liberal party member of Parliament from Cornwall, Charles Conybeare, who wound up assisting, even joining the resistance efforts of evicted tenants in Donegal and was for his trouble arrested, convicted, and jailed on the charge of criminal conspiracy. Since the "clinching evidence" turned on Conybeare giving "three cheers for the Plan of Campaign," one might reasonably infer that he was punished for the crime of identifying with the disaffected Irish by being treated as one.[13] Another Liberal party politico, George Lansbury, was motivated to organize a Radical club delegation to the Plan of Campaign by a preexisting Irish identification, which has a special pertinence for **Dracula.** Having moved as a boy to the Whitechapel neighborhood of the East End—the haunt of Dracula in London and the ground of certain of his racial affiliations—Lansbury lived, in his words, "among what may be described as a mixed population—Irish and Jews and foreigners, of all nationalities."[14] Here Ireland became the center of a radiating countercultural web of subaltern loyalties and adherences spun right in the heart of the metropole:

> The Irish boys at our school were all 'Fenians'; consequently, when the wall of Clerkenwell Prison was blown down and three Irish martyrs executed in Manchester because a police officer was accidentally killed, very great excitement prevailed in our classes and playground. The teachers tried to make us understand how wicked the Irishmen had been on both occasions, but my Irish friends would have none of it, and when a few months later T. D. Sullivan's song *God Save Ireland* came out, we boys were shouting it at the tops of our voices every playtime.[15]

The last sentence adumbrates a developing solidarity between elements of the English and Irish communities in England, a bond that proved crucial to the Home Rule policies of Stoker's politi-

cal favorites and found still more strenuous expression in the Plan of Campaign that they opposed.

By having the English Seward place the final, ultimately successful push against Dracula under the sign of the Plan of Campaign, Stoker looks to rivet text and context, history and fantasy, literary and geopolitics from both ends. On one side, through the association of the Plan, and more specifically English participation in the Plan, with the happy resolution of a hibernicized nightmare of blood, Stoker offers his support, characteristically encrypted, for those advanced Liberals who seized the occasion to fashion links with the moral force Irish independence movement, fulfilling the political posture implicit in "The Voice of England." On the other side, insofar as these elements sought a resolution to the Irish crisis in a self-conscious revision of England's ethnic attitudes, Seward's replication of this gesture further attests to the self-reflexive turn the vampire hunt has taken.

The construction of the novel's denouement, the pursuit and execution of Dracula, illustrates the last point compellingly. When the vampire fighters arrive at Galatz, looking for the box containing the Count, they are directed to the office of Immanuel Hildesheim, whose presence elicits an outburst of anti-Semitic vitriol from Jonathan Harker (**D** 302). In keeping with the dream logic of the novel, this racist fulmination magically conjures forth an objective correlative with direct bearing upon Little England's quest: the man to whom Hildesheim directs them, Petrof Shinsky, immediately turns up dead, the victim of a murder with apparent racial overtones ("'This is the work of a Slovak,'" the women cry; 303). To avoid being caught up in a Balkan "whirlpool" of racial animosity and outrage, Harker must flee the scene with his cohorts, forsaking any immediate prospect of locating his wife's tormentor. The men's response to this setback, phantasmatically effected by their own lingering racism, is to begin "taking Mina again into [their] confidence" (303). Given her telepathic function, this decision is particularly significant because it serves to close the circuit, to complete the connection, between the society of Little England and their vampiric other. At this point, the men finally agree to finish the process of admitting alterity in their midst, to assume the "hazardous" "chance" of racial self-exposure (303). This attitude proves as conducive to their ultimate goal as their blood anxiety has been counterproductive.

With her "man's brain" and "woman's heart," her mixed blood and iconic purity, her undead and yet unvanquished spirit, Mina is not only a hybrid figure but also, through sheer force of over-determination, a symbolic figure of hybridity; and it is she, tellingly, who puts Little England back on the trail lost in connection with her husband's anti-Semitic lapse. Her determination of the proper route to follow, the river course, merely transposes onto the terrain of action adventure her earlier directions as to the proper ethico-political course to follow. Once again, the narrative and symbolic syntax prompts the discovery that the waterway to finding and defeating Dracula flows inward.

To render this lesson still more forcibly, while keeping the attendant social critique as muted as possible, Stoker contrives to make the final narrative destination, the killing of Dracula, purposively anti- and ante-climactic at the same time. The end of Dracula is anti-climactic because there is no prolonged or gripping death struggle. Dracula seemingly dies at a touch and disappears in the same motion. As Mina records it, "It was like a miracle; but before our very eyes, and almost in the drawing of a breath, the whole body crumbled into dust and passed from our sight" (325). Noting that the collective "butchery" promised by Van Helsing fails to meet expectations, Auerbach and Skal opine that "Dracula's supposed death is riddled with ambiguity" (325). On the contrary, a definite message can be gleaned from the manner in which Dracula's death defies expectations. The body of the vampire does not in the end offer even the minimal resistance necessarily exerted by an independently objectified being. Unsustainable, even as dust, he bears the insubstantiality of a mirage, an internally generated phantom. Mina's phraseology seems chosen to insinuate the imaginary status of Dracula. He vanishes "in the drawing of a breath" because he is a function of breath, metaphorically considered, an emanation of the soul.

In this light, the fate of Quincy Morris may be seen as the terminal and summary instance of the mirroring of vampire and vampire fighters. Received in the very act of slaying Dracula, Morris's death wound serves as a ritual token of Dracula's symbolic value for the members of Little England: it signifies that their effective extermination of the vampire and what he represents can only transpire through the eradication of a blameworthy part of their collective self. That the sacrificial embodiment of this part is an Anglo-American, the ethno-national group inheriting world-imperial domination from the British, suggests that a more broadly colonialist supremacism is at last emerging as the guilty attribute. This brings us to the ante-climactic aspect of Dracula's demise. While the reader might infer that Mina's all-important scar—the mark of her pollution by and subjection to the hibernicized monster—disappears on the instant of Dracula's passing, the spectacle of its disappearance is explicitly paired instead with the end of Morris. Dracula has been gone for some time—indeed, his gypsy allies have since departed—when Morris in his death throes bears witness to the regenerated purity of Mina's visage: "'Look! Look! . . . See! The snow is not more stainless than her forehead! The curse has passed away!'" (326). Timing, as we know by now, is everything in the symbolic economy of **Dracula.** The timing here, the coincidence of Mina's cleansing not with the vampire's destruction but with its *subjective correlative,* indicates that "the curse" consists less in the taint of blood immixture than in the estimation of such immixture as taint. In other words, Mina carries the *stigmata* of her Irish hybridity until the moment, symbolically enacted in Morris's death, when the social *stigma* of that hybridity dissipates.

Jonathan Harker's closing "Note," seven years on, confirms as much on several levels—fact, import, and ethos—all of which converge in the person of the Harkers' first-born child, who signals the renewal of Little England on other terms. The *fact,* first of all, that "the boy's birthday is on the same day as that on which Quincy Morris died" (326) positions him as the redemptive effect of Morris's "gallant" performance as ritual scapegoat in the destruction of the evil doppelgänger. Mina herself draws some such inference in her "secret belief that some of [Morris's] spirit has passed into [her son]," in what amounts to a clear reversal of the vampiric "curse" whose passing is heralded by Morris's death (326). As opposed to Dracula's outright appropriation of the spirit through the lethal ingestion of another's blood, Morris has achieved a *partial* transmission of spirit through the shedding of his own blood. The yoking of the Christian ideal with the politics of hybridity, initiated by Mina, is thus sustained through the coda of the novel.

The *import* of Morris's death is memorialized in the naming of the Harker child. His parents give him a "bundle of names" intended to link the "little band of men together" (326). By this act, he becomes not just the symbolic heir of Little England as a whole but a living emblem of that radical connectivity which proved the ethical correlative of the Little Englanders' triumph, their means of destroying the vampire in themselves. Quincy, the name the boy is called, becomes by extension the master signifier of that connectivity, upon which the first Quincy's death put the seal. In a certain sense, even Dracula himself finds a place in the xenophilic community that young Harker embodies.

As a number of critics have noted, Mina's dark tryst with Dracula means that the blood of the vampire now flows in the veins of her golden child. Some have seen this genetic residuum as an ironic portent of ongoing or recrudescent racial menace, "an element of horror . . . left over, uncontained," in the words of Daniel Pick.[16] Others see this result as ironic evidence that, as Stephen D. Arata puts it, "the position of vampire and victim have been reversed. Now it is Dracula whose blood is appropriated and transformed to nourish a failing race. . . . The English race invigorates itself by appropriating those racial qualities needed to reverse its own decline."[17] The former position sees the nightmare of *Dracula* continuing *for* British imperialism; the latter sees the nightmare *of* British imperialism continuing, with Stoker's license. Before we accept this Hobson's choice, however, it is well to remember that insofar as *both* the vampire and Mina Murray Harker are coded Irish in the novel, and undecidably Anglo/Celtic-Irish in either case, this final admixture of blood need not be construed as bearing any significance, as making any objective difference in a *racial* or *ethnic* sense. And this ultimate in-difference is by no means an accident of allegory. To the contrary, Stoker has characteristically reappropriated a well-worn Gothic convention, here the secret ineradicability of vampiric infection, to index what is unconventional about his novel: that it is not finally about blood distinction but blood consciousness. The dominant, seemingly opposed readings of the coda have joined in mistaking the novel's critical object for its ideological objective, a tribute to Stoker's dense, socially motivated cryptology.

The characters themselves, however, do point the way beyond this error by the end of *Dracula*. Arata claims that Harker "unwittingly calls attention" in the closing note to the presence of Dracula's blood in his son and heir.[18] But since Harker clearly neither forgets nor suppresses the incident of his wife's vamping—"Seven years ago we all went through the flames" (326)—his unwittingness can be seen to arise from a comparative unconcern or lack of anxiety about the index of "blood." Indeed, Harker's ease of mind on this

score is the political burden of the novel's happy ending. *It is precisely in relinquishing the mania or obsession with blood that the men of Little England have freed themselves from the enthrallment with vampirism, which is but the Gothic literalization of that mania. To accept the influx of Dracula's blood, his racial otherness, is to escape the influence of Dracula's vampirism, his racist obsession with blood as the vehicle of identity.* The vampire fighters have, in Harker's words, gone "through the flames," the Christian symbol of purgation, and it is they who have been purified, not of Dracula's blood, which they only encountered in the process, but of their own liability to blood "hate." In Lacanian terms, the men of Little England have graduated from the Imaginary register, which is defined by an antagonistic struggle for an always elusory self-identity, here presumed to reside in blood; and they have graduated to the Symbolic register, wherein identity is understood to be the aftereffect of a social relationality inscribed in the signifier, here an aptly polyeponymous name capable of linking a group of people together. Projected onto the geopolitical scale, this shift from an Imaginary of blood to a Symbolic of social articulation or interlinkage represents a theoretical model of the shift that Stoker desired and his political hero Gladstone made a Liberal policy goal: from emulous rivalry among the various parties to the Irish Question to coexistence within a multinational state embracing Home Rule for its several constituencies.

Quincy Harker, finally, is the culmination of Mina's role as universal mother, on which basis she has served as the principal exponent of the *ethos* of radical social connectivity celebrated in the novel. Accordingly, the child provides an occasion for punctuating the narrative with a reaffirmation of Mina's preeminence, not just as an iconic presence but as a transformative agency. The task falls to the official spokesman and authority figure of the group, Van Helsing, who holds young Harker, rather like a symbolic prop, upon his knee: "'This boy will some day know what a brave and gallant woman his mother is. Already he knows her sweetness and loving care; later on he will understand how some men so loved her, that they did dare much for her sake'" (327). As he has done before, Van Helsing manages to cast Mina simultaneously as a hyperfeminine ideal, here troped in terms of maternal "sweetness and loving care," and as a gloriously androgynous bearer of masculine virtue, here troped along martial rather than the usual intellectual lines. While the men "did dare so much for her sake," Mina does not occupy the traditional feminine pedestal of treasured object, but proves "brave and gallant" in her own right, a positive force in the struggle against vampirism. One effect of this unconventional gender combination is to suggest that Mina's surpassing courage consists *in* her maternalism itself, in her willingness to acknowledge her imbrication with even the most threatening forms of otherness and to predicate her ethical posture on that radical connectivity. It is in following Mina's heroic lead, in letting go the racialist impetus of their manly ideal, that the men of Little England become the heroes that they are too readily presumed to be all along. And it is by following this lead that the "hard men" of young Harker's generation might have resolved the Irish Question on the principles of domestic cosmopolitanism, first advocated in Stoker's *Address,* twenty-five years before *Dracula,* instead of resolving the Irish Question twenty-five years after *Dracula,* on principles of tribal bloodletting worthy of the vampire at his worst.

Notes

1. Janet Oppenheim, *"Shattered Nerves"* (New York: Oxford University Press, 1991), 141-80.

2. For a discussion of this traditional identification, see Joan Copjec, *Read My Desire* (Boston: MIT Press, 1994), 128-29.

3. As in contemporary slasher films, the heroine (Mina) actually exceeds stereotyped gender expectations in ways that the female victims (Lucy and her mother) do not. See Carol J. Clover, "Her Body, Himself: Gender in the Slasher Film," *Representations* 20 (Spring 1987): 187-228.

4. Wolf takes her "whole argument" to be "dictated from afar by Dracula." See *ED* 367 n. 17.

5. See Oliver MacDonagh, *States of Mind* (London: Allen and Unwin, 1983), 34-51.

6. In Stoker's time, there was a Roman Catholic church called Mary, Star of the Sea, off Leahy's Terrace in suburban Dublin. See Don Gifford, *Ulysses Annotated* (Berkeley: University of California Press, 1988), 384.

7. The phrase *sweeter counsels* recalls another prominent appellation of Mary, "Our Mother of Good Counsel."

8. Moses, "The Irish Vampire," 87.

9. For a detailed anatomy of the role of religion in *Dracula,* see Moses, "The Irish Vampire," 89-96.

10. Tom Garvin, *Nationalist Revolutionaries in Ireland* (Oxford: Clarendon, 1987), 157.

11. Lyons, *Ireland since the Famine,* 188-94. In every other edition of *Dracula,* the *Plan of Campaign* is capitalized, so the Norton's lowercase rendering is surely an error.

12. Liz Curtis, *The Cause of Ireland,* 152.

13. Ibid., 152-53.

14. Ibid., 153.

15. Ibid., 153-54.

16. Pick, "'Terrors of the Night,'" 77.

17. Arata, *Fictions of Loss,* 129.

18. Ibid.

Abbreviations

D   Bram Stoker, *Dracula,* ed. Nina Auerbach and David Skal, Norton Critical Edition (New York: Norton, 1997).

ED   Bram Stoker, *The Essential Dracula: The Definitive Annotated Edition of Bram Stoker's Classic Novel,* ed. Leonard Wolf (New York: Penguin, 1993).

NPH   Bram Stoker, "The Necessity for Political Honesty," auditor's *Address to the Trinity College Historical Society,* first meeting, twenty-eighth session, November 13, 1872.

FURTHER READING

Criticism

Clemens, Valerie. "Dracula: The Reptilian Brain at the Fin de Siècle." In *Dracula: The Shade and the Shadow: A Critical Anthology,* edited by Elizabeth Miller, pp. 205-18. Westcliff-on-Sea, Essex, United Kingdom: Desert Island, 1998.

Examines Dracula *in light of turn-of-the-century concerns over rapid social, technological, and cultural change.*

Craft, Christopher. "'Kiss Me with Those Red Lips': Gender and Inversion in Bram Stoker's *Dracula.*" *Representations,* no. 8 (autumn 1984): 107-33.

Probes the ambivalent representation of same-sex eroticism in Dracula.

Fry, Carol L. "Fictional Conventions and Sexuality in *Dracula.*" *Victorian Newsletter,* no. 42 (fall 1972): 20-22.

Briefly identifies the classically Gothic melodramatic plot of the rake's pursuit and seduction of a virgin as rendered in Dracula.

Ingelbien, Raphael. "Gothic Genealogies: *Dracula,* Bowen's Court, and Anglo-Irish Psychology." *ELH* 70, no. 4 (winter 2003): 1089-1105.

Considers Dracula *as "an allegory of Ireland's social, political, and cultural upheavals at the end of the nineteenth century."*

Jackson, Rosemary. "Gothic Tales and Novels." In *Fantasy: The Literature of Subversion,* pp. 95-122. London: Methuen, 1981.

Studies Dracula *as "a culmination of nineteenth-century English Gothic," particularly considering the symbolic qualities of the vampire myth employed by Stoker in the novel.*

Lewis, Pericles. "Dracula and the Epistemology of the Victorian Gothic Novel." In *Dracula: The Shade and the Shadow: A Critical Anthology,* edited by Elizabeth Miller, pp. 71-81. Westcliff-on-Sea, Essex, England: Desert Island, 1998.

Examines the ways in which Dracula *prefigures postmodern critical notions of the "unreliability of individual perception."*

Nayder, Lillian. "Virgin Territory and the Iron Virgin: Engendering the Empire in Bram Stoker's 'The Squaw.'" In *Maternal Instincts: Visions of Motherhood and Sexuality in Britain, 1875-1925*, edited by Claudia Nelson and Ann Sumner Holmes, pp. 75-97. New York: St. Martin's Press, 1997.

Highlights thematic concerns with gender and empire in Stoker's story "The Squaw."

Pedlar, Valerie. "*Dracula*: A Fin-de-Siècle Fantasy." In *The Nineteenth-Century Novel: Identities*, edited by Dennis Walder, pp. 196-216. London: Open University Press, 2001.

Analyzes Dracula *in the contexts of nineteenth-century myth and fantasy writing, the conventions of Gothic literature, vampire folklore, and Freudian psychoanalysis.*

Roth, Phyllis. *Bram Stoker*. Boston: Twayne, 1982, 167 p.

Concise critical introduction to Stoker and his works that includes a psychoanalytical interpretation of Dracula, *a biographical summary, and an extensive bibliography.*

Schaffrath, Stephan. "Order-versus-Chaos Dichotomy in Bram Stoker's *Dracula*." *Extrapolation* 43, no. 1 (spring 2002): 98-112.

Elucidates the symbolic conflict between order and chaos depicted in Dracula.

Senf, Carol A. Introduction to *The Critical Introduction to Bram Stoker*, edited by Carol A. Senf, pp. 1-41. Westport, Conn.: Greenwood Press, 1993.

Surveys the defining characteristics of Stoker's fiction.

Stade, George. Introduction to *Dracula*, by Bram Stoker, pp. v-xiv. New York: Bantam Books, 1981.

Recapitulates the modern critical tendency to interpret the "prevailing emotion" of Dracula *as "a screaming horror of female sexuality."*

Stewart, Garrett. "'Count Me In': *Dracula*, Hypnotic Participation, and the Late-Victorian Gothic of Reading." *Lit: Literature Interpretation Theory* 5, no. 1 (1994): 1-18.

Theoretical discussion of Dracula *as the aesthetic terminus of the late-Victorian Gothic romance.*

Temple, Philip. "The Origins of *Dracula*." *Times Literary Supplement* (4 November 1983): 1216.

Observes several possible anecdotal and geographical sources for Dracula.

Tilley, Elizabeth. "Stoker, Paris and the Crisis of Identity." *Literature and History* 10, no. 2 (autumn 2001): 26-41.

Investigates the Paris setting of Stoker's short story "The Burial of the Rats" and its relation to garbage, sanitation, and middle-class identity.

Twitchell, James B. "Dr. Jekyll and Mr. Wolfman." In *Dreadful Pleasures: An Anatomy of Modern Horror*, pp. 215-16. Oxford: Oxford University Press, 1985.

Regards "Dracula's Guest" as "one of the best werewolf stories ever written."

Valente, Joseph. "'Double Born': Bram Stoker and the Metrocolonial Gothic." *Modern Fiction Studies* 46, no. 3 (fall 2000): 632-45.

Concentrates on topical references to Anglo-Irish relations and the psycho-symbolic use of the doppelgänger *motif in Stoker's story "The Dualitists; or the Death Doom of the Double Born."*

Varnado, S. L. "The Daemonic in *Dracula*." In *Haunted Presence: The Numinous in Gothic Fiction*, pp. 95-114. Tuscaloosa: The University of Alabama Press, 1987.

Views Dracula *as a dramatization of the "cosmic struggle between the opposing forces of darkness and light, of the sacred and the profane."*

Weissman, Judith. "Women and Vampires: *Dracula* as a Victorian Novel." *Midwest Quarterly* 18, no. 4 (July 1977): 392-405.

Interprets Dracula *as a novel of "sexual terror." Weissman interprets the female vampire as a symbol of "the sexually straightforward and insatiable woman" who is threatening to the sexually insecure man.*

Williams, Anne. "Why Are Vampires Afraid of Garlic?: *Dracula*." In *Art of Darkness: A Poetics of Gothic*, pp. 121-34. Chicago: University of Chicago Press, 1995.

Examines the significance of the tools—"the rosary, a branch of the flowering wild rose, and the Host, as well as ⋯ [g]arlic, the crucifix, and the stake"—used by vampire hunter Van Helsing.

Wolf, Leonard. *The Essential* Dracula. New York: Plume, 1993, 484 p.

Places Dracula *within the literary and historical contexts of Gothic fiction.*

OTHER SOURCES FROM GALE:

Additional coverage of Stoker's life and career is contained in the following sources published by Thomson Gale: *Authors and Artists for Young Adults*, Vol. 23; *Beacham's Encyclopedia of Popular Fiction: Biography & Resources*, Vol. 3; *Beacham's Guide to Literature for Young Adults*, Vol. 5; *British Writers*, Vol. 3; *Concise Dictionary of British Literary Biography, 1890-1914*; *Contemporary Authors*, Vols. 105, 150; *Dictionary of Literary Biography*, Vols. 36, 70, 178, 304; *DISCovering Authors*; *DISCovering Authors: British*; *DISCovering Authors: Canadian*; *DISCovering Authors Modules: Most-studied Authors and Novelists*; *DISCovering Authors 3.0*; *Literature and Its Times*, Vol. 1; *Literature Resource Center*; *Novels for Students*, Vol. 18; *Reference Guide to English Literature*, Ed. 2; *St. James Guide to Horror, Ghost & Gothic Writers*; *Short Story Criticism*, Vol. 62; *Something about the Author*, Vol. 29; *Supernatural Fiction Writers*; *Twayne's English Authors*; *Twentieth-Century Literary Criticism*, Vols. 8, 144; *World Literature and Its Times*, Vol. 4; and *World Literature Criticism*.

HORACE WALPOLE

(1717 - 1797)

English novelist, biographer, memoirist, historian, essayist, playwright, and letter writer.

One of the most flamboyant personalities in eighteenth-century English letters, Walpole is often considered the outstanding chronicler and correspondent of his era. According to biographer W. S. Lewis (see Further Reading), "Walpole is the man who brought the art of letterwriting to the highest point it reached in our language." The *Letters,* which date from 1732 to 1797 and number in the thousands, are noted for their remarkable content as well as their distinctive style. While the detailed description they provide of English politics and society in Walpole's time is unsurpassed, they also possess stylistic charm and wit which make them highly entertaining prose. In addition to this achievement, Walpole is widely recognized as one of England's first art historians, an influential revivalist of Gothic architecture, and the author of *The Castle of Otranto* (1764), a work which pioneered the introduction of supernaturalism and mystery into the romance and is thus regarded as the first Gothic novel.

BIOGRAPHICAL INFORMATION

Walpole was born into a family of old Norfolk stock which could be traced back to the last king of the Britons. His immediate family came into wealth during his father's political career. Sir Robert Walpole, who held many influential posts including secretary of war and treasurer of the navy, served during the reign of George II as England's first prime minister and became the first Earl of Orford. Because Horace was considerably younger and both physically and temperamentally different from the other children of Sir Robert and Catherine Shorter Walpole—and because his parents had a notoriously strained marriage—there was considerable speculation over Horace's paternity. He, however, was unaffected by the gossip and remained fervently loyal to both of his parents until their deaths. Conditions in the Walpole home enhanced Horace's tendencies toward impetuosity and self-indulgence. Lady Walpole, a reputedly vain and capricious woman, compulsively pampered her youngest son, and the atmosphere of the Walpole home can perhaps best be summed up by the family motto: "Fan qua sentiat" ("Say what you think"). From 1727 to 1734 Walpole attended Eton, which proved a much more stable environment than his family's estate. Here he became close friends with Thomas Ashton, Richard West, and Thomas Gray. Referring to themselves as the Quadruple Alliance, the four schoolmates prided themselves on their intellectual precocity and delved into Latin classics as well as French and English literature, which they read, translated, and parodied. Along with Gray,

Walpole entered Cambridge, but he did not take a degree; in 1739 he left school to make the Grand Tour of the Continent with Gray as a traveling companion. They toured for two years but eventually quarreled and returned to England separately. Much of the strain on their friendship stemmed from the class differences between them: while Gray was a scrivener's son, Walpole was the prime minister's, which admitted him to elite social circles and enabled him to spend without consideration of cost. While on the Continent he was elected to Parliament, and he served in that body intermittently until 1768. His terms were characterized by brief, fervent bouts of enthusiasm amidst an overriding sense of apathy. Despite his occasional passion over a particular issue, he was generally more interested in the drama of the political scene than actual policymaking. Although Walpole classified himself as a "settled Whig"—that is, one opposed to the bulk of power residing in any single branch of government or class of society—he once described his political objective as being "at the liberty of pleasing myself without being tied to a party."

In 1747, the year in which he published *Aedes Walpolianae*, a catalog of Sir Robert's art collection and the first book on a private art collection in England, Walpole moved into a former coachman's cottage near Twickenham. He named this residence Strawberry Hill and began remodeling it in 1753, a project which grew in extravagance year by year. The original Strawberry Hill was a fairly modest dwelling; Walpole turned it into a late-medieval castle designed in the Gothic style. The architectural "committee" responsible for the castle's appearance consisted of Walpole and two of his friends, John Chute and Richard Bentley. Their primary goal was to create a structure that reflected the beauty of older English architecture, but which also captured a viewer's imagination and sense of make-believe. The result was a museum-like tribute to Gothic detail as well as to Walpole's unbridled determination to make his fantastic conception a reality. The completed Strawberry Hill exhibited lavish examples of Gothic ornamentation, including stained-glass windows, balustrades, loggias, and hidden stairways. Unfortunately, since neither Walpole nor his associates were experienced engineers, many parts of Strawberry Hill were structurally unsound. For example, during Walpole's lifetime alone the battlements had to be replaced three times. Although Strawberry Hill became the object of ridicule in some quarters because of its outlandish appearance, it inspired an architectural fad, as

many members of the upper class began to add Gothic touches to their homes. Walpole also established a private press at Strawberry Hill in 1757 which operated for thirty-two years and is still recognized for publishing one of the most impressive lists of titles of any private press in England, including Walpole's works and the poems of Thomas Gray. The estate ultimately became an elaborate showcase for Walpole's extensive collections of armor, coins, books, art, and bric-a-brac, which were viewed by ticket-holding visitors. In 1842 the contents of Strawberry Hill were sold in a widely publicized auction which lasted over a month; Strawberry Hill itself now serves as a training college for teachers. In spite of changes made in the house and gardens, much of its original splendor remains and contemporary visitors may still perceive the fanciful, if eccentric, imagination responsible for its design and creation.

In 1765 Walpole made the first of four extended trips to Paris, where he was received by the pinnacle of French society. Members of the French upper class were widely known for their scathing wit and expertise at verbal assault: thus, Walpole, who was despised by many of his fellow Britons for these very qualities, became the toast of Parisian society. While in Paris, he was bedridden with a severe case of gout—to which he finally succumbed at age eighty—and was visited by an illustrious parade of well-wishers. Walpole was befriended by Madame du Deffand, the grand dame of French society, who was twenty years his senior and with whom he corresponded until her death in 1780. Deffand fell in love with Walpole, who had never shown any romantic interest in women, and expressed her emotions in letters to him. Although Deffand's letters to Walpole survived, he requested that his be destroyed after his death. Biographers and critics consider this an unfortunate loss and speculate that this correspondence would have shed light on Walpole's generous and compassionate nature, a dimension of his personality which has received little attention. Throughout his life Walpole was always devoted, sometimes irrationally, to a select group of friends, and this was especially true during his later years. Particularly close to him near the end of his life were the Berry sisters, Agnes and Mary, daughters of one of his Strawberry Hill neighbors. After Walpole's death it was rumored that he had wanted to marry Mary, so charmed was he by her intelligence and wit. However, biographers conclude that this was most unlikely considering his stalwartly negative stance on marriage and their age differences—Walpole was seventy and Miss

Berry was in her early twenties. Nevertheless, the Berry sisters lived at Little Strawberry Hill, a cottage on Walpole's estate, for many years and Mary became literary executrix of his papers upon his death in 1797, editing his works under her father's name in accordance with the prejudices of the age.

MAJOR WORKS

The only fictional work for which Walpole is widely known is his novel *The Castle of Otranto*. Although considered a seriously flawed work, *The Castle of Otranto* is credited with introducing a number of important innovations that influenced the development of the Gothic novel, which enjoyed a great vogue during the late eighteenth and early nineteenth centuries. According to Walpole, *The Castle of Otranto* was inspired by a dream in which he was in a castle and a gigantic armorclad hand appeared to him at the top of a staircase. After two months of continuous, almost fevered, writing, Walpole completed the story, but published it anonymously under the pretense that it was an Italian manuscript written during the Last Crusade and translated by one William Marshal. Some early reviewers accepted it as a medieval text and praised it as possessing surprisingly "modern" qualities. Other commentators were not convinced or amused by this claim: the novel was generally faulted as being preposterously unbelievable and insulting to its readers. However, the negative critical reception of *The Castle of Otranto* did not prevent it from becoming extremely popular, which encouraged Walpole to reveal his authorship in the second edition. In his preface he defined the work as "an attempt to blend the two kinds of romance, the ancient and the modern." The former, he explained, relied upon imagination and improbability, with the result frequently being grossly incredible: the latter attempted to copy nature, but often lacked imagination. He concluded that these elements must be adequately balanced in order to create a plausible, yet interesting, narrative. Walpole was largely successful in accomplishing his objective. An admirer of legends of the Middle Ages, he incorporated their fairy-tale elements and chivalric code into a storyline which featured characters who were contemporary in speech and thought. His use of a Gothic castle and its array of machinery (trap doors, vaults, dungeons, rattling chains, etc.) was original not only in its inclusion but in its offhanded presentation. In *The Castle of Otranto*, statues bleed, apparitions stalk the castle, and

ancestral portraits sigh, but all are accepted as natural occurrences by the characters. In addition to this technique, Walpole manipulated the forces of nature to accentuate the sense of ominousness. For example, a gust of wind extinguishes the heroine's candle at a critical moment and moonlight magnifies and plays tricks on the characters' perception of objects. Another important element of *The Castle of Otranto* is the introduction of what eventually became stock characters in Gothic literature: the handsome hero, the virginal heroine, sinister monks, and the nobleman in peasant's garb.

Walpole's lesser-known fictional works include *The Mysterious Mother* (1768), a drama in blank verse, and *Hieroglyphic Tales* (1785). The theme of *The Mysterious Mother*—incest—was so controversial that Walpole printed the work himself and distributed it only to selected friends. Although it has received relatively little critical comment, the drama has come to be recognized as an important forerunner of Gothic drama. Of *The Mysterious Mother* Bertrand Evans (see Further Reading) wrote: "Elements of setting, character, machinery, and technique, combined for a single purpose, make *The Mysterious Mother* the first play in the Gothic tradition." The *Hieroglyphic Tales* are considered Walpole's most peculiar fictional effort. By his own admission the *Tales* were "written extempore and without any plan." In these early examples of automatic writing, Walpole completely defied fictional conventions of his day as well as prevailing moral taste to create works rife with incest, scatology, and unwitting cannibalism, and populated by concubines, dead children, and such fantastic elements as giant hummingbirds and carts made of giant pistachio shells. The effect is one of delirium and surrealism with—some critics claim—a detectable undercurrent of Walpole's obsessions and psychological disturbances.

CRITICAL RECEPTION

Critics generally consider Walpole's letters the masterwork for which he is most deservedly known to posterity. The primary purpose of the letters was to entertain Walpole's readers: their secondary purpose was to inform. Therefore the letters are marked by a highly distinctive style—witty, colorful, and vividly descriptive—but they are not always factually accurate. A harsh critic of dry and uninteresting writing by his contemporaries, Walpole sought to avoid similar weaknesses in his own prose and concentrated on developing seemingly artless but riveting narratives which came alive through carefully selected and embellished detail. While most critics agree that Walpole's vivid imagination and strongly-held opinions make the letters less than objective portrayals of his era, a significant number have harshly attacked what they consider exaggeration or distortion in his correspondence. In the twentieth century, critics reevaluated Walpole's work and began to defend the significance of his letters as one of the most trustworthy and indispensable sources available for a thorough depiction of society, politics, and manners in eighteenth-century England.

General critical assessment maintains that, in spite of its important contributions to the Gothic tradition, *The Castle of Otranto*'s shortcomings are too serious to overlook. The novel suffers from a convoluted and confusing plot, insufficient character development, and stilted dialogue, all of which discourage and virtually prohibit reader involvement. One prevalent criticism is that the work is too rapidly paced, with the Gothic devices occurring in such quick succession that little of the sense of mystery Walpole wished to create is present. Nevertheless, these defects have not obscured *The Castle of Otranto*'s influence upon novelists who have received more recognition than Walpole. Both Clara Reeve and Ann Radcliffe, prominent Gothic novelists, as well as Sir Walter Scott, acknowledged their indebtedness to Walpole's work, with Reeve (see Further Reading) calling her acclaimed novel *The Old English Baron* "the literary offspring of *The Castle of Otranto*" and Scott praising *The Castle of Otranto* as "not only . . . the original and model of a peculiar species of composition, attempted and successfully executed by a man of great genius, but . . . one of the standard works of our lighter literature."

PRINCIPAL WORKS

The Beauties: An Epistle to Mr. Eckardt, the Painter (poetry) 1746

Aedes Walpolianae; or, A Description of the Collection of Pictures at Houghton Hall in Norfolk, the Seat of the Right Honourable Sir Robert Walpole, Earl of Orford (catalog) 1747

A Letter to the Whigs, Occasioned by the "Letter to the Tories" (essay) 1747

A Letter from Xo Ho, a Chinese Philosopher at London, to His Friend Lien Chi at Peking (satire) 1757

A Catalogue of the Royal and Noble Authors of England, with Lists of Their Works. 2 vols. (biography) 1758

A Dialogue between Two Great Ladies (satire) 1760

Anecdotes of Painting in England, with Some Account of the Principal Artists, and Incidental Notes on Other Arts. 4 vols. (art history) 1762-71

The Opposition to the Late Minister Vindicated from the Aspersions of a Pamphlet Entitled "Considerations on the Present Dangerous Crisis" (essay) 1763

The Castle of Otranto: A Story (novel) 1764

Historic Doubts on the Life and Reign of King Richard the Third (essay) 1768

The Mysterious Mother: A Tragedy (play) 1768

A Description of the Villa of Horace Walpole, Youngest Son of Sir Robert Walpole, Earl of Orford, at Strawberry-Hill, near Twickenham (catalog) 1774

Hieroglyphic Tales (short stories) 1785

Memoires of the Last Ten Years of the Reign of George the Second. 2 vols. (memoirs) 1822

Memoirs of the Reign of George the Third. 4 vols. (memoirs) 1845

Last Journals, from 1771 to 1783. 2 vols. (journals) 1859

Letters of Horace Walpole. 19 vols. (letters) 1903-25

Horace Walpole's "Fugitive Verses" (poetry) 1931

The Yale Edition of Walpole's Correspondence. 48 vols. (letters) 1937-83

Memoirs and Portraits (memoirs) 1963

Selected Letters (letters) 1973

PRIMARY SOURCES

HORACE WALPOLE (ESSAY DATE 1764)

SOURCE: Walpole, Horace. "Translator's Preface." In *Castle of Otranto, A Story*, pp. iii-ix. Dublin, Ireland: J. Hoey, J. Exshaw, P. Wilson, S. Cotter, W. Sleater, J. Potts, S. Watson, J. Hoey, junior, J. Williams, and J. Sheppard, 1764.

In the following "Translator's Preface" to The Castle of Otranto *Walpole offers a fictional account of the "discovery" of the manuscript, presented as a medieval document.*

The following work was found in the library of an ancient Catholic family in the north of *England*. It was printed at *Naples*, in the black letter, in the year 1529. How much sooner it was written does not appear. The principal incidents are such as were believed in the darkest ages of Christianity; but the language and conduct have nothing that savours of barbarism. The stile is the purest *Italian.* If the story was written near the time when it is supposed to have happened, it must have been between 1095, the æra of the first crusade, and 1243, the date of the last, or not long afterwards. There is no other circumstance in the work, that can lead us to guess at the period in which the scene is laid: The names of the actors are evidently fictitious, and probably disguised on purpose: Yet the *Spanish* names of the domestics seem to indicate that this work was not composed, until the establishment of the *Arragonian* Kings in *Naples* had made *Spanish* appellations familiar in that country. The beauty of the diction, and the zeal of the author [moderated, however, by singular judgment] concur to make me think that the date of the composition was little antecedent to that of the impression. Letters were then in their most flourishing state in *Italy,* and contributed to dispel the empire of superstition, at that time so forcibly attacked by the reformers. It is not unlikely that an artful priest might endeavour to turn their own arms on the innovators; and might avail himself of his abilities as an author to confirm the populace in their ancient errors and superstitions. If this was his view, he has certainly acted with signal address. Such a work as the following would enslave a hundred vulgar minds beyond half the books of controversy that have been written from the days of *Luther* to the present hour.

This solution of the author's motives is however offered as a mere conjecture. Whatever his views were, or whatever effects the execution of them might have, his work can only be laid before the public at present as a matter of entertainment. Even as such, some apology for it is necessary. Miracles, visions, necromancy, dreams, and other preternatural events, are exploded now even from romances. That was not the case when our author wrote; much less when the story itself is supposed to have happened. Belief in every kind of prodigy was so established in those dark ages, that an author would not be faithful to the *manners* of the times, who should omit all mention of them. He is not bound to believe them himself, but he must represent his actors as believing them.

If this *air* of *the miraculous* is excused, the reader will find nothing else unworthy of his perusal. Allow the possibility of the facts, and all the actors comport themselves as persons would do in their situation. There is no bombast no

similes, flowers, digressions, or unnecessary descriptions. Every thing tends directly to the catastrophe. Never is the reader's attention relaxed. The rules of the drama are almost observed throughout the conduct of the piece. The characters are well drawn, and still better maintained. Terror, the author's principal engine, prevents the story from ever languishing; and it is so often contrasted by pity, that the mind is kept up in a constant vicissitude of interesting passions.

Some persons may perhaps think the characters of the domestics too little serious for the general cast of the story; but besides their opposition to the principal personages, the art of the author is very observable in his conduct of the subalterns. They discover many passages essential to the story, which could not be well brought to light but by their naivete and simplicity: In particular, the womanish terror and foibles of *Bianca,* in the last chapter, conduce essentially towards advancing the catastrophe.

It is natural for a translator to be prejudiced in favour of his adopted work. More impartial readers may not be so much struck with the beauties of this piece as I was. Yet I am not blind to my author's defects. I could wish he had grounded his plan on a more useful moral than this; that *the sins of fathers are visited on their children to the third and fourth generation.* I doubt whether, in his time, any more than at present, ambition curbed its appetite of dominion from the dread of so remote a punishment. And yet this moral is weakened by that less direct insinuation, that even such anathema may be diverted by devotion to St. *Nicholas.* Here the interest of the Monk plainly gets the better of the judgment of the Author. However, with all its faults, I have no doubt but the *English* reader will be pleased with a sight of this performance. The piety that reigns throughout, the lessons of virtue that are inculcated, and the rigid purity of the sentiments, exempt this work from the censure to which romances are but too liable. Should it meet with the success I hope for, I may be encouraged to re-print the original *Italian,* though it will tend to depreciate my own labour. Our language falls far short of the charms of the *Italian,* both for variety and harmony. The latter is peculiarly excellent for simple narrative. It is difficult in *English to relate* without falling too low or rising too high; a fault obviously occasioned by the little care taken to speak pure language in common conversation. Every *Italian* or *Frenchman* of any rank piques himself on speaking his own tongue correctly and with choice. I cannot flatter myself with having done justice to

ABOUT THE AUTHOR

FREDERICK S. FRANK ON *THE MYSTERIOUS MOTHER*

Unlike the first Gothic novel, the first Gothic drama consigns its characters permanently to the outer darkness. *The Mysterious Mother* is not only the darkest work that Walpole himself ever wrote, it is probably the darkest tragedy written on incest or any other subject of sexual transgression in the entire eighteenth century. In later forms of the high Gothic, the soul often dies before the body dies and evil supplants good. Surely, this tragic fact is what moved the publisher of the 1798 edition of the play to celebrate Walpole's achievement in these terms: "Of the present tragedy we may boldly pronounce, that for nervous, simple, and pathetic language, each appropriated to the several persons of the drama; for striking incidents; for address in conducting the plot; and for consistency of character uniformly preserved through the whole piece; it is equal, if not superior, to any play of the present century" (*Mysterious Mother*, Advertisement from the Publishers, 174).

SOURCE: Frank, Frederick S. Introduction to *The Castle of Otranto: A Gothic Story and The Mysterious Mother: A Tragedy*, by Horace Walpole, edited by Frederick S. Frank, pp. 11-34. Peterborough, Ontario: Broadview, 2003.

my author in this respect: His stile is as elegant, as his conduct of the passions is masterly. It is pity that he did not apply his talents to what they were evidently proper for, the theatre.

I will detain the reader no longer, but to make one short remark. Though the machinery is invention, and the names of the actors imaginary, I cannot but believe, that the ground-work of the story is founded on truth. The scene is undoubtedly laid in some real castle. The author seems frequently, without design, to describe particular parts. *The chamber*, says he, *on the right-hand; the door on the left-hand; the distance from the chapel to Conrad's apartment*: These and other passages are strong presumptions that the author had some certain building in his eye. Curious persons, who have leisure to employ in such researches, may possibly discover in the *Italian* writers the foundation on which our author has built. If a catastrophe, at all resembling that which he describes, is believed to have given rise to this work, it will contribute to interest the reader, and will make the castle of *Otranto* a still more moving story.

TITLE COMMENTARY

The Castle of Otranto

THE CRITICAL REVIEW (REVIEW DATE JANUARY 1765)

SOURCE: A review of *The Castle of Otranto: A Story*, by Horace Walpole. *The Critical Review* 19 (January 1765): 50-1.

In the following excerpt from a negative review of The Castle of Otranto, *the critic expresses disapproval of the gross absurdity of the supernatural elements and suggests that the anonymously-published novel is the work of a modern, not medieval, author.*

The ingenious translator of this *very curious* performance [**The Castle of Otranto**] informs that it was found in the library of an ancient catholic family in the north of England; that it was printed at Naples, in the black letter, in the year 1529; and that the style is of the purest Italian; he also conjectures, that if the story was written near the time when it is supposed to have happened, it must have been between 1095, the era of the first crusade, and 1243, the date of the last, or not long afterwards. . . .

Such is the character of this work given us by its judicious translator; but whether he speaks seriously or ironically, we neither know nor care. The publication of any work, at this time, in England composed of such rotten materials, is a phenomenon we cannot account for. That our readers may form some idea of the absurdity of its contents, we are to inform them that Manfred, prince of Otranto, had only one son, a youth about fifteen years of age, who on the day appointed for his marriage was 'dashed to pieces, and almost buried under an enormous helmet, an hundred times more large than any casque ever made for human being, and shaded with a proportionable quantity of black feathers.' This helmet, it seems, resembled that upon a statue of Alfonso the Good, one of the former princes of Otranto, whose dominions Manfred usurped; and therefore the helmet, or the resemblance of it, by way of poetical justice, dashed out his son's brains.

The above wonder is amongst the least of the wonderful things in this story. A picture comes out of its panel, and stalks through the room, to dissuade Manfred from marrying the princess who had been betrothed to his son. It even utters deep sighs and heaves its breasts. We cannot help thinking that this circumstance is some presumption that the castle of Otranto is a modern fabric; for we doubt much whether pictures were fixed in panels before the year 1243. We shall not affront our readers understanding so much as to describe the other monstrosities of this story; but, excepting those absurdities, the characters are well marked, and the narrative is kept up with surprising spirit and propriety.

JOHN LANGHORNE (REVIEW DATE FEBRUARY 1765)

SOURCE: Langhorne, John. A review of *The Castle of Otranto, a Story,* by Horace Walpole. *The Monthly Review* 32 (February 1765): 97-9.

In the following excerpt from a laudatory review of The Castle of Otranto, *Langhorne applauds the vivid writing and dramatic power of the novel. This review, written when the work was supposed to be the work of a medieval author, contrasts sharply with a scathing review written by Langhorne for the same periodical three months later when the identity of the author was revealed.*

Those who can digest the absurdities of Gothic fiction, and bear with the machinery of ghosts and goblins, may hope, at least, for considerable entertainment from [*The Castle of Otranto*] . . . : for it is written with no common pen; the language is accurate and elegant; the characters are highly finished; and the disquisitions into human manners, passions, and pursuits, indicate the keenest penetration, and the most perfect knowledge of mankind. . . .

The principal defect of this performance does not remain unnoticed. That unchristian doctrine of visiting the sins of the fathers upon the children, is certainly, under our present system, not only a very useless, but a very insupportable moral, and yet it is almost the only one deducible from this story. . . . However, as a work of genius, evincing great dramatic powers, and exhibiting fine views of nature, *The Castle of Otranto* may be read with pleasure. To give the reader an

ABOUT THE AUTHOR

SIR WALTER SCOTT OFFERS HIGH PRAISE FOR WALPOLE AND *THE CASTLE OF OTRANTO*

The Castle of Otranto is remarkable, not only for the wild interest of the story, but as the first modern attempt to found a tale of amusing fiction upon the basis of the ancient romances of chivalry. . . .

This romance has been justly considered not only as the original and model of a peculiar species of composition, attempted and successfully executed by a man of great genius, but as one of the standard works of our lighter literature. . . .

The style of *The Castle of Otranto* is pure and correct English of the earlier and more classical standard. . . . Description, for its own sake, is scarcely once attempted in *The Castle of Otranto*; and if authors would consider how very much this restriction tends to realise narrative, they might be tempted to abridge, at least, the showy and wordy exuberance of a style fitter for poetry than prose. It is for the dialogue that Walpole reserves his strength; and it is remarkable how, while conducting his mortal agents with all the art of a modern dramatist, he adheres to the sustained tone of chivalry which marks the period of the action. This is not attained by patching his narrative or dialogue with glossarial terms, or antique phraseology, but by taking care to exclude all that can awaken modern associations. In the one case, his romance would have resembled a modern dress, preposterously decorated with antique ornaments; in its present shape, he has retained the form of the ancient armour, but not its rust and cobwebs.

SOURCE: Scott, Sir Walter. "Walpole." In *Lives of the Novelists.* 1811. Reprint edition, pp. 177-96. London: Oxford University Press, 1906.

analysis of the story, would be to introduce him to a company of skeletons; to refer him to the book will be to recommend him to an assemblage of beautiful pictures.

PERCY LUBBOCK (ESSAY DATE 26 MAY 1923)

SOURCE: Lubbock, Percy. A review of *The Castle of Otranto: A Story,* by Horace Walpole. *The Nation and The Athenaeum* 33, no. 8 (26 May 1923): 267-68.

In the following excerpt from a review of The Castle of Otranto, *Lubbock concludes that the novel is of no interest to the general reader, its plot and characterization being too trivial, unsubstantial, and tedious. Lubbock asserts that this work is of interest only because of its historical importance and is correctly relegated to the classroom as an example of early Gothic fiction or the eighteenth-century Romantic revival.*

It is certainly hard on [Walpole], the trick that a later age has played with his Gothic romance [*The Castle of Otranto*]. Gray said it made the dons at Cambridge afraid to go to bed in the dark, Scott found a "wild interest" in it, Macaulay spoke of its unflagging excitement; and the end has been, not merely that it excites and frightens nobody, not only that it lies unread, but worse—that it is relegated to the very place of all others which is least congenial to Horace Walpole. It is handed over to the schools, to the critical handbooks, to the literary lecture-rooms; in these *The Castle of Otranto* lives on vigorously, but this is its only life. It is never mentioned, never thought of anywhere else; but as soon as the lecturer reaches the "romantic revival" of the eighteenth century we know what to expect—punctually the epoch opens with Horace Walpole's tale of terror. He invented, we always understand, a "new form" in fiction, and his invention was symptomatic of the great new turn of thought that was changing the world of Pope into the world of Coleridge; and so *The Castle of Otranto,* ceasing to be terrible, remains historic, and doubtless it will continue to open the age of romance as long as there are handbooks and lectures on English literature in which to do so. Such is the company into which the fastidious author appears to have fallen irredeemably. As a collector and a wit and a letter writer, he may enjoy a society more to his mind; but as a romancer, no—as a romancer he belongs exclusively to the frumpish inelegance of the schools. He would rather be forgotten outright. . . .

Can we do anything, even now, to retrieve his situation? . . . [Read] the story straight through—and say whether you find the story attractive in any way on its unsupported merit. It may be that the answer is surprising, if the experiment is made for the first time. Taken on its own merit, the story has an interest, neither wild indeed nor unflagging, but an interest as a piece of writing carefully studied and mannered, a neat exercise in an artificial tone. There is no crudity and no violence in its accent; it seems to be describing the adventures of a well-bred and courtly company in a rococo stage-pastoral, a world which at times will gracefully unbend to the humours and extravagances of its domestic servants. It is a pleasing and familiar effect, classical in its disciplined taste. It may be a shock to discover, on listening more closely, that these distinguished people are enduring agonies, experiencing portents, plunging into disasters such as "words cannot paint"—the author, staggered by the succession of enormities, can find no other phrase. But their style is not seriously ruffled by their tortures; they are still classical in their sufferings, and with a noble resignation they meet their doom, models of antique deportment in their despair and their extinction. It is not exciting, it is not terrifying, it is rather dull; but it has all the proprieties of an urbane tradition.

And is this, then, the spirit-shaking fiction that inaugurated a new method of romance? After all, *The Castle of Otranto* must remain what it has been for so long, the text of the lecturer; for its respectable manners, though well maintained, are not so striking as to restore it to the casual liberal reader. Its interest as a tale is a very thin matter compared with its interest as a document; but this latter is heightened, perhaps, by the attempt to read it as a tale. For the startling novelty of its method, that to which it owes its prominence in the history of taste, unexpectedly disappears if it is not specially sought; unless you are purposely looking for it to point a moral, the Gothic rudeness and grimness of the *Castle* is easily missed. The dismal horrors that were once so medieval have turned to the baroque in their decorative exuberance; not a hollow groan, not a clanking chain, not a hair-raising shriek in the story, but is now the very echo of an age that comfortably toyed with marvels, persuading itself to a pleasing shudder. The revival of romance?— . . . it carries us back to the days when the imagination of man was so bright, so clear, so complacent, that it had actually, for its own relief, to create a little pretence-obscurity and mystery in one of its polished corners. We have changed all this so thoroughly—such vapours of the pit now curl and swirl in our haunted minds—that we may claim to have discovered, at last and again, the recesses of the grotesque and the mysterious, the places where the antic sits and grins. Perhaps it is we who are inaugurating a Gothic revival; at least we have plenty to shudder at that was never dreamed of at Strawberry Hill.

As for Horace Walpole, the moral he may point in the schools, or part of it, is the very long way a very little matter will go when it is really new. It was really a new idea to use the supernatural once more in fiction as a means of making your flesh creep; and Horace used the supernatural so inexpertly that we now hardly notice it is there; but in its day it frightened dons from their rest and struck even Scott with its gruesome power. Horace handled his marvels precisely as Mr. Anstey and Mr. Wells handle theirs; only he asked of them exactly the opposite effect. To bring the supernatural into your story without precaution, to tumble it forth into life that is unprepared and unattuned—this is the way to use it for burlesque and satire; taken for granted, blandly precipitated into normal life, the effect of a miracle is richly comic. Horace Walpole thought that it might become tragic and solemn by no other arts; and he was right: it could become both for a time, since the idea was a new revival. And so a gigantic helmet dropped from heaven into a castle-yard, a picture groaned, a statue shed blood from its nose; and for the space of a generation and more these prodigies met the demand of their author, crept upon his readers with delicious thrills. Enough, *The Castle of Otranto* had its turn, and more than its turn, in the genial world; let it remain henceforward in the handbooks, for ever heralding an historic movement.

EMMA CLERY (ESSAY DATE 1994)

SOURCE: Clery, Emma. "Against Gothic." In *Gothick Origins and Innovations*, edited by Allan Lloyd Smith and Victor Sage, pp. 34-43. Atlanta, Ga. and Amsterdam: Rodopi, 1994.

In the following essay, Clery explores the significance of the change in critical perception of The Castle of Otranto *from positive to negative following the disclosure of the novel's true authorship, noting particularly the potentially subversive nature of the work.*

In February 1765 a critic in the *Monthly Review* said of *The Castle of Otranto*:

Those who can digest the absurdities of Gothic fiction, and bear with the machinery of ghosts and goblins, may hope, at least, for considerable entertainment from the performance before us: for it is written with no common pen; the language is accurate and elegant, the characters are highly finished; and the disquisitions into human manners, passions and pursuits, indicate the keenest penetration, the most perfect knowledge of mankind.[1]

In May 1765 the same critic in the *Monthly Review* wrote:

While we considered [*The Castle of Otranto* a translation] we could readily excuse its preposterous phenomena, and consider them as sacrifices to a gross and unenlightened age. But when, as in this edition, [it] is declared to be a modern performance, that indulgence we offered to the foibles of a supposed antiquity, we can by no means extend to the singularity of a false tale in a cultivated period of learning. It is, indeed, more than strange that an Author, of a refined and polished genius, should be an advocate for re-establishing the barbarous superstitions of Gothic devilism!

And he went on to complain about the author's attempt to defend in his preface 'all the trash of Shakespeare . . . what that great genius evidently threw out as a necessary sacrifice to that idol the *caecum vulgas,* the ignorant masses he would adopt in the worship of the true God of Poetry'.[2]

What we have here is one of the great doubletakes in the history of book-reviewing. Three months divide the two judgements. The incitement was the appearance in the interim of a second edition with a new preface and the initials H. W. *Otranto* stood revealed as a modern scandal rather than an ancient curiosity, a sinister hoax rather than a naive genuine article. Most interesting for present purposes is the reminder that the founding text of the tradition of gothic fiction as we see it was a double text for the first audience. What does it mean, that a work is today installed in all its unitary and canonical splendour at the head of a literary genus, when the same work, as a historical event, provoked such a profound doubleness, disjunction, or even disfunction, incoherence, in response?

How are we to understand this initial hiccup in *Otranto*'s reception? How much importance should we attach to it? From the perspective of the present that seeks to establish the essential coherence of a gothic aesthetic it must register as mere surface noise. At the most basic level, a critical discourse that employs 'Gothic' as a useful genre classification, presupposes 'Gothic' as the 'already read', the already known. It cannot imagine, or has no interest in imagining, a position from which a modern fiction employing the marvellous, like *Otranto,* figures as a disruption of norms and expectations. By disruption, I don't mean the tired 'gothic versus neo-classicism' formula. This still posits a 'Gothic' in place as a retrospective unity. I'm talking about a horizon within which 'Gothic' does not exit as given entity, stable and reassuringly objective. Where, instead, Walpole's experiment of updating superstition for modern consumption can be glimpsed only differentially, interpreted only in so far as it affirms or negates what existed before. A literary work addresses itself to what Hans Robert Jauss calls the horizon of expectation of the reader. It 'predisposes its audience to a very specific kind of reception by announcements, overt and covert signals, familiar characteristics, or implicit allusions.'³ From its first pages it arouses expectations which can then be confirmed intact, disorientated, reorientated or fulfilled ironically in the course of the reading.⁴ What is stressed in this version of literary history is dialogism, the constitutive role of the historical reader in establishing the work's meaning. The meaning of a text is not immanent and fixed, but spun out through the process of interaction. Such a perspective grants real hermeneutic value to the double-take of the critic from the *Monthly Review* and allows that he was, in effect, judging two entirely different works. One, a curious relic by 'Onuphrio Muralto, Canon of the Church of Otranto' translated by a certain 'William Marshall, Gent.'; the other, identical in almost every respect to the first, the work not only of a living author, but one who has inherited one of the best-known names in the country.

The question that next presents itself, is why the first of these works should be allowed and the second disallowed. Again, projections of a preconstituted 'gothicism' which confounds critical orthodoxies, can only obscure by their essentialism. There is a logic that joins together the reviewer's two disjunct verdicts and it can be at least partially reconstructed from the terms used in the articles. A systematicity, a discourse, subtends the move from enthusiastic appreciation to sour grapes. The preface to *The Order of Things*, where Foucault introduced his theory of discourse, famously cites a Chinese encyclopedia as discussed by Borges, with its alien and fabulous taxonomy of animals, including among the classifications, 'belonging to the Emperor', 'frenzied,' 'embalmed', 'innumerable', and 'having just broken the water pitcher'. I won't pretend that I can uncover anything as arresting in the *Monthly Review*, but one of the procedures of discursive discipline described by Foucault, the principle of exclusion, is especially relevant here. The articles bring together a number of, for us, mysteriously disconnected elements under two categories of fiction, the commendable and the prohibited. They could be arranged in two columns like this: *commendable*: antique object (even with 'gothic absurdities' attached, contemporary parallel, Ossian); translation (mediation with the past, contextualising preface quoted at length in reviews); verisimilitude (with reference to the representation of character); *prohibited*: modern use of the marvellous; famous author (MP and son of Prime Minister); 'trash of Shakespeare' (appealing to the vulgar). The opposition could be construed in the following way. An antiquity which is firmly situated as a product of the past by the apparatus of translation but at the same time is rather like a modern novel of manners is commendable. A modern fiction that exploits the marvellous and is written by a man with political connections to appeal to the basest instincts of the audience is prohibited.

Now, rather than continuing to discuss the reviews in isolation, I want to turn to Walpole's two prefaces, and try to show how the binary system I've sketched draws its coherence as a discourse from a dialogic exchange with the prefaces. The discourse is summoned into voice by the familiar signals of the first preface, only to be undermined by the second. I should mention that in the second edition of **Otranto**, only the second preface was printed, therefore assuming a knowledge of the first, but from the third edition in 1755 onwards they were printed together, as they are today.

Lack of space forbids subtlety, so I will say straight away that I see the first preface as an invocation of the discourse of material and social improvement used by the reviewer. The twist is, that when Walpole eventually comes clean about the authorship, this preface will be revealed as a parody in advance of the terms in which the reviewer will reject the work. The second twist is, that its account of the work's origins in the dark ages will turn into an allegory of the present. Let me show how this happens with a few specific references to the text:

PREFACE TO THE FIRST EDITION

The following work was found in the library of an ancient Catholic family in the north of England. It was printed at Naples, in the black letter, in the year 1529. How much sooner it was written does not appear. The principal incidents are such as were believed in the darkest ages of Christianity; but the language and conduct have nothing that savours of barbarism. The style is the purest Italian. If the story was written near the time when it is supposed to have happened, it must have been between 1095; the æra of the first crusade, and 1243, the date of the last, or not long afterwards. There is no other circumstance in the work that can lead us to guess at the period in which the scene is laid: the names of the actors are evidently fictitious, and probably disguised on purpose: yet the Spanish names of the domestics seem to indicate that this work was not composed until the establishment of the Arragonian kings in Naples had made Spanish appellations familiar in that country. The beauty of the diction, and the zeal of the author [moderated however by singular judgment] concur to make me think that the date of the composition was little antecedent to that of the impression. Letters were then in their most flourishing state in Italy, and contributed to dispel the empire of superstition, at that time so forcibly attacked by the reformers. It is not unlikely that an artful priest might endeavour to turn their own arms on the innovators; and might avail himself of his abilities as an author to confirm the populace in their ancient errors and superstitions. If this was his view, he has certainly acted with signal address. Such a work as the following would enslave a hundred vulgar minds beyond half the books of controversy that have been written from the days of Luther to the present hour.

The solution of the author's motive is however offered as a mere conjecture. Whatever his views were, or whatever effects the execution of them might have, his work can only be laid before the public at present as a matter of entertainment. Even as such, some apology for it is necessary. Miracles, visions, necromancy, dreams, and other preternatural events, are exploded now even from romances. That was not the case when our author wrote, much less when the story itself is supposed to have happened. Belief in every kind of prodigy was so established in those dark ages, that an author would not be faithful to the *manners* of the times who should omit all mention of them. He is not bound to believe them himself but he must represent his actors as believing them.

'Letters were then in their most flourishing state in Italy, and contributed to dispel the empire of superstition . . .'. The trope of the spread of learning driving out superstition is, of course, a ubiquitous feature of the language of enlightenment. With technological determinism á la Marshall McLuhan, it places the printing press at the centre of world historical progress. The present, witnessing an unprecedented dissemination of print and rapid expansion of the reading public, represented the glorious conclusion of this progress. The trope was, in fact, habitually applied to modern times and, in Britain, most often joined to elaborate panegyrics of English liberty and English institutions, and to denunciations of those institutions raised on superstition, notably the Catholic Church and the despotic forms of government found abroad. Walpole, with what will appear in retrospect a transparent irony, projects the contemporary struggle between light and darkness into a murky Italian past.

The potential irony then intensifies. 'It is not unlikely that an artful priest [ie Onuphrio Muralto, the author of this work] might endeavour to turn their own arms on the innovators; and might avail himself of his abilities as an author to confirm the populace in their errors and superstitions.' Onuphrio Muralto, it will emerge, is Horace Walpole; and it is precisely as an 'artful priest', a propagator of the 'barbarous superstitions of gothic devilry' that he will be condemned. Like the priest, he is hijacking the primary instrument of reform, the press, and reintroducing fabulous lies by means of the widely-circulated form of popular fiction.

Here the discourse of socio-historical improvement intersects with debate on the power of fiction and the proper methods of directing it to useful and moral ends. The critics, straight-faced and earnest, will reverse against Walpole his teasing assertion in the preface that, 'Miracles, visions, necromancy, dreams, and other preternatural events, are exploded now even from romances'. As the *Monthly Review* puts it, the 'singularity of a false tale' is incompatible with 'a cultivated period of learning'. Or the *Critical Review*: 'The publication of any work, at this time, in England, composed of such rotten materials, is a phenomenon we cannot account for'. However, with the transposition of the discourse of improvement into the fiction controversy, 'superstition', the other-to-be-subjugated, is subsumed by a much nearer anxiety, the threat of unregulated consumerism.

Like superstition, hedonistic consumption is a manifestation of the passions without the guidance of reason. In the view of the discourse of improvement, which is sometimes called the discourse of civic humanism, the economic passions, which include the love of luxury and are the basis of national prosperity, need to be reigned in and coordinated for the public good under the rational direction of wise governors. This view was scandalously challenged by Bernard Mandeville who argued in *The Fable of the Bees* that the private vices of greed and luxury would translate into the public benefits of a healthy national economy and strength abroad without the need for moral or political intervention, a position not far from the *laissez-faire* and 'invisible hand' of Adam Smith. I want to suggest that Walpole's prefaces represent a similar scandal, disguised in the first instance and later confirmed by the second edition. And naturally the scandal would be magnified by the fact that the author was himself in a position of political power (as it was, 30 years later, in the case of 'Monk' Lewis).

Mimicking the shocked tones of the civic humanist, he observes in preface number one: 'Such a work as the following would enslave a hundred vulgar minds beyond half the books of controversy that have been written from the days of Luther to the present hour'. 'To the present hour' exactly—for the statement lexically hooks into a literary critical discourse that speaks of the reading public's 'enslavement' by authors of fiction who calculatingly manipulate the passions, and Walpole obliquely confesses himself guilty, of just this crime. Neither are the remarks about 'entertainment' or 'faithful to the manners of the times' as innocent as they seem. A work of the distant past may be presented as pure entertainment, since it can contain no useful moral for the enlightened present; but this is far from being the case with a modern work of fiction, which must justify and redeem its fall from truth to illusion with a clear moral function. Walpole will go on to refuse a moral function outright in the second preface, and already in the first he obligingly draws attention to this heterodoxy, pointing out, in the role of translator, the 'author's defect' in not finding a more useful moral than that *'the sins of the fathers are visited on their children to the third or fourth generations'* (a moral, though, not without interest). In the same fashion, the detached stance of the antiquarian who simply offers the public a record of 'things as they were' disguises the amoral modern author, happy to cater to the regressive public taste for the marvellous, because he accepts, without judgement, 'things as they are'.

If we move on now to the second preface, we can see the way this position of economic amoralism is articulated in aesthetic terms:

PREFACE TO THE SECOND EDITION

The favourable manner in which this little piece has been received by the public, calls upon the author to explain the grounds on which he composed it. But before he opens those motives, it is fit that he should ask pardon of his readers for having offered his work to them under the borrowed personage of a translator. As diffidence of his own abilities, and the novelty of the attempt, were his sole inducements to assume that disguise, he flatters himself that he shall appear excusable. He resigned his performance to the impartial judgment of the public; determined to let it perish in obscurity, if disapproved; nor meaning to avow such a trifle, unless better judges should pronounce that he might own it without a blush.

It was an attempt to blend the two kinds of romance, the ancient and the modern. In the former all was imagination and improbability: in the latter, nature is always intended to be, and sometimes has been, copied with success. Invention has not been wanting; but the great resources of fancy have been damned up, by a strict adherence to common life. But if in the latter species,

Nature has cramped imagination, she did but take her revenge, having been totally excluded from old romances. The actions, sentiments, conversations, of the heroes and heroines of ancient days were as unnatural as the machines employed to put them in motion.

The author of the following pages thought it possible to reconcile the two kinds. Desirous of leaving the powers of fancy at liberty to expatiate through the boundless realms of invention, and thence of creating more interesting situations, he wished to conduct the mortal agents in his drama according to the rules of probability; in short to make them think, speak and act, as it might be supposed mere men and women would do in extraordinary positions. He had observed, that in all inspired writings, the personages under the dispensation of miracles, and witnesses to the most stupendous phenomena, never lose sight of their human character: whereas in the productions of romantic story, an improbable event never fails to be attended by the most absurd dialogue. The actors seem to lose their senses the moment the laws of nature have lost their tone. As the public have applauded the attempt, the author must not say he was entirely unequal to the task he had undertaken; yet if the new route he has struck out shall have paved a road for men of brighter talents, he shall own with pleasure and modesty, that he was sensible the plan was capable of receiving greater embellishments than his imagination or conduct of the passions could bestow upon it.

In a very well known passage, the author speaks of a 'new route' in fiction, and of a 'blend of the two kinds of romance, the ancient and the modern'. The idea of a blend is based on the perceived deficiencies of these two existing types. Modern fictions are overly mimetic, cramped by their imitation of nature. Ancient fictions are too wildly improbable, in particular their delineation of character is too unnatural, Walpole seems to be suggesting, to allow a modern reader a proper point of identification. Both the proposal to salvage the extravagances of the past, and the criticism of an aesthetic of nature that really amounted to an ethic, are controversial. But how do they engage with the social and economic issues just mentioned?

First, I should say, by context. The preface quickly launches into a digression of three or four pages addressed to Voltaire, (establishing that Shakespeare is Walpole's model and defending the presence of comedy in the tragedies from the criticisms of the Frenchman). Walpole's rehabilitation of genre hybridism in Shakespeare parallels Elizabeth Montagu's contemporary, influential rehabilitation of the preternatural in Shakespeare. In both these instances, the exemplary function of literature is discounted. Walpole and Montagu ignore the objection that drama which included gross improbabilities like ghosts and fairies, or promiscuously mixed comedy and tragedy, threatened to lapse from the role of instruction and elevation to mere unredeemed entertainment, from didacticism to aimless affectivity. Conversely, when Walpole and Montagu's revaluations are resisted and condemned, it is rationalised as resistance to a groundling's-eye-view of the drama, the passive, uncritical, sensuous pleasure of the spectacle. Not incidentally, Walpole's argument is framed in terms of rank, as the right of the fictionalised domestic servant to laugh, 'however grave, important, or even melancholy, the sensations of princes or heroes may be'.

This lengthy aside of Walpole's on drama illuminates the libertarian language used in the passage quoted. The powers of fancy in fiction have been dammed up and cramped, in his view, by the same prescriptions, the same critical strictures, aimed at Shakespeare. The subordination of fiction to moral instrumentality is refused. In place of this function 'boundless realms of invention' are evoked, prompting ideas of the infinite vistas of commercial expansion. The absolute value of freedom is novelty, 'creating more interesting situations'; suggesting the central place of the fashion system in that most commercially up-and-coming literary form, the novel. Walpole spotted a gap in the market. He decided to try to reconcile the 'powers of fancy' with 'the rules of probability'. The success of the first edition has vindicated his venture, and encouraged him to reveal his authorship and point the way for 'men of brighter talents' to build on his entrepreneurial foundations.

But this vision of liberty is not without its tensions. The remark that 'the great resources of fancy have been dammed up by a strict adherence to common life', removes the notion of moral instrumentality at the same time as it metaphorically introduces an idea of economic instrumentality by representing fancy as a property, a form of mineral wealth. More immediately, the author's deferential address to 'the public' masks a more complex relation involving both antagonism and dependency. On the one hand, there is the memory of the claim that 'such a work as the following would enslave a hundred vulgar minds', relocated in present fears concerning the addictive, pathological pleasures of fiction, and the extraordinary powers wielded by the novelist over the sensibilities of his or her readers. On the other hand, there is the reverse possibility, raised by the simple observation 'the public have applauded

the attempt', that fiction, having asserted its autonomy from moral ends, its social uselessness, may become in turn a slave to the whims of the audience, or the law of supply and demand, reinstrumentalised by the operations of the market, (reformed) as a commodity.

This possibility is raised more provocatively in the final sentence of the preface: 'Such as [*Otranto*] is, the public have honoured it sufficiently, whatever rank their suffrages allot to it.' An elaborate way of saying, 'this is a bestseller, so stuff the critics'. A hierarchical, judgemental conception of taste is superseded by 'kitchen taste' relating to a 'culinary' or entertainment art, based on a gustatory model, subjectivist and non-evaluative, as in 'each to his own taste'. The word 'rank' does double service here: not only indicating the indifference of the author to critical hierarchy, but also playfully mauling the cherished correlation of social rank and the proper exercise of taste. The rather forced use of 'suffrages' may, too, be an attempt to crank up the level of critical reaction one degree closer to hysteria, its radical political connotations overlaying the radical prospect of a 'republic of consumption'.

The two prefaces of *The Castle of Otranto* raise the spectre of a thoroughgoing transformation in the relation between literary fiction and society; not in order to analyze or resolve the difficulties involved in such a transformation, certainly; more, if I can change the metaphor, to wave it like a red flag in the face of the opposition. But we find there not only a proposal for a new kind of reading matter, but the outlines of a new mode of fiction reading, one which still largely determines our expectations today.

The reading I offer is, I think, incompatible with the assumptions of genre criticism. That said, I wouldn't question the interpretative value of the term 'gothic' when applied to works of the 19th and 20th century, when self-consciousness in the writing of fantastic or supernatural fictions has reached a level such that 'gothic' becomes determinate as the name for a species of writing. But it seems to me that when applied to earlier works, 'gothic' can only serve to widen the cause of ontology, the search for essences. I wonder if we wouldn't be better off examining some of the categories in which contemporary commentators actually placed the works—the 'terrorist system of novel-writing' for instance, or most often, 'modern romance', a term which for the 18th century was instilled with the fascination of paradox.

Frontispiece of Horace Walpole's *A Description of Strawberry Hill,* in which Walpole delineates his Gothic castle.

In the first edition, **The Castle of Otranto** is subtitled, 'A Story'. On the title page of the second edition this has been changed to 'A Gothic Story'. For the reader of today, this supplement has no resonance. As a consequence of overuse or misuse, the term has no elasticity. It is merely what we expect to see. The main point I want to establish in the paper is that in its historical moment this word is absolutely full, taut, with meaning; invested, in fact, with all the significance I've allotted to the interaction between author and critic and the interplay between one preface and the other. 'Gothic' in this place is no ordinary sign—as an adjective, as a representation, it would be properly applied to the *first* edition of **Otranto**—it would be used as the reviewer uses it, to delimit the work of a past era. Instead, 'gothic' is introduced precisely in the place where it shouldn't be, where it doesn't fit, rupturing coherence, severing a modern fiction from its function as an index of enlightenment, an anti-sign, a negativity, semantically dislocated but ominous with a futurity that figures as regression. The future of autonomous fiction that cannot escape the condition of a commodity.

What I hope I've shown is that **The Castle of Otranto** interprets its own project in material terms, most specifically with reference to class hierarchy and the development of a consumer society. It's my belief that the works written and published prior to the canonization of gothic have a lot to tell us about the social causes and consequences of that aesthetic conversion.

Notes

1. *Monthly Review* (Feb. 1765), pp. 97-99.

2. *Ibid,* (May 1765), p. 394.

3. *Towards an Aesthetic of Reception,* trans. Timothy Bahti (Brighton: Harvester Press, 1982), p. 23.

4. *Ibid,* p. 23.

MICHAEL GAMER (ESSAY DATE 2001)

SOURCE: Gamer, Michael. Introduction to *The Castle of Otranto,* by Horace Walpole, pp. xiii-xxxv. London: Penguin, 2001.

In the following essay, Gamer discusses how The Castle of Otranto *has been received by critics from the eighteenth century through the twenty-first century, and explores Walpole's vision as evidenced in the novel.*

1. Reception

Since its first publication in 1764, **The Castle of Otranto** has rarely, if ever, been out of print, and over 130 editions precede this one.[1] Few books of fiction have surpassed its sustained popularity in the history of literary publishing; even fewer can claim so central an influence on the history of the novel or on late eighteenth-century prose romance. Appearing a quarter of a century before Gothic fiction became a popular literary form, Walpole's story is startling for the way in which it assembles, almost prophetically, an array of generic devices recognizable to any reader familiar with *Frankenstein* (1818), *Northanger Abbey* (1818), *Wuthering Heights* (1847) or *Dracula* (1897). The fatal prophecy against Manfred's house, the supernatural visitations attending it, and the Draconian attempts of Manfred to combat both found their way into countless late eighteenth- and early nineteenth-century fictions, including those of Anna Letitia Barbauld, Clara Reeve, Ann Radcliffe, Matthew Lewis, W. H. Ireland, Charlotte Dacre and Charles Robert Maturin. In addition, the book's breathless pace and mysterious opening, packed with unexplainable happenings and sinister portents, anticipate later detective and sensation fiction. Most influential and evocative of all, of course, has been the icon of the castle, transformed in Walpole's handling from a locus of safety into a place of sexual transgression and supernatural visitation, of secret passageways and political intrigue. With its adjacent monastery, it is a place that harbours guilty secrets and unlawful desires, a fortress not for keeping people out but for keeping them in. Modern readers, therefore, will find in Walpole's Gothic structures the prototypes not only for other Gothic fictions like *The Mysteries of Udolpho* (1794) and *Melmoth the Wanderer* (1820), but also for twentieth-century films as popular and disparate as *Nosferatu* (1922), *Rebecca* (1940), *Alien* (1979) and *The Name of the Rose* (1986).

Yet in its immediate reception and in the many appraisals that have followed, critical responses to **The Castle of Otranto** and to its author have been consistently mixed, characterized by a recognizable blend of pleasure and bewilderment, admiration and discomfort. Early nineteenth-century anthologies of the British novel, for example, included Walpole's romance almost without exception; yet when Anna Letitia Barbauld chose in 1810 to include it in her monumental series *The British Novelists,* she began by pointing uneasily to its popularity with younger readers and by expressing reservations about its cultural value. Walpole's 'slight performance', as she called it, may have been 'one of the first of the modern productions founded on appearances of terror' and may have shown 'a livelier play of fancy' than most of its successors, but these virtues did not entirely excuse the supernatural fiction that it apparently had inspired: 'it is calculated to make a great impression on those who relish the fictions of the *Arabian Tales,* and similar performances . . . Since this author's time, from the perusal of Mrs Radcliffe's productions and some of the German tales, we may be said to have "supped full with horrors".'[2]

A year later, another essay on Walpole and **The Castle of Otranto** appeared, this time published in an Edinburgh edition of the novel edited by Walter Scott.[3] Like Barbauld, Scott expressed reservations about the source of **Otranto**'s popularity and its frequent recourse to the supernatural before moving on to more enthusiastic praise; but there the similarities between the two essays ended. No longer (as in Barbauld's description) a slight, spirited work written by a dilettante in eight days, **The Castle of Otranto** in Scott's treatment constituted a daring synthesis of historical realism and unfettered imaginative liberty. Scott, therefore, presents Walpole as at once an eccentric dreamer, an insightful antiquarian, and a gifted

ABOUT THE AUTHOR

H. P. LOVECRAFT ON WALPOLE'S INFLUENCE ON THE GOTHIC

Fond of mediaeval romance and mystery as a dilettante's diversion, and with a quaintly imitated Gothic castle as his abode at Strawberry Hill, Walpole in 1764 published the *Castle of Otranto;* a tale of the supernatural which, though thoroughly unconvincing and mediocre in itself, was destined to exert an almost unparalleled influence on the literature of the weird. . . .

Such is the tale; flat, stilted, and altogether devoid of the true cosmic horror which makes real literature. Yet such was the thirst of the age for those touches of strangeness and spectral antiquity which it reflects, that it was seriously received by the soundest readers and raised in spite of its intrinsic ineptness to a pedestal of lofty importance in literary history. What it did above all else was to create a novel type of scene, puppet-characters, and incidents; which, handled to better advantage by writers more naturally adapted to weird creation, stimulated the growth of an imitative Gothic school which in turn inspired the real weavers of cosmic terror—the line of actual artists beginning with Poe. This novel dramatic paraphernalia consisted first of all of the Gothic castle, with its awesome antiquity, vast distances and ramblings, deserted or ruined wings, damp corridors, unwholesome hidden catacombs, and galaxy of ghosts and appalling legends, as a nucleus of suspense and daemoniac fright. . . . All this paraphernalia reappears with amusing sameness, yet sometimes with tremendous effect, throughout the history of the Gothic novel; and is by no means extinct even today, though subtler technique now forces it to assume a less naive and obvious form. An harmonious milieu for a new school had been found, and the writing world was not slow to grasp the opportunity.

SOURCE: Lovecraft, H. P. "The Early Gothic Novel." In *Supernatural Horror in Literature.* 1945. Reprint edition, with a new introduction by E. F. Bleiler, pp. 23-9. New York: Dover, 1973.

and imaginative historian. Tapping 'that secret and reserved feeling of love for the marvelous and supernatural, which occupies a hidden corner in almost every one's bosom',[4] Walpole's antiquarian knowledge, Scott argued, had allowed him the coup of introducing apparitions seamlessly into a carefully historicized setting:

> The association of which we have spoken [that of overcoming rational disbelief in the supernatural] is of a nature peculiarly delicate, and subject to be broken and disarranged. It is, for instance, almost impossible to build such a modern Gothic structure as shall impress us with the feelings we have endeavoured to describe. It may be grand, or it may be gloomy; it may excite magnificent or melancholy ideas; but it must fail in bringing forth the sensation of supernatural awe, connected with halls that have echoed to the sounds of remote generations, and have been pressed by the footsteps of those who have long since passed away. Yet Horace Walpole has attained in composition, what, as an architect, he must have felt beyond the power of his art. The remote and superstitious period in which his scene is laid, the art with which he has furnished forth its Gothic decorations, the sustained, and, in general, dignified tone of feudal manners, prepare us gradually for the favourable reception of prodigies, which, though they could not really have happened at any period, were consistent with the belief of all mankind at that time in which the action is placed.[5]

Coming from a writer traditionally credited with inventing the historical novel—whose estate Abbotsford was modelled, in many ways, on Walpole's own Strawberry Hill—Scott's tribute probably should not surprise us. That Scott should agree with Barbauld (herself an early theorist and practitioner of supernatural fiction[6]) in so many particulars while differing so markedly on *Otranto*'s cultural significance, however, is at once unexpected and yet typical of the book's varied critical reception. It remains one of the few works of fiction to draw strong praise and censure from so many authors of note, boasting famous dismissals by William Hazlitt and Thomas Babington Macaulay and encomiums from writers as different from one another as Lord Byron and Ann Yearsley.[7] Scott's celebration may be the one more often quoted in scholarly essays and editions, but twenty-first-century readers will find themselves surprised by the justness of Barbauld's observations, particularly her fascination with the volume's slightness and theatricality and her representation of it as 'the sportive effusion of a man of genius, who throws the reins loose upon the neck of his imagination'.[8] If readers have found difficulty finding stable footing when reading Walpole's romance, their uneasiness has stemmed at least in part from its unsettling combination of careful historicism and imaginative outrageousness, of solemnity and burlesque.

In addition to these difficulties of irony and tone, *The Castle of Otranto*'s first reviewers were forced to cope with the ruse of its initial publication. Anxious over the book's reception, Walpole had disguised its first edition by publishing it under the pseudonym of 'William Marshall, Gent.' and by having Thomas Lownds print and sell the work rather than doing so at his own press at Strawberry Hill. Walpole then added a bogus Preface that still reads as one of the work's triumphs, burlesquing scholarly tone and gleefully attending to minute details of the forgery. Writing in the persona of Marshall, Walpole declares *Otranto* to be an English translation of a sixteenth-century text printed in Naples in 1529 and written by one 'ONUPHRIO MURALTO, Canon of the Church of St. NICHOLAS at OTRANTO' (see p. 1). He then proceeds to give this genealogy an extra twist, surmising Onuphrio Muralto to have taken as the source of his narrative a tale originally written during the Crusades. Walpole's Preface even provides an account of the work's probable religious and political origins, speculating it to be a document of the Italian Counter-Reformation: 'It is not unlikely that an artful priest . . . might avail himself of his abilities as an author to confirm the populace in their ancient errors and superstitions' (see p. 5). The sum is a fabrication whose complex historicism is typical of Walpole's sense of humour, since to pull off the forgery in convincing fashion he must impersonate an eighteenth-century Catholic English country gentleman translating a militant sixteenth-century Neapolitan priest appropriating (for religious and political ends) a thirteenth-century local history. With this elaborate frame and a few additional observations on its dramatic excellence and the difficulties of translating Italian into English, *The Castle of Otranto* appeared in masquerade on Christmas Eve of 1764.

The immediate response was not auspicious. Perhaps suspicious of the book's holiday publication date, the *Critical Review* reacted defensively. It flatly condemned the book's subject matter and, after displaying its own command of antiquarian knowledge, cavalierly refused to judge its authenticity: 'whether he speaks seriously or ironically, we neither know nor care. The publication of any work, at this time, in England composed of such rotten materials, is a phœnomenon we cannot account for'.[9] The *Monthly Review* chose a more charitable course, recommending the book as a historical curiosity and as 'a work of genius, evincing great dramatic powers, and exhibiting fine views of nature'.[10] When Walpole's second edition showed the work to be a modern production with pretensions to literary innovation, however, the *Monthly* was forced to recant its judgement:

> While we considered it as [a translation from an ancient writer], we could readily excuse its preposterous phœnomena, and consider them as sacrifices to a gross and unenlightened age.—But when, as in this edition, the Castle of Otranto is declared to be a modern performance, that indulgence we afforded to the foibles of a supposed antiquity, we can by no means extend to the singularity of a false taste in a cultivated period of learning. It is, indeed, more than strange, that an Author, of a refined and polished genius, should be an advocate for re-establishing the barbarous superstitions of Gothic devilism![11]

No doubt the *Monthly*'s irritation stemmed from a dislike of being made to look foolish. Still, its response is worth examining for what it yields about the literary culture into which Walpole published his romance. Strikingly, none of the immediate responses to *The Castle of Otranto* allowed for the possibility that a cultivated mind could enjoy reading, let alone be capable of writing, such a book. In the above quotation, the *Monthly Review*'s objections arise out of assumptions about its role as a respectable and enlightened literary journal. The reviewer, John Langhorne, appears especially keen to separate his own 'period of cultivated learning' from past ages, and especially from *Otranto*'s culture of chivalry and its 'barbarous superstitions of Gothic devilism'. What is interesting here is the way in which imagining this kind of gulf between superstitious past and enlightened present brings with it other assumptions about readerly pleasure. From the *Monthly*'s relative position of enlightenment, it is unwilling on some fundamental level to believe that rational readers or writers can take pleasure in supernatural representations. Its first review, therefore, had instead presented *The Castle of Otranto* as a historical curiosity, and within this framework had invited readers to discern a recognizable human nature transcending history and overcoming the most egregious superstition. Put another way, the *Monthly Review*'s stance of finding pleasure in *Otranto*'s 'fine views of nature' while being repulsed by its barbarism allowed for the accompanying belief that noble, laudable aspects of human nature could transcend the centuries while other, less desirable aspects could not.

The *Monthly*'s applause in its first review had arisen, then, from the narrative of historical

progress it had been able to impose on Walpole's book. In doing so, it wielded a story that recurs in critical writing frequently during the second half of the eighteenth century, shaping debates about the function of the supernatural not only in fiction but also on the stage.[12] We find it operating even in the responses of Walpole's own circle of friends—as with George 'Gilly' Williams, who felt *Otranto*'s archaic setting and subject matter to be so patently absurd and innately uninteresting that 'no boarding-school Miss of thirteen could get half through without yawning'.[13] We see it also in the accounts of more flexible and sympathetic readers like William Mason, who could not fathom the idea that the book was a modern production. Writing to Walpole immediately after the publication of the book's second edition, Mason confessed that, 'When a friend of mine to whom I had recommended *The Castle of Otranto* returned it me with some doubts of its originality, I laughed him to scorn, and wondered he could be so absurd as to think that anybody nowadays had imagination enough to invent such a story.'[14] In the face of such statements, we can begin to grasp how completely the assumptions of readers like Mason could be challenged by the revelation that *The Castle of Otranto* was not an ancient text but a 'Gothic story' (the subtitle Walpole affixed to *Otranto*'s second edition) by a modern author. To understand the particular nerves that Walpole's book struck we need to consider the social position of its inventor and his relation to this historically specific question of 'imagination', since Walpole brought both to bear on his attempts to transform how his contemporaries read prose fiction and understood its function.

2. The 'Master of Otranto'

With the appearance of its second edition, *The Castle of Otranto* ceased to be written by a zealous priest from bygone times. Its author became instead a living, mature man of forty-seven years of age, a Member of Parliament of nearly twenty-five years' standing, and the son of a celebrated Prime Minister. Part of *The Castle of Otranto*'s contemporary reception, then, has always been tied to Walpole's notoriety as a public figure, since readers and reviewers alike were forced to ask what it meant for a man of such eminence to write such a book. Educated at Eton and Cambridge, Horace Walpole had grown up during the height of Robert Walpole's power. As Walpole's biographers have suggested, his social position no doubt helped to render his time at Eton free of the usual bullying and brutality associated with the school in the eighteenth century, and made his Grand Tour a heady, exuberant and formative experience.[15] While travelling in Italy in 1740 with his childhood friend Thomas Gray, Walpole mixed with its best society, befriending diplomats like Horace Mann and taking great pleasure in purchasing works of art for his father's extensive collection at his country estate Houghton in Norwich. Elected to Parliament while abroad, Walpole arrived back in England in September of 1741 expecting to take his seat in the House of Commons and his place among London's élite. His first speech six months after his arrival, however, could hardly have accorded less with his expectations. In that time, Robert Walpole's government had fallen after over two decades in power. Consequently, Walpole's first address was in defence of his father who, in the wake of his resignation, faced multiple allegations of corruption. With this reversal of fortune, Horace Walpole's involvement in parliamentary matters over the next decades was intermittent and behind the scenes. Rather than acting as a direct participant in affairs of state, he moved between the role of periodic strategist and pamphleteer and that of perpetual observer and chronicler. Steadfastly loyal to his father's memory, his first book was a catalogue of the paintings Robert Walpole had collected and housed at Houghton, entitled *Aedes Walpolianae,* written in 1743 and printed privately in 1747. Walpole's later *Memoirs,* begun in 1751 and forty-one years in the writing, constitutes a textual version of this lifelong work of defending the family's political legacy.[16]

Over the next years Walpole wrote primarily as a gentleman author and elegant essayist, publishing when it suited him and taking pleasure in helping to publish the works of his friends. Three of his early poems—'**Epistle to Thomas Ashton from Florence**', '**The Beauties**' and an Epilogue to *Tamerlane*—appeared in 1748 in the first volumes of James Dodsley's *Collection of Poems,* which also featured Gray's first published work. After this joint appearance, Walpole spent considerable energy over the next decade persuading Gray to publish more poetry and overseeing its production and reception. The *Elegy Written in a Country Churchyard* appeared in 1751 to great applause; *Designs by Mr. R. Bentley, for Six Poems by Mr. T. Gray* (featuring elaborate rococo illustrations by Walpole's friend Richard Bentley) appeared two years later. It is no accident that when Walpole opened the Strawberry Hill Press in 1757, he chose *Odes by Mr. Gray* (1757) as its first published work.

In spite of this sustained interest in writing and publishing poetry, however, Walpole emerged in the 1740s and 1750s primarily as a prose writer—one capable of moving between savage parody, graceful elegance and pointed observation. His first essays, written for magazines such as the *Museum* and the *World,* were determinedly frivolous and deliberately at odds with the moral essays of Samuel Johnson and with the serious tone of periodicals like the *Gentleman's Magazine.* The '**Advertisement to the History of Good Breeding**' and '**On the Relative Simplicity of Gothic Manners to Our Own**', for example, indulged in parody and burlesque. Others, like the '**Scheme for Raising a large Sum of Money by Message Cards and Notes**', were at once more outrageous and more intellectual, and showed Walpole developing ideas that would prove central to the literary and aesthetic projects that culminated in *The Castle of Otranto*:

> The notion I have of a *Museum* is an Hospital for every Thing that is *singular;* whether the Thing have acquired Singularity, from having escaped the Rage of Time; from any natural Oddness in itself; or from being so insignificant that nobody ever thought it worth their while to produce any more of the same Sort. Intrinsic Value has little or no Property in the merit of *curiosities* . . . If the Learned World could be so happy as to discover a *Roman*'s old Shoe (provided the Literati were agreed it were a Shoe, and not a leathern Casque, a drinking Vessel, a balloting Box, or an empress's Head Attire), such Shoe would immediately have the Entrée into any collection in *Europe.*[17]

This notion of singularity and uniqueness informs most of Walpole's writing and publishing in these years. The Strawberry Hill Press, moreover, provided him with a means of bypassing the usual channels of book printing and bookselling when he chose to do so. Abjuring both profit and politics when choosing manuscripts for publication, the press quickly acquired a reputation for publishing books fundamentally different from those available elsewhere.

In his own compositions Walpole appears often to have been driven by a similar desire for innovation even when writing anonymous partisan tracts for other presses. His successful political satire, *A Letter from Xo Ho, a Chinese Philosopher at London, to His Friend Lien Chi at Peking* (N. Middleton, 1757), anticipated later works like Robert Southey's *Letters from England by Don Manuel Alvarez Espriella* (1807), while his *Catalogue of Royal and Noble Authors* (Strawberry Hill Press, 1758) was one of the first books of its kind. It was for his groundbreaking *Anecdotes of Painting* (Strawberry Hill, 1762), however, that Walpole became best known before the success of *The Castle of Otranto.* At once a treasure-trove of information and a sustained assessment of English painting, the book shows Walpole moving at ease between the minutiae of historical research and engaging, arresting writing. W. S. Lewis puts the matter succinctly: 'It was an instant success. Gibbon spoke of his "minute curiosity and acuteness." Strangers wrote to him with gratitude and volunteered additions and corrections for the next edition. It was no wonder that this work was so popular: it was new, informative, and entertaining . . . [and] laid the foundations for an historical study of the Fine Arts in England.'[18]

One of the difficulties readers have faced when attempting to come to grips with Walpole's writings and reputation has stemmed from his diversity of interests and this fondness of 'Singularity'. For nineteenth-century historian and essayist Thomas Babington Macaulay, Walpole's eccentricity and determination to be considered a gentleman author who wrote with ease on many subjects smacked of affectation and effeminacy. '[None] but an unhealthy and disorganized mind,' he argued, 'could have produced such literary luxuries.'[19] Likely the most influential assessment of Walpole ever written, Macaulay's account derives its persuasiveness from its ability to present Walpole's work and life as projections of a single set of affectations that, while assembled and put on like masks, nevertheless comprise Walpole's character.[20] Whether by reading Walpole's correspondence, wandering through Strawberry Hill, or perusing the volumes published by its press, one nevertheless imbibes the same aesthetic experience:

> The motto which he prefixed to this *Catalogue of Royal and Noble Authors,* might have been inscribed with perfect propriety over the door of every room in his house, and on the titlepage of every one of his books. 'Dove diavolo, Messer Ludovico, avete pigliate tante coglionere?' ['Where the devil, Sir Ludovico, did you collect so many imbecilities?'] In his villa, every compartment is a museum; every piece of furniture is a curiosity; there is something strange in the form of a shovel; there is a long story belonging to the bell-rope. We wander among a profusion of rarities, of trifling intrinsic value, but so quaint in fashion, or connected with such remarkable names and events that they may well detain our attention for a moment. A moment is enough.[21]

Deriving much of its rancour from his own sense of professionalism, Macaulay's distaste arises out of a belief not just that Walpole's interests are 'unhealthy', but that they also constitute an affront to artistic seriousness and therefore a deni-gration of appropriate authorship. Yet what Macaulay dismissed pejoratively as a 'profusion of rarities' in Walpole's life and works has been reappraised by twentieth-century literary historians as a body of innovative writing of unparalleled range, one typical of the generation of Samuel Johnson and Hester Thrale Piozzi and surpassing even that of Oliver Goldsmith. Between 1747 and his death in 1797, Walpole wrote and published several poems, a historical romance, a tragedy, a comic afterpiece, a book of art history, a bibliographic study, a memoir, a diary, a description of his own house, several catalogues of paintings, political pamphlets, fables and fairy tales. After his death his executors published what remains an authoritative political history of late eighteenth-century Britain and perhaps the most famous body of correspondence ever written.[22]

Even in the face of this voluminous output, it is fair to say that Walpole was equally famous in his lifetime for his achievements as a collector and architect. At the time of his death his collection of miniature and print portraits was arguably the best ever assembled in Britain. His villa Strawberry Hill, moreover, was without question the most famous house of its kind. Like *The Castle of Otranto,* which, though often called the first Gothic novel, was in many ways anticipated by the poetry of William Collins and novels like Tobias Smollett's *Ferdinand Count Fathom* (1753) and Thomas Leland's *Longsword* (1762), Strawberry Hill was more influential than entirely original. While not the first attempt to appropriate Gothic architecture into a domestic setting, it effectively revived Gothic as a popular architectural style.[23] In 1748 Walpole had purchased the original Chopp'd-Straw Hall and its five acres in Twickenham because of its nearness to London and its attractive location on the banks of the Thames. He did not start remodelling until 1751, and for that purpose commandeered the help of friends John Chute (who transformed much of the exterior) and Richard Bentley (who brought to Walpole's interiors the same extravagant flair with which he had illustrated Gray's poems). Calling themselves 'The Committee', the three transformed the house, quadrupling its original size in a little over a decade and adding battlements, turrets, cloisters, stained glass, fireplaces and other fixtures to give it the effect of a medieval castle. Their work, moreover, was decidedly unlike Robert Walpole's Palladian estate at Houghton, largely because Strawberry Hill's small size and irregular design dictated different choices of architectural style and materials. Where Houghton achieved its effects through stone, grand rooms and columns, Strawberry Hill used theatrical devices like *trompe-l'oeil* painting and materials like plaster and papier mâché. Writing to Horace Mann in 1750, Walpole explained that '[t]he Grecian is only proper for magnificent and public buildings. Columns and all their beautiful ornaments look ridiculous when crowded into a closet or a cheesecake house. The variety is little, and admits no charming irregularities.'[24]

By the end of its second stage of building in 1763, Strawberry Hill had already become a celebrated attraction, further gaining in reputation as the century closed. A telling measure of its popularity occurs in *The Ambulator: or, A Pocket Companion in a Tour Round London* (1800), which devotes five pages to Strawberry Hill while allocating only two to the British Museum.[25] While the steadily increasing stream of visitors to his villa forced Walpole later in his life to print rules for admission, he also openly encouraged the attention that the house conferred on him by twice printing a description of it and its contents.[26] This transformation of house into textual form was hardly accidental. As early as 1765 Walpole began to encourage friends and readers to associate Strawberry Hill with the setting of *The Castle of Otranto* by playfully referring to the villa as 'Otranto' and himself as 'The Master of Otranto'.[27] More importantly, he repeatedly associated the house with *Otranto*'s composition:

> Your partiality to me and Strawberry have I hope inclined you to excuse the wildness of the story. You will even have found some traits to put you in mind of this place. When you read of the picture quitting its panel, did not you recollect the portrait of Lord Falkland all in white in my gallery? Shall I even confess to you what was the origin of my romance? I waked one morning in the beginning of last June from a dream, of which all I could recover was, that I had thought myself in an ancient castle (a very natural dream for a head filled like mine with Gothic story) and that on the uppermost bannister of a great staircase I saw a gigantic hand in armour. In the evening I sat down and began to write, without knowing in the least what I intended to say or relate. The work grew on my hands, and I grew fond of it—add that I was very glad to think of anything rather than politics—In short I was so engrossed with my tale, which I completed in less than two months, that one evening I wrote from the time I had drunk my tea, about six o'clock, till half an hour after one in the morning, when my hand and fingers were so weary, that I could not hold the pen to finish the sentence, but left Matilda and Isabella talking, in the middle of a paragraph.[28]

The dream, pointedly, is 'a very natural dream' within the surroundings of Strawberry Hill, one that opposes Gothic story, Gothic villa and Gothic dream to their 'modern' and 'rational' counterparts. In this sense, Walpole's account of his romance's origin constructs a fairly elaborate analogy, one in which the same differences that distinguish Strawberry Hill from other eighteenth-century houses also distinguish *The Castle of Otranto* from other contemporary fiction. House and text stand, here and elsewhere, as analogous expressions of the same singular urge, serving as both excuse for, and vindication of, one another. It is within the surroundings of Strawberry Hill and this notion of complementarity that we should understand *The Castle of Otranto*'s choice of aesthetics and its narrative strategies, particularly its fondness for dreamlike setting and theatrical effect.

3. 'Two Kinds of Romance'

However much it might have begun as a random exercise in composition, *The Castle of Otranto* exhibits in its opening pages the purposiveness of a manifesto. Walpole's narrative of the book originating in a dream, suggestive as it has been to explorations of consciousness in Gothic fiction,[29] is more than counterbalanced by the critical accounts he provided in the book's second Preface and in his own correspondence. The story's opening lines, furthermore, with their strong allegiance to fairy tales, signal a departure from established forms of eighteenth-century fiction, while the miraculous events frequently invoke and subvert literary conventions in ways that smack of anti-romances like Charlotte Lennox's *The Female Quixote* (1752). Here, however, the conventions that are being subverted are not those of romance (as with Lennox) but those of formal realism. Walpole may open, for example, with an unwilling bride left at the altar, but he does not devote his ensuing pages (as one might expect in a novel) to providing that bride's 'history' or to describing the chain of individual motivations and contingent events that brought about the occurrence. Instead, he provides a supernatural spectacle—the groom Conrad 'dashed to pieces, and almost buried under an enormous helmet, an hundred times more large than any casque ever made for human being' (p. 18)—that obliterates the possibility of rational explanation and raises more questions than it answers. We see similar strategies at work as well in the book's almost allegorical handling of character. Even in the case of his most fully developed character, Manfred, Walpole spends considerably more time describing Manfred's strategic decisions than the internal processes that produce them. *The Castle of Otranto*'s supernatural agents, moreover, contribute to this strategy, actively thwarting the very kinds of characterization that form a staple of the fiction of Defoe and Richardson and even of the social satires of Henry Fielding, Charlotte Lennox and Tobias Smollett. All of Manfred's plotting and re-plotting, his gifts for calculating probabilities and responding to contingencies, fail because he is presented with a fixed narrative and fate that no amount of character, no attention to detail, and no amount of strategizing can avert.

If the ruse of Walpole's first Preface governed how *The Castle of Otranto*'s first edition was received, the critical discourse with which he opens the Preface to the second edition has proven equally influential with modern readers. Part of its persuasiveness is more than understandable; Walpole's description of the book, as 'an attempt to blend the two kinds of romance, the ancient and the modern' (see p. 9), does capture its innovative combination of supernaturalism and psychological realism, of chivalric romance and modern novel. His Epigraph, moreover, tellingly revises Horace's *Ars Poetica* to express *Otranto*'s aesthetic ends. While the original Horace translates roughly into 'Idle fancies shall be shaped like a sick man's dream so that neither foot nor head can be assigned to a single shape,' Walpole's rewriting of the Latin changes the meaning of the final words to 'nevertheless head and foot are assigned to a single shape'.[30]

What Walpole's critical statements do *not* adequately capture are the ways his text consistently transgresses the conventions of both fictional traditions rather than compromising between them—an assertion suggested elsewhere by Walpole in a letter to Madame du Deffand:

> Let the critics have their say: I shall not be vexed: it was not written for this age, which wants nothing but cold reason. I own to you, and you will think me madder than ever, that of all my works it is the only one in which I pleased myself: I let my imagination run: my visions and my passions kindled me. I wrote it in defiance of rules, critics, and philosophies: and it seems to me all the better for that.[31]

Stated in the terms of his second preface, Walpole's 'defiance' arises from his belief that the critical 'rules' separating ancient and modern romance are more artificial than any fiction that could result from their indiscriminate mixing. In the place of such strictures he offers the counter-

Illustration from *The Castle of Otranto,* c. 1790.

argument that his generic mixture of the supernatural and the mundane, of broad comedy and classical tragedy, is both appropriate and natural because it functions as a formal expression of medieval consciousness and culture. A modern critic, E. J. Clery, describes the various historicisms at work here nicely: 'Rationally speaking, ghosts and goblins are not *true*, but when they appear in the literary artifacts of past ages, they are *true to history*, accurate representations of an obsolete system of belief: a stance we might call *exemplary historicism*.'[32] Walpole puts this matter of the nature of history more ironically, provocatively insisting within *The Castle of Otranto*'s historicized setting, 'My rule was nature' (p. 10).

Writing within the literary culture of the 1760s, Walpole's confident celebration of *The Castle of Otranto*'s 'nature' owes a considerable debt to Richard Hurd's *Letters on Chivalry and Romance* (1762), a text that helped to revive the status of medieval 'Gothic' literature and architecture in the second half of the eighteenth century. Published only two years before Walpole's romance, Hurd's study had argued for the fundamental similarity of Homeric epic and 'Gothic' metrical romance. From this 'remarkable correspondency', Hurd had proceeded to make a striking defence of the formal logic of the Gothic:

> When an architect examines a Gothic structure by Grecian rules, he finds nothing but deformity. But the Gothic architecture has its own rules, by which when it comes to be examined, it is seen to have its merit, as well as the Grecian . . . The same observation holds of the two sorts of poetry. Judge of the *Faery Queen* by the classic models, and you are shocked by its disorder: consider it with an eye to its Gothic original, and you find it regular. The unity and simplicity of the former are more complete: but the latter has that sort of unity and simplicity, which results from its nature. The *Faery Queen*, then, as a Gothic poem, derives its METHOD, as well as the other characters of its composition, from the established modes and ideas of chivalry.[33]

Walpole's appropriation of key ideas in Hurd's *Letters* has understandably been important to modern assessments[34] of *The Castle of Otranto*, providing a sense of its intellectual underpinnings and anticipated readership. As the attacks on Voltaire in its second Preface suggest, Walpole was more than willing to repackage Hurd's arguments in the language of anti-French sentiment and in the logic of cultural nationalism. Given Macaulay's later condemnation of Walpole as 'the most Frenchified English writer of the eighteenth century',[35] his recourse to national chauvinism here strongly suggests a desire to mitigate reader and reviewer censure that might have otherwise resulted from the initial ruse of its first edition. The criticisms of Voltaire, after all, could just as easily have been directed against his own countrymen David Garrick and Nahum Tate, whose popular stage versions of Shakespeare had frequently purged scenes perceived to be at odds with the overall tone of the play in question.

Apart from this decision to represent his romance as homage to the natural genius of the national Bard, other political currents run through *The Castle of Otranto* as well. Walpole's account of the book's composition as a kind of therapy against a particularly bad year in Parliament has been well documented,[36] as have been the correspondences between Manfred's tyranny and aspects of Walpole's own life, particularly George III's treatment of Walpole's cousin Henry Seymour Conway. Other commentators have called attention to the almost Oedipal family violence that pervades the text, finding in Manfred's political downfall a kind of political exorcism by Walpole of his father.[37] It is when we remind ourselves of Walpole's fondness for masquerade and ventriloquism, however, that we begin to sense the extent of Walpole's deep play in *The Castle of Otranto*

with issues of defiance and transgression, whether literary or political. For if the character of Manfred raises questions concerning the nature of Walpole's identification with the psychology of power, then Walpole's impersonation of the translator 'William Marshall, Gent.' presents us with an equally striking piece of political theatre. Walpole's politics throughout his life were resolutely Whig, in part out of loyalty to his father and in part because of his innate suspicion of power and those who held it. Yet within the fiction of *The Castle of Otranto*'s first edition, Marshall is unquestionably Tory and likely an old Jacobite supporter of the Stuart monarchy. Standing at the head of 'an ancient catholic family in the north of England' (p. 5), Marshall discovers, translates and publishes a tract of the Italian Counter-Reformation. The story, furthermore, dramatizes the restoration of a wrongfully ousted ruler and the downfall of a usurping house after three generations in power, one in which Manfred's position as the grandson of the usurper Ricardo corresponds nicely to George III's position as the grandson of the first Hanoverian king of Great Britain. Given the horror Walpole expressed in his correspondence during the 1745 Jacobite rebellion, his reasons for choosing a figure like Marshall are difficult to ascertain. Unlike the 'artful priest' he supposedly translates, Marshall functions in Walpole's representation as neither a figure of allegory nor an object of ridicule, and falls equally far from embodying Jacobite parody or from functioning as a fictional means of acting out fantasies of political defiance. He does, however, form part of Walpole's sense of aesthetic subversion and knowing impropriety—what Macaulay criticized as perversion and what recent commentators have characterized as an obsession with surface, performance and counterfeiting.[38]

For Susan Sontag, Strawberry Hill (and Gothic fiction more generally) embodies the essence of 'camp' because each displays a nostalgic affection for its source materials and a self-conscious 'love of the exaggerated, the "off"'.[39] Such 'off' moments in *The Castle of Otranto* have been noted by even its earliest readers. They occur in the book's superfluous details (as when Bianca notes that no one has slept in the chamber below them 'since the great astrologer that was your brother's tutor drowned himself' (p. 38)), in its habit of setting conventions against one another (as when the chivalry-mad Theodore unchivalrously pledges himself both to Matilda and to Isabella because he cannot tell the two heroines apart), and in its crucial scenes (as when the statue of Alphonso the

Good ludicrously bleeds from its nose). Such occasions most often show Walpole gesturing to literary conventions yet refusing to wield (or oppose) them with propriety. Responding to these unstable moments in the text, readers as far-ranging as Clara Reeve, Walter Scott and William Hazlitt all noted that Walpole's ghosts often undermined the very effects they were supposed to produce. They appeared too often, or else were too large, too substantial, too *corporeal*. Hazlitt's distaste is especially telling. Calling Walpole's supernatural 'the pasteboard machinery of a pantomime', he characterizes it as too obtrusive and too artificial to produce authentic terror in its reader. Lacking appropriate sublimity and seriousness, Walpole's ghosts 'are a matter-of-fact impossibility; a fixture, and no longer a phantom'.[40] Such formulations nicely anticipate the critical assessments of Robert Miles and Jerrold Hogle, who, while differing from one another in the questions they ask of Walpole's texts, none the less isolate Walpole's self-consciousness about questions of authenticity as emblematic of Gothic writing more generally.[41] For Miles, Walpole's romance is not only about uncovering correct genealogies; it also thematizes such questions of lineage by putting forward a false account of its own origins and then insisting on its veracity. Hogle finds a similar practice of counterfeiting—and a similar nostalgia about literary and class origins—in Walpole's ghosts, which parade as medieval Italian spirits while gesturing with every action to Shakespeare. Hogle's term, 'the Ghost of the Counterfeit', recalls not only Macaulay's disgust for Walpole's 'masks within masks' but also Sontag's notion that *The Castle of Otranto* presents us not with ghosts but rather with 'ghosts'—what Hazlitt calls 'chimeras . . . begot upon shadows and dim likenesses'.[42]

It is this sense of inherent irony and self-conscious artifice—that one is somehow not meeting with characters and things but rather with performances of characters and representations of things—that has so often produced the revulsion of critics like Macaulay and the excitement of writers like Sontag. Addressing Walpole's habit of infusing his text with allusions to Shakespeare and other works, Robert Mack finally attaches the word 'parody' to Walpole's text—but not 'parody' in its usual sense:

> *Otranto* is parody not in the sense that it seeks to deride or to mock the characteristics and language of Shakespearean drama, but parody rather in the more etymologically precise sense of the word. It is a literal *para-odos,* a complementary 'song' to be heard not in place of, but alongside the original. It asks its readers to carry their knowledge of the

entire corpus of Shakespeare's drama to the work so that those very readers can themselves fill in the narrative gaps in the volume with the resonance of a shared theatrical tradition.[43]

The same can be said for the position of theatre and performance in *The Castle of Otranto* as well. While Walpole's first reviewers sensed that they were reading an eighteenth-century forgery and not a medieval romance, because of small historical errors in the text, twenty-first-century readers will discover *Otranto*'s eighteenth-century origins in the sentimental and overblown acting styles of its character-performers. The blushes, sighs and fainting spells of Walpole's heroines, and the dark brow and moody stalking of Manfred, are as much a part of the theatre of Garrick as is the spectacle in which Manfred's servant reports the death of Conrad:

> The servant, who had not staid long enough to have crossed the court to Conrad's apartment, came running back breathless, in a frantic manner, his eyes staring, and foaming at the mouth. He said nothing, but pointed to the court. The company were struck with terror and amazement. The princess Hippolita, without knowing what was the matter, but anxious for her son, swooned away.
>
> (p. 18)

This focus on sentiment and emotional gesture—on representing the *expression* of emotional conflict rather than on describing its internal processes—provides us with another way of understanding the self-consciousness of Walpole's narrative style and characterization. That an inveterate theatre-goer and author of an acclaimed tragedy (*The Mysterious Mother*) and a successful comic afterpiece (*Nature Will Prevail*) should construct character theatrically rather than novelistically should not surprise us. Similar observations can be made about *Otranto*'s narrative structure. Its five chapters and general fidelity to the classical unities of the drama make it resemble a five-act tragedy far more than an eighteenth-century romance. Certainly Walpole cultivated the association; in his first Preface to *Otranto* he noted playfully: 'It is a pity that he did not apply his talents to what they were evidently proper for, the theatre' (p. 7).

Responding to Walpole's cue, we may wish to attend to the seemingly endless ghosts, counterfeits and masks in *The Castle of Otranto* by investigating the degree to which they are informed by a logic of performance and by the cultural history of Georgian theatre and opera. For Charles Beecher Hogan and Anne Williams, such a suggestion opens up a number of fruitful possibilities for understanding how and why Walpole's book has troubled its readers for so long. Locating the aesthetics of *The Castle of Otranto* in *opera seria*, Williams reimagines Strawberry Hill and the romance it inspired as essentially theatrical: 'For Walpole, Gothic is always just that, performances, its structures always full of imitation, disguise, and *travesti*.'[44] Looking to late eighteenth-century dramas of spectacle and the invention of melodrama in the early nineteenth century, Hogan's assessment is equally sweeping and suggestive. 'The grandfather of the Gothic novel,' he concludes, 'was also the grandfather of the Gothic play.'[45]

We might wish to reverse this pronouncement, however, when we consider *The Castle of Otranto*'s sustained popularity and influence. Commentators on Walpole and the Gothic have often been puzzled by the seemingly inexplicable gap between the publication of *Otranto* (1764) and the later popularity of Gothic fiction and drama in the 1780s and 1790s, wondering why such an explosively popular genre should have taken nearly twenty years to gain its hold on British imaginations. Examining its publication history a final time, we see only one significant span of years (1767-81) in which no printing of *The Castle of Otranto* occurred—perhaps the only time the book might ever have been out of print. This single dry spell was ended by the stage success of Robert Jephson's *The Count of Narbonne* (1781), an adaptation of *The Castle of Otranto* to which Walpole contributed many hours of his time hoping for its success. He was not disappointed. Performed twenty-one times during its initial run, *The Count of Narbonne* was the hit of the 1781-2 theatrical season and held the stage for the next two decades. With Jephson's success, a fresh edition of *The Castle of Otranto* was called for in 1782, and thereafter the book experienced a similar, sustained popularity: it received fourteen printings in English between 1782 and 1800; spawned numerous imitations; and acquired its status as a foundational work of Gothic fiction. Certainly the Gothic novel gave rise to the Gothic play, but the suggestion here is that Jephson's adaptation invited readers to do more than merely take up Walpole's romance again and read it alongside its theatrical representation. The sustained popularity of both points to a symbiosis between Gothic text and Gothic drama—one that anticipates the Gothic's later returns in film and digital media, and that is present since the first Gothic 'revival' of the genre Jephson and Walpole helped to construct.

Notes

1. See A. T. Hazen, *A Bibliography of Horace Walpole* (New Haven: Yale University Press, 1947), pp. 52-67; and W. S. Lewis, Introduction to Walpole, *The Castle of Otranto*, ed. W. S. Lewis (London and New York: Oxford University Press, 1964), pp. vii-viii.

2. See [Anna Letitia Barbauld, 'Horace Walpole', The British Novelists, ed. A. L. Barbauld, 50 vols. (London: F. C. & J. Rivington et al., 1810), Vol. 22, pp. i-iii.] By 'German tales' Barbauld refers not only to German works popular in Britain in the 1790s, like K. F. Kahlert's *The Necromancer, or a Tale of the Black Forest* (1794) and Gottfried August Bürger's oft-translated poem *Lenore* (1774), but also to English celebrations of German supernaturalism like Matthew Lewis's *The Monk* (1796) and Charlotte Dacre's *Zofloya* (1805).

3. See [Walter Scott, Introduction to *The Castle of Otranto* (Edinburgh: James Ballantyne, 1811), pp. iii-xxxvi. Extract.] Scott later reprinted the essay for *Ballantyne's Novelist's Library*, ed. and intro. Walter Scott, 10 vols. (London: Hurst, Robinson & Co., 1821-4).

4. See [Walter Scott, Introduction] p. xvii.

5. Ibid., pp. xx-xxi.

6. Barbauld's *Miscellaneous Pieces in Prose* (London: J. Johnson, 1773), written with her brother John Aiken, contains a theoretical essay on suspense ('On the Pleasure Derived from Objects of Terror') and a supernatural short story ('Sir Bertrand, a Fragment').

7. See Appendix: Early Responses to *The Castle of Otranto* [, in *The Castle of Otranto*, with an introduction by Michael Gauer, New York: Penguin Books, 2001.]

8. See [Anna Letitia Barbauld, 'Horace Walpole'] p. i.

9. See [Review of *The Castle of Otranto*, Critical Review 19 (January 1765), pp. 50-51. Extract.] p. 51.

10. See [Review of *The Castle of Otranto*, Monthly Review 32 (February 1765), pp. 97-9. Extract.] p. 99.

11. See [Review of *The Castle of Otranto* (2nd edition), Monthly Review 32 (May 1765), p. 394.] p. 394.

12. See especially Robert P. Reno, 'James Boaden's *Fontainville Forest* and Matthew Lewis's *The Castle Spectre*: Challenges of the Supernatural Ghost on the Late Eighteenth-Century Stage', *Eighteenth-Century Life* 9 (1984), pp. 95-106; and Further Reading, Clery.

13. See Further Reading, Lewis, *The Yale Edition of Horace Walpole's Correspondence* (hereinafter referred to as *Correspondence*), Vol. 30, p. 177.

14. Ibid., Vol. 28, p. 5.

15. See Further Reading, Kallich, Ketton-Cremer, and Mowl.

16. By Walpole's injunction, the manuscripts of the *Memoirs* were not published until nearly three decades after his death.

17. *Museum* 2 (1746), pp. 46-7.

18. See Further Reading, Lewis, *Horace Walpole: The A. W. Mellon Lectures in the Fine Arts 1960*, p. 155.

19. See [Thomas Babington Macaulay, Review of *Letters of Horace Walpole, Earl of Orford, to Sir Horace Mann*, Edinburgh Review 58 (October 1833), pp. 227-58. Extract.] p. 227.

20. Ibid., esp. p. 227: 'His features were covered by mask within mask. When the outer disguise of obvious affectation was removed, you were still as far as ever from seeing the real man.'

21. Ibid., p. 239.

22. See Further Reading, Ketton-Cremer and Lewis (*Correspondence*).

23. As a revived architectural style, Gothic was first popularized by the engravings that appeared in Thomas and Batty Langley's *Gothic Architecture, Improved*, which was first published in 1741 under the title of *Ancient Architecture*. Walpole criticized the Langleys' attempts to graft Gothic decorations on to classical forms. Other early attempts, like those of Lord Brooke at Warwick Castle, failed in Walpole's mind for similar reasons, while Saunderson Miller's work at Wroxton simply collapsed.

24. Walpole to Horace Mann, 25 February 1750 (*Correspondence*, Vol. 20, p. 127).

25. See *The Ambulator: or, A Pocket Companion in a Tour Round London* (London: J. Scatcherd, 1800), pp. 14-15, 198-202.

26. See Walpole, *Journal of the Printing-Office at Strawberry Hill*, ed. Paget Toynbee (London: Constable & Houghton Mifflin, 1923). Under 1784 the entry reads 'printed a page of rules for admission to see my House', but does not indicate how many copies were printed. See also Walpole, *A Description of the Villa of Mr. Horace Walpole* (Twickenham: Strawberry Hill, 1774; 2nd edition, 1784).

27. See Walpole to William Cole, 9 March 1765 (*Correspondence*, Vol. 1, p. 88); Walpole to Horace Mann, 18 November 1771 (ibid., Vol. 23, pp. 349-51); and Walpole to Mme du Deffand, 27 January 1775 (ibid., Vol. 6, p. 145). Angry over Walpole's refusal to believe his forgeries genuine, Thomas Chatterton later wrote a long diatribe against the 'Baron of Otranto', which formed the basis of the later controversy over Walpole's role in Chatterton's death (ibid., Vol. 15, pp. xvi-xvii).

28. Walpole to William Cole, 9 March 1765 (*Correspondence*, Vol. 1, p. 88). See also Walpole, *A Description of the Villa of Mr. Horace Walpole*, p. iv.

29. See Further Reading, Guest, Harfst, Kiely and Punter.

30. This was first noted in W. S. Lewis, Introduction to *The Castle of Otranto*, pp. 12-13.

31. Walpole to Mme du Deffand, 13 March 1767. This translation quoted from Stephen Gwynn, *The Life of Horace Walpole* (London: Thorton Butterworth, 1932), p. 191.

32. See Further Reading, Clery, p. 54.

33. Richard Hurd, *Letters on Chivalry and Romance*, ed. Edith J. Morley (London: Henry Frowde, 1911), pp. 94, 118-19.

34. See Further Reading, Clery, Guest and Kiely.

35. See [Thomas Babington Macaulay, Review] p. 233.

36. See Further Reading, Fothergill, Ketton-Cremer and Samson.

37. See Further Reading, Harfst and Haggerty.

38. See Further Reading, Hogan, Hogle, Sedgwick and Williams.

39. See Further Reading, Sontag, p. 108.

40. See [William Hazlitt, *Lectures on the Comic Writers* (1819), *The Complete Works of William Hazlitt*, ed. P.P. Howe (London and Toronto: J.M. Dent, 1930-33), Vol. 6, p. 127. Extract.]

41. See Further Reading, Miles and Hogle.

42. See [William Hazlitt, *Lectures*]

43. Robert Mack, Introduction to Walpole, *The Castle of Otranto and Hieroglyphic Tales* (London: J. M. Dent, 1993), p. xx.

44. See Further Reading, Williams, p. 115.

45. See Further Reading, Hogan, p. 237.

Further Reading

Books and Articles:

Clery, E. J., *The Rise of Supernatural Fiction 1762-1800* (Cambridge: Cambridge University Press, 1995). This material history of Gothic and supernatural fiction devotes two chapters to Walpole and *Otranto*: Ch. 3, 'The Advantages of History', places Walpole's hoax with the first edition in the context of popular antiquarianism in the 1760s and the various historicisms it practised; Ch. 4, 'Back to the Future', reads *Otranto* within contemporary re-imaginings (Richard Hurd, James Stuart and Adam Smith) of chivalry and feudalism as 'a distinctive stage in historical evolution with a prevailing mode of subsistence giving rise to characteristic social, intellectual and political structures' (p. 68).

Fothergill, Brian, *The Strawberry Hill Set: Horace Walpole and His Circle* (London: Faber & Faber, 1983). A biographical account of Walpole, focusing on his many friendships.

Guest, Harriet, 'The Wanton Muse: Politics and Gender in Gothic Theory after 1760', *Beyond Romanticism: New Approaches to Texts and Contexts, 1780-1832*, ed. Stephen Copley and John Whale (London and New York: Routledge, 1992), pp. 118-39. This article focuses on early theories of Gothic; on their ambivalent gendering and how they define a 'territory of . . . pleasure in terms that do not readily yield their political affiliation' (p. 119). These early theories provided a marked contrast to those affiliated with Gothic texts in the 1790s.

Haggerty, George E., 'Literature and Homosexuality in the Late Eighteenth Century: Walpole, Beckford and Lewis', *Studies in the Novel* 18 (1986), pp. 341-52. Explores the relation between Gothic fiction and the homosexuality of three of its primary eighteenth-century male practitioners.

Harfst, Betsy Perteit, *Horace Walpole and the Unconscious: An Experiment in Freudian Analysis* (New York: Arno, 1980). This published dissertation 'attempts to expose the unconscious repressions which could have been responsible for the erratic behavior of Horace Walpole . . . and to determine the relationship between these repressions and his romantic works' (p. i).

Hogan, Charles Beecher, 'The "Theatre of Geo. 3"', *Horace Walpole: Writer, Politician, and Connoisseur*, ed. Warren Hunting Smith (New Haven and London: Yale University Press, 1967), pp. 227-40. This article establishes Walpole's interest in both reading plays and attending the theatre as a foundation for reading *The Castle of Otranto*, ultimately arguing that '[t]he grandfather of the Gothic novel was also the grandfather of the Gothic play . . . Far more than *The Mysterious Mother* or *Nature Will Prevail* its form is dramatic; so is its theme; so are its characters' (p. 237).

Hogle, Jerrold, 'The Ghost of the Counterfeit and the Genesis of the Gothic', *Gothick Origins and Innovations*, ed. Allan Lloyd Smith and Victor Sage (Amsterdam and Atlanta: Rodopi, 1994), pp. 23-33. This playful essay interprets Walpole's (and Gothic fiction's) obsession with forgeries and counterfeited signs through the work of Jean Baudrillard, Gilles Deleuze and Félix Guattari, focusing particularly on their contention that with the advent of mercantile and capitalist culture one sees a widening gulf between sign and signifier.

Kallich, Martin, *Horace Walpole* (New York: Twayne, 1971). This study of Walpole's literary historical importance gives primacy to his published writings rather than to his letters.

Ketton-Cremer, R. W., *Horace Walpole: A Biography*, 3rd edition (London: Methuen, 1964). First published in 1940, this remains the most recent standard biography of Walpole.

Kiely, Robert, *The Romantic Novel in England* (Cambridge, MA: Harvard University Press, 1972). This book devotes its opening chapter to *The Castle of Otranto*, stressing the book's relation to epic and eighteenth-century politics, and its interest in Catholicism and the irrational.

Lewis, W. S., *Horace Walpole: The A. W. Mellon Lectures in the Fine Arts 1960* (London: Rupert Hart-Davis, 1961). Five readable and cogent introductory lectures on Walpole's 'Family', 'Friends', 'Politics', 'Strawberry Hill' and 'Works'.

Lewis, W. S., ed., *The Yale Edition of Horace Walpole's Correspondence*, 48 vols. (New Haven: Yale University Press; London: Oxford University Press, 1937-83). The monumental edition of Horace Walpole's correspondence.

Miles, Robert, *Gothic Writing, 1750-1820: A Genealogy* (London and New York: Routledge, 1993). Defining Gothic as a heterogeneous aesthetic crossing the genres, this book devotes a chapter to Walpole's (and the Gothic's) self-reflexive fixation upon questions of lineage and descent.

Mowl, Timothy, *Horace Walpole: The Great Outsider* (London: John Murray, 1996). This most recent biography of Walpole takes issue with earlier treatments of Walpole's homosexuality by W. S. Lewis, R. W. Ketton-Cremer and others; it is most persuasive in its treatment of Walpole's Grand Tour and his relationship with Lord Lincoln.

Punter, David, *The Literature of Terror: A History of Gothic Fictions from 1765 to the Present Day: Volume 1: The Gothic Tradition* (London and New York: Longman, 1980; 2nd edition, 1996). A foundational study of the Gothic from both Freudian and Marxist approaches, treating its persistent themes, its relation to other contemporary aesthetic movements, and its various transformations and their contexts.

Samson, John, 'Politics Gothicized: The Conway Incident and *The Castle of Otranto*', *Eighteenth-Century Life* 10 (1986), pp. 145-58. Countering the widespread assumption that Walpole wrote *The Castle of Otranto* as an escape from politics, this essay argues that 'the book evinces a startling infusion of the characters, events, and ideas in Walpole's political life in 1764' (p. 145).

Sedgwick, Eve Kosofsky, *The Coherence of Gothic Conventions*, 2nd edition (New York: Methuen, 1986). This book provides an account of the relation between Gothic conventions and the ways in which its practitioners wield language and structure narrative.

Sontag, Susan, 'Notes on Camp', *Against Interpretation* (New York: Farrar, Strauss & Giroux, 1966). Also printed in *A Susan Sontag Reader*, intro. Elizabeth Hardwick (Harmondsworth: Penguin Books, 1983), pp. 105-19.

Williams, Anne, 'Monstrous Pleasures: Horace Walpole, Opera, and the Conception of Gothic', *Gothic Studies* 2 (April 2000), pp. 104-18. This article explores Walpole's fondness for opera and grounds *The Castle of Otranto* and the Gothic in operatic travesty, theatricality and subject matter.

FURTHER READING

Biographies

Lewis, Wilmarth Sheldon. *Horace Walpole: The A. W. Mellon Lectures in the Fine Arts.* 1960. National Gallery of Art, Washington, Vol. 9. Bollingen Series 35, Pantheon Books, 1961. 215 p.

Authoritative biography by a foremost Walpole scholar.

Mowl, Timothy. *Horace Walpole: The Great Outsider.* London: John Murray, 1996, 274 p.

Full-length biography of Walpole.

Criticism

Beers, Henry A. "The Gothic Revival." In *A History of English Romanticism in the Eighteenth Century.* 1899. Reprint edition, pp. 221-64. New York: Henry Holt & Company, 1916.

Finds it impossible to take The Castle of Otranto *seriously as a work of literature and difficult to understand the respect accorded to the work.*

Birkhead, Edith. "The Beginnings of Gothic Romance." In *The Tale of Terror: A Study of the Gothic Romance.* 1921. Reprint edition, pp. 16-37. New York: Russell & Russell, Inc., 1963.

Chapter from what is widely regarded as a key early analysis of Gothic literature. Contends that The Castle of Otranto *was not a serious contribution to literature, but supports the now commonly accepted belief that the novel was the inspiration for later works of Gothic romance.*

Bleiler, E. F. "Horace Walpole and *The Castle of Otranto*." In *Three Gothic Novels*: The Castle of Otranto, Vathek, The Vampyre, edited by E. F. Bleiler, pp. vii-xviii. New York: Dover Publications, Inc., 1966.

Provides details of Walpole's biography that pertain to The Castle of Otranto *and surveys public and critical reaction to* The Castle of Otranto *since the time of its first publication.*

Clark, Kenneth. "Ruins and Rococo: Strawberry Hill." In *The Gothic Revival: An Essay in the History of Taste*, third edition, 1962. Reprint edition, pp. 46-65. New York: Harper & Row, Publishers, 1974.

Discusses Walpole's creation of Strawberry Hill as the preeminent example of the Gothic fashion. He finds Walpole's sham castle not merely a local absurdity, but the culmination of the aesthetic taste of his period.

Conger, Syndy McMillen. "Faith and Doubt in *The Castle of Otranto*." *Gothic* 1 (1979): 51-9.

Restates René Descartes' assertion that "radical doubt, left to itself, can come full circle to become primitive faith," and maintains that "[f]rom its first exemplar, The Castle of Otranto, the Gothic novel has been a fascinating combination of radical doubt and primitive articles of faith like animism, ancestor worship, and belief in ghosts, giants, or devils."

Davenport-Hines, Richard Treadwell. "The Dead Have Exhausted Their Power of Deceiving." In *Gothic: Four Hundred Years of Excess, Horror, Evil and Ruin*, pp. 115-50. New York: North Point Press, 1998.

Provides contextual information surrounding Walpole's composition of The Castle of Otranto, including Walpole's political writings and the construction of his Gothic "castle," Strawberry Hill.

Evans, Bertrand. "The First Gothic Plays." *Gothic Drama from Walpole to Shelley*, pp. 31-48. Berkeley: University of California Press, 1947.

Provides a detailed discussion of the themes and techniques of The Mysterious Mother.

Frank, Marcie. "Horace Walpole's Family Romances." *Modern Philology* 100, no. 3 (February 2003): 417-35.

Maintains that "[i]n both Otranto and The Mysterious Mother, incest blocks inheritance, a narrative combination that points not to an intrafamilial or intrapsychic conflict, but rather to a sociopolitical context, which I read as a clash between aristocratic and bourgeois models of the family."

Haggerty, George E. "Fact and Fancy in the Gothic Novel." *Nineteenth-Century Fiction* 39, no. 4 (March 1985): 379-91.

Discusses Walpole's innovations in blending "opposing modes of literary expression"—fact and fancy—in The Castle of Otranto and how this legacy affected later works in the Gothic tradition. Asserts that "[b]y introducing into the novel material that emerges so specifically from private fantasy . . . Walpole brought into focus both the seeming limitations of the novel form as it emerged in the eighteenth century and the terms under which those limitations were to be overcome."

Kahn, Madeleine. "'A By-Stander Often Sees More of the Game Than Those That Play': Ann Yearsley Reads *The Castle of Otranto*." *Bucknell Review* 42, no. 1 (1998): 59-78.

Examines poet Ann Yearsley's assessment of The Castle of Otranto as expressed in her poem "To the Honourable H_____e W_____e, on Reading 'The Castle of Otranto.' December, 1784."

Kiely, Robert. "*The Castle of Otranto*: Horace Walpole." In *The Romantic Novel in England*, pp. 27-42. Cambridge, Mass.: Harvard University Press, 1972.

Examines The Castle of Otranto and The Mysterious Mother in detail as characteristic works exhibiting the strengths and weaknesses of Gothic fiction. Asserts that

Gothic and Romantic fiction evolved because of the inability of Neoclassical literature to explore the complexities of human nature.

McKinney, David. "'The Castle of My Ancestors': Horace Walpole and Strawberry Hill." *British Journal for Eighteenth-Century Studies* 13 (1990): 199-214.

Probes the reasons Walpole "chose the Gothic style for his house" and included "stage-set designs as an attempt to create the atmosphere of a medieval castle," thereby "determining [his] vision for Strawberry Hill."

Mehrotra, K. K. *Horace Walpole and the English Novel: A Study of the Influence of* The Castle of Otranto, *1764-1820*. 1934. Reprint edition. New York: Russell & Russell, 1970, 197 p.

Discusses eighteenth-century conceptions of the novel and of the moral purpose of fiction, and demonstrates the ways in which The Castle of Otranto violated those rules.

Morrissey, Lee. "'To Invent in Art and Folly': Postmodernism and Walpole's *Castle of Otranto*." *Bucknell Review* 41, no. 2 (1998): 86-99.

Argues that "Gothic follies, and The Castle of Otranto, dispense with conventional proportions, on the one hand, and show that Enlightened people, on the other, are subject to a 'milling confusion' that prevents them from seeing the truth."

Mudrick, Marvin. "Chamber of Horrors." In *Books Are Not Life but Then What Is?*, pp. 303-09. London: Oxford University Press, 1979.

Argues that The Castle of Otranto merits consideration not only as the inspiration for later works in the Gothic tradition, but for what it reveals about the nightmares and subconscious fears of Walpole's age.

Reeve, Clara. "Preface to the Second Edition." *The Old English Baron: A Gothic Story*. 1778. Reprint edition, edited by James Trainer, pp. 3-6. London: Oxford University Press, 1967.

Preface to Reeve's novel in which she discusses the influence of The Castle of Otranto on her work, and the flaws in Walpole's novel that she hopes to avoid in hers.

Varma, Devendra P. "The First Gothic Tale: Its Potentialities." In *The Gothic Flame: Being a History of the Gothic Novel in England: Its Origins, Efflorescence, Disintegration, and Residuary Influences*, pp. 42-73. London: Arthur Barker, 1957.

Provides one of the most extensive discussions of the literary influences upon Walpole's work and Walpole's influence on other writers. Also examines in detail the structure of The Castle of Otranto and Walpole's presentation of his characters.

OTHER SOURCES FROM GALE:

Additional coverage of Walpole's life and career is contained in the following sources published by Thomson Gale: *British Writers*, Vol. 3; *Dictionary of Literary Biography*, Vols. 39, 104, 213; *Literary Movements for Students*, Vol. 1; *Literature Criticism from 1400 to 1800*, Vols. 2, 49; *Literature Resource Center*; *Reference Guide to English Literature*, Ed. 2; *St. James Guide to Horror, Ghost & Gothic Writers*; *Supernatural Fiction Writers*, Vol. 1; and *Twayne's English Authors*.

EDITH WHARTON

(1862 - 1937)

(Full name Edith Newbold Jones Wharton) American short story writer, novelist, essayist, and autobiographer.

Wharton is best known as a novelist of manners whose fiction detailed the cruel excesses of aristocratic society in the United States at the beginning of the twentieth century. Her carefully crafted, psychologically complex novels, novellas, and short stories reflect concern for the status of women in society as well as for the moral decay she observed underlying the outward propriety of the upper classes. While her subject matter, tone, and style have often been compared with those of her friend and mentor Henry James, Wharton has achieved critical recognition as an original chronicler of the conflict between the inner self and social convention. Aside from her numerous tales of the supernatural, collected as *Ghosts* in 1937, Wharton's writings generally eschew overt Gothic machinery, while many nevertheless evoke the pervasive and elemental sense of foreboding and psychological terror typically associated with the genre. Among her most well-known works, the tragic novella *Ethan Frome* (1911) features an ominous mood of preternatural dread that underscores the self-destructiveness and alienation of its main character. Noted stories that demonstrate Wharton's fascination with the supernatural include "The Eyes," "Pomegranate

Seed," and "Bewitched," works that were gathered and printed in her late volume of ghost tales.

BIOGRAPHICAL INFORMATION

Born into a wealthy New York family, Wharton was privately educated by governesses and tutors both at home and abroad. At an early age she displayed a marked interest in writing and literature, a pursuit her socially ambitious mother attempted to discourage. Nevertheless, Wharton finished her first novella at the age of fourteen and published a collection of verse two years later. From the perspective of an upper-class initiate, she observed the shift of power and wealth from the hands of New York's established gentry to the nouveau riche of the Industrial Revolution. Wharton considered the newly wealthy to be cultural philistines and drew upon their lives to create many of her best-remembered fictional characters and situations. In 1885 she married Edward Wharton. Becoming dissatisfied with society life and disillusioned with marriage, however, Wharton sought fulfillment in writing. Many of her stories and poems originally appeared in *Scribner's Magazine,* and both her first short story collection, *The Greater Inclination* (1899), and her novel *The House of Mirth* (1905) were well received by critics and readers. Suffering from ill health and forced to contend with her husband's growing mental instability, Wharton was granted a divorce in 1912. Soon after, she established residence in France. During World War I, Wharton organized relief efforts in France. With her financial support, an ambulance unit, a workroom for female garment workers, and a sanatorium for women and children with tuberculosis were established there. The French recognized her philanthropy by awarding her the Cross of the Legion of Honor, and she was made Chevalier of the Order of Leopold in Belgium for her work on the behalf of Belgian orphans. In the United States, her energetic fund-raising activities were aided by "Edith Wharton" committees in New York, Boston, Philadelphia, Washington, and Providence during the war. While her war novella *The Marne* (1918), generated little positive critical interest, Wharton became the first female recipient of the Pulitzer Prize for her novel *The Age of Innocence* (1920) in 1921. In 1927, Wharton was nominated to receive the Nobel Prize for literature. During the final years of her life, Wharton continued to write short stories and novels, many of which reflect her growing disillusionment with postwar America and the Jazz Age. Several of her finest short stories featuring supernatural themes were also published during this time, these and other of her noted works of Gothic fiction were collected at the end of her life, while her final novel, *The Buccaneers* (1938), remained unfinished at her death in St. Brice-sous-Foret in 1937.

MAJOR WORKS

Wharton's most celebrated works of fiction include the novels *The House of Mirth* and *The Age of Innocence,* as well as her novella *Ethan Frome*. Of these, her longer novels are thought to be especially effective at piercing the veil of moral respectability that sometimes masked a lack of integrity among the rich. In *The House of Mirth* an intelligent and lovely girl must lose her status as a member of the leisure class if she is to avoid moral ruin. Lily Bart rebels against the standards of her social group enough to smoke, gamble, and be seen in public with married men; however, her sense of decency keeps her from marrying a wealthy but vulgar suitor merely to secure her fortune. Her other opportunity consists of a young lawyer who makes fun of the "high society" his modest but adequate means entitle him to observe. When the first proposes, she turns him down; when the second proposes, it is too late—he finds the distraught Lily dead of an overdose of sleeping pills. Written after World War I, *The Age*

of Innocence, another novel about Old New York society, again showcases passionate characters hemmed in by their desire to keep their membership in a dispassionate social group. Newland Archer is engaged to marry an acceptable and attractive girl, but falls in love with Ellen Olenska, a European divorcee. Olenska had married a Polish Count, a villain from whom she escaped with the eager aid of his secretary. Equally passionate but seeking to reestablish her honor in New York society (which is not sure she is acceptable), Olenska encourages Archer to keep his commitment. To make it easier for him, she returns to Europe. A third work of social criticism, *Ethan Frome* is also notable for its enveloping atmosphere of decay and gloom, and reflects several of the Gothic themes that Wharton explored more fully in her short stories. Set in the aptly-named village of Starkfield in the hill country of rural New England, *Ethan Frome* portrays a world that offers no satisfactory escape from a loveless marriage. Wharton shows how the title character suffers when he is caught between two women—his wife, Zeena, on whom he depends for economic survival, and his true love, a younger relative of his wife's who has come to their farm. Near the conclusion of the novella, Ethan and his beloved realize that there is no escape from their predicament. When their attempt at suicide fails, they become invalids in the hands of Zeena.

Wharton gave full play to the literary allure of supernatural horror in her short stories, which included numerous ghost stories, as well as several works featuring Gothic tropes displaced into the milieu of the psychological and the domestic. One of her earliest works of short fiction, "The Fullness of Life" (1893) is an afterlife fantasy. In it, the spirit of a deceased wife finds herself attracted to another spirit she perceives to be her soul mate. After much deliberation, however, she decides to wait instead for the death of her husband so that they may be rejoined. With "The Moving Finger" Wharton moved more fully into the genre of the macabre. In the story, a man decides to have a painting of his dead wife altered so that the two may age together. He perceives this as her wish, but as time proceeds the painting seems to mysteriously change on its own, signaling the wife's realization of her husband's impending death. In "The Lady's Maid's Bell" the ghost of a former maid continues to serve her mistress. Seeking to protect the woman, an invalid, from an encroaching danger, the dead maid's spirit rings her bell, but to no avail. Wharton's supernatural stories written after her relocation to France are thought to bear affinities with the stories of Henry James, Wharton's close friend. Both writers remarked on their interpretation of the supernatural as an extension of the subconscious, particularly in its projection of the guilt or fear stimulated by the collapse of human relationships. In "Afterward" a vengeful spirit from the past returns to strip Ned Boyne of the fortune he has made years ago under questionable circumstances. This ghost of a young man Boyne once knew in America appears in England, where the story's protagonist has retreated with his new-made wealth. Both are never heard from again. In the hallucinatory story "The Eyes" the protagonist Andrew Culwin is haunted by a pair of repulsive, disembodied eyes. Only much later does he realize that the eyes are apparitions from the future, a phantasmal projection of his own wizened conscience as it looks back upon his youthful indiscretions and self-deception. In "The Triumph of Night" the protagonist Faxon becomes plagued by obsessive feelings of guilt after failing to respond to a nightmarish vision in which he sees his friend's death planned by a greedy uncle. "Kerfol" depicts a ruined French estate haunted by the spirits of dogs, animals murdered by the previous owner in revenge for what he wrongly believed was his wife's adultery.

Particularly in her later stories, Wharton employed the supernatural to project various aspects of the human psyche ranging from fear and guilt to joy and longing. In "Bewitched" a married man becomes infatuated with the spirit of a dead girl, a witch whom his wife believes has entranced him with black magic. "Miss Mary Pask" features a more jubilant tone than is typical of Wharton's ghosts stories, describing its narrator's meeting with an old friend whom he only belatedly realizes has already died. With "A Bottle of Perrier" Wharton produced a tale of psychological terror influenced by the writings of Edgar Allan Poe and centered on a murderous relationship between master and servant. "Mr. Jones" is perhaps Wharton's most Jamesian piece. It tells of a house dominated by the spirit of a former caretaker whose rule was so formidable that it continues to control the dwelling and those living in it. The protagonist of "After Holbein," Anson Warley, is confronted with the specter of death and the realization that his dilettantish life has been wasted. Among Wharton's most well-received stories, "Pomegranate Seed" evokes the mythological tale of Persephone in recounting the story of a spirit that continues to send letters to her living husband while terrifying her perceived rival, the man's second wife and the story's narrator, Charlotte Ashby.

CRITICAL RECEPTION

During her lifetime many of Wharton's works of fiction were lauded with high critical and popular esteem. *The House of Mirth* became a best seller in 1905 and provoked much discussion in the United States, where it was hailed as one of the best novels ever produced by an American author. *The Age of Innocence* was likewise highly acclaimed as one of Wharton's finest works, and earned her a Pulitzer Prize in 1921. Despite these successes, Wharton's fiction was for most of the twentieth century dismissed as the work of an outdated novelist of manners whose settings, style, and slow-moving pace belonged to the nineteenth century. By the end of the twentieth century, however, feminist scholars, genre critics, and mainstream audiences began to regard Wharton's writings with a much higher degree of distinction and appreciation, rehabilitating her reputation and suggesting the significance of her place in literary history between the moral and psychological fiction of the late nineteenth century and the iconoclastic realism of the early twentieth-century's Lost Generation. Wharton's ghost stories, in particular, have been linked to new insights into the overall thematic concerns of her work. In the 1937 preface to her collection *Ghosts* Wharton wrote: "the 'moral issue' question must not be allowed to enter into the estimating of a ghost story. It must depend for its effect solely on what one might call its thermometrical quality; if it sends a cold shiver down one's spine, it has done its job and done it well." While Wharton's own thoughts on her ghost stories appealed to a relatively straightforward test of audience response, contemporary scholars, without questioning the chilling effectiveness of her ghost tales, have subjected these works to more rigorous critical standards. Several have studied Wharton's adapted use of Gothic conventions in her ghost stories for the purposes of social critique, focusing on her career-long examination of class divisions in American society during the early decades of the twentieth century in conjunction with her use of psychological terror. A juxtaposition of feminist and Gothic concerns have also appeared frequently in contemporary critical estimations of Wharton's ghost stories. Of principal interest has been Wharton's fictional alignment of patriarchal value systems, capitalist-bourgeois repression of women, and the machinations of Gothic fantasy in not only her supernatural fiction, but also in her novels *The House of Mirth* and *The Age of Innocence.*

PRINCIPAL WORKS

"The Fullness of Life" (short story) 1893; published in the journal *Scribner's Magazine*

The Decoration of Houses [with Ogden Codman, Jr.] (nonfiction) 1897

The Greater Inclination (short stories) 1899

The Touchstone: A Story (novella) 1900; published in England as *A Gift from the Grave: A Tale*

Crucial Instances (short stories) 1901

The Valley of Decision: A Novel (novel) 1902

Sanctuary (novella) 1903

†*The Descent of Man, and Other Stories* (short stories) 1904

Italian Villas and Their Gardens (essays) 1904

The House of Mirth (novel) 1905

Italian Backgrounds (memoirs) 1905

The Fruit of the Tree (novel) 1907

Madame de Treymes (novella) 1907

The Hermit and the Wild Woman, and Other Stories (short stories) 1908

‡*Tales of Men and Ghosts* (short stories) 1910

Ethan Frome (novella) 1911

The Reef: A Novel (novel) 1912

The Custom of the Country (novel) 1913

#*Xingu, and Other Stories* (short stories and novella) 1916

Summer: A Novel (novel) 1917

The Marne (novella) 1918

French Ways and Their Meaning (essays) 1919

The Age of Innocence (novel) 1920

The Glimpses of the Moon (novel) 1922

A Son at the Front (novel) 1923

Old New York (novellas) 1924

The Mother's Recompense (novel) 1925

The Writing of Fiction (criticism) 1925

‖*Here and Beyond* (short stories) 1926

Twilight Sleep (novel) 1927

The Children (novel) 1928

Hudson River Bracketed (novel) 1929

§*Certain People* (short stories) 1930

The Gods Arrive (novel) 1932

A Backward Glance (autobiography) 1934

**The World Over* (short stories) 1936

Ghosts (short stories) 1937; also published as *The Ghost Stories of Edith Wharton*

The Buccaneers (unfinished novel) 1938

Collected Short Stories. 2 vols. (short stories) 1967

Edith Wharton Abroad: Selected Travel Writings, 1888-1920 (travel essays) 1995

The Uncollected Critical Writings (criticism) 1997

* This collection includes the short story "The Moving Finger."
† This collection includes the short story "The Lady's Maid's Bell."
‡ This collection includes the short stories "Afterward" and "The Eyes."
# This collection includes the short stories "Kerfol" and "The Triumph of Night."
‖ This collection includes the short stories "Bewitched" and "Miss Mary Pask."
§ This collection includes the short stories "A Bottle of Perrier," "After Holbein," and "Mr. Jones."
** This collection includes the short story "Pomegranate Seed."

PRIMARY SOURCES

EDITH WHARTON (ESSAY DATE 1973)

SOURCE: Wharton, Edith. "Preface." In *The Ghost Stories of Edith Wharton.* 1973. Reprint edition, pp. 7-11. New York: Scribner, 1997.

In the following preface to her Ghosts, *first published in 1937 (also published as* The Ghost Stories of Edith Wharton), *Wharton discusses ghosts, belief in ghosts, and the various techniques employed by authors of ghost stories.*

Do you believe in ghosts?" is the pointless question often addressed by those who are incapable of feeling ghostly influences to—I will not say the *ghost-seer*, always a rare bird, but—the *ghost-feeler*, the person sensible of invisible currents of being in certain places and at certain hours.

The celebrated reply (I forget whose): "No, I don't believe in ghosts, but I'm afraid of them," is much more than the cheap paradox it seems to many. To "believe," in that sense, is a conscious act of the intellect, and it is in the warm darkness of the prenatal fluid far below our conscious reason that the faculty dwells with which we apprehend the ghosts we may not be endowed with the gift of seeing. This was oddly demonstrated the other day by the volume of ghost stories collected from the papers of the late Lord Halifax by his son. The test of the value of each tale lay, to the collector's mind, not in the least in its intrinsic interest, but in the fact that someone or other had been willing to vouch for the authenticity of the anecdote. No matter how dull, unoriginal and unimportant the tale—if someone had convinced the late Lord Halifax that it was "true," that it "had really happened," in it went; and can it be only by accident that the one story in this large collection which is even faintly striking and memorable is the one with an apologetic footnote to the effect that the editor had not been able to trace it to its source?

Sources, as a matter of fact, are not what one needs in judging a ghost story. The good ones bring with them the internal proof of their ghostliness; and no other evidence is needed. But since first I dabbled in the creating of ghost stories, I have made the depressing discovery that the faculty required for their enjoyment has become almost atrophied in modern man. No one ever expected a Latin to understand a ghost, or shiver over it; to do that, one must still have in one's ears the hoarse music of the northern Urwald or the churning of dark seas on the outermost shores. But when I first began to read, and then to write, ghost stories, I was conscious of a common medium between myself and my readers, of their meeting me halfway among the primeval shadows, and filling in the gaps in my narrative with sensations and divinations akin to my own.

I had curious evidence of the change when, two or three years ago, one of the tales in the present volume made its first curtsy in an American magazine. I believe most purveyors of fiction will agree with me that the readers who pour out on the author of the published book such floods of interrogatory ink pay little heed to the isolated tale in a magazine. The request to the author to reveal as many particulars as possible of his private life to his eager readers is seldom addressed to him till the scattered products of his pen have been collected in a volume. But when **"Pomegranate Seed"** (which I hope you presently mean to read) first appeared in a magazine, I was bombarded by a host of inquirers anxious, in the first place, to know the meaning of the story's title (in the dark ages of my childhood an acquaintance with classical fairy lore was as much a part of our stock of knowledge as Grimm and Andersen), and secondly, to be told *how a ghost could write a letter, or put it into a letterbox*. These problems caused sleepless nights to many correspondents whose names seemed to indicate that they were recent arrivals from unhaunted lands. Need I say there was never a Welsh or a Scottish signature among them? But in a few years more perhaps there may be; for, deep within us as the ghost instinct lurks, I seem to see it being gradually atrophied by those two world-wide enemies of the imagination, the wireless and the cinema. To a generation for whom everything which used to nourish the imagination because it had to be won by an effort, and then slowly assimilated, is now served up cooked, seasoned and chopped into little bits, the creative faculty (for reading should be a creative act as well as writing) is rapidly withering, together with the power of sustained attention; and the world which used to be so *grand à la charté des lampes* is diminishing in inverse ratio to the new means of spanning it; so that the more we add to its surface the smaller it becomes.

All this is very depressing to the ghost-story purveyor and his publisher; but in spite of adverse influences and the conflicting attractions of the gangster, the introvert and the habitual drunkard, the ghost may hold his own a little longer in the hands of the experienced chronicler. What is most to be feared is that these seers should fail; for frailer than the ghost is the wand of his evoker, and more easily to be broken in the hard grind of modern speeding-up. Ghosts, to make themselves manifest, require two conditions abhorrent to the modern mind: silence and continuity. Mr. Osbert Sitwell informed us the other day that ghosts went out when electricity came in; but surely this is to misapprehend the nature of the ghostly. What drives ghosts away is not the aspidistra or the electric cooker; I can imagine them more wistfully haunting a mean house in a dull street than the battlemented castle with its boring stage properties. What the ghost really needs is not echoing passages and hidden doors behind tapestry, but only continuity and silence. For where a ghost has once appeared it seems to hanker to appear again; and it obviously prefers the silent hours, when at last the wireless has ceased to jazz. These hours, prophetically called "small," are in fact continually growing smaller; and even if a few diviners keep their wands, the ghost may after all succumb first to the impossibility of finding standing room in a roaring and discontinuous universe.

It would be tempting to dwell on what we shall lose when the wraith and the fetch are no more with us; but my purpose here is rather to celebrate those who have made them visible to us. For the ghost should never be allowed to forget that his only chance of survival is in the tales of those who have encountered him, whether actually or imaginatively—and perhaps preferably the latter. It is luckier for a ghost to be vividly imagined than dully "experienced"; and nobody knows better than a ghost how hard it is to put him or her into words shadowy yet transparent enough.

It is, in fact, not easy to write a ghost story; and in timidly offering these attempts of mine I should like to put them under the protection of those who first stimulated me to make the experiment. The earliest, I believe, was Stevenson, with "Thrawn Janet" and "Markheim"; two remarkable ghost stories, though far from the high level of such wizards as Sheridan Le Fanu and Fitz James O'Brien. I doubt if these have ever been surpassed, though Marion Crawford's isolated effort, "The Upper Berth," comes very near to the crawling horror of O'Brien's "What Is It?"

For imaginative handling of the supernatural no one, to my mind, has touched Henry James in "The Turn of the Screw"; but I suppose a ghost novel can hardly be classed among ghost stories, and that tale in particular is too individual, too utterly different from any other attempt to catch the sense of the supernatural, to be pressed into the current categories.

As for the present day, I have ventured to put my own modest "omnibus" under the special protection of the only modern ghost evoker whom I place in the first rank—and this dispenses with the need of saying why I put him [Walter de la Mare] there. Moreover, the more one thinks the question over, the more one perceives the impossibility of defining the effect of the supernatural. The Bostonian gentleman of the old school who said that his wife always made it a moral issue whether the mutton should be roasted or boiled, summed up very happily the relation of Boston to the universe; but the "moral issue" question must not be allowed to enter into the estimating of a ghost story. It must depend for its effect solely on what one might call its thermometrical quality; if it sends a cold shiver down one's spine, it has done its job and done it well. But there is no fixed rule as to the means of producing this shiver, and many a tale that makes others turn cold leaves me at my normal temperature. The doctor who said there were no diseases but only patients would probably agree that there are no ghosts, but only tellers of ghost stories, since what provides a shudder for one leaves another peacefully tepid. Therefore one ought, I am persuaded, simply to tell one's ghostly adventures in the most unadorned language, and "leave the rest to Nature," as the New York alderman said when, many years ago, it was proposed to import "a couple of gondolas" for the lake in the Central Park.

The only suggestion I can make is that the teller of supernatural tales should be well frightened in the telling; for if he is, he may perhaps communicate to his readers the sense of that strange something undreamt of in the philosophy of Horatio.

GENERAL COMMENTARY

MARGARET P. MURRAY (ESSAY DATE AUGUST 1989)

SOURCE: Murray, Margaret P. "The Gothic Arsenal of Edith Wharton." *Journal of Evolutionary Psychology* 10, nos. 3-4 (August 1989): 315-21.

In the following essay, Murray illustrates how Wharton uses horror in the Gothic tradition to highlight women's experiences, particularly with regard to power and identity.

Throughout Edith Wharton's life, we find several recurring themes related to her own emotional problems were not resolved in her novels. One of these themes is her ambivalence towards her femininity. However, she was an adept student of literature as well as a gifted author, and her strong literary background allied with her talents as writer enabled her eventually to put to rest, one by one, her own ghosts, through a careful manipulation of a genre familiar to her as a scholar: The Gothic. Nothing could have suited Edith Wharton, the writer's, deepest needs and fears more than the Gothic story. Only this genre and its Edwardian evocation of atmosphere and style would answer the needs of Edith Wharton, the Lady.

Many Gothic critics, such as Jack Sullivan, contend that a ghost story should not be reduced to a simple Freudian case reading (6), which can become little more than an act of vandalism perpetrated on a work of art. A Freudian study strips it of its atmosphere, which is probably the single most important characteristic of the tale of terror. Wharton would agree with this theory. She tells us in the preface to her ghost stories that a ghostly tale "must depend for its effect solely on what one might call its thermometrical quality: if it sends a shiver down one's spine, it has done its job and done it well" (4).

Thus Wharton takes a Gothic story out of the realm of "how and why." Any attempt to establish psychological cause and effect can tear the thin, extoplasmic tissue which chills. In the best tales of terror the explanation is totally irrelevant; the damage is already done; the reader is cold. However, we can't overlook what Freud tells us regarding storytelling in general:

> A happy person never fantasies (sic), only an unsatisfied one. The motive forces of fantasies are unsatisfied wishes and every single fantasy is the fulfillment of a wish, a correction of unsatisfying reality.
>
> (qutd. in Punter 409)

Freud's theory gives us a deeper insight into Wharton's creative drive. Her personal and social dissatisfaction, demonstrated through her themes, is well-documented. A quick perusal of the history of the Gothic tale explains why the most logical vehicle for her "correction of unsatisfying reality" became the Gothic tale.

In a Gothic tale, we are presented with motifs and images designed to terrify. Why they terrify can be explained by the Jungian theory of universal archetypes and the collective unconscious. Jung maintains that there are certain primordial images "universally present in the preconscious makeup of the human psyche" (69). This preconsciousness can be seen as a "preracial memory," exemplified in various mythical prototypes which are and have been extant throughout the history of mankind. Whether Wharton read Jung or not is irrelevant. When she tells us in the preface, "it is in the warm darkness of the pre-natal fluid far below our conscious reason that the faculty dwells with which we apprehend the ghosts. . . ." (1), we are able to see her instinctive appreciation of the tools which build the Gothic tale.

Gothic tales may be divided into two categories: the tale of terror and the tale of horror. Varma says of the former: "the Gothic spirit makes humble obeisance before the great Unknown. . . ." and thus a tension is kindled between the human and the divine (16). From this tension comes terror and in terror, there is a dark beauty. The reader is in the presence of something greater than himself, which is awesome and beautiful: but the ambiguity of the mechanism which evokes the presence raises fear or terror.

In horror, the mechanism is no longer ambiguous. There is no divine tension. Varma continues: "The difference between Terror and Horror is the difference between awful apprehension and sickening realization: between the smell of death and stumbling against the corpse" (130). Wharton is able to use Terror most adeptly but in **"Pomegranate Seed"** she completely masters the subgenre of horror.

Wharton's works in the Gothic spanned her career. The first, **"The Dutchess at Prayer,"** was written in 1900 during the Edwardian Gothic renaissance when the literature of alienation, paranoia, and nightmare came to be called the literature of power. Part of that power lies in its ability to move the soul by evoking the "unteachable" and the "unknowable" (Sullivan 10). The Edwardian ghost story was also characterized by stylictic sophistication. "Eschewing Gothic hyperbole, the best stories have elegant surfaces that gradually imply or reveal something not so elegant; the chills are evoked with care and control" (Sullivan 8). Here, as H. P. Lovecraft states, "'atmosphere is the all important thing'" (qutd. in Sullivan 8).

What we are given is a genre tailor-made for an author so careful and controlling she edits her own biographical material and writes her own epitaph.

A striking parallel exists between her examination of the displaced wife in *The Fruit of the Tree* and her later use of this theme in **"Pomegranate Seed."** Justine Brent, the second wife in *The Fruit of the Tree*, is supplanted by the dead Bessie Amherst. But the Bessie who supersedes her is not the woman who was, but the figment of the guilt-stricken imagination of their mutual husband, John Amherst. Justine cannot fight a ghost, particularly the ghost of a creature who never existed. Justine becomes just one more powerless, hopeless woman.

When Wharton reworks the theme twenty-three years later, she has arrayed her Gothic weaponry. Moving the plot reversal into the realm of the supernatural, she is able to assert her mastery over the societal restrictions that reduce women to mere shadow dancers on the fringe of a male-defined world. If women must remain in the shadows, then let the shadows come alive. In **"Pomegranate Seed"** exactly this happens: for it is in this tale of the nether world that Wharton unveiled her omnipotent woman.

In her preface Wharton tells us it is easier for her to imagine ghosts "wistfully haunting a mean house in a dull street than the battlemented castle with its boring stage properties" (3), and such is the house of Ken and Charlotte Ashby. Osbert Sitwell felt "ghosts went out when electricity came in"; (qutd. in Preface 3). Wharton strongly disagreed, and to make her point, there are more electric lights in **"Pomegranate Seed"** than this reader cares to count. What she did believe is that the reader must meet her "halfway among the primeval shadows" (Preface 2). It is through "the states of mind inherited from an earlier phase of race-culture" (Wharton, **WF** [**The Writing of Fiction**], 38), that we respond to the universal archetype in Gothic fiction.

Wharton tells us "the creative mind thrives best on a reduced diet," (qutd in Wolff 25), and **"Pomegranate Seed"** is certainly that. There are no Gothic mechanisms or motifs. **"Pomegranate Seed"** demands an alert reader because Wharton plunges right into the pit in the first paragraph.

In **The Writing of Fiction,** she tells us, "every phrase should be a signpost" (37). The Ashby home had been a "sanctuary" from the "soulless roar" (200). Now it is not. Charlotte must deal with the soulless in her own home, which has become no haven, but an antechamber of the abyss. And since a mortal has no power over ghosts, we see the hopelessness of the situation right away. In this simple evocation of the atmosphere of the doomed, we are immediately faced with a horror which "contracts and freezes the soul" (MacAndrew 125).

Margaret McDowill notes that "neither Ken nor Charlotte is equal to the spiritual demands imposed upon them by extraordinary circumstances" (139), but this is not the point. If redemption were possible through a battle of good and evil" **"Pomegranate Seed"** would be a tale of terror. Instead, it is a tale of horror, indicated by the "signposts" which identify the Ashby home as an entranceway to the underworld.

The second signpost comes when Charlotte realises the malevolence of the grey letters as soon as she sees one. In the Gothic lexicon, "grey is the most subtle of symbolic adjectives. It is the color of . . . fear" (Downey 89). Charlotte identifies it as "peculiar," and it always arrives after dark (201). Whenever Ken receives the letters he is "emptied of life" (202) and they take him "far away" (203) from her. Thus, as Wharton outlines in **The Writing of Fiction,** "the preliminary horror [is] posited" (39). Afterward, the only other symptoms of distress are a few more letters (nine in total). But

Wharton keeps to her credo regarding the tale of horror, by "harping on the same string—the same nerve . . ." (39), which she tells us in the same place, does the trick. And she is right.

Wharton has turned on all the lights, left no shadows and given us a tale of contemporary horror. She is in the realm of "literature of power" in that she is "evoking the unknowable and unteachable" (Sullivan 10). Through her prose style she involves the reader on an atavistic level. Through our preracial consciousness, we know that something unspeakable is going on here. She has also, in this tale, answered the critics who think her prose doesn't stand the test of time. A young mother comes home, thumbs through her children's homework, and realizes in the course of her day something is wrong in her marital paradise. She plans a second honeymoon for her husband and herself, anticipating the advice of the contemporary marriage counselor. Problems ensue; she telephones mother. She hops in a taxicab, goes to mother's house, places a few more phone calls, trying to solve the problems, to no avail. Mother and she hop back into a cab, go home and call the police, "as if . . . it could do any good" (230). All these modern solutions are to no avail because her antagonist is impervious to the light of scientific development. Her anatagonist may be met only in the "pre-natal fluid." Her ghost, as McDowell points out, has "an archetypal dimension reaching beyond the purely abnormal to the universal" (135).

The third signpost comes when Charlotte, who is totally cognizant of the problem, tries to explicate the "unteachable": "on the other side of the door something I can't explain, can't relate. . . . Something as old as the world, as mysterious as life." (205). Her nemesis is unseen, but there is no doubt there is a ghost. Penzoldt, in his study of the supernatural in fiction notes "invisibility is an important quality of the gods of all known religions" (46). This theomorphic trait "is more terrifying than any other, especially if it asserts its presence through all the other senses" (47). To make sure we haven't missed these signs, Wharton follows up with her own omnipresent "premonition of something inexplicable, intolerable, to be faced . . . when she opened the door . . ." (203).

Charlotte knows that "her husband [is] being dragged away from her into some mysterious bondage . . ." (217). He has "the clutch of a man who felt himself slipping over a precipice," and he looks at her "as if salvation lay in [her] face . . ."

(218). But it is too late. He has already kissed the letter: he has accepted Elsie's summons from the underworld. (This act of a lover's obeisance to a death image can be further clarified by looking at the role of women in the love-death archetype.)

Elizabeth MacAndrew provides invaluable information on the roles of women in the Gothic tale. Women, she tells us, are not split in half, as a male Doppelgänger is, in Gothic fiction. Whether she takes the form of seductress or gentle inspiration, she is in touch with the earth:

> In its positive form, the female spirit ties the male to the earth, keeping him in touch with it. . . . In its malignant aspect, . . . it tempts, seduces, lures men to inevtiable destruction, and draws its power from the same tie with the earth.
>
> (179)

Whether the woman is good or bad is therefore irrelevant. What is pertinent is, she is strong. Charlotte is the inspirational tie, but what good is that when she ties Kenneth to Mother Earth? Mother Earth is Elsie. This imagery explains R. W. B. Lewis's suggestion that Elsie "has assumed the role of Pluto and has summoned her spouse to . . . cohabit with her in the land of the dead" (Introduction xvi). In Lewis's reading she is the consort of Pluto, which identifies Elsie as the *Magna Mater,* Kore/Demeter. This image broaches the first archetypal aspect of Elsie, whose other incarnation is the *femina alba.*

Aniela Jaffe, through her work in Jung's theory of the collective unconscious explains there is a persistent transcultural image of "a lady in white," the *femina alba,* who is a harbinger of doom and who, in her radiant appearance is identified as the goddess Aphrodite. We must remember:

> All archetypal contents are two-fold and ambiguous. In the unconscious the opposites are not yet separated: an unconscious content becomes conscious only through discrimination of its latent opposites. When the two sides stand face to face they can be comprehended and the conscious mind can grasp them.
>
> (90)

Jaffe quotes Karl Kerenyi, a mythologist:

> Aphrodite is not only the goddess of love, in secret she is the queen of the underworld or of death. . . . In Greek southern Italy there are superb works of art which show how Persephone . . . can appear in the guise of Aphrodite.
>
> (90)

Jaffe demonstrates the universality of this archetype by citing the image of Frigg (or Freya) in the Germanic pantheon. She is literally, "the Beloved" of the sky-god who receives the souls of the dead. As the goddess of death she is called Hel, and in this incarnation, she is horrific.

More significant was Erda (or Hertha). "This earth mother was divided into the shining radiant Freya for she encompassed both: light and darkness, life and death" (91) It is in the persons of "Aphrodite-Persephone, Freya-Hel, [that] the goddess of love and the goddess of death are opposite aspects of the one primordial mother" (90). Jung himself notes, "these mythologies express the ultimate concerns of the psyche" (xxx).

There is, textually, proof of the convergent natures of Charlotte and Elsie. Persephone ate only a few pomegranate seeds. Her meager meal was enough to keep her locked in the netherworld for the length of the growing season. The twelve months become the twelve years of Ken and Elsie's mariiage. The seeds are transformed into letters, the impotent recipient of which is ken. But Elsie does not call him back for the short time of the growing season in the myth. There are nine she has strayed into the territory of her mirror image, Charlotte. As the dual natures converge, Charlotte, unconsciously, defends her own preconscious image when she berates Ken for being "too unstable" to bear the burden of a great love. She challenges his fidelity not on the grounds that he has emotionally deserted her, but that he has "already forgotten Elsie twice within a year" (212). Charlotte's nascent duality is further evidenced when she tells Ken time is "only a word" (213). To an immortal this is true; to a mere human being, time is a measure of mortality. Charlotte knows this to be true, because almost immediately, she characterizes herself as "unhuman" (213).

Justine Brent's hellish dream world has become the prehistoric realm of the *Magna Mater.* In this nether world Ken becomes an insignificant pawn in the battle, not of sister against sister, but of an ancient, primordial world versus the electrified, motorized, industrialized world. The power of the *femina alba* will not be denied. The authorial voice has elicited no sympathy for Ken. The emotional focus is entirely on Charlotte, who plans vacations, speaks to servants, visits mother, schemes, pleads; she acts and interacts. Ken only reacts—to letters and to Charlotte. John Amherst's egocentric vision is trampled by Wharton's illumination of life in the prenatal bath. Ken is the symbolic bagatelle awarded to the conquering power.

Through the language of the unconscious, Wharton was able to address the dichotomy between herself as an accomplished woman and her fictional powerless women. Such a focus enabled her to stop distancing herself from her own womanhood. In slaying the ghost of her ambivalence regarding her own gender, she was able to create an omnipotent woman: Charlotte-Elsie, who is Aphrodite-Persephone.

Wharton evoked an atmosphere of horror which traces its lineage to the Edwardian Gothics, who were much admired by her. Yet, for all **"Pomegranate Seed"**'s Edwardian style, she never lets the reader forget that the setting is most contemporary. She did not use a single Gothic mechanism, but never leaves the Gothic genre. Even though she makes a point of mentioning "skyscrapers, advertisements, telephones, [radios], airplanes, movies, motors and all the rest of the twentieth century" (205), she never lets the reader forget the timeless nature of fear.

Works Cited

Downey, June E.: *Creative Imagination: Studies in the Psychology of Literature.* New York: Hartcourt, Brace& Co., 1929

Jaffe Aniela: *Apparitions: An Archetypal Approach to Death Dreams and Ghosts.* Irving, Texas: Spring Publications, 1979.

Jung C. G.: *Psyche and Symbol.* Ed. Violet S. deLaszlo, Garden City, New York: Anchor Books, 1958.

Lewis, R. W. B.: "Introduction," *The Selected Short Stories of Edith Wharton,* by Edith Wharton. New York: Charles Scribner's Sons, 1968. vii-xxvii.

MacAndrew, Elizabeth: *The Gothic Tradition in Fiction.* New York: Columbia University Press, 1979.

McDowell, Margaret B.: "Edith Wharton's Ghost Stories." *Criticism* XII (Spring 1970): 133-52.

Penzoldt, Peter: *The Supernatural in Fiction.* New York: Humanities Press, 1965.

Punter, David: *The Literature of Terror.* London and New York: Longman, 1980.

Sullivan, Jack: *Elegant Nightmares.* Athens, Ohio: Ohio Univ. Press, 1978.

Varma, Devendra P.: *The Gothic Flame.* London: Arthur Baker Ltd., 1957.

Wharton Edith: *The Fruit of the Tree.* New York: Scribner's 1907.

———: *The Ghost Stories of Edith Wharton.* New York: Charles Scribner's Sons, 1985.

———: "Pomegranate Seed." *Ghost Stories* 199-230.

———: "Preface." *Ghost Stories* 1-4.

———: *The Writing of Fiction.* New York: Octagon Books Inc., 1966.

Wolff, Cynthia Griffin: *A Feast of Words.* New York: Oxford University Press, 1977.

MONIKA ELBERT (ESSAY DATE MARCH 1995)

SOURCE: Elbert, Monika. "The Transcendental Economy of Wharton's Gothic Mansions." *American Transcendental Quarterly* 9, no. 1 (March 1995): 51-67.

In the following essay, Elbert asserts that in her Gothic, domestic ghost stories, Wharton—like the Transcendentalists—offers an alternative to the perceived greed, corruption, and compulsion inherent in a capitalist society.

Ghosts, to make themselves manifest, require two conditions abhorrent to the modern mind: silence and continuity.
—Edith Wharton, Preface to *The Ghost Stories of Edith Wharton*[1]

"Outside there," she thought, "skyscrapers, advertisements, telephones, wireless, airplanes, movies, motors, and all the rest of the twentieth century; and on the other side of the door something I can't explain, can't relate to them. Something as old as the world, as mysterious as life. . . ."
—Charlotte Ashby in Wharton's "**The Pomegranate Seed**" 205

In her ghost stories Edith Wharton is really not diverging significantly from the social critique of her other stories or novels.[2] However, instead of depicting mansions peopled with social climbers, Wharton creates mansions haunted by ghosts who stand in the way of social climbers. In fact, her depiction of a class structure in disarray and of the individual's alienation from an overwhelming business ethic is as pronounced in her Gothic tales as in her novels of Old New York. However, there is a slight twist: the ghosts outside, in the shape of bad business partners, mismatched lovers, unfaithful friends, and abused and disgruntled servants, are not half as terrifying as the ghosts within, a quandary which Charlotte Ashby faces and attempts to articulate (in the epigraph above), as she leaves the bustle of the city to discover the territory within. Ultimately, Wharton allows spiritual concerns to triumph over economic circumstances and suggests that there is a world elsewhere: in the process, she reaffirms the vision of the American Transcendentalists. Here is a Realism tinged with the idealism of the American Renaissance writers.

Behind the Gothic quandary is Wharton's ambivalence towards French and Old New York aristocracy: she is as obsessed with her confusion about her allegiance to European or New England origins as her Transcendental predecessors. On the one hand, she loathes the old order and wants the structures torn down; on the other, she is terrified of disorder and chaos: "[Wharton] was simultaneously appalled by the shams of her class and contemptuous of classes beneath her" (Conn 173); moreover, being so conservative, she felt that "disruption anywhere in the system threatens the disintegration of the entire culture. . . . Since anarchy represented for Wharton the worst of all possible outcomes—certainly worse than death—restraint always declared itself a better strategy than reform" (174). Not surprisingly, the inception of the Gothic novel corresponded with the burgeoning of industrialization and class fluctuations, and, similarly, Wharton's writing of Gothic stories corresponded with a growing consumer culture and mass technology: "The ideology of the gothic novel is the legitimization of burgeoning capitalist power, a dark fairy-tale assurance that the propertied, after surviving their troubles, could maintain their ascendancy in terms of political and economic powers" (Bernstein 161). Beneath the terror of Wharton's Gothic mode is her own ambivalence towards the servants in her life and towards the issue of class and culture in general.[3]

Wharton, in her Gothic stories, shows the corruption of the old aristocracy and the compulsiveness of the nouveaux riches; in so doing, she subverts and undermines the economic foundations of Western capitalism, as much as Thoreau did in escaping from the world of work to his Walden sanctuary. One finds the same dilemmas of a capitalistic economy in many of Wharton's ghost stories, most notably in **"A Bottle of Perrier," "The Lady's Maid's Bell," "The Looking Glass,"** and **"All Souls',"** i.e., the tensions between the leisure class and the servant class, and the leisure class' increasing atrophy of the will, their alienation from nature and the countryside, as well as the discrepancy between rational and imaginative vision.

Many of the pacts made between master/mistress and servant in Wharton's gothic fiction center on duplicitous appearances and economic necessity: thus, for example, in **"The Looking Glass,"** Cora tells a lie to the bedridden Mrs. Clingsland to make her final days less oppressive: in fact, she concocts a dead lover's letters in order to pacify one of those "discouraged . . . grand people" in one of those "grand houses" (232). The servant-nurse ostensibly wanted to keep the greedy, fraudulent clairvoyants away from Mrs. Clingsland, who wanted to resurrect her youthful good looks and lover; i.e., the servant wanted to protect her from a bad business deal, but by having a dying man concoct the letters for her, Cora feels guilty—the servant who has transgressed her boundaries—and also vindicated: "For it was true

I'd risked my soul, and that was something she couldn't pay for; but then maybe I'd saved hers, in getting her away from those foul people, so the whole business was more of a puzzle to me than ever" (148). Ironically, feeling guilty for lying and for selling her soul, Cora manages to wheedle one hundred dollars out of Mrs. Clingsland to have masses read for the repose of the dead letter-writing man's soul, and she feels some comfort in that the priest had been "a sort of accomplice too, though he never knew it" (250). Here, as in most of Wharton's Gothic tales, the spirit is weighed against money, and strangely enough, the terms are often interchangeable, though the servant's province is more often than not more allied with the soil (the country) and the soul, even if s/he doesn't wield much power in the marketplace world. Thus, the protagonists in **"Afterward"** and in **"The Triumph of Night"** suffer because of a bad business transaction (deception or self-deception on their part), and the protagonist in **"All Souls'"** is weighed down by her possessiveness and by her dependence on modern luxuries. Implicit in Wharton's attack is the sentiment behind Thoreau's admonition in the "Economy" section of *Walden* that humankind needs to simplify and get back to basic necessities to find meaning in life.

Though the vision of ghosts allows the Wharton protagonists to escape (temporarily) the rampant materialism surrounding them, inhabiting the Gothic edifices leads to stasis, a clinging to the past, and finally to illness, if not to death, if the inhabitants cannot imagine another cultural construct. The visions of the past are not organic, but solipsistic; the masters use their servants to bridge the gap between past and present, body and spirit, but the servants do not eradicate the past, nor can they connect the master to a primeval, agrarian past, but rather, they serve as a constant reminder of the present. Thus, in **"A Bottle of Perrier"** the master Almodham attempts to recapture the past by pursuing his archaeological interests in the desert, but the servant murders him; similarly, Sara Clayburn in **"All Souls'"** attempts to find shelter in her old "Colonial" house, but her servants possess her mind, and she is left without any social or mental stability. In the latter case, the "coven" of servants, like Cora in **"The Looking Glass,"** offered the potential of viewing anew, though ostensibly, the servants appear to be the medium to some irretrievable past for the wealthy mansion-owner.

In some ways, though, Wharton is more of a Romantic than the Realist James, more Emersonian than Jamesian, in suggesting that enlightenment might come from the silence within, when one is removed figuratively, in one's psychic home or mansion, or literally, from society, but the fears and neuroses which characterize her protagonists cannot be overcome through a simple sojourn in the country. Indeed, the business mentality of contemporary New York weighs heavily upon Wharton, and she looks for meaning to counteract the loudness of American technological civilization, in the mythology of the European past—in the many abandoned villages and haunted castles of her ghost stories. In other words, she turns aesthetic in her tastes and longings.

Considering that the Gothic was a European art form (on both the literary and architectural levels), it is not surprising that Wharton should feel at home with it, since she is ambivalent about all that is European. She resembles the Transcendentalists, especially Emerson, in both affirming and denying her allegiance to an aristocratic European past, while trying to establish her American identity. She manifests the anxiety of influence, as surely as Emerson does in "The American Scholar." The only other critic to consider Wharton's Transcendental affinities, Toby Widdicombe, does a close reading of Wharton's **"The Angel at the Grave"** as a "problematic memorial to Transcendentalism" (47). He asserts that "If Wharton is considered the doyenne of realism, then the story, with its focus on the philosophical problems inherent in Transcendentalism, overturns expectations" (47). One of those problems, evident in the story, is the Transcendental belief that one needed to create something new, while reappraising the genius of the past (55). Certainly, Wharton was also caught in this bind, as I mention earlier in describing her allegiance to the "old" and "new" European and American culture.

At times Wharton is downright elitist about her mythologized European past, especially aesthetically speaking, when she advises writers not to "disown" the past, not to waste the "inherited wealth of experience" (154); she praises Proust, for example, for his ability to combine originality with respect for the past and reads his strength as "the strength of tradition" (*Writing of Fiction* 154). She attacks young contemporary writers for their "lack of general culture" and of "original vision" as they "attach undue importance to trifling innovations" (154). Wharton did not think much about contemporary American writers; in fact, in a letter to Comte Arthur de Vogue, who wanted to be introduced into cultural circles in America, she regrets that she cannot recommend any authors' names to him, even though she has "several men of science" to recommend: "but the new America is so little literary that I do not know to whom I should direct you" (October 1919). She sees the world of intellect divided between the scientist and the writer, with the scientist (Emerson's version of the Materialist) faring remarkably better. She writes to John Jay Chapman that he and she are the "only valid survivors" of "a milieu litteraire" (8 October 1919).

Moreover, Wharton is nostalgic about her own personal European past, as she reminisces fondly about her childhood in *A Backward Glance.* Suffering a financial setback after the Civil War, the father let "his town and country houses for six years to some of the profiteers of the day," and, ironically, the family goes "to Europe to economize" (44). This is actually the reverse situation of the rich American couple who go ghost-hunting in an old Tudor mansion in Wharton's ghost story, "**Afterward**":

> . . . [the mansion's] remoteness from a station, its lack of electric light, hot water pipes, and other vulgar necessities—were exactly those pleading in its favor for two romantic Americans perversely in search of the economic drawbacks which were associated, in their tradition, with unusual architectural felicities.
>
> (48)

In her own life, Wharton's family was forced to move to Europe for six years, and from this crucial period of her life, she gathered sustenance from the traditions of the past.

> Happy misfortune, which gave me for the rest of my life, that background of beauty and old-established order! I did not know how deeply I had felt the nobility and harmony of the great European cities till our steamer was docked at New York.
>
> (44)

Wharton juxtaposes the eyesore of New York ("the shameless squalor of the purlieus of the New York docks") with "the glories of Rome and the architectural majesty of Paris" (44).

It is this sense of being lost in America which allies her with fellow expatriates, James and T. S. Eliot. Towards the end of her life, though, she realizes that one urban center is like another, as she describes a veritable modern Wasteland:

> Paris is simply awful—a kind of continuous earthquake of motor busses, trams, lorries, taxis, & other howling & swooping & colliding engines, with hundreds of U.S. citizens rushing about in them & tumbling out of them at one's door—&, through it all, the same people placidly telephoning one to come to tea.
>
> (To Bernard Berenson, 23 May 1920)

To escape the commotion and the American tourists (who seem synonymous with noise) in Paris, Wharton escapes to the natural landscape of her country getaway: "The country—the banlieue

even—is divine, & my humble potager gushes with nightingales" (23 May 1920).

It is no wonder that with this malaise of modern culture weighing upon her, Wharton finally spends the last years of her life not in a sprawling urban center like Paris but in a country villa, Pavillon Colombe, outside Paris. In many ways, she lives her last years as her protagonist in "**All Souls'**" (Mrs. Clayburn) does: isolated and outside the realm of modern communication. When Wharton hears about the death of a family friend, she writes to Dr. Beverly Robinson about the gap in communications:

> The news of Anna's death comes as a great shock to me, for I had not heard of her illness. Since I have given up Paris, & live entirely in the country, I sometimes miss a letter or newspaper containing news of friends at home, and thus remain for weeks in ignorance of what has happened to them.
>
> (21 January 1921)

This self-imposed isolation causes all news from the outside to seem garbled, fantastic, and fragmented; thus, as the ghosts without are held in check, the ghosts within loom large for the aging Wharton.

Wharton invites both the protagonist and the reader to explore the power of the imagination in order to validate one's private space in the face of overwhelming odds. The wireless, telegraphs, telephones, movies, the constant static, "white noise," of everyday life prevent the protagonist from encountering the "silence and continuity" of oneself alone (stripped of the accouterments of modern culture).[4] One is reminded here as elsewhere in Wharton's Gothic tales of Thoreau's need to shut himself off from news, telegrams, and trains in an effort to ward off the debilitating effects of civilization and to "live deliberately." To Wharton, too, modern channels of communication cut off one's life-line to an inner self: on a trip to New York, after settling down in France, she comments about the crippling effects of her sojourn, paralyzing, that is, in terms of her self-expression:

> The fact is, my wonderful New York fortnight reduced me to absolute inarticulateness—of tongue and pen. . . . moreover, I had acquired [in New York] a proficiency in telephoning and telegraphing which seemed to have done away with my ability to express myself in any less lapidary style.
>
> (Letter to Corinne Robinson, 2 March 1914)

In her Gothic fiction, Wharton forces the skeptic and the non-introspective reader to believe and to move within the realm of the unconscious: she asks us to suspend belief or disbelief momentarily and seduces us into the realm of ghosts, to a higher understanding of self. She invites us to move from the "soulless" roar of the city to the "soulful" existence within the home one creates (e.g., "**Pomegranate Seed**"), even if that requires some painful psychic experiences—or an encounter with a ghost. Essentially, Wharton asks the reader to return to some primitive, psychological state: she explains that "No one with a spark of *imagination* ever objected to a good ghost story as 'improbable'. . . . Most of us retain the more or less shadowy memory of ancestral terrors, and airy tongues that syllable men's names" (**The Writing of Fiction** 38-39). The belief in ghosts, according to Wharton, has its origin in "states of mind inherited from an earlier phase of race-culture" (**Writing** 38).

In telling her life's story, Wharton discusses how her reading of ghost stories was crucial to the development of her imagination. In her autobiographical sketch "**Life and I**," Wharton recounts the story of her childhood encounter with death and the underworld: she "fell ill of typhoid fever, and lay for weeks at the point of death" (1079). In her later Gothic stories, one can find traces of this moment of fear she experienced as a child, when the two worlds of body and spirit—of the physician's diagnosis and scientific advice and of the magic of children's fairy tales—seemed to collide. She was in Germany, in the Black Forest, a natural setting for ghosts, at the time, and two little playmates lent her a book of ghost stories which terrified her: "To an unimaginative child the tale would no doubt have been harmless; but it was a 'robber story,' and with my intense Celtic sense of the supernatural, tales of robbers and ghosts were perilous reading" (1079). This particular story brought on a relapse of the fever (perhaps the fever intensified the reaction), and for many years after, she lived in "a world haunted by formless horrors" (1080). This nameless horror lasted for eight years, until she was seventeen or so, and even as a woman of twenty-seven, she "could not sleep in the room with a book containing a ghost-story" (1080) and found herself burning books of this kind.

The fear of something "on the other side of the door" which the protagonist Charlotte Ashby articulates ("**Pomegranate Seed**" 205) is similar to Wharton's threshold experience with death and her initiation into terror—"something as old as the world, as mysterious as life." This fear, since it was wrought at a time of sickness, could have been her awakening to mortality, or to the secrets of her unconscious, as she was left alone for many hours. The stimulus of the ghost story exacerbated this apprehension, this recognition of life beyond the body. Indeed, it was after this experience that she could no longer sleep at night because her "terror"—"some dark undefinable menace"—was "forever dogging [her] steps," and when she took walks with her nursemaid, she would return terrified at the thought that something was pursuing her, "I could feel it behind me, upon me; and if there was any delay in the opening of the door I was seized by a choking agony of terror" (1080). This symbol of the opening and closing door—bridging the external life to one's unconscious—becomes prominent in Wharton's ghost stories.

The collision of two realms—spiritual and material—was ultimately liberating for Wharton and her characters because it sparked her creative potential; Wharton reveled in the chaos and unbounded freedom of the moment of collision. One of the reasons Wharton so admired Nietzsche was his abandonment of rules, his predilection for the unbounded, the chaotic: "He has no system, and not much logic, but wonderful flashes of insight, and power of breaking through conventions that is most exhilarating" (To Sara Norton, 7 July 1908). Wharton praises Nietzsche for his "get-[ting] back to a wholesome basis of naked instinct." According to R. W. B. Lewis, Wharton greatly admired Emerson for his influence on Nietzsche: "Nietzsche, she said, was Emerson's chef-d'oeuvre" (236). In the letter praising Nietzsche, Wharton laments the split between body and soul which Christianity has created, "There are times when I *hate* what Christianity has left in our blood—or rather, one might say, taken out of it—by its cursed assumption of the split between body and soul." Interestingly enough, this is the same kind of distress felt by Emerson in "The Transcendentalist," where he describes the separation of body and spirit in his discussion of the Materialist and Idealist, and by Thoreau in his chapter of *Walden*, "Higher Laws," where he feels compelled to devour a woodchuck raw: "I found in myself, and still find, an instinct toward a higher, or, as it is named, spiritual life, as do most men, and another toward a primitive rank and savage one, and I reverence them both" (257).

Wharton attempts to go beyond the eternal binary opposition of body-soul, and this is what makes her both Transcendentalist and modern. Thus, in her ghost stories, she shows the dangerous consequences of bifurcating the world of spirit and matter, and one can make the case that Wharton creates pagan ghosts rather than Christian ghosts to initiate the reader into her own conflicts between the spiritual and material realms. Though the context may be ostensibly Christian, as in "**All Souls'**," the ghosts are, psychologically seen, the passions which have been repressed in the individual psyche; they are not aroused by the Christian remembrance of the dead, but in the ritualistic evocation by a coven of witches who feel close to the earth. Indeed, All Souls' is the evening upon which the veil between life and death is the thinnest, when the realms between body and spirit are not totally distinct, and Wharton is provocative in allowing Sara's transformation to occur on this very evening. Bereft of the luxuries of modern communication (the material), Sara is forced to contend with her own voice, or spirit, by herself. Ghosts most often manifest themselves in Wharton's Gothic when a character experiences a psychological crisis in development—whether that be an inappropriate marriage (involving class differences or emotional incompatibilility, e.g., "**Kerfol**," in which the eternal bachelor-narrator recreates the drama of an unhappy marriage), a mid-life crisis (e.g., "**Pomegranate Seed**"), an encounter with illness ("**The Lady's Maid's Bell**"), with aging ("**The Looking Glass**"), or with death ("**All Souls'**"), or the adolescent search for one's profession ("**The Triumph of Night**"). Wharton's repeated use of the Persephone myth in her ghost stories shows her coming to terms with her childhood terror of mythical descent into the underworld, into the unconscious.[5]

For Wharton the stasis of life—in Old New York—could be overcome by other-worldliness. An overly intrusive business world or a scientifically determined milieu necessitates a ghost. One of the prerequisites for the appearance of a ghost in Edith Wharton's world (of the ghost stories) is a deep sense of ennui emanating from a routine business life, which is often intertwined with a disintegrating married life. Often such characters try to re-establish their history by purchasing an old haunted house, but the ghosts they meet are their own bugaboos, taken from the depths of their unconscious. Thus, for example, in "**Afterward**" Mary and Ned Boyne attempt to escape their American past and the drudgery of work: Mary Boyne had been "exiled" from New York when her husband's engineering business forced them to move to the "*soul-deadening* ugliness of a Middle Western town" (50); finally, after much hard work, her husband enjoys a "prodigious windfall" of a particular mine which puts them "in possession of life and the leisure to taste it"

(50). With their newly acquired American fortune, they seek an old secluded house in Europe (in old England), but they tell the real estate agent that it must be haunted. Ironically, while the husband writes his long-planned book on the "Economic Basis of Culture," his deceased business partner from the past, whom Boyne has deceived and ruined, comes back to haunt him and finally to destroy him: the New World ghost returns to the Old World to have his vengeance. Meanwhile, the wife, who waits patiently, years even, for the return of her husband, whom the ghost has taken hostage, finds herself "domesticated with the Horror, accepting its perpetual presence as one of the fixed conditions of life" (71). All her visions of painting and gardening disappear as she becomes the harshest critic of culture, by dropping out of the work world and social life altogether: "She watched the routine of daily life with the incurious eye of a savage on whom the meaningless processes of civilization make but the faintest impression" (71).

This watching and being watched are crucial factors in Wharton's Gothic, and the visual motif may be read in several ways. On the most obvious level, the protagonists feel haunted by something which they cannot fathom: in "**Kerfol**" and in "**A Bottle of Perrier**," for example, the characters feel eyes gazing at them from behind the window as they traverse the courtyards. Of course, the most nightmarish vision of being watched occurs as a result of technology—as Wharton would show in such stories as "**All Souls'**." Moreover, Wharton shows, even in her non-Gothic fiction, as in the aptly titled "**Atrophy**," that the disjunction between seeing and being, between public and private, added much to twentieth-century anxiety, ironically through such illusory images provided by the media (film, newspaper, and literature):

> You took up the morning paper, and you read of girl bandits, movie star divorces, "hold-ups" at balls, murder and suicide and elopement, and a general welter of disjointed disconnected impulses and appetites; then you turned your eyes onto your own daily life, and found yourself as cribbed and cabined, as beset by vigilant family eyes, observant friends, all sorts of embodied standards, as any white muslin novel heroines of the sixties!
> ("Atrophy" 501)

In such a world, there is nowhere to escape public and private scrutiny, even though the wish to be invisible is there.

On another level, the gaze of the eyes does not so much represent the gaze of the other as it does the protagonists' own moral conflict, their own guilt for putting personal business interests above those of their friends; thus, in "**The Triumph of Night**," George Faxon, recuperating from his nervous breakdown, reads of his friend's death and feels utter remorse: the friend's obituary "stared up at him as if with Rainer's dying eyes" (128). In "**The Eyes**" the protagonist Culwin seeks his soul in the eyes of others, for he is haunted by his own soul—as reflected in his eyes; in the darkness of night, he has visions of eyes that "hung there and drew me. I had the *vertige de l'abime*, and the red lids were the edge of my abyss" (37). To his horror, he finds the eyes are his. Nonetheless, as a good post-Darwinian character, he tries to deny these "hallucinations" through the power of science, explaining them away by attributing the "illusion" to the flicker in the fireplace or the reflection of the mirror. Moreover, he suggests that his ghosts would have disappeared with "a pair of spectacles" (31). He feels that he is "afflicted by an optical or a digestive delusion" (31) but decides not to go to a doctor because he wanted to pursue the eyes' "interesting double life" (31).

Always beneath the scientific vision of Wharton's non-believing Gothic protagonists is a wish for another realm beyond the physical/empirical; in fact, she follows an American tradition that is not simply Gothic, in making claims for a double vision which encompasses binary oppositions and destroys traditional categories of thinking. Thoreau and Emerson, with their Transcendental beliefs, explore similar spiritual realms and similar out-of-body experiences. Thoreau, for example, speaks of a "certain doubleness" which makes him as "remote" from himself as from another: "However intense my experience, I am conscious of the presence and criticism of a part of me, which, as it were, is not a part of me, but spectator, sharing no experience, but taking note of it" (*Walden* 180). Similarly, Emerson discusses the nature of his dreams in terms of ghostly apparitions and marvels at the easy reconciliation between subjectivity and objectivity in these dreamscapes:

> Their [the dreams'] double consciousness, their sub- & ob- jectiveness is the wonder. I call the phantoms that rise the creation of my fancy but they act like volunteers & counteract my inclination. They make me feel that every act, every thought, every cause, is bipolar & in the act is contained the counteract. If I strike, I am struck. If I chase, I am pursued. . . .
>
> (*Jrnl.*, 20 April 1838)

However, in his essay, "The Transcendentalist," Emerson, in his attack upon the marketplace, shows the discrepancies between the materialist's and idealist's views and the contradictions which surface through this double vision: "The worst feature of this double consciousness is, that the two lives, of the understanding and of the soul, which we lead, really show very little relation to each other; never meet and measure each other" (254). Moreover, Emerson feels that behind every material fact are levels of some higher spiritual meaning or meanings: ". . . the highest minds of the world have never ceased to explore the double meaning, or shall I say the quadruple or the centuple or much more manifold meaning, of every sensuous fact" ("The Poet" 260). Like her predecessors Emerson and Thoreau, Wharton is deeply concerned with the binary oppositions resulting from the rampant materialism of American culture.

Indeed, Wharton prefers the "ghost-feeler," "the person sensible of invisible currents of being in certain places and at certain hours" over the rational "ghost-seer" who relies upon his senses for truth ("**Preface**" 1). Though she believes that "deep within us . . . the ghost instinct lurks" (2), she feels that science and technology are robbing us of this instinct; she chastises those who need scientific or rational data to "believe" in ghosts. For her, "To 'believe' . . . is a conscious act of the intellect," but superior to this realm is the unconscious: "it is in the warm darkness of the prenatal fluid far below our conscious reason that the faculty dwells with which we apprehend the ghosts we may not be endowed with the gift of seeing" ("**Preface**" 1).

Many of Wharton's ghost stories revolve around ocular deception in the marketplace: a belief in the physical realm with one's earthly eyes or an obsession with one's professional (but superficial) identity, but finally, the deceived party is made to see the ugly reality of his business ethics through his encounter with the supernatural. Thus, for example, in "**The Eyes**," every time the protagonist, Culwin, cheats or deceives another character (often by being non-committal), he is haunted by dreams of eyes: "What turned me sick was their expression of vicious *security*. I don't know how else to describe the fact that they seemed to belong to a man who had done a lot of harm in his life, but had always kept just inside the danger lines" (34, emphasis mine). Though he initially attempts to explain the phenomenon by applying "scientific principles," he ultimately is undone by them, for they are his own eyes. There is often a relationship between the narrator telling the story and the ghost story he tells. For example, the dilettante-author Culwin in "**The Eyes**" makes his ghost public and finally realizes his mistake.

He has discouraged an artist disciple (Gilbert) of his from a life of the imagination. By telling him that he cannot write, he relegates him to a tedious life on Wall Street: "He vegetated in an office, I believe, and finally got a clerkship in a consulate, and married drearily in China. I saw him once in Hong Kong, years afterward. He was fat and hadn't shaved. I was told he drank" (45). Similarly, in **"The Triumph of Night,"** George Faxon, out of a job and on his way to a secretarial job in the country, could have saved his alter-ego Frank Rainer from the manipulations of his Wall Street uncle, but instead, he ignores the signs of the ghost lurking over the mercenary uncle's figure. Faxon suffers a nervous breakdown and is forced to retreat into solitude, away from the work-world. His doctor diagnoses the problem as "overwork" and advises him "to be quiet for a year. Just loaf and look at the landscape" (126).[6] Faxon ultimately realizes that if he had not fled the ghost, he "might have broken the spell of iniquity, the powers of darkness might not have prevailed" (127).

The most horrific of Wharton's ghost stories, **"All Souls',"** suggests that it is not so much ghosts as modern civilization which terrifies man. It is the most modern of men or women who become most victimized by the apparitions; thus, while the servants, the people who live on the land and are close to early traditions, can live in the world of ghosts, the newcomer, the idle rich man or the marketplace success, is most uprooted. As in the other servant-master Wharton ghost stories, two tensions emerge. There is a disjunction between the new business mentality and an old domestic, agrarian ideal, and there is the attendant rift between social classes, between servant and master (with the dynamics often upset, so that the servant is more master of the situation than the master, who is portrayed as paralyzed or diseased and whose intellectual powers atrophy as he loses touch with his hands and body). The narrator of **"All Souls'"** (significantly, the title suggests the universality of the soul's link with the supernatural), the cousin of Sara Clayburn, the woman who encounters the ghost, insists that ghosts didn't go out when "electric lights came in" (252). She also suggests that it is people like Sara who are most susceptible to ghosts, simply because they suffer from a lapse of the imagination, as they rely heavily on the false light of technology and logic: "it's generally not the high-strung and imaginative who see ghosts, but the calm matter-of-fact people who don't believe in them, and are sure they wouldn't mind if they

did see one? Well, that was the case with Sara Clayburn and her house . . ." (252). In fact, the narrator's obsession with explaining her haunted cousin's fate may emanate in part from her own "matter-of-fact" rational self, which puts her at the same risk as her "modern" cousin. The cousin-narrator clearly expresses that of all the relatives she is "more likely than anybody else to be able to get at the facts, as far as they can be called facts, and as anybody can get at them" (252). Ostensibly, the cousin-narrator and Sara suffer (initially—before Sara's breakdown) from the same practical, level-headed outlook on life.

However, the narrator makes the point that one need not retrace one's steps back to England to discover a ghost; in fact, she sounds a great deal like Hawthorne pleading the case that New England would offer as much material for his romances as Old England. However, once again, the turn of the screw is that the real ghost story, the real terror, belongs to the modern New Englander. Wharton's narrator explains the misconception as she evokes a parody of the traditional ghost story: "As between turreted castles patrolled by headless victims with clanking chains, and the comfortable suburban house with a refrigerator and central heating where you feel, as soon as you're in it, *that there's something wrong,* give me the latter for sending a chill down the spine!" (252). The real horror then is the wasteland of urban sprawl and suburban uniformity; the frustration comes from not being able to break the continuity of meaningless gestures and conventions.

As Sara Clayburn's surname suggests, the class to which Sara belongs is rather rigid and unyielding; however, the steadfastness that traditionally belongs to the land-owning class is slipping away, and ironically, it is the servant/working class who are in control in this setting. After her husband's death, Sara Clayburn continues to inhabit her husband's Connecticut Colonial estate, which has housed three generations of Clayburns. Though the Clayburns have been considered a "good influence" on the countryside, it is also obvious that they have exploited the land and perhaps usurped power: "There was a lot of land about it, and Jim Clayburn, like his fathers before him, farmed it, not without profit, and played a considerable and respected part in state politics" (254). It is obvious that one does not need European history to reclaim the sins of the fathers—that New England history does just as well. Though the Clayburn estate was built in circa 1780, it "was open, airy, high-ceilinged, with electricity, central heating, and all the modern appliances" (252), and the past and present clash in Sara's All-Souls' night breakdown.

The Clayburns, indeed, seem excessively civilized, in the most corrupt sense of possessing the most modern accouterments and in subjugating the wills of the townspeople and servants. It is rather ironic, then, when Sara suffers from a fall and finds herself totally dependent on the servants, who abandon her for an evening (and who, according to the rational narrator, go off on an All Souls' witch's vigil, at the prompting of a ghost). Left to her own devices, Sara becomes a bundle of nerves as she is cut off from civilization, as surely as the house's electricity and telephone lines are cut for the night. She awakens to a house of "Silence. A deep nocturnal silence in that day-lit house" (258) and is terrified by the equally silent snow outside: "It [snow] was still falling, with a business-like regularity, muffling the outer world in layers on layers of thick white velvet and intensifying the silence within. A noiseless world . . ." (259). She is temporarily crippled from her fall, so she crawls to the kitchen for sustenance, and, literally groping in the dark, she finds something much more terrifying than the female ghost she encountered earlier in the morning. If, at first, the terrifying silence of being alone is disturbing, the encounter with the bodiless voice is maddening: the silence is broken by "a man's voice, low and emphatic, and which she had never heard before" (264). Her earlier fears emanated from the too white landscape, with its "business-like" monotony, and the white noise of silence: "Her previous terrors had been speculative, conjectural, a ghostly emanation of the surrounding silence" (264), but now she is struck to the core by this strange unintelligible voice. It is none other than the blasting of the radio: the voice of the "invisible stranger" is "passionately earnest, almost threatening" and is incomprehensible to her (he was speaking "a language unknown to her" (264). Significantly, she loses consciousness, not at the sight of a ghost, but at the sight of the monster of the twentieth century—the deadening radio: "in the middle of the perfectly scoured table stood a portable wireless, and the voice she heard came out of it" (264). (It is the same feeling of contempt that Thoreau describes in the "Economy" section of *Walden* towards the telegraph, the railroad, and the transatlantic cable.) The horror of it is that the electrical current is ostensibly cut, but still there is noise and no silent realm to which to retreat.

In the end, Wharton's ghost stories suggest that there is a higher realm of knowing than what the practical world of business teaches us. In the post-Darwinian, post-Freudian milieu of Wharton's settings, all reality becomes suspect, and there is no particular way to interpret the phenomenon of ghosts. In the preface to her ghost stories, Wharton chides the type of ghost-seeker emerging in England, the type of person who wants to "validate" or "authenticate" the appearance of a particular ghost in a particular mansion. That pseudo-empiricist is uninteresting to her. For her, "the warm darkness of the prenatal fluid" ("**Preface**" 1) is associated with the ghost-seeing power or intuitive faculty, but this "ghost instinct" is "being gradually atrophied by those two worldwide enemies of the imagination, the wireless and the cinema" (2). Ultimately, Wharton seems to suggest that the pre-Darwinian ghost is still significant, that some other mode of perceiving reality is deep within each individual and is linked to some distant universal past. Or in Emersonian terminology, one could say that Wharton looks back to a Transcendentalist ethos. To Emerson, the reality of the Materialists is based on "experience," while that of the Idealists is founded on "consciousness"; the former group "think from the data of the senses," whereas the latter "perceive that the senses are not final, and say, 'The senses give us representations of things, but what are the things themselves, they cannot tell'" ("The Transcendentalist" 239). While the Materialist is weighed down by the "external world," the Transcendentalist, much like Wharton's ghost-feeler, "believes in miracle, in the perpetual openness of the human mind to new influx of light and power; he believes in inspiration . . ." (243).

In this context, one should recall the words of a doubter, the bachelor-narrator of "**Kerfol**," who, with his fortune, can afford to buy a solitary and romantic but dilapidated old house in Brittany, especially since the owners are "dead broke, and it's going for a song" (80). He begins to be absorbed by the atmosphere of the place, "Certainly no house had ever more completely and finally broken with the present. . . . I wanted only to sit there and be penetrated by the weight of its silence" (81). Overcome "by the pressure of the invisible," he experiences the collision of past and present values, of material and spiritual realms, and begins to see anew as he recreates and relives the history of the former inhabitants: "I was beginning to want to know more; not to *see* more—I was by now so sure it was not a question of seeing—but to feel more: feel all the place had to communicate" (81-82). Once again, Wharton has been able to convert yet another skeptical protagonist (and simultaneously, the reader) from "ghost-seer" to "ghost-feeler."

Notes

1. Wharton, *Ghost Stories*, 3. Further references to Wharton's ghost stories are to this edition, unless otherwise indicated. "A Bottle of Perrier" is cited from the Lewis collection of short stories. *The Ghost Stories of Edith Wharton* (Scribner's, 1973) is somewhat different from the original Appleton-Century edition of Wharton's *Ghosts* (1937). Among other changes in the reprint are the inclusion of "An Autobiographical Postscript" from "Life and I" and the substitution of "The Looking-Glass" for "A Bottle of Perrier" (McDowell 313).

2. Cf. Judith Fryer; though she does not speak about the ghost story at great length, she does mention that the ghost stories as well as the major novels share an underlying dichotomy: Wharton explored "the issues of social order and the wildness of individual abandon . . ." (199).

   See also Margaret McDowell, who examines Wharton's later ghost stories in an effort to understand Wharton's relationship with the past and to explore Wharton's concern with "the intimate connection of body with spirit" (293), especially as it relates to aging and death.

3. For a discussion of Wharton's complex relationship with her servants, see Erlich, who discusses one of Wharton's most intimate (and earliest) relationships— with her nanny: "Wharton regarded her nanny as a benevolent goddess who wrapped her in a cocoon of safety, but even good care proffered by a nursemaid is a commodity purchased by parents who renounce this role for themselves" (7).

   Cf. also Carol Singley, who analyzes Wharton's Gothic story "A Bottle of Perrier" in terms of "the interrelations of sexuality, class, race, and power as functions of both the female and male gothic" (272); significantly, Singley chooses a Wharton Gothic story dominated by males to show that Wharton ". . . not only critiques patriarchal power and the damaging sexual relations it spawns, but she offers a fleeting glimpse of what these new, revisionary relations may be" (272-273).

4. For a discussion of the use of the letter, the cable, and the telegraph as a structural and dramatic device in Wharton's novels, see Jean Frantz Blackall's informative essay; she focuses on the telegram as emphatic and representative of the "authoritative voice, or the intrusive presence of its sender" (164).

5. For readings of the Persephone myth in Wharton, see Candace Waid, who analyzes mother-daughter relationships using the myth of Persephone as well as the position of the woman writer (195-203). See also Josephine Donovan for a discussion of the Demeter-Persephone myth in terms of the mother-daughter dynamics in Wharton's fiction (43-83), and see also Erlich (42-25).

6. This fear of the "rest cure" might be a manifestation of Wharton's own fears of inertia, since, as a young woman, Wharton was sent to Philadelphia for S. Weir Mitchell's famous "rest treatment" (Lewis 82-84). Like Faxon, too, she felt that she was constantly under surveillance during the treatment; in Lewis's words, she felt that "ghostly presences were peering in on her morning and night" (84).

Works Cited

Bernstein, Stephen. "Form and Ideology in the Gothic Novel." *Essays in Literature* 18 (Fall, 1991): 151-165.

Blackall, Jean Frantz. "The Intrusive Voice: Telegrams in *The House of Mirth* and *The Age of Innocence*." *Women's Studies* 20 (Dec. 1991): 163-168.

Conn, Peter. *The Divided Mind: Ideology and Imagination in America, 1898-1917*. New York: Cambridge University Press, 1983.

Donovan, Josephine. *After the Fall: The Demeter-Persephone Myth in Wharton, Cather, and Glasgow*. University Park: Pennsylvania State University Press, 1989.

Emerson, R. W. *Emerson in His Journals*. Ed. Joel Porte. Cambridge, Massachusetts: Belknap Press, 1982.

——. "The Transcendentalist" and "The Poet." *Ralph Waldo Emerson: Selected Essays*. Ed. Larzer Ziff. New York: Penguin, 1982: 239-258, 259-284.

Erlich, Gloria C. *The Sexual Education of Edith Wharton*. Berkeley: University of California Press, 1992.

Fryer, Judith. *Felicitous Space: The Imaginative Structures of Edith Wharton and Willa Cather*. Chapel Hill: University of North Carolina Press, 1986.

Lewis, R. W. B. *Edith Wharton: A Biography*. New York: Harper & Row, 1975.

McDowell, Margaret B. "Edith Wharton's Ghost Tales Reconsidered." *Edith Wharton: New Critical Essays*. Eds. Alfred Bendixen and Annette Zilversmit. New York: Garland, 1992. 291-314.

Singley, Carol. J. "Gothic Borrowings and Innovations in Edith Wharton's 'A Bottle of Perrier.'" *Edith Wharton: New Critical Essays*. Eds. Alfred Bendixen and Annette Zilversmit. New York: Garland, 1992. 271-290.

Thoreau, Henry David. *Walden and "Civil Disobedience."* New York: Penguin, 1983.

Waid, Candace. *Edith Wharton's Letters from the Underworld: Fictions of Women and Writing*. Chapel Hill, North Carolina: University of Chapel Hill Press, 1991.

Wharton, Edith. *A Backward Glance*. New York: Scribner's, 1933.

——. "A Bottle of Perrier" and "Atrophy." *The Collected Short Stories of Edith Wharton*. Vol. II. Ed. R. W. B. Lewis. New York: Scribner's, 1968. 511-531, 501-510.

——. "Life and I." *Novellas and Other Writings*. Ed. Cynthia Griffin Wolff. New York: The Library of America, 1990. 1071-1096.

——. *The Ghost Stories of Edith Wharton*. New York: Scribner's, 1973.

——. *The Letters of Edith Wharton*. Eds. R. W. B. Lewis and Nancy Lewis. New York: Collier, 1988.

——. *The Writing of Fiction*. New York: Charles Scribner's Sons, 1925.

Widdicombe, Toby. "Wharton's 'The Angel at the Grave' and the Glories of Transcendentalism: Deciduous or Evergreen?" *American Transcendental Quarterly* 6:1 (1992): 47-57.

KATHY A. FEDORKO (ESSAY DATE 1995)

SOURCE: Fedorko, Kathy A. "The Gothic Text: Life and Art." In *Gender and the Gothic in the Fiction of Edith Wharton*, pp. 1-21. Tuscaloosa: University of Alabama Press, 1995.

In the following essay, Fedorko maintains that "the Gothic in her fiction allows Wharton both to mirror and to revise issues that inform her life as well as the genre."

Wharton's conflicting and conflicted views of women and men and feminine and masculine reflect a complicated interweaving of family and social environment, historical time, and individual psychology. These conditions and the gender tension they foster in turn provide the impetus for Wharton to use and recast Gothic conventions and narratives in her fiction as a way to dramatize psychic conflict. Indeed, as a dreamlike interaction among parts of the self, the Gothic in her fiction allows Wharton both to mirror and to revise issues that inform her life as well as the genre: an ambivalent terror of/attraction to the supernatural and the threatening; a fascination with incest; a fearful ambivalence about marriage, about breaking out of social restraints, about being "different"; and an attraction to houses as signs of self and to the "abyss" as a state of being beyond the rational. Wharton's handling of these issues distinctly evolves throughout her career. In the process, Wharton progressively imagines a fe/male self, moving from gender-bound women and men in the Gothic-marked fiction written early in her career to characters in the later fiction who struggle toward or even attain a degree of gender mutuality.

Family and Society

Wharton's autobiographies—the published version, *A Backward Glance* (1934) and the unpublished version, "Life and I"[1]—and her autobiographically colored nonfiction *French Ways and Their Meaning* and *The Writing of Fiction* document the personal and professional struggles that drew Wharton to a Gothic perspective. "Life and I" also vividly dramatizes that perspective, for in it Wharton remembers her child self as a Gothic heroine—trapped in suffocating interiors, suppressed by patriarchal restraints embodied by her mother, isolated by her writing and tortured by her acute sensibilities, but at the same time pleasurably, even erotically, charged by those sensibilities. As a passionate, secret lover of words and literature, Wharton felt herself to be the isolated, emotionally orphaned heroine, alone in her "other side," a supernatural world where

the flow and energy of words brought ecstatic release while producing inordinate guilt because she was so "different" ("**Life**" 23, 36). This intermingling of eroticism and fear, pleasure and pain, is the quintessential Gothic psychology.

"**Life and I**" demonstrates Wharton's uneasiness with the patriarchal value system that tells women they are worthwhile only if they are attractive, especially to men, and that they risk being excluded if they are intelligent or strong willed or in any other way "unfeminine."[2] "To look pretty" is one of the "deepest-seated instincts of my nature," Wharton writes there. Her clarification of this instinct identifies her as both gazed-at (female) art piece and (male) artist: "I say 'to look pretty' instead of 'to be admired,' because I really believe it has always been an aesthetic desire, rather than a form of vanity. I always saw the visible world as a series of pictures, more or less harmoniously composed, & the wish *to make the picture prettier* was, as nearly as I can define it, the form my feminine instinct of pleasing took" ("**Life**" 1-2).

Wharton's earliest memory, with which she begins *A Backward Glance*, is of being dressed beautifully while walking with her father and realizing for the first time the value of being a "subject for adornment" (2). Yet at the same time, in "**Life and I**," she confesses humiliation about being laughed at by her brothers for her red hair and the "supposed abnormal size" of her hands and feet; she was, she felt, "the least good-looking of the family" and therefore intensely conscious of her "physical short comings" (37).

Though pronouncing at a young age that when she grew up she wanted to be "the best dressed woman in New York" like her mother, Wharton felt herself no match and no daughter for the elegant Lucretia Jones (**BG** 20). While she recalls her "tall splendid father" as "always so kind," with strong arms that "held one so safely," and her childhood nurse Doyley as "the warm cocoon" in which she "lived safe and sheltered," she remembers that her mother's abounding interest in flounced dresses and ermine scarves was accompanied by her indolence and capriciousness, that her mother stressed politeness and reserve rather than nurturing (20, 26). This model of old New York womanhood upheld the patriarchy with her "shoulds" and "musts," her withering judgmental demeanor, and her physical reserve, an outcome, perhaps, of her own "internalized oppression" that she encouraged in her daughter (Wehr 18). Sandra Gilbert describes Wharton's situation in her comment that "the more fully the mother represents culture, the more inexorably she tells the daughter that she cannot have a mother because she has been signed with and assigned to the Law of the Father," the law that means "culture is by definition both patriarchal and phallocentric" ("Life's" 358).

Even speaking was a hazardous business for the precocious, acutely sensitive young Edith, because, in Wharton's view, her mother scorned verbal imperfection and risk taking. Over sixty years later the daughter writes, "I still wince under my mother's ironic smile when I said that some visitor had stayed 'quite a while,' and her dry: 'Where did you pick *that* up?'" (**BG** 49). The anger is palpable in the memory that "my parents—or at least my mother—laughed at me for using 'long words,' & for caring for dress (in which heaven knows she set me the example!); & under this perpetual cross-fire of criticism I became a painfully shy self-conscious child" ("**Life**" 37). And a shy adult. For throughout *A Backward Glance* runs the theme of her "incorrigible shyness" that she blames time and again for missed opportunities of intimacy. The mute girl is mirrored in the passive female Gothic character, holding her tongue, afraid to question, unable to defend herself.[3]

It is worth remembering that "the image of the repressive mother is the daughter's *creation*" and that Wharton's autobiographies should not be assumed to be factual documents (Fryer 359-60 n.4).[4] Although there are hints in *A Backward Glance* about Lucretia's difficult childhood, we have no "backward glance" from Lucretia to counter her daughter's perspective and to help us understand her own childhood pain and losses. Still, however skewed Wharton's memories of her mother, her perception was that she was rejected by a cold mother who criticized and restrained more than she accepted and nurtured. From her Wharton learns the intense self-criticism, the self-hating voice, that women internalize from patriarchal judgment of them as inadequate. Wharton's reiteration in "**Life and I**" that she "frankly despised" little girls clearly seems to include herself (12). This "self-hater" turns up in her Gothic short stories as the female victim who colludes in her own destruction and as the villainous male who oppresses the passive woman (Wehr 20).[5]

As a child Wharton is beset by "the most excruciating moral tortures" instilled by her internalized mother ("**Life**" 2). She illustrates this point with an anecdote about telling a little boy in her dance class that their dance teacher's mother looks like an old goat. When she admits to the teacher that she made the remark, she gains a scolding and the tormented sense that her own mother would have thought her "naughty" not to have known how to do the "right" thing ("**Life**" 7). Noting that she had two "inscrutable beings" to please, God and her mother, and that her mother was the most inscrutable of the two, Wharton confesses that "this vexed problem of truth-telling, & the impossibility of reconciling 'Gods' standard of truthfulness with the conventional obligation to be 'polite' & not hurt anyone's feelings" plunged her into a "darkness of horror" (6-7).

Wharton's intense moral anxiety resembles the impetus for traditional Gothic fantasy of the eighteenth century, springing as it did from uneasiness about "problems of personal moral responsibility and judgement, questions of restrictive convention, and a troubled awareness of irrational impulses which threatened to subvert orthodox notions of social and moral propriety" (Howells 7). Wharton's girlhood, as she perceives it, thus is haunted by a late nineteenth-century version of the "grim realities" of eighteenth-century womanhood that inspired Ann Radcliffe's and Fanny Burney's Gothic, "the restraints on her freedom, all the way to actual imprisonment; the mysterious, unexplained social rituals; the terrible need always to appear, as well as always to be, virtuous; and, over all, the terrible danger of slippage from the respectable to the unrespectable class of womanhood" (Moers 206-207).

Bourgeois men were actors in the eighteenth-century world, and women were passive possessions whose good behavior was often the deciding factor in their material well-being. Female respectability involved passive obedience to male authority, since women were seen as "inescapably Other" (Day 95). Societal emphasis on reason and repression of feeling, the "male" sphere, made that which was repressed, the "female" sphere, all the more threatening and thereby in need of destruction or imprisonment. The rebellious Gothic probed fears, spoke the unspeakable, meddled in the taboo, like rape, sex among the clergy, and, especially, incest. Social institutions like the church and the family, symbolized by the ruined church or castle, were considered claustrophobic and hypocritical because they suppressed and denied part of human experience.

Initially Wharton's "devastating passion" for "making up" stories as a child was a way of finding release from a threatening, confining, judgmental world into a supernatural one ("**Life**" 11).

The sound and sight of words produced "sensuous rapture," regardless of her inability to understand them (10). She writes in **"Life and I"** that words "sang to me so bewitchingly that they almost lured me from the wholesome noonday air of childhood into some strange supernatural region, where the normal pleasures of my age seemed as insipid as the fruits of the earth to Persephone after she had eaten of the pomegranate seed" (10). Wharton might well be describing immersion in *le sémiotique,* Julia Kristeva's term for a pre-Oedipal, preverbal, sensual state associated with the maternal voice and bodily rhythms. The sensuousness of language thus provides the young Wharton with a haunted maternal bower, a "secret garden."[6]

Even when Wharton learns the meanings of words, it isn't intellectual discourse but rather the language of erotic secrecy and mystery, of supernatural otherworldliness that pervades her descriptions of immersion in books. She feels a "secret ecstasy of communion" with the books in her father's library: Coleridge; Goethe's *Faust* and *Wilhelm Meister; The Duchess of Malfi; The White Devil;* the "Song of Solomon"; Irving's *Tales of the Alhambra,* no small dose of the romantic, the erotic, the Gothic (*BG* 69). These "enraptured sessions" with poetry, philosophy, religion, and drama become part of her "secret retreat" within her where she "wished no one to intrude" (70). "Words and cadences haunted it like song-birds in a magic wood," nurturing the way her mother did not (70). Her father's library becomes analogous to "my strange inner world," conflating the symbolic and spiritual, the paternal and maternal (72). In Wharton's Gothic, startling, disorienting, and often erotic discoveries take place in libraries, as intellectual knowledge is expanded by intuitive, uncanny awareness.[7]

Wharton's dilemma as female child and woman is that intellectual knowledge and activities endow male-identified power at the same time that they estrange her from her female self as it has been defined by her society and her mother. Discovering Sir William Hamilton's *History of Philosophy* in her brother's room gives the young Wharton the hope that "now I should never be that helpless blundering thing, a mere 'little girl,' again!" (**"Life"** 32-33). But her intense intelligence and engagement with language also increase her sense of abnormality. As she confesses, "it humiliated me to be so 'different'" (36). The social ramifications of difference were clear. According to an 1882 story in the *Newport Daily News* the engagement between Edith Jones and Harry Stevens, when she was nineteen, was broken because of "an alleged preponderance of intellectuality on the part of the intended bride" (Lewis, *Biography* 45).

Her own writing intensified Wharton's gender conflict. This public, and thereby unfeminine, act was met with silent disapproval: "My literary success puzzled and embarrassed my old friends far more than it impressed them, and in my own family it created a kind of constraint which increased with the years. None of my relations ever spoke to me of my books, either to praise or blame—they simply ignored them; and among the immense tribe of my New York cousins, though it included many with whom I was on terms of affectionate intimacy, the subject was avoided as though it were a kind of family disgrace, which might be condoned but could not be forgotten" (*BG* 143-44). In having her own writing avoided as though it were a "family disgrace," Wharton faced the quintessential woman writer's dilemma. Writing is a fearful, "naughty" thing to do, for it involves honesty of feeling, assertiveness, and noticing and talking of things not polite to acknowledge. Like sex, it is fraught with guilt, this uncontrolled, unladylike, other-worldly act. Hélène Cixous, in urging women to "write her self," shows that Wharton's dilemma is still a current one for women: "Where is the ebullient, infinite woman who, immersed as she was in her naiveté, kept in the dark about herself, led into self-disdain by the great arm of parental-conjugal phallocentrism, hasn't been ashamed of her strength? Who, surprised and horrified by the fantastic tumult of her drives (for she was made to believe that a well-adjusted normal woman has a . . . divine composure), hasn't accused herself of being a monster? Who, feeling a funny desire stirring inside her (to sing, to write, to dare to speak, in short, to bring out something new), hasn't thought she was sick?" (**"The Laugh"** 876).[8]

The denial by silence of Wharton's writing by her extended family and their dread of creativity is not unlike the denial of intense and sometimes supernatural experiences by characters in her Gothic stories. Their attempted suppression of disorienting awareness is undermined when the reader joins Wharton in an act of voyeurism and recognition as the story plays itself out.[9]

Her family relationships and experiences were not Wharton's only impetus for using Gothic conventions and narratives in her fiction as a way to tell the disallowed story of female sexuality and power. Her Victorian/Post-Victorian Anglo-Saxon society, with its penchant for ignoring what it considered inappropriate human experience, was an impetus as well. In *French Ways and Their Meaning,* Wharton describes maturity in a society as the ability to face primal terrors. "Intellectual honesty, the courage to look at things as they are," she writes, "is the first test of mental maturity. Till a society ceases to be afraid of the truth in the domain of ideas it is in leading-strings, morally and mentally" (58-59).

One of the main aspects of life to which Wharton refers in the phrase "things as they are" is sexuality. The French, she observes, are criticized by Anglo-Saxons for talking and writing freely about sexuality, as if to do so were "inconsistent with . . . purity and morality." Wharton notes approvingly that the French just take sex for granted "as part of the great parti-coloured business of life" (60, ellipsis mine).

Wharton felt that Anglo-Saxon literature had been no better than the society at acknowledging female sexuality in particular. In *The Writing of Fiction* she argues that English novelists create women whose passion is banked by prudery. Scott, for instance, "became conventional and hypocritical when he touched on love and women," substituting "sentimentality for passion" and reducing his heroines to "'Keepsake' insipidities" (5). Thackeray, Dickens, Brontë, and Eliot were also affected by the "benumbing" restraints of their time (63).

Wharton's own portrayal of passionate women in her novels was hindered not only because, as Elizabeth Ammons argues, she felt the American woman she wrote about "was far from being . . . a whole human being" but also because her society, her background, and the very form of realism resisted such portrayal (3, ellipsis mine). In *A Backward Glance,* Wharton recounts that early in her career she had a reader protest, "have you never known a respectable woman? If you have, in the name of decency write about her!" (126) Those were the days, she remembers, when an editor stipulated that no "unlawful attachment" should appear in her projected novel and when her friend Charles Eliot Norton warned that "no great work of the imagination has ever been based on illicit passion" (126-27). But decades later the situation remained unchanged. The *Saturday Evening Post, Liberty,* and *Collier's* wouldn't publish *Hudson River Bracketed* and *The Gods Arrive* because of the "illicit liaison" in them, and the editor of *Delineator,* which finally did publish them, commented that "the situation, that of a man and woman unmarried and living together, is a little startling for magazine publication" (Lewis, *Biography* 502).

Wharton's anger about the problem of portraying sexuality in literature surfaced most heatedly when she chided younger novelists for not realizing that portraying whole people, complete with passions, had been difficult for their predecessors. In a 1931 letter to Sinclair Lewis she rebukes him for the depreciatory comments he had made about Howells in his Nobel acceptance address; Wharton points out that Howells had to contend with a country "reeking with sentimentality and shuddering with prudery" (Dupree 265). She returns to the matter in *A Backward Glance,* commenting bitterly that "the poor novelists who were my contemporaries . . . had to fight hard for the right to turn the wooden dolls about which they were expected to make believe into struggling suffering human beings. . . . The amusing thing about this turn of the wheel is that we who fought the good fight are now jeered at as the prigs and prudes who barred the way to complete expression" (127, ellipsis mine).

Contemporary critical discussion of realism has shown that the difficulty of portraying passions in realistic fiction that Wharton pinpointed (and a reason why she relied on a Gothic subtext to show passion constrained) is a problem inherent in the form. The dilemma is the very strength of realistic fiction, Leo Bersani has argued; its recreation of social structures militates against a full portrayal of the forces that would deny their validity. "The technical premises of realistic fiction—the commitment to intelligible, 'full' characters, to historical verisimilitude, to the revealing gesture or episode, to a closed temporal frame—already dooms any adventure in the stimulating improbabilities, of behavior which resists being 'placed' and interpreted in a general psychological or formal structure" (67). Because it keeps characters coherent, "the containment of desire is a triumph for social stability" (73).

Feminist criticism has enlarged the conversation about how this "containment of desire" in deference to "social stability" is a culturally created gender issue, a containment of the "natural" feminine/maternal by the "symbolic" masculine/paternal. Often "submerged meanings" appear in women's writing as surreal or uncanny eruptions in and interruptions of the text (Gilbert and Gubar, *Madwoman* 72). Grace Poole's intrusion into Jane's story in *Jane Eyre* is one of the most discussed examples. A novel such as *Villette,* as well, which seemingly doesn't recognize the Romantic or Gothic, nonetheless can be said to possess a "buried letter of Romanticism" and "the phantom of feminism" conveying "the discourse of the Other, as the novel's unconscious . . . struggles for articulation within the confines of midnineteenth-century realism" (Jacobus, "Buried Letter" 42, 59; ellipsis mine).

Brontë's texts have been called examples of "new" Gothic in that intense feeling and extrarational experience are not only contained in "marvelous circumstance" but interpenetrate the "ordinary world" and thereby enlarge the sense of reality in the novels, especially the reality of women (Heilman 123, 121). Traditional Gothic male villains are deconstructed when "dark magnetic energy" characterizes female protagonists (127). Such a view privileges the realist form with which Wharton was comfortable in her novels but into which, like Brontë, she interwove a Gothic text to accommodate the gender tension central to her life as a writer.

The Abyss

Wharton's sense of being an outsider, the "separated one," as a precocious child and a woman writer, uncomfortable with the male-identified power of writing and the intellect while at the same time lured by the nourishing female-identified "rich world of dreams" and the sound and sight of words, helps explain her use of mystical/supernatural rather than "realistic" language to describe her creative process, the goddess's descent into the soul, as she puts it (Wilt 19; "Life" 12; *BG* 198). The moment of creation is akin to the mysterious moment just before sleep when "one falls over the edge of consciousness" (*BG* 198). Similarly, the storytelling process "takes place in some secret region on the sheer edge of consciousness" where characters haunt the brain and names spectrally appear without characters (205). The creative act is "like the mystic's union with the Unknowable" (121) or "that mysterious fourth-dimensional world which is the artist's inmost sanctuary (*WF* 119)."[10]

Wharton's language of creativity—the "unknown depths," the "sheer edge of consciousness," the mysterious and the spectral—is the language of her Gothic as well. Characters anxiously facing the dark abyss of preternatural knowledge or entering a mysterious life removed from society in the Gothic stories and the Gothic-marked novels replicate Wharton's creative process of entering the "unknown depths." Wharton's Gothic thus enacts the writing process as a plunge into awareness beyond the realistic, where the unexpurgated "real" story is told, the "unla-beled, disallowed, disavowed" of which her patriarchal mother and society would not approve (Stein 126).

The omnipresent Gothic abyss traditionally threatens damnation, a fall into "the demonic underworld" that leads to "the rejection of human identity and the embracing of the monstrous" (MacAndrew 49; Day 7). Rather than this chaotic loss of humanity, the abyss as Wharton uses it is a plunge into a realm that threatens loss of the controlled self at the same time that it promises new understanding. And what realm could be more frightening and yet more alluring for this unmothered daughter of the patriarchy than the feminine/maternal darkness, with its overwhelming intimacy and primal power?

Wharton acknowledges the occult power of the maternal when she places the faculty for apprehending ghosts in "the warm darkness of the pre-natal fluid far below our conscious reason" (*G* vii). Her Gothic portrayals of inner journeys into threatening knowledge take characters into maternal places: houses, cabins, caves. Within the place within the mind of the character, an abyss opens, threatening annihilation at the same time that it promises self-awareness if s/he can acknowledge the experience.[11]

Facing the abyss is crucial to Wharton's Gothic, for the willingness of characters to face the maternal darkness indicates their willingness to understand the inner life, the loss of the known self that has opened before them. Arrogant intellectual men in her Gothic fiction are usually those least willing to acknowledge what they have seen in the abyss and most apt to ignore or deny their experience with the darkness. Wharton seems to be mirroring her sense of the limitations of her own rationality, of the patriarchal symbolic, her sense that, emphasized at the expense of respect for the maternal erotic darkness, such logocentrism becomes tyrannical and repressive.[12] Since the characters, especially in the stories, are themselves too timid to fully assimilate what they have experienced, Wharton depends on the reader to decipher their lost knowledge. Thus the woman's story is heard despite the attempts of the male narrator or other (usually male) character to deny or suppress it.

Contemporary feminist criticism of the Gothic argues that what draws a woman in particular to the "forbidden center" of the Gothic mystery is not threatened incest within the Oedipal plot, a reading that privileges the male reader, but rather "the spectral presence of a dead-undead mother, archaic and all-encompassing, a ghost signifying the problematics of femininity which the heroine must confront" (Kahane, "Gothic Mirror" 336).[13] The "ubiquitous Gothic precipice on the edge of the maternal blackness" thus draws female characters to a confrontation with the mysteries of identity (340).

Sexual maturity, the secret knowledge and power of the mother, is both feared and desired. "Bad" women the heroine confronts in the Gothic text are the "monstrous" other parts of herself, and the parts of the mother, that she cannot accept—her passions, her ambitions, her energy (Stein 123ff.). The Gothic gives "*visual* form to the fear of self," the dark, knowing mother/self who might appear in the fiction as a mad woman or a freak or a sexual monster and therefore beyond the pale of respectable society (Moers 163). Wharton gives such "visual form to the fear of self" when Lily Bart has her disturbing vision of herself in the mirror early in *The House of Mirth* and in the mirror of her thoughts after Trenor's attempted rape. Wharton's own fear of her sexual self is reflected in the exaggerated mirroring of Lily's vaguely erotic activities by the omnivorously sexual Bertha Dorset.

Wharton's use of the abyss in her Gothic fiction as a character's disorienting confrontation with primal human emotion or experience recalls Jung's theory of individuation, "the process by which a person becomes a psychological 'individual,' that is, a separate, indivisible unity or 'whole,'" by assimilating knowledge from the unconscious as part of consciousness (9[1]:275). This process has been called an adaptation to inner reality as well as outer, to what one is "meant to be"; one recognizes the next step in what one is meant to be by looking for what attracts and frightens at the same time (Whitmont 48-49, 62). The "rebirth journey," as individuation has been called, brings to consciousness "the lost values of the psyche, which lie so largely in the realm of Eros, and by this means the human being becomes more complete" (Harding 245). The goal of the journey is an assimilation of gender selves, inner and outer worlds, consciousness with unconsciousness.[14]

Jung conforms with most androcentric Western theory in his association of consciousness with the masculine and unconsciousness with the feminine. "Psychologically the self is a union of conscious (masculine) and unconscious (feminine). It stands for the psychic totality" (9[2]:268). These realms accrue, however, the sexist associations of reasonable, reasoning masculine consciousness as opposed to feared, fearful feminine unconsciousness. In Jung's theory the male hero's plunge into the abyss of the unconscious involves confronting his "shadow," the hated, repressed side of the personality and thereafter the "anima," the archetypal image of the female in a man's unconsciousness, an awesome, organic power associated with the Terrible Mother or with a dual mother, part destructive, part creative (Wehr 59-67, 112-13). The ultimate encounter is thus with an Other that must be overcome to be assimilated.

Feminist archetypal critics have revised Jungian theory to make it more compatible with women's experiences as women themselves have written about them. The shadow a woman confronts often carries with it the gynophobia of the social world that fuses with the animus (the archetypal image of the male in a woman's unconscious) into "a masculine character who loathes the woman as much as she loathes herself" (Pratt, "Spinning" 104). Annis Pratt cautions that for women the rebirth journey entails psychological risk that is as likely to lead to madness as to renewal (*Archetypal* 142). But women may also overcome this self-destructiveness and assimilate a mother/self that engenders a sense of female power and erotic independence by accepting rather than fearing the life forces of sexuality, birth, and death. Thus "the woman's encounter with a feminine figure at the depths of her psyche . . . is more a fusion than an agon; the woman encounters a being similar to herself which empowers even as it exiles her from the social community," since she then becomes a woman unreconciled to a patriarchal world (Pratt, "Spinning" 106, ellipsis mine). In imagining this feminine archetype encountered in the inner world, women writers often draw on female-identified mythology: Demeter/Persephone, Celtic Grail legends, Ishtar/Tammuz rebirth legends, and witches and other wise women (Pratt, *Archetypal* 170). This is Wharton's practice in her Gothic-marked fiction.

While male reading of the Gothic places the "maternal blackness" beneath the ruined castle, "the crumbling shell of paternal authority," as imprisoning womb/tomb, feminist reading is more apt to identify the castle or other enclosure as the mother, "mother as nurturer, as sexual being, as body, as harboring a secret, as an indifferent hardness" (Fiedler 112; Holland and Sherman 289). The mother, especially for the woman reader, threatens nothingness, overwhelmingness, nonseparation (Holland and Sherman 283). The female Gothic character's entrapment in or exploration of a Gothic house is thus an extension of her relationship to the maternal body she shares (Kahane, "Gothic Mirror" 338).[15]

Kristeva's theory of the abject provides another way to read the abyss in Wharton's Gothic. Though Kristeva emphasizes the abject as a reiteration of *separation* from the maternal, her discussion of the self-awareness gained in the process of struggling against and being pulled into the abject sheds light on the response of Wharton's Gothic characters. Lying just on the edge of meaninglessness and nonexistence, the abject represents "our earliest attempts to release the hold of *maternal* entity even before ex-isting outside of her, thanks to the autonomy of language" (13). "The phantasmatic mother," constitutes, in the history of each person, "the abyss that must be established as an autonomous (and not encroaching) *place,* and *distinct* object, meaning a *signifiable* one," so that the person might "learn to speak" (100). In spite of this "placing," one does not "cease separating" from the abject; it retains the power to recreate the act of attempting to break away from the maternal entity punctuated by the pull back from it (13).

Reexperiencing the act of separation from the mother forces the limits of one's psychic world and the limits of self-knowledge. "The abject shatters the wall of repression and its judgments. It takes the ego back to its source on the abominable limits from which, in order to be, the ego has broken away. . . . Abjection is a resurrection that has gone through death (of the ego). It is an alchemy that transforms death drive into a start of life, of new significance" (15, ellipsis mine).

Such a definition of the abject as a rebirth into new understanding through the pull of the maternal abyss helps explain why Wharton's characters are both terrified of and attracted to extrarational experiences. Wharton's Gothic emphasizes the maternal abyss as "repellent and repelled" to those most frightened by it, yet Wharton also emphasizes that it is also a state of being that one must assimilate within oneself rather than reject or pull away from (6). In dramatizing primal experiences in her Gothic fiction—of ghosts, madness, and sexual threat—Wharton is courting disorder. She is pressing the limits of rationality and having her characters risk temporary egolessness for the sake of greater awareness, particularly of the feminine. She is speaking about those things considered unspeakable by her family and society—the erotic, the antisocial, the grotesque, the energetic, the

fearful—those emotions and conditions that, like the regression to the maternal, threaten to overwhelm one.[16]

Wharton dramatizes the power of the uncontrollable and overwhelming in her autobiographical account of recuperating, when she was nine years old, from a near-fatal bout of typhoid and of being given a book to read: "To an unimaginative child the tale would no doubt have been harmless; but it was a 'robber-story,' & with my intense Celtic sense of the super-natural, tales of robbers & ghosts were perilous reading. This one brought on a serious relapse, & again my life was in danger" (**"Life"** 17).

Thereafter, until she was a "young lady," she lived in "chronic fear" of an unexplained terror, "like some dark undefinable menace, forever dogging my steps" (17). Most terrifying was returning from daily walks outside with nurse, governess, or father and, while waiting for the door to her home to be opened, feeling the menace behind her, on top of her, and being "seized by a choking agony of terror" until she could escape inside (18). The memory suggests an overwhelming need to reconnect with the sheltering maternal body/house across the threshold. But the intensity of the "undefinable menace" that sends her to the mother also suggests an anxious fear of separation intensified by never having felt solidly connected in the first place. In Wharton's Gothic fiction, terror of the outside unknown is transmuted into terror of the internal unknown, within the house/mother rather than outside of it. Facing that terror is a courageous means of claiming and transforming it.

Wharton states, in **"Life and I,"** that until the age of twenty-seven or twenty-eight, she "could not sleep in the room with a book containing a ghost-story" (19). Using the progressive tense of recent occurrence, she admits, "I have frequently had to burn books of this kind, because it frightened me to know that they were down-stairs in the library!" (19). Such a sensational reaction to the threat posed by the supernatural—such books almost killed me and I subsequently burned them—reveals how much Wharton feared the uncontrollable and how much power she granted fiction as a means of recreating the terror of uncontrollable forces. Julia Briggs's idea that "by recounting nightmares, giving them speakable shapes and patterns" in "stories of the terrific unknown," we hope to "control them and come to terms with them" might well account for both

Wharton's autobiographical "confession" and her Gothic fiction that draws one into the "terrific unknown" (11).

In recasting the "abyss" as a restorative, regenerative place for those courageous enough to face it, Wharton reconceives its destructive power. Her several nervous breakdowns and her bouts of "occult and unget-at-able nausea" and overwhelming fatigue during the period when she was most conflicted about her identity as writer/wife/socialite/intellectual/homemaker made her familiar with the risks of the journey into the self (Wolff 52). Wharton's experience with the Weir Mitchell Rest Cure for her nervous collapse was more salutary than the experiences of Charlotte Perkins Gilman or Virginia Woolf, since she was encouraged to write during her time of separation from the outside world (Lewis, *Biography* 84). Nonetheless her imposed infantalization, during which she was barred from visitors yet felt "ghostly presences . . . peering in on her morning and night," reappears as a dominant theme in many of her Gothic stories (84). Walter Berry's comment in his letter of November 9, 1898, that he is "delighted to hear" that Wharton had "loosened the first stone in your cell toward an escape" suggests that Wharton saw herself as a prisoner during her "cure" (Beinecke).

Her visit with her dear friend Henry James during his period of despair in 1910 is another encounter with the abyss. She observes that his eyes are those of a man who "has looked on the Medusa," and as she sits beside him, she looks "into the black depths over which he is hanging—the superimposed 'abysses' of all his fiction" (Lewis and Lewis, *Letters* 202). Most notable for Wharton is that James is no longer in control of his emotions: "I, who have always seen him so serene, so completely the master of his wonderful emotional instrument . . . , I could hardly believe it was the same James who cried out to me his fear, his despair, his craving for the 'cessation of consciousness,' & all his unspeakable loneliness & need of comfort, & inability to be comforted!" (202, ellipsis mine).

Wharton later comments how "haunted" she has been by James's condition (203). The tension between complete mastery over one's emotions and being incapacitated by them is part of the gender-identified duality that Wharton dramatizes in her Gothic fiction. Ellen Olenska in *The Age of Innocence* is perhaps her most successful example of a character who exemplifies balance between the extremes, though it comes at the cost of "leaving home" for good. Because she has faced the

Medusa and the darkness of the abyss, Ellen possesses a maturity of mind and spirit that Newland Archer admires, even marvels at. He himself skirts the edge and the Medusa's gaze, thereby sacrificing the "flower of life" (*AI* 350).

Confronting the Medusa, without the deflecting mirror in which Perseus sought refuge, is one of Wharton's favorite ways of describing the act of facing powerful femaleness directly, unflinchingly. Yet the drama and tension of traditional female Gothic is in good part dependent on the *concealment* of female knowledge, the mysteries of birth, death, and sexuality, within the threatening maternal space of dungeon, castle, or haunted room. One female reader of the form, Leona Sherman, describes recreating in the Gothic a figurative confrontational dance with her mother about the essence of femaleness: "I know she knows but she won't tell me. I know I know, but I doubt because she won't tell me. She says one thing, but I see another on her face. I feel we can't really talk about what we know, because she would be calling her whole past life into question and endangering her present. She thinks the concealment necessary for my survival, and finally, she loves me and wants to protect me above all. The mysteries are the issues of sex and birth and death and, too, the necessity of concealing them" (Holland and Sherman 287).

Wharton describes in **"Life and I"** just such an evasive encounter with her mother about sexuality. I quote this much quoted passage in its entirety because Wharton's dramatic, even melodramatic, rendering of her request for information about the secret of sexuality so uncannily mirrors Sherman's description of a woman reading/recreating a Gothic story:

> . . . a few days before my marriage, I was seized with such a dread of the whole dark mystery, that I summoned up courage to appeal to my mother, & begged her, with a heart beating to suffocation, to tell me "what being married was like." Her handsome face at once took on the look of icy disapproval which I most dreaded. "I never heard such a ridiculous question!" she said impatiently; & I felt at once how vulgar she thought me.

> But in the extremity of my need I persisted. "I'm afraid, Mamma—I want to know what will happen to me!"

> The coldness of her expression deepened to disgust. She was silent for a dreadful moment; then she said with an effort: "You've seen enough pictures & statues in your life. Haven't you noticed that men are—made differently from women?"

> "Yes," I faltered blankly.

> "Well, then—?"

I was silent, from sheer inability to follow, & she brought out sharply: "Then for heaven's sake don't ask me any more silly questions. You can't be as stupid as you pretend!"

The dreadful moment was over, & the only result was that I had been convicted of stupidity for not knowing what I had been expressly forbidden to ask about, or even think of!

["**Life**" 34-35]

Wharton recreates herself here as the traditional Gothic heroine probing the dread-producing mother/castle for answers about "the whole dark mystery" of sexuality, but she leaves both uninformed and humiliated because she is so uninformed.

Perhaps because Wharton didn't believe, as Sherman posits, that the mother/Gothic denies the knowledge to the questing daughter because she "loves me and wants to protect me above all," in her own Gothic fiction Wharton turns the "Gothic denial" of "the whole dark mystery" of sexuality, birth, and death figured by the woman/mother on its head (Holland and Sherman 292, 287). By denying access to the mother and thereby to femaleness, both women and men wield patriarchal power, power defied by characters such as Charity Royall in *Summer* and Lady Jane Lynke in "Mr. Jones." More often, a character shrinks from rather than claims this powerful knowledge, and the reader is left with an awareness of the sacrifice that the character has made because of her or his timidity.

Notes

1. Cynthia Griffin Wolff posits that "Life and I" was written in 1920 or 1922 (417, n.3).

2. Wolff discusses the tension in Wharton between doing and being, between creating art and becoming a beautiful art object. See especially 40-43.

3. According to Wolff, Wharton's experiences taught her that "strong emotions of any kind were innately dangerous" (38). For the young Wharton nothing was worse than to be mute. "To be 'mute' . . . is to be vulnerable to pain," and words offered "the promise of an escape from loneliness and helplessness" (25-26, ellipsis mine). I argue that in the Gothic stories dangerous emotion is projected onto the dangerous man, preying upon the mute woman, whose imprisonment is partly a result of self-censorship. Although she doesn't mention the Gothic, Wolff discounts most of Wharton's ghost stories as inferior fiction.

4. Wolff also notes that the inclination "to fall into the formula of nasty mother and clever daughter" ignores the complexity of the relationship between Lucretia and Edith Jones (32). Erlich posits that Wharton's image of her mother may well have been "a projection of the child's need for punishment rather than an accurate description," but she acknowledges that whatever the "historical truth," Wharton's "internalized mother" was a "persecutory figure" (25, 26).

5. As Pablo Freire writes, "The oppressed suffer from the duality which has established itself in their innermost being. They discover that without freedom they cannot exist authentically. Yet, although they desire authentic existence, they fear it. They are at one and the same time themselves and the oppressor whose consciousness they have internalized" (32).

6. Several critics have noted that Wharton's use of "secret garden" in connection with her writing probably refers to Frances Hodgson Burnett's 1911 children's classic of the same name. What is important for my purposes are the similarities *The Secret Garden* bears both to Wharton's childhood and to her Gothic. At the beginning of the novel, two emotionally abandoned children, Mary and Colin, are angry, pale, and lonely, living together in what Mary calls a "queer house," where "everything is a kind of secret. Rooms are locked up and gardens are locked up" (159). Both think the other is a ghost when they first meet, both live in their own world of stories and dreams. Together they enter the secret, neglected garden, care for it, and are rejuvenated by the activity. This plot resembles Wharton's Gothic heroes/heroines entering the spirit of the mother in a mysterious enclosure and being shaken and changed by the encounter.

7. Erlich calls Frederick Jones's library Wharton's "emotional center" (32). She notes that Wharton even makes the connection in "Life and I" between the library and her self or body and that books and libraries are thereafter "libidinized" (34, 154). Carol J. Singley and Susan Elizabeth Sweeney discuss Wharton's anxiety about reading, in her father's library, books forbidden by her mother. They quote Paula Berggeren as even suggesting that in disobeying her mother Wharton is figuratively gazing on her "father's nakedness" in the library (185).

8. Gilbert and Gubar also identify the "anxiety of authorship" that a woman writer experiences because of "her culturally conditioned timidity about self-dramatization, her dread of the patriarchal authority of art, her anxiety about the impropriety of female invention" (*Madwoman* 50). Singley and Sweeney discuss how Wharton expresses her anxiety about reading and writing in the narrative of "Pomegranate Seed." My sense of Wharton's gender discomfort in relation to writing differs slightly but significantly from both of these useful studies. I believe Wharton felt anxious about writing not only because she was a woman but because speech and writing *do* have the potential to be aggressive, harmful acts regardless of which gender engages in them. Lucretia Jones's power to wound with words was an early model for her daughter of this potential. Thus although the culturally constructed anxiety Wharton felt about writing influenced her projective creation of menacing intellectual men in her Gothic fiction, she is also responding to her discomfort with destructive verbal power.

9. Howells refers to readers of the Gothic as "literary voyeurs" (15-16), and Wolstenholme extensively discusses this quality of the Gothic experience.

10. Fryer discusses the haunted quality of Wharton's creative process (158-59).

11. Wolff talks about Wharton's realization that good art develops from the artist's courage to plunge into the primal depths and confront "his most secret self" (9). Wolff stresses Wharton's need to outgrow and reject her relationship with her mother, however, while I see

Wharton attempting to assimilate and recreate her maternal relationship and using the Gothic abyss as a locus of this interaction.

12. A key characteristic of ghost stories by American women, according to Lynette Carpenter and Wendy K. Kolmar, is that they not only expand "reason" to include the supernatural but more often replace reason with sympathy as the key interpretive faculty (13).

13. Fleenor notes that "this confrontation can be seen in a literary context as the confrontation of the female author with the problem of being an author, not the father of her work but the mother of it" (16).

14. Jung's tendency to ignore socially derived, sexist assumptions in the construction of his archetypes, which I discuss earlier, also colors his theory of individuation; this emphasizes the importance of feminist archetypal criticism of women's rebirth journeys as portrayed in their writing.

15. Kahane points out that the maternal body carries such "archaic fantasies of power and vulnerability" because society encourages it with its cultural divisions ("Gothic Mirror" 350).

16. Tzvetan Todorov discusses the fantastic as a means of combating social and internal censorship. The function of the supernatural in particular "is to exempt the text from the action of the law, and thereby to transgress that law" (159).

Abbreviations

AI	*The Age of Innocence*
BG	*A Backward Glance*
CI	*Crucial Instances*
CP	*Certain People*
CSS	*Collected Short Stories*
DM	*The Descent of Man and Other Stories*
EF	*Ethan Frome*
G	*Ghosts*
GA	*The Gods Arrive*
HB	*Here and Beyond*
HM	*The House of Mirth*
HRB	*Hudson River Bracketed*
HW	*The Hermit and the Wild Woman and Other Stories*
"Life"	*"Life and I"*
S	*Summer*
WF	*The Writing of Fiction*
X	*Xingu and Other Stories*

FURTHER READING

Bibliographies

Garrison, Stephen. *Edith Wharton: A Descriptive Bibliography.* Pittsburgh, Pa.: University of Pittsburgh Press, 1990, 514 p.

Provides a descriptive bibliography.

Lauer, Kristin O. and Margaret P. Murray. *Edith Wharton: An Annotated Bibliography.* New York: Garland Pub., 1990, 528 p.

Offers an annotated bibliography.

Biographies

Benstock, Shari. *No Gifts From Chance: A Biography of Edith Wharton.* New York: Charles Scribner's Sons, 1994, 546 p.

Biography of Wharton.

Coolidge, Olivia. *Edith Wharton, 1862-1937.* New York: Charles Scribner's Sons, 1964, 221 p.

Biography of Wharton.

Dwight, Eleanor. *Edith Wharton: An Extraordinary Life.* New York: Abrams, 1994, 296 p.

Biography of Wharton.

Lewis, R. W. B. *Edith Wharton: A Biography.* New York: Harper & Row, 1975, 592 p.

Definitive biography of Wharton.

McDowell, Margaret B. *Edith Wharton.* Boston: Twayne, 1976, 158 p.

Provides a biographical and critical overview of Wharton's life and career.

Singley, Carol J., editor. *A Historical Guide to Edith Wharton.* New York: Oxford University Press, 2003, 302 p.

Offers a biographical and critical examination of Wharton.

Wolff, Cynthia Griffin. *A Feast of Words: The Triumph of Edith Wharton.* New York: Oxford University Press, 1977, 453 p.

Offers a biographical and critical analysis of Wharton's career.

Criticism

Banta, Martha. "The Ghostly Gothic of Wharton's Everyday World." *American Literary Realism* 27, no. 1 (fall 1994): 1-10.

Probes Wharton's fiction as it responds to modern society through "ethnographic surrealism," a form of cultural study focused on the discovery of primitive knowledge and particularly evident in her Gothic short story "Afterward" and novella Ethan Frome.

Beer, Janet, and Avril Horner. "'This Isn't Exactly a Ghost Story': Edith Wharton and Parodic Gothic." *Journal of American Studies* 37, no. 2 (August 2003): 269-83.

Argues "that some of Wharton's ghost stories contain a further dimension, beyond allusion, where they shift into a parodic and humorous strain that enables her to engage self-reflexively with the Gothic tradition."

Dyman, Jenni. *Lurking Feminism: The Ghost Stories of Edith Wharton.* New York: Peter Lang, 1996, 199 p.

Book-length study of Wharton's short Gothic fiction that concentrates on the incipient feminist awareness demonstrated in these works.

Elbert, Monika M. "T. S. Eliot and Wharton's Modernist Gothic." *Edith Wharton Review* 11, no. 1 (spring 1994): 19-25.

Argues that in her short story "A Bottle of Perrier" Wharton emulates the mytho-historical and rationalist modernism of T. S. Eliot's Waste Land.

———. "Wharton's Hybridization of Hawthorne's 'Brand' of Gothic: Gender Crossings in 'Ethan Brand' and

'Bewitched.'" *American Transcendental Quarterly* 17, no. 4 (December 2003): 221-41.

Compares the use of Gothic conventions associated with male desire in Wharton's short story "Bewitched" and Nathaniel Hawthorne's "Ethan Brand."

Kaye, Richard A. "'Unearthly Visitants': Wharton Ghost Tales, Gothic Form and the Literature of Homosexual Panic." *Edith Wharton Review* 11, no. 1 (spring 1994): 10-18.

Studies male homosexuality depicted as a supernatural threat in five stories by Wharton: "A Bottle of Perrier," "The Triumph of Night," "The Eyes," "Afterward," and "Pomegranate Seed."

Singley, Carol J. "Gothic Borrowings and Innovations in Edith Wharton's 'A Bottle of Perrier.'" In *Edith Wharton: New Critical Essays,* edited by Alfred Bendixen and Annette Zilversmit, pp. 271-90. New York: Garland, 1992.

Argues that in her short stories Wharton "follows a tradition of Ghost Fiction by British and American women writers . . . which deals in varying ways with the missing or longed-for mother."

OTHER SOURCES FROM GALE:

Additional coverage of Wharton's life and career is contained in the following sources published by Thomson Gale: *American Writers; American Writers: The Classics,* Vol. 2; *American Writers Retrospective Supplement,* Vol. 1; *Authors and Artists for Young Adults,* Vol. 25; *Beacham's Encyclopedia of Popular Fiction: Biography & Resources,* Vol. 3; *Concise Dictionary of American Literary Biography, 1865-1917; Contemporary Authors,* Vol. 132; *Dictionary of Literary Biography,* Vols. 4, 9, 12, 78, 189; *Dictionary of Literary Biography Documentary Series,* Vol. 13; *DISCovering Authors; DISCovering Authors: British Edition; DISCovering Authors: Canadian Edition; DISCovering Authors Modules: Most-studied Authors* and *Novelists; DISCovering Authors 3.0; Encyclopedia of World Literature in the 20th Century,* Ed. 3; *Exploring Short Stories; Feminism in Literature: A Gale Critical Companion; Literature and Its Times,* Vols. 2, 3; *Literature and Its Times Supplement,* Vol. 1; *Literature Resource Center; Major 20th-Century Writers,* Eds. 1, 2; *Major 21st-Century Writers; Modern American Women Writers; Novels for Students,* Vols. 5, 11, 15, 20; *Reference Guide to American Literature,* Ed. 4; *Reference Guide to Short Fiction,* Ed. 2; *St. James Guide to Horror, Ghost & Gothic Writers; Short Stories for Students,* Vols. 6, 7; *Short Story Criticism,* Vols. 6, 84; *Supernatural Fiction Writers; Twayne's United States Authors; Twentieth-Century Literary Criticism,* Vols. 3, 9, 27, 53, 129, 149; *20th Century Romance and Historical Writers;* and *World Literature Criticism.*

OSCAR WILDE

(1854 - 1900)

(Full name Oscar Fingal O'Flahertie Wills Wilde; has also written under the pseudonyms Sebastian Melmoth and C. 3. 3.) Anglo-Irish playwright, novelist, essayist, critic, poet, and short story writer.

Wilde is one of the foremost figures of late nineteenth-century literary Decadence, a movement whose members espoused the doctrine of "art for art's sake" by seeking to subordinate moral, political, and social concerns in art to matters of aesthetic value. This credo of aestheticism, however, indicates only one facet of a man notorious for resisting any public institution—artistic, social, political, or moral—that attempted to subjugate individual will and imagination. In contrast to the cult of nature purported by the Romantic poets, Wilde posed a cult of art in his critical essays and reviews; to socialism's cult of the masses, he proposed a cult of the individual; and in opposition to what he saw as the middle-class façade of false respectability, he encouraged a struggle to realize one's true nature. Wilde's only novel, *The Picture of Dorian Gray* (1890), is typically considered one of the defining literary works of the Decadent movement. Exhibiting the author's fascination with human perversity, the novel also features numerous Gothic themes and techniques as it details in elaborate, ornamental prose the moral degeneration of its morbidly narcissistic protagonist. Other writings by Wilde noted for their use of Gothic elements include two satirical short stories, "The Canterville Ghost" (1887) and "Lord Arthur Savile's Crime," and the biblically-inspired drama *Salomé* (1893).

BIOGRAPHICAL INFORMATION

Wilde was born in Dublin, where he received his early education. As a student at Dublin's Trinity College and later at Oxford University in London, he was influenced by the writings of Walter Pater, who, in his *Studies in the History of the Renaissance* (1873), urged indulgence of the senses, a search for sustained intensity of experience, and stylistic perfectionism in art. Wilde adopted such aestheticism as a way of life, cultivating an extravagant persona that was burlesqued in the popular press and music-hall entertainments, copied by other youthful iconoclasts, and indulged by the avant-garde literary and artistic circles of London wherein Wilde was renowned for intelligence, wit, and charm. Wilde published his first volume, *Poems*, in 1881. In 1884 he married Constance Lloyd, the daughter of a wealthy Dublin family, and thereafter promoted himself and his ideas with successful lecture tours of the United States, Canada, and Great Britain. In the late 1880s Wilde and his family settled in London, and he continued to crusade for aestheticism as a book reviewer and as the editor of the periodical

Woman's World. "The Canterville Ghost," the first of Wilde's short stories to appear in print, was published in *Court and Society* in February 1887. In addition to this work, three subsequent short stories written by Wilde appeared in various London magazines that same year and were later collected as *Lord Arthur Savile's Crime, and Other Stories* (1891). His novel *The Picture of Dorian Gray* was published during a period of great creativity and productivity for Wilde that extended from 1888 to 1895. Most of his highly regarded critical essays, collected in *Intentions* (1891), also appeared during this time. Shortly after the publication of this collection, Wilde attained the greatest critical and popular success of his lifetime with the plays *Lady Windermere's Fan* (1892), *A Woman of No Importance* (1893), *An Ideal Husband* (1895), and *The Importance of Being Earnest* (1895). Meanwhile, during the 1890s, Wilde met and became infatuated with Lord Alfred Douglas, son of the Marquess of Queensbury. His relationship with Douglas, the Marquess's violent disapproval of this relationship, and his own ill-advised legal action against the Marquess scandalized London. *The Importance of Being Earnest* was in production at the time of Wilde's 1895 trial on charges of "gross indecency between male persons." His conviction and subsequent imprisonment led to ignominy for Wilde and obscurity for his works. He continued to write during his two years in prison, producing the poems in *The Ballad of Reading Gaol, and Other Poems* (1898) and the essay *De Profundis* (1905). Upon his release, however, Wilde was generally either derided or ignored by literary and social circles. At the time of his death in 1900 the scandal associated with Wilde led most commentators to discuss him diffidently, if at all. While critical response no longer focuses so persistently on questions of morality, Wilde's life and personality still incite fascination. Biographical studies and biographically oriented criticism continue to dominate Wilde scholarship.

MAJOR WORKS

A writer far from exclusively concerned with the supernatural, Wilde nevertheless made several experiments with Gothic subjects during his relatively brief professional literary career. Wilde's first collection of prose, *The Happy Prince, and Other Tales* (1888), displays his early penchant for ornamentation and stylistic grace in his writings and largely predates his Gothic concerns. Often described as fantastic due to their exotic characters and setting, these stories feature characters who take responsibility for their own actions, are conscious of the suffering of those around them, and are capable of generosity and forgiveness as well as selfishness and cruelty. Containing both social and literary satire, the works collected in *Lord Arthur Savile's Crime, and Other Stories* parody what he considered American naïveté, the cultural and social snobbery associated with the British aristocracy, as well as many of the contrivances of Gothic fiction. Among these pieces, "The Canterville Ghost" is a story about an American family who rents a haunted castle in England but steadfastly refuses to believe in the increasingly indignant ghost who inhabits it. Often dismissed as simplistic and melodramatic, this story nonetheless evinces Wilde's fascination with the supernatural and the dark side of human nature. Wilde further explored these themes in "Lord Arthur Savile's Crime." In this story, Lord Arthur, who is soon to be married, meets a palm reader who predicts that he will commit murder. Because Arthur believes in predestination, he feels obliged to fulfill the prophecy before allowing himself to marry. Like the family in "The Canterville Ghost," Arthur is unable to acknowledge or accept the existence of evil in himself and others. At the end of the story, after killing the palm reader by throwing him in the Thames, he heaves a "deep sigh of relief" before happily marrying his fiancée. The title figure of Wilde's novel *The Picture of Dorian Gray*, in evident fulfillment of his impulsive wish to remain young while a painted portrait of himself grows old in his place, retains his youthful attractiveness while signs of age and debauchery appear in the painting. Detailing a period of eighteen years in Dorian's life after the completion of his portrait by the painter Basil Hallward, *The Picture of Dorian Gray* chronicles the young aristocrat's involvement in the unspecified "ruin" of a number of individuals, his revels in rare, beautiful, and costly objects, his experimentation with drugs and alcohol, and finally his descent to murder. During this time his portrait, hidden from view in Dorian's attic, mysteriously ages and becomes repulsive, reflecting the effects of Dorian's excesses, while Dorian himself remains young and attractive. His ultimate attempt to destroy the painting results in his own death; the portrait then resumes its original appearance, and the hideous corpse found lying before it is only with difficulty identified as that of Dorian Gray. A thematic departure for Wilde, the one-act drama *Salomé* joins a biblical subject with Decadent themes. Retelling the story of the prophet John the Baptist's death due to the passion of a Judean princess, *Salomé* has been categorized as an eroticized Gothic tragedy that explores themes of unrequited love and forbidden desire. Wilde's stylized and urbane social dramas of the 1890s, including *An Ideal Husband* (1895) and *The Importance of Being Earnest* (1895) are finely crafted comedies of manners sparkling with wit and abounding with quotable epigrams. Generally devoid of Gothic concerns, these dramas are usually considered Wilde's crowning literary achievements.

CRITICAL RECEPTION

Wilde's novel *The Picture of Dorian Gray* created a sensation on its first appearance, when it was widely interpreted as advocating the immoral behavior of its protagonist. The subject of extensive analysis in ensuing years, the novel has been assessed as a moral fable, a Gothic horror tale, a catalog of Decadent concerns owing much to Joris-Karl Huysmann's *A rebours* (1884; *Against the Grain*), a study of Victorian art movements, and a fictional dramatization of Paterian ideas about art and morality. While a number of critics have read the novel purely as a morality tale on the hazards of indulgence and self-absorption, others accept Wilde's viewpoint that the suffering and belated wisdom of the protagonist are incidental to the work's artistic form. Conceding a departure from his own literary principles, Wilde freely admitted that the book does indeed contain a moral, which he summarized as: "All excess, as well as all renunciation, brings its own punishment." Critics interested in the Gothic elements of the novel have frequently studied these in conjunction with the work's aesthetic and ethical concerns. Lewis J. Poteet has explored the affinities between *The Picture of Dorian Gray* and its Gothic precursor, Charles R. Maturin's *Melmoth the Wanderer*, a work he argues constructs both the structural and thematic patterns of Wilde's novel. According to Poteet, both works share such features as the depiction of a "radical bifurcation of nature and art" illustrated in the seductive and corruptive effects of social knowledge, a distinctive doubling of characters, and a shared use of supernatural horror to convey a theme of moral retribution. Kenneth Womack has interpreted the novel as a late-Victorian study in Gothic subversion. Highlighting the essential moral hollowness of Dorian Gray, who in his debauched, hedonistic, and narcissistic behavior sacrifices his spiritual being to empty aesthetic pleasures, Womack suggests that the novel principally employs its supernatural device of Dorian's aging portrait for the purposes of social critique centered on the figure of the aesthete. Donald Lawler has also examined the juxtaposition of Gothic and aesthetic elements in *The Picture of Dorian Gray*. In Lawler's estimation, Wilde's writings frequently appropriate a Gothic sensibility as a means of exploring the outer limits of human behavior, and that Wilde, in effect, endeavored to "gothicize" art and aesthetics in his novel and other works. Lawler has additionally explored Wilde's drama *Salomé* as "a gothically inverted worship of death" concentrated on the figure of the enraptured princess and symbolized in the sexualized imagery associated with her call for the head of John the Baptist. Overall, despite such modern assessments, Wilde is not usually considered a Gothic writer, but rather one whose unique blend of Decadent aesthetic concerns, literary supernaturalism, and interest in human perversity lends itself well to Gothic interpretation. While the critical reception of Wilde's writings remains complicated, in part because his works have had to compete for attention with his sensational life, the Gothic vein remains a viable and robust critical approach to one of the more fascinating and diverse literary figures of the late nineteenth-century period.

PRINCIPAL WORKS

Poems (poetry) 1881

The Happy Prince, and Other Tales (short stories) 1888

The Picture of Dorian Gray (novel) 1890; first published in the journal *Lippincott's Monthly Magazine*; revised edition, 1891

A House of Pomegranates (short stories) 1891

Intentions (essays) 1891

*Lord Arthur Savile's Crime, and Other Stories (short stories) 1891

Lady Windermere's Fan (play) 1892

Salomé (play) 1893

A Woman of No Importance (play) 1893

An Ideal Husband (play) 1895

The Ballad of Reading Gaol, and Other Poems [as C.3.3.] (poetry) 1898

†De Profundis (letter) 1905

PRIMARY SOURCES

OSCAR WILDE (STORY DATE MAY 1887)

SOURCE: Wilde, Oscar. "The Sphinx without a Secret." In *100 Ghastly Little Ghost Stories*, edited by Stefan Dziemianowicz, Robert Weinberg, and Martin H. Greenberg, pp. 438-44. New York: Barnes & Noble, 1993.

The following story was originally published under the title "Lady Alroy" in Saunder's Irish Daily News *in May, 1887. Wilde changed the title to "The Sphinx without a Secret" when the story was collected and published in* Lord Arthur Savile's Crime and Other Stories *in 1891.*

One afternoon I was sitting outside the Café de la Paix, watching the splendour and shabbiness of Parisian life, and wondering over my vermouth at the strange panorama of pride and poverty that was passing before me, when I heard someone call my name. I turned round, and saw Lord Murchison. We had not met since we had been at college together, nearly ten years before, so I was delighted to come across him again, and we shook hands warmly. At Oxford we had been great friends. I had liked him immensely, he was so handsome, so high-spirited, and so honourable. We used to say of him that he would be the best of fellows, if he did not always speak the truth, but I think we really admired him all the more for his frankness. I found him a good deal changed. He looked anxious and puzzled, and seemed to be in doubt about something. I felt it could not be modern scepticism, for Murchison was the stoutest of Tories, and believed in the Pentateuch as firmly as he believed in the House of Peers; so I concluded that it was a woman, and asked him if he was married yet.

"I don't understand women well enough," he answered.

"My dear Gerald," I said, "women are meant to be loved, not to be understood."

"I cannot love where I cannot trust," he replied.

"I believe you have a mystery in your life, Gerald," I exclaimed; "tell me about it."

"Let us go for a drive," he answered, "it is too crowded here. No, not a yellow carriage, any other colour—there, that dark green one will do"; and in a few moments we were trotting down the boulevard in the direction of the Madeleine.

"Where shall we go to?" I said.

"Oh, anywhere you like!" he answered—"to the restaurant in the Bois; we will dine there, and you shall tell me all about yourself."

"I want to hear about you first," I said. "Tell me your mystery."

He took from his pocket a little silver-clasped morocco case, and handed it to me. I opened it. Inside there was the photograph of a woman. She was tall and slight, and strangely picturesque with her large vague eyes and loosened hair. She looked like a clairvoyante, and was wrapped in rich furs.

"What do you think of that face?" he said; "is it truthful?"

I examined it carefully. It seemed to me the face of someone who had a secret, but whether that secret was good or evil I could not say. Its beauty was a beauty moulded out of many mysteries—the beauty, in fact, which is psychological, not plastic—and the faint smile that just played across the lips was far too subtle to be really sweet.

"Well," he cried impatiently, "what do you say?"

"She is the Gioconda in sables," I answered. "Let me know all about her."

"Not now," he said; "after dinner," and began to talk of other things.

When the waiter brought us our coffee and cigarettes I reminded Gerald of his promise. He rose from his seat, walked two or three times up and down the room, and, sinking into an armchair, told me the following story:—

"One evening," he said, "I was walking down Bond Street about five o'clock. There was a terrific crush of carriages, and the traffic was almost stopped. Close to the pavement was standing a little yellow brougham, which, for some reason or other, attracted my attention. As I passed by there looked out from it the face I showed you this afternoon. It fascinated me immediately. All that night I kept thinking of it, and all the next day. I wandered up and down that wretched Row, peering into every carriage, and waiting for the yellow brougham; but I could not find *ma belle inconnue*, and at last I began to think she was merely a dream. About a week afterwards I was dining with Madame de Rastail. Dinner was for eight o'clock; but at half past eight we were still waiting in the drawing-room. Finally the servant threw open the door, and announced Lady Alroy. It was the woman I had been looking for. She came in very slowly, looking like a moonbeam in grey lace, and, to my intense delight, I was asked to take her into dinner. After we had sat down, I remarked quite innocently, 'I think I caught sight of you in Bond Street some time ago, Lady Alroy.' She grew very pale, and said to me in a low voice, 'Pray do not talk so loud; you may be overheard.' I felt miserable at having made such a bad beginning, and plunged recklessly into the subject of the French plays. She spoke very little, always in the same low musical voice, and seemed as if she was afraid of someone listening. I fell passionately, stupidly in love, and the indefinable atmosphere of mystery that surrounded her excited my most ardent curiosity. When she was going away, which she did very soon after dinner, I asked her if I might call and see her. She hesitated for a moment, glanced round to see if anyone was near us, and then said, 'Yes; to-morrow at a quarter to five.' I begged Madame de Rastail to tell me about her; but all that I could learn was that she was a widow with a beautiful house in Park Lane, and as some scientific bore began a dissertation on widows, as exemplifying the survival of the matrimonially fittest, I left and went home.

"The next day I arrived at Park Lane punctual to the moment, but was told by the butler that Lady Alroy had just gone out. I went down to the club quite unhappy and very much puzzled, and after long consideration wrote her a letter, asking if I might be allowed to try my chance some other afternoon. I had no answer for several days, but at last I got a little note saying she would be at home on Sunday at four and with this extraordinary postscript: 'Please do not write to me here again; I will explain when I see you.' On Sunday she received me, and was perfectly charming; but when I was going away she begged of me, if I ever had occasion to write to her again, to address my letter to 'Mrs. Knox, care of Whittaker's Library, Green Street.' 'There are reasons,' she said, 'why I cannot receive letters in my own house.'

"All through the season I saw a great deal of her, and the atmosphere of mystery never left her. Sometimes I thought that she was in the power of some man, but she looked so unapproachable that I could not believe it. It was really very difficult for me to come to any conclusion, for she was like one of those strange crystals that one sees in museums, which are at one moment clear, and at another clouded. At last I determined to ask her to be my wife: I was sick and tired of the incessant secrecy that she imposed on all my visits, and on the few letters I sent her. I wrote to her at the library to ask her if she could see me the following Monday at six. She answered yes, and I was in the seventh heaven of delight. I was infatuated with her: in spite of the mystery, I thought then—in consequence of it, I see now. No; it was the woman herself I loved. The mystery troubled me, maddened me. Why did chance put me in its track?"

"You discovered it, then?" I cried.

"I fear so," he answered. "You can judge for yourself."

"When Monday came round I went to lunch with my uncle, and about four o'clock found myself in the Marylebone Road. My uncle, you know, lives in Regent's Park. I wanted to get to Piccadilly, and took a short cut through a lot of shabby little streets. Suddenly I saw in front of me Lady Alroy, deeply veiled and walking very fast. On coming to the last house in the street, she went up the steps, took out a latch-key, and let herself in. 'Here is the mystery,' I said to myself; and I hurried on and examined the house. It seemed a sort of place for letting lodgings. On the doorstep lay her handkerchief, which she had dropped. I picked it up and put it in my pocket. Then I began to consider what I should do. I came to the conclusion that I had no right to spy on her, and I drove to the club. At six I called to see her. She was lying on a sofa, in a tea-gown of silver tissue looped up by some strange moonstones that she always wore. She was looking quite lovely. 'I am so glad to see you,' she said; 'I have not been out all day.' I stared at her in amazement, and pulling the handkerchief out of my pocket, handed it to her. 'You dropped this in Cumnor Street this afternoon, Lady Alroy,' I said very calmly. She looked at me in terror, but made no attempt to take the handkerchief. 'What were you doing there?' I asked. 'What right have you to question me?' she answered. 'The right of a man who loves you,' I replied; 'I came here to ask you to be my wife.' She hid her face in her hands, and burst into floods of tears. 'You must tell me,' I continued. She stood up, and, looking me straight in the face, said, 'Lord Murchison, there is nothing to tell you.' . . . 'You went to meet someone,'

I cried; 'this is your mystery.' She grew dreadfully white, and said, 'I went to meet no one.' . . . 'Can't you tell the truth?' I exclaimed. 'I have told it,' she replied. I was mad, frantic; I don't know what I said, but I said terrible things to her. Finally I rushed out of the house. She wrote me a letter the next day; I sent it back unopened, and started for Norway with Alan Colville. After a month I came back, and the first thing I saw in the *Morning Post* was the death of Lady Alroy. She had caught a chill at the Opera, and had died in five days of congestion of the lungs. I shut myself up and saw no one. I had loved her so much, I had loved her so madly. Good God! how I had loved that woman!"

"You went to the street, to the house in it?" I said.

"Yes," he answered.

"One day I went to Cumnor Street. I could not help it; I was tortured with doubt. I knocked at the door, and a respectable-looking woman opened it to me. I asked her if she had any rooms to let. 'Well, sir,' she replied, 'the drawing-rooms are supposed to be let; but I have not seen the lady for three months, and as rent is owing on them, you can have them.' . . . 'Is this the lady?' I said, showing the photograph. 'That's her, sure enough,' she exclaimed; 'and when is she coming back, sir?' . . . 'The lady is dead,' I replied. 'Oh, sir, I hope not!' said the woman; 'she was my best lodger. She paid me three guineas a week merely to sit in my drawing-room now and then.' . . . 'She met someone here?' I said; but the woman assured me that it was not so, that she always came alone, and saw no one. 'What on earth did she do here?' I cried. 'She simply sat in the drawing-room, sir, reading books, and sometimes had tea,' the woman answered. I did not know what to say, so I gave her a sovereign and went away. Now, what do you think it all meant? You don't believe the woman was telling the truth?"

"I do."

"Then why did Lady Alroy go there?"

"My dear Gerald," I answered, "Lady Alroy was simply a woman with a mania for mystery. She took these rooms for the pleasure of going there with her veil down, and imagining she was a heroine. She had a passion for secrecy, but she herself was merely a Sphinx without a secret."

"Do you really think so?"

"I am sure of it," I replied.

He took out the morocco case, opened it, and looked at the photograph. "I wonder?" he said at last.

OSCAR WILDE (LETTER DATE 26 JUNE 1890)

SOURCE: Wilde, Oscar. "To the Editor of the *St. James's Gazette*." In *The Artist as Critic: Critical Writings of Oscar Wilde*, edited by Richard Ellmann, pp. 238-41. New York: Random House, 1969.

In the following letter, published in the St. James's Gazette *two days after that newspaper published a vicious attack ("A Study in Puppydom," June 24, 1890) on* The Picture of Dorian Gray, *Wilde responds to the critic's derisive evaluation of his work and defends his novel.*

In your issue of today you state that my brief letter published in your columns is the "best reply" I can make to your article upon *Dorian Gray.* This is not so. I do not propose to fully discuss the matter here, but I feel bound to say that your article contains the most unjustifiable attack that has been made upon any man of letters for many years. The writer of it, who is quite incapable of concealing his personal malice, and so in some measure destroys the effect he wishes to produce, seems not to have the slightest idea of the temper in which a work of art should be approached. To say that such a book as mine should be "chucked into the fire" is silly. That is what one does with newspapers.

Of the value of pseudo-ethical criticism in dealing with artistic work I have spoken already. But as your writer has ventured into the perilous grounds of literary criticism I ask you to allow me, in fairness not merely to myself but to all men to whom literature is a fine art, to say a few words about his critical method.

He begins by assailing me with much ridiculous virulence because the chief personages in my story are "puppies." They *are* puppies. Does he think that literature went to the dogs when Thackeray wrote about puppydom? I think that puppies are extremely interesting from an artistic as well as from a psychological point of view. They seem to me to be certainly far more interesting than prigs; and I am of opinion that Lord Henry Wotton is an excellent corrective of the tedious ideal shadowed forth in the semi-theological novels of our age.

He then makes vague and fearful insinuations about my grammar and my erudition. Now, as regards grammar, I hold that, in prose at any rate, correctness should always be subordinate to artistic effect and musical cadence; and any peculiarities of syntax that may occur in *Dorian Gray* are deliberately intended, and are introduced to show the value of the artistic theory in question. Your writer gives no instance of any such peculiarity. This I regret, because I do not think that any such instances occur.

As regards erudition, it is always difficult, even for the most modest of us, to remember that other people do not know quite as much as one does oneself. I myself frankly admit I cannot imagine how a casual reference to Suetonius and Petronius Arbiter can be construed into evidence of a desire to impress an unoffending and ill-educated public by an assumption of superior knowledge. I should fancy that the most ordinary of scholars is perfectly well acquainted with the *Lives of the Caesars* and with the *Satyricon.* The *Lives of the Caesars,* at any rate, forms part of the curriculum at Oxford for those who take the Honour School of *Literæ Humaniores*; and as for the *Satyricon,* it is popular even among passmen, though I suppose they are obliged to read it in translations.

The writer of the article then suggests that I, in common with that great and noble artist Count Tolstoi, take pleasure in a subject because it is dangerous. About such a suggestion there is this to be said. Romantic art deals with the exception and with the individual. Good people, belonging as they do to the normal, and so, commonplace, type, are artistically uninteresting. Bad people are, from the point of view of art, fascinating studies. They represent colour, variety and strangeness. Good people exasperate one's reason; bad people stir one's imagination. Your critic, if I must give him so honourable a title, states that the people in my story have no counterpart in life; that they are, to use his vigorous if somewhat vulgar phrase, "mere catchpenny revelations of the non-existent." Quite so. If they existed they would not be worth writing about. The function of the artist is to invent, not to chronicle. There are no such people. If there were I would not write about them. Life by its realism is always spoiling the subject-matter of art. The supreme pleasure in literature is to realise the non-existent.

And finally, let me say this. You have reproduced, in a journalistic form, the comedy of *Much Ado about Nothing,* and have, of course, spoilt it in your reproduction. The poor public, hearing, from an authority so high as your own, that this is a wicked book that should be coerced and suppressed by a Tory Government, will, no doubt, rush to it and read it. But, alas! they will find that it is a story with a moral. And the moral is this:

All excess, as well as all renunciation, brings its own punishment. The painter, Basil Hallward, worshipping physical beauty far too much, as most painters do, dies by the hand of one in whose soul he has created a monstrous and absurd vanity. Dorian Gray, having led a life of mere sensation and pleasure, tries to kill conscience, and at that moment kills himself. Lord Henry Wotton seeks to be merely the spectator of life. He finds that those who reject the battle are more deeply wounded than those who take part in it. Yes; there is a terrible moral in *Dorian Gray*—a moral which the prurient will not be able to find in it, but which will be revealed to all whose minds are healthy. Is this an artistic error? I fear it is. It is the only error in the book.

GENERAL COMMENTARY

DONALD LAWLER (ESSAY DATE 1994)

SOURCE: Lawler, Donald. "The Gothic Wilde." In *Rediscovering Oscar Wilde,* edited by C. George Sandulescu, pp. 249-68. Gerrards Cross, England: Smythe, 1994.

In the following essay, Lawler examines The Picture of Dorian Gray, Salomé, *and* The Sphinx, *asserting that these three works share "a gothicized aestheticism whose obsessive beauty-worship expresses itself in a symptomatic fixation with art's decorative character—and . . . a reliance on the Gothic as expressing, determining, and resolving the artistic requirements of each work."*

As the 1880s were ending and the Aesthetic Movement modulating into the Decadence, Oscar Wilde was concluding a series of essays, later to be collected as *Intentions,* that contributed a radical aesthetic to this movement of which he had become the unacknowledged leader. Having made a case for aestheticizing Victorian manners and mores in 'The Decay of Lying', Wilde began turning the tables on art in 'The Portrait of Mr. W. H.', by offering a fictional resolution to the problem of Shakespeare's sonnets, showing that faith alone brings art to life, whereas empirical demands for proof cause faith to become deceitful, seeking foolish correlatives of itself in forgery. Wilde's gothic transactions with aestheticism that were to follow in the early 1890s, invite critical inquiry that addresses both their revisionary and gothic character. This paper brings into focus Wilde's uses of the gothic[1] in three major works, in three different structural genres: *Dorian Gray,* a novel; *Salome,* a one-act play; and a long poem, *The Sphinx.* From a critical perspective, they form an odd sort of trilogy, connected by shared interests, common themes, and treatments—especially a gothicized aestheticism whose obsessive beauty-worship expresses itself in a symptomatic fixation with art's decorative character—and sharing a reliance on the gothic as expressing, determining, and resolving the artistic requirements of each work.[2]

Wilde appropriated gothic resources of expression, effect, even genre-framing for exploring the limits and contradictions of his own arguments for aestheticizing life. In this series of works the once 'Great Aesthete' explores the destructive effects of art, especially in the familiar romantic idealization of beauty as well as in a synaesthesia of art for life, an advanced form of Romantic idealism's disillusion with worldly commerce.

I propose to begin as did Wilde with **Dorian Gray** in which he first explored and reshaped the expressive resources of the gothic for telling the story of Dorian Gray.[3] In so doing, Wilde displayed his exceptional powers of inventive synthesis, theatrical intuition, and stylistic ingenuity to their best advantage. The gothic informs every important aspect of the novel to the extent that references will be limited to a few representative instances of the novel's more innovative and influential gothic features.[4]

Wilde's contribution to exploring new worlds of gothic influence and revelation was to gothicize art in **Dorian Gray**. More precisely it was the romantic aesthetic worship of art and beauty that he gothicized, locating it at the juncture between the two great forces of the revised, 1891 novel: the archetypal moral allegory of the wages of sin complemented by an aesthetic allegory that interrogates two, art-related delusions. The first is Basil's artistic error of painting a confessional portrait that proclaimed his own love for his subject. The second is Lord Henry's aesthetic doctrine that living may be refined into an art-form. Dorian's supplement to that axiom is the delusion that Henry's aesthetic vision is achievable with a wish-fulfilled perpetual youth stolen from Basil's portrait and by aestheticizing life through art, leading to a spiritualization of the senses.

The encryption of the gothic begins with Basil Hallward's romanticized portrait that awakens a narcissism in Dorian, who sees himself through the eyes of the artist's 'idolatry'. Basil's admission to Henry that he had erred artistically by putting too much of himself into the painting includes his aesthetic apologia exposing a more ambitious motive of the artist for his subject than an invita-

tion to vanity. Dorian has 'suggested to me a new manner in art,' and Basil then adds, 'I can now recreate life in a way that was hidden from me before' (14). That statement departs from Romantic idealism to foreshadow the gothic world.[5] Unlike previous gothic stories, the invention of the gothic world in this one is a cooperative venture in three stages, dispersed over the first three chapters. Basil provides the occasion in a life-size, realistic portrait of his ideal Dorian. Henry adds the catalytic temptation in his philosophy of pleasure declaimed as Dorian poses on Basil's platform, while the painter adds the final touches to the picture. These remaining brush strokes are critical because they are a record of Dorian's expression as he recognizes in his repressed appetites ways to a knowledge of good and evil with the power of transforming his life. Basil paints on, 'conscious only that a look had come into the lad's face that he had never seen before' (20), as Dorian experiences a conversion to Henry's philosophy of self-realization through affirmation and pursuit of appetites: 'The only way to get rid of a temptation is to yield to it' (21). Dorian is easily caught in the network of Henry's epigrams—'Nothing can cure the soul but the senses, just as nothing can cure the senses but the soul.' The novel makes no claims about Dorian being smart, but he had a perfect profile, which after all both Henry and the author preferred to mere intelligence in their favorites.

Thus, Basil's portrait of an ideal Dorian becomes a recording of Dorian's fall from innocence and grace. These are the strange combinations and conjunctions of influences reflected in the portrait that were to have such a profound and lasting influence on Gray. Henry's temptation speech established the basis for Dorian's legitimizing his appetites by redefining them as questing for experience and therefore as a kind of knowledge rather than as matters for denial, repression, and shame. In gothic terms, Gray's wish to exchange lives with the portrait is his expression of the classic desire of the gothic protagonist/antagonist to re-create himself, this time by bartering his soul for a life in art, appropriating the appearances of the artist's icon, while his soul animates the picture that will then begin to age. The painting's reflecting the true condition of Gray's soul is the price of his admission to the gothic world.

Dorian Gray never does understand the rules of the world he hoped to live in, but they are obviously not what he expected. In the gothic world, they never are. The interactive magical picture is not merely the focus of the gothic world in the novel: it *is* the gothic world and with its invention Wilde gothicizes art and the beauty-worship of aestheticism, just as Mary Shelley gothicized science and the mad scientist in *Frankenstein*.[6] The consequences of Dorian's wish that gothicizes art resonate throughout every remaining action of the novel. Nothing is left untouched by it.

Dorian's new opinions of art, mostly appropriations from Lord Henry, nonetheless diverge from his mentor's even as early as the Sibyl Vane affair. Dorian's rejection of Sibyl is the direct result of her abandonment of a life or more accurately a love in art for the real thing, once she had experienced it. Her declaration as a contemporary Lady of Shalott strikes at the heart of Dorian's aesthetic idealism. With the loss of Sibyl's influence and his gradual estrangement from Basil, Gray indulges his appetites, believing his sins justified by his quest for self-understanding and self-fulfillment. These may have been precepts of Henry's philosophy of the Dandy; but once acted upon, understanding becomes self-loathing. Dorian also enacts and therefore transforms Henry's doctrine of aestheticizing life, only Dorian really attempts it as an extended exercise in redesigning his instinctive behaviour, sense impressions, and even the structure of both brain and mind through art.[7] This is the main purpose of the notorious eleventh chapter, of its central location, of its literal cataloguing of the exotica of art, and of its position immediately preceding Basil's murder. Chapter eleven presents two contradictory views of Dorian's extended experiments in self-reconstruction. First, it implies that Gray artificially controls and refines his responses. Second, it shows that Gray's method for applying art to life and recreating himself is a delusion. He is, rather, a collector and a dilettantish one at that. His only artistic creation, most ironically, is his gothic revision of Basil's portrait, which Gray achieves through his misbehaviour, contextualized in the diary of his life as updated daily in the picture (120).

Even Gray's delusions of a life in art are permanently gothicized after he reveals the condition of his soul to Basil in the gothic portrait and then murders him. Gray who once had lived to savour and raise every new experience to the level of a sonnet, a fugue, or a watercolour could think of nothing thereafter but escape from guilt and of course his emblematic conscience, even if that meant abandoning art and dandyism for ugliness, violence, and crime.[8] Gray is hounded by an impressive variety of secularized, contemporary Wildean furies in addition to the portrait: from the avenging but luckless James Vane to the various arts in which Gray seeks both consolation and escape. Gray's fascination with the painting quickly becomes a morbid obsession, and as other gothic herovillains, he becomes the enthralled captive of the gothic world he has created, ending in hysteria and near-madness.

The phrase 'Gothic art' is used by Wilde but once and in Chapter eleven of the novel, prefaced by Dorian's conviction that 'life itself was the first, the greatest of the arts, and for it all the other arts seemed to be but a preparation' (100) and contextualized by Dorian's increasingly hallucinated mental state (102). In the story of Gray's failure to aestheticize the life of a dandy, Wilde represents art as having been transformed into the talisman of gothic thinking in which the moods and atmospheres created by art recreate, reinforce, and sustain the nightmare originating in the picture. Once Dorian's imagination has been gothicized, he cannot free himself from it. Instead of promoting the ideal of Dorian's 'new scheme of life', elaborated in Chapter eleven, 'that would have its reasoned philosophy and its ordered principles, and find in the spiritualizing of the senses its highest realization' (101), gothicized imagination subverts Gray's agenda for aestheticizing life and spiritualizing the senses into parodies as foul as the picture of Basil's original icon of beauty and inspiration had become.[9]

* * *

After finishing **Dorian Gray,** Wilde turned his attention to other projects: another essay, perhaps a reparational homage to Ruskin in '**The Soul of Man under Socialism'** and the first of his derivations of the French well-made play that became **Lady Windermere's Fan.** His work on that social comedy was soon interrupted by **Salome,** a topic that Wilde had been considering for more than a year. In addition to obvious and well-recognized French influences and Wilde's decision to write out of his system a sexual tragedy before completing a more polite sexual and social comedy, it appears that he was also interested in exploring further potentials of gothicized art for three related interests represented but not foregrounded in the novel: sexual passion (unfulfilled, repressed, and perverse), the supernatural (especially the scriptural and prophetic), and the tragic.[10]

The controversies surrounding the play must have exasperated even the showman in Wilde since its performance was limited to the original French version in Paris during Wilde's lifetime.[11] Nevertheless, **Salome,** without doubt, was intended by Wilde to be shocking and controversial, and in that he could not have been disappointed. In the play, Wilde extends the influence of gothicized art to scripture, dramatizing freely from the narratives of Matthew (14:1-12) and Mark (6:14-29). Wilde wants his scriptural materials to exercise influences in the play roughly analogous to myth or legend in Greek tragedy, within the context of a gothic mode modulated by the rich economy of symbolist drama. Together they develop the mood and tonal unity of the drama, transforming the biblical account of Salome and the death of John the Baptist from an erotically charged imbroglio of mismatched desire into a gothically inverted worship of death. Herod's recoil at Salome's necrophilic foreplay with the head of the Baptist as the stage empties and darkens may be the most subtly complex dramatic action Wilde invented, and its power, drawing upon the convergence of the play's gothic elements, is superbly theatrical.[12]

The decorative and descriptive symbolism Wilde uses repeatedly in the play forecasts an approaching gothic storm of sexual emotion and reaction. The repetitive technique may have been inspired by Maeterlinck, but it also derives surely from the uses of aesthetic and decorative effects in **Dorian Gray**.[13] In **Salome**, subtle dramatic variations and inversions of dialogue, scenery, lighting, acting as dramatic equivalents of balladic refrains (according to Wilde), promote premonitions of the gothic. It is not necessary to recognize these as patterns repeated from the novel, partly because foreknowledge of events leading to Salome's dance and its outcome for the Baptist bears a parodic similarity to dramatic irony—the gothic is a parodic form—producing resonances for the audience with every word and action of the characters.

The argument from unrequited or denied sexual passion involves the major players of the drama in a complex dance of transformations, leading to the deaths of all but the original guilty parties, Herod and Herodias, whose incestuous marriage occasioned the arrest of the Baptist for preaching against Herodias's adultery. The overlapping romantic entanglements among characters produce several perverse and inverse passions that build toward Salome's awakened lust for the prophet. It is her sudden, irresistible passion that Wilde requires of his biblical Juliet, whose virginal innocence is attested by the other characters in that stylized dialogue Wilde uses to frame the symbolist associations he unpacks from some of his earlier stories.[14] Wilde required Salome's passion to flame out of an early indifference to the

attentions that her budding sexuality wins for her. Even Herod's leering admiration that awakens a sense of her own sexual power does not affect her beyond making her more wary. Rather than appearing intimidated by Herod's amorous interest, Salome realizes that a weakness of character expressing itself in voyeurism gives her a degree of power over him that she will soon exploit. Would Salome and Herodias have discussed Herod's Inclination? Salome remains coyly indifferent to the attentions of Narraboth, the young Syrian captain of the guard; but then she is a princess, and Wilde never has her forget it. Her detachment matches that of Dorian Gray at the beginning of the novel, a quality the author apparently found attractive and perhaps personally challenging. And yet she responds immediately to the sound of Iokanaan's chthonic voice, a monotone that intimidates Herod if not Herodias, who suffers no illusions that the Baptist speaks with any supernatural authority. The appearance of the Baptist evokes Salome's libido, moving her to adopt the language and manner of an aggressive courtship of the prophet. Young and impetuous, Salome grows more perverse with each rebuffed advance. Acceleration of Salome's enthralled passion for the prophet can be measured by the Baptist's features that her passion fetishizes: the black hair, the white body, and finally the red lips. Salome's contradictory passion and denial statements express youthful petulance and confusion at failing to arouse even Iokanaan's human interest in her let alone an erotic response. Her passion focuses at last upon the lips of the prophet as the symbol of his power and prophetic office.[15] Thereafter, Salome is obsessed with kissing the mouth of the Baptist. His contemptuous rejection of her as unworthy of notice seems to motivate her the more, as it warps her judgment.

Salome's immortal dance is the central action of the play, her art gothicized by a purpose we foreknow to be death, but which turns out to be something even worse. Salome dances for the head of the Baptist, a man she loves so madly that she will take his life in order to possess him. That desire beckons the gothic entry into the drama, an arrival more anticipated than experienced.[16] The dance is a powerful scene in any venue, and yet it is all but unwritten in the play. The unveiling of the scorned woman dancing her temptation before the enthralled desire of Herod is left, like the sins of Dorian Gray, to the reader's (and the dancer's) powers of invention. Salome's dance becomes the first measure of her moral insanity— once a category of psychology understood by

Victorians. Moreau's image of Salome dances also before our mind's eye, a visual double and another painted allusion, as Wilde's image performs her own version of this most intentional of dances. And yet, if this be the obligatory scene of the play, it is neither the climax nor the quintessentially gothic scene that biblical history teaches us to expect, a point that confirms Wilde's theatrical instincts.

There are three powerful scenes yet to follow in which the gothic character of the play defines itself. In another of Wilde's bargaining scenes, Herod's haggling over the promised reward neatly reverses the power roles of the King and his step-daughter. In her monotonal responses, interrupted by Herod's prolix, Pilate-like attempts at saving both face and conscience, Salome assumes the imperative style of the Baptist, thereby parodying it. The final scene begins with the head of Io-kanaan brought to Salome on a charger, in payment of Herod's debt and the double revenge of two scorned women, Herodias and her daughter.

Having altered the scriptures thus far for dramatic effect, Wilde places his personal imprint on the Salome legend in the conclusion, producing an unusual climax for a gothic plot. Salome's dramatic apostrophe to the severed head and missing body of the Baptist is indeed worthy of a prose Browning. Salome's perverse eroticism, outdoes even Swinburne in the gothic power of its interrogation of the Baptist's prophetic and implicitly Christian asceticism by Salome's Dionysian carnality. In a sense, Salome's monologue was prefaced by her awakened libido at the sight of the Baptist, who represents power, supernatural authority, her own lost innocence and frustrated desire. More than one reader has remarked on the parallelism between Salome and Iokanaan, and that sense of shared identity emphasizes Wilde's gothic representation of the revulsion of the flesh at what is described in **Dorian Gray** as 'this monstrous soul-life'. Iokanaan had spiritualized his senses by denying and demonizing them and the world to which they belong. Salome apparently wins her monologistic debate with the Baptist but at the price of becoming enough like him to suggest the transposition of Dorian and his picture.

The play ends with two more strong dramatic moments. First we hear the voice of Salome sounding like the disembodied voice of the Baptist in her Maenad-like, triumphant peroration: 'They say that love hath a bitter taste. [. . .] But what of that? What of that? I have kissed thy mouth, Iokanaan.' Only in possessing the head of the Baptist does Salome think to possess his lips of power and prophecy, both metaphors of the man. Herod's disgusted, and fearful reflex is one of those moments of ironic and even cynical reversal that Wilde loved to construct in his prose poems: 'Kill that woman!'. The genius in that reflexive instant lies in the way Wilde forces dramatic recognition of both the appropriateness of the sentence and concurrently its impulsive, arbitrary, and hypocritical wrongness. The play closes with Salome crushed to death but thereby released by Herod from a state of Dionysian sexual frenzy that has disgusted the Tetrarch (although apparently not Herodias, whose last words are 'I approve of what my daughter has done') and is supposed to appall the audience as well. The conclusion like that of other gothic plots remains ambiguous, inviting revisionary, even contradictory interpretations. Nor should we mistake the play's and the gothic's heteroglossal preferences, if I may appropriate Bakhtin's ingenious and fashionable term.[17]

* * *

The Sphinx, Wilde's long unfinished poem, had its beginnings in Paris, according to Ellmann, in 1874 (36, 90-91), inspired by Poe, Swinburne, and Browning. The idea was put aside but taken up again at Oxford in 1878, after Wilde had finished '**Ravenna**', when it would have suited his purpose of establishing himself as a young poet of promise to follow the Newdigate Prize poem with another from a similar perspective: a set piece featuring youthful, Byronic reflections on a vaguely classical subject graced by curious historical and learned ornamentation. Though ambitious enough for fame, a youngish Wilde perhaps sensing unrealized potentials put it back in the trunk. He may have had another go at it in the early eighties while back in Paris but with no better result. Finally, some time in the early nineties, probably following the publication of the original **Salome,** Wilde completed the poem, in Paris, of course.

I suggest that Wilde returned for this last time to his unfinished sphinx because he saw how it could be revived and completed by applying a gothic aesthetic that had produced such sensational effects in both **Dorian Gray** and **Salome.** The gothic provided the means for realizing the unfulfilled potentials of the various drafts, and this revised, final version of **The Sphinx** was published at last in an ornate edition designed by Charles Ricketts in 1894, at least a year after it was completed.

Although Wilde's **Sphinx** is more Greek than Egyptian in form, both mythic traditions are mingled together freely in the poem. Hermaphroditic, the sphinx symbolizes a pagan ideal of uniting a primitive animism with animal worship, an early representation of mystery religion, and a forerunner of the great mystery religion, Christianity, bridging the historic evolution of mind and soul. Wilde connects the mythological sphinx—perhaps for contemporary and later readers a relic of an incredible age of monsters out of the fossil rocks, somehow symbolized by the early generations of Greek and Egyptian gods, swarming with monstrous mutations—to the Old and New Testaments in which the land of Egypt, a refuge for Joseph and Israel only to become a slave state, later serves as a haven for the holy family fleeing the tyranny of another Herod.

Wilde's sphinx dwells in a private Victorian collection of antiquities, a curiosity, a silent messenger of Greco-Egyptian myth and the chaos that informed it, surrounded by the upholstery of late Victorian imperial England. It is a displacement that inspired Victorian and later stories of supernatural terror and whose gothic potentials are obvious. The location is also a metaphor for the aestheticized history of the sphinx, a fantastic biography of mythic and legendary rumours, appropriately chaotic and contradictory, whose primary effect is the gothicized, nightmare-like state of an overly stimulated imagination, such as we encounter in **Dorian Gray** and **Salome**. Indeed, our interlocutor's late descriptions of the sphinx have the distinct flavour of Wilde's gothicized art.[18] The characteristic heaping up of aesthetic ornamentation also serves purposes similar to the gothicized art of **Dorian Gray**. Different forces creating the gothic world of each work, however, do indeed produce related but different effects. Dorian's intentional wish creates his gothic world of art, but it is the speaker's enthralled, perverse sexual fantasies that lead him into the sphinx's circle of desire and devolution.

The speaker's long, monologic interview with the sphinx, the many questions put to the mute statuette whose mythic voice has not been heard in twenty centuries, seem to break an enchantment of silent isolation and bring the symbol back to a kind of life, at least in the gothicized imagination of the speaker.[19] The sphinx yet has power, it seems, of speaking as a gothic artifact through the imagination of the questioner. In this respect, Wilde's sphinx appears to be a significant departure from Rossetti's reflections on the great bull that Layard had excavated from Nineveh and brought as the spoils of science to the British Museum. Wilde wants the sphinx to be a relic of an altogether different sort of history, not natural but mythic and pre-human. **The Sphinx** offers a gothic archaeology of a human soul rather than of a city, and the secret of the sphinx's savage antiquity lies in the imagination of the speaker as a primitive retention of pre-conscious mind. The life of the sphinx is stored in the imagination of the speaker rather than at a national gallery or in his private collection. The statuette speaks to those who understand its unconscious iconography.[20]

The interrogation of the sphinx produces a fantastic psychoanalysis of the god's ancient promiscuous life. The probing questions and increasingly morbid emphasis on the sphinx's mythic indiscretions gradually reveal to the reader the erotic fantasies of the speaker in the guise of an inquiry into the perverse sexual preference of sphinxes in which passion is linked with cruelty and even murder, both aspects of erotic passion in **Dorian Gray** and **Salome**, and both traditionally energizing forces of the gothic. However, grotesquely, the sphinx symbolizes for the speaker a demi-god at liberty to indulge in its impulses and appetites freely and without guilt, as matters of preference and involving nothing of moral restraints or absolute prohibitions, both of which, when viewed by Wilde's contemporary anthropology, were considered decayed remnants of tribal taboos.

The speaker's renunciation of the sphinx as false in a complex echoing of Keats raises questions about our speaker's stability, similar to those about Gray. First, the rejection is also a self-indictment of one whose imagination has been gothicized by the sphinx's seductive silence, ancient at the crossroads of historic and cosmic time yet revenant in its power to energize our speaker's imaginative avatar. The sphinx seems therefore relevant historically as gothicized imagination: not merely its symbol but its reification, realized in the monstrous archetype from which the speaker cannot completely escape. Yeats's famous concluding lines to 'The Second Coming' may have a special relevance, perhaps even special reference to Wilde's revenant sphinx: 'what rough beast, its hour come round at last . . .' We also have license to recall Herod's reflexive dismissal of Salome's necrophilia.[21]

Wilde's connection of the sphinx with Christianity may not be as gratuitous as Ellmann suggests. Developing from **Dorian Gray** and **Salome**, it anticipates Wilde's later meditations on the aesthetic Christ as an artist of religion. Each symbol—the sphinx statuette and crucifix—exercises power over the speaker's imagination in this poem, although the crucifix is rather a late-comer. Yet each symbol betrays albeit differently the humanism that was at this point in Wilde's life central to his speculative thinking. The primitive animistic power of the sphinx in its chaotic mixture of animal and human pre-consciousness becomes historically parallel to the irrational, that is to say, the historically unfulfilled archetype of the crucified god whose humanity and divinity appear locked in unresolvable antithesis. In the poem if the sphinx is too savage to lift the narrator above the primitive avatar of human imagination, the crucifix is too complex a symbol of the human in the divine and the divine potential of the human to be realizable. Claims by both symbols offer the speaker little to choose but a cold conscience, itself the remnant of tribal guilt. At the centre of the circle of fear and desire are the contradictory symbols: the woman/animal and the man/god, each representing a now gothicized myth, one ancient and bestial the other historical and divine through which, Wilde's interlocutor implies, human imagination has been tangled in problematic contradictions. Arousing himself from his gothic reveries, our speaker, still a student in his 'students cell', finds himself obliged to choose between the loathsome mystery of the sullen sphinx whose power to 'wake in me each bestial sense' and the powerless crucified God who 'weeps for every soul that dies, and weeps for every soul in vain'. Can there be escape from this nightmare if the sphinx must be renounced by a dying or poisoned soul? The waking world appears to offer only despair in place of guilt, suggesting that the difference between two worlds linked by imagination is insufficient to relieve the burden of a gothic life of desire that eventually kills the soul.

* * *

Wilde's uses of the gothic mode in three major works helped produce two masterpieces and transformed an unfinished work into a dramatic monologue of the conflicted presentations of carnal passion and spiritual enervation.

Wilde's first deployment of the gothic mode seems to have arisen from the inspiration for **Dorian Gray** to deconstruct Wilde's own aesthetic philosophy of life as represented in his stories and essays of the late eighties and early nineties. To a significant extent, the foundations of **Dorian Gray, Salome,** and **The Sphinx** as decadent masterpieces seem dependent upon Wilde's decision to use the gothic as the most effective means for resolving artistically the competing claims of the

aesthetic, sexual, tragic, and supernatural aspects of works representing portions of his own inner life. Since the works were to be realized through sequences of effects, like the phasmatropic projection of Victorian picture cards set into a synchronized motion, Wilde required a form that emphasized powerful engagement of reader reaction through his manipulation of imagery, symbols, legendary or mythic structures and secondary or imagined emotions. Traditionally, appeals of this kind have been especially suited to the gothic because the genre offered models for expressing those hidden, complex relationships among the sexual, psychological, and supernatural declensions of mind encoded in the exotic and decorative powers of art.

Wilde's use of the gothic was a brief, brilliant episode in an experimental phase of his career during which he assayed and reshaped conventions of the major structural genres *en route* to his greatest success as a comedic dramatist. Wilde was not to return to the gothic. Perhaps after prison and social martyrdom, reflected so powerfully in **The Ballad of Reading Gaol,** neither the gothic nor the tragic were available options to his art because he had experienced both real tragedy and the fulfillment of his own imagination of disaster. As Lord Henry once put it: 'the only things that one can use in fiction are the things that one has ceased to use in fact' (64).

Notes

1. Given the persistence of a critical superstition that the gothic novel died in the 1820's, I am obliged to declare such reports have been grossly exaggerated and to affirm its survival despite critical interment: 'it had a limited run (nearly everyone dates it from *Otranto* in 1764 to either *Melmoth* in 1820 or Hogg's *Confessions of a Justified Sinner* in 1824)' (Geary 2).

   Day's definition of gothic literature identifies characters' experience of an enthralled state of fear and desire as the distinctive power of the genre, and it will serve our needs in this essay. Although emphasizing the fate of characters in gothic plots, this approach is a variant of reader-response in the Aristotelian tradition. The primary cause of the characters' enthralled condition is a kind of hubris: the desire for something contrary to nature, often associated with the supernatural or forbidden sex.

   In his Preface to the second edition of *The Castle of Otranto*, H. Walpole explained that his new type of romance had been invented to energize the fiction of his age by representing two powerful, instinctive forces omitted from contemporary novels: the will to believe in a supernatural (and the fear of it at the same time, most often expressed as dread of the demonic) and the desire for a sexual freedom proscribed by social mores and religion. The gothic internalized the conflict of these forces through the power of romance or fantastic narrative to engage readers' primary emo-

WILDE

tions of awe, fear, wonder, and desire. Walpole also established alliances with the tragic and the didactic, traits that have remained affiliated with the gothic ever since.

The transmission of the gothic to the present has produced too many distinct sub-types even to mention let alone discuss, but these discrete species range from gothic science fiction (*Frankenstein* to *Jurassic Park*) to gothic fantasy (*Varney the Vampire* to *Twin Peaks*) and include domesticated gothics like *The Picture of Dorian Gray,* and exotics like *Salome,* and *The Sphinx.*

2. The premise of this approach of *Dorian Gray, Salome,* and *The Sphinx* is that they are each in the gothic mode, meaning that they commonly share an experimental use of the gothic in conjunction with other well-documented formal elements of plotting and style. Wilde's use of the gothic has been noted, albeit in passing, by many scholars (Buckler, Charlesworth-Gelpi, Cohen, Ellmann, Hyde, Kohl, Nassaar, Régnier, San Juan) but not formally addressed. It seems to me that many features of Wilde's three works that have perplexed critics as 'strange' (a favoured term) and even ineffable are more readily understandable as expressive of the gothic.

3. References in my text are to the revised, 1891 version of the novel. However, in the original, *Lippincott's* version (1890), gothic sensationalism amplified the effect of the moral allegory, of Dorian's growing depravity and eventual indirect suicide. Although it was not Wilde's intent, his original use of the gothic contributed to a widespread misinterpretation of that finale as the despairing but repentant act of a justified sinner: a misreading Wilde himself realized his text supported. The revised version, although it does not close out moral allegory, reinforces the relationship between art and the gothic world of nightmare and anxiety.

4. Wilde selected the gothic because he needed a literary mode that would promote the best features of a complex narrative that included a fantastic premise with supernatural resonances (the soul-bargaining and the magical picture), a complex allegory (moral, aesthetic, historical, autobiographical), and multivalent sexual passions while producing a more tragic than pathetic or sentimental impression. Wilde developed his gothic fantastic treatment of the living painting to emphasize his ingenious scheme of gothicising art and everything associated with art in the novel, but especially the decorative uses of art. The result of these and the other conjunctions within the context of a gothic narrative was to produce a style of discourse, design, and symbolic emphasis that was immediately identified as the distinctive idiom of British Decadence. The key to this idiom, I believe, is Wilde's gothic treatment of art and its many associations, but especially as an intensely decorative and ornamental mode.

5. 'To recreate life' is the gothic signature of such overreachers as Drs Frankenstein and Jekyll. It does not matter to the gothic that Basil intended no more than recreating life aesthetically. The tragic pattern is already established for Dorian to complete, proving Basil's error fatal not only for the painter but also, eventually, for Sibyl Vane and Dorian.

6. Wilde gothicizes art in the novel and in the other texts we examine only for the duration of the plot and not in some ontologic sense. Nevertheless, Wil-

de's vision of the gothic potential of art does take its place permanently in the repertory of the gothic. Just as *Frankenstein* defines the condition of gothic science, so does *Dorian Gray* establish a gothicized art that is retained as a resource in the genre.

7. It is probable that Wilde derived Dorian's method of attempting to spiritualize the senses from contemporary thinkers like G. H. Lewes and Wilhelm Wundt. We find traces in references to Henry's quasi-scientific studies of individual and group behaviour, the importance of hereditary influences on Dorian equated with personal influences (Henry, Basil, and Sibyl) and the influences of art. These reflect theories of Lewes and Wundt on parallel psychic and physical causation that informed their debate with Huxley and the Darwinists over a purely materialist model for development and influence of human consciousness.

The key notion for Lewes was 'psychic causality', an idea that first Henry and then Dorian mis-appropriate as a formula for reconstructing an aestheticized self, built up by repeated exposures to artistic effects that would produce acquired dispositions. Unfortunately for Gray's scheme of becoming the artist of his own life, since art had been gothicized in the painting by his own wish, everything aestheticized becomes thereby gothicized as well.

8. See *Dorian Gray* 143: to Dorian the image of the closed circle of hallucinated desire and fear is an apt representation of his gothicized mind. At this point art enthrals rather than enchants because the linkage of art with evil, of dandyism and aestheticism with the gothic world has become a self-replicating pattern.

9. A few representative examples will do: the morning after Basil's murder Gray awakens peacefully in his sunlit bedroom, then but 'gradually the events of the preceding night crept with silent, bloodstained feet into his brain' (125). The bloodstains foreshadow the changes in the picture. Later, when Gray seeks escape from consciousness in London's opium dens, 'the moon hung low in the sky like a yellow skull' (142). This moment comes just before he encounters his nemesis, James Vane. It may be worth an aside to note that Wilde's idea for costuming *Salome* was to dress the entire cast in yellow.

10. Themes of perverse sexual passion, supernaturalism of one sort or another, and tragic deaths have been associated with the gothic novel since *The Castle of Otranto* and were also linked in some of Wilde's poetry and later stories like 'Mr W. H.' and those in *A House of Pomegranates.*

11. The text I use is the English language translation, originally botched so badly by Alfred Douglas that Wilde finally did a complete revision, after having rejected Aubrey Beardsley's offer to make a new translation of his own. In a somewhat more radical if eccentric way, the play's transmission history forms the rough equivalent of mediated narratives in gothic stories.

Refusal to approve a license for the English version while the play was in rehearsal caused a great controversy over censorship, and drew from Wilde a threat to renounce his English citizenship and defect to France where he would be free from interference. Had he done so rather than heed George Archer's counsel not to leave under fire, he would have left an intellectual hero, at least in Europe, and literary and cultural history would have been changed. It is tempting to speculate how different Wilde's life could have been. As it was, Wilde stayed, and a similar motive later kept Wilde from taking his chance to leave England for France after the collapse of the first trial.

12. It should be noted that *Salome* performed is far more effective than *Salome* read, although admittedly the experiences differ. For instance the theatrical effect of the repetitious, stylized dialogue, punctuated by the symbolist imagery encountered in the speech of every character but Herodias and Iokanaan can be mesmerizing in the theatre, especially as the erotically and gothically derived tensions build toward a culturally foretold climax. Indeed, no small portion of the play's success is the result of Wilde's genius for playing his characters against his audience's expectations derived from both scriptural authority and other artistic representations.

13. Wilde's gothic invasion of the world of art from the novel to the play included the power to gothicize the imaginations of those who invoke emotionally charged decorative effects or seem obsessed by them: allusiveness is an attribute of genres. This helps to account for the otherwise gratuitous foreboding shared by the choric characters with the principals. Hence anything that a gothicized art may incorporate either directly or by association becomes a rumour of some aspect of the gothic world.

The power of gothicized art, as we have already seen, haunts the imagination of the characters and, thereby, affects the reader's imagination. By using the power of a gothic aesthetic, Wilde had at his disposal for drama a proved and effective way for exercising an audience's response and for energizing their imaginations without need of explanations. Gothic appeals to readers' secondary fears and desires, for example, are experienced as reflexes of imagination, needing no conceptual recognition.

14. Those parodic prose-poems with biblical subjects were given in Wilde's aestheticized, archaic idiom. The moon that serves symbolic duty in poems, stories, and the novel, rises to the level of influence in *Salome* and serves also as a thematic barometer, changing from white to red to black. There is the symbolism associated with Salome's little white feet—possibly imported from 'The Fisherman and His Soul' because of their sexual fetishism there—that fascinate the Syrian captain and even his gay admirer, the 'Page of Herodias'. Flower and bird symbols abound in 'The Nightingale and the Rose', and a bird out of *The Happy Prince and Other Tales* may have precursed the white doves associated with the early, virginal Salome before the moon turns red.

15. Iokanaan hardly engages Salome in dialogic exchange; and he does not have a pleasant word to say to or about anyone. He offers only a few words about the Christ who is to follow but who remains distantly off stage. The Baptist appears as the last Old Testament prophet.

Salome, however, finds him irresistible, perhaps, because he denies himself to her, or perhaps for no reason at all beyond an inexplicable attraction. It is the sort of tragic fatality about which Basil speaks in the novel. If the fisherman (of 'The Fisherman and His Soul') could fall in love with a woman's feet because the mermaid had none and Dorian be enchanted by Henry's voice, it would not be uncharac-

teristic in Wilde for Salome to be smitten by Iokanaan's voice, hair, skin, and at last mouth.

Religion is not so much gothicized in *Salome* as marginalized. However, scripture in its translated discourse, to the extent that it is aestheticized in the play, does reveal a parodic, gothic potential for Wilde as it did in the prose poems. Matthew and Mark are, after all, revised by Wilde for a gothic, dramatic purpose.

16. Here is another instance of Wilde's innovative use of gothic conventions or practice.

17. Perhaps the literary and dramatic conclusions need to be critically separated for the moment. As the performance ends, the audience is supposed to agree with Herod's outrage at Salome's necrophilia and blasphemy but be shocked at his arbitrary order to kill Salome—at least this may be assumed about the majority of Wilde's contemporary audiences. Readers who dramatize the text internally enjoy the burden of electing to reread the conclusion where they will find not only signs of authorial sympathy for the admittedly mad Salome but traces of another working myth—that of Cupid and Psyche—behind the Dionysian construction that is foregrounded.

There is, then, more than one irony to Herod's command. Salome has ended her monologue: 'If thou hadst looked at me thou hadst loved me, and the mystery of love is greater than the mystery of death. Love only one should consider.' What a lesson for him! Perhaps what Salome thought she was getting in Iokanaan was a god to equal her passion rather than a desiccated prophet. Herod's response is to deplore Salome's 'crime against an unknown God'. It is a statement with more reflexive than direct meanings. In the myth of Cupid and Psyche, Cupid was the unknown god.

Historically, another Herod was to pass another death sentence, this time on the very unknown god this Herod condoles. And, of course, the 'unknown God' alludes to St Paul's famous 'Areopagus Sermon' in Athens (Acts 17:22-31) that led to the conversion of many.

18. Wilde reintroduces from *Dorian Gray* the drawing room of a collector of ancient and fabled curiosities, especially ones that would have been associated with anthropological study of primitive customs, religious rituals, and sexual rites that James G. Frazer had just analyzed in *The Golden Bough. The Roots of Religion and Folklore* (1890). Wilde's interlocutor may remind us of Gray in both his youth and debauched imagination, but there seems something of the amateur anthropologist in him also, more like the Victorian gentleman-scientist of Robert Browning's 'A Tocatta of Galuppi's', perhaps, than Wilde's decadent brat. Once again Wilde imports a work of art to be wished into a kind of hallucinated, gothic life that then reflects the true condition of the protagonist's guilty soul.

In the 1944 MGM film adaptation of *Dorian Gray*, not only does the sphinx appear in Basil's studio, in the painting, and in Dorian's study but also the poem is quoted several times as a basis for representing the statuette as one of the gods of Egypt with the power of granting Dorian Gray's wish for endless youth and for exercising an ancient evil influence over the lad in what was a rather creative reversal of the historical declension of influences in the texts.

19. The sphinx has long since turned to stone and has no longer a voice of her own. Her previously reputed conversations with humans having been riddling invitations to death make us wonder whether this her silence is now another form of riddle.

20. In *Dorian Gray*, this very argument for the survival of imagination and conscience as transformed remnants of the emotional and irrational life of primitive cultures is one phase of the theme of gothicized influence. The idea fascinated Wilde, perhaps because he was one who had learned to search for and recognize influences that had shaped his own life, especially we may suppose, his sexual life. This interest may have originated with Pater and later been reinforced by the growing influences of post-Darwinist psychology and the newer cultural and primitive anthropology. The theme appears in stories like 'Lord Arthur Savile's Crime', 'Mr. W. H.', and *Intentions* before it became gothicized in *Dorian Gray, Salome,* and *The Sphinx*.

21. Wilde's reversal of the argument of *Salome* in the poem is worth noting. Instead of the female princess who is the victim of the gothic world created by her sick desire for Iokanaan, the speaker's morbid and carnal curiosity elaborated through his double-edged confessional interview, exercises in him appetites so feral that no human of Wilde's class could have entertained them without shame, even in a conditional state.

References

Behrendt, P. F. *Oscar Wilde. Eros and Aesthetics*, New York, St Martin's Press, 1991.

Buckler, W. '*The Picture of Dorian Gray*. An Essay in Aesthetic Exploration', *Victorians Institute Journal* 18 (1990), 135-174.

Charlesworth-Gelpi, B. *Dark Passages: The Decadent Consciousness in Victorian Literature*, Madison, University of Wisconsin Press, 1965.

Cohen, P. K. *The Moral Vision of Oscar Wilde*, Cranbury, New Jersey and London, Associated University Press, 1978.

Day, W. P. *In the Circles of Fear and Desire*, Chicago, University of Chicago Press, 1987.

Ellmann, R. *Golden Codgers*, New York, Oxford University Press, 1973.

———. *Oscar Wilde*, New York, Knopf, 1988.

Gagnier, R. *Idylls of the Marketplace*, Palo Alto, Stanford University Press, 1986.

Geary, R. F. *The Supernatural in Gothic Fiction*, Lewiston, New York, Mellon University Press, 1992.

Hyde, H. *Oscar Wilde*, New York, Ferrar, 1975.

Kohl, N. *Oscar Wilde. The Works of a Conformist Rebel*, trans. D. H. Wilson, New York, Cambridge University Press, 1989.

Nassaar, C. S. *Into the Demon Universe. A Literary Exploration of Oscar Wilde*, New Haven, Yale University Press, 1974.

San Juan, Jr., E. *The Art of Oscar Wilde*, Princeton University Press, 1967.

Walpole, H. 'Preface', *The Castle of Otranto*. Ed. W. S. Lewis, Oxford, Oxford University Press, 1969.

Wilde, Oscar. *Complete Works*, London, Collins, 1969.

———. *Letters*, Ed. R. Hart-Davis, London, Hart-Davis, 1962.

———. *The Picture of Dorian Gray*, Ed. D. Lawler, New York, Norton, 1987.

Worth, K. *Oscar Wilde*, New York, Grove Press, 1983.

TITLE COMMENTARY

The Picture of Dorian Gray

ST. JAMES GAZETTE (REVIEW DATE 24 JUNE 1890)

SOURCE: "A Study in Puppydom." In *A Norton Critical Edition: Oscar Wilde*: The Picture of Dorian Gray, edited by Donald L. Lawler, pp. 67-71. New York: W. W. Norton & Company, 1988.

In the following essay, first published in the St. James's Gazette *on June 24, 1890, the critic derides* The Picture of Dorian Gray *as poorly written, derivative, immature, and immoral.*

Time was (it was in the '70's) when we talked about Mr Oscar Wilde; time came (it came in the '80's) when he tried to write poetry and, more adventurous, we tried to read it; time is when we had forgotten him, or only remember him as the late editor of *The Woman's World*—a part for which he was singularly unfitted, if we are to judge him by the work which he has been allowed to publish in *Lippincott's Magazine* and which Messrs Ward, Lock & Co. have not been ashamed to circulate in Great Britain. Not being curious in ordure, and not wishing to offend the nostrils of decent persons, we do not propose to analyse **The Picture of Dorian Gray**: that would be to advertise the developments of an esoteric prurience. Whether the Treasury or the Vigilance Society will think it worth while to prosecute Mr Oscar Wilde or Messrs Ward, Lock & Co., we do not know; but on the whole we hope they will not.

The puzzle is that a young man of decent parts, who enjoyed (when he was at Oxford) the opportunity of associating with gentlemen, should put his name (such as it is) to so stupid and vulgar a piece of work. Let nobody read it in the hope of finding witty paradox or racy wickedness. The writer airs his cheap research among the garbage of the French *Décadents* like any drivelling pedant, and he bores you unmercifully with his prosy rigmaroles about the beauty of the Body and the corruption of the Soul. The grammar is better than Ouida's; the erudition equal; but in every other respect we prefer the talented lady who broke off with "pious aposiopesis" when she touched upon "the horrors which are described in the pages of Suetonius and Livy"—not to mention the yet worse infamies believed by many scholars to be accurately portrayed in the lost works of Plutarch, Venus, and Nicodemus, especially Nicodemus.

Let us take one peep at the young men in Mr Oscar Wilde's story. Puppy No. 1 is the painter of the picture of Dorian Gray; Puppy No. 2 is the critic (a courtesy lord, skilled in all the knowledge of the Egyptians and aweary of all the sins and pleasures of London); Puppy No. 3 is the original, cultivated by Puppy No. 1 with a "romantic friendship." The Puppies fall a-talking: Puppy No. 1 about his Art, Puppy No. 2 about his sins and pleasures and the pleasures of sin, and Puppy No. 3 about himself—always about himself, and generally about his face, which is "brainless and beautiful." The Puppies appear to fill up the intervals of talk by plucking daisies and playing with them, and sometimes by drinking "something with strawberry in it." The youngest Puppy is told that he is charming; but he mustn't sit in the sun for fear of spoiling his complexion. When he is rebuked for being a naughty, wilful boy, he makes a pretty *moue*—this man of twenty! This is how he is addressed by the Blasé Puppy at their first meeting:

> "Yes, Mr. Gray, the gods have been good to you. But what the gods give they quickly take away. . . . When your youth goes, your beauty will go with it, and then you will suddenly discover that there are no triumphs left for you. . . . Time is jealous of you, and wars against your lilies and roses. You will become sallow, and hollow-cheeked, and dulleyed. You will suffer horribly."

Why, bless our souls! haven't we read something of this kind somewhere in the classics? Yes, of course we have! But in what recondite author? Ah—yes—no—yes, it *was* in Horace! What an advantage it is to have received a classical education! And how it will astonish the Yankees! But we must not forget our Puppies, who have probably occupied their time in lapping "something with strawberry in it." Puppy No. 1 (the Art Puppy) has been telling Puppy No. 3 (the Doll Puppy) how much he admires him. What is the answer? "I am less to you than your ivory Hermes or your silver Faun. You will like them always. How long will you like me? Till I have my first wrinkle, I suppose. I know now that when one loses one's good looks, whatever they may be, one loses everything. . . . I am jealous of the portrait you have painted of me. Why should it keep what

ABOUT THE AUTHOR

JULIAN HAWTHORNE ON *THE PICTURE OF DORIAN GRAY*

Mr Oscar Wilde, the apostle of beauty, has in the July number of *Lippincott's Magazine* a novel or romance (it partakes of the qualities of both), which everybody will want to read. It is a story strange in conception, strong in interest, and fitted with a tragic and ghastly climax. Like many stories of its class, it is open to more than one interpretation; and there are, doubtless, critics who will deny that it has any meaning at all. It is, at all events, a salutary departure from the ordinary English novel, with the hero and heroine of different social stations, the predatory black sheep, the curate, the settlements, and Society. Mr Wilde, as we all know, is a gentleman of an original and audacious turn of mind, and the commonplace is scarcely possible to him. Besides, his advocacy of novel ideas in life, art, dress, and demeanour had led us to expect surprising things from him; and in this literary age it is agreed that a man may best show the best there is in him by writing a book. Those who read Mr Wilde's story in the hope of finding in it some compact and final statement of his theories of life and manners will be satisfied in some respects, and dissatisfied in others; but not many will deny that the book is a remarkable one, and would attract attention even had it appeared without the author's name on the title page.

SOURCE: Hawthorne, Julian. "The Romance of the Impossible." *Lippincott's Monthly Magazine* (September 1890): 79-80.

I must lose? . . . Oh, if it was only the other way! If the picture could only change, and I could be always what I am now!"

No sooner said than done! The picture *does* change: the original doesn't. Here's a situation for you! Théophile Gautier could have made it romantic, entrancing, beautiful. Mr Stevenson could have made it convincing, humorous, pathetic. Mr Anstey could have made it screamingly funny. It has been reserved for Mr Oscar Wilde to make it dull and nasty. The promising youth plunges into every kind of mean depravity, and ends in being "cut" by fast women and vicious men. He finishes with murder: the New Voluptuousness always leads up to blood-shedding—that is part of the cant. The gore and gashes wherein Mr Rider Haggard takes a chaste delight are the natural diet for a cultivated palate which is tired of mere licentiousness. And every wickedness or filthiness committed by Dorian Gray is faithfully registered upon his face in the picture; but his living features are undisturbed and unmarred by his inward vileness. This is the story which Mr Oscar Wilde has tried to tell; a very lame story it is, and very lamely it is told.

Why has he told it? There are two explanations; and, so far as we can see, not more than two. Not to give pleasure to his readers: the thing is too clumsy, too tedious, and—alas! that we should say it—too stupid. Perhaps it was to shock his readers, in order that they might cry Fie! upon him and talk about him, much as Mr Grant Allen recently tried in *The Universal Review* to arouse, by a licentious theory of the sexual relations, an attention which is refused to his popular chatter about other men's science. Are we then to suppose that Mr Oscar Wilde has yielded to the craving for a notoriety which he once earned by talking fiddle-faddle about other men's art, and sees his only chance of recalling it by making himself obvious at the cost of being obnoxious, and by attracting the notice which the olfactory sense cannot refuse to the presence of certain self-asserting organisms? That is an uncharitable hypothesis, and we would gladly abandon it. It may be suggested (but is it more charitable?) that he derives pleasure from treating a subject merely because it is disgusting. The phenomenon is not unknown in recent literature; and it takes two forms, in appearance widely separate—in fact, two branches from the same root, a root which draws its life from malodorous putrefaction. One development is found in the Puritan prurience which produced Tolstoy's "Kreutzer Sonata" and Mr Stead's famous outbursts. That is odious enough and mischievous enough, and it is rightly execrated, because it is tainted with an hypocrisy not the less culpable because charitable persons may believe it to be unconscious. But is it more odious or more mischievous than the "frank Paganism" (that is the word, is it not?) which delights in dirtiness and confesses its delight? Still they are both chips from the same block—"The Maiden Tribute of Modern Babylon" and *The Picture of Dorian Gray*—and both of them ought to be chucked into the fire.

Not so much because they are dangerous and corrupt (they are corrupt but not dangerous) as because they are incurably silly, written by simpleton *poseurs* (whether they call themselves Puritan or Pagan) who know nothing about the life which they affect to have explored, and because they are mere catchpenny relevations of the non-existent, which, if they reveal anything at all, are revelations only of the singularly unpleasant minds from which they emerge.

LEWIS J. POTEET (ESSAY DATE SUMMER 1971)

SOURCE: Poteet, Lewis J. "Dorian Gray and the Gothic Novel." *Modern Fiction Studies* 17, no. 2 (summer 1971): 239-48.

In the following essay, Poteet surveys possible connections between The Picture of Dorian Gray *and Charles Robert Maturin's* Melmoth the Wanderer, *maintaining that "Wilde in fact may be said to have written a version of Gothic novel, giving the form contemporary dimensions."*

The Picture of Dorian Gray, Oscar Wilde's only novel, was written and published during the same burst of creative energy that produced the essays collected in *Intentions* (1891).[1] Yet it has rarely been studied in connection with them or with any native English novelistic tradition; it has usually been treated as a curious, anomalous artifact of aestheticism, deriving more from the French than from anything else. In fact, Graham Hough is typical in treating the novel as a bad imitation of K.-J. Huysmans' *A Rebours*. He bases this judgment on the identity of the unnamed "yellow book" which Dorian Gray reads in Chapter X and whose influence on his life is detailed in Chapter XI, and he says rather ungenerously that the "yellow book," which he identifies with *A Rebours*, "probably remains anonymous because Wilde owed too much to it and was not overanxious to advertise his sources."[2] The most recent full-length study of Wilde's work, too, calls Huysmans' novel the "main inspiration" of *Dorian Gray*.[3] These attributions of influence have been made again and again despite Wilde's clearly caustic deprecation of Huysmans in a letter to Robert Ross (*Letters*, p. 520).[4] He does, to be sure, mention Huysmans in answer to a question about the "yellow book": "The book in *Dorian Gray* is one of the many books I have never written, but it is partly suggested by Huysmans's *A Rebours*. . . . It is a fantastic variation on Huysmans's over-realistic study of the artistic temperament in our inartistic age" (*Letters*, p. 313). But he has been taken to mean that his own novel is the "fantastic variation"; what he says is that it is the "yellow book" which Lord Harry sends Dorian. In another letter, answering the same question, he writes, "The book that poisoned, or made perfect, Dorian Gray does not exist; it is a fancy of mine merely" (**Letters,** p. 352) as if to counter the mistaken, if commonplace, association with Huysmans.

Wilde may indeed have owed Huysmans more than he acknowledged, but a close look at both books uncovers important differences. *A Rebours* is, as Wilde says in the description of the "yellow book" in **Dorian Gray,** "a novel without a plot"; **Dorian Gray** is definitely a novel with a plot, beginning with Dorian's temptation and his rash vow, moving through his progressive loss of "natural" innocence and his artificialization of his life to his crime, the murder of Basil Hallward, and his own death. *A Rebours* is an intensely psychological study of a single protagonist, seen through his own eyes; Wilde divides the reader's attention among three main characters and a "living" portrait. The protagonist of *A Rebours* is not criminal; Dorian is. He does not even inspire unsavory rumors, as Dorian does, for society is irrelevant to the exploration of his personal aesthetic. In fact, the direct influences of *A Rebours* on **Dorian Gray** are pretty much limited to Chapters X and XI, in which Dorian encounters the "yellow book" and imitates the protagonist by collecting sensations—musical, artistic, gemological, religious. But even this is only one of several exercises in Dorian's progressive initiation into aestheticism: it has its appropriate place, I suggest, in a larger scheme.

Behind the larger scheme of the book lies a native, English Romantic literary tradition, that of the Gothic novel, the form which a recent scholar calls "the serious romance" and which he says the novels of Godwin, Ann Radcliffe, Charles Maturin, Mary Shelley, Dickens, the Brontës, and R. L. Stevenson best represent.[5] Instead of making generalizations about the Gothic novel in general, we may most usefully inquire into the relationship of Wilde's novel to it by looking closely at the Gothic novel that was most likely to be on his mind when he wrote **Dorian Gray.** Charles R. Maturin, one of the Gothic novelists most successful and prolific in the Romantic period, was an ancestor of Wilde; in fact, Wilde mentions his novel *Melmoth the Wanderer* and acknowledges the family relationship with some pride—Maturin was his grand-uncle (**Letters,** p. 520). Wilde may have helped his friends Robert Ross and More Adey to write an "anonymous biographical introduction

to a new edition of the novel in 1892" (**Letters,** p. 555n), about a year after **Dorian Gray** was published.

And *Melmoth the Wanderer* does provide many of the larger patterns with which Wilde shapes his novel, so that Wilde in fact may be said to have written a version of Gothic novel, giving the form contemporary dimensions. From *Melmoth* and other Gothic novels and legends which provided material for them (the Faust legend, for example), Wilde takes the overall movement from rash vow (the bargain with the devil) to condemnation. Melmoth's pact with the devil is for vaguely specified ends, giving him the power of a magician over the world of spirits and demons and the power to move about the earth freely, not limited to place or time as are ordinary men. Thus, in the most explicit statement about his bargain, he cries out before his condemnation to hell, "no one has ever exchanged destinies with Melmoth the Wanderer. I have traversed the world in the search, and no one, to gain the world, would lose his own soul" (III, 327), Dorian makes a pact, the implications of which are tied in with Wilde's aesthetic theory, as we shall see; he is increasingly the subject of gossip and rumor because, like Melmoth, he moves about secretly and is associated with debauchery and disaster (*Melmoth* II, 180ff, 275). Wilde takes from Maturin's novel Dorian's eternal youth—Melmoth, though "then . . . considerably advanced in life, to the astonishment of his family, . . . did not betray the slightest trace of being a year older than when they last beheld him" (I, 35-36). He also follows Maturin by making Dorian suddenly age at the moment of his damnation, just as, after Melmoth's dream of damnation, "now the lines of extreme age were visible in every feature. His hairs were as white as snow, his mouth had fallen in, the muscles of his face were relaxed and withered—he was the very image of decrepit debility" (III, 328-332).

From *Melmoth* and other Gothic novels, Wilde accepts the radical bifurcation of nature and art; he puts to original uses the Gothic novelist's conventional plot pattern in which an innocent child of nature is corrupted by the artificialities of society. In *Melmoth,* the child of nature is Immalee: "Her drapery consisted only of flowers, whose rich colours and fantastic grouping harmonized well with the peacock's feathers twined among them, and altogether composed a feathery fan of wild drapery, which in truth, beseemed an 'island goddess'" (II, 187-188). After her "seduction" into the cruel arts of society and a knowledge of the inconsistency and cruelty of man to man in society, Immalee finds nature no longer friendly but threatening (II, 210-221, 249-256). On her "nuptial" trip with her tempter and demon-lover, she finds nature hostile:

> I feel as if I were traversing some unknown region. Are these indeed the winds of heaven that sigh around me? Are these trees of nature's growth, that nod at me like sceptres? How hollow and dismal is the sound of the blast!—it chills me though the night is sultry!—and those trees, they cast their shadows over my soul!
>
> (III, 57)

This vision of nature inverted, of a sort of anti-nature, would not have been distasteful to the author of "The Decay of Lying," but of course Wilde's attitude to nature and art is not precisely that of Maturin. The point is that Wilde keeps the concepts in opposition and connotatively loaded as the Gothic novelist had, particularly as he describes Dorian's progress from child of nature in the first chapter to disillusioned aesthete at the end. At the beginning, he is described with profuse nature imagery:

> The studio was filled with the rich odor of roses, and when the light summer wind stirred amid the trees of the garden there came through the open door the heavy scent of the lilac, or the more delicate perfume of the pink-flowering thorn. . . . Dorian "looks as if he was made of ivory and rose-leaves. . . . He is some brainless, beautiful creature, who should be always here in winter when we have no flowers to look at."
>
> (II, 1, 3-4)

Dorian's vow preserves his beauty but commits him to the superiority of art over nature, and he cultivates the artificial. He finds nature increasingly neither beautiful nor ugly, but dull and without meaning. Ultimately, his natural beauty gone, he lies dead, identifiable only by his rings (II, 272).

The Gothic novel is also almost certainly an influence on the passage, in Chapter XIV, in which Wilde describes how Dorian gets rid of the body of the murdered Hallward. The torture devices, the dark caverns, the mysterious diabolical machines of the Inquisition which are suggested in *Melmoth* are adapted as Dorian forces Campbell, a young scientist whom he has compromised in some unexplained way, to bring his "heavy chest, and the irons, and the other things that he required for his dreadful work" (II, 209) of dissolving the body.

But most important, Wilde would have been able to find the suggestion in *Melmoth* of the portrait device. The young narrator of that novel first encounters the Wanderer in a portrait:

> John's eyes were in a moment, and as if by magic, rivetted on a portrait that hung on the wall, and appeared, even to his untaught eye, far superior to the tribe of family pictures that are left to moulder on the walls of a family mansion. It represented a man of middle age. There was nothing remarkable in the costume, or in the countenance, but *the eyes,* John felt, were such as one feels they wish they had never seen, and feels they can never forget.
>
> (I, 20)

As in *Dorian Gray,* the portrait of old Melmoth is given mysterious and terrifying associations. The young narrator thinks he sees "the eyes of the portrait, on which his own was fixed, *move*" (I, 23). He discovers that his uncle asked in his will that the portrait be destroyed, as if by that act the obscure curse of the Wanderer might be driven off (I, 26-27). When young Melmoth tries to destroy it, obeying the will, he finds hints that it may have a life of its own:

> He seized it;—his hand shook at first, but the mouldering canvas appeared to assist him in the effort. He tore it from the frame with a cry half terrific, half triumphant,—it fell at his feet, and he shuddered as it fell. He expected to hear some fearful sounds, some unimaginable breathings of prophetic horror, follow this act of sacrilege, for such he felt it, to tear the portrait of his ancestor from its native walls. He paused and listened;—there was "no voice, nor any that answered;"—but as the wrinkled and torn canvas fell to the floor, its undulations gave the portrait the appearance of smiling. Melmoth felt horror indescribable at this transient and imaginary resuscitation of the figure.
>
> (I, 93-94)

It is not only in *Melmoth,* of course, that this concentration on a portrait is to be found; Eino Railo has traced the history of the portrait motif through Gothic literature from Walpole to Wilde, with particular attention to works by Poe and Rossetti.[6] But in Maturin's attribution of a sort of life to the portrait, which to destroy is in some way fearful to the living, we have the most direct suggestion of Wilde's symbol in a book he knew well.

Wilde certainly puts the portrait to more significant use than Maturin. He makes it a structural, unifying element in his novel, and he spins out of it whole levels of meaning never attained in *Melmoth.* Most studies of *Dorian Gray* have recognized the portrait's function as Dorian's "double," the figure which embodies the subconscious, darker, evil side of his nature. This psychological allegorizing, the "doppelgänger motif," has been shown to be a basic technique of the novelistic romance.[7] In studying it, Eino Railo calls this "parting of good and evil as though into two separate entities in the same individual and [the idea of] veritable doubles" an "extremely vital theme of terror in romantic literature."[8] In *Melmoth*, for example, Moncada, a character in one of the internal narratives, finds himself inescapably involved with a parricide, who acts as a catalyst to his own unrealized darker potentialities—"I dreaded him as a demon, yet I invoked him as a god" (II, 42). A recent analysis of the "double" which goes beyond mere identification explains it as originating in a "verbal distinction . . . between personality and character, the former as in some way the conscious product of the latter." In the nineteenth century, this critic says, writers began to treat the self as "binary or double-decked" and naturally tended to "anthropomorphize each part."[9] According to this analysis, Wilde's use of the portrait, however more sophisticated than in *Melmoth,* is still relatively simple:

> The artist transfers to the canvas, as by magic, the entire personality of his sitter, thus creating the latter's double. . . . The portrait represents the evil half of his being. . . . In this manner Wilde brings to light an idea that had probably always lain behind the portrait-theme—that the picture constituted in some mysterious way the sitter's double, living a parallel life and reflecting his personality. . . . What the author is actually arguing is simply that a vicious life leaves its own marks.[10]

While this scheme may point up Wilde's place in a tradition, it oversimplifies the psychology of the artist in *Dorian Gray.* The essays in *Intentions,* particularly the two parts of "The Critic as Artist," describe the creative personality not in terms of conscious and subconscious but as in process of multiple realizations of the possibilities of the self. In one of his fanciful descriptions of the book, Wilde suggests, similarly, that the different characters may represent not just two but several versions of one person: "that strange coloured book of mine . . . contains much of me in it. Basil Hallward is what I think I am: Lord Henry what the world thinks me: Dorian what I would like to be—in other ages, perhaps" (*Letters,* p. 352).

Wilde was not so much drawn, I suggest, to the "doubling" of certain characters in the Gothic novel as to the far more central technique of focusing on a strong-willed central protagonist whose goals are not narrowly defined. What stands out, after all, about Melmoth and Ambrosio (hero of *The Monk,* 1794) and even Manfred (*The Castle of Otranto,* probably the first Gothic novel) is both their self-absorbed, narcissistic egomania and the fluidity of their aims. They seek variously to possess the souls of innocent victims and the bodies of women (Melmoth, Ambrosio, and Manfred) or exclusive and perpetual control over a kingdom through a dynastic triumph (Manfred), or power over dark powers (Melmoth and Vathek); but the exact object of their ambitions is never as important as the exercise of the will itself. What better fictional model could Wilde have had for the artist- and critic-figure of the *Intentions?* His self is described as a creative, dynamic one, not a simple character with fixed attributes. He is active and forceful; his art is the product of his conscious will; but he uses the will not to "express" a static personality, good or evil, but rather as an agent to flux:

> The soul that dwells within us is no single spiritual entity, making us personal and individual, created for our service and entering into us for our joy. It is . . . sick with many maladies, and has memories of curious sins.
>
> (IV, 180)

> He will realise himself in many forms, and by a thousand different ways, and will ever be curious of new sensations and fresh points of view. Through constant change, and through constant change alone, he will find his true unity. . . . What people call insincerity is simply a method by which we can multiply our personalities.
>
> (IV, 197)

It is perhaps not quite accidental that Wilde's character of the artist is derived from sources contemporary with the Gothic novel—specifically, Keats, whose letters Wilde loved to quote, and whose definition, in one of the best-known of them, of his own poetical "character" distinguishes it from the Wordsworthian in that it "is not itself—it has no self—it is everything and nothing—It has no character."[11]

It is my contention, then, that with the portrait-motif as with the other structural elements derived from the Gothic novel, Wilde expresses and tests the theory of art and the artist of the *Intentions.* This dimension in the novel is suggested by Richard Ellmann when he writes, "Dorian sells his soul not to the devil but, in the ambiguous form of his portrait, to art."[12] It is not merely "art" in the abstract, though; it is specifically to the theory of art expounded in the *Intentions* that Dorian makes his rash vow: "If it were I who was to be always young, and the picture that was to grow old! For that—for that—I would give everything!" (II, 31). Dorian's dilemma is embodied in the paradox repeated throughout the dialogues, a paradox derived ultimately from Keats' Odes—man, mortal and mutable, creates works of art which are immortal. Dorian tries by an extraordinary exercise of the will to resolve the paradox, to become a work of art. He is tempted into this venture by a sort of "devil," the aesthetic critic Lord Henry, who preaches a version of the dialogues' main tenet, the artistic possibilities of multiple realizations of the self: "I believe that if one man were to live out his life fully and completely, were to give form to every feeling, expression to every thought, reality to every dream—I believe that the world would gain such a fresh impulse of joy" (II, 21-27). Dorian's vow and his subsequent exploration of art, music, travel, and the whole range of sensation, not excluding opium, sex (Lord Henry's conquest of Dorian, and Dorian's of Campbell, are described with many hints of the seduction of a younger by an older man), and finally murder, are thus to be taken as the story of an artist in the framework laid down by **"The Critic as Artist"**:

> In his search for sensations that would be at once new and delightful, and possess that element of strangeness that is so essential to romance, he would often adopt certain modes of thought that he knew to be really alien to his nature, abandon himself to their subtle influences, and then, having, as it were, caught their color and satisfied his intellectual curiosity, leave them with a . . . curious indifference that is not incompatible with a real ardor of temperament.
>
> (II, 159)[13]

He is an artist in life, not only in paint or in words, for he tries to give his life the beautiful changeableness of the artist and artist-critic of Wilde's dialogues.

Dorian Gray is, then, both artist and work of art; in fact, in Wilde's version of romantic, the two are one. As artist, Dorian seeks to apply aesthetic criteria in a pure form to all of life, even—in the Sybil Vane affair—to love, loving the actress only so long as her art is perfect and spurning her when, touched by real love, she loses her sense of form. As work of art, Dorian illustrates the Wildean notion of the independence of the work of art from conditions of creation and the artist's preconceptions, for initially Basil Hallward and Lord Henry "create" Dorian. Basil Hallward creates the emblem of his beauty—the portrait— which precipitates his narcissistic recognition of his own beauty and his rash vow; Lord Henry "creates" his personality by tempting him with a vision of the artistic possibilities of confident and aggressive self-development. But Dorian goes far beyond Lord Henry's instruction, for he really acts, while Lord Henry merely speculates on the possibilities. And Dorian bewilders Basil, who is basically Victorian in his morality, with a complete amorality. Dorian in effect takes over the creation of the work of art from Basil, for *he* is himself the work of art in the new scheme, and his artistic experiments in living make him more and more different from whatever the "real" Dorian Gray, who sat for Basil's portrait, may have been. In a sense, he also undertakes a repainting of the portrait, for his experiences modify the expression on the canvas, making it more and more old, cruel, and brutal. But these changes in the canvas—often explained as the conventional "voice of conscience" in Dorian—actually reflect the life of Dorian filtered through the judgment of Basil, the Victorian moralist, to whom Dorian's search for sensation is a wallowing in sin. After all, Basil used "realism . . . of method," painting Dorian "in his own dress and in his own time" (II, 138). It is typical Wildean puckishness that at one level the entire portrait device is an elaborate joke at the expense of representational painting.

Dorian's rash bargain, then, is ambiguous in the same way as the bargain made by the protagonist of the Gothic novel. Melmoth's deal with the devil elevates him above normal men; he dares more, he achieves more, than they do. He tests the bounds of the spiritual universe. He sees the world of men from a special perspective, outside time, and can compare generations and societies as most men cannot. He is a martyr to this special knowledge. He is damned, for the price of his greater knowledge and experience is his soul. Similarly, Dorian dares to live by an aesthetic more purely aesthetical than most men are willing to attempt. His rejection of the moral evaluation of behavior is complete. Wilde is, like most late Victorians, skeptical of metaphysical systems; and for his version of Gothic novel, even the pretended belief in the world of demons which characterizes the works of Walpole, Beckford, and Maturin is impossible. But he can substitute a contemporary version. The aesthetic dandy, cynical, amoral, and defiant of conventional morality, keenly interested in the contemporary French writers of "little yellow books" who so shocked the Victorian middle class, was a perfect "demon" to flaunt before the respectable late-century reading public. And from Wilde's point of view, the only spiritual world with any meaning is the aesthetic one. It is thus appropriate for Dorian's vow to be in the service of art.

But Wilde is at once both honest about the possibilities of such a pure aestheticism and true to the Gothic tradition of the moralistic ending. He gives the moralists their spokesman in Basil Hallward and his terrifying portrait; he acknowledges the likelihood that Dorian is excessively individualistic ("You worshiped yourself too much"—III, 190); and he recognizes the sterility of the absolute affirmation of art, as the dead Dorian can only be identified by his rings (II, 272). Above all, Dorian's ultimate self-hatred as he accepts the moralists' view of his life and his consequent attack on the portrait (which turns out to be suicide)—all this is not so much a denial of the aesthetic as it is both an acknowledgment that in its pure form it is not ready for the world, or the world for it, and also an experiencing of the decadent's final thrill—*le frisson nouveau*—death. **Dorian Gray**, like *Melmoth*, seems insincerely moralistic at the end; both were conceived, however, as tests, experiments in the juxtaposition of opposites, to be ended only by a doom made necessary precisely by the irreconcilability of the opposing forces.

The Gothic novel, itself a fin-de-siècle genre of the eighteenth century, cast off the conventional eighteenth-century homage to realism, credibility, and responsibility to an aesthetic of taste, reaching beyond accepted novelistic approaches to life and character to explore with brilliant if erratic flashes a psychological universe. Horror in the Gothic novel is almost never genuine; its effects are overstated in a calculated way; characters are rarely believable or consistent. It is not hard to see why the Gothic novel appealed to Oscar Wilde. In it he found implicit and explicit attitudes toward a realistic, moralistic Establishment aesthetic similar to the one he faced. It gave him a form through which he could test his own anti-Victorian aesthetic in a protagonist whose very woodenness is a function of his being partly allegorical and whose damnation is as inescapable as it is irrelevant to the "truth" of his theories. For the "truth" of **Dorian Gray** is to be found, like the "truth" of *Melmoth the Wanderer*, in the resonances and tensions of the work, rather than in any fidelity to the ordinary life of the society from which its author came.

Notes

1. All parenthetical references in the text to Oscar Wilde's works are to the edition by Robert Ross (New York: Bigelow, Brown, & Co., 1909); to the letters, to the edition by Rupert Hart-Davis (London: Rupert Hart-Davis Ltd., 1962); to *Melmoth the Wanderer*, to the edition Wilde probably helped edit (London: Richard Bentley & Son, 1892).

2. Graham Hough, *The Last Romantics* (London: Methuen & Co., 1961), p. 195.

3. Epifanio San Juan, Jr., *The Art of Oscar Wilde* (Princeton: Princeton University Press, 1967), p. 53.

4. Wilde writes, "*En Route* is sheer journalism. It never makes one hear a note of the music it describes. . . . The style is . . . worthless, slipshod, flaccid."

5. Edwin Eigner, *Robert Louis Stevenson and Romantic Tradition* (Princeton: Princeton University Press, 1966), pp. 5-6.

6. Eino Railo, *The Haunted Castle: A Study of the Elements of English Romanticism* (London: George Routledge & Sons, Ltd., 1927), pp. 304-307. I am indebted to Edouard Roditi's *Oscar Wilde* (Norfolk, Conn.: New Directions Books, 1947), for pointing out the possibility of the influence of Maturin on Wilde. He also suggests a number of analogues in other nineteenth-century uses of the portrait motif (pp. 113-118).

7. Eigner, pp. 21-22.

8. Railo, pp. 186-188.

9. Richard Ellmann, *Yeats: The Man and the Masks* (New York: E. P. Dutton & Co., 1948), pp. 72-73.

10. Railo, p. 307.

11. John Keats, *Letters* (London: Oxford University Press, 1935), pp. 227-228.

12. Richard Ellmann, "Romantic Pantomime in Oscar Wilde," *Partisan Review*, (Fall, 1963), 353.

13. On possible sources for the concept of murder as a fine art, see De Quincey's "On Murder, Considered as one of the Fine Arts," *Collected Works*, XIII (London: A. & C. Black, 1897), 9, and Wilde's own "Pen, Pencil, and Poison" (IV, 61 ff).

KENNETH WOMACK (ESSAY DATE 2000)

SOURCE: Womack, Kenneth. "'Withered, Wrinkled, and Loathsome of Visage': Reading the Ethics of the Soul and the Late-Victorian Gothic in *The Picture of Dorian Gray*." In *Victorian Gothic: Literary and Cultural Manifestations in the Nineteenth Century*, edited by Ruth Robbins and Julian Wolfreys, pp. 168-81. New York: Palgrave, 2000.

In the following essay, Womack argues that "[a]n ethical reading of" The Picture of Dorian Gray "reveals the ways in which the novelist exploits the fantastic elements inherent in the Victorian Gothic as a means for fulfilling his decidedly moral *aims."*

As a literary phenomenon, the Victorian gothic manifests itself in *fin-de-siècle* literature both as a subversive supernatural force and as a mechanism for social critique. Envisioning the world as a dark and spiritually turbulent tableau, the fictions of the late-Victorian gothic often depict the city of London as a corrupt urban landscape characterized by a brooding populace and by its horror-filled streets of terror. In *The Three Impostors* (1895), for instance, Arthur Machen offers a desolate, hyper-eroticized portrait of London and its invasion by a chemically altered degenerate race of pagan beings. In one of the more chilling portrayals of London's citizenry,

Marie Corelli's *The Sorrows of Satan* (1896) narrates the Devil's progress through the city's ethically bankrupt environs as he searches for someone—indeed, *anyone*—with the moral strength to resist his temptations. He does not succeed. At the conclusion of *The Sorrows of Satan,* the Devil ascends the steps of Parliament, walking arm-in-arm with its acquiescent ministers. The characters in Richard Marsh's *The Beetle* (1897) encounter a similarly troubled London cityscape. In the novel, a desperate and lonely Robert Holt wanders the city in search of lodging only to confront the supernatural insect, metaphor for London's spiritual vacancy in the form of a giant beetle. Finally, in *The Lodger* (1923), Marie Belloc Lowndes depicts the mean streets of 1880s London in her fictional account of Jack the Ripper's murderous exploits in the city's notorious East End. The novel's chilling atmosphere of suspense, fear and horror—as with other works in the genre—underscores the manner in which the Victorian gothic provides a critique of the moral and spiritual value systems of London and its forlorn inhabitants. Each volume also narrates—in one form or another, human, insect or otherwise—the corruption of the soul.

In *The Picture of Dorian Gray* (1890), Oscar Wilde likewise investigates the ethics of the soul through his own well-known portrait of aesthetic narcissism and *fin-de-siècle* decadence. Yet in the novel's Preface, Wilde writes that 'no artist has ethical sympathies. An ethical sympathy in an artist', he coyly adds, 'is an unpardonable mannerism of style' (1991, 69). During the novel's initial serialization, the popular press severely rebuked *The Picture of Dorian Gray* for its ostensible lack of moral import. A reviewer in the 30 June 1890 edition of the *Daily Chronicle* described the novel as 'unclean' and a 'poisonous book' with 'odours of moral and spiritual putrefaction'. In a 5 July 1890 notice in the *Scots Observer,* yet another reviewer complained about the novel's 'false' morality, 'for it is not made sufficiently clear that the writer does not prefer a course of unnatural iniquity to a life of cleanliness, health, and sanity' (cited in Beckson 1998, 271). Wilde swiftly replied to the growing horde of critics, arguing, rather ironically, that *The Picture of Dorian Gray* was in fact *too* moral: 'All excess, as well as all renunciation', Wilde soberly concluded, 'brings its own punishment' (cited in Ellmann 321). While the novelist's contradictory stances regarding his narrative's ethical properties seem purposefully beguiling, few critics deny the moral fable that functions at the core of *The Picture of Dorian Gray.* Although Colin McGinn, for example, evaluates the novel in terms of its humanist agenda in *Ethics, Evil, and Fiction* (1997), he neglects, as with other Wilde critics, to consider the role of the Victorian gothic as the mechanism via which Wilde achieves his moral aims regarding the soul and its function as the repository for humanity's notions of goodness and evil—the essential qualities that define our perceptions about the interpersonal fabric of the self.[1]

An ethical reading of Wilde's novel reveals the ways in which the novelist exploits the fantastic elements inherent in the Victorian gothic as a means for fulfilling his decidedly *moral* aims in *The Picture of Dorian Gray.* Ethical criticism, with its reliance upon contemporary moral philosophy, affords readers with a paradigm for considering the contradictory emotions and problematic moral stances that often mask literary characters. Ethical criticism also provides its practitioners with the capacity for positing socially relevant interpretations by celebrating the Aristotelian qualities of living well and flourishing. As Martha C. Nussbaum reminds us in *The Fragility of Goodness: Luck and Ethics in Greek Tragedy and Philosophy,* the ethical study of literary works offers a powerful means for interpreting the ideological and interpersonal clashes that define the human experience. The ethical investigation of literature, she writes, 'lays open to view the complexity, the indeterminacy, the sheer difficulty of actual human deliberation'. Such humanistic criticism, she adds, demonstrates 'the vulnerability of human lives to fortune, the mutability of our circumstances and our passions, the existence of conflicts among our commitments' (1986, 1314). By focusing our attention upon the narrative experiences of literary characters, ethical criticism provides a powerful mechanism for investigating the interconnections between the reading experience and the life of the reader.

An ethical reading of Wilde's novel—concerned, as it is, with the soul and our perceptions regarding the nature of goodness—demands that we devote particular attention to these issues and their relevance to such a reading of *The Picture of Dorian Gray.* In her important volume of moral philosophy, *The Sovereignty of Good,* Iris Murdoch elaborates upon the concept of goodness and the ways in which our personal configurations of it govern human perceptions regarding the relationship between the self and the world. Murdoch's paradigm for understanding goodness functions upon the equally abstract notions of free will and moral choice. 'Good is indefinable',

Murdoch writes, 'because judgments of value depend upon the will and choice of the individual' (1985, 3). Postulating any meaning for goodness, then, requires individuals to render personal observations about the nature of this precarious expression and its role in their life decisions. Although Murdoch concedes that goodness essentially finds its origins in 'the nature of concepts very central to morality such as justice, truthfulness, or humility', she correctly maintains, nevertheless, that only individual codes of morality can determine personal representations of goodness (89). 'Good is an empty space into which human choice may move' (97), she asserts, and 'the strange emptiness which often occurs at the moment of choosing' underscores the degree of autonomy inherent in the act of making moral decisions (35). Individuals may also measure their personal conceptions of goodness in terms of its foul counterpart, evil, which Murdoch defines generally as 'cynicism, cruelty, indifference to suffering' (98). Again, though, as with good, evil finds its definition in the personal ethos constructed by individuals during their life experiences in the human community.[2]

Because such ontological concepts remain so vitally contingent upon personal rather than communal perceptions of morality, Murdoch suggests that their comprehension lies in the mysterious fabric of the self. 'The self, the place where we live, is a place of illusion', she observes, and 'goodness is connected with the attempt to see the unself, to see and to respond to the real world in the light of a virtuous consciousness' (93). In Murdoch's philosophy, goodness manifests itself during the *healthy* pursuit of self-awareness and self-knowledge. The soul, as the product of such an intrapersonal quest, functions as the repository for goodness and evil, as well as the essential material that comprises the self. Moral philosophers often conceive of the soul as a vast entity that consists of our innate emotional senses and desires. In *Love's Knowledge: Essays on Philosophy and Literature*, Nussbaum elaborates upon the concept of the soul, which she sees as 'shaped and structured by the needs and interests of an imperfect and limited being. Its characterization of what truth and value are is distorted by the pressure of bodily need, emotional turmoil, and the other constraining and limiting features of our bodily humanity' (1990, 248). The soul operates as a conflation of sorts between bodily desires and individual value systems, and the harmony between these two elements produces a kind of moral beauty. Robert E. Norton describes the soul's

capacity for moral beauty as 'both the motivation and manifestation of virtue' (1995, 48) and associates 'moral purity and goodness with a kind of beauty of soul' (1995, 96). As the essence of a given individual's humanity, then, the soul consists of spiritual and emotional components that define the sensual and virtuous qualities of our selves.

'To choose a style', Nussbaum writes in *Love's Knowledge,* 'is to tell a story about the soul'. For Wilde, the literary style of **The Picture of Dorian Gray** manifests itself in his appropriation of the Victorian gothic as his novel's narrative means. 'Form and style are not incidental features', Nussbaum argues. 'A view of life is *told*. The telling itself—the selection of genre, formal structures, sentences, vocabulary, of the whole manner of addressing the reader's sense of life—all of this expresses a sense of life and of value, a sense of what matters and what does not, of what learning and communicating are, of life's relations and connections' (1990, 259, 5). In this manner, the Victorian gothic's supernatural elements make possible Wilde's narration of Basil Hallward's artistic rendering of Dorian Gray, the painting of whom functions as the basis for the ethical debate that undergirds much of the novel: should we, as human beings, pursue our id-driven desires for sensual gratification and external beauty for the price of a hideous soul? Wilde employs the paradoxical Lord Henry Wotton as the voice of **The Picture of Dorian Gray**'s moral deliberations and Dorian's soul as the object of Lord Henry's intellectual whimsy. In addition to calling into question the ethics of the aristocracy in his novel, Wilde avails himself of the Victorian gothic as a means for engendering a philosophical discourse on good and evil, as well as on the mysterious properties of the human soul.[3] An ethical reading of **The Picture of Dorian Gray** not only allows us to speculate about Wilde's moral aims in his depiction of Dorian's increasingly repulsive soul, but also to interrogate the Victorian gothic as an ethical construct in itself.

As with the novel itself—which John Stokes describes as being from 'that bottomless pile of Gothic stories' (1996, 37)—the character of Dorian Gray combines elements of aesthetic decadence with the Victorian gothic. As he roams through the 'dim roar' of the novel's desolate London setting, Dorian vacillates between states of pronounced ennui and musical euphoria (Wilde 1991, 71). As Basil completes the portrait, for instance, the eternally posing Dorian complains of boredom: 'You never open your lips while you are painting', he tells the artist, 'and it is horribly dull standing on a platform and trying to look pleasant' (1991, 83). Conversely, Wilde punctuates Dorian's most intense life experiences, particular his aesthetic ones, with musical images. Talking to Dorian, Wilde writes, 'was like playing upon an exquisite violin. He answered to every touch and thrill of the bow . . . with all the music of passion and youth' (1991, 99). Dorian's beauty informs every aspect of his *persona,* from his external appearance to his capacity for inspiring confidence in every person he encounters: 'Yes, he was certainly handsome', Wilde writes, 'with his finely-curved scarlet lips, his frank blue eyes, his crisp gold hair. There was something in his face that made one trust him at once. All the candour of youth was there, as well as youth's passionate purity. One felt that he had kept himself unspotted from the world' (1991, 83). As an exquisite combination of youthful good looks and a pleasant outward demeanor, Dorian enjoys the worship of nearly everyone he meets, especially Basil and Lord Henry.

While Dorian ultimately subscribes to Lord Henry's ontology of new Hedonism, Basil proffers the moral philosophy that the young aesthete clearly—given the novel's tragic conclusion—*should* have accepted. Devoted both to his craft as well as to his subject, Basil espouses a theory of moral beauty simply too realistic for Dorian to imbibe, stricken, as he is, with his ostensibly fleeting good looks. In sharp contrast with the *fin-de-siècle* decadence that surrounds him, Basil's philosophy of the soul argues for a healthy balance between our inner and outer selves, between our spiritual centres and the external images that we present to the world. 'The harmony of the soul and the body', Basil cautions, 'we in our madness have separated the two, and have invented a realism that is vulgar, and ideality that is void' (1991, 79). In his portrait of Dorian, Basil clearly attempts to strike a balance between these two vital elements, so much so that he initially refuses to exhibit his latest creation and unleash it upon an aesthetically absorbed late-Victorian society. Basil fears, correctly, that the painting will consume 'my whole nature, my whole soul, my very art itself' (1991, 75). Perhaps even more troubling, the artist confesses that Dorian's 'personality has suggested to me an entirely new manner in art, an entirely new mode of style' (1991, 78). This all-encompassing sense of artistic style, a kind of decadence in itself, frightens the painter even more, for he perceives the unsettling wave of aestheticism that characterizes *fin-de-siècle* London, particularly evidenced by Lord Henry's mind-set.[4]

Unlike Basil, who champions a theory of moral beauty founded upon a balance between body and soul, Lord Henry advocates the separation between these two forms of experience. Lord Henry, in the words of Amanda Witt, 'cultivates the attitude of observing his own life, rather than actually living it' (1991, 91). At times a caricature of the disinterested upper class, Lord Henry subscribes to a range of effected homilies and aphorisms. In one instance, he proudly proclaims that 'there is only one thing in the world worse than being talked about, and that is not being talked about'. The philosophy of new Hedonism that he delineates in the novel—and which Dorian, to his detriment, literally and figuratively absorbs—can only function by separating fully the spiritual from the corporeal self.[5] 'Beauty, real beauty', Lord Henry remarks, 'ends where an intellectual expression begins' (1991, 72), adding that 'Beauty is a form of Genius—is higher, indeed, than Genius, as it needs no explanation' (1991, 88). Lord Henry's decadent philosophy challenges its subscribers to elevate their desires for aesthetic experience and fulfillment over interpersonal consequences, to achieve a total separation between their ethical obligations to their community and their needs for self-indulgence: 'I believe that if one man were to live out his life fully and completely, were to give form to every feeling, expression to every thought, reality to every dream', Lord Henry observes, then 'I believe that the world would gain such a fresh impulse of joy that we would forget all the maladies of mediævalism, and return to the Hellenic ideal—to something finer, richer, than the Hellenic ideal' (1991, 85).

Lord Henry's late-Victorian philosophy of new Hedonism also proposes a striking counterpoint to notions of goodness as espoused by such contemporary moral philosophers as Murdoch, Nussbaum, McGinn and others. In Murdoch's ethical paradigm, the concept of goodness relates to a given individual's capacity for perceiving the 'unself', or that person living within us who attempts to approach the world with a 'virtuous consciousness'. Such a lifestyle possesses the possibility of producing a beautiful soul. In Lord Henry's philosophy, however, what matters is 'one's own life', as opposed to the lives of the others with whom we live in community. New Hedonism, at least in Lord Henry's postulation, urges its adherents to pursue pleasure at any cost.

'Individualism', Lord Henry argues, 'has really the higher aim' than endeavouring to share in the ethical codes of one's society (1991, 134). The philosophy of new Hedonism also eschews morality in favour of pleasurable experience. Although some experiences initially may be spiritually distressing or ethically unsatisfying, Lord Henry contends that their iteration should produce nothing but pleasure once the individual has inured his or her conscience to the soul-purging qualities of such experiences, no matter how sinful they may prove to be. 'Moralists had, as a rule, regarded it [experience] as a mode of warning, had claimed for it a certain ethical efficacy in the formation of character, had praised it as something that taught us what to follow and showed us what to avoid', Lord Henry remarks. 'But there was no motive power in experience', he adds. 'All that it really demonstrated was that our future would be the same as our past, and that the sin we had done once, and with loathing, we would do many times, and with joy' (1991, 118).

Delivered with the confidence and verbal precision of his station, Lord Henry's aesthetic philosophy proves too enticing for the naïve and impressionable Dorian to ignore and serves as the catalyst for the Faustian bargain that he strikes in the novel. 'A new Hedonism', Lord Henry tells the young aesthete, 'that is what our century wants. You might be its visible symbol. With your personality there is nothing you could not do. The world belongs to you for a season' (1991, 88). Yet Dorian, inspired by Lord Henry's philosophy, dares to possess the world for more than a mere season. While staring at his portrait, 'the sense of his own beauty came on him like a revelation. He had never felt it before' (1991, 90). Fearing the day when time finally robs him of his youthful good looks, Dorian initially vows to kill himself when he grows old. For Dorian—with Lord Henry's theory of beauty still ringing in his ears—living in anything other than a state of exalted beauty seems simply unfathomable:

> There would be a day when his face would be wrinkled and wizen, his eyes dim and colourless, the grace of his figure broken and deformed. The scarlet would pass away from his lips, and the gold steal from his hair. The life that was to make his soul would mar his body. He would become dreadful, hideous, and uncouth.
>
> (1991, 90)

Dorian soon finds himself unable to distinguish between himself and the picture, describing it as 'part of myself' and the 'real Dorian' (1991, 93-4). Unbeknownst to himself at the time, Dorian enters into a supernatural bargain of sorts when he wishes he could change places with the picture: 'If it were only the only the other way!' he pleads. 'If it were I who was to be always young, and the picture that was to grow old! For that—for that—I would give everything!' (1991, 90).

The ethics of his Faustian transaction and of his absorption of Lord Henry's philosophy only become known to Dorian after his brief association with Sybil Vane, an aspiring young working-class actress from London's East End. Night after night, Dorian watches as she performs in various Shakespearean plays, taking on a myriad of fictional identities while remaining, in Dorian's envious words, 'more than an individual' (1991, 115), a beautiful soul in her own right. Unconcerned with her lower-class origins, Dorian falls in love with the youthful actress: 'Sybil is the only thing I care about', he tells Lord Henry. 'What is it to me where she came from? From her head to her little feet, she is absolutely and entirely divine. Every night of my life I go to see her act, and every night she is more marvelous' (1991, 114). In short, Dorian admires Sybil for her ability to create genuine, beautiful souls upon the stage. He reveres her capacity for taking fictional characters and imbuing them with the physical and spiritual aspects of real life that Dorian, whose external beauty depends on stasis for its endurance, simply cannot grasp. Yet Dorian's love for Sybil collapses after she gives a lifeless performance in *Romeo and Juliet*. After the play, Sybil appears 'transfigured with joy' because her incipient relationship with Dorian had freed her 'soul from prison'. Before encountering Dorian, the only reality that she knew existed on the stage; after meeting Dorian, however, 'suddenly it dawned on my soul what it all meant', she explains, vowing to give up the theatre and its artificiality (1991, 140-1). Dorian subsequently chastises Sybil for her change of heart, for her implicit denial of Lord Henry's philosophy.

After he leaves a distraught Sybil in her dressing room, Dorian strolls alone among London's desolate gothic streets: 'He remembered wandering through dimly-lit streets, past gaunt black-shadowed archways and evil-looking houses', Wilde writes. 'Women with hoarse voices and harsh laughter had called after him. Drunkards had reeled by, cursing, and chattering to themselves like monstrous apes. He had seen grotesque children huddled under doorsteps, and heard shrieks and oaths from gloomy courts' (1991, 143). When he returns home after experiencing his dark night of the aesthetic soul, Dorian perceives a change in Basil's portrait of him, 'a touch of cruelty in the mouth' that had not existed there previously (1991, 144). Suddenly remembering his wish for eternal youth and its spiritual consequences, Dorian decides to return to Sybil in order to forestall the spiritual demolition of his soul. As he bathes in the warm glow of his romantic feelings for the young actress, Dorian repeats her name over and over again to the music of singing birds. 'I want to be good', he later tells Lord Henry. 'I can't bear the idea of my soul being hideous' (1991, 149). After he learns of Sybil's suicide, however, Dorian chooses to devote himself entirely to a lifestyle of hedonism in the tradition of Lord Henry's philosophy. Having already tasted the pleasures of decadence, Dorian resolves to avail himself of sin with the knowledge that he can do so without being challenged by a guilty conscience: 'Eternal youth, infinite passion, pleasures subtle and secret, wild joys and wilder sins—he was to have all these things', Wilde writes. 'The portrait was to bear the burden of his shame' (1991, 157). In this fashion, the picture becomes Dorian's ethical *doppelgänger*, his wilful sacrifice for a decadent lifestyle and the means via which he will preserve his youth.

Dorian embarks upon his life of debauchery with the aid of a book given to him by Lord Henry. Essentially a handbook for decadent living, the volume—a yellow, paper-covered French novel—influences Dorian's progress toward total spiritual and ethical ruin.[6] 'The whole book seemed to him', Wilde writes, 'to contain the story of his own life, written before he had lived it' (1991, 174). With his new Hedonist education at the hands of Lord Henry complete, Dorian engages in a protracted life of crime and corrosive sensuality in gothic London. At the age of 25, Dorian's aristocratic social standing begins to erode when an exclusive West End club threatens to blackball him. In addition to consorting with thieves and coiners, Dorian brawls with foreign sailors in the Whitechapel area. Suddenly the subject of numerous rumours and upper-class gossip, Dorian becomes associated with scandals involving the suicide of a 'wretched boy in the Guards' (1991, 193); the disappearance of Sir Henry Ashton, who fled England in disgrace; and the diminished reputations of the young Duke of Perth and the son of Lord Kent. 'Women who had wildly adored him, and for his sake had braved all social censure and set convention at defiance', Wilde writes, 'were seen to grow pallid with shame or horror if Dorian Gray entered the room' (1991, 186-7).

In addition to his chosen life of crime and social iniquity, Dorian feeds his exaggerated licentious desires during his search for new arenas of sensual fulfillment. In one instance, he considers joining the Roman Catholic communion, not for spiritual reasons, but rather, because the 'Roman ritual had always a great attraction for him' (1991, 178). Dorian also becomes an avid collector of beautiful objects and searches for yet other venues for assuaging his aesthetic needs. At one juncture in the novel, Dorian devotes himself entirely to the study of music, constructing an elaborate room with a vermilion-and-gold ceiling and walls of olive-green lacquer in which to serenade himself with the pleasing strains of Schubert, Chopin and Beethoven. As a collector of sensual objects, Dorian accumulates perfumes from the Far East, painted gourds from Mexico, rare and expensive jewelry, tapestries and embroideries once housed in the palaces of Northern Europe, and various ecclesiastical vestments. Dorian assembles his orgy of material possessions to provide himself with a 'means of forgetfulness', Wilde writes, with 'modes by which he could escape, for a season, from the fear that seemed to him at times to be almost too great to be borne' (1991, 185). Hidden in the attic above his palatial London home lies the picture, which grows even more ghastly as Dorian's evil exploits continue to mount. At 38, Dorian soothes his fears in opium dens in remote London, where 'the heavy odour of opium met him', Wilde writes. 'He heaved a deep breath, and his nostrils quivered with pleasure' (1991, 224). All the while, Dorian earns glowing praise for his decadent lifestyle and his lack of meaningful social or artistic endeavour from Lord Henry, his hedonist master and tutor.[7] 'You are the type of what the age is looking for, and what it is afraid it has found', Lord Henry tells him. 'I am so glad that you have never done anything, never carved a statue, or painted a picture, or produced anything outside of yourself! Life has been your art. You have set yourself to music. Your days are your sonnets' (1991, 248).

Dorian's life of debauchery begins to collapse, however, with the confluence of his murder of Basil and his dogged pursuit by James Vane, Sybil's vengeful brother. Dorian kills Basil after the artist insists that the aesthete show him the picture of Dorian's rotting soul. Basil reacts in horror as he glimpses the portrait of Dorian's foul inner life being slowly corroded by 'the leprosies of sin' (1991, 199). After he stabs the artist to death for condemning his evil lifestyle, Dorian stares disinterestedly at Basil's lifeless body as a woman on the street sings in a hoarse voice. By murdering Basil, Dorian attempts to rid himself once and for all of the artist's irritating moral influence. As Stephen Arata observes in *Fictions of Loss in the Victorian fin de siècle,* 'The contrast between the lovely Dorian and the hideous portrait can be taken to stand for the difference between Henry's ethic and Basil's' (1996, 64). In this instance, Henry's hedonistic philosophy wins out yet again. Dorian finally begins to re-evaluate his decadent existence after experiencing James's stubborn effort to exact revenge for the untimely death of his sister. After spotting him in a London opium den, James follows Dorian to a social occasion at the home of the Duchess of Monmouth. James startles Dorian into a 'death-like swoon' after pressing his face against the window of the conservatory. 'The consciousness of being hunted, snared, tracked down, had begun to dominate him', Wilde writes (1991, 233-4), and Dorian conceals himself in the Duchess's house.

After the Duchess's brother accidentally kills James during a shooting-party the next day, Dorian experiences a 'cataleptic impression'—a cognitive, philosophical phenomenon that, according to Nussbaum in *Love's Knowledge,* 'has the power, just through its own felt quality, to drag us to assent, to convince us that things could not be otherwise. It is defined as a mark or impress upon the soul' (1990, 265). Relieved to have survived James's efforts at revenge, Dorian resolves to devote himself to goodness. 'I wish I could love', he tells Lord Henry. 'But I seem to have lost the passion and forgotten the desire. I am too much concentrated on myself' (1991, 238). Despite Lord Henry's considerable protests, Dorian demonstrates his intentions to adopt an ethical lifestyle by opting not to destroy the innocence of Hetty Morton, a girl in the village near the Duchess's estate. Shocked by his sudden change of heart, Dorian 'determined to leave her as flower-like as I had found her' (1991, 243). As Dorian symbolically rises from the piano—the producer of the sensual music that served as the soundtrack for his evil life—he confesses to Lord Henry that 'I am going to be good' and that 'I am a little changed already' (1991, 249). Yet when he later checks the picture for evidence of his ethical renewal, he discovers 'no change, save that in the eyes there was a look of cunning, and in the mouth the curved wrinkle of the hypocrite', Wilde writes. 'The thing was still loathsome—more loathsome, if possible, than before' (1991, 252).

Rather than being the product of a genuine shift in moral attitude, Dorian's aspirations toward goodness result from his own vanity, as well as from his apprehension regarding the potential loss of the self that he adores above all others in his community. In this manner, the novel's *faux* cataleptic impression confronts readers—and perhaps Dorian himself—with an unusual ethical construct, the anti-epiphany. Stultified by his own hypocrisy and his 'mask of goodness', Dorian chooses to destroy his decaying soul: He 'would kill the past, and when that was dead he would be free', Wilde writes. Dorian 'would kill this monstrous soul-life, and without its hideous warnings, he would be at peace' (1991, 253). Taking up the knife that he used to murder Basil, Dorian stabs at the picture. After servants hear an agonized cry and a 'crash', they enter the attic and discover a splendid portrait of their master in all 'his exquisite youth and beauty. Lying on the floor', Wilde writes, 'was a dead man, in evening dress, with a knife in his heart. He was withered, wrinkled, and loathsome of visage' (1991, 254). By attempting to eradicate the picture that serves as a record of his unethical life, Dorian succeeds in destroying himself. While the novel's *deus ex machina* conclusion, a virtual cliché of gothic fiction in general, suggests a number of narrative possibilities,[8] Dorian's supernatural demise nevertheless results directly from his Faustian bargain and the ethically vacuous existence that he deliberately pursues.

In **The Picture of Dorian Gray,** Dorian's adherence to Lord Henry's hedonist philosophy clearly manifests itself in his spiritual and physical destruction. Dorian's soul expires, William Buckler astutely observes, because of the 'inevitable consequence, not of aestheticism, but of an ugly, self-deceiving, all-devouring vanity that leads the protagonist to heartless cruelty, murder, blackmail, and suicide' (1991, 140). Wilde employs the Victorian gothic as the express means through which he characterizes the corrosion and ultimate demise of Dorian's soul. Because Wilde relies on the supernatural and the grotesque as means for narrating Dorian's spiritual digression in **The Picture of Dorian Gray,** the Victorian gothic clearly operates as an ethical construct in Wilde's novel. Ethical criticism, with its interest in exploring the trials and tribulations of human experience and their intersections with the act of reading, simply affords us with a mechanism for recognizing a given writer's humanistic agenda. In *The Realistic Spirit: Wittgenstein, Philosophy, and the Mind,* Cora Diamond argues that through ethical criticism 'we can come to be aware of what makes for deeper understanding and an enriching of our own thought and experience; we can come to have a sense of what is alive, and what is shallow, sentimental, cheap'. The ethical critique of literature reminds us, moreover, that 'it is our actions, our choices, which give a particular shape to the life we lead; to be able to lead whatever the good life for a human being *is* is to be able to make such choices well' (Diamond 1991, 303, 373). In *The Picture of Dorian Gray,* Wilde avails himself of the Victorian Gothic in a stunning depiction of what transpires when human beings make ineffectual choices and sacrifice their own senses of moral beauty by elevating the aesthetic pleasures of the body over the spiritual needs of the soul.

Notes

1. In 'Ethics and Aesthetics in *The Picture of Dorian Gray,'* Michael Patrick Gillespie offers yet another ethical critique of Wilde's novel, although, as with McGinn, he fails to consider the role of the Victorian gothic as the engine of the novelist's moral debate regarding the sanctity of the human soul, opting instead to read the novel in terms of the ethical nature of its aesthetic elements: 'Through the actions of its characters', Gillespie writes, *The Picture of Dorian Gray's* 'discourse establishes within us a sense of the wide-ranging aesthetic force that ethics exerts upon a work of art. Furthermore, Wilde's novel gives us the opportunity to enhance the mix of our aesthetic and ethical views by extending our sense of the possibilities for interpretation beyond those delineated by our immediate hermeneutic system' (1994, 153-4).

2. For a useful definition of 'ethics' and discussion of its emergence as a viable reading paradigm during the past decade, see Geoffrey Galt Harpham's chapter on 'Ethics' in Frank Lentricchia and Thomas McLaughlin's *Critical Terms for Literary Study* (2nd edn, 1995). 'Understanding the plot of a narrative', Harpham writes, 'we enter into ethics. Ethics will always be at the flashpoint of conflicts and struggles', he continues, 'because such encounters never run smooth' (1995, 404). As Wayne C. Booth observes in *The Company We Keep: an Ethics of Fiction*, 'the word "ethical" may mistakenly suggest a project concentrating on quite limited moral standards: of honesty, perhaps, or of decency or tolerance'. In Booth's postulation of an ethical criticism, however, 'ethical' refers to 'the entire range of effects on the "character" or "person" or "self". "Moral" judgments are only a small part of it' (1988, 8).

3. In *Fictions of Loss in the Victorian fin de siècle,* Stephen Arata rejects the notion that Wilde appropriates an ethical rhetoric in *The Picture of Dorian Gray,* contending that 'here as elsewhere Wilde rejects humanistic notions of the organic and autonomous individual' (1996, 61). Yet a comparison of Wilde's divergent characterizations of the competing ethics of Lord Henry and Basil suggests otherwise. Wilde clearly derides Lord Henry's ambiguous philosophy of new Hedonism through its expositor's pompous and malformed discourse, while arguing in favour of Basil's theory of moral beauty through the devastation, and ultimately the death of, Dorian's soul.

4. In this instance, Basil clearly fears the rise of aestheticism because he senses the erosion of the ethical and cultural value systems of his community, a process that William Greenslade describes as 'degeneration' in *Degeneration, Culture, and the Novel, 1880-1940.* 'Such fears at the *fin de siècle* were at work shaping institutional practices—medical, psychiatric, political—and their assumptions', Greenslade writes. 'Degeneration facilitated discourses of sometimes crude differentiation: between the normal and the abnormal, the healthy and morbid, the "fit" and "unfit", the civilized and the primitive. Degeneration', he adds, 'was, in part, an enabling strategy by which the conventional and respectable classes could justify and articulate their hostility to the deviant, the diseased, and the subversive' (1994, 2). Despite his espousal of a new Hedonism, Lord Henry also registers anxiety about the lower classes and the disenfranchised in *The Picture of Dorian Gray.* As an anti-Hedonist, Basil ironically demonstrates little affinity for the practices of degeneration and proves to be remarkably tolerant of the lower classes, particularly evinced by his enthusiastic approval of Dorian's relationship with Sybil.

5. In *Oscar Wilde and the Poetics of Ambiguity,* Gillespie reminds us of the illogic inherent in Lord Henry's philosophy, an anti-ethical system with little concern for consistency or reason. 'As the novel progresses', Gillespie writes, 'one finds that each of these points of view contributes to a more detailed illumination of the discourse and in doing so blunts inclinations to privilege any one of these perspectives over the others. New Hedonism in fact defines itself only through the symbiotic support of multiple systems of values, and any effort to view it in isolation would prove reductive' (1994, 61).

6. In *Oscar Wilde,* Richard Ellmann speculates about the book's identity. At his trial, Wilde conceded that the mystery book was Joris-Karl Huysmans's *À Rebours* (1884), although it also has thematic similarities to Walter Pater's *Studies in the History of the Renaissance* (1873). According to Ellmann, in the first draft of *The Picture of Dorian Gray* Wilde entitled the book *Le Secret de Raoul,* by Catulle Sarrazin. 'This author', Ellmann writes, 'was a blend of Catulle Mendès, whom he had known for some years, and Gabriel Sarrazin, whom he met in September 1888, and the name of 'Raoul' came from Rachilde's *Monsieur Vénus'* (1988, 316).

7. In *Oscar Wilde: Myths, Miracles, and Imitations,* John Stokes notes the interesting similarities in the interpersonal dynamics of the relationships between Lord Henry and Dorian and between Wilde and Lord Alfred Douglas, the novelist's youthful lover and aesthetic protégé (1996, 11).

8. For a thorough analysis of *The Picture of Dorian Gray's* sudden and mysterious conclusion, see McGinn's *Ethics, Evil, and Fiction.* 'What Wilde has done is to condense the general theme of his book into this final scene', McGinn argues, 'giving it literal expression, so that Dorian's odd ambiguous status, suspended between life and art, is represented' (1997, 135).

Bibliography

Arata, Stephen. *Fictions of Loss in the Victorian fin de siècle.* Cambridge: Cambridge University Press, 1996.

Beckson, Karl. *The Oscar Wilde Encyclopedia.* New York: AMS, 1998.

Booth, Wayne C. *The Company We Keep: an Ethics of Fiction*. Berkeley: University of California Press, 1988.

Corelli, Marie. *The Sorrows of Satan, or the Strange Experience of One Geoffrey Tempest, Millionaire: a Romance*. Oxford: Oxford University Press, 1996.

Diamond, Cora. *The Realistic Spirit: Wittgenstein, Philosophy, and the Mind*. Cambridge: MIT, 1991.

Ellmann, Richard. *Oscar Wilde*. New York: Vintage, 1988.

Gillespie, Michael Patrick. 'Ethics and Aesthetics in *The Picture of Dorian Gray*'. *Rediscovering Oscar Wilde*. Ed. C. George Sandulescu. Gerrards Cross: Colin Smythe, 1994. 137-55.

Greenslade, William. *Degeneration, Culture, and the Novel, 1880-1940*. Cambridge: Cambridge University Press, 1994.

Harpham, Geoffrey Galt. 'Ethics'. *Critical Terms for Literary Study*. Eds Frank Lentricchia and Thomas McLaughlin. 2nd edn. Chicago: University of Chicago Press, 1995. 387-405.

Lowndes, Marie Belloc. *The Lodger*. Oxford: Oxford University Press, 1996.

Machen, Arthur. *The Three Impostors*. New York: Knopf, 1930.

Marsh, Richard. *The Beetle*. New York: G.P. Putnam's Sons, 1976.

McGinn, Colin. *Ethics, Evil, and Fiction*. Oxford: Clarendon Press, 1997.

Murdoch, Iris. *The Sovereignty of Good*. 1970. London: Ark, 1985.

Norton, Robert E. *The Beautiful Soul: Aesthetic Morality in the Eighteenth Century*. Ithaca: Cornell University Press, 1995.

Nussbaum, Martha C. *Love's Knowledge: Essays on Philosophy and Literature*. New York: Oxford University Press, 1990.

Stokes, John. *Oscar Wilde: Myths, Miracles, and Imitations*. Cambridge: Cambridge University Press, 1996.

Wilde, Oscar. *Plays, Prose Writings, and Poems*. New York: Everyman's Library, 1991.

FURTHER READING

Biography

Laver, James. *Oscar Wilde*. London: Longmans, Green & Co., 1954. 32 p.

Succinct biography of Wilde. Includes a bibliography.

Criticism

Backus, Margot Gayle. "Homophobia and the Imperial Demon Lover: Gothic Narrativity in Irish Representations of the Great War." *Canadian Review of Comparative Literature/Revue Canadienne de Littérature Comparée* 21, no. 4 (March-June 1994): 45-63.

Explores the underlying motifs of demonized homosexuality and "the Gothic reunion of the self with some incomprehensible, unspeakable thing from which it has been divided" in The Picture of Dorian Gray *and several other contemporaneous works of Anglo-Irish fiction.*

Charlesworth, Barbara. "Oscar Wilde." In *Dark Passages: The Decadent Consciousness in Victorian Literature*, pp. 53-80. Madison: University of Wisconsin Press, 1965.

Biographical reading of The Picture of Dorian Gray.

Clark, Bruce B. "A Burnt Child Loves the Fire: Oscar Wilde's Search for Ultimate Meanings in Life." *Ultimate Reality and Meaning* 4, no. 3 (1981): 225-47.

Calls The Picture of Dorian Gray *the most important of Wilde's works in explicating his thoughts on reality and literary meaning.*

Clausson, Nils. "'Culture and Corruption': Paterian Self-Development versus Gothic Degeneration in Oscar Wilde's *The Picture of Dorian Gray*." *Papers on Language and Literature* 39, no. 4 (fall 2003): 339-64.

Argues that in The Picture of Dorian Gray *Wilde endeavored to merge a Gothic plot of decadence and degeneration with themes of self-development and (homo)sexual liberation inspired by the writings of Walter Pater.*

Cohen, Philip K. "The Crucible: *The Picture of Dorian Gray* and *Intentions*." In *The Moral Vision of Oscar Wilde*, pp. 105-55. Rutherford, N.J.: Fairleigh Dickinson University Press, 1978.

Suggests that in The Picture of Dorian Gray *Wilde fully explored the potential tragedy that was circumvented in his satiric short story "Lord Arthur Savile's Crime," maintaining that in the essays of* Intentions *Wilde sought to establish a middle ground between the repression and hypocrisy portrayed in the story and the hedonistic abandon depicted in the novel.*

Dickson, Donald R. "'In a Mirror That Mirrors the Soul': Masks and Mirrors in *Dorian Gray*." *English Literature in Transition: 1880-1920* 26, no. 1 (1983): 5-15.

Considers "the notion of mirror images that reflect masks of characters" with regard to the subtle aesthetic design of The Picture of Dorian Gray.

Dryden, Linda. "Oscar Wilde: Gothic Ironies and Terrible Dualities." In *The Modern Gothic and Literary Doubles: Stevenson, Wilde and Wells*, edited by Laurence Davies, pp. 110-45. Basingstoke, England: Palgrave Macmillan, 2003.

Analyzes The Picture of Dorian Gray *within the genre traditions of Gothic horror and literary Decadence, particularly highlighting affinities between Wilde's novel and Robert Louis Stevenson's* The Strange Case of Dr. Jekyll and Mr. Hyde.

Ericksen, Donald H. "*The Picture of Dorian Gray*." In *Oscar Wilde*, pp. 96-117. Boston: Twayne Publishers, 1977.

Discusses the sources, plot, critical reception, characterization, imagery, language, and setting of Wilde's novel.

Gomel, Elana. "Oscar Wilde, *The Picture of Dorian Gray*, and the (Un)Death of the Author." *Narrative* 12, no. 1 (January 2004): 74-92.

Interprets The Picture of Dorian Gray *as it traces parallels between the narrative themes of fin de siècle Gothic fantasy and postmodern theory concerning authorship, identity, and textuality.*

Jullian, Philippe. "Dorian Gray." In *Oscar Wilde*, translated by Violet Wyndham, pp. 213-23. London: Constable, 1969.

Enumerates some of the diverse literary and social influences on The Picture of Dorian Gray *and summarizes the effect of the novel's publication on Wilde's career and personal reputation.*

Kohl, Norbert. "Culture and Corruption: *The Picture of Dorian Gray.*" In *Oscar Wilde: The Works of a Conformist Rebel,* translated by David Henry Wilson, pp. 138-75. Cambridge: Cambridge University Press, 1989.

Attempts to account for the "continued interest in and varied reception of Dorian Gray*" through an examination of the novel's origins, structures, setting, themes, and characterizations.*

Oates, Joyce Carol. "*The Picture of Dorian Gray:* Wilde's Parable of the Fall." In *Contraries: Essays,* pp. 3-16. New York: Oxford University Press, 1981.

Contends that "Wilde's novel must be seen as a highly serious meditation upon the moral role of the artist," regarding its theme as "the Fall—the Fall of innocence and its consequences, the corruption of 'natural' life by a sudden irrevocable consciousness (symbolized by Dorian's infatuation with himself)."

Pappas, John J. "The Flower and the Beast: A Study of Oscar Wilde's Antithetical Attitudes toward Nature and Man in *The Picture of Dorian Gray.*" *English Literature in Transition* 15, no. 1. (1972): 37-48.

Examines The Picture of Dorian Gray *for expressions of antipathy toward nature as well as toward the place of humans in the natural world.*

Riquelme, John Paul. "Oscar Wilde's Aesthetic Gothic: Walter Pater, Dark Enlightenment, and *The Picture of Dorian Gray.*" *Modern Fiction Studies* 46, no. 3 (fall 2000): 609-31.

Investigates The Picture of Dorian Gray *as a novel that blends various literary sensibilities, tropes, and structuring principles, including Gothic doubling, Paterian aestheticism, mythic allusion, and the technique of chiaroscuro.*

Zeender, Marie-Noëlle. "John Melmoth and Dorian Gray: The Two-Faced Mirror." In *Rediscovering Oscar Wilde,* edited by C. George Sandulescu, pp. 432-40. Gerrards Cross, England: Smythe, 1994.

Compares the themes, characterizations, and centralizing motif of the two-faced mirror in Wilde's The Picture of Dorian Gray *and Charles Robert Maturin's* Melmoth the Wanderer.

Ziolkowski, Theodore. "Image as Motif: The Haunted Portrait." In *Disenchanted Images: Literary Iconology,* pp. 78-148. Princeton, N.J.: Princeton University Press, 1977.

Includes commentary on The Picture of Dorian Gray *in a chapter devoted to supernatural occurrences involving portraits in fiction.*

OTHER SOURCES FROM GALE:

Additional coverage of Wilde's life and career is contained in the following sources published by Thomson Gale: *Authors and Artists for Young Adults,* Vol. 49; *Beacham's Guide to Literature for Young Adults,* Vol. 15; *British Writers,* Vol. 5; *British Writers: The Classics,* Vols. 1, 2; *British Writers Retrospective Supplement,* Vol. 2; *Concise Dictionary of British Literary Biography, 1890-1914; Contemporary Authors,* Vols. 104, 119; *Contemporary Authors New Revision Series,* 112; *Dictionary of Literary Biography,* Vols. 10, 19, 34, 57, 141, 156, 190; *DISCovering Authors; DISCovering Authors: British Edition; DISCovering Authors: Canadian Edition; DISCovering Authors Modules: Dramatists, Most-studied Authors,* and *Novelists; DISCovering Authors 3.0; Drama Criticism,* Vol. 17; *Drama for Students,* Vols. 4, 8, 9; *Exploring Short Stories; Literature and Its Times Supplement,* Vol. 1; *Literature Resource Center; Novels for Students,* Vol. 20; *Reference Guide to English Literature,* Ed. 2; *Reference Guide to Short Fiction,* Ed. 2; *St. James Guide to Fantasy Writers; Short Stories for Students,* Vol. 7; *Short Story Criticism,* Vols. 11, 77; *Something About the Author,* Vol. 24; *Supernatural Fiction Writers; Twayne's English Authors; Twentieth-Century Literary Criticism,* Vols. 1, 8, 23, 41; *World Literature and Its Times,* Vol. 4; *World Literature Criticism;* and *Writers for Children.*

INDEXES

The main reference

Austen, Jane 1775-1817 **1**: 2, 7, 35, 37, 74-76, 80, 217, 220, 324, 333, 353, 354, 453, 466; **2: 25-47**

lists the featured author's entry in volumes 2 and 3 of Gothic Literature; *it also lists commentary on the featured author in other volumes of the set, which include topics associated with* Gothic Literature. *Page references to substantial discussions of the author appear in boldface.*

The cross-references

See also AAYA 19; BRW 4; BRWC 1; BRWR 2; BYA 3; CD-BLB 1789-1832; DA; DA3; DAB; DAC; DAM MST, NOV; DLB 116; EXPN; FL 1, 2; LAIT 2; LATS 1; LMFS 1; NCLC 1, 13, 19, 33, 51, 81, 95, 119, 150; NFS 1, 14, 18, 20, 21; TEA; WLC; WLIT 3; WYAS 1

list entries on the author in the following Gale biographical and literary sources:

AAL: Asian American Literature

AAYA: Authors & Artists for Young Adults

AFAW: African American Writers

AFW: African Writers

AITN: Authors in the News

AMW: American Writers

AMWR: American Writers Retrospective Supplement

AMWS: American Writers Supplement

ANW: American Nature Writers

AW: Ancient Writers

BEST: Bestsellers (quarterly, citations appear as Year: Issue number)

BG: The Beat Generation: A Gale Critical Companion

BLC: Black Literature Criticism

BLCS: Black Literature Criticism Supplement

BPFB: Beacham's Encyclopedia of Popular Fiction: Biography and Resources

BRW: British Writers

BRWS: British Writers Supplement

BW: Black Writers

BYA: Beacham's Guide to Literature for Young Adults

CA: Contemporary Authors

CAAS: Contemporary Authors Autobiography Series

CABS: Contemporary Authors Bibliographical Series

CAD: Contemporary American Dramatists

CANR: Contemporary Authors New Revision Series

CAP: Contemporary Authors Permanent Series

CBD: Contemporary British Dramatists

CCA: Contemporary Canadian Authors

CD: Contemporary Dramatists

CDALB: Concise Dictionary of American Literary Biography

CDALBS: Concise Dictionary of American Literary Biography Supplement

CDBLB: Concise Dictionary of British Literary Biography

CLC: Contemporary Literary Criticism

CLR: Children's Literature Review

CMLC: Classical and Medieval Literature Criticism

CMW: St. James Guide to Crime & Mystery Writers

CN: Contemporary Novelists

CP: Contemporary Poets

CPW: Contemporary Popular Writers

CSW: Contemporary Southern Writers

CWD: Contemporary Women Dramatists

CWP: Contemporary Women Poets

CWRI: St. James Guide to Children's Writers

CWW: Contemporary World Writers

DA: DISCovering Authors

DA3: DISCovering Authors 3.0

DAB: DISCovering Authors: British Edition

DAC: DISCovering Authors: Canadian Edition

DAM: DISCovering Authors: Modules

> **DRAM:** Dramatists Module; **MST:** Most-Studied Authors Module;
>
> **MULT:** Multicultural Authors Module; **NOV:** Novelists Module;
>
> **POET:** Poets Module; **POP:** Popular Fiction and Genre Authors Module

DC: Drama Criticism

DFS: Drama for Students

DLB: Dictionary of Literary Biography

DLBD: Dictionary of Literary Biography Documentary Series

DLBY: Dictionary of Literary Biography Yearbook

DNFS: Literature of Developing Nations for Students

EFS: Epics for Students

EXPN: Exploring Novels

EXPP: Exploring Poetry

EXPS: Exploring Short Stories

EW: European Writers

FANT: St. James Guide to Fantasy Writers

FL: Feminism in Literature: A Gale Critical Companion

FW: Feminist Writers

GFL: Guide to French Literature, Beginnings to 1789, 1798 to the Present

GLL: Gay and Lesbian Literature

HGG: St. James Guide to Horror, Ghost & Gothic Writers

HLC: Hispanic Literature Criticism

HLCS: Hispanic Literature Criticism Supplement

HR: Harlem Renaissance: A Gale Critical Companion

HW: Hispanic Writers

IDFW: International Dictionary of Films and Filmmakers: Writers and Production Artists

IDTP: International Dictionary of Theatre: Playwrights

LAIT: Literature and Its Times

LAW: Latin American Writers

JRDA: Junior DISCovering Authors

LC: Literature Criticism from 1400 to 1800

MAICYA: Major Authors and Illustrators for Children and Young Adults

MAICYA: Major Authors and Illustrators for Children and Young Adults Supplement

MAWW: Modern American Women Writers

MJW: Modern Japanese Writers

MTCW: Major 20th-Century Writers

NCFS: Nonfiction Classics for Students

NCLC: Nineteenth-Century Literature Criticism

NFS: Novels for Students

NNAL: Native North American Literature

PAB: Poets: American and British

PC: Poetry Criticism

PFS: Poetry for Students

RGAL: Reference Guide to American Literature

RGEL: Reference Guide to English Literature

RGSF: Reference Guide to Short Fiction

RGWL: Reference Guide to World Literature

RHW: Twentieth-Century Romance and Historical Writers

SAAS: Something about the Author Autobiography Series

SATA: Something about the Author

SFW: St. James Guide to Science Fiction Writers

SSC: Short Story Criticism

SSFS: Short Stories for Students

TCLC: Twentieth-Century Literary Criticism

TCWW: Twentieth-Century Western Writers

WCH: Writers for Children

WLC: World Literature Criticism, 1500 to the Present

WLCS: World Literature Criticism Supplement

WLIT: World Literature and Its Times

WP: World Poets

YABC: Yesterday's Authors of Books for Children

YAW: St. James Guide to Young Adult Writers

The Author Index lists all of the authors featured in the Gothic Literature *set. It includes references to the main author entries in volumes 2 and 3; it also lists commentary on the featured author in other author entries and in other volumes of the set, which include topics associated with Gothic Literature. Page references to author entries appear in boldface. The Author Index also includes birth and death dates, cross references between pseudonyms or name variants and actual names, and cross references to other Gale series in which the authors have appeared. A complete list of these sources is found facing the first page of the Author Index.*

A

Atwood, Margaret (Eleanor) 1939-
2: 1–24
See also AAYA 12, 47; AMWS 13; BEST 89:2; BPFB 1; CA 49-52; CANR 3, 24, 33, 59, 95, 133; CLC 2, 3, 4, 8, 13, 15, 25, 44, 84, 135; CN 2, 3, 4, 5, 6, 7; CP 1, 2, 3, 4, 5, 6, 7; CPW; CWP;

DA; DA3; DAB; DAC; DAM MST, NOV, POET; DLB 53, 251; EWL 3; EXPN; FL 1, 5; FW; INT CANR-24; LAIT 5; MTCW 1, 2; MTFW 2005; NFS 4, 12, 13, 14, 19; PC 8; PFS 7; RGSF 2; SATA 50; SSC 2, 46; SSFS 3, 13; TCLE 1:1; TWA; WLC; WWE 1; YAW

Austen, Jane 1775-1817 **1: 2, 7, 35,** 37, 74–76, 80, 217, 220, 324, 333, 353, 354, 453, 466; **2: 25–47**
See also AAYA 19; BRW 4; BRWC 1; BRWR 2; BYA 3; CD-BLB 1789-1832; DA; DA3; DAB; DAC; DAM MST, NOV; DLB 116; EXPN; FL 1, 2; LAIT 2; LATS 1:1; LMFS 1; NCLC 1, 13, 19, 33, 51, 81, 95, 119, 150; NFS 1, 14, 18, 20, 21; TEA; WLC; WLIT 3; WYAS 1

B

Baillie, Joanna 1762-1851 **1:** 339–41, 390; **2: 49–77**
See also DLB 93; NCLC 71, 151; RGEL 2

Beckford, William 1760-1844 **1:** 146, 181, 241, 260–61; **2: 79–102**
See also BRW 3; DLB 39, 213; HGG; LMFS 1; NCLC 16; SUFW

Brontë, Charlotte 1816-1855 **1:** 347, 350–52, 358; **2: 103–30**
See also AAYA 17; BRW 5; BRWC 2; BRWR 1; BYA 2; CD-BLB 1832-1890; DA; DA3; DAB; DAC; DAM MST, NOV; DLB 21, 159, 199; EXPN; FL 1, 2; LAIT 2; NCLC 3, 8, 33, 58, 105, 155; NFS 4; TEA; WLC; WLIT 4

Brontë, Emily (Jane) 1818-1848 **1:** 263–64, 331, 347, 358–59; **2: 131–51**
See also AAYA 17; BPFB 1; BRW 5; BRWC 1; BRWR 1; BYA 3; CDBLB 1832-1890; DA; DA3; DAB; DAC; DAM MST, NOV, POET; DLB 21, 32, 199; EXPN; FL 1, 2; LAIT 1; NCLC 16, 35; PC 8; TEA; WLC; WLIT 3

Brown, Charles Brockden 1771-1810 **1: 62, 212, 250, 284,** 519, 523; **2: 153–78**
See also AMWS 1; CDALB 1640-1865; DLB 37, 59, 73; FW; HGG; LMFS 1; NCLC 22, 74, 122; RGAL 4; TUS

C

Carter, Angela (Olive) 1940-1992 **2: 179–200**
See also BRWS 3; CA 53-56; 136; CANR 12, 36, 61, 106; CLC 5,

41, 76; CN 3, 4, 5; DA3; DLB
14, 207, 261, 319; EXPS; FANT;
FW; MTCW 1, 2; MTFW 2005;
RGSF 2; SATA 66; SATA-Obit
70; SFW 4; SSC 13, 85; SSFS 4,
12; SUFW 2; TCLC 139; WLIT
4

Collins, (William) Wilkie
1824-1889 **1:** 4, 18, 20, 86–89,
263, 290, 300, 354, 497; **2:**
201–28

See also BRWS 6; CDBLB 1832-
1890; CMW 4; DLB 18, 70,
159; MSW; NCLC 1, 18, 93;
RGEL 2; RGSF 2; SUFW 1;
WLIT 4

D

Dickens, Charles (John Huffam)
1812-1870 **1:** 87, 94, 161, 260,
262, 347, 350, 352, 357–59, 365;
2: 229–56

See also AAYA 23; BRW 5;
BRWC 1, 2; BYA 1, 2, 3, 13,
14; CDBLB 1832-1890; CLR
95; CMW 4; DA; DA3; DAB;
DAC; DAM MST, NOV; DLB
21, 55, 70, 159, 166; EXPN;
HGG; JRDA; LAIT 1, 2; LATS
1:1; LMFS 1; MAICYA 1, 2;
NCLC 3, 8, 18, 26, 37, 50, 86,
105, 113, 161; NFS 4, 5, 10,
14, 20; RGEL 2; RGSF 2; SATA
15; SSC 17, 49; SUFW 1; TEA;
WCH; WLC; WLIT 4; WYA

Dinesen, Isak 1885-1962 **2: 257–78**
See also CLC 10, 29, 95; EW 10;
EWL 3; EXPS; FW; HGG; LAIT
3; MTCW 1; NCFS 2; NFS 9;
RGSF 2; RGWL 2, 3; SSC 7, 75;
SSFS 3, 6, 13; WLIT 2

du Maurier, Daphne 1907-1989 **1:**
436; **2: 279–92**

See also AAYA 37; BPFB 1; BRWS
3; CA 5-8R; 128; CANR 6, 55;
CLC 6, 11, 59; CMW 4; CN 1,
2, 3, 4; CPW; DA3; DAB; DAC;
DAM MST, POP; DLB 191;
HGG; LAIT 3; MSW; MTCW 1,
2; NFS 12; RGEL 2; RGSF 2;
RHW; SATA 27; SATA-Obit 60;
SSC 18; SSFS 14, 16; TEA

F

Faulkner, William (Cuthbert)
1897-1962 **1:** 35, 212, 519; **2:**
293–320

See also AAYA 7; AMW; AMWR
1; BPFB 1; BYA 5, 15; CA 81-

84; CANR 33; CDALB 1929-
1941; CLC 1, 3, 6, 8, 9, 11, 14,
18, 28, 52, 68; DA; DA3; DAB;
DAC; DAM MST, NOV; DLB 9,
11, 44, 102, 316; DLBD 2;
DLBY 1986, 1997; EWL 3;
EXPN; EXPS; LAIT 2; LATS 1:1;
LMFS 2; MAL 5; MTCW 1, 2;
MTFW 2005; NFS 4, 8, 13;
RGAL 4; RGSF 2; SSC 1, 35,
42; SSFS 2, 5, 6, 12; TCLC 141;
TUS; WLC

G

Godwin, William 1756-1836 **1:** 2,
20, 22–25, 27, 76, 78–79, 81–83,
85, 87, 98–101, 165, 181, 249–50,
254–57, 261, 330, 362, 411,
432–33; **2: 321–39**

See also CDBLB 1789-1832;
CMW 4; DLB 39, 104, 142,
158, 163, 262; HGG; NCLC
14, 130; RGEL 2

Goethe, Johann Wolfgang von
1749-1832 **1:** 2, 3, 45, 232, 241,
308, 313–14, 319, 432; **2: 341–62**

See also CDWLB 2; DA; DA3;
DAB; DAC; DAM DRAM, MST,
POET; DC 20; DLB 94; EW 5;
LATS 1; LMFS 1:1; NCLC 4, 22,
34, 90, 154; PC 5; RGWL 2, 3;
SSC 38; TWA; WLC

H

Hawthorne, Nathaniel 1804-1864
1: 60, 62, 69, 124, 180–81, 284,
290–96, 370, 519, 523; **2: 363–86**

See also AAYA 18; AMW; AMWC
1; AMWR 1; BPFB 2; BYA 3;
CDALB 1640-1865; CLR 103;
DA; DA3; DAB; DAC; DAM
MST, NOV; DLB 1, 74, 183,
223, 269; EXPN; EXPS; HGG;
LAIT 1; NCLC 2, 10, 17, 23,
39, 79, 95, 158; NFS 1, 20;
RGAL 4; RGSF 2; SSC 3, 29,
39; SSFS 1, 7, 11, 15; SUFW 1;
TUS; WCH; WLC; YABC 2

Hoffmann, E(rnst) T(heodor)
A(madeus) 1776-1822 **1:** 2,
232–33, 301–5, 429, 439; **2:**
387–420

See also CDWLB 2; DLB 90; EW
5; NCLC 2; RGSF 2; RGWL 2,
3; SATA 27; SSC 13; SUFW 1;
WCH

Hogg, James 1770-1835 **1:** 2, 19,
28–29, 80, 86, 158, 165, 318, 326,
453; **2: 421–39**

See also BRWS 10; DLB 93, 116,
159; HGG; NCLC 4, 109;
RGEL 2; SUFW 1

I

Irving, Washington 1783-1859 **1:**
182, 262, 504, 522; **2: 441–60**

See also AAYA 56; AMW; CDALB
1640-1865; CLR 97; DA; DA3;
DAB; DAC; DAM MST; DLB 3,
11, 30, 59, 73, 74, 183, 186,
250, 254; EXPS; LAIT 1; RN-
CLC 2, 19, 95; GAL 4; RGSF 2;
SSC 2, 37; SSFS 1, 8, 16; SUFW
1; TUS; WCH; WLC; YABC 2

J

James, Henry 1843-1916 **2: 461–80**

See also AMW; AMWC 1;
AMWR 1; BPFB 2; BRW 6; CA
104; 132; CDALB 1865-1917;
DA; DA3; DAB; DAC; DAM
MST, NOV; DLB 12, 71, 74,
189; DLBD 13; EWL 3; EXPS;
HGG; LAIT 2; MAL 5; MTCW
1, 2; MTFW 2005; NFS 12, 16,
19; RGAL 4; RGEL 2; RGSF 2;
SSC 8, 32, 47; SSFS 9; SUFW 1;
TCLC 2, 11, 24, 40, 47, 64;
TUS; WLC

K

King, Stephen (Edwin) 1947- **1:**
398; **2: 481–505**

See also AAYA 1, 17; AMWS 5;
BEST 90:1; BPFB 2; CA 61-64;
CANR 1, 30, 52, 76, 119, 134;
CLC 12, 26, 37, 61, 113; CN 7;
CPW; DA3; DAM NOV, POP;
DLB 143; DLBY 1980; HGG;
JRDA; LAIT 5; MTCW 1, 2;
MTFW 2005; RGAL 4; SATA 9,
55, 161; SSC 17, 55; SUFW 1,
2; WYAS 1; YAW

L

Le Fanu, Joseph Sheridan
1814-1873 **1:** 31, 38, 86, 89–90,
139, 173, 232–33, 260, 290,
335–36, 376–77, 379, 382–84; **3:**
1–29

See also CMW 4; DA3; DAM
POP; DLB 21, 70, 159, 178;
HGG; NCLC 9, 58; RGEL 2;
RGSF 2; SSC 14, 84; SUFW 1

W

Walpole, Horace 1717-1797 **1:** 2,
20, 27, 31, 45–46, 48, 51, 57, 80,
87, 99, 112, 129, 155, 162, 221,
241, 249, 252, 254–55, 261, 270,
277, 290, 322, 326, 354, 402–3,
454, 459, 461, 479, 492, 494–95,
497–98, 501–5, 520; **3:** 429–55
   See also BRW 3; DLB 39, 104,
   213; HGG; LC 2, 49; LMFS 1;
   RGEL 2; SUFW 1; TEA

Wharton, Edith (Newbold Jones)
1862-1937 **1:** 213; **3:** 457–86
   See also AAYA 25; AMW; AMWC
   2; AMWR 1; BPFB 3; CA 104;
   132; CDALB 1865-1917; DA;

DA3; DAB; DAC; DAM MST,
NOV; DLB 4, 9, 12, 78, 189;
DLBD 13; EWL 3; EXPS; FL 1,
6; HGG; LAIT 2, 3; LATS 1:1;
MAL 5; MAWW; MTCW 1, 2;
MTFW 2005; NFS 5, 11, 15,
20; RGAL 4; RGSF 2; RHW;
SSC 6, 84; SSFS 6, 7; SUFW;
TCLC 3, 9, 27, 53, 129, 149;
TUS; WLC

Wilde, Oscar (Fingal O'Flahertie
Wills) 1854-1900 **1:** 31–31, 34,
133, 158, 160–62, 166, 169, 253,
363–64; **3:** 487–518
   See also AAYA 49; BRW 5;
   BRWC 1, 2; BRWR 2; BYA 15;

CA 104; 119; CANR 112; CD-
BLB 1890-1914; DA; DA3;
DAB; DAC; DAM DRAM, MST,
NOV; DC 17; DFS 4, 8, 9, 21;
DLB 10, 19, 34, 57, 141, 156,
190; EXPS; FANT; LATS 1:1;
NFS 20; RGEL 2; RGSF 2; SATA
24; SSC 11, 77; SSFS 7; SUFW;
TCLC 1, 8, 23, 41; TEA; WCH;
WLC; WLIT 4

The Title Index alphabetically lists the titles of works written by the authors featured in volumes 2 and 3 of Gothic Literature *and provides page numbers or page ranges where commentary on these titles can be found. English translations of foreign titles and variations of titles are cross referenced to the title under which a work was originally published. Titles of novels, dramas, nonfiction books, and poetry, short story, or essay collections are printed in italics; individual poems, short stories, and essays are printed in body type within quotation marks.*

A

INDEX

SUBJECT INDEX

SUBJECT INDEX

SUBJECT INDEX

SUBJECT INDEX

SUBJECT INDEX

SUBJECT INDEX

T

SUBJECT INDEX